INTERNATIONAL
ENCYCLOPEDIA OF
HOSPITALITY MANAGEMENT

INTERNATIONAL ENCYCLOPEDIA OF HOSPITALITY MANAGEMENT

Chief editor
Abraham Pizam

ELSEVIER
BUTTERWORTH
HEINEMANN

AMSTERDAM • BOSTON • HEIDELBERG • LONDON • NEW YORK • OXFORD
PARIS • SAN DIEGO • SAN FRANCISCO • SINGAPORE • SYDNEY • TOKYO

Elsevier Butterworth-Heinemann
Linacre House, Jordan Hill, Oxford OX2 8DP
30 Corporate Drive, Burlington, MA 01803

First published 2005

British Library Cataloguing in Publication Data
A catalogue record for this book is available from the British Library

Library of Congress Cataloging in Publication Data
A catalog record for this book is available from the Library of Congress

ISBN 0 7506 5996 3

For information on all Elsevier Butterworth-Heinemann publications
visit our website at http://books.elsevier.com

Typeset by Newgen Imaging Systems Pvt Ltd, Chennai, India
Printed and bound in Great Britain

Contents

Editorial team

Peter Harris
Accounting and Finance
Oxford Brookes University, UK

Zheng Gu
Accounting and Finance
University of Nevada, Las Vegas, USA

Randall Upchurch
Club Management and Timeshare Management
University of Central Florida, USA

Deborah Breiter
Event Management
University of Central Florida, USA

Patti Shock
Event Management
University of Nevada, Las Vegas, USA

David Stipanuk
Facilities Management
Cornell University, USA

Gill Maxwell
Human Resources Management
Glasgow Caledonian University, UK

Darren Lee-Ross
Human Resources Management
James Cook University, Australia

Dimitrios Buhalis
Information Technology
University of Surrey, UK

Alan Stutts
Lodging Management
American Intercontinental University, USA

Stowe Shoemaker
Marketing
University of Houston, USA

Linda Shea
Marketing
University of Massachusetts, USA

Dennis Reynolds
Restaurants and Foodservice Management
Washington State University, USA

J. Stephen Taylor
Strategic Management
University of Strathclyde, UK

Arie Reichel
Strategic Management
Ben-Gurion University, Israel

Contributors

Jim Ackles
Tharaldson Energy Group, USA

Debra Adams
Arena4Finance Ltd, UK

Julie Adams
Southern Cross University, Australia

Benjamin del Alcazar
University of Malaga, Spain

Sekeno Aldred
Center for Effective Public Policy, USA

Judy Allen
Judy Allen Productions, Canada

Robert Allender
Energy Resources Management,
Hong Kong SAR, China

Tommy D. Andersson
Goteborgs University, Sweden

Helen Atkinson
University of Brighton, UK

Rodolfo Baggio
Bocconi University, Italy

Billy Bai
University of Nevada, Las Vegas, USA

Patricia Baldwin
Club Corporation, USA

Seyhmus Baloglu
University of Nevada, Las Vegas, USA

Deborah Barrash
University of Nevada, Las Vegas, USA

Paul Beals
University of Denver, USA

Suwathana Bhuripanyo
Coca-Cola Co., Thailand

David Biel
Houston's Restaurants, USA

Kemal Birdir
Mersin University, Turkey

Ruth Blackwell
Leeds Metropolitan University, UK

David Bojanic
University of Massachusetts, USA

Frank Borsenik
University of Nevada, Las Vegas, USA

Debbi Boyne
Meeting Demands, USA

Jackie Brander Brown
Manchester Metropolitan University, UK

Deborah Breiter
University of Central Florida, USA

Anthony Brien
Lincoln University, New Zealand

Dimitrios Buhalis
University of Surrey, UK

Cathy Burgess
Oxford Brookes University, UK

Sally-Ann Burriss
Southern Cross University, Australia

Liping A. Cai
Purdue University, USA

Grant Cairncross
Southern Cross University, Australia

Debra F. Cannon
Georgia State University, USA

Bonnie Canziani
University of North Carolina – Greensboro, USA

Amanda Kay Cecil
Indiana University, USA

Benny Chan
The Hong Kong Polytechnic University,
Hong Kong SAR, China

Eric S.W. Chan
The Hong Kong Polytechnic University,
Hong Kong SAR, China

Steven Chan
The Hong Kong Polytechnic University, Hong
Kong SAR, China

William N. Chernish
University of Houston, USA

Julia Christensen Hughes
University of Guelph, Canada

Olgun Cicek
Skyline College, United Arab Emirates

Candice Clemenz
University of West Florida, USA

Paolo Collini
Trento University, Italy

Catherine Collins
University of Surrey, UK

Jennifer T. Condon
Newmarket International, Inc., USA

Malcolm Cooper
Ritsumeikan Asia Pacific University, Japan

Jerry Daigle
Orange County Convention Center, USA

Agnes Lee DeFranco
University of Houston, USA

Adrian Devine
University of Ulster, UK

Frances Devine
University of Ulster, UK

Ron Dowell
Southern Cross University, Australia

Suzette Eaddy
National Minority Supplier Development Council,
USA

Roman Egger
Salzburg, Austria

Raymond Clinton Ellis, Jr
University of Houston, USA

Dominique Faesch
Ecole Hoteliere de Lausanne (EHL), Switzerland

Trish Fairbourn
Southern Cross University, Australia

George Fenich
University of New Orleans, USA

Raymond Ferreira
Georgia State University, USA

Reed Fisher
Johnson State College, USA

William Fisher
University of Central Florida, USA

Jose Manoel Gandara
Federal University of Paraná, Brazil

Morgan Geddie
University of Houston, USA

Don Getz
University of Calgary, Canada

Jim H. Gilkeson
University of Central Florida, USA

Pat Golden-Romero
University of Nevada, Las Vegas, USA

Ian Graham
The Hotel Solutions Partnership, UK

Susan Gregory
Eastern Michigan University, USA

Kurt Gruber
Island One Resorts, USA

Zheng Gu
University of Nevada, Las Vegas, USA

Chris Guilding
Griffith University, Australia

Sigal Haber
Tel-Aviv University, Israel

Mine Haktanir
Eastern Mediterranean University, Turkish
Republic of Northern Cyprus

Robert Harrington
Nicholls State University, USA

Peter Harris
Oxford Brookes University, UK

Shelly T.I. Harris
The Harris Group, USA

Michael Haushalter
Orlando, Florida, USA

Flavia Hendler
University of Nevada, Las Vegas, USA

Rom Hendler
Venetian Resort Hotel and Casino, Las Vegas,
USA

G. Keith Henning
University of Calgary, Canada

M.T. Hickman
Richland College, USA

Tyra W. Hilliard
The George Washington University, USA

Nicole Marie Holland
Londonderry, NH, USA

Connie E. Holt
Widener University, USA

Sonja Holverson
Ecole Hôtelière de Lausanne (EHL), Switzerland

William R. Host
Roosevelt University, USA

Judy Hou
Ecole Hôtelière de Lausanne (EHL), Switzerland

Krista Hrin
Brock University, Canada

Dieter Huckestein
Hilton Hotels Corporation, USA

Michael Hughes
Tradeshow Week, USA

David Inaneishvili
Hotel Kämp, Finland

Aviad Israeli
Ben-Gurion University, Israel

Robert F. Jenefsky
Ecole Hôtelière de Lausanne (EHL), Switzerland

Colin Johnson
San Jose State University, USA

Eleri Jones
University of Wales Institute, UK

Juli Jones
Convention Industry Council, USA

Tom Jones
University of Nevada, Las Vegas, USA

Jay Kandampully
Ohio State University, USA

Bomi Kang
University of Nevada, Las Vegas, USA

Kurtulus Karamustafa
Erciyes University, Turkey

Tammie Kaufman
University of Central Florida, USA

Gillian Kellock Hay
Glasgow Caledonian University, UK

Ashish Khullar
University of Massachusetts, USA

Hyunjoon Kim
University of Hawaii, USA

Sherri Kimes
Cornell University, USA

David Kirk
Queen Margaret University College
Edinburgh, UK

Jaksa Kivela
The Hong Kong Polytechnic University,
Hong Kong SAR, China

Frederick J. Kleisner
Wyndham International, Inc., USA

Bozidar Klicek
University of Zagreb, Croatia

Sheryl F. Kline
Purdue University, USA

Metin Kozak
Mugla University, Turkey

Vira Krakhmal
Oxford Brookes University, UK

Robert Kwortnik
Cornell University, USA

Jerry LaChappelle
Harrah's Entertainment, Inc., USA

Carolyn Lambert
Pennsylvania State University, USA

Conrad Lashley
Nottingham Trent University, UK

Rob Law
The Hong Kong Polytechnic University,
Hong Kong SAR, China

Stephen LeBruto
University of Central Florida, USA

Suna Lee
University of Nevada, Las Vegas, USA

Darren Lee-Ross
James Cook University, Australia

Eric O. Long
Waldorf Astoria Hotel, USA

Erwin Losekoot
University of Strathclyde, UK

Paul Lynch
Queen Margaret University College
Edinburgh, UK

Ann Lynn
Ithaca College, USA

Wm. Michael Lynn
Cornell University, USA

Angela Maher
Oxford Brookes University, UK

Hilary C. Main-Murphy
Ecole Hôtelière de Lausanne (EHL), Switzerland

Alan Marvell
Bath Spa University College, UK

Gillian Maxwell
Glasgow Caledonian University, UK

Karl Mayer
University of Nevada, Las Vegas, USA

Vivienne McCabe
Southern Cross University, Australia

Ian McDonnell
University of Technology, Sydney, Australia

G. Michael McGrath
Victoria University, Australia

Brumby McLeod
University of Nevada, Las Vegas, USA

Una McMahon Beattie
University of Ulster, UK

Edward A. Merritt
California State Polytechnic University, USA

Brian Miller
University of Delaware, USA

Juline E. Mills
Purdue University, USA

Asad Mohsin
University of Waikato, New Zealand

Marco Mongiello
University of Westminster, UK

Christopher Muller
University of Central Florida, USA

James Murphy
University of Western Australia, Australia

Eunha Myung
University of Nevada, Las Vegas, USA

Kathy Nelson
University of Nevada, Las Vegas, USA

Richard Nelson
Hyatt Hotels Corporation, USA

John Nightingale
Leeds Metropolitan University, UK

Peter O'Connor
IMHI (Cornell–ESSEC), France

Fevzi Okumus
The Hong Kong Polytechnic University,
Hong Kong SAR, China

Barry O'Mahony
Victoria University, Australia

William O'Toole
University of Sydney, Australia

Ruth Owen
University of Surrey, UK

Ioannis S. Pantelidis
University of Surrey, UK

Alexandros Paraskevas
Oxford Brookes University, UK

H.G. Parsa
Ohio State University, USA

David V. Pavesic
Georgia State University, USA

Gabriele Piccoli
Cornell University, USA

Annemarie Piso
Leeds Metropolitan University, UK

Jeff Pope
Curtin University of Technology, Australia

Josephine Pryce
James Cook University, Australia

Samantha Quail
Glasgow Caledonian University, UK

Carola Raab
University of New Hampshire, USA

Arie Reichel
Ben-Gurion University, Israel

Dennis Reynolds
Washington State University, USA

Paul Reynolds
University of South Australia, Australia

Noel Richards
James Cook University, Australia

Chris Roberts
University of Massachusetts, USA

Marco Antonio Robledo
University of the Balearic Islands, Spain

Stephani K.A. Robson
Cornell University, USA

Pimrawee Rochungsrat
James Cook University, Australia

Glenn Ross
James Cook University, Australia

Chantal Rotondo
ARDA International Foundation, USA

Denney G. Rutherford
Washington State University, USA

Naz Saleem
Bilkent University, Turkey

Steve Sasso
University of Massachusetts, USA

Udo Schlentrich
University of New Hampshire, USA

Raymond Schmidgall
Michigan State University, USA

Peter Schofield
University of Salford, UK

Junwon Seo
Hilton Grand Vacations Company, USA

Kimberly Severt
University of Central Florida, USA

Margaret Shaw
University of Guelph, Canada

Linda J. Shea
University of Massachusetts, USA

Atul Sheel
University of Massachusetts, USA

Patti J. Shock
University of Nevada, Las Vegas, USA

Stowe Shoemaker
University of Houston, USA

Mariana Sigala
University of the Aegean, Greece

Aram Son
James Cook University, Australia

Beverly Sparks
Griffith University, Australia

David Stipanuk
Cornell University, USA

Sandy Strick
University of South Carolina, USA

Alan T. Stutts
American Intercontinental University, USA

Alex Susskind
Cornell University, USA

Nancy Swanger
Washington State University, USA

Irene Sweeney
International Hotel Management Institute,
Switzerland

Joy Talbot-Powers
RCI, USA

Cheng-Te (Carlos) Tan
Daxon Technology, USA

Karen Tang
University of Surrey, UK

Masako Taylor
Taylor Associates, Japan

J. Stephen Taylor
University of Strathclyde, UK

Mustafa Tepeci
University of Mersin, Turkey

Lyle Thompson
Burnaby, BC, Canada

Nils Timo
Griffith University, Australia

Horatiu Tudori
Ecole Hôtelière de Lausanne (EHL), Switzerland

Randall S. Upchurch
University of Central Florida, USA

Gary Vallen
Northern Arizona University, USA

Jean-Pierre van der Rest
Leiden University, The Netherlands

Cynthia Vannucci
Metropolitan State University, USA

Constantinos S. Verginis
The Emirates Academy of Hospitality
Management, United Arab Emirates

Gerard Viardin
The Marquette Hotel, Minneapolis, USA

Richard Vickery
Metropolitan State College, USA

Peter Walton
ESSEC Business School, France

Rod Warnick
University of Massachusetts, USA

Karin Weber
Hong Kong Polytechnic University,
Hong Kong SAR, China

Paul Weeks
Southern Cross University, Australia

Paul A. Whitelaw
Victoria University, Australia

Charles Whittaker
Oxford Brookes University, UK

Karl Wöber
Vienna University of Economics and Business
Administration, Austria

James Wortman
University of Houston, USA

Chiemi Yagi
University Education Center, University of the
Ryukyus, Japan

Ian Yeoman
Scotland National Tourism Agency, UK

Darla Zanini
ARDA International Foundation, USA

Dina Marie V. Zemke
University of New Hampshire, USA

Acknowledgments

This 'labor of love' project could not have been done without the hard work and complete dedication of the 15 section editors who comprise the editorial team of this encyclopedia. During the past 18 months these volunteers have spent collectively thousands of hours in identifying and selecting entries for their respective sections, assigning entries to authors, making sure that the deadlines for completion were met, reviewing the entries and making the appropriate revisions, and submitting their final product to the Chief Editor. Thus, this book can be considered as a compilation of their creative genius and complete mastery of the field of hospitality management.

My total gratitude and admiration is also extended to the 218 authors who gave freely of their time and volunteered to write the 728 entries of this encyclopedia. They are the true heroes of this project and to them this book is dedicated.

On the publishing side, I wish to express my deepest appreciation to Ms Sally North, who entrusted me with this sacred project, had confidence in my ability to bring it to fruition, and guided me patiently through the complex web of publishing such a colossal composition.

Special acknowledgments are due to Ms Shirley Russo, my research assistant, who spent numerous hours in proofreading and formatting the entries, and to the faculty and staff of the Rosen College of Hospitality Management at the University of Central Florida for their full support and understanding during the past 18 months.

Last, but not least, many thanks and appreciation to my wife, Esther, to whom I have been a 'ghost husband' during the many months that I worked on this project.

Abraham Pizam
Chief Editor

Introduction

The objective of this encyclopedia is to serve as an authoritative source of scientific and professional reference for students, researchers, and practitioners interested in the growing field of hospitality management.

In designing the encyclopedia the Chief Editor was guided by three principles. First, that the entries should be representative of the main sectors of the hospitality industry. Thus, great care was taken to include entries relevant to the lodging, foodservice, events, clubs, and timeshare sectors of the hospitality industry. Second, that the entries should reflect all the major managerial disciplines prevalent in the hospitality industry. Therefore, important entries were incorporated which are common in the disciplines of accounting and finance, marketing, human resources, information technology, strategic management, and facilities management. Third, that the entries should denote the global and cross-cultural nature of the hospitality industry. For that reason, the entries were written by authors who practice or teach hospitality management in different countries around the world.

The end result is a single volume that is composed of 728 entries containing some 362,000 words that were written by 218 authors from 23 different countries. The entries are alphabetically arranged and signed by their authors. At the end of each entry is a list of up to ten relevant and up-to-date references, including electronic references and suggested websites. Though this encyclopedia is by no means an all-encompassing reference book that covers every single aspect of hospitality management as practiced in every country around the world, it is nevertheless a serious attempt to describe, define, and analyze the major issues relevant to the international and multi-sectoral hospitality industry.

Not all entries are of the same size. An entry's length represents its importance and complexity. Entries that are the most important and/or complex command around 2000 words, while those that deal with the least significant or complex subjects are allocated only 200, with entries of around 1000 words between the two. Since the aim was to produce an encyclopedia rather than a dictionary, all entries not only define concepts, but describe their use, review past research and practice, and analyze their strengths and weaknesses.

The easiest and most convenient method of using this encyclopedia is by searching through the alphabetically arranged list of entries that appears at the beginning of the book. Alternatively, one can look up a concept or subject in the index at the end of the volume, which gives in bold type the location of a main entry that describes the concept/subject as well as cross-referencing it (in regular type) with other entries that discuss the same concept/subject from different perspectives.

It is the sincere wish and hope of the Chief Editor that this encyclopedia will become an essential tool in the scientific development and professionalization of the field of hospitality management, for generations to come.

List of entries

Entries A–Z

A

À la carte

The literal interpretation of à la carte is 'from or off the card to order.' The course structure for all modern menus is governed technically by the à la carte menu. This classic format is based on the original French à la carte menu form, which in former times comprised 16 courses – with or without a choice in each course for guests to choose from. Each menu item was individually priced. The classic French à la carte chronological course structure is as follows: appetizers; soups; farinaceous dishes; eggs; fish and shellfish; entrées; grills; roasts; vegetables; salads; cold buffet items; sweets; ices; savories; cheeses; and chocolates, fruits, and bonbons.

In its modern and reduced format the à la carte menu has all the dishes that are offered to the guest listed, described, and individually priced. The à la carte menu is designed to enable guests to choose the meal according to their needs and tastes. An à la carte menu therefore should provide:

- A full listing and description of menu items available to the guest on a 'to order' basis
- A separate price for each menu item listed
- Menu items that are prepared and cooked to order
- A choice of menu items within each course
- A limitation of menu items offered in accordance with operational scope
- A representation or interpretation of the type of operation or cuisine/dining theme offered.

Note: The menu term 'entrée' is used in the United States to denote the main course or the main dish on the menu, whereas in Europe, Australia, and elsewhere it is used to denote appetizers or starters.

Reference

Greenstein, L. (1993) *A la carte: A Tour of Dining History*. Weimar, TX: Culinary & Hospitality Industry Publication Services.

JAKSA KIVELA
THE HONG KONG POLYTECHNIC
UNIVERSITY, HONG KONG SAR, CHINA

Accommodation, demand for

Development of the hotel sector comes as a result of a healthy tourism industry attracting international leisure visitors, coupled with an expanding economy which stimulates demand for business and leisure both domestically and through inbound business tourism (Travel Tourism and Intelligence, 2001).

There have been fundamental changes in the demand for hospitality accommodation during the past two decades. These have been in response to general socio-economic trends, in particular:

- Increasing prosperity and/or increased leisure time in developed economies (e.g., the introduction of the 35-hour working week in France in the 1990s has impacted directly on the demand for hospitality, as customers are taking short break holidays starting on a Thursday evening).
- Changes in the structure of family life (e.g., dual careers, smaller families holidaying together).

- Increasing urbanization.
- The transition from an industrial society to an information society.

These, however, are generalizations, and do not exclude certain paradoxes, such as market segments which are 'dollar-rich and time-starved.' To satisfy such a clientele requires new hospitality products involving technology and high value-added. Such trends have made demand more heterogeneous, and spread throughout the year.

As the hospitality industry is an important subset of tourism, its customers have become increasingly sophisticated and well-traveled, as international travel has become more 'democratized' and available to wider sectors of society This growth, from 25 million international arrivals in 1945 to 699 million in 2000, is forecast to more than double by 2020 to 1.6 billion (World Tourism Organization, 1999, 2000, 2002).

Changes in hospitality demand in response to such increases may be analyzed by geographic and market segments. Although the WTO (World Tourism Organization, 2002) suggests that Europe will remain the major tourist destination over the next 20 years, major growth in demand will be in Asia, particularly South-East Asia. Travel and demand for hospitality accommodation is still largely in response to a wish for 'sun and sea,' which brings, e.g., North and East Central Europeans to Mediterranean resorts.

Historically, international hotel companies have often responded to demand opportunities by developing luxury properties for international business leaders (a follow-the-client strategy), which largely ignored domestic markets. In terms of numbers, the latter, however, are usually several times as large as international markets. There is evidence, however, of what may be termed a 'convergence theory,' as large hotel chains such as Accor and Six Continents expand both with luxury hotels for the international business market, and budget and mid-tier hotels for the domestic market. These hotels are often developed through strategic alliances and joint ventures, as for example by Accor in Hungary and Poland.

By market segment, there have been major changes in the demand for hospitality accommodation. International business travel has developed into one of the most profitable market niches, especially with the development of the MICE market (meetings, incentives, conventions, and exhibitions). Research has correlated the demand for hotel accommodation with the rise in the service sector in national economies (Todd and Mather, 2001). One of the most significant changes in recent years has been the demand for 'mass customization' and for personalization, with business guests turning to boutique hotels in preference to the standardized product offered by the chains.

In what may be termed mid-sector mass markets, demand is now more informal, with growth in the budget, 'hard-budget,' and backpacker sectors. There is also evidence of increasing demand from clients for environmentally respectful hotels, especially among clients emanating from Scandinavian countries and Germany.

References

Todd, G. and Mather, H. (2001) Structure of the hotel industry in the new Europe. In Pricewaterhousecoopers, *New Europe and the Hotel Industry*. London: Pricewaterhousecoopers.

Travel and Tourism Intelligence (2001) *International Hotel Industry, Special industry sector report*. London: Travel and Tourism Intelligence.

World Tourism Organization (1999) *Tourism: 2020 Vision Executive Summary Updated*. Madrid: WTO.

World Tourism Organization (2000) *Tourism Market Trends: Europe*. Madrid: WTO.

World Tourism Organization (2002) *Tourism Highlights 2001*. Internet version: www.world-tourism.org. Madrid: WTO.

COLIN JOHNSON
SAN JOSE STATE UNIVERSITY, USA

Accommodation, supply of

Hospitality accommodation is difficult to define with precision, which presents problems in comparing statistics between countries and in identifying trends. Accommodation may include hotels, guest-houses, lodging-houses, bed and breakfast, inns, pensions, motels, and 'auberges.' In the United States, the industry is often referred to as lodging properties. Go and Pine (1995) use the general definition of 'lodging firms, including motels, in competition, and producing goods and services of a like function and nature.' Accommodation may be commercial, non-commercial or social in character, and may include not only hotels but also holiday camps, holiday villages, sanatoria, and villas and apartments for rent.

There is no universally accepted definition of what constitutes 'a hotel.' The most common definition, by the World Tourism Organization (WTO), refers to the category of 'hotels and similar establishments' thus:

> ... are typified as being arranged in rooms, in number exceeding a specified minimum; as coming under a common management; as providing certain services, including room service, daily bed-making and cleaning of sanitary facilities; as grouped in classes and categories according to their facilities and services provided ... (World Tourism Organization, 1994)

Although this definition is far from perfect and open to different interpretations in different countries, the WTO maintains that the total number of accommodation establishments covered in national statistics should represent at least 95% of total overnight stays in hotels and similar enterprises. This can provide at least a measure of consistency in reporting between countries. The WTO has calculated growth in hotel rooms at approximately 2.3% per year throughout the 1990s, and that by the end of 2000 there were approximately 16.3 million hotel rooms worldwide (Johnson, 2002).

In recent years, several major trends have affected the supply of accommodation and therefore the structure of international hotel companies, including increasing concentration and consolidation, the increased importance given to branding, and the impact of technology.

The major companies are indeed getting bigger. In 2001, the largest company, Cendant Corporation, controlled almost 550,000 rooms and was twice as large as the major hotel company (Holiday Inn) 25 years earlier. International companies now control an increasing proportion of the worldwide hotel stock: at the end of 2000, approximately 32% (Johnson, 2002). Owing to the effects of globalization, the industry has seen increasing competition, but with the continued dominance of major brands through companies

emanating from the United States. Branding is becoming increasingly important by generating higher market share, allowing hotels to charge premium prices, providing higher investor returns, and establishing customer loyalty (Travel and Tourism Intelligence, 2001).

As in other sectors, technology is playing an increasingly important role in the industry, through reservation systems, Internet procurement and the use of technology for customer relationship marketing (CRM). Additional important trends include the development of multiple brands by major operators, and the increasing importance of non-equity forms of involvement, to ensure global distribution of brand names. These factors have resulted in the increasing development of strategic alliances and partnerships, especially by major players in the industry. As a result, companies may have several forms of involvement (e.g., foreign direct investment, management contracts with minority equity, and franchising) in the same market. The decision they face, therefore, is where to compete and where to cooperate (Contractor and Kundu, 1998).

References

Contractor, F.J. and Kundu, S.K. (1998) Franchising versus company-run operations: modal choice in the global hotel sector. *Journal of International Marketing*, 6 (2), 28–53.

Go, F. and Pine, R. (1995) *Globalization Strategy in the Hotel Industry*. London: Routledge.

Johnson, C. (2002) Locational Strategies of International Hotel Operators in Eastern Central Europe. Doctoral thesis, Fribourg University, Switzerland.

Travel and Tourism Intelligence (2001) *The International Hotel Industry, Special industry sector report*. London: Travel and Tourism Intelligence.

World Tourism Organization (1994) *Tourism Market Trends: Europe*. Madrid: WTO.

COLIN JOHNSON
SAN JOSE STATE UNIVERSITY, USA

Account aging

Accounts receivable represents money owed to a hotel by its customers. To monitor how customers are paying their bills, hotels need to age the accounts and perform an aging schedule. This schedule is a table that lists the names of the customers, the unpaid account balances, and the number of days the accounts are outstanding. Unpaid account balance is the amount of funds that customers owe or have not paid to the hotel.

Normally, the days are categorized into 0–30 days (current), 31–60 days, 61–90 days, 91–120 days, and over 120. Some hotel companies may categorize these accounts in 45 days intervals. The aim of the hotel is to keep all accounts 'young' so that they will not be aged. An aged account has a higher probability to become a delinquent account.

Once the amounts of these categories or columns are totaled, estimated percentages of uncollectable, based on historical data, are multiplied to the totals to estimate the dollar amount that may be delinquent. This trend of accounts receivable balances, uncollectable amounts, and credit terms, should be tracked over time and analyzed so that the liquidity of the hotel company will not be compromised.

References

Cote, R. (1991) *Understanding Hospitality Accounting II.* Lansing, MI: Educational Institute of the American Hotel and Motel Association.

Weygandt, J., Kieso, D., and Kell, W. (1996) *Accounting Principles.* New York: John Wiley & Sons.

AGNES LEE DEFRANCO
UNIVERSITY OF HOUSTON, USA

Activity-based pricing

The hospitality industry can greatly benefit from the application of activity-based pricing, a new prototype for improving profitability by reducing pricing mistakes and emphasizing revenue maximization. Activity-based pricing (ABP) is a pricing method that combines market research data with cost accounting information to establish prices for products and services that result in designed profits (Daly, 2002).

The ABP concept emphasizes that profits can be maximized through knowing how much of a product's price is profit and through the elimination of pricing errors. Many companies sell products at an unintentional loss because they do not fully understand the costs related to the products and customers (Daly, 2002). For example, one method that the lodging industry uses to maximize room revenues is yield management. This technique forecasts demands for market segments that will generate the highest room rates, but it does not incorporate precise product and customer costs.

While most marketing departments of hospitality firms seem adequately equipped to estimate how many products and services they can sell at various prices, without complete cost information they cannot determine whether maximized revenue equals optimal profits. Faulty cost information can have devastating effects, because functions such as budgeting, cost control, product pricing, or any kind of financial analysis are based on the firm's cost information.

In highly competitive market conditions, hospitality operators cannot afford to be ignorant of their full costs. ABP can improve a company's profitability by providing the marketing and accounting departments with information that allows them to cooperatively establish accurate prices. The ABP process incorporates a technique called activity-based costing to determine comprehensive cost information for individual products/services and customers.

Using activity-based costing to conduct ABP

Activity-based costing (ABC) is an approach that was originally created for the manufacturing industry. ABC has major advantages over other costing methods through its ability to trace overhead costs to individual products, which allows for the calculation of operating profits for each unit produced (Cooper, 1989; Turney, 1991; Cooper and Kaplan, 1992; Garrison and Noreen, 1997). The general conditions that make manufacturing companies good candidates for the application of ABC systems, such as a diversity of resource consumption, a highly competitive environment, and the fact that product and resource consumption are not correlated with traditional cost allocation methods, also exist in the hospitality industry.

Kaplan and Cooper (1988) demonstrated that traditional contribution margin analysis could be greatly enhanced by the use of ABC, because over the past three decades, the costs that have seen the greatest increases in many businesses are overhead costs. Today's hospitality firms are both capital- and labor-intensive, where undistributed costs represent a large percentage of total costs. Although direct costs are distributed to profit centers in the hotel industry, overhead costs most often remain undistributed (Geller and Schmidgall, 1997). Furthermore, the restaurant industry generally does not allocate or trace overhead costs to individual menu items. The restaurant industry commonly establishes menu prices and manages menus by using contribution margin analyses (Bell, 2001).

ABC is conducted using a two-step process (O'Guin, 1991). First, all activities and their costs are identified. ABC uses three major categories of activities that drive expenses at the product level and that can be traced to individual products. The three categories are costs at the unit level, costs at the batch or production level, and product-sustaining costs. Unit level cost measures the expenses that are consumed proportionally with the number of units produced. For example, in the hospitality industry unit level costs are incurred every time a customer arrives and certain activities must be conducted, such as checking the customer in or seating him or her in the restaurant. Batch-related activities are performed each time a batch of goods is produced. Examples of batch-related activities for the restaurant business include purchasing, baking, and supervision. The third category includes activities that are performed to enable individual products to be produced and sold, which are labeled as product-sustaining activities. Hospitality industry examples are recipe research and testing, cost control, and staff training.

The second step in ABC costing traces activities back to the product or services that trigger them. Costs are then assigned based on the resources that products or services consume. Overhead costs are traced to certain products/services, which are then revealed in a 'Bill of Activities.' The total product cost is the total cost of all activities involved in producing a particular product or service. Finally, each product receives a unique value based on its individual consumption of resources.

Once ABC costs are calculated, accounting and marketing can cooperatively apply ABP by considering the relationships between volume, price, and cost. For example, if a restaurant wants to introduce a new menu item, management can forecast the number of items that it expects to sell at various price levels. Next, management can consider the relationships between cost and volume, based on a forecasted ABC cost for the menu item in conjunction with the relationship between price and volume. Finally, price can be determined at the point where total profits are maximized (Daly, 2002).

References

Bell, D. (2001) Food and Beverage Cost Control (course packet). Las Vegas: University of Nevada, Las Vegas, Department of Reprographic Services.

Cooper, R. (1989) The rise of activity-based costing – Part 4: What do activity-based cost systems look like? *Journal of Cost Management*, Spring, 38–49.

Cooper, R. and Kaplan, R.S. (1992) Activity-based systems: measuring the costs of resource usage. *Accounting Horizon*, 1–11.

Daly, J.L. (2002) *Pricing for Profitability: Activity-Based Pricing for Competitive Advantage*. New York: John Wiley & Sons.

Garrison, R.H. and Noreen, E.W. (1997) *Managerial Accounting*, 8th edn. New York: Irwin McGraw-Hill.

Geller, A. and Schmidgall, R.S. (1997) Should overhead costs be allocated? In R.S. Schmidgall, *Hospitality Industry Managerial Accounting*, 4th edn. Lansing, MI: Educational Institute of the American Hotel and Motel Association, pp. 285–293.

Kaplan, R.S. and Cooper, R. (1988) Measure costs right: no longer. *Journal of Management Accounting Research*, Fall, 2–15.

O'Guin, M. (1991) *The Complete Guide to Activity-Based Costing*. New York: Prentice Hall.

Turney, P.B. (1991) *Common Cents. The ABC Performance Breakthrough*. USA: Cost Technology.

CAROLA RAAB
UNIVERSITY OF NEW HAMPSHIRE, USA

Affiliate resort

According to industry research conducted by Interval International and Resort Condominiums International (major exchange companies), one of the more predominant reasons for purchasing a timeshare is the possibility of exchanging the purchased interval on a local, regional, national, or international level. However, it must be understood that this exchange process typically is done on an equivalency basis, meaning that unit weeks (i.e., intervals) are assigned a value based on demand, quality, pricing, etc. In short, this means that an individual owning an interval of lesser value will not be able to exchange outright for an interval of higher value without purchasing an equivalent unit week.

The basic premise underlying the exchange process is that a collection of timeshare resorts (either single site or multi-site) enter into an agreement with an exchange company to offer their owners the option of exchanging their interval (commonly a week) with another member that is seeking to swap their interval. It is this agreement between the timeshare developer and the exchange company that is known as an affiliation agreement. The affiliation agreement simply means that the developer has the right, at the point of sale, to offer the exchange company's services to this new owner as an additional service. Therefore, the owner makes a voluntary decision to buy into the exchange process by paying an annual fee to this exchange company for their services.

Reference

American Resort Development Association (2002) *The Timeshare Industry Resource Manual.* Washington, DC.

PIMRAWEE ROCHUNGSRAT
JAMES COOK UNIVERSITY, AUSTRALIA

Agency theory

The appropriate framework for understanding the contractual relationship, for instance, between a hotel operating company and a hotel owning company, is agency theory (Rodríguez, 2002). The agent is represented by the operating company, the principal is represented by the owning company and the two parties' relationship is mediated by a hotel management contract. Agency theory explains how to best organize these relationships in which the owning company (the principal) delegates the work to the operating company (the agent) who performs that work. More specifically, the focus of the theory is on the contract between the principal and the agent and the ways in which the contract can be made most efficient from the point of view of the principal. In determining the most efficient contract, agency theory makes certain assumptions about people, organizations, and information. It assumes that agents and principals will act in their self-interest to maximize their own welfare, and hence identifies two barriers to effective contractual performance – adverse selection and moral hazard (Fama and Jensen, 1983). Adverse selection is the condition under which the principal cannot ascertain if the agent accurately represents his ability to do the work for which he is being paid. Moral hazard is the condition under which the principal cannot be sure if the agent has put forth maximal effort.

References

Fama, E. and Jensen, M. (1983) Separation of ownership and control. *Journal of Law and Economics*, 26, 301–326.

Rodríguez, A.R. (2002) Determining factors in entry choice for international expansion. The case of the Spanish hotel industry. *Tourism Management*, 23 (6), 597–607.

KURTULUS KARAMUSTAFA
ERCIYES UNIVERSITY, TURKEY

Aims and objectives

Successful hospitality businesses have built their achievements by deciding very early on answers to the following questions: What will our business be? What should our business be? Who are our customers? And how do they consider value? For a hotel or a restaurant, on the face of it, the answers may seem to be simple, but the more these questions are examined, the more complex they become. The truthful answers to these questions may be considered to be our aims.

We must derive the methods of getting there. These can be considered the objectives. They can be considered the fundamental strategy of a business. The objectives must be operational. They must be capable of being converted into specific targets and goals. They must be capable of becoming the basis, as well as the motivation, of work and achievement.

In any business there will be multiple objectives, and the role of management is to balance a variety of needs and goals to achieve the aims. According to Drucker (1983, p. 93):

> Objectives are not fate; they are direction. They are not commands; they are commitments. They do not determine the future; they are means to mobilize the resources and energies of the business for the making of the future.

Reference

Drucker, P.F. (1983) *Management*. London: Pan Business Books.

PAUL REYNOLDS
UNIVERSITY OF SOUTH AUSTRALIA,
AUSTRALIA

Alarm annunciators

Annunciator panels or terminals are used to pinpoint the specific location of a fire. The alarm annunciator panel is located in a control center, such as the security office, engineering office or at a main entrance to allow trained personnel to identify the exact location, or zone, of the fire. Annunciators can monitor from 8 to 64 points and can be mounted on racks, panels, walls or desks. Some annunciators are flame- or explosion-proof and most of them come with standby power supply. The alarm annunciator at the control center is required to be audible and visible to alert employees, who might be away from their desk or concentrating on another task. Regulations in the Life Safety Code limit the size of the floor area that can be included in an alarm zone.

Reference

Puchovsky, M. (2000) A brief introduction to sprinkler systems for Life Safety Code users. In R. Cote (ed.), *Life Safety Code Handbook*. Quincy, MA: National Fire Protection Association, pp. 967–980.

CAROLYN LAMBERT
PENNSYLVANIA STATE UNIVERSITY, USA

Alliances

Organizations may cooperate with other organizations in pursuit of their objectives. The term 'alliance' is an umbrella term for a wide range of cooperative arrangements that can encapsulate suppliers, buyers, and competitors. As such, it covers many collaborative organizational forms including franchising, management contracts, joint-ventures, marketing, and purchasing consortia.

Primarily, alliances offer organizations a basis for creating a degree of stability in their external relationships and a method to secure access to resources or competences possessed by other organizations that support the attainment of strategic objectives. This might be in the form of particular operational expertise or knowledge regarding a particular market or competitive context. This is frequently the case where international hotel chains enter a new country in partnership with an indigenous hotel organization. Joining an alliance with local businesses permits firms to internalize market knowledge and expand local service capacity simultaneously. Moreover, the new country often serves as a platform that enables smooth penetration to neighboring countries (Preble *et al.*, 2000). Numerous international hospitality organizations like Hilton International or Sheraton form alliances with local chains in their penetration strategy to new markets. In this case, the major motivation involves exposure to local knowledge on the legal-political environment; the market; trade policies; access to qualified local executives and employees; as well as sharing financial risk via joint investments in property (equity alliance). Such alliances also enable international hospitality organizations to reap the benefit of economies of scale.

A recent trend in strategic alliances in hospitality involves agreement between an international hospitality organization, real estate investors, and hospitality managing corporations. In this 'triangle' shape of alliance, the hotel property is owned by the realtor; the hospitality chain grants its brand name and sometimes also access to international reservation systems; and the management company actually manages the hotel often according to the specifications of the brand recognized hospitality organization.

While alliances might be formed to achieve specific objectives and be dissolved on their attainment (i.e., joint ventures), or a more flexible open-ended network (Jarillo, 1993) type arrangement (e.g., a marketing consortium) they can often be used as a prelude to a more permanent arrangement such as a merger or takeover. Franchises and management contracts when used as a means of 'technology transfer' are good examples of the former, while marketing consortia, such as 'Leading Hotels of the World' is an obvious example of the latter. According to Chathoth and Olsen (2003) alliances may function on the basis of formal or informal agreements and can be classified into two categories – equity and non-equity alliances. Equity alliances demonstrate a mutual financial commitment and often imply a long-term commitment to the partnership. On the other hand, non-equity alliance allows for greater strategic flexibility as partners may decide to terminate an agreement and either act on their own or form an alternative alliance without the need to deal with shared equity.

According to Preble et al. (2000), franchising has become the world's leading form of strategic alliance. Franchising enables the franchisor to penetrate new markets and increase market share either domestically or globally with limited financial investment. The need for such a form of alliance is also apparent from the franchisee side,

often a single ownership operation that cannot take advantage of economies of scale. Clearly, the growing power of international hotel organizations leaves the single unit hotel without the adequate resources to attract guests, unless securing special non-imitable resources.

Alliances epitomize what de Wit and Meyer (1998) refer to as the 'embedded organization perspective' and represent an alternative arrangement to internal hierarchies (stand-alone firms) and market arrangements (external contracting). They are therefore seen as a solution to the problem of strategic coordination across the traditional boundaries of what we typically consider to constitute the 'organization'. In addition, the increasing prevalence of alliances highlights the need for hospitality organizations to proactively consider network level strategies in addition to the traditional focus upon business- and corporate level strategies.

Similarly, designing a network of outsourcing may represent another form of strategic alliance. Specifically, numerous hotels sign an agreement with suppliers to serve previously in-house services supplied by the hotel. Food and beverage services, safety and security measures, and even cleaning services are outsourced. The internalization process of such services into the core services of the hotel represents a high degree of confidence in suppliers that are considered as partners in hospitality services. The network of interorganizational partnership is also evident in the case of regional or county-wide marketing efforts. Such partnerships (marketing consortia) are formed in order to share marketing expenses or promote a particular destination, usually in the case of crisis or declining demand. Such alliances are based on the realization that sharing marketing efforts and resources may benefit all organizations that would be considered as competing under different circumstances. Another common alliance involves the creation of strategic marketing alliances where hotels, car rental companies, and airlines merge their reservation systems and marketing campaigns to protect or gain market share. The proliferation of Internet reservation systems and the growing usage of online reservations often justifies the formation of such consortia.

A different type of marketing consortia on a more modest, often on a regional, basis is evident in the case of rural tourism. The growing trend of small-scale rural tourism, mainly 'bed and breakfast' operations and small tourist attractions, often formed to solve unemployment problems, calls for the formation of alliances. Joint marketing efforts are used to create a shared 'brand' that distinguishes the region and to design packages of lodging and leisure activities that emphasize the competitive advantage of the region.

Chathoth and Olsen (2003) conceptualized strategic alliance as a process involving the following steps: (1) the strategic alliance decision criteria, usually based on resource and capabilities; (2) organizational complementarily – how to access the benefit potential of complimentarily strategic resource; and (3) governance of strategic alliances – the form of governance the allying firms choose during their inception and evolutionary phases.

References

Chathoth, P.K. and Olsen, M.D. (2003) 'Strategic alliances: a hospitality industry perspective', *International Journal of Hospitality Management*, 22 (4), 419–434.

de Wit, B. and Meyer, R (1998) *Strategy: Process, Content, Context*, London: International Thomson Business Press.

Jarillo, J.C. (1993) *Strategic Networks: Creating Borderless Organization*. Oxford: Butterworth-Heinemann.

Preble, J.F., Reichel, A., and Hoffman, R.C. (2000) 'Strategic alliances for competitive advantage: evidence from Israel's hospitality and tourism industry', *International Journal of Hospitality Management*, 19 (3), 327–341.

ARIE REICHEL
BEN-GURION UNIVERSITY, ISRAEL
J. STEPHEN TAYLOR
UNIVERSITY OF STRATHCLYDE, UK

Application service provider (ASP)

An ASP is an information technology service firm that deploys, manages, and hosts remotely a software application through centrally located servers in a rental or lease agreement. The service provision is made usually through the Internet or Virtual Private Networks (VPN). Usually the client pays a flat fee to sign up and a monthly fee for access to the application, training, expert support, and upgrades. Other payment schemes are based on usage rates (fees per transaction, number of screen clicks, or amount of computer time).

ASP benefits can be classified into bottom-line and top-line ones. Bottom-line benefits are cost-saving measures, thus enabling hospitality and tourism firms to better manage their resources. By sharing research and development costs with others, firms can maintain up-to-date systems at an affordable cost. Top-line benefits involve creating value, improving customer service, and enabling firms to add value to their services, enhancing their competitiveness and ultimately their profitability.

Initially hospitality and tourism firms were reluctant to adopt the ASP model, mainly due to the perception of data control loss, current telecommunication infrastructure problems, interface challenges with legacy systems and data transfer security. Problems are gradually being overcome and the model seems to receive greater acceptance.

References

Paraskevas, A. and Buhalis, D. (2002) Outsourcing IT for small hotels: the opportunities and challenges of using application service providers. *Cornell Hotel and Restaurant Administration Quarterly*, 43 (2), April, 27–39.

Rambler, M. and McGrew, G. (2000) The case for ASPs: opportunities and challenges with the ASP model, *Lodging*, December.

ALEXANDROS PARASKEVAS
OXFORD BROOKES UNIVERSITY, UK

Apprenticeship

Apprenticeship involves combining practical work with structured training leading to nationally recognized qualifications. Hospitality apprentices can learn in fields such as Front Office, Housekeeping, Food and Beverage or Cookery. In Australia, it seems the most popular hospitality apprenticeships are in the field of cookery, where hospitality apprentices enter into formalized agreements with employers known as 'training agreements.' Apprentices are paid a training wage adjusted to reflect the amount of time spent learning off-the-job and employers have access to public training funds to assist with training apprentices (Dockery *et al.*, 2001).

The apprenticeship method of instruction involves phases of modeling, coaching, scaffolding, and fading (Billet, 1994):

- *Modeling* involves an expert, such as a qualified chef, executing a task so that apprentices can observe this task being accomplished.
- *Coaching* is a process of observation and monitoring as apprentices carry out activities. Experts provide hints, feedback, clues, and tricks of the trade. The content of coaching is immediately related to the specific events or problems that arise from the apprentice completing the task.
- *Scaffolding* refers to the support that experts provide for the apprentices, through joint problem-solving, giving opportunities to acquire knowledge/skills and assisting with tasks that are too difficult for the apprentice to complete.
- *Fading* consists of a gradual removal of support until apprentices are able to conduct the task autonomously.

References

Billet, S. (1994) Situated learning in the workplace – having another look at apprenticeships. *Industrial and Commercial Training*, 26 (11), 9–16.

Dockery, A.M., Kelly, R., Norriss, K., and Stromback, T. (2001) Costs and benefits of new apprenticeships. *Australian Bulletin of Labour*, 27 (3), 192–204.

SALLY-ANN BURRISS
SOUTHERN CROSS UNIVERSITY,
AUSTRALIA

Arbitration

A method of dispute settlement in which an independent third party (e.g., industrial or labor tribunal) considers the arguments of both sides in a dispute and then makes a decision that is legally binding on the parties. Arbitration differs from other forms of dispute settlement such as mediation or conciliation (where an arbitrator attempts to find a compromise) because its decisions are legally binding (Davis, 2001). Some commentators advocate arbitration as a safety valve to avoid lengthy disputes. Others see merit in both and encourage parties to use mediation prior to arbitration. Many national regulatory systems require that dispute settlement provisions be incorporated in industry/workplace agreements and labor contracts. Arbitration-driven dispute resolution may result in a larger number of short work stoppages whereas mediation is likely to result in a smaller number of strikes that may occur for longer periods as each side attempts to gain the upper hand. However, the actual effectiveness of either approach is difficult to demonstrate. Hospitality and hotel employers generally join employer associations (such as hotel associations) that represent their interests during arbitral proceedings in industrial tribunals, though larger hotels are increasingly using their own internal HRM departments to conduct tribunal work (Woods, 2002).

References

Davis, E. (2001) *Australian Master Human Resources Guide 2002*. Sydney: CCH Australia Ltd.

Woods, R.H. (2002) *Managing Hospitality Human Resources*, 3rd edn. Lansing, MI: Educational Institute of the American Hotel and Lodging Association.

NILS TIMO
GRIFFITH UNIVERSITY, AUSTRALIA

Architectural plans

Architectural plans are drawings developed by architects, engineers or consultants to provide instructions for contractors and trades personnel. They may also be used to determine the amount of construction materials needed and to evaluate the travel patterns of building inhabitants. There are several types of architectural plans:

Plan view

The plan view is obtained when a building or room is cut horizontally 3' above the finished floor. The view shows all of the major equipment or furniture located in the room. This plan may be used to show equipment or furniture layouts, electrical or lighting systems, to calculate floor-coverings and to analyze travel patterns.

Elevation

An elevation is a vertical view of an exterior wall or an interior room. Exterior elevations show the building height, the size and height of windows, construction materials, roof lines, and orientation of the building. Interior elevations show the height of walls, equipment or furniture; window types and heights, and the height relationship of adjacent pieces of furniture or equipment.

Section

A section view is generally a vertical cut through a building or piece of equipment. Section views can show wall thickness, roof construction, stair construction or equipment construction.

Plot/survey

A plot view is a horizontal view of an entire property, showing the location of the building, contour lines, and landscaping. The plot view can be used to assess the topography, determine where rain water will drain, and the best location for parking. A survey view shows the legal boundary lines of the lot. This view also shows the distances from the property line to the building.

Detail

A detail view is used to show specific features of construction, such as cabinet drawers, decorative trim or furniture design. When the blueprint scale is too small for a tradesperson to use, a detail is drawn using a scale large enough for instruction. The detail drawing should clarify the understanding of the specified furniture or equipment.

Reference

Borsenik, F.D. and Stutts, A.T. (1997) *The Management of Maintenance and Engineering Systems in the Hospitality Industry*, 4th edn. New York: John Wiley & Sons.

CAROLYN LAMBERT
PENNSYLVANIA STATE UNIVERSITY, USA

ARDA international foundation

The American Resort Development Association was founded in 1969 to represent the interests of the resort industry in the United States. Today, with almost 1000 corporate members, ARDA is recognized internationally as the foremost organization promoting the resort development and vacation ownership industry.

In the midst of ARDA's growth, the timeshare segment of the industry believed that more resources were needed to address their unique needs. The International Timeshare Foundation (ITF) was founded in May 1982 to enhance the timesharing industry and help insure its longevity through research, technical studies, and education. With a membership of 54 Directors and Fellows and an endowment of over $1 million, the ITF has pursued its goals of industry education, research, and enhancement. During the past 14 years, the Foundation has provided funding for a number of significant research programs and through its think-tank sponsorships, brought critical issues affecting the future of vacation ownership to the attention of industry leaders.

As the industry grew, the Foundation's leaders began to think about ways to create an even stronger and more effective Foundation. In 1996, ARDA and the ITF decided to unify resources and create a more efficient entity to fulfill mutual goals. A strategic planning session was conducted in November 1996 and future trends of the resort development industry were identified. These include increased globalization, greater public awareness, more product diversity demands, larger and more affluent markets, limited availability of qualified personnel, constant technological changes, broadening of financing including more public financing and scrutiny, greater services by developers, and the enforcement of ethics and standards in new markets.

In response to these trends and needs, ARDA allowed the International Timeshare Foundation, a 501(c) (6) organization, to lapse and then in April 1997, incorporated the ARDA International Foundation (AIF). This new, nonprofit organization, established as a 501(c) (3) organization, is devoted to meeting the industry's research and education needs (see Table 1). More specifically, the AIF is devoted to identifying consistent, ongoing industry benchmarks, expanding research, offering professional development opportunities for those within the industry, analyzing technological change and its impact, and enhancing the public's knowledge of the timeshare industry. The vision for the ARDA International Foundation is for it to function as a research grant-making entity, not an implementing one, thereby keeping staff and overhead costs to a minimum.

While ITF's past efforts provided basic support, the AIF's ability to fund expanded programs requires a significant increase in funding. In order to fully invest in new initiatives, a minimum of $6 million additional endowment was needed. This amount, in addition to the $1 million existing endowment corpus provided through the original Foundation Directors and Fellows, will provide a stable and predictable base for sustaining the public education and research initiatives. 'The Time for the Timeshare Industry,' a capital campaign to raise these funds, was created. Cristel DeHaan gave a substantial amount of money to assist in the creation of new educational projects and programs for vacation ownership professionals and there are ongoing fundraising events and activities to help ensure that the AIF has the resources it needs to provide the necessary research studies and programs that ARDA members rely on and outside of the industry companies look to for future opportunities.

The current ARDA International Foundation mission is to '*Support, conduct and disseminate research and technical studies that will enhance and improve knowledge for the public and the industry, and develop educational resources that will optimize operations, value, acceptance and service for the industry and the public.*'

Among the many valuable services available to Association members, the educational arm of the ARDA International Foundation continues to serve the professional and educational needs

Table 1 Comparison of 501(c)(3) and 501(c)(4), (6), and (7) status

501(c)(3)	501(c)(6)
Organizational requirement	No requirement (or less stringent)
Assets must be dedicated to charitable purposes	No requirement to dedicate assets
Social activities must be insubstantial	Social activity may be anything less than 'primary'
Legislative activity must be insubstantial, or <20% if election made	No limit on legislative activity as long as it furthers the exempt purpose; legislative expenditures may limit the deductibility of dues
Absolute prohibition against political activity	Political activity permitted, but taxed
Must serve public purposes	Can serve the business purposes of the members
Donations are deductible as charitable contributions by donors on their tax returns	Donations not deductible as charitable contributions – businesses sometimes deduct as advertising; dues may be deductible as business expense
Eligible for low-cost non-profit bulk mailing permit	Not eligible for lowest bulk mail rates
Must take care to generate enough public support to avoid classification as a private foundation	Not an issue under (c)(6)
Exempt from federal income tax unless the organization has unrelated business income	Exempt from federal income tax unless the organization has unrelated business income

of the resort industry. Participation in the AIF Education programs signify professional awareness, enhance workplace performance and foster self-esteem. For industry professionals, participation in these programs demonstrates to consumers, state regulators, the media, and fellow industry professionals a commitment to quality and the ARDA Code of Standards and Ethics.

Anyone involved in the vacation ownership industry requires detailed knowledge of the industry's operational, legal, and regulatory frameworks. The following programs exist to create learning opportunities for people currently in the industry and others who seek to enter it. Toward this goal, AIF offers: publications covering the industry's ethical, legal, regulatory, and operational intricacies; study courses; tests which assess industry knowledge; and recognition of continuing educational efforts.

A timeshare industry resource manual has been created that is used as a general textbook covering all aspects of the industry, including marketing, sales, financing, resort management, state and local regulatory laws, and ARDA's Code of Ethics as well as much more. Based on the manual is an ARDA Qualification Exam that is given both to students and to professionals already serving in the industry. Passing the exam shows that the individual demonstrates a personal commitment to quality, industry knowledge, integrity, and pledges to adhere to the ARDA Code of Standards and Ethics.

Following the Qualification Exam are the two highly coveted professional designations, the Associate Resort Professional (ARP) and the Registered Resort Professional (RRP), which individuals apply for based on their experience and continuing education within the industry. The Associate and Registered Resort Professionals are awarded by ARDA to those industry leaders who have demonstrated their commitment to high ethical and professional standards through long-term participation in the educational and industry-related activities. A prerequisite for all individuals seeking these designations is active ARDA Advantage Plus membership (passing the ARDA Qualification Exam and maintaining individual membership to ARDA) and a minimum of five years of full-time industry employment.

A certain amount of credits is necessary to gain the designations and credits are earned through participation in educational and industry-related activities as well as tenure. Individuals must have demonstrated their commitment to high ethical and professional standards.

There is also a certification for supervisors, the Certified Timeshare Supervisor, that is based on programs developed with the American Hotel and Lodging Association. The hands-on series helps supervisors meet management's objectives for productivity and quality guest service, solve everyday workplace challenges, and gain respect, trust, and support from the people who work for them. The workbook provides a case-study approach to building supervisory skills and is designed for those in supervisory or management roles in the resort industry.

Another extremely important program of the ARDA International Foundation is the conduct of consistent, on-going surveys and research studies of the industry. Studies conducted include a Worldwide Timeshare study, a US Economic and a Financial Performance study. The Foundation is also greatly interested in setting up the process to collect specific industry data on a regular basis that will be analyzed by an independent economist. These independent reports on the industry will be released to the public, semi-annually, at first.

The Foundation also supports ARDA's Research Library, offering a compilation of recent industry research covering a broad range of topics from the state of the timeshare industry to fractionals to a market profile of future timeshare buyers.

Reference

http://www.arda.org. Accessed 8 January 2004

DARLA ZANINI
ARDA INTERNATIONAL FOUNDATION, USA

ARDA resort owners coalition

The ARDA Resort Owners Coalition is one of the American Resort Development Association's most successful and influential programs that brings together opposite sides of the timeshare industry, the developer and the consumer, to work together in achieving benefits for everyone. The ARDA is a national association in the United States that serves as the vacation ownership industry's sole lobbying, educational and information source. The ARDA Resort Owners Coalition (ARDA–ROC) is a nonprofit program, dedicated to preserving, protecting, and enhancing the ownership of vacation resort property. The coalition is comprised of timeshare owners dedicated to protecting the economic interests that owners have committed to their vacation experience. This goal is achieved by monitoring and responding to legislative and regulatory activity in all 50 states and Washington, DC that has an impact on timeshare owners. Since its inception in 1989, ARDA–ROC has served as an indispensable funding resource waging legislative battles across the United States. The influence of ARDA–ROC's grassroots network, as well as its team of attorneys and legislative representatives who specialize in tax, banking, and consumer issues, reaches from state governments to the nation's capital.

The coalition's growth has been remarkable. In 1994, just five years after it was established, ARDA–ROC membership grew to 130,000 owners. At the end of 1998, ARDA–ROC members numbered more than 330,000. The coalition members voluntarily contribute $3.00 a year to promote a legislative agenda at the local, state, and federal levels beneficial to timeshare owners. One state's actions can set a dangerous precedent and spread to other states if not dealt with effectively. Therefore, a successful outcome for owners in one state can be seen as a victory for all timeshare owners.

ARDA–ROC benefits the developer's owner relations, the Association's legislative efforts on the part of consumer protection, and thus, the industry itself. ARDA–ROC plays a critical educational role to the industry through three distinct methods. First, ARDA–ROC contributes to the industry by educating homeowners association (HOA) boards of directors via promotional materials like the short video *ARDA–ROC: Protecting Your Vacation for $3.00*, which explains the program's benefits. ARDA can provide assistance in highlighting the major benefits that come from participation when

educating the Board, and then secure the Board's approval to place the request for the voluntary contribution on the owner's assessment. Second, ARDA–ROC includes a letter in the member's annual assessment from ARDA or a company representative explaining the purpose and benefits of ARDA–ROC. The companies then simply forward the collected funds to ARDA–ROC. Third, ARDA communicates industry information to resort owners to make them feel involved, and more vested in their vacation ownership purchase. By engaging in this process, the members become aware of the sophistication of the industry, as they receive updates through their resort company on the Association's efforts for the industry. Other methods of communication include updates from ARDA–ROC's newsletter, meetings, and press releases in owner communications. Other ancillary materials that may be provided from ARDA are the ARDA–ROC audit and its funding history and there is an ARDA–ROC section of the American Resort Development Association's website, www.arda.org that can be used as a reference and has frequent updates and information for owners.

As federal and state governments search for creative ways to raise revenue, the vacation ownership industry becomes an attractive target for 'revenue enhancement' programs. The coalition funds an online computer-tracking system which monitors regulatory activity in all 50 states. ARDA State Affairs provides state legislative updates regarding the Association's efforts on these issues. ARDA–ROC keeps its owners aware of these events through its newspaper, *The ARDA–ROC Report*. ARDA–ROC also conducts research studies which are used to benefit timeshare owners. These studies serve to educate legislators about the economic benefits that timeshare owners provide to the community and the state and enhance the ability of our specialists in taxes, banking and consumer affairs conveying the message of vacation ownership to legislators. Legal analyses are also conducted to explore new ways to combat negative legislative efforts that could adversely affect timeshare owners.

In its short life, ARDA–ROC has achieved many meaningful legislative victories. ARDA–ROC was (a) successful in defeating the South

Carolina Department of Revenue's proposal to apply a 7% sales tax on exchanges – a significant legislative victory; (b) succesful in New Hampshire against an attempt to impose an 8% room and meals tax on timeshare maintenance fees; (c) passed legislation in Florida expediting HOAs' foreclosure on delinquent assessment liens – this law helps preserve the integrity and financial soundness of timeshare homeowners associations; and (d) successful in spearheading the enactment of the Homeowners Association Clarification Act of 1997, protecting timeshare reserves, carryover, and prepaid assessments from being unfairly taxed. This was the culmination of a lengthy hard-fought battle with the IRS. Without the enactment of this Act, many HOAs would have been taxed on their reserves and likely forced to levy special assessments on owners. In recent years, ARDA–ROC efforts in Washington, DC also have been successful in defeating efforts to eliminate the federal tax provision that generally permits an owner to deduct the interest on a time-share loan. Many battles undoubtedly lie ahead and the coalition's legislative record will be tied closely to its ability to grow and swiftly respond to every challenge.

Reference

http://www.arda.org. Accessed 8 January 2004

CHANTAL ROTONDO
ARDA INTERNATIONAL FOUNDATION, USA

Artificial intelligence (AI)

A branch of computer science focusing on the automation of intelligent behavior, such as reasoning, learning, and problem-solving. AI seeks to construct intelligent machines; formalize knowledge and mechanize reasoning; make use of computational models to understand behavior of people, animals, and intelligent agents; make it possible to work with computers as easily as with friendly experts. Areas of AI are: (a) knowledge representation and articulation (representation of the world in an efficient and expressive manner); (b) learning and adaptation (extraction of knowledge from instructions, experience, and data); (c) deliberation, planning, and acting (making decisions and controlling them); (d) speech and language processing (capability to communicate in and translate written and spoken language); (e) image understanding and synthesis (analysis of images and video, and customized presentation of information); (f) manipulation and locomotion (replication and surpassage of natural hands), etc.; (g) autonomous intelligent agents and robots (creation of entities capable of interacting with the environment); (h) multi-agent systems (agents capable of working together); (i) cognitive modeling (replication of human cognition); (j) mathematical foundations (formalization of methods and techniques). AI went through a period of success followed by failure, and is becoming a steadily growing and maturing technology now. AI could help tourists to better plan their trips and choose the most appropriate services from huge information sources, and also support hospitality management.

References

Doyle, J. and Dean, T. (1995) Strategic directions in artificial intelligence. *ACM Computing Surveys*, 28 (4), 653–670.

Russel, S. and Norvig, P. (1995) *Artificial Intelligence: A Modern Approach.* Englewood Cliffs, NJ: Prentice-Hall.

BOZIDAR KLICEK
UNIVERSITY OF ZAGREB, CROATIA

Association Market

By definition, associations are groups of people who find strength in numbers while sharing common interests of industry, profession, charitable activity, hobbies, or philanthropic action (ASAE, 2003a). Associations are a subset of a type of organization typically referred to as 'nonprofits.' Outside the United States nonprofits are often called nongovernmental organizations (NGOs) or civil society organizations. Like the greater classification of nonprofits, associations may in fact charge fees, generate revenue, and generate a profit. The difference is that nonprofits, unlike businesses, do not exist to make money for owners or investors (BoardSource, 2002). Instead profits made by these types of organizations are reinvested back into the organization.

Most nonprofit organizations and associations are also structured as tax-exempt organizations under the US Internal Revenue Code (IRC). This means that the organization is exempt from paying income tax on income earned from activities related to its tax-exempt purpose. The two primary IRC classifications under which associations fall are 501(c) (6) and 501(c) (3). 501(c) (6) is the most common classification for associations because this section governs trade associations, business leagues, and chambers of commerce. To be classified as 501(c) (6), an organization must possess the following characteristics:

1. It must be an association of persons having some common business interest and its purpose must be to promote this common business interest.
2. It must be a membership organization.
3. It must not be organized for profit.
4. No part of its net earnings may inure to the benefit of any private shareholder or individual (ASAE, 2004).

As of April 2002, the US Internal Revenue Service (IRS) recognized 71,032 organizations as tax exempt under section 501(c) (6) of the Internal Revenue Code (ASAE, 2004).

Some associations are organized under section 501(c) (3), although this section of the tax code is technically for charities, foundations, and other donor-based organizations. To be classified as 501(c) (3), an organization must possess the following characteristics:

1. It must be organized and operated exclusively for one of the following purposes: charitable, religious, educational, scientific, literary, testing for public safety, fostering national or international amateur sports competition, or the prevention of cruelty to children or animals.
2. No part of its net earnings may inure to the benefit of any private shareholder or individual.
3. It may not attempt to influence legislation as a substantial part of its activities and it may not

participate at all in campaign activity for or against political candidates (ASAE, 2004).

There are many more 501(c) (3) organizations than 501(c) (6), but most would be considered 'charities' or generically referred to as 'nonprofits' rather than 'associations.' Most associations are membership-based trade associations or business leagues organized under 501(c) (6).

Size and scope of the association industry

More than 147,000 associations exist in the United States, representing nearly every industry, profession, charity, hobby, cause, and interest. This figure is estimated to include more than 127,340 local, state, and regional associations, 20,285 national associations, and 2409 international associations headquartered in the United States. The association field is growing, with as many as 1000 new associations being formed each year. Nine out of 10 American adults belong to an association, and one out of four belongs to four or more associations, according to a 1998 study conducted by the American Association of Retired Persons (AARP) (ASAE, 2003b).

Associations are big business in the United States, employing 295,000 people. In fact, more people work for nonprofit organizations than for the federal government and all 50 state governments combined (8.6 million versus 6.8 million). Washington, DC is home to more associations than any other city (3500), with New York City (1900) and Chicago (1500) in second and third place (ASAE, 2003b).

Association educational programs

Ninety-five percent of associations offer educational programs to their members. Convention planning and other convention activities are the second most prevalent activity, in which 89% of associations engage. Other common association activities include using websites and e-mail to share information with members (81%), and public information activities (79%) (ASAE, 2004).

Although many people perceive that associations are funded primarily through membership dues, the reality is that membership dues represent less than 36% of total revenue for most associations today (ASAE, 2003a). Educational programs and conventions are important financial activities for associations, accounting for nearly one-third of association revenue (Connell, 2002, p. 22).

Because they are nonprofit organizations, associations are sometimes underestimated as a valid target market for goods and services. Associations have spending power, as associations' annual budgets now exceed $21 billion. As mentioned above, a significant part of associations' time and budgets are dedicated to offering educational programs to members in the guise of meetings, conventions, and trade shows. In fact, membership education and training is the largest overall budget item for associations, accounting for $3.6 billion per year or about 18% of the average association's budget (ASAE, 2004).

Not only do associations spend significant money offering educational programs to members, but association members spend in excess of $10 billion per year to participate in educational programs offered by associations. Association-sponsored meetings and conventions account for more than 26 million overnight stays in hotels each year (ASAE, 2004).

Association events

The meetings industry is estimated to be a $98 billion industry, weighing in as the 23rd largest contributor to the Gross National Product. Association meetings and events account for a large part of this industry, with associations spending more than $66.4 billion annually on conventions, expositions, and seminars (ASAE, 2004). While associations hold a smaller number of meetings with fewer total annual attendees than corporations, association meetings and conventions account for a much larger share of total expenditures than corporate meetings (Meetings & Conventions, 2002, p. 6).

Association meeting budgets are estimated at $1.4 million annually (Meeting Professionals International, 2004). Common association events include conventions, educational seminars, and trade shows. These events are frequently held concurrently as part of a major convention program, although they may be held at different times and in different locations. A majority of associations hold major conventions, to which membership and sometimes non-members are invited. A convention is 'an event where the primary activity of the attendees is to attend educational sessions, participate in meetings/discussions, socialize, or attend other organized events. There is a secondary exhibit component' (Convention Industry Council, 2004). Attendance at conventions is usually voluntary, although conventions for professions whose members are required to earn some kind of continuing education units (CEUs) may be more likely to attend as association conventions are often geared toward providing specific educational programming geared toward the members' needs. Eighty percent of association members say that meetings are critical to their profession (Meetings & Conventions, 2003, p. 26). A 2002 survey indicated that 75% of associations hold an annual convention, while 12% have conventions twice a year, and 5% hold conventions every other year. Only 11% of associations surveyed said they do not hold a convention at all (Meetings & Conventions, 2002, p. 36).

The program content of an association convention may be based on information gathered from program or education committees, member (and non-member) surveys, focus groups, sampling techniques, evaluations of previous events, and association staff departments who have special insight into topics and trends of interest to the association's members. Other sources of program information may include industry suppliers, an association's credentialing program, computer bulletin boards, responses to a call for programs, chapter meeting agendas and evaluations, and the programs of meetings held in complementary industries or professions (Cox, 1997, p. 302).

An association convention is comprised of an agenda of meetings and events of various sizes and types. Depending on the learning objectives for each session, an association convention may include one or more general sessions, various breakouts or educational workshops, an exhibition or trade show, guest programs, and social events (Cox, 1997, p. 303). A general session, also sometimes called a keynote session or plenary session, is open to all convention participants. The general session speaker is often a high level association or industry person or a celebrity. The general session topic and speaker often set the tone for the entire convention and the title and topic of the opening general session may be tied to the theme of the convention.

An association convention usually has a number of concurrent breakouts, workshops, or seminars that allow attendees to customize their learning by following certain programming 'tracks' or their own areas of interest. The number of concurrent breakout sessions held is determined by the number of attendees, the availability of meeting rooms of appropriate size and location for breakouts, and the variety of educational interests that the attendees have. Breakouts may be more or less interactive, depending on the needs of the audience and the skill of the presenter(s).

An association convention may also include an exhibition or trade show as a component of convention programming. An exhibition is 'an event at which products and services are displayed. The primary activity of attendees is visiting exhibits on the show floor. These events focus primarily on business-to-business (B2B) relationships' (APEX, 2004). A trade show is similar to an exhibition, except that it exhibits 'products and/or services held for members of a common or related industry. Not open to the general public' (APEX, 2004). Thus, a trade show may be open only to people registered for and attending an association's convention. If there is a demand for access to a trade show, some associations will have a 'Show Only' registration fee that allows people to attend the trade show portion of a convention, but not the educational programming or social events.

Depending on the number of exhibition booths needed in a trade show or exhibition, the event may require a significant amount of function space. Standardized exhibit booths are 10 ft × 10 ft or 8 ft × 10 ft, so a trade show with 100 10 ft × 10 ft exhibit booths will require 10,000 net square feet of space just for the exhibit booths themselves. To account for additional trade show floor space for aisles, food areas, exhibitor lounge, and other show floor needs, this net square foot figure is typically doubled: a 10,000 net square foot show will require approximately 20,000 gross square feet of function space (Connell, 2002, p. 370). Because trade shows are so space-intensive, this type of event is often held in a convention center or in a hotel that has an exhibit hall. Most convention centers have meeting space of various sizes in addition to several exhibit halls. Because most association conventions have the additional programming of general sessions and smaller breakouts, convention centers are made for – and are often the best fit for – association conventions. A smaller trade show using table top exhibits, which consist basically of 6' or 8' rectangular tables with table cloths and skirts, may be held in a hotel ballroom or pre-function space.

There is a growing tendency for convention attendees to bring guests with them to an association convention. For this reason, guest programs that provide the spouse, partner, child, or guest of an attendee with opportunities for social interaction and recreation have become an important part of association conventions. Such guest programs can boost meeting attendance, add value to the meeting experience, and enhance the image of the association (Connell, 2002, p. 239). As a side benefit, active guests who are engaged in activities planned especially for them are less likely to draw association members and convention attendees away from the educational programming provided for attendees' benefit (Cox, 1997, p. 304).

Because networking can be as much a motivation for attendance at an association convention as education, most conventions contain a variety of social events, including luncheons, dinners, receptions, and parties. In a recent survey, half of association meeting planners surveyed said that special events held at a trade show or conference were *very important* to the organization's overall mission: 8.4% said the special events were *critical* to the organization's mission (Event Solutions, 2004, p. 92). From the attendee's perspective, 69% of meeting attendees said that meals and snacks were *very important* or *somewhat important* at meetings; 41% said that entertainment was *very/somewhat important* (Meetings and Conventions, 2003, p. 26). Thus, the power of special events, social events, and networking opportunities should not be overlooked as an important part of association conventions and meetings.

References

American Society of Association Executives (ASAE) (2004) *About Associations.* Dated 23 March, retrieved 16 July 2004, from http://www.asaenet.org/asae/cda/index/1,1584,ETI17733_MEN3_NID4067,00.html

American Society of Association Executives (ASAE) (2003a) *Starting an Association.* Retrieved 16 July 2004 from http://www.asaenet.org/asae/cda/index/1,ETI16465,00.html

American Society of Association Executives (ASAE) (2003b) *Associations in a Nutshell.* Retrieved 16 July 2004 from http://www.asaenet.org/asae/cda/index/1,ETI10471,00.html

BoardSource (2002) *What is the Nonprofit Sector?* Retrieved 14 July 2004 from http://www.boardsource.org/FullAnswer.asp? ID=82.

Connell, B. (2002) *Professional Meeting Management,* 4th edn. Chicago, IL: Professional Convention Management Association Education Foundation.

Convention Industry Council (CIC) (2004) *APEX Industry Glossary.* Retrieved 16 July 2004 from http:// glossary. conventionindustry.org/default.asp

Cox, J.B. (1997) *Professional Practices in Association Management.* Washington, DC: American Society of Association Executives (ASAE).

Event Solutions (2004) *2004 Black Book.* Tempe, AZ.

Meeting Professionals International (MPI) (2004) *FutureWatch 2004.* Retrieved 23 March 2004 from http://www.mpiweb.org/media/home/futurewatch2004.pdf

Meetings & Conventions (2003) *2003 Meeting Attendee Survey.* New York: M&C.

Meetings & Conventions (2002) *2002 Meetings Market Report.* New York: M&C.

TYRA W. HILLIARD
THE GEORGE WASHINGTON UNIVERSITY, USA

Atmospherics

The term 'atmospherics' refers to the study of the physical environment where some activity occurs. The physical environment is defined as the material surroundings of a place. For example, a physical environment may be the lobby of a hotel or the swimming pool/spa area of a property. Atmospherics studies the effect that the physical environment has on people's behaviors.

Early research in the field of environmental psychology focused on how the physical environment affected behavior in workplace, educational, and penal institutional/correctional settings. Mehrabian and Russell (1974) suggest that a combination of environmental factors and personality characteristics will result in an individual's emotional response to the physical stimuli encountered in an environment. This emotional response will influence the individual's behavior in the environment, leading the individual to approach, to avoid, to explore, to affiliate with others, or to take other actions.

Research on the effect of 'atmospherics' in business is a relatively recent phenomenon. The term 'atmospherics' was first proposed by Kotler, referring to the study of a retail store's atmospheric effects on consumer behavior (Turley and Milliman, 2000). The concept is that consumer behavior can be changed or controlled by manipulating elements in the physical environment. Most of the research in atmospherics has been conducted in retail settings to determine the factors that elicit an approach or avoidance behavior from potential store patrons. Once store patrons enter the store, retailers assess the effects of several environmental variables on the customer's behavior inside the store, including the length of time spent in the store and effects on store revenue.

Elements of atmospherics

One way of looking at the atmospheric effects of an environment is the 'Servicescapes' framework. Mary Jo Bitner (1992) proposed a framework for examining the effect of the physical environment on human response in a services delivery situation. Her 'Servicescapes' framework identifies several environmental variables, divided into three general categories: (1) ambient conditions, (2) space/function, and (3) signs, symbols, and artifacts. Individuals perceive these variables, as well as other people, in the environment, resulting in internal responses that lead to external behaviors.

'Ambient conditions' are the conditions that affect the five senses: touch, taste, smell, vision, and sound. Ambient conditions include such factors as odor, lighting, color, background noise, flavor, and texture. 'Signs, symbols, and artifacts' include such items as signage in a space, artwork, general style of decoration, personal items belonging to individuals within a space, or the attire of people within a space. This dimension changes constantly as people enter and leave a space.

The space/function dimension of the physical environment is the layout of an area, as well as the equipment and furniture within the area. Some of the interesting aspects of the space/function dimension include spatial arrangements of objects and/or furniture in the space and the presence of other people in the space. Our interactions with others and with our environment may be influenced by the dimensions (size, largeness, smallness) of the physical environment, by the placement of objects within the physical environment, or by our proximity to other people in the environment.

Atmospherics in the hospitality industry

Services product design and marketing originally focused on the traditional 'Four Ps' of the marketing mix – product, price, promotion, and place (distribution). While the four factors are still applicable in the services industries, they are incomplete, particularly in the hospitality industry. Services marketing and management requires consideration of four additional characteristics of services – intangibility, inseparability, variability, and perishability – that are not typical in product marketing. The customer becomes part of the service-creation environment and the physical surroundings become part of the product itself. The product is evaluated while the customer is still in the service environment, rather than at a later time as is often possible with a tangible product. The employees

and other customers at a restaurant or hotel also become part of the product, as the customer interacts or is affected by them. Understanding the overt and subtle effects of the environment and managing them properly is important to provide the best product possible for the right customers.

References

Bitner, M.J. (1992) Servicescapes: the impact of physical surroundings on customers and employees. *Journal of Marketing*, 56, 57–71.

Mehrabian, A. and Russell, J.A. (1974) *An Approach to Environmental Psychology*. Boston, MA: Massachusetts Institute of Technology.

Turley, L.W. and Milliman, R.E. (2000) Atmospheric effects on shopping behavior: a review of the experimental evidence. *Journal of Business Research*, 49, 193–211.

DINA MARIE V. ZEMKE
UNIVERSITY OF NEW HAMPSHIRE, USA

Attendee

A combination of delegates, exhibitors, media, speakers, and guests/companions who attend an event. Attendee scope includes where attendees come from. It is directly related to the spending characteristics of attendees, who fall into each of these categories:

- *International:* Draws a national and international event audience; 15% or more of event delegates reside outside of event host country.
- *National:* Draws a national event audience; more than 40% of delegates reside outside of a 400 mile (640 km) radius of event venue.
- *Regional:* 60% of delegates reside within a 400 mile (640 km) radius of the event venue; delegates may reside in a multi-state area and/or a regionally homogeneous international area.
- *State/province:* More than 80% of delegates reside in event state/province (or event-sponsoring state/province when held in state/province other than home state/province; more than 20% of delegates reside outside a 50 miles (80 km) radius of the event site; state/provincial audiences are less inclined to

use air travel and local auto rental than regional audiences.

- *Local:* 80% of delegates reside within a 50 miles (80 km) radius of the event site; local audiences typically do not require overnight accommodations.

Reference

APEX Glossary, http://glossary.convention-industry. org/

SANDY STRICK
UNIVERSITY OF SOUTH CAROLINA, USA

Attitudes, behavior, and reasoned action

Attitudes, behavior, and reasoned action all relate to the way people behave in the workplace. This is critically important in the intensive service context of the hospitality industry.

More formally, attitudes are defined as 'a mental state of readiness, learned and organized through experience, exerting a specific influence on a person's response to people, objects and situations with which it is related' (Ivancevich, Olekalns, and Mattesson, 1997, p. 752). Attitudes shape the way the world is viewed and how people organize themselves in response to external stimuli. Originally, the word attitude related to the physical orientation of an object – for example, the 'attitude' of an airplane refers to the angle the plane adopts as it is about to land. However, in recent times, it has more generally been used to refer to our emotional orientation, even feelings, towards things as shaped by our opinions.

Behavior is the broad set of actions undertaken to fulfill various needs and wants. It is formally defined as 'anything a person does, such as talking, walking, thinking or daydreaming' (Ivancevich, Olekalns *et al.*, 1997, p.752). Behavior does not necessarily have to be conscious or planned. For example, we can do things out of habit without even being aware that we are doing them.

Finally, and in contrast to doing things out of habit, our reasoned actions are those behaviors which we consciously decide to do in order to meet our specific goals. The 'theory of reasoned action' was initially proposed by Fishbein and Ajzen in the mid-1970s. According to them, the central factor is the individual's intention to perform a behavior and that one's intentions capture one's attitude towards the behavior, one's perception of control in the situation and one's understanding of acceptable behaviors (subjective norm). For a detailed discussion on this theory see Ajzen (1991).

Whilst our attitudes have a major influence on our behavior, particularly in hospitality (Deery, 2002), a variety of other factors have a major impact on the development of our attitudes (Ashkansay, 2002). Generally, they are learned both from our own experiences and the general socialization process wherein we tend to adopt the views and perspectives of the important people in our life such as parents, older relatives, significant peers, and school teachers. Recent research has further indicated that how we develop these attitudes can also be a function of our personality and psychological type, which in turn are a function of our genetic composition. This is particularly the case with how we acquire and interpret information and then express our understanding of that information in our behaviors.

For example, whilst some people have an inherent and natural ability to see things in a broad context, others are more adept at seeing things in fine, highly specific, detail. Given that one's perception is one's reality, this can lead to people developing attitudes that may reflect a broad understanding of the wider context, whilst others may prefer to see things in terms of specific details. In a similar fashion, some people have an inherent and pervading desire to express themselves in a very structured logical and pragmatic fashion. In contrast, others may have a preference to express themselves in a fashion which is reflective of a desire for harmony and comfort rather than logic and order.

The ongoing debate about the role and impact of genetics (nature) and socialization (nurture) on our attitudes, behavior, and reasoned action will provide further insight and understanding of why we work and deal with ourselves and others in the way that we do. However, at this stage, we have sufficient understanding of these functions to identify their consequences for our work, particularly in the hospitality industry.

However, this should not be interpreted as a form of determinism in which one's attitudes and behaviors predetermine them to a particular form of employment or industry. Rather, our knowledge of these phenomena should help inform employment decisions and professional and personal development agendas (Deery and Jago, 2001). Whilst playing to one's strengths is considered a good strategy, rounding out and broadening one's skill base is also a good thing with regard to long-term career progression. If you can reflect upon why you think and behave in a particular way, and then understand why, you must be in a better position to influence, even modify, your behavior to help you achieve your goals.

In hospitality, this self-awareness and discipline can be of considerable advantage. Hospitality work tends to involve long hours with bursts of intense activity driven by a combination of production and customer interaction pressures. Whilst some people are considered 'naturals' in this environment, others, who still have a commitment to hospitality, may struggle to cope in this environment and consequently find themselves under-achieving in the industry. However, if these people are able to recognize that their actions and behaviors in these situations are a function of their attitudes, which are in turn a function of their socialization and genetic make-up, then they can embark upon a program to modify their attitudes by way of 're-learning' and adjusting their attitudes towards the situation. In turn, they can also develop specific strategies to help them deal with the stresses and pressures that challenge their effectiveness in the workplace.

Whilst it is clearly not possible to alter our genetic make-up at this stage, it is possible to alter our attitudes and thus behavior and reasoned action. We can do this by firstly, thinking about our actions and planning them and fundamentally by thinking about why we behave in the way we do and why we have the attitudes that we have. By applying ourselves to developing new ways of interpreting information and considering other perspectives, we will be able to alter our attitudes. In turn, our new-found attitudes may lead us to engage in new forms of behavior, and finally, a more considered and thoughtful approach to pursuing our goals can lead to changes in our planned actions.

References

Ajzen, I. (1991) The theory of planned behavior. *Organizational Behavior and Human Decision Processes*, 50, 179–211.

Ashkansay, N.M. (2002) Studies of cognition and emotion in organizations: attribution, affective events, emotional intelligence and perception of emotion. *Australian Journal of Management*, (27), Special Issue, 11–20.

Deery, M. (2002) Employee work attitudes, mobility and promotional opportunities in the accommodation sector. *11th Annual CHME Research Conference, Leeds, Council for Hospitality Management Education*. Leeds Metropolitan University.

Deery, M. and Jago, L.K. (2001) Hotel management style: a study of employee perceptions and preferences. *Hospitality Management* 20, 325–338.

Ivancevich, J., Olekalns, M., and Matteson, M. (1997). *Organizational Behavior and Management*, Sydney: Irwin.

PAUL A. WHITELAW
VICTORIA UNIVERSITY, AUSTRALIA

Attribution theory

Attribution theory (Heider, 1958) attempts to explain how individuals interpret causes of behavior based on their past knowledge and experiences. They can attribute behavior either to internal factors such as ability, skill or effort, or to external factors such as rules, policies or environment. This is known as our locus of control and can influence our behavior at work. For example, if a customer complains about poor service from their waiter, the restaurant manager might agree that the waiter has been slow and rude (internal attribution). Alternatively, they might attribute this to the restaurant being overcrowded or short-staffed (external attribution). The attribution of these events might then influence how the restaurant manager deals with the waiter.

Employees with an internal locus of control are more likely to believe that they can influence their own performance and therefore are more likely to be satisfied in their work. However, there are international differences: Berry *et al.* (1992) highlighted that locus of control varies across cultures, with employees in Far Eastern countries more likely to have an external locus than Western countries.

References

Berry, J.W., Poortinga, Y.H, Segall, M.H., and Dasen, P.R. (1992) *Cross Cultural Psychology: Research and Application.* Cambridge: Cambridge University Press.

Heider, F. (1958) *The Psychology of Interpersonal Relationships.* New York: John Wiley & Sons.

GILLIAN KELLOCK HAY
GLASGOW CALEDONIAN UNIVERSITY, UK

Attrition clauses

Most hotel contracts today have attrition clauses that set forth the fees that an organization must pay if it fails to use the sleeping room block commitment it has previously booked. This clause contains formulas that stipulate the amount of liquidated damages for which the organization will be held liable. The attrition fee is based on the difference between the total room nights booked by the organization and the total number of rooms actually used. There is often a 10% attrition allowance before fees are imposed. The amount is generally multiplied by an agreed upon percentage of the room rate to calculate the fee due in terms of lost profit for the facility. Experienced meeting planners require language that stipulates that rooms resold by the hotel are not included in the penalty fee. The contract should contain an audit provision requiring the hotel to provide complete housing lists, daily reports, city ledgers, and any other documents to support attrition claims before the group is required to pay an attrition fee. This documentation will help identify additional rooms that should be credited to the block, as well as the number of room nights sold by the hotel or taken off the market for renovations or repair or invoiced to other groups or individuals as attrition, cancellation or no-shows. It should also be stipulated that attrition charges will be calculated as cumulative, not by room night. If attrition occurs, the group may also have to pay the hotel function room rental charges and lose or pay for complimentary concessions that were made based on anticipated attendance and revenue.

Reference

Connell, B., Chatfield-Taylor, C., and Collins, M.C. (eds) (2002) *Professional Meeting Management.* Chicago: Professional Convention Management Association.

CYNTHIA VANNUCCI
METROPOLITAN STATE UNIVERSITY, USA

Auto closing device

A fire door is impaired when chocked or blocked open and it is unattended. Opening a fire door and walking through it, or holding it open for material to pass through it, is not an impairment as long as someone is there to close the door when done. For safety and security, hotels may install an auto-closing device on each fire door. It is a device that automatically takes the fire door back to the closed position.

When a guest walks out from a room, the auto closing device will start its function by closing the door automatically. It also serves a security purpose. Furthermore, when fire breaks out on a hotel guest floor and the hallway fills with smoke, the auto-closing device can prevent the spread of fire and smoke through the hallway by containing it in the compartment of origin. It can provide a safer place for the guest, i.e., inside the guestroom awaiting rescue. The material commonly used for fire doors is timber. The material must withstand fire for 30 or 60 minutes and be approved and certified by the relevant authority.

References

http://www.pppl.gov/eshis/PPPL_docs.shtml.
Allen, D.M. (1983) *Accommodation and Cleaning Services*. London: Hutchinson.

BENNY CHAN
THE HONG KONG POLYTECHNIC
UNIVERSITY, HONG KONG SAR, CHINA

Automated mini bar

Mini bars have been in use for some time, consisting of a refrigerator in the guest's room containing drinks and other items (snacks, sun cream or disposable cameras), which the guest can consume if they wish. The guest is then charged for those items consumed. Manual systems rely on the mini bar being restocked daily, and the consumption noted. An automated mini bar has sensors that record the removal of items. These sensors are linked to a computer, which records the removal of each item. This produces information about consumption that is added to the guest's bill, as well as a list of items to be restocked by the hotel staff.

Automated mini bars have the advantage of reducing the demand for room service. They can be locked, for instance when children are staying in the room. They ensure that items are added to the guest's bill immediately, reducing the risk of a guest checking out before the consumption is noted and charged for.

In some systems the sensors may be triggered by guests moving the items, which can lead to guests being charged for items they have not consumed. This can then lead to complaints and arguments from customers.

References

Braham, B. (1988) *Computer Systems in the Hotel and Catering Industry*. London: Cassell.

O'Connor, P. (2000) *Using Computers in Hospitality*, 2nd edn. London: Cassell.

JOHN NIGHTINGALE
LEEDS METROPOLITAN UNIVERSITY, UK

Average check

Meeting customer needs is the primary purpose of any organization. To achieve that goal, organizations strive to understand the nature of their customers first. Average check (also referred to as 'guest check average') is one of the common tools available to the foodservice industry to measure the amount of money spent per customer. This information is extremely useful in managing a restaurant. Average check is used in foodservice operation for various purposes, including allocating labor dollars, forecasting unit sales, assessing employee productivity, measuring the effectiveness of suggestive selling, effective usage of floor space in the dining area, calculating cost percentage per meal, comparative analysis across operational units, etc. In on-site foodservice operations, average check is sometimes translated into 'average transaction.'

Average check is calculated by dividing total revenues by total number of customers.

$$\text{Average check} = \text{Total revenues}/\text{Total number of checks (guests)}$$

The denominator remains unchanged but the numerator can vary with managerial needs. For example, by using total revenues for a meal period as the numerator, one may arrive at average check per meal period. Similarly, one may calculate average check per day, per week, per month, per quarter, as well as per unit of operation, per shift, per wait staff person, or per available seat. It is one of the most commonly used and effective comparative analysis tools in the foodservice industry.

Reference

Ninemeier, J.D. (1999) *Planning and Control for Food and Beverage Operations*. Orlando, FL: Educational

Institute of the American Hotel and Motel Association.

H.G. PARSA
OHIO STATE UNIVERSITY, USA

Average daily rate

The average daily rate is a measure of the hotel's staff in selling available room rates. Average daily rate or ADR is calculated by dividing total room sales by the number of rooms sold. Average daily rate is used in projecting room revenues for a hotel and is a factor in calculating gross revenue from room sales. A front office manager will calculate an average daily rate even though room rates within a property vary significantly from single rooms to suites, from individual guests to groups and conventions, from weekdays to weekends and from busy to slack seasons. If the supply of hotel rooms is limited considerable attention is focused on improving the average daily rate. In the United States, 1993 was the first year the hotel industry turned a profit since 1985. As the economy recovered from recession, demand picked up. With no new supply of hotels rooms, all demand in growth went straight to increasing occupancy and improving average daily rate. In the United States the increase in average daily rate did not surpass inflation until 1994.

Reference

Stutts, Alan T. (2001) *Hotel and Lodging Management – An Introduction.* New York: John Wiley & Sons, .

ALAN T. STUTTS
AMERICAN INTERCONTINENTAL
UNIVERSITY, USA

Awareness, trial, and usage

A grouping of three types of questions, *awareness, trial,* and *usage,* is used in marketing research to determine some of the behavioral characteristics of consumers. *Awareness* refers to the presence of the product or brand in the consumer's mind. This variable is measured in a variety of ways, ranging from simply asking a survey respondent if he or she is aware of a specific product or brand through asking the respondent to list the types of products or brands that come to mind. The second method is particularly powerful because it elicits the respondents' 'salient,' or top-of-mind, items.

Trial refers to the types of questions that ask the consumer if he or she has ever used the product or brand in the past. Questions may include if respondents have used the product in the past, if they are current users, and if they intend to or would be willing to use the product in the future.

Usage of the product may refer to both the frequency of use as well as the way the product is used. Frequency may be split into categories, such as Light, Medium, or Heavy users, or may be grouped by the number of times a product is used over a set period of time (e.g., number of times per month, per year, or per week). Usage questions should also ask how the respondent uses the product or service. Hospitality applications of usage questions may include the occasion or reason for a visit to a hotel or restaurant and the types of services that are consumed while at the hotel or restaurant.

Reference

Lewis, Robert C. and Chambers, Richard E. (2000) *Marketing Leadership in Hospitality Foundations and Practices,* 3rd edn. New York: John Wiley & Sons.

DINA MARIE V. ZEMKE
UNIVERSITY OF NEW HAMPSHIRE, USA

B

Back flow prevention

All water distribution systems are designed to keep the water flowing from the distribution system to the customer. However, when hydraulic conditions within the system deviate from the 'normal' conditions, water flow can be reversed. When this back flow happens, contaminated water can enter the distribution system. Back flow can be prevented by the installation of a device or assembly that uses valves, in different configurations, to prevent polluted or contaminated water from reversing direction and flowing backwards.

In the case of hotels or restaurants, the devices are used to prevent the property's water system from over pressurizing and forcing the water back into the municipality's system. In the United States and most other countries, laws and/or regulations require that water suppliers protect their water systems from contamination. In most cases, regulations exempt single-family residences used solely for residential purposes from assembly requirements. However, residences used for other purposes, including hotels, are required to install and maintain back flow prevention assemblies.

Generally the back flow prevention assembly is installed in the main water line to a building just after the water meter. Typically, annual or bi-annual testing of the assembly is required by the appropriate agency or fines can be incurred, including having the water turned off at the meter.

Reference

Stipanuk, D.M. (2002) *Hospitality Facilities Management and Design*, 2nd edn. Lansing, MI: Educational Institute of the American Hotel and Lodging Association.

JIM ACKLES
THARALDSON ENERGY GROUP, USA

Back-of-the-house in hotels

So named in a hotel or lodging business because the interaction between guests and employees is less common. Such areas include housekeeping, engineering and maintenance, accounting, and human resources. While housekeeping personnel interact with guests it is not part of their primary duties as it is for front desk and bell staff. Back-of-the-house employees may not directly serve the guest by taking an order, assisting with registration, or delivering luggage to a guestroom. However, the back-of-the-house employee indirectly serves the guest by: cleaning the guestroom; cleaning the public areas of the hotel; repairing building systems upon which the guests depends such as electrical, plumbing and heating, ventilation and air conditioning; maintaining the aesthetics which may have brought the guest to the hotel such as the grounds and recreational facilities; providing guidance and direction to the management of the hotel in the recruitment, selection, and training of new managers, supervisors, and employees; managing the compensation programs and evaluation procedures for all hotel employees; correcting an error in a guest account; or insuring the smooth operation of the hotel through a accounting system that insures the hotel's vendors are paid in a timely manner, compilation and production of the payroll for the hotel, budget preparation, and the production of the profit-and–loss statement, all of which are essential in determining which services the hotel can provide to a guest.

Reference

Stutts, Alan T. (2001) *Hotel and Lodging Management – An Introduction.* John New York: Wiley & Sons.

ALAN T. STUTTS
AMERICAN INTERCONTINENTAL
UNIVERSITY, USA

Back-of-the-house in restaurants

'Back-of-house' or 'back-of-the-house' is a rather archaic term, having survived over the centuries. It was first used in the Middle Ages in England to describe the area of an inn where food was prepared, which was normally located outside and to the rear, and therefore was called the back of house area. Its modern interpretation is similar, as it is commonly used to describe the areas of a restaurant, which are normally off-limits to the guests, e.g. the kitchen. The term also applies to hotels where the areas include the laundry and other support areas.

The modern application lies with the delineation of back-of-house employees – cooks, for example – from front-of-house employees – servers. Today the two groups often have a sense of identity based on the job functions that correspond to the place in the restaurant where they work (front *vs.* back). Such differences are underscored in operations where tipping is found: front-of-house employees are usually the recipients of such gratuities while back of house employees are not. Bourdain (2000) contends that these groups are different also in intangible ways and the resulting tension between them contributes to the restaurant industry's élan.

Reference

Bourdain, A. (2000) *Kitchen Confidential.* New York: Ecco Press.

JAKSA KIVELA
THE HONG KONG POLYTECHNIC
UNIVERSITY, HONG KONG SAR, CHINA

Back office systems

Back office systems are the IT business applications that support the internal business functions of hospitality organizations. Like the customer-facing (front office) ones, these applications are instrumental in the fulfillment of the hospitality or tourism enterprise's mission – from product to service and everything in between. They are usually software packages such as Business Performance Management tools, Enterprise Resource Planning, Supply Chain Management and Sourcing or individual applications such as inventory management, purchasing or e-procurement, menu and recipe management (for catering operations), human resources management (e-recruitment, e-training, employee scheduling, and payroll), energy management, preventative property maintenance, and accounting.

Customer-centric strategies require back office systems to have some level of integration with front office systems (mainly the PMS in the case of hotels and the CRM system of the enterprise) in order to provide a complete outlook on customer interactions and the connected business processes.

Investment in back office systems is a point of significant concern for hospitality and tourism enterprises. A number of large enterprises have found that outsourcing these applications to third parties offers good return on investment (ROI) and allows them to focus on their primary activities related with customer service. The ASP model of outsourcing can also be appropriate for back office applications.

References

O'Connor, P. (2000) *Using Computers in Hospitality.* London: Cassell, pp. 190–207.

Paraskevas, A. and Buhalis, D. (2002) Outsourcing IT for small hotels. *Cornell Hotel and Restaurant Administration Quarterly*, 43 (2), 27–39.

ALEXANDROS PARASKEVAS
OXFORD BROOKES UNIVERSITY, UK

Balance sheet

The balance sheet is a statement showing a business's financial position at the end of an accounting period. It portrays the financial position of the organization at a particular point in time. The balance sheet lists all the assets, liabilities, and owner's equity of an entity as of a specific date. It is classified into major groupings of assets and liabilities in order to facilitate analysis, for example, current assets, fixed assets, current liabilities, non-current liabilities. The balance sheet is like a snapshot of the entity. For this reason it is also called the statement of financial position. The balance sheet is useful to financial statement users because it indicates the resources the entity has and what it owes.

A simple example of a business's balance sheet is given below:

SUNSET RESTAURANT
Balance Sheet as at 30 June 200X, in pounds sterling

Current assets	
Cash at bank	12,376
Beverage (non-alcohol) inventory	4,135
Alcohol inventory	11,351
Food inventory	8,120
Other stocks inventory	540
Accounts receivable	2,375
Total current assets	38,897
Non-current assets	
Restaurant building	523,000
Less building write-off	(98,000)
Equipment	328,540
Less accumulated depreciation	(35,800)
Total non-current assets	717,740
Total assets	756,637

Current liabilities	
Interest payable	7,846
Accounts payable	10,749
Total current liabilities	18,595
Non-current liabilities	
Bank loan	535,000
Total non-current liabilities	535,000
Total liabilities	553,595
Net assets	203,042
Owner's equity	
Capital	110,000
Retained earnings	93,042
Total owner's equity	203,042
Owner's equity	203,042

Within the balance sheet, important terms are: current assets; fixed (or non-current) assets; current liabilities; long-term liabilities; working capital and owner's equity.

Current assets normally have a life of one year or less and represent future economic benefits controlled by the business as a result of past transactions or other events and are not intended for continuing use in the business. Current assets include cash and inventory (stock) that will be converted to cash or consumed. Current assets also include prepayments and marketable securities. The conversion to cash or consumption is expected to occur within one year or the normal operating cycle of the entity, whichever is longer.

A fixed asset is an item that has physical substance and a life in excess of one year. Fixed assets are intended to be retained in the business beyond the period of current operations and for the purpose of earning revenue and are not intended for resale to customers in the ordinary course of business. Fixed assets are those assets that are intended for use on a continuing basis for the purpose of the business's activities. Fixed assets are usually referred to as property, plant, and equipment.

Current liabilities are obligations payable within one year or the normal operating cycle of the business. A current liability requires payment out of a current asset, or the incurrence of another short-term obligation. Current liabilities are obligations that are expected or could be required to be discharged on demand or within one year. Examples are accounts payable, such as telephone and bank interest payments, and accrued expenses payable, such as salaries and taxes.

Long-term liabilities are amounts that fall due after the expiration of the next normal operating cycle, that is, typically after one year. They can also be described as an obligation payable in money, goods or services for a period in excess of one year. Long-term liabilities are presented under non-current liabilities in the balance sheet. They are liabilities that do not need to be discharged within 12 months of the balance date. For example, if a loan has been taken out over 10 years, that portion not due within the first year is included in long-term liabilities.

Working capital is described as current assets less current liabilities, properly called net working capital. Working capital is a measure of the long-term investment required to finance the day-to-day operations at a given level of activity; current assets minus current liabilities. Working capital is also seen as a measure of a business's liquidity. Sources of working capital are net income, increases in non-current liabilities, increases in shareholder's equity, and decreases in non-current assets.

Owner's equity is the financing provided by the owner (or owners) and the operations of the business. It is the interest of the owner(s) in the assets of the business represented by capital contributions and retained earnings. Owner's equity is the residual interest of the owner(s) in the net assets (assets less liabilities) of the entity, and may be thought of as the owner's residual claims against the net assets of the entity. Thus owner's equity is a residual claim or interest – a claim to the assets remaining after the debts to creditors have been discharged.

References

Gaffikin, M., Walgenback, P.H., Dittrick, N.E., and Hanson, E.I. (1990) *Principles of Accounting*, 2nd Australian edn. Sydney: Harcourt Brace Jovanovich.

Harrison, Walter T. and Horngren, Charles T. (2003) *Financial Accounting*, 5th edn. Harlow: Pearson Technology Group.

Hoggett, J. and Edwards, L. (2000) *Financial Accounting in Australia*, 4th edn. Sydney: John Wiley & Sons.

Parker, R.H. (1992), *Macmillan Dictionary of Accounting*, 2nd edition, UK: London: The Macmillan Press Ltd.

Siegel, J.G. and Shim, J.K. (1987), *Dictionary of Accounting Terms*. New York: Barron's Educational Series.

JEFF POPE
CURTIN UNIVERSITY OF TECHNOLOGY,
AUSTRALIA

Baldrige award

The Malcolm Baldrige National Quality Award is an internationally-recognized prize given by the United States Commerce Department to businesses in manufacturing, services, small businesses, education, and health care for excellence in quality. The Baldridge Award is highly prestigious. Applicants are subjected to rigorous review of their performance in areas such as leadership, strategic planning, customer and market focus, information and analysis, human resources management, process management, and the business's results.

The only hospitality company that has won a Baldrige Award to date is the Ritz–Carlton Hotel Company, which won it for the first time in 1992. The company focused on achieving 100% guest loyalty with defect-free performance, reducing employee turnover, making its strategic planning process more systematic, and developing processes and tools for quality improvement. Tools to measure processes and quality were developed using statistical control techniques that were previously rarely used in the services industries. Ritz–Carlton's attention to continuous improvement, a hallmark of all quality management programs, led to their winning the award for a second time in 1999.

References

For more information on the Malcolm Baldrige National Quality Program, go to the Award's

website at http://www.quality.nist.gov/index.
html. Accessed 25 May 2004.
A summary of the award-winning submission
from Ritz–Carlton Hotels is available at
http://www.quality.nist.gov/1999_Application_
Summaries.htm. Accessed 25 May 2004.

DINA MARIE V. ZEMKE
UNIVERSITY OF NEW HAMPSHIRE, USA

McKeown, P.G. (2003) *Information Technology and
the Networked Economy.* Boston, MA: Thomson
Course Technology.

ROB LAW
THE HONG KONG POLYTECHNIC
UNIVERSITY, HONG KONG SAR, CHINA
STEVEN CHAN
THE HONG KONG POLYTECHNIC
UNIVERSITY, HONG KONG SAR, CHINA

Bandwidth

A channel is a crucial component of telecommunications. It is the path through which information passes between the sending and receiving
ends, and bandwidth describes the width of the
channel (McKeown, 2003). The amount of data
that the channel can transmit at one time is
directly proportional to the size of the bandwidth. Explicitly, data transmission rate is predominantly determined by the transmission
channel capacity, usually expressed in bits per
second (bps). In other words, bandwidth represents the data rate, and the term refers to how
fast data flow on a telecommunication channel.
Intuitively, bandwidth is like the measurement of
the diameter of a water pipe through which
water can pass through. To increase the volume
of water passing through the pipe, one must
increase the diameter of the pipe.

In the context of hospitality, bandwidth is
considered as the communication capacity
(Kasavana *et al.*, 1997). As communication rate
increases, bandwidth-intensive applications such
as high-quality Internet multimedia will be benefited from rapid downloading and good quality
graphical images. Hotels and guests therefore
will be able to distribute and access better quality
multimedia information much faster via the
Internet.

References

Kasavana, M.L., Knutson, B.J., and Polonowski, S.J.
(1997) Netlurking: the future of hospitality
Internet marketing. *Journal of Hospitality and
Leisure Marketing,* 5 (1), 31–44.

Banquet event order (BEO)

The banquet event order (BEO) is sometimes
referred to as simply an event order or the function sheet. It is the basis of a property's internal
communication system between the various
departments and the catering department. It is
also the basic building block upon which the
catering department's accounting and record-
keeping systems are constructed. A BEO is prepared for each meal and beverage function, and
copies are sent to each department that will be
directly or indirectly involved with the events.
Usually all departments receive a copy of each
BEO a week or more before the catered function
is held. This ensures that all department heads
have enough time to schedule and complete their
necessary activities that support the events.
BEOs are usually numbered sequentially for easy
reference. It is important to assign an identifying
number to each BEO so that department heads
can resolve any discrepancy easily and quickly.
For instance, if banquet set-up is unclear about
a particular event's requirements, it can call the
catering office for additional information regarding BEO #175. This is much easier and more
accurate than using clients' names or other forms
of identification, all of which can be garbled and
misinterpreted after two or three phone calls.
A BEO should include who is responsible for
what and specify the cost for every item or service. The BEO acts as the primary means of
communication within the facility, letting each
department know what their responsibility is for
each function. Each sheet should be signed by
the meeting planner acknowledging it was read
and making any necessary changes.

The typical BEO contains the following information:

- BEO number
- Function day(s) and date(s)
- Type of function
- Client name with a line for a signature
- Client's address
- Client contact person, or person in charge
- Person who booked the event and the authorized signature(s)
- Name of function room assigned to the event
- Beginning time of the function
- Expected ending time of the function
- Number of guests expected
- Number of guests to prepare meals for
- Agreed upon menus
- Style of service (American, French, etc.)
- Function room set-up instructions (placement of bars, buffet tables, etc.)
- Any special instructions (such as centerpieces, parking details, miscellaneous labor charges, sleeping room blocks, linens, table sets, bar arrangements, props, entertainment, electrical and/or engineering needs, unique underliners, VIPs, and other special amenities)
- Agreed upon prices to be charged
- Master billing account number
- Billing instructions
- Reference to other BEOs or other relevant records
- Date the BEO was completed
- Signature of person preparing (or approving) the BEO
- A list of departments receiving a copy of the BEO.

Function sheets should include the following information:

- Group name
- Program name
- Day(s) and date(s) of meeting
- Name and code number of each function
- Meeting room name and floor
- Room set-up time
- Beginning and ending time of each function
- Expected attendance
- Number of speakers
- Head table set-up

- Staging instructions
- Audiovisual requirements
- Special requirements such as computer set-up, floral decorations, special table linens or colors, signage, event posted on the reader board, etc.
- Food and beverage requirements including menus, scheduled breaks for refreshing the room, name of contact person in charge of the event.

It is important to have as much detailed information as possible, including diagrams, equipment, tables, placement, etc.

References

Krug, S., Chatfield-Taylor, C., and Collins, M. (eds) (1994) *The Convention Industry Council Manual*, 7th edn. McLean, VA: The Convention Industry Council.

Shock, Patti J. and Stefanelli, John (2001) *On Premise Catering: Hotels, Convention and Conference Centers and Clubs*. New York: John Wiley & Sons.

PATTI J. SHOCK
UNIVERSITY OF NEVADA, LAS VEGAS, USA

Bargaining power

This refers to the relative power that either a guest or supplier has over the firm and its ability to negotiate transactions. Buyers have power if they buy in bulk and can therefore dictate terms, or if the product represents a large percentage of the buyer costs, making the buyer highly price-sensitive (Porter, 1980). In such cases, the firm's bargaining power is weak. It may have to concede terms and/or conditions. Suppliers have power if there are few firms supplying the product or if there is no reasonable substitute for it, or if the hotel or restaurant is of little importance to the supplier, making the supplier insensitive to the hospitality firm's needs. In such cases the firm is again in a weak bargaining position and will likely have to make concessions such as paying a higher price or accepting limitations in either selection, quality or delivery terms. A firm's bargaining power is enhanced if these conditions shift in their favor. For example, tourists often spend a large portion of their vacation budget on lodging, making them highly price-sensitive for this product. In periods of low occupancy hotels are often willing to lower their prices significantly in order to sell rooms to these price-conscious buyers (Israeli and Reichel, 2003). However, as a supplier of rooms when occupancy rates are high the hotel's bargaining power is increased, allowing it to maintain a fairly firm position on room rate. Thus bargaining power is predicated upon the relationship between the quantity desired, the percentage of the total buyer cost, and product availability.

References

Israeli, A.A. and Reichel, A. (2003) Hospitality crisis management practices: the Israeli case, *International Journal of Hospitality Management*, 22 (4), 353–372.
Porter, M.E. (1980) *Competitive Strategy*. New York: The Free Press.

CHRIS ROBERTS
UNIVERSITY OF MASSACHUSETTS, USA

Barriers to entry

Barriers to entry block new hospitality competitors from entering the local industry. Since new hotels or restaurants bring additional capacity and the desire to gain market share, the result often reduces profitability for existing firms. This threat of entry can be reduced through seven major types of entry barriers: (1) economies of scale, (2) product differentiation, (3) capital requirements, (4) switching costs, (5) access to distribution channels, (6) competitive advantages such as proprietary products, locations, access to raw materials, etc., and (7) government policy (Porter, 1980). If a firm is operating within a local industry, high barriers are desired to block new entrants. Existing competitors can raise barriers through favorable supplier contracts, market dominance, offering unique products and/or

services or by lobbying government for restrictions on building policies or licensing costs. Brand strength can act as a barrier, causing a potential entrant to reconsider entry because of the strength of the associated marketing power and customer identification with the existing brand. Macro-level forces such as a weakened economy (high interest rates, lack of venture capital for loans, etc.) or the unavailability of raw materials such as land or labor also act as industry level barriers to entry. In the hospitality industry, entry barriers are not particularly high. Opening a restaurant requires a relatively modest investment and would-be hotel operators can usually find financing (Harrison, 2003).

References

Harrison, J.S. (2003) Strategic analysis for the hospitality industry, *Cornell Hotel and Restaurant Administration Quarterly*, April, 139–152.
Porter, M.E. (1980) *Competitive Strategy*. New York: The Free Press.

CHRIS ROBERTS
UNIVERSITY OF MASSACHUSETTS, USA

Barriers to exit

Exit barriers are economic, strategic and/or emotional reasons that keep hospitality firms competing even thought they might be earning low or even negative returns on investments (Porter, 1980). Such costs are viewed to outweigh poor performance. Examples of such barriers include specialized assets with high costs to transform or with limited other use (such as a hotel or aircraft), fixed costs (labor agreements), or strategic relationships that attach high importance to being in the business and would significantly impact image, marketing ability, access to capital, etc. For example, a hotel building has limited reuse other than that of a hotel. The rooms are generally too small for residential living and the building infrastructure too complex for convenient redesign. Office space or light manufacturing operations generally prefer larger, more open areas and do not require as many bathroom or electrical facilities. While the front-of-the-house in restaurants can be converted to new purposes, other types of businesses rarely need the specialized industrial production facilities in the back. The cost to convert such space often outweighs retaining the space as it was initially created. With such high costs to transform the facilities for other purposes, hospitality firms frequently find it more acceptable to continue current operations.

Reference

Porter, M.E. (1980) *Competitive Strategy*. New York: The Free Press.

CHRIS ROBERTS
UNIVERSITY OF MASSACHUSETTS, USA

Basic elements of cost

Most business accounting systems classify costs in groupings of 'material,' 'labor,' and 'expenses' that relate to the resources consumed. For example, in a restaurant operation, basic cost elements would typically include food and beverages (material), wages, salaries, and overtime (labor), cleaning supplies, energy, insurance, advertising and depreciation (expenses). With respect to accommodation activities of a hotel we would also see other expenses such as guest supplies, laundry, travel agents' commission. This signifies that if we were to inspect the records of a hotel company, we would find expense accounts with headings such as those listed above. This type of cost classification is generally used in the routine presentation of profit and loss (income) statements.

Presenting cost information in the basic elements provides the basis to begin to assess business performance in terms of, e.g., calculating each separate element of cost as a percentage of sales revenue and determining various profit levels.

Costs can also be classified according to their behavior. For example, costs can be classified into fixed and variable. Fixed costs do not change in total as a hotel's level of activity changes (e.g., rent and insurance stay the same even though a hotel's occupancy rate may have doubled). Variable costs change in line with a hotel's volume of activity,

e.g., if a restaurant's volume of wine sales doubles, the cost of wine purchases would double.

References

Harris P.J. and Hazzard, P.A (1992) *Managerial Accounting in the Hospitality Industry*, 5th edn. Cheltenham: Stanley Thornes.
Jagels, M.G. and Coltman, M.M. (2003) *Hospitality Management Accounting*, 8th edn. New York: John Wiley & Sons.

CHRIS GUILDING
GRIFFITH UNIVERSITY, AUSTRALIA

Beliefs and attitudes

A belief is a descriptive thought that a person holds about an object or phenomenon (Kotler *et al.*, 1999). The term 'attitude' refers to an individual's preference, inclination, views or feelings towards some phenomenon or object (Churchill, 1995). Thus, attitudes and beliefs are part of a consumer's psychological makeup. Consumers' attitudes are learned, are characterized by their consistency and responsiveness (Hanna and Wozniak, 2001), and can be very difficult to change (Kotler *et al.*, 1999).

Beliefs and attitudes are important concepts in marketing science, since it is generally held that a person's beliefs and attitudes are related to his/her behavior. Thus, marketers are interested in people's overall beliefs and attitudes toward not only a product or service itself, but also with regard to specific brands and brand features (Churchill, 1995).

Unfortunately, consumers' beliefs and attitudes are not directly observable (Hanna and Wozniak, 2001) by marketers. Thus, Fishbein and Ajzen (1975) used a multi-attribute model to study attitudes, which hypothesized that consumer attitudes are a function of both a person's belief about an object, and a person's evaluation of those beliefs.

References

Churchill, G.A., Jr. (1995) *Marketing Research: Methodological Foundations*, 6th edn. Orlando,

FL: The Dryden Press, Harcourt Brace Publishers, pp. 339–342.

Fishbein, M. and Ajzen, I. (1975) *Beliefs, Attitude, Intention, and Behavior: An Introduction to Theory and Research*. Reading, MA: Addison-Wesley.

Hanna, N. and Wozniak, R. (2001) *Consumer Behavior: An Applied Approach*. Upper Saddle River, NJ: Prentice-Hall, p. 174.

Kotler, P., Bowen, J., and Makens, J. (1999) *Marketing for Hospitality and Tourism*, 2nd edn. Upper Saddle River, NJ: Prentice-Hall, pp. 196–197.

KARL MAYER
UNIVERSITY OF NEVADA, LAS VEGAS, USA

Benchmarking

Benchmarking is the comparing and measuring of a hospitality firm's business processes against the best practices of those processes by *any* organization in *any* industry in the entire world (Tucker *et al.*, 1987). The objective of benchmarking is to accelerate organizational learning in order to achieve a break-through in performance. To engage in this approach to self-improvement, a firm must first identify its own value-adding activities or processes that create its value chain. Then specific areas should be pinpointed for improvement. Next, star performing firms in any industry are examined to identify what it is they do to create their outstanding results. The focus is upon practices, processes, and operational methods for it is these aspects that enable a firm to identify how to apply their findings to their own activities. A weakness of this approach is that adopting the best practices of another may permit the firm to improve performance – and perhaps even match that of the benchmarked firm – but it rarely leads to superior results. Benchmarking should be done against non-competing firms so that innovative concepts are uncovered and unworthy practices are more easily identified and avoided.

Reference

Tucker, G.T., Seymour, M.Z., and Camp, C.C. (1987) How to measure yourself against the best. *Harvard Business Review*, January–February, 2–5.

CHRIS ROBERTS
UNIVERSITY OF MASSACHUSETTS, USA

Benchmarking performance

Through the widespread use of uniform accounting systems, such as the Uniform System of Accounts for the Lodging Industry (USALI), it has become feasible to collate and assemble data into statistical reports comprising profit and loss statement results and other operating data in order to benchmark performance against industry norms. This has primarily been pioneered and developed by the leading professional accounting and hospitality consulting firms which initially produced the information internally, for their own commercial purposes, from a growing base of data gathered from individual clients. These firms later recognized the significant potential public relations and marketing value of making the reports available externally to a wider audience of potential clients, industry operators (prepared to pay for them) and other interested parties, e.g. universities and college libraries. Thus, the overall outcome is that hospitality decision-makers are enabled to carry out operational planning and control activities more effectively through the additional access to external benchmark reports, rather than by the sole reliance on internally generated budgeted and past performance results.

The collection and analysis of data, and the presentation of information continues to become more detailed and refined. For instance, it is now possible to benchmark operating performance against competitive sets at a local, regional, national, and international basis.

References

Deloitte (annually) *HotelBenchmark Survey*. London: Deloitte & Touche.

PKF (annually) *Country Trends: Hotel Performance and Profitability in Europe, Middle East, Africa and South Asia*. London: PKF.

TRI Hospitality Consulting (annually) *United Kingdom Hotel Industry*. London: TRI Hospitality Consulting.

PETER HARRIS
OXFORD BROOKES UNIVERSITY, UK

Benchmarking in property management

Originally a benchmark was a mark in a wall used as a point of reference against which other measurements could be compared, and today the computer industry still uses the term benchmarking to mean the comparison of the speed or other attribute of various computer systems or components against a nominal standard. In the hospitality and other industries, however, benchmarking does not refer to standards, but rather to a specific process formalized by Robert Camp at the Xerox Company in the 1970s, namely 'the search for industry best practice that leads to superior performance.' Camp himself abbreviated this definition to 'finding and implementing the best practices.'

Benchmarking can be of an entire company, a broad functional area, or the smallest business process. It can be carried out against the best organization in the world, against a direct competitor, against non-competing companies, or against an internal or related group. Unlike simply trying to see what one's competitors are doing, or even trying to reverse-engineer their products, benchmarking seeks to discover the *best* practices. Since they do not involve seeking the very best practices, let alone adapting and implementing them, simply carrying out a comparative study, or simply copying other organizations' practices, or simply assessing performance are not benchmarking.

Hotels may benchmark utilities usage and costs as well as property operations, maintenance services, and costs. Utilities are often measured as consumption per unit area or per guest. POM services may be measured in a variety of ways including service measures (e.g., time to respond to a request) as well as efficiency measures (e.g., number of work orders per unit time.

References

Camp, R.C. (1989) Benchmarking: the search for industry best practice that leads to superior. *Performance*, Milwaukee, WI: ASQC Quality Press.

Stipanuk, D.M. (2002) *Hospitality Facilities Management and Design*, 2nd edn. Lansing, MI: Educational Institute of the American Hotel and Lodging Association, pp. 61–64.

ROBERT ALLENDER
ENERGY RESOURCES MANAGEMENT,
HONG KONG SAR, CHINA

Biases in consumer decision-making

Consumers are often biased in their decision-making. A bias is a tool that we cognitively use to ease the decision-making process. Many types of bias exist and all people have biases to varying degrees.

Bias as a result of context effects

When a decision needs to be made, the most important information in the decision may be compared against a background of other information that provides a 'frame,' or context, for the decision (Kardes, 1999). When consumers make a decision about adding features to a house that they are having built, the features, which may be very expensive, seem inexpensive when compared to the total cost of the project. Another example would be the cost of a bottle of water. The normal cost of a one-liter bottle of a branded mineral water in the grocery store is approximately $1.50. However, the same bottle of water costs $7.00 when purchased at an after-hours nightclub at a hotel/casino. People who would be outraged to see the water at a cost of $7.00 in the grocery store casually pay this amount because it is being purchased in the context of the nightclub, particularly after the individual has paid a $20 cover charge to enter the club.

This context effect leads to bias in decision-making behavior. The process that is happening is a shift in the reference point of the decision-maker. Kahneman and Tversky (1984) provide a description of the phenomena of the choices made under risky or less-risky conditions. People tend to induce risk aversion in a gain situation, but tend to seek risk when in a losing situation. Some of the hallmarks of human decision-making are the tendencies to overweight the probabilities of sure things and improbable events.

Bias as a result of the simulation heuristic

Heuristics are short-cuts that humans use in decision-making. It is not always possible to give a decision our full attention, so heuristic devices are used to help make decisions quickly and with a lower amount of effort (Kardes, 1999). Heuristics may also be referred to as 'underprocessing,' since they do not involve the full effort of processing that is possible. It is believed that the brain is rewarded for minimizing the effort put into a task with increased levels of pleasure-inducing chemicals. There are three basic heuristics that we use to simplify decision-making: representativeness, availability, and anchoring-and-adjustment.

The representativeness heuristic analyzes how much we believe A resembles B. We then project B's characteristics onto A. This is a typical example of a racial or social stereotype, where we see a characteristic in a person and assign that person other characteristics our minds. Examples are often discussed when a person exhibits a certain set of characteristics and people then try to determine what the person's job is.

The availability heuristic is manifested by the ease with which we think of something. In other words, if the object or situation is salient, or comes to the top of our mind, we are likely to think of it to the exclusion of other options. Tversky and Kahneman (1974) also refer to this as the 'bias of imaginability,' which is related to making illusory correlations.

The anchoring-and-adjustment heuristic involves starting at an initial value, and then adjusting it to arrive at a final answer. Different starting points yield different answers, though, which are always biased toward the initial values. This may also be called 'phenomenon anchoring' (Tversky and Kahneman, 1974). This is virtually identical to the concept of framing in decision-making, which was previously discussed.

Another type of heuristic is the 'simulation' heuristic (Kardes, 1999). The simulation heuristic is a device that we use to decide whether something is likely to happen. Basically, if we can imagine it happening, we will believe that it is more likely to happen. Gregory et al. (1982) conducted four experiments where subjects were asked to imagine a structured scenario. The scenarios included winning a contest, getting arrested, and buying cable television service. After the imagining phase was complete, the subjects were surveyed to elicit their belief that the scenario would befall them. The researchers reported a belief in probability that the event would happen. In addition, in a test of actual behavior, a follow-up survey was conducted among home-owners that found that many of the subjects who imagined purchasing cable television service actually did so after the experiment.

Self-serving bias

Self-serving bias is a form of attributional bias (Folkes and Kiesler, 1991). Attributional bias occurs when the consumer views themselves more positively than is actually the case and believes that their own contributions are more worthy than those of others.

Self-serving bias influences people's perceptions of success and failure. If a person experiences a success, they are likely to attribute the success to their own abilities. However, if a failure is experienced, the person is more likely to attribute the failure to the actions of others, bad luck, or other difficulties. Consumers have these biases when making product decisions. Folkes and Kotsos (1986) studied the reactions of buyers and sellers of faulty apparel and of auto repairs. They found that the buyers of the product or service blamed the problems on the clothing manufacturer or the auto mechanic. The sellers of the clothing blamed the customer for the problems experienced with the clothing, while the auto mechanics blamed the drivers for mechanical breakdowns. The causes for the responsibility or blame differ based on the viewpoint of the decision-maker.

Schindler (1988) conducted studies to evaluate the consumer's opinion of receiving a good deal on a purchase. He found that the shopper attributed the 'good deal' to their own cleverness, even though the deal was a result of the salesperson's error. Prices have two consequences for the shopper – utilitarian consequences and ego-expressive consequences. The ego-expressive consequences lead some people to feel like a 'smart shopper' if they received a good deal, or a 'sucker' if they did not feel that they received a good deal. The ego-expressive consequence can have an influence on customer satisfaction. Schindler studied the reference point versus the paid price for an object and the subject's satisfaction with the deal. If the subject felt that they were responsible for the good deal received, then satisfaction was increased over that of the other conditions in the experiment. Marketers can enhance this feeling by 'dangling' discounts in front of the shopper (Schindler, 1989).

Certain segments of consumers are more likely to be strongly affected by the ego-expressive consequences of being a smart shopper (Schindler, 1989). Studies have been conducted examining the use of discount coupons. Not only are the people we would normally assume to be coupon shoppers in this group (e.g., housewives not employed outside the household) but additional characteristics are suggested. For example, the type of person who enjoys 'beating the system' and who is gregarious and has access to high social contact is likely to engage in this type of shopping. This person may also hold a social position that is maintained by their ability to obtain and discuss (brag about) the good deals they find.

Other types of bias

Numerous other types of bias exist. Bias in decision-making that is the result of the perseverance effect occurs when a person continues to believe something is true, even when the facts are proven to be false (Kardes, 1999). This is probably due to the ease with which current beliefs are held and the resultant brain chemical rewards that are not present when making the mental exertion of changing our beliefs. Bias as a result of the perseverance effect is often in evidence during the political campaign season. If one candidate runs a 'smear' campaign of negative publicity against another candidate, the electorate hears and often believes the negative message. Even if the message is proven to be untrue, most people will still believe in the negative message.

Bias is also formed as a result of the dilution effect (Kardes, 1999). Important information can be received and recalled if it is delivered in small packets. However, if too much information is received, a consumer may be biased in their judgment of product or service because of over-emphasis on the other information presented. Judgment is clouded by over-reliance on irrelevant information. This can lead to a negative assessment of a situation, but may also be a good way to 'bury' negative information that is required to be divulged. For example, drug companies advertise medication on television and radio. The United States Food and Drug Administration requires the list of possible side effects of the medication to be read during the advertisement. The long list of potential side effects that most drugs have dilutes the perceived risks of the side effects. However, the major benefit that the drug can provide may be lost amidst all of the negative side effects that are mentioned.

Finally, the vividness of a message can lead to bias in decision-making. Vivid, unique images and sounds tend to attract our attention. An option in a product or service choice that is presented in the most unique manner is likely to receive more of our attention time than other, more congruent or similar options. This effect is also known as the 'figure-ground' principle, where novelty commands more attention than other options because something new or unexpected is occurring. Consumers who prefer new experiences (novelty-seekers) may tend to be biased in favor of products and services that are presented more vividly and uniquely than competing products.

References

Folkes, V.S. and Kiesler, T. (1991) Social cognition: consumers' inferences about the self and others. *Handbook of Consumer Behavior* (T.S. Robertson and H.H. Kassarjian, eds). Englewood Cliffs, NJ: Prentice-Hall.

Folkes, V.S. and Kotsos, B. (1986) Buyers' and sellers' explanations for product failure: Who done it. *Journal of Marketing*, 50, 74–80.

Gregory, W.L., Cialdini, R.B., and Carpenter, K.M. (1982) Self-relevant scenarios as mediators of likelihood estimate and compliance: Does imagining make it so? *Journal of Personality and Social Psychology*, 43, 89–99.

Kahneman, D. and Tversky, A. (1984) Choices, values, and frames. *American Psychologist*, 39, 341–350.

Kardes, F.R. (1999) *Consumer Behavior and Managerial Decision-making*. Reading, MA: Addison-Wesley.

Schindler, R.M. (1988) The role of ego-expressive factors in the consumer's satisfaction with price. *Journal of Consumer Satisfaction, Dissatisfaction, and Complaining Behavior*, 1, 34–39.

Schindler, R.M. (1989) The excitement of getting a bargain: some hypotheses concerning the origins and effects of smart-shopper feelings. In T.K. Srull (ed.), *Advances in Consumer Research, 16*. Provo, UT: Association for Consumer Research, pp. 447–453.

Tversky, A. and Kahneman, D. (1974) Judgment under uncertainty: heuristics and biases. *Science*, 185, 1124–1131.

DINA MARIE V. ZEMKE
UNIVERSITY OF NEW HAMPSHIRE, USA

Biennial timeshare

A biennial timeshare gives the purchaser the use of a fixed week every other year. The primary reason that developers started to offer a timeshare in an every other year format was to meet certain consumers' financial needs that normally could not afford an annual timeshare. Typically the biennial owner is classified as an 'odd' or an 'even' owner.

If an owner isn't going to use the week that they own, or if the owner wants to use it to exchange elsewhere, the owner can enter their week into the exchange company's reservation system. Once this week is deposited into the exchange company's 'bank' the owner has typically two years in which to request an exchange against the deposited week. It is important for the biennial owner to understand that the depositing process, otherwise known as 'banking', means the occupancy rights to that week belongs to the exchange company. The bottom line is that once a week is deposited it cannot be used by the original owner due to this transfer to the exchange company. In short, this means that it is the exchange company's right to distribute the deposited week to another interested owner within the exchange company's membership network.

References

http://www.timeshareparadise.com/timeshareweb/glossaryIndex/B.htm
http://www.thetimesharebeat.com/glossary.htm

PIMRAWEE ROCHUNGSRAT
JAMES COOK UNIVERSITY, AUSTRALIA

Bluetooth

A world-wide standard in short-range radio communication technology that enables computers, mobile telephones, personal digital assistants (PDA), and other electronic devices to be connected without wires, cables or infrared to each other or to the Internet (http://www.bluetooth.com). The technology has been developed and promoted by the Bluetooth Special Interest Group (SIG). The group is a trade association comprising some of the largest communication companies, which include 3Com, Agere, Ericsson, IBM, Intel, Microsoft, Motorola, Nokia, and Toshiba.

It uses radio waves at a frequency of 2.4 Gigahertz to establish short-range networks, up to 10 m in distance, with other similar devices. Once a network has been formed the systems in the network then communicate without any interference from the user and switch frequencies automatically in order to prevent another similar device from interfering with the network. This allows multiple networks to be established simultaneously. Applications in hospitality include automated check-in for guests, controlled door access with a PDA acting as a virtual key, billing of services via the guest's computer or PDA, in-room wireless printing and access to the Internet and e-mail.

References

Bisdikian, C. (2001) An overview of the Bluetooth wireless technology. *IEEE Communications Magazine*, 39 (12), 86–94.

Takada, Y., Kishimoto, M., Kawamura, N., Komoda, N., Oiso, H., Yamasaki, T., and Masanari, T. (2003) An information service system using Bluetooth in an exhibition hall. *Annales des Telecommunications – Annals of Telecommunications*, 58 (3–4), 507–530.

ALAN MARVELL
BATH SPA UNIVERSITY COLLEGE, UK

Booth

A booth is one or more standard units of exhibit space. In Europe, a *booth* is known as a *stand*. In the US, a standard unit is generally known to be a 10 foot × 10 foot space (one standard booth unit, equaling 100 net square feet. This would be 3 meters by 3 meters in metric). A booth is a specific area assigned by management to an exhibitor under contractual agreement. If an exhibitor purchases multiple units side-by-side or back-to-back, the combined space is also still referred to as 'a booth.' These exhibitors are companies or organizations who buy booth space for the length of the trade show or exhibition. Not all booths are priced the same to exhibitors. There are premium locations on the trade show floor where some booth locations are automatically more visible to attendees, making them more desirable and more costly. There are

four basic booth types: the standard booth has access from one side; the perimeter booth, which is up against the wall of the facility; the peninsula booth which is at the end of a row and has access from three sides; and the island booth which has access from four sides.

Reference

APEX Glossary, http://glossary. conventionindustry.org

GEORGE FENICH
UNIVERSITY OF NEW ORLEANS, USA
KIMBERLY SEVERT
UNIVERSITY OF CENTRAL FLORIDA, USA

Brand

The American Marketing Association defines a brand as a name, term, sign, symbol, or design, or a combination of them, intended to identify the products or services of one seller or group of sellers and to differentiate them from those of competitors. A product or service's brand reveals its functional, pleasure and symbolic values as a reflection of the buyer's self-image. The brand summarizes all the attributes, values and principles infused into the product or service. Under the trademark laws, the seller is granted exclusive rights to the use of the brand name in perpetuity. In the context of the hospitality industry, a brand identifies the service provider or establishment. There is no legal difference between manufacturers' brands and service brands. Hospitality brands such as Marriott, Hilton, Westin, and Ritz–Carlton identify a specific set of attributes that take the shape of a definite and unique, though intangible, service. Structurally, hospitality brands are handicapped in creating images of themselves and usually use slogans to represent their attributes and benefits and to differentiate themselves. Popular examples are: 'Bring yourself. We will take care of the rest' used by Holiday Inn, and Four Seasons Hotel's 'Welcome to the Extraordinary.'

References

American Marketing Association: http://www. marketingpower.com/live/mg-dictionary-view329.php

Kapferer, Jean Noel (1994) *Strategic Brand Management: New Approaches to Creating and Evaluating Brand Equity*. New York: The Free Press, pp. 27–30.

ASHISH KHULLAR
UNIVERSITY OF MASSACHUSETTS, USA

Branding

It is very popular today to describe everything and anything for consumption in the marketplace as a 'brand.' The business writer Tom Peters even coined the phrase 'The Brand Called You!' to suggest that individuals share characteristics with consumer products (Peters, 1997).

There is much more to creating and managing a brand than this simplistic view would suggest. The Egyptian pharaohs used brands such as scarring from hot irons or healed wounds to leave a mark on slaves, cattle, or other living property as proof of ownership. Royal families have used heraldic crests and seals to differentiate family from foe. Early Christians used the cross as a way of clandestinely signaling shared beliefs.

Branding as a marketing tool is perhaps as old as commerce itself. Craftsmen, in an attempt to guarantee the authenticity of their handiworks, would leave a mark or '*griffe*' (translated as a claw) on the goods they produced. In the earliest examples, potters would press their thumbprints into the bottoms of bowls and cups to signify that the work was genuine. Later, smiths would etch an identifying image or even sign their names to their work; Paul Revere was one such 'branded' silversmith when he practiced his craft during the time of the American Revolution.

The earliest example of a government's recognizing the value of a commercial brand is generally considered to be the ale brewer Bass & Co.'s red triangle, which the British Patent Office, Trade Marks Branch, granted as 'Registered Trade Mark No. 1' on 31 January 1888. Interestingly, the German water bottler, Apollonaris, also claims the use of a similar red triangle as its trademark, with the two companies still honoring each other's non-competitive use of the mark.

Today, a brand is more than just the trademark, logotype, or a registered name. 'A brand is the product or service of a particular supplier which is differentiated by its name and presentation' (Murphy, 1990). Brands are a 'gestalt' of messages and images created to connect with the consuming public. It can certainly be argued that a product is not a brand, even while many of the strongest brands are consumer products. A product may be something made in a factory, or it could be a service provided and instantly consumed at the point of purchase. A brand, on the other hand, is a *promise* from a company or service provider made to a consumer that creates a lasting image in the mind of that consumer. The power of a brand means that one does not have to actually purchase a brand to have a lasting image of it. The strongest brands can gain legal claim to the creation of '*secondary meaning*,' where the logo or trademark creates a symbolic imagery that takes on a life beyond any physical representation, e.g. the Nike 'Swoosh' or the 'Golden Arches' of McDonald's.

During the last half of the twentieth century, first advertising, then marketing, and eventually anything to do with public relations became significantly more sophisticated in crafting a message that would resonate with the consuming public. *Brand management* has become a significant part of the work of senior company executives. While it was customary for companies to take advantage of their 'good will' in the marketplace, the first time one corporation paid a quantifiable premium for another's 'brand equity' occurred when the UK consulting firm Interbrand helped Grand Metropolitan calculate a value for the brand assets of Pillsbury (which included Burger King, Green Giant, and the Pillsbury Doughboy) during the 1980s. Today Interbrand publishes an annual list of the world's strongest brands, which typically includes restaurant-related companies such as McDonald's, Starbucks, Krispy Kreme, and Coca-Cola (see http://brandchannel.com for a yearly updated list).

These global companies become strong because the market value of a brand is reflected in a firm's ability to capture price premiums above the intrinsic value of the products it sells. Hamburgers, coffee, donuts, or soft drinks are commodity products, available on any street corner around the world. They gain significant equity only when they are sold as Big Macs, Tall Mocha Lattes, 'Hot Donuts Now,' or in a distinctive red can.

Finally, the primary objective for any brand is to enhance customer loyalty to the firm. This is accomplished through increasing customer frequency of use, positive brand positioning in relation to competitors, and forging a consumer's personal association with the brand. The stronger the emotional attachment, the more trustworthy a brand's promise becomes, and the greater the likelihood is that a customer will return to buy that product again. This equity, as demonstrated in the literature (e.g., Rust, Zeithaml, and Lemon), is reshaping much of corporate strategy in the emerging global economy. Thus, this 'branding' is when the historical value of a brand, showing 'proof of ownership,' becomes equally shared between the producer and the consumer.

References

Murphy, J.M. (1990) *Brand Strategy*. New York: Prentice-Hall, p. 1.

Peters, T. (1997) The Brand Called You! *Fast Company*, 10, August/September, 83.

Rust, R.T., Zeithaml, V.A., and Lemon, K.N. (2000) *Driving Customer Equity: How Customer Lifetime Value Is Reshaping Corporate Strategy*. New York: The Free Press.

CHRISTOPHER MULLER
UNIVERSITY OF CENTRAL FLORIDA, USA

Break-even analysis

Sometimes referred to as cost-volume-profit analysis, break-even analysis considers the interaction among fixed costs, variable costs, and revenue. When revenue is sufficient to cover both variable and fixed costs exactly, but insufficient to provide any profit (i.e., profit is zero), the operation is at the break-even point (BEP). The key assumptions are that fixed costs remain constant and that variable costs change at a constant rate with sales. Moreover, the technique requires that those costs that have fixed and variable components will be addressed accordingly. Related analyses can be performed using total revenue, number of orders, or number of covers.

The BEP calculation is expressed as follows:

$$BEP = \text{Net income } \$0$$
$$= \text{Revenue} - \text{Fixed costs} - \text{Variable costs}$$

The utility of break-even analysis is apparent in the following example: consider a fast casual restaurant that has an average check of $7.58. Variable costs per cover, based on this amount, equal $3.16. Fixed costs for the period under analysis are $183,526. The operator wants to determine the number of covers required to reach BEP. Since the amount of each check available to cover fixed costs is $4.42, BEP is calculated by dividing the total fixed expenses by this amount ($183,526 / 4.42 = 41,522). Thus, BEP equates to 41,522 covers.

The analysis can also be examined graphically, as depicted below. In the example in Figure 1, each cover in excess of the BEP represents $4.42 in profit.

Reference

Reynolds, D. (2008) *Foodservice Management Fundamentals*. Hoboken, NJ: John Wiley & Sons.

DENNIS REYNOLDS
WASHINGTON STATE UNIVERSITY, USA

Breakout sessions

Breakout sessions occur during the course of a meeting agenda, in which participants may choose the session most relevant to their needs or be assigned to a number of smaller sessions occurring simultaneously. Unlike plenary (general) sessions, which are convened for the entire group of participants in attendance at a meeting, breakout sessions are convened to target the interests or skill level of a sub-set of meeting participants. The sessions may provide the opportunity for more in-depth presentations on a particular topic, or for exercises or hands-on activities. The particular format of the breakout session – panel, presentation, and workshop – will vary depending on the specific objectives to be achieved. They will likely take place in smaller meeting spaces aside from the plenary meeting space and should be arranged to facilitate the purpose of the breakout session, whether in classroom style for presentations or conference style for discussions. It is important for these spaces to be easily accessible to meeting participants. Breakout sessions vary in length, complexity and subject matter and are an excellent way to vary the method, setting, and environment during the course of a larger meeting. Breakout sessions are also called concurrent sessions.

Reference

Price, C.H. (1989) *The AMA Guide for Meeting and Event Planners*. New York: AMACON.

SEKENO ALDRED
CENTER FOR EFFECTIVE PUBLIC POLICY,
USA

Budget methods

Budgets are a quantitative expression of a proposed plan of action. Widely used by hospitality managers for directing and controlling operations, such plans may be presented in a variety of forms. For example, 'traditional' static budgets are based on one particular planned volume of activity, such as the numbers of covers in a restaurant,

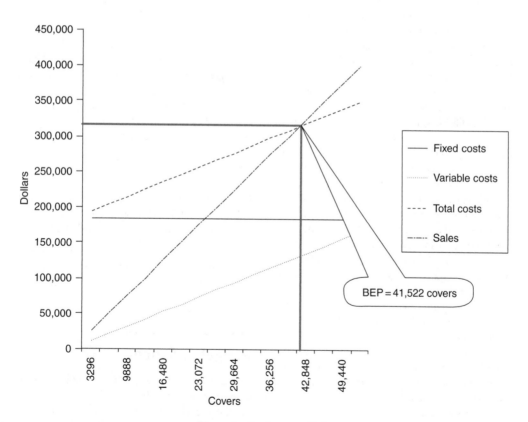

Figure 1   Break-even analysis

which is consistent with the achievement of an organization's strategic objectives. Irrespective of subsequent changes in actual activity levels, selling prices or cost drivers, and as their name implies, static budgets are not adjusted after they have been determined. Consequently, despite providing management with a clear and constant focal point, static budgets can quickly become 'out-of-date.' Furthermore, they may provide only limited useful information to assist management's understanding of the underlying causes of variances between budgeted and actual performance. It is perhaps not too surprising then that organizations are increasingly supplementing – or even replacing – static budgets with other planning tools.

For example, flexible budgets depict a range of activity levels within which management considers an organization may operate, and also within which they believe cost and revenue behavior patterns will remain relatively stable. As flexible budgets provide management with useful sensitivity analysis information by reflecting the reaction of key revenues and costs to changes in an organization's volume of activity (for example, changes in hotel room occupancy levels), they can enable a more effective assessment of the performance of an organization when the actual activity level achieved differs from that incorporated within the static budget. In order to provide such information though, an organization's budgeted revenues and costs must first be analyzed into their fixed and variable components. Once this is achieved, the variable revenues and costs can then be 'flexed' to reflect the costs and revenues that should have been achieved at the actual level of activity, while the fixed elements are maintained at their set amount. The resulting variances identified between the appropriately flexed budget and an organization's actual performance can then provide management with more valuable insights into the real reasons for the difference(s) between budgeted and actual performance.

In order to cope more effectively with the complexities and uncertainties of the emerging information age, hospitality managers are also increasingly choosing to utilize rolling budgets and forecasts. Typically, rolling budgets are established for a full 12-month period by adding, as appropriate, a month or quarter in the future as the current month/quarter ends. As a result, they encourage managers to be always looking forward and anticipating possible future developments for a full 12-month period. Rolling forecasts, meanwhile, especially focus on critical business processes and on changes in key external indicators. Typically prepared in a summarized format, these forecasts can be updated quickly when required – and not only in relation to the traditional annual planning cycle. Given the likely effort involved in re-working these rolling budgets and forecasts, however, it is important that management regularly assess the relative benefits to be obtained from such 'updates' – which benefits are likely to be most significant when an organization is operating in a relatively volatile and hostile market environment.

References

Brander Brown, J. and Atkinson, H. (2001) Budgeting in the information age: a fresh approach. *International Journal of Contemporary Hospitality Management*, 13 (3), 36–143.

Jagels, M.G. and Coltman, M.M. (2003) *Hospitality Management Accounting*, 8th edn. New York: John Wiley & Sons.

Harris, P.J. (1999) *Profit Planning*, 2nd edn. Oxford: Butterworth-Heinemann.

Hope, J. and Fraser, R. (1997) Beyond budgeting . . . breaking through the barrier to the third wave. *Management Accounting*, December, 20–23.

Horngren, C.T., Bhimani, A., Datar, S.M., and Foster, G. (2002) *Management and Cost Accounting*, 2nd edn. Harlow, UK: Pearson Education.

JACKIE BRANDER BROWN
MANCHESTER METROPOLITAN
UNIVERSITY, UK

Budget variances

The analysis of budget variances enables hospitality managers to 'drill-down' into the cause(s) of differences between actual and budgeted performance levels. Sales variances, for instance, focus on the impact of differences in sales volume and selling prices on an organization's profit. In order to enhance the usefulness of this analysis, sales variances are typically expressed as (contribution) margin variances. This means that any profit effect due to changes in variable direct costs is 'removed' by deducting the standard rather than actual variable cost of sales from the revenue actually earned. Thus the total sales margin variance for a period for an organization represents the difference, on a standard cost basis, between the actual and budgeted contributions. Where actual contribution exceeds budgeted contribution, this is viewed as being a favorable variance – whereas if budgeted contribution is greater than actual contribution, this is termed an unfavorable or adverse variance. Significantly, the total sales margin variance can be further analyzed into a number of useful sub-variances.

More specifically, the sales margin price sub-variance, in a restaurant, estimates the impact on an organization's profits arising from changes in the actual menu selling price(s) achieved. In order to determine this variance, the difference between the actual unit contribution margin and the standard unit contribution margin for a period must first be established. Both of these contribution margins should be based on standard costs, thus ensuring that the variance calculation is not 'corrupted' by any changes in the actual cost of sales. The contribution margin difference calculated should then be multiplied by the actual volume of sales activity achieved for a period – thus ensuring the full impact of any variation in selling price is applied to the whole of the actual sales level achieved. Typical causes associated with a sales margin price variance include mis-estimating demand strength, and reacting to competitors' price changes.

The sales margin volume sub-variance, meanwhile, assesses the effect of changes in the level of sales activity on an organization's profits. In this regard the difference between the actual and budgeted volumes of sales activity, such as the number of restaurant covers sold for a period, must first be established. This volume difference should then be multiplied by the standard contribution margin (standard selling price less standard variable cost of sales). By utilizing the standard contribution

margin, the standard selling price is necessarily incorporated within the calculation – and thus the sales volume variance established will not be 'contaminated' by any changes in the actual selling price. The relative impact of the primary components of a sales margin volume variance can also be determined by analyzing two further sub-variances – a sales quantity variance, in the case of a restaurant, relating to the number of covers, and a sales mix variance, relating to the pattern of menu item selection. These variances further assist management in determining how much of a sales margin volume variance is primarily due to the impact of a change in sales quantity, and how much is attributable to a change in sales mix. The sales quantity variance reflects the difference in contribution, on a budgeted sales mix basis, between the actual and budgeted volume of sales activity for a period. Typical causes underlying a sales quantity variance include mis-estimating the relevant market size and/or the organization's share of that market. The sales mix variance corresponds to the difference in contribution, at the actual sales volume level, between the budgeted sales mix and the actual sales mix achieved. As indicated in the restaurant example, above, a common factor associated with a sales mix variance is a change in customer demand patterns.

Helpful variances in relation to a wide range of variable organization costs can also be calculated. Typically a total variance for e.g. food cost of sales is calculated by comparing the actual expenditure incurred with the flexed budgeted cost for the actual level of activity achieved. Where the actual cost incurred exceeds the budgeted cost, this is viewed as being an unfavorable or adverse variance – whereas if the budgeted amount is greater than the actual spend, this is termed a favorable variance. Importantly, this total food cost variance can also be further analyzed into two underlying sub-variances: a food price related (expenditure) variance, and a food quantity related (efficiency) variance.

Expenditure variances are usually determined by first calculating the difference between the actual price paid and the standard price per relevant cost unit. This difference is then multiplied by the actual cost units used during the period – thus ensuring that the price variance is applied in full to all the cost units actually consumed. Common reasons for an expenditure variance include actual quality and/or skill levels paid for being different from that expected. Efficiency variances, in the meantime, focus on the difference between the actual cost units used in a period and the standard amount of cost units that should have been consumed for the actual level of activity achieved. This difference is then multiplied by the standard price for a cost unit – thereby ensuring that the variance is not unduly affected by changes in the actual price paid. Typical causes for an efficiency variance may again include the impact of actual quality and/or skill levels obtained, as well as changes in production and/or service delivery methods.

References

Drury, C. (2001) *Management Accounting for Business Decisions*, 2nd edn. London: Thomson Learning.

Harris, P.J. (1999) *Profit Planning*, 2nd edn. Oxford: Butterworth-Heinemann.

Horngren, C.T., Bhimani, A., Datar, S.M., and Foster, G. (2002) *Management and Cost Accounting*, 2nd edn. Harlow, UK: Pearson Education.

Jagels, M. and Coltman, M. (2003) *Hospitality Management Accounting*, 8th edn. New York: John Wiley & Sons.

Schmidgall, R.S. (2002) *Hospitality Industry Managerial Accounting*, 5th edn. Lansing, MI: Educational Institute of the American Hotel and Lodging Association.

JACKIE BRANDER BROWN
MANCHESTER METROPOLITAN
UNIVERSITY, UK

Budgetary control

Operating budgets are meaningless unless they assist in controlling the business and hence maximize profits (or minimize costs). The objectives of control are to:

- Safeguard assets
- Ensure accuracy and reliability of data
- Promote efficiency
- Encourage adherence to prescribed managerial policies.

Use of the Uniform System of Accounts for the Lodging Industry or similar enables departmental reports to be produced for managers for both actual and budgeted ('standard') results. These should also include both financial and non-financial ratios that will then allow common-size comparisons to be made. Variances are calculated by monetary or numerical and percentage amount and are used by managers to identify areas for concern. The process is:

- Identification of variances, and determination of which are significant.
- Analysis of these and identification of the causes.
- Establishment of action to be taken.

Methods of control may be both physical or via systems, with increased technology such as EPOS (point of sale) systems aiding in the control of food and beverage. This may often be more tightly controlled than labor, although they account for a similar proportion of costs. However, managers should be aware which costs are variable in nature and therefore more controllable, and which are more fixed in nature and hence less manageable. If the reasons for the variances are unable to be solved then it may be necessary to re-forecast the budget using flexible budgetary techniques.

References

Burgess, C. (2001) *Caterer and Hotelkeeper Guide to Money Matters for Hospitality Managers*. Oxford: Butterworth-Heinemann.

Schmidgall, R. and de Franco, A. (1998). Budgeting and forecasting – current practice in the lodging industry. *Cornell Hotel and Restaurant Administration Quarterly*, December, 45–51.

CATHY BURGESS
OXFORD BROOKES UNIVERSITY, UK

Budgetary preparation

Budgets form a detailed operating plan that looks at all aspects of the hospitality business for the forthcoming financial year. It guides the firm towards its objectives, perhaps with the aid of a balanced-scorecard approach by making plans for the future that are then converted to financial and statistical information. The process for establishing the various aspects of the master budget requires the involvement of all managers within the organization. The benefits of budgeting are:

• Provides a strategic plan to assist in achieving objectives
• Establishes standards of performance
• Demonstrates the financial impact of management decisions
• Managers identify their own responsibility to the business.

There are three parts to a master budget – the operating, capital expenditure, and cash budgets.

Operating budgets

Operating budgets predict the profit and loss results for the forthcoming period (usually a financial year). Once a budget has been established comparisons may be made with actual results and variances analyzed (budgetary control). Flexible budgetary techniques may also be used to update figures or test alternative courses of action.

The advantages and disadvantages of an operating budget are:

Advantages	Disadvantages
Commitment and motivation of managers	The time taken and the cost of this time
Looks at alternatives	May be unexpected events that affect later results
Sets targets and standards	Information must remain confidential
If predicted volumes change, new sales and costs can be predicted using flexible budget techniques	Managers may treat cost budgets as separate from revenues, and hence over-spend if revenues are not achieved
Looks forward and considers both internal and external factors	

There are two approaches to budgeting – 'bottom up' and 'top down', with the bottom up approach resulting in a greater level of commitment from managers. Potentially, however, the sum of all the departments may not add up to the total unit requirements of head office. The approach is still somewhat hierarchical and often does not match current approaches to management with their emphasis on flexibility and empowerment.

In order to be effective operating budgets are prepared by departmental managers using the Uniform System of Accounts for the Lodging Industry or similar to give detailed figures for all volumes, sales, costs and hence profits or costs. These may be by month or in some cases (for instance, volumes) may be predicted by day for the entire financial year. The main steps towards achieving a successful operating budget are:

• Planning for attainable goals and objectives
• Comparing actual to budget and analyzing the differences (variances)
• Taking corrective action if required.

Sources of data are limiting factors, historical data, national, regional, and local economic indicators, the impact of price changes and marketing decisions, corporate level changes and managerial experience to produce the sales, costs and profits required. Departmental managers generally have knowledge of all these areas and their involvement via a responsibility accounting approach will lead to an increased commitment to achieving the actual results.

In diagrammatic form this may be shown as in Figure 1.

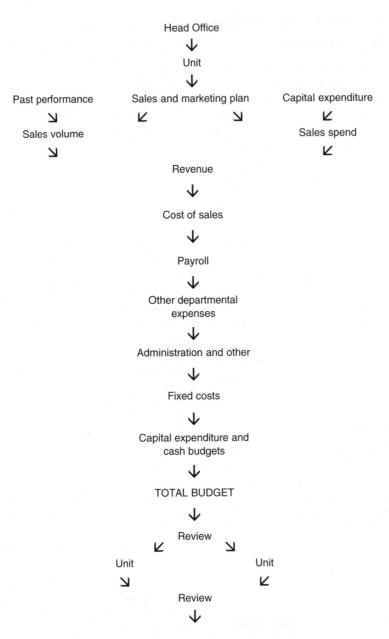

Figure 1   Budgeting process for a leisure hotel

Zero-based budget

Zero-based budgeting is used colloquially to mean the preparation of a budget from a nil-base – usually where little or no historical sales or cost information is available – for instance, for a new project or product. It is constructed by considering first volumes and average spends and then the costs associated with these (variable costs). Finally fixed costs are added to the budget.

The advantages and disadvantages of a zero-based approach to budgeting are:

Advantages	Disadvantages
Gives detailed information	Time, effort, and paperwork involved
Involves managers	Implies standard methods of budgeting are not good enough
Concentrates on monetary figures rather than percentages	
Identifies inefficiencies and duplication	

Capital expenditure budget

A capital expenditure budget is prepared to replace fixed assets, expand the business or for health and safety reasons, not all of which may be financially beneficial. This may impact on the operating budget in terms of revenues, operating costs and depreciation, and on the cash budget. There are different approaches to planning capital expenditure that may depend on the economy and the strategy of the company, but in all cases there must be a feasibility study as part of the process. Accurate predictions of capital expenditure are important because:

- The organization can commit substantial sums of money
- The purchase affects a long period with potential uncertainty
- It is almost impossible to reverse
- It may result in success or failure of the business.

A capital budget forecasts all aspects of the balance sheet, including fixed assets, working capital, and financing.

Cash budget

Cash is not necessarily the same as profits – businesses may be operationally profitable but due to high finance charges and/or slow payment by debtors may be technically insolvent. The cash budget forms one part of the master budget, together with the operating and capital expenditure budgets and are used for monitoring cash flows, planning acquisitions and refurbishments, investing surplus cash or borrowing if required, at optimum rates.

There are two approaches:

- *Direct* – uses receipts (cash and credit sales) less payments and calculates surpluses or deficits
- *Indirect* – the 'adjusted net income' approach that emphasizes external sources of cash; it takes profits and adds or subtracts the changes in assets and liabilities to achieve a forecasted balance.

Calculating cash flows is dependent on knowledge of existing cash balances, the ability to borrow, the level of risk, efficiency of systems and historical experience. The frequency of calculating these depends on the company and on the amount of cash available – established businesses may often only plan cash on an annual basis whereas new businesses may wish to plan their cash flows on a monthly basis.

References

Adams, D. (1997) *Management Accounting for the Hospitality Industry – a Strategic Approach.* London: Cassell.

Brander Brown, J. and Atkinson, H. (2001) Budgeting in the information age: a fresh approach. *International Journal of Contemporary Hospitality Management*, 13 (3), 136–143.

De Franco, A. and Schmidgall, R. (1999) Cash budgets and their uses in the lodging industry. *Bottomline*, June–July, pp. 43, 44, 47–52.

Pyrhh, P. (1973) *Zero-based Budgeting.* New York: John Wiley & Sons.

Uniform System of Accounts for the Lodging Industry, 9th edn. (1996) Lansing, MI: Educational Institute of the American Hotel and Motel Association.

CATHY BURGESS
OXFORD BROOKES UNIVERSITY, UK

Building codes

Building codes regulate construction methods and materials to protect the safety and welfare of people. Three major model building codes existed in the United States prior to 1994. These were the National Building Code (NBC), developed by the Building Official and Code Administrators International (BOCA), the Southern Building Code (SBC), developed by the Southern Building Code Congress International (SBCCI), and the Uniform Building Code (UBC), published by the International Conference of Building Officials (ICBO). Any municipality or state could adopt one of these three codes or they could develop their own set of regulations, which is why they are termed 'model' codes. Since they are codes, they are not enforceable until they are adopted. Codes provide minimum standards for occupancy classifications, types of construction and construction materials, interior finishes, accessibility, and fire protection systems. In 1994, the three organizations joined to form the International Code Council (ICC) to establish a uniform code. All three codes are now written in the same format so the order of topics is similar. Additionally, the intent is to phase out the three model building codes and incorporate all of the standards into one International Building Code.

References

Fisette, P. (2003) Decoding building codes. Retrieved 2 January 2003 from University of Massachusetts, Building Materials and Work Technology. Web site: http://www.umass.edu/bmatwt/publications/articles/building_codes.html

http://www.iccsafe.org/index.html

CAROLYN LAMBERT
PENNSYLVANIA STATE UNIVERSITY, USA

Building components

Major building components include items such as foundations (located under or at ground level), structural framing (usually steel but can be wood in smaller structures) or bearing walls (often poured concrete or concrete block but sometimes wood as well) providing the above ground physical support for the structure, curtain walls or other types of exterior façade or fenestration (glazing) (providing a weatherproof exterior for the building), the roof (consisting of a roof deck and weatherproof covering), interior walls (often with a steel or wood framing covered with drywall), and various elements of mechanical, electrical, and plumbing systems. Some properties may also have items such as parking (either in a ground level structure or in a parking garage) and possibly extensive grounds and landscaping. In addition, there are various elements of FF&E (furniture, fixtures, and equipment) including paint, wall coverings, carpet, foodservice equipment, dining tables and chairs, and guestroom furnishings. Components such as foundation and structural framing require little maintenance and hopefully little in the way of replacement investment over time. Interior walls, building systems, and FF&E may require substantial maintenance attention and cost on an ongoing basis. Other elements, such as roofing, may require little ongoing maintenance but substantial periodic replacement costs.

Reference

http://www.loanofficer.us/construction_terminology.htm

DAVID M. STIPANUK
CORNELL UNIVERSITY, USA

Burnout

Burnout is one of the more pernicious yet commonly misunderstood effects of work stress. Work stress among hospitality industry employees can be understood as both a psychological and a physical condition, and typically results from a perceived threat or demand neither easily dealt with nor circumvented. Stressors may be external or internal forces, which strain the consequential adverse effect upon the employee; burnout may then follow. This syndrome represents a state of exhaustion caused by chronic stress, and evidences a number of physiological, behavioral and cognitive consequences; physical problems may include chronic low levels of energy, frequent headaches, nausea, sleeplessness, and marked changes in eating habits. Psychological symptoms may include anxiety, fear, emotional liability, and out-of-character signs of defensiveness and heightened sensitivity to any perceived criticism. Within the hospitality industry work context burnout may frequently manifest itself in concentration problems, physical illnesses, absenteeism, and lack of interest in cooperating with others.

Major sources of damaging stress leading to burnout in hospitality industry work life include role conflict (wherein an employee has to choose between competing expectations and demands), and role overload or underload (wherein too much or too little work is assigned); disempowerment, diminished social support, and job insecurity (which might also involve the threat of unemployment) are also causal agents. Burnout may also be symptomatic of the hospitality employee's alienation from their work and from co-workers, and is commonly associated with uninteresting work, as well as unpredictable or unmanageable work levels; it might also be engendered by dysfunctional communication processes involving a range of individuals, including hotel general managers, line managers, subordinates, fellow hospitality industry employees, and even guests. The syndrome might further be elicited by the assignment of too much responsibility with little or no corresponding support or guidance for the employee.

Maslach et al. (2001) point out that employees suffering burnout can evidence a number of cognitive and behavioral patterns: they may become less energetic and less enthusiastic about their work; they may also indicate signs of depression as well as emotional and physical lassitude. Many such employees within the hospitality industry may find fault within their work environment, including those co-workers with whom they formerly enjoyed cordial and productive associations. Whilst the quantity of work performed may not diminish, the quality often does. Rigidity may also characterize this syndrome; individuals evidence a heightened preference for rules and procedures, often because exhaustion allows little or no flexibility to consider any other approach. It is also the case that an employee exhibiting this condition may, over time, have a negative impact upon the emotional health and competency of co-workers within any hotel or hospitality context. Burnout is also said to be more likely to strike workers who are dedicated and committed to their work, to such an extent that all other aspects of life become neglected. Such individuals may have performed a great deal of voluntary overtime, taken work home on a regular basis, and would prefer to be in the office on weekends and public holidays.

It was not until the late 1970s that many in the psychological and medical communities began to realize that burnout was a serious health issue, and was clearly not the usual experiences associated with moderate levels of work stress. The phenomenon of burnout has now been investigated widely in the workplace. Certain occupational groups, notably those dealing with people-problems, have a high incidence of burnout; the helping professions (Maslach et al., 2001) and also managers (Garden, 1989) are among those whose members have been found more vulnerable to this syndrome. The syndrome has been measured by way of the Maslach Burnout Inventory (Maslach et al., 1996), consisting of four sub-scales assessing the elements of emotional exhaustion (the feeling of being drained and empty, occasioned by excessive psychological and physical demands), depersonalization (insensitivity and pessimism, together with a reduced sensitivity regarding those with whom they work), personal accomplishment (the perception that one's actions are of no effect), and personal involvement (the perception of being cut off from others, dissociation); this inventory has now been successfully employed in a variety of employment contexts.

Methods of addressing or ameliorating hospitality industry burnout, focusing on the individual, need to include specific stress reduction techniques as well as general strategies aimed at lifestyle modification. Individual approaches encompass the recognition of stress symptoms, the development of methods to modify burnout's physical and physiological symptoms, the development of a support network among friends and relatives, and the regular practice of a preferred method of relaxation. Organizational means of addressing burnout include regular hospitality workplace audits aimed at eliminating or at least reducing those stressors commonly known to cause burnout; these should involve the fostering of participative decision-making, workload control, role clarity, the development of an empowering organizational climate, and the careful management of organizational change throughout the hospitality industry. Whilst some workers may feign burnout for ulterior motives, many more attempt to hide the condition; such attempts, however, assist neither the hospitality employee nor the organization. Addressing the problem of debilitative work stress, at both the organizational and the individual level, is the only effective solution for worker burnout (Maslach *et al.*, 2001).

Relatively little hospitality workplace research has been completed involving either burnout or even stress among staff and managers (Ross, 1995, 2003). Yet burnout is an ever-present possibility for members of the hospitality industry; those whose work involves people and interpersonal problem-solving, and also those who have an aspiration to high levels of service quality within a fiercely competitive business environment ought to be aware of the initial signs of this incapacitating syndrome. Whether during induction programs, in regular training, or in promotion orientations, methods by which debilitating work stress can be mitigated at the individual level should be introduced. Finally, structural elements and processes in the hospitality work environment such as role conflict, workload misassignment, or inattention to the organizational change process ought to be managed more competently and perceptively, so that burnout in this industry is minimized.

References

Garden, A. (1989) Burnout: the effect of psychological type on research findings. *Journal of Occupational Psychology*, 62 (2), 223–234.

Maslach, C., Jackson, S.E., and Leiter, M. (1996) *Maslach Burnout Inventory Manual*, 3rd edn. Palo Alto, CA: Counseling Psychologists Press.

Maslach, C., Schaufeli, W.B., and Leiter, M.P. (2001) Burnout. *Annual Review of Psychology*, 52, 397–422.

Ross, G.F. (1995) Work stress and personality dispositions among hospitality industry employees. *International Journal of Contemporary Hospitality Management*, 7 (6), 9–13.

Ross, G.F. (2003) Workstress response perceptions among potential employees: the influence of ethics and trust. *Tourism Review*, 58 (1), 25–33.

GLENN ROSS
JAMES COOK UNIVERSITY, AUSTRALIA

Business centers

Business centers within hotels provide services to business travelers who require an office away from the office. It is now an expectation that a range of facilities and services are provided to meet their business needs. Depending on the type of guest that a hotel targets, its business center may be open 24 hours a day, and according to Gee (1994, p. 362), it can provide: equipment such as computers, facsimile machines, printers, pager systems etc.; services such as audiovisual services, secretarial services, translation services, desktop publishing services etc.; and facilities such as private offices, meeting rooms, lounges and libraries.

Today, various survey findings report that up to 85% of business travelers require the use of some type of office equipment (copier, PC, printer and/or fax machine) while registered in a hotel. Nearly 60% of these travelers indicate that a hotel's ability to offer these services has a bearing on their choice of accommodation. Even while claiming to be on vacation, 35% of professionals will seek the use of hotel business services at least once during the course of their lodging.

Hotel and lodging properties are rapidly moving to business centers with free usage of fax, printing, and copying equipment. A slightly higher room rate may often be justification enough to the traveler who is provided with an efficient working environment.

References

Baker, S., Bradley, P., and Huyton, J. (1994) *Principles of Hotel Front Office Operations London*. London: Cassell.

Chuck, Y. (1994) *International Hotel Management USA*. Lansing, MI: Educational Institute of the American Hotel and Motel Association.

IRENE SWEENEY
INTERNATIONAL HOTEL MANAGEMENT
INSTITUTE SWITZERLAND, SWITZERLAND

Business environment

Hospitality includes the provision of accommodation and food and beverage services within a wide range of establishments and occasions. Paul Morrison, editor of the *Australian Journal of Hospitality Management*, has noted that these include hotels, motels, clubs, casinos, restaurants, fast food outlets, bars, special event catering, and other services, farm and bed and breakfast establishments, but also in-flight, shipping, rail, school, hospital, college and armed forces catering services (Morrison, 1996). He also suggested that while some patrons are bona fide tourists, the majority are undertaking leisure or commercial activities. This definition of the coverage of the hospitality industry led him to state that it is the hospitality industry not the tourism industry that provides most of the employment and creates the associated wealth attributed to tourism.

The business environment for those firms, government departments, and associations engaged in the hospitality industry is, as might be expected, similar in its generic aspects to that faced by any other industry, while containing a few specific components relating to the nature of that industry (Ansoff, 1987). These generic aspects are the macroeconomic environment, market opportunities, the political environment concerning enterprise and competition, policies towards foreign investment, trade, and exchange controls, taxes, and financing, and the social environment including labor markets, physical and social infrastructures, and national and regional cultures (White and Rudall, 1999; Hope, 2004).

The internal business environment for the larger contemporary hospitality organizations includes *inter alia* production, marketing, facility management, purchasing, finance, information technology, and human resource management divisions, while as with other industries smaller firms may not be as internally differentiated. For any hospitality business to perform effectively however, interdependent individuals and groups within them must establish working relationships across those boundaries that exist. Individuals and groups depend on one another for information and support facilities so that action can be coordinated and complementary (White and Rudall, 1999, 13).

The external business environment of the firm is most often largely uncontrollable by management. Factors such as demography, economic conditions, level of competition, industry structure, social and cultural forces, political and legal forces, and technological level impact on the ability of the firm to provide its services to its intended clients and to sustain its internal business environment. Equally, external microenvironmental factors of the market, suppliers, competitors and intermediaries all influence the behavior of the firm in the business environment. External factors perceived as causing change in the business environment are generally identified as pertaining to two main categories: regulatory frameworks and local business culture and structures (Correia and Wilson, 1997). Changes of a regulatory nature (i.e., in rules and procedures, tariff barriers) may be linked to the nation joining a trading bloc such as the European Community or NAFTA and to government intervention in the economy (foreign ownership rules, monetary policy), while changes of a business nature may be linked to such trends as concentration in the industry and the economic health of client industries, as well as to culturally based ways of conducting business.

Assessment of these environmental influences in recent times has shown that the business environment for the hospitality industry has become increasingly hostile and rather complex, even though turbulence has at times stayed relatively low (Ansoff, 1987). On the other hand, the advent of such environments as the European Union-type Single Market or the global hotel chain have been recognized as inevitable and their ramifications are now faced predominantly with a moderate degree of optimism within such markets and by smaller players in the industry, as it is now widely believed that keeping market shares or conquering a niche market or realizing a successful alliance are possible in most business environments. Also, a firm may have some influence on the politico-legal forces in its environment through direct representations and industry association lobbying.

Factors that affect the impact of internal or external environments are the size of the firm and the complexity of its organizational structure. Another factor that influences the attention given by managers to internal or external environments is the predominance of certain types of business culture within the firm, or the non-existence of a business culture. The functional role played by the firm in the hospitality industry also influences the impact of internal or external environments. Internal environments are viewed by some managers as filters and by others as contaminators of the information provided by external environments. Some managers stress the complementarities between impersonal and personal business environments, impersonal environments being looked at as conveyors of generic information, meaning information that is in the public domain, or about factors which, in principle, evolve gradually, and also as means to feed an attitude of general awareness. While personal environments would convey specific information, meaning more or less secret information that cannot be found on printed sources and is transmitted only by word-of-mouth, or specific and detailed information that can help in clarifying ideas or implementing specific business strategies.

References

Ansoff, H.I. (1987) *Corporate Strategy*, rev. edn. London: Penguin.

Correia, Z. and Wilson, T.D. (1997) Scanning the business environment for information: a grounded theory approach. *Information Research*, 2 (4). Available at: http://informationr.net/ir/2-4/paper21.html

Hope, C. (2004) The impact of national culture on the transfer of 'best practice operations management' in hotels in St Lucia. *Tourism Management*, 25, 45–59.

Morrison, P. (1996) Editorial. *Australian Journal of Hospitality Management*, 3 (1), iii.

White, C. and Rudall, L. (1999) Dimensions and measurement of internal serviced quality in the hospitality industry. *Australian Journal of Hospitality Management*, 6 (2), 13–22.

MALCOLM COOPER
RITSUMEIKAN ASIA PACIFIC
UNIVERSITY, JAPAN

Business level strategy

Business level strategy is defined as the approach taken by an organization to compete in its chosen markets. A business level strategy can be competitive – battling against all competitors to secure competitive advantage – and/or cooperative advantage – working with one or more players to gain advantage against other competitors. Porter (1980) classified strategies into two generic types aimed at a broad segment of market.

- *Low-cost leadership:* Based on efficient cost production that enables the company to charge a lower price for its product than its competitors and still make a satisfactory profit. Factors that underline low-cost structure include economies of scale and learning experience effects. To illustrate: Accor hotels cater to large segment of the population and strive to keep costs low, while providing clean, functional, and comfortable rooms.
- *Differentiation:* Refers to the ability to provide unique value to customers and create brand loyalty that lowers customer sensitivity to price. To illustrate, Marriott has been adding services available to guests once they have checked in, including in-room services and toiletries. Pursuing both differentiation and low cost may create sustainable competitive advantage.

Porter also identified a third option, called *focus strategy*, in which companies target a narrow segment of market. Firms can *focus* on a particular segment through either low-cost leadership (Motel 6) or differentiation (Ritz–Carlton). Firms that do not pursue a distinct generic strategy are *stuck in the middle* (Harrison and Enz, 2005).

References

Harrison, J.S. and Enz, C.A. (2005) *Hospitality Strategic Management: Concepts and Cases*. New Jersey: John Wiley & Sons.

Porter, M.E. (1980) *Competitive Strategy*. New York: The Free Press.

SIGAL HABER
TEL-AVIV UNIVERSITY, ISRAEL

Business Management Institute (BMI)

The Business Management Institute, most frequently referred to as BMI, is the comprehensive educational program of the Club Managers Association of America (CMAA). Designed as a series of courses, BMI offers continuing education specifically for club managers.

The Club Managers Association of America began in 1927 when managers of independent clubs across the country expressed a desire to unite for the purpose of discussing issues of mutual interest. Throughout the organization's evolution, visionary members suggested a focus on education. It was not until 1955, however, that CMAA offered its first highly structured five-day educational program, held at the University of Houston.

In 1986 Joe Perdue was recruited by CMAA to develop what would become BMI, a program originally envisioned by club manager Chris Borders. Perdue led the development of course programs and content, and the first BMI course was offered in 1988 at Georgia State University. The growth and success of the program over the years is widely acclaimed.

BMI currently consists of five hierarchical courses that serve managers ranging in experience from entry level to senior level club professionals; additionally, eight elective programs are available. All BMI courses are intensive one-week learning experiences taught by university faculty and industry experts at seven leading universities throughout the United States. BMI today exists as an educational role model for other professional organizations. It boasts of over 5000 graduates and serves as a stepping-stone for club managers who aspire to the prestigious designation of Certified Club Manager (CCM).

References

Morris, R. (2001) *Club Managers Association of America 1927–2002, Celebrating Seventy-Five Years of Service*. Virginia Beach, VA: Donning Company Publishers.

Perdue, Joe (ed.) (1997) *Contemporary Club Management*. Lansing, MI: Educational Institute of the American Hotel and Motel Association.

CANDICE CLEMENZ
UNIVERSITY OF WEST FLORIDA, USA

Business process reengineering (BPR)

Business processes are activities that transform a set of inputs into a set of outputs. BPR has been propelled due to recent ICT developments and the proliferation of the Internet (Hammer and Stanton, 1995). Many hotels redesigned their inter- and intraorganizational processes to increase efficiency and facilitate interaction and interconnectivity (Buhalis, 2003). Hospitality distribution is a good example of BPR, where hotels redesign best processes to reach their customers and partners. In contrast to continuous process improvements, BPR requires process designers to start from a clean slate, disassociating themselves from current thinking and focusing on a new course of action.

Successful BPR projects require:

- Senior management commitment and support
- Appropriate manpower and equipment
- Well-defined core business processes as well as project scope and objectives
- Adequate funding
- Technological innovation and solutions considered
- Assumptions and preconceptions challenged.

Factors for BPR failure include:

- Inappropriate change management
- Leaders losing focus on the scope and goals of the initiative

- Difficulty in monitoring the progress of change.

Technological developments and the Internet will continually force hospitality organizations to review their working processes and to radically re-engineer the nature of their business.

References

Buhalis, D. (2003) *eTourism: Information Technology for Strategic Tourism Management*. Harlow: Prentice-Hall.

Hammer, M. and Stanton, S.A. (1995) *The Re-engineering Revolution: A Handbook*. New York: HarperBusiness.

DIMITRIUS BUHALIS
UNIVERSITY OF SURREY, UK
RUTH OWEN
UNIVERSITY OF SURREY, UK

Business risk

Business risk varies across industries as well as across firms within a given industry. Demand variability or seasonality, input cost fluctuations, sales price volatility, operating leverage and a firm's ability to keep up with competition and to adapt its sales price to absorb cost fluctuations are some factors that can influence a firm's business risk. Such factors depend partly on a firm's industry characteristics. However, a firm's management may also control these factors to some extent. For instance, the seasonality in a ski resort's demand may be industry-specific. However, the management may successfully reduce such demand volatility by organizing pre-season and post-season festivals, thereby stretching the seasons. The firm-specific aspect of business risk may also be eliminated via diversification by the firm's equity holders.

References

Brigham, E.F. and Gapenski, L.C. (1993) *Intermediate Financial Management*, 4th edn. Orlando, FL: The Dryden Press.

Weston, J.F. and Brigham, E.F. (1993) *Essentials of Managerial Finance*, 10th edn. Orlando, FL: The Dryden Press.

ATUL SHEEL
UNIVERSITY OF MASSACHUSETTS, USA

C

Capital assets pricing model

The Capital assets pricing model (CAPM) developed by Sharpe (1964) and Lintner (1965) describes the relationship between risk and required rate of return. The CAPM proposes that the required rate of return on a risky asset is composed of the risk-free rate of return plus a risk premium, which is the excess market return over the risk-free rate multiplied by the level of systematic risk of the asset. Systematic risk, often denoted as beta, is a measure of a stock's covariance with the capital market.

According to the CAPM, hospitality investors expect to be compensated for bearing the systematic risk. Here, the unsystematic risk of a hospitality firm, which is the stock volatility caused by firm-specific events, such as labor disputes or lawsuits, is irrelevant. Unsystematic risk can be eliminated via diversification and hence plays no role in determining the hospitality investor's expected return. Symbolically, the CAPM for determining the required rate of return for a particular hospitality security i, can be described as:

$$R_i = R_f + \beta_i (R_m - R_f)$$

where R_i is the required return for security i, R_m is the return on the market portfolio, R_f is the risk-free rate, and β_i is the estimated beta for security i.

References

Lintner, J. (1965) Security prices, risk and maximal gains from diversification. *Journal of Finance*, 20 (4), 587–615.

Sharpe, W.F. (1964) Capital asset prices: a theory of market equilibrium under conditions of risk. *Journal of Finance*, 19 (3), 425–442.

HYUNJOON KIM
UNIVERSITY OF HAWAII, USA

Career planning and development

Career planning and development is the 'lifelong process of working out a synthesis between individual interests and the opportunities (or limitations) present in the external work related environment, so that both individual and environmental objectives are fulfilled' (Van Maanen 1977, p. 36). It is a continual process that affects both the individual and the hospitality organization. For the individual in the hospitality industry it involves career planning and career outcomes and encompasses such issues as job change, mobility, and stages of a career. Whilst for the hospitality organization it is concerned with and influences human resource planning. The demise of the traditional hospitality organizational career, with its vertical progression, has affected an individual's career development, with the trend now being to develop core skills, increase marketability and develop employability. The focus is one of continuous personal development, building out from core jobs, sideways moves, cross-functional movement, and job growth and development. These changes have impacted on hotel general managers within the hospitality industry, with Ladkin (2002) arguing that a gradual shift is being seen from the traditional skill base (such as food and beverage) to more managerial and business skills together with the need for international experience and language skills. In the development of a career in the hospitality industry networking and using industry contacts are key career planning strategies.

References

Ladkin, A. (2002) Career analysis: a case study of hotel general managers in Australia. *Tourism Management*, 23 (4), 379–388.

Van Maanen, J. (1977) *Organizational Careers: Some New Perspectives*. London: John Wiley & Sons.

VIVIENNE McCABE
SOUTHERN CROSS UNIVERSITY, AUSTRALIA

Cash flow

Cash flow is the term often used to describe the inflow and outflow of liquid assets from operations. A cash flow statement is one of the top three financial statements used in foodservice operations, along with income (profit and loss) statements and balance statements. An income statement indicates profit and loss for a specified accounting period. A balance statement shows the assets and liabilities of an organization at a given time. Neither of these shows the amount of funds available to meet current financial obligations, which is the purpose of a cash flow statement. For that reason, most financial institutions insist on healthy cash flow statements as an indication of their ability to meet current obligations.

According to generally accepted accounting principles, cash flow statements can be prepared by the *direct method* or the *indirect method*. The direct method takes into consideration only the cash receipts and payments from operations. The indirect method considers all receipts and payments irrespective of the source. A cash flow statement begins with net income from the earlier period. It is followed by cash inflows from operational sources, investment activities, etc. It will then include cash outflows used to meet operational, financial, legal, and other obligations. Net cash available to meet immediate operational needs is also identified.

Reference

James Keiser and Frederick J. DeMicco with Robert Grimes (2000) *Contemporary Management Theory: Controlling and Analyzing Costs in Foodservice Operations*, 4th edn. Columbus, OH: Prentice-Hall.

H.G. PARSA
OHIO STATE UNIVERSITY, USA

Cash flow statement

The cash flow statement provides an overview of the cash inflows and outflows of an organization. While the profit and loss (income) statement can provide one perspective on the organization's profit performance, it fails to provide an indication of the organization's cash flows. This is because the profit and loss statement is prepared on the basis of accrual accounting and not cash flow accounting. One example of why the profit reported in the profit and loss statement does not represent cash flow is the fact that depreciation of fixed assets is included as an expense in the profit and loss statement. There is, however, no cash flow associated with depreciation. It merely represents the allocation of the cost of an asset that might have been purchased several years earlier. The statement of cash flows can thus be seen to provide useful supplementary information to that provided in the profit and loss statement. In the statement of cash flows example presented below, cash flow from operations represents the normal trading operations' cash receipts minus the cash payments associated with normal trading activities. The remainder of the terms used in the statement are relatively self-explanatory.

ABC Hotel
Cash Flow Statement the year ending
31 December 200X, in US$

	$	$
Net cash flow from operations		210,000
Cash flow from investments and for servicing finance:		
Interest on loan capital	(5,000)	
Drawings	(125,000)	
		(130,000)
		80,000
Investing activities:		
Fixed assets purchased	(54,000)	
Proceeds from fixed assets sales	22,000	
		(32,000)
		48,000
Sources of finance:		
Capital introduced	18,000	
Loan raised	4,000	
		22,000
Net cash flow for the year		70,000

References

Harris, P.J. (1999) *Profit Planning*, 2nd edn. Oxford: Butterworth-Heinemann.

Jagels, M.G. and Coltman, M.M. (2003) *Hospitality Management Accounting*, 8th edn. New York: John Wiley & Sons.

CHRIS GUILDING
GRIFFITH UNIVERSITY, AUSTRALIA

Casinos

Casino hotels have been one of the most rapidly growing and expanding sectors of the lodging industry over the past 15 years. Casino hotels vary in size from small limited service hotels in small markets such as remote Native American reservations (Eagle Pass, Texas and some areas of North and South Dakota), or smaller riverboat jurisdictions in Iowa and Louisiana, to large opulent hotels worthy of five-star or diamond ratings as are found in Las Vegas and Connecticut. Four of the seven largest hotels (rooms-wise) in the world are casino hotels. These large casino hotels can be found amongst the commercial casino brand names that many of us are familiar with: MGM Grand, Venetian, and Park Place Entertainment (to be renamed Caesars as of January 2004); and Native American casinos such as Foxwood's and Mohegan Sun, both of which are in Connecticut.

There are many reasons for the growth of hotels in the casino industry. Perhaps the paramount reason is the location of the population center from which the players come. One needs only to look at the two premiere gaming markets in the United States: Las Vegas and Atlantic City. The primary population centers for Las Vegas are Los Angeles and San Francisco. Both are located over 275 miles from Las Vegas. Atlantic City boasts that 25% of the population of the United States lives within a gas tank's drive of Atlantic City. This disparity in distance has led to a disparity in the number of hotel rooms each city has. Since a 550-mile roundtrip in a single day is possible, but certainly undesirable, Las Vegas casinos have built 129,000 hotel rooms to accommodate their guests. Since most of the players who frequent Atlantic City casinos live less than 150 miles away, the casinos have opted to provide 8–12 hour bus tours for their patrons. Consequently, even with the newly opened (July 2003) Borgata Resort/Casino, Atlantic City has only 30,000 hotel rooms, which is small considering that they are the second largest gaming jurisdiction in the United States.

Some of the other reasons are: competition (every casino is striving to draw customers, many of whom are clamoring for new casinos, concepts, themes, decorations, shows, etc.), consolidation (sometimes it is the only way to achieve a desirable location), partnerships (the casinos and the Las Vegas Visitors and Convention Bureau are trying to make Las Vegas, the premier convention city in the United States, if not the world; toward this end, Mandalay Bay Casino has just completed a 1.6 million square foot stand-alone convention center), and finally, replacement (in the casino industry the customers have loudly proclaimed that old is not necessarily better).

Casino hotels have long realized the importance of the lodging industry. There have been many discussions between casino operators and well-known hotel companies regarding the lodging operations of a casino hotel. Currently, there are two prestigious lodging companies actively partnering with casino companies. The Hyatt Corporation is an active partner in the Lake Las Vegas Resort. When the Mandalay Bay Corporation was looking to partner with a hotel company, who would be able to successfully deal with their high-roller clientele, they contacted the Four Seasons Corporation of exclusive luxury hotel fame. This led to a unique partnership; Mandalay Bay operates the casino and most of their hotel, while Four Seasons handles only the exclusive high-roller customers. Four Seasons has nothing to do with the casino operation. This is a win–win for both companies since Mandalay Bay is able to use the Four Seasons name in their advertising and has the benefit of their expertise, while Four Seasons now has access to a market they otherwise might never have.

Casino hotels go against the trends of the traditional lodging industry. In the past two years, a number of cataclysmic events have seriously wounded the lodging industry. These events are: the terrorist attacks of 9/11, the war in Afghanistan, the SARS epidemic, a poor economy, and the war in Iraq. These events have led to governmental controls which, while deemed necessary for international security, have further negatively affected an already skittish traveling public. Less international travel, less domestic air travel, and vacationing closer to home have all contributed to less hotel demand; yet the casino industry continues to grow and expand. One of the hotel industry's most respected daily current events reporters, www.hotelon-line.com, reports almost daily on a new casino opening or a new casino hotel tower being built. One of the reasons casinos are able to be pro-active is that their revenue is not tied just to hotel revenue.

The casino industry itself gambles on human nature and that it will not change. Even during difficult times, financial or otherwise, people seem to pursue escapism and entertainment in the form of gambling. Barring significant scandals that would erode the gambling public's confidence, casino hotels seem likely to continue to grow, both in size and number. While traditional lodging concepts and barometers are not always applicable to casino hotels, conversely, some of the technology and practices developed by the large casino hotels are being adopted by larger traditional hotel operations. The future development of these relationships will be of interest.

Reference

Stutts, Alan T. (2001) *Hotel and Lodging Management – An Introduction.* John Wiley & Sons, New York.

JAMES WORTMAN
UNIVERSITY OF HOUSTON, USA

Centralization

An organization structure where elements of a system are united and consolidated under a single center. This type of organization can be applied to computer systems, networks, employees, and business facilities, as well. Centralization arose in the 1980s, when computers became able to establish better control in organization departments. The advantages of centralization are: increased organization of a system, cost reduction due to standardization of equipment and procedures, and increased efficiency. The downside is inflexibility and slow implementation of structural changes. Decentralization denotes organizational structure where administrative control is distributed towards system elements or local sub-centers or groups. Decentralization enables increased communication among local parts of the organization and decreases formal communication. Implementation of decentralization is, generally, slightly more risky than that of centralization. These risks include neglect, mismanagement, and loss of objectivity. Computer systems could enhance both of these strategies, and also combine them, in a complex way, in a business organization. The way to decentralize or centralize a company's operations, facilities, or management policies must be derived from a careful analysis of the company's existing state, immediate needs, and future goals. Hotel reservation systems are sometimes made for smaller individual hotels, while for hotel chains they have centralized reservation facilities. When several reservation systems should be integrated, their infrastructure could be organized according to the decentralization principles.

References

Buhalis, D. (2003) *eTourism: Information Technology for Strategic Tourism Management*. Harlow: Prentice-Hall.

George, J.F. and King, J.L. (1991) Examining the computing and centralization debate. *Communication of the ACM*, 34 (7), 63–72.

BOZIDAR KLICEK
UNIVERSITY OF ZAGREB, CROATIA

Centralized guestroom HVAC

Centralized guestroom HVAC systems utilize fan coil units installed either vertically (usually adjacent to a window) or horizontally (usually immediately over the entry area within the room). The fan coil units consist of a copper pipe with fins to enhance heat transfer and a drip pan and drain to collect condensate that may occur during cooling operation. There is also a fan to circulate air through the unit and out into the room and a filter to remove airborne dust. The fan coil units are connected to pipes which deliver chilled or hot water to the rooms. Rooms with 2-pipe fan coil units can only deliver heat (if the pipes are connected to the boiler) or cold (if the pipes are connected to the chiller) with the connection decision made based on the climate season (chiller connection in common cooling seasons and boiler in common heating seasons). Some 2-pipe units have an electric heating coil to provide space heating. Rooms with 4-pipe fan coil units can deliver heat or cooling depending on the choice of the guest. Two of the pipes provide supply and return for hot water while the other two provide this for cold water. Control of fan coil units is provided by the guestroom thermostat.

References

ASHRAE (1999) Hotels, motels, and dormitories. *ASHRAE Applications Handbook*, ch 5. Atlanta, GA: American Society of Heating, Refrigeration and Air Conditioning Engineers.

Stipanuk, D.M. (2002) *Hospitality Facilities Management and Design*, 2nd edn. Lansing, MI: Educational Institute of the American Hotel and Lodging Association, pp. 238–240.

DAVID M. STIPANUK
CORNELL UNIVERSITY, USA

Chain restaurants

Chain (also called *multi-unit*) restaurant companies dominate the modern retail landscape, but for all intents and purposes the chain restaurant segment is a post-World War II phenomenon. There were multi-unit operators prior to 1950, but they were few and far between. Since 1954, chains have been slowly growing to the point of now representing more than one out of every two dollars in US foodservice sales.

One early example of a multi-unit restaurant chain was the Harvey Restaurant Company. Created in the late nineteenth century, Harvey restaurants were available to travelers stopping in railroad stations as the new intercontinental trains moved from East to West. Men, women, and their families were greeted by 'Harvey Girls' wearing standard blue pinafore uniforms in clean and familiar dining rooms offered in the genteel 'tea house' style of the time.

Probably the greatest contribution to the ideas we now accept as defining the chain restaurant came from industry pioneer Howard Johnson. He began quite modestly, selling ice cream to beachgoers at a traffic circle on US Highway 1 in Quincy, Massachusetts in the early 1920s. Demand was great, and he offered broader menu options such as hotdogs, fried clams, and saltwater taffy. Visitors from up and down the East Coast asked if they could sell his products in their home markets, which gave Johnson the opportunity to expand his brand recognition through licensing and the use of innovative franchising models. He identified his restaurants with strong architectural designs, including an orange roof with turquoise trim, and the brand icon of Simple Simon and the Pieman from the children's nursery rhyme. As his empire expanded along Route 1 from Portland, Maine, all the way to Miami, Florida, Johnson became acutely aware of the harm inconsistencies at one operator could cause across his system. Howard Johnson was completely focused on operational excellence, and it is generally accepted that he was the first to describe each of the units in his system as being like a 'link in a *chain of restaurants*.'

During the 1950s the combination of Baby Boom demographics, the advent of the Eisenhower Interstate Highway System, and a growing affluence created a fertile market for the efficiencies that chain restaurants encompassed. First to catch on to this market were the fast food/quick service companies, especially Kentucky Fried Chicken, McDonald's, and Burger King. Many others entered and left the market as the times changed and views on how and where people dined evolved. With each passing year, consumers have become more accustomed to having their meals in a chain restaurant, with a corresponding decline in the impact of independent operations. Today more than nine out of every ten hamburgers eaten away from home are ordered in a chain restaurant setting.

In 1978 D. Daryl Wyckoff and W. Earl Sasser offered this definition, which with the minor change to three units, is still in common use: '*Restaurant chains* are two or more eating establishments at separate locations under common ownership or related through other legal entities (e.g. franchising) which, as the dominant activity, provide prepared food for consumption on or off premises' (Wyckoff and Sasser, 1978).

By the end of 2002 there were in the United States over 4000 chain companies that fit this definition, 39 of them doing more than $1 billion in sales annually. These chains include everything from the giant international hamburger companies to small local franchisees with three or four units in a single suburban market. In fact, some large restaurant franchisee companies are publicly listed corporations with revenues in the hundreds of millions of dollars annually. Other chains are privately held corporations, partnerships, or even entrepreneurial sole proprietorships. There are as many different ways to operate as a multi-unit chain restaurant company as there are people interested in creating them.

The largest chain restaurant companies employ many thousands of workers each, generating more than USD 200 billion in sales annually. Leading companies in the QSR segment include McDonald's, Burger King, Kentucky

Table 1   Chain restaurant leadership, 1975–1999

1975	1999
McDonald's	McDonald's
Kentucky Fried Chicken	Burger King
Burger King	Wendy's
A & W Root Beer	Taco Bell
Howard Johnson's	Pizza Hut
Pizza Hut	KFC
Tastee Freez	Subway
Hardee's	Dairy Queen
Sambo's Restaurants	Domino's Pizza
Burger Chef	Applebee's

Fried Chicken, Taco Bell, Pizza Hut, and Wendy's. In the full service casual theme segment, leading companies include Red Lobster, Applebee's, and Olive Garden. From 1975 until 1999 – 25 years of sustained growth in the chain restaurant industry – all but four leading companies stayed in positions of leadership. Three companies on the original list are completely gone (Howard Johnson's, Sambo's Restaurants, and Burger Chef), replaced by a new breed of restaurant concepts (Wendy's, Taco Bell, Subway, and Applebee's) (Table 1).

References

Bernstein, C. and Paul, R. (1994) *Winning the Chain Game: Eight Key Strategies*. New York: John Wiley & Sons.

Wyckoff, D.D. and Sasser, W.E. (1978) *The Chain-Restaurant Industry*. Lanham, MD: Lexington Books, p. xxiii.

CHRISTOPHER MULLER
UNIVERSITY OF CENTRAL FLORIDA, USA

Change management

In all sectors, organizations have to respond to external and internal environmental factors and improve on performance. Change management is usually seen as the planned organizational response to these two objectives. External factors include political, economic, social, and technological events or circumstances which influence the environment in which an organization functions. These can operate at both a macro and a micro level, either affecting the sector as a whole or sub-sections or specific organizations within it. Within the hospitality and tourism sector these include the impact of regional conflicts, regional or global recession, demographic changes, property prices, increased leisure spend, increasing globalization, the emergence of markets and new business centers in newly industrialized countries, and the increasing use of the Internet by both businesses and individuals. Internal factors can be such things as a change in ownership as a result of mergers and acquisitions, procedural or policy changes to reinforce brand differentiation or customer focus, restructuring to achieve greater job flexibility, expansion or downsizing. The key to change management is not only to be able to respond to these drivers of change but also to anticipate them.

Theories of change management can be divided two ways: either by the nature of the change; planned change or emergent change; or by the methods and systems used to achieve that change; hard systems or soft systems (Senior, 2002). Planned change models are largely based on the work of Kurt Lewin (1951). He developed a three phase model of change management which stressed that for change to take place there has to be an 'unfreezing' of the present behaviors and attitudes, to reinforce the need for change, then activities or processes such as restructuring, training or staff redeployment to 'move' or change the status quo within the organization, and finally a 'refreezing' of the new behaviors and standards to ensure that embedding of the changes. Most other models of planned change follow a similar pattern, albeit with a varying number of steps.

Alternatively, the emergent approach to change believes that nowadays the forces for change are so complex and constant that it is impossible to fully plan the change process. This is particularly pertinent for the dynamic business environment in which international hospitality organizations operate. Also, with constant change the timescales for change programs make 'refreezing' obsolete, as each change program is lapped by the next initiative. Instead, change should be a process of continuous adaptation and improvement throughout the organization. The emergent change approach also stresses the role of power and organizational politics during

change which are often overlooked in change management models.

In relation to hard or soft systems approaches to change, hard systems models emphasize the detailed diagnosis of the change situation, generation, and selection of options and the planned implementation of the change. Although this approach is useful for clearly defined changes such as implementing a new computer system, it is less helpful when hospitality managers are confronted with more complex changes, especially changes where staff behaviors, attitudes, and values need to be addressed. The interface between the sub-systems of foodservice and production is an obvious example where worker attitudes and behaviors are in an almost constant state of flux. The soft systems approach therefore focuses on developing organizational capacity for change and using methodologies associated with organizational development such as action research, team building, culture change and quality initiatives. These approaches stress the importance of participation and communication during the change process. However, Dunphy and Stace (1993) pointed out that it is not always possible or advisable to involve staff and that the selection of the correct strategy for change management is contingent on the nature of the change itself.

One of the main issues in change management is anticipating and understanding stakeholder responses to change and consequently, overcoming resistance to change. Although from an organizational point of view resistance to change is usually seen as a negative event, as it slows down the progress of change, it can be seen as a natural reaction, especially when there is a high level of uncertainty and employees fear reorganization, relocation or even redundancy.

Kotter and Schlesinger (1979) suggested six strategies for overcoming resistance to change. These strategies were:

- *Education and communication:* Making sure that all stakeholders understood the need for change and the actual details of the change process and how it would impact on them.
- *Participation and involvement:* Kotter and Schlesinger recognized that if employees were consulted at an early stage of planning the change they were less likely to resist.

- *Facilitation and support:* Where it was unlikely that employees would be accepting of the proposed change, for example in a redundancy situation, change managers must ensure humane treatment to help the employee come to terms with the implications of change.
- *Negotiation and agreement:* Where resistance was a result of a specific sticking point, change managers may wish to amend their plans to gain agreement and buy-in.
- *Manipulation and cooptation:* When time is short or where confidentiality is paramount, for example, it may be necessary to limit the flow of information and therefore the ability of opposing factions to mount any resistance to the change.
- *Explicit or implicit coercion:* In some instances it may be necessary to force through an unpopular change and rebuild support after the event. Many hospitality managers adopt this 'business process engineering' approach. That is, change decisions are made and implemented swiftly. Disgruntled employees often quit their jobs but are soon replaced by new recruits particularly where labor supply outstrips demand. Moreover, this is a typical scenario in mid-quality hotels where much operation work has been deskilled.

Finally, it is important throughout the change process to consider the ethical dimensions of change management. Many change programs are a result of a desire to improve customer service, service quality or overall organizational performance. To achieve this, many change models stress the importance of alignment of organizational and individual goals and values. In reality, this may mean the acceptance of negative outcomes for the individual and the sublimation of considerable personal stress and anxiety into increased performance and attitude change. It is therefore vital that those who are leading a change program have excellent interpersonal and leadership skills to support employees during the transition period.

References

Dunphy, D. and Stace, D. (1993) The strategic management of change. *Human Relations*, 46 (8), 905–918.

Kotter, J.P. and Schlesinger, L.A. (1979) Choosing strategies for shange. *Harvard Business Review*, March–April.

Lewin, K. (1951) *Field Theory in Social Science*. New York: Harper & Row.

Senior, B. (2002) *Organisational Change*, 2nd edn. Harlow: Prentice-Hall.

GILLIAN KELLOCK HAY
GLASGOW CALEDONIAN UNIVERSITY, UK

Characteristics of service

Increasingly, products from the hospitality industry are becoming more difficult to differentiate. Operators are clever and quick to duplicate the tangible efforts of their competition. The similarities in the menu variety at Applebee's and Chili's or the guestrooms at Hawthorne Suites and Spring Hill Suites or the travel experience purchased through Expedia and Travelocity are all examples of this phenomenon. Consequently, the marketplace is left with homogeneity of the physical product being offered. To a greater extent, hospitality organizations must recognize service characteristics (intangibles) that enable them to differentiate their products (tangibles) in the marketplace to sustain long-term success. Presented here are the characteristics that are unique to the production and delivery of services by hospitality firms where success is achieved through differentiation from their competition.

The following are 13 distinguishable characteristics of service. To achieve world-class service, it is important for hospitality professionals to understand how these characteristics interact with their service delivery system so they can focus on factors that are salient to their customers.

Service is an experience for the customer

The interaction between the customer and the service provider will leave an impression on the customer. The effect of the interaction between the service provider and the customer will either enhance or detract from the customer's satisfaction of the tangible product.

Service is a performance by an employee or product

An employee, the product, or a mechanical device can provide the service transaction to the customer and because the service is intangible it can be transmitted in multiple ways. The lack of consideration of the customer's perspective will often lead to a less than satisfactory outcome (Powers and Barrows, 1999).

When service is delivered, the guest and service provider are both part of the transaction

Services purchased by customers often involve the interaction between the service provider and the customer. Typically, the transaction requires the customer to be a participant in the experience (Shea, 2001).

Service quality is difficult to control and evaluate

Often the service transaction occurs without close supervision thus making it difficult to control the service provider's actions. Since there are no physical remains of the service once it has been delivered, evaluating its quality requires receiving feedback from the customer. To ensure that the service is consistent requires a service commitment from the organization that includes consistent service training for employees as well as continual feedback from customers.

The customer and the organization often measure quality of service differently

Consumers often view service quality as the effectiveness of the service, whereas organizations view service quality as the efficiency with which it is produced. Consumers value reliability, responsiveness, assurance, and empathy of the services being delivered. Organizations look for productivity, costs, and consistency. Often the method of evaluating quality of services between the consumer and the organization are not congruent.

When service is delivered, there can be no recall of the guest's experience

There is an aspect of time that is associated with the delivery of service. Additionally, since service is the intangible part of the organization's output there are no opportunities for the organization to recall and evaluate the quality of the service delivered. This requires management to develop service providers that have the ability to deliver service consistently under different and changing environments (Powers and Barrows, 1999).

Estimating the cost of service delivery is difficult

Unlike the production of tangible goods, it is difficult for hospitality organizations to quantify specific costs associated to the delivery of services. This is because the delivery of services often spans a variety of tangible products being offered concurrently. This challenge is exacerbated by the nominal expense of selling an additional unit of service and the extreme variability of demand (Lovelock, 1996).

Excess production of service cannot be placed in inventory

Economies of scale cannot be realized in the production of services. Since demand fluctuates and production cannot be stockpiled, hospitality service providers are not able to take advantage of consistent and steady production that result in a cost reduction associated with the manufacturing of tangible products.

Service delivery and demand can be individually customized

Since service production and consumption are simultaneous, hospitality organizations have great latitude to customize the service being delivered. Offering varying levels and types of services to the consumer can lead to a better match of their needs while increasing opportunities to raise revenue potential.

Successful service delivery can be achieved with different viewpoints

The management of the service philosophy within hospitality can be structured as a series of tasks that must be delivered without variation or as a strategy that is expected to focus on the customer's need and will vary between customers and service providers (Powers and Barrows, 1999).

Service as a task

The delivery of service is viewed as a series of tasks that can be scripted and given to the employees through training. In this viewpoint of service, employees are assumed to always follow the delivery of service in a consistent manner. The rationale for this approach is to eliminate opportunities for variation among the service providers and offer ease in evaluating employee performance.

Service as a strategy

Organizations who adopt this viewpoint are less concerned that employees follow a scripted pattern of the delivery of the service. Rather, employees are hired because of their abilities and personalities, and are empowered to provide service that meets the needs and expectations of the customer. It is expected that the service delivery may vary within and among employees. Empowering employees to make the right decisions will lead to service that meets or exceeds the needs and expectations of customers.

Service is often provided as a value added to a physical product

In most hospitality products the services are provided to customers as an added value or incentive to purchase the physical product. Receiving the service provided in a restaurant, on an airplane, renting a car would have no value if they did not accompany a meal, the airplane or automobile respectively.

Service has an aspect of time

Often, the delivery of service adds value to the physical product as noted above, therefore, service must be delivered at the time and speed that is appropriate to the consumption or delivery of the physical product. However, hospitality organizations can add value to the service proposition by varying the time the service is available so that it better meets the needs of the customer, such as restaurants having extended hours or brunches during weekends and holidays (Lovelock, 1996).

When purchasing services there is limited or no ownership

When purchasing services from a hospitality organization, the purchaser has limited or no ownership of the service provided. Once the service transaction is complete, there is little or no ability to enjoy the use of the service again in the future.

Managing the service delivery in any hospitality organization is difficult but often proves to be the only sustainable competitive advantage available to the business in a hyper-competitive marketplace. Failure to understand these characteristics of service will lead to a failure to recognize and meet the needs of the consumer.

References

Lovelock, C. (1996) *Services Marketing*, 3rd edn. Upper Saddle River, NJ: Prentice-Hall.

Powers, T. and Barrows, C. (1999) *Introduction to Management in Hospitality*, 6th edn. New York: John Wiley & Sons.

Shea, L.J. (2001) Marketing service products. In Brian Miller (ed.), *The Hospitality Industry: A Dynamic Experience*. Dubuque, IA: Kendall/Hunt Publishing.

BRIAN MILLER
UNIVERSITY OF DELAWARE, USA

Check-out

This is the last stage of the guest cycle and is one of the last contacts that a guest has with the hotel. The main objective here is to settle the guest account, to update room status information, and to create a guest history record. It is also important here to establish if the guest has enjoyed his or her stay. Due to changes in technology there are other check-out options available, namely express check-out and self check-out. *Express check-out* involves the front office slipping express check-out forms under the doors of guestrooms before 6a.m., which gives the guest (who has given credit card details at check-in) a chance to authorize the front desk to charge his/her card. This means the guest does not actually have to queue at the front desk at the busy time in the morning. *Self check-out* involves the guest actually checking him or herself out of the system through terminals located in the lobby area or via in-room systems which may be connected to the front office computer. Like express check-out, the guest should have given credit card details at check-in.

Reference

Kasavana, M.L. and Brooks, R.M. (1995) *Front Office Procedures*, 4th edn. Lansing, MI: Educational Institute of the American Hotel and Motel Association.

IRENE SWEENEY
INTERNATIONAL HOTEL MANAGEMENT
INSTITUTE SWITZERLAND, SWITZERLAND

Cleaning schedule

Scheduling is the housekeeping department's most important management function. Without a clear and well thought out schedule every day may present one crisis after another. Regardless of the size and structure of a housekeeping department most housekeeping departments are responsible for cleaning guestrooms, corridors, public areas (i.e. lobby and public restrooms), pool, patio, management offices, storage areas, linen and sewing rooms, laundry room, back-of-the-house areas, meeting rooms, dining rooms, banquet rooms, convention exhibit halls, hotel operated shops, game rooms, and exercise rooms. Since the housekeeping department is responsible for cleaning so many different areas of the hotel, scheduling the work of the department must be done with a systematic, step-by-step approach. Scheduling includes: creating inventory lists of all items within each area that will need housekeeping's attention; determining the frequency or number of times the items on the inventory lists are to be cleaned; creating performance standards which clearly state not only what must be done but detail how the job must be done; identifying productivity standards that describe the acceptable quantity of work to be done by the departments' employees; and providing appropriate equipment and supply inventory levels to insure that the employees have the necessary equipment and supplies to get their jobs done.

Reference

Tucker, Georgina and Schneider, Madelin (1975) *The Professional Housekeeper*. New York: Cahners Publishing Company.

ALAN T. STUTTS
AMERICAN INTERCONTINENTAL
UNIVERSITY, USA

Clicks and mortar

The term *clicks and mortar* (alternatively known as *bricks and clicks*, *surf and turf*, *cyber-enhanced retailing* and *hybrid e-commerce*) refers to supplementing physical outlets of traditional *bricks and mortar* businesses with e-commerce capabilities on the Web. Steinfield (2002) offers a conceptual framework which identifies potential sources of synergy between physical and virtual channels: common infrastructure, common operations, common marketing and sales, common buyers, and other complementary assets, e.g. existing supplier and distributor relationships, experience in the market, and a customer base. This enables the business to take better advantage of an innovation like e-commerce (Afuah and Tucci, 2001). Management strategies to achieve synergies and avoid channel conflicts include: goal alignment, explicit coordination and control, and capacity development. Four benefits can be achieved through cost savings, improved differentiation through value-added services, enhanced trust, and market extension. In the world of retailing tangible products, it is increasingly recognized that Internet-only businesses, the so-called 'dot-coms', are unlikely to displace traditional channels for business to consumer (B2C) commerce. In the hospitality industry the role of trust in consumer purchasing is paramount and the use of the Web to capitalize on strongly-branded products, e.g. international chain hotel brands, in responding to the needs of carefully researched markets cannot be underestimated.

References

Afuah, A. and Tucci, C. (2001) *Internet Business Models and Strategies: Text and Cases*. New York: McGraw-Hill Irwin.

Steinfield, C. (2002) Understanding click and mortar e-commerce approaches: a conceptual framework and research agenda. *Journal of Interactive Advertising* [Internet], 2 (2), Spring 2002. Available at http://www.jiad.org. Accessed 11 August 2003.

ELERI JONES
UNIVERSITY OF WALES INSTITUTE, UK

Club board of directors

The governing function of private clubs is assigned to a board of directors otherwise known as a board of governors. A club's board is comprised of directors and club officers (i.e., president, vice-president, treasurer, and secretary. These positions are typically elected on a rotating two-year basis so that there is never a complete replacement of the entire board in any given year. The primary reason for this rotational design is to maintain continuity of the goals established by the board with the intent to maintain overall club functionality. Members of the board are elected either by (a) an election by the club's membership, or (b) by an election held by the present board officers. In an effort to preserve the consistent provision of club services the

board of directors sets forth club bylaws concerning club operation, fiduciary responsibilities of the club as reflected in financial statements, operational and reserve budgets, membership nomination, committee of standing committees, and in some settings the hiring of key management personnel such as the recreational professionals (i.e., tennis, aquatic, golf, clubhouse manager, and general manager). Relative to the general manager, the board accepts the responsibility of reviewing the general manager's performance on an annual basis.

References

White, Ted and Gerstner, Larry (1991) *Club Operations and Management*. Van Nostrand Reinhold: New York.

Perdue, Joe (1997) *Contemporary Club Management*. Lansing, MI: Educational Institute of the American Hotel and Motel Association.

RANDALL S. UPCHURCH
UNIVERSITY OF CENTRAL FLORIDA, USA

Club Corporation (ClubCorp)

ClubCorp is a renowned developer of private clubs and golf courses throughout the world. Founded in 1957, Dallas-based ClubCorp has approximately $1.6 billion in assets. Internationally, ClubCorp owns or operates nearly 200 golf courses, country clubs, private business and sports clubs, and resorts. Among the company's nationally recognized golf properties are Pinehurst in the Village of Pinehurst, North Carolina (the world's largest golf resort, site of the 1999 and 2005 US Opens); Firestone Country Club in Akron, Ohio (site of the 2003 World Golf Championships – NEC Invitational); Indian Wells Country Club in Indian Wells, California (site of the Bob Hope Chrysler Classic); the Homestead in Hot Springs, Virginia (America's first resort, founded in 1766); and Mission Hills Country Club in Rancho Mirage, California (home of the Kraft Nabisco Championship).

The more than 60 business clubs and business and sports clubs include the Boston College

Club; City Club on Bunker Hill in Los Angeles; Citrus Club in Orlando, Florida; Columbia Tower Club in Seattle; Metropolitan Club in Chicago; Tower Club in Dallas; and the City Club of Washington, DC. The company's 19,000 employees serve the nearly 210,000 member households and 200,000 guests who visit ClubCorp properties each year.

Reference

http://www.clubcorp.com/thecompany/, 10 January 2004

PATRICIA BALDWIN
CLUB CORPORATION, USA

Club entertainment

A critical part of club member satisfaction is directly related to process of entertaining club members. This is important to note because well-designed entertainment entices the members to utilize the club while enhancing the perception that the club is an exciting place to be. Designing club entertainment is not a haphazard process, instead the design and deployment of an entertainment program requires a thorough assessment of club members' needs, wants, and expectations. This is a challenging and rewarding process because entertainment can range from children's programs, graduation parties, honeymoon celebrations, weddings, holiday parties, to debutante celebrations, each of which requires unique planning, physical arrangements, ambience, and personnel requirements.

Entertainment can be of two varieties. First is the special event type of entertainment that is a one-time event or cyclic event that is largely conducted using internal staff, club members, or management. Examples of special events are bingo tournaments, card tournaments, and youth reading programs. Second is static entertainment that supports normal clubhouse or private area operation. Examples would be televisions in the lounge, reading room, grill, shuffle board, online interactive games or stock market services. All planned entertainment must

be approved by the appropriate club committee and overseen by management.

References

Perdue, Joe (1997) *Contemporary Club Management*. Lansing, MI: Educational Institute of the American Hotel and Motel Association.

White, Ted and Gerstner, Larry (1991) *Club Operations and Management*. Van Nostrand Reinhold: New York.

RANDALL S. UPCHURCH
UNIVERSITY OF CENTRAL FLORIDA, USA

Club fitness programs

The primary objectives of a private club's physical fitness program are the improvement of the general health and well being for those individuals that choose to engage in a structured physical fitness program. The secondary benefits of a member fitness program encompass enhanced social interaction with other club members, a means of allowing members to entertain clients while promoting the club, and a means of interacting with family members in a private setting. It should also be understood that a club fitness program primarily caters to club members; however it is not unusual for a club to provide fitness training for employees. When offered to the members, fitness programs can be offered in a clinic format, group arrangement, or in an individual design. If the fitness program extends beyond the normal services offered to the members as a whole, the participating member is expected to pay an additional fee for the services rendered. Access to fitness facilities is a direct function of the member's membership status. If the member is a 'full or regular' member, he or she has access to clubhouse services, fitness facilities, and all recreational services (e.g., golf, tennis, aquatics). Some clubs offer athletic memberships, which limit the member to limited fitness facilities, which in most cases includes weight and aerobic facilities, tennis courts, and the aquatic areas.

Common fitness programs include general physical conditioning (including weight training), aquatics, and tennis. In each case, the club should hire and assign a 'professional' who has educational training and experience in the concepts and activities specific to the fitness program at hand. Member-focused fitness programs can include active sports programs, recreational activities, food and beverage, and educational components. In addition, concentrating on general member health ranging from weight management, stress management, and nutritional concerns can also enhance fitness programs. To achieve these latter fitness programs it is not uncommon to find the club's recreational department working with the food and beverage department to educate the members on nutritional concerns relative to daily diets and proper food handling and preparation procedures.

When the club fitness program focuses on employees it can be used to enhance worker productivity while personally benefiting the individual's state of health. There are benefits and challenges in offering a fitness program to the employees. The most obvious challenge is in scheduling access to the facilities for employee use due to the fact that simultaneous access can become an issue if management allows employees to use the facilities during posted access hours normally allotted for members. Another challenge is in making sure that employees are aware and understand the liabilities surrounding use of the fitness equipment. The upside of allowing employee access to fitness training and equipment is that it is believed that worker productivity and commitment increases as a direct result of fitness and wellness training. As opposed to club member fitness training, the common format of delivery is group education relative to fitness training followed by unsupervised use of fitness facilities. In short, there is no individualized training offered to employees due to the cost-prohibitive nature of such services.

The oversight of a club's fitness program varies with the type of fitness services and how responsibilities are assigned to each of the fitness areas. In some club settings the athletic directors of the respective fitness areas (e.g., aquatics, tennis, physical fitness) communicates with an assigned athletic committee (i.e., aquatic, fitness, tennis) relative to policies and procedures. In other clubs this structure might be downsized where an athletic director communicates with a single athletic committee.

The physical fitness area of a club encompasses a fitness area, exercise area, sports area, and spa areas. The fitness area is the most robust in terms of equipment of all the fitness areas with enough space to allow for warm-up and stretching activities, bulk weight training or progressive weight training, cardiovascular training, and cool-down routines. The stretching area offers sufficient room on non-absorbent mats so that an individual can 'warm-up' their muscles prior to engaging in weight lifting or aerobic activities. The main cardiovascular area typically contains stationary bicycles, stair-masters (step master), rowing machines, cross-country ski machines, and treadmills. In addition, it is not unusual for this area to provide entertainment for the individual's pleasure. Such devices include large screen televisions, area music or personal audio devices, and reading materials (e.g., newspapers and journals). The weight training area is frequently subdivided into a free weight area and progressive resistance training equipment. In general, both can be used for bulk training or isometric training and either system allows the member to exercise the body's major muscle groups.

The exercise room is often a separate room that offers flooring that exerts low impact upon the joints. This room is mirrored so that the member and the instructor can observe proper exercise movements. In an effort to entertain the member, many clubs provide music that is meant to please and stimulate the senses. The sports area typically requires sufficient square footage to accommodate indoor sports activities such as basketball, volley ball, squash, racquet ball, handball, and volleyball. It should be noted that the sports area as well as the exercise areas also serve as a means for the member to relax, socialize, entertain business guests, and promote the club's finest features. The spa area of the club is the one area of the club in which the member can be pampered following a workout regimen or simply as a means to relax after a long day. The spa area of a club can include a sauna, steam room, or a whirlpool.

The staff structure of a fitness area is largely dependent on the type and array of fitness services offered. In clubs that offer a fitness area as described above it is not uncommon to find a fitness director, assistant director, fitness instructor(s), personal trainer(s), and locker room attendants.

Reference

Perdue, Joe (1997) *Contemporary Club Management.* Lansing, MI: Educational Institute of the American Hotel and Motel Association.

RANDALL S. UPCHURCH
UNIVERSITY OF CENTRAL FLORIDA, USA

Club management

Club management is a profession that involves managing all of the different areas and departments in a club. A club manager generally supervises the following departments and/or staff: accountant/comptroller, upscale dining, casual dining, banquets, lounge/bar, maintenance, locker rooms, kitchen, membership, aquatics, and tennis. If the manager is a general manager then the golf program/golf professional and golf course maintenance/golf course superintendent also report to the general manager. The manager implements the policies set by the Board and oversees the operation of the club.

Club managers need skills in multiple areas. They must be service-oriented in order to interact well with members. They must have good supervisory skills because they have many departments and employees working at the club. Financial skills are a must because operational and capital budgets are planned and monitored by the club's manager. Personnel and legal skills are a must to keep the club operating efficiently. Knowledge in food and beverage is mandatory since all clubs provide some type of dining. Managers of golf or athletic clubs should have some knowledge of the sports and activities they will be overseeing. It should be enough knowledge so that they can interact with the professionals working in those departments.

Reference

Perdue, Joe (1997) *Contemporary Club Management.* Lansing, MI: Educational Institute of the American Hotel and Motel Association.

RAYMOND R. FERREIRA
GEORGIA STATE UNIVERSITY, USA

Club manager certification programs

In an effort to keep private club management current with trends and issues in the private club industry, the Club Managers Association of American (CMAA) offers professional development courses that lead to educational and professional designations. This type of program is important to note because a private club manager's success within a club setting requires a willingness and commitment to professional development. The professional development programs offered through CMAA are multi-level courses that are designed for entry level to senior management. The Business Management Institute (BMI) is unique in that it represents an industry and multi-university (Cornell University, Georgia State, Michigan State, University of Nevada – Las Vegas, California State Polytechnic, and the University of Arizona) agreement to offer certification courses on topics that are pertinent to leadership in private country clubs. Each level of the Business Management Institute focuses on different topics with each level offering a 5-day seminar on the topics of: Basic Club Management Concepts (BMI-I), The Leadership Edge (BMI-II), The Chief Operating Officer (BMI-III), Managerial Excellence (BMI-IV), Strategies for Tomorrow (BMI-V), The Team Dynamic (BMI-VI). In addition, the Business Management Institute program offers elective courses that enhance the BMI courses. The elective courses include sports management, food and beverage management, culinary orientation, and culinary update for club managers. In addition to the Business Management Institute, CMAA offers professional development courses through an annual world conference on club management, leadership and legislative conferences, and local chapter education opportunities.

Reference

Perdue, Joe (1997) *Contemporary Club Management.* Lansing, MI: Educational Institute of the American Hotel and Motel Association.

RANDALL S. UPCHURCH
UNIVERSITY OF CENTRAL FLORIDA, USA

Club Managers Association of America (CMAA)

The Club Managers Association of America (CMAA) is a nonprofit membership organization whose mission is to 'advance the profession of club management by fulfilling the educational and related needs of its members.' Having celebrated its 75th anniversary in 2002, CMAA is a progressive association with a membership of over 6000 dues-paying club professionals who belong to more than 50 regional chapters throughout the United States and around the world. CMAA serves to unify an otherwise fragmented industry, and it has played a pivotal role in evolving the job of a club manager into a highly respected profession.

The Club Managers Association of America (CMAA) is the professional Association for managers of membership clubs. CMAA has more than 3000 country, city, athletic, faculty, yacht, town, and military clubs. The objectives of the Association are to promote and advance friendly relations between and among persons connected with the management of clubs and other associations of similar character; to encourage the education and advancement of its members; to assist club officers and members, through their managers; and to secure the utmost in efficient and successful operations. The Association's Club Foundation supports the advancement of the club management profession. CMAA's budget is $7.5 million. The staff numbers 36.

The following 2003 quick facts noted on the CMAA website indicate the impact of the private club industry to the hospitality and tourism industry. Seventy-nine percent of CMAA members are golf and country clubs, 13% of all private clubs are classified as city clubs, gross revenues equaled $10.16 billion in 2003, food and beverage revenues totaled $3.26 billion, and the average annual club income was $3.98 million, private clubs employ over 263,000 employees, club payrolls equal $4 billion, private clubs raised about $153 million in charities in 2001, donated $8.3 million in student scholarships, most private clubs offer student scholarships within their respective states, the economic impact of private clubs averaged $1.61 million to local communities, private clubs spent about $1.79 million within state economies, and private clubs pay on average $132,449 in property taxes.

Historical development

Although associations of club managers had begun to form in the cities of Boston and New York, it was not until 1926 that 'Colonel' Clinton G. Holden, manager of the Olympia Fields Country Club, called for a national club managers association. He began by sending letters to club managers across the country, inviting them to join the National Association of Club Managers. One hundred members attended the organization's first convention in January 1927, at which time Holden was elected as the first CMAA president. A year later the Board of Directors changed the name of the organization to the Club Managers Association of America.

In spite of early challenges posed by the Depression and wars, the club industry and CMAA prospered over time. Along with an increasing number of new chapters and a growing membership base, CMAA evolved to include a professional development program, an annual club management conference, professional certifications known as CCM (Certified Club Manager) and MCM (Master Club Manager), a charitable foundation, and enhanced benefits and services. The CMAA headquarters staff expanded gradually to keep up with the needs of a growing membership, moving offices in 1987 to their present location on King Street in Old Town Alexandria, Virginia.

An educational focus

Although not always by unanimous decision, CMAA maintained education as a central theme of the organization throughout the years. And the commitment to education has never been stronger than it is today. Professional development opportunities are currently available for club managers through the following venues: the BMI, World Conference on Club Management, annual leadership/legislative conference, and monthly or quarterly chapter education sessions.

BMI, founded in 1988, currently offers five core courses geared for managers of varying experience levels, and a choice of eight electives. Classes are offered in week-long increments at various university locations throughout the United States, and rosters generally fill quickly. The Business Management Institute is the backbone of CMAA's educational initiative, and a source of pride as a model for effective continuing education within the hospitality industry.

Charitable support

Confronted with the rising costs associated with its educational programs, the CMAA Board of Directors established The Club Foundation in 1988 to endow the association's educational pursuits in perpetuity. Continuing and expanding high-quality education for club managers, funding of club-related research, and scholarships for college students interested in club management, are just a few of the initiatives supported by The Foundation. The Campaign for Excellence was introduced by CMAA in 1990 with the goal of raising $3 million for The Club Foundation; the goal was quickly achieved and The Foundation Endowment continues to grow.

Value-added services

Premier Club Services (PCS) began in 1994 to provide additional support for club managers through innovative products/services designed to increase club managers' knowledge base. PCS offers books, manuals, white papers, etc., which help managers to operate their clubs more efficiently and to more effectively interact with their governing boards. PCS also keeps club managers abreast of legislative and regulatory issues that stand to impact private clubs.

In 1988 the International Wine Society started as a sub-group of the larger CMAA organization. The Society offers CMAA members, who are also wine enthusiasts, an opportunity to share knowledge of wine and food. Some of the group's activities include wine tours, an annual black-tie dinner, and wine auctions.

CMAA embraced technology in 1995 when it entered the 'dot.com' world with the creation of ClubNet, the name of the organization's website located at www.cmaa.org. The website quickly became the organization's main source to disseminate up-to-date information on various topics of interest to club managers. It enhanced networking among members and even serves as a resource for job seekers and job recruiters. As CMAA members embrace the future, ClubNet is one of the vehicles that will enable the organization to maintain its successful strategy of continually delivering more services and greater value to its members worldwide.

References

Morris, R. (2001) *Club Managers Association of America 1927–2002: Celebrating Seventy-Five Years of Service.* Virginia Beach, VA: Donning Company Publishers.

Perdue, Joe (ed.) (1997) *Contemporary Club Management.* Lansing, MI: Educational Institute of the American Hotel and Motel Association. http://www.cmaa.org, 15 February 2004.

CANDICE CLEMENZ
UNIVERSITY OF WEST FLORIDA, USA

Club membership categories

By the very nature of the private club industry, membership within any given private club is a very coveted title. Due to the popularity of being a member of a private club, existing members give great detail to protect the overall composition of their club. In short, the existing members view their existing club as an exclusive community that mirrors a common value system. It should be understood that the following definitions apply to an equity club type of operation versus that of a non-equity club. Another understanding is that the following membership classifications are designed with the specific purpose of satisfying the needs of the club membership. It should also be understood that not all equity clubs will offer these classifications, however these membership categories are readily accepted within the private equity club sector.

When a club member is scheduled to be out of the country for an extended period of time (e.g., a year or more) an *absentee* membership can be granted in accordance with the club's bylaws. This category is a perfect example of how a club must remain cognizant of member usage needs, so by offering this classification the absentee member might be entitled to reduced monthly dues as a direct result of not utilizing club services.

An *associate* membership, also known as a non-resident membership, applies to out-of-state members that desire to use the club on a seasonal (e.g., infrequent) basis. Due to a lower usage pattern, this type of club member pays lowered initiation fees and monthly dues as set forth in the club's bylaws.

A *clergy* membership is offered to local clergy. Under a clergy membership the member does not have voting rights or hold office. In most cases this type of membership is associated with no initiation fees and a lowered dues structure.

A *founder* membership applies to an individual or individuals that provided the funds that established the club. Naturally by this definition there are very few individuals that would fall into this classification. The granting of a founding membership must be in accordance with the club's bylaws. A founding member has voting rights relative to club operations, and they pay dues (monthly or annual).

Some clubs offer a *golf* membership for individuals who want nothing more than to use the golf course facilities of the club. For many private clubs the mere presence of full golf facilities is a major attractor for local residents either located near or within the immediate community. The preference of golf-related activities cannot be discounted based on the notion that a golf member often does not have access to clubhouse services (e.g., food and beverage services). There are initiation fees and monthly fees that correspond with this classification.

Honorary memberships are offered to individuals that are respected leaders in the community. The primary purpose of offering an honorary membership is an act of goodwill. Members that fall in this category may be entitled to lower dues but with restricted voting rights.

A *junior* membership applies to individuals who are under a specified age as noted in the club's bylaws. This classification only applies to the children of club members. A junior membership plays an important role in maintaining a constant stream of interest within those families that have been loyal members. Therefore, the junior membership is primarily a marketing tool to maintain a certain membership level. Individuals holding a junior membership do not have voting rights relative to club operations.

A *regular* membership within an equity club means that members pay an initiation fee to join a club of preference with either none or at least a partial part of the initiation fee being refunded upon the member's separation from the club. In addition, there are monthly dues (on top of initiation fees) that are required as part of membership. The regular member has full access to the clubhouse and all recreational services offered by the club. This type of membership is influential because the member exercises voting rights relative to club conduct.

A *reciprocity* membership is an agreement between clubs that are commonly geographically remote. A reciprocity membership is essentially a reciprocal agreement between two private clubs whereby members of either club can use the other club's services, at times convenient to the member, while the member is in the area.

A *senior* membership is available to individuals that have been members for a specified number of years and have reached a certain age. A senior membership is a sign of respect to members who have stayed loyal to the club for a number of years. There are monthly dues for this type of membership; however they are at a reduced rate in comparison to a regular membership.

The *social* membership classification appeals to those individuals who seek out social functions within the club while not desiring to use recreational services (i.e., golf course, tennis, racquet, etc.). This type of member is commonly restricted to using the services offered within the clubhouse, which basically means that the social member is not entitled to use the recreational services offered at the club. Given that the social member is not entitled to use full club services, the initiation fees and monthly dues that apply to this membership category are less than that for 'regular' membership.

The *surviving spouse* classification is a special membership where the surviving spouse of a member assumes the membership classification of the deceased member. In some cases the surviving spouse classification is entitled to reduced dues. However, at some clubs the surviving spouse classification is restricted in terms of voting privileges.

Some clubs offer a *temporary* membership category in cases where visiting dignitaries are in the area. The main intent of this 'temporary' classification is offered as a professional courtesy with no initiation fees or monthly dues being levied. When a temporary membership is offered it is often done so to establish goodwill and to bring recognition to the club.

References

Perdue, Joe (1997) *Contemporary Club Management.* Lansing, MI: Educational Institute of the American Hotel and Motel Association.

White, Ted and Gerstner, Larry (1991) *Club Operations and Management.* New York: Van Nostrand Reinhold.

JUNWON SEO
HILTON GRAND VACATIONS COMPANY, USA

Club membership nomination

In general, the initial step in gaining membership is to submit a formal application to the club. Before an application will be considered the prospective member must be sponsored by a club member. The role of this member sponsor is critical to the receipt and acceptance of this inquiry given the selective nature of the application process. The sponsoring member ensures that all the necessary information is contained in the application and then forwards the application to club management or to the membership committee. In many clubs the prospective member's application is sent out for scrutiny to the club membership. This is important to note because the club's members can accept or reject the applicant based on personal reasons, stature in the community, fit with values of the club, or some other pertinent reason. In all cases, the general consensus of the membership is strongly considered before the membership committee levies their vote for approval or rejection. It is interesting to note that clubs in England traditionally use the 'black ball' system, whereby each member is given a black and a white ball to be used in a secret ballot. A black ball indicates rejection and a white ball indicates acceptance. If any prospect receives a black ball then the applicant is rejected.

References

Perdue, Joe (1997) *Contemporary Club Management.* Lansing, MI: Educational Institute of the American Hotel and Motel Association.

White, Ted and Gerstner, Larry (1991) *Club Operations and Management.* New York: Van Nostrand Reinhold.

JUNWON SEO
HILTON GRAND VACATIONS COMPANY, USA

Club membership process

The club industry consists of all private clubs, both equity and non-equity, that provide services and amenities to individuals with similar interests and desires for social and recreational purposes. Access to a private club is restricted to members, their immediate families, and guests of the members. To join a club a candidate for membership must be sponsored by a current member. In addition, the applicant has to provide letters of recommendations from other members that are in good standing. The application is then carried forward to management or the membership committee for consideration. As such, the member that forwards the nomination must be a strong advocate for the applicant. The candidate or nominee for membership is then evaluated by the membership committee to ensure that the candidate is a good 'fit' for the club and the applicant meets the criteria for club membership. In some private clubs the candidate may have to meet and interview with the board members. Some clubs do not have enough members to make them economically viable so they allow the public to use the club for a fee after giving priority of usage to members (e.g., priority tee times on a golf course). This type of club is referred to as a semi-private club.

Reference

Perdue, Joe (1997) *Contemporary Club Management*. Lansing, MI: Educational Institute of the American Hotel and Motel Association.

RAYMOND R. FERREIRA
GEORGIA STATE UNIVERSITY, USA

Club officers

The governing body of a private club is comprised of a group of club officers who preside over the club's operation. This policy-making function is clearly delineated within the club's charter as recorded with the state in question. In form with this policy-making function there are certain functions that are position-specific. The president performs the function of directing the club officers within their policy-making capacity for the club. In this role the president is a very influential person within the club membership structure because he or she directs the club's chief operating officer (i.e., the club general manager) in the implementation of the club officer's directives. The vice president serves in an advisory function to the president and replaces the president when he or she cannot attend a board meeting. The secretary sets the meeting agendas, records all meeting minutes, and distributes meeting reports to the board members. The treasurer files reports of the club's financial status as disseminated from the finance/budget committee. The sergeant in arms is given the role of ensuring that the board of directors follows proper rules of conduct, which is formally Robert's Rules of Order. (Robert's Rules of Order is America's foremost guide to parliamentary procedure and is used extensively by more professional associations, fraternal organizations, and local governments than any other guide.)

References

Perdue, Joe (1997) *Contemporary Club Management*. Lansing, MI: Educational Institute of the American Hotel and Motel Association.
White, Ted and Gerstner, Larry (1991) *Club Operations and Management*. New York: Van Nostrand Reinhold.

ARAM SON
JAMES COOK UNIVERSITY, AUSTRALIA

Club professionals

The skills required to run a private club correspond directly to the complexity of services offered through the club's departments. The common departments found in a private country club include the clubhouse and the recreational divisions of aquatics, tennis, and golf. In addition to these recreational departments a private club also requires professionals in the areas of grounds and within the executive office.

The clubhouse is the main hub of all social activities that transpire at a private club. Given that the clubhouse is the social hub for the club, management must offer a wide array of food and beverage, and special catered events to meet the needs of their membership. It is this role that requires finely honed skills surrounding food and beverage preparation and management and culinary skills. Perhaps the most influential person in satisfying members' culinary tastes is the executive chef.

The executive chef is charged with managing the food production and beverage services for all the club's food facilities and beverage outlets. Given the culinary flair that is expected at a private club, the executive chef is often trained by a culinary institute of great stature either nationally or internationally. In most cases, the executive chef is charged with budget development and monitoring, recipe development, costing of food products, vendor relations, purchasing of perishables and non-perishables, liquor purchasing, and wine selection. In addition, executive chefs can offer seminars that are of interest to their members on a culinary or wine topic of interest. This type of service is above and beyond the normal dues structure, meaning that the members pay for this type of experience.

Another person that is critical to the delivery of quality service within the clubhouse is the assistant general manager, also known as the clubhouse manager. The primary assistant general manager duties include enacting duties assigned by the general manager as well as managing the daily operation of the clubhouse. On the latter function, the assistant general manager is responsible for staffing, motivating, and terminating clubhouse staff (i.e., servers, kitchen help, etc.). The assistant general manager should hold a bachelor's degree in a business-related discipline. This professional manages in the absence of the general manager, approves budgets, hires, trains, terminates, oversees lodging room units, housekeeping, maintenance, and security department where applicable. This person also oversees club safety and security issues, but most importantly maintains contact with members and ensures optimal member satisfaction.

Commonly the aquatics director is knowledgeable of water polo, water ballet, snorkeling, and scuba diving. The duties of an aquatics director entail management of daily aquatic center operations, maintenance of aquatic facilities, and supervision of aquatics staff. In some clubs the aquatic director also assumes the duties of a fitness director. As a fitness director this professional is responsible for fitness equipment maintenance, exercise program set-up and monitoring, and in some cases personal training. The aquatics/fitness director should hold a bachelor of science degree or higher in a discipline related to physical fitness.

The primary golf professional at a private club is called the golf director or golf pro. The golf pro should hold a PGA designation and have years of experience as an assistant golf pro. The golf pro is responsible for developing the golf department budget as well as hiring, training, and managing all golf staff. The golf pro is commonly given the duties of designing, promoting, and directing all golf activities; prepares annual and monthly golf operation budgets; orders golf merchandise; supervises the maintenance of all golf equipment; supervises golf pro shop personnel; provides golf lessons; designs and conducts golf clinics; supervises all on-course staff; organizes golf tournaments; collects and accounts for all golf charges and fees; and enforces all policies surrounding golf play.

The grounds superintendent of a private club plays a critical role in the maintenance of the grounds and in staffing grounds personnel. The grounds superintendent should hold a bachelor of science degree in biology- or a chemistry-related program given the critical nature of applying herbicides, pesticides, and compliance with state and federal regulations. This person has budget responsibilities for all activities surrounding golf course maintenance. Furthermore, the grounds superintendent supervises the planting, fertilizing, turf management, shrub and lawn maintenance, nursery maintenance; supervision of all equipment maintenance personnel; maintains records concerning daily, monthly, and annual maintenance activities; maintains strict accounting of expenditures for variables and capital expenditures; selects and prepares fertilizers and other chemical applications to meet state and federal guidelines; maintains proper irrigation and drainage systems; keeps the golf course in optimal playing condition; and maintains active personnel records.

The tennis professional at a private club handles the daily management of tennis facilities which includes hiring, training, and performance appraisal of tennis staff. In addition, the tennis pro should have served as a tennis pro assistant and hold a sports-related bachelor of science degree. This person also has budgetary responsibilities for all tennis facilities and staff, conducts personal training, and monitors the repair of tennis equipment.

The last but not least to be mentioned is the club's general manager. The general manager, or chief executive officer, of a private equity club plays a pivotal role in communicating operational concerns with the club's board of directors. As such, the general manager is responsible for the daily management of the club. This general manager's duties also include the staffing of the club's departments, development of the annual operation and capital expenditure budget, general responsibility for club financial record oversight, and member relations. As part of the basic duties assigned to him/her, the general manager: implements policies established by the board of directors; coordinates short-range and long-term business plans; establishes personnel policies that promote service quality; coordinates development of capital and operating budgets; serves as an ex-officio member of club committees where assigned; and constantly engages in the highest level of member relations as possible on a daily basis. Given the broad range of skills required, the general manager should hold a bachelor of science degree from a business-related program.

References

Perdue, Joe (1997) *Contemporary Club Management*. Lansing, MI: Educational Institute of the American Hotel and Motel Association.
White, Ted and Gerstner, Larry (1991) *Club Operations and Management*. New York: Van Nostrand Reinhold.

CHENG-TE (CARLOS) TAN
DAXON TECHNOLOGY INC., USA

Club reciprocity

One of the most unique benefits associated with being a member in the private club industry is that of reciprocity. When private clubs enter into a reciprocity agreement the respective members have the right to use the facilities and services of a reciprocal club while traveling in the area.

Reciprocal agreements can be made at the local, national, or international level. When planning to exercise their reciprocal usage rights the member must notify management of the receiving club of the time and duration of their travel plans. Another example of a reciprocal agreement is when a private club is undergoing a major renovation that requires the club to close down over an extended period. In this instance a reciprocal use agreement is sought so that club members do not experience a discontinuation of services while the renovation process is taking place. However, the entire club does not have to be under renovation for this type of agreement to be put into effect. A reciprocity agreement can also be exercised when club services are only partially under renovation. For instance, in cases where the clubhouse or the golf course is under renovation, a member can share the clubhouse or golf course of a local private club that has entered into such a reciprocal use agreement.

Reference

Perdue, Joe (1997) *Contemporary Club Management*. Lansing, MI: Educational Institute of the American Hotel and Motel Association.

RANDALL S. UPCHURCH
UNIVERSITY OF CENTRAL FLORIDA, USA

Club types

The private club industry is stratified by facilities that cater to unique user needs surrounding social, recreational, and financial needs. In answering these needs, in most cases private clubs are logically located in an area where people choose to recreate, socialize, or conduct business. The following are brief definitions that delineate the different club types.

City club

A club that typically offers its members food and beverage service. A city club usually is located in a downtown or urban location. In addition to member dining areas, a city club usually has a variety of meeting rooms. Most city clubs are more formal than country or golf clubs because of its emphasis on business entertainment. Some established clubs have overnight lodging accommodations. In almost all instances, a city club offers one or more restaurants, beverage outlets, serve lunch and dinner, and cater special parties for their members.

Country club

A club that typically offers its members and families a variety of activities and services. A country club is usually located in the country or suburbs because of the large amount of land needed for the golf course. In addition to a golf course a country club usually has tennis courts, a swimming pool, golf driving range, short game practice area, and a golf pro shop. The clubhouse usually accommodates a casual dining area (grill), upscale dining (main dining room), ballroom, board room (meeting room), and locker rooms. Other sports activities/areas at some country clubs are fitness centers, croquet and other lawn games, equestrian centers, skeet shooting areas, archery, cross country skiing, etc.

Yacht club

A club that is typically on a body of water with members who have an interest in boating (sailboats or powerboats). Some yacht clubs are exclusively for sailboats, while some are for a specific class or type of boat (e.g., Laser, Thistle, etc.). Most yachts clubs today allow both sailboats and powerboats. Clubs usually provide marina services, such as dry docking, refueling, boat maintenance, boating lessons, etc. Most yacht clubs usually have a clubhouse providing food and beverage service and locker rooms. Some also have a swimming pool and other sports facilities.

Golf club

A club that is similar to a country club but usually only has golf as its sole recreational activity.

The clubhouse is usually smaller than that at a country club with small member dining areas and a limited meeting/ballroom area.

Health club

Health clubs are positioned to address the needs of a time-compressed society and stressful lifestyle of its membership by offering access to personal use of fitness equipment and physical conditioning programs. In most cases, personal trainers can be obtained by paying for these services.

City-athletic club

A city club (business food and beverage) that usually has sports facilities. This type of club is usually located in the city and has extensive indoor and outdoor sports programs. Typical activity areas at this type of club are fitness centers, exercise classes, tennis, squash, racquetball, swimming pool, massage services, barber/beauty shops, ice-skating, etc.

Member-owned club

A club that is usually owned by its members which means that the members have invested in the club. This club is usually governed by a Board of Directors or Board of Governors who typically set policies and procedures. The club's manager usually reports to the Board and is responsible for implementing the rules, services, and amenities that the majority of members desire.

Corporate club

A club owned by a company, partnership, or individual. Most of these clubs offer similar products and services as member-owned club. The main difference is governance of the club and it is typically run to make a profit or be an amenity for another product the owner has. One of the largest companies that own and manage clubs for a profit is ClubCorp.

Developer club

A club usually started by a real estate developer. The initial purpose of most developer clubs is to offer an amenity (the club) to individuals interested in purchasing a home in the development. Usually real estate lots in a club development are more appealing, therefore more valuable and produce more revenue for the developer. The club is usually sold or given to the members (becoming a member-owned club at that time) after the developer sells and develops the majority of the real estate lots in the development.

Military club

A club usually open to a specific branch of the military for its officers and enlisted personnel (e.g., Army Navy Club, etc.)

University club

A club usually open to faculty, staff, alumni, and students of a specific university. Some clubs that have the name of the University Club in a city (e.g., Houston and Dallas, Texas) are not directly affiliated with a specific school, but may be near one or have the name because of the prestige associated with it.

Equity club

A club where the members or shareholders receive a portion or all of the up-front fees paid when a member resigns or leaves the club. This club usually has two components to the upfront fee that a candidate for membership pays when they join the club. The first component is the initiation fee which the club receives and it is usually used for capital projects at clubs. The second portion is the equity portion and this amount is usually used to pay the equity that a resigning member is entitled to. In some cases the equity portion may increase, stay the same, or decrease over time. While at some clubs the equity portion is set by the Board or owner, there are some clubs that allow it to float based on market conditions or what the resigning member is willing to accept.

Non-equity club

Clubs that do not have any liability to resigning members for repayment of upfront joining fees. Non-equity clubs are able to use all of the initiation fees collected for capital projects or any operating deficits.

Semi-private club

A semi-private is a mixed use club that caters to both the general public and private members. In general, these clubs are less glamorous than equity clubs, while still offering food and beverage services, as well as golfing.

Reference

Perdue, Joe (1997) *Contemporary Club Management*. Lansing, MI: Educational Institute of the American Hotel and Motel Association.

RAYMOND R. FERREIRA
GEORGIA STATE UNIVERSITY, USA

Clubhouse

The clubhouse is part of the club's physical structure that offers a centralized place where club members can meet and socialize. Depending on the type of the club, the clubhouse can be rather austere in ambience and furnishing up to the most lavishly adorned facilities with granite, marble, antique displays, libraries, smoking rooms, card room, formal dining, informal or casual dining facilities, bar and cocktail lounge, piano bar, small to large meeting rooms, aerobic rooms, fitness areas, and a spa. This is not an exhaustive list because the range and quality of the club's facilities is a direct reflection of the club members' desires. Due to the influence of socializing within a private club, the food and beverage function is critical to the clubhouse experience. Therefore, the assistant general manager, otherwise known as the clubhouse manager, ensures the attractiveness of the dining rooms and meeting rooms, maintains the highest quality of food preparation and presentation, and promotes the highest level of service during all food and beverage events. From this perspective, the clubhouse plays a critical role in the establishment of loyalty via member satisfaction and in promoting the club to non-members.

References

Perdue, Joe (1997) *Contemporary Club Management*. Lansing, MI: Educational Institute of the American Hotel and Motel Association.

White, Ted and Gerstner, Larry (1991) *Club Operations and Management*. Van Nostrand Reinhold.

ARAM SON
JAMES COOK UNIVERSITY, AUSTRALIA

Coaching

Coaching can be a cost-effective alternative to formal training in the development of services/experiences staff in hospitality organizations. Coaching has been defined in hospitality as 'a directive process by a manager to train and orient an employee to the realities of the workplace and to help the employee remove barriers to optimum work performance' (Woods and King, 1996).

This was refined by Weiss (2000), who distinguished between coaching and consulting. Coaching focuses more on the personal development needs of employees, enabling them to perform at a higher level in the organization while consulting focuses on helping employees achieve a particular desired organizational result. Given the unique nature of services, coaching can be very effective in developing empowered employees.

Weiss (2000) sets out seven elements that coaches may have to deal with:

1. The individual's contribution to the service situation
2. The individual's level of competence and/or knowledge in the role
3. Resistances or deficits in motivation
4. Interpersonal issues
5. The individual's credibility
6. The individual's career aspirations
7. The effect of non-work concerns on workplace performance.

Coaching is particularly important in organizational change and when particular competencies are desired or needed in an organization. It can also be an effective way of socializing employees.

References

Weiss, D.S. (2000) *High Performance HR: Leveraging Human Resources for Competitive Advantage*. Toronto: John Wiley & Sons.

Woods, R.H. and King, J.Z. (1996) *Quality Leadership and Management in the Hospitality Industry*. Lansing, MI: Educational Institute of the American Hotel and Motel Association.

G. KEITH HENNING
UNIVERSITY OF CALGARY, CANADA

Co-branding

Co-branding occurs when brands from different organizations (or distinctly different businesses within the same organization) combine to create an offering in which each plays a driver role. One of the co-brands can be a component or an ingredient brand (McDonald's New Premium Salads with Newman's Dressings) or an endorser (Fairmont Hotels offer the Porsche Experience). While the offering can capture more than one source of brand equity and enhance the value proposition and point of differentiation, there are risks associated with it. The design and implementation of co-branding efforts is complex and the returns in terms of finances and brand building cannot be pre-determined. Forces affecting one brand can result in a blurring of the other brand. The key to successful co-branding is to find a partner brand that will enhance the offering by complementary associations. It is important to consider the individual brand associations, ways to leverage them, benefits for each brand, and how the alliance will fit into their existing business models. Achieving effective, complementary associations can enhance and strengthen the overall position of both brands.

References

Aaker, David A. and Joachimsthaler, Erich (2000) *Brand Leadership*. New York: The Free Press, pp. 141–142.

Fairmont Hotels. http://www.fairmont.com.

ASHISH KHULLAR
UNIVERSITY OF MASSACHUSETTS, USA

Cognitive dissonance

During the post-purchase evaluation stage of the consumer decision process, a buyer may experience cognitive dissonance. Cognitive dissonance refers to doubts that may occur shortly after the purchase of a product or service when the buyer questions whether or not he or she made the right decision in purchasing the product. The consumer typically ponders the question of did I make a good decision? Did I buy the right product or service? Did I get a good value? Hospitality and tourism companies generally minimize these questions with several strategies. Cognitive dissonance may be reduced through effective communication with the consumer and following-up with the consumer after the purchase. Frequent flyer and other loyalty programs help resolve dissonance as they are designed to give something back to the customer, hence improving the value of the product or service. Hospitality providers may also reduce consumer uncertainty by quickly responding to and rectifying any problems identified by the consumer as a result of a purchase as well as offering satisfaction or money-back guarantees or service warranties.

Reference

Kotler, P. and Armstrong, G. (1999) *Principles of Marketing*, 8th edn. New Jersey: Prentice-Hall.

JULINE E. MILLS
PURDUE UNIVERSITY, USA

Collective bargaining

Collective bargaining refers to bipartite negotiations between parties (hospitality managers and employees) who bargain directly with one another, usually unaided by either a mediator or industrial tribunal (Heys, 2001). In some countries collective bargaining can occur with direct legislative support and intervention where industrial legislation provides procedures for bargaining, such as recognizing the role of bargaining agents (trade unions), allowing either party to take industrial action during a 'protected' bargaining period (protected from common law damages under tort), and an obligation by the parties to bargain in 'good' faith by attending meetings, providing information, and negotiating the agenda in good faith. The process can occur formally through an employee bargaining unit and employees and their unions at a departmental, unit or higher company level (multinational hotel chain), or informally without recourse to a formal system of rules.

In the UK and Australasia, collective employee participation may take the form of a Joint Consultative Committee (JCC) and usually involves hotel employees, associated union and hotel management representatives at the bargaining table. Participants represent discreet sections of work. JCCs are a step in the collective barging process, and involve a formal and structured approach to employee consultation. This is a broad term referring to the process of communicating ideas between employers and employees. Consultation can occur formally through a JCC in collective bargaining to informal consultation using newsletters etc. with employees at each hotel department level.

Reference

Heys, A. (2001) *Australian Master Human Resources Guide 2002*. Sydney: CCH Australia Ltd.

DARREN LEE-ROSS
JAMES COOK UNIVERSITY, AUSTRALIA

Combined heat and power (CHP)

CHP refers to the simultaneous production of heat (hot water or steam) and power (electricity). There are two primary types of CHP units. In one type, water is heated in a boiler and the resultant steam is used to turn the blades of a turbine. The turbine is connected to a generator that produces electricity and the heat generated can be recovered for use at the property. Natural gas is the preferred fuel source because of its cost and availability in the United States. However, propane and other fuels may be employed. A second type of CHP unit uses an engine or turbine driving a generator with heat captured from the engine. The engine-captured heat from both types of CHP may be used for water heating, space heating or to power an absorption chiller. Some of these devices are sized to provide electricity and domestic hot water for hotels, motels, and even restaurants. The advantage of these devices to an operator includes the ability to generate electricity and heat in a remote location not served by utilities, or in areas where the power supply is unstable. It may also be cost-effective to a hospitality operator when comparisons are made to current electric utility charges. However, cost increases in fuel used to power these devices may diminish their appeal.

Reference

District Heating and Cooling. http://www.chp-info.org/content.html.
International District Energy Association http://www.districtenergy.org/.

TOM JONES
UNIVERSITY OF NEVADA, LAS VEGAS, USA

Comfort zones and human comfort

Comfort zones delineate specific combinations of temperature and relative humidity (RH) ranges where statistical tests have shown 80% of the tested population to be comfortable. These zones are different for winter and summer conditions. Higher RH necessitates cooler dry bulb temperatures to be in the comfort zone. It is more energy-efficient for a facility to have a lower temperature with a more humid environment during the winter, and a dryer but higher dry bulb temperature during the summer.

Dry bulb (DB) temperature measures the ambient air either indoors or outdoors on an ordinary thermometer. The temperature measuring device of choice should be shielded from radiation (e.g. direct sunlight) to insure accurate measurement of the temperature.

Wet bulb (WB) temperature is the minimum temperature reached with the thermal sensing element encased in a water wetted wick in an air stream. The wet bulb temperature is always below or at the dry bulb temperature. The closer the WB to the DB the higher the RH.

The temperature and humidity ranges defined as the comfort zone are rather wide. The winter comfort zone is between 68 °F (20 °C) with 90% RH and 76 °F (24 °C) with 25% RH. The summer conditions are between 74 °F (23 °C) with 90% RH to 81 °F (27 °C) with 25% RH. Additional factors influencing comfort include room air movement, activity level in the room, clothing worn by room occupants, and the temperature of the room surfaces.

References

Honeywell Engineering Manual of Automatic Control for Commercial Buildings (1997) Minneapolis: Honeywell.
Stipanuk, D.M. (2002) *Hospitality Facilities Management and Design*, 2nd edn. Lansing, MI: Educational Institute of the American Hotel and Lodging Association.

CONNIE E. HOLT
WIDENER UNIVERSITY, USA

Commercial home

Commercial home refers to the provision of commercial hospitality within a home setting. The traditional private home setting is highly significant as a temporal and cultural construct, suggesting a relationship between the host and the home setting. For the host, the home setting will have various associations, such as security, affection, perhaps tyranny, or a retreat. The home and its artifacts act as a reflection of the householder's personality. A successful commercial home experience therefore will partly depend on the extent to which the guest can engage with the home setting. The type of home setting can be classified as of three types: traditional, virtual reality, and 'backdrop.' Traditional is where the private home setting is strongest, for example, host families, bed and breakfasts, self-catering properties, small family-run hotels, or religious retreats. Virtual reality is where the home setting as a construct is reproduced artificially, for example, timeshare accommodation, town house or country house hotels. Backdrop homes refers to the use of the home setting and its associations for commercial purposes, for example, a house used as a visitor attraction, or a house used as a film set.

Reference

Lynch, P.A., Johns, N. and Cunnell, D. (2003) *Best Practice In Self-Catering Accommodation in Scotland: Analysis and Results*. Report for Association of Self-Caterers, Highlands and Islands Enterprise, Scotland.

PAUL LYNCH
QUEEN MARGARET UNIVERSITY COLLEGE,
EDINBURGH, UK

Commitment

According to Cullen (2001) commitment is the extent to which an employee identifies with an organization and is committed to its goals and objectives. Higher levels of employee commitment have been linked to higher levels of productivity and service quality, a vital factor in a service industry like hospitality. The use of power has also been linked with commitment, with positive management styles being associated with commitment, whereas more coercive styles are associated with compliance rather than commitment. As a result, committed employees tend to need less supervision, although this may be confusing cause and effect. The challenge for hospitality managers is building a culture of commitment within an industry traditionally perceived as a poor employer, with long hours and poor rewards. Levels of organizational commitment amongst employees may vary according to sector and nationality. For example, levels of commitment may be higher for employees of international, luxury hotel chains, as the strong brand image represents a company to be proud of, whereas, smaller, local hotels might struggle to

keep employees who feel that they have little to offer them in terms of career development.

Reference

Cullen, N.C. (2001) *Team Power: Managing Human Resources in the Hospitality Industry*. Upper Saddle River, NJ: Prentice-Hall.

GILLIAN KELLOCK HAY
GLASGOW CALEDONIAN UNIVERSITY, UK

Common-size statements

In order to undertake meaningful comparisons of financial results between businesses of different sizes or scale of operations, it is important the comparisons are assessed on a like-for-like basis, i.e. on a level playing field. For example, assume a company that owns two similar restaurants, with seating capacities for 40 and 75 persons, wishes to compare the operating performance of each establishment, one against the other. If the larger of the two restaurants were to achieve higher levels of revenue, costs and profits this, by itself, is unlikely to give a clear indication of the relative operating efficiency of the two establishments, because under normal conditions the larger establishment would be expected to generate higher revenues and, therefore, higher profits. Thus, notwithstanding the seating capacity of the restaurants, in terms of assessing efficiency, the problem of differing levels of business alone prevents an equitable comparison between the two establishments. However, the question of 'how do the two establishments compare in terms of operating efficiency,' e.g. costs and profits achieved as a percentage of revenue, or cost and profit per euro of revenue generated, addresses the level (scale) of business issue by focusing on the 'relative' (percentage relationship) level of business rather than the 'absolute' (numerical) value of the level of business.

In terms of implementation, the issue of operating efficiency can be addressed by the presentation of profit and loss statements in what is termed 'common-size' format. Total revenue is taken to represent 100% and the various individual expense items are expressed in 'relative' terms as percentages of the total revenue. In the case of a multiple department hospitality business such as a hotel, the individual department revenues are regarded as 100% and the associated direct department expenses are expressed as percentages of their particular department revenue, whilst the undistributed operating expenses (overhead) are expressed as percentages of total revenue. The individual department revenues are subsequently expressed as percentages of total revenue, commonly referred to as sales mix (or business mix). An alternative approach, as implied earlier, is to present the common-size profit and loss statement in terms of the cash value of costs and profit per euro of revenue generated. Clearly, the preferred method will depend on the context and purpose of the analysis.

With regard to hotels, however, the nature of the business offers another approach to the presentation of common-size profit and loss statements, based on the 'per available room' (PAR) concept. In this case, the various hotel revenues, expenses, and profits contained in the profit and loss statement are presented line-by-line, in PAR terms, by dividing each line item by the number of available rooms in the particular hotel property under review. For example, if the annual profit statement of a 200-room mid-market hotel showed rooms department revenue £4,000,000, rooms department payroll £480,000, and other rooms department expenses (guest supplies, laundry, travel agent commission etc.) £360,000, the PAR common-size format for the statement would show RevPAR (revenue per available room) £20,000, CostPAR (cost per available room) – payroll £2400, and CostPAR – other expenses £1800. The same principle is applied line-by-line to the food and beverage department, other operated departments (such as telephone department and leisure center), and the undistributed operating expenses (overhead), down to gross operating profit (GOP).

The process of dividing the various revenues and expenses by the number of available rooms neutralizes the influence of capacity (size) and allows a hotel's financial results to be compared (benchmarked) against (say) other mid-market hotels (with differing numbers of rooms) PAR results in the same company. Alternatively, a hotel's results could be benchmarked against

hospitality industry norms published by leading accounting and hospitality consulting firms. These firms not only produce annual industry statistics for their own commercial purposes, but also benefit data contributors and others by making available valuable annual performance indicators and analysis of industry trends. Thus, once preparation of the PAR profit and loss statement is complete the results can be compared on an intra-company and/or industry basis using comparative analysis techniques.

The rationale for applying PAR as the basis for presenting the common-size format of hotel profit and loss statements is that room capacity, rather than (say) restaurant capacity, is normally the main 'driver' of a hotel business and, therefore, broadly considered to be the lowest common denominator. An alternative approach is to present the common-size profit and loss statements based on 'per occupied room' (POR). However, compared with the per occupied room basis which only considers capacity utilization (room occupancy), the per available room approach is regarded as a more comprehensive as it incorporates both capacity utilization and total capacity (room occupancy and total room stock).

References

Fay, C.T., Rhoads, R.C., and Rosenblatt, R.L. (1976) *Managerial Accounting for the Hospitality Service Industries*, 2nd edn. Dubuque, IA: Wm. C. Brown.

Harris, P.J. (1999) *Profit Planning*, 2nd edn. Oxford: Butterworth-Heinemann.

Harris, P.J. and Brander Brown, J. (1998) Research and development in hospitality accounting and financial management. *International Journal of Hospitality Management*, 17 (3), 161–181.

Jagels, M.G. and Coltman, M.M. (2003) *Hospitality Management Accounting*, 8th edn. New York: John Wiley & Sons.

Pannell, Kerr & Foster (annually) Country Trends: Hotel Performance and Profitability in Europe, Middle East, Africa and South Asia. London: PKF.

PETER HARRIS
OXFORD BROOKES UNIVERSITY, UK

Communication

Communication is the exchange of information and understanding. It is not a one-way process with information passing from sender to receiver, but rather a means of information processing that is socially constructed with both sender and receiver interpreting the message in accordance with their needs and motivations. Effective communication is vital for organizational success and is positively correlated with employee job satisfaction and performance. Communication is particularly important for service encounters, as without effective communication, service quality will suffer. However, there is always a balancing act between enough communication with a customer to ensure friendliness and warmth, but not so much that staff appear impolite and disrespectful. Within the global hospitality industry, there are several factors that complicate the communication process; hospitality managers might work for foreign-owned companies, deal with non-native guests or customers, manage a multi-cultural and multi-lingual workforce, and collaborate with other managers around the world. They therefore have to be able to deal with a multiplicity of communication behaviors in many different contexts, languages or cultures. Cultural differences mean that people will interpret the same communication very differently, with some nationalities favoring direct, unambiguous messages, whereas others prefer more ambiguous, vague communication that is less likely to cause offence.

Reference

Cullen, N.C. (2001) *Team Power: Managing Human Resources in the Hospitality Industry*. Upper Saddle River, NJ: Prentice-Hall.

GILLIAN KELLOCK HAY
GLASGOW CALEDONIAN UNIVERSITY, UK

Comparative statement analysis

Comparative statement analysis is an effective technique for the comparison of financial results with either past or budgeted results, or industry norms. For example, the comparison of actual results with budgeted results is carried out as follows:

$$\text{Actual result} - \text{Budgeted result} = \text{Absolute variance}$$

If a hotel achieves actual room sales revenue for a month of £68,600 against a budget of £70,000 the comparison will show an 'absolute' (numerical) variance of $-£1400$ (£68,600–£70,000). The absolute revenue variance of $-£1400$ is denoted by a 'minus' sign due to the rooms sales revenue shortfall of £1400 against budget. However, in order to improve the understanding of the absolute variance resulting from the revenue shortfall, it is necessary to determine the 'relative' (percentage) variance by:

$$(-£1400/£70,000) \times 100 = -2\%$$

and presented as follows:

	Actual	Budget	Absolute Var.	Relative Var.
Room sales revenue	£68,600	£70,000	$-£1400$	-2%

The room revenue variance of $-£1400$ represents a 2% shortfall against budget, thus providing additional insight into the relative comparison by relating the absolute variance as a proportion of the budgeted rooms revenue. Therefore, although the magnitude of the £1400 may be a considerable sum in absolute cash terms, it represents only 2% shortfall against budget, thereby providing management with a more informed and balanced view of the financial result. *Note:* relative variances should always be expressed as a percentage of the predetermined standard (or benchmark), in this case the budgeted rooms sales revenue.

References

Jagels, M.G. and Coltman, M.M. (2003) *Hospitality Management Accounting*, 8th edn. New York: John Wiley & Sons.

Harris, P.J. (1999) *Profit Planning* 2nd edn. Oxford: Butterworth-Heinemann.

Harris, P.J. and Hazzard, P.A. (1992) *Managerial Accounting in the Hospitality Industry*, 5th edn. Cheltenham: Stanley Thornes.

PETER HARRIS
OXFORD BROOKES UNIVERSITY, UK

Compensation

Compensation is most usually a monetary payment to an employee paid under a 'no fault' scheme by way of reparation for personal loss or injury arising in the employee's employment (Vitale, Bare and Skene, 2001). Monetary compensation for workplace injury or illness or psychological injuries has been an accepted form of dealing with workplace injury; however, today there is greater emphasis on prevention and rehabilitation strategies to help individuals return to work. Compensation is paid irrespective of whether the employee was negligent or not (with some exceptions including intoxication and self-inflicted injuries). The notion of injury is broadly defined and can extend to items of personal property, which may have been damaged as a result of a personal injury. In many countries, there are mandatory workers' compensation schemes and employers who fail to comply risk heavy non-compliance penalties. Emphasis is on the implementation of risk assessment strategies in order to control workplace hazards and risks. In the hospitality industry, areas of work that are generally considered high risk include rooms (back and stretch injuries), kitchens (slips, sprains, and heat), and cleaning (chemicals and repetitive train). Assessing the actual extent of employer duty of care and liability for workers is crucial because of the increasing use of agency staff and subcontractors (Woods, 2002).

References

Vitale, P., Bare, M., and Skene, G. (2001) *Australian Master Human Resources Guide 2002*. Sydney: CCH Australia Ltd.

Woods, R.H. (2002) *Managing Hospitality Human Resources*, 3rd edn. Lansing, MI: Educational

Institute of the American Hotel and Lodging Association.

NILS TIMO
GRIFFITH UNIVERSITY, AUSTRALIA

Competencies

Core competencies are the collective learning in the hospitality firm, especially how to coordinate diverse production skills and integrate multiple streams of technology throughout the hotel or restaurant. In addition, it is about the organization of work and the delivery of value, communication, involvement, and a deep commitment to working across organizational boundaries (Prahalad and Hamel, 1990). Most often, core competencies are process or skills rather than physical assets or technologies. They are the central skill sets used by the firm to produce its products. For example, for the 3M Company it is the ability to work with adhesives. For the Sony Corporation it is the ability to miniaturize so as to lower design and production costs. For Pepsi it is the production of soft drink beverages. For Holiday Inn it is the ability to work with massive customer databases. For numerous organizations in the service industry core competencies include functional aspect of service (how) rather than technical (what) (Gronroos, 2000). Competencies are built over time through the complex integration of organizational activities and are difficult to imitate.

References

Gronroos, C. (2000) *Service Management and Marketing*. Chichester: John Wiley & Sons.

Prahalad, C.K. and Hamel, G. (1990) The Core Competence of the Corporation, *Harvard Business Review*, 68 (3), 79–91.

CHRIS ROBERTS
UNIVERSITY OF MASSACHUSETTS, USA

Competency profiling

Competencies in a hospitality organization may refer to desired personal attributes and behaviors (e.g. the ability to organize, listen, and react to the needs of others) and the knowledge and skill (e.g. the ability to operate machinery safely or to be computer and numerically literate) required to bring about improved performance and to provide value to the customer.

Shellabear (2004) defines Competency Profiling as 'a method used to identify specified skills, knowledge, attitudes and behavior necessary to fulfilling a task, activity or career'. He identifies levels of competency profiling for many commercial organizations to involve:

- *Novice* – a basic level of understanding, but the employee has not performed the task before
- *Apprentice* – the employee has performed the task with help or has understanding and limited practical experience
- *Competent* – the employee has depth of understanding and consistently performs the task to the required standard
- *Expert* – the employee consistently performs the task to the required standard and looks at ways of improving ways of working, has in-depth understanding and could train others.

The competencies of skill, knowledge, attitude, and behavior can be identified for any task in a hospitality organization. Take the task of 'serving a drink to a customer' – the server's competencies can be graded or profiled according to the level of novice, apprentice, competent, or expert.

Reference

Shellabear, S. (2004) Competency profiling: definition and implementation. *Dancing Lion Training and Consultancy.* www.dancinglion. co.uk. Accessed 5 April 2004.

FRANCES DEVINE
UNIVERSITY OF ULSTER, UK
ADRIAN DEVINE
UNIVERSITY OF ULSTER, UK

Competitive advantage

This is the set of factors or capabilities that allow a hotel or restaurant consistently to outperform its rivals (Porter, 1985). Not all hospitality firms have a competitive advantage. Businesses may enjoy a sustained competitive advantage if their capabilities are valuable and rare, lack substitutes, and are difficult to imitate. Usually the advantage is a process or skill but occasionally it can be an asset. For example, Hyatt has created a competitive advantage through the use of innovative architectural design of their hotel buildings. In contrast, location might become a competitive advantage (Barney, 1991). The Plaza Hotel in New York City is the only hotel that can occupy that prestigious corner lot on Fifth Avenue across from Central Park. A competitive advantage may be created through an accumulation process that includes time, an interconnectedness of capabilities, steady investment, a building upon past successes, and shrouding the advantage from the view of competitors. If hidden from view it is generally more difficult to imitate. Processes are typically easier to shield than assets. Once the set of factors or capabilities become less valuable or rare, have a substitute or can be imitated the advantage loses its competitive strength.

References

Barney, J.B. (1991) Firm resources and sustained competitive advantage. *Journal of Management*, 15, 649–661.

Porter, M.E. (1985) *Competitive Advantage: Creating and Sustaining Superior Performance.* New York: The Free Press.

CHRIS ROBERTS
UNIVERSITY OF MASSACHUSETTS, USA

Competitive position

A firm's competitive position can be looked on as how successfully a company competes in the marketplace relative to its competitors. Thus, the competitive position concept is concerned with how strongly the firm holds its present position and if it is positioned to maintain or improve this position in the future. The resource-based view asserts that a strong competitive position is created by firms committing tangible and intangible resources, which become a bundle of unique products and capabilities. A defensible competitive position can be formed when this process creates value to the customer and cannot be easily imitated by competitors.

The approach of the resource-based view to a competitive position is more closely aligned with the service nature of hospitality firms. Specifically, the competitive position of hospitality firms is a process of linking systems and competencies that create a portfolio of product and service offerings. Within this process, managers make resource allocation decisions to implement competitive methods addressing 'what' portfolio of products and services will be offered, 'how' these will be offered and implemented to maximize value to the customer, and 'how' this portfolio can be consistently delivered to maintain a strong competitive position relative to industry or segment competitors.

References

Hitt, M. and Hoskisson, R. (2001) *Strategic Management: Competitiveness and Globalization*, 4th edn. Cincinnati, OH: South-Western College Publishing.

Olsen, M., Tse, E., and West, J. (1998) *Strategic Management in the Hospitality Industry*, 2nd edn. New York: John Wiley & Sons.

ROBERT HARRINGTON
NICHOLLS STATE UNIVERSITY, USA

Competitive strategy

A competitive strategy of an organization is, generally, conceived of as a comprehensive master plan of 'what' an organization intends to accomplish and 'how' it plans to implement and achieve its mission, goals, and objectives. The formulation of what an organization intends to achieve is referred to as strategic ends. Types of strategic ends include mission statements, business purpose, key strategic goals, market share objectives, financial target objectives, and key result areas. The formulation of how an organization intends to achieve its mission, goals, and objectives is referred to as strategic means.

Strategic means can be described as strategies, policies, alternatives, programs, and action plans. Strategic ends and means make up the overriding competitive strategy for a firm. When properly formulated, the competitive strategy maximizes the competitive advantage for the firm and minimizes any competitive disadvantage.

The competitive strategy of a firm has three general levels: corporate strategy, business strategy, and functional strategy. For hospitality firms, it is of particular importance to consider the multiple levels of competitive strategy. Hospitality business units and the knowledge base within them are geographically and departmentally dispersed. Competitive strategies can best be achieved when this dispersed knowledge and differences in guest expectations are integrated into corporate, business unit, and functional strategy.

References

Brews, P.J. and Hunt, M.R. (1999) Learning to plan and planning to learn: Resolving the planning school/learning school debate. *Strategic Management Journal*, 20, 889–913.

Olsen, M., Tse, E., and West, J. (1998) *Strategic Management in the Hospitality Industry*, 2nd edn. New York: John Wiley & Sons.

ROBERT HARRINGTON
NICHOLLS STATE UNIVERSITY, USA

Computer

An electronic machine, which comprises hardware and software as the major components (Capron, 1998). Hardware refers to the collection of chips and other electronic devices of a computer system, which are the identifiable and movable elements. In order to drive the operations of hardware components, a set of computer programs known as software is needed to control the electronic devices. A typical computer processing cycle consists of four stages: input, process, output, and storage. An input device gets computer accessible data, and transfers the data to a processing unit. The electronic circuit of the processing unit then transforms input data to information. After that, an output device produces the user-required information in a human comprehensible form. Lastly, an internal or external storage device can store data and information.

Computers can be broadly classified as personal computers, mobile devices, midrange servers, mainframes, and supercomputers. In the hospitality industry, computers are widely used from back office to front office (Kasavana and Cahill, 1997). Examples of back office computer applications include human resources, accounting, inventory control, and purchasing management. Reservations, food and beverage management, and banqueting are some examples of front office computer applications.

References

Capron, H.L. (1998) *Computers: Tools for an Information Age.* New York: Addison-Wesley.

Kasavana, M.L. and Cahill, J.J. (1997) *Managing Computers in the Hospitality Industry.* Lansing, MI: Educational Institute of the American Hotel and Motel Association.

ROB LAW
THE HONG KONG POLYTECHNIC UNIVERSITY,
HONG KONG SAR, CHINA

Computer reservation system (CRS)

Computer reservation systems are primarily used for inventory management by airlines, hotels, and other tourism and hospitality enterprises. Enhanced and sophisticated CRS configurations and functionality offer companies an integrated solution for several processes including managing sales, bookings, customer relationship management and service, other marketing practices, yield management, payments and accounting even at a one-to-one customer basis (Sigala *et al.*, 2001). Integrated CRSs aim to organize companies internally by enabling organizational reengineering/restructuring changes that in turn streamline processes and foster functional efficiency and effectiveness. Moreover, the term central reservation system refers to the CRS developed by hotel chains for centralizing the reservation process of all their affiliated properties and enabling multi-chain management. The major benefits of such systems are operational efficiencies and staff reductions.

Braham (1988) briefly outlined the processes, functionalities, and benefits of a CRS as follows:

- Flexible inventory booking capability
- Immediate availability update
- Overbooking management
- Complete and detail reservations screen
- Individual and group reservations and blockings
- Travel agency information entry, activity reports and commission handling
- Guest information enquiry
- Reservations linked to city ledger
- Advance deposit posting and auditing
- Request for deposit and deposit received
- Modifications and cancellation confirmations
- Free-form comments field on all reservations
- System generated confirmation numbers on all reservations
- User identification
- Confirmations printed automatically or on demand
- Forecast reports
- Current and future dates to five years historical information
- Detailed inventory control
- No-shows reports and handling (charging and billing)
- Customer information – past, present, future – retained in system.

The primary reason for using computers in the handling of reservations is to increase yield metrics, but this entirely depends on the level of systems integration (Sigala *et al.*, 2001). This is because computer reservation systems not only help tremendously in processing reservations, but they also support decision-making in marketing and sales (e.g. yield management, discount policies, the creation of guest records etc.). Integration between CRSs and distribution channels can improve efficiency, facilitate control, reduce personnel, and enable more rapid response time to both customers and management requests, whilst enabling personalized service and relationship marketing (Braham, 1988;

O'Connor, 1999; Sheldon, 1997). Overall, most CRSs tend to serve several business functions as follows (Buhalis, 2003):

- Improve capacity management and operations efficiency
- Facilitate central room inventory control
- Provide last room availability information
- Offer yield management capability
- Provide better databases access for management purposes
- Enable extensive marketing, sales and operational reports
- Facilitate marketing research and planning
- Travel agency tracking and commission payment
- Tracking of frequent flyers and repeat hotel guests
- Direct marketing and personalized service for repeat hotel guests
- Enhance handling of group bookings.

Overall, Braham (1988) and Sigala *et al.* (2001) analyzed the levels of integration at which hotels can exploit CRSs and identified the benefits that such systems integration can provide as follows:

- *Integration with external reservations networks:* Examples here would be airline global distribution systems, or partners' corporate reservation systems. Traditionally, third party reservation systems such as hotels.com operated by obtaining guaranteed allocations of rooms from hotels in advance that could then be sold directly to travel agents and the public. However, inventory allocation does not allow the sale of the last available room and disadvantages efficient multi-channel distribution and yield management strategies. To optimize occupancy and average room rates, seamless integration between company and external reservation systems is required so that real-time room and rate inventory is made available to all distribution channels.
- *In-house reservations networks:* Hotel chains and consortia integrate their CRSs with each property-based reservation system. Seamless connectivity allows cross-selling between hotel properties and multi-unit distribution strategies. Nowadays, intranets are increasingly used for this purpose.

- *Single-property reservations systems:* These systems handle reservations that come from different sources, e.g. telephone, letter, fax etc., solely for a hotel property. This level of integration refers to the internal integration of the reservation system with other business systems.
- *Property management system (PMS):* Integration between the CRS and PMS is required for enhancing guest services by enabling CRM (customer relationship marketing) practices, express check-in/out procedures as well as for increasing operational procedures, e.g. housekeeping, staff scheduling, just-in-time procurement.

Through terminals and systems interconnections, enhanced CRS configurations can allow direct access to stock and price inventories to intermediaries and/or final customers for checking availability, making bookings and payments. A CRS can support the coordination and cooperation along the distribution chain and may result in the development of dynamic and powerful distribution networks. The global distribution systems, e.g. Amadeus, emerged from the integration of several airline CRS systems. However, through CRS interconnections as well as the collection, analysis and use of information gathered through the distribution chain, GDSs have nowadays evolved to critical and significant travel distribution networks offering ubiquitous one-stop-shop travel solutions even directly to customers, e.g. travelocity.com. Research reveals that CRS exploitation can lead to operational efficiencies and strategic/competitive systems integration and expertise exploitation. Research in the hospitality industry also revealed that firms exploiting information generated by electronic reservation systems gain greater strategic and operational benefits in yield management, e-marketing strategies as well as productivity benefits from ICT investments (Sigala *et al.*, 2001).

To conclude, CRSs are central to the hospitality industry and are becoming the digital nervous system of the hospitality value chain. Due to the current technological advances and economic development, CRSs face several challenges including: their immigration to customer-centered services and infrastructure for providing personalized guest services and CRM practices; adoption of wireless solutions for guests and hotel staff services, e.g. reservations, check-in/out on the move, mobile control and monitoring of occupancy rates; linkages to other electronic systems of partners or third parties for enabling coopetition models (coopetition being a judicious mixture of cooperation and competition by which businesses can gain advantage) and boosting synergies.

References

Braham, B. (1988) *Computer Systems in the Hotel and Catering Industry*. London: Cassell.

Buhalis, D. (2003) *eTourism. Information Technologies for Strategic Tourism Management*. Harlow: Prentice-Hall.

O'Connor, P. (1999) *Tourism and Hospitality Electronic Distribution and Information Technology*. Oxford: CAB International.

Sheldon, P. (1997) *Tourism Information Technology*. Oxford: CAB International.

Sigala, M., Lockwood, A., and Jones, P. (2001) Strategic implementation and IT: gaining competitive advantage from the hotel reservation process. *International Journal of Contemporary Hospitality Management*, 17 (3), 364–371.

MARIANNA SIGALA
UNIVERSITY OF THE AEGEAN, GREECE

Concept mapping

Concept mapping is a technique that provides a more complete understanding of relationships among ideas, concepts, and even business operations. As Jonassen *et al.* (1993) note, the traditional approach to concept mapping involves linking related ideas unidirectionally and expanding the number of ideas while brainstorming or investigating complex clusters of interrelated ideas. Concept mapping is also instrumental in analyzing units on the basis of dimensional attributes.

It is this latter application that offers utility to restaurant operators. For example, suppose an operator is considering entering a new market. It would be useful to him or her to know what type of restaurants are currently operating in that market, separating each on the basis of cuisine style

and average entrée price while also considering the size of each restaurant in the analysis. As shown in Figure 1, such a map readily identifies gaps in the market. Here the size of each unit is depicted by the diameter of the associated data point and the color equates to the type of cuisine.

As useful as it is, this analysis ignores a key component: quantity of food. For example, what if some of these restaurants serve only tapas? Thus, the concept map requires the addition of another vector to permit analysis on the basis of all characteristics under consideration: average check, quality of food, quantity of food, type of cuisine, and restaurant size. Rotated accordingly, the concept map depicted here on a two-dimensional basis (due to the limitations of printed media) offers an ideal example (Figure 2).

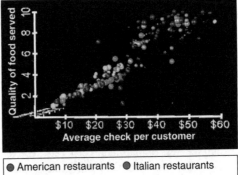

Figure 1 Quality of food served *vs.* average check

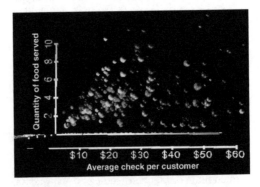

Figure 2 Quantity of food served *vs.* average check

This extension of the traditional concept map provides a wealth of information that has many applications. Furthermore, it can be refreshed routinely to provide an operator with the information necessary for repositioning a given unit or for adding new one.

Reference

Jonassen, D.H., Beissner, K., and Yacci, M.A. (1993) *Structural Knowledge: Techniques for Conveying, Assessing, and Acquiring Structural Knowledge*. Hillsdale, NJ: Lawrence Erlbaum Associates.

DENNIS REYNOLDS
WASHINGTON STATE UNIVERSITY, USA

Concierge

The concierge assists the guest with most problems concerning accommodations, handles their mail, and facilitates special requests with the front desk agent and other hotel personnel.

There is an interesting etymology to the word concierge. One school of thought suggests that the Latin root is *conserves*, or fellow slave. The Old French derivation that can be traced back to feudal times, *comte des cièrges*, or keeper of the candles, needed to know where all the functions in the palace would take place as they were in charge of maintaining the candles for each event. Over time, the *comte des cièrges* became the person in charge of catering to every whim and desire of a palace's visiting nobility.

In the Middle Ages, the *concièrges* were the keepers of the keys of noted government buildings and castles. There is even a famous prison in Paris named the Concièrgerie in honor of the warden who kept the keys and assigned cells to the inmates.

As the beginning of the 20th century, the international tourism industry experienced a tremendous boom, in large part due to the increasing popularity of rail and steamship travel. Switzerland's grand hotels, in working to satisfy the needs of these travelers, created the 'hall porter' position. These first-ever modern concierges were responsible for everything from meeting the guests at the station in a horse-drawn carriage to assisting them with every detail of their stay.

The ability to respond to a guest's request is critical to guest satisfaction. As the level of services to guests increases in volume or complexity, the creation of a separate department may become necessary.

The guest services department provides directions to points of interest, specialty shops, and shopping centers, recommendations for off-premise restaurants, tickets to the theater, reservations for tours, assistance with the purchase of airline tickets, help in locating the nearest religious services, assistance in setting up golf tee times, and other services.

The guest services department may consist of a single person, the concierge, or an entire department of employees who report to the concierge, including the concierge assistant, the bell captain, the bellmen and baggage porters, and the doormen.

Typically the concierge reports to the front office manager. The concierge assistant, bell captain, and doorman report directly to the concierge. The concierge establishes policies and procedures and writes job descriptions, training manuals, and procedures for all areas of guest services, including bell service, doorman service, guest paging, baggage and package handling, guest tour and travel services, and special guest requirements. Additional responsibilities include assisting guests with the many unscheduled guest service needs (theater tickets, car rentals, sightseeing tours, travel information, etc.); coordinating with the assistant manager, the senior assistant front office manager, and other departments; supervising and coordinating the parking of guest cars, and the coordinating with the laundry manger to ensure quality laundry and valet service.

Reference

Stutts, Alan T. (2001) *Hotel and Lodging Management – An Introduction*. John Wiley & Sons, New York.

GERARD VIARDIN
THE MARQUETTE HOTEL, USA

Concurrent sessions

Within a meeting or convention agenda, concurrent sessions are two or more plenary or breakout sessions which run concurrently, or at the same time as others, with the understanding that participants will select or be assigned to those sessions. Concurrent sessions are much the same as breakout sessions. Concurrent sessions typically differ in complexity, themes, subject matter, and/or target audience, but also typically run on an identical time schedule to assure that break times and transitions to other sessions are not disrupted. While concurrent sessions are different in context, they are designed to bring people together with a common interest or need and provide educational enhancement for participants. Concurrent sessions are typically in a conference-style format and typically serve groups of 150 or more and last between 1 and 1.5 hours. Group discussions may also be incorporated into the session. The number of participants per session varies depending on the size and scope of the overall meeting or event. By utilizing concurrent sessions, meeting planners can provide options for attendees and are better able to meet event objectives. Concurrent sessions are based more on logistical factors as opposed to the substantive factor of the meeting.

Reference

Fenich, G. (2004) *Meetings, Expositions, Events and Conventions: An Introduction to the Industry.* Englewood Cliffs, NJ: Prentice-Hall.

SEKENO ALDRED
CENTER FOR EFFECTIVE PUBLIC
POLICY, USA
KIMBERLY SEVERT
UNIVERSITY OF CENTRAL FLORIDA, USA

Condominium

A condominium describes the absolute ownership of an apartment in a multi-unit building based on a legal description of the air space the unit actually occupies. Common areas such as the land, the physical structure, the lobby and any amenities are owned jointly by all condominium unit owners. Common charges and fees for operational and managerial expenses are allocated among the owners of the condominiums based on the square foot percentage of each owner's unit.

The term 'condominium hotel' is a relatively new term used by the hotel industry and refers to those buildings whose suites are individually owned but are collectively marketed and operated as a hotel. Typically, condominium hotels offer housekeeping, front office and security services, but have limited or no food and beverage facilities. What further distinguishes condominium hotels is that the units are normally rented for a minimum stay of one week. Typically, investors in condo hotel suites are motivated by tax write-off opportunities, personal free use of their unit during a limited period of time each year and the potential profit share derived from the yearly rental of their unit to vacationers.

Reference

Gentry, Robert A., Mandoki, Pedro and Rush, Jack (1999) *Resort Condominium and Vacation Ownership Management: A Hospitality Perspective.* Lansing, MI: Educational Institute of the American Hotel and Motel Association.

UDO SCHLENTRICH
UNIVERSITY OF NEW HAMPSHIRE, USA

Conference

A meeting characterized by its participatory nature, a conference is designed for the discussion of subjects related to a specific topic or area that may include fact-finding, problem-solving, and consultation. It is an event used by any organization to meet and exchange views, convey a message, open a debate, or give publicity to some area of opinion on a specific issue. No tradition, continuity or specific period is required to convene a conference. Although not generally limited in time, conferences are usually of short duration with specific objectives. Conferences are generally on a smaller scale than congresses and/or conventions and do not have exhibits. They may also be described as assemblies of a large number of individuals that discuss items of mutual interest or engage in professional development through learning and sharing. Conferences may be held in a variety of venues, including conference centers, conference hotels, convention centers, universities, and resorts. A conference may be organized by an association, a corporation, a for-profit company, a non-profit organization or any other entity that wants to produce it.

References

Goldblatt, Joe, and Nelson, Kathleen (2001) *The International Dictionary of Event Management*, 2nd edn. New York: John Wiley & Sons.

Krug, S., Chatfield-Taylor, C., and Collins, M. (eds) (1994) *The Convention Industry Council Manual*, 7th edn. McLean, VA: The Convention Industry Council.

PATTI J. SHOCK
UNIVERSITY OF NEVADA, LAS VEGAS, USA
DEBORAH BREITER
UNIVERSITY OF CENTRAL FLORIDA, USA

Conference center

A conference center is a facility dedicated as an adult learning environment and designed for the comfort of the meeting participant. In order to conform to the 'universal criteria' of best practices as established by the International Association of Conference Centers (IACC), it should provide ergonomic furniture, state of the art audiovisual and computer equipment, leisure time activities, and offer unique and plentiful food and beverage choices. Most conference centers are also residential and provide guestrooms, although it is not a requirement of the IACC.

Conference centers in the United States surfaced in the 1960s, when entrepreneurs renovated mansions and estates into executive meeting sites. Those led to purpose-designed meeting space and guestroom facilities with companies such as Marriott, Hilton, Starwood, and Aramark

soon leveraging their catering operations into full property management (Flynn and Kephart, 2000). In addition, conference centers may be owned and operated by corporations for in-house staff training and education, managed by a university, or privately owned.

Often times the fees for a conference center are based on a CMP or complete meeting package. This is usually a per person/per day fee, covering the cost of the sleeping room, food and beverage, meeting space rental, and audiovisual equipment.

References

Flynn, M.J. and Kephart, L. (2000) *Hotel Companies Turn Focus to Conference Centers. Hotel & Motel Management*, 215 (4), 76.

International Association of Conference Centers (2003) Universal criteria. Retrieved 18 September 2003 from http://www.iaccnorthamerica.org/about/inde.cfm?fuseaction=memcrit.

WILLIAM R. HOST
ROOSEVELT UNIVERSITY, USA

Conference plan

A conference plan is a roadmap for the overall programming of different sessions held during a conference. The plan takes into account the broad goals and specific objectives of the conference organizer or producer. It helps in the development of individual session content and plays an important role in the overall success of the individual sessions. Sessions for meetings, conferences, and training events are all different in context and purpose, but the development for each is much the same. One key element in the plan is to require the session content developer to submit an outline that includes measurable objectives for the session. This outline will assist the planner in keeping the development of instructional material on track for the session. Having measurable objectives provides structure for presenters and allows the planner to coach presenters who are inexperienced or not proficient in developing presentations. By incorporating measurable objectives into the conference plan, it makes evaluations easier and more logical for the presenter and the attendee while enabling the meeting planners to evaluate the overall effectiveness and success of the session.

Reference

O'Toole, W. and Mikolatis, P. (2002) *Corporate Event Project Management.* New York: John Wiley & Sons.

GEORGE FENICH
UNIVERSITY OF NEW ORLEANS, USA
KIMBERLY SEVERT
UNIVERSITY OF CENTRAL FLORIDA, USA

Confirmed reservation

A confirmed reservation is that which is made by a guest prior to their arrival at the hotel and is made with enough time for the hotel to respond to the request. Prospective guests who have a reservation for accommodations that is honored until a specified time represent the critical element in no-shows. Confirmations can be given over the telephone but this is not as good a method as putting the response in writing. The letter of confirmation has certain advantages, i.e. it allows the hotel to inform the guest of the details of the request and includes information such as the rate(s) quoted, gives information on cancellation procedures, suitable methods of payment, and any special requests made. A confirmed reservation will only be held until the cancellation hour deadline after which the reservation will be released for sale to the next interested customer.

Various types of travelers with confirmed reservations – corporate, group, or pleasure – have varying no-show rates. For example, corporate confirmed reservations may have a 1% overall no-show rate. Group travelers may have a 0.5% no-show rate, with no-shows all coming from one or two particular bus companies. Pleasure travelers may have a 10% no-show rate. The detailed investigation of each of these categories will suggest methods for minimizing no-show rates.

References

Bardi, James (2003) *Hotel Front Office Management,* 3rd edn. New York: John Wiley & Sons.
Kasavana, M. (1981) *Effective Front Office Operations.* New York: Van Nostrand Reinhold.

IRENE SWEENEY
INTERNATIONAL HOTEL MANAGEMENT
INSTITUTE SWITZERLAND, SWITZERLAND

Conflict

The Marxist approach presupposes that conflict is inherent in the employment relationship because both employers and employees are trying to maximize a return for their efforts. Neither party can be fully compensated for this.

In a less political sense, work-related conflict is a generic term that usually refers to various forms of inevitable organizational conflict (Heys, 2001). There are a number of ways of classifying these conflicts. For example, vertical conflict is that which occurs between managers and workers and concerns power differentials. Horizontal conflict occurs between people at approximately the same organizational level. Other ways of describing conflict include overt and covert. The former is often collectively based and organized and usually refers to strikes, go-slows, picketing, stop-work meetings, etc. Covert conflict is individually based and unorganized and usually refers to absenteeism, sick leave, absence without leave, sabotage, poor productivity and work attitude etc. It is usually recognized that the causes of conflict are complex (e.g. different responses to managerial decision-making) or from general causes relating to the way in which we work in industrial society (e.g. the effects of mass production, boring and repetitive work, alienation, stress etc.). According to Woods (2002) conflict in hotels often relates to poor departmental decision-making, poor work climate, and perceived inequity in the treatment between individuals. Increasingly, hotels are introducing people skills training for managers in order to enhance inter-personal communication skills.

References

Heys, A. (2001) *Australian Master Human Resources Guide 2002*. Sydney, Australia: CCH Australia.

Woods, R.H. (2002) *Managing Hospitality Human Resources*, 3rd edn. Lansing, MI: Educational Institute of the American Hotel and Lodging Association.

NILS TIMO
GRIFFITH UNIVERSITY, AUSTRALIA

Congress center

A congress center plays a key role in the MICE (meetings, incentives, conventions, and exhibitions) industry and makes a vital economic contribution to a destination. It is an important consideration in meeting planners' site selection, with its size, the type, and expertise of management being specific selection criteria. Referred to as convention centers in North America, congress centers in Europe are facilities that are designed to accommodate multiple groups of varying sizes and primarily host congresses and meetings. They consist of one or more fixed-seat theatres, a ballroom, and a large number of smaller meeting rooms for breakout sessions. Congress centers typically have catering facilities and are non-residential in nature (i.e., they do not provide sleeping rooms). Until recently, the majority of congress centers in Europe did not have dedicated exhibition space, with exhibitions traditionally being held in separate trade fair buildings. However, as associations in Europe have begun to realize the revenue potential of exhibitions concurrently run with congresses, existing congress centers are adding exhibit halls and new centers include them in their initial design, either as part of the center or being linked via a bridge or walkway. Centers' entrance lobbies are often utilized to facilitate attendee registration while interior lobbies typically serve as pre-function areas for receptions and cocktail parties. Congress centers are often located in a city's central business district, in close proximity to hotels and other support facilities, and have easy access to transport modes and tourist infrastructure.

Congress centers cater for a wide variety of events. Primarily designed to host large congresses and conferences they also accommodate exhibitions (trade and consumer shows), banquets, dances, business breakfasts and lunches, and product launches. Congress centers in Europe also often host cultural events, given the inclusion of fixed-seat theatres in their design that is attributable to the fact that European associations typically host more plenary sessions than North American ones. However, many of these events are seasonal in nature and combined with the intense competition among venues may result in substantial and predictable gaps in the event schedule. Therefore, center facilities may also be used by the local community and tourists during the peak tourist seasons, especially as there is a need to justify the often substantial public investments.

The various types of events hosted by congress centers give rise to the ballroom and meeting room space designation, with space being described in terms of the number of people that can be accommodated for different events, for example, banquet style, cocktail style, theatre or classroom style.

In recent years many new congress centers have been built in Europe and in the Asia–Pacific region, often due to a government's policy to promote economic regeneration, particularly in deprived areas. The construction of congress centers has assisted in the revitalization of numerous communities and regions, both physically and economically. As congress centers are non-residential, they require several hotels in close proximity to accommodate congress delegates, in addition to restaurants and shopping facilities. As a consequence of their construction, the image of the destination may be enhanced and enable its repositioning, resulting in further economic and social benefits.

The creation of employment opportunities, both by the congress center itself and supporting services, the stimulation of growth in related economic activities, and increased direct and indirect spending in the community, together with the multiplier effect represent primary economic benefits. An enhanced destination image, increased civic pride and the availability of facilities for use by the community are key social benefits resulting from the congress center construction.

Despite the numerous benefits congress centers can bring to a destination, they are often viewed as loss generators, due to the high cost of development of both the center and the supporting infrastructure, and the high level of debt servicing on-going repayment costs for the construction. Furthermore, there may also be potential losses in the operation of the centers.

The operation and ownership of congress centers can be either public or private. The majority of centers are publicly owned, either by local or state government. Government typically passes legislation that determines how the center will be financed, who will finance it, and other policies relating to the center's operation. Since the 'public' owns them, the interests of residents have to be balanced with commercial interests. This can at times create conflicts when congresses compete with events aimed at the public for space during a particular time. In contrast, privately owned congress centers are held by companies or corporations with an entrepreneurial orientation with the prime objective of profit generation. While the government does not directly finance private congress centers, they may provide financial incentives.

The management of a convention center has a significant impact on operating efficiency, economic impact, and overall success of a center. As is the case for ownership, the majority of congress centers are also publicly managed. It is important to note that management is not synonymous with ownership; for example, a publicly owned convention center may contract private management to operate the center. The key objective of publicly managed congress centers is to maximize their benefit to local residents while privately managed congress centers are operated like business enterprises. There are distinct advantages and disadvantages associated with either form of ownership and management, primarily relating to efficiency, profitability, and staffing.

In view of the substantial increase in the number of congress centers in recent years, the competition for business has become intense. There is much emphasis on architectural design of new congress centers, incorporating the use of natural materials, environmentally friendly practices, and views of the surrounding area. The quality of foodservice is also becoming an important promotional feature for some congress centers in Asia–Pacific, with catering services being in-house, in contrast to North America where catering is typically contracted. The availability of advanced audiovisual services is also becoming more vital to professional congress organizers and delegates. Innovative marketing and management strategies are required more than ever to succeed in such a competitive environment that is set to continue.

References

Fenich, G.G. (2002) Convention center ownership and management: the case of the United States. In K. Weber and K. Chon (eds), *Convention Tourism: International Research and Industry Perspectives*. New York: Haworth Press, pp. 139–153.

McCabe, V. (2000) *The Business and Management of Conventions*. Milton, Qld: John Wiley & Sons.

Petersen, D.C. (2001) *Developing Sports, Convention, and Performing Arts Centers*, 3rd edn. Washington, DC: Urban Land Institute.

KARIN WEBER
THE HONG KONG POLYTECHNIC UNIVERSITY,
HONG KONG SAR, CHINA

Consortium

A consortium is a group of companies that form a partnership to accomplish a certain task. For instance, in the late 1990s organizations formed procurement consortia to achieve buying power within their respective industry, reduce procurement costs, and streamline their supply chains. The underlying assumption was that if multiple organizations bought products as one entity, a better price could be achieved because of the increased volume. Procurement consortia are also known as online exchanges (Sawhney and Acer, 2000).

Purchasing was one of the more obvious areas for consortia because of the immediate savings recognized from large purchases (Cleary, 2001). These consortia frequently act as independent organizations collectively owned by the interested parties. For example, in 2001 Marriott International and Hyatt Hotels formed a buying consortium. They named the consortium Avendra. The consortium streamlines many of the repetitive procurement tasks across each individual hotel property. By late 2002, the consortium was generating profits (Browning, 2003).

Consortia are not limited to purchasing. In fact, many large players formed consortia for research and development and information systems years prior to forming consortia for procurement. Procurement consortia came to light in the late 1990s because of the technological advances in software and the Internet.

References

Browning, L. (2003) Hotel supply company controlled by Marriott shows a profit. *New York Times*, 9 May, p. C4 (retrieved on 22 April 2004 from EBSCO Host Research Databases).

Cleary, M. (2001) Room service. *Interactive Week*, 8 (3 March), 22 (retrieved on 22 April 2004 from EBSCO Host Research Databases).

Sawhney, M. and Acer, J. (2000) Dangerous liaisons. *Business*, 2.0 (24 October) 5, 138 (retrieved on 22 April 2004 from EBSCO Host Research Databases).

BRUMBY McLEOD
UNIVERSITY OF NEVADA, LAS VEGAS, USA

Constructive dismissal

In Australia and a few other countries of British heritage, the term refers to the abrupt termination of an employee's common law contract of employment that initially appears as if the employee resigned, but in reality, under certain circumstances, may be regarded as a dismissal by the employer. Circumstances amounting to constructive dismissal at common law include attempts by the employer to change workers' duties or location and a reduction of wages and other benefits without appropriate consultation (Vitale, Bare and Skene, 2001). This is known as a 'fundamental unilateral variation to employees' terms and conditions.' Other situations may include false accusations of theft and 'forced resignation' where the employer threatens to dismiss the worker if they fail to accept a particular ultimatum. However, there is no clear picture of what actually constitutes a forced resignation.

Employers imposing unreasonable performance standards upon particular workers also constitute grounds for constructive dismissal. Furthermore, a ruling of constructive dismissal may result if the employer gives unreasonable cautions or inappropriate disciplinary warnings to the employee. In sum, the term constructive dismissal refers to employers engaging in any behavior calculated to destroy or damage the relationship of confidence and trust between themselves and employees with the purpose of forcing them from the workplace. In the hospitality industry, cases of constructive dismissal are rare due to the limited amount of legal employee protection given to the majority of the workforce (employees working short-term and part-time).

Reference

Vitale, P., Bare, M., and Skene, G. (2001) *Australian Master Human Resources Guide 2002*. Sydney: CCH Australia.

NILS TIMO
GRIFFITH UNIVERSITY, AUSTRALIA

Consumer buying (decision) process

At every second of the day consumers are being bombarded with marketing information and promotional messages. Messages from television advertisements to website banners may reaffirm information about a product, showcase new products that are being launched, identify special product/service promotions, as well as notify consumers about special discount offers. Consumers therefore must constantly answer the question of 'which product/service should they purchase?' In order to arrive at a decision, the consumer goes through a process called the *consumer buying decision process*. This process is a useful tool that hospitality and tourism companies use in order to more accurately understand the buying behavior of their customers. To understand consumer buyer behavior is to understand how the customer interacts with the marketing mix inputs, that is, the four Ps of price, place, promotion, and product.

The consumer buying process is a five-stage purchase decision process that includes (1) need/want recognition, (2) information search, (3) an evaluation of alternatives, (4) purchase, and (5) postpurchase evaluation. Need recognition is the result of an imbalance between an actual and a desired personal state. Need recognition also occurs when the consumer recognizes that he/she has an unfulfilled want. Need recognition may be triggered by the knowledge that a current product is not performing properly, when the consumer is running out of a product, or when another product seems superior to the one currently used. Once a need or want is recognized, the consumer then begins to conduct an information search. Information search is the process of recalling past information stored in the memory and/or the process of seeking information in the outside environment. Sources of information may be *marketer-dominated* as in advertisements or personal selling efforts, *nonmarketer-dominated*, as in word-of-mouth communication from friends or acquaintances, or *neutral*, such as independent rating services. From this search process a set or group of brands will emerge from which the buyer can choose, often referred to as a consideration or evoked set, that a buyer views as possible alternatives. The consumer will then evaluate the alternatives generated that may potentially meet his/her needs. Product attributes are analyzed using some cutoff criteria or ranking of the importance of the product/service attributes as predetermined by the consumer. After evaluation the consumer will then make a product/service purchase that suits the recognized need/want. In the purchase stage, a consumer selects a product/service and a seller or service provider. Post-purchase evaluation will then follow. For certain types of purchases, a buyer may experience cognitive dissonance. Cognitive dissonance refers to doubts that may occur shortly after the purchase of a product when the buyer questions whether or not he or she made the right decision in purchasing the product. The consumer typically ponders the question of did I make a good decision? Did I buy the right product? Or did I get a good value? The hospitality and tourism company generally minimizes these questions through effective communication with the consumer, following-up with the consumer after the purchase and rectifying any problems identified by the consumer as well as offering guarantees or warranties.

The stages that a consumer typically passes through in the consumer buying decision process are demonstrated in the following example. A family of four recognizes that they are not spending enough time with each other and decides to purchase a winter vacation to meet that need. The family starts the internal search process based on past experience and knowledge about winter vacation destinations. They may continue an external search for information about potential holiday destinations, availability of hotel accommodations, flight schedules, and holiday activities for the family. This information search involved talking to friends and family, obtaining holiday brochures, and surfing the Internet. The family evaluated the alternative vacation possibilities and made a final decision about which vacation to purchase. The family then purchased the vacation whether as a single purchase through a travel agent, or by making several individual purchases such as hotel accommodations, car rental, and airline tickets separately. The family then goes on vacation and evaluates the destinations. If the family members are satisfied with the vacation, they may decide to take this vacation again or recommend it to other family members or friends. If the vacation experience has been an unhappy one, then the negative aspects of the vacation may be related to discouraging family and friends them from making the same purchase.

In some situations the consumer buying decision process moves very quickly, such as in the repeat purchasing of a familiar brand of convenience product. However, in other situations, each stage of the consumer buying decision process can be clearly observed. In addition, cultural, social, individual, as well as psychological factors will affect all steps. It must also be noted here that impulse buying is not a consciously planned buying behavior but involves a powerful urge to buy something immediately. In addition, not all decision processes culminate in a purchase, nor do all consumer decisions always include all of the five stages of the consumer buying decision process. Finally, individuals involved in a group buying decision may exert more or less influence at different stages of the process.

Understanding the consumer buying decision process is important for hospitality and tourism companies as it highlights that a possibility exists to influence the consumer prior to the actual purchase taking place and at each stage in the process. The hospitality and tourism company should identify all the sources of information the consumer is likely to use when coming up with alternatives. The organization should also determine what criteria and strategies consumers use to evaluate alternatives and how best to ensure that the company's product/service message is used as a source of information by the consumer. Further, the consumer buying decision process highlights that the purchase of a hospitality product/service does not end with the sale. If the consumer's expectations about the product are not realized then future sales to that consumer may be lost. Negative word-of-mouth to family and friends may also discourage other people from purchasing the company's products/services in the future, ultimately affecting sales and profitability of the firm. Finally, the consumer buying decision process is important as if a marketer can identify consumer buyer behavior, he or she will be in a better position to target products and services at them. Without a sound knowledge of the reasons why consumers purchase its goods/services, a hospitality and tourism company cannot expect to create marketing strategies and promotional plans that work.

References

Brown, L. and McDonald, M.H.B. (1994) *Competitive Marketing Strategy for Europe*. Basingstoke: Macmillan.

Cateora, P.R. (1993) *International Marketing*, 8th edn. Homewood, IL: Irwin.

Dibb, S., Simkin, L., Pride, W.M., and Ferrell, O.C. (1994) *Marketing – Concepts and Strategies*, 2nd European Edition. Boston, MA: Houghton Mifflin.

Kotler, P. and Armstrong, G. (1999) *Principles of Marketing*, 8th edn. Englewood Cliffs, NJ: Prentice-Hall.

Lewis, R. and Chambers, R. (1989) *Marketing Leadership in Hospitality*. New York: Van Nostrand Reinhold.

Smith, P.R. (1996) *Marketing Communications – An Integrated Approach*. London: Kogan Page.

JULINE E. MILLS
PURDUE UNIVERSITY, USA

Consumer rights under the purchaser deposit

The laws of some jurisdictions require that all or a portion of the funds or other property received by a developer of a timeshare plan from a purchaser of a timeshare interest in the timeshare plan must be deposited in an escrow account with an independent escrow agent prior to completion of the purchase transaction.

The purchaser is entitled to the return of the funds or other property if the developer defaults under the purchase contract, including the developer's inability to deliver the accommodations and facilities of the timeshare plan as promised. Some jurisdictions permit developers to access purchaser funds or property prior to meeting the conditions for releasing the funds or property by providing an alternative assurance covering the purchaser funds or property. Alternative assurances can include such arrangements as the posting of a letter of credit or obtaining a security bond in the full amount of the funds or property that are deposited in the escrow account. Funds or property covered by the alternate assurance are released as the conditions for release from escrow are met, and any funds collected in excess of the amount of the alternate assurance must be deposited in the escrow account until the total amount of funds or property covered by the alternate assurance is again below the alternative assurance limit.

Reference

See *Fla. Stat.* §721.08 (2 October 2003). http://www.flsenate.gov/statutes/index.cfm? App_mode=Display_Statute&Search_String= &URL=Ch0721/SEC08.HTM&Title=->2000->Ch0721->Section percent2008.

KURT GRUBER
ISLAND ONE RESORTS, USA

Contextual effects in consumer behavior

Contextual effects relate to an area of marketing known as consumer behavior. Contextual refers to the environment surrounding a situation and effects refer to the response of the consumer to that surrounding environment. Ultimately, marketers are interested in the impact material surrounding an advertisement, product, or service will have on the consumers' interpretation. Marketers try to influence behavior. The situation in marketing might be an advertisement. The environment might be the type of magazine. For instance, the Four Seasons might advertise in *Architectural Digest* because the magazine has a reputation for luxury and wealth. The type of magazine impacts the interpretation of the Four Seasons advertisement. Even articles and other advertisements within the magazine influence perception of the advertisement by the consumer. Many television and radio advertisements are aired during specific types of programming to minimize or maximize the contextual effects.

Reference

Hawkins, D.I., Best, J.B., and Coney, K.A. (2001) *Consumer Behavior: Building Market Strategy*, 8th edn. New York: McGraw-Hill/Irwin, p. 299.

BRUMBY MCLEOD
UNIVERSITY OF NEVADA, LAS VEGAS, USA

Contingency theory

Originating in the 1960s, contingency research into organizational structure continues to exert an important influence on strategic management thinking to this day. In essence, contingency theory asserts the existence of a connection between some aspect of organizational structure and some aspect of the situation. Situational factors – referred to as 'contingency factors' – include environmental instability, technology, size, and strategy.

Research into the link between the environment and organizational structure includes seminal contributions by Burns and Stalker (1961) and Lawrence and Lorsch (1967). For example, the research by Burns and Stalker demonstrated that a stable environment required a mechanistic structure, while a dynamic environment demanded a more organic structure. Consequently the type of organizational structure that was deemed to be appropriate was contingent on the type of external environment in which the organization operated.

In a similar vein, research by Woodward (1965) demonstrated that the type of technology deployed by an organization influenced the appropriate organizational structure. Here organizations deploying process technologies were found to adopt mechanistic type structures, while those using more craft-based technologies adopted organic organizational structures. McDonald's Corporation is a good example of the former, while Ritz–Carlton is an example of the latter.

Research into the influence that organization size exerts upon structure was conducted in the famous Aston Studies: increasing organizational size leads to an increase in the structural differentiation of the organization in terms of both horizontal structure (number of divisions and sections within these) and vertical structure (number of levels in the hierarchy). As structural differentiation increases, so does the complexity of the coordination required, and this leads to an increase in the ratio of managers and administrators to total employees (i.e. increased administrative intensity). However, this will be offset by increasing formalization and increasing homogeneity within divisions and thus ultimately economies of administration arise.

The link between strategy and structure was the theme of Chandler's pioneering study (1962) of the growth of American industrial firms. He demonstrated that as the strategies of these organizations developed and changed, their structures changed (albeit lagged) to match. Therefore the growth of the multi-divisional structure (M-form) was driven by the increasing diversity in products and markets served by these organizations. The structural changes occur because the old structure has caused inefficiencies that have become detrimental to the survival of the organization. Chandler proposed a process or sequence to illustrate the necessary change: First, a new strategy is formulated. Second, new administrative problems emerge. Third, the organization's economic performance declines. Fourth, a new appropriate structure is invented. Fifth, profit returns to its previous level. In sum, Chandler's famous dictum, 'structure follows strategy,' simply states that organizational structure is contingent upon an organization's strategy.

The issue of structure and strategy is also manifested in the stages of an organizational development approach that argues that successful corporations tend to follow a pattern of structural development as they pursue growth strategies. The assumption is that the new structure, as originally proposed by Chandler (1962), is expected to be followed by a better performance. Accordingly, most organizations begin with a simple structure of the entrepreneurial firm in which every member does everything. This is common in small-scale bed-and-breakfasts or family hotels. As the organization grows, its operations and scope require organization according to functional lines with marketing, production, and finance operations. This seems to be the case for independent hotels that are not part of a chain. With continuing success and growth strategy, the hospitality organization may add new services, expand into different locations or even venture out into entirely new unrelated products and services. Clearly, this strategy requires a new structure: divisional structure. The divisional structure requires a central headquarters and decentralized operating divisions – each organized along functional lines.

It seems that the ever-changing and turbulent environment of the end of the twentieth century and the trends of this century may require a new, more *flexible structure that fits the prevailing external conditions.*

Overall, structural contingency theory can be considered to be a functionalist theory in that organizational structure is seen as producing (causing) certain outcomes such as effectiveness, innovation, and so on. Organizations are thus seen as being required to adopt the structural form that fits with the contingency factors if they are to be effective. For some researchers this was seen as being overly deterministic and led to the development of the concept of strategic choice (Child, 1972), which argued that management has more discretion in decision-making than contingency theory implies.

References

Burns, T. and Stalker, G.M. (1961) *The Management of Innovation*. London: Tavistock.

Chandler, A.D. (1962) *Strategy and Structure: Chapters in the History of the American Industrial Enterprise*. Boston, MA: MIT Press.

Child, J. (1972) Organizational structure, environment and performance: the role of strategic choice. *Sociology*, 6, 1–22.

Lawrence, P.R. and Lorsch, J.W. (1967) *Organization and Environment: Managing Differentiation and Integration*. Boston, MA: Division of Research, Graduate School of Business Administration, Harvard University.

Woodward, J. (1965) *Industrial Organization: Theory and Practice*. London: Oxford University Press.

J. STEPHEN TAYLOR
UNIVERSITY OF STRATHCLYDE, UK

Continuous improvement

The concept of continuous improvement gained prominence with the onset of the total quality management (TQM) movement, with the term used in relation to processes that involve everyone in an organization working in an integrated effort towards improving performance at every level (Rickards, 1999, p. 145). In a hotel, for example, continuous improvement would involve every department from housekeeping to the front office, guest services to food and beverage operations as well as support areas.

As part of a company's emphasis on quality, these processes aim at getting work done with minimum errors. The application of statistical control techniques is used in striving to achieve zero defects. For example, a restaurant could strive for zero errors in having no guests return their orders because of being prepared incorrectly. One control technique could involve the logging of how many returns occur and for what reasons.

According to management guru Peter Drucker (1999, p. 81), continuous improvement ultimately transforms an organization by leading to product and service innovation. Continuous improvement eventually leads to fundamental change.

References

Drucker, P. (1999) *Management Challenges for the 21st Century*. New York: Harper Business.

Rickards, T. (1999) *Creativity and the Management of Change*. Oxford: Blackwell Business.

DEBRA F. CANNON
GEORGIA STATE UNIVERSITY, USA

Contract of employment

A legal term describing the (common law) of contract in which the employment relationship between an employer and an employee is determined and the conditions set out (De Cieri and Kramar, 2003). A contract of employment has expressed terms in relation to the rights of each party that specifies and defines the nature of the employment relationship such as hours of work, duty, pay, holidays etc. A contract also has implied terms written into it (through the application of common law), such as the employer duty to indemnify the employee, to pay wages for work performed, and to provide a safe workplace. Employees have a duty to obey lawful instructions, to look after the property of the employer, and a duty of fidelity. In many industrial jurisdictions, the (common law) contract of employment has to be applied in the context of other statutory mechanisms such as industrial awards, industrial determinations, and employment statute that may also set out mandatory employment conditions. Statute law prevails over common law contracts of employment to the extent of any inconsistency. In the hospitality industry written employment contracts are frequently not provided for seasonal workers. However, theoretically this does not compromise the rights and liabilities of both hotel employer and employee.

Reference

De Cieri, H. and Kramar, R. (2003) *Human Resource Management in Australia: Strategy, People, Performance*. Sydney: McGraw-Hill.

DARREN LEE-ROSS
JAMES COOK UNIVERSITY, AUSTRALIA

Contribution margin

In conceptual terms, contribution margin is the amount contributed by a product to meet an organizational objective after paying for raw materials. It can be calculated by deducting the cost of all variable expenses from the revenues generated by a product. Products with higher levels of contribution margins are given greater importance in menu-planning decisions. Contribution margin is calculated not only at the individual product level but also at aggregate levels. For example, one could calculate contribution margin for a meal period such as breakfast. In on-site foodservice operations such as university foodservices, where several meals are offered in a day, contribution margin can be calculated for each meal period. Such information can be used in identifying 'profit leaders' or 'loss leaders' to make appropriate corrective actions.

Contribution margin is used extensively in making menu engineering decisions such as selecting a food item for a menu, setting price levels for food items, selectively promoting menu items to improve overall profitability, etc. Contribution is also used in determining such particulars as management compensation or managerial bonus calculations. In the foodservice industry, achievement of consistently high contribution margin is seen as an indication of sound management practices.

Reference

Pavesic, David (2003) *Fundamental Principles of Restaurant Cost Controls*. Columbus, OH: Prentice-Hall.

H.G. PARSA
OHIO STATE UNIVERSITY, USA

Controllable and non-controllable costs

Conventional wisdom requires managers to be responsible only for costs and revenues over which they have control. Measuring financial responsibility requires a distinction to be made between costs that can be driven by a unit and costs that are not under the control of a unit. Most costs in an organization are controllable by someone. However, the term 'controllable' refers to a responsibility center and not to the organization as a whole. Cost are controllable for a responsibility center when they are under the influence of the manager of the center.

A cost is controllable if the amount of cost incurred is significantly influenced by the action of the manager of the responsibility center. However, sometimes costs are controllable by more than one manager. The cost of the output of an organizational unit is often only partially a function of the unit's decisions. The average cost per night in a hotel, for example, is a function of number of clients, efficiency of people in charge of cleaning the rooms and several other factors. For a rooms division manager the only controllable costs are those related to the efficiency of the personnel in the services provided within his or her area of competence. In other words, controllable costs are those directly affected by the management of the organizational unit. These include direct costs and overheads allocated on the basis of 'level of usage' (e.g. the cost of laundry charged accordingly

with the actual usage of linen) because the manager is driving the level of services required. At the same time, general overheads allocated on a 'volume-based system' (e.g. the administrative cost) are controllable only by the department where resources are actually used (the administration department) and therefore other centers should not be held accountable for these costs. Often the physical amount of resources and prices of resources are controlled by different organizational units, because the purchasing function is carried out by a specialist unit and consumption is carried out by another unit. Therefore, controllable costs should be split between those two units. In these cases, standard prices are used in order to compare actual costs with the budget.

The distinction between controllable and non-controllable is sometimes partially artificial: cost and revenues are often affected by many factors controlled by several organizational units within the organization. The cost of food in the restaurant is a function of the overall demand because the rate of waste per unit goes up when the number of customers falls and, therefore, part of the so-called variable cost is affected by factors that are not under the control of the responsibility center. However, the responsibility system requires costs and revenues to be regarded as managed exclusively by a unit because, in principle, joint responsibility is difficult to account for.

For the purpose of management control, only controllable costs are important. Allocating to a responsibility center expenses that are not controllable by the center might be useful for producing information for decision-making (e.g. the full cost of a product), but is misleading for measuring responsibility. Therefore, the accounting system plays an important role in selecting controllable and non-controllable costs. A responsibility center's accounting reports should be based on controllable costs only. Therefore, cost accounting systems should be designed in order to serve different purposes (control, decision-making, inventory evaluation).

References

Drury, C. (2000) *Management and Cost Accounting*, 5th edn. London: Thomson Learning.

Fay, C.T., Rhoads, R.C., and Rosenblatt, R.L. (1976) *Managerial Accounting for the Hospitality Service Industries*, 2nd edn. Dubuque, IA: Wm. C. Brown.

Hilton, R.W. (2002) *Managerial Accounting: Creating Value in a Dynamic Business Environment*, 5th edn. Boston, MA: McGraw-Hill/Irwin.

PAOLO COLLINI
TRENTO UNIVERSITY, ITALY

Controllable costs in foodservice

Controllable costs are among the most commonly watched numbers in the foodservice industry. As the name suggests, controllable costs are those expenses that fall *directly* under the control of unit management. Common examples of items with controllable costs include food, beverages, labor, paper, linens, glassware, cleaning supplies, and services. Unit management often has direct control over the rate of usage of these products and services. Two of the most prominent controllable costs are food and beverage cost and labor costs. Since these two costs contribute nearly 70% of the controllable costs in a typical restaurant, they are often referred to as prime costs.

Most foodservice organizations make controllable costs a primary consideration in calculating compensation. The lower the percentage of controllable costs, the greater the possibility of achieving higher net profits. A word of caution is, however, in order: Not all controllable costs are under the control of unit management. In some instances unit management may have only partial control over selected costs. A case in point would be a unit where product usage is dictated by operational policies such as minimum labor coverage, assigned management labor, contractual services, etc.

Reference

Coltman, Michael M. (1989) *Cost Controls for the Hospitality Industry*. New York: John Wiley & Sons.

H.G. PARSA
OHIO STATE UNIVERSITY, USA

Convention

An event where the primary activity of the attendees is to attend educational sessions, participate in meetings/discussions, socialize, or attend other organized events. There (may be) is a secondary exhibit component. Normally organized by an association, the convention is usually an annual or biannual event for members. The convention program would likely include several different kinds of sessions: general sessions, keynote addresses, and break-out sessions. There would also be meetings of the association leadership, such as board meetings and committee meetings. Very often, special events, such as awards ceremonies, are also included in convention programming. Attendees pay a registration fee that covers general sessions and other scheduled events, including some meals. Conventions may be held in a variety of venues, depending upon the size of the audience. Sometimes they are held in convention centers, sometimes in convention hotels, sometimes in conference centers. Delegates will arrange their own travel to the convention and reserve their own hotel rooms. The convention producer may negotiate a special room rate for delegates at one or more hotels. Top destinations in the United States for conventions are Chicago, Orlando, and Las Vegas. Conventions generate profit for associations.

References

Morrow, S.L. (2002) *The Art of the Show*. Dallas, TX: Education Foundation, International Association for Exhibition Management.

Robbe, D. (2002) *Expositions and Trade Shows*. New York: John Wiley & Sons.

DEBORAH BREITER
UNIVERSITY OF CENTRAL FLORIDA, USA

Convention catering

Receptions, banquets, breakfasts, luncheons, refreshment breaks, and hospitality suites are an important part of any meeting. They serve as a focus for social interaction to meet new associates, renew old acquaintances, exchange ideas, and develop positive attitudes for the overall meeting experience. Costs of food and beverage functions can have a major impact on a meeting budget. The facility's catering and/or convention services departments usually start working on arrangements for the food functions of large events from 12 to 18 months prior to the meeting. Smaller meetings may start with arrangements 3 months in advance.

Banquet event order

A banquet event order should include all of the details of each particular event from set-up to teardown, including who is responsible for what. The caterer needs to know the history of each group, as well as current requirements and special needs. The history of past events, including attendance patterns and meal selections, is important information for the facility and the planner. For example, if historically only 50% of attendees eat breakfast the guarantee should be adjusted accordingly. The facility staff should provide preliminary information on local laws and regulations that may affect the function. An example would be the legal hours in the locality for liquor consumption. Another critical area is union work regulations that can limit the number of guests that wait staff can serve at a banquet or the number of musicians you must hire for a particular sized event. Another consideration is union pay scales and overtime rules. In the United States, many facilities are reluctant to negotiate prices more than 6 months in advance of an event due to the fluctuations in food prices. However, it is possible to negotiate prices as much as a year in advance if planners agree on a percentage ceiling above current prices.

Guarantees

Functions can be charged by signed guarantees, collected tickets or quantities consumed. Guarantees are normally required 48 hours in advance of a function, to allow the facility enough time to order food and call in the necessary servers to work the banquet. A complex menu with special food orders may require a longer lead time.

Oversets

Tables are usually set with 3–5% more covers than the number guaranteed (the percentage is negotiable).

Gratuities

Gratuities or *service charges* vary from one facility to another and normally range from 17 to 20% of the net price of the function. They are mandatory charges, unlike *tips*, which are discretionary. Service charges may also be levied against non-food items, such as audiovisual charges. If any portion of the service charge goes to the hotel instead of the service staff, it is considered subject to sales tax in the United States.

Food selection

In planning food for meetings, it is necessary to have a basic understanding of different foods because attendees have become much more health-conscious in recent years. Food and beverage affect the brain's ability to produce substances that may have stimulating, energizing or calming effects. For example, alcoholic beverages produce a delayed sluggishness, or if one has difficult material to present at a first morning session, one should select a breakfast with juices, fruit, coffee, cereal with milk, toast, bagels or muffins, keeping sugary foods to a minimum since research shows that sugar has a calming, not an energy-boosting effect. Protein foods should be served first, then the carbohydrates. The food selections provided to attendees will have as much effect on their mental awareness, retention, and sharpness as the methods of presentation used.

References

Shock, Patti J. and Stefanelli, John (2001) *On Premise Catering: Hotels, Convention and Conference Centers and Clubs*. New York: John Wiley & Sons.

Krug, S., Chatfield-Taylor, C., and Collins, M. (eds) (1994) *The Convention Industry Council Manual*, 7th edn. McLean, VA: The Convention Industry Council.

Hildreth, Richard A. (1990) *The Essentials of Meeting Management*. Englewood Cliffs, NJ: Prentice-Hall.

PATTI J. SHOCK
UNIVERSITY OF NEVADA, LAS VEGAS, USA

Convention center

The term convention center is typically used to identify a facility that consists of exhibition halls and meeting rooms, and is used to host conventions, trade shows, consumer events, and other large meetings and assemblies. In the United States and some other countries, the primary purpose of convention centers is to generate economic activity. Hosting an annual convention for an association, for example, can bring thousands of doctors, engineers, or other professionals to a city for several days. These delegates attend educational sessions and exhibitions. They also generate millions of dollars of revenue for local hotels, restaurants, retail establishments, transportation companies, and various other businesses.

Convention centers are built in various shapes and sizes, and sometimes encompass several city blocks. Exhibition space usually contains moveable walls that can create exhibit halls of varying sizes, each having loading dock access. Electrical and other utilities for exhibit booths are provided from floor boxes and/or ceiling connections throughout the halls. Meeting space typically consists of multiple breakout rooms that total 20–40% of the exhibition space. Other common architectural elements include registration areas, prefunction spaces, and food courts. Convention centers can be a part of a hotel complex, but most of the larger ones are freestanding venues.

In Europe and some other parts of the world, convention centers are called congress centers and they are usually used to host meetings without exhibitions. Congress centers often contain one or more fixed-seat theaters, since they host more diplomatic and plenary sessions than their North American counterparts. Exhibitions in Europe are traditionally held in separate, often remote trade fair buildings because many members of professional associations believe that the commercialism of an exhibition detracts from the dignity of their events (Petersen, 1996).

Conference centers are a related concept used to identify meeting facilities with nearby guestrooms. They are designed to host seminars and conferences for less than 100 people, and they are often a part of a hotel or resort complex. Conference centers are usually privately owned, unlike freestanding convention centers, which are almost always owned by governmental entities.

Prior to building or expanding a convention center, a consultant is often hired to perform a feasibility study. This includes an analysis of the intended target market(s), such as trade shows, association conventions, or consumer events. Clear and realistic determination of intended markets helps provide community leaders with answers on whether to build, and how to manage and operate, the proposed facility (Graham and Ward, 2003).

Feasibility studies also evaluate factors that impact competitiveness, such as the relative desirability of the locale. Throughout the world there are what are considered to be destination cities. When events are scheduled in locales such as San Francisco or New Orleans, for example, delegate attendance is almost always strong. Certain cities have highly desirable images, deserved or not, and people want to go there. Inordinate success has also been experienced in high-intensity airline hub cities such as Chicago and Atlanta primarily due to their ease of access (Jewell, 1998). A city's inventory of convention-class hotel rooms in the vicinity of the convention center is another important competitive factor.

The financial analysis portion of a feasibility study typically includes a review of financing options, construction costs, and operating costs of the facility, as well as the economic impact of the projected event activity. Construction financing is often provided by bonds, which are backed by hotel taxes and/or other government revenue sources. It is common to subsidize a portion of the annual operating cost of convention centers, since it is generally accepted that they act as loss leaders.

Unlike a private-sector real estate project, the feasibility of building or expanding a convention center is not contingent on cash flow or profitability. The primary motive for the development of a convention center is to attract nonresidents whose spending will infuse new money into the local economy and create new jobs, increased sales, and more tax revenues (Petersen, 1996). Additional tax revenues come from hotel and sales taxes, as well as property taxes on new hotels, restaurants, and other business properties that support convention center activities. An analysis of incremental tax revenues versus tax expenses can be a useful tool in the development decision.

While most freestanding convention centers in North America are owned by governmental entities, there are at least three general business models for how they are managed. Some facilities are managed by government departments, others by quasi-governmental authorities or public corporations, and still others by private management companies. Some of the reasons that governmental bodies decide not to manage their facility with in-house personnel include the recognition that they may not have the skill sets necessary to be successful in a highly competitive marketing and sales environment; and/or that they want management to be independent from the inherent bureaucratic restrictions in governmental purchasing and human relations.

The marketing and sales processes for a new or expanded convention center typically begin well before construction is completed, since many conventions and trade shows are booked 4–6 years in advance. Based on the established mission and strategic plan, the convention center and the local convention and visitors bureau usually work together to promote and sell the city as a preferred convention destination. Booking a large event is a major task that can take many years and require the orchestrated support of local hotels, businesses, public safety officials, and other community leaders.

The detailed event planning process usually begins 12–18 months prior to the event, and it includes the show organizers and their service contractors working closely with convention center operations personnel to coordinate floor plans, work requirements, and schedules. Event

move-in (and likewise move-out) activities can take several days and employ thousands of workers, many provided by local union halls. Service contractors deliver freight, assemble exhibit booths, and install carpeting. Convention centers usually provide electrical, telecommunications, lighting, audio, and room set-up services. When the event opens, convention centers then provide food services, parking management, building security, janitorial, and other services.

In order to ensure long-term success, a convention center should establish and maintain effective community partnerships to complement its marketing and operations activities. It should also hire and retain capable management, marketing, and operations personnel that regularly meet or exceed the expectations of show organizers, exhibitors, and attendees.

References

Graham, Peter and Ward, Ray (2003) *Public Assembly Facility Management: Principles and Practices* (Limited Review Edition). Coppell, Texas: International Association of Assembly Managers.

Jewell, Don (1998) *Privatization of Public Assembly Facility Management.* Malabar, FL: Krieger Publishing Company.

Petersen, David C. (1996) *Sports, Convention, and Entertainment Facilities.* Washington, DC: ULI – the Urban Land Institute.

JERRY DAIGLE
ORANGE COUNTY CONVENTION
CENTER, USA

Convention Industry Council

The Convention Industry Council (CIC) is an organization composed of the following 31 associations that represent more than 98,000 individuals and 15,000 firms and properties involved in the meetings, convention, and exhibitions industry.

- Air Transport Association of America (ATA)
- American Hotel and Lodging Association (AH & LA)
- American Society of Association Executives (ASAE)

- Association for Convention Operations Management (ACOM)
- Association of Destination Management Executives (ADME)
- Alliance of Meeting Management Companies (AMMC)
- Center for Exhibition Industry Research (CEIR)
- Council of Engineering and Scientific Society Executives (CESSE)
- Exhibit Designers and Producers Association (EDPA)
- Exposition Services and Contractors Association (ESCA)
- Healthcare Convention and Exhibitors Association (HCEA)
- Hospitality Sales and Marketing Association International (HSMAI)
- Insurance Conference Planners Association (ICPA)
- International Association of Assembly Managers (IAAM)
- International Association of Association Management Companies (IAAMC)
- International Association of Conference Centers (IACC)
- International Association of Convention and Visitor Bureaus (IACVB)
- International Association for Exhibition Management (IAEM)
- International Association of Speakers Bureaus (IASB)
- International Congress and Convention Association (ICCA)
- International Special Events Society (ISES)
- Meeting Professionals International (MPI)
- National Association of Catering Executives (NACE)
- National Coalition of Black Meeting Planners (NCBMP)
- National Speakers Association (NSA)
- Professional Convention Management Association (PCMA)
- Religious Conference Management Association (RCMA)
- The Society of Corporate Meeting Professionals (SCMP)
- Society of Government Meeting Professionals (SGMP)
- Society of Incentive and Travel Executives (SITE)
- Trade Show Exhibitors Association (TSEA)

CIC was formed in 1949 to provide a forum for member organizations seeking to enhance the industry. It facilitates the exchange of information and develops programs to promote professionalism within the industry and educates the public on its profound economic impact. CIC is a forum for leadership to productively and cohesively move the industry in an ever-changing economic and political environment.

Through its programs, CIC enables delegates from the meeting, convention, and exhibition industry to review the state of the industry and its role in today's economy. CIC's most notable programs include:

- Certified Meeting Professional (CMP) program
- APEX – the Accepted Practices Exchange initiative
- Coalition Campaign to Advance Face-to-face Meetings
- Industry publications
- CIC Hall of Leaders
- Website resource guide for the industry.

Certified Meeting Professional (CMP) program

The Certified Meeting Professional (CMP) program was launched in 1985 to enhance the knowledge and performance of meeting professionals, promote the status and credibility of the meeting profession and advance uniform standards of practice. The requirements for certification are based on professional experience and a rigorous examination. At present the CMP community numbers over 8000 and represents every sector of the industry – from corporations and associations to government and institutional organizations.

The CMP program aims to increase the professionalism of meeting managers in any component or sector of the industry by:

- Identifying a body of knowledge in the meeting management profession

- Establishing the level of knowledge and performance required for certification
- Stimulating the advancement of the art and science of meeting management
- Increasing the value of practitioners to their employers
- Recognizing and raising industry standards, practices and ethics
- Maximizing the value received from products and services provided by CMPs.

APEX – accepted practices exchange

APEX is an industry-wide initiative spearheaded by CIC that brings together all stakeholders in the development and implementation of industry-wide accepted practices, which create and enhance efficiencies throughout the meeting, convention, and exhibition industry. APEX is uniting the entire meeting, convention, and exhibition industry in the development and eventual implementation of voluntary standards, which will be called *accepted practices*.

When the approved accepted practices are implemented, the initiative will result in:

- Eased communication and sharing of data with suppliers and customers
- Enhanced quality of service provided to customers
- Clear definitions and terms for relationships with suppliers and customers
- Streamlined systems and processes that significantly reduce duplication of efforts, increase efficiencies of operations, and result in cost-savings
- Acknowledged measures of comparison and evaluation for improved decision-making
- Better educated, more professional employees
- Companies remaining competitive with the implementation of the practices.

Coalition campaign to advance face-to-face meetings

With numerous advances in technology and a fluctuating political and economic situation, the CIC has initiated a coalition campaign to promote the importance of face-to-face meetings, conventions, and exhibitions. The core message of the campaign is that technology is beneficial in strengthening relationships, but nothing can replace face-to-face interaction when initiating and strengthening relationships.

The coalition campaign targets business leaders to educate them on the importance of face-to-face interaction. Through various media, the promotion seeks to increase involvement in conventions, meetings, and exhibitions throughout the country.

Industry publications

The CMP Candidate Handbook, *The Convention Industry Council Manual*, and the CIC Economic Impact Study are among CIC's publications. *The Convention Industry Council Manual*, 7th edn. is a comprehensive resource designed for managing the basic components of a successful meeting. It was written by some of America's leading meeting-, convention-, and exhibition-planning professionals. *The Convention Industry Council Manual* contains detailed information on effectively organizing, planning, publicizing, managing, and budgeting for group events of any size. This step-by-step working guide features an extensive collection of checklists, forms, and glossary of industry terms.

CIC hall of leaders

Since 1985, the CIC has honored the industry's outstanding leaders and innovators with the bi-annual Hall of Leaders awards. Nominations are submitted by CIC member organizations and the general industry community. A selection committee appointed by the CIC chooses the recipients, who are inducted at a gala awards ceremony. A bronze plaque bearing the likeness of each honoree is permanently housed at the Washington, DC Convention Center and at McCormick Place in Chicago, Illinois.

Only those who have substantively contributed to the industry and whose efforts continue to shape it qualify for nomination. The nominee must also prove his or her contributions through a range of actions that have impacted meetings, conventions, and exhibitions.

Website resource guide for the industry

The CIC website, www.conventionindustry.org, provides industry professionals with CIC news, event schedules, and industry information.

Reference

www.conventionindustry.org

JULI JONES
CONVENTION INDUSTRY COUNCIL, USA

Convention service manager

(1) The convention service manager is the facility manager who is responsible for planning and servicing meetings and conventions held at a hotel, conference center, convention center or other meeting property. The convention service manager provides the liaison between the meeting planner and all of the departments at the facility, and is responsible for meeting room set-up, including tables, chairs, décor, audiovisual equipment, etc. In some facilities, the convention service manager also performs the duties of a catering manager, seeing to banquets, receptions, etc. This is called a *uniserve* property. Conversely, at a *duoserve* property, the logistics of the event are handled by the convention service manager with a separate catering manager to handle food and beverage requirements. In either case, the convention service manager is the primary contact with ultimate responsibility for the success of an event.

A convention service manager's title may vary, depending on the facility. Other titles include conference services coordinator, event services manager, and operations manager. Once the sales department confirms the event has been booked, a convention service manager is assigned to handle all group needs from initial planning to the post-meeting report. The convention service manager will create a timeline to proactively anticipate the needs of the group. If the event includes an exhibit area, the convention service manager will work with the meeting planner and the designated official show service contractor to ensure that proper floor plans and fire code approvals are obtained.

(2) A person who works for a convention and visitors bureau (CVB), and services meetings and conventions, which book their hotel(s) through the CVB. The convention service manager at a convention and visitors bureau assists the meeting planners in selecting hotel(s) once they have selected the destination.

Reference

Connell, B., Chatfield-Taylor, C., and Collins, M.C. (eds) (2002) *Professional Meeting Management*. Chicago: Professional Convention Management Association.

PAT GOLDEN-ROMERO
UNIVERSITY OF NEVADA, LAS VEGAS, USA

Convention and visitors bureau (CVB)

A membership organization representing a city or urban area in the solicitation of business and tourism travelers is known as a convention and visitors bureau (CVB). These organizations promote the image of its community and market the destination to tourists and to groups hosting meetings, conventions, and trade shows.

They provide information about hotels, special event venues, and other host facilities, conduct sales tours (also known as familiarization or FAM trips) and promote local service providers and vendors to the planner. CVBs assist groups with preparations, may lend support throughout the meeting and aid in the marketing of the event to the attendees. In addition, a bureau provides valuable research data to local governments regarding tourism and convention attendance, spending, and revenue generated. For the tourist, a convention and visitors bureau encourages visitors to its historic areas, cultural events, and recreational attractions.

Once a potential customer is identified, the CVB staff creates a 'lead sheet' with planner contact information and details about the potential meeting. This lead is distributed to various hotel and supplier members for their follow-up. It is important to remember that while the CVB 'sells' the city, it cannot negotiate contracts or prices for its members.

In some cases the bureau coordinates housing for large conventions using multiple hotels and may coordinate ground transportation to move attendees to and from the convention center, hotels, and special attractions.

Most CVBs are 'nonprofit' membership organizations. The various suppliers to the industry – hotels, restaurants, attractions, transportation and tour companies, caterers, equipment rental companies, security services, and other suppliers – pay an annual membership fee for the services of the bureau. CVBs also receive funding through local and state agencies, hotel room occupancy taxes, the sale of various publications and guides, providing convention services, and holding sponsored events and trade shows. Most CVBs belong to the International Association for Convention and Visitors Bureaus.

References

Connell, B., Chatfield-Taylor, C., and Collins, M.C. (eds) (2002) *Professional Meeting Management.* Chicago: Professional Convention Management Association.

Montgomery, R.J. and Strick, S.K. (1995) *Meetings, Convention and Expositions: An Introduction to the Industry.* New York: Van Nostrand Reinhold.

WILLIAM R. HOST
ROOSEVELT UNIVERSITY, USA

Cook–chill

Producing food in bulk, cooling it rapidly, and holding it under refrigeration for later reheating and service is called cook–chill production. This process allows a foodservice operation to use fewer skilled personnel to produce a wide range of food products that can be taken from inventory as required and, if necessary, distributed to other locations. Large facilities such as health care institutions, correctional facilities, and centralized kitchens for school systems often use cook–chill production, although the practice is also being applied in smaller venues such as hotels and restaurants with great success.

In a cook–chill production system, food products are prepared in bulk in a central location, packaged while hot, and quickly chilled to an internal temperature of 0–3 °C (32–37 °F) using specialized cooling equipment such as blast chillers and tumble chillers. Once chilled, food can be held under refrigeration for up to 30 days or more, depending on the product. When required, the chilled food is taken from the refrigerated inventory and, as close to the time of service as possible, rethermalized to an internal temperature of 65 °C (149 °F) and plated. Once reheated, chilled food that has not been consumed must be discarded.

Reference

Light, N. and Walker, A. (1990) *Cook–Chill Catering: Technology and Management.* New York: Elsevier Applied Science.

STEPHANI K.A. ROBSON
CORNELL UNIVERSITY, USA

Cook–freeze

The process of preparing, packaging, and freezing a food product for later distribution and reheating is called cook–freeze production. Typically undertaken in a central production facility, cook–freeze allows skilled personnel to prepare a wide range of products in quantity, hold them in inventory, and then ship them while still frozen to another location for reheating ('rethermalization') by less skilled staff just prior to service. Cook–freeze food products have been used for many years by health care institutions, transportation industries, and commercial foodservice operations.

In cook–freeze production, food products are cooked in bulk and packaged while hot into either single portions or bulk packs. The packaged food is then blast-frozen to a final temperature of −18 °C (0 °F) within 80 minutes and held at that temperature for up to two months. (Products may be held even longer at $-30\,°C$ $(-22\,°F)$.) It is common to use, at the point of service, a convection or microwave oven to bring the product to a safe internal temperature of $80\,°C$ $(176\,°F)$ within 30 minutes, after which the dish can be plated and served.

While many foods respond well to being frozen after cooking, some recipes require modification so that starch-based sauces will not separate or lose their texture upon rethermalization.

Reference

Light, N. and Walker, A. (1990) *Cook–Chill Catering: Technology and Management*. New York: Elsevier Applied Science.

STEPHANI K.A. ROBSON
CORNELL UNIVERSITY, USA

Corporate event market

Small and big businesses alike have learned the value that comes from holding and hosting corporate events. While the reasons for having a corporate event and event styles and structures may vary from business to business and industry to industry – done right – corporate events can help fast track a company's business growth and success no matter its size. And, as a business grows in size and stature, so does their need for corporate events.

In the past, corporate events were mainly used as a medium for imparting internal corporate communication such a company's future plans, prospects, policies, and procedures. Business enterprises used corporate events as a means to foster goodwill between employees and management, encourage company support, raise morale, demonstrate leadership, provide training, and to show employee and customer appreciation. Basic corporate event needs were generally handed in-house, held in the office or at a local hotel, and produced with the help of audiovisual company and basic equipment.

As technology evolved and companies grew, corporate events developed a more sophisticated style. Companies began holding meetings and corporate events further afield, in a variety of venues and logistically became more complex. Corporations seeking new ways to stand out from their competition, lead in market share, entice top performers to work with them, and retain key personnel started turning to event planning and meeting professionals to help them achieve their goals and objectives through the staging of corporate events.

Today, corporate events have become dynamic sales, marketing, and public relations tools used by businesses of all sizes. Corporate events are being used as means to solicit new business, create a corporate or brand image, retain and build loyalty with existing suppliers and customers in addition to being used to elicit peak performance from employees and produce camaraderie and teamwork among co-workers. The corporate event bar has been raised dramatically and the competition to craft something new that will help businesses create public awareness as well as industry and media buzz is high.

Corporations are continuing to outsource the planning of their corporate events to meeting and incentive houses and have opened the door to communication companies, special event experts, and advertising and public relation firms as well. Corporate companies are also bringing in highly accomplished event planners to work with them exclusively – setting up their own internal event planning divisions. Event specialists, skilled in business development, creativity, communications, strategic planning, budget management, event orchestration, execution, and who are masters of meeting a diverse range of corporate objectives became in great demand. Schooling and specialized training grew to meet this need.

Companies today are actively pursuing, identifying, and analyzing new business and marketing opportunities that can be achieved through the application of corporate events and the scope of corporate events is widening.

Traditional corporate events

Traditional corporate events include:

- Board meetings
- Business meetings

- Client appreciation events
- Conferences
- Conventions
- Corporate shows
- Employee appreciation events
- Trade shows.

Board meetings are typically held in an office and require a minimum of audiovisual support. Meetings can range from a couple of hours in duration to several days. Participants are generally senior executives and board members.

Informal business meetings can take place at corporate head office, in branch offices, at a local restaurant or in a supplier's or client's place of business. Hotels are typically used to host more formal business meetings. The number of participants can vary greatly depending on the nature of the meeting and if any outside guests (e.g. suppliers, clients etc.) are involved. Staging, audiovisual, and print material can be required.

Client appreciation events can be held at the company worksite – enabling the corporation to showcase their facility and their staff members – and be informal or formal in nature. Sample in-house client appreciation events can include catered barbecues, wine and cheese receptions, and the like. Client appreciation events can also be held out of the office and be quite diverse, e.g. boat cruises, dinner theatre evenings, golf tournaments, attending prestige sporting events in a corporate tent, reception and dinner followed by a formal presentation in a private venue or hotel etc.

Conferences generally involve bringing the branch offices together for a meeting one or two times a year. They can be held locally, nationally or internationally. The number of attendees is greater and depending on the company size can range in the hundreds to the thousands. Staging, speech writing, lighting, audiovisual, and production of print material for handouts is often required. Mandatory group activities – such as golf tournaments, beach Olympics, teamspirit activities, off property dining – are often a critical corporate event component with participants being carefully assigned to designated groups (playing together or being seated together). A welcome reception to launch the conference and a farewell dinner to close it are generally included features.

Corporations may send selected delegates to attend an industry *convention*. Within the convention these same corporations may also hold their own mini meetings and corporate events and also host others they want to spend time/bond with at specially planned meals or activities. For example, at one financial convention, a company interested in creating an opportunity to spend some quality time with specific attendees arranged to host a private theme event – invitation only – scheduled to take place the evening participants were on their own for dinner, which would be at their own expense. The corporate event was strategically designed to be enticing, keep their guests entertained, and at their event exclusively (they supplied transportation to and from the venue).

An example of a *corporate show* would be a new car display for the media, dealer, selected clients, open to the general public or a combination of all of them. Depending on the guest list, company objectives and event structure, a corporate show could take place in a day, over a series of days, and in multiple locations, e.g. a cross-country road show. Event requirements could be extensive.

Employee appreciation events can be held at the company worksite and staged to get departments mixing and mingling. They can be either informal or formal. Sample in-house employee appreciation events can include catered picnics, softball games, holiday parties, and after-work celebrations. Alcohol is generally not freely served unless safe transportation for employees has been pre-arranged. Employee appreciation events can also be held out of the office and be quite diverse, e.g. catered barbecues in local parks, boat cruises, dinner theatre evenings, golf tournaments, reception and dinner followed by a formal presentation in a private venue or hotel etc.

Corporate companies taking part in *trade shows* customarily reserve booth space and are responsible for the set-up, décor, staffing, handout material, and presentation. They may bring in event expertise to help them design a booth that will attract attendee interest, pull in new business, help them build their database, position themselves in the industry and set themselves apart from their competition.

Expanded corporate event market

- Custom training seminars involving emotional and physical challenges
- Executive retreats
- Gala fundraising events
- Incentive travel and premium programs
- Naming rights
- Product launches
- Product placement
- Special events
- Teleconferencing.

Custom training seminars involving emotional and physical challenges may include ropes courses, rock climbing, white water rafting, climbing and jumping off telephone poles – all examples of physical team building challenges that have become a standard part of corporate meetings. Training in mindfulness, taking part in equine experiences where it is not about the horse but overcoming fears and self doubt, finding self awareness through private desert journeys, meditation, creative expression and how to reduce stress at home and at work through spa and yoga teachings are the other side of events that are starting to be built into corporate meetings. Development in personal growth areas that will benefit employees and companies professionally and personally are becoming an important part of company meetings.

To lessen work distractions while conducting board meetings some corporations book *executive retreat* getaways, which usually involve one or more overnights and can involve upscale play (golfing, fly-fishing or skiing, adventure sports) as well as structured meeting time. Some companies do exclusive takeovers of small luxury spas or resorts while others whisk executives to select properties that out of the way.

Gala fundraising events: Companies know the benefits that can come with corporate sponsorship and having their name tied to a worthy cause. In the past nonprofit organizations were the ones soliciting partnership but now corporate companies are often the parties prompting the producing of fundraising events that are custom created to raise their profile, get media play, fit in with their public image and corporate culture and do good.

Incentive travel programs are limited only by an event planner's imagination and a company's budget. Incentive events can take place locally or around the world. They are usually rewards for top sales performance and the event must have cachet and must create an experience that a participant would not be able to duplicate on their own. Teaser programs (marketing the event internally) are important to keep the momentum going. *Premiums* are also being used as stand-alone incentive programs or to compliment a travel event (part of the teaser campaign or in room nightly gifts during the incentive). Top premium gift choices are those that can be used at home, such as flat screen or plasma television sets. These are examples of top reward gift items that produce sales results. Some companies will do a mix of both, as there is value to having top performers together sharing ideas and sales techniques. For the incentive winner there is public acknowledgement of their success, winning serves to enhance their professional reputation, and most companies allow incentive winners to bring a spouse or partner with them. An incentive program can be pure pleasure or business elements can be built into it (for tax reasons).

New buildings, landmarks, and special events alike are selling their *naming rights* to corporations. In exchange for funds, the corporation receives pubic awareness of their name, publicity, goodwill, and access to one of their targeted client markets through hosting private events at the facility that has been named after them. For example, a financial company may buy the naming rights of a well-known festive arts event. The art company receives must needed funds and corporate company obtains name recognition/branding in newspaper ads, radio and television promos, and all print material such as programs distributed at the performance. The corporate client also has the opportunity to invite select clientele to opening night with a private pre or post party with principal cast members attending or sponsor a premier party for seasoned ticket holders who are potential clients.

Product launches can be low key or multi-million dollar themed extravaganzas filled with special effects. The style of the event will be determined by the product, corporate image, the excitement the company wants to generate, and the budget. Product launches can be filled with theatre and drama, especially if the corporation launching the product has promoted themselves as being leaders in their industry with a cutting edge image. They are going to want to have a corporate product launch that projects that to the public – a ho hum affair will not produce the results.

Corporate events are becoming vehicles for *product placement*. For example, at one music industry function the lids of soft drink containers were fashioned from mini working CDs that featured a new recording artist who was being promoted. The artist was not being launched at the event, but event elements were carefully structured to tie in as much product as possible. Both movies and television today are becoming corporate events, with product imbedded into the production. The shows provide marketing possibility and spin-off event opportunities. If a major sponsor's product is being featured on a show or in a movie, the sponsor has been presented with the perfect fit for a screening party to select guests who could be existing clients, suppliers, employees or targeted new customers.

A company may hold a *special event* to commemorate a company milestone, honor a guest, company employee, executive or be activity-based. These types of corporate events can take the form of a formal awards presentation, a televised event or custom-designed event, e.g. a sporting or entertainment event in which they will figure prominently.

With technology today, corporate meetings can take place electronically – *teleconferencing*. Event planners today need to be on top of what is current and new. They need to understand how teleconferencing and webcasts work and when it is beneficial to recommend them. They can be time-saving and financially viable options when it is not possible to bring everyone together. They are a part of today's corporate events but they are not replacing face-to-face meetings and company get-togethers.

Event objectives must be determined at the outset. An event can have more than one objective and a number of events can provide the means to achieving it. To judge the success of an event, a company must be able to see a return on their investment, and that does not have to be monetary, as the examples above illustrate. Planners must know the company objectives and have a clear understanding of the company vision before they can begin strategically to plan which style of corporate event will bring the desired outcome and what event elements they will need to include to take their image, give it form and turn it into reality.

References

Allen, Judy (2000) *Event Planning: The Ultimate Guide to Successful Meetings, Corporate Events, Fundraising Galas, Conferences, Conventions, Incentives and Other Special Events*. Toronto: John Wiley & Sons.

Allen, Judy (2002) *The Business of Event Planning: Behind-the-Scenes Secrets of Successful Special Events*. Toronto: John Wiley & Sons.

Allen, Judy (2003) *Event Planning: Ethics and Etiquette: A Principled Approach to the Business of Special Event Management*. Toronto: John Wiley & Sons.

Allen, Judy (2004) *Marketing Your Event Planning Business: A Creative Approach to Gaining the Competitive Edge*. Toronto: John Wiley & Sons.

Allen, Judy (2004) *Your Stress Free Wedding Planner: Experts Best Secrets to Creating the Wedding of Your Dreams*. Naperville, IL: Sourcebooks, Inc.

Allen, Judy (2005) *Savvy Time Management Strategies: Tips and Techniques for Event Planning, Hospitality and Travel Industry Professionals*. Toronto: John Wiley & Sons.

JUDY ALLEN
JUDY ALLEN PRODUCTIONS, CANADA

Corporate level strategy

As they grow, organizations often pursue businesses outside their core business areas through intrapreneurship, mergers, and acquisitions or joint ventures. Corporate growth strategy typically evolves from concentration to some form of *vertical integration* or *diversification* (Porter, 1985). *Vertical integration*, which expands an organization's involvement in multiple stages of the industry supply chain, can be accomplished through either *backward integration* (e.g., a restaurant that acquires a bakery supplier) or *forward integration* (e.g., a hotel chain that becomes a travel distribution service provider). *Diversification* refers to growth through entry into different industries. Diversification that stems from common markets, functions served, technologies or services to achieve synergy, is referred to as *related diversification*. Examples of related diversification include hotel companies that branch out into a variety of related businesses, including real estate. *Unrelated diversification* is not based on commonality among the corporation's activity. For example: Cendant Corporation is a conglomerate with holdings in industries such as hospitality and retail mortgage. Conglomerates place significant demands on corporate level managers due to increased complexity across industries. A decline in profits of multi-business corporations may result in *restructuring* that involves reducing the business definition and focusing on the things the organization does well. This strategy, also known as *turnaround strategy* can be implemented through workforce reductions, sale of assets to reduce debts, and outsourcing (Harrison and Enz, 2005).

References

Harrison, J.S. and Enz, C.A. (2005) *Hospitality Strategic Management: Concepts and Cases*. New York: John Wiley & Sons.

Porter, M.E. (1985) *Competitive Advantage*. New York: The Free Press.

SIGAL HABER
TEL-AVIV UNIVERSITY, ISRAEL

Corporate meeting

A corporate meeting is an officially sanctioned and required meeting for employees of a specific corporation. Corporate meetings are often held off site of the corporate location and require employees to travel to the meeting. Expenses associated with the meeting, such as transportation, meals, and hotel accommodations are paid for by the corporation. Corporate meetings differ from association meetings in that attendance is required for corporate meetings and not required for association meetings.

Corporate meetings play an important part in the development and success of businesses around the world. The Meetings Market Report published bi-annually in *Meeting & Conventions Magazine* shows there were 844,100 corporate meetings in 2001 and 51,500,000 people attended corporate meetings. The total expenditures for corporate meetings in 2001 were $10.3 billion. Corporate meetings have a tremendous economic impact on the hospitality industry.

There are a variety of corporate meetings, which include but are not limited to: incentive events, training seminars, sales meetings, and board of director meetings. An incentive event is a corporate sponsored meeting to reward performance of employees. Training seminars are structured learning sessions for employee while sales meeting focus on motivating staff and introducing new products. Board of director meetings focus on the leadership of the organization by setting long-term goals and objectives.

References

Allen, J. (2000) *Event Planning: The Ultimate Guide to Successful Meetings, Corporate Events, Fundraising Galas, Conferences, Conventions, Incentives and Other Special Events*. Ontario: John Wiley & Sons.

Goldblatt, J. and Nelson, K. (2001) *The International Dictionary of Event Management*, 2nd edn. New York: John Wiley & Sons.

PAT GOLDEN-ROMERO
UNIVERSITY OF NEVADA, LAS VEGAS, USA
KIMBERLY SEVERT
UNIVERSITY OF CENTRAL FLORIDA, USA

Cost of goods sold

In the foodservice industry, cost of goods sold (COGS) is typically considered to be the sum of food and beverage expenses. It is the cost of items used to generate all food and beverage revenues over a specified time period. To determine the COGS for a given establishment, inventory at the beginning and end of a particular time period must be calculated. An establishment must also keep track of all food and beverage purchases during that time period. COGS calculations are done separately for food and beverage categories, and sometimes COGS are calculated for sub-categories within these areas (e.g., wine, spirits, bottled beer, draft beer, meat, produce, dairy, fish, frozen products, etc.). The general calculation for COGS is

COGS = Beginning inventory + Purchases
    − Ending inventory

There are, it should be noted, a number of adjustments that need to be made to each category of COGS to extract the exact COGS for a given time period. Such adjustments might include employee meal costs, products transferred to or from the kitchen/bar, products transferred to or from other foodservice operations, and complimentary products given to customers. All of these adjustments will either increase or decrease net COGS for food or beverage.

Reference

Virts, W.B. (1987) *Purchasing for Hospitality Operations.* Lansing, MI: Educational Institute of the American Hotel and Motel Association.

DEBORAH BARRASH
UNIVERSITY OF NEVADA, LAS VEGAS, USA

Cost of sales

Cost of sales refers to the cost of stock items sold during the accounting period. In a hotel, the items comprising the cost of sales would include food stocks purchased and *consumed* in the production of food sold through the restaurant and also the cost of beverage stock sold in the bar. Where there is a shop in the hotel complex, cost of sales would also include the cost of all merchandise sold in the shop. However, food provided to staff as part of their remuneration is a labor cost i.e. part of wages and salaries and, as such, is not available for consumption by customers. Therefore, in order to obtain a more accurate indication of the true cost of food consumed by customers, the cost value of staff meals should be deducted from cost of sales and added to labor cost.

Cost of sales parallels the notion of 'cost of goods sold,' which is a term used in manufacturing industries. In a car manufacturing plant, cost of goods sold would include the cost of all the materials (components, metal, plastic, etc.) that are physically assembled in the car manufacturing process.

The following example shows how the cost of sales can be calculated in a restaurant:

Cost of opening stock balance	$12,000
Total purchases of stock	180,000
	192,000
Less: returns to suppliers	3,000
Net stock available for sale	189,000
Less: closing balance of stock	14,000
	175,000
Less: staff meals	5,000
Net cost of sales	170,000

References

Harris, P.J. and Hazzard, P.A. (1992) *Managerial Accounting in the Hospitality Industry*, 5th edn. Cheltenham: Stanley Thornes.
Schmidgall, R.S. (2002) *Hospitality Industry Managerial Accounting*, 5th edn. Lansing, MI: Educational Institute of the American Hotel and Lodging Association.

CHRIS GUILDING
GRIFFITH UNIVERSITY, AUSTRALIA

Cost strategy

A cost strategy is when a firm intends to become the low-cost producer in its industry or competitive group. The cost strategy creates a competitive advantage when industry rivals and new entrants cannot duplicate established cost advantages. Porter (1985) describes two types of cost strategies: cost leadership and cost focus. The strategic basis following cost leadership requires a broad scope and that a firm becomes the cost leader rather than one of many in an industry. Cost leadership can be derived through the pursuit of economies of scale, the use of technology, access to particular suppliers and distribution channels, or other factors. A cost focus strategy refers to a narrow target market or scope. This narrow focus can refer to either a particular segment within an industry or a regional focus.

The cost strategy has created a cost advantage and an important competency for many large firms in the hospitality industry. Firms such as McDonald's, Motel 6, and Southwest Airlines are examples of well-known hospitality organizations that have achieved significant success following a low-cost strategy. Research in the foodservice industry indicates that a cost or efficiency strategy can result in high performance for the firm.

References

Olsen, M., Tse, E., and West, J. (1998) *Strategic Management in the Hospitality Industry*, 2nd edn. New York: John Wiley & Sons.

Porter, M.E. (1985) *Competitive Advantage*. New York: The Free Press.

ROBERT HARRINGTON
NICHOLLS STATE UNIVERSITY, USA

Cost–benefit analysis

Cost–benefit analysis is a managerial tool used to assess the potential benefit of current or future investments. This technique could be used in many ways. The primary objective of conducting cost–benefit analysis is to understand the return, realized or potential, of current investments. For example, every equipment-purchase decision at a foodservice organization must be preceded by a cost–benefit analysis. Similarly, most restaurant organizations prefer to do such analysis before expanding business operations or operating hours. Growth plans done without proper cost–benefit analysis may lead to disastrous consequences. In the early 1980s, for example, a restaurant company had expanded from a single-unit operation to an over-500-unit operation in less than six years. Such an uncontrolled growth phenomenon resulted in business failure and the eventual bankruptcy of the company.

In financial terms, cost–benefit is also called 'ROI' (return on investment). ROI is an excellent tool. It can be used to compare the performance of various projects within a company or across the industry. Especially when ROIs are compared across the industry, a foodservice organization may gain competitive advantage by adjusting its cost–benefit numbers.

Reference

Keiser, James and DeMicco, Frederick J. with Grimes, Robert (2000) *Contemporary Management Theory: Controlling and Analyzing Costs in Food-service Operations*, 4th edn. Columbus, OH: Prentice–Hall.

H.G. PARSA
OHIO STATE UNIVERSITY, USA

Cost-informed pricing methods

A number of surveys of business pricing practices indicate that *cost-plus pricing* is a technique used by a large number of firms. According to these studies, a majority of businesses set prices on the basis of the cost of a product or service plus a margin for profit. The cost is typically a standard, or fully allocated, cost concept based on some assumed level of output. The margin for profit is usually a percentage mark-up that can be expressed as follows:

$$\text{Mark-up} = \frac{\text{Price} - \text{Cost}}{\text{Cost}}$$

where the numerator is called the profit margin. Solving the mark-on equation for price provides the expression that determines price in a cost-plus pricing system:

$$\text{Price} = \text{Cost} \, (1 + \text{Mark-up})$$

Although empirical evidence shows widespread application of cost-plus techniques, many doubts are cast over the approach. It ignores demand, denies the existence of competition, and exaggerates the accuracy of allocated costs. Therefore, the approach is used because:

- It may be the best alternative available as setting prices is a very complex decision process. Faced with this complexity, management has developed different methods of simplifying the pricing process.
- It is regarded as only an approximation of price; generally, competitive conditions are also taken into account.
- It is a means of comparing prices of different products rather than a way of making a pricing decision.
- Most business firms attempt to pursue more than one goal; maximizing profits – at least in the short-term – may not actually be the company's objective. Hence, cost-plus pricing as a means for survival may be quite reasonable.
- Cost-plus pricing may reduce the hazards of price warfare.

Cost-plus pricing formulas take a number of forms that differ amongst industries and even between firms within an industry. This variation may be caused by differences in accounting methods and differences in the relative importance of overhead cost and selling expenses. Cost, however, does not determine a (selling) price as it merely determines the profitability of producing a product or service. The ideal pricing policy is simultaneously profit-based, cost-conscious, market-oriented, and in conformity with any other aims a business may have.

Full cost or average cost pricing is just a name for a number of pricing procedures that allocate all costs to individual products or services and, hence, are decisive for the final prices (Figure 1).

Two main principles exist in the calculation of price, which is based either on average variable or on average total cost. In a rigid full cost pricing system, all costs are calculated into the cost of each product according to a predetermined process of allocation. All other systems are flexible full cost (e.g. using different criteria for different products). In addition, total or partial allocation methods can be distinguished with regard to the types of overhead that are allocated to the different products (Fog, 1993). Although derived from manufacturing industry, full cost-plus pricing can be applied to fast food restaurant operations as the high volume and limited choice of similar products essentially reflects a production activity.

Direct cost-plus pricing implies establishing selling prices at a certain percentage above the direct, or traceable, costs of the product or service. This percentage mark-up is designed to cover an allowance for indirect costs (i.e. the overheads associated with operations) and to provide for net profit (Figure 2).

In manufacturing, the direct cost procedure has validity when the indirect costs of each product line is essentially the same and when the assets employed by product lines are similar. Some managers argue that if their product lines have different margins, losses of one product line are counterbalanced by gains of the other product line. This reasoning is dangerous, for these differences will only be equalized if the sales quantities of each product line are in the proportion originally assumed when the sales prices were set.

Whilst direct cost-plus pricing evolved from batch production industry activities, it is equally applicable to conference, banqueting, and special event business.

Gross margin pricing can be used when the material cost is the only direct cost that can be identified (when labor and expense costs can only be identified as indirect costs, i.e. overhead or burden).

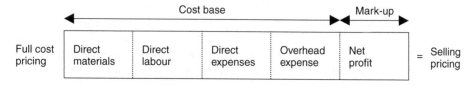

Figure 1 Full cost plus pricing (adapted from Harris and Hazzard, 1992)

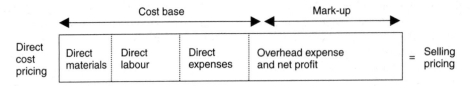

Figure 2 Direct cost-plus pricing (adapted from Harris and Hazzard, 1992)

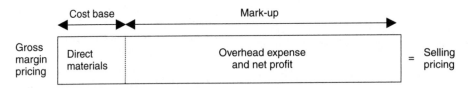

Figure 3 Gross margin pricing (adapted from Harris and Hazzard, 1992)

The pricing procedure involves the calculation of direct materials per product plus a mark-up percentage to cover overhead expense and net profit (Figure 3). When the range of products or services is heterogeneous, such as in a restaurant, it is quite often very complex and uneconomical to estimate the direct labor and expense costs per type of product on an item-by-item base.

To solve this problem, total direct materials costs are computed after which the necessary sales revenue is established to cover total overhead expense and desired net profit.

Direct materials	90,000
Overhead expense	110,000
Net profit	25,000
Required sales revenue	225,000
Gross profit percent $(135,000/225,000) \times 100 =$	60%
OR Mark-up percent $(135,000/90,000) \times 100 =$	150%

Note: In any given situation, gross profit and mark-up are the same figure in absolute money terms, but are different percentages because the figure is related to different bases, i.e. gross profit percentage relates to selling price and mark-up relates to cost.

However, the use of an established uniform average gross profit or mark-up percentage may lead to problems if prices and activity levels of products within an entire product range differ

substantially. Consequently, there may be a need to apply a mix of gross profit margins.

The price of selling a final product or service may be different from the price of a factor of production (i.e. a production cost). Therefore, management must measure what contribution it would get if it met the competitive market, or going price. Unfortunately, it is sometimes impossible to predict this spread. *Contribution pricing*, for that reason, emphasizes the contribution margin by delineating the behavior of variable and fixed cost.

A typical form of variable cost pricing involves adding a mark-up on direct and indirect variable cost so that a gross profit is made which can contribute to the recovery of overhead costs and net profit. Nonetheless, there is a danger in focusing all attention on variable cost and contribution margin. First, when products have identical contribution margins there may be a temptation to treat them as equals in pricing. This may lead to incorrect decisions when products absorb different types of overhead. Second, fixed costs are labeled as irrelevant and omitted from consideration. Thus, when variable costs are exceptionally small, the link between cost and selling price becomes very vague and indirect. Last, the contribution margin provides no means to qualify or analyze the specific components of the direct cost whether it consists largely of materials cost or of conversion cost. Therefore, it does not allow an examination of the extent to which invested capital supports the direct costs.

If the contribution margin from a going rate price is insufficient, means should be sought to reduce the direct and indirect variable costs, to withdraw the product or service from the market, or to investigate other alternatives. Nevertheless, the contribution approach may be the best known alternative to full cost-plus pricing.

Market and competitive conditions may force businesses to sell below 'full' cost and competitively or passively accept the *'going' rate*. To meet such 'market' price, management adjusts costs in order to secure a sufficient level of profit. For this purpose, a direct costing system could be used. However, to meet the going rate, a constant mark-up is usually impractical. Finally, not all demand at the going price should be accepted. Thus, before a firm can agree to meet 'going' prices, it must have knowledge of its absolute price floor. This floor is the direct or the out-of-pocket cost.

References

Dean, J. (1951) *Managerial Economics*. Englewood Cliffs, NJ: Prentice-Hall.

Dorward, N. (1987) *The Pricing Decision: Economic Theory and Business Practice*. London: Harper and Row.

Fay, C.T., Rhoads, R.C., and Rosenblatt, R.L. (1976) *Managerial Accounting for the Hospitality Service Industries*, 2nd edn. Dubuque, IA: Wm. C. Brown.

Fog, B. (1993) *Pricing in Theory and Practice*. Copenhagen: Handelshøjskolens Forlag.

Guilding, C. (2002) *Financial Management for Hospitality Decision-makers*. Oxford: Butterworth-Heinemann.

Harris, P.J. and Hazzard, P.A. (1992) *Managerial Accounting in the Hospitality Industry*, 5th edn. Cheltenham: Stanley Thornes.

Kotas, R. (1999) *Management Accounting for Hospitality and Tourism*, 3rd edn. London: International Thompson Press.

JEAN-PIERRE VAN DER REST
LEIDEN UNIVERSITY, THE NETHERLANDS

Cost–volume–profit analysis

Cost–volume–profit (CVP) analysis describes the relationships between costs, revenues, profit (income), and volume. It is based on the definition of Profit = Total revenue − Total cost. Since total revenue as well as total cost depends on volume, the definition of profit can be expressed as:

$$Profit = p \times Q - v \times Q - F$$

where:

p is price per unit
Q is volume
v is variable cost per unit
F is fixed cost

CVP analysis can be used to solve equations with one unknown parameter and to answer questions such as:

- If price, volume, variable cost per unit, and fixed cost are known, what will the profit then be?
- If volume, variable cost per unit, fixed cost as well as desired profit are known, what price must then be charged?
- If price, variable cost per unit, fixed cost, as well as desired profit are known, what is then the necessary volume?

CVP analysis is the basis for 'break-even charts' and can be applied to all levels of decision-making, such as:

- *Product level:* What number of guests is required for a banquet to be profitable?
- *Production unit level:* What room sale is necessary to make a hotel profitable?
- *Firm level:* What average room occupancy is necessary to make a hotel chain profitable?

The simple form of CVP model assumes linearity, i.e. that price per unit, fixed cost, and variable cost per unit do not vary with volume. The model also assumes that it is possible to categorize total cost into the two categories fixed cost and variable cost, which often is difficult to apply to a practical situation. These assumptions are, however, only necessary to hold true for a limited relevant range around the solution, which often is an acceptable approximation and a realistic assumption. Other assumptions are that productivity and the methods of production and service remain unchanged.

A break-even chart, also known as a cost–volume–profit (CVP) chart, illustrates how revenue, cost, and profit vary with the volume of activity. It is possible to use the chart to determine the 'break-even volume' (i.e. how many units must be produced/sold in order to achieve full cost recovery) as well as 'break-even sales' (i.e. what turnover figure is critical in order to break even). Although a break-even chart is based on the same simplistic assumption as CVP analysis, it can be a very useful tool to illustrate and communicate the effects of business volume on profit and business risk.

The CVP chart can be further developed. Since contribution margin can be defined as the difference between revenue per unit and variable cost per unit, it is possible to describe how profit depends on volume by just describing total contribution and fixed costs. The 'break-even volume' is then defined as the volume where total contribution equals fixed costs. The chart also illustrates how profit and business risk depends on volume. It is, however, not possible to determine 'break-even sales' with this type of break-even chart.

As referred to earlier, the simple form of CVP analysis comprises a number of assumptions and limitations, and it is important to draw these together. For instance, the model assumes a single product or service business. Where this is not so then it is assumed that the given sales mix remains constant as sales revenue changes. Also, volume of activity is assumed to be the only factor that determines cost behavior. Clearly, there are numerous factors, other than volume, that affect revenue and costs. These include seasonal factors; quality of management and staff; employee relations; working methods and practices; political situation; economic cycle; and training and development policies. These, and other variables, are widely acknowledged as influencing cost and revenue behavior. However, their lack of inclusion in CVP analysis is primarily due to the difficulties encountered when attempting to quantify the extent of their influence. In addition, the model assumes that selling price per unit will not change; variable costs are directly proportional to sales revenue; fixed costs remain constant; cost prices remain unchanged e.g. food and beverage prices, serving staff wage rates; productivity remains unchanged; methods of production and service are unchanged. The importance of fully understanding the implications underlying the simple form of CVP is that, by being aware of the assumptions and limitations of the model, managers are enabled to make more informed decisions.

However, a cost driver can be any factor that correlates with total cost. Activity-based costing (ABC) is an approach to cost analysis where much emphasis is placed on finding the most precise cost drivers.

Volume of production/service, such as the number of rooms occupied, number of restaurant covers, is the most commonly used cost driver, but time may also be a relevant cost driver. Number of banquets may explain the cost of a catering department better than number of customers served and, thus, be a more precise cost driver.

References

Drury, C. (2000) *Management and Cost Accounting*, 4th edn. London: Van Nostrand Reinhold.

Graham, I.C. and Harris, P.J. (1999) Development of a profit planning framework for an international hotel chain: a case study. *International Journal of Contemporary Hospitality Management*, 11 (5), 198–204.

Harris, P.J. (ed.) (1995) *Accounting and Finance for the International Hospitality Industry*. Oxford: Butterworth-Heinemann.

Horngren, C.T., Foster, G., and Datar, S.M. (2000) *Cost Accounting: A Managerial Emphasis*, 10th edn. London: Prentice-Hall International.

Johnson, H.T. and Kaplan, R.S. (1991) *Relevance Lost: The Rise and Fall of Management Accounting*. Boston, MA: Harvard Business School Press.

TOMMY D. ANDERSSON
GOTEBORGS UNIVERSITY, SWEDEN

Credit card guarantee

All guaranteed reservations are assured a room and the charge for the room is credit card guaranteed, by which the payment for the room is guaranteed should the guest not check in. Credit card guaranteed reservations are the most common form of guaranteed reservation, especially for city center hotels. Credit card guarantee is an assurance to the guest that the hotel will hold a hotel room reservation until a specific time of the day, usually 6 p.m. to 7 p.m. for city center hotels. After that time the hotel, unless otherwise agreed with the guest, has the right to release the room and sell it to another customer. From the hotel point of view, credit card guarantee reservations are a system that guarantees the hotel payment for no-show reservations. Unless a credit card guaranteed reservation is cancelled by the guest before a stated cancellation hour, the hotel will charge the guest's credit card for the amount of the room's rate, or a stated no-show charge. Typically the front desk assigns rooms to credit card guaranteed reservations throughout the day as accommodations become available. On days when a credit card guaranteed reservation is on file and it has been determined that sell-out is possible, the front desk protects these reservations with rooms but does not actually assign them room numbers.

References

Kasavana, M.L. and Brooks, R.M. (1998) *Front Office Procedures*, 5th edn. Lansing, MI: Educational Institute of the American Hotel and Motel Association.

Dix, C. and Baird, C. (1988) *Front Office Operations*, 4th edn. Harlow: Longman.

CONSTANTINOS S. VERGINIS
THE EMIRATES ACADEMY OF HOSPITALITY
MANAGEMENT, UNITED ARAB EMIRATES

Critical incidents technique

Service failures occur at critical incidents, or 'moments of truth,' in the service encounter, when customers interact with a firm's employees. It is important to provide service personnel with the authority and the recovery tools necessary to correct service failures as they occur. The timeliness and form of response by service providers to service failures will have a direct impact on customer satisfaction and quality perceptions.

The critical incidents technique can be defined as a set of procedures for systematically identifying behaviors that contribute to success or failure of individuals or organizations in specific situations. Organizations should encourage customers to provide feedback concerning their service encounters. Some of the popular methods for customer feedback are: toll free numbers, comment cards, and surveys. In addition, employees should be encouraged to report any service failures and detail their responses. This is often difficult to do because employees have a fear of retribution or punishment. In terms of successes, some firms provide customers with tokens that can be given to an employee who demonstrates exemplary performance. Finally, a third party could be contracted to observe a firm's operations and comment on critical incidents. One popular approach used by hotels and restaurants is to hire a firm that conducts a 'mystery shopping' program. Trained professionals will stay at hotels or dine at restaurants and evaluate the experience. These programs could also be run through the corporate headquarters.

Service failures can be assigned to one of three categories: service delivery system failures, customer needs failures, and unsolicited employee actions. The first category, *system failures*, refers to failures in the core service offering of the firm. These failures are the result of normally available services being unavailable, unreasonably slow service, or some other core service failure that will differ by industry. For example, a hotel's pool may have a leak and be closed, a customer may have to wait a long time for the shuttle to an airport rental car agency, or an airline might mishandle a passenger's luggage.

The second category, *customer needs failures*, are based on employee responses to customer needs or special requests. These failures come in the form of special needs, customer preferences, customer errors, and disruptive others (i.e., disputes between customers). For example, a hotel guest may want to have a pet in the room, a customer may want to be switched to a window seat on an airliner, a customer at an event may lose his or her ticket, or a customer in a restaurant may be smoking in a non-smoking section.

The third category, *unsolicited employee actions*, refers to the actions, both good and bad, of employees that are not expected by customers. These actions can be related to the level of attention an employee gives to customers, to unusual actions that can be performed by employees, to an action's reinforcement of a customer's cultural norms, or an employee's actions under adverse conditions. For example, a hostess in a restaurant could anticipate the needs of a family with a small child, a hotel front desk clerk could give a free upgrade to a guest who waited in line too long, a flight attendant could ignore passengers with children, or a cruise employee could help to evacuate passengers during a crisis.

When customers complain, firms are presented with the opportunity to recover from service failures. *Service recovery* occurs when a firm's reaction to a service failure results in customer satisfaction and goodwill. In fact, customers who are involved in successful service recoveries often demonstrate higher levels of satisfaction than customers who do not report service failures or complain. The following is a list of popular service recovery strategies:

- *Cost/benefit analysis:* Service firms should compare the costs of losing customers and obtaining new customers with the benefits of keeping existing customers. Most firms place a high value on retaining customers. However, some guests take advantage of satisfaction guarantees and complain on every occasion. Hotel chains, like Doubletree, maintain a database on complaints and will flag chronic complainers.
- *Actively encourage complaints:* It is better to know when customers are not satisfied so that action can be taken to rectify the situation. It is important to note, that while unhappy customers may not complain to service firms, they will often complain to their family and friends. Hospitality and travel firms use comment cards and 'toll free' numbers to encourage customers to provide feedback. Also, service personnel are trained to ask customers if everything was satisfactory when they check out or pay the bill.
- *Anticipate the need for recovery:* Service firms should 'blueprint' the service delivery process and determine the 'moments of truth,' or critical incidents, where customers interact with employees. The process can be designed to avoid failures, but recovery plans should be determined in the event a failure occurs.
- *Respond quickly:* The quicker the response in the event of a service failure, the more likely recovery efforts will be successful. Once a customer leaves a service establishment, the likelihood of a successful recovery falls dramatically. Based on this principle, firms like Marriott Hotels and Resorts provide service hotlines at each hotel in order to resolve problems quickly.
- *Train employees:* Employees should be made aware of the critical incidents and provided with potential strategies for recovery. For example, some hotel training programs use videotaped scenarios of service failures to show employees' potential problems and the appropriate solutions.
- *Empower the front line:* In many cases, a successful recovery will hinge on a front-line employee's ability to take timely action and make a decision. Firms should empower employees to handle service failures at the time they occur, within certain limits. For example, Ritz–Carlton allows its employees to spend up to $1000 to take care of dissatisfied customers.

Reference

Reid, R. and Bojanic, D. (2001) *Hospitality Marketing Management*, 3rd edn. New York: John Wiley & Sons, pp. 47–49.

DAVID BOJANIC
UNIVERSITY OF MASSACHUSETTS, USA

Critical success factors

The critical success factor (CSF) approach has been in existence for some considerable time, mainly in the information systems field, and in later years, its application was extended to the generic management field. Critical success factors can be defined as the limited number of areas in which 'things must go right' in order to ensure predetermined 'goals' are achieved. Furthermore, it is important to determine suitable 'measures' to monitor and control the results of CSFs. Thus, CSFs represent priority areas for on-going information provision and form the basis for a company's management decision-making. The approach is based on a framework of 'goals–CSFs–measures' called 'CSF analysis.' For example, in a hotel business, if the goal is to improve room revenue, then the key elements (critical success factors) to be managed are essentially the number of rooms sold and the room rate charged, thus involving the measurement of room occupancy, average room rate, and RevPAR to monitor the results.

The CSFs will normally vary from company to company within an industry and among the individual managers within companies, thus, they are related to the specifics of a particular manager's situation.

References

Brotherton, B. and Shaw, J. (1996) Towards an identification and classification of Critical Success Factors in UK Hotels Plc. *International Journal of Hospitality Management*, 15 (2), 113–135.

Geller, A.N. (1985) Tracking the critical success factors for hotel companies. *Cornell Hotel and Restaurant Administration Quarterly*, February, pp. 76–81.

MINE HAKTANIR
EASTERN MEDITERRANEAN UNIVERSITY,
TURKISH REPUBLIC OF NORTHERN CYPRUS

Cross-selling

Cross-selling techniques exist in almost every field. Cross-selling relates to sales activities that identify, suggest, and sell related items such as accessories or services to a prospective or existing customer. There are many different types of cross-selling, for example, if a customer is buying a laptop, the sales person might recommend a carrying case and/or extended warranty to go with that purchase. Other examples are mailings and on-pack messages that offer free samples or savings coupons of other products that are perceived as adding value to the initial purchase. Cross-selling not only introduces customers to other products that can have an impact on the company's '*share of customer*'[1] but it also helps the company to attract new customers.

The foundation of cross-selling is based on the already established relationship between the company and its customers. Companies can capitalize on the present bond by building upon this relationship with cross-selling techniques. It is important to emphasize on the existing relationship first, and then make the new offer appear to be a continuation by keeping the same or similar name, copy style, graphics, and offer structure.

References

Howe, Lee, Acito (2003) Power in cross selling – a proven approach. Booz Allen and Hamilton Teleservicing Cross-Selling Research. http://www.boozallen.com.

Kotler, P. and Armstrong, G. (2001) *Principles of Marketing*, 9th edn. Upper Saddle River, NJ: Prentice-Hall, pp. 18, 600–606.

Rothfeder, J. (2001) Connecting the dots on cross-selling. Available at http://www.pcmag.com/; available from www.eu-marketingportal.de.

JUDY HOU
ECOLE HÔTELIÈRE DE LAUSANNE (EHL),
SWITZERLAND

[1] *Share of customer:* in contrast to market share, share of customer refers to the percentage of a particular customer's business a firm gets over that customer's lifetime of patronage.

Customer centricity

Customer centricity is the capacity of organizations to focus on providing customers opportunities to be involved in every aspect of the business.

It is achieved when customers are able to access and interact with multiple areas of the business at both the tactical and strategic levels of the organization. The organization is committed to the conviction that the customer is at the center of all that they do. They involve the customer in their organization with a great amount of communication and trust. An organization that is truly customer-centric does not hold the more limited view of serving the customer, but rather views the customer as a partner in the organization.

An organization is customer-centric if it:

- Addresses customer issues fully and resolves them completely.
- Ensures that all employees adopt an external focus.
- Grants employees the authority and tools to decide the right way to treat customers.
- Gives the customer the choice to interact with the organization in ways that are to their benefit.
- Supplies customers with goods and services that they will want.
- Let customers decide how the business is organized.
- Accords customers the ability to dictate the organization's policies.

Reference

Stauffer, D. (2001) What customer-centric really means: seven key insights. *Harvard Management Update Newsletter*, 6 (8), 1–3.

BRIAN MILLER
UNIVERSITY OF DELAWARE, USA

Customer complaint behavior

The study of customer complaint behavior and complaint resolution has been receiving increasing attention in the marketing literature for over three decades. Although most of the literature has been related to 'product buyers' complaint behavior, service-related studies have begun to emerge recently. Based on the review of current literature, it is possible to classify customer complaint studies into three areas: (1) the nature and causes of complaints, i.e. why some people complain and some don't, and when and how they complain if they tend to complain; (2) complaint and post-complaint behavior; and (3) firms' responses to complaints. Among the many questions that the consumer complaint behavior research investigates, some appear to be vital and useful to marketing professionals. Most marketers wonder why some dissatisfied customers are reluctant to complain and whether complaint behavior is due to some clearly defined factors such as cultural traits.

Based on the findings of several studies from the 1970s, Stephens and Gwinner (1998) cite that about two-thirds of customers do not report their dissatisfaction. If a customer does not complain, it remains a concern to the management as the firm loses the opportunity to remedy any problems and improve the product and enhance quality through customer feedback. It also damages the firm's reputation because of negative word-of-mouth. A dissatisfied customer can either take action or stay silent. Since a silent majority seems reluctant to show their dissatisfaction explicitly, one may wonder if the firms should encourage customers to complain. Some, like Nyer (2000), argues that encouraging the dissatisfied customers to complain is beneficial to the firms. If so, what can the firms do to facilitate the process and to address the issues of complaint handling and resolution?

Causes of complaint and complaint behavior

According to several studies as cited by Bennett (1997), major causes of customer complaints are failure to meet customer expectations and discourtesy by company staff. The study cites that almost 50% of the complaints were motivated by the desire to vent frustration. Bennett (1997) argues that customers who were extremely hostile and aggressive when making complaints were actually less likely to be lost as customers of the business in future than were people who appeared nervous and subdued when expressing dissatisfaction.

It is rather difficult to profile a complaining customer. Some argue that complaint behavior is a personality trait. A highly competitive and easily irritated person with aggressive nature is more likely to complain explicitly and aggressively although his or her post-complaining behavior is unclear. Baron and Byrne (1994) (cited in Bennett, 1997) point out that an individual with high self-esteem is perceived to be good, capable, and worthy whereas a person with low self-esteem is considered inept and useless. This means, an individual with low self-esteem lacks confidence, including when making purchase decisions, and is less likely to complain.

Singh (1988) describes the phenomenon of customer complaint behavior 'as a set of multiple behavioral and non-behavioral responses, some or all of which are triggered by perceived dissatisfaction with a purchase episode.' According to Singh, such a behavior can be categorized into three: voice responses, private responses, and third party responses. An example for the first case is seeking redress, and thus going on venting dissatisfaction. In the second case, an example of a private response is negative word-of-mouth and/or withdrawal of future custom. The third involves such actions as reporting to the consumer protection agency or taking legal action.

Cultural trait can also play an important role in complaint behavior. It is considered that Western culture is rather individualistic and Eastern cultures such as Chinese and Koreans are more towards collectivist. Individualist culture values independence and self-sufficiency whereas the members of collectivist culture tend to behave according to social norms, which are often designed to maintain social harmony in the group. Liu and McClure (2001) argue that the members of individualistic culture is more likely to engage in voice behavior such as seeking redress and the latter in private behavior such as negative word-of-mouth. It is also argued that customers who voice dissatisfaction are more likely to be retained as customers and vice versa. There are a few studies that attempt to examine the cross-cultural nature of complaint behavior. Heung and Lam (2003), based on their examination of Asian diners, found that most Chinese diners do not complain, but engage in negative word-of-mouth and exit behavior. The complaint intentions of Chinese diners were also quite low and passive in communicating their dissatisfaction. As cited in Bennett (1997), a customer's complaint behavior is likely to be influenced by the individualism–collectivism (conceptualized as a continuum) dimension of their cultural identity.

There are several other factors that influence the inclination to complain and complaint behavior. Stephens and Gwinner (1998) cite numerous studies on the factors influencing consumer complaint behavior. These factors are claimed to be demographics, personal value, personality traits, and attitudes towards complaining. Moreover, situational factors and product-related factors such as the role of provider responsiveness, the cost of complaining, price and importance of the product, and consumer experience are also claimed to influence the complaint behavior.

Post-complaint behavior and complaint resolution

Recently, firms have recognized the importance of complaint resolution and customer relationship management. However, the majority of the firms still seem to lack an effective system for customer complaint handling. The manner firms respond to customer complaints also affects the consumer choice of firms. Customer satisfaction derived from complaint handling by firms is relatively less than expected, particularly in the service sector. Firms that have a reputation for consistently remedying consumer complaints are more likely to develop customer loyalty and over a time, increase in market share (Blodgett et al., 1995).

Complaint behavior is said to derive from customer dissatisfaction and therefore seeking justice. Hui and Au (2001), based on a study of customers' perception of justice, focus on three complaint-handling strategies: voice, compensation, and apology. The authors claim that voice, compensation, and apology have a positive effect on perceived fairness of complaint handling process. It is said that by giving the customer an opportunity to express their dissatisfaction makes them consider the conflict resolution process to be fairer. Compensation is also said to affect the conflict resolution process as well as the outcome. Like voice, it is also believed to carry a symbolic assertion of respect and expression of sincere regret by the company. It is believed that apology produces more favorable effects on post complaint behavior than excuses and avoidance.

One aspect of the study of Hui and Au (2001), however, is its cross-cultural nature where the authors examined the perception of justice in Canada and the People's Republic of China. The authors claim that voice has a stronger effect on perceived fairness of the complaint handling process for Chinese customers than for Canadians because granting voice to collectivist society can raise their social status. But, compensation is said to have a stronger effect on perceived fairness of the complaint handling process and outcome for the Canadian customers than for Chinese customers.

In order to manage the post-complaint consequences, firms need to develop appropriate strategies. Some argue that firms should encourage dissatisfied customers to vent and make voice responses, avert private responses, and avoid third party responses. So it seems preferable to let the customers express their displeasure by venting verbally rather aggressively. Also, an expression of apology by the company employees can also mean a lot to the dissatisfied customer. The employees need to listen apologetically when customers go on venting since customers usually feel angry and will not think rationally.

On experiencing dissatisfaction, one can respond in a variety of ways. The model suggested by Blodgett et al. (1995) enables us to develop several hypotheses linking such factors as likelihood of success (response or outcome), attitude towards complaining, and product importance as independent variables. Here, the dependent variables are redress-seeking behavior, pre- and post-redress negative word-of-mouth behavior, re-patronage intentions, and positive word-of-mouth behavior.

Maxham and Netemeyer (2002) believe more than one factor is involved in generating perception of justice: interaction with the firm's staff,

complaint handling procedure, and the outcome of the recovery process. It means, there is a three-dimensional approach to perceived justice: distributive, procedural, and interactional justice. This is, in fact, an extension to the works of Blodgett et al. (1995). By distributive justice, the authors mean the degree of fairness or the extent at which customers feel they have been treated fairly in terms of the final outcomes. It is claimed that distributive justice positively affects satisfaction with the recovery process. Procedural justice refers to the perceived fairness of firms' policies and procedures regarding the recovery process. In most cases, firms' policies and procedures, or lack of them, restrict the implementation of recovery strategy. Here the authors claim that the procedural justice positively affects satisfaction with the recovery as well as overall satisfaction with the firm. Lastly, interactional justice is also claimed to have positive effects on the satisfaction of the recovery. Interactional justice refers to such elements as, but not limited to, courtesy, honesty, respect, and genuine interest in fairness.

In the service sector, complaint-handling process is not entirely different from other sectors but the service recovery process requires special attention. Customer turnout is costly because the cost of finding and serving new customers is claimed to be more expensive than retaining the existing customers. Blodgett et al. (1995) think one possible strategy involves recovering from failures fairly. In services businesses such as hospitality, marketers' dilemma is how to determine the desired level of service. However, with careful analysis of complaints and appropriate actions taken to remedy the problems together with an effective recovery program, service firms can survive in an extremely competitive environment.

Lapidus and Schibrowsky (1994) believe customer satisfaction can be enhanced and product service can be improved through an effective customer relationship management (CRM). In this regard, positive and careful evaluation of customers' complaints becomes an important part of the CRM strategy. Here, the authors propose an aggregate complaint handling system where those service dimensions perceived by a significant number of consumers as falling below an acceptable level are considered for careful analysis. Then the authors suggest a quality function deployment (QFD) tool (borrowed from the Japanese manufacturing sector) known as the House of Quality for service analysis leading to developing a new service strategy.

Under this approach, problem identification starts with unsolicited customer complaints or a planned 'focus group' interview and or critical incidence technique (CIT). An aggregate assessment of consumer discontent would then help develop a strategy to improve the situation. Such an approach is also called 'defensive marketing strategy' because it would help retain the existing customers. The advantage over individual complaint analysis is that it focuses on the long-term benefits by attacking the source of the problem rather than attacking the symptoms.

Conclusion

Obviously, the causes of customer complaint behavior are numerous and profiling the complainants is a difficult task. Also, the silent majority, who are reluctant to show dissatisfaction explicitly, may simply take their custom elsewhere or engage in negative word-of-mouth behavior. Therefore, it becomes important for firms to provide an environment in which they are able to express their feelings and to complain. This means the first step of a complaint resolution process is to create an atmosphere that encourages dissatisfied customers to seek redress, both implicitly and explicitly. A strategic approach to complaint handling and resolution process should be developed under the umbrella of a CRM strategy. An aggregate analysis of customer complaints can help identify the fail points both in manufacturing and service sector establishment. Future studies in the area of profiling and segmenting the complainants would be extremely useful. Data mining would particularly be useful for analyzing complaints in company data warehouses. A comparative study of complainants and complaint behavior of product buyers and service buyers can also help marketers develop appropriate strategies for complaint handling and resolution.

References

Bennett, R. (1997) Anger, catharsis, and purchasing behavior following aggressive customer complaints. *Journal of Consumer Marketing*, 14 (2), 156–172.

Blodgett, J.G., Wakefield, K.L., and Barnes, J.H. (1995) The effects of customer service on consumer complaining behavior. *Journal of Service Marketing*, 9 (4), 31–42.

Heung, V.C.S. and Lam, T. (2003) Customer complaint behavior towards hotel restaurant services. *International Journal of Contemporary Hospitality Management*, 15 (5), 288–289.

Hui, M.K. and Au, K. (2001) Justice perceptions of complaint-handling: A cross-cultural comparison between PRC and Canadian customers. *Journal of Business Research*, 52 (2), 161–173.

Lapidus, R.S. and Schibrowsky, J.A. (1994) Aggregate complaint analysis: a procedure for developing customer service satisfaction. *Journal of Service Marketing*, 8 (4), 50–60.

Liu, R.R. and McClure, P. (2001) Recognizing cross-cultural differences in consumer complaint behavior and intentions: an empirical examination. *Journal of Consumer Marketing*, 18 (1), 54–74.

Maxham, J.G. III and Netemeyer, R.G. (2002) Modeling customer perceptions of complaint handling over time: the effects of perceived justice on satisfaction and intent. *Journal of Retailing*, 78 (4), 239–252.

Nyer, P.U. (2000) An investigation into whether complaining can cause increased consumer satisfaction. *Journal of Consumer Marketing*, 17 (1), 9–19.

Singh, J. (1988) Consumer complaint intentions and behavior: definitional and taxonomical issues. *Journal of Marketing*, 52, 93–107.

Stephens, N. and Gwinner, K.P. (1998) A cognitive emotive process model of consumer complaint behavior. *Journal of the Academy of Marketing Services*, 26 (3), 172–189.

NAZ SALEEM
BILKENT UNIVERSITY, TURKEY
SEYHMUS BALOGLU
UNIVERSITY OF NEVADA, LAS VEGAS, USA

Customer expectations

General model of customer expectations

The concept of customer expectations is intertwined with that of service quality. From the beginning of the 1960s when marketing started a fundamental shift from product orientation to customer orientation, customers have been considered to be the focal point of all marketing actions. With the rapid advent of a service economy, profit-making businesses and nonprofit organizations alike attach a greater emphasis on managing customers than managing brands or products. A company's success or failure in managing customers rests with its ability to provide and sustain the level of service quality that meets and exceeds the expectations of its customers.

The role of customer expectations in service quality was first conceptualized by Parasuraman, Berry, and Zeithaml (1985) in their widely quoted gaps model and a measurement instrument SERVQUAL. Using this instrument, the service quality is measured through the comparison customers make between their expectations and their perception on these five dimensions:

1. Tangibles: the physical facilities, equipment, and appearance of service personnel.
2. Reliability: the ability to perform the promised service dependably and accurately.
3. Responsiveness: the willingness to help customers and to provide prompt service.
4. Assurance: the knowledge and courtesy of employees and their ability to inspire trust.
5. Empathy: the caring, individualized attention the firm provides to its customers.

The importance of customer expectations has been well acknowledged, and it is widely accepted that expectations serve as standards with which actual performance of the service provider and the experience of customers (i.e., *perceived service*) are compared. However, the nature of the standards has been approached from different angles. In one approach, the standards are defined as the predictions made by customers about their experience. They represent an objective calculation of probability of performance, or an estimate of anticipated level of performance. These standards are termed *predictive expectations*. Another approach is to interpret the standards as *ideal or desired expectations*, defined as the level at which customers want the service provider to perform.

In light of different views of what the standards should be, Zeithaml, Berry, and Parasuraman (1993) proposed a comprehensive conceptual model that articulated the nature and determinants of customer expectations of service. The model retains the understanding of *desired expectations* and introduces the term *desired service*, defined as the level of service customers hope to receive. It consists of what customers believe 'can be' and 'should be.' The comparison made by a customer between *desired service* and *perceived service* leads to the assessments of service quality. Zeithaml, Berry, and Parasuraman contend that such comparison was the intended understanding of customer expectations in their original 1985 gaps model.

The 1993 conceptual model of customer expectations also retains the understanding of *predicted expectations*, through which Zeithaml, Berry, and Parasuraman incorporated the concept of customer satisfaction into their new model of customer expectations. They differentiate customer satisfaction from service quality assessments in that the former results from the comparison made by customers between *predicted service* – defined as the level of service customers believe they are likely to get – and *perceived service*, while the latter results from the comparison between *desired service* and *perceived service*. In the model of customer expectations, Zeithaml, Berry, and Parasuraman added a new type of standards termed *adequate service*. They posit that customers' assessments of service quality are based on not only what they desire but also what they deem acceptable, and the difference between the two types of standards (*desired service* versus *adequate service*) is the zone of tolerance. The zone of tolerance may become wider or narrower depending on a number of influences. Some of these antecedents include the number of available alternatives, the price of the service, urgency or other situational factors and an individual's predisposition toward service quality.

While the empirical proof and applications are abundant of comparing *desired service* with *perceived service* to assess service quality, and of comparing *predicted service* with *perceived service* to gauge customer satisfaction, one recent study questioned the usefulness of using *adequate service* as standards or measurement of customer expectations. Caruana, Ewing and Ramaseshan (2000) conducted an experiment to determine, among other objectives, whether respondents could distinguish between *desired expectations and minimum (adequate) expectations*. They found that the addition of *minimum expectations* appears to have added little incremental value to the measurement of service quality. Their experiment also raised new questions as to the diagnostic usefulness resulting from the simultaneous collection of expectations and perception scores. They suggest that collection of data about expectations and perceptions is best done separately. The former can be conducted on a less frequent basis than the latter.

Applications in hospitality and tourism

Applications of the concept of customer expectations in hospitality and tourism disciplines are dominated by the essence of the original SERVQUAL model. They focus on the comparison between *desired service* and *perceived service*. Representative of such applications are the two measurement scales of LODGSERV developed by Knutson, Stevens, Wullaert, Patton, and Yokoyama (1989), and DINESERV by Knutson, Stevens and Patton (1995). Both scales were developed using US samples, and mirrored the five dimensions of the SERVQUAL. The specific service items of each dimension were developed in the US lodging and restaurant contexts. The LODGSERV scale and specific service items are as follows.

- *Reliability*
  - equipment works
  - dependable and consistent
  - quickly correct problems
  - services on time
- *Assurance*
  - trained and experienced employees
  - guests feel comfortable
  - company supports employees

- knowledgeable staff
- reservationists are knowledgeable
- *Responsiveness*
  - prompt service
  - staff shift where needed
  - do special requests
- *Tangibles*
  - neat personnel
  - quality food and beverage
  - attractive room
  - décor reflects concept
  - attractive public areas
  - up-to-date equipment
- *Empathy*
  - guests feel special and valued
  - no red tape
  - sympathetic employees
  - sensitive employees
  - convenient hours
  - anticipate guests' needs
  - complimentary services
  - healthful menus

The five dimensions and their specific service items of the DINESERV are as follows.

- *Tangibles*
  - visually attractive parking areas and building exteriors
  - visually attractive dining area
  - staff members who are clean, neat, and appropriately dressed
  - décor in keeping with its image and price range
  - menu that is easily readable
  - attractive menu that reflects the restaurant's image
  - dining area that is comfortable and easy to move around in
  - rest rooms that are thoroughly clean
  - comfortable seats in the dining room
- *Reliability*
  - serve in the time promised
  - quickly correct anything that is wrong
  - be dependable and consistent
  - provide an accurate guest check
  - serve food exactly as ordered
- *Responsiveness*
  - employees help each other maintain speed and quality of service during busy times
  - employees provide prompt and quick service

- employees give extra effort to handle special requests
- *Assurance*
  - employees who can answer guests' questions completely
  - make guests feel comfortable and confident in their dealings with employees
  - personnel who are both able and willing to give information about menu items, the ingredients, and methods of preparation
  - make guests feel personally safe
  - personnel who seem well-trained, competent, and experienced
  - managers support employees so that they can do their job well
- *Empathy*
  - employees who are sensitive to individual needs and wants rather than always relying on policies and procedures
  - make guests feel special
  - anticipate individual needs and wants
  - employees who are sympathetic and reassuring if something is wrong
  - employees seem to have the customers' best interests at heart

The LODGSERV and DINESERV developed by Knutson *et al.* provide a score that indicates the desired or ideal level of performance by hotels and restaurants with regard to each of the service items, as well as an index that indicates the desired or ideal level of performance with regard to each of the five dimensions. To assess the service quality of a particular hotel or restaurant, a randomly selected group of its customers would be asked to rate each of the items according to their actual experience of the performance provided. The resultant ratings would then be compared with the desired score and index. Following the methodology employed in the United States, Patton, Stevens, and Knutson tested the LODGSERV scale in Japan, Hong Kong, Taiwan, Australia, and the United Kingdom. The five overall dimensions remained valid in these markets. Some service items were not applicable in one or more markets.

The concept of customer expectations is applied to travel services as well. Lam and Zhang (1999) assessed customer expectations and perceptions of services provided by travel agents in Hong Kong.

They tailored the SERVQUAL scale to the unique setting of the retailing travel services and arrived at five dimensions that were somewhat different from the SERVQUAL. Their dimensions and specific service items are as follows.

- *Responsiveness and assurance*
  - willing to help
  - prompt service
  - employee's consistent courtesy
  - never too busy to respond
  - understanding of customer's needs
  - instilling confidence in customers
  - reliability
  - provision of exact service
  - solving customer problem
  - completion of promised tasks
  - provision of service right
  - telling when service is performed
- *Empathy*
  - convenient operating hours
  - individual attention by the company
  - personal attention by employees
  - having customer's best interest
- *Resources and corporate image*
  - adequate capacity
  - sufficient resources
  - employee's product knowledge
  - promotion strategies to project image
  - projection of quality service image
- *Tangibility*
  - appealing office décor
  - advanced reservation technology
  - neat employees

Customer expectations and branding

As a concept intertwined with the measurement of service quality, the study of customer expectations has evolved with that of service quality, and in many instances propels and even outgrows the latter. Its significance to both marketing academia and practitioners becomes increasingly magnified, as a wider spectrum of industries embrace the shift from transaction marketing to relationship marketing, and recognize the service quality as a determining factor in customer satisfaction and loyalty.

At the turn of the new century, branding began to take central stage in contemporary

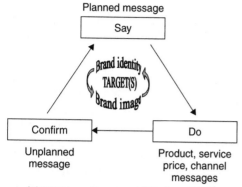

Planned message

Say

Brand identity
TARGET(S)
Brand image

Confirm

Do

Unplanned
message

Product, service
price, channel
messages

Adapted from Duncan and Moriarty (1997)

Figure 1   The Say–Do–Confirm model (after Duncan
and Moriarty, 1997)

marketing. The concept of customer expectations is the foundation on which branding is studied and practiced. Understanding the needs and wants of consumers and delivering products and services to satisfy them are at the heart of successful marketing. A leading school of thought on branding is the customer-based brand equity (CBBE) model. Its basic premise is that 'the power of a brand lies in what customers have learned, felt, seen, and heard about the brand as a result of their experience over time (Keller, 2003).' In examining the branding practices in the lodging industry, Cai and Hobson (2004) proposed an integrated approach to communicating brand messages in building strong hotel brands, as in Figure 1.

The 'Say–Do–Confirm' model integrates customer expectation and other marketing concepts of segmentation, targeting, and positioning in the context of branding. It represents the efforts in advancing the study of customer expectations in hospitality and tourism disciplines.

References

Cai, L. and Hobson, P. (2004) Making hotel brands work in a competitive environment. *Journal of Vacation Marketing*, 10 (3), 197–208.
Caruana, A., Ewing, M., and Ramaseshan, B. (2000) Assessment of the three-column format

SERVQUAL – an experimental approach. *Journal of Business Research*, 49 (1), 57–65.
Duncan, T. and Moriarty, S. (1997) *Driving Brand Value*. New York: McGraw-Hill.
Keller, K. (2003) *Strategic Brand Management*. Upper Saddle River, NJ: Prentice-Hall.
Knutson, B., Stevens, P., and Patton, M. (1995) DINESERV: measuring service quality in quick service, casual/theme, and fine dining restaurants. *Journal of Hospitality and Leisure Marketing*, 3 (2), 35–43.
Knutson, B., Stevens, P., Wullaert, C., Patton, M., and Yokoyama, F. (1989) The service scoreboard: a service quality measurement tool for the hospitality industry. *Hospitality Education and Research Journal*, 14 (2), 413–420.
Lam, T. and Zhang, H. (1999) Service quality of travel agents: the case of travel agents in Hong Kong. *Tourism Management*, 20, 341–349.
Parasuraman, A., Zeithaml, V., and Berry, L. (1985) A conceptual model of service quality and its implications for future research. *Journal of Marketing*, 49, 41–50.
Patton, M., Stevens, P., and Knutson, B. (1994) Internationalizing LODGESERV as a measurement tool: a pilot study. *Journal of Hospitality and Leisure Marketing*, 2 (2), 39–56.
Zeithaml, V., Berry, L., and Parasuraman, A. (1993) The nature and determinants of customer expectations of service. *Journal of the Academy of Marketing Science*, 21, 1–12.

LIPING A. CAI
PURDUE UNIVERSITY, USA

Customer lifetime value

A key component of relationship marketing is keeping loyal customers. The costs associated with taking care of loyal customers decline over time, while sales from loyal customers increase (Reichheld, 2001; Shoemaker and Lewis, 1999). Customer lifetime value, a common way to quantify this customer loyalty, highlights the importance of keeping good customers.

Shoemaker and Lewis (1999) provide a detailed explanation of calculating customer lifetime value. In essence, they estimate how much a customer will spend with a company over their lifetime minus the costs of supporting the customer and providing the products and services. Important parts of this calculation are the probability that the customer will stay with the company and how much the customer will spend.

References

Reichheld, F.F. (2001) *Loyalty Rules! How Today's Leaders Build Lasting Relationships*. Boston, MA: Harvard Business School Press.

Shoemaker, S. and Lewis, R.C. (1999) Customer loyalty: the future of hospitality marketing. *International Journal of Hospitality Management*, 18 (4), 345–370.

JAMES MURPHY
UNIVERSITY OF WESTERN AUSTRALIA,
AUSTRALIA

Customer loyalty

One definition suggested by Shoemaker and Lewis is illustrative of the emotional side of loyalty, as compared to the frequency side. They state that loyalty occurs when:

> The customer feels so strongly that you can best meet his or her relevant needs that your competition is virtually excluded from the consideration set and the customer buys almost exclusively from you – referring to you as their restaurant or their hotel. The customer focuses on your brand, offers, and messages to the exclusion of others. The price of the product or service is not a dominant consideration in the purchase decision, but only one component in the larger value proposition.

Reichheld proposes a second definition of loyalty:

> A loyal customer is one who values the relationship with the company enough to make the company a preferred supplier. Loyal customers don't switch for small variations in price or service, they provide honest and constructive feedback, they consolidate the

bulk of their category purchasers with the company, they never abuse company personnel, and they provide enthusiastic referrals.

Loyalty is important because it provides critical inoculation across multiple areas. For instance, loyal customers are less likely to ask about price when making a reservation. They are also less likely to shop around; hence, competitive offers face a higher hurdle. The customer becomes more forgiving when you make a mistake because there is good will equity. In fact, loyal customers are more likely to report service failures. *Loyalty begets loyalty*. Further, marketing and sales costs are lower as well as transactions costs.

References

Reichheld, Kurt (2002) Letters to the Editor. *Harvard Business Review*, 80 (11), 126.

Shoemaker, Stowe and Lewis, Robert (1999) Customer loyalty: the future of hospitality marketing. *Hospitality Management*, 18, 349.

STOWE SHOEMAKER
UNIVERSITY OF HOUSTON, USA

Customer relationship management/marketing (CRM)

The concept of customer relationship on a one-to-one basis is not new to business. In fact, one-to-one relationships were prevalent over the centuries. Having direct contact with the person with whom one was doing business was commonplace. As a result, specific bonds of trust were established between farmers, traders, merchants, shopkeepers, artisans, and their customers. This trend continues and the economy of the twenty-first century is becoming increasingly customer-centric. Building long-term, loyal relationships with customers is the key to profitability. Obviously, the marketer's objective is eventually to maximize the dollar value of transactions. Rather than following that objective based on the classical combination of product, price, place, and promotion, marketers view the customer relationships as a primary asset that should be cultivated and grown in order to reduce the effects of ever-increasing competition and potential pressure on pricing. Nevertheless, it is difficult to conceive and implement a strategy built on customer relationship management (CRM) without having a sound understanding of principles of relationship marketing and accepting that services have to apply this new paradigm.

The analysis of each of the three key words can offer the basis for a definition. Customer relationship management is about (1) being customer-oriented, i.e. deliver quality and value as expected and perceived by the guest; (2) putting a strong emphasis on mutually profitable relationships between the service firm and its clients; and (3) being able to communicate, organize, and manage the whole organization accordingly. Hence, CRM is a company-wide business strategy designed to reduce costs and increase profitability by encouraging customer loyalty. It brings together information from all data sources within an organization (and where appropriate, from outside the organization) to give one, holistic view of each customer in real time. CRM extends the concept of selling from a discrete act performed by a salesperson to a continual process involving every person in the company. It allows front-line employees in such areas as sales, customer support, and marketing to make quick yet informed decisions on everything from cross-selling and upselling opportunities to target marketing strategies to competitive positioning tactics.

It is possible to distinguish between two forms of CRM that have evolved in time. One version focuses primarily on managing the information flow between the hotel and guest and represents a technology-driven solution to sales and marketing management. It grew out of the information technology development in North America, including data aggregation and consolidation, data-warehousing, data mining, and sales force automation. The other version, developed primarily in Northern Europe out of services marketing, focuses more on aligning the organization's resources in such a way that ongoing relationships are formed, maintained and, where possible, enhanced (Schultz, 2000). Thus, the primary focus of CRM is on building customer loyalty

and retention and answering the question: 'How must we fundamentally change what we do and how we do it to create lifetime customers?' If the Nordic School version of CRM is generally developed, implemented, and managed by the sales and marketing people, in North America it is the information technology group that manages the process.

With the current state of information technology, and high customer service expectations, it is practically impossible to consider the service process issues without addressing technology, but it is important to remember that customer relationships – interpersonal relationships – are the ultimate driving force. Thus, by combining the North American approach with the Nordic School, CRM is best suited to help hotels use people, processes, and technology gain insight into the behavior and value of customers. This insight allows for improved customer service, increased efficiency of voice reservations, added cross-sell and upsell opportunities, improved close rates, streamlined sales and marketing processes, improved customer profiling and targeting, reduced costs, increased share of customer wallet, and overall profitability.

A successful CRM and customer retention strategy in the hotel industry is fundamentally dependent on the implementation at the property level. It is important to train front-line employees to capture information from as many offline touch points as possible, in combination with online data capture and effective collaboration with intermediaries. Training is vital to ensure consistency and cleanliness of guest information. This information should be immediately available to front desk receptionists, call center agents, pit bosses, concierge and housekeeping staff, and so on.

When conceiving and developing its relationship marketing strategy, the hotel should define the appropriate CRM decisions and consider the four foundations needed when focusing on customer retention strategies: (1) the core service, (2) the relationship customization, (3) the service augmentation, and (4) the relationship pricing (Berry and Parasuraman, 1991). These foundations are not independent of one another and can be used in combination or simultaneously.

First, the ideal core service is one that attracts the customers by meeting their needs, cements the business through its quality, components, and long-term nature, and provides a base for selling of additional services over time. The goal of CRM decisions at this level is to 'keep the promise' by delivering the perfect, irreproachable core service to all the clients. It is the mandatory step for strengthening customers' trust, their confidence in the firm's fundamental reliability and integrity.

Second, for customizing the relationship the organization has to keep track of and learn about specific characteristics and requirements of individual customers. Thus, the firm becomes able to tailor service to the situation at hand by applying database marketing. The hospitality version of this technology allows for extensive analysis of guest history, reservation databases, guest comment cards, preference for ancillary services (e.g. fine dining, spa, golf, banqueting, function space for corporate meetings, etc.), information requests and other sources of guest data.

One of the crucial issues for the service firm involved in relationship customization is its ability to create 'listening posts' within the organization – formal and informal communications channels to record both guest preferences and complaints (any problems and their resolution). The database marketing has to provide the necessary information for fundamental activities such as customer profitability segmentation and targeted marketing. Essentially the idea is that not all customers are equally profitable, and determining the profitability of different market segments can help the firm to decide where to invest its limited resources to build loyalty with highly profitable customers. This type of segmentation can be used to determine levels of service provided – the more profitable segments are typically given more personal or customized service. The difficult part for hospitality firms is to be confident in the numbers they get, e.g. costs and potential revenues, used to determine segment profitability, and to decide whether to focus on short-term or long-term profitability. For example, a particular customer or customer segment may not be profitable today, but its long-term potential may support the decision of a short-term investment.

The relationship customization is the critical moment for the company to understand if there are opportunities for having repeat visits, i.e. a profitable long-term relationship, as well as return on service augmentation strategies (see below, the third foundation). The hotel strives to differentiate the guests by calculating and comparing the customer lifetime value and to organize them into a pyramid of segments with the most valuable clients at the top. The concept of lifetime value (LTV) is a measure of how much someone is worth to the hotel company and how long they will contribute to its revenue. The goal of all hotel frequency (loyalty) programs, and ideally the goal of all hotels, is to maximize LTV.

From the customer's point of view, profitability segmentation, while logical, may not seem fair. Customers may resent receiving a lower level of service (e.g. automated versus face-to-face service encounter) than they had previously received, knowing that others are still getting customized and personal service. This is particularly true if they perceive that they are receiving less service than before, or if they are being asked to pay for service they previously received for free.

The third foundation for relationship strategies is about service augmentation. It gives the firm the opportunity to differentiate its service from the competitors by building non-core, genuine ancillary services that are valued by the target market. It is possible to distinguish between different forms of augmented services as applied by hotels: new amenities and features, guarantee for service quality, preferred guest clubs, etc. The benefits behind them can be linked to guests' comfort, confidence in quality of services provided, or prestige and self-esteem.

Finally, the relationship pricing foundation consists of the application of differential pricing by giving a price incentive to repeat customers to consolidate their business with one service supplier. The most well known form of relationship built on such bases are the frequent flyer and frequent guest programs. Although the price incentive can be defined in various ways, e.g. upgrades, free trips or room-nights, special price for the spa access, etc., the objective remains the same: to encourage customer repeat business by rewarding it.

Following the four foundations of customer retention strategies, the hospitality firm has to decide on the appropriate level of retention strategy, i.e. the specific strategies and tactics to build relationships and tie clients closer. The retention strategies can be classified into four levels (in ascending order): (1) financial bonds, (2) social bonds, (3) customization bonds, and (4) structural bonds (Zeithaml and Bitner, 2003). The higher levels forge stronger bonds with customers and are more difficult for competitors to imitate. Leading hospitality firms often employ multiple relationship strategies, possibly at all four levels, simultaneously.

A retention strategy based on financial bonds (level 1) rewards repeated purchases or customer longevity financially, e.g. frequent guest, frequent flyer programs. Other incentives for the repeated clients consist of bundled services and cross-selling actions developed internally or within partnerships with other service providers, e.g. hotels and car rental; hotels, fine dining restaurants and museums, etc. Financial bonds also can be built on stable pricing guarantees, or lower price increase than those paid by new customers. Hotel managers and guests can often misunderstand the financial bonds strategy and assume that it simply means the organization charges lower rates or applies a continuous rate discount based on purchase frequency only. Financial incentives do not generally provide long-term, sustainable advantages to a firm, as they cannot differentiate it from its competitors in the long run, unless combined with another relationship strategy.

A level 2 strategy combines the financial incentives with social or interpersonal bonds between the customer and the organization's employees. Customers become individuals whose specific needs and wants the hospitality firm seeks to understand. Clearly, the implementation of social bonds requires customer identification for every service purchase. Interpersonal bonds are common among professional service providers and personal care providers, but also in business-to-business relationships where customers develop relationships with salespeople or relationship managers. A particular case can be the one of country clubs, extended stay lodging, health clubs, or senior residence where customers interact with each other though developing social bonds among themselves rather than with the service firm.

Level 3 strategies focus on building ties through service customization, although involving social ties and financial incentives. The assumption is that customers who receive individualized service, suited to their own particular needs and circumstances, will be more satisfied and less vulnerable to competitors. The investment of time on their part to educate a new service provider regarding their needs also makes it more difficult to switch. The two-way communications with the client, backed by an effective learning process, represent a sustainable source for anticipation and service innovation. Intimate knowledge of individual customers and the development of 'one-to-one solutions' are the foundations for other customization ties such as mass-customization and customer intimacy.

Structural bond strategies (level 4) are the hardest to imitate and involve all the other three categories of bonds between the customer and the firm. These strategies are the most difficult from which a customer can disengage, since they also include a structural component often based on shared systems or technology. Structural bonds are common in the business-to-business context, where partners share processes and equipment, agree and participate to joint investments, and implement integrated information systems. The relationships between hotel companies and distributors (virtual or 'bricks and mortar') represent a good example of new developments of structural ties.

Customer relationship management is a philosophy of doing business (B2C and B2B), a strategic orientation that focuses on keeping and improving current customers rather than on continuously investing in acquiring new customers. Thus, CRM is to establish, nurture, and enhance relationships with the customers and other partners, at a profit, so that the objective of the partners involved is met. This goal is achieved by a mutual exchange and fulfillment of promises.

References

Berry, L.L. and Parasuraman, A. (1991) *Marketing Services: Competing Through Quality*. New York: Simon & Schuster Adult Publishing Group.

Schultz, D.E. (2000) Learn to differentiate CRM's two faces. *Marketing News*, 20 November.

Zeithaml, V.A. and Bitner, M.J. (2003) *Services Marketing: Integrating Customer Focus Across the Firm*, 3rd edn. New York: McGraw-Hill.

HORATIU TUDORI
ECOLE HÔTELIÈRE DE LAUSANNE (EHL),
SWITZERLAND

Customer relationship management in foodservice

Customer relationship management (CRM) is a management philosophy or a strategy that calls for the reconfiguration of a firm's activities around the customer. More specifically, CRM requires cross-functional integration of operations, marketing, and technology. CRM differs from traditional marketing initiatives in that, while the latter take a predominantly short-term, transactional approach, CRM focuses on maximizing revenue from each customer over the lifetime of the relationship by getting to know each customer intimately (Wilson *et al.*, 2002). CRM is also, by definition, a cross-functional philosophy that calls for substantial business integration (Markus, 2000). In a foodservice context, then, the operator – usually chains – no longer merely markets to customers, but rather fosters a relationship with them through programs that span marketing, operations, information systems, accounting and other organizational functions.

Day *et al.* (1998) neatly summarize the benefits of using CRM in the context of the service industry, which have direct application in foodservice. First, by developing a closer relationship with customers, a restaurant chain may gain a competitive advantage and, through increased switching costs, may be able to defend it. Over time, individual customers typically educate the chain about their individual needs, wants, and preferences, a costly process they may be reluctant to repeat with a rival (Peppers and Rodgers, 1994). Thus, getting to know customers intimately creates a barrier to imitation of the leader's strategy.

Second, effective CRM can lead to greater customer satisfaction. Properly implemented, an effective customer–company dialogue facilitates the tailoring of menu items and service styles closely to individual needs, and encourages the development of food options or items and services (e.g. takeout) to meet changing needs or even anticipate future needs.

Third, CRM techniques increase the restaurant company's efficiency in terms of marketing resources. By using available data to develop accurate profiles of profitable customers, a firm can be more effective in targeting high-potential prospects. McDonald's has done this artfully in targeting the 'large users' – males between the ages of 18 and 24.

Finally, developing a closer relationship with customers is thought to increase customer loyalty, and loyal customers are thought to continue patronizing the foodservice outlet with reasonable consistency (Dowling, 2002). While the value of loyalty is currently under debate (Reinartz and Kumar, 2002), restaurant companies remain behind the curve compared with lodging companies, who have been fostering loyalty through frequent traveler rewards programs for a long time. More importantly, because the restaurant product is characterized by co-production (i.e. the guest is intimately involved in the creation of the experience), and because restaurant guests are eager to provide information about their needs and preferences, foodservice is a perfect candidate for the unobtrusive application of CRM. Thus, for foodservice operators it seems that using CRM is the logical next step.

The above arguments offered by CRM proponents suggest that, for foodservice companies, CRM leads to higher profitability due to increased sales, declining customer acquisition costs, and the increasing profitability of customers who are willing to pay a premium for 'better' food and service.

Some authors warn that substantial investments in CRM are not right for everyone (Gronroos, 1990). In a single unit, for example, it is relatively easy to keep in touch with customers' preferences. Successful CRM implementation requires significant investments in technology, process redesign, and people because of the significant increase in the amount of information that must be managed as a chain's scale and scope increase. An international restaurant chain or a regional multi-unit operator must manage significantly larger amounts of data than a small independent operator to achieve a similar relationship with its customers.

In sum, customer relationship management in foodservice, often connected to customer loyalty programs, can be defined as the process through which operators gather and analyze data about their customers. This consumer-driven data is then used by operators to help make decisions about how better to understand and manage their customers' purchasing behavior and preferences. Data for CRM can come from a variety of sources, such as point-of-sales systems, customer-profile forms, or data gathering companies such as Gazelle Systems. The main premise behind CRM is that a better understanding of your customers will provide you with the ability to better meet their needs, in turn breeding long-term loyalty to your business.

Common applications of CRM vary, ranging from putting customers on mailing lists (to receive general information and offers of interest) to very specific service-related offerings, such as recording guest preferences for table type, table placement, or smoking. CRM programs can go as far as informing service staff about customers' food allergies, drink preferences, birthdays, and the like.

We believe that CRM holds tremendous promise for restaurant and foodservice operations. While still relatively novel, CRM has begun to build a tradition in other industries that can inform future development in the foodservice industry. We caution managers to learn critically from the experience of other industries rather than blindly mimic other industries' 'best practices.' An apt example is offered by reward programs, a mainstay and a cost of doing business in the airline and hotel industries. Should restaurants introduce 'frequent diner cards'? Before rushing to say yes, we need to understand why we are doing so. Is a frequent diner program a tool to increase demand? If there is demonstrable evidence of its positive effect on consumption, then a frequent-diner program may be very valuable to a firm. Is it a tool to gather reliable consumption data and support a CRM strategy? If so, we caution restaurateurs! With respect to the information systems currently present in most restaurants, a bit of process and organizational change may yield the same information with no need to increase cost in an industry characterized by razor-thin margins. Asking the tough questions and clearly understanding which CRM orientation best fits a company will enable managers to reap the highest payoff from this promising strategy.

References

Day, J., Dean, A.A., and Reynolds, P.L. (1998) Relationship marketing: its key role in entrepreneurship. *Long Range Planning*, 31 (6), 828–837.

Dowling, G. (2002) Customer relationship management: in B2C markets, often less is more. *California Management Review*, 44 (3), 87–104.

Gronroos, C. (1990) Relationship approach to marketing in service contexts: the marketing and organisational behaviour interface. *Journal of Business Research*, 20, 3–11.

Markus, M.L. (2000) Paradigm shifts e-business and business/systems integration. *Communications of the AIS*, 4, (10), 1–24.

Peppers, D. and Rodgers, M. (1994) The only business to be in is the business of keeping customers. *Marketing News*, 28 (3), 6.

Reinartz, W. and Kumar, V. (2002) The mismanagement of customer loyalty. *Harvard Business Review*, July, pp. 4–12.

Wilson, H., Daniel, E., and McDonald, M. (2002) Factors for success in customer relationship management systems. *Journal of Marketing Management*, 18, 193–219.

GABRIELE PICCOLI
CORNELL UNIVERSITY, USA
ALEX SUSSKIND
CORNELL UNIVERSITY, USA

Customer satisfaction

Customers' reactions to service experiences are a main concern of foodservice operators. A large body of research examines the influences and outcomes of service experiences for customers. There are four main categories of issues that influence consumers' perceptions of customer service processes: (a) perceptions of service and product quality; (b) perceived performance of products and services; (c) customer complaint behavior; and (d) perceived or real interaction between customers and service providers.

First, customers' perceptions of service and product quality can be examined by considering the foodservice 'Big Three': food, service, and décor. Food is a tangible element and customers evaluate food on the basis of flavor, texture, aroma, presentation/appearance, portion size, temperature, and overall perceived quality. While none of these elements is likely to lead to satisfaction or dissatisfaction by itself, customers process their perceptions of these elements relative to their expectations. For example, a steak that was ordered medium rare but is served medium might be served hot in an attractive presentation, and be flavorful and very tender, but if it is slightly overcooked when served a guest must then evaluate the impact of the cooking temperature on his or her level of satisfaction. Is this one element sufficient enough to create dissatisfaction, or is the larger package sufficiently satisfying?

Consider next the second piece of the 'Big Three,' service. Service is much less tangible than food quality. Effective service delivery involves a combination of reliable communication, timing, accessibility, and conviviality. These elements in the correct proportion should lead to a seamless service experience for customers. Similar to the evaluation of a food product, when evaluating service delivery no one element is more likely than another to dominate the service experience, but particular elements of service delivery may be more noticeable than others. Take as an example the slightly overcooked steak mentioned above. Let's say that the guest decides to complain to his or her server about the doneness of the steak. In order for this to happen, the server will need to be available to the customer to determine the problem, offer a suitable correction along with a sincere apology, and ensure that the solution is implemented quickly. If the customer

feels that the server did not accomplish the suggested remedy, customer satisfaction regarding both food quality and service will likely be negatively influenced no matter which unmet element was the more dominant.

The last of the 'Big Three' factors that influence customer satisfaction is the décor or the environment in which the service experience takes place. Issues such as lighting, color schemes, table layout and spacing, hard and soft finishes, noise level, music/entertainment, and other ambient factors set the stage for the effective delivery of service elements. A perfectly cooked steak delivered seamlessly will not be as satisfying to customers if the environment and décor do not enhance the consumption of the food and service.

As noted above, the 'Big Three' also influence customers' perceptions of service experiences. On a daily basis, foodservice operators deal with a variety of customers seeking a variety of food and beverage services. While each foodservice patron has specific needs and expectations for each service episode, it is understood that, at a minimum, the customer's expectations of the service episode should be met. Inevitably, customers experience elements of the service process that do not meet their expectations, inextricably connecting customer satisfaction with the perceived performance of the 'Big Three.'

When a service failure occurs, a customer can opt to: (a) lodge a complaint in order to influence or adjust the service delivery process, or (b) terminate the service experience unsatisfactorily. Given this seemingly difficult decision, a customer must first be willing and able to complain (a function of efficacy expectations) and, second, believe that his or her complaint will lead to adjustments that compensate for the dissatisfaction (a function of outcome expectations).

Complaints generally occur in three forms: *voice* responses, *private* responses, and *third party* responses. Voice responses occur when individuals seek redress through a personal exchange with a seller. Private responses occur when individuals engage in word-of-mouth communication through others (not a seller) about their dissatisfying experience. Third party responses occur when individuals appeal to an outside party to redress the dissatisfaction, such as a newspaper, the Better Business Bureau, a 'watchdog' organization, or a lawyer.

As noted above in the description of the 'Big Three,' an individual's propensity to complain about a dissatisfying service experience is contingent upon the perception that he or she is able effectively to voice a complaint to redress the dissatisfying experience (again, a function of self-efficacy). One's complaint efficacy is then connected to the perception that the effort in voicing the complaint(s) will lead to a renewed sense of satisfaction (outcome expectancy again). A given individual's response to dissatisfying experiences will therefore vary (self-regulation). In effect, one's ability or desire to complain about dissatisfying experiences is based on elements posited in self-efficacy theory, where efforts or action come about through a perception of mastery or ability in the voicing of complaints. Individuals who consume restaurant services more frequently are more likely to identify gaps between their expectations and the delivery of services (i.e. service failures) and to have more experience in formulating complaints and in turn evaluating service providers' ability to handle complaints satisfactorily (Susskind, 2000).

Lastly, customer satisfaction is ultimately a result of interaction between service providers and customers. Research indicates that employees' positive perceptions of service processes are linked with customers' positive perceptions of service experiences. Similarly, attribution theory (Fiske and Taylor, 1984) suggests that both customers and service providers try to make sense of a service experience by assigning attributions to the causes and effects of the service elements. It is from these perceptions and attributions that both customer orientation and customer satisfaction most likely arise. For an extensive review of the antecedents and consequences of customer satisfaction in service-based organizations, refer to the meta-analysis conducted by Szymanski and Henard (2001).

References

Fiske, S.T. and Taylor, S.E. (1984) *Social Cognition*. Reading, MA: Addison–Wesley.

Susskind, A.M. (2000) Efficacy and outcome expectations related to customer complaints about service experiences. *Communication Research*, 27 (3), 353–378.

Szymanski, D.M. and Henard, D.H. (2001) Customer satisfaction: a meta-analysis of the empirical evidence. *Journal of the Academy of Marketing Science*, 29, 16–35.

ALEX SUSSKIND
CORNELL UNIVERSITY, USA

Cycle menus

Cycle menus (rotating menus/cyclical menus) are generally used for on-site foodservice and volume catering, such as in hospitals, industrial operations, shipping, and large venue catering. The recipes are usually standardized for a set use, quality and quantity of ingredients, method of preparation and cooking, and method of service. Cycle menus are designed for specific periods. The average cycle with most institutional operations is 28 days, after which the whole cycle or sequence of menus is repeated. Some operations run their cycles for five-day or seven-day periods before they are repeated. Again, the menu format, menu quality, menu price, and cycle period are developed for the specific needs of the operation. Since cycle menus are repeated, the menu structure and the choice of dishes must be carefully selected. The menu planner must avoid repetition. Careful attention to nutrition and season of the year should be observed. It would not do, for example, to offer winter-type dishes in the middle of summer. Attention to kilojoules, proteins, carbohydrates, fats, minerals, and vitamins must be given in operations that have captive audiences – such as hospitals or correctional facilities. Regular customers need well-balanced, nutritious meals. Dietary and religious needs must also be assessed and catered to.

To augment the standard cycle menu, many operators add a *plat du jour* or special of the day. This dish should be quite different from the ones featured on the regular menu. A *plat du jour* feature may be used to:

- Offer a different choice to regular customers
- Feature a special cuisine or event
- Take advantage of seasonal availability/quality/ produce
- Test the market for future menu items
- Feature and test a particular selling price range.

Reference

McVety, P.J., Ware, B.J. and Levesque, C. (2001) *Fundamentals of Menu Planning*. New York: John Wiley & Sons.

JAKSA KIVELA
THE HONG KONG POLYTECHNIC
UNIVERSITY, HONG KONG SAR, CHINA

D

Daily operations report

The night auditor prepares the daily operations report, a summary of the day's business from which the general manager and different department heads can review revenues, receivables, operating statistics, and front office cash receipts and disbursements; departmental reports on revenue and expenditures; and a credit report, which lists guest accounts remaining unpaid three days after billing, and any unusually large guest charges or balances. This report contains a summary of a hotel's financial activities during a 24 hour period. The daily operations report provides a means of reconciling cash, bank accounts, revenue, and accounts receivable. The report also serves as a posting reference for various accounting journals and provides important data that must be input to link front and back office computer functions. Also included in the daily operations report are rooms statistics and occupancy ratios and comments and observations from the accounting staff. For example, statistics about the number of guests using the hotel's valet parking services take on added significance when remarks indicate that valet sales are down while occupancy is up. The front office manager may assume that the front office staff is not properly promoting available guest valet parking services. Typically information provided by the daily operations report is not restricted to the front office manager or hotel general manager. Copies of the daily operations report are generally distributed to all department and division managers in the hotel.

Reference

Stutts, Alan T. (2001) *Hotel and Lodging Management – An Introduction.* New York: John Wiley & Sons.

ALAN T. STUTTS
AMERICAN INTERCONTINENTAL
UNIVERSITY, USA

Data envelopment analysis

Hospitality managers attempting to assess unit level productivity have embraced several methods. At the department level, for example, front-of-house restaurant managers have looked at meals served per hour while housekeeping managers have assessed rooms cleaned per labor hour. Such partial-factor measures facilitate meaningful comparisons when applied to the same operation over multiple operating periods or when used to compare similar operations. Unfortunately, these measures have limited utility because they reflect only certain aspects of labor utilization. Even worse, such measures may not correlate to actual operational efficiency.

Fortunately, an analytic technique born from a study of the efficiency of educational programs solves the shortcomings of the various approaches used to assess productivity in hospitality operations. Data envelopment analysis (DEA) is a benchmarking technique based on linear programming that explicitly considers multiple outputs and inputs, producing a measure of performance. As Charnes, Cooper and Lewin (2001) describe fully, this non-parametric (mathematical programming) approach optimizes on the basis of each individual observation, calculating a piecewise frontier occupied by the most efficient units. Moreover, DEA integrates the variables simultaneously – including discretionary input variables that are under management's control and non-discretionary variables that are uncontrollable. Through an iterative calculation process, DEA produces a single relative-to-best productivity index that relates all units under comparison.

Applied to a restaurant chain, for example, DEA allows for the assessment of contingent productivity, which takes into account the differing environmental or situational factors of each restaurant under comparison. Thus, operators can use the best-performing units as the bases for evaluation. Furthermore, the number of applicable input and output variables DEA allows is limited only by the number of restaurants in a comparative set; analyzing a chain with hundreds of restaurants would permit the inclusion of dozens of variables, assuming each input had an oblique relationship to one or more of the output variables.[1]

Extending the example further, consider a small mid-scale restaurant chain with 15 units (see Table 1). For the given month, the average profit-per-front-of-house labor hour is $4.75. Thus, any store with profit per labor hour above this number might be considered efficient. Moreover, if regression analysis was used to predict what sales should be, based on the single independent variable and using the small data set, the dotted line shown in Figure 1 would be determined.

The regression equation underlying this line would serve historically to project what level of profit unit n might be expected to produce as a linear function of monthly labor hours. (The reverse prediction model might also be used.) Such parametric approaches are intended to formulate a single regression plane through the data. The associated assumption is that a 'normal' restaurant should occupy a coordinate on this plane. Put another way, the operator would predict the 'typical' value of the output variable, say profit, by using the values of the various input variables.

Productivity assessment is, however, predicated on maximizing output while using a limited number of inputs most effectively. Thus,

Table 1 Average monthly labor hours and profit for a small restaurant chain

Location	Monthly labor hours	Monthly profit
1	2,483	10,460
2	2,190	12,593
3	1,973	9,453
4	1,463	6,842
5	2,382	10,869
6	2,594	11,611
7	1,523	6,368
8	1,765	10,299
9	2,054	9,666
10	2,108	10,559
11	1,867	9,854
12	1,650	6,270
13	2,159	7,971
14	2,434	11,373
15	1,688	8,499

striving to meet an average is not a sound objective. Non-parametric techniques such as DEA provide a more effective technique. In short, DEA allows us to optimize the output measure for each restaurant given the inputs used. The same technique can also help determine how inputs might be minimized. In either case, the focus is where it should be – on the individual variable(s) for each individual restaurant that may be affecting that unit's productivity.

The other critical component of DEA, which is starkly underscored when DEA is compared with parametric approaches, is that DEA requires no assumptions about functional form. For example, a linear-regression analysis produces a straight line. Such a linear analysis requires assumptions about the data, such as that the error terms (the difference between the actual data point and the regression estimation) are independently and normally distributed, whereas DEA requires no assumptions about functional form. As shown in Figure 1, the optimal frontier resulting from the DEA analysis demonstrates which units (2, 4, and 8) are 100% efficient on the basis of profit and labor hours, given this population.

The real advantage of DEA lies in the ability it gives analysts to integrate several inputs and outputs – while still allowing them to calculate

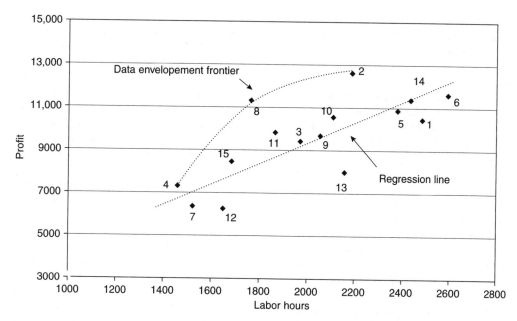

Figure 1 Simplified comparison of DEA and regression analysis (using data from Table 1)

which unit is most efficient given its own set of variables, which are then compared with others in the set. Consider a chain of restaurants where size (as measured in number of seats) and parking availability vary considerably among units. As Reynolds (2003) explains, a simply partial-factor productivity analysis using sales per seat might yield results that would not reflect the impact of parking availability. If we assess each unit on the basis of both of these input variables as a function of sales, however, DEA will show which units are more productive given the dual constraints of number of seats and parking availability. Thus, the multi-unit operator could assess unit level productivity for any unit based on that unit's specific parameters.

As an example of how DEA-related values are calculated, consider a restaurant that is evaluated using two output variables, Y_1 and Y_2, and three input variables, X_1, X_2, and X_3. Its efficiency (P_1) is calculated as:

$$P_1 = \frac{U_1 Y_1 + U_2 Y_2}{V_1 X_1 + V_2 X_2 + V_3 X_3}$$

In applying DEA, the weights (U_s and V_s) are estimated separately for each restaurant to yield the maximum attainable efficiency. Moreover, when the weights estimated for the first restaurant are applied to corresponding outputs and inputs from other units in the analysis, the ratio of weighted outputs to weighted inputs is less than or equal to 1. On a more general basis, assuming that the number of outputs and inputs is infinite, the maximum efficiency of restaurant c as compared with that of n other restaurants is calculated as follows:

$$\text{Maximum } P_c = \frac{\sum_{r=1}^{s} U_r Y_{ro}}{\sum_{i=1}^{m} V_i X_{io}}$$

$$\text{subject to } \frac{\sum_{r=1}^{s} U_r Y_{rj}}{\sum_{i=1}^{m} V_i X_{ij}} \leq 1 \quad \text{for all } j = 1, \ldots, n$$

$$U_r, V_i > 0; \quad r = 1, \ldots, s; \quad i = 1, \ldots, m$$

where

Y_{rj} is the rth output for the jth restaurant,
X_{ij} is the ith input for the jth restaurant,
U_r and V_i are the variable weights estimated and used to determine the relative efficiency of c,
s is the number of outputs, and
m is the number of inputs.

Since DEA seeks optimization contingent on each individual restaurant's performance in relation to the performance of all other units, those with the greatest productivity have a productivity score (P) of 1, suggesting 100% efficiency. These optimal units lie on a multi-dimensional frontier; the efficiency frontier 'envelops' the inefficient units within and quantifies the inefficiency by a relative score of less than 100% and a relational measure on each output and input. Referring back to Figure 1, then, the two-dimensional frontier would transcend only a single plane; however, this number would increase for every additional variable added during the analysis. While difficult to conceptualize and especially to imagine when describing a model with a frontier that occupies a dozen or more dimensions, such an approach provides very useful efficiency information.

The final technical point that is important in understanding the subtleties of DEA pertains to the model specification. There are four general model types, the major differences among which are worth noting. The first and most commonly used model type is the CCR model, which was named for those who proposed it – Charnes, Cooper, and Rhodes – in 1978. This ratio model wields an objective evaluation of overall efficiency on the basis of the population being considered and identifies values associated with the variables corresponding to the inefficient units. The key assumption of the CCR model is that the associated frontiers have constant return-to-scale characteristics. Thus, such a model might be most appropriate when this assumption is reasonable given the variable specifications.

The BCC model, named for Banker, Charnes, and Cooper, is also frequently applied but distinguishes between technical and scale inefficiencies by estimating pure technical efficiency given the respective scale inefficiencies. It also identifies whether increasing, decreasing, or constant returns to such scales are possible. In contrast to the CCR model, the BCC model is appropriate when output maximization is achieved through a proportional (but not necessarily constant) reduction in inputs. This method, therefore, requires mathematical constructs not present in the CCR model.

The third type is called 'multiplicative,' and it is unique because multiplicative models provide a piecewise log-linear or a piecewise Cobb–Douglas envelopment. Multiplicative models can include a convexity constraint, which is sometimes useful given the transformed data space.

Additive models, the fourth and final type, relate the efficiency results to concepts found in econometrics, including the concept of Pareto optimality. At the risk of oversimplifying things, this model type uses unique geometric interpretations of the data and, as a result, is dependent on the units of measurement. As with the other models, the decision to choose such a model specification should reflect the variable definitions as well as the problem parameters.

DEA has been applied in a variety of fields. Specifically to the service industry, research has included productivity analysis using DEA in multi-unit foodservice enterprises and hotels (e.g., Anderson, Fok, and Scott, 2000; Reynolds, 2004) as well as in such arenas as banking and even public libraries. Each of these applications demonstrates the utility of the method and opens the door to more research, encompassing a greater number of potential inputs and outputs.

References

Anderson, R.I., Fok, R., and Scott, J. (2000) Hotel industry efficiency: an advanced linear programming examination. *American Business Review*, 18 (1), 40–48.

Charnes, A.C., Cooper, W.W., Lewin, A.Y., and Seiford, L.M. (eds) (2001) *Data Envelopment Analysis: Theory, Methodology, and Application*. Norwell, MA: Kluwer Academic Publishers.

Charnes, A.C., Cooper, W.W., and Rhodes, E. (1978) Measuring efficiency of decision-making units. *European Journal of Operations Research*, 2, 429–449.

Reynolds, D. (2003) Hospitality-productivity assessment using data envelopment analysis. *Cornell Hotel and Restaurant Administration Quarterly*, 44 (2), 130–137.

Reynolds, D. (2004) Multiunit restaurant productivity assessment using data envelopment analysis. In Z. Gu (ed.), *Management Science*

Applications in Tourism and Hospitality. New York: Haworth Press, pp. 19–26.

DENNIS REYNOLDS
WASHINGTON STATE UNIVERSITY, USA

[1] The accepted practice for determining for determining an adequate number of business units (i.e., units of analysis) is as follow: The number of outputs multiplied by the number of inputs must be less than double the number of business units.

Data mining

Data mining helps organizations achieve new insight and actionable knowledge from their business data. It is a process that employs a combination of machine learning, statistical analysis, modeling techniques, and information technology to discover hidden facts, previously unknown patterns of behavior, and trends. Companies can use this knowledge to make business decisions in their marketing, sales, customer service, production, credit, and finance activities more quickly, more accurately, and with higher confidence.

Data mining can lead to better management decision-making in areas such as planning, matching inventory to customer requirements, customer targeting, and improving marketing and operating processes more generally.

As a marketing tool, data mining is often used to study customers and their purchasing behavior in order to look for patterns that describe the behaviors and permit businesses to perform market segmentation in new ways. Through intelligent segmentation and response analysis data mining has helped companies to retain customers and to become more relevant, by designing products and services that meet the needs of customer 'segments' and to communicate with them more effectively. Moreover, it helps to improve customer relationships through profiling, profitability, value, and loyalty analysis.

References

Introduction to data mining. Available at http://www.the-data-mine.com

Kotler, P. and Armstrong, G. (2001) *Principles of Marketing*, 9th edn. Upper Saddle River, NJ: Prentice-Hall, pp. 132–135.
Loveman, G. (2003) Diamonds in the data mine. *Harvard Business Review*, July, 109–115.

JUDY HOU
ECOLE HÔTELIÈRE DE LAUSANNE (EHL),
SWITZERLAND

Data warehouse

The information systems of most companies are designed primarily for transaction processing. In general, the systems of these companies are not particularly well integrated, nor are they designed for the type of analysis required for strategic and tactical decision-making purposes. A data warehouse is, essentially, a copy of the data contained in a company's operational databases, transformed and reorganized specifically for query and analysis purposes. This, in turn, enables data mining – the analysis of data for relationships that have not previously been discovered – often using advanced artificial intelligence tools. An example is the Australian Tourism Data Warehouse, a system for storing tourism product information, in a standardized and integrated system (in a single repository) for access by interested parties worldwide. Subscribers then have the ability to: access a wide range of product and destination information from a single source in a common format; analyze that data using data mining tools; publish data through individual websites without external links; and publish in a variety of languages. Data warehousing and data mining are critical for the implementation of CRM in hospitality.

Reference

Daniele, R., Mistilis, N., and Ward, L. (2000) Partnership Australia's national tourism data warehouse: preliminary assessment of a destination marketing system. In D. Fesenmaier, S. Klein and D. Buhalis (eds), *Information and Communication Technologies in Tourism 2000*, Vienna: Springer, pp. 353–364.

G. MICHAEL MCGRATH
VICTORIA UNIVERSITY, AUSTRALIA

Database marketing

Database Marketing is the process of building, maintaining, and using a company's own customer database and other database (products, suppliers, resellers) for the purpose of contacting and transacting with customers. Database marketing is the most sophisticated selling process in the marketing world today. It is the basis for direct marketing and ultimately relationship marketing.

Database marketing has been around for 20 or 30 years. Historically, database marketing was accomplished using a marketing customer information file (MCIF) system, a proprietary stand-alone database. There was much preparatory work, as one had to load data periodically, monthly or quarterly usually by keypunching the data into files. Then the files were taken and entered into the database. It contained a limited amount of data and the data became outdated rather quickly. However, as the cost of storage decreased and the advent of other technological advances increased, database capabilities have also increased so now it is possible for a database to hold millions of records. This has enabled firms to create and keep a great deal of information about their customers. They have also been able to add data on their customers from other sources, which further helps with marketing activities. For instance, it is now possible for an airline to share its database with a hotel company so both can undertake a joint promotion to a specific city.

Database marketing is often referred to as direct marketing. The term target marketing is also often applied, relating to focusing in on a given group of customers or 'segment.' By categorizing customers into various segments that have common needs, database marketing tools can be applied directly to the different segments and deliver a different message and a different solution to each one.

References

Carr, M. (1994) Database marketing: talking direct to our listening customers. *Marketing Intelligence and Planning*, 12 (6), 12–14.

Kotler, P. and Armstrong, G. (2001) *Principles of Marketing*, 9th edn. Upper Saddle River, NJ: Prentice-Hall, pp. 132–137, 143–144, 626–627.

Rowe, W.G. (1998) Relationship marketing and sustained competitive advantage. *Journal of Market Focused Management*, 2, 281–297.

Schoenbachler, D.G., Gordon, G.L., Foley, D., and Spellman, L. (1997) Understanding consumer database marketing. *Journal of Consumer Marketing*, 14 (1), 5–19.

Shacklett, M. (2000) Database marketing. *Credit Union Magazine*, 66 (12).

JUDY HOU
ECOLE HÔTELIÈRE DE LAUSANNE (EHL),
SWITZERLAND

Database systems

In the context of database management, data are stored and organized by fields and records. A field (sometimes known as an attribute) is the single unit of information, such as the surname of a hotel employee. A record (also called a tuple) is a collection of related fields. For instance, an employee record contains all information fields that are relevant to a specific hotel employee. Furthermore, a file (also known as a table) has multiple records that are pertaining to a specific topic. To demonstrate, the employee file of a hotel contains all employee records. Lastly, a database comprises all related files. A hotel database, among others, consists of employee files, room files, customer files, and payment files. According to Date (2000), a database system is basically a computerized file-keeping system, and the database itself is a repository of computerized data files.

In hospitality, databases support most business functions and applications. An advantage of database systems application to the hospitality industry is the personalization of products and services (Law, 1998). The selective capability of a database system makes it easy for the hospitality practitioners to maintain a direct contact with customers. This, in turn, helps establish the two-side loyalty connection.

References

Date, C.J. (2000) *An Introduction to Database Systems.* Reading, MA: Addison-Wesley.
Law, R. (1998) Hospitality data mining myths. *FIU Hospitality Review*, 16 (1), 59–66.

ROB LAW
THE HONG KONG POLYTECHNIC
UNIVERSITY, HONG KONG SAR, CHINA

Daypart

A daypart is a subsection of the day during which meals in a restaurant are served. There once was a time when conventional meal periods defined the service times of restaurants – breakfast, lunch, and dinner. Many restaurants, primarily in the full service and quick service segments, specialized in one or two of these meals. Typically these were combined into either breakfast/lunch or lunch/dinner, with one of the meals being the focus. In contrast to this business model, the one followed by the mid-scale coffee shop restaurant segment often meant serving on a 24-hour schedule, with the three meals blended together into one 'all-day' menu.

During the 1970s, restaurant companies – concerned with maximizing the use of restaurant facilities – became concerned with productivity. Since most quick service restaurants (QSR) were busiest during lunch, with considerably less customer traffic during dinner, many companies looked for ways to increase revenues at existing restaurants. Menu prices in QSR had increased steadily with inflation, but the top end of market price acceptance was being reached. With the creation of hand-held sandwiches suitable for breakfast dining, such as the McDonald's Egg McMuffin®, these companies were able to expand into a third meal period. At about the same time, other companies looked to extend their operating hours into the after-dinner, late-night periods.

As this trend evolved during the 1980s and 1990s, customers became more and more accustomed to finding restaurants open and ready to serve them, whenever the impulse moved them, in what has become known as different dayparts.

The sociological changes accompanying the 'dot.com' economy also changed the public's daily schedules. With the advent and rapid growth of the fast casual segment around 2000, represented by companies such as Starbucks and Panera Bread, meal times became less defining, with offerings being described instead by customer seasonality, such as 'drive time' on the way to work, mid-morning, the 'chill-out hours' between 2 p.m. and 5 p.m., and 'after dinner.' Today it is not uncommon for restaurants to target customers in four or more dayparts instead of emphasizing the old fashioned two meals.

Reference

Miller, K. (2004) *The 2004 Restaurant and Foodservice Market Research Handbook.* New York: Market Research.

CHRISTOPHER MULLER
UNIVERSITY OF CENTRAL FLORIDA, USA

Decentralized guestroom HVAC

Decentralized guestroom HVAC equipment is installed through the exterior wall of the guestroom and consists of an electrically powered unit capable of providing either space cooling only or space cooling and heating. Space cooling is provided using a conventional refrigeration cycle. Space heating may be provided by an electric heater or by reverse operation of the refrigeration cycle for units that are heat pumps. Generally, the units are controlled using controls integral to the units themselves, not a thermostat in the room.

Packaged terminal air conditioners (PTAC) or packaged terminal heat pumps (PTHP) are terms used to describe types of decentralized guestroom HVAC units. PTHP units may use air or water as heat sources or heat sinks. Water sources for some PTHP units have been groundwater but more common have been water circulated throughout the property with heat removed or added to this as needed.

Split systems have the compressor unit installed separately from the evaporator with a length of refrigerant piping between the two. This means that the compressor may be installed on a roof or on an outdoor balcony while the evaporator may be installed on the wall in the room. Split systems operate more quietly than typical PTAC/PTHAP units.

References

ASHRAE (2000) Decentralized cooling and heating. In *ASHRAE Applications Handbook*, ch. 5. Atlanta, GA: American Society of Heating, Refrigeration and Air Conditioning Engineers.

ASHRAE (2000) Room air conditioners, packaged terminal air conditioners, and dehumidifiers. In *ASHRAE Systems and Equipment Handbook*, ch. 46. Atlanta, GA: American Society of Heating, Refrigeration and Air Conditioning Engineers.

DAVID M. STIPANUK
CORNELL UNIVERSITY, USA

Decision-making

Decision-making is the process of determining and selecting alternative solutions that can help to achieve intended objectives in hospitality organizations. Making decisions is one of the primary responsibilities of hospitality managers and it can occur at individual, group, and organizational levels. Hospitality managers make two types of decisions that are programmed and non-programmed decisions. The former is repetitive and routine, like making shifts in the F&B department, while the latter is novel and unstructured decisions, like a hotel group deciding to open a new hotel brand. To explain how programmed and particularly non-programmed decisions are made, various decision-making models have been proposed, such as the rational model, the bounded-rational model, the process model, the political model, and the garbage can model. Each model is based on a different set of assumptions and offers unique insight into decision-making in organizations (Miller *et al.*, 1999; Okumus, 2003). The literature gives much emphasis to the role and style of leaders/managers when making decisions. Individual versus group decision-making styles also receive much attention since both have advantages and limitations. Several techniques of improving decision-making have been suggested, such as providing training programs for managers and using brainstorming, the Delphi Technique, the Nominal Group Technique, and Computer Group Problem-solving Technique. Okumus (2003) notes that the literature on decision-making in the hospitality management field is limited and therefore he invites future research studies into this key area.

References

Miller, S.J., Hickson, D.J., and Wilson, D.C. (1999) Decision-making in organizations. In S.R. Clegg, C. Hardy, and W.R. Nord (eds), *Managing Organizations: Current Issues*. London: Sage Publications, pp. 44–62.

Okumus, F. (2003) Decision-making in tourism and hospitality organizations. In S. Kusluvan (ed.), *Managing Employee Attitudes and Behaviors in the Tourism and Hospitality Industry*. New York: Nova Science Publishers, pp. 631–639.

FEVZI OKUMUS
THE HONG KONG POLYTECHNIC
UNIVERSITY, HONG KONG SAR, CHINA

Decision support system

A decision support system (DSS) is an interactive system that enables decision-makers to use databases and models on a computer in order to solve ill-structured problems. A DSS consists of problem-solving technology containing people, knowledge, software, and hardware to facilitate improved decision-making. Special types of DSS are expert systems, which integrate and use decision rules and weights from domain-specific experts, and group decision support systems (GDSSs) involving multiple decision-makers. Analytical models commonly used in decision support systems are forecasting, simulation or optimization models. These models are either developed with a general programming language or with a statistical or mathematical standard software package.

In hospitality management decision support systems frequently occur in the form of travel recommendation systems, in order to support customers in their accommodation and/or travel decision-making process, or as management information systems (MISs), in order to support hospitality managers in their business decisions. Decision support systems have been successfully introduced for agent counseling, budget allocation problems, site selection analysis, and yield management systems for hotel and other tourism suppliers. While DSSs help hospitality managers to make decisions, they do not replace managerial judgment. An ideal DSS allows a manager to combine his or her experience and intuition with the consistent objectivity of a computer-based model.

References

Turban, E. and Aronson, J.E. (2000) *Decision Support Systems and Intelligent Systems*, 6th edn. London: Prentice-Hall.

Wöber, K.W. (2003) Information supply in tourism management by marketing decision support systems. *Tourism Management*, 24 (3), 241–255.

KARL WÖBER
VIENNA UNIVERSITY OF ECONOMICS AND
BUSINESS ADMINISTRATION, AUSTRIA

Deeded timeshare ownership

A type of interest in a timeshare plan in which the owner receives the right to use the accommodations and facilities of the timeshare plan during the term of the timeshare plan together with an ownership interest in the underlying property included in the timeshare plan. At such time as the timeshare plan terminates, the owner of a deeded ownership interest will continue to own an interest in the underlying property as a co-tenant along with all other owners of deeded timeshare interests in that underlying property. The purchaser of a deeded ownership interest is conveyed the interest through the execution and delivery of deed of conveyance, such as general warranty deed or quitclaim deed, similar to the conveyance of any other interest in real property. Consequently, a deeded ownership is governed by the same laws and principles applied to traditional real estate transactions, such as mortgage lending and taxing laws and accounting rules. In general, a deed is a written contract that provides legal title after the contract price has been paid in full after the execution of the contract or completion of construction, whichever occurs later. This type of interest is also referred to as a timeshare estate.

References

See, e.g., *Fla. Stat.* §721.05(32) (2 October 2003). http://www.flsenate.gov/statutes/index.cfm? App_mode=Display_Statute&Search_String= &URL=Ch0721/SEC05.HTM&Title= ->2000->Ch0721->Section percent2005

KURT GRUBER
ISLAND ONE RESORTS, USA

Departing the guest

Departing a guest typically involves at least three members of a hotel's staff – front desk, bell, and airport courtesy van driver and/or doorman when a guest is ready to check out of his/her room at a hotel. The front desk aspects include:

- Inquiring about the quality of products and services that have been provided to the guest.
- The guest returning room keys to the hotel if the hotel is still utilizing hard keys rather than electronic keys and locks.
- Both the guest and the front desk reviewing a hard copy of the guest's folio for completeness and accuracy.
- The guest determining the method of payment and the front office receiving payment.
- Inquiring of the guest the need for additional reservations.
- Preparing a copy of the folio and related documents for the guest and for the night audit.

- Communicating the guest's departures to housekeeping and other departments in the hotel if necessary.

Both the front office cashier and the guest should review the folio for accuracy, including the room fee and tax for the number of lodging nights, and incidentals including personal phone calls, food, beverage, and other purchases in the hotel. The front desk cashier should also inquire as to whether any late charges were incurred at a hotel restaurant or with any other hotel department. After determining how the guest will pay, the front desk brings the guest's account balance to zero. A guest's account balance must be settled in full for an account to be considered zeroed out.

Reference

Stutts, Alan T. (2001) *Hotel and Lodging Management – An Introduction.* New York: John Wiley & Sons.

ALAN T. STUTTS
AMERICAN INTERCONTINENTAL
UNIVERSITY, USA

Depreciation of fixed assets

Fixed assets, with the exception of land, are subject to depreciation. The word 'depreciation' has two principal meanings. In contemporary accounting it means an allocation of the cost of an asset over its useful life. In other circumstances, it means a reduction in the value of an asset.

More specifically in accounting terms, depreciation is a measure of the wearing out, consumption or other loss of value of a fixed asset arising from use, the passing of time or obsolescence (being out-dated or superseded). Depreciation involves the systematic allocation over time of the historical cost (the purchase price) or other measure of an asset in financial statements. In order to make the allocation it is necessary to estimate not only a historical or current replacement cost but also the asset's useful economic life and its residual value.

The purpose of depreciation is to allocate the cost of a tangible operational asset over its useful life. The calculation of depreciation expense requires three amounts for each asset:

1. Acquisition cost.
2. Estimated useful life to the business.
3. Estimated residual value at the end of the asset's useful life to the business.

Of these three amounts, two (useful life and residual value) are estimates. Therefore depreciation expense is an estimate. Residual value must be deducted from acquisition cost to compute depreciation expense. This value represents that part of the acquisition cost that is expected to be recovered by the user upon disposal of the asset at the end of its estimated useful life to the entity.

Accountants have not been able to agree on a single, best method of depreciation because of significant differences among businesses and the assets that they own. As a result, several different depreciation methods are commonly used in financial statements. The different depreciation methods are based on the same concept; each method allocates a portion of the cost of a depreciable asset to each future period in a systematic and rational manner. Nevertheless, each method allocates to each period a different portion of the cost to be depreciated. The most common depreciation methods are: straight line; accelerated depreciation, also known as declining balance or diminishing value; units of production.

Straight line depreciation is the method that allocates the cost of an operational asset in equal periodic amounts over its useful life. The *accelerated depreciation* method results in higher depreciation expense in the early years of an operational asset's life and lower expense in the later years. *Declining balance depreciation* is the method that allocates the cost of an operational asset over its useful life based on a multiple of the straight line rate. Units of production depreciation is the method that allocates the cost of an operational asset over its useful life based on its periodic output related to its total estimated output. In practice, restaurants and other hospitality businesses use either the straight line of depreciation method or the declining balance method. Other methods are more applicable to manufacturing businesses.

References

Henderson, S. and Peirson, G. (1988) *Issues in Financial Accounting*, 4th edn. Melbourne: Longman.

Libby, R., Libby, P.A., and Short, D.G. (1998) *Financial Accounting*, 2nd edn. New York: Irwin McGraw-Hill.

Parker, R.H. (1992) *Macmillan Dictionary of Accounting*, 2nd edn. London: Macmillan.

Siegel, J.G. and Shim, J.K. (1987) *Dictionary of Accounting Terms*. New York: Barron's Educational Series.

JEFF POPE
CURTIN UNIVERSITY OF TECHNOLOGY,
AUSTRALIA

Destination management company

A destination management company (DMC) is a liaison between the out-of-town client and all of the services of a destination that the host property does not offer. DMCs range from those that provide very specialized services to full service firms capable of handling all logistics. For instance, some companies provide only ground transportation (such as buses, limos, and vans), while others can handle personally, or can subcontract, everything a client needs. Full service firms can book entertainment, plan theme parties, coordinate tours and spouse programs, and handle off-site events (including catering) at museums and other local attractions.

Full service firms can also provide personnel. For instance, exhibitors may want to hire local models to work exhibit booths. Trained registration personnel can also be hired. And 'moving décor,' such as costumed models, caricature artists, and celebrity look-a-likes, can be used to help carry out an event's theme. Generally speaking, it is much cheaper for the out-of-town corporate and association clients to hire these persons locally than to pay transportation and per-diem maintenance for company employees.

Destination management companies are oftentimes used to secure props for theme parties.

For instance, a DMC can see to it that a 1960s party has a vintage Mustang or Corvette display. This intermediary can also coordinate appropriate balloon art and pyrotechnics displays.

Many out-of-town clients are willing to pay a local destination management company to provide guidance in an unfamiliar area. It is very difficult for a client to judge the quality of services available if he or she has never visited the area. This intermediary can relieve the client of this burden. Furthermore, it can handle negotiations and oversee every detail, thereby ensuring a successful event.

Clients whose events are held in a different area every year prefer working with destination management companies. These intermediaries have made it easy for clients to indulge this preference by locating themselves in major convention cities. In fact, some national firms, such as USA Hosts, have local offices in several major convention cities that provide one-stop service for large corporate clients as well as favorable quantity-discount prices for this service.

Of course, there are independent DMCs that work only one part of the country. Because of their specialized approach, clients may find them to be the best option. The Association for Destination Management Executives (ADME) can be visited at: http://www.adme.org.

Reference

Shock, Patti J. and Stefanelli, John (2001) *On Premise Catering: Hotels, Convention and Conference Centers and Clubs*. New York: John Wiley & Sons.

PATTI J. SHOCK
UNIVERSITY OF NEVADA, LAS VEGAS, USA

Destination management system

A destination management system (DMS) assists a destination management organization (DMO) to collect, coordinate, and disseminate computerized information about a particular region. The system offers support to the reservation function for local tourism attractions, facilities, and products. Most DMS developments have been led by public tourist organizations as these are traditionally charged with information provision and marketing. Destination management systems emerge as major promotion, distribution, and operational tools for both destinations and small and medium-sized tourism and hospitality enterprises (SMTEs) locally.

SMTEs dominate the tourism provision and contribute a considerable proportion of benefits. However, most small hotels find difficult to establish their online presence and to communicate effectively with their clientele. Hence, destination management systems have developed as interfaces between destination tourism enterprises (including principals, attractions, transportation, and intermediaries) and the external world (including tour operators, travel agencies, and ultimately consumers). Their contribution to strategic management and marketing is demonstrated by their ability to integrate all stakeholders and to reach a global market. A DMS can offer considerable benefits, including:

- Increase business for the destination and local suppliers
- Generate revenue for the DMO and SMTEs through reservations and value-added services
- Improve communications and relationships with both individual travelers and targeted groups
- Reduce costs associated with communications and distribution.

References

Buhalis, D. (2003) *eTourism: Information Technology for Strategic Tourism Management*. Harlow: Prentice-Hall.

WTO (2001) *eBusiness for Tourism: Practical Guidelines for Destinations and Businesses*. Madrid: World Tourism Organization.

DIMITRIOS BUHALIS
UNIVERSITY OF SURREY, UK

Destination marketing

Destination marketing aims at creating positive images to promote tourist destinations for social and economic benefits. A destination can be a geographically defined area but it also varies in scope depending on the perceptions of tourists. Depending on travel motivations and destination offerings, people visit destinations for various reasons such as seeking knowledge, getaway, relaxation, urban life, rural and pastoral peace, and authentic and unique experience. Destination marketing promotions can be done at various levels: local, regional, national, and international. In the United States, the convention and tourist bureaus play an important role in planning and developing destination marketing activities. In other countries or regions, government tourist offices design, coordinate, and administer tourism policies that exert influence on how destinations are introduced and promoted to various markets. Both public and private sectors may seek different interests in destination marketing efforts. Local residents' attitudes and support toward tourism development in the area are essential to ensure successful marketing campaigns for the destination. Sustainability of tourist destinations is at the top of the development agenda.

To market destinations effectively and fully understand tourists' destination choice, various scholarly research approaches have emerged. From the perspective of destination image, destination marketers are concerned with how to create positive images to affect actual and potential tourists' destination choice. The destination branding approach brings in the synergy effect of a cluster of destinations, such as co-branding. Destination marketers are seeking innovative ways to build tourists' loyalty to the destination.

References

Buhalis, D. (2000) Marketing the competitive destination of the future. *Tourism Management*, 21 (1), 97–116.

Gartrell, R.B. (1988) *Destination Marketing for Convention and Visitor Bureaus*. Dubuque, IA: Kendall/Hunt Publishing.

Morgan, N., Pritchard, A., and Pride, R. (2003) *Destination Branding: Creating the Unique Destination Proposition*. Oxford: Butterworth-Heinemann.

Seaton, A.V. and Bennett, M.M. (1996) *The Marketing of Tourism Products: Concepts, Issues, and Cases.* Boston, MA: International Thomson Business Press.

BILLY BAI
UNIVERSITY OF NEVADA, LAS VEGAS, USA

Destination marketing organization

The travel and tourism industry has become a significant contributor to the economic growth and stability of cities, states, provinces, regions, and nations. Tourism is a comprehensive industry providing hotels, restaurants, attractions, transportation, and auxiliary services (retail, tour guides, recreation, etc.) to pleasure and business travelers. These autonomous suppliers are often seen as one entity by consumers based on the totality of their experience at a destination (Williams and Palmer, 1999). Synergy between tourism suppliers can be developed through the use of destination marketing organizations (DMOs). The tourism industry is also characterized by a divergent set of promotional needs. Research has shown that cooperation between destination stakeholders rather than on individual brands will influence the growth of a destination (Prideaux and Cooper, 2002).

Destination marketing organizations market their geographic areas to travel trade intermediaries, individual and group travelers on behalf of the tourism organizations (hotels, restaurants, attractions, transportation, and auxiliary services) in their destination. Examples of DMOs include government agencies at the national, state, territory, region, county, or city levels. There are also private sector DMOs that represent large tourism organizations that own/manage multiple operations such as Disney Worldwide and Ski Country USA that may not be owned by the same corporation or entity. There are also quasi public–private DMOs that are funded with public tax dollars and membership dues. These organizations may be convention and visitor bureaus (CVB) or tourism authorities. One of the missions of a CVB is to make sure there is a good selection of tourism products and service suppliers in their area. CVBs then work on behalf of these tourism suppliers in attracting travelers to the destination. CVBs may be membership-driven, with members paying dues, or tax-driven, with all tourism businesses in the destination represented, or a combination of the above.

Destination marketing organizations funded by tax dollars operate through various government agencies at all levels of government. At the national level the British Tourist Authority (BTA), which markets Britain abroad, merged with the English Tourism Council, which promotes domestic travel and operates under the name VisitBritain (Barrett, 2003). The US Travel and Tourism Administration (USTTA) has worked under a regionalization perspective so they can pool resources, demonstrate US diversity, and the economic benefits of tourism can be focused and measured more efficiently (Ollendorff and Wynegar, 1988). In recent years these countries as well as others have built alliances with other levels of government and the private sector to market their destinations.

Destination marketing organizations out of economic necessity have built relationships with tourism suppliers and even competing destinations to pool resources and present a unified travel experience. These quasi public/privately funded DMOs have become more commonplace as tax dollars appropriated for tourism marketing have been diminished. California's travel-and-tourism industry has initiated a self-assessment system approved by an industry-wide referendum. The revenues are earmarked for supporting the state tourism plan approved by the California Travel and Tourism Marketing Commission (Seal, 1999). In Estes Park, Colorado Innkeepers Association has implemented a voluntary bed tax to support the city's tourism marketing plan (Gregory and Koithan-Laudeerback, 1997).

The success of a tourism destination product depends on a network of independent and interdependent organizations. Each member provides a piece of the tourism picture with their unique products and services. Some of these DMO programs include cooperative advertising, tour product development, regional marketing conferences and trade shows and travel missions. DMOs also may assess market size and performance, and prime market value, and identify future opportunities for tourism-related business development (Ollendorff and Wynegar, 1988).

The proliferation of World Wide Web sites now offers new opportunities for DMOs to promote a composite of its members through cooperative Web address. There is opportunity to move away from a mass marketing approach that relied on toll-free (freephone) numbers and brochures to customize information that fits the changing information channel offered through the Internet. These tourism-related websites have led the way in promoting and distributing to consumers their products and services (Palmer and McCole, 2000). Many DMOs have developed and promoted their websites with varying levels of information and interactivity. Interoactivity provides a way for multiple suppliers to seamlessly connect their services, providing travelers one-stop-shopping for their travel needs. As travelers become more aware of the Internet in their search for travel opportunities it becomes clear that DMOs to increase their share of the national, regional, and state market must have strong brand recognition that is supported by a single marketing body and a single destination brand (Prideaux and Cooper, 2002).

References

Barrett, Lucy (2003) Putting England back on the map. *Marketing Week*. 3 April, p. 19.

Gregory, Susan and Koithan-Laudeerback, Kathy (1997) Marketing of a resort community. *Cornell Hotel and Restaurant Administration Quarterly*, 38 (6).

Ollendorff, Max and Wynegar, Don (1988) Regional cooperative marketing programs in tourism: Why re-invent the wheel? *Business America*, 109 (4), 4,6.

Palmer, Adrian and McCole, Patrick (2000) The role of electronic commerce in creating virtual tourism destination marketing organizations. *International Journal of Contemporary Hospitality*, 12 (3), 198.

Prideaux, Bruce and Cooper, Chris (2002) Marketing and destination growth: a symbiotic relationship or simple coincidence? *Journal of Vacation Marketing*, 9 (1), 35–52.

Seal, Kathy (1999) California tourism initiative pools marketing funds. *Hotel and Motel Management*, 214, (6), 71.

SUSAN GREGORY
EASTERN MICHIGAN UNIVERSITY, USA

Developer rights under the purchaser deposit

The laws of some jurisdictions require that all or a portion of the funds or other property received by a developer of a timeshare plan from a purchaser of a timeshare interest in the timeshare plan must be deposited in an escrow account with an independent escrow agent prior to completion of the purchase transaction. These purchaser's funds and property are safeguarded in the escrow account and may not be delivered to or accessed by the developer until certain conditions are met or certain events transpire such as: (i) the purchaser's right to cancel the purchase contract during any statutorily-required cancellation period has expired; (ii) construction of the accommodations and facilities of the timeshare plan have been completed as promised to the purchaser; (iii) the developer can deliver title to or use of the timeshare interest free and clear of any encumbrances or such encumbrances have been subordinated to the rights of the timeshare purchasers in the plan; (iv) the purchase transaction between the developer and the purchaser has been completed and ownership or use has been transferred to the purchaser. The developer is also entitled to receive the purchaser's funds or other property if the purchaser cancels the purchase after the statutorily-required cancellation period or otherwise defaults under the terms and conditions of the purchase contract.

References

See *Fla. Stat.* §721.08 (2 October 2003).
http://www.flsenate.gov/statutes/index.cfm?
App_mode=Display_Statute&Search_String=

&URL=Ch0721/SEC08.HTM&Title=
->2000->Ch0721->Section percent2008

KURT GRUBER
ISLAND ONE RESORTS, USA

Deviance

This term is generally associated with traditional practice and morality and refers to negative behavior that contravenes accepted norms. In the workplace, deviance involves a departure from formal or informal procedures, standards, codes of conduct, and/or rules and regulations (Delbridge, Bernard, Blair, Peters and Butler, 1991). Examples of workplace deviance include aggression, harassment, insubordination, tardiness, absenteeism, theft, fraud, obscenity, sabotage, and the consumption of drugs or alcohol within the workplace. Deviant behavior can be directed at an organization or at individuals within an organization. In the hospitality sector the reliance on human capital for service delivery means that deviant behavior by employees can result in customer dissatisfaction with the service experience and a reduction in customer loyalty. Consequently, the effects and costs of deviant behavior are magnified within the hospitality industry. Some studies suggest that deviant behavior is common in the hospitality industry because several factors conspire to produce it. The chief culprits are said to include:

- Mainly short-term, seasonal and part-time jobs
- Relatively unskilled and low paid jobs
- Autocratic, despotic, and unsupportive styles of management
- Low union membership
- Entrepreneurial nature of front-line employees
- Orientation to work of hospitality employees (Robinson and Bennett, 1995).

References

Delbridge, A., Bernard, J.L.R., Blair, S., Peters, S., and Butler, S. (eds) (1991) *The Macquarie Dictionary*, 2nd edn. Sydney: The Macquarie Library, p. 485.

Robinson, S.L. and Bennett, R.J. (1995) A typology of deviant workplace behaviors: a multi-dimensional scaling study. *Academy of Management Journal*, 38 (2), 555–572.

BARRY O'MAHONY
VICTORIA UNIVERSITY, AUSTRALIA

Diffusion models

The diffusion of innovations is the aggregate of the individual adoption process whereby an individual passes from knowledge, to formation of an attitude, to a decision to adopt or reject, to implementation of the new idea, and to confirmation of the decision (Rogers, 1983). It refers to the process and rate at which various groups of individuals adopt an idea or innovation in a given society. Diffusion represents the demand side of the product life cycle (where the supply or production side is represented).

Adopter groups

Individuals within a social system adopt new concepts and ideas at different times and can be categorized sequentially according to the relative order in which they adopt. Adopter groups are identified as innovators, early adopters, early majority, and laggards or non-adopters (Rogers, 1983). Innovators represent about 5% of the population, the early adopter category adds another 15%, the early and late majorities represent 34% each, leaving laggards and non-adopters with the final 10%. The result is a normal bell-shaped curve indicating adoption over relative time. Adopter groups can be described by their personal characteristics, socio-economic status, exposure to communications, and by their subsequent influence on others. For instance, innovators are relatively young, cosmopolitan individuals who rely on scientific sources of information. Because they tend to be non-social, they serve a limited role in influencing others to adopt. The early adopters are high in socio-economic status, seek interpersonal sources of information, are gregarious, and are socially and politically connected both formally (professional associations) and informally (known for their expertise in a product or service category) to other individuals and groups. They are the most important group for hospitality and other marketers to reach, as they are often considered to be opinion leaders, and others look to them in forming their own opinions and attitudes about products, services and ideas. The early majority group is above average socio-economically and emulates the early adopters. They rely on mass communications for information. The late majority emulates the early majority as well as others in the late majority. Finally, laggards and non-adopters tend to be older, more conservative individuals who are most hesitant to try new products and services or adopt new ideas.

Communication channels

Communication channels through which information travels are categorized as interpersonal or mass media in nature. Interpersonal channels usually involve a face-to-face exchange between two or more individuals. These can be marketer-dominated sources (sales personnel, travel agents) or non-marketer dominated (friends, family) forms of word-of-mouth communication. Mass media channels include radio, television, newspapers, and direct mail, and may be marketer-dominated (advertisements) or neutral sources (destination or hotel rating guides). Channel usage by different adopter categories also determines the flow of communication and differentiates between the categories on the basis of the awareness and the dissemination of information. The use of Internet communications, common in the hospitality field, is of particular interest because it can be considered a source of both interpersonal and mass communication among e-consumers (Shea *et al.*, 2004). Furthermore, it is a rather informal non-marketer dominated form of communication (even within formal organizations) that itself had not yet diffused throughout the population when diffusion/adoption theories were initially developed and studied. The use of the Internet in the form of e-mails, researching hospitality services such as airline tickets, and to some extent websites, adds a new dimension to available methods of communication among networks of individuals and groups, both formal and informal.

Diffusion rates and direction

As noted, not all individuals in a social system adopt an innovation or an idea at the same time. Rather, they adopt in a time sequence, and they are classified into adopter categories on the basis of when they employ the idea. The diffusion effect is the cumulatively increasing degree of influence upon an individual to adopt or reject an innovation, resulting from the activation of peer networks about an innovation in the social system. The speed and extent of the diffusion effect depends on the degree of interconnectedness of adopter groups. It is the communication flow, dissemination of information and interconnectedness that ultimately determine the rate of diffusion.

Rogers (1983) posited three theories of the direction of diffusion: the trickle down, trickle up, and trickle across theories. The classical model posits a trickle down process whereby information and influence flow sequentially from the top down through socio-economic classes within a social system. Later, a two-step flow of communications model was proposed as a second theory. Known as the trickle across theory, it implies a layer of opinion leaders (early adopters) who seek out information and influence others within formal and informal, social, and work groups. Finally, a third theory referred to as the trickle up process suggests that some innovations begin at the lower end of the socio-economic population and move upward through the classes. The three diffusion processes are depicted in Figure 1.

The conceptual equivalent of the trickle down process for hospitality or any other business could be viewed as the movement of information or ideas from top management filtering through layers of managers and employees. The trickle across process implies the receipt of information by opinion leaders in an organization with subsequent passage to others. Finally, the trickle up process suggests that lower level employees pass information to those in higher-ranked positions. Diffusion models traditionally have implicated strategies for marketer-dominated communications. Word-of-mouth communication has been a part of the model since its inception; however, considering the speed and extent of diffusion through the Internet, this non-marketer-dominated (in some cases)

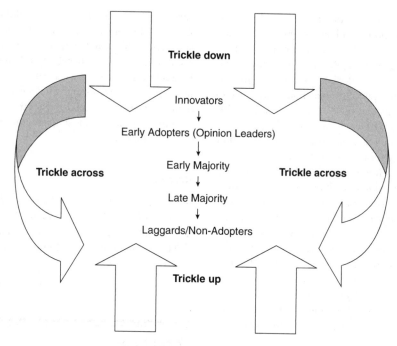

Figure 1 Three diffusion models

communication channel introduces a unique element to this process. It is well accepted by marketing scholars and managers that non-marketing dominated sources of information, including negative word-of-mouth messages are given substantial consideration in forming opinions and making purchase decisions – particularly in the context of services (Richins, 1983). Furthermore, as noted by Ritson (2003), with help from the Internet, this 'viral marketing' (spread of information through the Internet) allows a customer to damage and potentially destroy multinational organizations when posting complaints on Internet venues.

Marketers in the hospitality and tourism disciplines can use diffusion theory as an effective strategic planning tool. It is particularly useful in the design and timing of communications strategies.

References

Richins, M.L. (1983) Negative word-of-mouth by dissatisfied consumers: a pilot study. *Journal of Marketing*, 47 (1), 68–78.

Ritson, M. (2003) Prepare for a virtual battering if you fail to deal with complaints. *Marketing*, March, 16.

Rogers, E. (1983) *Diffusion of Innovations*, 3rd edn. New York: The Free Press.

Shea, L.J., Enghagen, L.K., and Khullar, A. (2004) Internet diffusion of an e-complaint: a content analysis of unsolicited responses. *Journal of Hospitality and Tourism Marketing*, 17 (2/3).

LINDA J. SHEA
UNIVERSITY OF MASSACHUSETTS, USA

Dining room turnover

Foodservice operators calculate *turnover* – how frequently seats or tables are occupied by new customers in a given time period – to increase revenue flow. Seat turnover is the number of times a seat is used by different individuals during a particular meal period or time; table turnover is the number of times a table is used by different parties during a particular meal period or time.

Consider a restaurant that has 100 seats, is open for four hours, and serves 200 diners during those four hours. Its seat turnover would be $200/100 = 2.0$ turns per seat. Table turnover is equally simple to calculate: If a restaurant has 30 tables, is open for four hours, and serves 90 parties during those four hours, its table turnover would be $90/30 = 3$ turns per table. These calculations help operators measure how well their restaurants use seating capacity.

Table turnover is generally higher than seat turnover, depending on discrepancies in a restaurant's mix of party and table sizes. Larger tables generally turn over more slowly than smaller tables because serving larger parties requires more time. Obviously, turnover will be lower in a fine dining restaurant than in a fast casual restaurant due to longer preparation and service times. Some restaurants feature banquet-style seating at large tables for all customers, in which case seat turnover will be higher than table turnover.

Reference

Kimes, S.E. (1989) The basics of yield management. *Cornell Hotel and Restaurant Administration Quarterly*, 30 (4), 15.

SHERRI KIMES
CORNELL UNIVERSITY, USA

Direct billing

Overall, direct billing allows less money to be taken out of the traveler's pocket, and less work for departmental secretaries. When an invoice is direct billed it is sent to the office of the controller where it is processed. The department will receive a photocopy of the invoice that was debited to their account, with a document number stamped at the bottom. Only certain businesses are typically set up for direct billing. For example, in the lodging business, many companies or guests may not want to settle their bills at the end of their stay with cash, check, money order, or even credit card. They would apply for a line of credit with the hotel and have established the line. Upon approval, they agree to pay for the charges incurred during their stay and a bill will be sent to them by the hotel at a later date. This is not only an advantage to the clients but can also be beneficial to hotels. Choice Hotels International has a central direct billing system for tour operators and wholesalers that allow them to make one consolidated electronic payment on a monthly basis. This simplifies the accounting processes for Choice.

References

Stutts, A.T. (2001) *Hotel and Lodging Management: An Introduction.* New York: John Wiley & Sons.
Tech Talk (August 2002) Hotel and Motel Management. www.hotelmotel.com

AGNES LEE DEFRANCO
UNIVERSITY OF HOUSTON, USA

Direct costs

Direct costs are expenses directly related to operations that result in menu-item production. These costs may be controllable or non-controllable in nature, but often direct costs are controllable. Direct costs in foodservice operations pertain to items such as food, labor, paper, linens, glassware, essential contractual services, etc. Costs for items such as payroll, marketing, depreciation, taxes and interest, legal fees paid, overhead, and building rent are not considered direct costs. Though these costs are important for unit operations, they are not related *directly* to production activities. Sometimes costs that are not directly related to operations are referred to collectively as 'overhead costs.'

Frequently, direct costs are analyzed to assess the effectiveness of resource utilization in an organization. A lower percentage of direct costs indicates excessive overhead and thus ineffective resource utilization. Organizations therefore tend to minimize indirect costs in order to maximize resource utilization. Greater understanding of the nature of direct costs and their role in foodservice operations is essential for maximizing unit revenues.

Reference

Coltman, Michael M. (1989) *Cost Controls for the Hospitality Industry*. New York: John Wiley & Sons.

H.G. PARSA
OHIO STATE UNIVERSITY, USA

Direct mail marketing

Direct mail marketing refers to the individualized advertising that is sent through traditional mail; the individualized component created from knowledge of the consumer through database marketing. The data on the consumer allows the marketing message to be customized to the consumer. Direct mail marketing is often called database marketing or one-to-one marketing. Direct mail marketing involves segmentation and customization.

Typically, direct marketing consists of the offer, the audience, and the promotion. The offer consists of an appealing product at an appealing price. The audience is comprised of potential or previous customers that have indicated that they are open to receiving such offers. The promotion is the benefit-oriented message sent via a particular media type. In this case, the media is mail. All direct marketing efforts should measure the response rate of an offer. By tracking the response rate, the organization sponsoring the direct marketing efforts can improve upon future marketing efforts because they know who responded, what they bought, when they bought it, and how much they spent. The database is the key factor behind direct marketing efforts.

Reference

Baier, M.B., Ruf, K.M., and Chakraborty, G. (2002) *Contemporary Database Marketing: Concepts and Applications*. Evanston, IL: Racom Communications, p. 26.

BRUMBY MCLEOD
UNIVERSITY OF NEVADA, LAS VEGAS, USA

Disciplinary action

Any management action intended to control, punish, modify or inhibit undesirable employee behavior. In some countries there are legislative provisions requiring employers to implement or adopt a fair internal grievance and disciplinary procedure (also known as procedural adequacy/fairness), while in others there is none. However, where hospitality organizations have a strong HRM focus, there is usually a formal disciplinary code or procedure to be followed. Adoption of this code has a number of advantages, including certainty for employees of what needs to be accomplished in the event of an issue arising. Also, where both employers and employees have negotiated or agreed on a set of principles, the more likely courts and tribunals will deem them to be fair. Additionally, if employees have contributed to shaping the workplace grievance procedure they will be more likely to accept outcomes without recourse to legal representation (Ntatsopoulos, 2001).

Effective disciplinary codes or procedures in the hospitality industry have three overall aims, including prompt resolution, fair and reasonable outcomes which consider the interests of all those affected, and promotion of harmony within the workplace. In many hotels, the grievance procedure forms part of the employee handbook and is an internal process. In some countries/states or industrial jurisdictions, tribunals may also play a role in resolving conflict and disciplinary issues through mediation (Woods, 2002).

References

Ntatsopoulos, J. (2001) *Australian Master Human Resources Guide 2002*. Sydney: CCH Australia Ltd.
Woods, R.H. (2002) *Managing Hospitality Human Resources*, 3rd edn. Lansing, MI: Educational Institute of the American Hotel and Lodging Association.

DARREN LEE-ROSS
JAMES COOK UNIVERSITY, AUSTRALIA

Disconfirmation theory

Disconfirmation theory involves a subjective before and after evaluation of a service after consumption. Prior to using a product or service, a consumer has certain expectations about it. These expectations become a basis against which to compare actual performance and experience. After consuming the product or experiencing the service, customers determine how well the product 'measures up' to their initial expectations and so decides whether product performance is better than, equal to or worse than expected. The extent to which perceptions of the performance or experience 'match' expectations determines the type of disconfirmation (Oliver, 1980):

- Positive disconfirmation results when perceived performance or experience exceeds expectations.
- Negative disconfirmation occurs when expectations are not met by the product or service.
- Zero disconfirmation (also, known as confirmation) ensues when performance matches expectations.

A substantial proportion of the 'hospitality experience' is comprised of intangible or service-type elements. Therefore, an understanding of this theory is of paramount importance for hospitality managers and front-line workers.

Currently, many hotels seek to 'delight' customers rather than simply ensure their expectations are matched with experiences of service delivery. In order to achieve this outcome consistently, other issues of service recovery, 'justice' and 'moments of truth' are also important. However, these notions are all underpinned by disconfirmation theory.

Reference

Oliver, R. (1980) A cognitive model of the antecedents and consequences of satisfaction decisions. *Journal of Marketing Research*, 17 (3), 460–467.

JOSEPHINE PRYCE
JAMES COOK UNIVERSITY, AUSTRALIA

Discrimination

Discrimination in the hospitality industry is based on gender, age, ethnicity, color or political opinion. Discrimination in the workplace has not always been unlawful, according to Rutherford (2002), and it was as recent as 1964 in the US that a federal statute addressed discrimination. Equal employment opportunity legislation in many countries (including the United States, the UK, Australia and New Zealand) has sought to implement anti-discrimination policies. Davidson and Griffin (2000) identify the following types of legislative discrimination approaches that are also applicable to the hospitality industry:

- *Anti-discrimination approach:* An approach that advocates equal opportunities for all people, regardless of identity difference, through the removal of discriminatory process in the workplace.
- *Direct discrimination:* Specific actions that are taken because of identity group membership (for example, where someone is refused appointment to a position based on gender or race etc.).
- *Indirect discrimination:* This results from situations where rules or practices disadvantage members of identity groups more than they do the majority group.
- *Equal employment opportunity:* The creation of conditions that allow all workers or potential applicants to have equal chance to seek and obtain employment, promotion and employment benefits.

Sexual harassment is considered to be gender-based discrimination.

References

Davidson, P. and Griffin, R.W. (2000) *Management – Australia in a Global Context*. Brisbane: John Wiley & Sons.
Rutherford, D.G. (2002) *Hotel Management and Operations*, 3rd edn. New York: John Wiley & Sons.

ASAD MOHSIN
UNIVERSITY OF WAIKATO, NEW ZEALAND

Discriminatory pricing

Contrary to common belief, discriminatory pricing has nothing to do with social biases. Discriminatory pricing is a method of setting prices at different levels based on the elasticity of demand of individual market segments. Price differentiations are not sustained by a difference in costs or quality but rather are the result of unique characteristics of individual market segments. Discriminatory pricing methods permit the charging of lower prices to price-sensitive customers and asking full prices from inelastic market segments (Kotler *et al.*, 2003). Several basic conditions have to exist in order to apply price discrimination successfully. First, various market segments must be identifiable and appreciate services differently; and, second, firms practicing price discrimination should know their costs well not only to maximize revenues but, more importantly, profits. Third, a firm should deal in perishable products, and have the ability to sell products in advance according to fluctuating demands. Finally, price discriminatory approaches must be well comprehended and accepted by the customer.

Price discriminatory methods have become standard operating procedures for many hospitality firms. For example, the hotel industry applies yield management practices to balance demand and supply by charging various room rates to different market segments. Hotels and airlines charge higher prices during peak seasons and lower prices during off-season for the same room and same plane seat leveraging the price elasticity. The same hotel company may charge less for senior citizens and may even offer a free room for children. In the restaurant industry, offering free drinks to ladies on Thursday nights is an example of discriminatory pricing. Similarly, tour operators and cruise lines offer different prices for the same tour package and cruise route depending on the duration left for the departure of a cruise ship. This practice benefits from the customers' willingness to pay higher prices for last minute plans. Customers who are willing to plan in advance often benefit from these discriminatory pricing practices. At the same time, business travelers often pay higher prices when they cannot plan too far in advance to follow the restrictions associated with the discriminatory pricing. Often organizations that offer various levels of services with the same core product or different bundled packages may use discriminatory pricing practices effectively.

Discriminatory pricing should always apply methods that are beneficial to the customers and to the hospitality firm. Therefore, firms must always offer sufficient benefits in exchange for restrictions and provide sufficient information about how to obtain price discounts.

Reference

Kotler, P., Bowen, J., and Makens, J. (2003) *Marketing for Hospitality and Tourism*, 3rd edn. Upper Saddle River, NJ: Prentice–Hall.

H.G. PARSA
THE OHIO STATE UNIVERSITY, USA
CAROLA RAAB
UNIVERSITY OF NEW HAMPSHIRE, USA

Dismissal

Wrongful dismissal (discharge or termination) includes 'unfair' and 'unlawful' dismissal. Unfair dismissal is the termination of employment deemed to be 'harsh, unjust or unreasonable' using a number of criteria expressed as questions (De Cieri and Kramar, 2003). For example, was there a valid reason for the termination, was the employee notified, were opportunities granted for employee responses to the reason and was adequate warning was given to employee to improve performance?

Unlawful termination or dismissal is deemed to be so for reasons prescribed in related legislation. Examples include dismissal on grounds of race, gender, political orientation, union membership, 'whistle blowing' etc. Unlike reemployment, reinstatement involves no loss of entitlements accrued as a result of service, as well as any earnings lost during the period that the employee was dismissed. Continuous service is maintained as if the contract of employment was not severed in the first place.

Bona fide dismissal refers to the termination of an employee according to the terms of the contract of employment or according to statute, where a valid reason exists to terminate the contract of employment or where it is illegal to continue employing the person (e.g. when the employment requires a license, qualification or accreditation, and the employee has lost it), such as a hotel employee holding a bus license for pick-up and delivery of guests. Bona fide dismissal falls into categories of 'on notice,' 'summary,' 'redundancy,' and 'retrenchment.'

Reference

De Cieri, H. and Kramar, R. (2003) *Human Resource Management in Australia: Strategy, People, Performance*. Sydney: McGraw-Hill.

NILS TIMO
GRIFFITH UNIVERSITY, AUSTRALIA

Distinctive capabilities

Distinctive capabilities are unique and integrative bundles of a firm's tangible and intangible resources that allow the firm to perform distinctive tasks or activities. These capabilities emerge over time and are central to the processes of the firm. Distinctive capabilities are derived through a complex interaction of resources and are frequently developed within functional areas or from a specific part of functional areas of the firm. A portfolio of resources and distinctive capabilities serve as a potential source of competitive advantage. Examples of functional areas include marketing, human resources, operations, finance, distribution, information systems, or research and development.

Management must identify the distinctive capabilities and resources that are essential for success when implementing and executing appropriate competitive methods. In addition, organizational structure, processes, and culture need to be supported to sustain distinctive capabilities.

Continually rising guest expectations as well as copying of capabilities by competitors makes distinctive capability a moving target for hospitality firms. Hospitality firms should continually develop and renew their distinctive capabilities as well as ensure that these capabilities are matched with appropriate competitive methods for strategic intentions to become realized.

References

Hitt, M. and Hoskisson, R. (2001) *Strategic Management: Competitiveness and Globalization*, 4th edn. Cincinnati, OH: South-Western College Publishing.
Olsen, M., Tse, E., and West, J. (1998) *Strategic Management in the Hospitality Industry*, 2nd edn. New York: John Wiley & Sons.

ROBERT HARRINGTON
NICHOLLS STATE UNIVERSITY, USA

Distribution channels

A distribution channel is the vehicle utilized to make a product or service available to the consumer. In hospitality, a successful channel management strategy consists of selling inventory at the highest possible rates, while pushing reservations through the lowest cost channels. Those are challenging tasks, which require an understanding of the wide array of distribution options available, their sales models, and how they interact.

One of the clear difficulties in discussing distribution channels is the lack of standardized definitions to describe them. The terms may overlap and the industry is not uniform in its nomenclature (Lewis and Chambers, 1999). Consequently, the reader may encounter different names to describe some of the concepts presented here. The terms 'operator' and 'supplier' will be used interchangeably to designate the supplier of the hospitality product (hotel rooms, airline tickets, rental cars, etc.).

Hospitality distribution channels

In hospitality, particularly in the lodging industry, the traditional main distribution channels were the call center and the travel agencies. Over time, other channels were created. For the most part, these new channels acted as intermediaries between the property and the global distribution system (GDS)/travel agent. The advent of the Internet led to profound changes in hospitality distribution. New business models were created, as well as online-based reservations networks, which allowed worldwide exposure to products while avoiding intermediaries such as the GDSs. For detail on this important and complex matter in today's hospitality environment see the section on 'Internet Channels.' An overview of the various channels is presented next.

Call center

This is a central location phone bank, also called *central reservation office* (CRO). In its simplest form, it consists of a telephone and a reservation agent. Generally, call centers have the ability to place multiple reservations at the same time through central computer reservation systems (CRSs), usually through an 800 number. Hotel companies may have call centers that serve many different properties within the corporation. Airlines and car rental companies usually have one centralized call center in each of the different countries where they operate, all interlinked through the CRSs. Centralized call centers have the advantage of providing consistent service and decreasing the company's costs, such as management and training. Multi-branded companies, however, may have different call centers and, in some cases, different CRSs within their system, mostly due to mergers and acquisitions.

The term 'CRS reservations' is sometimes used to refer to the reservations originating from the call center, even though the CRS serves as an intermediary between most other channels and the property management system (PMS). There are companies that provide third party call centers (e.g. Utell), which may handle all incoming calls or overflowing calls in periods of high demand. They may also provide central reservation services for companies that do not have their own CRS.

Global distribution systems

These are technologies that allow worldwide real-time distribution. A global distribution system

(GDS) contains a database with information on travel products (air, hotel, rental car, etc.), such as schedules, prices, availability, and descriptions. Users are able to access information as well as book and/or purchase the hospitality products. As explained by Burns (2000), 'The GDS originated as private networks listing only air flights for use by travel agents. In the . . . years since their inception, they have grown to serve a worldwide clientele who use nearly 500,000 access points with a full array of travel services.'

The four major GDS systems are Sabre, Galileo/Apollo, Amadeus, and Worldspan. Those systems, however, were built on older technological platforms and do not interface directly with most property management systems (PMSs). Intermediaries, the switching companies, provide interfaces between the suppliers and the GDSs. The supplier pays fees per reservation to a GDS and to the switching companies. Because accessing information from a GDS requires a physical GDS terminal and specific training in codes and search techniques, the GDSs are usually used by travel agents and not by the end consumer (Ader *et al.*, 2000). Some operators used the term GDS to refer to the travel agents, mostly because they used to be the main users of the GDSs.

Travel agents

Travel agents act as intermediaries between the customer and the supplier. The role of the travel agent is to provide information to the customer as well as to effectuate the booking and purchase of the hospitality product. Examples of travel agents are Carlson Travel, Thomas Cook, and International Leisure Corporation. They access rates and place reservations in a variety of ways. The most common is through a global distribution system (GDS). Travel agents may also contact a property directly, through wholesalers, or by accessing the Internet. The traditional travel agents are also referred to as 'brick-and-mortar' travel agents. Travel agents typically work on commission, i.e., they sell rooms at a negotiated rate or at the prevailing rate, and receive a percentage of the sale from the suppliers.

Meeting planners, group travel agents, and corporate travel agents

Meeting planners and group travel agents, also simply called 'third parties' or 'third party meeting planners,' are companies that specialize in providing business travel services, such as meeting planning, incentive travel, and convention services. Their roles may overlap, but generally these third parties prescreen hotels, negotiate rates, and organize events, working with travel agents or acting as specialized travel agents in order to cater to corporate group travel needs. Examples of third parties are Carlson Marketing Group, PGI HRT, and Krisam. Corporate travel agents perform similar roles, but they are part of a corporation (e.g. American Express, Sony, etc.) and attend exclusively to the corporation needs.

National, state, and local tourism agencies

These agencies promote tourism in certain geographic areas. They may be sponsored by the state or constitute business associations with the common goal of providing information and promoting travel in certain regions. Tourist agencies advertise resources, tourist attractions, and help customers to plan their trips providing maps, guides, and effectuating bookings, generally though destination management systems (DMSs). They are usually located either in strategic target markets (e.g. the Spanish Office of Tourism, in Los Angeles) or in entrance or strategic points (e.g. the Los Angeles Convention and Visitors Bureau).

Tour operators and wholesalers

According to Lewis and Chambers (1999), tour operators and wholesalers differ from the previous channels in that they take nominal possession, or secure an allotment, of the suppliers inventory to sell to the public. Wholesalers, also called consolidators, can often negotiate for deeply discounted rates because they buy large volumes or have access to a surplus inventory of deeply discounted tickets and hotel rooms that

they are free to sell at slightly marked-up prices. Their advance purchase agreements for hotel rooms also mean that consolidators are often able to provide inventory when other resources list products as sold out. The wholesalers obtain rates and availability directly from the supplier and create packages with different accommodation and transportation options, such as airlines, cruise lines, railroads, car rentals, and bus companies, which are sold directly to the consumer or through travel agents. Examples of wholesalers are America West, GoGo Tours, and Mark Travel.

Tour operators offer discounted packages, which may include meals and tours, and may specialize in certain markets or destinations. Motorcoach tours are typical tour operator products. The Japanese Tourist Bureau (JTB) is an example of a tour operator.

Consortia, affiliations, and reservation companies

These are associations with common marketing efforts. In the United States, the term 'consortia' normally refers to a conglomerate of travel agencies. In some other countries, particularly in Europe, 'consortia' refer to entities that provide chains or individually owned and operated hotels with access to global distribution systems and representation services, acting as intermediaries between the supplier and the travel agents. Affiliations and reservation companies have similar roles. However, as Lewis and Chambers (1999) explain, the strength of the association and entry requirements may vary among consortia, affiliations, and reservation companies. Membership in a consortium is a quality statement. The properties become associated to a third party brand and there are entry requirements, even though the hotels still keep an individualized image. An example of a consortium is the 'Leading Hotels of the World.' There are also entry requirements and certain consistency among the members in affiliations. The hotel name, however, is secondary, and the affiliation brand becomes the flagship for the members. Best Western Hotels is an example of an affiliation. There are virtually no entry requirements for reservation companies. Hotel companies use reservation services when they wish to delegate GDS distribution and reservation processing, as well as broad Internet distribution, to a third party. Unirez, Utell, and TRUST International are examples of reservation companies. Most reservation companies are also known as representation companies, because they usually provide representation services.

Representation companies

These companies act as sales organizations, representing hotels through their sales force, the representatives, in regional offices located in different geographical areas. Representation companies eliminate the supplier's need for establishing sales offices in certain markets. European Hotels Representation and David Green Organization are examples of representation companies. A special case of representatives are the 'junket reps,' individuals who have a casino clientele and work with casinos that are promoting gambling trips. Junket reps are particularly active in international markets.

Internet channels

These channels involve the online dispersal and purchase of travel products, and include Internet counterparts of the traditional channels. These companies interact with the customer in different ways, forming complex and dynamic distribution arrangements. The online reservation environment has two major players: hotel companies and third party travel companies. Most dot-commers currently use the so-called 'merchant model,' which consists of a certain mark-up over rates to sell rooms in lieu of commissions and fixed fees used in traditional GDS-based channels. Internet channels also use innovative sales strategies, such as 'name your own price auctions' and opaque models. For further details see 'Internet Channels.'

References

Ader, J.N., LaFeur, R.A., and Falcone, M.J. (2000) *Internet Travel*. New York: Bear Sterns Equity Research.

Buhalis, D. and Laws, E. (2001) *Tourism Distribution Channels*. London: Thomson.

Burns, J. (2000) Understanding and maximizing a hotel's electronic distribution options. *Hospitality Update*. Retrieved 10 May 2004, from http://www.hotel-online.com/News/PressReleases2000_4th/Oct00_ElectronicDistrib.html

Hotel Consolidators (n.d.). Retrieved 10 May 2004, from http://www.freetraveltips.com/Online/Hotel_Consolidator.htm

Kotler, P., Bowen, J., and Makens, J. (1999) *Marketing for Hospitality and Tourism*, 2nd edn. Upper Saddler River, NJ: Prentice-Hall.

Lewis, R.C. and Chambers, R. (1999) *Marketing Leadership in Hospitality: Foundations and Practices*. New York: John Wiley & Sons.

FLAVIA HENDLER
UNIVERSITY OF NEVADA, LAS VEGAS, USA
ROM HENDLER
VENETIAN RESORT HOTEL AND CASINO,
LAS VEGAS, USA

Distribution channels in foodservice

In the United States, food away from home generates over $400 billion in sales a year (National Restaurant Association, 2004). In order to generate these sales, operators purchase over $170 billion in products from their distributors (Dlahoba, 2002). Foodservice supply chain members procure, move, and transform raw materials into products and services for foodservice customers. The relationships among supply chain members are key to the efficient movement of product.

A supply chain is the network of internal and external functions and processes that are associated with procuring, moving, and transforming basic raw materials into a product or service for an end-user. In the restaurant industry this means getting food products from farmers and processors to manufacturers, consolidators, and brokers, who distribute their products to wholesalers and distributors, who in turn deliver the products to individual restaurant operators. An integral part of the supply chain is the flow of information among all members of the distribution network (Figure 1).

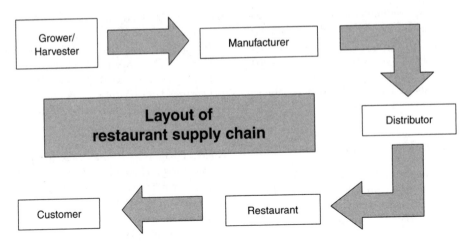

Figure 1 Restaurant supply chain

Restaurant operators typically order from at least one broadline distributor, who sells multiple product types. In addition, operators purchase specialty items from local beverage, alcohol, produce, dairy, meat, and seafood distributors. Office and restaurant supplies and cleaning and paper products may also be ordered through separate specialized vendors.

Broadline distributors order and stock up to 180,000 different products, but the individual distribution centers (DCs) may stock only 5000–10,000 items (Norkus and Merberg, 1994). The purchasing department of a large distributor must procure products from hundreds of different manufacturers, consolidators, and brokers. They accumulate orders from multiple restaurant operators to place accurate orders with each of their suppliers. Wholesalers, consolidators, and brokers purchase products directly from manufacturers and from each other. Distributors negotiate with vendors successfully when they can develop accurate product order history and compute more accurate forecasts for as many of their customers as possible. Many broadline distributors have also developed their own brands that compete directly with manufacturers' products. These products are then marketed to foodservice operators at lower prices than traditional 'name-brand' products.

Manufacturers represent the next stage in the supply chain. They transform raw ingredients purchased from farmers and processors into products for sale to foodservice distributors. Since many food commodities are seasonal, manufacturers may forward-buy some products to ensure lower prices and availability. With the onset of rapid and inexpensive international transportation, many commodities can be procured year-round. Manufacturers must take these long-term storage, processing, and transportation costs into account when pricing these products for distributors.

The final stage in the supply chain is the farmer or rancher. Large conglomerates that manage multiple locations and have greater economies of scale have purchased many of the small family farms in the US. Those that remain receive subsidies from the government to ensure an adequate and stable supply of certain products for US consumption. By concentrating power in the hands of a few large companies, manufacturers and processors are losing their flexibility to negotiate when purchasing raw ingredients.

Trading on commodity markets like the Chicago Mercantile Exchange determines the prices for many raw ingredients, such as butter, cheese, chicken, and beef. Some prices are determined using a derivative formula. Traders, who never take possession of product, make money when markets are volatile, so prices tend to change frequently based on the trader's perception of supply and demand.

Pricing of produce is based on the quality of and demand for each product. There is a difference between a produce grower and produce harvester. The growers plant the seeds, take care of the crop while it is in the ground, and make sure it is of the highest quality; the harvesters remove the product from the ground and pack it for shipment. Many growers do not harvest their own crops because the equipment for this task is very specialized and expensive.

The relationship between restaurant operators and their major distributors is usually adversarial. Operators haggle for reduced prices. Distributors attempt to gain a larger and more profitable portion of the operators' business. Restaurant operators have three main objectives in developing a relationship with a distributor: price, service, and quality. In determining the pricing structure for a specific restaurant, distributors must consider the average order size, the distance and ease of service between the warehouse and the restaurant, the frequency of deliveries required, and the payment reliability of the restaurant operator. The level of service the distributor can provide is based on size and number of delivery windows, site delivery requirements (such as unloading into specific areas of storage, stairs or elevators), order size, the order-entry mechanism (such as fax, phone, or electronic) and rebate recovery programs available. Finally, product condition, yield, and consistency measure the quality of the products delivered to the restaurant operator.

Restaurant operators and broadline distributors operate on a 'cost-plus' basis. Volume, frequency, and speed of delivery determine the 'plus' portion of the arrangement. Operators who negotiate this type of contract gain access to the 'invoice cost' of manufacturers' products. They then pay distributors a specified premium on this invoice cost for the majority of their purchases.

When independent operators begin relationships with broadline distributors, they become 'street' accounts for sales representatives. Sales representatives are compensated based on gross profit generated for the distributor. If operators agree to purchase 70–80% of their products from a given distributor, the operator will qualify as a 'program' or primary vendor account. Street accounts and program accounts qualify for different cost-plus arrangements and are managed very differently by distributors. A street account might receive a cost-plus 35% arrangement, while a primary vendor account may receive a cost-plus 8–14% arrangement. Distributors receive higher margins from restaurant operators when the average order size is reatively small. Distributors also receive higher margins on lower cost-per-case products compared to more expensive products, even though the dollar amount per case might be the same.

References

Dlahoba, Ihor (2002) Despite calamities, the industry grows: The ID Top 50. *ID*, March, 24–60.

National Restaurant Association and Deloitte & Touche (2004) *2004 Restaurant Industry Forecast*. Washington, DC: National Restaurant Association.

Norkus, Gregory X. and Merberg, Elliot (1994) Food distribution in the 1990s. *Cornell Hotel and Restaurant Administration Quarterly*, 35 (3), 50–63.

DEBORAH BARRASH
UNIVERSITY OF NEVADA, LAS VEGAS, USA

District heating/cooling plants

Some municipalities have heating and/or cooling plants with large loops running through the downtown part of the city. For example, steam, hot water, and sometimes chilled water from one central plant is run through the city loop and is delivered to many buildings that do not have their own central plants. Instead, each building on the loop relies upon heat or cold from these central plants to provide building services. Using a district plant reduces a hotel's first cost during new construction or when an existing heating or cooling plant requires replacement. See also Combined Heat and Power Cogeneration.

References

District Heating & Cooling. http://www.chp-info.org/content.html

International District Energy Association http://www.districtenergy.org/

JIM ACKLES
THARALDSON ENERGY GROUP, USA

Diversification

Within strategic management, diversification research most likely constitutes the largest single area of focused activity. Diversification refers to changes in a firm's scope of operations in terms of products/services offered and markets served. More precisely, it refers to a movement *away* from the original technology used and/or types of customers targeted. The primary focus of research in this area has been the relationship between diversification and economic performance. More specifically, do more diversified firms perform better or worse than less diversified firms?

While interest in diversification has been driven by observations as to the nature of the growth and rise of large corporations, it has also been fuelled by the two major waves of acquisitions and mergers in the 1960s and 1970s in the United States and elsewhere. The outcome of this activity was the creation of large conglomerates with varied interests across a wide range of industries. This led consultancy firms such as the Boston Consulting Group to develop analysis tools such as the growth/share matrix to specifically address the increased complexity faced by executives of diversified firms.

Chandler's (1962) study of the relationship between strategy and structure represents the earliest study that examined diversification as a growth strategy, with the emphasis here being on the effects on organizational structure. However, the first formal attempt to coherently map this process was Ansoff's (1965) product/market matrix (although he used the term 'missions' instead of markets), which differentiated between horizontal, concentric, conglomerate, and vertical diversification using the concepts of degrees of newness in markets served and the degree of relatedness of the underlying technology used.

More recently, these forms of diversification were categorized as different types of corporate level strategies. Specifically, if a hospitality organization prefers to remain within the core business even during penetration into the global arena, it will be classified as a business level concentration strategy. If, on the other hand, the decision calls for entering unrelated areas of service or production while maintaining the hospitality core operation as a relatively independent unit (SBU), then it would be considered a corporate level diversification strategy. The diversification into different realms of business activity is often presented as a means of lowering risk. Clearly, relying only on the hospitality segment in case of a sharp change of consumer preferences or geopolitical crises could result in a major threat to the survival of the organization. Diversifying into other industries is thus expected to carry the hospitality subunit through the crisis or declining demand periods. The degree of relatedness determines the classification of the diversification strategy as either 'concentric' or 'conglomerate.' While concentric diversification is expected to utilize shared knowledge of related industries held by the organization executives and employees, conglomerate diversification is designed to present corporate level executives with the opportunity or challenge of demonstrating their abilities to utilize managerial acumen in diverse products or services in different market segments and environments.

A growth strategy through concentric diversification into a related industry is considered when the organization has a strong competitive position, but industry attractiveness is low. Diversification of hospitality organization into the catering or restaurant sectors can be viewed as 'concentric' when the customer base is similar and the organization utilizes its proven strengths in the hospitality business to secure the appropriate competitive position in related industries. Concentric diversification often constitutes a search for synergy, the concept that success in several related businesses will be greater than the sum of success in each operation separately. Managerial know-how, appropriate service orientation of employees or marketing distribution channels that are applied to two or more related businesses may contribute to the creation of synergy for the diversification of the hospitality organization. As a service-based industry, it seems that the quality and expertise of hospitality organizations may serve as an inimitable resource that can contribute to the creation of synergy and to the success of a well-designed concentric diversification strategy.

In the 1970s, using secondary data about diversification – building upon Chandler's theme of the relationship between strategy and structure – doctoral work by Scott, Wrigley, Rumelt, Thanheiser, and Channon represents a significant stage in the development of strategic management (Spender, 2001). In addition to establishing an emphasis upon quantitative methods and the topic of diversification, it marked a shift away from the earlier focus on the needs of practitioners and the adoption into mainstream strategic management of microeconomic concepts such as rational, profit maximizing decision-makers, full information and equilibrium theory.

With the emergence of the 'resource-based view' in the 1980s, strategy scholars once again turned to the topic of diversification. Wernerfelt and Montgomery (1988) produced empirical evidence demonstrating that firms with more closely focused operations (i.e. less diversified) performed better than diversified firms. Research by Chandler (1990) claimed that the lower performance of diversified firms was a result of a breakdown of communications and loss of control. This, he argued, was due to management having insufficient product-specific knowledge of the divisions under their control. As such, this would tend to support Penrose's (1959) contention that resource relatedness is critical in supporting successful growth through diversification.

From the 1980s onwards there has been a shift in corporate behavior towards an emphasis on managing related businesses. In the hospitality sector examples include ITT's divestment of the Sheraton chain and Forte's unsuccessful defense strategy of the Granada takeover bid which involved a proposal for the radical separation of its restaurant concerns from those of its hotel portfolio on the grounds that a 'pure' hotel-based strategy would result in superior performance. However, diversification activity remained evident during the 1990s, with the growth strategies of both Whitbread plc (UK) and Bass (now Intercontinental plc) in the hospitality sector representing explicit efforts to diversify their interests away from a traditional reliance on a core business of brewing. It remains to be seen whether diversification will once again become a significant issue in corporate development in future years.

References

Ansoff, H.I. (1965) *Corporate Strategy*. New York: McGraw-Hill.

Chandler, A.D. (1962) *Strategy and Structure: Chapters in the History of the American Industrial Enterprise*. Boston, MA: MIT Press.

Chandler, A.D. (1990) *Scale and Scope: The Dynamics of Industrial Capitalism*. Cambridge, MA: Harvard University Press.

Penrose, E. (1959) *The Theory of the Growth of the Firm*. Oxford: Blackwell.

Spender, J.-C. (2001) Business policy and strategy as a professional field, in H.W. Volberda and T. Elfring (eds), *Rethinking Strategy*. London: Sage, pp. 26–40.

Wernerfelt, B. and Montgomery, C.A. (1988) Tobin's q and the importance of focus in firm performance. *American Economic Review*, 78 (1), 246–250.

J. STEPHEN TAYLOR
UNIVERSITY OF STRATHCLYDE, UK

Domain name

All websites have a Web address of the form (e.g.) http://www.hilton.com. In this case, hilton.com is the domain name. The first part of the address shows that the information is to be transferred using HyperText Transfer Protocol, and it is part of the World Wide Web. Domain names always end with the name of a top level domain – in this case '.com' indicating that this is a commercial site. Other top level domains indicate either a country (e.g. uk for the UK) or a type of site (e.g. .edu for a US education institution). For a list of the possible top level domains, see http://www.webopedia.com.

One can register a domain name through a range of agencies (go to www.google.com and search for Domain Name Registration). It is possible to register any domain name you wish, provided nobody else has previously registered it. Domain name registrations are not permanent, and expire after a fixed period of time. Some people register a domain name similar to the name of a famous organization (e.g. www.mcdonalds.net) in the hope of being able to sell the name later. This process is known as cyber-squatting.

References

Nielsen, J.J. (ed.) (2000) *The Internet All In One Desk Reference for Dummies*. New York: Hungry Minds.

O'Connor, P. (2000) *Using Computers in Hospitality*, 2nd edn. London: Cassell.

JOHN NIGHTINGALE
LEEDS METROPOLITAN UNIVERSITY, UK

Downsizing

Downsizing involves a deliberate reduction in the size of the permanent workforce in response to declining demand, a merger or acquisition (i.e., which has resulted in redundancies), increased operational efficiencies, or pressure to reduce labor costs. Downsizing strategies include termination and layoffs (in which employees are forced to leave on either a permanent or temporary basis) and enhanced attrition (in which employees are provided with incentives to voluntarily depart). In unionized environments terminations and layoffs are typically based on seniority, but may also be based on position or skill set (i.e., particularly in the case of redundancies or skill obsolescence). In many jurisdictions, severance pay must be provided to compensate for the termination of the employment contract. In contrast to these forced strategies, enhanced attrition involves incentivizing employees to reduce their hours, take an unpaid leave of absence, quit, or retire. Such incentives may include offering departure bonuses, outplacement services, and in the case of early retirement programs, enhancements to pensions and medical benefits. While downsizing can provide the organization with short-term cost savings, it can also result in lost expertise and organizational memory deficits, reductions in loyalty and productivity, and work overload and increased stress for those who remain. Increased selection and training costs can also be incurred once business volumes resume.

Reference

Armstrong, M. (2001) *A Handbook of Personnel Management Practice*, 8th edn. London and Milford, CT: Kogan Page.

JULIA CHRISTENSEN HUGHES
UNIVERSITY OF GUELPH, CANADA

Drayage

Drayage is the term used to encompass the activities of delivery of exhibit materials from the dock to an assigned exhibit space, removing empty crates, returning crates at the end of show for re-crating, and delivering materials back to dock for carrier loading. It entails the labor and equipment necessary to move a shipment, including the storage of empty cartons and crates for the duration of the event. Drayage can be as simple as having a hotel bellman unload a car and take exhibit materials to the hotel ballroom or as complex as unloading products and exhibits using specialized labor and equipment, such as dollies or forklifts. Drayage is provided by the official show contractor and often involves minimum time labor calls and/or equipment rentals, so it can become very expensive. Information must be obtained from the facility as to the maximum size and weight of packages that they will accept, as well as elevator, loading dock and door measurements, and floor load capacities. On site storage facilities can be a hotel package room or a remote warehouse or marshalling yard, where shipments are kept until delivered to the facility on move-in day. Crate storage areas during show days are called *boneyards*.

References

APEX Glossary. http://glossary.conventionindus-try.org/

Krug, S., Chatfield-Taylor, C., and Collins, M. (eds) (1994) *The Convention Industry Council Manual*, 7th edn. McLean, VA: The Convention Industry Council.

GEORGE FENICH
UNIVERSITY OF NEW ORLEANS, USA

Duty of care

In Australia and a few other countries of British heritage, the term refers to the employer's duty towards others, as recognized by common law, to take reasonable care for the safety of others usually in the form of:

• Provision of a safe workplace
• Provision of a safe system of work
• Provision and maintenance of safe plant and equipment
• Provision of competent staff to manage and supervise the business.

The duty of care is part of the common law known as tort (the tort of negligence). Negligence is associated with causing another person injury or harm unintentionally but carelessly. Evidence necessary for establishing a breach of the duty of care include:

• The risk was foreseeable
• There was a reasonably practicably means of avoiding the risk and it was preventable
• The person suffered a foreseeable injury
• The employer owed a duty of care and the failure to eliminate the risk showed a lack of reasonable care.

The questions of what constitutes 'reasonable' is determined by reference to community standards and expectations. Furthermore, the risk of injury must be 'real' rather than fanciful and the employer must have failed to take reasonable steps (De Cieri and Kramar, 2003). Implications of occupational health and safety issues for the hospitality industry are significant, especially relating to equipment safety in food preparation areas and the overall condition of internal fixtures and fittings used by customers (electrics, floor coverings etc.).

Reference

De Cieri, H. and Kramar, R. (2003) *Human Resource Management in Australia: Strategy, People, Performance*. Sydney: McGraw-Hill.

NILS TIMO
GRIFFITH UNIVERSITY, AUSTRALIA

E

Earnings per share

The earnings per share ratio is considered to be an important measure of corporate performance and is normally required to be shown in the published profit and loss account for a business:

$$\text{Earnings per share} = \frac{\text{Profit after interest and tax}}{\text{Number of ordinary shares in issue}}$$

Alternatively it can be explained as the net profit attributable to each ordinary share in issue. When preference shares have been issued the preference dividend is subtracted from the profit after interest and tax. The more equity increases, in terms of the number of shares issued, the greater the dilution of the earnings per share. This would indicate that additional funding from loan sources would serve to improve the resulting earnings per share value. Although this is true, it should be remembered that loan finance carries its own risks, associated with the commitment to pay interest and the repayment of the capital sum. Increases in earnings per share can be achieved by reinvesting annual earnings to achieve an increase in profit without the requirement for additional shares to be issued.

Earnings per share tends to reflect the degree of profit stability experienced by organizations. Therefore, in the case of businesses with high operating leverages, fluctuating demand and resultant profit instability, such as hotels, earnings per share is inclined to be relatively volatile.

References

Dyson, J.R. (2003) *Accounting for Non-accounting Students*. London: FT Prentice-Hall.

Schmidgall, R.S. (2002) *Hospitality Industry Managerial Accounting*, 5th edn. Lansing, MI: Educational Institute of the American Hotel and Lodging Association.

DEBRA ADAMS
ARENA4FINANCE LTD, UK

Economies of scale

The term *economies of scale* refers to a firm's ability to reduce the cost of producing one unit of goods or services as the volume of production increases. Mass production and economies of scale were central concepts in the development of modern economic theory. In his book *An Inquiry into the Nature and Causes of the Wealth of Nations* (1776), Adam Smith, a Scottish economist and philosopher, laid the foundations of mass production and economies of scale. According to Smith's theory, scale economies and economies of scale are requirements for success in post-industrial revolution economic markets.

Most classifications of economies of scale focus on two major categories: real economies and pecuniary economies. The former refers to the physical dimension, meaning the ability to increase capacity without increasing fixed costs. The latter refers to the financial dimension, the ability to lower the prices that the firm pays for its inputs. This broad categorization can be further subdivided into production economies, technical economies, marketing economies, and others. The outcome of economies of scale is a decrease in unit cost, because more units are produced at the same (fixed) cost. Economies of scale are an important component of firm efficiency and success. Firms with a lower cost structure can offer their goods and service at a more competitive price and thus ultimately improve their performance.

Economies of scale became a leading philosophy in modern economic societies. This philosophy argues that in order to become efficient and competitive, organizations will have to adopt scale economics, grow large, and thus further reduce production cost and per unit cost. As a result, businesses will be able to provide goods and services at a competitive price and, at the same time, maintain a profit margin. History has shown that the concept of economies of scale (or scale economics) has become critical to survival in certain industries. The automobile industry, for example, relies heavily on economies of scale for competitive pricing and, therefore, economies of scale serve as an entry barrier to new competition. Firms in the automobile industry with limited economies of scale could not compete in the industry, because their unit cost would be high relative to the competition.

In the hospitality industry economies of scale can originate from different sources. For example, economies of scale can result from the ability to share marketing and sales infrastructure for increasing capacity. A central reservation system (CRS) might serve as an example for economies of scale. When a CRS has been implemented, the infrastructure is shared by a large number of hotels, thus reducing the per unit cost of a reservation (Burns, 1997; Coyne and Burns, 1996). Economies of scale in the hospitality industry can also result from the utilization of central management teams, acquisition of raw materials, and production and labor utilization. As noted by Israeli and Uriely (2000), the ability to achieve economies of scale is one of the primary factors behind the formation of large corporations in the hospitality industry. Therefore, the majority of high-end hotels have a large room capacity which can, with appropriate management control, create a situation of economies of scale. Specifically, a large hotel can distribute its fixed costs across a large number of rooms. Consequently, the cost per room is lower than average, and potential profit margin is high.

Despite the appealing nature of economies of scale and the potential benefits they may generate for firms, there are some cases in which the process of economies of scale is reversed or not applicable. One example is provided by Arnold (1994), who investigated the lodging industry before, during and after the Gulf War in 1991. Generally, the dominant strategy of hotels was to utilize economies of scale. However, between 1989 and 1991, in the period prior to the Gulf War and during the war itself, hotels experienced an increase in operating profits that was faster than either inflation or revenues. It would not be illogical to expect the industry to be satisfied with those results. However, the analysis of operating profitability per occupied room indicated one reason that the industry has been suffering. The fear of losing market share caused hotels to use a strategy of cutting room rates in an effort to induce travel and increase occupancy. While expenses have increased at the rate of inflation, the strategy of reducing rates has led not to economies of scale, but to a converse situation. While hotels have managed to increase their total income, incremental profit margin per occupied room has been shrinking. Furthermore, rate cutting has proven problematic, as it has not supported the ability to generate benefits from economies of scale.

Another example is a study by Poorani and Smith (1995), which demonstrated that the bed and breakfast (B&B) sector is another interesting exception in the context of economies of scale. Improving profitability has been a key issue in the hospitality industry, and economies of scale are an important component in that effort. In contrast to the hospitality industry, the B&B sector is characterized by innkeepers who choose innkeeping as either a second career or as a way to satisfy personal career goals. Consequently, while economies of scale are practically a prerequisite for profitability in the hospitality industry, in the B&B sector profitability may not be the primary reason for operation, and thus economies of scale are not a prerequisite for success.

References

Arnold, D. (1994) Profits and prices: a lodging analysis. *Cornell Hotel and Restaurant Administration Quarterly* 35 (1), 30–33.

Burns, J.D. (1997) Getting the most out of CRS and GDS. *Hotel & Motel Management*, 21, 38, 48.

Coyne, R.M. and Burns, J.D. (1996) Global connectivity. *Hotel & Motel Management*, 211, 28–29.

Israeli, A. and Uriely, N. (2000) The impact of star ratings and corporate affiliation on hotel room prices. *Tourism and Hospitality Research*, 2 (1), 27–36.

Poorani, A.A. and Smith, D.R. (1995) Financial characteristics of bed-and-breakfast inns. *Cornell Hotel and Restaurant Administration Quarterly*, 36 (5), 57–63.

AVIAD ISRAELI
BEN-GURION UNIVERSITY, ISRAEL

redundant facilities and personnel. Furthermore, the mergers increased the product and service offerings and thus strengthened the economies of scope of the merged firms. Improved financial performance, which was partially attributed to economies of scope, was also identified.

References

Canina, L. (2001) Acquisitions in the lodging industry – good news for buyers and sellers. *Cornell Hotel and Restaurant Administration Quarterly*, 42 (6), 47–54.

Lynch, R. (2003) *Corporate Strategy*. New York: Prentice-Hall.

AVIAD ISRAELI
BEN-GURION UNIVERSITY, ISRAEL

Economies of scope

The term refers to the ability to join resources and produce two or more distinct products or services from the same company compared with providing them from two different companies (Lynch, 2003, p. 496). The result is a lower product cost, as all the products are produced at the same (fixed) cost.

In the hospitality industry economies of scope can originate from strategic alliances, joint ventures or mergers. For example, consider a hospitality company that forms a strategic alliance with a car rental company. As part of this alliance, the companies use the same central reservation system (CRS) to support both hotel and car reservations. Consequently, reservation cost of hotel rooms and rental cars generate a joint reservations system and a general cost reduction in reservations transactions.

Strategic alliances, joint ventures, and mergers are gaining popularity in the hospitality industry (Canina, 2001). In 1993 only two mergers occurred in the American hospitality industry, and their total value was about $30 million. In 1998, the number rose to 11 mergers, valued at $25 billion. The findings suggest that these mergers generally reduce costs by eliminating

Efficiency ratios

In addition to understanding profitability, the other key aspect of overall organizational performance is efficient use of resources and assets. Asset turnover or asset utilization contributes to overall performance (measured by ROCE) in combination with Net Profit/Sales Revenue ratio.

The asset turnover or *asset utilization* ratio is therefore a key measure of effectiveness; it relates the assets employed in the business to the income or sales revenues generated from the use of those assets. It reflects the intensity with which assets are employed or used, and as such, it gives an indication of the productivity of the business.

Sales revenue ÷ Total Assets, represented as number of times
e.g. £350,000 ÷ £222,000 = 1.58 = 1.6 times

This ratio is expressed as *times per annum*, which means the number of times the asset value is turned over in a year, but it can more easily be interpreted as the value of sales revenue generated from each £ invested in assets. In the example above the company is generating £1.6 of sales from every pound invested in assets.

If an organization has low ratios of sales to assets it is implied that some substantial under-utilization of assets is occurring. However, as with profitability, the level of utilization will vary between different sectors of the industry, for example, city center full service hotels will have a much lower utilization ratio when compared to a budget hotel operation; this of course will be counteracted by higher profitability. Asset utilization is arguably a prime determinant of the level of future profits. However, it is important to observe this ratio as a trend, as factors such as large capital investment projects which will lead to improved service quality can diminish the ratio score, and sustained under-investment in the assets of the business will improve this ratio but to the detriment of the business profitability long term. More specific ratios can be used to explain trends in the asset utilization ratios, such as occupancy percent and RevPAR (revenue per available room). Further analysis is also possible to understand how effectively different classes of assets are being used by evaluating fixed asset turnover, inventory turnover, and accounts receivable turnover, the latter two being part of the working capital.

Fixed asset turnover is similar to asset utilization, but only includes fixed assets. This ratio enables the isolation of short-term assets and liabilities from the overall picture of productivity. It is calculated as:

Sales Revenue ÷ Average Fixed Assets, represented as number of times
e.g. £350,000 ÷ £196,000 = 1.78 = 1.8 times

The final two ratios in this section help explain the overall picture of productivity but are focused on short-term assets and effective management of working capital.

Inventory turnover (stock turnover) measures the average speed by which stock (or inventory) is bought and sold, in other words, how long on average an organization holds stock before selling it. Stock turnover can be expressed in two ways: times per annum or number of days. It is

calculated as:

Cost of Sales ÷ Average Stock = Stock Turnover, represented as number of times
e.g. £140,000 ÷ 9635 = 14.5 = 14 times

This can be converted to days by dividing it into the number of days in the year:

e.g. 365 ÷ 14.5 = 25.1 = 25 days

When interpreting this ratio it is important to remember that different types of stock will have different lifespans and it is normal, for example, for food stock turnover to be much faster than beverage, which has a longer shelf life.

Accounts receivable turnover (this is also called *debtor turnover* or *debtor collection period*), measures the length of time it takes for an organization to collect the money from its customers. It provides an indication of the efficiency of the accounts receivable (debtors) department and reflects the nature of the customer base. The mix of different types of customers, i.e. cash or credit, business or private, their terms of business, and the speed by which they pay, will all be factors in this ratio. It is calculated as follows and can be presented in two ways:

Credits Sales ÷ Average Debtors,
e.g. 100,000 ÷ 23,800 = 4.2016 = 4.2 times

This can be converted to days by dividing it into the number of days in the year:

e.g. 365 ÷ 4.2 = 86.9 = 89 days

It is important with all ratios to evaluate this ratio as part of a trend, and to understand the factors that contribute to improved or diminished performance.

References

Adams, D. (1997) *Management Accounting for the Hospitality Industry: A Strategic Approach*. London: Cassell.

Jagels, M. and Coltman, M. (2003) *Hospitality Management Accounting*, 8th edn. New York: John Wiley & Sons.

Glautier, M.W.E. and Underdown, B. (1997) *Accounting Theory and Practice*, 6th edn. London: Pitman Publishing.

Harris, P. (1999) *Profit Planning*, 2nd edn. Oxford: Butterworth-Heinemann.

HELEN ATKINSON
UNIVERSITY OF BRIGHTON, UK

Eighty-six

The number '86' is fundamental to the rich food-service vernacular. Chapman (1998) explains that the numerical expression was made popular by short-order cooks to inform food servers they were out of a specific dish. Hence, after the last slice of cherry pie was served, the cooks would yell, '86 cherry pie!'

The terms is also applied when customers are asked to leave a bar or restaurant. Typically as the result of behavior associated with intoxication, a manager may tell the bartender to '86' the guest in question. The term has extended to use in other sectors, too. The military, for example, uses the term to mean eliminate or destroy ('86 the enemy's headquarters'). It is evident in contemporary colloquialism where it is used as a slang term to denote the end of a relationship ('My girlfriend just 86'd me.')

Given the term's ubiquity, its origins are interesting. Some assert that it stems from the original specifications for grave digging: '8' feet long and '6' feet deep. Another belief is that the first chain steakhouse, Delmonico's, had a very popular item that was listed as number 86 on the menu and frequently sold out. While Delmonico's is credited with having the first printed menu in the US, this explanation is questionable since the menu was not that long and, according to records, did not have numbers next to items.

Perhaps the most likely explanation dates back to prohibition. Many believe the term had one of the following three origins. The first pertains to a street-car line that ran from 14th to 86th, where '86th' was the end of the line. Another relates to a bar with a backdoor opening onto 86th Street. When a raid was imminent, the operator would yell '86' to instruct everyone to leave using the back exit. Similarly, Chumley's Bar at 86 Bedford St in New York City is reputed to have been a popular – albeit illegal – drinking establishment. At the threat of a raid, the word was spread to leave '86.'

Reference

Chapman, R.L. (1998) *Dictionary of American Slang*. New York: HarperCollins.

DENNIS REYNOLDS
WASHINGTON STATE UNIVERSITY, USA

Eighty–twenty customer pyramid

Developed in the late 1800s by the Italian economist Vilfredo Pareto, the 80–20 rule or Pareto's Principle argues that 20% of a population often account for 80% of an occurrence. In a business context, this means that 80% of a company's business stems from 20% of its customers (Newell, 2000). Management's task is finding and keeping this lucrative 20%.

The lucrative 20% are sometimes termed 'barnacles,' because they tend to stay with a business over their lifetime, while the 80% are sometimes termed 'butterflies' because they tend to give their business to a variety of firms. Reichheld (2001) suggests marketing programs should be designed to collect barnacles rather than to lure butterflies. Treated right, the loyal former will stick around for a lifetime. The latter tend to flit around from deal to deal.

Successful companies identify potential barnacles and target their marketing programs towards attracting and keeping these loyal customers. Correspondingly, they also design programs that shoo away the butterflies (Reichheld, 2001).

References

Newell, F. (2000) *Loyalty.com: Customer Relationship Management in the New Era of Internet Marketing*. New York: McGraw-Hill Professional Books.

Reichheld, F.F. (2001) *Loyalty Rules! How Today's Leaders Build Lasting Relationships.* Boston, MA: Harvard Business School Press.

Shoemaker, S. and Lewis, R.C. (1999) Customer loyalty: the future of hospitality marketing. *International Journal of Hospitality Management,* 18 (4), 345–370.

JAMES MURPHY
UNIVERSITY OF WESTERN AUSTRALIA,
AUSTRALIA

Electric power purchasing

Hotels normally purchase their electricity from a local electric utility. Their purchase involves a charge for the electricity itself, measured in kilowatt-hours or KWH, and the peak demand for electricity, measured in kilowatts or KW.

Utility rates may vary by season as well as by time of day. These variations reflect the differing costs to produce and delivery electrical energy. One common way that utilities adjust their rates to reflect changing costs is via the fuel clause adjustment – an additional charge or credit on top of the base rate reflecting the costs of fuel (or purchased electricity) to the utility.

Normally, hotels are on a 'secondary' electric power rate with electricity supplied at 480 volts or less. That is, the meter is set on the customer's side of a transformer that is owned by the utility company. Primary power customers (over 480 to 13,400 volts) take power from a utility meter that is in the line before the customer owned transformer.

The primary power customer pays a lower kilowatt-hour rate than secondary power customers do, but primary customers must pay for the transformer or pay for a replacement if the existing one fails. Primary power can be a dramatic energy saving for hotels that can qualify for the rate; usually only very large full service properties, large convention centers or resort properties.

JIM ACKLES
THARALDSON ENERGY GROUP, USA

Electronic commerce (e-commerce)

Electronic commerce (e-commerce) is simply defined as the practice of buying and selling products and services by means of computers, utilizing technologies such as the Web, electronic data interchange, e-mail, electronic fund transfers, and smart cards. Paper-based systems are no longer required and the business processes are optimized to make the best use of the technology available. A shopping card is a piece of software that acts as an online store's catalogue and ordering process which electronically exists on end-users' computers either at home or at work. Typically, it is the interface between a seller's website and its deeper structure. e-Commerce allows potential customers to select goods and services, review what they have chosen, make necessary modifications, and complete the purchasing process accordingly (Buhalis, 2003). Although e-commerce in a broad sense means using various telecommunication tools for making transactions, in reality most hospitality operators use such systems as the Internet, Extranet, intranet, and electronic data interchange to facilitate and fulfill transactions.

Having been accepted as the biggest single transformation that has happened in the last few generations, e-commerce encompasses all forms of online electronic trading, including business-to-business (B2B) and business-to-consumer (B2C) transactions. B2B supports the use of computer applications referring to electronic trade or partnering between organizations and businesses over the electronic marketplace. This type of e-commerce is quickly becoming an important driver of the new economy and it is likely to become a critical method for doing business in the near future as a result of its perceived importance within the supply chain management. As opposed to B2B e-commerce between organizations alone, B2C refers to electronic trade between businesses and consumers/end-users. Businesses promote their products and services on the Internet where potential customers are given the opportunity to complete the shopping transaction online. Credit cards are the main method of payment for B2C e-commerce. It is estimated that the total value of the B2B transactions is much larger than that of the B2C transactions although consumer confidence is increasing rapidly.

In recent years, an increasing number of businesses have adopted e-commerce technologies to sell customers their products or buy products and services from a variety of businesses in diverse industries as a part of the management of their supply chains. The application of e-commerce includes many major industries such as books (e.g. www.amazon.com) or music sites (e.g. www.mp3.com).

In the past few years, e-commerce has expanded rapidly and this growth is expected to continue in the future because developments in information technologies have brought products and services on the screen together whilst consumers gain confidence in purchasing online. It seems clear from developments in the use of information technologies that the boundaries between 'c-commerce' (conventional commerce) and 'e-commerce' will become increasingly blurred in the future and that service providers will be more likely to use multi-channel strategies. This is because using e-commerce has become a very common process.

Within the context of hospitality operations, it has become possible to make all arrangements for a holiday or travel in a few seconds (O'Connor, 1999). Using the Internet as an electronic medium, it gives suppliers (hotels, motels or holiday villages), intermediaries (travel agencies, GDSs), and customers (end-users, guests or visitors) obvious advantages over traditional marketing methods applied in the hospitality industry.

First, benefits for hospitality businesses include the provision of faster, cheaper, more convenient choices, offering as well as wider and more detailed material and richer advertisement contents (Rimmington and Kozak, 1997). The service providers have the opportunity to reach their potential customers immediately with no barriers of time and distance and to offer them various options and choices for accompanying an online shopping activity. Sellers can use better yield management for distressed inventory and advertise special offers. Customers can now

make a price comparison with different businesses supplying similar products without directly interacting with their representatives (Connolly *et al.*, 1998). The e-commerce developments will change the way hotels do business in the future and will be of strategic importance.

Accordingly, many hospitality businesses have already established their marketing strategies. They are using the electronic marketplace to provide a wide range of benefits for customers. Through e-commerce technology, customers are provided with the opportunity to choose their desired products and services and order them online without spending much time for face-to-face communication (Lin, 1998). People are allowed to search and purchase hospitality products 24 hours a day, 7 days a week, and 365 days a year. Given this, customers are now able to sit at home or in their office and browse comfortably without being pressured and having to wait in the office of travel agencies. In a few minutes, they are able to see the pictures of hotels where they are likely to stay, make their bookings, pay fees by credit cards, and get electronic tickets in return. Both hoteliers and information technology service providers will be the key players in this type of electronic marketplace where traditional intermediaries are expected to either modernize or disappear.

References

Buhalis, D. (2003) *eTourism: Information Technologies for Strategic Tourism Management*. Harlow: Prentice-Hall.

Connolly, D.J., Olsen, M.D., and Moore, R.G. (1998) *Competitive Advantage: Luxury Hotels and the Superhighway*. Research Report. Paris: International Hotel and Restaurant Association.

Lin, L. (1998) Computer-based information technologies and their impact on the marketing of international tourism industry. In D. Buhalis, A.M. Tjoa and J. Jafari (eds), *Information and Communication Technologies in Tourism*. Vienna: Springer-Verlag, pp. 318–327.

O'Connor, P. (1999) *Electronic Information Distribution in the Tourism and Hospitality*. Wallingford, UK: CAB International.

Rimmington, M. and Kozak, M. (1997) Developments in information technology: Implications for the tourism industry and tourism marketing. Anatolia. *International Journal of Tourism and Hospitality Research*, 8 (3), 59–80.

METIN KOZAK
MUGLA UNIVERSITY, TURKEY

Electronic data interchange (EDI)

Electronic data interchange (EDI) allows the transfer of data using networks, particularly the Internet. There are various EDI standards approved by the American National Standards Institute (ANSI), e.g. X12. However, EDI can be expensive and a new cheaper standard AS2 has been developed which enables smaller companies with limited budgets to exploit the benefits of EDI. A hospitality supply chain networks companies supplying hospitality products. EDI can be used to provide easy and cheap interaction for business-to-business (B2B) commerce and the secure sharing of data. EDI is becoming increasingly important as an easy mechanism for hospitality companies to buy, sell, and trade information. Yip and Law (2002) recommend the adoption of EDI to add value to services and achieve successful e-commerce. Adding value to products and services is facilitated by a shift towards a more collaborative business model. Integration of supply chains enables collaboration between the supply chain partners. The Internet can enable automation of supply chains and provide organizations with real-time information. It can help to reduce costs and improved productivity by identifying process enhancement opportunities. Often lower specification extranets are used instead.

References

Yip, L. and Law, R. (2002) User preferences for web site attributes: a study of the Hong Kong Disneyland. *Asia Pacific Journal of Tourism Research*, 7 (1), 36–44.

Laudon, J.P. and Laudon, K.C. (2003) *Management Information Systems*, 8th edn. Upper Saddle River, NJ: Prentice-Hall.

ELERI JONES
UNIVERSITY OF WALES INSTITUTE, UK

Electronic locking systems

In the late 1960s and throughout the 1970s, there were efforts to develop a room access system that would not require a traditional metal key. In England, Unique introduced a card access system that met with some acceptance in the United Kingdom and on the Continent. They were unable to establish a successful presence in the United States. During that period of time Vingcard, based in Oslo, Norway, produced a mechanical key card which was the predecessor to the contemporary electronic room access card. In New York City, Saflok was under development at the Hilton Hotel at the Rockefeller Center (now known as the New York Hilton and Towers). The inventor, Leslie Ellison, had hoped to persuade Vice President and General Manager Alphonse Salomone to bring the financial support of the Hilton organization in development of the electronic locking system. The Hilton organization provided the 38th floor as a 'laboratory' for the development of the card access system. However, ultimate development and distribution of the lock was through other financial and manufacturing sources.

ADT installed the first online, hard-wired key card access system in the Algonquin Hotel in New York City in the 1970s. The retro-fitting of a property to hard-wire was an expensive project and ADT made that single installation before deciding to discontinue development of such a system for the lodging industry. Other organizations, notably Marlok and Vingcard, have continued to provide the online option.

There has been a preference for stand-alone systems where the lockset in each door has a memory that permits reading of the card when introduced into the lock unit. (This may be accomplished by proximity, swipe or insertion of the card.) The lock is powered by a battery and the card is programmed at the front desk for a specific room. When the card is introduced into the lock, the memory chip will recognize it as the appropriate 'level' for entry; or deny entry when the card does not carry the proper access code.

In the online, hard-wired installation, the card is programmed at the front desk and a simultaneous message is transmitted to the lockset in the door to the assigned room. Recent developments permit changing of the room access remotely by the use of infrared or radio frequency technology in addition to the hard-wire.

During the 1990s, many lodging organizations mandated the installation of an electronic card access system. As a result, over 85% of the lodging industry in the United States has such an installation. Spurred by the installation of such systems by American-based hotel corporations in foreign locations, there have been widespread installations in many foreign properties.

The smartcard has been developed in Europe and in Asia, and is slowly receiving acceptance in the American market. Unlike the magnetic-stripe card which has wide acceptance in the United States, the smartcard has an embedded integrated circuit chip (this usually has the appearance of a small gold square) in the card which may be programmed for a multiplicity of uses. These may include the function as a regular credit or debit card as well as a card that can be programmed for the guestroom and other facility services (i.e. health club, concierge, or club floor, etc.).

Developments over the years have enhanced the electronic card system. An audit function is available whereby the number of entries to the room are recorded. This will give a record of entries by staff as well as the guest. This has been very effective in reducing the number of room thefts as staff entering the room during a given period of time is fully recorded.

Most recent developments include the use of infrared to determine whether a person is present within the guestroom. This eliminates the possibility of staff personnel walking into an occupied room when they fail to receive a response to the announcement of a hotel service seeking entry.

Bluetooth technology (developed in Sweden) has evolved along with the growing use of cell phones. With an enabling device in the owner's cell phone, short range radio signals are used to transmit data between the cellular phone and the electronic lock. Upon entering a facility, the property management system (PMS) will recognize the enabled device and the reservation is automatically confirmed without the necessity of standing in line at the front desk. Upon approaching the room, the guest uses the cell phone to signal the lockset in order to open the door and to access the guestroom. Several US manufacturers are now working with this concept and exploring different channel capabilities.

Recent developments in room access card systems have focused on the use of biometric technology. This has introduced systems where a fingerprint, palm print, retina scan or voice identification and activation may be employed. In the opening years of the twenty-first century, there has not been a significant move by the lodging industry to biometrics. The economy in the post 9/11 era has not been supportive of introduction of new systems in addition to existing electronic card access systems. This will undoubtedly receive greater attention as the economy improves over the next several years.

Reference

Ellis, Raymond C. and Stipanuk, David M. (1999) *Security and Loss Prevention Management*, 2nd edn. Lansing, MI: Educational Institute of the American Hotel and Motel Association.

RAYMOND CLINTON ELLIS, JR
UNIVERSITY OF HOUSTON, USA

Electronic mail (e-mail)

As Campbell (1998) states, only three or four times in recent history has a technological innovation totally changed the way that humans communicate with each other. One of these is electronic mail, or as it is more usually known by its abbreviation, e-mail. In 1971 Ray Tomlinson, an American computer engineer who worked for BBN, a company hired to build the precursor to the Internet, invented electronic mail. He also decided on the now ubiquitous @ as the locator symbol in an email address.

E-mail is sent cheaply via a network from one computer to one or many other computers at near instantaneous speed, with an email address available to all with access to a computer. Because of its asynchronicity (e-mail is a form of asynchronous computer mediated communication) it is receiver friendly, as the receiver can deal with it at a time of their choosing, unlike a telephone call, which can be intrusive.

For these reasons it is a popular tool for hospitality marketers who can effectively and efficiently use it to advise a target market of upcoming product offers designed to appeal to that market. However, overuse of unsolicited commercial e-mails (spam) may incur recipients' wrath.

References

Campbell, T. (1998) The first email message. *Pretext Magazine*, March 1998 available at http://www.pretext.com/mar98/contents.htm.

Wilson, D. (2002) *Managing Information: IT for Business Processes*. Oxford: Butterworth-Heinemann.

IAN MCDONNELL
UNIVERSITY OF TECHNOLOGY SYDNEY,
AUSTRALIA

Electronic marketing (e-marketing)

Electronic marketing (e-marketing/Web marketing) uses the Internet/World Wide Web (the Web) to market products and services in 'marketspace' – the virtual equivalent of the global marketplace. e-Marketing is more than the migration of traditional 'one to many' marketing onto the Web. It provides advantages from flexible proactive 'many to many' communications and narrowcasting *in extremis*. e-Marketing radically changes how hospitality firms operate, requiring a paradigm shift towards dialogue with content created by, and for, individuals using information from customers not about them (Hoffman and Novak, 1997). e-Marketing provides low-cost gateways enabling small and non-brand businesses to compete globally alongside brands. However, brand importance for Web-based hospitality purchasing cannot be underestimated. A website is a fundamental requirement for e-marketing, but does not guarantee success – businesses must attract, engage and retain users to learn about them and support customized interaction. Growing consumer access to, and greater trust in, the Web 'points to a scenario of "Universal Connectivity" in which the challenge . . . is to . . . improve customer relationship management and hence bookings/revenue . . . on-line' (DCMS/DTI, 2003, p. 29). Web-enabled customer relationship management systems require considerable financial investment but forge rich customer relationships, cutting the time and energy normally associated with database marketing.

References

Hoffman, D.L. and Novak, T.P. (1997) A new marketing paradigm for electronic commerce. *The Information Society*, 13 (1), 43–54.

DCMS/DTI (2003) *e-Commerce Impact Study of the Tourism Sector. Summary Report*, March 2003. Available at http://www.ukonlineforbusiness. gov.uk/cms/resource/file/Tourism-Summary-Report.pdf. Accessed 20 August 2003.

ELERI JONES
UNIVERSITY OF WALES INSTITUTE, UK

Electronic procurement (e-procurement)

Electronic procurement (e-procurement) streamlines the purchase and delivery processes (e.g. from product ordering to payment by the firm's bank) by integrating them into the Internet for increasing operational efficiencies and creating competitive advantages. Since the Internet is an open shared platform, businesses of any size can gain access to e-procurement, in contrast to expensive and proprietary electronic data interchange (EDI) procurement systems. e-Procurement has the following advantages:

- One-stop shopping from numerous suppliers
- Dynamic pricing
- Increased auditing, i.e. detailed purchasing reports and purchases' authorization control system
- Just-in-time
- Automated paperless ordering
- Chain approved purchases for brand consistency
- Financial benefits through fast product/supplier search/comparison, purchase aggregation, and streamlined processes (Hoek, 2001).

e-Procurement takes place in e-marketplaces classified as:

- Exchanges (many-to-many), e.g. www.hotel-supplies.com
- Sell-side (one seller-many buyers), e.g. www.dairy.com
- Buy-side (one buyer-many sellers)
- Public (open to all)
- Private (open to invited trades only).

Several market mechanisms are used (e.g. e-auctions, reverse auctions). Hospitality firms can use e-procurement for day-to-day supplies (e.g. cleaning material, food and beverage) and for strategic supplies (e.g. technology, furniture). All hotels (branded, managed, and independent) can equally benefit from e-procurement.

e-Procurement shifts the focus from the engineering of internal processes to the coordination of dynamic supply chain networks that deconstruct traditional chains and develop coopetition (e.g. avendra.com, developed by five competing hotel chains to support central procurement). Such e-procurement partners become involved in: advanced production/demand planning and scheduling by sharing information; as well as flexible usage of all available resources.

References

Hoek, R. (2001) e-Supply chains – virtually non-existing. *Supply Chain Management: An International Journal*, 6 (1), 21–28.

Poirer, C. and Bauer, M. (2001) *e-Supply Chain: Using the Internet to Revolutionize Your Business*. New York: Berrett–Kohler.

MARIANNA SIGALA
UNIVERSITY OF THE AEGEAN, GREECE

Emotional labor

Hochschild's (1983) seminal work points out the emotional dimensions of service work, and the potential stress arising from having to display emotions that support the service encounter but which are not genuinely felt. Hochschild provides case studies using cabin crew to suggest that service workers who are consistently required to display one emotion whilst feeling another, experience stress and labor that is genuine toil. In hospitality operations, the emotional displays of front-line employees are required to match the expectations of their customers. In many cases these organizations require what Mann (1998) describes as the 'Have a Nice Day culture'. Although some see this approach to service interactions sweeping the world, others like doctors, accountants, and solicitors, need emotional displays that are seen as serious-minded. In other cases, say as in the case of police officers (Lashley, 2001) or debt collectors (Hochschild, 1983), workers may have to deliver 'Have a Rotten Day' emotions.

That said, the 'have a nice day' approach is one shared by large numbers of people working in hospitality services. Many service organizations suggest a strong service culture in which staff performance is seen as a key feature of the offer to customers. 'A strong service culture means that staff are happy and pleased to help, enjoy their work, like the company and will always deal pleasantly with customers' (Mann, 1999, p. 22). Conversely, organizations are unlikely to be tolerant of displays of the wrong emotions. Displays of temper or aggression, frustration and anger, or whatever is deemed to be inappropriate, are not tolerated. Hence employees are frequently in a position of having to display one set of emotions when they actually feel other emotions, say when dealing with an unreasonable customer.

Employees have to exercise 'emotional management' in their interactions with customers, managers, and other staff. Hospitality employees particularly are required to display emotions that are appropriate to the job. 'In the hand' culture, smiling, and patience with customers is expected, even when they are unpleasant and insulting. When dealing with angry and aggressive people the natural response is to become angry oneself, but neutralizing involves adopting a quiet and calm manner. In other cases, emotions are expressed and released 'back of the house' where these displays would not be allowed 'front of the house.' Many hospitality retail employees will display the 'right emotions' in front of the customer, but then release their anger in the kitchen or non-public areas.

At heart, emotion management requires acting. The way that each organization defines service and the appropriate service performance alters the details of the 'act,' but in many ways requires the same techniques so as to hide what one feels and fake what one doesn't (Mann, 1999). Even people who are naturally cheerful will have times when they do not feel cheerful, welcoming, hospitable, pleasant or friendly, but they will be expected to manage the emotional performance required by their employer.

Looking to the techniques used by professional actors shows that there are two main approaches. The first, the technical school, involves the actor adjusting his or her physical appearance to display the emotion(s) required. This surface approach to displaying the emotions does not need the hospitality service worker to actually feel the emotion, they just create the impression they do. Whilst this is less demanding of the individual it is difficult to continuously display these appearances over a prolonged period, or when the person is tired, or their feelings are opposite to those intended. The second approach requires

the actor to produce the feeling required by calling on a past experience or imaging how it would feel to have these experiences. Often hospitality service workers use this approach when dealing with a client. They imagine how it would feel if they were in the customer's place. So there is an attempt to get the service worker to empathize with the customer; treating the customer as a guest in one's own home is an example of this technique being encouraged (Lashley and Lee-Ross, 2003).

The problem that most employees face is that emotional management requires emotional labor, as each person works on making the appropriate emotional display required in their work. Mann (1999, p. 69) reminds us that emotional labor has three components; 'It involves the faking of emotion that is not felt, and/or hiding of emotion that is felt. This emotion management is performed in order to meet social expectations – usually as part of the job role.' Emotional labor, therefore requires the faking of emotions or the hiding of emotions felt typically in work situations. Mann defines three potential situations regarding the match between emotions felt and emotional display, particularly in work roles. *Emotional harmony* is said to exist in situations where the individual actually feels the emotion required of the display rules and social expectations. In this case, no emotional labor is taking place because the individual does not have to hide or fake emotions. *Emotional dissonance* takes place when the emotions displayed for the purposes of the job role are not the emotions felt. Mann identifies a third state as *emotional deviance* which occurs when the person displays the emotions felt, but these are not ones that are expected to be displayed. Again this does not require emotional labor because individuals do not have to display emotions that they are not feeling, though they may find that they are in a disciplinary dispute with the employer.

Emotional labor is supplied, as we have seen when emotional dissonance occurs, that is a person acting within the confines of the expected displayed emotions, provides a display of emotions that are not felt. Here stress stemming from this emotional dissonance can lead to 'Have a Nice Day Syndrome' (Mann, 1999, p. 84), that is the psychological effects of providing emotional labor. Mann suggests that the effects of working in a situation where emotional dissonance is an almost permanent feature of the work experience are likely to produce stress related behavior. Emotional laborers such as hospitality workers are likely to be less satisfied with their jobs, more likely to leave or be absent from work, suffer minor illnesses, complain of being 'burnt-out', and 'have an increased susceptibility to serious conditions like coronary heart disease' (Mann, 1999, p. 85).

References

Hochschild, A.R. (1983) *The Managed Heart: Commercialization of Human Feeling.* Berkley, CA: University of California Press.

Lashley, C. (2001) *Empowerment: HR Strategies for Service Excellence.* Oxford: Butterworth-Heinemann.

Lashley, C. and Lee-Ross, D. (2003) *Organization Behaviour for Leisure Services.* Oxford: Butterworth-Heinemann.

Mann, S. (1998) *Psychology Goes to Work.* Oxford: Purple House.

Mann, S. (1999) *Hiding What We Feel, Faking What We Don't: Understanding the Role of Emotions at Work.* Shaftesbury: Element.

CONRAD LASHLEY
NOTTINGHAM TRENT UNIVERSITY, UK

themselves to this service, even if it is not affecting their work performance. Alternatively, supervisors or managers may recommend an employee to an EAP on the basis that work performance has declined below an acceptable level.

It is necessary for hospitality organizations to provide an EAP as a cost-effective means of reducing staff turnover and keeping employees productive on the job. In a service-based industry, customers prefer to see familiar, happy faces and thus, keeping employees on the job and smiling, is an imperative. As Nankervis *et al.* state (2002, p. 433), 'EAPs are found in organizations that exhibit a genuine concern for their employees. Managers in such organizations show a readiness to invest in their people programs: they demonstrate a commitment to the well-being of their staff.'

References

Arthur, A.R. (2000) Employee assistance programmes: the emperor's new clothes of stress management? *British Journal of Guidance and Counselling*, 28 (4), 549–559.

Nankervis, A., Compton, R., and Baird, M. (2002) *Strategic Human Resource Management*, 4th edn. Melbourne: Nelson Thomson Learning.

TRISH FAIRBOURN
SOUTHERN CROSS UNIVERSITY, AUSTRALIA

Employee assistance program

An employee assistance program (EAP) can be defined as a voluntary, confidential scheme that provides assessment, counseling, and therapeutic services for employees (and their dependants) who are experiencing a wide range of personal, emotional and psychological problems (Arthur, 2000). An outside contractor would normally be engaged to provide this broad range of consulting and counseling services.

Counseling services may either be by telephone, face-to-face, or even Web-based. According to Nankervis *et al.* (2002), employees may refer

Employee orientation and mentoring

Employee induction or orientation is the beginning of the training and development process of new employees. According to Stone (1998, p. 335), it can be defined as, 'The systematic introduction of the new employees to their jobs, co-workers and the organization.' Whilst job information is essential, it is also just as important for the employee to be socialized into the organization and to be made to feel welcome in those critical first few days and weeks. Kennedy and Berger (1994) maintain that the highest turnover rates are found in new employees and that orientation programs should also deal with the emotional needs of new employees, helping them reduce their anxiety and making the new job transition easier. With the tourism and hospitality industry suffering from high turnover rates, proper induction of employees is imperative to try to combat this issue.

Mentoring is a further process of employee development that involves less experienced employees aligning themselves with more senior, experienced employees in order to learn skills. The mentor will pass on their experience, give advice or instruction, and open up career opportunities (Stone, 1998). Mentoring can be both formal (where a mentor is assigned to an upwardly mobile employee), or informal, where a relationship develops over time. Mentoring is a useful practice in hotel corporate traineeship programs.

References

Kennedy, D.J. and Berger, F. (1994) Newcomer socialization: oriented to facts or feelings? *Cornell Hotel and Restaurant Administration Quarterly*, 35 (6), 58–71.
Stone, R.J. (1998) *Human Resource Management*, (3rd edn. Brisbane: John Wiley & Sons.

TRISH FAIRBOURN
SOUTHERN CROSS UNIVERSITY, AUSTRALIA

Employee participation

Employee participation deals with the involvement of workers in the work issues that affect them in their jobs. This concept could also be referred to as employee involvement but is not often used. At its simplest, employee participation could be merely being told by supervisors and managers of what is going on (with no opportunity for two-way communication), and at its most complex it could be employee ownership (industrial democracy).

Wang (1974) developed a four-part participation scale, from information-giving at one end, through consultation then joint decision-making,

to self-management at the other end of the continuum. Participation can be either direct, where the individual worker is involved, or indirect, where the workers are represented by a nominated person or group. The employee participation/industrial democracy movement had its zenith in the 1980s and 1990s (refer to the General Motors' 'Saturn Project' cited by Mills, 1994, p. 131), but the movement has waned in the new millennium.

These days in the hospitality industry the most mentioned form of employee participation tends to be 'empowerment,' yet one needs to recognize that this is at the lower end of the employee participation continuum. Currently there is a debate whether the practice of empowerment is really empowering employees or is just another form of management control.

References

Mills, D.Q. (1994) *Labor-Management Relations*, 5th edn. New York: McGraw-Hill.
Wang, J.J. (1974) A worker participation matrix. *Personnel Practice Bulletin*, 30 (3), 264–277.

RON DOWELL
SOUTHERN CROSS UNIVERSITY, AUSTRALIA

Employee relations (ER)

Employee relations is a term often used interchangeably with industrial relations and human resource management to describe particular human resource management (HRM) or industrial relations (IR) philosophies and approaches. The debate concerning whether to use ER, or HRM or IR can be located in the continuing debates about the nature and direction of workplace change, even though there is considerable discussion about what all three terms mean.

Arbitration and third party labor regulation

Historically, labor regulation and trade unions formed the dominant paradigm to understanding workplace behavior and the role of trade unions in collectively organizing workers. Under this paradigm, labor regulation was understood in the context of third party arbitration. Orderly and compulsory arbitration was meant to be a substitute for strikes and lockouts and unbridled managerial prerogative. Academic debate has focused on the role of trade unions and the state in fostering a 'collectivist' approach to employment regulation emphasizing the interaction between regulation institutions, employers, and trade unions. Increasingly however, there is growing HRM literature that argues for the primacy of the role of HRM in shaping the employment relationship. The HRM approach is often considered 'unitarist' and associated with strong managerial prerogative. Some researchers use the term 'ER' to describe a form of employment management at workplace level that relies on human resource management practices in order to manage conflict and avoid the intrusion of third parties such as unions in the employment relationship. This debate takes on added significance when viewed against the backdrop of declining employee collective 'voice' mechanisms such as trade union workplace representation in negotiations and emergence of HRM. Employee relations practices come in 'hard' and 'soft' versions. Each is seen as having either a short-term or long-term impact on business strategy and the extent to which they are integrated into broader business strategies is a matter of debate.

'Soft' and 'hard' versions of HRM

According to Legge (1995), HRM comes in both 'hard' and 'soft' models, suggesting that the differences between the two are largely incremental. The soft model of HRM is seen as a form of 'developmental humanism' where employees are considered as 'assets' whose intellectual and creative skills contribute to a competitive advantage, associated with HRM practices that are values-based and built on cooperation, consensus, and mutual trust (Legge, 1995, p. 66). This integrative approach emphasizes the development and nurturing of human capital in order to achieve

strategic 'fit' through adopting a qualitative approach to HRM practices thereby enhancing competitive advantage. The emphasis is on behavioral approaches. HRM practices adopted here include employee consultation mechanisms, emphasis on training, skill formation, career planning, adoption of high performance work systems and job security as means for enhancing employee commitment, loyalty, and 'high trust' underpinning quality and flexibility as competitive advantage (Guest, 1987).

The 'hard' version of HRM is defined as 'utilitarian humanism' where cost minimization is paramount, requiring close surveillance, supervision, and control of employees (Legge, 1995, p. 66). The 'hard' approach has a preference for unitarist values that emphasizes high managerial control. The HRM adopted here takes a 'low trust' quantitative approach that sees human resources as a cost factor of production to be systematically measured and monitored where the focus is on increasing efficiency and reducing labor costs (Legge, 1995). This approach favors cost minimization HRM practices such as low investment in skill/training, adoption of individualized or performance pay systems, use of dismissals as a disciplinary measure, and higher use of temporary and casual forms of labor. Employee and union consultative mechanisms at the workplace are avoided or resisted. Union relations under these two HRM models range from 'sophisticated' (union inclusion or incorporation) to 'macho' style union exclusion strategies. Many hospitality organizations subscribe to this approach.

Individualism, ER, and HRM practices

Globalization, deregulation, and changing employer HRM strategies favoring non-union or union exclusionary practices are seen as weakening of the institutions of labor market regulation. Along the way, there has also been an on-going reappraisal of collectivism and the representative role of trade unions in conjunction with a greater emphasis on HRM. Human resource management has been defined as encompassing 'a distinctive approach to employment management which seeks to achieve competitive advantage through the strategic deployment of a highly committed capable workforce, using an integrated array of cultural, structural and personnel techniques' (Storey, 1995, p. 5). Managerial decisions to pursue individual employment outcomes (e.g. individual employment contracts) are usually founded on the premise that there are common interests, bonds, and values between management and labor that foster 'high trust' workplace relations whilst promoting individual self-interest and individual rewards.

A demise of collectivist employment relations?

A number of researchers have expressed concern that ER practices are increasingly likely to be dominated by hard HRM practices. Generally, under individualism, employer strategies are associated with attempts to either bypass or exclude trade unions and deal directly with employees through individual contracts thereby exercising greater managerial prerogative on a range of matters that were once the subject of collective negotiation. Research in the UK suggests little evidence linking individualized non-union working arrangements with high-trust HRM strategies. For example, Sisson (1993) has labeled workplaces in the UK in the individualized non-union sector as 'bleak houses,' characterized by poor employee consultation practices with little or no employee involvement, higher incidences of 'unorganized conflict' (such as employee turnover and absenteeism), and a higher level of dismissals or enforced redundancies. Many hospitality organizations suffer from these unfortunate outcomes. Sisson argues that these firms were less likely to have implemented HRM/employment policies or grievance mechanisms and experienced a higher level of accidents brought about by a greater failure to comply with occupational health and safety requirements. These companies were also more likely to regularly use temporal and flexible forms of labor (Sisson, 1993). Individualism is also a closed bargaining process. Individualism often has little to do with 'genuine' individual

bargaining and is essentially standardized contracts used to by-pass third party intervention in order to secure changes in work practices via unilateral managerial decision-making. Small to medium-sized firms have traditionally had low union density, and debates about ER and the introduction of new HRM practices that might lead to de-unionization or union avoidance is generally a debate that is confined to larger unionized workplaces in both public and private sectors. It has been argued by some that the relationship between HRM and individualism is more about breaking down existing collectivist forms of labor regulation than the emergence of a 'new' employee relations model of the type suggested by 'soft' HRM (Legge, 1995).

In practice it is difficult to demonstrate a pure approach. HRM may have both a collectivist and individualistic persona. At a corporate level, there is often a strong emphasis on collective goals and a strong corporate culture, whereas at workplace level there may be an emphasis on individual responsibility, accountability, and performance (Guest, 1987). In order to cut through the maze, Blyton and Turnbull (1998) suggest that ER encompasses:

> focus on and define the distinctive characteristics of the employment relationship; to locate that relationship with the broader nature of economic activity; to analyze the structural bases of conflict and accommodation between employer and employee; to consider the influence of the wider society; and to develop an interdisciplinary approach using concepts and ideas derived from sociology, economics, psychology, history and political science. (p. 28)

The state plays a significant role in adjudicating the two approaches. For example, over the past two decades, regulation of labor has decreased in many industrialized countries with a greater emphasis on labor flexibility and deregulation of wages and conditions (such as through enterprise bargaining). This is seen in terms of greater deregulation of industrial and employment regulation in favor of increasing usage of workplace agreements and contracts and growing use of non-union workplace agreements. With a decline in trade union membership and

Table 1 Differences between the disciplines of industrial relations and human resource management from an ER perspective

Feature	Industrial relations	Human resource
Definition	Broadly defined as the study of employment relations in a multi-disciplinary/ interdisciplinary manner emphasizing the role of state, unions and employers management approach	Defined as a function of managerial control over internal labor markets linked to broader business objectives than the more limited historic personnel
Major emphasis	Emphasizes the legitimate role of conflict of interest and collective bargaining and third parties in the employment relationship	Emphasizes human growth potential, direct, cooperative management– employee relationships (but not to the exclusion of bargaining and other forms of conflict resolution)
Levels of analysis	Analyzes multiple levels of management, employee/union and state interaction	Focuses on the firm as the unit of Analysis
Extent of debate	Exhibits a pluralist approach emphasizing the role of state, unions, and employers	Exhibits a unitarist approach emphasizing the primary role of Management
Public policy contribution	Provides critiques of public policy in labor market/industrial relations areas	Not yet a significant contributor to public policy debates but is developing in this area
Teaching locus	Liberal arts degree/commerce degree base	Business school (B.Bus. MBA and Executive short course base)

Adapted from Boxall, and Dowling. (1990)

the greater emphasis on the decentralization of the employment relationship and the growing importance of HRM, it can be argued that the regulation of the employment relationship has gradually shifted from a pluralist to a unitarist perspective. The increasing debate over the use of the term ER is an attempt to locate this shift in the modern context. A significant shortcoming of the ER approach, however, remains its inability to adequately conceptualize and resolve workplace conflict. Despite greater emphasis on HRM strategies in the ER literature, debates over power, control, and conflict continue to significantly shape our understanding of the workplace.

ER in the hospitality and hotel industry

According to Price (1994), UK hotels have generally suffered from poor personnel practices creating conditions associated with 'low pay, low trade union density, occupational segregation, low levels of personnel professionalism, weak internal labor markets, and flexible and peripheral forms of labor' (p. 45), this is despite the growth in hospitality employment and increased educational qualifications. The reasons may be many, but the absence of the type of labor market 'push–pull' factors such as labor scarcity, greater demand for skills, organized labor, etc. that would normally push wages upwards may be some explanations. Studies by Guerrier and Lockwood (1989), Price (1994), and Lucas (1995) (UK hotels) and Hort and Timo (2003) (Australian hotels) suggest global trends. Hoque's study (2000) of larger UK hotels suggests attempts at introducing high performance work systems, though there are no consistent patterns. Table 1 attempts to illustrate the intellectual origins and conceptual differences between the HRM and IR approaches.

References

Blyton, P. and Turnbull, P. (1998) *The Dynamics of Employee Relations*. London: Macmillan.

Boxall, P. and Dowling, P. (1990) Human resource management and the industrial relations tradition. *Labor and Industry*, 3 (2/3), 195–214.

Guerrier, Y. and Lockwood, A. (1989) Core and peripheral employees in hotel operations. *Personnel Review*, 18 (1), 9–15.

Guest, D. (1987) Human resource management and industrial relations. *Journal of Management Studies*, 24 (5), 503–521.

Hoque, K. (2000) *Human Resource Management in the Hotel Industry: Strategy, Innovation and Performance*. London: Routledge.

Hort, L. and Timo, N. (2003) A survey of enterprise agreement making in the Australian hotel industry. In J. Burgess and D. MacDonald (eds), *Developments in Enterprise Bargaining in Australia*. Croydon, VA, Australia: Tertiary Press, pp. 239–255.

Legge, K. (1995) *Human Resource Management: Rhetoric and Realties*. London: Macmillan.

Lucas, R. (1995) *Managing Employee Relations in the Hotel and Catering Industry*. London: Cassell.

Price, L. (1994) Poor personnel practice in the hotel and catering industry: does it matter? *Human Resource Management Journal*, 4 (1), 44–62.

Sisson, K. (1993) In search of HRM. *British Journal of Industrial Relations*, 31 (2), 201–210.

Storey, J. (ed.) (1995) Human resource management: still marching on, or marching out? In J.Storey (ed.), *Human Resource Management*. London: Routledge, pp. 3–32.

NILS TIMO
GRIFFITH UNIVERSITY, AUSTRALIA

and obligations that employers and employees have already created, such as wages and employment conditions. In some areas of the hospitality industry (particularly in the seasonal tourist sector) employees do not commonly receive a written contract of employment. This position is compounded by the lack of trade union representation in the industry. Employees are therefore often unaware of procedural and substantive rules.

Another example of substantive rules is employee handbooks that set out additional rights and obligations (Woods, 2002). Upon engagement, many employers have employee handbooks or policy manuals that set out additional responsibilities, employment information etc. that the employee is expected to abide by during employment. Many hotel employee manuals specify for example the standard of grooming to be expected by employees, additional employment information, grievance procedures, health and safety information, hours of work, departmental rules and procedures, leave provisions, etc.

References

Wood, J., Wallace, J. and Jeffane, R. (2001) *Organisational Behaviour: A Global Perspective*, 2nd edn. Sydney: John Wiley & Sons.

Woods, R.H. (2002) *Managing Hospitality Human Resources*, 3rd edn. Lansing, MI: Educational Institute of the American Hotel and Lodging Association.

DARREN LEE-ROSS
JAMES COOK UNIVERSITY, AUSTRALIA

Employee rules

According to Wood, Wallace and Jeffane (2001) rules and regulations refer to the processes that control and define employment rights and obligations. Procedural rules refer to those processes that govern the way in which rights are created and distributed, usually by tribunals, such as deciding how a tribunal will deal with a wages claim etc. Substantive rules refer to the rights

Employee satisfaction

The study of the customer service employee has begun to move slowly to the forefront of organizational research, providing a better understanding of employees' reactions to their service-related duties. It is safe to say that managers and employees in service-based organizations understand that customer satisfaction and service quality are crucial to success in the service sector. This proposition alone does not, however, create behavior that produces satisfying customer service experiences for managers, customer service employees, or their customers.

Employee satisfaction with job-related activities is viewed in the literature as an attitudinal element that relates past events and rewards to current feelings about a job and can be described as 'a personalistic evaluation of conditions existing on a job' (Schneider and Snyder, 1975). To describe how service-process constituents respond to service experiences, scholars have coined the term *customer orientation* to represent an employee's commitment to the service process and to the customers themselves. Research indicates that employees who are more satisfied with their jobs show a higher commitment to guest service and the service process. Brady and Cronin (2001) presented their own model highlighting the extent to which service employees' customer orientation affects consumers' perceptions of a service organization's performance, presented as overall service quality, satisfaction, and perceived value. They showed that elements of employee performance, the quality of physical goods, and 'servicescape' quality influenced consumers' perceptions of overall service quality, connecting employees' job-related satisfaction to customers' positive reactions to the service experience.

For employees, providing customer service is an organizational behavior that is influenced by the organization, its management, their co-workers, and customers. To perform customer service activities employees must possess both motivation and aptitude. As such, individuals display varying levels of proficiency for customer service behavior with varying frequency, realizing intrinsic and extrinsic rewards accordingly. This is further complicated because each service episode is unique and is influenced by forces both internal and external to the organization such as customers, employees, and the organization itself. While the examination of intrinsic and extrinsic factors that influence employee satisfaction is a worthy topic in its own right, this article will focus henceforth on three environmental/organizational influences that are instrumental in fostering employee satisfaction: co-worker support, supervisory support, and customer orientation.

The discussion is predicated on workers being motivated to perform their service-related duties, having a basic level of commitment to their respective organizations, and holding a belief that they receive fair pay for their efforts.

First, given the broad range of support elements present in service-based organizations, where employees, customers, and management each take part in the service process, it is necessary to further clarify the role that organizational support functions play in service-based organizations. Susskind, Kacmar, and Borchgrevink (2003) proposed that organizational support be viewed from two perspectives, those of co-workers and supervisors. This extended view builds upon the traditional definition of support as a set of perceptions that gauge the extent to which employees perceive an organization as being concerned about or committed to their well-being (Eisenberger, Huntington, Hutchinson, and Sowa, 1986). In service-based organizations, the majority of customer-server interactions occur on the front lines as part of product/service delivery and consumption. This is a key distinction of support functions in service-based organizations. Having a strong base of support when performing work-related duties is likely to build satisfaction among employees.

Co-worker support is a function of the extent to which employees believe their co-workers are willing to provide them with work-related assistance to aid in the execution of their service-based duties. In most instances, co-workers' perceived support is vital to the accomplishment of work-related tasks. Perceived support influences more than just tangible issues such as pay or comfort, strongly affecting morale and other psychological factors. Co-worker support (whether formal or informal in nature) is usually void of hierarchical differences, likely supplements the formal support offered by supervisors and managers, and should be based upon espoused organizational standards for service delivery. Supervisory support, on the other hand, is a function of individuals' beliefs that supervisors offer them work-related assistance to aid in the performance of their jobs. Employees receiving adequate support from their superiors will most likely view that support as an organizational function, consistent with Wayne, Shore, and Liden's (1997) finding that the quality of leader-member exchange has a strong effect on perceived organizational support offered to co-workers. The findings of Susskind *et al.* (2003) suggest that multi-level support is a necessary element of a service environment and when absent will likely affect the service delivery process.

Having a sense of support and a commitment to one's customers can enhance the development of employee satisfaction. Managers of service-based organizations have considerably less contact with their customers than their employees do, which should prompt them to recognize the important role employees play in the customer service process. If employees believe they are as important to an organization as the customer, and their significance as an internal customer is institutionalized into organizational practices, they are more likely to view positively their customer service duties through performance efficacy promoted by their supervisors. Internal customer perceptions differ from support functions because it is possible to enjoy the support needed to perform service-related duties without being rewarded with a sense of importance in the service process.

References

Brady, M.K. and Cronin, J.J. (2001) Customer orientation: effects on customer service perceptions and outcome behaviors. *Journal of Service Research*, 3, 241–251.

Eisenberger, R., Huntington, R., Hutchinson, S., and Sowa, D. (1986) Perceived organizational support. *Journal of Applied Psychology*, 71, 500–507.

Schneider, B. and Snyder, R.A. (1975) Some relationships between job satisfaction and organizational climate. *Journal of Applied Psychology*, 60, 319.

Susskind, A.M., Kacmar, K.M., and Borchgrevink, C.P. (2003) Customer service providers' attitudes relating to customer service and customer satisfaction in the customer-server exchange (CSX). *Journal of Applied Psychology*, 88 (1), 179–187.

Wayne, S.J., Shore, L.M., and Liden, R.C. (1997) Perceived organizational support and leader-member exchange: a social exchange perspective. *Academy of Management Journal*, 40, 82–111.

ALEX SUSSKIND
CORNELL UNIVERSITY, USA

Employee selection techniques

Employee selection has been defined as a 'process of narrowing down the pool of potential job candidates and choosing the one person (or people) that best meets the requirements of the job' (Christensen Hughes, 2002, p. 17). These requirements – also referred to as the job specification – may include personal competencies, prior work experience, and formal qualifications deemed necessary to be able to competently perform the job. Effective selection processes allow both the candidate and the organization to properly assess the degree to which the candidate fits the job specification and are in keeping with all applicable legislation. Formal selection procedures typically involve several stages of assessment including pre-screening, interviewing, testing, and reference checks.

Pre-screening helps to ensure that only those meeting the stated minimal requirements proceed to the more labor-intensive interviewing stage. Application forms or resumés can be assessed on the basis of both content and presentation. In addition, applicants can be unobtrusively screened (e.g., for their interpersonal skills) when dropping off their application or waiting for their interview. Some hospitality employers also provide online pre-screening tools, requiring potential candidates to assess their suitability prior to applying.

Those who successfully pass the pre-screening stage should be interviewed. Ideally, interviews occur face to face, but if distance is a factor, they can also be carried out over the phone or through video-conferencing. Interviews require careful planning in terms of both the questions to be asked and the interview format. Interview questions should be specifically developed to help assess the extent to which the candidate possesses the stated job requirements. Interview formats can vary based on the degree of structure, question type, the number of people involved, and tone.

With structured interviews the same questions are asked of every candidate in the same order. While somewhat rigid, this approach can be helpful for ensuring consistency as well as for documenting why one candidate was ultimately deemed most appropriate. Unstructured interviews use a few general open-ended questions and follow points of interest as they arise. While more interesting, unstructured interviews can take longer to conduct, be more difficult to assess, and interviewers can be more susceptible to bias (e.g., be overly influenced by first impressions or non-job-relevant factors). Semi-structured interviews involve a combination of the above.

There are four standard types of interviewing questions: fact-based, opinion-based, problem-solving, and behavioral-based. Fact-based questions help clarify details that may be stated or missing from the candidate's resumé (e.g., What were you doing between 2003 and 2004?) Opinion-based questions probe the candidate's personal views (e.g., What aspects of the job are you most/least interested in?). Problem-solving questions provide potential insight into the candidate's approach for dealing with difficult situations (e.g., If a customer complained to you about . . . , what would you do?). Finally, behavioral-based questions probe an actual situation the candidate has previously encountered. Behavioral-based questions are based on the belief that the best predictor of future performance is past performance (Janz *et al.*, 1986). An example of behavioral-based questioning is: 'Tell me about a time when you experienced a significant conflict with a co-worker? What led up to it? What did you do about it? What was the outcome?'

Successful candidates typically go through several interviews. The first interviewer may be either the HR manager, the immediate supervisor, or if a private employment agency is being used, the headhunter. If successful, the candidate will proceed to subsequent interviews involving those with whom he or she will potentially be working. Some hospitality organizations also include customers in the interviewing process. Such interviews can be serialized (i.e., a series of coordinated one-on-one interviews) or panel-based (i.e., several interviewers meet with one candidate at the same time). The candidate may also be asked to participate in a multiple-candidate interview (i.e., where several candidates are interviewed together), which can be helpful for assessing interpersonal skills.

Finally, interviews can vary by tone. In the supportive interview, the candidate is interviewed in a pleasant room, free of distractions, and deliberately put at ease through casual banter before the formal questions begin. In contrast, in the stress interview, which is designed to assess how well the candidate can perform under pressure, the candidate is deliberately made to feel ill at ease and defensive. Questions are rapid, direct, and confrontational. Such an approach should only be used when ability to perform in a highly stressful environment is the overriding requirement of the job.

As part of the selection process, candidates may also be asked to take a written test or participate in a simulation. Some larger organizations have assessment centers that are dedicated to implementing such tests. Testing can be used to assess such factors as intelligence, personality, conceptual ability, knowledge, interpersonal skills, psychological type, language skills, cultural sensitivity etc. Candidates may also be tested for general physical health as well as for substance abuse (e.g., illicit drugs). Employers using tests need to ensure that they are both valid (job-related) and reliable (accurate) and in keeping with all applicable employment legislation.

Once the most suitable candidate has been identified, the final step may include a reference check. Some estimates suggest that as many as 80% of North American employers use telephone references and another 13% use some other format, such as reference letters (Dessler and Turner, 1992, p. 177). Reference checks can be particularly effective for verifying employment facts (positions held, dates employed) and education credentials. They can be less effective for exploring the quality of job performance, as candidates will typically only provide the contact information for people who regard them highly, and previous employers may be reluctant to share negative information with someone they do not know. Concern with legal action has led some organizations to implement policies restricting the amount of information provided through reference checks. In fact, within many European countries (Belgium, France, Germany), employers are forbidden by law to 'make unfavorable statements about former employees' (Belcourt *et al.*, 1996, p. 631).

Once the selection decision has been made, a formal offer of employment should follow. Only once the offer has been negotiated and formally accepted, should the unsuccessful candidates be informed that the job has been filled.

References

Belcourt, M., Sherman, A.W., Bohlander, G.W., and Snell, S.A. (1996) *Managing Human Resources*. Scarborough: Nelson.

Christensen Hughes, J. (2002) Recruitment and selection issues and strategies within international resort communities, in N. D'Annunzio-Green, G.A. Maxwell, and S. Watson (eds), *Human Resource Management: International Perspectives in Hospitality and Tourism*. London: Continuum.

Dessler, G. and Turner, A. (1992) *Human Resource Management in Canada*. Scarborough: Prentice-Hall.

Janz T., Hellervik, L., and Gilmore, D. (1986) *Behavior Description Interviewing*. Boston, MA: Allyn and Bacon.

JULIA CHRISTENSEN HUGHES
UNIVERSITY OF GUELPH, CANADA

Employer association

The term refers to a collective association of employers, usually organized on an industry basis, to represent the collective interests of employers. Employer associations not only represent their members in industrial issues, but may also be active at an economic and political level. For example, the activities of the *Australian Chamber of Commerce and Industry* (ACCI) include advocacy to government across a number of issues including economy and investment, workplace safety and the environment, taxation, and regulation, education, and training. The ACCI is also represented on a range of statutory and business boards and committees nationally and internationally. Employer associations range from small with only several members to groups that represent 10,000 companies and employ up to 1 million staff. Clearly, large associations have the potential to wield tremendous power and influence on the government (Davis, 2001).

Employer associations tend to be less cohesive than trade unions as their membership is drawn from businesses that also compete commercially with one another. Examples are local and national hotel associations. Typically, members of local or regional hotel associations are comprised of hospitality organizations but also of firms, which benefit from indirect tourist income. These can include retail outlets, petrol (gas) stations, and other service providers. National hospitality employer associations have a more homogeneous membership base.

Reference

Davis, E. (2001) *Australian Master Human Resources Guide 2002*. Sydney: CCH Australia.

DARREN LEE-ROSS
JAMES COOK UNIVERSITY, AUSTRALIA

Employment law

Employment law derives from historical interpretations and the reliance upon the application of precedent – that is, judicial interpretations handed down from one court to another. The common law is important in regulating the employment relationship and the activities of unions. The common law contract of employment sets out the rights and duties of employers and employees known historically by the term 'master and servant' (Heys, 2001). Union activities are also often influenced by a part of the common law known as 'tort'. This is used to regulate different forms of civil wrongs, arising from such issues as intimidation, conspiracy to induce a person to breach their contract of employment, economic loss, property damage, trespass, and restraint of trade. Tort law is often used by hospitality employers against unions during industrial disputes as a vehicle for pursuing compensation and cost recovery for economic loss caused by union strike activity. Statute law refers to the mechanism by which government through a parliament or other governmental system enacts legislation that sets out rights and obligations of employers and employees. Generally, statute law overrides common law to the extent of any inconsistencies that may be contained in the latter.

Reference

Heys, A. (2001) *Australian Master Human Resources Guide 2002*. Sydney: CCH Australia.

NILS TIMO
GRIFFITH UNIVERSITY, AUSTRALIA

Empowerment

Generally regarded as a method for promoting greater employee involvement, empowerment is argued to lead to greater organizational success through engaging the employee in the decision-making process. The focus is on providing employees with opportunities to have greater freedom, autonomy and self-control over various aspects of their work, whilst at the same time being encouraged to think creatively and take risks to respond quickly to work situations.

Empowerment was first introduced within the hospitality industry as a response to the changing nature of service markets (Maxwell, 1997). Contemporary issues such as customer purchasing sophistication, increased levels of competition, and a drive for quality coupled with a decrease in skills and available labor resulted in many organizations looking to their employees to take more responsibility for quality and service.

Lashley (1997) further states that empowerment is found in a variety of forms:

- *Empowerment through participation:* Delegation of decision-making from the management arena, for example the use of autonomous working groups, staff consultative committees.
- *Empowerment through involvement:* Management gain through reflecting on employees' experiences, ideas and suggestions, for example creating and using suggestion schemes and team briefings.
- *Empowerment through involvement:* Increased commitment to goals and employee job satisfaction, for example profit-sharing schemes, job rotation.
- *Empowerment through delayering:* Reducing the number of ranks of management hierarchy in an organization, for example job redesign, re-training.

Beardwell and Holden (2001) identify various organizational and individual benefits derived from empowerment. Empowered employees may display higher levels of commitment through increased job satisfaction, ownership, self-confidence, acquisition of new knowledge and skills and the promotion of team working. A higher understanding of business needs can bring about organizational improvements, as employees are more responsive to customer needs. Organizational benefits also include increases in quality and reduction in costs, reduced staff turnover, and increased communication and loyalty. Organizations are also better equipped to respond to changes in customer demand.

Successful empowerment is dependent on various factors including:

- The employee feels personally effective.
- The employee is able to determine outcomes.
- The employee has a degree of control over certain aspects of working life.
- Full training is provided as to boundaries of control.
- Management is fully supportive and willing to devolve responsibility.
- The culture of organization is supportive of errors.

The importance of the culture of the organization is further explained by Dobbs (1993, pp. 55–57). He referred to this as a 'hospitable climate' whereby several factors must be in place to support the empowered employee. Employees must be actively and willingly engaged in their jobs, and innovation and curiosity are encouraged. Furthermore, employees must be provided with the information required to carry out their role and finally employees must understand that they are accountable for their behavior and the resultant organizational impact. Iverson (2001) states that to maximize the benefits of empowerment, hotel managers must become coaches and facilitators, their role will be altered by the presence of empowered staff and the management perspective will no longer be one of control. She also states that involving staff in goal setting at all levels and ensuring that all employees feel the support of senior management will reap positive benefits. Employee roles will also be challenged and empowerment will only be viewed positively if the employees can see the personal benefit or worth associated with their additional responsibility.

However, most forms of employee empowerment are limited on the level of power that is actually given to employees and tend to concentrate on work-based contribution rather than strategic decisions, e.g. employees may be encouraged to decide how to respond to customer complaints directly. Problems with empowerment can arise when the structure and culture of an organization are at odds with the concept of empowerment. Lashley (1997, p. 11) suggests that problems with empowerment will arise when 'company policy, customer moods and expectations may impact on perceptions of satisfaction and may be areas beyond the server's control.' Thus not only are empowered employees burdened with additional stress to anticipate what will delight the customer but they may also be pressurized to offer this delight at the same time as maintaining costs within company policy. Further, if the boundaries within which employees are empowered to make a decision are clouded then confusion can arise amongst employees and managers. Ownership of problems and creation of solutions through empowerment will not be possible if managers are reluctant to give up power or indeed if the employees themselves are not willing to work in an empowered environment (Iverson, 2001).

Within the hospitality sector examples of empowerment are found mainly in customer-facing roles. The reception staff may be allowed to discount room rates or offer free upgrades dependent on factor such as time of day, occupancy rates, and so on. Restaurant staff may have authority to decide when to reduce a customer's bill as a result of a complaint. However, someone, normally in higher authority, has often decided the guidelines with which these decisions can be made. For example, Ritz–Carlton employees at all levels within the organization are empowered to decide when and how they spend an amount of money (up to $2000) on satisfying a disgruntled guest or to delight an important customer.

Marriott Hotels have been seen to be one of the leading hospitality companies in terms of empowering staff (Maxwell, 1997). In a study of the employees of the Glasgow Marriott Hotel, employee satisfaction in relation to their empowered roles was clear. This was evidenced through figures such as: 71% (of respondents') satisfaction with the ability to make decisions themselves and 67% satisfaction with accepting personal responsibility. Furthermore, employees identified the following factors as being personal advantages achieved through empowerment: job satisfaction (69%), improved customer service (65%), speedier decision-making (63%), and personal development (53%). Thus it can be clearly seen that the employees of the Glasgow Marriott Hotel had a positive experience of empowerment, as Maxwell (1997, p. 61) states this positive empowerment was achieved through 'investment in staff through a constant process of review of their perceptions and subsequent refinement of their management.'

References

Beardwell, I. and Holden, L. (2001) *Human Resource Management: A Contemporary Approach.* Harlow, UK: Pearson Education.

Dobbs (1993) as cited in Maxwell, G. (1997) Empowerment in the hospitality industry, in M. Foley, J. Lennon, and G. Maxwell (eds), *Hospitality, Tourism and Leisure Management – Issues in Strategy and Culture*. London: Cassell.

Iverson, K. (2001) *Managing Human Resources in the Hospitality Industry: An Experimental Approach*. Englewood Cliffs, NJ: Prentice-Hall.

Lashley, C. (1997) *Empowering Service Excellence: Beyond the Quick Fix*. London: Cassell.

Maxwell, G. (1997) Empowerment in the hospitality industry. In M. Foley, J. Lennon, and G. Maxwell (eds), *Hospitality, Tourism and Leisure Management – Issues in Strategy and Culture*. London: Cassell.

DEBRA F. CANNON
GEORGIA STATE UNIVERSITY, USA
SAMANTHA QUAIL
GLASGOW CALEDONIAN UNIVERSITY, UK

Energy management

Energy management encompasses decisions about all aspects of an organization's energy usage. It is above all a management discipline, one that should be brought to bear on decisions regarding energy engineering, energy accounting, energy cost control, energy conservation, and energy efficiency.

Energy management requires a high degree of competence in the management of capital, the management of technology, and the management of human effort. As with other management disciplines, its objective is not to minimize costs, but rather to maximize value. To achieve this, deliberate energy management decisions should be made at the very conception of any new building, renovation project, energy-related equipment purchase, or initiation or change in any energy-related operating decision. For example, the appropriate energy management decisions regarding the selection of systems that will convert energy sources from one form to another (e.g. electricity to chilled water, gas to steam), transport that energy to where it is needed (distribution systems for chilled water, steam, and electricity), and finally provide the service the end-user requires (space cooling or heating, illumination) will affect an organization's ability to maximize value over the life of those systems and the facilities they serve.

These same decisions will also determine the energy forms that will need to be purchased thereafter (fuel selection), and how price and reliable supply of those energy forms could impact the organization's very viability. Contracts and other arrangements to purchase that energy come under energy management, as does the function of verifying quantities received and invoices submitted and paid for that energy. Maximizing value also entails managing the tradeoff between some less expensive energy sources whose use is polluting and unsustainable, and some more expensive energy sources whose use can further an organization's goals regarding corporate social responsibility (CSR) and community goodwill.

Energy efficiency, the measure of the number of units of production out for a given number units of energy in, is an important goal of energy management. It relates especially to ensuring that energy converting and consuming plant and equipment is operated and maintained properly. There are a number of equally important energy management functions, including energy conservation (eliminating waste), energy accounting (determining, through the use of an energy information system, where energy is being used, and how the cost of that energy is contributing to the organization's business objectives), and energy knowledge management (imparting necessary information and skills, and ensuring these are then embodied within the organization's strategies, policies, and practices).

Reference

www.energystar.gov

ROBERT ALLENDER
ENERGY RESOURCES MANAGEMENT,
HONG KONG SAR, CHINA

Energy management system

Energy management systems allow hoteliers to take control of lighting, temperature, and electricity to minimize costs while at the same time maintaining guest comfort. For example, energy management systems can automatically reduce heating in unoccupied rooms until allocation to a guest, at which point they can quickly be returned to an acceptable temperature. Similarly, while the guest is not physically present in the room, heating and power can automatically be placed into stand-by status to minimize energy usage and cost. Electronically controlled systems allow more precise control to be maintained over temperatures than with the previous mechanical systems. For example, temperatures can be kept accurate to within ± 0.2 °C, as opposed to ± 3 °C with older mechanical thermostats, which means that average temperatures can be reduced, leading to energy savings of up to 10%. While older systems work by using the guest's key card as a physical trigger in a special holder by the bedroom door, more advanced systems operate by detecting movement or body heat. Room services are only activated when the guest presence is detected in the room, and the use systems of this type can generate savings of between 30 and 60%.

References

Collins, G. and Malik, T. (1999) *Hospitality Information Technology: Learning How to Use It*, 4th edn. Dubuque, IA: Kendall/Hunt Publishing.

Levy, J. (1998) *Technical Hotel Management*. Geneva, Switzerland, www.jlevy.ch.

O'Connor, P. (2003) *Using Computers in Hospitality*, 3rd edn. London: Continuum International.

PETER O'CONNOR
IMHI (CORNELL–ESSEC), FRANCE

Enterprise resource planning (ERP)

Enterprise Resource Planning (ERP) software was designed to automate and model the core business functions of an enterprise. It uses data and processes from logistical management, financial, and human resources. The main goal of ERP is to integrate information across the enterprise to eradicate the intricate and costly links between computer systems that do not communicate effectively with each other (Chan, 1999). Most business processes involve receiving an order from a customer, shipping, and billing the requested products (Koch, 2001). When utilizing ERP, the customer service representative will have all the necessary information, including customer's credit rating, order history, inventory of the company, and shipping schedules; this information can be viewed by authorized employees within the company as the information is stored in one single database. Thus, the overall process passes through each department and is completed automatically. Employees can view the process at any stage, monitoring the order. The end product is customer satisfaction with the timely and accurate processes of ERP (Koch, 2001).

ERP is useful in the hospitality industry because it enables the user to do many functions simultaneously. For instance, with a hotel conference center the conference coordinator can book a group in for a function via computer, thus informing foodservices whose computer will generate menus, in turn informing the shipping/receiving department that food would need to be ordered. From there the information would be forwarded to the food distribution center and the overall product would be shipped back to the hotel conference center in time for the function that was pre-planned.

References

Chan, S. (1999) The impact of technology on users and the workplace. *New Directions for Institutional Research*, 103 (3), p. 19.

Koch, C. (2001) What is ERP? *Darwinmag*, retrieved 29 August 2003 from http://www.darwinmag.com/learn/curve/column.html?ArticleID=39.

KRISTA HRIN
BROCK UNIVERSITY, CANADA

Entrepreneurism

Kirby (2003) defines entrepreneurism as a building and creation process beginning with little or nothing and moving to something. The hospitality industry is dominated by small to medium-sized enterprises chiefly because of low barriers to entry and because many people mistakenly believe that running a small hotel business is easy to do successfully. Franchises may be an attractive option for those who wish to limit risk but still want to operate a hospitality business. In either case, the above individuals may be described as entrepreneurs.

Entrepreneurs have psychological traits which often predispose them, amongst other things, toward creativity, engaging in risk-taking business behavior and having a strong inner locus of control. Often entrepreneurs are status-conscious and dislike 'taking orders' from others, preferring to 'be their own boss.' Additionally, some tend towards extroversion. Running one's own hospitality operation allows these individuals to engage in extrovert behavior, such as occupying the role of 'mein host.'

However, entrepreneurism in the hospitality industry is not limited to owner/mangers. Some evidence suggests that front-line workers share similar psychological traits and behavioral tendencies with their employers. 'Performing' at the customer interface for reward (tips) is a typical example of entrepreneurial behavior.

Reference

Kirby, David A. (2003) *Entrepreneurship*. Maidenhead: McGraw-Hill.

DARREN LEE-ROSS
JAMES COOK UNIVERSITY, AUSTRALIA
NOEL RICHARDS
JAMES COOK UNIVERSITY, AUSTRALIA

Entrepreneurship

Entrepreneurship in restaurants and foodservice suggests an interest in starting, owning, and operating a profitable independent or franchised operation. Entrepreneurship covers the full range of the restaurant business including, but not limited to:

- Concept
- Conducting analyses
- Understanding entrepreneurial potential
- Financial planning, borrowing, and control
- Franchising
- Location and property analysis
- Ownership and management.

Concept, advertising, innovation, and promotion includes knowledge of how to target a market, generate ideas for new or improved products or services, develop a budget, select the media, design a campaign, and assess results.

Marketing analysis includes assessing market potential, determining market niche and segmentation, forecasting sales, and describing sales strategies.

Entrepreneurial potential describes the characteristics and behavior of a successful entrepreneur.

Financial planning, borrowing, and control includes creating a business plan that will meet the lending standards of a financial institution; determining sources of capital and costs involved in financing business operations; developing operating budgets which project income, expenses, and profitability; and analyzing cash flow statements.

Franchising refers to an interest in researching the opportunity of franchising, including acquisition, operation, and profitability.

Location and property analysis is the function of analyzing business locations, using market research, and determining suitability of the property.

Ownership and management involves such concepts as administrative organizational structure, staffing, front-of-house operations, and back-of-house operations.

Entrepreneurship has become a major force in the global economy – this is especially true in the hospitality industry and, more specifically, the restaurant and foodservice sector. Viewed from the perspective of workers as a form of on-the-job training in itself, restaurants and the foodservice industry can constitute an apprenticeship providing a springboard for entrepreneurship rather than relegation to a career of low-paid work. Such a springboard suggests that an entrepreneur who is willing to take risks can overcome many of the barriers to entry inherent in non-foodservice operations and become successful without formal education. In fact, Smith and Miner (1989) defined two typologies of entrepreneurs according to personality, background, and behavior: craftsmen entrepreneurs and opportunistic entrepreneurs. These two types of entrepreneurs display many opposite personality qualities in their behavior and orientation.

Craftsmen entrepreneurs usually lack formal education in the field, lack depth in managerial experience, and have blue-collar backgrounds. They often enjoy being immersed in operations and doing planning and administrative work. Craftsmen typically are not concerned about social involvement, may lack social awareness, and do not interact or communicate effectively. Craftsmen usually prefer autocratic management styles by giving orders and making decisions without regard for others' input. Such entrepreneurs have a high aversion to risk-taking and display a high degree of rigidity and lack confidence. Businesses led by craftsmen usually operate without long-range plans and typically experience low growth rates. Craftsmen measure their success by customer satisfaction and are usually content with making a comfortable living.

Opportunistic entrepreneurs often have a high level of formal education, bring an extensive variety of management experience to a job, and come from middle-class backgrounds. These entrepreneurs prefer democratic, decentralized management styles and emphasize marketing efforts. Opportunistic entrepreneurs are highly socially aware and are very much involved in social relationships. They tend to be trend-oriented in predicting the future of their organizations. The key measures and indicators for success include profit, personal income, and business growth.

Even as research on entrepreneurs is increasing, there remains considerable variety in the definitions and criteria used to determine entrepreneurial status. Among the criteria used to differentiate entrepreneurial organizations from others are that the organization is typically 2–8 years old and has between 2 and 19 employees.

Bygrave and Zacharakis (2004) estimates that some 460 million people worldwide were either actively involved in entrepreneurial ventures or were owner–managers of a new business in 2002. Pertaining to these millions, what factors differentiated the successful from the unsuccessful? In general terms, those entrepreneurs who most accurately identify an opportunity offer the most promise. Yet these people realize success in their ventures only if they can create organizations – restaurants, for example – that allow the concept to tap successfully the target market.

In more specific terms and with direct implications for restaurateurs, there are two success factors that are critical. The first is planning. As Rainsford and Bangs (1992) note, lack of planning is the major reason leading to failure in the restaurant business. This includes business and strategic planning.

The second critical success factor is capitalization. In reviewing bankruptcy filings made by unsuccessful restaurant operators in the United States, the most common problem operators reported was undercapitalization. Despite a rule of thumb that restaurateurs should be prepared to operate with a negative cash flow for up to six months after opening, many believe that they will not face the same challenges as others.

Most venture capital investors agree that the opportunity at the core of any entrepreneurial activity must be evident enough to justify an investment but not so obvious that too many will enter the market at the same time. This is a difficult situation. After all, too ambiguous an opportunity may result in poor planning and lack of investor interest. Perhaps Mark Twain articulated the entrepreneur's bane best: 'I was seldom able to see an opportunity until it had ceased to be one.'

References

Bygrave, W.D. and Zacharakis, A. (eds) (2004) *The Portable MBA in Entrepreneurship*. Hoboken, NJ: John Wiley & Sons.

Rainsford, P. and Bangs, D.H. (1992) *The Restaurant Planning Guide*. Chicago: Upstart Publishing.

Smith, N.R. and Miner, J.B. (1989) Type of entrepreneur, type of firm, and managerial motivation: implications for organizational life cycle theory. *Strategic Management Journal*, 4, 225–240.

EDWARD A. MERRITT
CALIFORNIA STATE POLYTECHNIC
UNIVERSITY, USA
DENNIS REYNOLDS
WASHINGTON STATE UNIVERSITY, USA

Entry strategies

In setting up a new business, entrepreneurs try to overcome entry barriers and break into the competitive arena. A variety of strategies exist for penetrating into the market either by innovation or development of an offering similar to an existing product or service.

Depending on the circumstances, entrepreneurs employ various strategies for entering into the hospitality industry, including acquisition, intrapreneurship, purchase of a franchise, cooperation with a hotel management firm such as Hilton (Brymer, 1995), joining a referral association such as Best Western, or joining a confederation of several businesses to discuss and decide on issues of common interest, such as quality of service among hotels located in a specific area. Acquisition indicates a high level of ownership and control over the new operation. The others show relatively lower levels of ownership and control and are based primarily on exploiting brand name and marketing resources of well-established business entities. It should be noted, however, that intrapreneurship incorporates all kinds of minor employee-initiated improvements, both in products and processes, that continue to be in the organization's control and ownership. In contrast, intrapreneurship also incorporates strategic moves such as spin-offs, characterized by relatively low levels of control and ownership of the organization over the new operation (Morrison *et al.*, 1999).

References

Brymer, R. (1995) *Hospitality Management: An Introduction to the Industry*. Dubuque, IA: Kendall/Hunt Publishing.

Morrison, A., Rimmington, M. and Williams, C. (1999) *Entrepreneurship in the Hospitality, Tourism and Leisure Industries*. Oxford: Butterworth-Heinemann.

SIGAL HABER
TEL-AVIV UNIVERSITY, ISRAEL

Environmental determinism

Within the various strategic management schools of thought identified by Mintzberg (1990), the environmental school offers the least scope for management choice. Drawing upon biology, this school in its most extreme form conceives of the external environment as effectively selecting from the population of firms those that 'fit' and rejecting those that do not. Thus the environment is seen as being dominant and deterministic, with strategy essentially a reactive process whereby the organization is largely passive.

The origins of the environmental school reside in contingency theory, which recognized the importance of the external environment as an influence of organizational strategy. While strategists generally recognize the environment as an important influence on organizations, most would reject the extreme influence as is embodied in environmental determinism. Generally speaking, strategists take a more optimistic view of the influence managers can have on selecting and shaping the external environment of an organization. Increasingly, strategy academics conceive of the external environment as being something that organizational members 'enact' (Weick, 1995) rather than as being something that is imposed upon them. This challenges the whole idea of 'the environment,' which underpins the concept of environmental determinism.

References

Mintzberg, H. (1990) Strategy formation: schools of thought, in J.W. Fredrickson (ed.), *Perspectives on Strategic Management*. New York: Harper and Row, pp. 105–235.

Weick, K.E. (1995) *Sensemaking in Organizations*. Thousand Oaks, CA: Sage.

J. STEPHEN TAYLOR
UNIVERSITY OF STRATHCLYDE, UK

Environmental management

Hotel facilities managers as well as others at the property are often responsible for the overall environmental programs at their hotels. These programs are aimed at reducing negative environmental impacts of operation. These impacts can be internal involving employees and customers as well as external involving the local, regional, and global environment.

Environmental management responsibilities generally include the following:

- Waste minimization
- Energy conservation and management
- Management of fresh water resources
- Wastewater management
- Hazardous substances
- Involving staff, customers, and communities in environmental issues.

Waste minimization should be a part of the overall solid waste management program of the operation. Solid waste management is the management and final handling of matter that has passed its useful life. Solid waste includes various materials including paper and cardboard, yard wastes, food wastes, glass, metals, plastics and other solid materials, but also includes semisolid, liquid, and even gaseous wastes in containers. Solid waste may also be defined as hazardous and non-hazardous. Hazardous waste is defined in various ways, but generally requires special handling and disposal because it causes some hazard to human health or the environment. Non-hazardous waste is generally defined as solid wastes, and can include various sources such as municipal wastes, household wastes, industrial and commercial wastes that are non-hazardous.

Waste minimization activities can be thought of as involving waste reduction, waste reuse, and waste recycling.

Waste reduction refers to reducing the volume of wastes or pollutants prior to discharging them into the environment. Instead of controlling a waste, means are sought to produce less of the waste or, better yet, produce none at all. Source reduction of excess packaging is one important area of waste reduction. A common practice within the hotel industry is to create procurement policies which encourage suppliers to reduce or even reuse packaging. Purchasing product in bulk or in concentrate for later dilution is also an attractive option to reduce wastes at their source.

Waste reuse is an efficient form of waste management, which focuses on extending the life cycle of a particular product or material before disposal. Reusing a product is generally more efficient than recycling because fewer resources are used and less pollution is produced. For example, refilling (or reusing) glass bottles takes two-thirds less energy than recycling the bottles.

However, this may not be the case if the energy saved in reusing is lost through the transportation or washing. Another common example in a hotel environment is the reuse of old towels which may no longer be up to guest standards. Generally these towels are cut down, dyed a specific color depending on their end-use and reused by various departments before they are finally disposed of.

Waste recycling is the practice of collecting and reprocessing waste materials after its useful life for reuse in the same or different product. This generally refers to the sortable and separable consumer products such as cans, bottles, plastics, organic wastes, newspapers and other paper products. In an industrial setting, recycling is more often referred to as *resource recovery*. For materials to be candidates for recycling, they must be properly diverted from the regular waste stream for future collection, sorting, and reprocessing. In recent years, the scarcity of raw materials and the rising cost of conventional waste disposal has led to an upsurge in the amount of waste being recycled. The extent to which waste recycling takes place depends on the cost and scarcity of producing or extracting new raw material from source, the cost and ease of recycling the material into a new product, and the political and social climate which can determine the acceptability of recycling.

Energy conservation and management involves efforts to reduce the amount of energy used at the property. This not only has an environmental benefit but also can achieve some significant cost savings. It can also involve attempting to purchase renewable energy. Major opportunities in energy conservation come from increased equipment efficiency, reducing operating hours of equipment, reducing loads consuming energy, and recovery of waste energy.

Energy conservation items that have proven cost-effective include use of more energy-efficient lighting, installation of occupancy sensor based controls for guestroom HVAC operation, photocell control of lighting operation, use of economizer/'free cooling' modes in the operation of HVAC equipment, and installation of ozone-based laundry equipment (which uses low temperature wash cycles and less water than conventional systems). There are literally hundreds of potential energy conservation options available and most operations will find the paybacks on most of these to be under 4 years.

Management of fresh water resources and of wastewater is somewhat intertwined. Most action to reduce usage of water will reduce the quantity of wastewater. Maintenance to repair leaks, use of water-saving devices, and recycling or reuse of water are all options here. For operations that are treating their own wastewater, ensuring that the treatment methods are operating in an optimal manner and that discharged wastes have a minimal negative environmental impact is clearly important.

Hazardous substances are potentially present in cleaning supplies used at the operation as well as with potential discharges such as oil, grease, and fuels and with disposal of items such as fluorescent lamps and ballasts. Efforts to reduce the use of hazardous substances as well as to dispose of these in ways that have minimal environmental impact are needed.

Involving staff, customers, and the community can open the door for the property to have a positive influence on all of these groups. Staff have been found to respond very favorably to environmental programs by their employers. Some customers have expressed preferences for 'green' hotels. The community can also be served by environmental programs with the efforts of hotels sometimes helping to create recycling services that go beyond the hotel boundaries. Some hotels further involve the community by providing leftover food to local homeless shelters.

One way to approach environmental management is through the implementation of a formal EMS or environmental management system. An EMS is a continual cycle of planning, implementing, reviewing and improving the processes and actions that an organization undertakes to meet its business and environmental goals. Most EMSs are built on the 'Plan, Do, Check, Act' model. This model leads to continual improvement based upon:

- Planning, including identifying environmental aspects and establishing goals (Plan)
- Implementing, including training and operational controls (Do)
- Checking, including monitoring and corrective action (Check)
- Reviewing, including progress reviews and acting to make needed changes to the EMS (Act).

The benefits of developing an EMS may include cost savings, increased competitiveness, enhanced public image, and better management of environmental obligations.

References

Hill, Marquita K. (1997) *Understanding Environmental Pollution*. Cambridge: Cambridge University Press, p. 25.

Jones, G., Hollier, G., Forbes, J., and Robinson, A. (1992) *The HarperCollins Dictionary of Environmental Science*. New York: HarperCollins.

Stipanuk, D.M. (2002) *Hospitality Facilities Management and Design*, 2nd edn. Lansing, MI: Educational Institute of the American Hotel and Lodging Association. pp. 91–122.

www.epa.gov/ems/.

LYLE THOMPSON
BURNABY, BC, CANADA

Environmental management in hotels

Environmental management refers to the management of an organization in such a way as to minimize the impact of that organization on the environment. Conceptually, environmental management is related to the principles and practices of sustainability. A sustainable organization may be defined as one that can satisfy its own needs, without diminishing the opportunities available to future generations. In practice, environmental management can cover a range of activities, from the simple process of saving money, through the better management of resources and the reduction of waste, to the total design of a business on sound principles of sustainability. The need for environmental management has been emphasized by international agreements on sustainable development, covering topics such as emissions (such as carbon dioxide and chlorofluorocarbons), social/cultural protection, and global stewardship. These principles have now been incorporated into the policies of many countries. However, the translation of these policies into action by businesses has been more problematic. A majority of companies have done very little to curb their use of resources. Some companies have actively engaged in a series of initiatives that reduce environmental impact, on the basis that they save money. A minority of companies have gone further than this, embracing environmental management for ethical reasons and with cost as a secondary factor.

The hotel industry has moved into environmental management relatively recently, probably because of dual factors. First, it is a common perception that hotels have a low environmental impact (at least in comparison with heavy industry). Second, because of the image of a hotel as a place of comfort and luxury, hoteliers are often nervous of appearing to be concerned mainly with cutting costs. Thus, for example, asking hotel guests if they wish to reuse their towels or if they would prefer fresh ones may appear to be reducing the level of service. However, a number of hotel chains and independently managed hotels now fully subscribe to environmental

management. Furthermore, organizations such as the International Hotels Environment Initiative have encouraged hotels to work together to improve standards throughout the industry.

An additional factor is the growth in green consumerism and, more specifically, in the emergence of the green tourist. A significant market segment is emerging of people who consider environmental practices when choosing a holiday or business destination, a hotel, and an airline. Whilst this segment is small at the moment, there are signs that it is growing. One response by hotel operators and tourist destinations to the growth of the green consumer has been the developing of environmental awards and badges, which allow hotel operators and tourist destinations to promote their environmental credentials.

A typical environmental management program will start with an audit of existing performance in relation to the use of all resources such as energy (particularly heating, air conditioning, and hot water), water and food. Second, a record of the level of emissions of combustion products, fumes, solid and liquid wastes, packaging materials, dangerous emissions, traffic, and noise should be taken. Based on the outcome of this audit, targets for the reduction of these impacts should then be agreed, together with a planned program of change designed to achieve these targets. The program of change may cover everything from staff awareness training through to capital investment in new plant and machinery. Finally, regular monitoring of performance against these targets will measure progress. In choosing which activities to tackle first, it makes sense to start with those that can be achieved with zero or low cost and that can be achieved relatively easily. This both engages staff in the processes of environmental management and increases levels of confidence, making it possible to go on and tackle more difficulty or complex projects. A key factor in the success of environmental management programs is the presence of a champion at a senior level in the organization.

Standards of performance may be externally audited, using procedures such as the International Standards Organization standard for environmental management. Based on this internationally agreed standard, an environmental management system includes:

- An environmental policy statement
- A plan, covering an identification of environmental impacts, legal requirements, objectives and targets, an environmental management program
- An implementation plan, identifying responsibilities within the organization, awareness raising, training needs, a communication policy, documentation systems and operational control
- Checking and corrective action covering monitoring, corrective action, records, audit procedures
- A regular management review process.

These procedures are certified by an external body, in a similar way to total quality management systems.

References

Capra, F. and Pauli, G. (1995) *Steering Business Toward Sustainability*. Tokyo: United Nations University Press, pp. 1–14.

IHEI (1996) *Environmental Management for Hotels*, 2nd edn. Oxford: Butterworth-Heinemann.

Kirk, D. (1996) *Environmental Management for Hotels*. Oxford: Butterworth-Heinemann.

Webster, K. (2000) *Environmental Management in the Hospitality Industry*. London: Cassell.

ISO (2002) *Environmental Management, the ISO 14000 Family of International Standards*. Geneva: International Organization for Standards.

Wilson, G.A. and Bryant, R.L. (1996) *Environmental Management*. London: UCL Press.

DAVID KIRK
QUEEN MARGARET UNIVERSITY COLLEGE
EDINBURGH, UK

Environmental management system

With an environmental management system (EMS), a hospitality firm can manage environmental risks and opportunities more systematically and efficiently. Although environmental management systems can be different for different types of organizations, depending on their size, products, and the nature of their business, etc., common components include the identification of environmental impact and legal obligations, the development of a plan for management and improvement, the assignment of responsibilities, and the monitoring of performance. BS7750, launched in 1992, was the world's first EMS standard. In 1993, another EMS standard was published by the European Union (EU), called 'Eco-Management and Audit Scheme' (EMAS). This is a voluntary EU regulation that enables interested parties to implement a formal EMS, evaluate their programs, and work towards continuous improvement in environmental performance. Thereafter, national EMS standards proliferated, eventually leading to the development of the ISO 14000 standards. In the ISO 14000 series, ISO 14001, commonly known as the most important EMS standard, defines EMS as a management system that includes organizational structure, planning activities, responsibilities, practices, procedures, processes, and resources for developing, implementing, achieving, reviewing, and maintaining environmental policies. To be successful, an EMS not only requires the ongoing leadership and support of the senior management, but also relies on the involvement of operations staff, accountable for environmental performance, which must be sufficiently motivated and encouraged to carry out their environmental responsibilities.

References

United Nations Education Program (1997) *Environmental Management System – Training Resources Kit*. United Nations Environment Programme, International Chamber of Commerce, and the International Federation of Consulting Engineers, the Version 1.0.

ISO (1996) *International Standard ISO 14001 Environmental Management Systems – Specification with Guidance for Use*. Geneva: International Organization for Standardization.

ERIC S.W. CHAN
THE HONG KONG POLYTECHNIC
UNIVERSITY, HONG KONG SAR, CHINA

Environmental scanning

Environmental scanning (ES) is an integral part of the strategic management process. It entails a constant examination of the external environment to detect changes that may affect the organization either directly or indirectly. Okumus (2004) defines environmental scanning as the employment of systematic methods by an organization to monitor, gather information and forecast external forces and developments not under the direct control of the organization.

According to Reichel and Preble (1984), formal ES begins with the identification of a relevant trend or external forces from the viewpoint of the organization. It would seem that the selection of the external force to be monitored and analyzed depends on the perspective of the hospitality organization. Clearly, a domestic chain will have a different focus and set of priorities than a global firm. In other words, while the process in each domestic market of a global chain might be similar to the ES of a domestic chain, there are additional global environmental forces such as regional economic crises or geopolitical crises that are significant from the global perspective and are an integral part of the global ES process.

A normative-prescriptive approach for ES would suggest checking a list of sub-environments to select those that are relevant. For example, it is possible to utilize the Harrison and Enz (2005) concept of the external environment for hospitality organizations. Their concept of the external environment is divided into the broad and operating environments. The operating environment is different for each firm, although similarities may exist among firms in the same industry (p. 33). The broad environment is not firm-specific and affects many firms and industries. It consists of socio-cultural trends, technological, political and economic influences. The operating environment consists of competitors, local communities, customers, the media, government agencies and administrators, financial intermediaries, unions, suppliers, and activist groups. Each one of these factors is further divided to specific environmental components. Socio-cultural influences, for example, may be further divided into attitude change, demographic shifts, changes in lifestyle patterns, changes in consumer tastes, new fads, public opinion and changes in leisure preferences.

A somewhat different concept of the environment is suggested by Okumus (2004): the 'general environment' and the 'task environment.' The general environment is referred to as the national and global context of political economic, social, technological, legal, and ecological conditions. The task environment is composed of suppliers, competitors, customers, regulators, and other interest groups (p. 125). Once the relevant environmental sectors are identified, the formal ES process calls for a constant search for information to examine current developments and attempt to predict future trends. The issue of deciding upon the relevant segments of the environment is referred to by Okumus (2004) as the scope of scanning activities. Accordingly, two approaches are identified: the outside-in approach and the inside-out approach. The first views the environment from a broad perspective. All elements or sub-environments are scanned, and the longer-term trends and development of alternative views as well as their implications are considered. The inside-out approach, in contrast, takes a narrow view of the environment and solely focuses on some (most relevant) elements in the outside environment. Gathering relevant information either through outside-in or inside-out perspectives is only a step toward the end result of ES: interpretation of the data on the relevant trends. Often referred to as environmental analysis or assessment, the interpretation is expected to classify the data into two major categories: environmental threats and environmental opportunities. Threats are trends interpreted as detrimental to the success of the organization, while opportunities are trends interpreted as helpful in terms of achieving the objectives of the organization.

ES can be done on an ongoing basis, as recommended by most prescriptive-normative models. It can also be conducted irregularly or periodically. Irregular scanning refers to crisis management, when the hospitality organization attempts to solve an immediate problem and the need for additional environmental information on the environment is apparent (Israeli and Reichel, 2003). In crisis situations managers are tested on their abilities to actually apply concepts such as ES, usually described as 'important.' Periodic systems are more sophisticated and focus on long-term issues.

Another distinction is often made between formal and informal ES. Formal ES involves assigning special personnel to the task and may result in the establishment of a special organizational unit dedicated to ES. The informal approach advocates constant alertness and attention to environmental data by all the members of the organization. Data gathering becomes an integral part of the job of each member. Relevant information is expected to flow from the bottom of the organization to the top decision-makers. This approach is similar to the concept of knowledge management.

Examining the challenges of employing a formal environmental scanning approach in hospitality organizations, Okumus (2004) identified the following deterrents:

- Difficulty in defining the external environment
- Difficulty in predicting the future
- Difficulty in collecting reliable data and accurately interpreting it
- Difficulty in distinguishing between opportunities and threats
- Issue of emergence or identification of opportunities and threats
- Problems with utilizing a formal and inside-out approach
- Dilemma of ES activities for short-term problems vs. long-term planning
- Difficulty in creating harmony between ES activities and company culture
- Survival and acceptance of ES units
- Finally, the crucial issue of organizational performance has to be considered.

Several studies have suggested that the adoption of ES leads to improved economic performance in hospitality organizations (for example, Costa and Teare, 2000). However, this issue is far from definite, as there are numerous other factors that account for successful performance. Furthermore, a sufficient number of longitudinal and in-depth studies that supply a clear-cut conclusion have yet to be conducted. Yet, the plethora of studies on strategic management and performance in numerous industries strongly support the approach that ES heightens the awareness of decision-makers to crucial environmental trends and promotes making the most of opportunities and avoiding threats.

References

Costa, J. and Teare, R. (2000) Developing an environmental scanning process in the hotel sector. *International Journal of Contemporary Hospitality Management*, 12 (3), 156–169.

Harrison, J.S. and Enz, A.C. (2005) *Hospitality Strategic Management: Concepts and Cases*. Hoboken, NJ: John Wiley & Sons.

Okumus, F. (2004) Potential challenges of employing a formal environmental scanning approach in hospitality organizations. *International Journal of Hospitality Management*, 23 (2), 123–143.

Reichel, A. and Preble, J. (1984) Environmental scanning for the hospitality industry. *Hospitality Education and Research Journal*, 9 (1), 38–53.

Israeli, A.A. and Reichel, A. (2003) Hospitality crisis management practices: the Israeli case. *International Journal of Hospitality Management*, 22 (4), 353–372.

ARIE REICHEL
BEN-GURION UNIVERSITY, ISRAEL

Equal employment opportunity

Equal employment opportunity (EEO) and affirmative action practices are based on a belief in universal human rights as expressed in the United Nations' Universal Declaration of Human Rights (1948). EEO is enshrined in anti-discrimination legislation that has been passed in many countries and attempts to ensure that all individuals have an equal chance for employment regardless of characteristics such as ethnic/national origin, religion, sex, age, and in some countries (i.e. Australia) sexual orientation

(De Cieri and Kramar, 2003). In other words, the aim of this legislation is to give legal support to the notion that all people in a society should have equal opportunities to enjoy the benefits of that society, including employment. Most industrialized nations have enacted EEO legislation but some variations of enforcement exist. In some cases this may only be achieved if groups who were previously disadvantaged now experience positive discrimination. This practice is known as 'affirmative action' and seeks to redress the balance, particularly for minorities and women in the workplace. In an increasingly global and service-oriented economy, effective diversity management is paramount for success. Moreover, ignorance can have significant costs in both financial and human terms. This is a key issue for the hospitality industry because of the significant numbers of women and minority groups employed (Woods, 2002).

References

De Cieri, H. and Kramar, R. (2003) *Human Resource Management in Australia: Strategy, People, Performance.* Sydney: McGraw-Hill.

Woods, R.H. (2002) *Managing Hospitality Human Resources*, 3rd edn. Lansing, MI: Educational Institute of the American Hotel and Lodging Association.

DARREN LEE-ROSS
JAMES COOK UNIVERSITY, AUSTRALIA

Ergonomics

Derived from the Greek *ergon* (work) and *nomos* (laws) to denote the science of work, ergonomics (or human factors) is a discipline that nowadays studies how the human body relates to its various environments. It is the application of scientific information concerning humans to the design of objects, systems, and environments for human use. Ergonomists' main concern is to ensure that work and leisure products, as well as physical environments are comfortable, safe and efficient for people to use. Ergonomics is relevant to everything that involves people. All human activities including work, sports, leisure, recreation, tourism, health and safety embody ergonomics principles, if properly designed. Ergonomics is a multi-disciplinary field involving numerous professionals such as engineers, designers, computer specialists, physicians, health and safety experts, and specialists in human resources. Ergonomists contribute to the design and evaluation of tasks, jobs, products, environments, and systems in order to make them compatible with the needs, abilities, and limitations of people. The basic human sciences involved in ergonomics are *anatomy*, *physiology*, and *psychology*. These sciences are applied by ergonomists to make the most productive use of human capabilities, and to protect and enhance human health and well being.

References

The Ergonomics Society. http://www.ergonomics.org.uk/ergonomics.htm. Retrieved 26 April 2004.

International Ergonomics Association. http://www.iea.cc/ergonomics/. Retrieved 26 April 2004.

JERRY LACHAPPELLE
HARRAH'S ENTERTAINMENT, INC., USA

Evaluative attributes

Consumers use three types of attributes to evaluate the quality of goods and services: search qualities, experience qualities, and credence qualities. Search qualities are more tangible attributes that a consumer can easily evaluate before purchasing a product such as color, style, price, fit, feel, and smell. Products high in search qualities include clothing, jewelry, and furniture. Experience qualities are attributes that cannot be judged until after purchase or during consumption, such as taste or durability. Restaurant meals and haircuts are examples of experience qualities. The third category of evaluative attributes, credence qualities, includes characteristics that the consumer may not be able to evaluate even after purchase and consumption due to their complexity. For example, few consumers have sufficient knowledge in medical services or mechanical services to be able to judge a medical diagnosis or an engine repair.

Consumers can evaluate most products by using a combination of search and experience qualities due to their tangible nature, while most hospitality and other services require consumers to focus on experience and credence qualities. Goods high in search qualities are the easiest for consumers to evaluate. Goods and services high in experience qualities are more difficult to judge and therefore most consumers exercise greater caution before purchasing them. Services high in credence qualities are the most difficult to judge and require different decision-making processes when deciding on services high in credence qualities.

Reference

Zeithaml, V. and Bitner, M.J. (2003) *Services Marketing: Integrating Customer Focus Across the Firm*, 3rd edn. New York: McGraw-Hill.

JENNIFER T. CONDON
NEWMARKET INTERNATIONAL, INC., USA

Event operations manual

Often referred to as 'the bible,' the event operations manual is used during an event to allow management and staff to easily use a master checklist. It is typically a three-ring binder with a colorful cover for easy identification. It should contain all schedules, checklists, task lists, a reference index, contact info for all staff, including the office phone, cell phones and hotel phone numbers where the staff are housed, contact information for all speakers, officers, and vendors, written procedures for locating lost persons or property, emergency services such as fire, ambulance, etc.. It normally includes an event summary including time, action, and location of each activity, a map of the venue, the production schedule, move-in, move-out information and set-up schedule, including date, action, suppliers, and crew list. The event operations manual also

contains information on catering services, including catering requirements for staff and crew, security information, photocopies of all credentials and inspections, and incident report forms. Additional information on rest room locations, parking information, shuttle bus information, and location of ATMs, media briefings, event fact sheet, and summary of event background should also be included.

Reference

O'Toole, W. and Mikolatis, P. (2002) *Corporate Event Project Management*. New York: John Wiley & Sons.

PATTI J. SHOCK
UNIVERSITY OF NEVADA, LAS VEGAS, USA

Event project management

Event project management is the adaptation of the project management methodology, as developed since the 1950s, to the management of events. The project management methodology has evolved into a formal system which can be described and improved. It includes areas of knowledge, tools, techniques, and processes. When project management was first formalized, it concerned the development of US Department of Defense contracts. Many of these tools, such as the scheduling of tasks, were adapted from operations research and scientific management. At the same time the collection of tools and techniques was used in civil engineering and construction. The project management of that time stressed certain techniques that were most relevant to these industries. They were characterized by a stable management environment.

It could be described as:

$$Requirements \rightarrow Process \rightarrow Result$$

Once the client's requirements were decided upon – such as expressed in an architect's drawing – the project manager went ahead and created the building as close to the plan as possible.

Therefore a large part of the work of a project manager concerned contract management and change control.

Contrast this to an event management environment, where change and uncertainty are common. When project management was applied to research projects and information technology development, the limitations of the construction/engineering model became obvious. Client requirements can be complex and changing for IT development. The product of a research project is often ill-defined and becomes more defined as the project develops. Project management evolved to encompass these fields. Event management, with its intangible outcomes, complexity of stakeholders and changing management environment, represents a further development possibility for project management. The point is that each new industry that joins the project management portfolio influences the project management methodology.

The areas of current project management that are found to be useful to event management are:

- *Scope definition:* The scope includes the amount of work needed to create the event or festival. This is useful as, too often, event management is regarded as just concerning the event itself and not the work need to design and implement it.
- *Work breakdown structure:* Arising from defining the scope is the breakdown of all the work into manageable units. The units can be assigned resources and a schedule for completion.
- *Task analysis:* Once the general areas of work have been defined, the individual tasks that must be completed can be discovered.
- *Scheduling:* To create an event is to work to a deadline. Therefore every task has to be completed by a certain time. This is the work schedule.
- *Responsibility chart:* The tasks need to be done by a person or a group of people. Therefore someone is assigned the responsibility to make sure the task is completed.
- *Resource analysis:* Each task will require a number of resources such as volunteers and equipment.
- *Risk management:* In a changing environment and the fact that the asset, i.e. the event or festival, is unique in some way, means there will

be many problems. Risk management as found in the project management methodology is perhaps the strongest reason for the adoption of project management. Risk management is relatively new to events. However it has been a foundation area of knowledge in project management. The fields of engineering, IT, and research projects have developed a sophisticated risk management process that can be easily adapted to event management.

- *Stakeholder management:* In some areas of event management there is a highly refined system for managing stakeholders. The management of sponsors is an example of this, with levels of sponsorship and the sponsor communication plan. Project management uses such a system for all the stakeholders.

These are a few of the key areas of project management that are useful to the management of events. Figure 1 illustrates how these key areas fit together to produces an event project management system.

O'Toole and Mikolaitis (2002) give a number of advantages of using a project management system:

- It provides a systematic approach to all events. By having a management system each event is a test of the system and a way to improve the management. Most event evaluation concerns the event itself.
- A project system has evaluation of the management of the event as one of its aims.
- It depersonalizes the event, that is to say it takes the event out of the hands of just one person.
- It facilitates clear communication; project management supplies common terminology across all areas of management.
- It fits in with the business practices of other companies and departments. Project management is one of the fastest-growing management systems in all areas of business.
- By employing it for an event, the event management finds it is easier to explain what they are doing to the stakeholders.
- It is an accountable system that can show the progress of the management; the event management can produce a report on the progress at any time, therefore the stakeholders such as

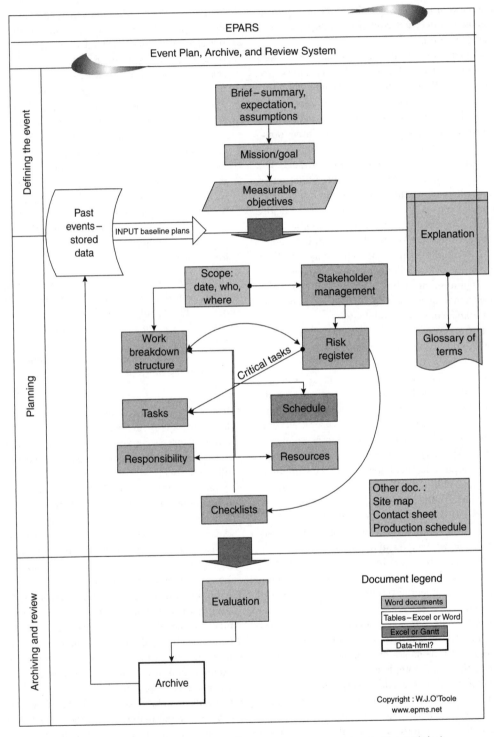

Figure 1   Event project management (from www.epms.net–reproduced with permission)

the government or sponsors do not have to wait until the event to find out the competency of the management.

- It creates transferable skills. The skill learned in working on an event can be used in other projects.
- It enables the event management to draw on other areas of knowledge – contract management. Logistics and decision optimization are an example of knowledge areas that can assist event management. By using project management these areas can be incorporated into the event management.

As events and festivals become more important to countries and their economies, governments are more aware of them and want a role in their development. The support of governments results in the need for a fully accountable management system. This is perhaps the strongest external driving force for the adoption of event project management. Governments around the world are concerned about management competency. Terrible disasters have occurred at some events and festivals and there is a move in some countries to legislate to control them. Risk management, as found in project management, is regarded by some countries as mandatory for events and festivals. Event project management provides the solution.

Large events are creating this new position of event project manager. Their position is often at the same level as the event director or producer. The latter has the creative role. Large sporting events will often have the project office as the controlling management body.

Some of the larger events that have incorporated event project management include the Grand Prix, the Sydney Olympics, the Masters Games, and the Asian Games.

References

Allen, Johnny, McDonnell, Ian, O'Toole, William, and Harris, Rob (2002) *Festival and Special Event Management*, 2nd edn. Brisbane: John Wiley & Sons.

Getz, D. (1997) *Event Management and Event Tourism*. New York: Cognizant Communication.

Gray, C. and Larson, E. (2000) *Project Management: The Managerial Process*. Boston, MA: Irwin/McGraw-Hill.

O'Toole, W. and Mikolaitis, P. (2002) *Corporate Event Project Management*. New York: John Wiley & Sons.

WILLIAM O'TOOLE
UNIVERSITY OF SYDNEY, AUSTRALIA

Evoked set

The evoked set is part of the alternative evaluation stage in consumer buying behavior when alternatives are considered for purchase. It can be viewed as a funneling process beginning with the *total set* of all brands or alternatives available from which a consumer can choose. The total set of available hotels in a large city contains many alternatives, as does the number of pizza or other fast food alternatives in certain geographic areas. Most consumers would not be aware of every alternative; hence, the total set for a particular consumer would be whittled down to a subset containing only those alternatives of which he or she is aware, or the *awareness set*. The consumer or tourism purchaser acquires information during the information search stage of the decision-making process, the consumer moves to evaluate various alternatives. In this stage, the consumer compares various brands or hospitality and tourism products and services that he or she feels are capable of meeting their needs or motives or solving the decision-making dilemma of what to do during a vacation, trip or travel event. The various brands or choices identified from the awareness set as viable options to be purchased during the alternative evaluation phase of the consumer buying process are referred to as the consumer's *evoked set*. They are, in effect, the only alternatives a consumer 'actually considers' buying.

The choice or evoked set is most always a subset of all of the various brands or choices of which the consumer is aware. For example, if a family is considering a family theme park vacation, all the various names or brands of theme parks might be considered including Disneyland, Disney World, Sea World, Six Flags, Kings Dominion, Universal Studios Theme Park, Hershey Park, Busch Gardens, and others. However, once the real choices are considered, it may be clear that the best choices for the family are in Orlando, Florida and the choice set narrows to Disney World, Sea World, and Busch Gardens. Thus, the family has moved to reduce the choice set to a smaller more managed evoked set of theme parks. The evoked set for services often includes self-provision. For instance, an alternative to going out to a restaurant may be to prepare and eat the meal at home. The exact size of the evoked set or choice set is likely to vary from consumer to consumer and the size of the choice set may depend upon the importance of the purchase and how long the consumer wishes to spend on comparing the various choices in the evoked set. However, the average number of alternatives in an evoked set is three, and rarely does it exceed six. For services, including hospitality services specifically, the average is less than three.

Advertising is critical in creating and maintaining the awareness and establishing the brand as one to be included in the choice set. If the consumer is not aware of an alternative, that alternative has a zero probability of being selected. Once an alternative is generated into the evoked set, its selection is dependent on how it measures against the other alternatives being considered. This requires knowledge of which attributes are most important to customers and how they perceive each competitor with respect to those attributes. Understanding how individuals apply decision strategies to arrive at a choice is critical. Marketers must also work beyond the initial choice set to further enhance the brand once the consumer(s) are on site and making additional choice decisions. Personal selling, promotional selling, suggestive selling, and a number of promotional techniques at the point of purchase can work to further consider brand extensions and multiple branded purchases of the goods or services. For example, when one considers a theme park visit and chooses the Disney World brand, Disney goes further with their branded choices by suggestive selling 'park hopper passes' to visit

additional brand-extended parks while in the Orlando area.

References

Belch, G.E. and Belch, M.A. (2001) *Advertising and Promotion – An Integrated Marketing Communications Perspective*, 5th edn. Boston, MA: McGraw-Hill Irwin.

Zeithaml, V.A. and Bitner, M.J. (2003) *Services Marketing Integrating Customer Focus Across the Firm*, 3rd edn. New York: McGraw-Hill.

ROD WARNICK
UNIVERSITY OF MASSACHUSETTS, USA
LINDA J. SHEA
UNIVERSITY OF MASSACHUSETTS, USA

Exchange company

Exchange is an increasingly important aspect of the timeshare offer, and has had a major impact on the increasing popularity of timeshare. Exchange companies act as brokers between timeshare owners. They give timeshare owners the opportunity to swap their timeshare for another week, in another resort, with confidence that they will experience similar quality.

The two principal exchange companies are Interval International (II) and Resort Condominiums International (RCI). They collective incorporate some 5400 resorts in their schemes. Virtually all timeshare resorts are members of one or other of these organizations. Where the resort is affiliated, a timeshare owner joins the exchange company at the time of purchase.

RCI (a subsidiary of Cendant Corporation (NYSE: CD), a provider of travel and real estate services) is a leading global provider of innovative products and services to the global travel and leisure industry. Founded in 1974 as an exchange service for condominium owners called Resort Condominiums International, RCI quickly became a driving force for growth within timeshare, and has been at the forefront of the vacation ownership industry ever since. Today, the company has over 3700 affiliated resorts located in 100 countries, with over 3 million members living in more than 200 countries. RCI's exchange systems offer consumers the ultimate flexibility in vacations with more quality resort destinations and leisure product choices in more countries than any other service. Since its inception, RCI has arranged exchange vacations for more than 54 million people worldwide.

As a growth partner to its business clients, RCI leverages core competencies in branding, networking, and partnering to unlock the value of leisure assets in vacation ownership, real estate, hospitality, travel tourism, and with affinities. The company consists of several major lines of business: RCI Community is an exchange network of 3 million timeshare owners worldwide who enjoy vacation experiences through RCI's traditional week-for-week and points-based timeshare exchange networks; RCI Consulting is a leader in providing professional guidance and comprehensive business solutions to new developers seeking to enter the timeshare and fractional industry. It also specializes in developing business and project strategies, program development, marketing, sales plans, and detailed financial overview; Holiday Network, with more than 80,000 units in more than 100 countries, is the world's largest and most diverse collection of holiday rentals. Accommodations available for rent include studios, multi-bedroom condominiums, summer homes, European villas and cottages, houseboats, and canal boats. Global Registry, LLC is an international service provider to the luxury leisure travel segment with core competencies in travel networks, concierge service, proprietary technology and quality assurance. In addition, RCI has a strategic alliance with Springer–Miller Systems, a leading provider of technology solutions to the hospitality industry. Through this alliance RCI is able to offer affiliates a sophisticated hospitality management system that is a fully integrated infrastructure for vacation ownership companies. RCI also has an ongoing strategic alliance with International Cruise and Excursions, Inc. (ICE), the leading provider of cruises to the vacation ownership industry. Together with ICE, RCI offers affiliates an array of value-added exchange services as an

incentive for their sales efforts, while members enjoy a wide range of the finest vacation options.

Since 1976, *Interval International* has been both a leader and a pioneer in the world of timesharing. The Interval International vacation exchange network consists of 2000 resorts in 75 countries, serving more than 1.5 million member families worldwide. Interval provides its members – vacation owners from around the world – with a variety of exchange services and other benefits. Membership is limited to owners at the resorts in II's network, all of which must meet rigorous criteria for quality. None of these resorts is owned or managed by Interval International. With 26 offices in 17 countries, Interval International is an operating business of IAC/InterActiveCorp, formerly known as USA Interactive. IAC/Inter ActiveCorp consists of IAC Travel, a division of the company that encompasses Expedia, Inc., Interval International, TV Travel Shop, Hotels.com and Hotwire.com. The other operating businesses of IAC are: HSN; Ticketmaster, which oversees Evite and Reserve America; Match.com, which oversees uDate.com; Entertainment Publications; Citysearch; Precision Response Corporation; and LendingTree. Interval offer a full support service to resort developers, including sales and marketing support, software support, purchasing services, operational services, reservation services, and consulting services.

Exchange companies act like a bank so that an owner who does not wish to use the week and/or resort purchased 'banks' the week owned with the exchange company. They are subsequently able to withdraw equivalent weeks at other times and/or at other resorts, which have been deposited by other owners.

Exchange companies have mechanisms for matching properties based upon a variety of factors which help to determine the value of different weeks in different resorts. Factors such as the size of the property, the duration of the stay, the time of year, resort quality, resort location are taken into account to arrive at relative values of properties in the system. Increasingly exchange companies are using a 'points system' as a kind of currency through which they can judge the relative value of the weeks concerned.

References

American Resort Development Association (2002) *The Timeshare Industry Resource Manual.* Washington, DC: ARDA.

http://www.intervalworld.com/iw/cs?a=60&p=about. Accessed 3 September 2003.

http://www.resortdeveloper.com/home/home.htm. Accessed 3 September 2003.

http://news.rciventures.com/OVER/setNI.html. Accessed 3 September.

CONRAD LASHLEY,
NOTTINGHAM TRENT UNIVERSITY, UK

References

Bocij, P., Chaffey, D., Greasley, A., and Hickie, S. (2003) *Business Information Systems: Technology, Development and Management for the e-Business.* Harlow, UK: Pearson Education.

McLeod, R. Jr and Schell, G. (2001) *Management Information Systems.* Upper Saddle River, NJ: Prentice-Hall.

ROB LAW
THE HONG KONG POLYTECHNIC
UNIVERSITY, HONG KONG SAR, CHINA
STEVEN CHAN
THE HONG KONG POLYTECHNIC
UNIVERSITY, HONG KONG SAR, CHINA

Executive information system

An executive information system (EIS) is a computer-based information system that assists executives to manage information for maintaining and achieving the overall business objectives (Bocij *et al.*, 2003). Executives normally refer to managers on the top level of a business hierarchy who can strongly influence the organization in strategic planning and policy setting. An EIS may or may not have a direct relationship with business decision-making. The system, however, will help executives with the necessary information system support, making them more productive in receiving and selecting the essential information that they need (McLeod and Schell, 2001).

In the unstructured and loosely defined hospitality context, executives often demand specialized information from a wide variety of resources in unlike formats. An EIS meets such a demand by pulling out, filtering, and processing the essential data from the internal and external data repositories. The EIS will then output the processed information in graphical on-screen displays. Examples of these displays include figures and tables that explain trends, ratios, and statistics. With such information, hotel executives can set policies, prepare budgetary plans, and compile strategic forecasts easily in a short time. An example of an executive information system in hospitality is the DA-5 EIP (www.hoteltechsolutions.com).

Executive recruiters/headhunters

The dollar costs to hospitality organizations of using executive recruiters may be high, but often guarantees, managerial time savings, and the ability to source top-management talent that hospitality organizations would be unable to access directly may make up for the cost.

Executive recruiters are one of three types of external employment agencies (Dessler, 2002). Others are governmental operations (useful for sourcing unskilled personnel) and those operated by professional and technical societies on behalf of their members.

Executive recruiters generally do not advertise, instead they approach individuals sourced through research and networks of contacts. Given the level of open cooperation between competitors in the hospitality industry, executive recruiters can, if necessary, keep both parties confidential until much later in the process than would otherwise be the case.

Executive recruiters search for and screen many applicants to find the most appropriate candidates (usually three to five candidates). They develop a profile of the ideal candidate that should take into account the unique job requirements and the culture of the hospitality organization through interviews with the client and an ongoing relationship with the client, often offering useful advice on selection matters. Executive recruiters use a variety of methods in screening potential employees including psychological testing, which can be important in service/experience provision situations.

Reference

Dessler, G. (2002) *A Framework for Management*, 2nd edn. Upper Saddle River, NJ: Prentice-Hall.

G. KEITH HENNING
UNIVERSITY OF CALGARY, CANADA

Exhibit prospectus

The exhibit prospectus is a marketing tool sent to exhibitors and potential exhibitors. It includes information about attendee demographics and other compelling reasons to exhibit in the show. Information in the prospectus includes:

- The name and address of the show organizer and the name of the meeting or show
- The name and exact titles of key personnel involved with the exhibition, including mailing addresses, telephone and fax numbers, and e-mail addresses
- Goals and objectives of the meeting
- Exhibit dates, exhibit facility, and location
- Background information on the meeting including a list of previous exhibitors, how many years it has been held, and locations of previous and future meetings
- Attendee demographics, including titles, and information from the most recent convention including attendance figures
- A copy of the program from the previous year.
- Additional marketing opportunities available to exhibitors, such as the official newspaper, other publications, availability of attendee mailing labels, hyperlink to show website, sponsorship opportunities, etc.
- A cost breakdown, a copy of the space contract, and well-defined information on space assignment methods. Many shows use a priority point system that gives exhibitors points for

things such as previous participation or size of booth area. For example, one point per year and one point for every 100 square feet of space occupied. Exhibitors with the most points are allowed priority to select the location of the booth on the show floor.

The prospectus also includes information on the exhibitor fees with a list of what is included in the booth fee, such as pipe and drape, booth sign, aisle cleaning, as well as the colors of aisle carpet and draping. Up to 25% of the booth fee may be required at the time of application, as a demonstration of good faith.

To enable exhibitors to make financial decisions prior to submitting a space application, rates for drayage, labor, and all official contractor services are quoted in the prospectus. Information is required on the space cancellation policy; background information on the show facility including photographs and diagrams; floor plan information including the price of each space; entrances and exits; post and column locations; location of registration area; ceiling height; aisle width; obstructions, balconies, air ducts, pipes, light fixtures, and elevators with location, dimensions, and capacities; and a listing of utilities available to booths including water, gas, phone, compressed air, electrical requirements, and locations of electrical hookups. Also needed are details of floor load restrictions, elevator and stair locations, loading dock area, security area, convention service desk location, dining area, storage areas, rest rooms and the exhibitor lounge. Also included is information on exhibit hours, installation and dismantle dates and hours. Restrictions or regulations on materials that may be prohibited due to fire safety codes are critical. For example, many facilities ban the use of helium for balloons or certain types of flammable adhesives may not be used in booth construction. Many facilities do not allow booths with ceilings or double decker booths.

References

Morrow, S.L. (2002) *The Art of the Show*. Dallas, TX: Education Foundation, International Association for Exhibition Management.

Robbe, D. (2002) *Expositions and Trade Shows.* New York: John Wiley & Sons.

PATTI J. SHOCK
UNIVERSITY OF NEVADA LAS VEGAS, USA

Exhibitions

The exhibition industry grew rapidly in the last quarter of the twentieth century to become one of the most important marketing and educational mediums in the global economy. Exhibitions provide unique face-to-face interaction between buyers and sellers and offer educational and networking opportunities for attendees. *Tradeshow Week*, a leading exhibition industry publication, has estimated that there are approximately 15,000 exhibitions held annually worldwide.

The rapid exhibition industry growth has been primarily fueled by two factors. First, corporations realized the value and efficiency of exhibitions. Second, attendance boomed as continuing professional education became a career necessity. Today, business-to-business exhibitions are an established and important part of most corporate marketing programs. According to a 2003 *Tradeshow Week* survey of corporate exhibitors, on average, exhibition and event marketing budgets account for 29% of the total corporate marketing budget. It is estimated that North American corporations spend $20 billion on their annual exhibition and event marketing programs.

Clearly modern exhibitions have roots traceable back to the most ancient marketplaces. But one of the first modern events is often cited as The Great Exhibition held in the Crystal Palace in London in 1851. The Great Exhibition was organized by Prince Albert, the husband of Queen Victoria, to display the economic and military power of Great Britain. In North America, nonprofit associations primarily ran the first exhibitions. Some of the longest-running exhibitions and conventions still held today include the American Psychiatric Association Annual Meeting and Exhibits, first held in 1844 and the American Pharmacists Association Annual Meeting and Exposition, held for the first time in 1852.

Today associations still play an important role in the exhibition and meetings industry. In fact close to 60 per cent of exhibitions are owned by associations. The remainder are owned and managed by for-profit media companies and independent show producers. In the 1970s, 1980s and 1990s for-profit media companies began to launch events to coincide with their trade publications. In the same period many of the leading for-profit media and show management groups also expanded via mergers and acquisitions and they continue to consolidate the industry today.

The value of exhibitions

The core value of exhibitions is that they are efficient marketplaces for buyers and sellers. Exhibition attendees gain value by meeting with a number of suppliers and vendors and comparing the offerings and the staff in each booth. Attendees also take advantage of educational and networking opportunities that are important parts of many exhibitions. Exhibiting companies are able to meet with hundreds of clients and prospects and display their goods and services in the span of just a few days. Finally, exhibitions are deemed cost-effective when compared with other marketing mediums and in terms of providing continuing corporate education and training.

Now in the early twenty-first century each industry tends to have one large 'horizontal' exhibition that covers nearly every aspect of the industry sector. Beyond this one large event are often dozens of other smaller, regional 'vertical' shows that focus on a particular region or industry specialty.

Convention centers

For many years North American municipalities invested significantly to build convention and conference centers to service the growing exhibition and meeting industry. Still today the convention center industry remains in the middle of a building and expansion boom. Since 1999, exhibit space supply has increased by 5% per year adding nearly 14 million square feet of new exhibit space in the United Sates and Canada to reach over 77 million square feet of exhibit space. Municipal leaders are attracted to the significant economic impact that exhibitions and meetings have on their cities and regions. According the International Association of Convention and Visitor Bureaus, the average exhibition attendee generates a local economic impact of over $1300 per event visit.

Exhibition outlook

The events of 11 September 2001 coupled with lobal economic downturn following the strong economy in the late 1990s made a sharp impact on the business events industry. Following 9/11 dozens of exhibitions were postponed and attendance dropped by 20 per cent at events held at the end of 2001 compared with attendance levels one year earlier.

Since then the industry has been recovering steadily. After years of business travel decreases and corporate marketing cuts, event producers continue to launch new shows. In fact, the number of exhibitions with over 5000 net square feet of exhibit space is expected to increase by 4.4% to 4779 sq ft in 2004. *Tradeshow Week* estimates that in 2004 total attendance at exhibitions held in the United States and Canada will reach 52 million. The exhibition industry also has a significant presence around the world, with significant growth in the number of exhibitions expected to continue in the emerging markets of Asia, Eastern Europe, and Latin America for many years.

Going forward, one of the key issues impacting exhibitions relates to competing with other marketing mediums and buyer commitments that may interfere with attracting high-quality attendees to shows. Exhibition producers know that attendance is the key issue. In fact, a recent *Tradeshow Week* survey of show producers found that a significant 80% have changed the way they promote the value of events to attendees since 2002. The most common changes have been enhancing educational opportunities, adding more

networking events, promoting the business value of attending, and spotlighting new products to be seen at shows. In short, exhibition producers are adding more value to the attendee experience.

The growth of the Internet as a communications, sales, and educational medium is often cited as a threat to traditional exhibitions and meetings. The first impact of the Internet has been positive in terms of lowering marketing costs for exhibition producers. Yet it has also impacted pre-negotiated hotel room blocks as attendees increasingly use Web-based hotel room wholesalers to search for lower rates.

Finally, the Internet is changing the exhibition floor experience, as attendees tend to be well informed about exhibitors' products and services well before the events are held. Because attendees are relatively well informed they are no longer going to events to simply learn about new products. They are attending to assess the quality of staff at exhibiting companies and make comparisons among participating exhibiting companies.

One of the main reasons why exhibitions have been so resilient as a marketing and educational medium for over 150 years is that trade exhibitions are essentially re-launched every year. This enables exhibition producers to react to industry shifts and turn challenges into solutions.

Generally speaking, there are two types of exhibitions. *Trade exhibitions* attract representatives from a certain industry or professional group and are generally closed to the public. The attendees learn about new products or services from the exhibiting companies. Products are displayed in booths usually measuring 100 sq ft ($10' \times 10'$) and demonstrations are offered to promote products to the attendees. (Trade expositions are also commonly referred to as trade shows or expositions.) The other type of exhibition is the *consumer show*. These shows are open to the general public and attract a local audience. Attendees pay a general admission fee. Examples are home, boat and recreational vehicle shows.

References

Trade Show Bureau (1994) *A Guide to the US Exposition Industry*.

Tradeshow Week (2003) *Tradeshow Week Executive Outlook Corporate Exhibitor*. March.

Tradeshow Week (2004) *Tradeshow Week Data Book*.

MICHAEL HUGHES
TRADESHOW WEEK, USA

Goldblatt, J. and Nelson, K. (2001) *The International Dictionary of Event Management*, 2nd edn. New York: John Wiley & Sons.

RICHARD VICKERY
METROPOLITAN STATE COLLEGE, USA
KIMBERLY SEVERT
UNIVERSITY OF CENTRAL FLORIDA, USA

Exhibits

Exhibit areas are called *exhibitions* or *trade shows*. Individual exhibit spaces are generally called *booths* in the United States and *stands* in Europe, although these terms are often used interchangeably. *Exhibits* refers to the materials relating to the products or services being promoted which are used for display in a booth or stand. Exhibits should be attractive, inviting, and informative to attendees in order to generate a good flow of traffic into the exhibit area. For exhibitors, a trade show provides a unique marketing opportunity for targeted customers and potential customers. Exhibits provide a value-added educational opportunity for attendees, allowing them to learn about the latest in products, services, and technology in a hands-on environment. Exhibits also provide a large revenue stream for the organization producing the show, such as associations, corporations or independent planners.

One of the first decisions for an exhibitor is deciding which show(s) to exhibit in. It is important to find out who will be attending the show in order to match the organizational marketing objective to the appropriate target market. Other considerations include the amount of exhibit space needed, the cost of show space rental, the cost of the booth itself, the cost of shipping, installation, staffing, and dismantle.

References

Fenich, G. (2004) *Meetings, Expositions, Events, and Conventions: An Introduction to the Industry, Preliminary Edition*. Upper Saddle River, NJ: Pearson Publishing.

Expenses

Expenses is the general term that refers to an outflow of assets that has occurred as a result of activities undertaken to generate revenue. In accrual-based accounting, we recognize an expense at the time it is incurred which may not coincide with the time cash is paid for the expense. In the hospitality industry 'expenses' encompass the whole range of expenditure required to operate a hotel or restaurant business, including the cost of sales (e.g. cost of food and drink items sold), employee wages and salaries, administration, energy, repairs and maintenance, marketing and advertising expense, rent expense, insurance expense, depreciation of assets.

Technically, accountants view an expense as having occurred when there is a consumption or loss of a future economic benefit in the form of a reduction in an asset or an increase in a liability, other than where the reduced economic benefit results from a distribution of wealth to owners. To qualify as an expense, the reduction in the asset or increase in the liability must have resulted from a past transaction or event that has resulted in a decrease of owner's equity. Purchasing an asset does not result in a decrease to owner's equity, however, as the asset is consumed, an expense should be recorded.

References

Uniform System of Accounts for the Lodging Industry, 9th edn (1996) Lansing, MI: Educational Institute of the American Hotel and Motel Association.

Schmidgall, R.S. (2002) *Hospitality Industry Managerial Accounting*, 5th edn. Lansing,

MI: Educational Institute of the American Hotel and Lodging Association.

CHRIS GUILDING
GRIFFITH UNIVERSITY, AUSTRALIA

Zeithaml, V.A. and Bitner, M.J. (1996) *Services Marketing*. New York: McGraw-Hill.

DINA MARIE V. ZEMKE
UNIVERSITY OF NEW HAMPSHIRE, USA

Experience economy

The 'experience economy' was proposed by Pine and Gilmore (1999). The service sector is becoming commoditized. For example, long-distance telephone service has moved from being marketed as a service to being viewed and purchased by consumers as a commodity. Little differentiation exists between long-distance providers, so telephone companies market their product almost exclusively on the basis of cost, and customers regularly switch when another competitor offers a better price. The challenge for marketers is 'why would customers pay increasing amounts for decreasing levels of service?'

The experience economy suggests that successful businesses in the future will strive to offer a distinct economic offering by 'experientializing' the service or product offering. Mundane transactions become experiences, offering an opportunity for customization and differentiation from the competition. Thus, a product that is a relative commodity may be transformed into an experience that provides the opportunity for increased profits and customer loyalty. One example is coffee. A cup of coffee may be a relatively mundane purchase, but Starbuck's experientializes the coffee purchase and consumption experience, allowing them to charge a great deal more for a cup of coffee.

References

Lovelock, C.H. (1995) Managing services: the human factor. In William J. Glynn and James G. Barnes (eds), *Understanding Service Management*. Chichester: John Wiley & Sons, pp. 203–243.

Pine, B.J. II and Gilmore, J.H. (1999) *The Experience Economy: Work is Theatre and Every Business a Stage*. Boston, MA: Harvard Business School Press.

Experimentation

Experimentation is a causal research method that can aid hospitality executives in decision-making. Using experiments, decision-makers can draw causal conclusions about the effects of various actions being considered. For example, experiments can be used to test the effects of changes in pricing, design, and other variables on actual consumption behaviors such as the amount of money consumers spend, or the number of visits to an establishment. However, despite its potential, experimentation is underused by hospitality firms because of the belief that experimentation is synonymous with laboratory research. While it is true that most basic research is experimental research conducted in a laboratory setting, it is possible to conduct true experiments investigating applied issues outside of the laboratory. Experimentation is a method, not a location.

True experiments have three characteristics. First, experiments have at least one treatment group and one comparison group. For example, one group of people can be exposed to a proposed advertisement for a product, while other people are exposed to the currently used advertisement. The comparison group can be either a different group of people, or the same group of people studied at a different time. Second, true experiments have at least one outcome measure. For marketers, this outcome measure should be sales or another measure of actual consumption behavior, not attitudes or reactions to the manipulated treatment. Finally, true experiments must have random assignment of subjects to the treatments. This means that each subject has an equal chance of getting into any treatment group. Random assignment distributes subjects' demographic and other personal differences evenly across the treatment groups, thus allowing the researcher to conclude that any differences in the outcome variable must be caused by the differences in the treatments. While random assignment to treatments can be challenging outside of the laboratory, it is not impossible. For example, restaurateurs can randomly assign patrons to different menu designs. In addition, the Internet provides many opportunities to randomly assign people to different promotional messages.

When designing and interpreting the results of experiments, marketing researchers must consider three types of validity that can affect the conclusions drawn from the results. These types of validity are statistical inference validity, internal validity, and external validity. Statistical inference validity insures that chance does not explain the observed differences among the treatment groups. Statistical inference validity can be improved by using appropriate alpha levels (the 'p-value') in statistical analyses, using large sample sizes, and decreasing the variability in the subjects and/or the way the treatments are delivered. Internal validity refers to the strength with which the researcher can conclude that the treatment caused the changes in the outcome variable. Confounded treatments (treatments that differ in more ways than those intended) are the threat to internal validity. Random assignment to treatments and keeping the people who deliver the treatments blind to the treatment are the best ways to increase internal validity. Finally, external validity is the extent to which the results of the experiment apply to the real world. External validity is threatened by differences between the real world and the people, treatments, outcomes, and context used in the research. The utility of marketing research is largely dependent upon the strength of external validity. Researchers can improve external validity by using samples, contexts, and outcome measures that are representative of the ones in the real world.

Descriptive and experimental research have a synergistic relationship. Ideally, decision-makers can use descriptive research – surveys, interviews, and focus groups – to develop a variety of potential courses of action. Then, these potential courses of action can be evaluated using experimentation. Experimentation is the ideal research tool for drawing causal conclusions about the effects of managerial actions on employee and consumer behaviors.

Reference

Lynn, A. and Lynn, M. (2003) Experiments and quasi-experiments: methods for evaluating marketing options. *Cornell Hotel and Restaurant Administration Quarterly*, 44 (2), 75–84.

ANN LYNN
ITHACA COLLEGE, USA

Expert systems

Expert systems, or knowledge-based systems, are a special type of decision support system (DSS) that uses knowledge of experts as input information. Essentially, these software applications mimic the logic of the decision processes of human experts. They offer software tools to incorporate inferential and deductive reasoning and heuristic manipulation of data. Expert systems encapsulate and process causal rules that have often been derived inductively from previous experimentation, market research or experience. Typically, these systems will use the rule base to suggest intelligent advice and explain the basis of its reasoning. Expert systems are commonly used in complex decision situations where objective quantitative information is rare or not available. Ideal expert systems allow combining the experiences and intuition of humans with the consistent objectivity of a computer-based model. In hospitality management, expert systems are most commonly applied to managerial decision problems (e.g. to forecast demand in a yield management system). However, recent developments also focus on the optimization of customer services, which are offered by Web-based tourist information and reservation systems. In fast-changing environments, where expert experiences are not suitable or available, neurocomputing and evolutionary programming technologies have also proved to be advantageous.

References

Jackson, P. (1999) *Introduction to Expert Systems*, 3rd edn. Harlow, UK: Addison-Wesley.

Moutinho, L., Rita, P., and Curry, B. (1996) *Expert Systems in Tourism Marketing*. London: Routledge.

KARL WÖBER
VIENNA UNIVERSITY OF ECONOMICS AND
BUSINESS ADMINISTRATION, AUSTRIA

Express check-out

To ease front desk volume during the peak periods of check-out, a hotel might initiate check-out activities before the guest is actually ready to leave. A common pre-departure activity involves producing and distributing guest folios to guests expected to check out. Front office staff, housekeeping staff, or even hotel security staff may quietly slip printed folios under the guestroom doors of expected check-outs before 6 a.m., making sure that the guest's folio can't be seen or reached from outside the room.

The front office will distribute an express check-out form with each pre-departure folio. Express check-out forms may include a note requesting guests to notify the front desk if departure plans change. Otherwise, the front office will assume the guest is leaving by the hotel's posted check-out time. This procedure usually reminds and encourages guests to notify the front desk of any problems in departure before the hotel's check-out time.

By completing the express check-out form, the guest is authorizing the front office to transfer his/her outstanding folio balance to the credit card voucher that was created during registration. If no credit card imprint was captured or if no credit was established at registration, the front office generally does not provide express check-out service. Having completed the form, the guest deposits the express check-out form at the front desk when departing. After the guest has left, the front office completes the guest's check-out by transferring the outstanding guest folio balance to a previously authorized method of settlement. Any additional charges the guest makes before leaving the hotel such as telephone calls, will be added to his/her folio before the front desk agent brings the account to a zero balance via account transfer. Due to the possible occurrence of late charges, the amount due on the guest's copy of the express check-out folio may not equal the amount applied to the guest's credit card account. This possibility is clearly stated on the express check-out form to minimize later confusion. When late charges are added to the account, a copy of the updated folio should be mailed to the guest so that she/he has an accurate record of the stay. In this way, the guest is not surprised when her/his credit card billing arrives with a different amount.

For an express check-out procedure to be effective, the front office must have captured accurate guest settlement information during registration. The front desk agent has to be sure to relay room status information to the housekeeping department as soon as an express check-out form is received.

Reference

Bardi, James A. (2003) *Hotel Front Office Management*, 3rd edn. New York: John Wiley & Sons.

ALAN T. STUTTS
AMERICAN INTERCONTINENTAL
UNIVERSITY, USA

External analysis

External analysis focuses on identifying and evaluating trends and events beyond the control of a single hospitality firm, such as increased foreign competition, population shifts, an aging society and advances in information technology (Costa and Teare, 2000; Nebel, 1991; Pearce and Robinson, 1991). External analysis helps a hospitality firm reveal key opportunities and threats confronting the organization so that managers can develop strategies to take advantage of the opportunities and avoid or reduce the impact of threats (Nebel, 1991). Empirical studies show that external analysis is fundamental to the competitive development of firms (Costa and Teare, 2000). Studies also demonstrate that to be successful, external analysis needs to be an important part of formal planning systems of a firm. Important outcomes of external analysis are: identification of events and trends in the external environment and the possible relationships between them; to support organizational development and design; and to provide an agenda for executive boards and management education (Costa and Teare, 2000).

The external environment should be divided into two parts when conducting an external analysis: the remote environment and the operating environment (Nebel, 1991). The remote environment of a hospitality firm consists of the following key factors: economic forces, political, governmental and legal forces, social, cultural, demographic and environmental forces, technological advancements/forces and competitive forces (Harrison, 2003; Woods, 1994). While a firm may not have control over these forces, management must carefully analyze all the external forces while conducting external analysis. Many factors in the remote environment may have an effect on a hospitality firm in varying degrees. Remote factors such as an economic expansion or recession, deregulation of the airline industry, increase in female business travel, advancements in teleconferencing technologies, and higher gasoline prices will certainly affect a hospitality business. Understanding and anticipating such trends will be indispensable aids for a firm when developing strategic plans. In analyzing customer profile, for example, a hospitality firm must try to know as much possible about its prospective clients. To begin with, guests should be classified into market segments based on their travel motives. Such classification is vital as the firm's marketing strategy will be based on this particular work. A guest classification of a hotel might include individual transient guests traveling for business, groups of guests on business, individual transient guests traveling for pleasure,

groups traveling for pleasure, and others. It is possible to classify a hotel's guests according to geographic, demographic, buying behavior, and sometimes even personality and life-style characteristics.

When developing strategic plans, some of the key areas to consider among remote environment forces are:

- *Economic forces*, such as availability of credit, level of disposable income, interest rates and inflation rates. Some relevant questions to ask at this phase of the analysis could be: the rate of increase in the cost of various factors of operation (e.g., wages, supplies, real estate, and building materials); influences of foreign currency exchange rates on sales and the economic developments and expectations for the future.
- *Social, cultural, demographic, and environmental forces*, such as number of special interest groups, population aging, population shifts, and environmental concerns. Here one should seek answers to questions regarding any emerging attitude changes and the social attitude with regard to the environment.
- *Political, governmental and legal forces* such as government regulations or deregulations, changes in tax laws, special tariffs and political action committees. Questions to ask at this stage are: What new laws are relevant to the hospitality industry? Are there any governmental policies that offer advantages (or challenges) to the hospitality industry?
- *Technological forces* such as the likely evolution in technologies that are critical to the success of hospitality firms, external technologies that might become critical to the performance of a firm, and technologies that are utilized and/or not utilized by major competitors. Some important questions to ask here are: What new service-production processes are being developed? What are the new service and product ideas? Are there any new manufacturing-process advances that might be relevant to the hospitality?
- *Competitive forces* such as major strengths and weaknesses of competitors and most likely responses of major competitors to current economic, social, cultural, demographic, geographic, political, governmental, technological,

and competitive trends affecting the hospitality industry.

The operating environment of a hospitality firm, on the other hand, relates to factors such as the structure, level, and intensity of competition in the industry, customers and shifts in customers' expectations and needs and wants, changes in the way suppliers act and operate, creditors and changes in the labor market in which the firm operates (Nebel, 1991). Major changes in factors in the operating environment of a hospitality firm directly influence how it operates. Competitive forces, customers, and labor markets are of particular importance to a hospitality firm's strategic planning (Nebel, 1991). To assess a hospitality firm's competitive position, one must carefully analyze factors such as location, market share, pricing, age and quality of facilities, competitors' actions, service levels, and marketing strategies. The end product of such a detailed analysis is a competitive profile of a hospitality firm compared to its immediate competition.

There are a number of sources of information a hospitality firm may benefit from for reliable and useful information while conducting external analysis (Pearce and Robinson, 1991). These sources include but are not limited to: (a) unpublished sources such as customer surveys, market research, and speeches at professional meetings, and (b) published sources such as periodicals, journals, reports and government document. There are also indexes, online databases, and library publications that might benefit managers who wish to conduct a sound external analysis.

References

Costa, J. and Teare, R. (2000) Developing an environmental scanning process in the hotel sector. *International Journal of Contemporary Hospitality Management*, 12 (3), 156–167.

Harrison, J.S. (2003) Strategic analysis for the hospitality industry. *Cornell HRA Quarterly*, April, 139–152.

Nebel, E.C. III (1991) *Managing Hotels Effectively: Lessons from Outstanding General Managers*. New York: Van Nostrand Reinhold.

Pearce II, J.A. and Robinson, R.B. (1991) *Formulation, Implementation, and Control of Competitive Strategy*, 4th edn. Homewood, IL: Irwin.

Woods, R.H. (1994) Strategic planning: a look at Ruby Tuesday. *Cornell Hotel and Restaurant Administration Quarterly*, June, 41–49.

KEMAL BIRDIR
MERSIN UNIVERSITY, TURKEY

Extranet

Extranets are private networks that use the Internet protocols and the public telecommunication system to share information, data or operations between trusted partners. Extranets facilitate business-to-business (B2B) communications as they connect external suppliers, vendors or customers. An extranet can be viewed as the external part of a company's intranet as it only allows partners to access data and processes. Extranets are firewall- and password-protected but can be accessed from multiple locations.

Extranets can be used widely by hospitality organizations for communications with regular partners. Extranets can be critical for developing and maintaining a network of distributors (such as a central reservation office, travel agencies, hotel room aggregators, tour operators, switch companies and global distribution systems). In addition, extranets can help procurement, especially with regular suppliers (such as food suppliers). Extranets can offer key benefits, such as increase of productivity, speed, staff collaboration, sharing of ideas and expertise throughout the value chain. However, extranets require a degree of interoperability and interconnectivity and that can be challenging.

References

Buhalis, D. (2003) *eTourism: Information Technology for Strategic Tourism Management*. Harlow: Prentice-Hall.

Laudon, J.P. and Laudon, K.C. (2003) *Management Information Systems*, 8th edn. Upper Saddle River, NJ: Prentice-Hall.

DIMITRIOS BUHALIS
UNIVERSITY OF SURREY, UK

F

Facilities engineering

The term refers to the design, specification, organization, building, and construction and use of machines and equipment in a hotel, foodservice or related area, structure or operation. Facilities generally include all of the installed materials of the property including building construction materials, the completed building itself, heating ventilation and air conditioning (HVAC) systems, plumbing and related water-handling systems, pumps, controls, electrical and electronic systems, telephone systems, lighting, waste and pollution, as well as exterior and interior materials and fittings. Engineering processes assure compliance with appropriate fire and life safety codes, regulations, and guidelines, architectural and design-related activities for buildings, public spaces, restaurants, meetings rooms, ballrooms, kitchen and food storage and preparation areas, guest sleeping rooms; application of appropriate specification of materials, equipment, systems, interfaces; installation, inspection, and approval are required as well as the design of maintenance procedures, schedules, and systems.

The basic goal of the facilities engineering design process is to produce a design of high technical quality which meets requirements in a cost-effective and timely manner. The primary characteristics of the design process which contribute to a highly quality engineered facility are: a clear definition of the objectives and customer needs; verification of existing field and location conditions; a specific plan for meeting the objectives and customer needs; approval or concurrence of the objectives before initiation of detailed design; multiple designs to allow refinement of the requirements; integration of pertinent constraints and information from similar designs, lessons learned or other design groups; identification of process logic and tasks requiring completion before proceeding to the next phase; progressive validation and acceptance of the design through a review and feedback process; and early and specific definition and implementation of requirements and design baselines.

Reference

Borsenik, Frank D. and Stutts, Alan T. (1997) *The Management of Maintenance and Engineering Systems in the Hospitality Industry*, 4th edn. New York: John Wiley & Sons.

WILLIAM N. CHERNISH
UNIVERSITY OF HOUSTON, USA

Facilities management

Facility management encompasses multiple disciplines to ensure functionality of the built environment by integrating people, place, process, and technology. The development, design, and application of systems to properly maintain, repair, and replace all of the elements relating to the physical components of a hospitality structure or operation are key aspects of facility management. Maintenance operations and space management are the primary areas of facility management. Facilities generally include all of the installed materials of the property, including building construction materials, the completed building itself, heating, ventilation and air conditioning (HVAC) systems, plumbing and related water-handling systems, pumps, controls, electrical and electronic systems, telephone systems, lighting, waste and pollution, as well as exterior and interior materials and fittings. Management activities involve routine functions ranging from repair of electrical and plumbing fixtures to preventive maintenance and replacement of building and equipment components on prescribed schedules. Facilities management requires implementation of appropriate computer or manual systems for tracking and prevention, responding to requests for work, for inventory of parts and spares, and for the costs associated with maintenance activities. In addition, the facility manager may include specification and oversight of contract firms for preventive maintenance, repair or replacement of specialized systems or components as part of their responsibility. The modern facility manager is facing issues including ergonomics, emergency response, smart buildings, and telecommunications.

Reference

Borsenik, Frank D. and Stutts, Alan T. (1997) *The Management of Maintenance and Engineering Systems in the Hospitality Industry*, 4th edn. New York: John Wiley & Sons.

WILLIAM N. CHERNISH
UNIVERSITY OF HOUSTON, USA

Facilities management associations

A number of associations provide technical, educational and professional services related to facilities operations. These associations include ASHRAE, BOMA, IFMA and CIBSE. The American Society of Heating, Refrigerating, and Air Conditioning Engineers (ASHRAE) is a key organization involved with facilities and equipment design and operation. ASHRAE strives to advance the arts and sciences of heating, ventilation, air conditioning, refrigeration, and related human factors. ASHRAE develops a number of publications dealing with the design and operation of building systems, including documents that are often the basis for building codes in the United States and elsewhere.

The Building Owners and Managers Association (BOMA) provides a significant facilities management role focusing on office buildings. BOMA is a primary source of information on office building development, leasing, building operating costs, energy consumption patterns, local and national building codes, legislation, occupancy statistics and technological developments. BOMA has chapters in the US and Canada as well as in a number of other countries.

The International Facilities Management Association (IFMA) provides education, training, and research involving offices and a number of other non-hospitality building types. In addition to chapters in the US and Canada, IFMA has chapters in 18 additional countries throughout the world.

The Chartered Institution of Building Service Engineers (CIBSE) is UK-based and serves a variety of needs for facilities professionals in the UK as well as other countries. CIBSE is dedicated to the development of better buildings through education, research, communication and maintaining an active role in determining governmental regulations and legislation.

References

www.boma.org
www.ashrae.org
www.cibse.org
www.ifma.org

DAVID M. STIPANUK
CORNELL UNIVERSITY, USA

Facilities operating and capital costs

The daily operation and continuing improvement of hotel facilities requires the investment of substantial amounts of money. The major categories for these investments are in property operations and maintenance, utilities, and capital expenditures.

Property operation and maintenance (POM) may be defined as procedures for managing physical assets, e.g., building exteriors and interiors, systems and equipment, to facilitate guest service, prevent problems, ensure safety and accessibility, and reduce non-productive and operational downtime.

The Property Operation and Maintenance Account of the Uniform System of Accounts for the Lodging Industry consists of 'payroll and related expenses' for the engineering/facilities department and a category of 'other expenses' that consists of purchased supplies and equipment, contract services, waste removal, and other expenses. POM costs typically range from 4 to 6% of total property revenues. Labor and benefits are typically 40–60% of these costs with contract services and supplies being the balance. Typical contract services are waste haulage, elevator maintenance, and items such as window cleaning on high rise structures.

Initial planning, design, and construction of a facility impact its subsequent operation and maintenance, i.e., the implementation of sound engineering and ecological practices in design and layout, the quality of construction and landscape materials and the choice of systems and equipment.

Utilities comprise the energy sources (electricity, gas, steam, and fuel) and water and wastewater services required by hospitality properties in their various mechanical, electrical, and plumbing systems. The Utility Cost budget category of the Uniform System of Accounts for the Lodging Industry includes the expenses for these utilities purchases as well as possible recoveries of these costs due to sales to others. There is also a provision in the Uniform System for chargebacks of these costs to departments incurring the costs (i.e. a leased restaurant space may be charged utilities related to its operation).

Utility budgets consume close to 3–6% of a property's revenue and vary with the age and size of the property, maintenance and operating procedures, systems and equipment type, and conservation practices. Hotels with extensive food and beverage facilities have almost double the utility costs of a limited service property with equivalent number of rooms. For almost all hotels, electricity is the largest component of the utility budget. For operations that are located in warm climates, water is likely to be the second largest component. Water costs include not only the purchased cost for potable water but also the costs for wastewater disposal.

Capital expenditures (CapEx) are funds spent to replace furniture, fixtures, and equipment (FF&E), purchase or improve physical assets such as buildings and fixtures, major equipment, vehicles, machinery or furniture. Examples of improvements include: replacing a roof, planning, designing, and constructing an addition, and *renovation*. CapEx tends to be a significant cost for companies with facility-driven products such as hotels. It increases as a property ages due to the increased investment in renovations and replacements, with significant increases often appearing at five to seven year intervals of the property life cycle.

CapEx may also be called *capital spending* or *capital expense*. Major assets that will be used in a business for more than a year are known as '*capital assets*' and are subject to differential depreciation treatment under the tax laws. Ownership structure may impact recorded CapEx rates in that private firms may increase operating budgets to cover major expenditures while public companies may record similar activities as capital expenses. Since CapEx levels impact the value of hotel appraisals as well as financing of new projects, reported CapEx rates do not necessarily coincide with actual expenditures on property renovation and enhancement. In similar fashion, planned and reported replacement reserves are often under-funded in comparison to actual CapEx requirements. Over the lifetime of hotel assets, 5 to 8% of the total revenue of the property is reinvested in the property via capital spending.

The terms 'renovation' and 'capital projects' are used interchangeably in the industry. Purists might reserve the term 'renovation' to focus on those activities that occur in the public spaces of the hotel and are visible to the guests while other 'capital projects' might include back-of-house changes such as replacing mechanical systems. In any event, capital expenditures at hotels generally involve the improvement of an existing facility, including major planned refurbishments and replacements of the physical assets, e.g., building exterior and interior and systems to enhance perceived value, extend *useful life*, upgrade safety features or combat *facility obsolescence*. The expenditures may be a response to change in use of the facility, legislative mandates, e.g., environmental codes or accessibility, or even changes in chain affiliation requiring brand image modifications or aesthetic improvements to satisfy new ownership. Other reasons for additional investments include to: enhance market position by addressing needs of current or new customers, match or surpass a direct competitor's features, upgrade the facility to a higher-rated category, alter systems to accrue long-term savings in operational expenses, and even repair structures damaged by natural phenomena such as hurricanes and earthquakes.

Over the life of a property, significant and regular modifications are made to enhance property appearance and resultant value. Levels of renovation projects range from minor renovation to major *restoration* projects. Rehabilitation of furnishings, commencing in years four or five of the property life cycle, involves such cosmetic enhancements as carpet, flooring, tile and window treatment changes. These retouches seldom alter the space's use or physical layout. Later renovation comprises major replacement of all furnishings, equipment, and finishes within a space and may include alterations in the physical layout of the space and/or upgrading existing systems. Total renovation generally requires demolition of the interior of a building or portion thereof, including the removal and subsequent replacement of electrical, plumbing, heating, ventilating and air conditioning systems, fixed equipment, floor coverings, and interior walls, or a complete new addition on the site. Properties undertaking significant renovation projects must choose between closing and losing customers to the competition or staying open and risking dissatisfaction due to guest exposure to the construction process.

Furniture, fixtures and equipment represent a common capital expenditure for hospitality operations. FF&E includes items such as moveable lighting and furniture, carpeting and pad, signage, laundry equipment, office furniture, food service equipment, and draperies and blinds. It does not include major building equipment such as HVAC components and items such as bathroom fixtures.

References

deRoos, J. (2002) Renovation and capital projects. In D.M. Stipanuk (ed.), *Hospitality Facilities Management and Design*, 2nd edn. Lansing, MI: Educational Institute of the American Hotel and Lodging Association, pp. 509–545.

Hassanien, A. and Losekoot, E. (2002) The application of facilities management expertise to the hotel renovation process. *Facilities*, 20 (7/8), 230–238.

Loosemore, M. and Hsin, Y.Y. (2001) Customer-focused benchmarking for facilities management. *Facilities*, 19 (13/14), 464–475.

Uniform System of Accounts for the Lodging Industry, 9th edn. (1996) The Property Operating and Maintenance Account of the Uniform System of Accounts for the Lodging Industry. Lansing, MI: Educational Institute of the American Hotel and Motel Association, pp. 118–123.

BONNIE CANZIANI
UNIVERSITY OF NORTH
CAROLINA – GREENSBORO, USA

Fairs

While festivals are about culture and celebration, fairs are more about trade, commerce, and education. Yet both types of special event are associated with having fun. 'Fair' can have multiple meanings, as in the following definitions:

- A gathering held at a specified time and place for the buying and selling of goods (i.e., a market)
- An exhibition[1] (e.g., of farm products or manufactured goods, usually accompanied by

various competitions and entertainments, as in a state fair); exhibitors may be in competition for prizes

- An exhibition intended to inform people about a product or business opportunity
- An event, usually for the benefit of a charity or public institution, including entertainment and the sale of goods (also called a bazaar).

The term 'festival' is sometimes incorrectly used as a synonym of 'fair', but fairs have a long tradition of their own, as periodic exhibitions and markets. Waters (1939) traced the history of fairs from the earliest days of human barter and trade. Although North Americans associate the word 'market' with a facility in which shopping is done, fairs were originally occasional markets. Every society had to have fairs, where goods were sold and traded at specific times, and usually in specific places that became markets or fairgrounds. The Latin word *feria*, meaning holy day (which evolved into holiday) is the origin of the English word 'fair.' They were often scheduled on church-sanctioned holy days.

Although fairs were often associated with religious celebrations, and now usually contain entertainment and amusements, fairs have more to do with productivity and business than with themed public celebrations. Indeed, Abrahams (1987) has argued that fairs and festivals are like mirror images. But he also suggests that in modern, urban society they have become almost synonymous because the old ways of production, as celebrated in fairs, have faded.

In the 1700s the British crossed the agricultural improvement society with the traditional trade fair/carnival and agricultural fairs were born (Ontario Association of Agricultural Societies: www.ontariofairs.com). The International Association of Fairs and Expos (IAFE) (www.fairsandexpos.com) notes that the first North American fairs were held in French Canada in the early 1700s, while in British North America the first was held in 1765 in Windsor, Nova Scotia, and it continues today. In 1807 the first fair was held in Massachusetts, in the form of an exhibit of sheep. IAFE says there are approximately 3250 fairs held annually in Canada and the United States, attracting an attendance of

about 150 million. The largest is the state fair of Texas in Dallas, hosting about 3.5 million visitors annually.

The most traditional fairs in North America are the numerous county and state fairs which are held annually on the same site, most of which continue to reflect rural and agricultural themes. Some are called 'exhibitions' or 'expositions' reflecting their educational orientation. Most fairs are operated by independent boards or agricultural societies, though many have close links with the host municipality. Typical elements of agricultural fairs and exhibitions include agricultural demonstrations and contests, sales and trade shows (farm machinery, etc.), amusements of all kinds, eating and drinking, parades, and a variety of entertainment. Education is also a vital program element. This type of fair is often called a 'show' in the United Kingdom, Australia and New Zealand.

Periodic fairs are mostly produced on permanent facilities dedicated to this function, but increasingly used to generate a portfolio of events over the entire calendar. Fairs are therefore closely associated with specific venues, and these have usually become important parts of community's entertainment, recreational and cultural infrastructure.

'World's fair' has a very specific meaning, derived from an international agreement in 1928 and regulated by the Bureau International des Expositions in Paris. BIE sets the policies for bidding on and holding world's fairs, which are often called Expos. Their nominal purpose has always been educational, with particular attention paid to technological progress, but some authors have described them as glorified trade fairs (Benedict, 1983).

There is a large body of literature on world's fairs, reflecting both their significance in economic and social terms and their popularity among Expo lovers. Competition to host them is often fierce, as cities and countries see them as an opportunity to attract attention and tourists, typically in concert with urban renewal or other development schemes. World's fairs are also major tourist attractions and their sites have often become permanent sites for tourist, cultural, and entertainment activities. Many world's fairs have left a legacy of landmark structures (e.g., the Eiffel Tower), urban renewal and parks.

References

Abrahams, R. (1987) An American vocabulary of celebrations. In A. Falassi (ed.), *Time Out of Time: Essays on the Festival.* Albuquerque, NM: University of New Mexico Press. pp. 173–183.

Benedict, B. (1983) *The Anthropology of World's Fairs.* Berkeley, CA: Scolar Press.

Waters, S. (1939) *The History of Fairs and Expositions.* London, Canada: Reid Brothers.

DONALD GETZ
UNIVERSITY OF CALGARY, CANADA

[1] 'Exhibition' is a term also used to describe trade shows/fairs and consumer shows, otherwise known as the exhibition industry.

Fast casual

Originally there were only two kinds of restaurants, *full service* and *limited service*. In a full service restaurant the diner was brought an entire meal from 'soup to nuts' in multiple courses. Alternately, in a limited service restaurant diners would be expected to help themselves in some way. This limited service meant that diners might be served by a waitress (or even the cook) at a counter and then take the check to a cashier near the door to pay, or perhaps push a tray along a cafeteria line and settle up at the end of the line. Diners would carry their own plates to their table of choice.

Then, self-service was introduced to make things quicker; here customers were expected to pay before they were served, carry their own food, and bus the table when they were done. Menu items were simply made in batches for high-volume, mass-market consumption. For two or three decades afterwards there were three restaurant categories: quick service, midscale/ family and full service. Beginning late in the 1980s a fourth segment emerged, eventually being identified as 'casual theme' restaurants. These were full service

places, but without all the stiffness and formality. They were fun, reasonably priced, had focused menu offerings, and were easy to use.

In the early twenty-first century a new group of offerings coalesced into the 'fast' or 'quick casual' segment. Food here is usually 'hand crafted' as in fine dining, but customers are responsible for some portion of their own limited service. In particular, they wait in line to order and pay in advance, and often carry their own trays to a table. This new hybrid offering has fast service, is casual in style and ambience, with generally more complex menu items than the quick service segment, but is offered at a price premium.

Reference

Salomon Smith Barney (2003) *Fast-casual Segment Handbook.* New York: Salomon Smith Barney.

CHRISTOPHER MULLER
UNIVERSITY OF CENTRAL FLORIDA, USA

Feasibility study

A feasibility study is an analysis that is most often conducted by a third party, that indicates whether a project is reasonable, meets the needs of the target market (the group of consumers to which the foodservice operator wants to appeal), and is financially viable, among other things. Such a study is generally conducted only after the concept underlying the restaurant operation is articulated. Moreover, this process of determining where it is feasible to locate a foodservice outlet and what precise form it should take is one of the most critical steps in profitably launching and operating a restaurant business. Properly conducted, a feasibility study pairs the right foodservice operation with a location that will support it.

Keiser *et al.* (2000) divide feasibility studies into two major sections: a market survey and a site analysis. A market survey includes evaluating the surrounding community's economics, performing a competitive analysis, and making volume projections (based on the given restaurant concept). A community's economics may be evaluated on demographics or psychographics, which may also be contrasted with prevailing ethnic or national food preferences. Other economic factors include the presence of major industries and firms, as well as the propensity of employees of such firms to dine out. Finally, the potential growth of the community must be assessed.

A competitive analysis entails completing a concept map, which may be built by compiling average checks for each of the nearby operations and then subdivided and mapped by cuisine type of market segment. Ideally, the related analyses will include other competitive indicators such as the profitability of nearby restaurants and the degree of market penetration realized by each one. Planned additional restaurants, with information pertaining to each one's potential effect on the market, should also be considered.

With information on the concept's menu type and offerings, general price parameters, facility size and volume capacity information (including often-neglected topics such as parking), and other service options (e.g., banquets), volume projections are then made based on the aforementioned information. This might include seat turnover and average check by daypart, the effects of seasonality, and ancillary revenue from take-out orders, banquets, and catering. As part of this section, the proportion of beverage sales should be evaluated and the related effect on profitability also considered.

Part and parcel of the market survey is the site analysis, which includes component analyses of location specifics, traffic patterns, visibility, legal constraints, and utilities. The most basic of the location specifics is the square footage requirement. If the concept requires a certain amount of kitchen space, and the volume information identified earlier requires a predetermined number of seats, then this information will produce a general guideline for the amount of space needed. Is there real estate available that can accommodate the concept's physical size? Too many operators know the challenges of sacrificing back-of-house space in order to make a location work – such compromises never survive the long-term effects on profitability (realized either in actual cash or as a function of employee or guest satisfaction).

Traffic patterns are the next consideration in a feasibility study. Prospective foodservice operators ignore the proverbial three most important attributes of a hospitality operation – location, location, and location – at their peril. What are the projected traffic counts? Is it easy to enter and exit the parking lot? If this is to be a destination restaurant, is it accessible to main roads? In addition to answering these questions, a feasibility study must also explore potential changes to local streets and surrounding main arteries that might affect traffic patterns.

Visibility is another key component of a site analysis. While restaurants located in alleys or in the basements of large buildings may be quaint, they do not benefit from strong site visibility. Possible future obstructions, such as those caused by new construction, must also be considered.

Legal constraints must also be considered. For example, it is vital to consider zoning regulations that might affect the feasibility of a restaurant in a given location. Another concern is local or state laws that may affect hours of operation, staffing, or parking. A related concern is liquor sales. What is required to obtain a liquor license if the concept calls for beverage service? Finally, the analysis should consider assessments and taxes that will ultimately speak to the restaurant's net profitability.

Finally, site analysis addresses utilities – the availability of and costs involved with respect to water, waste disposal, gas, electricity, etc. Possible restrictions should also be considered. For example, where must a dumpster be placed according to local ordinances does such placement provide accessibility to the waste-removal company?

Birchfield and Sparrowe (2002) note as well that the final recommendation provided in a feasibility study must be quantitatively based on the research conducted and the data collected. The resulting recommendation should also integrate holistically all the concerns identified while also noting opportunities – both present and projected. The final recommendation should, if the project appears feasible, include a pro forma for at least the first full year of operation. Comprehensive feasibility studies include multiyear forecasts as well as financial projections using contingency models. Furthermore, capital cost estimates must be included, along with a return-on-investment (ROI) analysis using the capital cost and pro forma information.

It is important to note that many aspects of a restaurant feasibility study relate or may be part of a comprehensive business plan. The differences, however, deserve mention. A business plan is not necessarily site-specific. A business plan is usually drafted, if not completed, by the operators. A feasibility study, on the other hand, is site-specific and is best performed by an objective third party. In some cases, a feasibility study will complement and may include many components of the business plan, restated to reflect the context of the analyses.

References

Birchfield, J.C. and Sparrowe, R.T. (2002) *Design and Layout of Foodservice Facilities.* New York: John Wiley & Sons.

Keiser, J., DeMicco, F.J., and Grimes, R.N. (2000) *Contemporary Management Theory.* Upper Saddle River, NJ: Prentice-Hall.

DENNIS REYNOLDS
WASHINGTON STATE UNIVERSITY, USA

Federacion Latinoamericana De Desarrolladores Turisticos (LADETUR)

The development of timeshare resorts within the Latin American marketplace has promoted the deployment of an association that specifically deals with legislative and educational concerns of Latin American countries regarding the development and conduct of timeshare developers. In a response to these advancing needs the Federacion Latinoamericana de Desarrolladores Turisticos (LADETUR) was formed to advance the state of understanding and development of timeshare operations.

Several initiatives were funded with LADE-TUR coordinating the work. The first initiative consisted of a review of the legislation affecting the timeshare industry in Latin American countries and the drafting of model legislation based on that review. Model legislation was drafted in early September 2000 and disseminated throughout the region. The second initiative was a market research study of the Latin American timeshare industry and its economic impact in the region. The third initiative will establish the LADETUR Education Institute; a comprehensive educational program aimed at industry staff residing in major timeshare markets throughout Latin America. Particular emphasis will be placed on delivering instruction in the sales and marketing and client services and operations areas.

Reference

http://207.199.153.42/mission/an_report2000.htm. Accessed 11 February.

RANDALL S. UPCHURCH
UNIVERSITY OF CENTRAL FLORIDA, USA

Festivals

Festivals are one of the most frequent and universal forms of cultural celebration, and while many are religious or traditional with long histories, the majority have been created in recent decades. Parades and processions are common elements in festivals, but those that are held on their own also display many celebratory elements. Many of the other major types of event, especially art and entertainment, are frequently found within or as the theme of festivals, and sport and recreational events also commonly add festive elements. Festivity is generally recognized as embodying gaiety, joyfulness, playfulness, or revelry and liberation from normal moral constraints, but these attitudes and behaviors are not exclusive to formal events.

Festivals are closely related to feasts, for example in the ancient custom of feasting at harvest times or in association with religious holy days. Falassi (1987, p. 2) has summarized contemporary English-language definitions of 'festival,' of which the most pertinent is 'a sacred or profane time of celebration, marked by special observances.' While traditional festivals often retain religious or mystical roots, contemporary festivals are primarily 'profane,' or secular. And although many traditional festival themes have been retained, including those related to the harvest, countless new themes have been established.

For a working definition that is concise and simple, the following was offered by Getz (1997):

A festival is a public, themed celebration.

Unless the public is invited to participate, the event is a private party. Merely selling tickets to the public might not be sufficient to qualify as a festival, as the celebration should be by and for the public. The object of celebration, which can be called the theme, is often explicitly recognized in the name, as in Festival of Music, or Tulip Festival. But many festivals with diverse programming are actually celebrations of the community itself. Falassi (1987, p. 2) noted:

Both the social function and the symbolic meaning of the festival are closely related to a series of overt values that the community recognizes as essential to its ideology and worldview, to its social identity, its historical continuity, and to its physical survival, which is ultimately what festival celebrates.

Turner (1969) described festivals as occasions that bring together and interpret or reinterpret the symbolic elements of a group or community, thereby laying the foundation of everyday life. Festivals and other 'cultural performances' in which cultural elements are displayed, are rich in meaning and provide a 'text' – the 'reading' of which can educate an observer about the host culture and community. As explained by Manning (1983, p. 4), celebration is performance: 'it is, or entails, the dramatic presentation of cultural symbols.' Celebration is public, with no social exclusion, is entertainment for the fun of it, and is participatory – actively involving the celebrant who takes time out of ordinary routine, and 'does so openly, consciously and with the general aim of aesthetic, sensual and social gratification.' Pieper (1973) said that only a religious celebration

could be a true festival, but that view is not widely held.

It is common to label events as 'community festivals' if their purpose is primarily to celebrate civic identity, pride or sharing. This type, generally represented by the International Festivals and Events Association often encompasses a broad program of events appealing to the whole community (e.g., parades, sports, fireworks, concerts, food) and increasingly many of them are also tourism-oriented. One of the main justifications for local government to get involved in producing or assisting such events, at least in the New World, is the absence of traditional events to mark the seasons and bring everyone together. As well, modern life involves so much moving about that communities typically lack a stable population and so the government (or a nonprofit organization) has to create a means of identity.

Festivals are also created by organizations with focused mandates. For example, the Arts Festivals network in the UK (www.artsfestivals.co.uk) describes the following thematic types of arts festival: opera; literature; early music; dance; new festivals; anniversaries and celebrations; festival commissions and premieres; family and children's events; classical music; theatre and performance; jazz and music world; community and street arts.

For-profit festivals are a growing trend, particularly for those with entertainment as the core, while tourism and economic development agencies also produce them as image-makers and tourist attractions. Corporate sponsorship is often vital, and the corporate presence at many festivals is intense, so the commercial world is closely identified with many festivals, even to the point of title sponsorship. Many others are linked to causes as fund raisers and profile raisers.

Festivals are increasingly featured in tourism development strategies and promotions. Robinson et al. (2004) discussed their role in cultural tourism, noting the substantial difference between those festivals that provide an authentic experience of the host culture and those 'placeless' events with generic themes or programs that are on the rise. When festivals are conceived and promoted as 'products' for tourists it raises fundamental issues related to the interpretation and ownership of the inherent cultural meanings.

Festivals and other events, according to Getz and Cheyne (2002), can attract special interest groups for satisfaction of intrinsic motives (based on the theme and specific program elements), plus they usually have generic touristic appeal as outlets for seeking and escaping behaviour. In addition, they can satisfy extrinsic motivators such as meeting work obligations or accompanying others. A review of pertinent motivational studies by Lee *et al.* (2004) confirmed that festival-goers in many settings are not only motivated by specific attractions but are engaged in cultural exploration and family togetherness, and seek novelty, escape, and socialization. The majority appear to have general, multiple interests rather than a specific motive for attending.

Many periodic festivals (such as Calgary's Stampede, the New Orleans Mardi Gras, or the Carnival of Venice) have achieved the status of 'hallmark' event. As defined by Getz (1997), these events help develop a positive destination image and assist in place marketing; they have achieved such fame that the festival and host city image become inseparable. The 'animation' role of festivals is easily in evidence at most static attractions, resorts, shopping areas, and other facilities that use programs of entertainment and special events to attract attention and keep people coming back.

As manifestations of culture and lifestyle, a number of important issues arise pertaining to festivals and tourism. Sociologists and anthropologists in particular have worried about the commodification of traditions as festivals evolve into, or are created as tourist attractions. On the other hand, festivals can help preserve and even revive dying customs and can expose and interpret culture to visitors, thereby providing authentic cultural experiences.

References

Falassi, A. (ed.) (1987) *Time Out of Time: Essays on the Festival*. Albuquerque, NM: University of New Mexico Press.

Getz, D. (1997) *Event Management and Event Tourism*. New York: Cognizant.

Getz, D. and Cheyne, J. (2002) Special event motives and behavior. In C. Ryan (ed.), *The Tourist Experience*, 2nd edn. London: Continuum, pp. 137–155.

Lee, C., Lee, Y., and Wicks, B. (2004) Segmentation of festival motivation by nationality and satisfaction. *Tourism Management*, 25 (1), 61–70.

Manning, F. (ed.) (1983) *The Celebration of Society: Perspectives on Contemporary Cultural Performance*. Bowling Green, KY: Popular Press.

Pieper, J. (1973) In *Time With the World: A Theory of Festivity*. Chicago: Franciscan Herald Press (translated by R. and C. Wilson from the 1963 German original).

Robinson, M., Picard, D., and Long, P. (2004) Festival tourism: producing, translating, and consuming expressions of culture(s). *Event Management*, 8 (4), 187–189.

Turner, V. (1969) *The Ritual Process*. Chicago: Aldine.

DONALD GETZ
UNIVERSITY OF CALGARY, CANADA

FIFO

This inventory valuation method calculates the value of ending inventory and cost of goods sold (COGS) based on the principle of 'first-in, first-out.' In a foodservice establishment, FIFO is a favored rotation method because it helps a kitchen use products before they deteriorate. When using the FIFO method, older products are used first, leaving newer products in inventory. This means that when valuing ending inventory, a manager will use the prices for the most recently purchased items. In contrast, because older products are used first, the value of COGS will be based on the prices of the older products. In times when prices are increasing, this method yields a high value for ending inventory and a low COGS. Since COGS is an expense, a lower COGS means that the operation will show a higher profit.

For example, suppose there are six cases of tomato sauce in beginning inventory. They were originally purchased for $22.00/case. During the month, an additional four cases of tomato sauce were purchased at a cost of $25.00/case. At the end of the month, there were three cases remaining in inventory. The COGS for tomato sauce is based on $(6 + 4) - 3 = 7$ cases. Under the FIFO inventory valuation method, these seven cases would be worth $(6 * \$22.00) + (1 * \$25.00) = \$157.00$ since the first six cases would have come from the beginning inventory and the remaining case would have come from the newly purchased cases.

Reference

Wild, T. (1998) *Best Practice in Inventory Management.* New York: John Wiley & Sons.

DEBORAH BARRASH
UNIVERSITY OF NEVADA, LAS VEGAS, USA

File Transfer Protocol (FTP)

FTP is an application protocol, based on the TCP/IP suite, which specifies the rules for transferring data files from one computer to another. FTP uses the client/server model of communication in which a computer user (a client) requests and is provided a service by another computer (a server). For example a hotelier is using FTP to upload (send) his Web pages to an Internet Web server. FTP operates among heterogeneous systems and allows users to interact with a remote server without regard for the operating systems in place.

Basic file transfer support is usually provided as part of a suite of programs that come with TCP/IP. However, several programs with a graphical interface have been developed and are available to the users. The FTP acronym is also used to indicate application programs based on the FTP protocol.

FTP is an authenticated protocol: the user connection to a server requires a user identification and a password; the term *anonymous FTP* represents a way to transfer files by logging in to an FTP server on the Internet as a public guest.

Using *anonymous* as user identification and own e-mail address as password, a customer can connect to a hotel server and exchange files.

References

Estabrook, N. and Pike, M.A. (1995) *Using FTP.* Indianapolis, IN: QUE Corporation.

Postel, J. and Reynolds, J.K. (1985) *File Transfer Protocol – RFC-959.* Internet Engineering Task Force, online: http://www.ietf.org/rfc/rfc0959.txt. Accessed August 2003.

RODOLFO BAGGIO
BOCCONI UNIVERSITY, ITALY

Financial accounting

Financial accounting is concerned with the maintenance of records that track the financial values of transactions made by a business, and the production of periodic statements that provide a summary of the performance and financial position of that business. The basis on which modern records are kept (double entry book-keeping) has been in use since the Middle Ages. This involves recognizing that any transaction will have an effect on the value of the business to the owners, and the way in which this value is stored. For example, a payment of expenses will both reduce the value of the business to the owner (reduce profit), and reduce its cash balances.

Financial accounting records economic transactions as they take place: it classifies and aggregates the transactions so that at any moment the accounting database is capable of giving a picture of the financial position. Formally, all businesses produce an annual performance statement (profit and loss account) and a statement of financial position (balance sheet) which summarize the aggregated data and are used to communicate this externally. Profit and loss accounts tend to reflect the kind of business, e.g. manufacturing or service industries, with hotel profit and loss accounts reflecting departments and related department and property level profitability information, whereas balance sheets tend to comprise a similar format regardless of the kind of business.

References

Horngren, C.T. and Sundem, G.L. (1996) *Introduction to Financial Accounting*, 6th edn. Upper Saddle River, NJ: Prentice-Hall.

Lewis, R. and Pendrill, D. (2004) *Advanced Financial Accounting*, 7th edn. London: Prentice-Hall.

PETER WALTON
ESSEC BUSINESS SCHOOL, FRANCE

Financial leverage

Financial leverage refers to the use of debt and/or preferred stocks by a firm in place of common equity to finance its assets. The use of financial leverage tends to raise a hospitality firm's return on equity (ROE) under favorable conditions. On the other hand, the use of financial leverage will raise a hospitality firm's financial risk. Financial risk of a firm is a part of its total risk, in addition to its usual business risk.

The higher a hospitality firm's degree of financial leverage (DFL) (percent change in earnings per share or EPS for each percentage change in earnings before interests and taxes or EBIT), the greater the fluctuation in its EPS as a result of changes in its EBIT. That is, *ceteris paribus*, a high DFL of a hospitality firm would imply that relatively small changes in its EBIT would lead to large changes in its EPS. Under adverse conditions, however, a small decrease in its EBIT will lead to a large decrease in its EPS as well as in its ROE. In general, whenever a hospitality firm's expected return on assets exceeds its cost of debt, the use of financial leverage will lead to an increase in the firm's ROE.

References

Brigham, E.F. and Gapenski, L.C. (1993) *Intermediate Financial Management*, 4th edn. Orlando, FL: The Dryden Press.

Weston, J.F. and Brigham, E.F. (1993) *Essentials of Managerial Finance*, 10th edn. Orlando, FL: The Dryden Press.

ATUL SHEEL
UNIVERSITY OF MASSACHUSETTS, USA

Financial risk

Financial risk of a hospitality firm is defined as the additional risk placed on its common stockholders when the firm is financed either by debt or by preferred stocks. Financial risk may be perceived as the risk of a hospitality firm in addition to its business risk, resulting from its use of financial leverage. Such risk-increasing effect of financial leverage is measured by the difference between the standard deviation of return on equity of a financially leveraged hospitality firm or a hospitality firm with debt financing, denoted as $\sigma_{ROE\ (L)}$, and the standard deviation of the return on equity of an un-leveraged all-equity or debt-free hospitality firm, denoted as $\sigma_{ROE\ (U)}$.

Financial risk and financial leverage are subjects of special interest in the hospitality industry because of the capital-intensive nature of hotel firms. Generally, the hotel sector of the hospitality industry is subject to high financial risk due to the fact that it is more leveraged with debt financing. On the other hand, being less fixed assets-intensive than the hotel sector, the restaurant sector of the hospitality industry uses less debt and hence experiences relatively low financial risk.

References

Brigham, E.F. and Gapenski, L.C. (1993) *Intermediate Financial Management*, 4th edn. Orlando, FL: The Dryden Press.

Weston, J.F. and Brigham, E.F. (1993) *Essentials of Managerial Finance*, 10th edn. Orlando, FL: The Dryden Press.

ATUL SHEEL
UNIVERSITY OF MASSACHUSETTS, USA

Fire protection

Fire protection has been a critical concern within the hospitality industry; and especially within the lodging segment, for many years. In recent years there has been a sharp reduction in fatal fire incidents involving a lodging facility within the United States. However, during that same period, there have been several fatal fires involving older properties in Europe and in fairly modern installations in Asia.

The effective control of major fire incidents has been the movement within the United States to facilities with automatic fire extinguishing systems (sprinklers), and with full smoke-detection and/or rate-of-rise heat detectors. There are few US jurisdictions where a new lodging unit does not have an automatic fire extinguishing system, whether it is 20 rooms on a single floor or several hundred rooms in a multi-storied building. This trend is being reflected in many foreign locations as American-based facilities are being installed with fire extinguishing systems.

In November 1980 the fatal fire at the MGM Grand in Las Vegas began a series of fatal arson fires which culminated on 31 December 1986 with the loss of 96 lives at the Hotel DuPont Plaza in San Juan, Puerto Rico. At this point the US Congress became involved as they moved toward enactment of the Hotel & Motel Fire Safety Act of 1990. In brief, the law required that employees of the federal establishment must stay in an approved lodging facility or travel reimbursement would be denied. The approved facilities must have hard-wired, single station smoke detectors in all spaces in a structure of four levels, or less, above ground level. Above the four levels, the structure must have both the smoke detection capability and a fire extinguishing system in order to qualify for federal employees' patronage. For reasons of potential litigation, meeting planners, travel agencies, and corporate travel offices quickly adopted these requirements, as well.

Throughout the decade of the 1990s, the lodging industry spent billions of dollars in new construction and as they retro-fitted properties to meet these specifications. In 1996, the industry had accomplished such a fine record that the National Fire Protection Association (NFPA) no longer carried a 'Hotel–Motel' line in its annual statistical report of fires in residential occupancies. The lodging industry had so sharply reduced fire incidents that the statistical instrument employed by NFPA would have charged the industry with fires that did not occur and fatalities that did not happen.

This fire protection effort in the United States was supported by the requirements in the Occupational Safety & Health Act (OSHA) for both emergency evacuation (Subpart E – Means of Egress – 1910.35 – 1910.40) and for fire protection training and systems (Subpart L – Fire Protection 1910.155 – 1910.165). Although directed to employees, this mandate also applied to the guest and the general public in a lodging establishment since they are in what are workplaces for the hotel employees. There has been outstanding progress in the training of staff from use of portable fire extinguishers, to search and rescue, to implementation of fire prevention, and to emergency evacuation procedures. Today, the traveling public is safer in a lodging establishment than in their own home.

Reference

Ellis, Raymond C. and Stipanuk, David M. (1999) *Security and Loss Prevention Management*, 2nd edn. Lansing, MI: Educational Institute of the American Hotel and Motel Association.

RAYMOND CLINTON ELLIS, JR
UNIVERSITY OF HOUSTON, USA

Fire seal

A fire door in a hotel is closed automatically by a fire system. When the door is closed, it is recommended that the gap between the door and frame should be no greater than 4 mm. No matter how narrow the gap, it forms an area of vulnerability for the passage of smoke and flames in a fire situation. Positive pressure is generated when a fire starts in a closed room, which causes smoke and gases to rapidly expand to other areas.

Fire seal is the material placed on the edge of the fire door to stop ingress of smoke during a fire. The expandable fire seal is used to seal the gap between the door and frame, reducing damage to the guestroom from the effect of fire and smoke. When exposed to heat, the fire seal begins a multi-directional expansion and swells up to several times of its original volume to fill any gap, joint or crevice in a construction where it is applied. The expansion of the seal prevents passage of flame, heat, smoke, and toxic gases that may be generated in case of fire.

References

http://www.astroflame.com/intumescent_fire_strip_install.html
http://222.chemtron.net/smokeseal-eng.htm
http://www.doorwaysplus.com/hagerseals.htm

BENNY CHAN
THE HONG KONG POLYTECHNIC UNIVERSITY,
HONG KONG SAR, CHINA

Fire sprinklers

Automated fire sprinklers are a component of a fire protection system, designed to protect against single fires in buildings. According to Mary Bellis (2004), Philip W. Pratt of Abington, MA was the inventor of the automatic sprinkler system and patented it in 1872. Two years later Henry S. Parmalee of New Haven, Connecticut improved upon the Pratt patent and created a better sprinkler system. Until the 1940s, sprinklers were installed almost exclusively in commercial buildings. However, with passage of time fire sprinklers became mandatory safety equipment, and today in most countries they are mandatory not only in commercial buildings but in all public buildings such as hospitals, schools, hotels etc. Sprinkler systems are required to include an automatic water supply that is reliable and adequate to meet the water requirements on a daily basis. The specific type of sprinkler system used is dependent on the types of fire hazard associated with different building types and uses. Standard spray sprinkler models include upright, pendant, or sidewall. Sprinklers may be installed behind special plates to match the ceiling background. In the United States regulations for the installation of sprinkler systems are addressed in NFPA 13, Standards for the Installation of Sprinkler Systems.

References

Bellis, Mary (2004) Fire Fighting Inventions. http://inventors.about.com/library/inventors/blfiresprinkler.htm Retrieved 28 April 2004.
Puchovsky, M. (2000) A brief introduction to sprinkler systems for Life Safety Code users. In R. Cote (ed.), *Life Safety Code Handbook*. Quincy, MA: National Fire Protection Association, pp. 967–980.

CAROLYN LAMBERT
PENNSYLVANIA STATE UNIVERSITY, USA

Fixed charges

A former term describing all the costs that appear below the current 'Income After Undistributed Operating Expenses' line – more commonly known as GOP or house profit – in the Uniform System of Accounts for the Lodging Industry (USALI). In the USALI these costs are captured under six rubrics:

1. Management fees
2. Rent, property taxes, and insurance (both building and contents and liability)
3. Interest expense
4. Depreciation and amortization
5. Gain or loss on sale of property
6. Income taxes.

The descriptor 'fixed' describes the charges from the perspective of the property manager, because the costs are the province of ownership and the operator cannot affect their magnitude. However, in terms of cost behavior, not all the expenses are fixed, including management fees (variable), rent (often semi-variable), and interest (semi-variable when a contingent interest component or 'kicker' is present). Fixed charges represent the overhead costs of hotel ownership and financing. As in the case of undistributed operating expenses, they are indirect costs that are not allocated to the revenue-generating departments under the Uniform System of Accounts for the Lodging Industry.

Reference

Uniform System of Accounts for the Lodging Industry, 9th edn. (1996) Lansing, MI: Educational Institute of the American Hotel and Motel Association.

PAUL BEALS
UNIVERSITY OF DENVER, USA

Fixed costs

Fixed costs normally remain constant within a 'relevant range' of activity and a specific period of time, e.g. one year. Examples of fixed costs in hospitality businesses, such as hotels or restaurants, include loan interest, rent, property taxes, insurance, and depreciation; representing the costs of occupying a hotel or restaurant property and referred to as 'fixed charges' in the Uniform System of Accounts for the Lodging Industry. Other examples of fixed costs can be marketing, and property operation and maintenance; these costs are regarded as fixed costs when, for example, an (annual) budget is set at a predetermined level. Also, administration expenses cost is, to a large extent, fixed in nature, though some elements such as credit card commission clearly vary with the level of activity. There are very few examples of costs that are fixed within an unlimited range of activity, which means that fixed costs normally turn into semi-variable costs as the specified range is increased.

Since fixed costs do not differ within a range of activity, the fixed cost per unit (per guest, per room, per cover) will decrease with an increasing volume. This is an important explanation to economies of scale advantages when cost efficiency normally increases with a higher volume.

References

Harris, P.J. (ed) (1995) *Accounting and Finance for the International Hospitality Industry*. Oxford: Butterworth-Heinemann.
Uniform System of Accounts for the Lodging Industry, 9th edn. (1996) Lansing, MI: Educational Institute of the American Hotel and Motel Association.

TOMMY D. ANDERSSON
GOTEBORGS UNIVERSITY, SWEDEN

Fixed costs in foodservice

Restaurant fixed costs typically do not change in the short-term. This means that they remain constant over the period of time being analyzed, regardless of changes in the restaurant business volume. As the number of patrons and total revenues change, fixed costs remain relatively constant. As volume and number of patrons change, however, the fixed costs per guest change. Examples of fixed costs include management salaries, rent, and insurance expense.

Accurately tracking fixed costs is key in a variety of functions, including menu pricing and breakeven analysis. Moreover, it is critical to budget for projected changes in fixed costs. For example, while building insurance is considered a fixed cost, it may increase at a given point during the fiscal year. Such increases should be reflected on the operating budget and consideration given for related effects.

Restaurant fixed costs can be divided into two categories: controllable and uncontrollable. Controllable fixed expenses – management salaries, for example – are considered within management's control since the unit level manager can determine number of managers and compensation for each manager. Depreciation, which is an uncontrollable fixed cost, is beyond management's purview since it is predetermined based on number and types of assets (and the depreciation methods used).

Reference

Deloitte & Touche LLP (1996) *Uniform System of Accounts*. Washington, DC: National Restaurant Association.

DEBORAH BARRASH
UNIVERSITY OF NEVADA, LAS VEGAS, USA

Fixed timeshare plan

An arrangement under which an owner receives a timeshare interest together with the right to use the accommodations and facilities at a timeshare property during the same specified period of time each year that the timeshare plan is in existence or for enough years to meet the requirements for regulation as a timeshare product. Depending on the nature of the timeshare plan, the owner of a fixed timeshare interest in a fixed timeshare plan may receive the same accommodation each time of use or may be assigned a different accommodation each time of use; however, the use will occur at the same time of the year. Generally, in a fixed timeshare plan there is not a requirement to use a complex reservation system, if one is needed at all, since the time of use is already determined. This fact equates to convenience for most consumers. Because the use is fixed and complex reservation systems are not needed, fixed timeshare plans present less complexities and costs for management. Conversely, there is also less opportunity for yield management resulting in more unreserved space and reduced revenue potential. It is possible to have mixed timeshare plans containing both fixed and floating timeshare interests.

Reference

American Resort Development Association (2002) *The Timeshare Resource Manual*. Washington, DC.

KURT GRUBER
ISLAND ONE RESORTS, USA

Flexible working

Flexible firms (with regard to human resources) are organizations that use their workforce with the aim of meeting industry demands – seasonal and other. The flexible firm was a concept first developed by Atkinson (1985) with the central concept being efficiency in the management of the workforce and being adaptive to ensure organization longevity (Volberda, 1999). This may include numeric flexibility, i.e. the ability to increase or decrease the workforce when required; functional flexibility, i.e. training the workforce to undertake multiple tasks; or outsourcing sections of the workforce, i.e. skills found and engaged from outside the organization to maximize the benefits of numeric and functional flexibility. Although all of these practices have advantages and disadvantages, they may not all be present in an organization at the same time.

The shamrock organization holistically brings together much of the flexible working organization. Generally it involves three three leaves: a *central core* that can include permanent, full-time critical employees; *temporary hires*, being part-time hires who are added and deleted as needed, allowing for numeric flexibility, and *independent contractors*, who are engaged to perform (specialist) key jobs and services as needed and can be thought of as outsourced labor (Handy, 1990). Most hospitality organizations could be described as operating within a shamrock frame at differing times and to differing degrees.

- Numeric flexibility is possibly the most focused aspect of human resource management. It forms part of the flexible firm and is achieved in a hospitality organization by the use of the contingent workforce – staff engaged on an 'as-needed basis' – therefore the number of employees varies (is flexible). The ability to use this workforce allows an organization to manage/cope with seasonal business trends, e.g. summer resorts increasing numbers in summer and decreasing in winter or vice versa. There are reported issues that a high use of contingent labor can result in increased employee turnover, due to the uncertainty of ongoing employment as viewed by an employee. An organization's desire to maintain numeric flexibility is the balance of the associated costs of recruitment as a result of turnover and the general thrust of flexibility. This desire is not always achievable in times of low unemployment. Some of these issues are: continual advertising (which may affect an organization's reputation), training, uniforms etc., each having direct and indirect costs. Numeric flexibility can be considered the temporary hires of the shamrock organization.

- Functional flexibility can be used within or outside numeric flexibility. When used within it, it refers to the workforce who may be either full-time or contingent, being able to undertake several functions. Potentially this allows the organization not only to increase and decrease the number of employees as demand requires, but also to manipulate the mix of employees that are needed. To achieve this, the hospitality organization cross-trains (multi skills) staff in a number of different roles so that the staff are more flexible in what they can do. For the employee this may provide the opportunity for increased hours of work and job security and increased job satisfaction. For the customer it may lead to increased customer satisfaction, and for the organization lower turnover and a reduced number of employees. Such an approach requires effective training systems, job/task rotation opportunities, and often sees a reduction in the number of distinct job titles (Cordery, 1989; Riley and Lockwood, 1997). Examples of this in hospitality organizations include hotel reservation staff cross-trained to work on the front desk or food waiters cross-trained as beverage waiters. Where functional flexibility is used outside the numeric workforce it potentially moves to the area known as outsourcing.
- Outsourcing can be used when an organization needs specific skills at certain times and does not wish to, or need to, engage them on a full-time basis. Naturally this does have linkage to functional and numeric flexibility. An example of this in the hospitality industry is where a hotel may no longer wish to maintain a full

housekeeping department so outsources this role to a specialist company that provides skilled staffing and resources, e.g. linen, etc. Another example is that of computer/IT services. A hotel may own its hardware but outsources the maintenance of this to a specialist computer company. Generally service agreements (including standards) are in place detailing the roles and responsibilities of each party. The benefit to the hospitality organization is that the required work is completed only when necessary, to an agreed standard, without the necessity of ongoing commitments (including associated costs) to often not fully used resources. Outsourcing also provides access to the latest processes, standards, trends etc. that often only a specialist contractor can provide. Although this can be considered a major advantage, the possibility of not being able to immediately fix a problem (although a service contract is in place) is something that some organizations are not prepared to risk, e.g. a computer breakdown during check-out with a 1 hour delay for an IT specialist to be on site. Alternatively, the location of the organization limits its ability to avail itself of such a system, e.g. a remote alpine resort may not consider outsourcing its housekeeping area due to potential road closures in winter that would not allow a contractor to get to the hotel. Outsourcing part of the workforce can be considered as the independent contractor section of the shamrock organization.

While hospitality organizations have in the past, and will continue in the future, to face the challenge of uncertainty of ongoing business for internal and external reasons, effective management of the human resources is seen as one way of trying to match business demands (financial and other), employee needs and satisfaction, and customer satisfaction.

References

Atkinson, J. (1985) Flexibility – planning for an uncertain future. *Manpower and Policy Practice*, 23 (3).

Cordery, John. L. (1989) Multi-skilling: a discussion of proposed benefits of new approaches to labor flexibility within enterprises. *Personnel Review*, 18 (3), 13–23.

Handy, Charles (1990) *The Age of Unreason.* Boston, MA: Harvard Business School.

Riley, Michael and Lockwood, Andrew (1997) Strategies and measurement for working flexibility: an application of functional flexibility in a service setting. *International Journal of Operations and Production Management*, 18 (4), 413–420.

Volberda, Henk W. (1999) *Building the Flexible Firm: How to Remain Competitive.* Oxford: Oxford University Press.

ANTHONY BRIEN
LINCOLN UNIVERSITY, NEW ZEALAND

Float timeshare plan

An arrangement under which an owner receives a timeshare interest together with the right to reserve the use of accommodations and facilities at a timeshare property during specified periods of time each year that the timeshare plan is in existence or for enough years to meet the requirements for regulation as a timeshare. The right to make a reservation is grouped according to such variables as season or unit location, with higher demanded times and locations commanding higher prices and more competition among owners for reservations. Depending on the timeshare plan, owners of interests in a floating timeshare plan may receive the same accommodation each time of use or may be assigned a different accommodation each time of use; however, the use may or may not occur at the same time of the year. Floating timeshare plans require rules for governing priority rights in making and confirming reservations and a reservation system to track and process reservations. Floating timeshare plans present more complexities and costs for management; however, there is greater opportunity for yield management resulting in more reserved space and higher revenue potential. It is possible to have mixed timeshare plans containing both fixed and floating timeshare interests.

Reference

American Resort Development Association (2002) *The Timeshare Resource Manual.* Washington, DC.

KURT GRUBER
ISLAND ONE RESORTS, USA

Focus groups

A focus group consists of a group of individuals brought together to discuss specific issues. The group is usually sized between 10 to 12 participants, although mini-focus groups of five to seven are common (Shoemaker, 2004). Participants in a focus group are frequently screened before they are selected to participate. The group is led through a series of topics, questions, and discussions by a moderator who is usually part of the research team. The purpose of using a focus group is exploratory; the focus group provides ideas and insights into a particular subject matter. The group is not used to infer about the population of interest, although focus group members might be representative of the population (Churchill, 2001). The focus group provides ideas and opinions to the organization. A focus group is frequently video taped or observed by other members of the research team, either openly or secretly (Salkind, 2003).

The moderator is critical to the focus group because that person leads the group through a predetermined series of questions, topics, or discussions. The moderator should possess the following characteristics. The moderator should be a quick learner in order to absorb and understand inputs from focus group participants. The moderator should also be fairly knowledgeable so the respondents do not feel that they have to teach the moderator. The moderator should not sound like a know-it-all either. The moderator needs to allow participants to feel comfortable in the group discussion so that true thoughts and feelings can be shared. The moderator needs to be an excellent listener in terms of content and implications. The moderator should be a facilitator, not an entertainer. The moderator should be somewhat flexible to allow the focus group to explore an issue more thoroughly. The moderator should be empathetic so that group participants are more comfortable in sharing. The moderator needs to be able to communicate the discussion to a client in a written report that provides meaningful action-oriented conclusions and recommendations (Shoemaker, 2004).

Focus groups are frequently used to conduct marketing research. They are used to develop consumer questionnaires since focus group participants are potential respondents. Focus groups are also a good research tool for learning how people use a product. They are also good for learning how people perceive a new product or concept. A focus group is also good for exploring complaints or problems that consumers have with a product. They are also good for exploring why people have certain views toward a product.

There are several benefits to using focus groups. Being part of a focus group lowers respondents' anxiety and provides a more comfortable setting for discussion. Focus groups allow the respondent to share the feelings and emotions behind their response to a question. Talking out the respondents thought processes assists the researcher in understanding motivations behind a response. Another benefit to surveys is that they are inexpensive compared to surveys.

On the other hand, there are several disadvantages to focus groups. One disadvantage is that members of the group influence one another by sharing their feelings aloud. This can cause homogeneous responses among the group. Additionally, the group setting may restrict the depth achieved in a one-to-one setting. Some of the disadvantages of focus groups can be counteracted by using multiple groups. In this way, characteristics of the participants and issues discussed within the focus group can differ across focus groups (Churchill, 2001).

References

Churchill, G.A. (2001) *Basic Marketing Research*, 4th edn. Mason: South-Western.

Salkind, N.J. (2003) *Exploring Research*, 5th edn. Upper Saddle River, NJ: Prentice-Hall.

Shoemaker, Stowe (2004) Personal communication, 25 March.

BRUMBY MCLEOD
UNIVERSITY OF NEVADA, LAS VEGAS, USA

Folio

This is an account statement upon which guest transactions (charges or payments) that affect the balance of the guest's account are recorded. There are four types of folios:

- *Guest folio* – accounts assigned to individual persons or guestrooms
- *Master folio* – accounts assigned to more than one person or guestroom; usually reserved for group accounts
- *Non-guest or semi-permanent folio* – accounts assigned to non-guest businesses or agencies with hotel charge purchase privileges
- *Employee folio* – accounts assigned to employees with charge purchase privileges.

Guest folios can also be 'split' for, e.g., a business guest who is getting their accommodation expenses paid. Room and tax charges can be posted to the room folio (A folio) and other charges can be posted to the incidental folio (B folio).

The accurate and timely processing of all these accounts assists the front office manager in maintaining hard copies of guests' financial transactions with the hotel. These accounts are collectively referred to as the hotel's accounts receivable – what guests owe the hotel. The accounts receivable consist of two categories, the guest ledger and the city ledger.

Reference

Kasavana, M.L. and Brooks, R.M. (1995) *Front Office Procedures*, 4th edn. Lansing, MI: Educational Institute of the American Hotel and Motel Association.

IRENE SWEENEY
INTERNATIONAL HOTEL MANAGEMENT
INSTITUTE SWITZERLAND, SWITZERLAND

Food code (THE)

The Food Code is published by the US Food and Drug Administration (FDA). Its purpose is to provide a model for local, state, tribal, and federal regulators for developing or updating their own food safety rules and to be consistent with national food regulatory policy. At the same time it also serves as a reference of best practices for the foodservice industry on how to prevent foodborne illness. The overall objective of the Food Code is to protect the public health and to provide food that is safe in foodservice operations. The Code includes recommendations for food handling methods, employee practices, equipment specifications, building plan reviews, and health inspections. The food code is published every four years and reflects the latest food safety knowledge. The last revision was published in 2001 and the next complete revision will be published in 2005. During the four-year interim period, a *Food Code* Supplement that updates, modifies, or clarifies certain provisions is being made available. Adoption of the Code is not mandatory. States may develop their own regulations and local county or city health departments can add requirements. The Food Code is enforced at the local level by health inspectors.

Reference

Food and Drug Administration (2001, December) The 2001 Food Code. Retrieved 27 August 2003 from http://www.cfsan. fda.gov/~dms/fc01-toc.html.

CAROLYN LAMBERT
PENNSYLVANIA STATE UNIVERSITY, USA

Foodborne illness

Foodborne illnesses are diseases transmitted to people through food. 'An outbreak of foodborne illness occurs when a group of people consume the same contaminated food and two or more of them come down with the same illness' (CDC, 2004). Table 1 contains a list of common foodborne-illness pathogens, along with their sources, symptoms, and methods of prevention.

The Centers for Disease Control (CDC) estimate that over 76 million people in the United States are sickened with a foodborne illness each year. Of those cases, over 300,000 require hospitalization and about 5000 result in death (Mead *et al.*, 1999, as reported by the CDC). Worldwide, the numbers are suspected to be much higher; however, because of variations in reporting methods or lack of reporting altogether, it is difficult to get an accurate estimate of the true magnitude of the problem. Table 2 breaks down by percentage of total infections the pathogens responsible for making people sick.

Development and implementation of an effective HACCP program (Hazard Analysis of Critical Control Points) by the operator may significantly reduce the risk of an outbreak of foodborne illness. In addition, food handlers must be thoroughly trained and constantly retrained in proper food safety and sanitation procedures. Food Safety Update (2001) offers five basic tips to increase the effectiveness of training programs. These include:

- *Promote participation:* Get employees involved in the training – the more interactively, the better.
- *Make it relevant:* People prefer listening to what's real over what's theoretical. Encourage storytelling; everyone has one.
- *Offer rewards:* What gets measured gets done. Create incentives that encourage people to do what's right.
- *Link food safety to performance:* Assess employees' knowledge of food safety and sanitation during the review process and reward them accordingly.
- *Lead by example:* Walk the talk. Managers must always provide the model they want their employees to emulate.

Beyond instituting meaningful training as a means of illness prevention, foodservice operators should encourage the development of good personal hygiene habits among those who handle food. Proper hand washing (which includes the use of soap, a nail brush, and at least 20 seconds of time) is one of the simplest, yet most effective, methods of stopping the transference of

Table 1 Common foodborne illness pathogens

Pathogen	Source	Symptoms/Onset	Prevention
Norwalk-like virus	Shellfish, beef, chicken, pork, salads, dressings, infected worker	Diarrhea, abdominal cramps, nausea, vomiting, fever; 10–51 hours	Thorough cooking, rapid chilling, proper hand washing, hold at below 40 °F (4 °C) or above 140 °F (60 °C)
Campylobacter	Raw milk, uncooked chicken, raw hamburger, water	Nausea, cramps, headache, fever, diarrhea; 1–10 days	Thorough cooking, use boiled/treated water
Salmonella	Undercooked poultry, eggs or foods containing such; meat, dairy products	Abdominal pain, diarrhea, chills, fever, vomiting, cramps; 6–72 hours	Thorough cooking; clean/sanitized hands, utensils, surfaces; prompt refrigeration
Clostridium perfringens	Soups, stews, gravies held at warm temperatures	Nausea, vomiting, pain, diarrhea; 6–24 hours	Thorough cooking, rapid chilling, hold at below 40 °F (4 °C) or above 140 °F (60 °C)
Giardia lamblia	Contaminated water, infected worker	Sudden diarrhea, cramps, nausea, vomiting; 1–3 days	Use boiled/treated water, proper hand washing
Escherichia coli	Contaminated ground beef; unpasteurized juice, milk, cider; water	Cramps, bloody diarrhea, fever, vomiting; 12–72 hours	Cook ground beef to 160 °F (71 °C); consume pasteurized products; use boiled/treated water; clean/sanitized hands, utensils, surfaces
Staphylococcus	Meats, salads containing proteins, sauces, reheated foods	Nausea, vomiting, cramps, diarrhea; 1–6 hours	Thorough cooking, hold at below 40 °F (4 °C) or bove 140 °F (60 °C), proper hand washing, open sores properly covered
Shigella	Moist foods, dairy products, salads, water, infected worker	Diarrhea, fever, vomiting, cramps; 1–7 days	Use boiled/treated water; clean/sanitized hands, utensils, surfaces
Listeria	Unwashed vegetables, unpasteurized dairy products, improperly processed meats	Flu-like symptoms with fever and nausea, pregnancy interruption; 4 days to 3 weeks	Thorough cooking, use pasteurized products, wash produce
Hepatitis A virus	Infected worker, water, seafood from polluted waters	Nausea, abdominal pain, weakness/discomfort, fever	Proper hand washing, use boiled/treated water, use reputable suppliers

Source: CDC (2004)

disease-causing pathogens from hands to food. 'Clean' (free of visible dirt) and 'sanitary' (free of disease-causing pathogens) are two very important words when it comes to protecting the public from foodborne illness.

Finally, it should be noted that a foodborne illness does not have to affect many people in order to be considered an 'outbreak.' In fact, an outbreak is defined as an incidence of foodborne illness that involves two or more people who eat a

Table 2 Estimated percentages of foodborne pathogens leading to illness in the United States

Pathogen	Percentage
Norwalk-like virus	66.7
Campylobacter	14.2
Salmonella	9.7
Clostridium perfringens	1.8
Giardia lamblia	1.4
Escherichia coli	1.3
Staphylococcus	1.3
Shigella	0.6
Listeria	<0.1
Hepatitis A virus	<0.1

Source: Mead *et al.* (1999), as reported by the Centers for Disease Control

common food, which is confirmed as the source of the illness through laboratory analysis (National Restaurant Association, 1992). The only exceptions, which qualify an outbreak on the basis of only a single incidence, are those that result from botulism or a chemical-caused outbreak.

References

CDC (Centers for Disease Control) (2004) *Foodborne Illness*. Available at http://www.cdc.gov/ncidod/dbmd/diseaseinfo/foodborneinfections_g.htm#whatoutbreak. Accessed 11 March 2004.

Food Safety Update (2001) Five basic training tips. *Food Safety Update*, 13.

Mead, P., Slutsker, L., Dietz, V., McCaig, L., Bresee, J., Shapiro, C., Griffin, P., and Tauxe, R. (1999) Food-related illness and death in the United States. *Emerging Infectious Diseases*, 5 (5). Available at http://www.cdc.gov/ncidod/EID/vol5no5/mead.htm. Accessed 21 August 2002.

National Restaurant Association (1992) *Applied Foodservice Sanitation*. New York: John Wiley & Sons.

NANCY SWANGER
WASHINGTON STATE UNIVERSITY, USA

Forecasting

Theoretically the term forecasting means planning for the future, but it is used colloquially in the hospitality business to mean short-term planning. It is a less formal process than budgeting (planning for a full financial year ahead), being operational in approach and predicting the coming days, weeks, and perhaps months. Budgets in hospitality and tourism firms tend to become outdated quickly due to changes in economic and political circumstances, weather conditions, markets activities and so on, and hence a more immediate short-term estimate of anticipated volume is required. This then allows the operation to adapt their selling strategies and to plan staffing levels, purchasing, stock movements, and cash flows. It is especially important where departments and/or businesses inter-relate such as the impact of tour businesses on flights and holiday accommodation or conference guests on rooms occupied, food and beverage, and leisure revenues and costs. In these cases small shortfalls in volume can have a significant effect on profits if not carefully managed. Forecasting and flexible budgeting techniques can also be used to assess the impact of changes in volume, sales mix, prices, and costs on the profits of a business.

References

Burgess, C. (2001) *Guide to Money Matters for Hospitality Managers*. Oxford: Butterworth-Heinemann.

Schmidgall, R. and de Franco, A. (1998) Budgeting and forecasting – current practice in the lodging industry. *Cornell Hotel and Restaurant Administration Quarterly*, December, 45–51.

CATHY BURGESS
OXFORD BROOKES UNIVERSITY, UK

Forecasting in foodservice/restaurants

Forecasting is one of the critical activities of any manager. In the hospitality industry, managers are expected to forecast revenue streams for both immediate and long-term needs. Some of the simple applications of forecasting include forecasting of revenues to schedule employees; forecasting of revenues to plan food and supply orders; forecasting of revenues to correspond with marketing efforts, etc. Forecasting can be accomplished by using sophisticated quantitative models or qualitative and intuitive managerial decisions. The choice depends on the complexity of the organization and the importance of the forecasting decision.

For example, to prepare an employee schedule for a typical work week, revenue forecasting can be accomplished by taking a moving average of the past four-week revenues and adjusting it to reflect changing circumstances. This is a very common practice in the foodservice industry. Similarly, forecasting can also be done using past-year sales for the same period and adjusting it for inflation or using statistical packages. Recently, a restaurant chain was able to save over one million dollars a year by implementing forecasting software in all of its units. Inaccurate forecasting leads to product and employee shortages or labor and product wastage.

Common methods of forecasting one may observe in the foodservice industry include: the adjustment method, the moving average method (these are illustrated below), the exponential smoothing method, regression models, and intuitive methods.

Adjustment method

The adjustment method involves taking some prior interval as a base period and adjusting it with a certain number determined by management. For example, some companies may use the percentage of general inflation in the economy as the adjustment factor. When introducing a new product, a company might use the percentage of additional sales expected from a new product as the basis of the adjustment factor. Other organizations may use managerial discretion to arrive at the adjustment factor to reflect local economic conditions.

Table 1   Forecasted revenues: adjustment method (adjustment factor = 10%)

Revenues	Jan	Feb	Mar	Apr	May	Jun
Last-year revenues (in thousands)	500	300	400	560	650	750
Projected revenues (adjusted by 10%)	550	330	440	616	715	825

Table 2   Forecasted revenues: moving average method

Revenues	Jan	Feb	Mar	Apr	May	Jun	Jul
Current	550	350	450	600	*450**	*500**	*490**
Forecasted (rounded up)					490	475	500

* = Actual revenues.

Moving average method

According to this method, the average of the past four accounting periods is selected as the basis for forecasting. If necessary, the newly calculated average is again adjusted to reflect managerial knowledge of local operations. The length of the accounting period may vary with the accounting practices of the organization. In the following example, revenues for May were projected to be 490 (the average of January, February, March, and April) while the actual revenues were 450. Revenues for June were projected by taking the average of the preceding four months (February, March, April, and May) while actual revenues were 500. Sales for July are again calculated by taking the average of the preceding four months (March, April, May, and June), which is 500.

Forecasting of food

Forecasting is used not only for financial purposes but also for placing purchase orders for food, paper, supplies etc. For example, restaurateurs often use forecasting to estimate the necessary purchase quantities of various food-related items. To accomplish this, restaurateurs first use one of the forecasting methods to determine forecasted sales. The second step would be to calculate the quantity of food needed. To determine the amount of food needed, restaurateurs must know the 'yield' factor for each food item. Yield factor is the amount of sales yielded by a unit of food. It could be sales per pound in the case of meats, or sales per case of lettuce, sales per bag of onions, sales per pound of flour, etc. Yield is calculated by dividing the total sales for (say) the past week by the amount of the product used.

Yield

$$= \frac{\text{4-week average sales}}{\text{4 week average product usage in Inventory Units}}$$

$$= \text{Dollars/Inventory Unit}$$

$$\text{Yield} = \frac{\$(36{,}000 + 30{,}000 + 28{,}000 + 42{,}000)}{(1200 + 980 + 850 + 1400)\,\text{lb}}$$

$$= \frac{\$136{,}000}{4430\,\text{lb}} = \$30.69/\text{lb}$$

Sales forecast = 4-week moving average (or any other method)

$= \$30{,}000$

Product needed = Sales forecast/Product yield

$$\text{Product needed} = \frac{\$30{,}000}{30.69\$/\text{lb}} = 978\,\text{lb}$$

Product needed = 1000 lb (rounded up) in Inventory Units

Purchase units = Cases (each case is 25 lb)

Product ordered = Product needed/Purchase unit weight

Product ordered = 1000 lb/25 lb/case

$= 40$ cases

All inventory units must be converted to purchase units before orders are placed. And all units are rounded up to the nearest whole number.

Forecasting menu items

Forecasting of menu items is slightly different from forecasting of raw food items. Some companies follow the percentage index method to forecast menu items for the day. According to this method, a restaurateur must know the percentage of each menu item compared with the total number of items sold. This can be calculated by taking the average number of menu items sold for the past four weeks and dividing it by the average number of specific menu items sold during that period. The second step would be to estimate the number of guests expected for a specific day. The third step involves multiplication of the total number of guests expected with the percentage index.

Example:

Shrimp Platter forecast for a Friday:

Percentage index

$$= \frac{\text{Total number of Shrimp Platters sold}}{\text{Total number of all items sold}}$$

$$= \frac{50}{350} = 14.28\%$$

$$\text{Total number of guests forecasted} = \frac{\text{Average of past 4 Fridays' sales}}{\text{Guest check average for past 4 Fridays}}$$

$$= \frac{\$3000/\text{day}}{\$7.50/\text{guest}}$$

$$= 400\,\text{guests/day}$$

Shrimp Platters forecasted

$$= \frac{\text{Number of guests forecasted per day}}{\text{Percentage index}}$$

$$= 400\,\text{guests/day} \times 14.28\%$$

$$= 57\,\text{Shrimp Platters}$$

References

Keister, D. (1997) *Food and Beverage Control.* Englewood Cliffs, NJ: Prentice-Hall.

Ninemeier, J. (2000) *Planning and Control for Food and Beverage Operations.* Lansing, MI: Educational Institute of the American Hotel and Motel Association.

H.G. PARSA
OHIO STATE UNIVERSITY, USA

Forecasting rooms availability

The hotel's reservations department is charged with two primary tasks; setting rates and selling rooms. Before successfully accomplishing either of these tasks, the reservations department needs an accurate count of the number of rooms available for sale. Knowing how many rooms are available for sale on a given date is a logical first-step for the task of selling rooms. Less clear, however, is the relationship between the number of rooms available for sale and the setting of rates for a given period. This second relationship forms the basis for the key objective of any hotel: to maximize revenues through yield management.

Yield management is the process of maximizing gross rooms revenues by carefully managing both the number of rooms sold for a given period (occupancy) as well as the average rate – known as average daily rate (ADR) or sometimes average room rate (ARR) – received for each room sold. Yield management is based heavily on the ability of the hotel to forecast the number of rooms available for sale in advance of the date in question.

The dual role of forecasting availability

The definition of yield management points clearly to the dual role of forecasting availability; maximizing rate through accurately estimating demand and maximizing rooms sold through systematic forecasting.

Yield management in the lodging industry rests on an irrefutable foundation; the rate charged for remaining rooms tends to increase with rising occupancy projections. In other words, hotels generally receive a higher rate from the last few rooms sold than they do from the first few rooms sold. The first rooms may have been sold (reserved) a year or more in advance, a period filled with uncertainty in terms of occupancy for the date in question. As such, hotels tend to discount room rates early in the cycle as they attempt to gauge their business levels for the date in question.

Through regular forecasts of the date in question, the hotel grows more and more confident in its understanding of the business levels it

will experience. As confidence grows and occupancy for the date becomes more and more certain, the room rate rises. In the end, the last rooms sold receive the highest rate. By raising rates, step-by-step, as the room forecast grows in accuracy, the hotel reaps maximum yield for the period in question.

Underlying the premise that rising occupancy gives way to rising rates is the logic that systematic forecasting of room availability affords the hotel less errors of fact with regard to under- or over-booking rooms sold.

It takes little to imagine the problems which might befall a hotel that incorrectly forecasts available rooms. A substantial error one way or the other can be costly to the hotel's bottom line. An error resulting in underbooking rooms available for sale can occur a number of ways. A few examples might include: a reservations department which holds more rooms for a group than they actually occupy, a heavier number of check-outs than forecast, or a high last-minute cancellation rate. Any of these examples will result in more available rooms than projected. And unsold rooms are costly!

Overbooking the hotel is equally costly. Examples of overbooking errors might include: projecting a higher number of check-outs than actually experienced, forecasting more no-shows and cancellations than occurred, or holding less rooms for a group room block than were actually required. While underbooking the hotel is costly to the bottom line, overbooking the hotel can be costly to good will and guest satisfaction. Certainly no guest wants to arrive for the night only to be told the reservation cannot be honored and the guest must be walked to another property because the hotel overbooked. (For more see entries on Overbooking, Walking, and No-show.)

Reservation types

The ultimate goal of every hotel is to achieve the 'perfect fill,' defined as a paid guest in every hotel room. To reach this elusive benchmark, however, the hotel needs to make some difficult (and often risky) decisions. One of the first steps in the decision-making process is to understand which types of reservations are acceptable to the hotel. Hotels seeking to reach perfect fill generally book a very high percentage of their rooms as guaranteed or advance deposit reservations. Conversely, they generally book very few non-guaranteed reservations. Some hotels refuse non-guaranteed reservations altogether.

Here is a quick look at the three classic types of reservations:

- *Advance-deposit reservations:* Advance-deposit reservations are another form of guaranteed reservation. However, rather than guaranteeing the room to a credit card or corporate account, an advance-deposit reservation requires the guest to send payment in advance. Payment may come in the form of a cashier's check, personal check, money order, or even authorized credit card payment. In any case, hotels that require advance-deposit reservations often establish more rigid cancellation policies (longer lead time for cancellations) in order for the guest to receive full refund.
- *Guaranteed reservations:* Reservations guaranteed against a guest's credit card or corporate account have higher credibility than non-guaranteed reservations. That's because the guest has something to lose if he or she fails to arrive. Depending on the hotel's cancellation policy, failing to arrive for a guaranteed reservation usually costs the guest or the corporate account a night's room and tax.
- *Non-guaranteed reservations:* Non-guaranteed reservations (sometimes called 6 p.m.-hold reservations) have no monetary promise associated with the reservation. Should the non-guaranteed reservation fail to materialize, the hotel has no recourse against the guest. As such, non-guaranteed reservations are very risky and uncertain reservations. Many hotels refuse to accept non-guaranteed reservations (though they may accept them on occasion as favors to particular guests or in unique circumstances). Because there is a very high no-show factor associated with non-guaranteed reservations, accepting such reservations impacts the hotel's ability to reach perfect fill.

Calculating availability

If guests never changed their minds, it would be very easy to fill hotels. The formula would

simply be:

Stayovers + Today's reservations
= Rooms committed

When the number of committed rooms equaled the number of rooms in the hotel, the hotel would be full. And since no guests were changing their minds, there would be no need to overbook the hotel in anticipation of a few cancellations or no-shows.

However, we do not live in a perfect world, and guests change their minds every day. While some guests check out a day or two earlier than originally planned (e.g. understays), others stay over additional nights (e.g. overstays). For whatever reason, some guests never arrive to honor their reservations (e.g. no-shows). Hopefully they call to cancel (e.g. cancellations), but many never do because they are too busy or forgetful to contact the hotel with their change in plans. Whatever the situation at a given hotel on a given night, the room availability formula is nothing more than a best-guess estimate.

Some hotels are able to better manage their room availability forecasting than others, and the reason is in the details. Careful tracking of incoming reservations coupled with a historical understanding of certain ratios and trends can substantially improve a property's forecasting accuracy. Well operated hotels strive to:

- Include as much information as possible on each reservation:
  - How recently was the reservation made?
  - Is the reservation part of a larger group? Or potentially made outside of the group's room block (Howe, 2002)?
  - If it is a corporate reservation, are other representatives of the company currently in-house?
  - How far is the guest traveling (weather problems, airline delays, etc.)?
- Begin forecasting room availability early in the day:
  - Calls to corporate offices confirming reservations must be accomplished by 5 p.m. at the latest.
  - Checking with in-house sales managers and administrative departments before the end of the work day may also provide insights for certain guest reservations.

○ Having a sense of room availability early in the day allows the reservations department to accept same-day and walk-in reservations.

• Uncover duplicate reservations:

○ Watch for spelling variations (e.g. McDonald, MacDonald, Mike Donalds).

○ Verify that the guest has not already checked-in at a sister, same-brand, property down the street or across town.

○ Look for reservations under the same name for tomorrow night or later in the week.

• Validate the reservation.

○ Verify that the guaranteed reservation is using a legitimate credit card number. Then authorize and approve the card.

○ Validate the credit status of all corporate guarantees. Is the company in good current standing with the hotel?

Tracking the accuracy of each reservation is an important step in forecasting availability because it places a higher confidence on each of the incoming reservations. However, no matter how carefully the hotel monitors its reservations, some guests will inevitably cancel or no-show. The net impact from each cancellation or no-show is an increase in the number of available rooms. Let's follow a running example for the 'Perfect Fill Hotel.' To start, we will assume:

○ The 'Perfect Fill Hotel' has 465 rooms.

○ Today is the third Tuesday following Labor Day.

○ Last night (Monday), we had 87.96% occupancy (409 rooms sold).

○ There are no rooms out-of-order or out-of-inventory.

○ Today we anticipate 249 rooms will depart.

○ The check-out hour is 11a.m.

○ We have 310 guaranteed reservations arriving today. There are no advance deposit reservations. There are no non-guaranteed reservations.

The forecasted room count for tonight is calculated as:

1	Occupied last night	409
	Less: Due to check out	249
	Equals: Stayovers	160

2	Stayovers	160
	Plus: Reservations	310
	Equals: Committed rooms	470
3	Rooms in hotel	465
	Less: Committed rooms	470
	Equals: Available rooms	−5

Based on this example, the Perfect Fill Hotel is overbooked by five rooms. Technically, there are more incoming reservations than rooms available. If every guest arrives as scheduled, the hotel will need to 'walk' five rooms to nearby properties.

But watch what happens to this equation when we forecast a 2% cancellation rate and a 1% no-show rate. Let's pretend the Perfect Fill Hotel knows that Tuesday evenings in late September have historically experienced 2% cancellation and 1% no-show rates. On any given day, however, such historical ratios may prove little better than educated guesses!

Looking back to the example, incoming reservations are reduced by no-shows and cancellations:

Reservations	310	
Less: Cancellations (2.0%)	−6	(rounded from 6.2)
Less: No-shows (1.0%)	−3	(rounded from 3.1)
Projected reservations	301	

The new 'projected' reservations figure affects sections 2 and 3 of the formula:

1	Stayovers	160
	Plus: Reservations	301
	Equals: Committed rooms	461
2	Rooms in hotel	465
	Less: Committed rooms	461
	Equals: Available rooms	+4

The net result is a hotel with four rooms left to sell. A big difference from the hotel overbooked by five rooms we saw moments before. Would you now sell these four rooms? Probably not. There are so many unanswered variables, that most hotel operators would wait a number of hours to see if a few cancellations actually do materialize.

One important variable for which hotel managers wait each day is the check-out hour. By 11a.m. or shortly thereafter, the hotel knows which rooms have not checked out that were scheduled to (overstays) and which did check out that were not expected to (understays). Indeed, availability forecasts usually add projections for overstays and understays into their formulas. In our continuing example, let's assume the hotel's historical experience with Tuesday mornings is that 2% of departures will overstay and zero% will understay. Overstays have the effect of reducing available rooms. Conversely, understays increase the number of rooms available.

1 Stayovers   160
   Plus: Overstays (2.0%)   +3 (rounded
                                 from 3.2)
     Less: Understays (0.0%)   −0
   Projected stayovers   163

The new 'projected' stayovers figure affects sections 2 and 3 of the formula:

2 Stayovers   163
   Plus: Reservations   301
   Equals: Committed rooms   464
3 Rooms in hotel   465
   Less: Committed rooms   464
   Equals: Available rooms   +1

The net result is a hotel with just one room left to sell. A quick review shows that forecasted room availability is impacted by no-shows and cancellations (both of which have the effect of increasing rooms available for sale) as well as by overstays and understays. Overstays have the effect of reducing the number of rooms available for sale; understays increase the rooms available for sale.

However, this is an artificially simple look at forecasting room availability. The reality is far more complex. Entire careers are devoted to forecasting availability, inventory, and revenue management. And as the Internet continues to grow, its impact on forecasting cannot be ignored. 'Hotel companies [are making] decisions on inventory management that were not necessary before [the advent of the Internet]'. Guests are learning to use distressed and last-minute inventory sites like site59.com, 11thhourvacations.com and lastminutetravel.com as a matter of routine. Hotels are experiencing higher cancellation rates as guests gravitate toward the following booking pattern; they make an initial reservation through normal booking channels, they wait patiently until the 'last-minute,' they book a better 'last-minute' deal online, they cancel the original reservation.

These are challenging times for the lodging industry. And forecasting rooms inventory is growing more and more difficult.

References

Dela Cruz, Tony (2002) Price vs. loyalty; cost-conscious guests and room inventory management fuel Internet booking tussle. *Hotel & Motel Management*, pp. 1, 52.

Howe, Jonathan (2002) Same old contract? Look again. *Meetings and Conventions*, p. 36.

Vallen, Gary and Vallen, Jerome (2000) *Check-in Check-out*, 6th edn. Upper Saddle River, NJ: Prentice-Hall.

Weinbach, Jonathan (2000) The late-bird special; new web sites peddle deals for impulsive fliers – we click for cheap seats. *Wall Street Journal*, p. W6.

GARY VALLEN
NORTHERN ARIZONA UNIVERSITY, USA

Forecasting rooms revenue

Hotels and resorts must set prices in an environment with highly perishable inventory which varies dramatically, and customers whose value may need to be carefully measured.

There are two approaches to forecasting rooms revenue available to hotel management. One of the simplest methods of forecasting rooms revenue involves an analysis of rooms revenue from past periods. Dollar and percentage differences are noted and the amount of rooms revenue for the budget year is predicted.

The second method of forecasting rooms revenue bases the revenue projection on past room sales and average daily rooms rates. A simple formula of multiplying rooms available by occupancy percentage by average daily rate reveals the forecasted rooms revenue. Occupancy percentage being the proportion of rooms sold to rooms available during a designated time period, average daily rate is derived by dividing net rooms revenue by the number of rooms sold and the number of available rooms is calculated by multiplying the number of rooms in the hotel by the number of days in the year the hotel is operating.

Various automation tools exist to assist in forecasting rooms revenue. It is key that the automation system should:

- Assist in determining overbooking at room-type level for optimal use of valuable inventory
- Stay pattern controls to enforce checkouts occur as anticipated to help maximize revenues on peak periods
- Shoulder date management that targets revenue potential on either side of peak periods.
- Measure and evaluate the value of prospective group business relative to other uses of the inventory
- Enable management of special events according to their revenue potential; and determine guests' value to one's business.

Reference

Bardi, James A. (2003) *Hotel Front Office Management*, 3rd edn. New York: John Wiley & Sons.

ALAN T. STUTTS
AMERICAN INTERCONTINENTAL
UNIVERSITY, USA

Fractional

The term refers to products that divide ownership and use of accommodations and facilities into larger increments of time, such as in 1/6th or 1/12th interests, rather than dividing the year into 1/52nd interests used in traditional timeshare plans. While legally there may be little distinction between fractional products and traditional timeshare products, fractional developers generally distinguish their product on the basis of such factors as purchaser income, a greater focus on the real estate underpinnings of the product, a more extensive amenity package, upscale accommodations, and different sales and marketing practices.

The purchaser of a fractional interest is usually in the market for a second home but does not want all-the-year-round use, maintenance obligations or high purchase price associated with acquiring and owning a second home. Use of a fractional product can take on many of the characteristics of other timeshare products by allowing the owner to exchange use or reserve different periods of time for use in different years. In some instances, the fractional interests are developed by bundling the lower-demanded times together with higher-demanded times with the lower-demanded times being subject to a floating plan and the higher-demanded times sold as fixed time.

Reference

American Resort Development Association (2002) *The Timeshare Resource Manual*. Washington, DC: ARDA.

KURT GRUBER
ISLAND ONE RESORTS, USA

Framing

'Framing' refers to positive or negative associations that accompany information. Framing occurs in two primary ways. First, the message that a company sends about a product or service is accompanied by images, sounds, or other stimuli associated with the product. These may have a positive or a negative effect on the customer. For example, a hotel company uses rock music in an advertisement, creating a 'frame' for the customer to evaluate the hotel. The rock music has a positive effect if the music makes the customer want to stay at the hotel, and a negative effect if the customer does not like rock music and thus finds the hotel unattractive.

Framing also includes the choice of language. For example, 'inexpensive,' 'economical,' and 'cheap' may be synonymous. A hotel might present itself as an 'economy' property rather than a 'cheap' one to avoid the negative connotations of cheapness.

Framing also occurs through outside context; prior exposure to a situation can influence the way that a current situation is perceived. An example is how we perceive the attractiveness of our spouse or significant other. Their attractiveness may diminish after viewing pictures of supermodels. The supermodels provide a temporary 'frame' against which we compare the attractiveness of our loved ones.

References

Kahneman, D. and Tversky, A. (1984) Choices, values, and frames. *American Psychologist*, 39, 341–350.

Kardes, F.R. (1999) *Consumer Behavior and Managerial Decision-Making*. Reading, MA: Addison-Wesley.

Peter, J.P. and Olson, J.D. (1999) *Consumer Behavior and Market Strategy*, 5th edn. Boston, MA: Irwin/McGraw-Hill.

DINA MARIE V. ZEMKE
UNIVERSITY OF NEW HAMPSHIRE, USA

Franchising

The word 'franchising' is derived from the French verb *franchir*, which means to make free or give liberty to, and often referred to freedom from some restriction, servitude or slavery. Franchising can be divided into two major categories: business format franchising and product/trade name format franchising. Business format franchising is defined by the International Franchise Association (IFA) as a marketing method in which the owner of a product or service, known as the 'franchisor', offers the right to operate and manage his product and service to others, the 'franchisees', in return for a fee and ongoing royalty payments. This is the preferred format of franchising in the hospitality industry. Product/trade name format franchising, on the other hand, concerns the

relationship between a franchisor and a franchisee in which the franchisor grants to the franchisee the right to distribute a product and/or use a trade name. This format is most frequently employed in the soft drink, automobile, and gasoline distribution industries.

History of franchising

In the Middle Ages, kings or local sovereigns granted rights to church officials, farmers, and tradesmen to collect taxes, brew ale, operate markets or hunt on their land and, in return, obtained a fee for these rights. Probably the earliest example of consumer goods franchising was recorded in 1850 when the Singer Sewing Machine Company granted agents the right to sell and repair its line of sewing machines within specific territories. Howard Johnson is recognized as the first person in the hospitality industry to use the franchising model. In the 1940s he expanded his original ice cream business into the Red Roof coffee shops and later expanded further into motor lodges.

In 1961, Ray Kroc acquired a limited service restaurant from Dick and Mac McDonald for $2.7 million. Today, McDonald's is the world's leading fast food retailer, operating over 30,000 restaurants in 119 countries and serving 47 million customers a day. Over 80% of McDonald's restaurants worldwide are owned and operated by local businessmen and women. Other pioneers adapted Ray Kroc's franchising business strategy of providing high standards of quality, friendly service, cleanliness, and value. In the hotel industry, companies such as Marriott, Holiday Inn, Hilton, and Accor have employed franchising as their primary growth strategy.

Although franchising was originally an American business strategy, it is now being adopted by companies all over the world. The French company Accor is Europe's leader of franchised hotels and restaurants, with nearly 4000 budget to upscale hotels worldwide. The British company Bass, which started out as a brewing company, has also entered the franchise market by acquiring established US brands such as Holiday Inns and InterContinental. Another British company, Allied Domecq PLC, acquired Dunkin' Donuts in 1989 and also owns

Baskin–Robbins and Togo's, a sandwich franchise brand.

A recent franchising phenomenon is multibranding, a strategy in which one company owns several franchise brands that it markets under one roof, for example, in the food courts of malls, in airports or in gas stations. This strategy was pioneered by the US company, Yum!Brands, proprietor of Kentucky Fried Chicken, Pizza Hut, Taco Bell, Long John Silvers and A and W. Although franchised fast food concepts have expanded rapidly worldwide, they have recently come under attack by consumers and government agencies for offering unhealthy, high calorie foods. This sector is now responding by offering healthier food options and consumer nutrition awareness programs.

The franchising system

The franchising system is designed to provide a formula for operating a successful business by providing a uniform product and service concept, thereby offering to the consumer a recognized standard of what to expect and a higher perceived value. A successful franchisor will have tested and specified all product and service delivery systems prior to launching the franchise program. In addition, franchisors assist franchisees during the launch of their new business and also provide continuous product, concept, and marketing assistance in order to ensure the long-term success of the franchise. William Rosenberg, founder of Dunkin' Donuts, said of franchising, 'In business for yourself, but not by yourself.'

The investment required for the acquisition of a franchise varies greatly depending primarily on the scale of the physical facility and whether the real estate is purchased or leased. Typical startup costs in the hospitality sector range from $150,000 to over $3 million.

Regulations

Although franchising is now recognized as a global business model, its initial growth began in the United States. The US Federal Trade Commission drafted the first regulations aimed at protecting franchise applicants. Franchisors are required to make an extensive disclosure document available to each potential franchisee before the franchisee signs a franchise agreement. This document is called a Uniform Franchise Offering Circular (UFOC). Its purpose is to provide prospective franchisees with information about the franchisor, the franchise system, and the agreements they will need to sign so that they can make an informed decision. The UFOC covers 23 important disclosure statements that give details about a franchise system's business experience, any outstanding litigation, fee and investment requirements, franchisee and franchisor obligations, territory and trademark regulations, restrictions on what the franchisee may sell, renewal and termination clauses, etc. Inaccuracies or misrepresentations by franchisors contained in UFOC documents may result in civil and/or criminal penalties.

Advantages and disadvantages of franchising

The primary advantages of franchising from the perspective of the franchisee are the provision of a recognizable consumer brand, tested product and service concepts, technical assistance in the areas of site selection, facility construction and interior design, training, marketing support, and financial controls. Franchisors often assist franchisee applicants in obtaining financing and/or lease agreements. Although all business models encompass a certain amount of risk, proven franchise concepts experience a considerably reduced level of failure. Given the extent of this support, even individuals without extensive experience in the hospitality industry can often acquire and successfully manage a franchise business.

The primary disadvantages of franchising from the perspective of the franchisee are that the franchisee must pay a royalty fee and must comply with vigorous quality and control procedures established by the franchisor. Conflict may arise between the franchisee and franchisor when territorial exclusivity is breached or when trademark issues or renewal rights are disputed.

The primary advantages of franchising from the perspective of the franchisor are that it enables a company to establish a large number of outlets in a relatively short period of time. In addition, although the franchisor provides the business concept, it is the franchisee that is required to obtain financing to pay for the land, physical facility, inventory and working capital. The franchisor's costs are primarily related to administrative and support expenses, such as pre-opening assistance, training, and quality control. Franchise companies are therefore leveraged to a lesser degree and are less vulnerable to cyclical fluctuations.

The primary disadvantages of franchising from the perspective of the franchisor are that, as its system grows, it is difficult to maintain high standards and effective communication with its franchisees. In addition, national and international growth often requires adaptation of the franchise system to local tastes and cultures.

Other franchise players

The International Franchise Association (IFA) is the most important membership organization, representing franchisors, franchisees, and suppliers. The association was founded in 1960 and is the world's oldest, largest and most important franchise organization. It has members from more than 100 countries. Its mission is to protect, enhance and promote all aspects of franchising. The association develops and administers education and certification programs, conducts research, and holds an annual convention. The association is based in Washington, DC.

The William Rosenberg International Center of Franchising at the University of New Hampshire maintains the largest financial database of US and international publicly listed franchise companies. The center publishes a monthly index that tracks the market performance of the top 50 US public franchisors and compares the performance of these companies against those in the S&P 500. In addition, the H. Wayne Huizenga School of Business and Entrepreneurship at Nova Southeastern University in Fort Lauderdale, Florida, offers executive education courses in the field of franchising.

Other key players in the franchise industry include consultants, search agencies, law firms, real estate and site finders, financing and leasing institutions, architectural and interior design firms, developers and contractors, and management companies.

The economic and social impact of franchising

The US franchise market generates nearly $1 trillion a year in revenue and thus accounts for over 45% of all retail sales. According to the International Franchise Association (IFA), there are an estimated 1500 franchise companies operating in the United States that conduct business through more than 320,000 retail units. Seventy-five industries use franchising to distribute goods and services to consumers. The largest franchise sectors are represented within the hospitality industry (fast food, limited and full service restaurants, and lodging). Franchising provides employment for more than 9 million Americans. Business format franchising has been the primary driver of the extraordinary growth experienced in the restaurant, hotel and recreation sectors of the hospitality industry.

In response to economic downturn cycles and corporate restructuring, many individuals have successfully made the transition from employee to employer by acquiring a franchise. Franchising plays an important role in providing employment to individuals without a higher education or specialized skills. It also provides first-time job seekers with an entry into the business world and provides the elderly with an opportunity to supplement their retirement benefits.

References

Justis, Robert T. and Judd, Richard J. (2002) *Franchising*, 2nd edn. Cincinnati, OH: Dame-Thomson Learning.

Rosenberg, William and Keener, Jessica B. (2001) *Time to Make the Donuts*. New York: Lebhar-Friedman Books.

UDO SCHLENTRICH
UNIVERSITY OF NEW HAMPSHIRE, USA

Franchising in restaurants

Some form of a franchise relationship has existed for as long as there has been a need to share power, commerce, and enterprise. In a franchise relationship, mutual benefit is gained when the opportunity for control and wealth are granted by a large entity (the franchisor) to a smaller one (the franchisee) in exchange for a pledge of fealty, a willingness to live by a set of defined rules, and a fee. The Roman Empire established regents and tax collectors as commissioned representatives across the far reaches of the empire, allowing them to keep a portion of any taxes they received while sending 'Caesar's share' back to Rome. In the Middle Ages, feudalism was built on the idea that 'royalties' (literally payments to the king) were the price to be paid by lower lords for the rights to manage and control tracts of land and workers. For over a millennium the Catholic Church as an enterprise has been constructed on the same model, with each parish being granted the rights to operate in a local market while sending a portion of all operating income to the Vatican. The American Revolution itself was nothing more than a franchisee/franchisor dispute once the colonies refused to pay the British Crown an increasing amount of royalties and fees for the use of an operating system.

Today the majority of franchise systems are not political or religious, but commercial in nature. Generally the franchise/commission business model used by the Singer Sewing Machine Company in the 1850s is considered to be the first example in the United States. When General Motors was formed in the early 1900s, management refined the franchise system to extend the reach of the company across most communities in the country – every respectable small town had a locally owned and operated Chevrolet dealership. Examples of franchising in hospitality from before 1940 include such ubiquitous snack and roadside offerings as Howard Johnson's, A and W Root Beer, Dairy Queen, and Tastee Freez. The real growth of restaurant franchising occurred during the 1950s and 1960s with the introduction of fast food restaurants such as Kentucky Fried Chicken, Burger King, and McDonald's.

Since then, the international restaurant industry has benefited greatly from this form of business ownership. Restaurant organizations are generally identified as comprising the single largest segment of the growing franchise industry, both in the US and the international marketplace. The International Franchise Association states that 'in 2000, most analysts estimated that franchising companies and their franchisees accounted for $1 trillion in annual US retail sales from 320,000 franchised small businesses in 75 industries. Moreover, franchising is said to account for more than 40% of all US retail sales' (International Franchise Association website). Quick service restaurants alone make up almost 100,000 of those businesses. Additionally, more than 100 US restaurant companies operate franchise businesses outside of their home markets, while many non-US companies have franchisees in the US marketplace.

Khan (1999) says, 'Simply defined, a franchise is a legal agreement in which an owner (franchisor) agrees to grant rights or privileges (license) to someone else ([the] franchisee) to sell their products or services under specific conditions.' This granting of rights and privileges increases costs for both sides in terms of control and profitability. The relationship comes down to this: franchising is a way of sharing power, control, and income between two organizations with similar but not necessarily identical goals and aspirations. A franchisor gives up some unit level profit and daily control to the franchisee acting as business owner. The franchisee gives up some profit in the form of royalties and fees and some control over menu and operating system design when acting as the licensee of a corporate brand. Together what they individually give up offers them the potential of gaining economies of scale and scope through the strength that comes from being associated with a larger organization. McDonald's was built on what Ray Kroc called 'the genius of the system.'

When a franchise system works well, with both sides enjoying the potential benefits that come from this power sharing, the opportunities for wealth accumulation and market power are greatly enhanced. If, on the other hand, a franchise system is built on an imbalanced power

Seven Basic Elements of Restaurant Franchising

1. A proven prototype restaurant
2. A distinctive and protected trade identity
3. Sufficient capitalization
4. A well designed offering document
5. A franchisee profile and screening system
6. A comprehensive operations manual
7. A franchise support system

Figure 1 Franchising in restaurant

relationship, the effect can be that both franchisor and franchisee lose more than they gain. In either case, all observers believe that the franchising model of business development and ownership will continue to grow during the twenty-first century.

References

Bradach, Jeffrey L. (1998) *Franchise Organizations.* Cambridge, MA: Harvard Business School Press.

International Franchise Association. http://www.franchise.org/resourcectr/faq/q4. asp.

Khan, Mahmood A. (1999) *Restaurant Franchising.* New York: John Wiley & Sons.

Salomon Smith Barney (2003) *Fast casual Segment Handbook.* New York: Salomon Smith Barney.

CHRISTOPHER MULLER
UNIVERSITY OF CENTRAL FLORIDA, USA

Free cash flow

Free cash flow (FCF) is defined as after-tax operating cash flow (OCF) minus additional investments in assets. It is free to distribute to creditors and shareholders because it is no longer needed for working capital or fixed assets investments. FCF of a particular period can also be calculated from the financing perspective. It is the increase in debt and stock minus the decrease in debt and stock and minus interest and dividend payments. FCF should be equal to cash flow to creditors and shareholders.

The value of a hospitality firm depends on its expected future FCF. A hospitality project's value is determined by the incremental FCF resulting from the project. Other things held constant, higher incremental future FCF leads to higher net present value (NPV) of the project, and hence higher probability of the project's acceptance.

Negative FCF can occur due to negative after-tax OCF, a bad sign of operation problems in a hospitality firm. On the other hand, a fast-growing hospitality firm can have positive after-tax OCF but negative FCF because the firm is making significant investments in assets to support the growth. In the second case, the negative FCF can be an indicator of growth opportunities rather than a signal of trouble.

References

Keown, A., Martin, J., Petty, W., and Scott, D. (2003) *Foundations of Finance: The Logic and Practice of Financial Management*, 4th edn. Upper Saddle River, NJ: Prentice-Hall.

Ross, S., Westerfield, R., and Jordan, B. (2004) *Essentials of Corporate Finance*, 4th edn. Boston, MA: McGraw-Hill.

ZHENG GU
UNIVERSITY OF NEVADA, LAS VEGAS, USA

Frequent guest programs

A frequency program is any program that rewards guests with points, miles, stamps, or 'punches' that enable the buyer to redeem such rewards for free or discounted merchandise.

Two questions that are often asked about frequency programs. One, are frequency programs the same as loyalty programs? And two, 'Do frequent guest programs build loyalty?' The answer to the first question is no, frequency programs are not the same as loyalty programs even though many firms call their frequent guest program a loyalty program. A loyalty program is a strategy undertaken by a firm to manage the three components of the Loyalty Circle (Process, Value, and Communication; see Shoemaker and Lewis, 1999) in order to create an emotional bond with the customer so that he or she gives a particular establishment a majority of their business, provides positive word of mouth, acts in partnership with the establishment, and spends more with the establishment than a non-loyal guest.

Frequency in itself does not build loyalty; it is loyalty that builds frequency. Frequency can create loyalty if the firm uses the information gathered on frequent visits to focus on the components of the Loyalty Circle; however, if the firm ignores this opportunity, then it ignores the emotional and psychological factors that build real commitment. Without that commitment, customers focus on the 'deal,' not the brand or product relevance. This focus on behavior makes bribing the customer the line of reasoning. Over time, the economics of bribery begin to collapse with greater and greater bribes, eventually eroding the brand image and diminishing product/service differentiation.

Reference

Shoemaker, S. and Lewis, R. (1999) Customer loyalty in hotels. *International Journal of Hospitality Management*, 18 (4), 345–370.

STOWE SHOEMAKER
UNIVERSITY OF HOUSTON, USA

Front-of-the-house in hotels

The divisions or departments of a hotel or lodging enterprise might be grouped in many ways. One such classification is front-of-the-house and back-of-the-house. In front-of-the-house departments employees have extensive guest contact. The rooms division has many such employees, including: reservationists; front desk agents; key, mail, information specialists; uniformed services; and other guest services. In addition, food and beverage employees have extensive guest contact through restaurants and lounges and are thus part of the front-of-the-house. Depending upon the classification of hotel or lodging enterprise, the employees assigned to recreational facilities will also have extensive guest contact and thus become a part of the front-of-the-house. More than half of all hotel guests make reservations. Whereas in the past reservationists basically took orders, now they may have extensive conversations with the guest and a real sales effort is part of their job. Among the departments most visible to the guest in the front-of-the-house is the front office. Front office personnel have more contact with guests than do staff in most other departments. The front desk is a focal point of activity for the front office and is prominently located in the hotel's lobby. Guests interact with personnel in this area to register, to receive room assignments, to inquire about available services, facilities, and the city or surrounding area, and to check out. Employees who work in the uniformed service department of the hotel or lodging enterprise, including bell attendants, door attendants, valet parking attendants, transportation personnel and concierges generally provide the most personalized guest service.

Reference

Stutts, Alan T. (2001) *Hotel and Lodging Management – an Introduction*. New York: John Wiley & Sons.

WILLIAM FISHER
UNIVERSITY OF CENTRAL FLORIDA, USA

Front-of-the-house in restaurants

Opposite of the 'back-of-the-house' is the 'front-of-the-house.' This common term is used to describe the public areas of a restaurant that are available to guests (e.g. dining rooms, bars). In a hotel setting, front-of-the-house includes the lobby area.

Front-of-the-house restaurant employees include food servers, bussers, bartenders, and hosts. Since these positions often receive gratuities in countries where tipping is practiced, they sometimes carry a certain prestige. Moreover, since employees working in the front-of-the-house deal directly with guests, they are perceived to embody the restaurant more concretely than those working in the back-of-the-house.

Which affects service more directly: front- or back-of-the-house? The answer rests largely on who is asked. Most chefs will argue that since the menu offerings are at the core of the operation, the back-of-the-house defines the very essence of the restaurant. Service is the other aspect of 'foodservice,' however; it can also be said that guests evaluate the caliber of an operation as much (or more) on the basis of the service provided by front-of-the-house employees, which may lead equally or more important to guests' overall dining experience.

Reference

Solomon, E. and Prueter, S. (1997) *Serve 'Em Right*. Greensboro, NC: Oakhill Press.

JAKSA KIVELA
THE HONG KONG POLYTECHNIC UNIVERSITY,
HONG KONG SAR, CHINA

Front office accounting

Front office accounting keeps track of financial data in folios for both guests and house accounts or city ledger. Folios provide support documentation and vouchers detail front office account postings. Computer systems minimize need for vouchers as most have interface capabilities from revenue centers.

The front office ledger is part of accounts receivable and includes a set of accounts for registered guests (the guest ledger) and a set of accounts for non-guests and unsettled guest accounts (the city ledger). Accounting collects city ledger and front office settles guest ledger. Guests present acceptable credit card or direct billing authorization at reservation or registration to establish charge privileges and line of credit. The night auditor identifies accounts near credit limits (high risk, high balance) and the credit manager intervenes and settles outstanding accounts of past guests.

The resolution of a folio posting error is done before close of business (night audit) and is supported by a correction voucher. Account allowances may be for compensation for poor service, rebates, and coupons and are documented by allowance vouchers requiring management signature.

Front office accounting also maintains transfers between folios, cash advances, front office cash sheets, and cash banks.

References

Jagels, M.G. and Coltman, M.M. (2003) *Hospitality Management Accounting*, 8th edn. New York: John Wiley & Sons.
Uniform System of Accounts for the Lodging Industry, 9th edn (1996) Lansing, MI: Educational Institute of the American Hotel and Motel Association.

STEPHEN LEBRUTO
UNIVERSITY OF CENTRAL FLORIDA, USA

Front office communications

In addition to memorandums, face-to-face conversations, and electronic communication, successful front-office communication includes log books, information directories, mail and telephone procedures and interdepartmental exchange of information.

The front desk typically keeps a log book, which enables the staff to be aware of important events and decisions that occurred during prior shifts. A log book is a daily journal which may chronicle unusual events, guest complaints or requests, and other events. Front desk agent's record in the log book throughout their shift and before the beginning of a shift the front desk supervisor and agents initial the log and review the log, paying particular attention to any activities, problems or situations that may require action. The log book is a management tool as well providing management with an understanding of the activity of the front desk and any ongoing issues.

The information directory is a tool for the front desk to communicate to guests answers to common questions that might relate to: local restaurant recommendations; transportation; directions to local business, shopping, places of worship, banks, ATMs, theaters, stadiums; information about hotel policies such as check-out time; and hotel facilities or recreational facilities nearby the property. As front desk agents access information not previously included in the directory it might be added. In addition, the front desk may refer guests to the reader board of daily events which might be posted on paper or viewed through a closed-circuit television system. A convention hotel may also have a group resumé book at the front desk. The book summarizes all of the group's activities, key attendees, recreational arrangements, arrival and departure, billing instructions and other key information.

The front desk also handles delivered mail and packages for the registered guests. Procedures for handling mail and packages varies but typically includes a time-stamp of all guest mail verifying when it arrived, verification that the addressee is currently registered, due to check in or already checked out and lastly notifying the guest. Typically guest mail that is not picked up or has arrived for a guest who has already checked out is time-stamped a second time and returned to its sender or sent to a forwarding address if one has been provided by the guest.

Guests may also receive registered letters, express packages, and other mail requiring signature. If the hotel permits the front desk agent to sign for such mail after doing so the agent typically records the items delivered in the front office mail signature book. The guest would also sign for the mail in the book at the time of pickup or delivery. Packages are typically handled as mail. If the package is too large to store at the front desk, it would be taken to a secure room. The package and its location should be recorded in the front office mail signature book.

Telecommunication services provided by a hotel front office for its guests are multiple. They include telephones, voice mailboxes, facsimile, wake-up services, email, and TDD (see below). Most hotels provide in-room local and long-distance service 24 hours a day. Modern

telephone systems are typically programmed to automatically turn on the guestroom message light when the guest is away from the room and a call is received from the front office computer. In addition it is very common for a hotel to provide its guests with a voice mailbox. Voice mailboxes are devices which can record messages for guests. A caller wishing to leave a message for a guest simply speaks into the phone; his or her message is then recorded by the voice mailbox system. To retrieve the message, the guest typically dials a special telephone number which connects to the voice mailbox. A key advantage of voice mail is that the message is captured in the caller's voice. This may be very important when the caller does not speak the local language clearly. This system also allows several guests to receive messages at the same time, thereby freeing the hotel operator(s) for other duties.

Facsimiles, another form of communication handled by the front office, should be treated like mail, but with special care. Since guests are typically waiting for these documents special handling is required. If an incoming fax has special delivery instructions, such as deliver immediately to a specific room, the front desk must be prepared to dispatch a member of the bell staff with the fax right away. Typically the front office maintains a fax log or combined fax and mail log for tracking purposes.

Wake-up services are a key communication and guest satisfier. Very often a component of the hotel's property management system can be programmed to receive and place the calls and play a recorded wake-up message. However, many hotels still prefer that the front desk agents or hotel operator place wake-up calls. In such cases, a clock used for wake-up purposes will often be found at the front desk or in the PBX (private branch exchange) area. This is known as the hotel clock and shows the official time of the hotel. Thus, the clock must be checked daily to be sure it is correct.

Many hotel business and leisure guests have e-mail capability and thus will want to send and receive e-mail communication. Thus, the telecommunication equipment in each guestroom and in other areas of the hotel should be configured to allow the guest to plug in a laptop and communicate with office, home or other corporate network.

A TDD is a specially designed piece of equipment for placing and conducting calls for those guests with a hearing and/or speech impairment. In the United States the Americans With Disabilities Act requires that hotels make available, upon request, a TDD for use by a guest who has impaired hearing or related communication disorder. It is also important that the front desk have a TDD device to handle in-house calls from hearing- or speech-impaired guests.

Front office communication also will include interdepartmental communications. The front office generally exchanges information with personnel in the housekeeping and engineering departments relative to room status, repairs, and work orders. In addition, the front office through the property management system compiles the guest's charges from food, beverage, room service, laundry/valet, gift shops, telecommunication, business center, valet parking, health and recreational facilities and banquets or catering on a daily basis.

Reference

Stutts, Alan T. (2001) *Hotel and Lodging Management An Introduction*. New York: John Wiley & Sons.

GERARD VIARDIN
THE MARQUETTE HOTEL, USA

Front office ledger

The front office ledger is a summary form of information gathered from front office account folios. The guest ledger, which is maintained at the front desk, consists of all of the charges made by guests registered in the hotel. Information contained in this ledger is from the accounts receivable ledger (money owed to the hotel), which comprises the guest ledger (also known as transient ledger, front office ledger, or rooms ledger) and the city ledger (also known as non-guest ledger). The guest ledger contains account information on guests who are registered at the hotel. The city ledger contains account information on non-guests who have charge privileges. During the cashier's shift, folios charged to the city ledger are filed by order of room number, other charges are filed by origin, such as coffee shop, gift shop, or banquet. Before a check is charged to the city ledger, the cashier should verify the calculations and tip computation, and be certain that it has been signed.

Occasionally the cashier is requested to transfer an amount from one guest account to another. Transfers also may occur between the guest ledger and the city ledger. In such cases, the cashier must fill out a charge credit slip with the amount, the name of the person being charged, and the name of the person being credited. This voucher must be validated for both transactions.

Reference

Kasavana, M.L. and Brooks, R.M. (1995) *Front Office Procedures*, 4th edn. Lansing, MI: Educational Institute of the American Hotel and Motel Association.

IRENE SWEENEY
INTERNATIONAL HOTEL MANAGEMENT
INSTITUTE SWITZERLAND, SWITZERLAND

Front office operations

The front office operations have gone through an evolution from manual, to electro-mechanical to computer-based. Up until the 1920s technology in the front office was non-existent and manual operations prevailed. Electro-mechanical operations were practiced through to the early 1970s and were the foundation for automated systems that began to be installed in the late 1970s.

Manual front office record-keeping systems relied on handwritten forms. Some small hotels still find this method of record-keeping sufficient to meet their information needs. However, the elements of handwritten systems have determined the structure of many front office processes. Techniques common to non-automated systems can be found in even the most advanced automated systems.

In a manual system reservation agents enter requests into a loose-leaf notebook or onto index cards. Non-automated hotels typically accept reservations for six months into the future and are unlikely to commit space beyond that time. Reservations confirmations, pre-registration activities, and occupancy forecasts are not common in a manual system. Reservation information is typically placed on a density chart or graph to illustrate future room availabilities and help managers identify high and low room demand periods. A density board is usually set up as a matrix, with days of the month for rows and number of available rooms for columns. As rooms are blocked or booked, the matrix cells that correspond to the dates of stay and number of rooms are colored in. These colored squares reflect the density or concentration of rooms reserved.

Upon guest arrival in a manual system, the guests are asked to sign a page in a registration book or complete a registration card. Room assignments are made using a manual card replacement technique involving a room rack and, sometimes, color coded flags indicating the housekeeping status for each room in the property. A room rack is an array of metal file pockets that displays guest and room status information in room number order. The registration card is often time-stamped during check-in and may be placed in the room rack to indicate occupancy.

At a manual check-in multiple copies of the guests registration card are distributed including the room rack, telephone operators and other personnel in the hotel that may need to provide services to the guest. The original registration card often doubles as a guest account folio. Revenue outlets send documentation of charges to the front desk for posting to guest folios. The revenue outlet also maintains a sales record of all charged transactions so that guest account postings can be cross-checked as part of the night audit. Although adding machines may be used to facilitate accounting procedures, monitoring guest activities within a manual process may become repetitive, cumbersome, and tedious.

At check-out in a manual system, guests settle their accounts and return their room keys; the cashier notifies the housekeeping department of departures. Registration cards or rack slips are removed from the room rack and marked to indicate departure. The registration card or rack slip may then be filed and serve as the hotel's guest history file. If the registration card was time-stamped at check-in, it is typically time-stamped at check-out.

Electro-mechanical front office systems rely upon both handwritten and machine-produced forms. Such systems were common in small and mid-size hotels in the early 1970s. The basic advantage over the manual system were the easy to read documents that detailed the steps of the transactions with each guest or an audit trail. Problems with the electro-mechanical systems were the complexity of operating the equipment and the frequency of maintenance problems.

Reservation with an electro-mechanical system were very similar to the manual system. Typically no more than six months was reserved into the future. Pre-arrival the front office would prepare registrations cards, guest folios, and information slips. Room assignments were still made using the room rack and in this system a room density board was also maintained.

However, upon arrival the guest would simply verify the previously recorded registration information and sign a pre-printed registration card. Copies were distributed to the room rack, the switchboard operator, and the information rack.

During occupancy while the paperwork of a guests stay was not reduced, mechanical and electronic cash registers and front office posting machines were used to process many of the records formerly processed by hand. This equipment enabled the front office to handle guest accounting transactions more accurately and rapidly. A night audit procedure based on posting machine records was used to verify account entries and balances.

The electro-mechanical system provided a more thorough audit routine at guest check-out that led to faster and smoother departures. Fewer discrepancies were experienced in guest accounts and front office personnel were able to efficiently reconcile guest accounts. Front office personnel were also able to relay room status information to housekeeping much more quickly than they could in a manual system.

In the late 1970s computer systems were first introduced into hotel front offices. Initially these systems were expensive, making them affordable only to the larger hotels or hotel companies. During the 1980s, computer equipment became less expensive, more compact, and easier to operate. User-friendly software packages evolved for various hotel functions and applications, which did not require extensive technical training required by the earlier systems. By the late 1980s computer systems were cost-effective for hotels of all sizes.

The software of the fully automated system impacts pre-arrival, arrival, occupancy and departure. Reservations software may directly interface with a central reservations network and automatically quote rates and reserve rooms according to a pre-determined pattern. The reservations software typically can generate letters of confirmation, produce requests for guest deposits, and handle pre-registration activities. Electronic folios can be established and pre-registration transactions can be processed for guests with confirmed reservations. A reservations software package may also generate an expected arrivals list, occupancy and revenue forecasts, and a variety of informative reports.

Information that is collected about an arriving guest that is collected during the reservation process may be automatically transferred from the computer's reservation record to the front desk. For walk-in guests, guest information is entered manually into the computer by front desk agent.

An arriving guest is presented with a computer-generated registration card for verification and signature. Online credit card authorization terminals enable front desk personnel to receive timely credit card approval. In addition, registration data, stored electronically in the computer, can be retrieved whenever necessary, thereby making a room rack unnecessary. Electronic guest folios are also maintained and accessed through the computer's memory. The fully automated system may also present an arriving and/or departing guest with an opportunity for self-check-in/check-out terminals. The arriving guest can insert a credit card into the terminal which reads the magnetic strip on the credit card and communicates with the reservation software. The reservation software locates the guest's reservation and returns the information to the terminal. After the guest verifies name, departure date, rate and room type, a room is assigned. The system may also provide the guest with a key if the hotel is utilizing electronic locks. If not, the guest is provided with a rooming slip including a room number and then can proceed to a special line at the front desk to receive a key.

A fully automated front office system replaces room racks, electro-mechanical, and electronic posting machines. As a guest purchases or incurs charges in the hotel the charges are electronically transferred to the front office computer from the point-of-sale location. These charges are then automatically posted to the proper electronic guest folio. Immediate posting, simultaneous guest account and departmental entries, and continuous trial balances free the night auditor to spend time on auditing, rather than focusing primarily on guest account balances.

Upon departure the guest is provided with a printed copy of his/her folio and can immediately verify whether it is complete and accurate. Depending on the method of settlement, the computer system may automatically post the transactions to appropriate accounts. For a guest account that requires billing, the system is capable of producing a bill to be sent to the guest. Once the guest's account is settled and the postings are considered complete, departed guest information is used to create an electronic guest history record.

A variation of the fully automated system is the involvement of an off-premise service bureau to provide a hotel with some of the benefits of automation without the hotel incurring all of the costs associated with the automated technology. However, for the most part service bureaus focusing on back office functions such as payroll processing and payroll accounting rather than front office activities.

Reference

Stutts, Alan T. (2001) *Hotel and Lodging Management – An Introduction*. New York: John Wiley & Sons.

ALAN T. STUTTS
AMERICAN INTERCONTINENTAL
UNIVERSITY, USA

Front office organization

The front office has the following functions:

- Sells guestrooms
- Registers guests, assigns guestrooms
- Processes future room reservations
- Coordinates guest services
- Provides information
- Maintains accurate room status information
- Manages all guest accounts and credit limits
- Produces guest account statements
- Completes a financial settlement with each guest upon departure.

The front office is the most visible department in a hotel and the front desk typically occupies a prominent place in the hotel's lobby. Guests come to the front desk to register, to receive room assignments, inquire about available services, facilities, and the city or surrounding area; and to check out. Since the front office may be the only contact a guest has with the hotel it is essential that the staff of the front office is organized, competent, and courteous. The front desk often serves as the focal point for guest requests regarding housekeeping, engineering, and information. Other services provided by the front office of a hotel handling guest and house mail, messaging services for the guest, and departing the guest from the hotel. Front office cashiers post charges and payments to guest accounts, all of which are later verified during an account auditing procedure. Front desk personnel also may verify outstanding accounts receivable, and produce daily reports for management.

Reference

Stutts, Alan T. (2001) *Hotel and Lodging Management – An Introduction*. New York: John Wiley & Sons.

ALAN T. STUTTS
AMERICAN INTERCONTINENTAL
UNIVERSITY, USA

Front office systems

Front office system is part of the property management system (PMS) that aims to facilitate the inter-action between hotel management and the guest. The system controls property management functions for reservations, front desk, cashier, housekeeping, and night audit management. Typical functions include control of room availability, room allocation, yield management, check-in, room status, postings to guest accounts, guest credit audits, advance deposits, guest history, check-out, currency exchange, room status, room and tax posting, operational reports, and system set-up. Reservations provide instant access to room availability and rate information, so that staff can easily book individual and group reservations. Integrated guest history allows for repeat guest recognition. Real-time updating of room availability provides accurate control of inventory that enables staff to achieve maximum occupancy. Check-ins and check-outs are handled efficiently. The front office system facilitates accurate transactions and personalized service. As part of the PMS this system is integrated with other systems such as food and beverage or sales and catering so that most postings occur automatically. The front office system is very important for customer satisfaction and retention as well as for market analysis, as it retains all information on guest transactions within the property.

References

Baker, S., Bradley, P., and Huyton, J. (1994) *Principles of Hotel Front Office Operations*. New York: Cassel.

Bardi, J. (1996) *Hotel Front Office Management*, 2nd edn. New York: Van Nostrand Reinhold.

IOANNIS S. PANTELIDIS
UNIVERSITY OF SURREY, UK

Full-time equivalent (FTE)

Many foodservice establishments hire both full-time and part-time employees to staff their operations, as part-time employees typically are less expensive than full-time employees. However, to compare one establishment's labor costs with another's, it is useful to have a consistent benchmark to use. For labor, this benchmark is full-time equivalent (FTE) employees. Total FTEs include the number of full-time employees who could have been employed if the reported number of hours worked by part-time employees had been worked by full-time employees and the actual number of full-time employees working at an establishment. By using FTEs, a restaurant company that operates multiple units can easily compare the number of employees being used across their restaurants. Typically, an FTE equates to 40 hours of work per week.

For example, if a restaurant employees 35 full-time employees who work 40 hours/week and 16 part-time employees who each work 15 hours/week, the number of FTEs for that establishment would be calculated as follows:

$$35 + (16 * 15)/40 = 35 + 240/40 = 35 + 6$$
$$= 41 \text{ FTEs}$$

Even though there are a total of 51 employees in the example, there are only 41 FTEs.

Reference

Kaplan, R.S. and Norton, D.P. (2004) *Strategy Maps: Converting Intangible Assets into Tangible Outcomes*. Cambridge, MA: Harvard Business School Press.

DEBORAH BARRASH
UNIVERSITY OF NEVADA, LAS VEGAS, USA

Furniture, fixtures, and equipment (FF&E)

Hotels and restaurants are furniture- and equipment-intensive forms of commercial real estate.

Furniture, fixtures, and equipment (FF&E) selection is generally coordinated with the theme and desired level of a hospitality property. The furniture and equipment component falls between 10% and 20% of the total project cost. Controlling costs related to FF&E requires careful attention to planned property design characteristics and preparation of detailed procurement specifications. Timely solicitation of bids or price quotations from competitive suppliers will further stabilize the costs of these physical assets.

Furniture, fixtures and equipment represent a common capital expenditure for hospitality operations. FF&E includes items such as moveable lighting and furniture, carpeting and pad, signage, laundry equipment, office furniture, food service equipment, and draperies and blinds. It does not include major building equipment such as HVAC components and items such as bathroom fixtures.

Reference

Rushmore, S. (2002) Hotel development cost can determine feasibility. Canadian Lodging Outlook *Hotel Online*, February. Retrieved 20 September 2003 from http:// www.hotel-onlonline.com/News/PR2002_2nd/Apr02_CanadianOutlookFeb.html.

BONNIE CANZIANI
UNIVERSITY OF NORTH CAROLINA –
GREENSBORO, USA

G

Game theory

Game theory can be a valuable tool for senior executives of hospitality organizations in their strategy process. This is because it offers mathematical techniques for problem-solving and competitive decision-making through the use of model building (Neumann and Morgenstern, 1944). Game theory, and in particular the game often referred to as 'the Prisoner's Dilemma', can be used in hospitality organizations particularly in decision-making, handling conflicts, competition, cooperation, joint ventures and strategic alliances between the organization and other companies. It is assumed that there are two or more players in a decision-making situation and the aim is to devise a plan that maximizes gains and minimizes losses (Brandenburger and Nalebuff, 1995). It offers a rigorous approach to predict what other players (hospitality organizations) would do in a well-defined situation and what possible results would be. By using the game theory hospitality firms can systematically examine various combinations of options that can alter the situation in their favor. According to game theory, in a business situation, success or failure of a hospitality company does not mean that other hospitality companies fail. In well-thought and articulated business situations, more than one hospitality company can win, which is often referred to as win–win situation. In short, predicting competitive behavior of other hospitality organizations and if possible achieving open or covert cooperation among major players can be beneficial for all parties.

References

Brandenburger, A.M. and Nalebuff, B.J. (1995) The right game: use game theory to shape strategy. *Harvard Business Review*, July–August, 57–71.

Neumann, J. and Morgenstern, O. (1944) *Theory of Games and Economic Behaviour*. Princeton, NJ: Princeton University Press.

FEVZI OKUMUS
THE HONG KONG POLYTECHNIC
UNIVERSITY, HONG KONG SAR, CHINA

Gap model of service quality

The Gap model of service quality was developed by Parasuraman, Berry and Zeithaml (1985), and more recently described in Zeithaml and Bitner (2003). It has served as a framework for research in services marketing, including hospitality marketing, for over two decades. The model identifies four specific gaps leading to a fifth overall gap between customers' expectations and perceived service.

The five gaps

Customers have expectations for service experiences and they use them to measure against the perceived service performance in their judgment of service quality. It is essential, then, that managers determine what those expectations are when designing the service. The first gap in service quality occurs when management fails to accurately identify customer expectations. It is referred to as the *knowledge gap*. Specifically, it is the difference in customer expectations and management's perception of customer expectations. Hotel managers, for instance, must know and understand what their guests expect from their stay, including all tangibles (the room, amenities, lobby features) and intangible components (availability of additional services, ease of check-in and check-out procedures). The size of the gap is dependent on the extent of upward communication (from customers to top management), the number of layers of management, the size of the organization, and most importantly, the extent of marketing research to identify customer expectations.

The second gap is referred to as the *design gap*. It is measured by how well the service design specifications match up to management's perception of customer expectations. The extent of this gap is dependent on management's belief that service quality is important and that it is possible, as well as the resources that are available for the provision of the service. A restaurant manager may understand customer expectations for being served within 20 minutes of ordering, but may not have the resources or the appropriate number of staff to insure that speed of service.

Gap 3 represents the variation in service design and service delivery. Known as the *performance gap*, its extent is a function of many variables involved in the provision of service. Since individuals perform the service, the quality may be affected by such factors as skill level, type of training received, degree of role congruity or conflict, and job fit. Some service providers do not have a high service inclination, despite training. Service recovery efforts along with extent of responsibility and empowerment also affect the size of this gap. The process is further complicated by the customer's participation in the service encounter. A customer may make a special request for a room type different from the one originally reserved, or request a menu item after the initial order has been completed, making it more difficult to perform the service as intended.

The fourth gap is called the *communications gap*. It is the difference between what is promised to customers, either explicitly or implicitly, and what is being delivered. Hospitality companies use advertising, personal selling, and sales promotion to inform, persuade, and remind guests about its products and services. Showing beautifully appointed hotel rooms, refreshing swimming pools, and luxurious lobby areas in an advertisement communicates to the target customers. The extent of communications between the company and the advertising agencies will affect the size of the gap. Over-promising is commonly responsible for the communication gap.

Each gap has a cumulative effect from the preceding gaps. Gap 5 is the total accumulation of variation in Gaps 1 through 4 and represents the difference between expectations and perceived service. Furthermore, consumers evaluate perceived service along five quality dimensions.

Dimensions of service quality

Service quality dimensions refer to the psychological dimensions that form the basis of a customer's perceived quality of a service. While numerous marketing researchers have attempted to define the specific dimensions of service quality, Parasuraman, Berry, and Zeithaml (1985) introduced the definition in their presentation of the Gap Model of Service Quality. They proposed that five specific dimensions of service quality exist and apply regardless of the service industry: reliability, responsiveness, assurance, empathy, and tangibles.

The most important service quality dimension to customers is *reliability*. Reliability is defined as the ability to perform the promised service dependably and accurately. In other words, it means doing what you say you will do. Customers have consistently stated that a company's ability to deliver promises is the most vital factor to providing service quality. Having a room ready upon check-in is an example of the reliability dimension.

Responsiveness is the willingness to help customers and to provide prompt service. Customers judge a company's responsiveness by assessing the amount of time it takes and the attentiveness that is offered in response to their requests, questions, complaints, and problems. Companies that use automated phone systems, regularly put customers on hold, or consistently have long wait times or long lines tend to be rated low on the responsiveness dimension. Responding quickly to requests or complaints leads to a higher rating on this dimension.

The third dimension of service quality is *assurance*. Assurance is defined as employees' knowledge and courtesy and the ability of the firm and its employees to inspire trust and confidence. The assurance dimension is particularly important in service industries offering high levels of credence qualities, such as auto repair and medical services. The importance of the assurance dimension increases in proportion to the risk, and the greater the inability for a customer to evaluate the service. The expertise of an endorser or a particular service provider for a cruise vacation may affect the level of confidence and trust a customer has toward that service.

Empathy is defined as the caring, individualized attention the firm provides its customers. Customers perceive the level of a company's empathy by the degree of personalized service offered. Customers want to be known on an individual basis and feel that the company understands and addresses their individual needs. When competing with companies that enjoy economies of scale, small companies can earn greater market shares by focusing on empathy. Showing concern for a guest whose luggage is lost is a way to improve the overall perceived service quality.

The final dimension of service quality is *tangibles*. Tangibles are defined as the appearance of physical facilities, equipment, personnel and communication materials. Service industries such as hotels and restaurants rely heavily on tangibles. Guest often judge the quality of a hotel experience on the quality of the physical environment and tangible amenities.

Each time they experience a service, guests are evaluating the hospitality organization. These customers judge the overall service quality by looking at its five dimensions during all interactions with service providers. Companies need to perform well on all dimensions of service quality to insure a positive overall evaluation.

References

Parasuraman, A., Zeithaml, V., and Berry, L. (1985) A conceptual model of service quality and its implications for future research. *Journal of Marketing*, 49, 41–50.

Zeithaml, V. and Bitner, M. (2003) *Services Marketing: Integrating Customer Focus Across the Firm*, 3rd edn. New York: McGraw-Hill.

Zeithaml. V., Parasuraman, A., and Berry, L. (1990) *Delivering Quality Service: Balancing Customer Perceptions and Expectations*. New York: The Free Press.

LINDA J. SHEA
UNIVERSITY OF MASSACHUSETTS, USA
JENNIFER T. CONDON
NEWMARKET INTERNATIONAL, INC., USA

General manager

The term general manager is applied to the top executive of a lodging enterprise who ultimately is responsible for the overall profitability and service performance of the operation and all of the enterprise's employees. The general manager represents the owner's interests, directs the activities of the departments, and may get involved in the day-to-day operation of individual departments. Short-term demands on the general manager revolve around the day-to-day operations issues of quality service and controlling costs/revenue. In the intermediate-term the general manager is responsible for the development and training of qualified subordinates and for implementing systems and programs to improve operational consistency and control. Long term, the general manager is seeking to develop organizational stability consistent with the enterprise's strategy. The general manager must manage effectively including planning, decision-making, organizing, staffing, controlling, directing, and communicating to develop a successful team. The effective general manager must know which key operating statistics reflect the profitability and efficiency of operations. Every general manager must work with key indicators that successfully measure the financial and operational success of each department director. The general manager is also the key link in the communication process. Department directors will take their lead or lack thereof from communications delivered by the general manager.

References

Bardi, James A. (2003) *Hotel Front Office Management*, 3rd edn. New York: John Wiley & Sons.

Stutts, Alan T. (2001) *Hotel and Lodging Management – An Introduction*. New York: John Wiley & Sons.

DIETER HUCKESTEIN
HILTON HOTELS CORPORATION, USA

General session

This is one session within a meeting, convention, congress, or conference that is open to all event participants. Also known as a plenary session, it is often designed to appeal to all event attendees. General sessions can be held for a variety of purposes, including a keynote speaker, a motivational speaker, or an association business meeting. Speakers at general sessions may be paid tens of thousands of dollars or may speak for free. There are usually no other events, activities, or meeting sessions scheduled during the same time as a general session. The organizations that hold general sessions in conjunction with their conventions or conferences may rely on the speakers to attract attendees.

Large general sessions often include complex multimedia extravaganzas or other unusual physical requirements. The numbers of people, variety of equipment, and types of activities drive the physical requirements for the selection of the site. Hotel ballrooms, auditoriums in convention centers or civic centers, theaters or other venues may be used to host general sessions. Theater-style seating is most appropriate for these events. Music is often used to open and close the session.

References

Connell, B., Chatfield-Taylor, C., and Collins, M. (eds) (2002) *Professional Meeting Management*, 4th edn. Chicago: Professional Conference Management Association Education Foundation.

Krug, S., Chatfield-Taylor, C., and Collins, M. (eds) (1994) *The Convention Industry Council Manual*, 7th edn. McLean, VA: The Convention Industry Council.

O'Toole, W. and Mikolatis, P. (2002) *Corporate Event Project Management*. New York: John Wiley & Sons.

M.T. HICKMAN
RICHLAND COLLEGE, USA

Generic strategies

Generic strategies are the building blocks of corporate strategy. However, such a structured approach to crafting business strategy is still in its infancy. Seventy years or so ago the governing argument of the industrial organization (IO) approach claimed that management could not influence industry conditions or its own performance (Mason, 1939), making business strategy essentially irrelevant because it is constrained or controlled by industry structural forces.

Porter (1991) was the first to depart from traditional IO theory, focusing on firm rather than on industry performance. Porter argued that the market environment could be influenced by firm actions and, therefore, strategy is a plan aimed at creating a competitive advantage. Porter argued that there two fundamental types of strategic plans exist: low-cost and differentiation. Low-cost strategies are primarily involved with process efficiency. The outcome of low-cost strategies is the ability to offer the product or service at a competitive price. Consequently low-cost strategies generate industry market share primarily from the price-sensitive market segment. The differentiation strategy is based on the ability to differentiate the product or service on the basis of subjective or objective attributes. By differentiating the product, the firm may be able to charge a premium and thus to secure market share in the industry.

Low-cost and differentiation are market-wide strategies. When an organization either cannot or does not wish to compete in the market-wide arena, the decision to focus on a particular market segment introduces the concept of scope to low-cost and differentiation firm strategies. Therefore, differentiation, low-cost and scope define the notion of two generic strategies that can be employed in the market or in a market niche. Therefore, within this framework offered by Porter, a firm can choose a generic strategy (low-cost or differentiation) in a broad market perspective or combine a generic strategy with a focus on a market niche (scope) resulting in four major constructs: low-cost, differentiation, low-cost–focus, and differentiation–focus.

Generic strategies serve as a game plan for many organizations. It should be noted, however, that organizations should commit to this game plan at all levels. For example, the selection of a low-cost strategy as a corporate strategy suggests that the firm must be efficient and cost conscious at all levels of operation and derive consistent departmental and functional strategies. Similarly, differentiation strategies should build and sustain a source of differentiation from competition and gain support from all levels of the organization. Another important aspect of the implementation of generic strategies regards the interpretations made by consumers. A firm that designs a low-cost strategy must ensure that consumers understand its strategic position and that the price-conscious segment in the market perceives the price as competitive and demands the product or service. Similarly, a firm that implements a differentiation strategy must ensure that consumers are knowledgeable of the differences between its product or service and that of the competition. Furthermore, the firm must make certain that these customers are not price-sensitive and are willing to pay the quoted premium for the differentiated product or service.

Roper (1995) used the framework offered by Porter to study the generic strategies employed by hotel consortia and found that from 29 firms 17 exhibited low-cost strategy. Only one hotel firm (Best Western) demonstrated a differentiation–focus strategy, and no consistent strategy could be identified for the remaining 11 hotels and they were thus considered as 'stuck in the middle' strategic types. Another finding was that functional strategies that support corporate differentiation strategy had implementation problems on the functional level and thus had also problems in sustaining the competitive position of differentiation. A low-cost strategy had relatively fewer problems when it was translated from the corporate level to operational requirements on the functional level. The finding

suggests that in the hospitality industry low-cost strategies are relatively easier to implement than differentiation strategies.

Some efforts have been made to extend the notion of generic strategies to the hospitality industry and to define industry-specific generic strategies. These efforts have generated different types of generic strategies, but the most consistent definition differentiates between two generic strategies in hospitality management: marketing-oriented and operations-oriented strategies (Olsen *et al.*, 1992, p. 57). These two generic strategies are specifically suited to the hospitality industry because they capture the individualized nature of the customer transaction in service industries and specifically in the hospitality industry (Lewis and Chambers, 1989). The marketing-oriented generic strategy implies that firms in the hospitality industry need a strategy to ensure repeat purchase by customers. One example of a marketing-oriented strategy is the design of customer loyalty programs that encourage repeat purchase via membership clubs or frequent member clubs. These strategies developed customer loyalty and increased the switching costs between brands in the airline industry and in the hospitality industry. In contrast, operations-oriented strategies are primarily involved in reducing the cost of the product or service and focusing on firm efficiency to attract customers. Regardless of the differences between these two generic strategies, their motto is to achieve the ultimate goal of firms in the hospitality industry, namely to increase the lifetime economic value of the customer to the firm.

References

Lewis, R.C. and Chambers R.E. (1989) *Marketing Leadership in Hospitality – Foundations and Practices.* New York: Van Nostrand Reinhold.

Mason, E. (1939) Price and production policies of large scale enterprises. *American Economic Review*, 29, 61–74.

Olsen, M.D., West J.J., and Tse, E.C. (1992) *Strategic Management in the Hospitality Industry.* New York: Van Nostrand Reinhold.

Porter, M. (1991) Towards a dynamic theory of strategy. *Strategic Management Journal*, Winter Special Issue, 12, 95–117.

Roper, A. (1995) The emergence of hotel consortia as transorganizational forms. *International Journal of Contemporary Hospitality Management*, 7 (1), 4–9.

AVIAD ISRAELI
BEN-GURION UNIVERSITY, ISRAEL

Global Alliance for Timeshare Excellence (GATE)

As the timeshare industry has expanded into international markets the need has surfaced for an educational and lobbyist voice within the international markets of Canada, Europe, Latin America, the Middle East, Australia, and South Africa. In a response to these advancing needs the Global Alliance for Timeshare Excellence (GATE) was organized. The primary focus of this association is to educate the consumer and to act on behalf of timeshare resort developers concerning legislative issues.

The GATE was established in 1999 by the leaders of timeshare associations in the United States, Canada, Latin America, Europe and the Middle East, Australia, and South Africa to promote the timeshare industry around the world. Each association retains its own identity, but collectively, the associations seek to cooperate on issues of common concern in order to advance the growth of the timeshare industry worldwide, the interests of their members, and the consumers they serve.

GATE seeks to serve as a resource to ensure that legislative and regulatory proposals are reasonable and conducive to the industry's business. GATE also seeks to serve as a resource and positive influence to encourage the industry to conduct its business in such a manner as to create positive public perception.

Reference

http://www.arda.org/about/gate.htm, 11 February 2004

RANDALL S. UPCHURCH
UNIVERSITY OF CENTRAL FLORIDA, USA

Global distribution system (GDS)

A global distribution system (GDS) can be defined as a centralized and permanently up-to-date database that is accessible to its subscribers through computing terminals. A GDS provides all kinds of tariffs and tourism services to subscribers everyday, allowing the users to make, change and cancel reservations, as well as to print tickets and avail themselves of any kind of rights related to services and products. Traditionally, travel agencies have been the main subscribers, with airline companies being the owners, creators, hosts or salesmen for GDSs. It be noted that this situation has been undergoing important alterations (Alcázar, 2002, 126–127).

The GDSs constitute at the present time the evolution and natural adaptation of the traditional computer reserve systems (CRS) to the market. The origin of these distribution systems comes from the 1960s in the United States as a consequence of the inefficacy of manual systems for the control of seat availability in the wake of the growth experienced by the aviation industry (Truitt *et al.*, 1991, 23). With the goal of creating an automated system for the capacity administration of their airplanes, American Airlines and IBM developed a joint program that became the SABRE, considered the first CRS (Vialle, 1995, 18). The original purpose of these systems was to facilitate through an automated system the storage and administration processes of all the information related to flights, lodging availabilty, and schedules or prices. Beginning in 1987 and as a consequence of the increase in demand for the application of such information to other types of tourism products (e.g. hotel rooms), and of the internationalization of their operations, CRS moved towards a new and enlarged concept which we know today as the global distribution systems.

Traditionally, inside the distribution channels a GDS operates as a retail wholesaler because its sales are addressed to the travel agencies. However, at the present time all the major players have developed direct access to consumers through the Internet, and as a result of this reorientation a GDS should now also be considered as a retailer.

GDS constitutes the main working tool for travel agencies, providing them all the necessary information to carry out their job, from the moment a client asks for a service until the potential sale and follow-through. The GDSs provides a valuable instrument for travel agencies, increasing their productivity. Moreover, this wholesale element in the distribution channel is also a very positive tool for hotel companies, airline companies, car rental business, etc. Some have argued, however, that the effectiveness of global distribution systems for hotel products has not been proven (O'Conner and Frew, 2000, 325). Disadvantages of this distribution channel include utilization costs, and the 'halo effect' may obscure the reality of its different effectiveness for different tourism products. The rise of computerized reservation systems sponsored by the hotels themselves, with a clear specialization in this kind of tourism product, has decidedly begun to revolutionize the way such central reservation systems operate.

The GDS industry is consolidated under the control of four powerful organizations, three of them – Galileo, Sabre, and Amadeus – comparable in dimension. The fourth element, Worldspan, keeps a certain distance from the others. Beyond these exist another five systems: Abacus Distribution Systems, Axes International Network, GETS, Infini Travel Information, and TOPAS. Parallel to these companies, however, whose origins are in the airline industry, another ninety-some regional reservation systems which emulate the original GDSs have important coverage. These regional systems (RICIRMSs – Regional Integrated Computer Reservation Management Systems), according to Buhalis's denomination (1993, 369), constitute a strategic tool for the small and medium-size companies of the tourism sector. These new developments in the organization of the tourism industry confront the GDSs with a panorama to which they must respond. The GDSs will have to develop new strategies that will allow them to continue being the nucleus of tourism distribution. To reach such a goal, providers of GDSs should understand, among others things, that they must: continue to evolve their technological experience; reduce utilization costs; simplify the utilization processes; enlarge the products and services range; establish strategic alliances with the new competitors; and develop a more effective relational marketing policy with travel agencies; etc.

References

Alcázar Martínez, B. del (2002) *Los canales de distribución en el sector turístico.* Madrid: Ed. Esic.

Buhalis, D. (1993) RICIRMS as a strategic tool for small and medium tourism enterprises. *Tourism Management,* 14 (5), 366–78.

O'Connor, P. and Frew, A.J. (2000) Evaluating electronic channels of distribution in the hotel sector. In D.R. Fesenmaier, S. Klein, and D. Buhalis (eds), *Information and Communication Technologies in Tourism 2000.* Vienna/New York: Springer, pp. 324–335.

Truitt, L.J., Teye, V.B., and Farris, M.T. (1991) The role of computer reservation systems. *Tourism Management,* 12 (1), pp. 21–36.

Vialle, O. (1995) *Los sistemas mundiales de distribución en la industria turística.* Madrid: World Tourism Organization.

JOSE MANOEL GANDARA
FEDERAL UNIVERSITY OF PARANÁ, BRAZIL
BENJAMIN DEL ALCAZAR
UNIVERSITY OF MALAGA, SPAIN

Global distribution systems: development and major players

A global distribution system (GDS) is an electronic reservation system and intermediary for all types of travel and tourism products that evolved from airlines' computer reservation systems. The four main GDSs provide the backbone of the travel distribution system. Figure 1 shows the evolution of simple computerized reservation systems for an individual airline to the global alliances that produced global distribution systems and the competitive advantages for their owners.

Figure 2 shows how the systems evolved. The reasons for this diminution in GDS numbers by mergers can be explained by:

- Economies of scale generated in marketing the service to agents.
- The great amount of research and development and cost needed to maintain competitiveness is more effective and efficient when shared.
- The larger the system, the greater the range of travel and tourism products that are available,

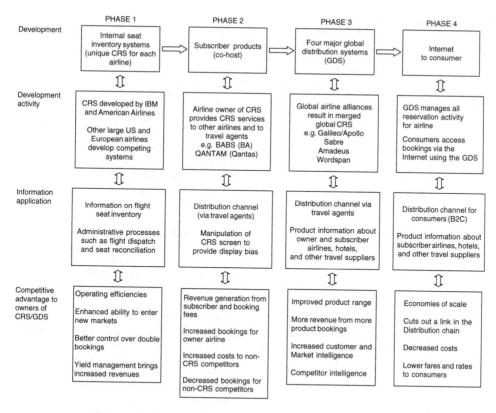

Figure 1   Phases of CRS/GDS development (based on Stonehouse *et al.*, 2001)

thereby increasing the global range of the GDSs.

- Increased market reach, as all GDSs were not represented in important markets.

Table 1 details the ownership and history of the major GDSs. Their respective market shares in 2002 are shown in Figure 3.

It is interesting to note that the GDSs have now moved from being simply an airline's computer reservation system to stand alone publicly owned companies that provide 'e' services to both marketing intermediaries (retail travel agents, tour wholesalers, general sales agents, and MICE organizations) and to travel principals such as airlines, hotels, tour operators and hire car companies. They now also deal direct to the consumer using online travel agencies such as Travelocity (owned by Sabre) and OneTravel.com (Amadeus).

However, in Buhalis and Licata's (2002) view, their future is threatened by principals' Internet presence (e.g. www.BritishAirways.com), new

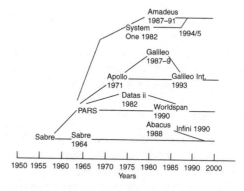

Figure 2   Evolutionary development of GDS technology (after Kärcher, 1996)

e-Mediaries who deal direct with the consumer via the Web – online travel agents such as Expedia (once owned by Microsoft) and Opodo (owned by a consortium of European airlines); and travel portals such as http://www.travelbyclick.com/ who may bypass GDSs. GDSs play a significant role for hospitality distribution as

Table 1   Major global distribution systems

GDS	Ownership	Number of agents	History	HQ
Galileo (known as Apollo in the USA)	Subsidiary of Cendant Corp., a conglomerate	47,000 agents	Founded by 11 major North American and European airlines	New Jersey USA
Amadeus	Publicly listed company since 1999. Three founder airlines currently hold 59.92%. Remaining shares held publicly	135,000 terminals	Founded by Air France, Iberia, Lufthansa, and SAS (no longer a shareholder). In 1995 merged with Continental's System One GDS. In 2000 launched airline IT to handle all CRS matters with BA and Qantas as first customers	Madrid, Spain
Worldspan	Delta Air Lines 40%, Northwest Airlines 34%, American Airlines, 26%	20,000 agencies	Formed in 1990 by a merger of CRSs of TransWorld Airlines, Delta, and Northwest. TWA became bankrupt in 2001 and its assets were taken over by AA, hence the AA shareholding	Atlanta, GA, USA
Sabre	Public company since 2000	38% market share	Started by American Airlines in 1964 and remained in the hands of AA until 1996 when it is split and 18% of its shares offered to the public	Texas, USA
Abacus	Sabre 35%, remainder various Asian airlines	9000, mainly in Asia–Pacific	Established in May 1988, by a consortium of Asian airlines. Sabre purchased 35% in 1998. It is arguable if Abacus is a GDS or a national marketing company for Sabre in the Asia–Pacific region, as in 1998 their 7300 Abacus travel agencies in 16 Asia–Pacific countries converted to a customized new version of the Sabre system	Singapore

Source: GDS web sites.

hitherto they have been providing the key mechanism for distributing hotel accommodation to travel agencies around the world.

References

Amadeus (2002) *Amadeus Facts and Figures – Travel Distribution Report*. Available at http://www.amadeus.com.pl/20_en/2030.php

Buhalis, D. (2003) *eTourism: Information Technology for Strategic Tourism Management*. Harlow: Prentice-Hall.

Buhalis, D. and Licata, M. (2002) The future of eTourism intermediaries. *Tourism Management*, 23, 207–220.

Kärcher, K. (1996) The four global distribution systems in the travel and tourism industry. *Electronic Markets*, 6 (2), pp. 20–25.

Stonehouse, G., Pemberton, J., and Barber, C. (2001) The role of knowledge facilitators and

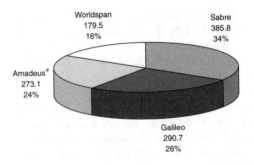

Figure 3   Global GDS market share (from Travel Distribution Report, 2002).

Note: *This figure represents the total number of air segments booked by travel agencies only, and does not include the ATO/CTO bookings that Amadeus maintains should be counted in its market share. With system user bookings included, Amadeus' air segments total 354.9 million, a 29% market share.

inhibitors: lessons from airline reservations systems. *Long Range Planning*, 34, 115–138.

Truitt, L.J., Teye, V.B., and Farris, M.T. (1991) The role of computer reservation systems. *Tourism Management*, 12 (1), 21–36.

IAN MCDONNELL
UNIVERSITY OF TECHNOLOGY, SYDNEY,
AUSTRALIA

Global strategies

The term *globalization* can be defined in the broadest sense as a process in which a complex of forces shift the world from a composition of countries, societies, and cultures toward a single world society or culture. Among these forces are the increasing significance of mass production, the development of mass communications, the development of commerce, the increased ease of travel, the increased popularity and use of the Internet, the development of popular culture, and the increasingly widespread use of English as an international language. Given the above, the term globalization refers to the world as the geographical unit of reference and suggests that occurrences in one part of the globe will potentially impact systems in another part.

Globalization is different from internationalization. Internationalization focuses on the expansion from a country of origin to other countries, and the main reference is to geographical coverage. Globalization, in contrast, is not measured as a function of geographical coverage, but as the ability to find a common dimension characterizing the people of the globe as a coherent group. Yip (2003) focuses on globalization and suggests that a global company does not have to be everywhere, but must have the capability to go anywhere, deploy any assets, access any resources, and maximize profits on a global basis.

In the 1990s the world saw a significant convergence of consumer needs and tastes, a drastic reduction of many barriers to free trade and investment, and accelerated development of communications technologies. This is not to say that every industry can become global, but there are some industries with a large global consumers' segment (Yip, 2003). For example, the international airline industry had a unique type of global customer. When making a reservation, most customers consider all airlines that fly the route they need and select one on the basis of quality, reliability, frequent flyer programs, and safety. Therefore, this industry serves as an example that demonstrates the significance of globalization. In food and beverage industries, there is also evidence of a developing global sector. Over relatively few years, the eating habits of the world population have converged to a uniform taste. For example, donuts were warmly embraced in Japan when cinnamon was introduced as a flavoring for donuts in this market. Today, the same recipe for making donuts is used throughout the world.

Despite the appealing benefits of globalization, our environment contains conflicting evidence about the stage of globalization as a universal concept in the business arena. On one hand, there is evidence to suggest that the process of globalization is strengthening in many industries, including transportation, electronics, communication, food and beverage, pharmaceutics, and others. On the other hand, catastrophic events in one part of the world, such as the September 11th terrorist attack in New York, impacted activities in other parts of the world and generated solidarity from people around the globe as if they were part of the same community. Even daily occurrences such as the stock market performance in one location impacts markets in another side of the globe. Furthermore, there are globally known products and services such as Coca-Cola and McDonald's that became a part of the global society. In contrast, some events lead us to believe that the concept of globalization is not advancing, and may even be on the decline. Among these are the highly publicized public protests at meetings of organizations that support globalization and the development of an anti-globalization culture in different countries around the world. In addition, the claim that globalization is responsible for poverty, unemployment, inequality, violent crime, failing families, and environmental degradation around the world is gaining currency.

A successful global strategy requires businesses to adopt a concept valued by customers around the world. Such a global common concept can be based on political, economic, socio-cultural, technological or ecological classification (Olsen *et al.*, 1992, pp. 284–285). When this global concept is identified, and the product or service addresses it effectively, the market segment is global and the product or service may also be global. As noted before, there are some industries with a growing global segment, but only a few examples of a true global product or service. Coca-Cola and McDonald's are considered to be products of a global market, which generally use consistent and common socio-cultural symbols of the global society.

A successful global strategy in the hospitality industry must first identify a global common dimension in the marketplace in order to become successful. Many international hotel chains are attempting to develop a global strategy (Littljohn and Roper, 1991). However, what they have achieved to date can be better described as a successful international, rather than global, strategy. For example, Accor and Holiday Inn have geographical coverage of over 60 countries and over 2000 hotels worldwide. Despite this, their product is not recognized globally in a uniform manner in different geographical markets (Israeli, 2002) and thus, they do not have a successful global strategy. With the increased geographical coverage of hotel chains, and with the attention of these firms to uniformity and standardization in the hospitality product, some global hospitality products and services may emerge.

References

Anonymous (2 September 2003) http://progressiveliving.org/globalization_defined.htm

Israeli, A. (2002) Star rating and corporate affiliation: their influence on pricing hotel rooms in Israel. *International Journal of Hospitality Management*, 21 (4), 405–424.

Littljohn, D. and Roper, A.J. (1991) Changes in international hotel companies' strategies. In R. Teare and A. Boer (eds), *Strategic Hospitality Management: Theory and Practice in the 1990s*. London: Cassell, pp. 194–212.

Olsen, M.D., Tse, E.C., and West J.J. (1992) *Strategic Management in the Hospitality Industry*. New York: Van Nostrand Reinhold.

Yip G.S. (2003) *Total Global Strategy II*. Upper Saddle River, NJ: Prentice-Hall.

AVIAD ISRAELI
BEN-GURION UNIVERSITY, ISRAEL

Globalization

The globalization of hospitality and tourism enterprises along with changing travel and immigration patterns has resulted in increasingly diverse customer and employee populations within the industry. As a result, today's hospitality managers must be skilled at managing a multi-cultural workforce, responsive to the diversity of their customers, and respectful of the local cultures in which they operate.

Research suggests that effectively managing a diverse workforce can lead to many benefits, including increased success in global markets, an enhanced ability to meet the needs of diverse customers, the ability to attract increased numbers of high-quality employees, increased creativity and higher-quality decision-making, increased organizational flexibility, and in some instances, reduced costs through lower rates of absenteeism and turnover (Cox and Blake, 1991). The term 'diversity management' refers to the organizational goals, policies, and practices that are put into place in order to help such benefits be realized. Diversity management typically includes the following (Christensen Hughes, 1999; Kandola, 1995; Mok, 2002):

- The explicit recognition of the strategic importance of employee and customer diversity by top management.
- Ensuring that all human resource management systems (e.g., recruitment, selection, orientation, training and development, rewards systems, communication strategies) are supportive of employee diversity and consistent with applicable legislation (e.g., local labor laws, human rights).
- The establishment of effective diversity training and development programs (e.g., multi-cultural awareness, language training).
- Data collection (demographics, attitude surveys) in order to track progress against established benchmarks and to identify areas for improvement.
- Providing incentives and holding managers accountable for the achievement of clearly defined goals in support of diversity.
- The establishment of processes for investigating allegations of harassment or discrimination.

While many domestic hospitality organizations (those that operate in only one country) have much to benefit from diversity management and can struggle with its implementation, the challenges for those doing business internationally can be even more considerable. National (and local) cultures can vary on a number of dimensions including: values (e.g., work ethic, time orientation, individualism/collectivism); religious beliefs (e.g., rituals, holidays, dress, customs); social structure (e.g., the role of the family, mobility, urbanization, social stratification); education (e.g., literacy, access); and communication (e.g., language, dialect, non-verbal communication, media, technology) (Belcourt et al., 1996). Political uncertainty and variations in legislative requirements only add to the challenge of managing in a culture other than one's own.

National culture can therefore have a considerable impact on human resource management practices. At the Four Seasons, a Canadian luxury hotel chain operating in 19 countries, cultural differences have been found to impact a number of important areas, including labor relations (i.e., the extent to which unionization is considered the norm), performance evaluation (i.e., the extent to which the focus is on the individual versus the group as well the directness of the feedback and whether merit or seniority is the determining factor in career progression), and training (i.e., the degree of structure and direction) (Belcourt et al., 1996).

In staffing an international operation, organizations typically deal with three types of employees: expatriates, host-country nationals, and third-country nationals (Belcourt et al., 1996). Expatriates or home-country nationals are employees from the company's home base, who are posted internationally (typically for a limited term); host-country nationals are employees native to the host country; and third-country nationals are from neither the home nor host country. Each employee type has its own advantages and disadvantages. Expatriates are typically highly skilled technically, very familiar with the home organization (i.e., its goals, culture, and systems), and interested in the personal development opportunity that an international posting can provide. Host-country nationals have intimate knowledge of the local culture, are adept at the language, cost less to

relocate, and help to satisfy the hiring expectations (formal or otherwise) of the host government. Finally, third-country nationals can bring broad experience, multilingualism, and an international outlook. Many international organizations employ a combination of these three types of employees, depending upon the needs of the business and the availability of local talent.

In instances where an expatriate or third-country national is deemed most appropriate, in addition to assessing fit with the technical requirements of the job, selection processes should determine the employee's tolerance for culture diversity, language, and communication skills, and the willingness of the employee to relocate. Research shows that the failure rate of US expatriates is in the range of 25–50%, costing on average US$40,000 to $250,000 per failure. The most common reasons for such failures are either the manager's or the spouse's inability to adapt (Belcourt et al., 1996, p. 632). Given the importance of the spouse's role in determining placement success, some organizations routinely interview the spouses of prospective candidates as part of their selection process.

Other recommended selection processes for overseas appointments include using interviewers who have had international experience themselves, asking problem-based questions that reflect situations unique to the host-country, the use of language proficiency tests (or assessments of ability to learn a second language), and psychological tests related to tolerance for novel situations and ethnocentrism. Ethnocentrism is defined by the *Oxford English Reference Dictionary* (1996) as 'the tendency to evaluate other races and cultures by criteria specific to one's own.' Research suggests that employees who exhibit high ethnocentrism experience higher rates of job failure in international assignments than those who do not (Belcourt et al., 1996, p. 637).

In order to assist expatriate and third-country nationals with the challenge of adapting to a new culture, organizations typically provide those selected for international assignments with training and development opportunities prior to departure. Such training may be related to a variety of topics, including: language (verbal and non-verbal), culture, social and business etiquette, laws, dress, history, geography, climate, diet, politics, currency, time zones, religion, tax implications etc. Assistance is typically also provided in attaining any required work permits. Once overseas, employees are ideally supported by senior managers who are expert in international concerns. McDonald's, for example, has five such managers who support local HR directors in 50 different countries (Belcourt *et al.*, 1996, p. 626). At the conclusion of an international assignment, expatriate employees are repatriated (i.e., retuned) to their home-countries.

References

Belcourt, M., Sherman, A.W., Bohlander, G.W., and Snell, S.A. (1996) *Managing Human Resources.* Scarborough: Nelson.

Christensen Hughes, J. (1999) The use of case studies to enhance diversity management effectiveness. In A. Lockwood (ed.), *Proceedings of the Eighth Annual CHME Hospitality Research Conference.* University of Surrey, vol. 2, pp. 403–421.

Cox, T.H. and Blake, S. (1991) Managing cultural diversity: implications for organizational competitiveness. *Academy of Management Executive,* 5 (3), 45–56.

Kandola, R. (1995) Managing diversity: new broom or old hat? *International Review of Industrial and Organizational Psychology,* 10, 131–167.

Mok, C. (2002) Managing diversity in hospitality organizations. In N. D'Annunzio-Green, G.A. Maxwell, and S. Watson (eds), *Human Resource Management: International Perspectives in Hospitality and Tourism.* London: Continuum.

Oxford English Reference Dictionary, 2nd edn (1996) (J. Perasall and B. Trumble, eds). Oxford: Oxford University Press.

JULIA CHRISTENSEN HUGHES
UNIVERSITY OF GUELPH, ONTARIO

Glocalization

Glocalization combines the word globalization with localization and refers to the concept that organizations should do business around the world, using methods that are appropriate for that particular country thereby creating a greater balance between global and local dimensions.

The premise of glocalization therefore is that a product or service is more likely to succeed when adapted specifically to each locality or culture it is marketed in. The proliferation of McDonald's restaurants worldwide is an example of globalization, while the restaurant chain's menu changes in an attempt to appeal to local palates are an example of glocalization.

Within the context of information technology communications (ICT) and the Internet the phrase 'Think Globally, Act Locally' is used to signify glocalization. This is so as the Internet expands a user's social world to people far away in different continents while at the same time binding users more deeply to the place where they live. Glocalized websites, such as www.visitbritain.com, offers local languages and adaptable interfaces targeted to specific user groups across the seven continents of the world.

References

Robertson, R. (1994) Globalization or localization. *Journal of International Communication,* 1 (1). Available at http://www.mucic.mq.edu.au/JIC/vol1no1/art1103.htm.

Solomon, C. (1996) Big Mac's Mcglobal HR secrets. *Personnel Journal,* 75 (4), 46.

JULINE E. MILLS
PURDUE UNIVERSITY, USA

Golf facilities

Golf facilities usually consist of a golf course, practice area, clubhouse, and a golf course maintenance area.

The golf course usually includes a layout of two 9-hole segments per 18-hole course, plus optional additional multiples of 9-hole segments. A regulation golf course offers par scoring between 69 and 73, three sets of tees or more, allowing overall course length to vary from approximately 5200 to 7200 yards, and holes rated according to the following array: four par 3s, ten par 4s, and three par 5s per 18 hole course. Most holes include common elements. The tee or tee box is the starting point for each hole; the fairway is the preferred landing and playing area between the tee and green; the rough is longer grass outside the perimeter of the fairway (not as desirable as the fairway for playing) with grass that is not as closely mowed as the fairway and typically lined with trees; the green is the putting surface, which contains the flagstick and cup (where the hole ends). Some holes include features designed to add difficulty to and/or enhance the aesthetics of the golf experience – most notably bunkers, which are sand areas located either in the fairways or around the greens, and water hazards, which run alongside or perpendicular to play.

Types of golf course design include:

- Core, whereby all 18 holes are designed together in cluster fashion.
- Single fairway continuous, whereby all 18 holes run end to end in one continuous loop.
- Single fairway with returning 9s, whereby the first 9 holes run end to end in one continuous loop and the second 9 holes run end to end in one continuous loop – with both 9s beginning and ending at the same central location (such as a clubhouse).
- Double fairway continuous, whereby the outgoing 9 holes run end to end in one direction and the returning 9 holes run end to end in the opposite direction (parallel to the outgoing 9).
- Double fairway with returning 9s, whereby four to five outgoing holes of the first 9 holes run end to end and the second four to five returning holes of the first 9 holes run end to end in the opposite direction (parallel to the outgoing four to five holes), then four to five outgoing holes of the second 9 holes run end to end and the second four to five returning holes of the second 9 holes run end to end in the opposite direction (parallel to the outgoing four to five holes) – with both 9s beginning and ending at the same central location (such as a clubhouse).

In addition to the golf course playing area, the golf course itself usually includes paved cart paths to facilitate traffic, benches, water fountains, ball washers/shoe scrapers, signage, lightening detection and warning systems, and weather shelters which are often combined with rest rooms and snack bars.

The practice area (range) designed to simulate golf course conditions – from tee, fairway, and bunker perspectives – is for golfers to practice a variety of golf shots. The practice area often includes a putting green and lesson area.

The clubhouse is often considered the element of the club experience that is central to the private club management experience. The clubhouse often features a golf pro shop offering supplies, equipment, apparel, accessories, golf car (cart) storage, caddie area, and bag storage, food and beverage outlets such as kitchen(s)/ dining areas, snack bars, and bar/lounge areas, locker rooms with dressing sections as well as shower/health/fitness areas, and often offers adjacent aquatics and tennis programs. Of particular importance to the clubhouse experience is the proper management of food and beverage services. In addition, to satisfy members the clubhouse manager must be knowledgeable of budgeting, budgetary controls, management of the foodservice experience, food preparation procedures, portion control processes, management of wines and spirits, product cost control procedures, management of the dining room experience, design and management of themed entertainment experiences, and member services etiquette.

The golf course maintenance facility is ideally located in a central location to the golf course to help facilitate productivity. It houses equipment and materials used in turf care including vehicles, tractors, mowers, trimmers, chemicals, fertilizers, soil, sand, and rock, a repair and maintenance area, a paint shop, an administrative office, locker room(s), and often times a sod farm. The management and maintenance of the golf course requires that the golf superintendent performs the following duties commonly associated with golf course maintenance:

- Determine golf course maintenance and improvement priorities in cooperation with the supervisor
- Determine watering, aeration, and topdressing requirements
- Identify turf and soil diseases
- Oversee and participate in the application of fertilizers, pesticides, insecticides, herbicides, and fungicides
- Oversee and participate in the mowing, watering, and maintenance of greens, tees, fairways, roughs, sand traps, and related golf course areas
- Maintain woody plants and trees on the golf course

- Inspect the course on a regular basis and make report
- Prepare and recommend an annual golf course maintenance budget
- Recommend purchase of equipment, supplies, and materials
- Assign, monitor, and review the work of permanently assigned employees, limited term employees, student workers, and/or other workers assisting with golf course maintenance activities
- Maintain effective working relationship with golf professionals and other golf course personnel
- Practice golf etiquette when scheduling golf course maintenance
- Use and operate a variety of equipment, such as riding and push mowers, manual and automated irrigation systems, thatchers, chemical sprayers, fertilizer spreaders, sod cutters, tractors, front-end loaders, and dump and pickup trucks
- Assure safe operation and use of equipment and tools
- Inspect, clean, and perform routine maintenance on equipment, tools, and golf course structures
- Assist groundkeeping staff or other workers, as needed
- Perform other duties as assigned by supervisor.

References

Mill, Robert C. (2001) *Resorts*. New York: John Wiley & Sons.

Perdue, Joe (1997) *Contemporary Club Management*. Lansing, MI: Educational Institute of the American Hotel and Motel Association.

State of Wisconsin (2003) *Bulletin MRS-SC-153 as a result of the Blue Collar Survey*. www.oser. state.wi.us/dmrs/documents/90470SPC.pdf

EDWARD A. MERRITT
CALIFORNIA STATE POLYTECHNIC
UNIVERSITY, USA

Golf professional classifications

The PGA of America offers the following membership classifications:

- *Master Professional:* Members of the Association who met the many stringent requirements prescribed by the Board of Directors for this classification, from 1972 until the program was suspended 1996 and replaced by PGA specialty certification. (Only 300 or so members ever attained this status.)
- *A-1:* Members of the Association who own/operate or supervise/direct a golf shop at a recognized golf club/course and engage in or supervise the teaching of golf at such facility.
- *A-2:* Members of the Association who own/operate or supervise/direct a golf shop at a recognized golf range and engage in or supervise the teaching of golf at such facility.
- *A-3:* Members of the Association who are exempt players on the PGA Tour, Senior PGA Tour, Buy.com Tour or LPGA Tour.
- *A-4:* PGA Members who direct the total golf operation of a PGA-recognized golf facility, including the golf shop, golf range, golf car operation (if applicable), and supervision of the head golf professional.
- *A-5:* All past presidents of the Association, regardless of their current occupation or profession.
- *A-6:* Those who are employed at PGA-recognized golf facilities or PGA-recognized golf schools as either golf instructors or supervisors of golf instructors.
- *A-7:* Those who are employed as a director of golf or head golf professional at a golf facility under construction.
- *A-8:* Assistants to Class A members of the Association who are head golf professionals, Master Professionals, Class A LPGA members or Class F members, provided they remain employed by the same Class F members for whom they were working at the time he/she was transferred to Class F.
- *A-9:* Those employed in professional positions in management, development, ownership, operation, and/or financing of golf facilities.
- *A-10:* PGA Members employed as golf clinicians.
- *A-11:* Members who become employed by the PGA of America, a PGA Section of the PGA Tour in an administrative capacity or employed by golf associations recognized by the PGA Board of Directors.
- *A-12:* Members of the Association who are employed as golf coaches at accredited colleges, universities, and junior colleges.

- *A-13:* Those employed as managers of an entire golf facility including golf operations, maintenance, clubhouse administration, food and beverage operation, and recreational activities.
- *A-14:* Those employed as director of instruction at PGA-recognized golf schools or PGA-recognized facilities.
- *A-15:* PGA members who own or manage golf products or services at a PGA-Recognized Retail Facility, provided such employment specifically excludes primary employment as a clerk. A PGA-recognized retail facility is defined as a stand-alone retail golf specialty store.
- *A-16:* Those employed in the design of golf courses as architects or PGA members who are employed in an ownership or management capacity as golf course builders.
- *A-17:* PGA Members employed in the management of all activities in relation to maintenance, operation, and management of a golf course. Members in this classification are required to satisfy the criteria of either a Golf Course Superintendent or Assistant Golf Course Superintendent as defined by the Golf Course Superintendents Association of America.
- *A-18:* Those employed in the reporting, editing, writing or publishing of golf-related publications in any form of media (inclusive of, but not necessarily limited to, newspapers, magazines, the Internet) or in the broadcasting or commentating about golf events on network television, cable networks, the Internet or any other form of related media.
- *A-19:* Members of the association who are employed in an executive, administrative or supervisory position with a golf industry manufacturer or golf industry distributor.
- *A-20:* Those employed by one or more golf manufacturing or distributing companies involved in the wholesale sales and distribution of golf merchandise or golf-related supplies to golf facilities, retail stores or any other golf outlets.
- *A-21:* Those employed within the coordination, planning, and implementation of golf events for organizations, businesses, or associations.
- *A-22:* Those employed in the provision of services as a rules official for recognized golf associations, recognized golf tours or recognized golf events.
- *A-23:* PGA Members employed in the business of club fitting must use a recognized fitting system or a comparable system, must have all the necessary equipment normally associated with club fitting and must have access to a PGA-Recognized Golf Range or a range at a PGA-Recognized Golf Course to monitor ball flight. A member employed in club repair must have an established place of business with all necessary equipment normally associated with club repair, or must service one or more golf tours or series of golf events.
- *A-24:* PGA Members primarily employed within the golf industry that are not eligible for another Active classification.
- *Class F:* Members of the Association who have failed to meet the recertification requirements.
- *Inactive:* Any member of the Association who is not eligible for one of the active classifications or Life Member classifications.
- *Life Member-Active/Life Member-Retired:* Members of the Association who are not eligible for classification as Active members and who have held a minimum of 20 years in an active classification (whether continuous or not).
- *Assistant Golf Professional:* An individual who is employed by or is under the direction of a head golf professional, director of golf or general manager as either a golf teacher or golf assistant (defined as individuals who spend at least 50% of the time working on club repair, merchandising, handicapping records, inventory control, bookkeeping and tournament operations).
- *Head Professional:* An individual whose primary employment is the ownership and operation of a golf shop at a PGA-recognized golf facility; or the supervision and direction of the golf shop and supervision of teaching at a PGA-recognized golf facility.

Additionally, the PGA of America offers these apprentice classifications:

- *Non-Member Head Professional Apprentice:* A person who owns and operates, or supervises and directs, a golf shop at a recognized golf club or course or Par-3 and engages in or supervises the teaching of golf at such facility.
- *Manager:* An individual who is employed full-time as a manager of one or more PGA members who are Directors of Golf, General

Managers or Head Professionals at PGA-recognized golf courses or PGA recognized ranges.

- *Assistant Professional Apprentice:* An individual who is employed by or is under the direction of a head golf professional, director of golf or general manager as either a golf teacher or golf assistant.

Reference

http://dev.pga.com/FAQ/membership/classifications.html. Accessed 10 August 2003.

EDWARD A. MERRITT
CALIFORNIA STATE POLYTECHNIC
UNIVERSITY, USA

Golf programs

The general belief is that the golf course is the primary attraction for the typical private club member. There are, indeed, other members who do not seek out a golf experience, however most research conducted attests to the fact that golf is the central focus for many clubs.

The golf facilities at a club usually consist of an 18-hole golf course, a pro shop, a driving range, a practice green, a short-game practice area, a bag storage area, a golf car storage area, and a maintenance storage area. Golf courses have at least 9 holes or multiple of 9 holes, with 18 holes being the most common number of holes at private clubs.

Private clubs have a variety of golf programs for members. Some members prefer to play golf for recreational purposes, while others enjoy the competitive nature of the sport and participate more often in the club's tournaments, championships, and handicap program. Lessons and teaching camps are fundamental in clubs in order to increase the golf ability of adults and children.

Most private clubs have a guest policy that restricts the times that guests can play, limit the number of times they can play, usually on a monthly or on an annual basis, and stipulate who is to be considered an out-of-town or in-town guest when usage is restricted based on residence.

At the time of check-in at the pro shop, most clubs require members to register their guests and sign the charge slip for the guest fee.

Many private clubs restrict usage of the golf course during peak periods (e.g., Saturday and Sunday morning, etc.) to the designated member in the household. This policy is to prevent over-crowding on the golf course. Spouses and children usually can play during non-peak periods. Some clubs restrict play to male members only during the peak time periods and do not allow females or the children of members to play at those times. This gender policy, which use to be common among clubs, is now found less often because of the number of female executives joining the club as the designated member.

During the week many private clubs designate time periods when the course is open for play only to organized club groups. The LGA (Ladies Golf Association) may have organized play by its group on a weekday morning and/or evening. The MGA (Men's Golf Association) may have its events on one weekday evening or one weekend morning. Juniors may have an organized activity on a weekday following school or on a weekend afternoon.

Most private clubs conduct a variety of golf tournaments each season, which typically include a club championship, invitational tournament, pro-am events, MGA events, LGA events, member–guest tournaments, men–women events, junior events, etc.

The club's handicap system allows individuals with different ability levels to play together and compete on an equal basis. The member must play on a regular basis and report each score so that fair and accurate handicaps can be determined. The handicap scores should be updated regularly and listed on the club's computer or posted on a bulletin board.

Outside golf tournaments are conducted at many private clubs. Some clubs may not allow any outside events, others may only allow a few outside tournaments a year, and certain clubs that are seeking additional revenues may aggressively pursue tournaments. An outside tournament is a tournament that is not organized primarily for members and invited guests. It may be organized by a company or organization that wants to host a golf tournament and banquet for a special event, such as a charity fund raiser, a corporate outing, etc. Generally the club hosts these events on a Monday, when most clubs are normally closed, therefore not inconveniencing the members. Organizers of outside events usually have to pay a greens fee for each participant, rent golf cars, pay a set fee for the driving range, host a lunch or dinner at the club, and pay for the food and beverage consumed on the golf course. A member of the club usually sponsors the outside event.

The golf instructional program at a private club is the foundation of the overall golf program. Instruction is a key to getting members to use the golf course and to frequent the club more often. Moreover, the instructional program is a good feeder into the other golf activities such as the MGA, LGA, and tournaments. Instructional programs should be viewed not as a one-time event just for beginners but as an ongoing process, from an introduction of the game as a beginner, to the intermediate skill level, to competing strategies, to the advanced skill level. There should be lessons for all ability levels and interests.

Golf lessons can be in the form of private lessons, group lessons, or clinics. The group lessons or clinics are also divided into age groups (adult and junior), sex (male and female), level (high, average, good, and advanced handicap), and topic (stroke improvement, playing strategy, and rules). Private lessons give members the individual attention that some desire, but at a high cost. Group lessons and clinics allow members to interact with other members, socialize, and improve their skill level; they are also less expensive and allow members to take more lessons for the same cost as private lessons. Lessons are usually at the driving range and short game practice areas. Many clubs are adding high-tech teaching centers with multiple cameras and computers to analyze the member's swing.

The future of the golf game lies in the junior programs at private clubs around the country. The junior golf program consists of group lessons, tournaments, clinics, games, educational activities, modified golf games, and supervision of juniors on the course. Summer clinics and camps are popular with children because they are out of school and the club usually has more tee times available during the weekdays. During the school year, club programs are usually run for juniors immediately after school. Many clubs carry junior size clubs to ensure success for children playing the game.

Reference

Perdue, Joe (1997) *Contemporary Club Management.* Lansing, MI: Educational Institute of the American Hotel and Motel Association.

RAYMOND R. FERREIRA
GEORGIA STATE UNIVERSITY, USA

Golf tournaments

The game of golf is a primary attractor of the sports-minded golf enthusiast. As such, private club managers should ensure that their golf offerings stimulate excitement, competitiveness, and social bonding for their golf members. In order to accomplish these outcomes, the following tournaments have proven to be very successful. This listing should not be taken to be totally inclusive of all possible golf tournament types, instead club management should poll their golf members to determine which tournaments would be the biggest draws.

- *Ace of Aces:* This tournament can be held monthly (or any given cycle) for a specified length of playing season. A low-gross score and low-net score qualifier game is held, with the winner of each competing in the Ace of Aces tournament at the end of the season.
- *Approach and putting:* This tournament requires each contestant to approach and hole three balls from 25, 50, and 100 yards off the green. Each ball should be played from a different direction with the winner holing the three different balls in the least amount of strokes.
- *Average stroke:* In this tournament, the player averages their gross scores for all 18 holes and then deducts half of their combined handicap from their total holes (18). Any half stroke is counted as a whole stroke in this tournament.

- *Best-ball:* This competitive tournament places three players against each other. Two of the players are partners that play their best ball against the score of the remaining member. It is assumed that the third member in this type of play is a better player.
- *Bingle–Bangle–Bungle:* This is an exciting and challenging tournament that assigns three points per hole. The scoring is determined as (a) one point for the ball closest to the green surface, (b) one point for the ball that is closest to the cup once all players are on the green, and (c) one point for the player who sinks the first putt.
- *Blind hole match:* This tournament involves the counting of play on designated holes that is determined by an individual after the playing team has left the first tee. A full handicap system is used during this type of tournament.
- *Blind low-net foursome:* In this style of play, all contestants play 18 holes with any partner of choice. At the conclusion of the 18 holes, a chosen person draws names and groups the players into foursomes. The net scores attained for each player are then added together for each team to determine the winning foursome with the best low-net score.
- *Blind partner:* After all players have left the first tee, a designated person pairs the players by a drawing. In doing so, none of the players knows who their partner is until all holes have been completed.
- *Bobs and Birds:* The Bobs portion of this tournament means that a player receives points for their tee shots on the green that are closest to the pin on par-3 holes only. Under the Birds portion of this game, a player is given points for birdies on any hole of play.
- *Chicago system:* Each player is assigned a point quota based on their assigned handicap as calculated using the Chicago system. Player points are assigned as: 1 point for a bogey; 2 points for a par; 4 points for birdie; and 8 points for an eagle. The winner is that player whose points for 18 holes most exceeds their assigned handicap.
- *Cross-country tournament:* The players start about a mile from the course and play 'cross-country.' The player is expected to play the ball wherever it lands. However, if the balls lands in an unplayable spot, the player is allowed to move it

with a two stroke penalty. The goal in cross-country is to finish at the hole nearest the clubhouse.
- *Derby tournament:* This 9-hole tournament is typically done with 15 players who are assigned a unique number. The choice of playing from scratch or full-handicap is the province of the event organizer. The order of play is done by the assignment number and this order is followed throughout the game. All players tee off from the same position and play by normal sequence of play rules. The elimination process begins with the three highest scoring players being culled out from remaining play for holes one and two. On the third and fourth holes the top two scoring players are eliminated from further play. From the fifth to the eighth hole, the player scoring the highest is eliminated from play. This process leaves only two players competing on the final ninth hole.
- *Driving contest:* This tournament is conducted on a straight and relatively flat fairway. Each player is given five drives with the best three that end on the fairway being counted.
- *Fewest putts:* All holes of play are counted, with the winner being the player that has the least amount of putts. All shots from the green count, with no putts being passed.
- *Handicap stroke:* All players play 18 holes at stroke play with prizes being given to players with the best gross score and net score. Under this tournament type a full handicap approach is employed.
- *Jack and Jill:* This is a mixed tournament where the low ball of the men and the low ball of the women are combined. In this game strokes are recorded as on the card and with a full handicap. The low scorer of the event is the winner.
- *Low-ball, low-total:* Under this tournament a player is given one-point for the best ball per hole and one-point for the low team score per hole.
- *Most threes, fours, and fives:* Scoring under this system is based on the number of strokes that the players takes on a hole-by-hole basis. The player with the most net threes, fours, and fives is considered the winner. This type of tournament is based on the full handicap system.
- *Obstacle tournament:* This golf event is played with obstacles on the course. Each hole has an

obstacle on it that the player must play around or through.

References

Perdue, Joe (1997) *Contemporary Club Management.* Lansing, MI: Educational Institute of the American Hotel and Motel Association.

White, Ted and Gerstner, Larry (1991) *Club Operations and Management.* New York: Van Nostrand Reinhold.

ARAM SON
JAMES COOK UNIVERSITY, AUSTRALIA

Grease trap

Every day, restaurants and food production businesses generate tons of cooking oil, grease, and food wastes. These wastes are in liquid state and are passed into the drainage system. However, these fat wastes can block the sewer system and cause waste water to back up into the restaurant. Furthermore, if the waste is not managed properly, it can cause major environmental problems. A grease trap is designed to capture food oils, fats, and greases coming from a restaurant and food production facility water drain lines. A grease trap prevents the discharge of grease into a sewer. Grease entering the trap is congealed by the water and settles into a perforated tray. A grease trap works by slowing down the flow of hot greasy water allowing it to cool with the fats and oils separating, solidifying, and rising to the top of the tank. By use of baffles inside the tank, the hardened grease is prevented from passing through the drain line. Food solids settle to the bottom of the trap. The tray must be removed at least once a week to be cleaned using hot water.

References

Allen, D.M. (1983) *Accommodation and Cleaning Services, Volume 1: Operations.* London: Hutchinson & Co.

http://www.foodgreasetrappers.com/id18_m.htm

BENNY CHAN
THE HONG KONG POLYTECHNIC
UNIVERSITY, HONG KONG SAR, CHINA

Green Globe 21

Green Globe 21 is a global benchmarking and certification program that facilitates sustainable travel and tourism for consumers, companies, and communities. It is based on Agenda 21 and principles for sustainable development endorsed by 182 governments at the United Nations Rio de Janeiro Earth Summit in 1992. There are four Green Globe 21 Standards: The Green Globe 21 Company Standard; the Green Globe 21 Standard for Communities; the International Ecotourism Standard; and the Design and Construct Standard. The Green Globe 21 Company Standard is available to operations in 20 different sectors of the travel and tourism industry.

The Standards requires an operation or community to achieve a baseline level of environmental and socially sustainable performance before it receives the Green Globe logo without the tick. The operation must also meet all of the requirements of the relevant Green Globe 21 Standard and be independently audited to be allowed to use the Green Globe logo with the tick.

Green Globe 21 provides a report to businesses on where its performance is positioned relative to the environmental and social benchmarks. Each year advice is provided as to whether an operation has improved or maintained its performance based on the original benchmarking assessment.

Reference

Parsons, C. (2003) *Green Globe 21: What We Do: About the Company.* Retrieved 1 October 2003 from http://www.greenglobe.org

LYLE THOMPSON
BURNABY, BC, CANADA

Green power energy purchasing

Green power is 'electricity that is generated from resources such as solar, wind, geothermal, biomass, and low-impact hydro facilities. Conventional electricity generation, based on the combustion of fossil fuels, is the single largest industrial source of air pollution' (www.epa. gov/greenpower/whatis.htm).

Green power pricing is an optional service at several utilities, allowing customers the option of purchasing all or part of a buildings energy load from renewable energy technologies. Participating customers usually pay a premium on their electric bill to cover the extra cost of the renewable energy. To date, in the United States more than 300 investor-owned utilities, municipal utilities, and cooperatives have either implemented or announced plans to offer a green pricing option.

Reference

Green Power Partnership: www.epa.gov/ green power

JIM ACKLES
THARALDSON ENERGY GROUP, USA

Gross operating profit (GOP)

Gross operating profit, or GOP, describes the current line 'Income After Undistributed Operating Expenses' under the Uniform System of Accounts for the Lodging Industry (USALI). Although sometimes criticized as a misnomer, since 'gross' and 'operating' suggest the measure more accurately describes profit at the departmental level (i.e. before deduction of undistributed operating expenses), the term is widely used and well understood in the hospitality industry. Gross operating profit has long been considered one of the most important measures of the property manager's performance. The level of GOP achieved is determined by management's revenue-generating ability, the sales mix the hotel is able to achieve, given its position in the market, and management's acumen in controlling costs. The GOP, when expressed as a percentage of revenue, can be a meaningful measure of property level management's control of departmental and undistributed operating costs, but may fail to give adequate attention to management's revenue-generating responsibilities. Experienced analysts, therefore, measure GOP on both a percentage and a dollars-per-available-room basis when judging the effectiveness of property level management. Benchmarking reports, prepared annually by a number of leading international hospitality consulting firms, primarily present statistical summaries of revenue, expense and profit data through to GOP.

Reference

Uniform System of Accounts for the Lodging Industry, 9th edn (1996) Lansing, MI: Educational Institute of the American Hotel and Motel Association.

PAUL BEALS
UNIVERSITY OF DENVER, USA

Gross profit and net profit

Profit is determined by deducting expenses related to a period from revenue for the same period. Two fundamental levels of profit are generally referred to in profit and loss (income) statements: gross profit, which is calculated by deducting cost of sales from sales revenue, and net profit, which is calculated by deducting total expenses from revenue.

The relative size of gross profit and net profit is often determined by referring to gross profit margin and net profit margin. Gross profit margin percentage is determined by dividing gross profit by operating revenue and multiplying by 100. Net profit margin percentage is determined by dividing net profit by revenue and multiplying by 100. The calculation of gross and net profit margins facilitates the comparison of profit levels across different-sized hotels.

The distinction between net profit and gross profit is highlighted through the following example:

ABC Hotel
Profit Statement for the year ended
30 December 200X, in US$

Sales revenue		45,000
Less: Cost of sales		<u>10,000</u>
Gross profit		35,000
Plus: Other revenue		<u>4,200</u>
Net revenue		39,200
Less: Other expenses:		
Employee benefits	15,000	
Administration	6,000	
Depreciation	1,500	
Other	2,400	<u>24,900</u>
Net profit		<u>14,300</u>

References

Harris P.J. and Hazzard, P.A. (1992) *Managerial Accounting in the Hospitality Industry*, 5th edn. Cheltenham: Stanley Thornes.

Schmidgall, R.S. (2002) *Hospitality Industry Managerial Accounting*, 5th edn. Lansing, MI: Educational Institute of the American Hotel and Lodging Association.

CHRIS GUILDING
GRIFFITH UNIVERSITY, AUSTRALIA

Gross profit in foodservice

Gross profit is the profit after the cost of goods sold (COGS) has been deducted from total revenues. In a foodservice operation, COGS is calculated for food and beverage products. After these expenses have been deducted from total food and beverage revenues, the operation is left with gross profit. Since the average food and beverage cost represents 25–40% of total costs in most US operations, the gross profit percentage is usually 60–75%.

For example, if a restaurant's revenue is $250,000 and its COGS is $75,000, then its gross profit would be $250,000 − $75,000 = $175,000. This would mean the restaurant's gross profit percentage is 70%.

It is important to note that while gross profit for COGS is a function of total sales, gross profit for food is calculated using food sales and gross profit for beverages is calculated using beverage sales. Building on the previous example, assume that food sales are $200,000 and beverage sales represent the remaining $50,000. If food cost is $66,000 and beverage cost is $9000, the gross profit percentage for food is 67% while the gross profit for beverages is 82%.

Reference

Deloitte & Touche LLP (1996). *Uniform System of Accounts*. Washington, DC: National Restaurant Association.

DEBORAH BARRASH
UNIVERSITY OF NEVADA, LAS VEGAS, USA

Group reservation

A group reservation is for a block of rooms in a lodging facility. The block of rooms could be for a convention, a meeting, a special event (wedding, party, etc.), a tour group, or various other reasons. A group reservation could be as small as five rooms to several thousand, depending on the size of the lodging facility. By booking rooms in large quantities, the group receives a lower rate. Conventioneers and/or group members are most often provided with reservation postcards by the marketing and sales department of the hotel. These cards can be presented at check-in and show the name of the convention or group and the official dates when the convention or group will convene at the hotel.

For a member of the group to receive this special rate they must identify themselves as a member of this group when making the reservation. When a group reservation is made a code is generated which is specific to that group and each reservation must include this code for tracking the group's reservations. To ensure that reservations get coded to the proper group and that the correct rates are offered, the person taking the reservation should always inquire if the person will be part of a group, convention or meeting.

Reference

American Hotel and Motel Association (1996) *Hospitality Skills Training Series: Front Desk Employee Guide*. Lansing, MI: Educational Institute of the American Hotel and Motel Association.

MORGAN GEDDIE
UNIVERSITY OF HOUSTON, USA

Groups

Groups are the building blocks of organizations and are designed to integrate job tasks and people effectively. Groups can comprise any number of people who interact with one another, are psychologically aware of one another, and who perceive themselves to be a group. Therefore, as well as the formal groups that are established by organizations, there are also informal groups, created by the members of these groups.

Formal groups are constructed by the organization to help with the implementation of plans and the achievement of organizational objectives. For example, within a hotel, employees will be grouped into departments such as housekeeping, banqueting, guest services etc. Within these departments, employees might be further divided into smaller groups to allocate specific tasks and responsibilities. This allows for division of work, allocation of responsibility, and organizational control. Also, short-life project groups would be included in this category, as they are established to address a particular organizational issue. Usually formal groups have a predetermined structure, roles and responsibilities and a designated leader or manager. Also, members are usually selected for membership using specific criteria such as job task or level of experience.

However, organizations also comprise informal groups. These are collections of individuals who come together within the workplace as a result of informal interaction to share interests, form identities, and establish informal control. In some sectors of the hospitality industry, informal groups are common and sometimes known as 'occupational communities.' They are based more on personal relationships and satisfy social and psychological needs rather than any formal task or remit. They can also cut across functions, hierarchical levels, and even geographical locations. Although not formally constituted, ground rules for behavior and informal leadership can still emerge through shared experience and understanding. These informal groups can influence the behavior and attitudes of group members and can even affect members' levels of productivity. They can be organized round such shared experiences as sporting interests, recruitment times, ethnic or national origin, age, gender or length of service. For example, immigrant workers of the same nationality might gravitate together when working in a hotel in a foreign country. Also, general managers may still have a special affinity with the department in which they started their career, and, by extension, the members of that department.

Despite the fact that these informal groups are not created by the organization, they can still have a huge influence on employee behavior. The influence of groups in the workplace was first identified by Elton Mayo during the Hawthorne Experiments of the 1920s and 1930s (Roethlisberger and Dickson, 1939). He recognized that informal groups could influence the output, attitudes, and motivation of employees. This developed into the human relations approach to management, expounded by Douglas McGregor and Edgar Schein amongst others, and emphasized the importance of social processes in the workplace. They stressed the importance of the group rather than the individual as a unit of analysis in organizational influence and maintained that people could be influenced by the norms of their informal work group in relation to attitudes to work and level of productivity.

Group norms are established when the group is sufficiently developed that it has established accepted patterns of behavior and working that are shared amongst members of the group. The group becomes a cohesive unit characterized by positive interaction, cooperation between members, low levels of conflict and shared goals. Groups at this phase of development are said to be in the 'performing' stage (Tuckman, 1965). Although the group will be performing effectively, it might be difficult for new members to join the group, especially if they challenge the group norms. For example, if a new member of staff joins a long-established team, it can cause conflict and disharmony, unless this person accepts the working practices and norms of the group.

Although establishing group norms can have a positive effect on group performance, groups can become overly cohesive to a point when they cease to be effective. This phenomenon was identified by Irving Janis (1982) as 'groupthink.' Members of groups suffering from groupthink are characterized as overly concerned with maintaining the unanimity of the group. As a result, they tend to minimize their own concerns about flawed group decisions, which prevents a more realistic appraisal of the group's course of action. For example, the senior management team of an international luxury hotel chain fails to act on repeated reports of poor customer satisfaction from general managers throughout the chain because as a group, they have decided that their strategy of cost-cutting is right for the organization. Usually, it takes a financial crisis or a change of personnel within the group for the groupthink consensus to be challenged.

One of the more recent developments in group dynamics within organizations is the creation of autonomous work groups. An autonomous work group (also known as self-managed or self-directed groups or teams) is a team of workers who work as a group to produce a significant part of the work process and have discretion over their choice of work methods and how tasks are allocated and rotated within the team. They usually also have responsibility for other vertically integrated aspects of the job, such as supervision, quality control, training, and team selection. This is usually introduced as a measure to increase work performance and employee job satisfaction. Indeed, Edgar Schein (1988) found that autonomous groups did give higher levels of quality and greater performance. However, autonomous groups do require an organizational culture where hierarchy, status, and control are set aside in favor of results, trust, and empowerment. This does not sit well with cultures where there is a high degree of power distance (Hofstede, 1980) as managers are seen as decision-makers and any attempt to involve employees in the decision-making process would be seen to indicate incompetence on the part of the manager. However, autonomous work groups have been introduced within a number of hospitality companies as a way of increasing employee empowerment and job satisfaction which in turn can impact on service quality and employee performance.

References

Hofstede, G. (1980) *Culture's Consequences: International Differences in Work-Related Values.* Beverly Hill, CA: Sage Publications.

Janis, J.L. (1982) *Groupthink*, 2nd edn. Boston, MA: Houghton Mifflin.

Roethlisberger, F.J. and Dickson, W.J. (1939) *Management and the Worker.* Cambridge, MA: Harvard University Press.

Schein, E. (1988) *Organizational Psychology*, 3rd edn. Englewood Cliffs, NJ: Prentice-Hall International.

Tuckman, B.W. (1965) Development sequence in small groups. *Psychological Bulletin*, 63 (6), 384–399.

GILLIAN KELLOCK HAY
GLASGOW CALEDONIAN UNIVERSITY, UK

Guaranteed reservation

A guaranteed reservation is one that is guaranteed by a credit card number, for hotel accommodations. In exchange for the guaranteed reservation, the hotel can charge the credit card certain fees if the reservation is not kept. When this type of reservation is made by a guest, it requires the hotel room to be held after the normal cancellation time. By guaranteeing the reservation the guest is saying I will definitely be there and please hold the room for me no matter how late I am checking in. The room is reserved with a credit card, a cash deposit or a corporate guarantee (if the company making the reservation has direct billing). A guaranteed reservation is an advanced booking which means that the room should be held the entire night for the guest and if the guest does not check-in, he/she will be charged for one night stay or lose their deposit. When taking a guaranteed reservation, the guest must be notified that he/she has made a guaranteed reservation and has until a specific time to cancel the reservation, after that time he/she will be charged for one night or lose their deposit if he/she cancels after the specified time or does not check in.

Reference

American Hotel and Motel Association (1996) *Hospitality Skills Training Series: Front Desk Employee Guide*. Lansing, MI: Educational Institute of the American Hotel and Motel Association.

MORGAN GEDDIE
UNIVERSITY OF HOUSTON, USA

Guest cycle

The guest cycle consists of four stages namely:

1. Pre-arrival
2. Arrival
3. Occupancy
4. Departure.

Pre-arrival is the stage where the guest chooses the hotel and makes the reservation. Important information is gathered at this stage, which allows the next stage to run smoothly. The arrival stage is when the guest actually arrives and registers at the hotel (check-in). Here the guest verifies the information gathered previously at the reservation stage, confirms method of payment, signs the registration card, and collects the key. The occupancy stage deals with security of the guest along with the coordination of guest services to ensure guest satisfaction and try to encourage repeat guests. The front desk plays an important part at this stage as this is the area where guests will make their requests or air their problems, to which the front desk agents need to respond in a timely and accurate manner. At this stage the front desk need to keep guest accounts up-to-date so that the final stage of the cycle runs smoothly. The final stage of the cycle is departure, which is when the guest is ready to check out. The main objective here is to settle the guest account, update room status information, and create a guest history record. In an attempt to ensure repeat guests it is important to find out if the guest has enjoyed their stay at this point.

Reference

Kasavana, M.L. and Brooks, R.M. (1995) *Front Office Procedures*, 4th edn. Lansing, MI: Educational Institute of the American Hotel and Motel Association.

IRENE SWEENEY
INTERNATIONAL HOTEL MANAGEMENT
INSTITUTE SWITZERLAND, SWITZERLAND

Guest history

To successfully return current guests and strategically market to new guests with similar characteristics, a hotel must maintain and evaluate data on all of its guests. The record of a guest's stay, called the guest history, becomes part of a file that can be used to determine when a guest might visit in the future, the type of accommodation the guest prefers, dining preferences, use of amenities or recreational facilities, and other, more personal data, including home address and telephone number, spouse's and children's names, birthday and so on. The guest history can be used by the hotel's sales and marketing department for promotional mailings soliciting repeat business or to target potential guests with similar profiles. Guest history is especially useful at the reservation stage (information already on file) and at the check-in (a guest can be greeted by a well informed receptionist). It is useful to management as it helps them to gain an insight into guest profiles and trends.

References

Kasavana, M.L. and Brooks, R.M. (1995) *Front Office Procedures*, 4th edn. Lansing, MI: Educational Institute American Hotel and Motel Association.

Renner, P. (1994) *Basic Hotel Front Office Procedures*, 3rd edn. New York: Van Nostrand Reinhold.

Stutts, Alan (2001) *Hotel and Lodging Management – An Introduction*. New York: John Wiley & Sons.

IRENE SWEENEY
INTERNATIONAL HOTEL MANAGEMENT
INSTITUTE SWITZERLAND, SWITZERLAND

Guest history file

Guest history files record customer's detailed historical stay information. The guest history database normally contains data such as arrival and departure dates, detailed revenue generated in rooms, food and beverage and extras, comments and special requirements during a stay of customer for each individual stay, and summarized (total number of reservations, total number of stays, total revenue generated) statistics. When new reservations are made, a property management system automatically searches the guest history database, determining if the guest has stayed at the property before. For repeat guests, the system calls up details from guest history, saving valuable time for both the reservations agent and customer. For new customers, a new guest profile needs to be created first. Guest history also indicates if customer is on a blacklist or had failed to honor reservations in past.

Most property management systems offer the ability to develop frequent stay guest programs. Many properties offer these programs in conjunction with frequent mile programs. Returning customers are able to use their frequent guest number when making a new reservation or check an existing reservation. Once the guest has met a predefined number of stays, most systems enable 'regular guest' indicators to be displayed on check-in and arrival reports. Modern property management systems allow properties and chains to keep accurate and tidy guest histories in order to enhance their marketing functions.

References

Baker, S., Bradley, P., and Huyton, J. (1994) *Principles of Hotel Front Office Operations*. New York: Cassell.

O'Connor, P. (2003) *Using Computers in Hospitality*, 3rd edn. London: Continuum International.

DAVID INANEISHVILI
HOTEL KÄMP, FINLAND

Guest operated interfaces

Depending on the computerized property management system that a hotel has installed, guests may be able to operate some of the automated devices within the hotel. It allows guests to have more control over the services they get. Examples of this include: in-room movie systems and fully automated guestroom vending machines. Guests may even be able to review their accounts through the guestroom television being connected to the guest accounting system. Through this system guests can receive information about events within the hotel and the local area or access airline schedules, local entertainment guides, news etc. all in the comfort of their own room.

Virtual reality, biometric identification systems, white noise – the world of academia is working hard to analyze how travel and lifestyle changes will shape the hotels of the future. The present and future may include: alarm clocks that increase the amount of light in a room rather than emitting a tone; rooms that are light-, noise- and temperature-sensitive in order to create a sleep profile tailored to each guest; keyless locks that are controlled by coded information gained through the scan of a guest's finger, palm or retina; windows replaced by guest-selected computer-generated scenes to create a more restful, relaxing in-room environment; choice of soothing white noise at the touch of a button to help guests unwind; in-room virtual reality entertainment centers; electronically controlled mattresses to provide guests with the right level of firmness and support; and in-room exercise amenities using tension lines and doorknobs so that guests can de-stress while they get fit in the privacy of their own room.

References

Kasavana, M.L. and Brooks, R.M. (1995) *Front Office Procedures*, 4th edn. Lansing, MI: Educational Institute of the American Hotel and Motel Association.

Stutts, Alan (1999) 'Hotel room of the future' combines traveler needs with modern technology, *Hotel Online Special Report*.

IRENE SWEENEY
INTERNATIONAL HOTEL MANAGEMENT
INSTITUTE SWITZERLAND, SWITZERLAND

Guest profile

In hospitality, a profile is a set of characteristics that define any business-related item, such as an individual customer, a travel agent, source, a company or a group profile. For example, an individual profile may include characteristics such as first name, last name, title, telephone, addressing information, gender, age, date of birth, nationality, VIP status level, e-mail address, negotiated rate code, comments and preferences, and membership number, if any. A company/ travel agent profile may include different characteristics, such as the company name, contact, addressing information, preferred correspondence language, preferred currency, e-mail addresses, industry code, volume of business, and negotiated rate codes. Group profiles are created to handle group events (conventions, meetings, parties, and weddings).

A group profile is distinguished from a company profile in that groups usually book for a specific time period, do not have standing rates, and do not have an ongoing relationship with the property or chain. Profile relationships are established between and among individuals, companies, groups, and travel agents for general information and to aid customer service. As usual, profile data are stored in the data store, by deploying various database management systems based property management systems (PMSs) with reservations and guest history features enabled. Profile information is updated and changed to reflect the customer's current data or status. Profiles are essential to the property management, as they provide information about the customers and companies who visit the property and how they use it (such as revenue generated). Profiles are used to analyze customer data, and target service to them.

References

Baker, S., Bradley, P., and Huyton, J. (1994) *Principles of Hotel Front Office Operations*. New York: Cassell.

O'Connor, P. (2003) *Using Computers in Hospitality*, 3rd edn. London: Continuum International.

DAVID INANEISHVILI
HOTEL KÄMP, FINLAND

Guest safety

Within the lodging sector of the hospitality industry, guest safety is a primary concern. This is also a concern in foodservice operations. Safety focuses on prevention of accidents or injuries.

Slips or falls are a major source of injury to the guest. Slips and falls may occur in the parking lot, on the walkways and roadways surrounding the lodging facility, in the entryway, lobby, food and beverage service units, public areas, meeting rooms, public restrooms, guestrooms, and guest bathrooms. Serious injuries may also be sustained in falls on stairways and escalators.

Under the category of 'bumped by or against,' guests may be struck by wheeled equipment (maid carts, luggage carts, food carts, golf carts, etc.), or by bumping against display units, building fixtures and features which are not properly 'highlighted.'

Staff must be trained to be more aware of conditions that could cause an accident and resultant injury to a guest, to another employee, or to the general public. While trite, the slogans continue to be relevant:

If you drop it, pick it up!
If you spill it, wipe it up!

Soap products must never be used for cleaning walking surfaces. An approved floor treatment product should be used. In inclement weather, mats should be promptly placed in entry and lobby areas and a mopping schedule must be maintained. There should be a regularly scheduled cleaning of public restrooms with a posted notation of the time of service.

In the event of an accident, a full report must be prepared with full detail as to time, the alleged cause of the incident, and the alleged injuries sustained. Witness statements and identification should be obtained and pictures when possible. Weather conditions, condition of footwear, clothing age, bifocals, or walking surface hazards should also be noted. The report must be brief, accurate, dated, and signed and without editorial comment by the reporter.

Reference

Ellis, Raymond C. and Stipanuk, David M. (1999) *Security and Loss Prevention Management*, 2nd edn. Lansing, MI: Educational Institute of the American Hotel and Motel Institute.

RAYMOND CLINTON ELLIS, JR
UNIVERSITY OF HOUSTON, USA

Guestroom floor configurations

It is important to plan guestroom floor configurations to determine an efficient floor plan for hotel guestrooms. Three common guestroom floor configurations are:

1. Slab configurations
2. Tower configurations
3. Atrium configurations.

In slab configurations, a single-loaded slab, where guestrooms are laid out on a single side of a central corridor, is suitable for narrow sites or for taking advantage of views. A double-loaded slab, where rooms are laid out on both sides of a central corridor, offers the most efficient options for elevator cores, exit stairs, and service functions, while offset-slabs offer interior core efficiency and more variety for facades. Tower configurations comprise a central core surrounded by a single-loaded corridor of guestrooms. Their exterior architectural treatment depends on the geometric shape of the plan. In an atrium configuration, first introduced by architect John Portman for the Hyatt Regency Atlanta in 1967, the guestrooms are arranged along single-loaded corridors, encircling a multi-storey lobby space. Most atrium hotels feature glass-enclosed elevators that allow hotel guests to overlook the hotel lobby. Many atrium designs are irregularly shaped to respond to various site constraints. Generally, the double-loaded slab is the most efficient, with about 70% of the gross floor area devoted to guestrooms, while the saleable space drops to 65 and 60%, respectively, in tower and atrium configurations.

Reference

Rutes, W.A., Penner, R.H., and Adams, L. (2001) *Hotel Design, Planning, and Development*. Oxford: Architectural Press.

ERIC S.W. CHAN
THE HONG KONG POLYTECHNIC
UNIVERSITY, HONG KONG SAR, CHINA

Guestroom occupancy sensors

There are three types on the market: infrared, ultrasonic, and a combination of both technologies. These devices detect the presence of people in a guestroom and are linked to the heating, refrigeration, and ventilation equipment that services the guest's room. They may also be linked to security and housekeeping functions, but their primary function is as an energy-saving device. When the guest is in the room, that guest has the ability to control the room's temperature through a thermostat in the room.

However, when the guest leaves, the occupancy sensor sends a signal to the heating and cooling system to move from a 'set point' temperature (i.e., guest-selected temperature) to a 'setback' temperature (i.e., a temperature the hotel has selected). This setback temperature is typically only 6–8 degrees Fahrenheit (3–4.5 degrees Celsius) from the guest's set point temperature. The moment the guest returns, the occupancy sensor notes the return and instantly the set point temperature is reinstated. The guest may note a slightly higher temperature in the room in the summer or a slightly lower temperature in the winter, but hearing the fan start up, assumes that the unit is just starting its cooling/heating cycle.

Reference

Stipanuk, D.M. (2002) *Hospitality Facilities Management and Design*, 2nd edn . Lansing, MI: Educational Institute of American Hotel and Lodging Association. pp. 242–245.

TOM JONES
UNIVERSITY OF NEVADA, LAS VEGAS, USA

H

HACCP (hazard analysis of critical control points)

HACCP is a program developed by the United States Food and Drug Administration early in the 1990s for the purpose of eliminating the contamination of food as it is produced, processed, and distributed to consumers. It is designed to be a 'farm-to-fork' approach for ensuring the safety of the food supply.

The general definitions of the terms central to HACCP, according to the NRA, are as follows: *Hazards* include microorganisms that can be grown at any point during the food production process (including storage and including those microorganisms or toxins that survive heating); chemicals that can contaminate food, food-contact surfaces, or food-handling utensils; physical objects not intended for consumption that enter food. A *critical control point* is any operation or process point (such as a preparation step or procedure) where a preventative or control measure can be applied effectively such that it eliminates, removes, or prevents a hazard.

The HACCP program is based on the identification, control, and elimination of food safety hazards through proven scientific methods at critical control points in the process. 'A critical control point is defined as a step at which control can be applied and is essential to prevent or eliminate a food safety hazard or reduce it to an acceptable level' (FDA, 2004).

In order to begin the process of developing an HACCP plan, the FDA (2004) suggests completion on the part of an operator of the following five preliminary tasks: assemble an HACCP team; describe the food and its distribution; describe the intended use and consumers of the food; develop a flow diagram that describes the process; and verify the flow diagram. Because developing an effective HACCP plan requires specialized expertise, operators are well advised to enlist local health department officials onto the HACCP team to help guide the process.

Upon completion of the preliminary steps, seven HACCP principles are applied. The University of Arizona cooperative Extension (2003) outlines those seven principles:

1. Analyze hazards. Potential hazards associated with a food and measures to control those hazards are identified. The hazard could be biological, such as a microbe; chemical, such as a toxin; or physical, such as ground glass or metal fragments.

2. Identify critical control points. These are points in a food's production, from its raw state through processing and shipping to consumption by the consumer, at which the potential hazard can be controlled or eliminated. Examples are cooking, cooling, packaging, and metal detection.

3. Establish preventive measures with critical limits for each control point. For a cooked food, this might include setting the minimum cooking temperature and time required to ensure the elimination of any harmful microbes.

4. Establish procedures to monitor the critical control points. Such procedures might include determining how and by whom

cooking time and temperature should be monitored.

5. Establish corrective actions to be taken when monitoring shows that a critical limit has not been met; for example, reprocessing or disposing of food if the minimum cooking temperature is not met.
6. Establish procedures to verify that the system is working properly. For example, testing time- and temperature-recording devices to verify that a cooking unit is working properly.
7. Establish effective record-keeping documenting the HACCP system. This would include recording of hazards and their control methods, the monitoring of safety requirements and action taken to correct potential problems.

Each of these principles must be backed by sound scientific knowledge, such as published microbiological studies on time and temperature factors for controlling foodborne pathogens.

After completing an HACCP review, a written plan is formulated identifying each of the control points within the operation and clearly outlining the procedures required to reduce or eliminate the risk of contamination to the food.

To maintain an HACCP program effectively, management must be very diligent in its execution and follow up. Constant training and retraining of employees is imperative to prevent breakdowns in the process. This can be aided by thoughtful integration of HACCP in all aspects of the operation. This may include standardized recipes that are written with HACCP in mind and receiving practices that integrate HACCP.

References

FDA (Food and Drug Administration) (2004) *Hazard Analysis and Critical Control Point Principles and Application Guidelines*. Available at http://vm.cfsan.fda.gov/~comm/nacmcfp.html. Accessed 12 March 2004.

National Restaurant Association (1995) *Serving Safe Food*. Washington, DC: National Restaurant Association.

University of Arizona Cooperative Extension (2004) HACCP. Available at http://ag.arizona.edu/maricopa/fcs/haccp/about.htm. Accessed 7 April 2003.

NANCY SWANGER
WASHINGTON STATE UNIVERSITY, USA

Hardware

The physical parts of a computer system, including electrical, electronic, magnetic, optical, and mechanical components. It is divided into machines (computers, displays, disk drives, keyboards) and media (floppy disks, optical disks, plastic cards). Hardware components of a computer are organized into two different structures: the central processing unit (CPU) and the peripheral devices. The central processing unit is built from a control unit that controls the execution of instructions, an arithmetic-logic unit that executes specific instructions, and a primary storage unit for immediate data and program holding. Peripheral devices are used for data and command input, output of information and secondary storage. Hardware devices include: palm devices, notebooks and desktop personal computers, mainframe computers, and different specific devices, which contain a processor. Peripherals are divided into input devices (keyboard, mouse, track ball, joystick, graphic tablet, light pen, touch-sensitive screen, bar code reader, optical character recognition devices, voice recognition devices, tills in restaurants), output devices (display, printer, plotter, microfiche), permanent storage devices (magnetic: hard and floppy disks; optical disks: CD and DVD). Beside office equipment, hardware serves a number of functions in hospitality: air conditioning, lighting, security. What is built upon the hardware is a program called the operating system that controls how the computer system works as a whole, and specific software, which solves particular problems.

References

Collins, G.R. and Malik, T. (1999) *Hospitality Information Technology: Learning How to Use It*. Dubuque, IA: Kendall/Hunt Publishing.

Zhou, Z. (2003) *e-Commerce and Information Technology in Hospitality and Tourism.* Clifton Park, NY: Delmar Publishers.

BOZIDAR KLICEK
UNIVERSITY OF ZAGREB, CROATIA

Haute cuisine ('High cookery')

The *Oxford English Dictionary* defines haute cuisine as cookery of a high standard, especially of the French traditional school. In this context, the term is often used to describe the classical French cuisine – *cuisine classique*, as prescribed by the great maître chef Auguste Escoffier in his classic work *Guide Culinaire*. It can be argued that Escoffier's *Guide Culinaire* is still the authoritative work on haute cuisine, which often requires an elaborate and skillful manner of preparing food. However, to have some understanding of the evolution of haute cuisine, at least in France, it is important to look back to the 1500s, and more specifically to Catherine de' Medici, 1519–89, the wife (1533) of the duc d'Orléans, who later became King Henry II of France. Catherine came to France from Italy and was the daughter of Lorenzo de' Medici, Duke of Urbino, a wealthy and powerful family. Despite her young age, when she went to France she took with her her entire household, which included some of the finest chefs in Europe at the time. Thus, it was Catherine de' Medici who introduced high-class cuisine to France.

Long after Catherine, great chefs like Antonin Carême, Jules Gouffé, and Urbian Dubois were instrumental in the development of complex French cuisine, which Escoffier simplified and refined at the turn of the nineteenth century. Most chefs today define haute cuisine as a culinary practice following a high standard that requires detailed, artistic, and expert preparation and presentation of food.

Reference

Cracknell, H.L. and Kaufmann, R.J. (2000) *The Complete Guide to the Art of Modern Cookery: The First Translation into English in Its Entirety of 'Le Guide Culinaire.'* New York: John Wiley & Sons.

JAKSA KIVELA
THE HONG KONG POLYTECHNIC
UNIVERSITY, HONG KONG SAR, CHINA

Health codes

Health codes are standards that have been developed to promote food safety and sanitation. Local health department officials enforce these codes during regular unannounced inspections of food-related businesses. The purpose of the inspections is to ensure that operators are following health codes in order to protect the public from practices that could result in foodborne illness. These codes not only regulate food handling, but also include specifications for facilities and equipment.

In general, inspectors evaluate the procedures for processing and handling food and the temperatures at which products are cooked, cooled, held, stored, and reheated. More specifically, health codes (NCDHD, 2004) may address areas dealing with:

- The general condition of food
- Storage conditions for potentially hazardous foods
- Proper food storage equipment
- Cross-contamination of foods
- The use of gloves when handling food or ice
- Employee hygiene – particularly hand washing
- Construction of food contact surfaces
- Chemical and mechanical sanitizing for dishwashing/surface cleaning
- The temperature and source of water
- Sewage
- Plumbing
- Properly stocked hand washing and toilet facilities
- Pest control
- Storage of toxic items.

An example of a health code would be the requirement to hold food at a temperature below 40 °F (4 °C) or above 140 °F (60 °C) to prevent the growth of bacteria.

Critical violations of health codes known to cause foodborne illness must be addressed within a certain amount of time – usually 10 days – after which a follow-up inspection is conducted to document and verify correction of the stated violations. If violations are severe enough at the time of the initial inspection or are not corrected by the date specified, the health official has the right to close down the establishment immediately in an effort to protect the public.

In the United States, inspections documenting violations of health codes are a matter of public record and many jurisdictions now have them available via the Internet. Some municipalities also incorporate a grading system and require that foodservice operations post their 'grade.' In Clark County, Nevada, for example, the health district conducts random inspections of local restaurants. An establishment receives an A grade if it has received no more than 10 demerits. A B grade is given to those establishments that receive 11 to 20 demerits, and a C grade is given to any establishment that receives 21 to 40 demerits. If an establishment receives more than 40 demerits, it is closed immediately. The grades are posted at the time of the inspection. The establishment has the option of requesting a reinspection before its next scheduled inspection.

An example from recent inspections in Clark County that resulted in the closure of an operation included violations such as a restaurant that did not have hot water. Another closure resulted from inadequate housekeeping practices that led to egregious pest and rodent infestation. Other violations, while not resulting in closure, are less common. For example, one operator was caught bringing food from the freezer located in his home's garage. Another used the three-compartment sink – normally used to wash dishes – as a soaking bin to defrost frozen poultry.

Health codes are developed by the state, county, or city responsible (depending on the locale). The respective codes are generally crafted using the Food and Drug Administration's 'Model Food Code.' The most recent version of this model, incorporating HACCP-based principles, was written specifically with foodservice operations in mind and is widely considered the best source of related information. The Model Food Code is not law, however, and there is no legislation that municipalities must use it. Nonetheless, most agencies find the code useful and adopt substantial portions of it to ensure uniformity across geographic boundaries. This also aids chain restaurant operators to conform more readily.

Specifically, the code offers recommendations on such topics as:

- Proper cooking temperatures for meat and fish
- Holding temperatures – including those for chilled items and items served hot
- Consumer advisories for raw or undercooked foods
- Methodologies related to the inspection of foodservice-operations
- Training guidelines for restaurant health inspectors
- Standards for refrigeration and dishwasher equipment.

Many argue that there is no adequate single set of health codes. The challenge is that too often the codes – regardless of their form or authorship – are subject to some degree of interpretation. Such subjectivity places the foodservice operator in a difficult position since violations may lead to financial penalties and loss in business even when the operator attempts to follow the respective code fully. Furthermore, a code may specify a certain practice that is not practical in a given situation and for which there is a better approach. Ultimately, however, the primary function of any health code and the responsibility of every foodservice operator is to protect public health.

Reference

NCDHD (North Central District Health Department) (2004) Food Inspection Violations Glossary. Available at http://www.ncdhd.us/food/glossary.html. Accessed 10 March 2004.

NANCY SWANGER
WASHINGTON STATE UNIVERSITY, USA

Hearing conservation

The term hearing conservation refers to implemented programs in the workplace designed to protect employees against hearing loss precipitated by exposure to high noise levels over an extended period of time.

The US Occupational Safety and Health Act mandates that employers must have a Hearing Protection Program (CFR 1910.95) implemented in any work environment that produces noise levels in excess of 85 decibels (db) over a time-weighted average of 8 hours.

The hearing protection program specifics mandate that employers must measure any work-site thought to produce high noise levels and implement a Hearing Protection Program when the 85 db limit is exceeded. The program (at a minimum) must consist of:

- Audiometric annual exams to include baseline tests
- Audiometric evaluation
- Engineering controls to lessen noise production (when noise levels are above 90 db)
- The issuance of personal protective equipment
- Employee training
- Record-keeping.

Reference

Noise and Hearing Conservation (n.d.) http://osha.gov/SLTC/noisehearingconservation/index.html.

JERRY LACHAPPELLE
HARRAH'S ENTERTAINMENT, INC., USA

Heat detectors

A heat detector responds to hot smoke and fire gases and is a component of a fire detection system. The three types of heat detectors are rate-of-rise, fixed temperature, and rate compensation. Rate-of-rise detectors react to rapid increases in the temperature, which activates the fire alarm. The actual temperature is not a factor so a slow-burning fire could go undetected unless a fixed temperature heat detector is also used. The fixed temperature detector contains a fusible element that melts rapidly at a set temperature and activates the fire alarm. Rate compensation detectors combine the techniques used for the fixed temperature and rate-of-rise detectors. If the air temperature is rising slowly, less than 40 degrees per minute, the detector will respond when the air temperature matches the rated temperature. If the air temperature is rising quickly, the detector responds based on the temperature rate-of-rise. These units are appropriate when temperatures normally fluctuate within a range and where a fixed temperature is critical. The unit will trigger a response based on either rate-of-rise or a preset temperature.

Reference

Puchovsky, M. (2000) A brief introduction to sprinkler systems for Life Safety Code users. In R. Cote (ed.), *Life Safety Code Handbook*. Quincy, MA: National Fire Protection Association, pp. 967–980.

CAROLYN LAMBERT
PENNSYLVANIA STATE UNIVERSITY, USA

High-tech high-touch

The hospitality and tourism industry is becoming more technology orientated due to Web-integrated technologies being used to improve customer relationships, streamline business processes, reduce paperwork, increase access to information and enhance productivity. Technology assists hotels to store, process, manipulate, and distribute information, formulating a high-tech environment. In order to meet the changing consumer requirements and to satisfy their needs, hotels use high-tech to provide personalized, value-added, real-time and high-quality services (high-touch) (Poon, 1993). The more high-tech the hospitality and tourism industry becomes the more consumers will expect real experience, high-touch or highly tailored individualized personalized service (Reiman, 2002). Hotel chains can use their systems to collect information about personal preferences and ensure that these are respected in future visits or other properties, increasing guests' appreciation and loyalty.

Although information technology cannot create competitive advantages or be a substitute for efficient employees, it can be used as a tool to create differentiation and assist employees to enhance service quality and customer satisfaction. The hospitality industry needs to focus on technologies that enhance the guest experience. This in turn can create customer satisfaction and ultimately provide a key source for gaining competitive advantage and business success.

References

Buhalis, D. (2003) *eTourism*. London: Pearson.

Poon, A. (1993) *Tourism Technology and Competitive Strategies*. Wallingford: CAB International.

Reiman, S. (2002) e-Stuff: in the rush for high tech, have we forgotten the high touch? *Interactive Marketing*, 3 (3), 218–229.

DIMITRIOS BUHALIS
UNIVERSITY OF SURREY, UK
CATHERINE COLLINS
UNIVERSITY OF SURREY, UK

Hiring crunch

The hiring crunch in the hospitality industry involves selecting individuals not only on merit but subject to other constraints such as skills availability, competition, and being able to manage high levels of turnover in the workforce. This is a challenge in an industry characterized by skilled labor shortages and a transient workforce. Rutherford (2002) states that the goal of selection is not to hire the best-qualified employee, but rather to hire the best employee for the job. The important point here is to match prospective employees to the organization and the job within the broader hospitality labor market context. Once these sometimes competing objectives have been satisfied, the hiring decision according to Tanke (2001) becomes a mere formality if job analysis, recruitment, and selection process have been dutifully carried out.

Consideration of the 'hire objective,' the job candidate's temperament, energy level, and emotional intelligence will help facilitate the hiring decision. However, hospitality managers also need to factor in other relatively uncontrollable issues before selection, such as staff reliability

and commitment. Indeed in the seasonal sector, many small to medium-sized hospitality firms employ staff using only a few selection criteria with 'availability' being key. Alternatively, some managers elect to use 'agency' workers during periods of high demand.

References

Rutherford, D.G. (2002) *Hotel Management and Operations*, 3rd edn. New York: John Wiley & Sons.

Tanke, M.L. (2001) *Human Resource Management for the Hospitality Industry*, 2nd edn. Melbourne: Delmar Thomson Learning.

ASAD MOHSIN
UNIVERSITY OF WAIKATO, NEW ZEALAND

Homeowners association

When a timeshare developer sells all or at least a majority (usually around 80% or 90% of all available inventory) of the timeshare units, ownership of the resort changes hands from the developer to that of a homeowners association (HOA). It should be understood that the exact point of changeover is mandated by state statute. At this point of turnover the homeowners' association elects a board of directors from the existing ownership base. The officers and directors of an association have a fiduciary relationship to the members who are served by the association. The powers and duties of an association include appropriate maintenance of the timeshare resort and proper tracking and investment of existing funds as collected through maintenance fees and annual member assessments. This definition clearly means that the homeowners association is charged with general interior maintenance, exterior maintenance, and upkeep of the resort grounds. However, it is much more likely that the board of directors will hire an outside management company to operate the resort, collect maintenance fees, etc.; sometimes the developer maintains management rights. The primary reason for delegating out this management function is that the owners commonly don't have the proper training in property management. Therefore, it is much more logical to outsource the property management function to a fully qualified management firm.

References

http://www.thetimesharebeat.com/glossary.htm. Accessed 27 January 2003.

http://www.flsenate.gov/Statutes/index.cfm? App_mode=Display_Statute&Search_String =&URL=Ch0720/SEC301.HTM&Title= ->2003->Ch0720->Section percent20301. Accessed 27 January 2003.

PIMRAWEE ROCHUNGSRAT
JAMES COOK UNIVERSITY, UK

Hospitality distribution terms and initials

This section provides a list of terms in hospitality distribution and their definitions.

- *ADS:* The terms Internet distribution system (IDS), e-distribution system, and alternative distribution system (ADS) denote the online dispersal and purchase of travel products. They consist of Internet-based reservations networks, which allow information to be instantly available worldwide, bypassing traditional intermediaries such as the GDSs. Travelweb and Hotelbook are examples of an ADS.
- *Brand erosion:* A potential decrease in the importance of brand and customer loyalty attributed to the intensive price-based strategies utilized by online third parties.
- *GDS provider service:* An intermediary between the operators and the switch companies (e.g. Synxis, Lexington). These services are reservation companies that allow suppliers to access the GDSs via the switch. They perform database update and content management services, which include exchanging information between operators and the switch, distributing rates to travel websites, and updating the hotel's online description.

- *Competitive information:* Information on rates, occupancy, RevPAR, and descriptions of hospitality companies, which is gathered by companies, specialized in providing competitive information (e.g. Travelclick). The information is aggregated and then distributed to members or sold as industry reports.
- *Connectivity:* The ability to make and maintain a connection between different systems. There are different levels of this ability. One-way connectivity means that when an entity books a reservation, the information is automatically placed in the PMS. One-and-a-half-way connectivity means that the entity that books the reservation also has the capability to effectuate changes and cancellations in real time. Two-way connectivity implies that in addition to the above the third party receives rates and availability in real time. As technologies develop, connectivity issues should disappear and hospitality systems should interface.
- *Destination management system (DMS):* A system created to cater to the distribution needs of a specific region and/or regional tourism agencies, which includes information for hotel, transportation, restaurants, and other tourism operations and attractions in a given geographical area. Destination management systems may be state or privately funded. These systems may also be called destination databases, destination marketing systems, or visitor information systems.
- *Electronic distribution system (EDS):* In hospitality, an electronic distribution system involves the electronic dispersal and purchase of travel products. The term embraces the global distribution systems, switches, and Internet distribution channels.
- *Hotel Distribution System (HDS):* Hotel Distribution System, LLC, normally referred to by the initials HDS, is a venture of Hilton Hotels Corporation, Hyatt Hotels, Marriott Hotels, Resorts and Suites, Six Continents Hotels, Starwood Hotels, and Pegasus. According to a Pegasus article (Pegasus solutions . . . , n.d.), HDS plans to provide Internet sites with the ability to sell hotel rooms at net rates via direct connections to hotel central reservations systems.

- *IDS:* See ADS above.
- *Links:* These are icons that possess the ability to direct an individual from one Web address to another. There are sites that simply provide links to operators' reservation pages. Examples are travelzoo.com and travelaxe.com. Operationally, these sites function as online advertising tools. Their look, however, is very similar to that of other travel service sites. In order to effectuate a booking, the customer clicks on a link and is directed to the supplier's site or to another intermediary site. They compete in the same markets as Internet distribution channels.
- *Rate parity:* The uniformity of retail rates across different channels of distribution that provide the same product. For example, a standard room for two nights, arrival on 29 January for two people, should be sold at the same price at a proprietary site, at a third party wholesaler, or through a GDS. If the same product was sold with different restrictions (e.g. non-refundable, non-transferable, or fully pre-paid), a different price could be applied to that product without affecting rate parity.
- *Rate integrity:* The trust in the fair price of a hospitality product. It is usually achieved when customers believe they would not find lower prices for a given product through other channels.
- *Rate transparency:* The perfect knowledge of the price for a specific hospitality product, due to the customer's ability to shop for rates across channels. The concept of rate transparency is similar to the concept of perfect information in economic theory.
- *Rate cannibalization:* A dilution in rates due to an increased rate transparency and a lack of rate parity. It occurs when customers shop for the same product through different channels and book at the lowest rate encountered, even though they would have booked at higher rates. In other words, there is demand for higher price levels. Rate cannibalization causes a decrease in revenues without increasing demand.
- *Onward distribution:* The dispersal of rates through a variety of distribution channels such as the GDSs and Internet sites.

- *Priority listing:* The order in which a website appears in a search engine listing. One of the strategies utilized by suppliers and third party sites in order to increase booking is to ensure that their sites have priority listing in the travel-related Web searches.
- *Rate erosion:* A term mainly used in online distribution to designate the decrease in rates caused by price-based selling strategies.
- *Seamless:* Seamless connectivity occurs when all the links in the distribution channel have access to the same inventory data. In order for this to happen, all systems have to be integrated and the information has to be updated in real time. In other words, there must be a two-way connectivity.
- *Switch:* An electronic device that enables different systems to communicate. This distribution technology links the CRS to the other channels, such as the global distribution systems, websites, corporate travel agents, tour operators and wholesalers, representation services, and property management system services. Large corporations may develop their own switch technology to access the GDSs, avoiding switch fees (e.g. The Marriott and Priceline). Most hotel companies, however, hire switch companies (e.g. Pegasus and Wizcom), which may also provide related activities such as reservation, representation, and financial services.
- *GDS provider:* A general term that refers to the entity that provides a hospitality company access to the global distribution systems, which may be the GDSs themselves, switch companies, or reservation companies. For example, an operator may select the GDS Worldspan to be its sole GDS provider, or contract Pegasus, which provides access to the main GDSs (Worldspan, Sabre, Amadeus, and Galileo), or a reservation company, such a Synxis, which uses the Pegasus switch to distribute inventory to the GDSs.

Reference

Pegasus solutions finalizes technology agreement with new online hotel discount venture HDS (n.d). Retrieved 15 May 2004 from http://www.pegs.com/newsroom/press/2002/040402.htm.

FLAVIA HENDLER
UNIVERSITY OF NEVADA, LAS VEGAS, USA
ROM HENDLER
VENETIAN RESORT HOTEL AND CASINO,
LAS VEGAS, USA

Hospitality strategic management

The term strategy is derived from the military, as part of war relations between nations and communities. Management theory adapted the term to competitive business situations between firms in terms of economic, technological or managerial dimensions. The meaning of strategy in the organizational context involves an amalgam of decisions, characterized by unique features, aimed at reaching the goals of the organization. Clearly, the desire to succeed in business and avoid failure requires formulation of strategies that determine exactly what the organization wants to achieve and what means are required to achieve these goals. It should be noted that in corporate strategy, not unlike military strategy, the actors may choose to cooperate rather than to be involved in head-on conflict. The literature offers numerous definitions of organizational strategy. It appears that common to all definitions is the realization that strategy involves significant decisions that can be detrimental to the future of the organizations. Additionally, these decisions always involve resource allocations and cannot be changed immediately or in the short term. As it emerges from the research, a more detailed definition of strategy includes the design and formulation of the goals and objectives of the entire organization, allocation of the resources needed to achieve these goals and the organizational processes dealing with the implementation of the decisions. A successful strategy is one that enhances the value of the organization in the long run through the development of sustainable competitive advantage. This advantage can be achieved if the organization manages to position itself in a preferred position in the competitive arena, often through the accumulation of unique resources.

According to Olsen and Roper (1998), the bulk of research on strategy in the hospitality industry has been of two types: Early work was, for the most part, conceptual, strategy-related models, developed in other sectors and applied to the hospitality industry, without empirical investigation actually being conducted. The second line of research was more empirical in nature, relying on hypotheses and frequently employed survey research methods. Several exploratory case studies were employed as well, resulting in the formulation of propositions that encouraged further research and theory building.

The conceptual, strategy-related approach can also be classified as normative, in the sense that the application of the concept to the tourism or hospitality organization, similar to all types of profit-making organizations, will significantly increase the likelihood of successful performance. Often, this normative approach is associated with what is known as the Harvard model. Over the years the model evolved into a process that includes the following stages or steps as applied to the hospitality industry. The first stage is determining the corporate vs. business level objectives and goals. This requires setting the hospitality corporate objectives, preferably in terms of explicit, measurable financial measures that determine the corporate future direction. Then the objectives of each hotel in the chain or profit center (or strategic business unit) are set, with an attempt to contribute to the attainment of corporate goals. The selection of goals and objectives is not trivial, particularly in the case of new entrepreneurial hospitality businesses (see for example, Haber and Reichel, 2004). The second stage involves examining the external environment of the hotel chain or of each property individually. Considerable attention has been given to this stage, generally with reference to environmental scanning and to threat vs. opportunity analysis. According to Harrison (2003), in the broad environment the hospitality industry has five major components: societal trends and influences, economic factors, technological advances, political and legal trends and influences, and major innovations in other industries.

Information on each component is expected to be used to create competitive advantage. Furthermore, the task environment includes external stakeholders with which the organization interacts, such as customers and suppliers.

Environmental scanning (ES) involves monitoring and forecasting the trends in the environment that are expected to affect the organization either directly or indirectly. It means that executives in the hospitality industry search, gather, and analyze relevant information either as an integral part of their job, or as members of a formal environmental scanning unit. According to Okumus (2004), ES appears to be the most written-about area in the field of strategic hospitality management. Yet, the often recommended formal model of ES for the hospitality industry fails to deliver the expected contribution to organizational performance. Okumus argues that hospitality organizations should not form formal ES units or recruit personnel specifically for this task, before critically evaluating the potential cultural and political problems and implications. Thus, 'everybody in a hospitality organization should be responsible for ES and try to continually identify and evaluate the patterns emerging within and outside the company' (p. 139). The main purpose of gathering environmental information is to distinguish between trends that are viewed as opportunities and trends that are seen as threats. This interpretation of trends is conducted from the viewpoint of the particular organization, be it a hotel chain or a particular hotel or subunit within the hospitality organization. An opportunity is a trend interpreted as positive or helpful in attaining the organization's goals and objectives. In contrast, a threat, as implied by the term, constitutes a potential threat to the attainment of the goals, or even to the survival of the organization. This distinction, often known as OT analysis, seems simple and straightforward. However, its application is often complex, mainly due to trends that can be analyzed simultaneously as opportunities and threats, and the inability often to predict environmental trends, particularly in today's turbulent geopolitical environment. Moreover, it is not always clear what trends are relevant to each hospitality organization. The issue of selecting the appropriate trends for data gathering and analysis is determined according to human judgment rather than by an objective mathematical model.

One of the most influential models in strategic management, as suggested by Porter (1985), relies heavily on the analysis of the organization within its environment, in this case, the industry. According to Porter, one of the crucial determinants of firm profitability is industrial attractiveness. In any industry, whether domestic or international, whether relating to products or services, the rules of competition are embodied in five competitive forces: entry of new competitors, threat of substitutes, bargaining power of buyers, bargaining power of suppliers, and rivalry among the existing competitors. The collective strengths of these five competitive forces determine the ability of firms in an industry to earn rates of return on investment in excess of the cost of capital due to their influence on the prices, costs, and required investment of firms in an industry. Yet, despite unfavorable industry structure, a firm may position itself well and may earn high rates of return through sustainable competitive advantage.

The next step in the normative model of strategic management involves the organizational internal environment analysis. This often includes gathering information about physical, financial, human, knowledge and learning, and organizational resources. Traditionally, the organizational internal environment was analyzed in terms of resources constituting the organizational strengths (S) in relation to its competitors vs. resources that manifest the organization's weaknesses (W). The contribution of analyzing internal resources and capabilities is also manifested in Barney's (1995) Resource Based Value theory (RBV). According to RBV, an organization can formulate a competitive strategy to achieve sustainable competitive advantage by gaining unique resources that cannot be obtained or duplicated by its competitors. As such, a hotel that enjoys a unique location and a stable, loyal high-quality personnel, as well as a long-established and solid quality image and positioning, can easily achieve and maintain competitive edge *vis-à-vis* other hotels in the relevant market segment that cannot imitate or gain such resources and capabilities. The two dimensions of environmental analysis, internal and external, serve as the basis for one of the most widely utilized concepts in organizational strategic management: SWOT analysis. The four cells of the models coherently depict the combination between environmental trends and organizational resources and capabilities. The normative approach calls for the adoption of a strategy that takes advantage of both the organization's strengths and the environmental opportunities.

At this point, a distinction is often made between the formulation of business level strategies and corporate level strategies. According to Harrison and Enz (2005), the most widely used business level strategies are the four generic strategies suggested by Porter (1985): overall cost leadership, overall differentiation, cost focus, and differentiation focus. Etap and Motel 6, both Accor subsidiaries, pursue overall cost leadership, while Marriot and Hilton are offered as examples of differentiation strategy. Harrison and Enz (2005) further argue that a focus strategy emphasizing lowest cost would be rare in the hospitality industry. Focus through differentiation is exemplified in the Four Seasons chain.

Corporate level strategies include concentration on a single business or market segment, vertical integration, related and unrelated diversifications, and mergers and acquisitions. Concentration strategy allows the organization to specialize in a single business and be in a better position to develop resources and capabilities to establish a sustainable competitive advantage. Yet, in the hospitality case, it entails a high dependency on changes in the tastes of guest segments and demand patterns. Vertical integration, aimed to control high transactions costs or create a barrier to entry, was not found to be a highly profitable strategy relative to other corporate level strategies (Harrison and Enz, 2005). Related or concentric diversification as applied to hospitality organizations is based on similarities among products, services or markets that are supposed to lead to synergy. Unrelated or conglomerate diversification requires expertise in numerous businesses in addition to hospitality and constitutes a considerable challenge from a managerial

perspective. Unfortunately, research does not indicate consistent positive results of such an ambitious strategy. Mergers and acquisitions are considered as a relatively rapid method of pursuing growth or diversification. In essence, most mergers are acquisitions of one organization by another, frequently leading to mixed results.

Although most of the aforementioned strategies are considered 'competitive' and assume a constant threat either from new entrants to the industry or from established competitors, research in hospitality management indicates that numerous organizations adopt cooperative strategies, generally in the form of strategic alliances. Cooperative business arrangements include licensing, R & D partnerships, technology transfers, franchising, and joint ventures. According to Preble, Reichel and Hoffman (2000) alliances offer hospitality organizations direct benefits, including quick access to new markets, internationalization, knowledge, circumvention or cooptation of regulatory barriers and lowering risk through shared costs and benefits from a partner's political connections. Often, alliances enable partner organizations to quickly gain economies of scale without considerable investment. In sum, strategic alliances must provide the partners with superior resources and/or skills they would not otherwise possess. Key resources obtained by hospitality organizations through alliances may include location, brand name, and customer base.

Once a strategy is formulated, whether at the business or corporate level, the process of implementation is detrimental to its success. According to Harrison and Enz (2005), strategy implementation is conducted through two main dimensions: The first is interorganizational relationships and management of functional resources. Interorganizational relationships basically refer to partnerships that include the aforementioned strategic alliances as well as mergers and acquisitions. The second dimension refers to organizational design and control. Basic organizational theory concepts such as formalization, specialization, and hierarchy of authority are some of the issues that have to be taken into consideration in adopting and designing the appropriate organizational structure and control method. In addition to interorganizational and organizational forms and controls, behavioral aspects have a significant role as either facilitators or barriers to successful implementation. Clearly, resistance to change can have a negative impact on strategy implementation. Non-compatible organizational cultures can easily hinder mergers between two or more hotel chains. Given the paramount role of the human resources in hospitality organizations *vis-à-vis* production organizations, service providers can easily affect the effectiveness of a given strategy through their encounter with guests. Even the most systematic and well-designed strategies are susceptible to failure if not appropriately understood or accepted by employees. Internal marketing can ease resistance to change and encourage employee cooperation (Gronroos, 2000).

Finally, most strategic management models emphasize the need for periodic evaluation of the adopted strategy and consideration of either minor or major changes if the organization's goals and objectives have not been met. Most changes are the result of environmental developments or internal processes, often related to availability or scarcity of resources required for the maintenance of the current strategy.

References

Barney, J.B. (1995) Looking inside for competitive advantage. *Academy of Management Executive*, November, 49–61.

Gronroos, C. (2000) *Service Marketing and Management: A Customer Relationship Management Approach*. Chichester: John Wiley & Sons.

Haber, S. and Reichel, R. (2004) Performance measures of small ventures: the case of the tourism industry. *Journal of Small Business Management* (forthcoming).

Harrison, J.S. (2003) Strategic analysis for the hospitality industry. *Cornell Hotel and Restaurant Administration Quarterly*, April, 139–153.

Harrison, S.H. and Enz, C.A. (2005) *Hospitality Strategic Management: Concept and Cases*. Hoboken, NJ: John Wiley & Sons.

Okumus, F. (2004) Potential challenges of employing a formal environmental scanning approach in hospitality organizations. *International Journal of Hospitality Management*, 23, 123–143.

Porter, M.E. (1985) *Competitive Advantage: Creating and Sustaining Superior Performance*. New York: The Free Press.

Preble, J.F., Reichel, A., and Hoffman, R.C. (2000) Strategic alliances for competitive advantage: evidence from Israel's hospitality and tourism industry. *International Journal of Hospitality Management*, 19, 327–341.

Olsen, M.D. and Roper, A. (1998) Research in strategic management in the hospitality industry. *International Journal of Hospitality Management*, 17, 11–124.

ARIE REICHEL
BEN-GURION UNIVERSITY, ISRAEL

Hotel accounting and finance terms

Outlined here are some of the terms used in the accounting cycle of guests.

- *Account allowance:* This is a reduction in a guest account folio for unsatisfactory service, a rebate on a discount voucher or if a correction is to be made to a posting, which has been made the previous day (after the night audit).
- *Account correction:* This is normally made on the same day that a transaction has been posted (before the night audit). It corrects errors that have been made to postings, e.g. if a wrong charge was posted to a room. Depending on the error it can either increase or decrease the guest account balance.
- *Account posting:* When guests make either payments or charges to their accounts the process is known as posting. It is the procedure used to record transactions made by the guests.
- *Account settlement:* This refers to when a guest account folio is brought to a zero balance, i.e. when the guest pays their account. Guests can pay their account in numerous ways, namely: by cash, by credit card, by direct billing arrangement (normally arranged before the guest stay) or a combination of the above.
- *Account transfer:* This involves transferring transactions from one account to another account. An example would be if one guest offers to pay for restaurant charges for another guest; the

posting would have to be transferred from one account to the other account.

- *Average daily rate:* This is the average rate that the hotel gets for rooms sold. It only produces an average rate as the rooms sold range from single to suite rates. The average daily rate is calculated by dividing the total rooms revenue by the total rooms sold.
- *Average rate per guest:* This is the average rate that the hotel gets per guest. Some rooms are double rooms, some are triple, and this rate indicates an average rate that each guest is paid. It is calculated by dividing the total rooms revenue by total number of guests.
- *Average room rate:* This is the same as average daily rate described above.
- *Call accounting system:* This is linked to the hotel computing system. It allows guests to make direct dial phone calls from their room without the assistance of an operator. It records each phone number dialed and the length of the call from guestrooms and posts the amount directly onto the guest account folio.
- *Revenue per available room:* This is used by hotels instead of calculating the yield statistic. It focuses on revenue per available room and is calculated by using either of the following formulae: actual room revenue divided by the number of available rooms; or occupancy percentage multiplied by average daily rate.

References

Abbott, P. and Lewry, S. (1991) *Front Office Procedures, Social Skills and Management.* Oxford: Butterworth-Heinemann.

Kasavana, M.L. and Brooks, R.M. (1995) *Front Office Procedures*, 4th edn. Lansing, MI: Educational Institute American Hotel and Motel Association.

IRENE SWEENEY
INTERNATIONAL HOTEL MANAGEMENT
INSTITUTE SWITZERLAND, SWITZERLAND

Hotel classification

To aptly classify the numerous types of 'lodging products' in today's hospitality environment, it is important to start from a basic presumption that incorporates the few characteristics common to all such products: they are basically 'boxes of air' that are rented to travelers for short periods of time. These boxes of air may appeal to different types of travelers, they may be decorated differently, and they may be in different locations, but most share those common characteristics. Classifying lodging products into similar types then becomes difficult when the number of variables is considered.

Classification variables

One of the first major variables to isolate is the *names* that are used to describe such products. Everyone is familiar with what hotels and motels are; but a resort is still a hotel, as is a lodge, inn, conference center, and even timeshare condos and assisted care facilities can fall under the same rubric.

Another variable refers to the types of *lodging company that operates or owns the property.* There are management companies that may or may not own the hotels, and similarly, there ore 'owning' companies that own and operate the properties. Additionally, there are franchising companies that sell the rights to a hotel's identity, image, and market presence to others. There also companies that link independent operations through a referral network and collections of independent properties that form a membership organization to afford them the same sorts of advantages the chain hotels enjoy.

The list that follows outlines the majority of these sorts of operators:

- *Independent hotels* (essentially, 'It's all mine!! And I operate it')
- *Chain hotels* (a regional, national or international series of similarly named hotels, regardless of ownership). These are usually:
  - Parent company hotels (where the company owns them)
  - Management contract hotels (someone else owns them, you may manage them)
  - Franchised hotels (you are the owner and 'rent' the name to someone else to operate). Cendant Corporation with more than

6000 lodging properties under such brand names as Days Inn, Howard Johnson, Ramada, and Super 8 is the largest of the franchise organizations. Others such as Choice Hotels International, Bass Hotels and Resorts and Hilton Hotels Corporation are also active franchisers and at the same time also have thousands of company-owned and operated properties.

○ Independent chains, referral groups, and branded distribution companies represent organizations that in various ways provide their memberships with many of the same benefits the large chains enjoy, mainly in terms of marketing, purchasing, and reservations.

Hotels can also be classified by the variable of which *type* of hotel they most resemble. Most of us can distinguish between a Motel 6 and a Four Seasons hotel just by virtue of the style and scope of construction, location, amenities and service, but what specific purpose do they serve? Both of them could fall under any (or any combination) of the following types:

• Commercial hotels
• Airport hotels
• Conference centers
• Economy properties
• Suite or all-suite hotels
• Residential hotels
• Casino hotels
• Resort hotels
• Bed and breakfast hotels.

This typology by itself can be confusing though, because commercial hotels can also be at airports; as can economies, all-suites, and conference centers. So more variables need to be considered.

Service levels are also commonly used variables used to distinguish hotels. From the bare-bones budget level 'room and a bath' motel with virtually no amenities other than the minimum legally necessary to full service and premium luxury levels, there are hotels with service for every pocketbook.

Perhaps the most useful classification system is that which divides up the lodging world by *brand segmentation*, which captures elements of what the traveler demands in a hotel, what that demand

necessitates in the way of construction, size, décor, service, amenities, personnel, and finally price. What the guest is willing to pay for that 'box of air' helps hotel operators isolate (segment) a category of products that will appeal to that traveler. Remember, the more the traveler wants in a lodging property and the fancier he/she wants the room to be, the more it is going to cost to provide and the higher the price will be. The most widely used brand segments usually are among the following eight:

1. Economy
2. Midscale without food and beverage
3. Midscale with food and beverage
4. Economy extended stay
5. Midscale or upscale extended stay
6. Upscale
7. Upper upscale
8. Premium luxury.

The Marriott Company operates as many as a dozen different types of hotels at the time of writing, that cover most price and service levels in the following list. They also serve the extended stay (or all-suite) market segment as well as the luxury vacation segment, which used to be known as time-share:

• Marriott Hotels Resorts and Suites
• JW Marriott Hotels and Resorts
• Renaissance Hotels and Resorts
• Courtyard by Marriott
• Residence Inn by Marriott
• SpringHill Suites by Marriott
• Fairfield Inn by Marriott
• Marriott Conference Centers
• TownePlace Suites by Marriott
• SpringHill Suites by Marriott
• Marriott Vacation Club International.

Marriott also owns and operates a group of hotels in the premium luxury market segment: the Ritz–Carlton collection of hotels that cater to the wealthy, high-end traveler who demands the utmost in luxury, fine food and beverage, and the absolute tops in service, along with décor and amenities that are not only second to none, but truly unique. You will notice that Marriott does not (as in the above list) tag 'by Marriott' to the brand. This is to keep the exclusivity associated with the Ritz–Carlton name, even though these hotels can benefit from Marriott's systems and management expertise.

A winner of the 1992 Malcolm Baldrige Quality Award, Ritz–Carlton has grown a 'culture of service' among its staff and offers guests a service guarantee that empowers all hotel employees to do whatever it takes to provide 'instant pacification' to guest problems or complaints. This level of service is expensive, and the exclusive image of the Ritz–Carlton is maintained without identification with the parent chain.

As demonstrated here, the classification of hotels can be a complex undertaking, with many variables coming into play. In the final analysis, though, the fundamental similarities of lodging properties lends them to a number of classification schemes that depend substantially on what the traveling public wants in a hotel. So, there can be no one classification scheme to fit all lodging definitions. A hotel can be full service, commercial, at an airport, and have a casino; we can find a number of variables in the lists previously developed that pertain to such an example, but does on word get it all? Probably not. Hotels should be evaluated based on their similarities, not how they might fit into a limited list.

Reference

Guralnik, David B. (1974) *Webster's New World Dictionary*, Second College Edition. Cleveland, NY: The World Publishing Company, p. 263.

DENNEY G. RUTHERFORD
WASHINGTON STATE UNIVERSITY, USA

Hotel consortia

Consortia are groupings of hotels, mostly independently owned, which share corporate costs such as marketing, while retaining independence of ownership and operations. Small businesses face particular problems in competition with large ones. Consortia can be local groups of hotels to promote a destination, or a group of independent non-competing hotels widely distributed geographically. In a 1996 survey reported in Powers and Barrows (1999), working in a consortium meant that in advertising expenditure in the United States, Best Western marketing consortium were fifth in terms of the total amount spent, after such global organizations as Hilton, Holiday Hospitality (now Six Continents), Sheraton, and Hyatt. Such cooperation provides independent hotels with greater visibility and access to a wider consumer base. The largest consortium is REZolutions, with 7700 hotel properties (1.5 million rooms) in 180 countries. This represents 10% of the world's hotel rooms. The organization was formed in 1997 by a merger between Utell International and Anasazi, and is based in Phoenix, Arizona, USA. Europe has 15 out of 25 of the largest consortia, but the United States's 10 represent 50% of the hotels and almost 75% of the world's hotel rooms. One of Europe's best known consortia is Best Western, with 4000 properties in over 100 countries, but the largest is Supranational Hotels, based in London, UK, with 827 hotels and 123,500 rooms. The focus of consortia is marketing, with common reservation systems, quality standards and logos leading to a unified sales effort without a loss of independent identity.

References

HCIMA (2002) *The Hospitality Yearbook*. London: HCIMA.
Medlik, S. and Ingram, H. (2000) *The Business of Hotels*. Oxford: Butterworth-Heinemann.
Powers, T. and Barrows, C.W. (1999) *Introduction to the Hospitality Industry*. New York: John Wiley & Sons.
Vallen, G.K. and Vallen, J.J. (2000) *Check-in Check-out*. Englewood Cliffs, NJ: Prentice-Hall.
Verginis, C.S. and Wood, R.C. (1999) *Accommodation Management*. Oxford: Butterworth-Heinemann.

ERWIN LOSEKOOT
UNIVERSITY OF STRATHCLYDE, UK

Hotel fire fighting team

A hotel fire fighting team, also known as an emergency response team or alarm response team, is established to verify the cause of fire alarms and respond accordingly. Generally, such a team consists of the duty assistant manager, duty engineer, the security officer nearest to the scene, and the assistant housekeeper. Some hotels may include the front office manager and the restaurant manager. The duty assistant manager is usually the team leader, who is responsible for assessing the situation and directing remedial measures. She/he is normally the only member of staff to make the initial decision to evacuate until fire fighters arrive. When notified about the location of the fire alarm from PABX or via the hotel's pager system, the team will rush to the scene and investigate the cause of the alarm. False alarm procedures such as finding the cause, resetting the internal alarm system, and recording the incident are followed if the alarm is verified as false. Upon confirmation of a real fire, apart from trying to put out and control a small supervised fire, the team will instantly notify the fire department and hotel operators for guest inquiries, and allocate duties as needed to other department heads and staff who report to the command post. In case of evacuation, the team will help hotel guests get to the appointed assembly place and carry out a roll call according to established procedures.

Reference

Burstein, H. (2001) *Hotel and Motel Loss Prevention – A Management Perspective.* Englewood Cliffs, NJ: Prentice-Hall.

ERIC S.W. CHAN
THE HONG KONG POLYTECHNIC
UNIVERSITY, HONG KONG SAR, CHINA

Hotel income statement

The income statement is often called a statement of earnings, a profit and loss statement, or a statement of operations. It reports on a period of time and the frequency can be daily, weekly, monthly, quarterly, or annually.

The income statement is used to: determine profitability, state total sales and various costs, and project trends. The key elements of the income statement are: revenue, which includes sale of goods and services; investment income and rental income; expenses, which are outflows to produce goods; cost of goods sold; labor; controllable expenses; and non-controllable expenses. Other gains and losses from incidental transactions or acts of nature are accounted for to get to the period income or loss. Income or loss is added or deducted from equity.

Income statements are prepared using a uniform system of accounts. A uniform system of accounts is a standardized accounting system that is industry-driven. It includes explanations and discussions and allows for comparison between other operations and self or industry averages. A uniform system of accounts can be used by any size operation and is designed for use at the property level.

Analysis of income statements can be done by horizontal analysis (comparative) or vertical analysis (common size). Comparative statements allow for comparing businesses of the same size or the business from different periods and common size statements, expressed in percentage terms, compare businesses of different sizes or to industry averages.

References

Jagels, M.G. and Coltman, M.M. (2003) *Hospitality Management Accounting*, 8th edn. New York: John Wiley & Sons.
Uniform System of Accounts for the Lodging Industry (1996) 9th edn. Lansing, MI: Educational Institute of the American Hotel and Motel Association.

STEPHEN LEBRUTO
UNIVERSITY OF CENTRAL FLORIDA, USA

Hotel management contracts and lease

Hotel management contracts

A management contract is a means by which a hotel operator runs a hotel on behalf of a third party owner. In this arrangement the responsibilities and rewards of owning and operating a hotel are divided in accordance with the contract drawn up between the parties. The owner may be an individual, a financial institution or other corporate body that wishes to own a hotel, usually as a long-term property investment.

The hotel owner typically benefits from the management expertise of the operator in that the latter brings skills and often economies of scale, which would otherwise not be available to an owner attempting to operate the hotel itself.

The benefits to the operator are that:

- It can expand its scope of operations and brand presence with little or no capital outlay.
- It is normally able to defray marketing and central management costs by way of a management charge through its 'base fee' and other charges.
- It further shares in any profits of the hotel alongside the owner.
- The risk and cost of ownership are avoided in part or in total, though, of course, the benefits of such ownership, such as capital gains, are foregone.

The variety of arrangements has, however, changed greatly over time. In the early days of management contracts, the remuneration of the operator consisted of a turnover-based fee and an incentive fee generally based on gross operating profit as defined in the Uniform System of Accounts for the Lodging Industry (1996). Additionally, the owner employed the staff and entered all contracts. Later owners began to realize that this left them with virtually all the risk, from downturns in trade and to the need to incur capital expenditure to maintain standards. Today it is not uncommon to see costs below the GOP level deducted, including insurance costs (previously considered attributable to ownership) and a replacement reserve for furniture and equipment (previously a requirement by the operator to ensure that funds were available, at the owner's expense, to maintain standards). Additionally, the operator may be required to bear a proportion of the capital costs of the building or fitting out itself, often based on the percentage of the profits received under the contract. In some cases the operator may be required to guarantee a minimum return, possibly subject to inflationary growth, to the owner on its invested capital.

In this way the gap between a management contract and a hotel lease is gradually being diminished, particularly as leases moved from a fixed annual rent, to one with a base rent to the owner plus a share of any profits earned above that level.

Hotel leases

Like management contracts, leases separate risks and rewards of the ownership of hotel property from those of its operation. At its simplest the hotel lease involves the owner receiving a fixed rent, usually indexed, over a period of time. The operator would then retain the profits (or losses) remaining after payment of the rent and the owner would be entitled to any capital gains (or losses) accumulating over the length of the lease. During the lease, the owner is normally responsible for structural repairs and the operator for the furniture, fittings, and equipment (FF&E). In this form a lease was similar to that of an office building, with the lessee responsible for general maintenance and the owner for major structural repairs.

The difficulty is that the hotel is the main vehicle for earning profits in a largely cyclical industry. Thus fixed or escalating rents could leave the hotel operator with losses in many years. From the owner's point of view, when operators went into losses, the security of their asset was compromised and the resale value tended to suffer at the very time when they needed to sell. At the same time the owner was not able to share in the superprofits at the top of the cycle. Hotels are, to all intents and purposes, single use properties and the operating income is the only security available.

As with management contracts, a range of income (and cost sharing) formulae have been used to try to reflect the relative risks of owners and operators, and match these with compensating rewards. These include:

- Rent based on a percentage of turnover
- Rent based on a percentage of gross operating profit (GOP) or other definition of profit
- A fixed base rent plus a share of profits after deducting such base rent
- The provision of FF&E and/or structural repairs reserves before determining the operator's share of profits

• Such reserves might be placed in escrow funds, though this ties up the capital of both parties and is generally not favored.

In recent years leases have become more common as operators seek to focus on operating skills, reduce exposure to property ownership, and improve their balance sheet gearing, since such long-term operating leases, generally, do not have to be capitalized under UK and US generally accepted accounting principles.

References

Eyster, J. (1980) *Hotel Management Contracts*, 2nd edn. Ithaca, NY: Cornell University Press.

Uniform System of Accounts for the Lodging Industry (1996) 9th edn. Lansing, MI: Educational Institute of the American Hotel and Motel Association.

CHARLES WHITTAKER
OXFORD BROOKES UNIVERSITY, UK

Hotel operating department ratios

Rooms department ratios

The rooms department for most lodging operations is the largest profit center and the most profitable for the hotel. Given its importance, ratios may effectively be used to measure its operating performance.

Occupancy

The most common ratio used to measure the guest activity is paid occupancy percentage. This ratio is calculated by dividing the number of rooms sold by the number of rooms available. The number used in the numerator is fairly straightforward, as only the number of rooms sold is used. The denominator is more challenging, that is, how is the number of available rooms determined? An out-of-order room cannot be sold neither can a room which is being renovated. How should complimentary rooms be treated in this calculation?

The Uniform System of Accounts for the Lodging Industry (1996) recommends the number of rooms available be determined by subtracting the number of guestrooms removed from the saleable inventory of guestrooms from the total number of guestrooms in the hotel.

An example to demonstrate the calculation of this ratio is as follows:

Guestrooms in lodging facility	200
Number of rooms sold	150
Rooms being renovated	5

$$\text{Paid occupancy (\%)} = \frac{150}{200 - 5}$$
$$= \frac{150}{195}$$
$$= 76.9\%$$

Separate paid occupancy percentages may be calculated for various markets, such as transient, regular, transient-group, and permanent guests. In addition, an occupancy percentage should be determined for complimentary rooms by dividing the number of complimentary rooms by the rooms available. Using the example above and assuming five rooms were provided to guests on a complimentary basis, the complimentary occupancy percentage is calculated as follows:

$$\text{Complimentary occupancy (\%)} = \frac{5}{195}$$
$$= 2.6\%$$

Average room rate

The average room rate (ARR), often referred to as the average daily rate (ADR), is determined as follows:

$$\text{ARR} = \frac{\text{Net room revenues}}{\text{Paid rooms sold}}$$

RevPAR

Another ratio that focuses on revenue but also includes occupancy is revenue per available room (RevPAR). It may be determined either by dividing net room revenues by the number of available guestrooms or by simply multiplying paid occupancy percent by the ARR. Thus, the significance of the RevPAR ratio is that it takes account of both room occupancy percentage and average room rate, thereby providing more balanced indicator of room sales performance.

Expenses

A number of room ratios should be calculated in relation to expenses of the rooms department. First and foremost are ratios in regards to labor, since labor costs are generally the largest expense of a rooms department. Labor ratios include salary expense percent, wages expense percent, and employee benefits percent. Each expense category should be divided by total net room revenue. In addition, each operating expense of the rooms department should be compared to total net room revenue and a ratio, expressed as a percentage, should be calculated. The suggested rooms department schedule according to the USALI (1996) lists 14 other expenses, such as, operating supplies, commissions, training, and uniforms. For example, the determination of operating supplies percent would be as follows:

$$\text{Operating supplies (\%)} = \frac{\text{Operating supplies expenses}}{\text{Total net room revenue}}$$

Generally, the various occupancy ratios and room revenue ratios are computed as often as daily. The expense ratios should be determined as frequently as the expense information is available. For many hotels the expense ratios will be calculated monthly.

Finally, these calculated ratios should be compared to a standard. The best standard is the plan (budget) for the period followed by the same ratio calculation for the prior periods.

Food and beverage department ratios

The food and beverage departments of full service lodging properties are often busy departments, but have relatively low profit margins. Therefore, it is important to measure the activity of these departments and to control their expenses.

The Uniform System of Accounts for the Lodging Industry (1996) treats the food and beverage operations of full service lodging operations as two separate departments. Many hotel operators continue to treat them as a single department. Of course, differences will result in some ratios whether the two departments are treated separately or as one. This discussion will follow the USALI and treat them as separate departments.

The food and beverage ratios to be presented include ratios measuring activity, revenue (sales), and expenses. First, the foodservice seat turnover measures the activity of the food department. It is calculated as follows:

$$\text{Foodservice seat turnover} = \frac{\text{Food covers}}{\text{Number of seats}}$$

This ratio should be calculated by meal part, generally breakfast, lunch, and dinner, and also by day of the week. In general, the greater the seat turnover the greater the activity.

Financial ratios focusing on revenues include average foodservice and beverage checks. These ratios are determined by dividing revenue for each area by the number of servings. The ratios, especially foodservice, should be calculated for each meal period and each day of the week. In general, the higher the ratio the better from a revenue perspective, though one must consider the price elasticity of demand for an operation's food and beverage sales.

The next two ratios are *cost of sales* percentages. For a beverage department, the beverage cost percentage is determined by dividing the cost of beverages sold by the total beverage sales. Many establishments compute separate percentages for their various beverage offerings, such as cocktails, beer, wine and spirits. The food cost percentage is determined by dividing the cost of food sold by total food sales.

Next, *labor cost* percentages should be computed for each department. The labor cost percentages should be calculated separately for salaries, wages, and employee benefits for each department. These percentages are determined by dividing the expense, such as foodservice salaries expenses, by total foodservice revenue. The major reason for separating salaries and wages is due to the amount of control management is able to exercise. Salaries generally are fixed while wages are variable. Thus, as sales increase the salaries expense percentage will decrease while the wages expense percentage should remain constant in regards to sales when wages are truly a variable expense. It may be desirable to separate employee benefits between the cost of benefits and the payroll tax expenses. Further, it may be useful to further separate these expenses on the basis of the amount of control exercised that is these expenses as they relate to salaries and wages.

Finally, all other *expenses* of the food and beverage departments should be compared individually to the total revenue of each department. Since the accounting department normally reports the expense numbers on a monthly basis, all the expense ratios should be computed monthly. These ratios should be computed as frequently as it is practicable so as to enhance management control over expenses in the food and beverage departments.

References

Guilding, C. (2002) *Financial Management for Hospitality Decision-Makers*. Oxford: Butterworth-Heinemann.

Jagels, M.G. and Coltman, M.M. (2003) *Hospitality Management Accounting*, 8th edn. New York: John Wiley & Sons.

Kotas, R. (1999) *Management Accounting for Hospitality and Tourism*, 3rd edn. London: International Thompson Press.

Schmidgall, R.S. (2002) *Hospitality Industry Managerial Accounting*, 5th edn. Lansing, MI: Educational Institute of the American Hotel and Lodging Association.

Uniform System of Accounts for the Lodging Industry (1996) 9th edn. Lansing, MI: Educational Institute of the American Hotel and Motel Association.

RAYMOND SCHMIDGALL
MICHIGAN STATE UNIVERSITY, USA

Hotel rate structures

The following terms are terms used when talking about rate structures. They refer to the rates charged for the room.

- *American plan:* This refers to a room rate that is all-inclusive. This rate includes the room charges as well as three meals per day. Also known as en pension and full board. This is a typical rate structure for a resort hotel.
- *Continental plan:* This refers to a rate that includes room charges plus breakfast. The type of breakfast included may vary according to the hotel. Continental breakfast which consists of a beverage, rolls, butter, and jam may be included with a supplemental charge for an English breakfast. Also known as *bed and breakfast*.
- *Day rate:* This is a rate calculated for a room that will be used for less than an overnight stay.
- *Demi pension:* This refers to a rate that includes room charges and two meals per day (usually breakfast and dinner). Also known as *modified American plan* (MAP) and *half board*. This rate structure may be suitable in a hotel that has a lot of guests who are away most of the day and return in the evening in time for dinner.
- *Double occupancy rate:* This rate is charged to a room that has more than one guest registered within.
- *En pension:* As for American plan above.
- *European plan:* This refers to a rate that includes room charges only with no meals included. Meals are priced separately. According to Kasavana and Brooks (1995), this rate is commonly used by non-resort hotels in the United States.
- *Full board:* As for American plan above.
- *Half board:* As for demi pension above.
- *Modified American plan:* As for demi pension above.
- *Rate range:* This refers to the range of values between the minimum and maximum rates charged by the hotel. The cost structure can help determine the minimum rate and the competition can help determine the maximum rate.
- *Rate spread:* This refers to the difference between the hotel's potential average single rate (PASR) and the potential average double rate (PADR). The PASR is calculated by dividing the single room revenues at rack rate by the number of rooms sold as singles. The PADR is calculated by dividing the double room revenues at rack rate by the number of rooms sold as doubles.

- *Room rate:* The amount that a hotel charges for overnight accommodation is known as the room rate. A standard rate will be designated to each room type and this rate is known as the rack rate.

References

Abbott, P. and Lewry, S. (1991) *Front Office Procedures, Social Skills and Management.* Oxford: Butterworth-Heinemann.

Dix, C. and Baird, C. (1988) *Front Office Operations.* London: Pitman Publishing.

Kasavana, M.L. and Brooks, R.M. (1995) *Front Office Procedures*, 4th edn. Lansing, MI: Educational Institute of the American Hotel and Motel Association.

IRENE SWEENEY
INTERNATIONAL HOTEL MANAGEMENT
INSTITUTE SWITZERLAND, SWITZERLAND

Hotel rating systems

Globally there are as many rating systems as there are countries. In most countries, the government ministry or department that is responsible for promoting tourism is responsible for the rating system. In the United States, The Mobil Travel Guide, a division of the Mobil Oil Corporation, uses a star rating system and the American Automobile Association (AAA) utilizes a diamond rating system. Under the diamond system of AAA a hotel applies for evaluation and can receive up to five diamonds, depending on the quality of the services and facilities it provides. In order to be listed in the AAA system, a hotel must meet a minimum of 34 basic operating criteria that include management, public areas, guestroom security, fire protection, housekeeping, maintenance, room décor, room ambience, and bathroom quality. Once a hotel is approved and included in the AAA system, it is revaluated at least once a year. AAA pays close attention to comments on listed establishments that are submitted by its members. Any complaints are compiled by AAA and forwarded to the listed hotel. In the AAA system of the more than 45,000

listings in AAA publications, the average ratio of member complaints is less than one per property. Globally many systems are often patterned after the AAA or Mobil rating systems. However, there is often considerable inconsistency between countries and often within countries. Often brand hotel companies operating internationally rely heavily on uniform standards that they have developed so as to ensure that their guests have a comfortable experience.

Reference

Stutts, Alan T. (2001) *Hotel and Lodging Management – An Introduction.* New York: John Wiley & Sons.

ALAN T. STUTTS
AMERICAN INTERCONTINENTAL
UNIVERSITY, USA

Hotel valuation methods

The methods used to value hotel properties can be broken down into three basic categories – those based on conditions in the marketplace at a given point in time (sales comparison), those based on cost to rebuild (replacement cost), and those based on the capitalization of future income flows (income capitalization).

In the United Kingdom the valuation issue has become problematic in that generally accepted accounting principles allow for the upward revaluation of original cost in financial statements, unlike the United States where historical cost must be used. Whilst such revaluation recognizes the long-term historical growth in property values and keeps observers aware of the current prices that the hotels might realize, it has the effect of improving the gearing of companies, since the increase in value is reported as part of shareholder's equity, i.e. by increasing reserves, albeit not distributable. Given the cyclical nature of the hotel industry and property values in general, this has resulted in some spectacular overvaluations and subsequent financial embarrassment, as companies borrowed against inflated figures reported. Explanations of the various methods of hotel valuation are provided below.

Sales comparison method

Under this method a range of prices should be gathered at which transactions of similar hotels have taken place in the recent past. Clearly these values can only be an indication, since no two hotels are identical. Hotels differ in location, construction, design, fitting out, and so on. Adjustments are therefore necessary to reflect these differences. Such adjustments are complex and rely on the knowledge and skill of the valuer. Normally, the valuer will not have access to the full background to other transactions and in such circumstances, it has been suggested that skill could be considered subjective (British Association of Hotel Accountants, 1993, p. 44). The value derived is generally translated into a value per room that can then be applied to other properties.

Rushmore (1992, p. 56) suggests that this approach is 'generally utilized to provide a range of value.' The British Association of Hotel Accountants (BAHA) takes a similar stance, stating that 'This method alone is not recommended and only has relevance in indicating a "benchmark" value (BAHA, 1993, p. 43).' However, the method appears to be more widely used than might be supposed and is frequently reported in press articles.

Hotel valuation: cost of replacement method

This method involves the calculation by professional quantity surveyors of what it would cost to rebuild the same hotel today. This figure is then reduced to recognize the loss of value over time through deterioration and obsolescence. The method depends heavily on the comparability of older hotels and modern building techniques – the greater this time gap, the more problematic the valuation. It is also subject to criticism in that the assessment of deterioration and obsolescence is by no means a scientific exercise.

The method ignores the income generating aspects of value. For this reason it is considered as inappropriate for valuing hotels and is ignored in an American Hotel and Motel Association

publication on hotel investment (Rushmore and deRoos, 1999). In the UK the Royal Institute of Chartered Surveyors in its Statement of Asset Valuation Practice No.1 suggests that this method is only appropriate for 'specialized properties' for which there is no market and could, generally, not be sold independently of the underlying operation (SAVP 2.8). This appears to conflict with the current UK accounting standard, which provides that valuation in the balance sheet should be the lower of replacement cost and net realizable value on the basis that this is 'the loss that the entity would suffer if it was deprived of the asset.'

Income capitalization methods

These methods are based on the assumption that a hotel has an economic value, which is equivalent to the present value of its future income flows. Thus, the hotel business is valued in the same way as an investment in gilt edged securities or an office generating a rental stream, except that the income flow is less certain and stable, being dependent upon trading conditions rather than contractual payments. The methods involve estimating the future trading profit (income) and cash flow of the hotel and discounting it back to the date of the valuation.

Discounted cash flow – unleveraged method

In the situation where an unleveraged investment is to be made, i.e. one without debt funding, the value can be derived by discounting back the projected cash flow of the property at an equity yield rate. This equity yield rate is defined as the yield that an investor would expect, taking into account a safe rate of interest that could be obtained (e.g. on gilt-edged investments), together with compensation for the extra effort and economic risks involved in a hotel investment and the expectations of property appreciation. Such data can be obtained by discussion with investors. An alternative is to examine recent transactions where the projected trading results and appraisal values are known. Generally valuers will have access to such data in the course of their work.

The method calculates the sum of:

1. The discounted projected annual cash flows over a 10 year period, and
2. The value at the end of 10 years derived by multiplying the projected income in year 11 by an appropriate capitalization rate, reduced by selling expenses such as brokers and legal fees, also discounted back.

Discounted cash flow – leveraged (simultaneous valuation) method

This method also uses a 10-year projection of income flows, but recognizes the impact of borrowing a portion of the funds rather than a full equity investment. The process for calculating the value can be summarized as follows:

1. Calculate the cash flow generated by operations based on a 10-year forecast.
2. Deduct the debt service from the annual income flow above.
3. Discount the annual net cash flow at the equity yield rate (or internal rate of return).
4. Calculate the terminal value of the income flows after year 10 by capitalizing the year 11 income pre-debt service.
5. Deduct the outstanding mortgage amount and estimated selling costs to arrive at the net value of the property at the end of year 10.
6. Discount the result of 5 above back to the valuation date at the equity yield rate.
7. Adding the current values of the income flows and the terminal value (together constituting the equity component) to the initial mortgage amount will give the total value of the property.

This method involves a circular argument, insofar as the initial debt included in arriving at the total value of the hotel is itself dependent upon that value. However, a method has been developed whereby an iterative calculation or an algebraic formula to give the same result is applied to calculate the current value of the property (Mellen, 1994; Rushmore, 1992, pp. 230–233).

Band of investment method

This method involves the calculation of a stabilized annual income from the hotel being valued. This might be set as a single typical year or, in the case of a new hotel building up business, the third year of that process. The stabilized annual income is likely to be based on past results of that or similar hotels and extrapolations of future expected performance.

The stabilized income flow is then capitalized at the weighted average cost of capital (WACC). The WACC is calculated as a weighted average of the cost of borrowed funds and of the equity needed to finance the hotel. Thus, a hotel costing £50 million might be financed by a mortgage debt of £30 million at an interest rate of 9% p.a. plus equity of £20 million at, say, 12.5%. The WACC would be:

Funds invested	Amount (£)	Rate (%)	Cost of capital (£)
Mortgage	30,000,000	9.0	2,700,000
Equity	20,000,000	12.5	2,500,000
Total	50,000,000		5,200,000
WACC		10.4	$= \dfrac{5.2\,m}{50\,m}$

Since individual hotels may be subject to rapid changes in income levels, due to new competition and other market forces, changes in customer taste etc., this method tends to be appropriate for properties with more stable situations.

References

British Association of Hotel Accountants (1993) *Recommended Practice for the Valuation of Hotels*. London: BAHA.

Nilsson, M., Harris, P.J., and Kett, R. (2001) Towards a valuation framework for hotels as business entities. *International Journal of Contemporary Hospitality Management*, 13 (1), 6–12.

Mellen, S.R and Castro, R.C. (1994) Simultaneous valuation: a proven capitalization technique for hotel and other income properties. *The Bottomline*, 19 (4), 24–29.

Royal Institute of Chartered Surveyors (1997) *Appraisal and Valuation Manual.* London: RICS Business Service.

Rushmore, S. (1992) *Hotels and Motels: A Guide to Market Analysis, Investment Analysis, and Valuations.* Chicago: Appraisal Institute.

Rushmore, S. and de Roos, J. (1999) Hotel valuation techniques. In L.E. Raleigh (ed.), *Hotel Investments: Issues and Perspectives*, 2nd edn. Lansing, MI: Educational Institute of the American Hotel and Motel Association.

CHARLES WHITTAKER
OXFORD BROOKES UNIVERSITY, UK

House limit

A house limit is a credit control mechanism used by the front desk when monitoring guest account folios. At check-in when guests present an acceptable credit card they are given charge privileges. This means that guests have the ability to charge to their rooms. The front desk will set a limit to which the guest can charge to their account and this limit is known as the house limit. The front desk must regularly check guest accounts that have been given these charge privileges to ensure that the house limit is not exceeded. The house limit of credit, a credit limit set by an individual hotel, can vary, depending on the amount of projected charges and the length of time allowed for charges to be paid. The credit rating of the individual or corporation in question will play a large part in assigning a credit limit.

House limits become particularly important with bill-to-account and direct billing whereby hotel guests, both corporate representatives and private guests, may also use the bill-to-account, a preauthorized account that allows guest to have their charges processed on a regular billing cycle without the use of a credit card to settle an account. Typically a list of people who are authorized to use the account as well as authorized positions within the corporation and identification cards with an authorization number are issued by the hotel.

References

Bardi, James (2003) *Hotel Front Office Management.* New York: John Wiley & Sons.

Kasavana, M.L. and Brooks, R.M. (1995) *Front Office Procedures*, 4th edn. Lansing, MI: Educational Institute American Hotel and Motel Association.

IRENE SWEENEY
INTERNATIONAL HOTEL MANAGEMENT
INSTITUTE SWITZERLAND, SWITZERLAND

Housekeeping

Housekeeping is the most important department in the hotel. The reason for this statement is simple: without housekeeping to clean the rooms, the reservationists, the front desk agents, and hotel sales departments would have nothing to sell. The public areas would soon become messy and littered, the glass and brass in these areas would become dirty and streaked, the restrooms in the public areas would begin to smell and run out of necessary items, the hallways on each floor would be dusty and dirty and the lobby would become uninviting. It needs little imagination to think of what different places in a hotel would look like if they were not cleaned every few hours or at least daily.

Housekeeping is usually one of the largest departments in a hotel. In spite of its importance, however, employees in this department are underpaid and overworked, which usually results in a very high turnover rate. This rate is generally ten to one hundred times the rate for other departments. This turnover rate costs the company thousands of dollars in recruitment, training, lost productivity and in some states, overtime costs. Successfully running such a department takes unique skills and a unique individual. In most lodging facilities this is the Executive Housekeeper.

This position is generally standard in most full service hotels. Many limited service operations have followed suit and have someone designated as the Executive or Lead Housekeeper. Many hotels have elevated the position to 'Executive

Staff level.' It should also be noted that along with the Executive Chef, the Executive Housekeeper is amongst the highest paid positions in many hotels. This is done, primarily, to retain and reward an employee who is performing an extremely necessary, difficult, and thankless job.

Housekeepers must be 'on the money' every time they do their job. Anything less than perfect is unacceptable. This is true whether we are profiling a luxury full service hotel or a budget limited service property. While certain expectations may vary with hotel type and room cost, the basic tenet of housekeeping remains true: the room must be spotlessly clean. In an informal survey of 250 college students (125 HRM, 125 non-HRM), 98% indicated that they would request another room if they found hair in the sink or bathtub/shower.

The room attendants (maids, housekeepers) perform very menial task: changing bed linens, scouring sinks, toilets, and bathtubs, dusting and re-arranging the furniture, and vacuuming floors and drapes, and all this is usually repeated some 16 times in a day. It is this type of repetitive menial task that leads to turnover. Further problems arise from the fact that there is usually a predominance of international employees for whom English is not their primary language; that they have to arrive before 6 a.m. and work if the previous night's occupancy rate was high but not if it was low; that they are paid only a minimum wage; that they must handle potentially dangerous chemical substances; undergo hazmat training; occasionally face erroneous accusations of theft and health concerns caused by the illness of a guest which could lead to secondary infections; that they must sometimes clean rooms that have been trashed or where someone has become violently ill. All these factors are inducive to high turnover.

Deep cleaning, which is normally accomplished with the assistance of a houseman, must be performed every two to three weeks. This usually includes the movement of all furniture, shampooing the carpets, vacuuming the drapes and whatever changeover (bedspread, shower curtain, etc.) or periodic maintenance is called for. Periodic maintenance would include things such as: inspections of all electrical appliances (hairdryers, lamps,

televisions, telephones) for frayed wires, loose connections, replacement of batteries in smoke detectors and remote controls, etc.

If the property carries a flag, such as a Hilton or Marriott, an additional factor comes into play, and that is the brand standard. Brand standards are those requirements the flag company places upon the operator of the hotel. This is true whether the hotel is corporately owned, franchised, or under management contract. Brand standards are required by the flag company in an attempt to guarantee to their customers a high consistency of product. Besides regular pre-announced inspections, mystery shoppers are employed to gauge degrees of compliance. From upper management through all the employee levels, additional stress is imposed not only to pass, but to achieve excellent grades during whatever inspection process is used.

Many of those in executive positions will have spent a part of their early career in housekeeping. The ability to manage successfully in such an environment will be an important indicator for promotion in the future. There is a saying 'You cannot manage what you have not done;' for this reason many of the management training programs operated by the larger hotel chains will have trainees working at quite menial levels for at least a couple of weeks before moving them on to supervision and management. Mundane, unglamorous, repetitive, and in some cases boring jobs must still be treated with passion in order to make a mark.

Reference

Tucker, Georgina and Schneider, Madelin (1975) *The Professional Housekeeper*. New York: John Wiley & Sons.

JAMES WORTMAN
UNIVERSITY OF HOUSTON, USA

Housing process

Housing for meetings attendees can be handled in four different ways. One way is for attendees to arrange their own room accommodations, which does not allow attendees or the organization to take advantage of group rates or other concessions. A second way is when the organization arranges for group rates with the hotel, and attendees respond directly to the hotel with a reservation request which can be using a card, a form, the telephone, a fax or the Internet. A third way is when attendees request room accommodations through an organization's in-house housing department which then supplies a housing list to the hotel. The fourth way is when a third party housing bureau, often the local convention and visitors bureau, manages housing requests from attendees and coordinates the final arrangements with the hotel or hotels involved. All except the first option require the organization to negotiate group room rates and book room blocks with one or more hotel properties.

When an organization contracts with a hotel or conference center for guest sleeping rooms, it asks the hotel to commit a certain number of rooms in a given pattern for the individuals that will be attending the meeting. That *room block*, once contracted for, is considered sold for that one time opportunity. Unless there are provisions in the contract that specifically state how and when the room block can be adjusted, the organization is bound to use and pay for those guestrooms.

The following information must be compiled prior to determining the size of the block and which method to use:

- Arrival and departure pattern, including the total number of rooms to be blocked for each night of the meeting
- Anticipated total number of attendees and the cumulative total of rooms reserved
- Recent historical meeting reports of total numbers of attendees
- Recent historical data on the actual room stays versus the number of rooms confirmed (commonly *called no-show reports*)
- Booking history reports that indicate when attendees typically make their reservations
- An explanation of the variance in attendance and room use, if necessary
- Location preferences with multiple hotels (all within walking distance of each other or convention center)

- Purchasing preferences for multiple hotels (single room rates at all hotels or a range of rates)
- Date(s) by which the room block may be revised
- Names of primary and additional contacts for the meeting
- Date housing opens and reservation requests can be processed
- Date housing closes and reservations can no longer be processed at the group rate (commonly called the cut-off date).

It is important for a meeting planner to have the above information when sleeping room rates are negotiated. If an organization selects the third option, by creating an in-house rooming department, housing lists are used to track accommodation requests from the attendees. In-house departments are normally only used for very large meetings or when an organization (corporation) is paying for guestrooms used by meeting participants.

Housing lists may also be utilized when an organization needs to track a special block of rooms within a meeting's larger room block, such as for on-site staff, association officers, speakers or other VIPs. Organizations that manage their own housing cite several reasons for doing so, including having total control over the housing process, having instant access to information regarding the remaining available rooms at each hotel, accurate and immediate information on complimentary rooms earned (generally one complimentary room for every 50 rooms sold), and meeting attendees usually appreciate the personal attention. The housing department will use a hotel reservation agreement form that specifies the room block, rates, and any special accommodations.

The housing list normally contains the following information:

- Name and date(s) of the meeting
- Name and address of the organization
- Contact information for the meeting manager
- Billing instructions specifying if the room charges and tax are to be paid by the individual or the organization and who is responsible for the payment of incidental charges such as telephone, minibar, laundry, room service, etc.

- Reservation guarantee or advanced deposits made
- Name of each individual requesting a room, with room type, arrival and departure dates, and any special needs.

Once the housing list is turned into the hotel, the hotel will process the reservations and return the confirmations to the organization's housing department for review.

Reference

Connell, B., Chatfield-Taylor, C., and Collins, M. (eds) (2002) *Professional Meeting Management*, 4th edn. Chicago: Professional Conference Management Association Education Foundation.

PATTI J. SHOCK
UNIVERSITY OF NEVADA, LAS VEGAS, USA

HTML (Hypertext markup language)

HTML is a set of rules and commands (called tags) used for encoding text files with formatting and linking information. These documents are stored on World Wide Web servers and are retrieved with a Web browser. The HyperText Transfer Protocol (HTTP) manages the communications between a Web browser client and a Web server, for example when a customer is asking to browse a hotel Web page. Besides the formatted text and the links to other documents, HTML allows embedding of more objects in a Web document: images, sounds, videos. Moreover, other programming languages (Javascript, VBscript, etc.) can be inserted in HTML documents to perform special operations like checking the availability or booking a hotel room. Linking of documents is accomplished by using a hypertextual technique: a sensitive area (text, picture, etc.) contains the full address of a computer file (Web page, image, sound file, or other document) to be retrieved.

The address, called URL (Universal Resource Locator), specifies the protocol with which the file must be retrieved, the computer name or IP address, and the full name and path of the file to be retrieved, e.g.: http://www.marriott.com/reservations/LookupReservation.htm.

Development and maintenance of HTML standards is coordinated by the World Wide Web Consortium (http://www.w3.org).

References

Baker, D.L. (2003) *HTML Complete Course*. New York: John Wiley & Sons.

Castro, E. (2002) *HTML for the World Wide Web, Fifth Edition with XHTML and CSS: Visual QuickStart Guide*, 5th edn. Berkeley, CA: Peachpit Press.

RODOLFO BAGGIO
BOCCONI UNIVERSITY, ITALY

Human capital

'Human capital sees people not as a perishable resource to be consumed but as a valuable commodity to be developed, people become more valuable when we invest in them. Moreover we can measure returns on that investment' (Friedman *et al.*, 1998, pp. 3–4). Human capital can be defined as the identification and recognition of a person's abilities, skills, training, education, and experience in their performance of productive labor. This labor contributes to the economic function of an enterprise from both a personal (wage earning) perspective and a management (employee as a resource) perspective.

Thus as an employer or user of human capital, an investment in training and education of those providing the labor is required. This investment may take the form of time spent training, dollars allocated to purchasing or teaching specific training programs and skills as well as time and resources spent on the identification of the specific skills required for a role or activity. As an employee or supplier of human capital the investment is in time, forgone leisure or other economic activities in the pursuit of skills or education, as well as the actual (dollars) cost of training. This investment is also reflected in the commitment to maintain those skills once acquired.

Prahalad and Hamel (1990), cited by Garavan *et al.* (2001), argue that competitiveness in organizational terms is directly attributable to the possession of certain core competencies, one of which is human capital. Thus during the early 1990s we saw the development of a resource based view of organizational competency. This resource based view identified these competencies as being firm (organization) specific and therefore difficult to replicate on a firm to firm basis. This variety of core competencies and by definition human capital allowed a discussion of the variability of success of organizations within the industry.

Garavan *et al.* (2001) cite a variety of authors in the identification of four key attributes of human resource management (HRM) of human capital.

1. Flexibility and adaptability.
2. Enhancement of individual competencies.
3. Development of organizational competencies.
4. Individual employability.

The recognition of these four attributes of the management of human capital not only leads to positive outcomes for the individual but also for the firm or organization. The appreciation of human capital (labor) will be improved and therefore lead to a sustainable competitive advantage.

Also contained within the definition of human capital are three important components, all relating to individual human capital.

Social capital is the development of social networks (professional and personal) on an individual level. These networks can take many forms, two of which are:

- Intra organizational networks, which allow the sharing of skills and knowledge between peers and also up and down the organizational hierarchical structure. This type of network will contribute to a person's success within an organization.

Inter-organizational networks, which allow the sharing of industry knowledge and practice and will ultimately increase a person's employability within an industry.

Instructional capital is the development, organization, and retention of institutional knowledge.

Thus it can be considered as the identification of organizational specific knowledge held by an individual and their ability to share this knowledge. Once a person leaves an organization their instructional capital is lost to the firm. Therefore it is imperative that this form of capital is shared via the use of social capital, so that all knowledge is shared by members of the organization.

Individual capital is the development of creativity and leadership. These are the 'personal' skills that may be both innate and learned and will allow an individual to make the most of their social and instructional capital.

Consideration of the above three components of human capital reveals that individual variations in the identification and use of these components can explain variations in individual performance in the workplace and within the industry.

The hospitality industry is defined by a wide range of economic activities all relating to the provision of goods and services (Walker, 1999). Thus we have the tangible products of hotel rooms, restaurants, public spaces etc. and the intangible product of service. The tangible product – the rooms, food and beverage, public spaces etc. – are all quantifiable according to industry standards and ratings. The use of human capital in this aspect of hospitality is formulaic, i.e. rooms are constructed to a certain building code and standard using a quantifiable skill or a set number of hours of a specific type of labor.

The intangible aspect of service is more problematic and it is reliant upon the use of individual human capital (labor) in the interpretation of the guest/organizational representative equation.

Whilst it can be argued that service standards are set and are perhaps even quantifiable (e.g. in its most basic form, answering a phone after three rings), in every case it is the individual interpretation of these standards that an organization in a service industry is relying upon. As we have seen from the individual components of human capital, not all individuals possess or develop each component in equal parts and thus the individuality of service occurs.

It is not only this individual and specific relationship of human capital and service that is problematic for the hospitality industry. Other features of the industry combine with issues of human capital management to make the management of a hospitality organization a very complex process.

The hospitality industry has the following characteristics:

- High staff turnover and thus the ongoing development and loss of instructional and social capital – these are a significant issue in the day-to-day management of an organization.
- Long irregular hours over a 7-day week cause individuals to react and deal with stress in different ways which will affect their performance.
- Hierarchical structure of many businesses resists the development of interorganizational networks and the sharing of organizational knowledge.
- The diversity of workforce in terms of culture, age, and gender as well as the diversity of skills required by individual departments results in a multitude of issues for the efficient management of human capital.

Therefore, the use and management of human capital is particularly relevant to the hospitality industry due to the use of intangibles in the product (service), the diversity of the workforce, and high staff turnover rates. These factors contribute to the constant review of training standards and education as well as a constant evaluation of the human capital available within the workforce.

References

Friedman, B., Hatch, J., and Walker, D. (1998) *Delivering on a Promise: How to Attract, Manage and Retain Human Capital.* New York: The Free Press.

Garavan, T., Morley, M., Gunnigle, P., and Collins, E. (2001) Human capital accumulation: the role of human resource management. *Journal of European Industrial Training*, 25 (2), 48–68.

Prahalad, L.K. and Hamel, G. (1990) The core competencies of the corporation. *Harvard Business Review*, May–June.

Walker, J. (1999) *Introduction to Hospitality*, 2nd edn. Englewood Cliffs, NJ: Prentice-Hall.

JULIE ADAMS
SOUTHERN CROSS UNIVERSITY, AUSTRALIA

Human resource accounting

Human resource accounting (HRA) has been defined by the American Accounting Association as 'the process of identifying and measuring data about human resources and communicating this information to interested parties.' HRA involves measuring the costs incurred by organizations in the recruitment, selection, hiring, training, and development of human resources. The process may also involve measuring the economic value of employees to hospitality organizations. Under conventional accounting systems investments in human resources are treated as expenses or operating costs and they are usually written off in the profit and loss account in the current accounting period. However, HRA is based on the premise that the costs associated with the acquisition and training of employees are not merely expenses, but rather the price of acquiring a 'human asset' that will give benefits in future accounting periods. The primary purpose of HRA is to provide better quality information at a reasonable cost to decision-makers. Introducing human capital variables into the traditional range of management decision-making variables may help management plan and control the use of human resources more effectively and efficiently. Some have also suggested that certain HRA information may be included in financial statements for use by investors and other outside parties.

Given the labor-intensive nature of the hospitality industry, HRA techniques can make a valuable contribution to cost-effective employment practices, which in turn will result in improved operational profitability.

References

Cascio, W.F. (1991) *Costing Human Resources.* Boston, MA: PWS/Kent.

Flamholtz, E.G. (1985) *Human Resource Accounting*. New York: Jossey-Bass.

ANGELA MAHER
OXFORD BROOKES UNIVERSITY, UK

Human resource development

Delahaye (2003) and Stacey (2003) contend that human resource development has become increasingly important because the traditional management belief that there were just two basic resources, time and money, is no longer true since knowledge has become an equally essential resource. Delahaye (2003) states human resource development crucially requires the direction, improvement, and management of both individual and organizational knowledge.

Initially human resource development was seen as primarily being the management of training and development, performance assessment and career and succession management (Baum, 1995). However the changes wrought by continuous external change from the mid-1990s onwards led to a wave of organizational reengineering which changed that view. Reengineering was a managerial response largely driven by financial cost saving imperatives and outsourcing and the flattening of organizational structures became strategies pursued with intense vigor and purpose – in fact, it has been argued some of these strategies were 'pursued too vigorously' (Delahaye, 2003, p. 205). In many cases as staff were retrenched or took early retirement their knowledge, much of it vital in helping an organization maintain a sustainable competitive advantage, went out the door with them.

Towards the end of the 1990s more emphasis was given to the importance of knowledge to an organization as a resource. This was inspired by organizational learning exponents like Senge (1992). Knowledge is located in a variety of places within an organization. It can be found within an organization's records and its database but the major pool of knowledge is found in the minds of staff (Delahaye, 2003). As a result the human resources manager needs to be aware that 'the most significant HRD task is the appropriate governance of the organization's knowledge resource' (Delahaye, 2003, p. 205).

Human resource development has four stages: needs investigation, design, implementation and evaluation. These systems provide feedback to individuals and, as a result, should also then offer single-loop learning and training. As a result a system is developed which makes a major contribution to the successful management of knowledge capital. Knowledge capital is something which, in turn, allows an organization the opportunity to obtain a competitive advantage in areas such as the effective and efficient servicing of a customer base.

The strategic management of knowledge capital through effective human resource development strategies allows an organization to develop what Prahalad and Hamel (1990) call *core competencies*. Attaining a core competency is something organizations less reliant on numerical flexibility can master more easily than those who are more reliant on it. In an industry such as tourism and hospitality, which requires a higher degree of numerical flexibility in its staffing arrangements than is the norm, the human resource developer's management of knowledge capital is a harder task.

The difficulty in analyzing how HRD is applied in the tourism and hospitality industry is that its labor markets are not heterogeneous. The internal labor markets of airlines, transport, and travel management organizations are fundamentally less reliant on numerical flexibility than hotels, resorts, catering, and event management organizations (Baum, 1995; Riley *et al.*, 2001).

The need for a degree of variability in these latter sectors of the tourism and hospitality industry raises the question 'can the employee commitment necessary for successful knowledge capital management co-exist with some employment insecurity?' This leads to the dilemma for managers of having to 'square the circle between needing employment flexibility and needing sustainable quality' (Riley *et al.*, 2001, p. 167). To try to achieve this, managers in the tourism and hospitality industry use three main strategies together or separately. First, they aim to achieve simplicity and standardization, a strategy often referred to as McDonaldization. It is argued this strategy has been adopted by organizations like McDonald's with its pre-packaged production line style of assembly, Formula 1 Motels with their mechanized check-in systems, and by London's Docklands Light Rail with its roboticized trains. It is also argued these strategies are incompatible with genuine empowerment (Baum, 1995) and with true employee commitment (Riley *et al.*, 2001), the latter of which is advantageous for managing and retaining knowledge capital. Second, they de-regulate job parameters, something that is driven by budget constraints, and they also adopt organizational downsizing which, like reengineering, is inimical to retaining and developing human knowledge capital, the most essential skill for human resource development, according to Delahaye (2003). Lastly, some organizations look to achieve sustainable flexibility through in-house and recognized external training and by adopting specifically customized hiring policies.

However, if tourism and hospitality organizations are to achieve service quality, attain human knowledge growth, reduce staff turnover costs, and achieve a resulting core competency that attains a sustainable market advantage then a mixture of human resource strategies such as job rotation, succession planning, genuine empowerment, and career progression need to be considered. These options are much easier for larger organizations like hotel chains. The Ibis chain of hotels in Australia, for example, is trialing front- and back-of-the-house job rotation for its staff so as to achieve a degree of functional flexibility while also trying to foster employee commitment through the attainment of a broader range of skills which hopefully will lead to knowledge capital retention and growth. Virgin Airlines is also similarly innovative in this regard.

Smaller organizations, who often make up the bulk of a nation's tourism and hospitality industry, clearly find it hard to offer career progression and have less capability to offer in-house or formalized training. Both are extremely important HRD and knowledge management tools. These organizations may need to use external training and job rotation more to keep human capital in an era when it is becoming vital to keep mature workers.

HRD practitioners need to use training and development, career planning and succession, and attain employee commitment to achieve human knowledge capital retention and growth. The task for tourism and hospitality human resource managers is to balance the dichotomy between their need for numerical flexibility and the need for continuous quality service. Retaining and encouraging human knowledge capital is essential to the latter but difficult as a result of the former.

References

Baum, T. (1995) *Managing Human Resources in the European Tourism and Hospitality Industry: A Strategic Approach.* London: Thompson International Business Press.

Delahaye, B.L. (2003) Human resource development and the management of knowledge capital. In R. Wiesner and B. Millet (eds), *Human Resource Management: Challenges and Future Directions.* Sydney: John Wiley & Sons, pp. 204–218.

Prahalad, C.K. and Hamel, G. (1990) The core competencies of an organization. *Harvard Business Review*, May–June, 79–81.

Riley, M., Ladkin, A. and Szivas, E. (2001) *Tourism Employment. Analysis and Planning.* Clevedon: Channel View Publications.

Senge, P.M. (1992) *The Fifth Discipline – The Art and Practice of the Learning Organization.* New York: Random House Publishing.

Stacey, R.D. (2003) *Strategic Management and Organizational Dynamics – The Challenge of Complexity.* London: Prentice-Hall/Financial Times Publishing.

GRANT CAIRNCROSS
SOUTHERN CROSS UNIVERSITY, AUSTRALIA

Human resource information systems

The request from the general manager to the human resources director of an international hotel chain could be 'provide me with a list of all employees in the Asia Pacific region who speak

English and French, who have worked for more than three years in an Asian country and who are ready to move into line management.' Dealing with such a request requires a well-designed and up-to-date human resource information system (Jaross and Walker, 2001). Smaller operations still utilize paper files on their staff, and these are quite adequate, but a computer-based system would be needed to obtain the information requested by the GM in the example here.

Good management practice and (sometimes) government regulations require certain data to be kept on employees, such as:

- Personal details
- Attendance analysis
- Training history
- Labor turnover analysis
- EEO
- Skills inventories
- Career and promotion tracking
- Compensation administration
- Accident reporting
- Performance appraisal.

Some firms design and develop their own systems, but there are ample consulting firms offering generic computerized human resource information systems (CHRIS). It is imperative for firms wishing to move up to a computerized human resource information system to conduct a needs analysis and then formalize their requirements in writing.

Reference

Jaross, M. and Walker, P. (2001) *Australian Master Human Resources Guide 2002*. Sydney: CCH Australia Ltd.

RON DOWELL
SOUTHERN CROSS UNIVERSITY, AUSTRALIA

Human resources management (HRM)

Human resources management (HRM) as an expression originated in the United States of America in the 1980s. It is now a widely used business expression, replacing the more dated term personnel management. However, HRM defies universal definition. Broadly, it is used to describe a contemporary approach to managing employees through a series of principles, policies, and practices that center on the individual employee as an organizational resource and investment.

Definition and explanation of human resources management

There are several definitions of HRM. One in particular captures the essence of HRM:

> The main dimensions of HRM [involves] the goal of integration [i.e. if human resources can be integrated into strategic plans, if human resource policies cohere, if line managers have internalized the importance of human resources and this is reflected in their behavior and if employees identify with the company, then the company's strategic plans are likely to be more successfully implemented], the goal of employee commitment, the goal of flexibility/adaptability [i.e. organic structures, functional flexibility], the goal of quality [i.e. quality of staff, performance, standards, public image]. (Guest, 1987)

McKenna and Beech (2002, p. 1) offer a succinct explanation that captures the fundamental scope of HRM:

> HRM seeks to maximize organizational performance through the adoption of best practice in the management of people . . . HRM can be viewed as an approach to personnel management that considers people as the key resource. It subscribes to the notion that it is important to communicate well with employees, to involve them in what is going on and to foster commitment and identification with the organization.

Characteristics of HRM

Several common threads can be identified to give HRM some distinction and meaning. These include: employee commitment, strategic integration, and achievement of business goals, all of which can be said to represent the main hallmarks of HRM. Other characteristics include long-term planning horizons, employee flexibility, employee development, unitarist employee relations, teamwork, more individualized contracts of employments and rewards, and, significantly, the involvement of line managers in HR activities and in developing a nurturing management style.

Above all, securing employee commitment – a departure from personnel management/ administration approaches centered on employee compliance and control – is arguably the most important aspect of HRM. Indeed it is a central principle of HRM for recognition of this principle leads to the other characteristics and necessitates a strategic perspective of HRM, often signaled in organizations' mission and value statements. Employee commitment is not important in itself, but because of its consequences: it may ultimately lead to enhanced business performance. Thus HRM does not center on employees for altruistic purposes but for more instrumental, business/management ends.

HRM models and functions

To facilitate practical application, HRM is often framed in terms of models and processes. One of the most influential models is the 'Harvard Framework' (Armstrong, 2001), which initiated in the United States. This model has several distinctive features. First, it includes internal and external perspectives (stakeholder interests) together with contextual factors influencing HRM, and so frames HRM both within and outside organizational parameters. Second, it focuses on the directions of HRM (policy choices), rather than specific HRM procedures or practices, and so elevates the horizons of HRM to a strategic level. Third, it relates HR effects (outcomes) to long-term consequences for and beyond organizations. It also indicates that these elements of HRM are inter-related and dynamic. Importantly, the Harvard model signals HRM as a general management concern, not the exclusive preserve of HR specialists.

Another model of HRM that is widely recognized is the 'hard' and 'soft' versions of HRM.

Hard HRM would apply to peripheral employees whereby employees are seen in rational-economic terms as a 'resource.' Therefore they are treated with a business focus first. Soft HRM would apply generally to core employees who would be seen as individual 'human resources' to be developed and nurtured for business performance. In practice, hard and soft HRM can co-exist in the same organizations, with differential terms and conditions of employment offered to different categories of staff. Generally, core employees would enjoy preferential employment packages.

HRM processes encouraging systematic approaches to specific activities are a common feature of HRM literature. For example, the HRM functions – or services as they are sometimes called – include the recruitment and selection process, the induction process, the human resource planning process, the negotiation process. Similarly, there are learning cycles, training cycles, empowerment cycles, and performance management cycles. Areas of HRM activities can be divided into three principal categories: employee resourcing, employee development, and employee relations.

Employee resourcing encompasses, for example, recruitment and selection, selection interviewing, induction, psychometric testing, job and competence analysis, outsourcing and human resource planning. The emphasis is on determining and procuring the appropriate quantity and quality of employees for the organization. Employee development focuses on mutual organization and employee needs in work experience, learning, development, and training in order that organizations themselves can develop. It encompasses organizational learning, learning theory, continuous learning, planning and evaluating training, coaching and mentoring, management development, career planning, and personal development planning for example. Employee relations centers as much on practices as on work relationships and issues. At its broadest it can include all issues involved in the reward (pay)–effort equation. Employee rewards and benefits, performance management, discipline, grievances, trade unions, employee participation and involvement in decision-making, and equality management at work can all be considered under the employee relations umbrella.

Not all HRM functions can be neatly divided into these three categories, so the boundaries between them should be viewed as porous. It is not the categories so much as the HRM function itself that is usually important to organizations. Underpinning and permeating HRM functions is organizational behavior, the study of individual and group behavior in organizations. Organizational behavior (OB) adopts a behavioral approach to the management and relationships of people at work. Understanding individual and group perceptions, values and behaviors is elemental to HRM with its declared focus on individuals and their needs. Therefore topics such as motivation, teamwork, role conflict and leadership are relevant. While HRM takes a largely business-centered approach to the management of employees, OB takes a person-centered approach; both are important to the effective management of employees.

HRM in the hospitality and tourism industry

The Harvard model of HRM, the flexible firm, hard and soft versions of HRM and the HR categories outlined above all have resonance in the hospitality and tourism industry. To understand the nature of HRM in the hospitality industry, it is important to understand the situational factors of hospitality work and different stakeholder points of view. In terms of the main situational factors, the sensitivity and vulnerability of hospitality and tourism markets due to varying economic, political, seasonal, and meteorological factors, lead to employment structures that rely heavily (and none more so than the restaurant sector) on a combination of core staff and large numbers of temporary employees who are often students, young and/or female. Young employees are often the predominant labor market in the fast food and club sectors of the industry.

From the perspective of hospitality employees, work can have a number of negative features:

- It is typically low paid and of relatively low status

- It has variable and unsocial hours
- It has unpredictable levels
- It can be stressful due to (physical) workloads, workplace violence, and dealing with customers.

Many jobs are part time and casual, and subject to the hard version of HRM. Full-time, core jobs often involve very long working hours, especially for managers. More positively, hospitality work offers:

- Job variety
- Low levels of supervision
- Personal incentives
- Teamwork
- Interaction with people
- Wide choices in the number of types of employer
- Pleasant work surroundings.

From the employer's point of view hospitality work:

- Is an important component in the sales mix
- Represents a high proportion of operating costs due to the labor intensity of hospitality service offerings
- Extends up to 24/7, in that work can be done 24 hours a day, seven days per week
- Has high levels of staff turnover
- Has a high proportion of female, young, and international staff, especially in the peripheral groups of staff
- Is market-sensitive
- Can be subject to intense competition.

Above all, for both employees and employers, hospitality work is characterized by the provision of service and the need for quality service. Many hospitality organizations, for example Hilton International, seek differentiation and competitive advantage though quality service, especially in mature marketplaces.

Yet hospitality jobs are often demanding and generally not well rewarded, hence employees may not be too motivated to consistently deliver the necessary quality service. The primary role of HRM can then become to mediate between the business and employee needs in order to encourage and facilitate quality service. In the absence of substantial financial rewards, for example, more intangible and intrinsic rewards such as teamwork and training can be offered. The range and balance of HRM policies and practices in hospitality organizations can have a significant impact on service quality. Second, HRM policies and practices will influence the leadership and management style of line managers that have an effect on employee service delivery. Third, the HRM philosophy and principles adopted by hospitality organizations contribute to an organization's culture which can play a large part in influencing service delivery.

Despite the heightened need for HRM in hospitality, the function has apparently not achieved its full potential around the world. In Australia, for example, a study of 483 hospitality firms indicates that service quality and staff commitment could be enhanced by human resource practices like performance appraisal and remuneration strategies in addition to training (Davies *et al.*, 2001). In the UK, the reputation of the hotel and catering industry generally as an employer is poor. In the small to medium-sized enterprises, which individually employ fewer than 250 people but comprise 97% of the UK tourism and hospitality workforce, HRM is acknowledged as having more potential than realization (Lee-Ross, 2000).

In developing economies HRM evidently needs to be utilized more. In Russia, for instance, one of the main challenges in its fast-expanding lodging industry lies in HRM (Swerdlow and Cummings, 2000). While in Latin America it is reported that under-developed employee performance, in respect of skills and motivation, is inhibiting the travel and tourism industry through poor standards of service (Pizam, 1999). Similarly, China has an expanding but under-developed tourism industry that has significant employee training and education needs in a country where the concept of customer service is not widely understood (Hanqin *et al.*, 2001). And in the Association of South East Asian Nations (ASEAN), the rate of growth of the tourism industry has outstripped training and development efforts, reducing the industry's competitiveness (Sadi and Bartels, 1999).

In contrast, evidence of good and best HRM practice in employee resourcing, development, and relations can be found in the hospitality industry.

For example, in North America's largest luxury hotel chain, Fairmont Hotels and Resorts which employs around 30,000 staff, strategic HRM has been the basis for developing a service culture that 'consistently delivers top service' (Langlois, 2001, p. 19). And Sodexho, an American-owned institutional catering firm employing 212,000 staff across the world, has executive coaching to improve management leadership skills.

Overall, the potential of HRM in the quality staff dependent hospitality industry has apparently not yet been fully realized. Generally, adoption of HRM seems patchy. While there is evidence of HRM approaches and practices, particularly in large organizations and in organizations operating in competitive labor markets, the challenge remains for hospitality businesses to equate HRM with business performance.

References

Armstrong, M. (2001) *A Handbook of Personnel Management Practice*, 8th edn. London and Milford, CT: Kogan Page.

Davies, D., Taylor, R., and Savery, L. (2001) The role of appraisal, remuneration and training in improving staff relations in the Western Australian accommodation industry: a comparative study. *Journal of European Industrial Training*, 25 (6/7), 366–374.

Guest, D.E. (1987) Human resource management and industrial relations. *Journal of Management Studies*, 21 (1), 503–521, quoted in Legge, K. (1995) *Human Resource Management: Rhetorics and Realities*. London: Macmillan, p. 65.

Hanquin, Z.Q., Lam, T., and Bauer, T. (2001) Analysis of training and educational needs of mainland Chinese tourism. *International Journal of Contemporary Hospitality Management*, 13 (6), 274–280.

Langlois, R. (2001) Business strategy starts with people. *Canadian Human Resources Reporter*, 14 (19), 19–25.

Lee-Ross, D. (ed.) (2000) *HRM in Tourism and Hospitality – International Perspectives on Small to Medium-sized Enterprises*. London: Cassell.

McKenna, E. and Beech, N. (2002) *Human Resource Management: A Concise Analysis*. London: Financial Times/Prentice-Hall.

Pizam A. (1998) The state of travel and tourism human resources in Latin America. *Tourism Management*, 20, 575–586.

Sadi, M.A. and Bartels, F.J. (1999) Recent developments in the Association of South East Asian Nations (ASEAN) tourist industry: manpower development, training issues and competitiveness. *Competitiveness Review*, 9 (1), 19–29.

Swerdlow, S. and Cummings, W.T. (2000) Toward a better cross-cultural understanding of US and Russian lodging employees: a discriminant analysis approach. *Journal of Hospitality and Tourism Research*, 24 (3), 336–350.

GILLIAN A. MAXWELL
GLASGOW CALEDONIAN UNIVERSITY, UK

HVAC equipment and systems

HVAC is an abbreviation for heating, ventilation, and air conditioning. HVAC systems in hospitality buildings serve to provide control of the interior temperature, humidity, air movement, and air quality within the structure. HVAC systems can be comprised of a number of components including boilers, chillers, centralized and decentralized guestroom HVAC units, larger roof mounted PTAC units, air handling units, and cooling towers.

A boiler is a pressure vessel designed to transfer heat (produced by combustion) to a fluid. Boilers in most hospitality buildings provide hot water for heating use only and are generally relatively low pressure (up to 160 psig) and low temperature (under 200 °F, 93 °C). A few operations produce steam in boilers to meet needs of laundry operations or cooking equipment (or because the building itself was constructed in an era when steam was used for heating needs). If steam is produced (or purchased from a district heating system) it is usually put though a heat exchanger and hot water is produced for domestic purposes at the property or for space heating. Whether a steam or hot water boiler is used, the water in the boiler loop is usually contained in a closed loop and is chemically treated to prevent rust, corrosion, and other problems.

Boilers commonly burn natural gas although they may also use fuel oil and even propane. Boilers in hospitality are commonly made of cast iron or steel although some modular designs may utilize copper or stainless steel. Boilers require a flue to safely discharge the exhaust gases from combustion as well as other safety controls.

A chiller is a device that creates chilled water for use in a centralized HVAC system. Most chillers use a vapor compression refrigeration system similar to that used by refrigeration equipment and air conditioners. These chillers may be reciprocating (for small applications), screw or reciprocating or scroll (for medium-sized applications) and screw or centrifugal for larger applications. It is also possible to have a chiller that uses heat as the primary energy source for its operation. Such chillers are referred to as absorption chillers. (The absorption chilling process is also used by some in room minibar units due to the quiet operation.) The chilled water is typically produced at between 44 and 50 °F (6 and 10 °C) and is circulated throughout the building using pumps. Heat rejection from the chiller is usually done using a cooling tower although heat rejection can also be done using a large fan coil rejecting heat to the air.

Efficiency of HVAC equipment usually expressed as the output of the equipment divided by the input. For building equipment, common measures of efficiency are:

- EER (energy efficiency ratio). This is the rated cooling capacity of a piece of cooling equipment (BTU per hour) divided by the watts consumed by the equipment. Typical values are 9–13.
- kW per ton (kilowatts per ton of refrigeration where a ton of refrigeration is 12,000 BTU per hour). Larger building cooling equipment such as building chillers are often rated in kW per ton, a 'reverse' efficiency measure where the input (kW) is divided by the output (tons of cooling). Typical values for modern chillers can be in the range of 0.45 to 0.6.
- COP (coefficient of performance). The rated heating capacity of a heat pump (BTU per hour) divided by the watts consumed by the equipment. Typical values are 2.5 to 3.5.

- Percent (%) boiler efficiency. Ranges of values from 75 to 95% can be found for modern equipment depending on the type of boiler.

Centralized and decentralized HVAC units are installed to condition the air in the guestrooms. Centralized units have fan coils and are connected to the building's boiler and chiller for supplies of hot water or chilled water. Decentralized units operate using electricity as their power source and provide heating or cooling independent of central utilities. Decentralized units mix fresh air with return air in the units themselves. Most centralized units rely up fresh air being supplied from the corridor under the guestroom door. Air is exhausted from guestrooms via the ventilation fan in the bathroom.

Some operations provide conditioned air to meeting areas and public spaces via packaged terminal air conditioners (PTAC) units. These are generally roof mounted. They provide space cooling and heating via the operation of a refrigeration system and gas heater or, in some instances, by connections with chilled and hot water supplies. Fresh air is introduced into the units from the roof area.

Another way to supply conditioned air to meeting rooms, ballrooms, corridors, and other public spaces is via air handling units. Air handling units consist of heating and cooling coils, filters, and fans. The heating and cooling coils are often supplied with hot water or chilled water although some may be what are called direct expansion (DX) utilizing a refrigeration evaporator in the air stream to create cooling. Fresh air is mixed with return air from building spaces, filtered, heated or cooled, and then returned to the spaces. Fresh air for the air handling units must be ducted from the outside and exhaust air from the building must be removed to the outside.

A cooling tower is a heat rejection device, which rejects heat to the atmosphere though the cooling of a water stream to a lower temperature. This cooling occurs by evaporation of water in the cooling tower. In hospitality buildings, cooling towers are common for rejection of heat from building chillers. They may also be used to reject heat from water source heat pumps and from water cooled foodservice refrigeration

equipment. Cooling towers can potentially be large consumers of water at the property as well as of electricity to operate pumps and fans.

Building management systems are installed in larger buildings to provide the facilities manager with the ability to monitor and control the distributed elements of the HVAC system from a central location. These systems allow for real-time measurement and viewing of key operating parameters of the systems. The systems also allow the facilities manager to control the operation of the system with such features as time of day operation, modification of desired operating conditions, and staging priority in terms of equipment operation.

References

ASHRAE (2000) Boilers. In *ASHRAE Systems and Equipment Handbook*, ch. 27. Atlanta, GA: American Society of Heating, Refrigeration and Air Conditioning Engineers.

ASHRAE (2000) Liquid chilling systems. In *ASHRAE Systems and Equipment Handbook*, ch. 38. Atlanta, GA: American Society of Heating, Refrigeration and Air Conditioning Engineers.

Stipanuk, D.M. (2002) *Hospitality Facilities Management and Design*, 2nd edn., ch. 8. Lansing, MI: Educational Institute of the American Hotel and Lodging Association.

www.ashrae.org

www.cti.org

DAVID M. STIPANUK
CORNELL UNIVERSITY, USA

HVAC loads

Any factors that require the HVAC system to use extra energy for heating or cooling to create comfort in a space are referred to as HVAC loads. HVAC loads can be categorized into transmission and conduction, solar, occupant, infiltration, ventilation, and appliance. Transmission and conduction loads involve the transfer of heat through walls, ceilings, windows, and other structural elements of a building. Solar loads refer to high indoor temperatures generated by sunlight entering a building through windows or heating the exterior surfaces of a building. Occupant loads are heat and moisture generated by the number of people present and what they are doing. Thus, when designing a HVAC system, a hotel's management must consider the number of customers and employees, and determine their activity level to create a comfort zone. Infiltration loads are caused because of the movement of air through window and door frames or open doors and windows. Ventilation loads, very similar to infiltration, are deliberately designed as part of a HVAC system to circulate cool and fresh air throughout a building. Appliance loads refer to all operating appliances inside a space that generate heat or moisture, such as computers, TV, water boilers, etc. To maintain a zone of comfort and save energy, HVAC loads should be controlled by closing curtains, windows, and doors; painting walls light; increasing the insulation value of walls and ceilings, etc.

Reference

Borsenik, F.D. and Stutts, A.T. (1997) *The Management of Maintenance and Engineering Systems in the Hospitality Industry*, 4th edn. New York: John Wiley & Sons.

ERIC S.W. CHAN
THE HONG KONG POLYTECHNIC UNIVERSITY,
HONG KONG SAR, CHINA

I

ICT and e-Hospitality

e-Hospitality is an umbrella term that incorporates the entire range of information communication technology (ICT) applications in the hospitality area. ICTs penetrate at a fast pace, by integrating the hotel operation; reshaping the marketing function; improving total efficiency; providing tools for marketing research and partnership building; enhancing customer services while providing strategic opportunities. Consumers increasingly expect ICT-enabled communications and interactions before, during, and after their visit. Hotels will be unable to perform their operations profitably without using technology extensively. The emergent ICTs provide unprecedented opportunities for hospitality organizations, as they assist the promotion of properties to a wide range of institutional and individual buyers around the world. ICTs are increasingly recognized as a means of achieving competitive advantage for the hospitality industry.

Managing internal operations

Hotels need ICTs to manage their inventory. Hotel chains in particular use group-wide systems to focus on the management for single properties as well as the distribution through a variety of electronic distribution channels. Most hotel properties around the world operate a *property management system* (PMS) that enables them to integrate their 'back-office' operations. As a result they can improve general administration,

as well as specific functions such as accounting; marketing research and planning; yield management; payroll; personnel management; and purchasing at individual properties. Increasingly these functions move on Intranet platforms, improving interfaces and allowing easier employee training.

PMSs were also introduced to facilitate the front office, sales, planning, and operation functions. This was achieved by employing a computer reservation system (CRS) to administrate a database with all reservations, rates, occupancy, and cancellations (Frew and Horam, 1999; O'Connor, 2000). PMSs and CRSs facilitate the following business functions:

- Improve capacity management and operations efficiency
- Facilitate central room inventory control
- Provide last room availability information
- Offer yield management capability
- Provide better database access for management purposes
- Support extensive marketing, sales, and operational reports
- Facilitate marketing research and planning
- Enable travel agency tracking and commission payment
- Enable tracking of frequent flyers and repeat hotel guests
- Allow direct marketing and personalized service for repeat hotel guests
- Enhance handling of group bookings and frequent individual travelers (FITs).

The proliferation of the Internet supported the development of a number of additional electronic distribution options. These include direct bookings to the hotel; hotel chains' own reservation central offices; independent reservation agents; hotel representation and consortium groups; airline CRSs and GDSs; hotel aggregators (such as Hotels.com) and destination management systems. For hotels to manage their distribution best they need two integral components, namely yield management and guest history. The yield management assists hotels to maximize both their occupancy and room rates contributing directly to their profitability. Revenue and yield management systems ensure that hotels optimize their revenue, by taking into consideration past and forecasted performance, as well as a wide range of additional factors. Revenue management systems are critical, particularly for large properties with numerous outlets and departments. Moreover, the guest history is effectively an early CRM software which records data for past guests and other intermediaries, assisting the personalization of the hotel.

Interconnecting partner systems and extranets

Hotels develop partnerships with a number of intermediaries to expand their distribution network. Hotel chains have therefore established central reservation offices (CROs) with sales agents that have access to property management systems. CROs allow both individual customers and travel trade to make reservations over the phone or Internet sites whilst they facilitate networking with a number of electronic intermediaries allowing onward distribution. Interconnectivity and interoperability between hotel CRSs and GDSs was a major problem, as each hotel and GDS has its own communication protocols and functions. Two major switch companies emerged, namely WIZCOM and THISCO, to provide an interface between the various systems and eventually to allow a certain degree of transparency.

Although CROs and GDSs currently dominate hotel bookings, the Internet emerges as the prime medium for receiving travel bookings from a wide range of intermediaries. GDSs have been problematic for hotel distribution as they allow only a fairly limited number of rates to be displayed. They abbreviate and truncate descriptions whilst they cannot display photographs, and take a lot of time to update data (O'Connor and Frew, 2000). Therefore, the Internet is much more suitable to promote hotel rooms and inventory whilst it provides the tools to increase revenue at a fraction of the traditional cost of booking. Interoperability of systems can support data and transaction exchanges to support hotels to expand their distribution network. Online bookings are showing dramatic growth and a number of online booking agencies and travel agencies, such as hotels.com, allthehotels.com, bookings.com, hrs.com, Travelocity, and Expedia, have been established as mainstream distribution. Internet hotel bookings are projected to rise dramatically in the near future and the hospitality distribution channel becomes more complex as most intermediaries establish links with other players in the marketplace.

Business-to-business (B2B) is also growing very fast. Marriott for example has begun to partner with large corporations to bring its website into their intranet's travel page creating a B2B environment and enhancing electronic collaboration. This enables corporations to benefit from special rates and added value benefits whilst it assists Marriott to increase it loyalty and profitability. The strength of the hotel brand and the fact that consumers have always relied on booking hotels directly, instead through intermediaries, are playing a critical role in developing B2B and B2C solutions in the marketplace. Effectively these systems are managed through extranets that facilitate interorganizational communication, allowing partners to share information and processes.

e-Procurement is also a successful application of extranets for the hospitality industry. Hotels are highly dependent on regular supplies of good quality and cost-efficient materials and ingredients. Eventually hotel e-procurement will integrate all aspects of the purchasing process electronically. As soon as the level of demand can be predicted from reservation levels and past data/experience, orders can be generated automatically, authorized by departmental heads, delivered and paid with little human involvement.

As a result, a number of B2B applications and companies emerged to serve this demand. For example, Avendra, a procurement company, was founded in early 2001 by Marriott International, Hyatt Hotels Corp., Club Corp., Six Continent Hotels and Resorts, and most recently Fairmont Hotels and Resorts. It is an independent company providing the largest, most comprehensive procurement network for the North American hospitality and related industries, with a market estimated at $80 billion annually. Ultimately Avendra aims to integrate systems of sellers and buyers in the hospitality industry in order to automate the entire purchasing process. Therefore, e-procurement pledges to end the hurdles of an inefficient buying system through cost controls, fully automated order processing, and corporate power to require properties to be compliant with purchasing policies. Finally, extranets are often used for other business functions such as human resources management. They can be developed to communicate with recruitment partners, social security, insurance, and pension organization. Six Continents, for example, have outsourced part of their recruitment to HCareers and use a specialized section on their website for their recruitment (e.g. http://sixcontinents.hcareers.com/jobs).

Hotels and the Internet

The proliferation of the Internet in the late 1990s and the revolution of technologies have introduced a wide range of new marketing tools. The Internet allowed hotels to develop their own websites and to display straight and clear information and photos of amenities and locations, as well as to facilitate online bookings. A number of hotel chains, including ACCOR, Marriott, and Thistle, receive a significant percentage of their reservations through their own websites, free of commissions and other charges. Hotels can reduce their distribution costs significantly by expanding their e-commerce. For example, Marriott has been able to save US$2 per Internet booking using its own booking engine instead of an outside source. Hilton saves US$25 on each website booking (compared with a traditional

travel agency booking) whilst Hyatt's cost for an online booking is US$3, compared with US$9 to book via the call center. More importantly, hotels can integrate their Web presence with their customer relationship management function by offering visitors the ability to store their personal profiles assisting the provision of personalized products and added-value elements.

The Internet also assists hospitality organizations to develop their value chain and to enhance a wide range of their *business functions*. In addition to e-commerce, e-sales, e-marketing, and e-procurement, hotels increasingly use the Internet for e-finance and e-accounting. This empowers hotels to use information and data from operational processes in order to automate their back office functions. In addition, e-HRM enables them to recruit and manage all their human resources issues online. By using the Internet they can attract employees and explain their policies, training program, and promotion opportunities. Marriott, for example, provides comprehensive information for employees and allows them to submit their CV electronically for consideration.

e-Hospitality futures: challenges for the future of hospitality

The hospitality industry gradually realizes that the ICT revolution has changed best operational practices and paradigms, altering the competitiveness of all hospitality actors in the marketplace. Hospitality corporations integrate their back and front office in a framework that takes advantage of the capabilities of the Internet as well as of intranets and extranets. Convergence of all technological devices gradually empowers greater connectivity, speed, transparency, and information-sharing. As a result, hospitality organizations are gradually focusing more on knowledge-based competition and on the need for continuous innovation, forcing management to stay abreast of the dynamic developments in the marketplace (Connolly *et al.*, 2000). Hospitality organizations are also attempting to increase their online bookings by promoting their Internet presence more aggressively and by capitalizing on partnership and collaboration marketing. As a result, multi-channel strategies are required to assist hotels to interconnect with the wide range of distributors in the marketplace. It is currently estimated that there are 35,000 websites from which consumers can book a hotel room. This raises a wide range of new challenges, including rate integrity, brand perception, segmentation, and value of customers. Stemming from the Internet, the emerging wireless devices and Bluetooth technology will allow consumers to interact with hotels constantly. This will increase transparency further and it will force hospitality organizations to rethink their pricing strategies.

The Internet has contributed unprecedented tools for communicating with consumers and partners and this has radical implications for hotel distribution. The hospitality industry must appreciate the 'high-tech high-touch' opportunity that emerges through the personalization of products, processes, and information. Hotels have the opportunity to cultivate relationships with their customers and adopt customer-centered approaches. Technology needs to simplify the way hotels look after every single need of their customer. By using ICT-enabled processes to coordinate all departments and services, as well as all properties for hotel chains, they are able to run the business more efficiently and to add value at each stage of consumer interaction. Innovative smaller properties gradually develop their online presence and are empowered to communicate their message with the world. Small and unique properties will be able to utilize ICTs strategically to demonstrate their specific benefits and to illustrate how they can innovate. By developing links with other properties they can also enhance their virtual size and compete with larger players. Larger hospitality organizations can benefit from economies of scale, multi-channel distribution strategies and from streamlining their operations through e-procurement. Larger hotels and chains will also be able to develop their globalized agenda and to ensure that their operations and strategies are coordinated worldwide, reinforcing their brand values and service promise. In any case, ICTs and the Internet will be critical for the competitiveness of both large and small hospitality organizations.

References

Anckar, B. and Walden, P. (2001) Introducing web technology in a small peripheral hospitality organisation. *International Journal of Contemporary Hospitality Management*, 13 (5), 241–250.

Buhalis, D. (2003) *eTourism: Information Technology for Strategic Tourism Management*. Harlow: Prentice–Hall.

Connolly, D., Olsen, M., and Moore, R. (1998) The internet as a distribution channel. *Cornell Hotel and Restaurant Administration Quarterly*, 39 (4), 42–54.

Connolly, D., Olsen, M., and Allegro, S. (2000) The hospitality industry and the digital economy, IH&RA Visioning the Future: Think Tank Event. Report, International Hotel and Restaurant Asscociation, Paris.

Frew, A. and Horam, R. (1999) eCommerce in the UK hotel sector: a first look. *International Journal of Hospitality Information Technology*, 1 (1), 77–87.

Marsan, J. (2001) Hotels technology survey. *Hotels*, February, 78–94.

Morrison, A., Taylor, S., Morrison, A., and Morrison, A. (1999) Marketing small hotels on the world wide web. *Information Technology and Tourism*, 2 (2), 97–113.

O'Connor, P. (2000) *Using Computers in Hospitality*, 2nd edn. London: Cassell.

Peacock, M. (1995) *Information Technology in Hospitality*. London: Cassell.

O'Connor, P. and Frew, A. (2000) Evaluating electronic channels of distribution in the hotel sector: a Delphi study. *Information Technology and Tourism*, 3 (3/4), 177–193.

O'Connor, P. and Horan, P. (1999) An analysis of web reservations facilities in the top 50 international hotel chains. *International Journal of Hospitality Information Technology*, 1 (1), 77–87.

DIMITRIOS BUHALIS
UNIVERSITY OF SURREY, UK

Incentive travel

Incentive travel is an important tool used to motivate, reward, and recognize corporate employees for outstanding performance, service, and commitment to an organization. This type of travel program intends to yield a positive return on investment, resulting in increased sales, reduction in turnover, improved morale, greater company loyalty, and enhanced customer service. Additionally, incentive travel can be an effective means to influence and create powerful alliances with valued customers.

Incentive travel can be organized two ways: *group programs*, where participants follow the same itinerary, or *individual incentives*, where participants choose the program based on established parameters. Most incentive trips take place at desirable or even exotic destinations creating a memorable, 'once-in-a-lifetime' experience. Travel packages such as these typically include first-class accommodations, exclusive transportation, recreational activities, entertainment, cultural opportunities, and sightseeing.

Corporations may seek the expertise of an *incentive travel house*. Due to the demand of this growing travel segment, this type of firm can leverage hospitality industry contacts to provide an affordable, attractive package. The services of these organizations range from full service planning and implementation to arranging logistical segments of travel. Potential leads and clients for this market can be acquired through the membership of the Society of Incentive Travel Executives (SITE).

Reference

Astoff, M. and Abbey, J. (2002) *Convention Sales and Services*, 6th edn. Las Vegas: Waterbury Press.

AMANDA KAY CECIL
INDIANA UNIVERSITY, USA

Independent restaurants

If asked to name a 'typical' restaurant, many people would describe a local, independent, full service eatery from their own neighborhood. It would be owner-operated and the owner would know many customers by name. The French use the terms 'chef/patron' and 'restaurateur' when referring to the proprietor of a restaurant. The proprietor is called the former if he or she operates from the kitchen and the latter if he or she operates mainly from the front-of-the-house.

The vast majority of restaurants around the world are independently owned and operated. These restaurants are 'independent' because they have no affiliation with regional, national, or international restaurants or other hospitality corporations (for more detail see Chain Restaurants; Franchising). Independent restaurants can be part of any segment of the industry, from quick service snack bars and coffee shops to the most elegant fine-dining establishments. They are also found throughout the event catering and on-site foodservice segments.

In most parts of the world, owning or operating independent restaurants is considered an 'easy entry/easy exit' business. By this we mean that, with a reasonably small amount of money, some relevant experience in cooking, service, or both, and a willingness to invest long hours of personal sweat equity, almost anyone can start a restaurant in one's local community.

David Birch, an MIT researcher on small business, identified independent restaurant businesses as 'income substitution' enterprises (Birch, 1987). People interested in foodservice open such restaurants to exercise control over menu design and composition, interior and kitchen design, the quality of the food they serve, and prices; they want to set their own work schedules for themselves and their employees; and they want to be able to target specific consumer markets.

Reference

Birch, David (1987) *Job Creation in America*. New York: The Free Press.

CHRISTOPHER MULLER
UNIVERSITY OF CENTRAL FLORIDA, USA

Indirect costs

Indirect costs cannot easily be associated with a particular department or area of a foodservice operation. In foodservice establishments located within hotels, casinos, or other retail spaces, indirect costs are allocated based on some other unit of measurement, like square feet, number of guests served over a given time period, or number of employees. Some examples of areas associated with these costs include maintenance, energy or utility usage, insurance, depreciation, administration, and security. Managers of this type of foodservice operation typically have no control over the indirect costs associated with their establishment.

The trend in most foodservice operations is to minimize the number of indirect-cost categories and to focus specifically on those cost categories over which unit level management has the most control. It is also important to note that some costs may be both direct and indirect; it depends on the context of the discussion and the level of analysis.

Reference

Schmidgall, R.S. (1986) *Hospitality Industry Managerial Accounting*. Lansing, MI: Educational Institute of the American Hotel and Motel Association.

DEBORAH BARRASH
UNIVERSITY OF NEVADA, LAS VEGAS, USA

Indoor air quality

Indoor air quality (IAQ) issues involve the exposure of a building's occupants to various air pollutants – particles, gases, and biological organisms, e.g., mold – and formulation of standards regarding ventilation and health protection. The public itself is demanding more attention be paid to this issue, e.g., smoke-free public areas are becoming more the norm across the United States. Central goals of formal IAQ movements are determining required levels of ventilation to sustain acceptable indoor air quality across a variety of facility designs, and assessing the effectiveness of IAQ control technologies in controlling human exposure to indoor pollutants. Ventilation rates and use of indoor pollutant sensors to control rates of ventilation and

air recirculation, as well as particle removal technologies, are currently in practice. Additional focus is on measuring emission data, determining acceptable levels of exposure for maintenance of occupants' health and comfort, and assessing performance of comparative air-cleaning technologies. Natural ventilation is becoming an increasingly popular way to ventilate buildings, based on the potential for energy savings, as are hybrid approaches that combine natural and mechanical features, such as fan-assisted natural ventilation. Research on building performance also addresses total building life, monitoring of outdoor air quality, and examining the relationship of building and indoor environmental characteristics with sick building syndrome symptoms and worker productivity.

References

ASHRAE Standard 62-2001: Ventilation for Acceptable Indoor Air Quality (2001). Atlanta, GA: American Society of Heating, Refrigerating and Air-Conditioning Engineers.
Selwitz, R. (2000) New coalition works to clear the air about air. *Hotel and Motel Management*, 215 (10), 8–9.

BONNIE CANZIANI
UNIVERSITY OF NORTH
CAROLINA – GREENSBORO, USA

Industrial tribunal

A generic term used in Australia and some other countries to describe various independent bodies and labor/wages boards created in order to prevent and settle legal disputes, fix wages and conditions of employment, and to resolve conflict (De Cieri and Kramar, 2003). Associated legislation serves to regulate industrial relations through registration of unions and employer associations. This ensures that employers are compelled to recognize the rights of unions to represent their members and, in turn, unions are compelled to recognize the rights of management. For example, in Australia, industrial tribunals established written determinations specifying the minimum terms and conditions of employment, such as hours of work, minimum pay and types of leave allowable. Compared with other developed nations, the Australian system was recognized as being egalitarian with pay differentials between high and low earners being less significant than in other developed economies. Until the 1980s, this system of awards and industrial tribunals was key in setting federal and state benchmarks for working conditions and pay.

More recently, the uniforming role of the industrial tribunal has been somewhat weakened with political pressure to move employment related negotiations to the organizational or enterprise level. This change is based on the notion that devolved negotiations restore the primacy of the relationship between managers and employees, improves competitiveness and restores the balance of power between parties.

In the hospitality industry, benefits of devolved negotiations to employees is questionable given the inherent bias of power in favor of management.

Reference

De Cieri, H. and Kramar, R. (2003) *Human Resource Management in Australia: Strategy, People and Performance.* Sydney: McGraw-Hill.

NILS TIMO
GRIFFITH UNIVERSITY, AUSTRALIA

Industry analysis

This is a process of assessing the profit potential of the lodging or restaurant industry in a market area (Rumelt, 1991). The purpose is to predict the future evolution of the local hospitality industry, to understand its competitors, and to use this information to craft a firm-specific competitive strategy. It is a process of first studying the general environment (economic, political, social demographics, technological, and regulatory) to identify broad trends or emerging changes. The next step is to conduct an industry assessment, measuring the attractiveness of the industry and relating any direct or indirect impacts of the general environment. While this

view captures potential macroenvironmental impacts, a deeper, micro-level analysis of the industry is revealed through an assessment of the forces that shape industry activity (Porter, 1978). These include the barriers to entry, the power of suppliers and customers, the threat of substitute products and the intensity of rivalry. High ratings on these five dimensions are favorable for existing firms as new businesses are discouraged from entering the industry. Low ratings make the industry more attractive to new investment and competition. Finally, an industry analysis is completed with an assessment of the competitive set; that is, a careful identification of the demand for the product, the overall market size, and an understanding of the firms that attempt to satisfy it.

References

Porter, M.E. (1978) How competitive forces shape strategy. *Harvard Business Review*, 56 (2), 137–145.
Rumelt, R.P. (1991) How much does industry matter? *Strategic Management Journal*, 12, 167–185.

CHRIS ROBERTS
UNIVERSITY OF MASSACHUSETTS, USA

Industry life cycle

This model proposes that hospitality products and services move through four successive stages: creation, growth, maturity, and decline. The time necessary to pass through the each stage varies. The model has been extended to describe individual hotel and restaurant firms and the entire hospitality industry as well, suggesting these businesses follow the same four stages (Hart *et al.*, 1984). Creation is the initial stage when the new business or product is introduced to the market. The majority of offerings do not make it past this stage (i.e., a spicy Mexican restaurant in northern Maine). It is during this period that the marketplace judges its initial value. Growth is marked by a rapid increase in size (volume of products sold such as the number of hotel rooms or when additional restaurants built) and maturity reflects a stabilizing of size (sales, number of employees, etc.). The maturity stage may linger for quite a while, creating a cash cow for the organization after it standardizes and streamlines operations. Decline occurs when the organization begins to shrink in size. Complete decline occurs when efforts to reenergize it fail or are not implemented. Unlike a biological entity, firms may occasionally move backward from decline through their own rejuvenating actions.

Reference

Hart, C.W., Casserly, W.G., and Lawless, M.J. (1984) The product life cycle: how useful? *Cornell Hotel Restaurant Administration Quarterly*, 25 (2), 54–63.

CHRIS ROBERTS
UNIVERSITY OF MASSACHUSETTS, USA

Information system (IS)

An information system (IS) is a computer-based system, which consists of hardware, software, users, data, processes, and procedures that work together to produce useful information that is related to the operation of a business organization. An IS can accept data resources as input, and then translates these resources into information as output. Specific instructions are provided for users to follow in order to accomplish an activity. An IS can support both short-term and long-range activities for users in an organization. By using an IS, managers can receive the updated information about the status of their business (Shelly *et al.*, 2002).

An IS can serve the purposes of planning, organizing, directing, and controlling. As a whole, an IS can assist hospitality managers to enhance operational efficiency and functional effectiveness, and to enable them to identify business opportunities. This, in turn, leads to the provision of better customer service. The most significant benefits that an IS can provide to a hospitality business are competitive advantages and personalized guest encounter (Ford *et al.*, 1995). The gained competitive advantages can lead to improved quality, while the guest encounter is important to guest satisfaction in a hospitality experience.

References

Ford, L., Ford, R.C., and LeBruto, S.M. (1995) Is your hotel MISsing technology? *FIU Hospitality Review*, 13 (2), 53–65.

Shelly, G.B., Cashman, T.J., and Vermaat, M.E. (2002) *Discovering Computers 2003: Concepts for a Digital World*. Boston, MA: Thomson Course Technology.

ROB LAW
THE HONG KONG POLYTECHNIC
UNIVERSITY, HONG KONG SAR, CHINA

In-house computerized reservation system

An in-house computerized reservation system can keep close track of reservations. Computer systems can tightly control room availability data and automatically generate many reservation-related reports including the number of expected arrivals per day, the number of guests choosing to stay over, and the number of guests departing on a particular day. Computerized systems also generate reports that summarize reservations by type of room, guest characteristics, and other factors. The major advantage of a computerized reservation system is the improved accuracy of room availability information. As a reservation agent inputs reservations and reservation modifications or cancellations into the system, the inventory of available rooms is immediately updated. In addition, if the front desk is part of the computer system, any front desk transaction involving guests who fail to check in, guests who leave early, or guests with no reservations who walk in will immediately update the computer's room availability.

A computerized reservation system can coordinate room sales in real time as salespeople, reservationists, and front office personnel have instant access to the most current information. Once all rooms in a specific category are sold, the computer can be programmed to refuse any further reservations in that category. Computerized reservation systems can be programmed to automatically suggest alternatives room types or rates, or even other nearby hotel properties. Systems may also display open, closed, and special event dates for an extended period of time. Open dates refer to available room days, while closed dates depict full-house forecasts. Special event dates can be programmed to alert reservation agents that a convention or large group is expected to occupy the hotel either before, during, or immediately following a caller's requested day of arrival. In addition, many hotel computer systems have a management override feature which enables overbooking.

A computerized reservation system tracks those reservations reaching the hotel directly from telephone, mail, hotel-to-hotel, e-mail, cable, and fax. A prospective guest may telephone a hotel directly, communicate via written request, which is more common for group tour and convention business, communicate a reservation from another member of a chain of properties while staying in an affiliated property, and (increasingly) communicate via e-mail or some similar form of communication.

As noted, global distribution systems such as airlines, car rental firms, and other businesses offer online reservation services through their Internet sites. This enables travelers from many different market segments to use their personal computers to book flights, reserve hotel rooms, and select rental cars. Vacation travelers, business travelers, corporate travel offices, and international visitors are all able to use the World Wide Web to arrange for their own travel and accommodation needs. The variety of potential guests accessing Internet sites to place reservations has prompted travel and hospitality companies to develop simple, user-friendly reservation procedures.

Hotels of all sizes have a presence on the internet. Chains often have a website focusing first on the brand and its features, then on the individual properties. Most chain Internet sites allow visits to the site to book reservations. It is also becoming more common for independent hotels to have websites. The independent hotel site may not be as sophisticated as the chain site but reservations are typically communicated to the hotel electronically to the property's computerized reservation systems.

While the degree of privacy and security of financial transactions over the Internet have prompted some concern, and in many cases this concern has been addressed with various modifications to the software protecting the Internet site. In addition to providing a user-friendly reservation process and securing transactions, online systems also perform important marketing functions for the hospitality company. Reservation features of many Internet sites enable users to access detailed pictures of individual hotels.

A computerized reservation system is also extremely valuable with group reservations. Group reservations can involve a variety of contacts: guests, meeting planners, convention and visitor bureaus, tour operators, and travel agents. Group reservations typically involve intermediary agents and thus the computerized reservation system must be able to carefully track these reservations. The group reservation may be given a special reservation identification code or reservation card to use to reserve rooms within the group's assigned block. The system applies reservations received from group members against the rooms held in the group's block, thereby reducing the number of rooms available within the block. The system identifies rooms for specific guests as booked, thus changing the room statuses from blocked to booked. The computerized reservation system allows a hotel reservation manager to verify the total number of rooms required for the group against what is available in the hotel. A computerized reservation system also permits members of the sales department to have access to verify general availability before booking the group. However, the group block should always be verified by the reservations manager to be sure the system inventory is up-to-the-minute before confirming the block to the group leader. Another feature of the computerized reservation system is providing the hotel manager with the possible effect of a group reservation in displacing non-group business.

In addition, the system establishes progress chart dates to evaluate the progress of conversions from blocked to booked rooms. Thus, at specific times the system may release rooms in a group's block to the available room inventory.

Typically with group reservations the computerized system can also track any special considerations given to a group through its contract, such as suites, complimentary rooms and, as previously noted, the group cut-off date for room availability. Hotel computer systems store reservation records electronically, thereby allowing the creation of waiting lists for high-demand periods. This feature contributes to the processing of group reservations and the implementation of revenue management strategies. The future time frame for tracking reservations is called the reservation horizon and most computer-based systems have horizons of two to five years. Because of the ability to store information, a reservation manager is able to provide to the sales department the history of a group in picking up rooms from a previous block before a new block with a prior group is finalized.

Reference

Stutts, Alan T. (2001) *Hotel and Lodging Management – An Introduction*. New York: John Wiley & Sons.

ALAN T. STUTTS
AMERICAN INTERCONTINENTAL
UNIVERSITY, USA

Integrated information systems

Integrated information systems are essential if modern information and communication technologies are to be used to their full potential within the tourism and hospitality industry. Essentially, systems are integrated if data are defined consistently and mean the same in each system. In addition, systems should be able to 'talk to each other,' in the sense that it must be possible to conveniently transfer data between them. Many large companies have been attempting to integrate their IS *within* their organizations since the 1960s. The evidence suggests they have had little success. e-Commerce applications demand that IS are integrated *between* companies and this adds an extra degree of difficulty to the integration task. The problem is particularly acute within the tourism and hospitality industry because of the number of companies involved, a lack of accepted standards, and because of the diffuse, geographically dispersed and autonomous nature of most of these companies, particularly the small-to-medium tourist enterprises (SMTEs).

Methods and technologies proposed as a means of addressing the integration problem have included databases, information engineering, strategic information systems planning, federated heterogeneous (meta) databases, enterprise resource planning (ERP) systems, data warehouses, and Web-based middleware based upon XML (Extensible Markup Language) standards. To a greater or lesser extent, problems have been experienced with all these techniques. Reasons identified for the failure of these integration ventures include technical obstacles, overly optimistic cost and schedule estimates, a lack of senior management support, poor communication and change management, inappropriate IT department structures and, possibly most important of all, a failure to adequately address people-related issues (especially power-political considerations).

Over the years, (data-centered) information engineering has proven to be a particularly popular approach. Here, IS are integrated by: (i) using formal conceptual modeling techniques to develop a corporate data model (CDM); (ii) constructing a set of subject databases (SDBs – groupings of data sets, with close affinities, derived from and consistent with the CDM); and (iii) building applications around the common set of SDBs. Theoretically, this approach makes a lot of sense and from the late 1970s through to the early 1990s (at least) it was the favored approach of a great many companies trying to truly integrate their information systems. The problem, though, is that it doesn't seem to work and, consequently, it has fallen out of favor – with data warehouses, middleware, and ERP systems correspondingly gaining in popularity in recent years.

New generation destination management systems (DMS) need to access data from the following sources: travel agents and tour operators; accommodation providers; airlines;

car rental agencies; event and attraction providers; government tourism agencies; restaurants; publicity, marketing, and promotion agencies; and, depending on customer requirements, many additional data sources. Also, given that a major objective of these systems is to find a best match between customer requirements and supplier offerings, access to online versions of guide books and other promotional material, plus the increasing number of personal (and organizational) websites, may assist substantially in this task. The problem here, though, is that the IS and websites of all these parties will, almost certainly, have been developed largely independently. Thus, methods and software tools are required to access, capture, and integrate data from these highly heterogeneous (and almost certainly inconsistent) sources.

Generically, the most popular integration approach involves defining a metadata schema (metaschema) – essentially, a model of the data to be manipulated within the DMS. The metaschema is so-named because it sits above the schemas (models) of the data sources it accesses. Mappings between the metaschema and its base schemas need to be specified and implemented and methods (automatic and manual) need to be developed to handle 'dirty data' – source data so inconsistent with the metaschema that no direct mappings are possible. Similarly, further methods need to be devised to cope with missing data. These data cleansing operations can be lengthy, complicated and costly, and the literature suggests that underestimating the resources required for this activity has been the cause of major cost and schedule overruns (if not outright failure) in a great many e-commerce applications (both within tourism and other areas).

Naturally, standards could greatly improve this situation and the wide adoption of XML (Extensible Markup Language) in recent years represents a major step forward here: particularly as a uniform language for data definition and message passing. XML has also been employed as the basis for a number of other significant recent standards developments, including WDSL (Web Services Description Language), the UDDI (Universal Description, Discovery, and Integration) standard services

registry, SOAP (Simple Object Access Protocol), and OASIS (a standard framework for trading partner data interchange). One of the remarkable aspects of these initiatives is the degree of agreement reached concerning core protocols – even between bitter rivals such as Microsoft, Sun, IBM, and Oracle. Recently released industry products based on these standards include Hewlett-Packard's e-speak, Microsoft's BizTalk, Oracle's Dynamic Services Framework, IBM's Application Framework for E-Business, and Sun's Open Network Environment (ONE). A further important initiative is the Semantic Web and one of the major standards development programs here is DAML (DARPA Agent Markup Language). Within tourism and hospitality, some efforts have been directed towards the development of a standard, industry-wide data model but the prospects of the widespread adoption of a single model at this point appear remote.

References

Carson, D. and Sharma, P. (2002) A model of tourism information: implications for information systems. *Information and Communication Technologies*. New York: Springer, 49–58.

Hendler, J. and McGuiness, D. (2000) The DARPA Agent Markup Language. *IEEE Intelligent Systems, Trends and Controversies*. November/December, 6–7.

Hsu, C. (1996) *Enterprise Integration and Modeling: The MetaDatabase Approach*. Norwell, MA: Kluwer.

Kaukal, M. and Werthner, H. (2000) Integration of heterogeneous information sources. *Information and Communication Technologies in Tourism 2000*. Vienna: Springer, pp. 81–92.

O'Leary, J.T. (2000) Data management in tourism: chaotic and Quixotic. *Information and Communication Technologies in Tourism 2000*. Vienna: Springer, pp. 57–166.

Stal, M. (2002) Web services: beyond component-based computing. *Communications of the ACM*, 45 (10), 71–76.

G. MICHAEL MCGRATH
VICTORIA UNIVERSITY, AUSTRALIA

Intelligent agents

Intelligent agents are software modules with an autonomy to perceive, reason, and adaptively act in their environments. They also possess the ability to cooperate with other agents to solve complex problems. Intelligent agents incorporate capabilities from object-oriented technology and knowledge-based systems, extending both of them. They enable distributed, dynamic, and large-scale applications like e-commerce and virtual enterprises. Agents can be divided into four basic forms: personal, application, system-level, and general business activity agents. Personal agents work with users to support presentation, organization, and management of user profiles, requests, and information collections. User agents (wizards) observe and monitor the action taken by the user in the interface and suggest more efficient ways of performing the task. Application agents are business-to-business e-commerce applications, networked from a large number of application agents. These agents are specialized to a single area of expertise and provide access to available information and knowledge sources and work cooperatively to solve complex problems. System-level supporting agents provide objects with transparent access to other application objects, transaction processing, permanent object storage, event-services and the like. General business agents perform a large number of general commercial support activities that can be customized to address the needs of a particular business organization such as information search agents, negotiation agents, marketing products and services agents, and legal advising agents. Applications might be: airline reservations; filtering external messages according to clients' needs, circumstances, and moods; identification of unique characteristics of consumers and matching them with individually designed or packaged products.

References

Buhalis, D. (2003) *eTourism: Information Technology for Strategic Tourism Management.* Harlow: Prentice-Hall.

Papazoglou, M.P. (2001) Agent-oriented technology in support of e-business. *Communication of the ACM*, 44 (4), 71–77.

BOZIDAR KLICEK
UNIVERSITY OF ZAGREB, CROATIA

Interactive systems

Interactive systems enable the provision of customized options and responses to users in a range of public access and self-service applications. Interactivity enables two-way communications and provides the ability to users to interrogate a system for accessing information or making reservations. Interactive hospitality websites can be used to support customer relationship management, brand building, and to provide multimedia enhancement of information (Gilbert and Powell-Perry, 2002). Interactive digital television is an emerging platform for the delivery of e-travel services, including hospitality products (Tate, 2001). Options can be presented in interactive telecommunications systems using pre-recorded databases of voice messages, e.g. for automated hotel switchboards, allowing customers to make selections, to input requisite data, e.g. account number, and to receive information, using digital phones as input devices. Interactive whiteboards can be used to support presentations allowing users to run computerized applications from the whiteboard, writing on the whiteboard in 'electronic ink' so combining the power of a projector, computer, and whiteboard. Systems are programmed with the most common requirements and default to human interaction when these are exhausted. Touchscreen technology combined with sophisticated graphics and text is widely used in interactive multimedia kiosk solutions, e.g. for exhibits in visitor centers and to provide information in hotel lobbies.

References

Gilbert, D. and Powell-Perry, J. (2002) Exploring developments in web based relationship marketing within the hotel industry. *Journal of Hospitality and Leisure Marketing*, 9 (3/4), 141–159.

Tate, P. (2001) Delivering e-travel services. *Travel and Tourism Analyst*, No. 4. 39–64.

ELERI JONES
UNIVERSITY OF WALES INSTITUTE, UK

Interactive television

The growth in interactive television has been made possible by the spread of digital services through satellite, cable, and terrestrial systems across the world. Digital services provide the opportunity to interact with television programs, from the choice of different commentaries and camera angles to home shopping, including the purchase of travel and tourism products, home voting, games, and also financial transactions. The technology also provides the capability for movies on demand, music and video games.

Interactive television offers the potential for multimedia presentations and video clips on demand. It can be seen by both individuals and family groups, often for much longer periods of time and in a more relaxed environment. The disadvantages of interactive television are that the service received depends on geographical location and access to the service. The television market is highly segmented in terms of viewing habits and socio-economic groups. An inter-active service is competing against other similar services, viewing other television channels or the use of the television for games and other video-based entertainment and media (Buhalis and Licata, 2002). In hospitality there is demand by clients for Internet connectivity and e-mail, made possible via interactive digital television. It can allow hotel guests to check their account status, view local tourism information, view hotel and restaurant menus, and arrange wake up facilities.

References

Buhalis, D. and Licata, M.C. (2002) The future eTourism intermediaries. *Tourism Management*, 23 (3), 207–220.

Marsan, J. (2001) Hotels technology survey. *Hotels*, February, 78–94.

ALAN MARVELL
BATH SPA UNIVERSITY COLLEGE, UK

Internal analysis

A major step in developing sound and successful strategic plans, internal analysis might simply be defined as a process to identify strengths and weaknesses on which a hospitality firm should base its strategies (Nebel, 1991). A strength is a resource, skill or other advantage that a firm serves or expects to serve compared to its major rivals. On the other hand, a weakness might be defined as a resource, skill, capacity limitation or deficiency that seriously decreases a firm's competitive performance (Nebel, 1991). A hospitality organization's internal strengths might include financial stability, a particular management capability, and a cost advantage over its major competitors. Internal weaknesses, on the other hand, might be obsolete facilities, high employee turnover, the lack of a certain management capability, and high departmental cost.

A straightforward approach considering strengths and weaknesses is to organize them around the major functions of the hospitality business (Nebel, 1991). For example, a hotel company may consider its major functions to be marketing, accounting and finance, hotel operations, hotel development, personnel, and food and beverage operations. Hospitality firms should develop relatively short lists of strengths based on their importance to influence the competitive environment. A strength should be judged in relation to its ability to improve a firm's competitive position. A strength must give a business some kind of competitive advantage. For example, a professionally competent executive chef should only be listed as a hotel's strength if his or her presence allows the hotel to gain an advantage over its competitors (Nebel, 1991). On the other hand, a weakness is something that a firm does poorly that could be a competitive disadvantage. It can also be something that a firm is incapable of doing that its competitors can do.

Lack of conference facilities, poor human resource management, high turnover rates and deteriorated brand names all might be considered as weaknesses depending on market conditions and competitor positions. Finally, a listing of strengths and weaknesses should be limited to those key factors that determine success or failure in a particular business. All aspects of what a hotel company or an individual hotel does are not equally important in its competitive struggle. Internal strengths and internal weaknesses should be limited to those areas that are critical to success or failure in the hotel business.

There are six major areas that a hospitality firm must carefully examine to identify potential strengths and/or weaknesses (Tse, 1988; Harrison, 2003). These areas are:

- *Marketing capability*, such as pricing, brand recognition and image acceptance, efficiency and effectiveness of marketing strategies, promotion and advertising activities of the firm.
- *Finance capability*, such as financial structure, liquidity, and cash flow. Some basic ratios, for example, are especially important to assess financial capabilities of hospitality firms. While airline companies should pay attention to load factors, for example, RevPAR (revenue per available room) is vital for hotel establishments.
- *Operations and technology base capability*, such as menu development and design systems, quality of service, equipment and facility sophistication and physical resources. Location of a hotel or a restaurant is for example especially critical in the hospitality industry.
- *Human resources capability* such as (and especially) management quality and style, level of employee turnover and effectiveness of training programs. According to Harrison (2003), 'it is part of the hospitality industry's character that among the most important resources a hospitality firm possesses are its human resources' (p. 149). As a result, analysis of human resources should be conducted at all levels of a hospitality firm. Moreover, being a 'people-intensive' (Nebel, 1991) industry, hospitality managers should especially possess high human relations skills such as listening, communication, and socialization skills.

- *Administrative capability*, such as planning and control systems, organization structure and management information systems. Especially important for hospitality managers is to be technology-driven and able to recognize, interact with, and utilize information technology resources, as 'tomorrow's hotel manager' is expected to be 'an information manager' (Olsen, 1996).
- *Research and development capability*, such as concept revitalization, environmental assessment, and top management commitment.

For an internal resource to be strategic, it needs to be 'value creating' (Harrison, 2003). As a result, a resource must:

- *Have economic value:* Installing a full-feature phone system, for example, is not a strength until guests perceive the system as an added value.
- *Be unique:* Acquiring a special kind of kitchen equipment that reduces energy consumption and food-preparation time would lead to competitive advantage only if other firms do not acquire the same equipment. Once the same system is acquired by the firm's major competitors, it's no more a unique advantage but only a norm in the industry.
- *Not have close substitutes:* In-seat entertainment systems in airlines might be difficult to substitute since it is an expensive investment. On the other hand, if the competitive advantage is to be sustainable, it must be costly or difficult to imitate. Unique brand names such as Hilton and Starbucks cannot be imitated. Well-trained, dedicated employees and unique managers and management systems are also expensive investments, require long-term dedication, and are hard to achieve.

An effective tool to diagnose a firm's key strengths and weaknesses is the 'Value Chain' approach developed by Michael Porter (Hitt *et al.*, 1996). It is a systematic way to carefully view a firm's product or service processes. Using the Value Chain, a firm can disaggregate its strategically important activities in order to understand its cost structure and its existing or potential sources of differentiation.

References

Harrison, J.S. (2003) Strategic analysis for the hospitality industry. *Cornell HRA Quarterly*, April, 139–152.

Hitt, M.A., Ireland, R.D., and Hoskisson, R.E. (1996) *Strategic Management: Competitiveness and Globalization*, 2nd edn. St Paul, MN: West Publishing Co.

Nebel, E.C. III (1991) *Managing Hotels Effectively: Lessons from Outstanding General Managers*. New York, NY: Van Nostrand Reinhold.

Olsen, M.D. (1996) Events shaping the future and their impact on the multinational hotel industry. *Tourism Recreation Research*, 21 (2), 7–14.

Tse, E.C. (1988) Defining corporate strength and weaknesses: is it essential for successful strategy implementation? *Hospitality Education and Research Journal*, 12 (2), 57–72.

KEMAL BIRDIR
MERSIN UNIVERSITY, TURKEY

Internal control

The primary concern of internal control is to safeguard the assets and profits of a business against losses, which occur through error or fraud. The main method of internal control is to install systems where any release of resources or assumption of costs is automatically subjected to checking by more than one person. This key element is known as 'separation of functions,' which means allocating different stages in the cycle of a transaction to different personnel. Thus, in a restaurant kitchen, if the chef orders from a supplier, a stores person should physically check the goods in to the business, and accounting personnel should check the invoice.

Such a system normally needs to be supported by manuals, which clearly assign responsibilities and identify which managers have authority to make decisions and for what purposes. Larger companies may have an internal audit department, which verifies periodically that the procedures are respected. External statutory auditors also have to evaluate the effectiveness of the system as part of reaching an opinion on the accuracy of the accounting records.

A viable internal control system is essential to allow central management to rely on the figures they receive as being an accurate reflection of what actually has taken place. In many countries the directors of listed companies now have to state in their annual report that they are satisfied with the adequacy of their internal controls.

References

Fenton, L.S., Fowler, N.A., and Parkinson, G.S. (1989) *Hotel Accounts and their Audit*, 2nd edn. London: Institute of Chartered Accountants in England and Wales.

Geller, A.N. (1991) *Internal Control: A Fraud-Prevention Handbook for Hotel and Restaurant Managers*. Ithaca, NY: Cornell University.

PETER WALTON
ESSEC BUSINESS SCHOOL, FRANCE

Internal marketing

Companies spend billions of dollars every year marketing their brands and/or trying to convince customers to choose their specific properties, yet consider this anecdotal example: Mike Leven, President of Days Inn, was chosen by the Hotel and Restaurant Program of the Washington State University as the 'Hotel Marketer of the Year.' Mr Leven flew into Seattle from New York and drove to Pullman, a long drive. As he arrived at the hotel, he was pleased to see the hotel marquee displaying 'Welcome, Mike Leven, Hotel Marketer of the Year.' When he approached the front desk, he learned that there was no reservation in his name. He commented that this didn't seem possible when the marquee sign was saying 'Welcome Mike Leven.' The clerk replied innocently that he didn't see the sign as he came through the back door.

Companies also have to spend millions more dollars in employee training so that products and services are delivered to the customers at the level promised. The former expenditure is intended to communicate with the external customers and is referred to as 'external marketing' and the latter expenditure spent on employee

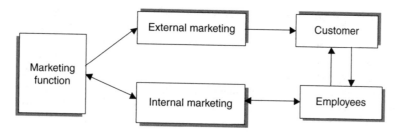

Figure 1 Schematic representation of the marketing function

training is referred to as 'internal marketing.' Kotler, Bowen, and Makens (2003) define internal marketing as 'marketing aimed internally at the firm's employee.' In the context of internal marketing, the employee is the 'customer' and the product is the job and its benefits. A leading scholar in services marketing, Leonard Berry described internal marketing as 'applying the philosophies and practices of marketing to people who serve the external customers so that (1) the best people can be employed and retained and (2) they will do the best possible work.'

Pride and Ferrell defined internal marketing in a traditional manner, as 'coordinating internal exchanges between the firm and its employees to achieve successful external exchanges between the firm and its customers.' As illustrated by the above definitions, internal marketing can be best described as the process by which an organization accomplishes its organizational objectives and societal commitments through effective communication of its goals and management of its internal customers (employees).

Internal marketing is one of the emerging but less understood areas of marketing. For the past few decades, marketing focus has been placed mostly on communicating with external customers. Importance of internal marketing was less emphasized, probably because it was less understood. External communications are effective in *attracting* customers to visit a hospitality business. When the guest makes the first visit to the business, the external marketing strategies are considered a success. After the first visit by a customer, it is the responsibility of the internal marketing to *retain* the customer. In other words, the purpose of external marketing is to attract

customers and the goal of internal marketing is to retain and convert them as repeat customers. Retention of repeat customers means greater profits for organizations. Research has shown that 5% increase in guest retention could lead to 25% to 125% increase in the bottom line. Thus internal marketing should be an integral part of organizations' overall marketing strategy. Effective implementation of internal marketing involves the following steps:

- Recognize the role of employees as internal customers
- Develop service culture that is appropriate to the organizational goals
- Institutionalize effective communication systems that allow free flow of ideas, concepts, and suggestions from the top to the bottom and vice versa
- Implement reward and recognition systems that support desired service goals
- Develop human resource practices that support internal marketing activities
- Coordinate the desired objectives of the external and the internal marketing systems
- Assess internal marketing systems periodically.

In spite of the preponderance of evidence supporting the importance of internal marketing, many hospitality firms fail to recognize it. Companies often learn that it is more challenging to implement internal marketing than external marketing. This point can be better illustrated from the following industry example.

Cameron Mitchell, the CEO of a 100 million dollar fine and casual dining, multi-concept restaurant company, was a patron one evening at a fine dining restaurant in town. His young son wanted a chocolate shake for dessert, which was not one of the choices on the menu. The waiter responded politely that it was not available. Mr Mitchell responded, 'Do you have milk? Do you have chocolate ice cream? Do you have a blender? You can make a milkshake.' The waiter communicated his dilemma with the manager. The manager came to the table and explained that it was not possible to custom-make desserts. At a subsequent managers' meeting Mr Mitchell described the incident and asked all his managers to do whatever was necessary to please guests. A week later, a similar thing happened to a restaurant manager, but this time it happened at one of the Mitchell company's restaurants. When this incident was reported, Mr Mitchell immediately implemented a company policy that every new employee would receive a chocolate shake during the first day of orientation to symbolize the point that his company would do everything possible to please its guests.

As this example illustrates, internal marketing is much more challenging to implement than external marketing. Here are some of the challenges often experienced by hospitality organizations while implementing internal marketing programs:

- Poor human resource practices that do not support the internal marketing activities
- Human resource practices that result in the selection of unqualified personnel and/or high employee turnover
- Lack of proper reward and recognition systems supporting internal marketing activities

- Lack of coordination between internal and external marketing activities
- Ineffective communication systems that do not allow upward movement of suggestions and ideas generated by the employees
- Absence of employee empowerment practices preventing them from fully realizing their potential as internal marketers.

There are limitations to internal marketing. It is effective only in the retention of existing customers and converting first time visitors to repeat customers. Unfortunately internal marketing is not very effective in attracting new customers. Internal marketing is also not recommended as the sole source of marketing while introducing new products or expanding into new markets. Internal marketing is cost effective when supported by external marketing. Unlike external marketing, the budget for internal marketing overlaps with that of the human resources as it strives to change the organizational culture. Therefore, it could become a challenge to assess the effectiveness of internal marketing without understanding the role of human resources and organization culture.

In summary, internal marketing is an important internal function of an organization. Internal marketing leads to greater retention of customer base and eventual higher profits for the organization. Development of appropriate human resource practices and supporting organization culture are essential for the internal marketing to be successful.

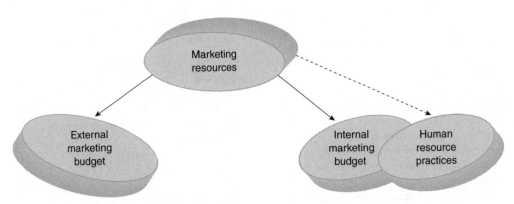

Figure 2   Schematic representation of distribution of marketing resources and the impact of human resource practices

References

Berry, Leonard L. (1984) The employee as a customer. *Journal of Retail Banking*. Reprinted in C.H. Lovelock (1984) *Services Marketing*. Englewood Cliffs, NJ: Prentice-Hall, pp. 271–278.

Kotler, P., Bowen, J., and Makens, J. (2003) *Marketing for Hospitality and Tourism*, 3rd edn. Upper Saddle River, NJ: Prentice-Hall.

Lewis, R. and Chambers, R.E. (1989) *Marketing Leadership in Hospitality*. New York: Van Nostrand Reinhold.

Pride, W.M. and Ferrel, O.C. (2003) *Marketing: Concepts and Strategies*, 12th edn. Boston, MA: Houghton Mifflin.

H.G. PARSA
OHIO STATE UNIVERSITY, USA

Internal rate of return (IRR)

The internal rate of return (IRR) method, also known as the *discounted rate of return*, belongs to the discounted cash flow (DCF) methods and is the rate that, when used to discount the future cash flows of a project, results in a net present value (NPV) of zero. Either the 'trial and error' method, or a proper computer algorithm, or the interpolation method (graphic solution), may be used to calculate it.

The IRR is usually calculated with a trial and error method, where different rates are applied to the NPV computation of a project. The higher the rate of interest used, the lower the NPV; therefore once a rate of interest (A) has been calculated, which brings the NPV to a positive result, and a different rate of interest (B) has been calculated, which brings the NPV to a negative result, the IRR falls between A and B.

The example in Figure 1 shows the trial and error method.

The formula for the interpolation method is as follows:

$$ IRR = A + \frac{a}{(a - b)} \times (B - A) $$

where:

A is a discount rate giving a positive NPV
B is a discount rate giving a negative NPV
a is the NPV when A is used
b is the NPV when B is used

The example in Figure 2 shows the interpolation method.

The IRR is recognized as 'the true interest rate' earned on an investment over its whole

	Year 2005	Year 2006	Year 2007	Year 2008	Year 2009
Additional cash flow due to the enlargement	230,000	320,000	350,000	400,000	460,000
DCFs using 15% rate of interest NPV = 129,500	200,000	241,966	230,131	228,701	228,701
DCFs using 25% rate of interest NPV = −117,400	184,000	204,800	179,200	163,840	150,733
DCFs using 20% rate of interest NPV = −5,800	191,670	222,222	202,546	192,901	184,864
DCFs using 19.766% rate of interest NPV = 0	192,040	223,091	203,736	194,413	186,677
Internal rate of return: 19.766%					

Figure 1 Trial and error method to obtain the IRR of a project (project to enlarge a hotel's capacity from 150 rooms to 175 rooms: outlay of $1m, paid in 2004)

	Year 2005	Year 2006	Year 2007	Year 2008	Year 2009
Additional cash flow due to the enlargement	230,000	320,000	350,000	400,000	460,000
DCFs with a 15% rate of interest NPV = 129,500	200,000	241,966	230,131	228,701	228,701
DCFs with a 20% rate of interest NPV = −5,800	191,670	222,222	202,546	192,901	184,864
Internal rate of return $= 15\% + \dfrac{129{,}500}{(5{,}800 + 129{,}500)} \times (20\% - 15\%) = 19.786\%$					

Figure 2 Interpolation method to obtain the IRR of a project (project to enlarge a hotel's capacity from 150 rooms to 175 rooms: outlay of $1m, paid in 2004)

	Year 2005	Year 2006	Year 2007	Year 2008	Year 2009
Additional cash flow due to the enlargement accepting the '1 million project'	230,000	320,000	350,000	400,000	460,000
Additional cash flow due to the enlargement accepting the '1$\frac{1}{2}$ million project'	330,000	470,000	525,000	600,000	650,000

	'1 million project'	'1$\frac{1}{2}$ million project'
Internal rate of return:	19.766%	18.795%
NPV, using a rate of interest of 15%:	$129,500	$153,760

Figure 3 Comparison of the IRR of two mutually exclusive projects (two projects of enlargement of a hotel's building are mutually exclusive: the first requires an outlay of $1m, the second requires $1.5m, paid in 2004)

economic life. Therefore this method is used in the decision to proceed with a project or not, comparing its IRR with a given rate of return (minimal return desired or maximum cost of capital applicable to finance the project).

If an investment is made abroad, the minimal return desired should be adapted by considering the different perception of risk in the different environment where the project takes place.

Nevertheless, IRR method has some limitations. It shows which interest rate is earned, but does not mention the cash value of the project, and hence the actual benefit for the shareholders is not immediately apparent. The example

in Figure 3 shows how comparison of the IRR of two mutually exclusive projects can result in a misleading outcome. (The higher IRR does not correspond with the higher NPV.)

This weakness of the IRR method lies in the assumption, that interim cash flows are reinvested to earn a return equal to the IRR itself (in the example it would be 19.766% for the one million project), whereas the NPV assumes that the interim cash flows are reinvested at the rate of interest used to discount (in the example it would be 15%).

In using the IRR method it should be noted that when there are negative future cash flows, more than one solution will be presented.

Caution should be exercised in such a situation because only one of these outcomes would be a reliable basis upon which to make a decision.

References

Drury, C. (2000) *Management and Cost Accounting*, 5th edn. London: Thomson Learning.

Horngren, C.T., Foster, G., and Datar, S.M. (2000) *Cost Accounting*, 10th edn. Upper Saddle River, NJ: Prentice-Hall International.

Lumby, S. and Jones, C. (1999) *Investment Appraisal and Financial Decisions*, 6th edn. London: Thomson Learning.

McLaney, E.J. (1994) *Business Finance for Decision-makers*, 2nd edn. London: Pitman Publishing.

MARCO MONGIELLO
UNIVERSITY OF WESTMINSTER, UK

International aspects of financial management

There are several issues that are not present in a domestic operating environment that must be addressed if a hotel operating or owning company is to manage its existing, or growth, portfolio, successfully. Amongst the most important are currency implications, tax and legal jurisdiction issues, investment appraisal and how these issues impact reporting and performance benchmarking.

Currencies pose a particular challenge. In a treasury (cash) sense, the goal is to have the right currency in the right bank account at the right time to meet obligations, whilst managing all other cash reserves to maximize net-of-tax earnings to the shareholder. This would appear to be a relatively easy task, but the cost of transfer of funds, the varying rates of tax on interest income, the varying rates of interest on funds deposited, together with differing approaches to exchange control, all mean that this 'simple' goal can consume significant time and effort to achieve. On the face of it, the development of the euro has simplified things in Europe, but of course in reality there still exist borders and central banks.

Taxes differ in each country – indeed in federal countries such as the United States and Germany, taxes vary at a state or county level. The goal in tax management is to achieve an ever lower effective rate of corporate tax – that is to say, to continually drive down the cost of corporate tax. This can be achieved through a variety of modes in which differentials in treatment are capitalized upon. Thus, it may be that the ownership of the brand is held by a subsidiary resident in a country with low rates of tax on licenses, whilst the physical asset of the hotel is held in a subsidiary in a country with low rates of capital gains tax.

The resultant network of legal entities will represent a corporate governance challenge. Boards of Directors need to meet perhaps physically in the country in which the legal entity resides, to make and document decisions in respect of that entity without necessarily having a holistic view of the overall network of entities. Care has to be taken to abide by the laws of each country and in most cases extreme care has to be taken to avoid the impression that the structures are artificial.

Having established a network, a web of legal entities for valid tax and legal reasons, the business is then faced with the challenge of reporting against the structure. Usually this calls, legitimately, for two sets of books because the managerial structure will not reflect the legal structure. Thus, brand management is generally organized geographically (e.g. Brand Manager, Northern Europe). Whereas the legal infrastructure actually reflects the fact, for example, that the brand is owned by a Dutch company and the asset is owned by an American company with the operating entity being located in the country of the hotel. This complexity means that management reporting has to be able to cut and dice the database of results into a meaningful output – meaningful to the brand manager as well as to the owner of the statutory books.

Returning to the first point, in most cases the business will be managed using a functional currency that is the actual currency of the country in which the parent company is based. However, the actual trading will be earned in and recorded in the currency in which the hotel based. So the two sets of books described above may both need to be expressed in two currencies. This requirement of an international business means that even the simplest business requires a sophisticated database and application allowing historic and projected results to be stored in one place in local currency and a separate reporting tool that allows such data to be aggregated and analyzed using historic, actual, and projected exchange rates – and all of this to take place at the click of a button.

In making investment decisions that involve a business investing in a foreign country, care also needs to be taken to ensure that the appropriate discount rate is used in investment appraisal. The general technique should be adjusted to recognize the risks associated with cross-border investment. Generally speaking, the techniques noted here continue to apply – they can be summarized as 'think local.' Thus the construction costs, the operating profit and loss should be projected in local currency with explicit assumptions of local inflation. The twist then comes with the discount factor which also should be the local WACC (weighted average cost of capital) rather than the offshore central WACC. This adjustment from the normal approach to investment appraisal ensures that the local cost of capital and local cost of debt are also factored into the investment appraisal by the offshore investor.

The diversity, which is at the heart of international operations, requires a very different set of human skills and competencies from those required by the domestic player – not to mention the requirement to understand and deal with the different cultural aspects that are represented by the rich tapestry of humanity around the world.

Reference

Graham, I.C. (1995) Financial management in an international environment. In P.J. Harris (ed.), *Accounting and Finance for the International Hospitality Industry*. Oxford: Butterworth-Heinemann.

IAN GRAHAM
THE HOTEL SOLUTIONS PARTNERSHIP, UK

International Hotels Environment Initiative (IHEI)

IHEI, the International Hotels Environment Initiative, is a program developed by the international hotel industry for the benefit of all hotels and the environment. The aim is to promote the benefits of environmental management as an integral part of running a successful, efficient hotel business. Focusing exclusively on hotels, IHEI keeps members informed about global environmental trends and provides hotel-specific guidance to assist hoteliers in tackling emerging issues.

IHEI is unique in that it is international, hotel-specific and not for profit. It was created in 1992, when a group of chief executives of 12 multinational hotel companies joined forces to promote continuous improvement in environmental performance by the hotel industry worldwide. Through this initiative, hotels pool resources and experience to produce self-help tools for use by the wider industry.

IHEI is a program of *The Prince of Wales International Business Leaders Forum* (IBLF) of which HRH The Prince of Wales is President. IHEI represents more than 8000 hotels around the world and over one million hotel rooms.

Green Hotelier is a magazine produced by IHEI which focuses on environmental trends and best practices in the international hotel industry. IHEI also offers an environmental benchmarking tool that allows hotels to compare their overall environmental performance with other hotels around the globe.

Reference

Borgers, J. (2003) About IHEI. Retrieved 1 October 2003 from http://www.ihei.org/HOTELIER/hotelier.nsf/content/i1html. www.ihei.org.

LYLE THOMPSON
BURNABY, BC, CANADA

International meeting

1 International/intercontinental: A meeting of an organization with multinational membership that is available to meet on more than one continent.
2 International/continental: A meeting of an organization with multinational membership that is available to meet on only one continent.
3 International/regional: A meeting of an organization with multinational membership that is available to meet in only a given region of one continent.

World meetings are open to all nations and meet worldwide. International meetings require more planning time than domestic meetings, due to the variety of special planning conditions, including the logistics of making long distance arrangements, budgeting complicated by foreign exchange currency risks, the availability of local services, such as technical support, and shipping and travel time to distant destinations. Logistical considerations include time differences, language barriers, the longer time needed for mailings, arranging for passports, visas and vaccinations, obtaining proper insurance coverage, finding suitable facilities and accommodations, locating required support services, international shipping procedures, customs regulations on importing/exporting meeting materials and giveaways, custom broker fees, special waivers for entertainers, regulations on paying meeting staff at the host hotel(s) in the meeting countries, and currency exchange and restrictions.

Reference

Goldblatt, Joe and Nelson, Kathleen (2001) *The International Dictionary of Event Management*, 2nd edn. New York: John Wiley & Sons.

PATTI J. SHOCK
UNIVERSITY OF NEVADA, LAS VEGAS, USA

Internationalization

Internationalization is defined as the process of expanding firm activities beyond the borders of its domestic markets. Historically, the primary motivation for internationalization among firms was the need to become more efficient. Efficiency in the context of the post-industrial revolution era is achieved when a firm becomes larger and thus generates economies of scale. Consequently, many firms searched for and found attractive markets in countries with higher market growth rates, developing consumer consumption, and growing discretionary income. Furthermore, the development of computer technology, communication technology, and new means of transportation all served as important enabling forces to internationalization. Today, internationalization has become one of the key preoccupations of firms. As barriers to international trade collapse in many parts of the world, managers become aware of new opportunities in an ever-changing global environment. For example, a uniform currency (the euro) is gaining a dominant position within the European market, Eastern European markets are developing rapidly, Asian markets are opening to the world, and the world business community has reached the General Agreement on Tariffs and Trade (GATT).

The decision of a firm to internationalize begins with a selection of the geographic market in which the firm will compete. This is a challenging task for most firms, because the selection is based on evaluation of a variety of issues such as trade barriers, tariffs, and restrictions on foreign ownership. Other differences that characterize regions include culture, physical environment, history, language, way of doing business, form of government, institutional agreements, cross-investment, intra-regional trade, trade policies and agreements, economic performance and prospects, and transportation infrastructure (Yip, 2000). Over time, international firms that generally consider all the elements in the geographic destination develop different strategies for each geographical market, each specially tailored for the specific market (Yip, 2003).

Examples can be found for both successful and unsuccessful international strategies. In the area of express delivery services, Federal Express (FedEx) dominates the market in the Americas, yet in other markets, such as Europe, FedEx is not successful, and the market is dominated by DHL. Wal-Mart has also encountered some difficulties in various international markets because it was considered too 'all-American.' In addition, Wal-Mart had to adjust its strategy in different markets to reflect the common practices in each location. For example, in the United States Wal-Mart does not accept postdated checks. In Brazil, however, postdating checks is a common practice with which Wal-Mart had to deal. Even MTV is adapting to penetrate international markets. In Asia, MTV is continuously trying to gain popularity by adjusting some of its media offerings and working with local partners to produce some of its programs.

Despite the challenges involved with internationalization, many studies have shown that internationalization improves the financial performance of firms and decreases overall risk (Reeb *et al.*, 1998). Another benefit stemming from internationalization is the ability to extend the product life cycle, where a product in the decline stage in one market and can be sold in another market where it is considered new or even innovative (Vernon, 1979). Finally, internationalization allows firms to shift their production and distribution to different locations when the terms in a specific location become unfavorable.

In the hospitality industry, internationalization efforts began at the turn of the century. The pioneers were the Ritz group in Europe and the Indian Taj hotel group. After the Second World War, Hilton, Sheraton and InterContinental Hotels began to acquire international properties to meet the demand of Americans traveling overseas. Many hotel chains are currently actively involved in internationalization efforts. Most notable are Accor with businesses in 68 different countries, InterContinental with 67, Holiday Inn with 63, Best Western with 62 and ITT Sheraton with businesses in 60 different countries (Olsen *et al.*, 1998, pp. 284–285).

Firms in the hospitality industry can develop an international strategy by using the following:

- *Franchising agreements* in which a franchiser grants a licensed privilege to a franchisee to do business. This agreement may include permission to use a brand name, products, operating systems, central reservation systems, and more. Franchising is used by Hilton International as a component of its international strategy.
- Management contracts in which management is separated from ownership, where a company can contract the management of its overseas operation to a management team in return for a fee. Sodehxo is one of the examples of a management contract company in the industry.
- *Strategic alliances* in which a linkage or a partnership forms between two or more companies that can benefit from greater market coverage, economies of scope or scale, increased visibility for the brand name or minimized capital investment. One such example is the strategic alliance between Accor and the Japanese Hokke Group. *Joint venture*, in which the multinational firm provides a partial equity stake to local businesses in order to secure their commitment to the agreement. Accor is actively involved in joint ventures in different Asian markets such as Korea, Vietnam, and Malaysia.
- A *wholly owned subsidiary*, in which the multinational firm has the sole equity stake in the foreign country. The Bass Company uses wholly owned subsidiaries in its internationalization strategy.

References

Olsen, M.D., West, J.J. and Tse, E.C. (1992) *Strategic Management in the Hospitality Industry*. New York: Van Nostrand Reinhold.

Reeb, D.M., Kwok, C.Y., and Baek, H.Y. (1998) Systematic risk of the multinational corporation. *Journal of International Business Studies*, 29 (2), 263–280.

Vernon, R. (1979) The product cycle hypothesis in a new international environment. *Oxford Bulletin of Economics and Statistics*, 41 (4), 255–267.

Yip, G.S. (2000) *Asian Adventure: Key Strategies for Winning the Asia-Pacific Region*. Cambridge, MA: Perseus Publishing.

Yip, G.S. (2003) *Total Global Strategy II.* Upper Saddle River, NJ: Prentice-Hall.

AVIAD ISRAELI
BEN-GURION UNIVERSITY, ISRAEL

Internet

The Internet can be defined as a computer network consisting of millions of hosts from many organizations and countries around the world transporting data across computers (Williams *et al.*, 1996). The Internet supports various functions such as the Worldwide Web (WWW), electronic mail (e-mail), Usenet, Gopher, Telnet, and File Transfer Protocol (FTP). The Web is similar to a global library with millions of books, directories, records, and movies open all day, every day of the year. The Internet encourages a new marketing approach for hospitality by supporting customers' involvement, as they benefit by examining in advance hotel facilities, attractions, and events at the destination. The Internet offers hoteliers the ability to show full-color virtual catalogues, provide on-screen reservation forms, offer online customer support, announce and distribute products easily. It also provides opportunities for extensive e-commerce and distribution as well as for obtaining feedback from potential or actual customers (Buhalis, 2003). As a result, the Internet technology has revolutionized the structure of the hospitality industry and is encouraging hospitality professionals to establish effective management and marketing strategies for the rapidly changing business environment worldwide.

References

Buhalis, D. (2003) *eTourism: Information Technologies for Strategic Tourism Management.* Harlow: Prentice-Hall.

Williams, P.W., Bascombe, P., Brenner, N., and Green, D. (1996) Using the Internet for tourism research. Information highway or dirt road? *Journal of Travel Research*, Spring, 63–70.

METIN KOZAK
MUGLA UNIVERSITY, TURKEY

Internet channels

The Internet has increased the reach and the efficiency of traditional distribution channels as well as provided new channels through Internet-based reservation networks. For the most part, two major types of players serve the online reservation industry: hospitality companies and third party travel companies. Malhotra and Desira (2002) stated: 'For the hospitality companies, the online booking business is a logical extension of their central reservation networks and brand support. It is in the arena of third party travel companies that we find unique product offerings, innovative business models, and along with them, challenging decisions for hotel operators as to how and when to use these companies.'

The different hotel reservation paths shown in Figure 1 provide an overview of how online and offline distribution systems interact.

The Internet channels that integrate the distribution systems represented in the figure will be described in detail. These channels will be classified according to how they access rates and inventory. For more information on offline channels, refer to 'Hospitality Distribution Systems,' and 'Hospitality Distribution Terms and Initials.'

Proprietary sites

A proprietary site is the hospitality company's or the property's Web page. Sales generated through proprietary sites are also called direct sales. In the proprietary site, the reservations are placed through the central reservation system (CRS), and thereby do not incur third party fees. The reservation booking-engine is interfaced with the CRS. Operators have a substantial interest in pushing reservations to their websites, due to the lower costs. It is estimated that for each room sold at a $220 rate, a hotel would pay a $22–$27 fee to traditional travel agents, or a $22.30–$26.80 fee per reservation to online travel agents (Shoemaker, 2004). The only costs incurred through a proprietary site would be those associated with site maintenance.

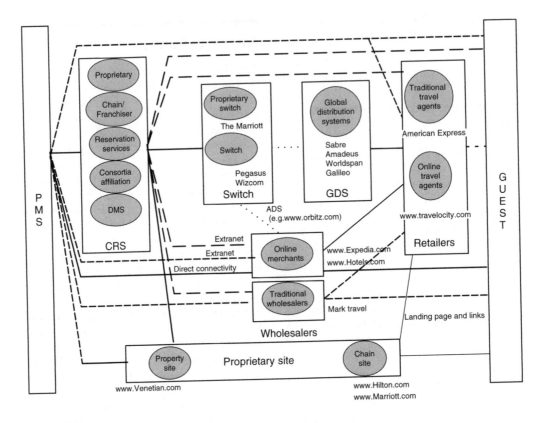

Key :

——————— Fully automated interface

———————· Manual (i.e. phone, fax, or e-mail) or semi-automated interface
(e.g., Extranet)

CRS – Central reservation systems

DMS – Destination management systems

GDS – Global distribution systems

Online travel agents – Travel agents that sell through online sites.

Online merchants – Third party sites who receive net rates directly from suppliers and distribute them online

PMS – Property mangement systems

Traditional travel agents – Brick-and-mortar travel agents

Traditional wholesalers – Brick-and-mortar wholesalers, who obtain rates directly from suppliers and distribute them through sales officers and travel agents

Figure 1   Hotel reservation systems (adapted from Carroll and Siguaw, 2003 and Carroll, 2004)

Third party sites

Third party, or secondary, sites are online retailers and wholesalers. Online wholesalers, also called online merchants, receive discounted rates which are either sold to affiliate websites or posted on the wholesaler's own website (HRN, Expedia, etc.). Online retailers simply reach the final customer.

The third party sites may work on commission, acting as online travel agencies. They may also utilize the merchant model, also known as mark-up, in which the third party marks up the net rate by a certain percentage. Examples of sites that utilize the merchant model are Orbitz, Travelocity, and Expedia. One of the disadvantages of the merchant model is that the suppliers cannot control the mark-up and therefore the end price, presenting challenges to rate integrity and yield management. Some sites utilize an opaque model (e.g. Priceline, Hotwire), hiding information on the product until the purchase is finalized. There are brand-opaque and price-opaque products. The brand-opaque products protect hotels rates by omitting the name or location of the product until the customers have made a purchase (e.g. Hotwire). The price-opaque products are mainly constituted by packages, in which the names of the suppliers are displayed but the prices are hidden in the bundled offerings (e.g. Travelworm). Opaque models can also occur in an auction or 'name-your-own-price' situation (e.g. Priceline). The main advantage of opaque models is that the customer cannot shop and compare prices for specific products. Opaque models protect the brand and operators tend to use them with deep discounts when they have distressed inventory. Most of the time, reservations are non-refundable and paid in full upfront.

Third party sites can access rates and effectuate transactions in a variety of ways. Since the information path determines the reservation cost structure, the sites are presented here according to how they access rates and availability:

- *Sites powered by the global distribution systems:* These sites obtain information directly from the GDSs. They usually develop their own interfaces to the GDSs (e.g. GetThere, powered by Sabre; Highwire, powered by Galileo; and Priceline, powered by Worldspan). They often pay lower GDS fees than a regular travel agent, due to GDS partnerships and/or high transaction volumes. There are also sites that were developed, or acquired, by the GDSs in an effort to reach guests directly (e.g. Travelocity, which is a Sabre subsidiary). However, the GDSs do not interface with most property management systems and therefore the reservations are processed through the traditional reservation structure. In other words, the reservations are referred from the GDS sites to a switch company.
- *Sites powered by the switch:* The switch companies developed their own sites that host occupancy and rate data, such as TravelWeb (owned by Pegasus, Hilton Hotels Corporation, Hyatt Corporation, Marriott International, Intercontinental Hotels Group, Starwood Hotels, and priceline.com), and Hotelbook (owned by Pegasus' Utell). Other third party sites may also obtain rates from the switch companies' sites (e.g. Orbitz, which is powered by Travelweb), thereby accessing a substantial array of travel products, while avoiding using the GDS terminals and associated fees.
- *Site powered by the supplier:* These sites interact directly with the supplier, without intermediaries. The information is exchanged as follows:
  - *Interface with the CRS:* Some sites are currently working on obtaining direct interfaces with property management systems. IAC's Newtrade interface is already able to directly connect Expedia.com to some PMSs. The fully automated direct interface between sites and PMSs, i.e., a two-way connectivity, is the ideal structure for both third party sites and the suppliers.
  - *Extranet:* The extranet is simply a page in the third party's intranet that is manually updated by the operators via the Internet. It is usually used by Internet wholesalers. Even though the use of an extranet is more efficient than a completely manual process, the third party cannot place the reservations in the PMS in real time. The reservations are usually faxed or e-mailed to the operator and then manually updated in the PMS.
  - *Landing page:* The landing page is an additional URL in the supplier website, customized to a third party site (e.g. lastminutetravel.com, travelzoo.com). It allows websites to be powered by the CRS. The rates are controlled through the property's booking-engine. The advantages of using a landing page are that there are no GDS fees, there is interface to the PMS, there is no labor involved to maintain the information, and the utilization is traceable. Developing those URLs, however, is time-consuming. In addition, too many landing pages may slow down the booking engine.
  - *Information updated manually by staff:* There are still some online wholesalers that obtain their rates and availability by either calling a company or simply by fax or e-mail. Even though the consumer perceives that online

reservations are complete when they finalize the online purchase, the reservations are manually transferred to the property and then placed in the PMS. This process is labor-intensive and subject to errors.

- *Affiliate websites:* These are sites that receive the rates and availability from online merchants or wholesalers. The numerous affiliate sites increase reach and exposure for suppliers and have the ability to cater to very specific markets. However, maintaining control over the content on these sites and enforcing contractual restrictions may be challenging. There have been instances when affiliate sites virtually copied a company's site, leading the customers to believe they were purchasing directly from the supplier. In addition, some affiliates and online wholesalers obtain rates from offline wholesalers, introducing obstacles to rate parity and revenue management.

References

Carroll, B. (2004) Internet marketing – examining key issues. Fourth Annual Conference for Hospitality Operations. *Lodging Hospitality*.

Carroll, B. and Siguaw, J. (2003) *Evolution in Electronic Distribution: Effects on Hotels and Intermediaries.* The Center for Hospitality Research at the Cornell University School of Hotel Administration.

Malhotra, N. and Desira, C. (2002) *Hotel Internet Distribution Channels.* San Francisco: HVS International.

Shoemaker, Stowe (2004) Personal communication.

FLAVIA HENDLER
UNIVERSITY OF NEVADA, LAS VEGAS, USA
ROM HENDLER
VENETIAN RESORT HOTEL AND CASINO,
LAS VEGAS, USA

Interval

The specific allotted period of time in which each owner/member of a common-interest subdivision may, based upon the use rules established by the common-interest, use and enjoy the property. Commonly used in dividing timeshare interests (interval ownership) into use periods. Traditional use periods are defined as a one week (seven night) period in which the occupant has exclusive rights to occupy a unit or piece of property. Once the intervals have been established the right to occupy a specific unit or parcel at a given time is defined by the use rules and reservation system established at the outset of the timeshare or interval ownership plan. Properties utilizing an interval ownership reservation system may include timeshare resorts, second homes, campground interests or recreational-subdivision lots. Interval time periods may be defined by a point-based system. In instances whereby a point-based system is utilized intervals are allocated as point values that correspond to periods of time for which the points may be redeemed. Intervals expressed in point values may be redeemed for greater or lesser periods of time as outlined in the use rules of the common-interests interval ownership plan. However, in no instance may the amount of points allocated as a whole, to the entire ownership base, be greater than the total point redemption value assigned to all of the intervals combined.

Reference

American Resort Development Association (2002) *The Timeshare Industry Resource Manual.* Washington, DC.

MICHAEL HAUSHALTER
ORLANDO, FLORIDA, USA

Intranet

An intranet disseminates information to employees of an organization using Internet hypertext protocol over private networked computers. It allows employees timely access to confidential company information and other tools (e.g. human resource records, e-learning, financial models, competitive intelligence, company news) that assist them to be more effective and efficient. It is also used as a communication medium among members of the organization. Intranets are usually WWW based and protected by firewalls and passwords to maintain confidentiality. They are not confined to one location. Like the Internet, they can be accessed around the world.

The data usually are generated by a hotel's property management system (PMS) and is accessible by staff on a need-to-know basis. The general manager of a property has access to all data on the intranet, housekeepers access to room status, marketing staff access to source of sales, average room rates, occupancy rates, and so on. The intranet is designed to deliver information where it can best be used. Intranets are usually linked to the WWW, which can be used to transfer data and to provide access for employees on the move. Other benefits of an intranet are facilitating staff collaboration, sharing of ideas and expertise, and communication of company policies.

References

Darwin Executive Guides. http://guide.darwin-mag.com/technology/web/intranet/index.html.

Burgess, S. (2002) *Managing Information Technology in Small Business: Challenges and Solutions.* Hershey, PA: Idea Group Publishing.

IAN MCDONNELL
UNIVERSITY OF TECHNOLOGY, SYDNEY,
AUSTRALIA

Inventory

Inventory describes goods to be sold in hospitality operations. In the food and beverage department inventory refers to food and beverage products, whilst in the rooms division inventory refers to room capacity. Inventory systems are used to facilitate control of the inventory. In the case of F&B, the system is used to order and monitor supplies, control interdepartmental transfers, monitor efficiency and market trends, by monitoring product sales. In the rooms division, the inventory is controlled by the front office system. Through this system rooms can be allocated to tour operators or other distributors such as online agents. Automated inventory systems allow your employees to create invoices, purchase orders, and packing slips and ships with standard inventory and sales-related reports. It allows tracking vendor orders and receipts, and monitoring stock levels. Stock levels are automatically adjusted and low stock levels are automatically highlighted. Items can be easily grouped together into assemblies and sold as a group. Customer's payments and balances can also easily tracked. Both systems (F&B and FO) are part of the property management system (PMS) and are integrated so that the information can be analyzed for market research and customer satisfaction purposes.

References

Davis, B. and Lockwood, A. (1994) *Food and Beverage Management.* Oxford: Butterworth-Heinemann.

Bardi, J. (1996) *Hotel Front Office Management,* 2nd edn. New York: Van Nostrand Reinhold.

IOANNIS S. PANTELIDIS
UNIVERSITY OF SURREY, UK

Inventory turnover analysis

One of the best tools to monitor inventory management is inventory turnover analysis. Inventory turnover can be calculated as:

$$\frac{\text{Food cost for the period}}{\text{Average inventory value for the period}}$$
$$= \text{Inventory turnover for the period}$$

For example, assume that a modest-sized midscale restaurant has weekly retail sales of $47,000 with an associated food cost of $16,450. For the targeted week, assume the average physical inventory was $17,312 (i.e., the inventory's beginning and ending valuations divided by two). The inventory turnover statistic for the period is:

$$\frac{16,450}{17,312} = 0.95 \text{ turns per week}$$

Of course, a single week's turnover statistic is not a valid benchmark for assessing overall inventory-management success. A more useful measure would be to calculate the inventory turnover statistic over a multi-week period. Such a calculation is easily applied to categories of food and beverages and even to individual food items in cases where problems with the inventory-management process are severe. Such analyses are especially helpful in identifying unexplained spikes in item-specific use, particularly for high-priced items.

The utility of the inventory turnover statistic is perhaps most obvious when comparing a single operation over time with a number of very similar operations. Even if an operator regularly achieves similar levels of turnover, anomalies may indicate cause for concern. In the table below, for example, the average monthly inventory turnover statistic for the hypothetical mid-scale restaurant is, at times, close to the target range of 3.5–4.5 for operations in this segment (Reynolds, 2003).

The data shown in Table 1 provide a good example of the turnover statistic's value, particularly when monitored over time. For the first six months of the period under scrutiny, the operator maintained relatively consistent inventory turnover (with turns per month between 3.6 and 3.9). For the next several months, however, a disturbing pattern emerged. The inventory turnover for months 7 and 8 was only 3.5 turns

Table 1 Inventory turnover statistics for Loyd's Grill and Tavern

Month	Turns per month
1	3.8
2	3.9
3	3.7
4	3.9
5	3.8
6	3.6
7	3.5
8	3.5
9	3.3
10	3.4
11	3.5
12	3.1

per month, and declined during the next four months.

This pattern of inconsistency signifies erratic inventory management, which is undesirable under any circumstances. Moreover, the decline beginning in month 7 may indicate an unexpected change in sales or reflect other operational problems; in either case, the information suggests that immediate investigation is warranted. Finally, the decline in turnover may be the result of employee theft or collusion in the inventory-valuation process. No matter what the cause of the decline, the periodic analysis is a bellwether that indicates management should investigate other operating statistics and performance measures to identify and remedy the problem. Granted, the cause may be innocuous, such as a change in vendor accompanied by a new delivery pattern. The point is to know when something out of the ordinary is happening, and to be prepared to do something about it (Reynolds, 1999).

These data also indicate the occurrence of a cyclical phenomenon in relation to the inventory turnover declines. That is, every three months the inventory turnover statistic takes a notable downturn. This can be explained if the same employee (or pair of employees) had a hand in the inventory process during those periods and is either making errors consistently or, more likely, is attempting to hide fraudulent activity.

A 'snapshot' approach is used when adequate historical data are available and a general measure is needed for a given period. Assuming there were no substantial changes during the past year, for example, an operator first calculates the average inventory value for the past 52 weeks. This number is used as the average inventory value in the denominator. The numerator, then, is the food cost for the given week. The resulting calculation provides a good indicator of the efficiency in managing inventory for the given week.

Owing to the related managerial adage and perennial objective of 'slow and old or fresh and fast,' inventory turnover analysis can aid operators in identifying problems related to inventory management and can directly help reduce the associated costs. The main caveat here is that more is not always better. For example, some operators may equate high inventory turnover to efficient use of resources. While it is true that higher inventory turnover statistics suggest that food is not sitting on the shelves for excessive lengths of time, it is also true that such statistics require very frequent food deliveries. Such a delivery schedule may unduly tax vendor relationships and may also produce higher labor costs associated with receiving and shelving these frequent deliveries. Thus, inventory turnover analysis must be performed thoughtfully, with overall efficiency and profitability always at the core of the operational analysis.

References

Reynolds, D. (1999) Inventory-turnover analysis. *Cornell Hotel and Restaurant Administration Quarterly*, 40 (2), 54–59.

Reynolds, D. (2003) *On-Site Foodservice Management: A Best Practices Approach*. Hoboken, NJ: John Wiley & Sons.

DENNIS REYNOLDS
WASHINGTON STATE UNIVERSITY, USA

Invitational tournaments

A planned invitational tournament instills excitement into a club's sports-minded members by creating an atmosphere of social bonding and competitive spirit. Of course, the downside of conducting a tournament at a club is that the sports facility in question is closed to regular membership play until the tournament is over. To avoid this type of conflict the club manager must gain, in advance, majority acceptance that the facilities will be closed during the period of tournament play. An invitational tournament can be conducted on a 'for members-only' basis or it can be open to an outside source such as the PGA tour. On the latter, it is not uncommon for non-equity (alias a corporate-owned club) to block off the entire club for a PGA invitational tournament. A good example of this would be the invitational tournament that is held each year at the Bay Hill Club in Orlando, Florida. In instances such as this the club usually makes arrangements for their members to play at other local clubs while the tournament is being held.

References

Perdue, Joe (1997) *Contemporary Club Management*. Lansing, MI: Educational Institute of the American Hotel and Motel Association.

White, Ted and Gerstner, Larry (1991) *Club Operations and Management*. New York: Van Nostrand Reinhold.

ARAM SON
JAMES COOK UNIVERSITY, AUSTRALIA

ISO 9000

While the vast majority of standards promulgated by the ISO (International Organization for Standardization, *not* International Standards Organization) are technical in nature, and intended for the use of engineers, two deal with the subject of management systems: ISO 9000, dealing with management of quality, and ISO 14000, dealing with management of environmental issues.

All organizations of any size have a management system, whether it is formalized and written down or not. Likewise, some part of this management system deals with ensuring that that organization's work is done to a certain quality level. The floor supervisor system, for example, is used by some hotels to see that guestrooms are cleaned and prepared to a certain quality. ISO 9000 is a family of standards providing a framework against which organizations can standardize their management of quality. One significant advantage of having such a framework is that each organization does not have to 'reinvent the wheel.' But the more important benefit of an international standard is that other parties wanting to do business with that organization, particularly customers and prospective customers, can operate with a high level of assurance that quality is uniform and being well managed. This is of particular value where organizations are doing business internationally. It is the growth of global trade that has fuelled the use of both the

ISO 9000 and ISO 14000 standards. Instead of a hotel company or its suppliers needing to send representatives to every company around the world that manufactures bed sheets to ensure it buys bed sheets that will arrive uniformly satisfactory, it can rely on a manufacturer's ISO 9000 certification to provide that assurance.

Reference

http://www.iso.org

ROBERT ALLENDER
ENERGY RESOURCES MANAGEMENT, HONG KONG SAR, CHINA

ISO 14000

ISO 14000 is a family of standards, guides, and technical reports covering environmental performance promulgated by the ISO (International Organization for Standardization, *not* International Standards Organization). ISO 14001 is the specific certification standard within the ISO 14000 family. It does not set environmental standards, nor does it measure environmental results. Rather, it covers the management systems used to control how an organization deals with environmental issues.

To obtain certification, companies are required to set up procedures to identify environmental aspects of all activities so that the impact of those activities can be determined. For the hospitality industry, this would include all supplies and resources used, including water, air and energy, and all waste produced, whether directly or indirectly. Participants then need to document plans to reduce those impacts, and to have a system for continual auditing.

For the hospitality industry, one significant driver for implementing ISO 14000 is the growing number of MICE (meetings, incentives, conventions, and exhibitions) customers requiring this certification of their suppliers. Another is that it provides a thorough risk management framework to ensure that potential risk exposures are being systematically evaluated and analyzed.

Senior management support is absolutely inescapable if ISO 14000 certification is to be achieved, making it an excellent tool for raising environmental decisions to the strategic level, where consideration can be given to risks, to long-term resource allocations, to competitive issues, and to existing operational factors.

References

http://www.iso.org.

ROBERT ALLENDER
ENERGY RESOURCES MANAGEMENT, HONG KONG SAR, CHINA

J

Job analysis

Job analysis is the process by which individual jobs are analyzed in order to determine the specific responsibilities, working conditions, and requirements of the position. A human resource specialist, the employee, the employee's supervisor, or an external consultant may conduct the job analysis. Methods used for gathering the information used in job analysis include interviews, surveys, observations, and journaling (i.e., having the employee record tasks undertaken as they are performed). Typical job analysis questions include:

- What is the major purpose of your job?
- What are your duties (both ongoing and episodic)?
- What types of decisions can you make without checking with a supervisor?
- What processes and resources do you use in the completion of your work?
- With whom do you interact and what is the nature of that interaction?
- What positions do you supervise?
- What education, experience, and skills are necessary in order successfully to carry out your responsibilities?
- What technology or equipment do you use?
- What are the major sources of stress in your job?
- What types of physical exertion are required?

An iterative process is typically used in finalizing the job analysis, with input from the employee and the employee's supervisor playing a pivotal role.

Job analysis information supports many important employee resourcing functions such as recruitment (i.e., for advertising the position and describing the responsibilities and nature of the job), selection (i.e., for identifying the minimal requirements – the job specification – on which to make the selection decision), performance evaluation (i.e., for identifying the performance criteria on which to assess performance), and pay scales (i.e., for ensuring pay equity between similar types of work). It can also provide useful information in support of improved job design leading to enhanced employee motivation and organizational effectiveness. Some of the specific concepts associated with job analysis – job description, job specification, job posting, and job design are further elaborated below.

A job description is a written summary of the major duties and responsibilities of the position. Job descriptions typically have several major components: identification information (e.g., title, department, reporting relationships); date last updated; job summary (i.e., a brief statement on the key purposes of the position and its importance to the organization); duties and responsibilities (i.e., a listing of all major functions and areas of accountability along with clearly defined standards of performance); and working conditions (i.e., hours and conditions of work). Job descriptions are used to communicate responsibilities and performance expectations to employees. They are also used to form the basis of job postings. While job descriptions serve many useful functions, they can be time-consuming to create and once created, difficult to keep up to date. One approach for ensuring that they are regularly updated is to have each employee review their own job description in advance of their annual performance review, and to make suggestions for change where appropriate. This ensures that not only do the job descriptions remain current, but that employees are reminded of their stated responsibilities and the performance standards on which their performance evaluation will be based.

A job specification is often included as part of the job description. It identifies the personal competencies, prior work experience, and formal qualifications considered essential in carrying out the responsibilities outlined in the job description. Personal competencies are typically designated as knowledge, skills, and attitudes. Prior work experience typically pertains to similar jobs done elsewhere, or pre-requisite types of experience (e.g., before becoming a dining room manager, one would ideally have worked as a waiter). Formal qualifications pertain to education and/or certification requirements. In determining what requirements to specify, every effort should be made to identify what is a required minimum, recognizing that employees can be trained and developed once on the job. In addition, it is important to keep in mind that the focus between these three areas (knowledge, skills, and attitudes) will vary depending on the nature of the job. For example, a job specification for an entry-level position in the hospitality industry may require little in terms of formal knowledge or education, but instead be heavily focused on interpersonal and communication skills as well as on positive job-related attitudes such as work ethic and customer-service orientation.

Job posting is a system for informing current and potential employees of available positions within the organization. Based on the information contained within the job description and job specification, a job posting typically includes a brief description of the major duties and responsibilities of the job, along with the minimum required personal competencies, prior work experience, and formal qualifications. Job postings can appear on company bulletin boards, and in newsletters and websites and can support both internal and external recruitment strategies. Well-written job postings can serve as an effective pre-screening device, helping potential candidates accurately assess their own appropriateness for the job. Internal job postings have been found to be particularly useful in large hospitality chains, for retaining employees interested in relocating.

Finally, job design pertains to the nature of the work itself, including the specific tasks to be performed, the working environment, and reporting relationships. Job design may be regarded as being primarily traditional or non-traditional in nature (Beer *et al.*, 1985). Traditional job design is based on the principles of scientific management and the work of Frederick Taylor, a noted US industrial engineer, who advocated that operational efficiency is enhanced by breaking down jobs into their simplest components and requiring employees to perform the same narrow tasks over and over again. Traditional job design requires employees to exercise little judgment, and to need few skills and training. In contrast, non-traditional job design embraces the concept of job enrichment, in which autonomous employees are given broad, meaningful jobs, in which they can make use of a variety of skills. Job enrichment has been associated with increased levels of extrinsic motivation, high-quality performance, high satisfaction, and low absenteeism and turnover (Hackman, 1977). Job analysis can be useful in helping identify positions that would benefit from increased job enrichment.

References

Beer, M., Spector, B., Lawrence, P.R., Mills, D.Q., and Walton, R.E. (1985) *Human Resource Management: A General Manager's Perspective.* New York: The Free Press.

Hackman, J.R. (1977) Job design. In J.R. Hackman and J.L. Suttle (eds), *Improving Life at Work: Behavioral Science Approaches to Organizational Change.* Santa Monica, CA: Goodyear Publishing.

JULIA CHRISTENSEN HUGHES
UNIVERSITY OF GUELPH, CANADA

Job specialization

In hotels, the traditional nature of job specialization (reservations, reception, wait staff, kitchen staff, housekeeping staff, and so on) means that many workers tend to do similar jobs within their workplace; jobs, therefore become rather mundane and routine, leading to less job satisfaction and motivation.

Quinn *et al.* (2003, pp. 161–163) suggest three job design strategies:

- Job enlargement increases the number of tasks that an employee does. This approach can be seen in the front office area of a hotel where staff are given a range of tasks across specializations (reception, reservations, communications, guest services).
- Job rotation expands skills through a variety of tasks, often in different areas. In hospitality, some organizations use cross-training as a job rotation mechanism.
- Job enrichment appears to be most effective in increasing worker motivation and satisfaction. Rather than focusing on skills and variety, this approach provides staff with more responsibility and decision-making. In hotel terms, this could equate with empowering front-line staff to take responsibility for delivering best-practice service to guests. However, Guerrier (1999) notes that in some organizations more specialization and less autonomy are considered beneficial.

Shadowing is where staff are provided an opportunity to work alongside other staff members. In many smaller hotels, shadowing often replaces structured orientation and training programs.

References

Guerrier, Y. (1999) *Organizational Behaviour in Hotels and Restaurants: An International Perspective.* London: John Wiley & Sons.

Quinn, R.E., Faerman, S.R., Thompson, M.P., and McGrath, M.R. (2003) *Becoming a Master Manager: A Competency Framework,* 3rd edn. New York: John Wiley & Sons.

PAUL WEEKS
SOUTHERN CROSS UNIVERSITY, AUSTRALIA

K

Key control

In the past, the concept of key control usually related to a metal key. In the United States there are fewer metal keys in use as the lodging industry has moved toward the electronic guestroom access card. However, there are sufficient metal keys in the international lodging industry and in 'back-of-the-house' operations in the United States to give special consideration to this area of security controls.

The key should not have identification of the property or the room or facility number controlled by the key. Coding has been successfully used to assist in such control. In addition, there are some control aspects in the use of the electronic access cards.

Management must make a decision as to the 'par' of keys to be retained per guestroom or storeroom; or other facility within a property. For example, there may be 12 keys per room. Three may be on the key deck at the front desk with three as back-up for large parties or families that may require more than three keys. The additional six are in an office safe; or may be retained in the accounting department safe. In Engineering, there are key blanks which permit any number of keys to be might be created for a single location. Key blanks must be secured and the key-machine must be secured and used by authorized staff, only. Special controls must be installed when an outside locksmith service is contracted.

A member of the Rooms Division supervisory staff should be assigned responsibility for issuing a requisition whenever a new key must be made. There must be accountability for every key that is created. Insofar as possible there should be a 'trail' on the keys that are being replaced. Have keys been taken by guests? If so, how many keys have to be missing before the lock on the guestroom is changed? Should it be after three, five or six? Beyond six is probably inadvisable from the point of defense. Indeed, even one missing key and the failure to change the lock may come back to 'haunt' one when such a key becomes involved in a criminal incident.

Establishments overseas are more likely to make an effort to have the key left at the front desk when the guest leaves the property. To that end, a large metal or wooden attachment may make it awkward for a guest to carry the key off the premises.

Keys for staff must be carefully controlled:

- Keys must never be removed from the premises
- Section master keys, floor master keys, grand master keys and e-keys (by-pass the dead-bolt on a key-operated lockset) must be strictly controlled.
- Keys should be issued daily and confirmed by staff signature. Similarly, the keys should be returned and signed in by a member of the security staff, the department supervision or other person named by management.

Controls for the key cards must relate to storage, inventory, use and re-use of the card. The great advantage of the card is that it can be instantly re-programmed and, when a lost card is reported, the replacement card will block entrance through use of the lost card.

Reference

Ellis, Raymond C. and Stipanuk, David M. (1999) *Security and Loss Prevention Management,* 2nd edn. Lansing, MI: Educational Institute of the American Hotel and Motel Association.

RAYMOND CLINTON ELLIS, JR
UNIVERSITY OF HOUSTON, USA

Kitchen fire suppression system

Kitchen fire suppression systems are designed to prevent fires from spreading to the duct system and ultimately the rest of the building. A kitchen fire suppression system is incorporated into the hood design and designed to sense fires in the food service equipment under the hood. When a fryer or char broiler ignites, the suppression system discharges a fire suppressant from the duct area on the cooking appliance involved. The original suppression systems used a dry chemical agent; however, wet chemicals were introduced in the early 1980s. In 1994 the Underwriter's Lab in the USA adopted UL 300, Fire Testing of Fire Extinguishing Systems for Protection of Restaurant Cooking Areas, because of new equipment and new frying oils. Wet chemical extinguishing systems, using an increased amount of extinguishing agent, were effective for the hotter fires.

Reference

Katsigris, C. and Thomas, C. (1999) *Design and Equipment for Restaurants and Foodservice.* New York: John Wiley & Sons, pp. 198–200.

CAROLYN LAMBERT
PENNSYLVANIA STATE UNIVERSITY, USA

Knowledge management

Although there is no universally accepted definition of knowledge management (KM), it can be defined as the process through which organizations generate value from their intellectual and knowledge-based assets. It is a concept in which an enterprise gathers, organizes, shares, and analyzes the knowledge of individuals and groups across the organization in ways that directly affect performance. Knowledge management can be described as a process that helps organizations find, select, organize, disseminate, and transfer important information and expertise necessary for activities such as problem-solving, dynamic learning, strategic planning and decision-making. It is basically about helping people communicate and share information.

Knowledge management envisions getting the right information, in the right context, to the right person, at the right time, for the right business purpose (Nohria, 2002).

The concept of knowledge is multifaceted: Knowledge is either *tacit* (residing in the minds of personnel) or *explicit* (meaning it can be captured in some physical and communicable form). It is *knowledge in products* – 'intelligent' or 'smart' products can command premium prices and be more beneficial to users; or *knowledge in people* – presumably the industry's most valuable asset, although the way people are actually treated and managed often belies this.

An effective knowledge management strategy should also benefit a company by doing one or more of the following:

- Fostering innovation by encouraging the free flow of ideas
- Improving customer service by streamlining response time
- Boosting revenues by getting products and services to market faster
- Enhancing employee retention rates by recognizing the value of employee knowledge and rewarding them for it
- Streamlining operations and reducing costs by eliminating redundant or unnecessary processes (Nohria, 2000).

Knowledge management, however, also presents challenges, including getting employees on board, allowing technology to dictate knowledge management, not having a specific business goal, recognizing that KM is not static, and that not all information is knowledge. The major problems encountered in KM generally occur because companies ignore the people and cultural issues. In an environment where an individual's knowledge is valued and rewarded, establishing a culture that recognizes tacit knowledge and encourages employees to share it is critical. In summary, knowledge management involves connecting people with people, as well as people with information.

The recent developments in information processing and knowledge production and transfer have several implications for the processes and relations in the hospitality and tourism industry. Yet, the application of knowledge management concepts to the hospitality sector has been slow compared to other fields, particularly in those sectors that have a strong service tradition. Despite the increasing importance of customer knowledge management, the concept appears to be ill-defined by companies across the hospitality and travel industry (Bouncken and Pyo, 2003). However, knowledge management has enabled numerous organizations of international repute comprehensively to change their approach and service delivery capability, both toward their internal employees and external stakeholders. A knowledge management system is useful only if it is accepted throughout a hotel or a tourism organization. This requirement should be noted in light of the fact that managing knowledge is becoming a business imperative for corporations that want to protect market share, explore future opportunities, and stay ahead of competition. Creating organizational competitive advantage requires developing and leveraging organizational knowledge of both the internal and external environments and the various levels within the organization.

Finally, knowledge management must be considered an underpinning objective of future research agendas so that the increasing intellectual capital in the hospitality and tourism sector can be transformed into industry capabilities. Among the instrumental objectives of hospitality and tourism policy such as the reinforcement of natural and cultural resources, sustainability, quality and efficiency, emphasis should also be placed on knowledge management.

References

Suresh, H. (2002) Knowledge management, the road ahead for success. *PSG Institute of Management Articles*. PSG Institute of Management, Peelamedu, Coimbatore, Tamil Nadu, India.

Bouncken, R.B. and Pyo, Sungsoo (2003) *Knowledge Management in Hospitality and Tourism*. New York: The Haworth Hospitality Press.

Nohria, N. (2000) *Knowledge Management*. New Delhi: McGraw-Hill.

OLGUN CICEK

SKYLINE COLLEGE, UNITED ARAB EMIRATES

L

Labor costs

Labor costs for foodservice establishments include wages paid to hourly employees, salaries paid to management and supervisory staff, and employee benefits for all employees. In the United States, average labor cost is typically 25–40%. Many foodservice employees are paid hourly wages and some also receive tips from customers. If hourly employees work more than 40 hours per week in the United States, they must be paid an overtime wage, which may vary between 1½ and 3 times their normal hourly wage. There are also a number of salaried employees – these employees are considered fixed-cost employees. This means that they will receive the same salary regardless of the number of hours they work and their salaries will not change over the short term. Business volume therefore does not affect this cost.

Employee benefits represent another significant component of labor costs for a foodservice operation. In addition to wages and salaries paid to employees, restaurant operators must pay federal and state taxes on all wages earned by these employees. Also, many employees receive additional benefits, which can include, but are not limited to, health insurance, vacation/sick pay, employee meals, and uniforms. Employee benefits can comprise over 15% of total labor costs for a foodservice operation.

Reference

Deloitte & Touche LLP (1996) *Uniform System of Accounts*. Washington, DC: National Restaurant Association.

DEBORAH BARRASH
UNIVERSITY OF NEVADA, LAS VEGAS, USA

Labor employment

Employment usually refers to the form of the contractual relationship between worker and employer. Employment in the hospitality industry is normally paid but there are significant exceptions. In some countries, including those that are industrialized, there is a high proportion of unpaid labor (International Labor Organization, 2001). This reflects the situation in hospitality where there are a large number of small entrepreneurs with unpaid family members. At least half the employment within the hospitality industry is within SMEs (small to medium-sized enterprises). However, since the 1970s there has been an expansion of branded chains which has created large multi-site organizations particularly within the fast food, themed bars, roadside catering, and budget hotel sectors (Lucas, 2004).

Demand for many hospitality services is subject to fluctuation on a daily and, often, seasonal basis. This creates unstable patterns of employment. These patterns of employment are compounded by certain service sector characteristics. The perishable nature of the product/service, the simultaneous occurrence of production and consumption, and the inseparability of the customer to the service process, combine together to create a just-in-time delivery of goods and services. This is further exacerbated by a range of external influences, such as economic, political, ecological, and meteorological factors (International Labor Organization, 2001), which create a climate of uncertainty. Taken together, these create a tendency within the industry to differentiate tenure of employment along a core–periphery divide. A small core of skilled full-time permanent employees is supported by a large pool of disposable labor which employers can access in times of demand. Core workers within the industry tend to be sourced from the primary labor market which is characterized by high levels of skill and permanence of employment, whereas peripheral workers are sourced from the secondary labor market which is characterized by less skilled, less valued, and often part-time or casual workers. The preference for unskilled work has created a deliberate strategy in certain parts of the industry to further casualize the workforce, in order to cheapen the cost of labor and simultaneously increase the pool of workers available.

Labor markets can be further segmented by a range of factors external to the organization: these include social class, access to educational opportunities, gender, age, ethnicity, culture, and disability. The emphasis of labor market segmentation theory is on the occupational rigidity that is created by social forces embedded in society. This can be clearly seen in the hospitality industry, where there is a preference for marginalized workers and a gendered occupational structure.

Most workers within the industry tend to be young and/or female. Indeed, the hospitality industry provides the point of entry for many young people into the world of employment as well as providing an opportunity for women to combine paid work with family responsibilities. The lack of jobs with organizational support for women with such responsibilities means that women are often forced to consider part-time, casual or temporary work within the industry. Women, therefore, find themselves in jobs which are low paid and lacking in security of tenure.

Over half of employment in the international hospitality industry is made up of women. Occupations are said to be feminized when women enter them in significant numbers. The feminization of labor is argued to be a process whereby the jobs performed by women become associated with low status and low rewards. There is debate about whether employers deliberately deskill jobs in order to offer them to women at lower rates of pay or, conversely, whether devaluation of jobs and their skill levels take place once they have been identified with women's work. (Wood, 1997). The value of skills can be determined by the cultural context in which employment takes place. In North West Europe, where direct customer service jobs in the hospitality industry tend to be perceived as less skilled, such jobs are more likely to be filled by young women, whereas in Southern and Eastern Europe, where there is a higher regard for such skills, there is a greater male presence (Baum, 1995). As cultural perceptions of skills change over time it would be expected that this would be reflected in the gender composition of employment in the hospitality industry.

Skill is argued to be a major determinant of occupational hierarchy within the hospitality industry. Employment is generally considered to consist of low and semi-skilled work, though there are exceptions to this within managerial and certain craft-based jobs at both a national and international level. This concentration of low-skilled workers within the industry has led to a pattern of recruitment and promotion strategies which can be understood within the features of a weak internal labor market.

Weak internal labor markets are characterized by the following factors: unspecified hiring standards, multiple points of entry, low skill specificity, no on-the-job training, a lack of fixed criteria for promotion, weak workplace customs, and pay differentials that vary over time (Riley, 1991). These characteristics lend themselves towards a reliance on external rather than internal sources of labor and, as such, create a vicious circle of high labor turnover and poor management practices.

Stronger internal labor markets tend to exist within some craft-based and managerial occupations in the industry. Within such internal labor markets the occupational skills tend to be more highly regarded and professionalized, which is reflected in greater opportunities for career progression. The extent to which this occurs may vary according to the cultural and economic contexts in which skills and employment are located. In some countries, however, there has been a blurring of occupational demarcation lines and skill differentials as a consequence of competitive pressures. This process is likely to be exacerbated by the pressures of globalization.

References

Baum, T. (1995) *Managing Human Resources in European Tourism and Hospitality: A Strategic Approach*. London: Chapman & Hall.

International Labor Organization (2001) *Human Resource Development, Employment and Globalization in the Hotel, Catering and Tourism Sector*. Geneva: ILO.

Lucas, R. (2004) Employment relations in the hospitality and tourism industries. London: Routledge.

Riley, M. (1991) *Human Resource Management: A Guide to Personnel Practice in the Hotel and Catering Industries*. Oxford: Butterworth-Heinemann.

Wood, R.C. (1997) *Working in Hotels and Catering*. London: International Thomson Business Press.

RUTH BLACKWELL
LEEDS METROPOLITAN UNIVERSITY, UK
ANNEMARIE PISO
LEEDS METROPOLITAN UNIVERSITY, UK

Labor turnover

There are three ways to calculate labor turnover. The first, as advocated by the United States Department of Labor, is as follows:

(Number of employee separations during the period/Total number of employees at the midpoint of the period) × 100 = Turnover rate

This method is considered inadequate because it assumes that employee separations will occur at equal intervals throughout the period of measurement. For example, assume that a restaurant has 28 employees at the beginning of the month

(the period for which the turnover statistic is needed). If 5 employees depart before the middle of the month, the turnover rate as calculated with this formula is just under 22%. If only one employee leaves in the beginning of the month and four leave near the end, however, the rate as calculated is less than 19%.

The second method allows for the often-subjective determination between the 'desired turnover' of undesirable employees and the 'undesired turnover' of desirable employees. This approach treats the resulting statistic as the *undesired turnover statistic*. The calculation is performed as follows:

[(Number of separations − Desired separations) /Average number of employees during the period] × 100 = Undesired turnover rate

This calculation appropriately takes the average number of employees during the period (as shown in the denominator). In essence, however, this method is useful only for managers who wish to justify some elements of the turnover problem. The truth is that turnover of any kind is undesirable. Although poor hiring decisions are occasionally made, resulting in so-called 'desired separations,' but nonetheless, even though such turnover may rid the restaurant of undesirable employees, it reflects problems in the human-resource management process.

The final method is the easiest and offers the greatest utility. The calculation is:

(Number of employee separations during the period/Average number of employees during the period) × 100 = Turnover rate

This statistic is not subject to interpretation and also allows for intra- and inter-unit analysis (in the case of multi-unit onsite operations).

Reference

Hinkin, T.R. and Tracey, J.B. (2000) The cost of turnover: putting a price on the learning curve. *Cornell Hotel and Restaurant Administration Quarterly*, 41 (3), 14–21.

DENNIS REYNOLDS
WASHINGTON STATE UNIVERSITY, USA

Laddering techniques

'Laddering' is a qualitative research technique that researchers and managers can use to understand the underlying reasons for people's behaviors. Laddering refers to in-depth interviewing and analysis methods used to elicit the salient characteristics that customers seek when they make a choice to purchase a product (Reynolds and Gutman, 1988). For example, the laddering technique can reveal the underlying reasons why customers choose a certain hospitality operation for a specific occasion over other alternatives. Understanding the relationship between a hospitality product's attributes and customers' desired benefits can provide hospitality marketers with information useful in targeting advertising and customer segmentation.

Consumers' values are connected to their behaviors through a cognitive conceptual structure (Gutman, 1982). This structure is often referred to as the 'means–end chain.' The central concepts of the means–end chain model are two linkages: the linkage of values and desired consequences and the linkage between consequences and product attributes. The means–end chain model is based on two fundamental assumptions about consumer behavior. First, consumers perceive and judge products as the 'means' to achieve a desired 'end-state' in a given product-use situation. Second, customers cope with the overwhelming choices of products by grouping products into categories. For example, when this concept is applied to the restaurant and lodging industry, customers might think of categories labeled 'hotels' and 'restaurants.' However, they might also produce categories such as the 'function' and 'type' of operations. Customers' categorization may also include groupings such as 'employee kindness' and 'clean environment' (Chong et al., 2002).

The 'laddering' interview technique can be used to examine the 'ends,' or values in the 'means–end chain,' that hospitality customers hope to fulfill when they make a choice to visit a hospitality operation. Laddering can also identify the categories that customers group the 'ends' in. The laddering interview consists of two steps: (1) eliciting salient characteristics, and (2) probing

to reveal the means–end structure (Hofstede et al., 1998). First, subjects are asked to identify attributes that distinguish different choice alternatives in a product class. This phase is used to identify the available competitive set of products or services. For example, knowing which restaurant or hotel attributes that customers use to infer the presence of desired consequences allows us to more clearly specify attribute development.

Next, the laddering interviewee is prompted to verbalize sequences of attributes, consequences, and values, which are referred to as ladders. Continuous probing is conducted by repeatedly asking a question such as 'Why is that important to you?' (Reynolds and Gutman, 1988). This dialogue compels the interviewee to consider the reasons behind his/her choices or judgment. These repetitive and probing questions reveal the means–end structure. For example, a hotel manager could learn about specific attributes that attract customers to his or her property or to that of a competitor. These attributes can serve as indicators for the creation of meaningful association between the choice of a hotel and the specific value that the customer wants to satisfy. The individual ladders, or means–end chains, for each interviewee are then aggregated and summarized in a hierarchical value map, which is also known as a consumer decision map.

Analyzing the laddering procedure

The first step in analyzing laddering data obtained from the interviewees uses a content analysis technique. Each idiosyncratic concept resulting from the laddering responses is categorized into one of three levels of abstraction – attributes, consequences, and values – in the means–end structure. Each element of the interviewees' responses should be included in one of these three categories. A number may be assigned to each element to make coding convenient.

It is important to remember that it is the relationship between the elements that is of interest, not the elements themselves. For example, a business traveler might prefer a certain hotel because its elegant atmosphere helps him or her to relax after a demanding day. Further, the business traveler may feel that relaxation increases his or her productivity, which results in a feeling of accomplishment. In this case, the elegant atmosphere of the hotel can be placed in the lower level of the ladder, which makes it an attribute. The relaxation property of the hotel occurs at a higher level of the ladder, which makes it a consequence. However, in this case the relaxation element is important because it leads to increased productivity as a second consequence and finally to a feeling of accomplishment, at a higher level of value.

Based on this type of content analysis, a summary table can be constructed representing the number of connections, or linkages, between the elements. There are direct and indirect linkages. For example, customers' responses reveal that an elegant atmosphere, previously identified as an attribute, allows for relaxation, which is a higher-level consequence. The frequency of total interviewee responses that link elegant atmosphere with relaxation is summed, and the total is assigned to the linkage between elegant atmosphere and relaxation. This relationship is an example of a direct linkage.

If an additional element lies between the two elements in the direct relationship, it becomes an indirect relationship. For example, if the relaxation property of the hotel falls between the attribute 'elegant atmosphere' and the consequence of 'increased productivity,' the link between the 'elegant atmosphere' of the hotel and the 'relaxation' consequence now represents an indirect relationship.

The values that are assigned based on the frequency of each of the linkages are then used to score each element in each ladder, producing a matrix called the implication matrix. The implication matrix is generated by specifying the occurrence frequency for each linkage. Each frequency represents the number of direct linkages between two adjacent levels as well as the indirect linkages between the qualitative concepts in the ladder offered by some of the respondents. A hierarchical value map (HVM) is constructed from the implication matrix. An HVM is developed by connecting all the chains that are formed by considering the linkages in the large matrix of relations among elements. This provides a well-organized summary of information derived in the interviews (Reynolds and Gutman, 1988).

References

Chong, Y.K., Raab, C., and Zemke, D.V. (2002) Means and chain model for restaurant attributes. *Proceedings of Seventh Annual Graduate Education and Graduate Students Conference in Hospitality and Tourism,* January 2002.

Gutman, J. (1982) A means–end chain model based on consumer categorization processes. *Journal of Marketing,* 46 (2), 60–72.

Hofstede, F., Audenaert, A., Steenkamp, J-B E.M., and Wedel, M. (1998) An investigation into the association pattern techniques as a quantitative approach to measuring means–end chains. *International Journal of Research in Marketing,* 15 (1), 37–50.

Reynolds, T.J. and Gutman, J. (1988) Laddering theory, method, analysis, and interpretation. *Journal of Advertising Research,* Feb/Mar, 11–31.

CAROLA RAAB
UNIVERSITY OF NEW HAMPSHIRE, USA

Late arrival

Any guest arriving after a designated hour of the day, typically 6 p.m. (1800 hours), is considered a late arrival. At that time a guest who did not guarantee his/her reservation may have it cancelled. A number of situations or circumstances can delay a guest's scheduled arrival. Guests frequently do not have the chance to change a non-guaranteed reservation to a guaranteed reservation by the time they realize they will arrive past the hotel's reservation cancellation hour. As a result, the hotel may not hold the room for the guest and may not have a room available when the guest arrives.

On the other hand, if reservations are carefully handled and sound forecasting procedures are followed, the property should not have to deny accommodations to a guest with a guaranteed reservation. The front office manager typically becomes actively involved when it appears the property will not have accommodations for a late arriving guest with a guaranteed reservation. The manager typically reviews all front desk transactions to ensure full occupancy; retakes an accurate count of rooms occupied, using all relevant data; compares the room rack, housekeeper's report, and guest folios for any discrepancy in occupancy status; reviews telephone due outs or guests expected to check out who have not yet checked out and confirms their departure time. If they do not answer the telephone, the rooms department visit the guestroom to verify continued occupancy, personally checking the current status of rooms listed as out of order and identifying rooms pre-blocked for one or two days in the future and register late arriving guests who will depart in time to honor the blocks.

Reference

Stutts, Alan T. (2001) *Hotel and Lodging Management – An Introduction*. New York: John Wiley & Sons.

ALAN T. STUTTS
AMERICAN INTERCONTINENTAL
UNIVERSITY, USA

Layout and design in foodservice facilities

Foodservice facilities are unique in that the design of the 'factory' is part of the product. Guests enjoy the physical elements of their dining experience as well as the food and service they receive, while the part of the design that they don't see is integral to the successful execution of their requests. For this reason, special care must be taken in creating the foodservice environment so that it balances the aesthetic experience with efficiency and efficacy.

Foodservice operations are almost all divided into two distinct physical components: the front-of-the-house, or those areas that a guest or customer sees; and the back-of-the-house, or those areas that are limited to employees. The design challenge for each component is to create a functional setting while at the same time expressing the unique personality of the operation. Because of significant differences in the design requirements of each component, two distinct groups of professionals are typically retained to create a single foodservice environment. Trained interior designers are often hired to create plans for front-of-the-house areas, while a professional foodservice consultant or food equipment dealer can assist the operator in laying out the most effective kitchen-related areas.

In the front-of-the-house, the main environmental concerns are that the placement of the furniture and fixtures – the layout – is functional for service, and that the dining room's colors, materials, textures, lighting, and sound – the design – is effective for creating the desired experience for the guest. A good front-of-the-house design will capitalize on the strengths of the building and its site, emphasizing scenic views or using existing columns or walls to create distinct dining environments within the space. It will also serve as a guide to guests, helping them understand what they might expect from the meal experience to come.

When determining the size of the front-of-the-house, it is common practice to allocate a fixed amount of space per seat, which varies depending on the type of experience desired. For fast food restaurants, it is not uncommon to allocate about 1 m^2 (10 sq ft) per seat to front-of-house areas, whereas a fine dining restaurant might allow as much as 2.5 m^2 (25 sq ft) per seat. This allocation is often adjusted to accommodate additional features such as a bar, a retail area, or demonstration cooking stations.

One of the main layout decisions in the front-of-the-house relates to the type and placement of seating. Freestanding tables give the operator the greatest degree of flexibility, but patrons may prefer booths, which allow them to regulate their privacy more effectively, increasing their comfort. To be profitable, an operation needs as many seats as possible in the available space. The challenge is that some seats are less desirable than others because of their proximity to kitchen or restroom entrances or other idiosyncrasies of the interior environment. In general, a good layout includes a mix of seating types that situates preferred table styles such as booths in higher traffic areas.

When planning the back-of-the-house, functionality and flexibility are the most important factors, allowing staff to produce a wide range of items with maximum efficiency during both busy and slow times. Selecting multi-purpose pieces of equipment, positioning equipment to minimize reach or steps, and even creating mobile elements that allow easy reconfiguration of the cooking line are all strategies that can enhance a foodservice facility's ability to respond to changing conditions.

Kitchen areas are generally divided into functional areas: storage, food preparation, cooking or production, serving, and sanitation (dish and pot washing). Good back-of-the-house design follows the principle of forward flow, which holds that goods should move through the kitchen in a continuous, forward-moving line without backtracking. The layout of each functional area will be dictated by how much preparation food items require, the volume of meals served, the complexity of the service, and the complexity of the menu.

In general, the higher the degree of preparation or service required by the operation, the more space will be required in the back-of-house. Back-of-the-house areas make up anywhere from 35–50% of the total foodservice area, although very simple or very sophisticated operations may vary outside this range. Foodservice operations that must store a wide range of goods or that receive infrequent deliveries will require substantially more back-of-the-house space than is typical.

References

Baraban, R.S. and Durocher, J.F. (2001) *Successful Restaurant Design*. Hoboken, NJ: John Wiley & Sons.

Birchfield, J.C. and Sparrowe, R.T. (2003) *Design and Layout of Foodservice Facilities*. Hoboken, NJ: John Wiley & Sons.

STEPHANI K.A. ROBSON
CORNELL UNIVERSITY, USA

Leadership, authority, power, and control

Often leadership is assumed to be synonymous with management or management style. However, although the terms may be used interchangeably within popular management literature, there is a fundamental difference. Leadership is the process of influencing the behavior of others by inspiring, influencing, and motivating them whereas management is about controlling and coordinating processes. Although traditionally the hospitality sector has been typified by an autocratic, task-centered approach to leadership, there is growing support for a more human relations approach, especially one that recognizes the importance of job satisfaction and employee motivation in delivery of good service. This is especially important within flatter organizational hierarchies and dynamic work environments where close supervision is no longer possible.

One of the key aspects of leadership is to understand the use of power. Power is the capacity for one individual or group to exert influence over another and to produce results or outcomes consistent with the former's interests and objectives. French and Raven (1959) identified five types of power:

- *Legitimate power*, where the individual's power comes from their position within the organizational hierarchy
- *Reward power*, when the individual has control over both tangible and intangible rewards, such as better shift patterns or better promotion opportunities, and can allocate these in recognition for achievement of results consistent with their preferred outcomes (this is an interesting issue in the hospitality sector, particularly for front-line staff where the customer wields reward power in the form of tips)
- *Coercive power*, the opposite of reward power, where the leader has the power to punish for non-conformance or poor performance
- *Charismatic or referent power*, where power derives from the regard in which the leader is held by followers, and their desire to maintain a positive relationship with the leader
- *Expert power*, where the leader's power is a function of their specialist knowledge or experience, as is often the case in a kitchen environment where there is strict demarcation of responsibilities and expertise, or in multidisciplinary teams where decision-making power might fall to different functional experts, regardless of their hierarchical authority, depending on the nature of the task.

It is important to recognize that these different sources of power are based on the subordinate's perception of the influence of the leader, rather than the actual ability of the leader to fulfill these roles. However, different cultures have quite different perceptions, based on their assumptions about the appropriate distribution of power. In some countries, legitimate power, that is power based on a person's position within the hierarchy, is considered to be the most appropriate basis of status and control. However, other cultures respect power based on expertise and knowledge rather than hierarchical control (Hofstede, 1980). With the hospitality industry changing its global profile in recent years, this can cause problems in multinational organizations where non-indigenous managers are sometimes required to adapt their leadership style to suit the perceptions of the host country or risk alienating staff.

There have been many attempts to explain the nature of leadership and categorize what makes an effective leader (Mullins, 2002). These range from early attempts to identify the requisite traits of a leader by studying the personal qualities of those who have been recognized as successful, collectively known as the trait approach to leadership. This approach is based on the assumption that leadership is an innate quality rather than a skill that can be nurtured and developed over time. Despite numerous studies, there has been very little agreement on either the qualities themselves or the nature of leadership.

Next studies looked at the responsibilities of the leader and how these are influenced by and can influence the group of subordinates. This functional approach to leadership has led to many initiatives to help managers to develop their leadership abilities. Another approach is to look at the behaviors of leaders and how these influence the subordinate satisfaction and performance. There is general agreement that behavior can be roughly divided into two categories: those behaviors associated with accomplishing the task, and those focused on the relationship the leader builds with their team. However, there is less agreement about the appropriate balance to these.

Another approach is to look at leadership style, or the way in which a leader typically behaves towards their subordinates. Within organizations generally and services industries specifically (including hospitality), the growing importance of employee commitment and satisfaction as a driver of organizational performance has precipitated a move away from more autocratic styles of leadership to more participative, inclusive styles. Leadership style focuses on the use of the different types of power outlined above, and recognizes that the reliance on legitimate and coercive power alone long term has a negative effect on employee morale and productivity. With better educational levels among employees, higher expectations of consultation and involvement and organizational reliance on emotional labor for service delivery, there is a growing recognition of a more democratic, inclusive style of leadership.

However, there is also growing recognition that there is no one best way of leading, and that often the appropriate style is contingent or dependent on the situation or environment in which the leader is working. Factors that might influence the choice of style include the nature of the task being undertaken by subordinates; the relationship between the leader and their subordinates; and the level of authority of the leader and the motivation and experience of the subordinates. These factors may have a singular or multiple effect on the leadership situation, with the interaction of several variables at one time.

The most recent work on leadership has drawn a distinction between transactional and transformational leaders (Burns, 1978). Transactional leadership emphasizes the efficient achievement work tasks and outcomes and is largely based on legitimate and reward power. Transformational leadership however, focuses on the use of charismatic power, to engender greater levels of employee commitment and motivation. Transformational leaders create a strong vision for the hospitality organization and a sense of mission among employees. This style of leadership has been highlighted as vital in today's fast-paced hotels, where flexibility, willingness to change and innovation are key determinants of organizational success.

References

Burns, J.M. (1978) *Leadership*. New York: Harper and Row.

French, W.L. and Raven, B.H. (1959) The bases of social power. In D. Cartwright (ed.), *Studies in Social Power*. Ann Arbor, MI: Institute for Social Research, University of Michigan Press, pp. 150–167.

Hofstede, G. (1980) *Culture's Consequences: International Differences in Work-Related Values*. Beverly Hills, CA: Sage Publications.

Mullins, L. (2002) *Management and Organizational Behaviour*, 6th edn. Harlow: Prentice-Hall.

GILLIAN KELLOCK HAY
GLASGOW CALEDONIAN UNIVERSITY, UK

Leadership in energy and environmental design (LEED)

The LEED (Leadership in Energy and Environmental Design) Green Building Rating System is a voluntary, consensus-based national standard for developing high-performance, sustainable buildings. Members of the US Green Building Council, representing all segments of the building industry, developed LEED and contribute to its improvement. LEED standards are currently available for new construction and major renovation projects.

LEED was created to:

- Establish a common standard defining a 'green building'
- Promote integrated, whole-building design practices
- Recognize environmental leadership in the building industry
- Stimulate green competition
- Raise consumer awareness of green building benefits.

LEED provides a framework for assessing building performance and meeting sustainability goals. Based on well-founded scientific standards, LEED emphasizes state of the art strategies for sustainable site development, water savings, energy efficiency, materials selection, and indoor environmental quality.

Reference

Leadership in Energy and Environmental Design. http://www.usgbc.org/leed/leed_main.asp.

JIM ACKLES
THARALDSON ENERGY GROUP, USA

Learning

Workers today and in the future will be required to learn and develop continuously. Wilson (1999) states that this learning will involve updating and learning new skills such as functional, interpersonal, and organizational skills. There are many ways in which people learn and a variety of interventions can be used to encourage learning. The following seeks to define some of the areas associated with learning.

Learning organizations are associated with the work of Burgoyne, Pedler and Boydell (1991). They argue that rather than viewing learning as a reaction to change, a learning organization encompasses the activities of learning at all levels. Therefore individual, team, and organizational learning activities produce a continuous focus on development and quality.

The philosophy of life-long learning as essential at all levels of staff and throughout an individual's career is increasingly popular in modern hospitality organizations. For example, the Club Managers Association of America (CMAA) provides learning and development programs for all levels of management from entry to senior management. Managers work towards professional qualification with the Certified Club Manager (CCM) designation. In the UK the government has supported the philosophy of life-long learning by setting up an organization called Learndirect whereby individuals and businesses are given advice and support to promote the continuous development of skills at all levels.

Action learning is the process whereby individuals learn skills through involvement in a team focusing on organization-specific problems. This is achieved through the use of questioning, analysis, and problem-solving techniques. As the individuals using this process are often working outside their normal area, there is the added advantage of learning about other processes or areas of the business whilst developing interpersonal skills and, of course, improving organizational effectiveness. For example, a member of the front office team may work in an action group with individuals from the sales and reservations teams to consider how to improve communication between the departments. The front office team member will learn about the other departments and assist in the creation of a solution for more effective communication; thus learning has taken place.

When discussing learning, we are essentially referring to learning within a working environment. Thus it is important to have an understanding of how adults learn. Knowles (1998) has identified the following as key characteristics of adult learning:

- Mature adults are self-directed and autonomous in their approach to learning
- They learn best through experiential methods
- They are aware of their own specific learning needs generated by life or work
- They have a need to apply newly acquired knowledge or skills to their immediate circumstances
- Learning should be seen as a partnership between trainers and learners, and learners' own experiences should be used as a resource (as cited in Simmonds, 2003, p. 75).

Consequently, when asking service staff to undertake a course of learning in wine service, an application of the learning in relation to the work environment should be identified, i.e. explaining to staff the advantages of obtaining these skills to both themselves and their job.

Often in the hospitality industry individuals learn by experience, practicing and displaying certain behaviors. For example a new bartender will learn the mix of cocktail ingredients and then practice how to blend these together whilst a room attendant will practice the various steps involved in making a bed. Many companies now identify key skills for all jobs within their organization to support and target learning. Hilton (UK) for example has defined the Technical and Behavioral Skills (TBS) required for all operations

roles and designed learning experiences around these. This is known as behavioral learning and is best suited to skill development. Attitudinal development is better achieved through cognitive learning. In this process learning is stimulated by explanation and understanding of concepts and theories which will then allow the learner to adapt their attitude to a given situation. For example, general managers may learn how to maximize staff productivity by gaining an understanding of motivational theories and the effect of leadership style on motivation.

With advances in technology and the increasing computer literacy of staff many organizations are now using e-learning to support skills development in the workplace. This is the process where information can be accessed through the use of CD-ROMs, multi-media and hypertext in an online environment either through the Internet or a company intranet (Reynolds *et al.*, 2000). This also has the benefit of allowing the learner to access learning in his or her own time and at a pace that suits the learner. It also allows the transfer of learning over geographical locations, increasingly relevant as a result of globalization. For example, in a global hotel chain a general manager in Hong Kong could participate in an online discussion forum on financial management with a general manager in the Bahamas.

When discussing learning it is appropriate to consider how learning takes place. Single loop learning is the process of learning to simply solve problems whereas double loop learning is not merely solving the problem but increasing learning by asking and understanding why the problem occurred in the first place. An example of single loop learning would be the case of a kitchen porter who attends chemical safety training to simply ensure the correct measures are used in the dishwasher. Double loop learning would occur if the learner was asked to consider what would happen if the correct measures were not used or if the chemicals were not stored properly.

Finally it is important to consider the ways in which people prefer to learn. Honey and Mumford (1986) categorize these preferred styles as follows:

- *Activist* – open-minded learners who like to be actively involved

- *Pragmatist* – practical learners who like to link learning to their work
- *Theorist* – logical learners who like to use diagrams and theories to learn
- *Reflector* – learners who like to observe and think about the learning they are undertaking.

For example, when learning cutting techniques in the culinary process activists would be keen to participate in the session and actually carry out the task of knife manipulation. They can be seen as tactile or kinesthetic learners as they process new information by touching or having physical contact in the task or behavior being learned. Reflectors would prefer to watch and listen; they are often referred to as auditory/visual learners.

References

Burgoyne, J., Pedler, M., and Boydell, T. (1991) *The Learning Company – A Strategy for Sustainable Development*. Maidenhead: McGraw-Hill.

Honey, P and Mumford, A. (1986) *The Manual of Learning Styles*. Maidenhead: Honey Knowles, M. (1998) Cited in Simmonds, D. (2003) *Designing and Delivering Training*. London: CIPD.

Reynolds, J. *et al.* (2002) How do people learn? Cited in Simmonds, D. (2003) *Designing and Delivering Training*. London: CIPD.

Wilson, J. (ed.) (1999) *Human Resource Development*. London: Kogan Page.

DEBRA F. CANNON
GEORGIA STATE UNIVERSITY, USA
SAMANTHA QUAIL
GLASGOW CALEDONIAN UNIVERSITY, UK

Learning environment

The concept of lifelong learning has a major impact on meetings and conventions. People who participate in seminars, training sessions, workshops, and other learning activities outside of a traditional classroom are examples of lifelong learners. They want an opportunity to increase their knowledge and skills while sharing their experiences and expertise. In order to facilitate their learning, the space in which the meeting is held needs to be conducive to information sharing and not set up barriers to communication. The learning environment should be comfortable and inviting. A room should be set up in consideration of the type of communication that will be used for the meeting. Other considerations are the acoustics, the ceiling height, the wall décor and/or coloring, lighting, windows, drapes, mirrors, audiovisual capabilities, and light and temperature controls. When interaction is desired, the group must be kept small. Distance between attendees affects interaction, and the outcomes are affected by culture. Some cultures are more comfortable up close and personal, others are more comfortable with more distance between them. Sight lines are important, if attendees cannot see the speaker or the stage they tend to disconnect. Sight can be obstructed by columns, shape of the room, or a too-tall centerpiece.

Reference

Hildreth, Richard A. (1990) *The Essentials of Meeting Management*. Englewood Cliffs, NJ: Prentice-Hall.

RICHARD VICKERY
METROPOLITAN STATE COLLEGE, USA

Learning organization

A 'learning organization' in the hospitality industry is one in which people at all levels, individually and collectively, are continually increasing their capacity to improve organizational actions through better knowledge and understanding. Learning in organizations takes place in three levels: individual, team or group, and organizational. Individual learning is a precondition for organizational learning, but it does not guarantee organizational learning. Senge (1990) suggested that teams are the fundamental learning unit in an organization. An organization learns through actions and interactions that take place between people who generally work in teams. Organizational learning increases greater capacity for organizational adaptation to changing internal and external environmental demands, a fuller utilization of the members' abilities and motivation, and higher level of job and personal satisfaction by organizational members (Senge, 1990). A learning organization can be achievable in the hospitality industry by systematic problem-solving, experimentation with new approaches, learning from one's own experiences and mistakes, learning from the experiences and best practices of others, and transferring knowledge quickly and efficiently throughout the organization (Cannon and Kent, 1995). Since the rate at which individuals and organizations learn might become the only sustainable competitive advantage, hospitality companies need to implement learning organizations in reality.

References

Cannon, D.F. and Kent, W.E. (1995) The secrets of becoming a learning organization. *Hospitality and Tourism Educator*, 7 (1), 9–12.

Senge, M.P. (1990) *The Fifth Discipline: The Arts and Practice of the Learning Organization.* New York: Doubleday.

MUSTAFA TEPECI
UNIVERSITY OF MERSIN, TURKEY

Legacy

A legacy is the long-lasting effect of an event or process. Bennett (1995) defined legacy systems informally as large hardware and software systems that we don't know how to cope with but which are vital to our organization. The Free On-Line Dictionary of Computing describes a legacy system as a computer system or application program which continues to be used because of the prohibitive cost of replacing or redesigning it, despite its poor competitiveness and compatibility with modern equivalents. The implication is that the system is large, monolithic, and difficult to modify. Legacy systems are critical information systems that significantly resist evolution to meet new and constantly changing business requirements and cost is a major factor.

However, the cost of maintaining a legacy system may eventually outweigh the cost of replacing the software and hardware. Many legacy systems used in the hospitality business today still rely on distributed networking and serial port interfaces for communication between applications. Besides being slow and unreliable, these old technologies require custom development for almost every application that uses them. Furthermore, these systems cannot benefit from the advances of new Web-based applications, mobile and wireless communication which have made storing and transferring data between systems much more efficient, faster, and more reliable.

References

Bennett, K.H. (1995) Legacy systems: coping with success. *IEEE Software*, January, 12 (1), 19–23.

The Free On-line Dictionary of Computing, FOLDOC, http://foldoc.doc.ic.ac.uk.

HILARY C. MAIN-MURPHY
ECOLE HOTELIERE DE LAUSANNE,
SWITZERLAND

Legionnaire's disease

Legionellosis is a form of pneumonia known as 'Legionnaire's disease' and is attributed to a bacterium named Legionella. The first indication of the disease was noted in the Bellevue Stratford Hotel, which was hosting a convention of the Pennsylvania Department of the American Legion. Guests or 'Legionnaires' succumbed to the illness after breathing in droplets of air and water that contained Legionella. Follow-up determined that the bacterium thrived in contaminated water found in the cooling tower in the hotel's air conditioning system. Subsequently, the bacterium has been found to be somewhat widespread and has also been found in potable water systems and in some water features as well.

Careful audits of water cooling and air conditioning systems have since lessened the number of recorded cases of this disease. Multiple venues in hotels exist as breeding grounds for these bacteria: air conditioning cooling towers, whirlpool spas, showers, and other plumbing systems. Legionellosis is not passed from person to person, nor is there evidence of infection from auto or home air conditioning units. Hotel operators have taken measures to reduce the potential of infection, including the management of water sources in contact with cooling towers and air circulation systems to reduce the growth of Legionella. The Centers for Disease Prevention and Control (CDC) in the United States monitor cases of Legionnaire's disease and offer recommendations for the management of systems known to be implicated in the transmission of this disease.

References

Legionellosis: Legionnaire's disease (LD) and Pontiac fever. Retrieved 2 January 2003 from http://www.cdc.gov/ncidod/dbmd/disease-info/legionellosis_g.htm.

The International Hotel and Restaurant Association (2002) Health alert: Legionnaire's disease. *Hotels* (November). Retrieved 20 September from http://www.hotelsmag.com/1102/1102ihra.html.

Minimizing the Risks of Legionnaires' disease – TM 13 (2003). London: Chartered Institute of Building Service Engineers.

Minimizing the Risks of Legionellosis Associated with Building Water Systems – Guidelines 12-2000 (2000) Atlanta, GA: American Society of Heating, Refrigerating, and Air-Conditioning Engineers.

BONNIE CANZIANI
UNIVERSITY OF NORTH CAROLINA –
GREENSBORO, USA

Les Clefs d'Or

Les Clefs d'Or (pronounced *lay clay door*), means 'keys of gold' in French. The crossed gold keys are the international symbol of the organization of that name. The keys displayed on a concierge's uniform lapels assure travelers they are dealing with a seasoned professional, one who is dedicated to serving the guests' every need.

In October 1929, three of the more prominent concierges met in Paris to exchange service tips and ideas. They found that together they could more effectively network and enhance guest services throughout their cities. As a result, many European countries created national concierge societies.

The end of the Second World War sparked a renewed interest in the need for these societies. Concierges throughout Europe created a chain of mutual assistance and friendship to help smooth the journeys of their clients who were traveling in post-war Europe. On 25 April 1952 delegates from seven European nations met in Cannes to hold the first ever 'Congress' and create L'Union Européene des Portiers des Grands Hotels. Ferdinand Gillet (then concierge at the Hotel Scribe, Paris) masterminded this effort and is considered the father of Les Clefs d'Or. Gillet served as president of this association until 1968.

In 1970, with the acceptance of Israel as a member country, UEPGH became UIPGH (Union Internationale des Portiers des Grands Hotels), signifying that not just Europe, but countries from around the globe, were joining forces.

Today, the UICH acronym stands for union Internationale des Concierges d'Hotels 'Les Clefs d'Or'. The word concierge appears in the name as a way to strengthen the brand-name recognition of UICH as a society of professional hotel concierges.

The USA section of Les Clefs d'Or was formally recognized on 21 November 1978, when the United States became the nineteenth member of UICH at a meeting in Vienna, Austria. Together, members of Les Clefs d'Or USA represent over 100,000 hotel rooms at more than 250 four- and five-star properties across the country. Les Clefs d'Or USA has more than 450 members in over 30 states.

Reference

Stutts, Alan T. (2001) *Hotel and Lodging Management – An Introduction.* New York: John Wiley & Sons.

ALAN T. STUTTS
AMERICAN INTERCONTINENTAL
UNIVERSITY, USA

Life cycle costing

Life cycle costing, also called total cost of owner-ship analysis, is a technique designed to systematically consider the full financial costs to an organization of a particular purchasing decision over the whole time period that the purchase, or its alternatives, will be relevant.

It is especially valuable where the operating, maintenance, training, and disposal costs (or salvage value) of one purchase choice are different from another. Reliability is another particularly complex but important factor in evaluating the overall cost of any purchase; the costs and implications of reliability issues to continuity of an organization's mission are often poorly understood. Tax and inflation ramifications also need to be considered.

In many cases original purchase price is only a small percentage of the total cost of ownership, yet the purchase decision commits the owner, without any flexibility, to as much as 95% of those total costs. The very fact that decision-makers go through the process of seeking to understand all the costs and implications of a purchase decision has been shown to improve the quality of decisions made.

While most commonly applied to capital purchases, life cycle costing can also aid in the evaluation of service contracts and the best selection of consumable supplies. In the hospitality industry, life cycle costing can be profitably applied to mundane purchases (e.g. light bulbs) just as readily as to complex purchases (e.g. outsourcing the housekeeping or laundry function).

In commercial situations life cycle costing would not normally include indirect or societal costs, but these costs are likely to be considered in increasing measure. The more commonly used term for this broader evaluation is life cycle assessment. Where applicable, however, the cost of insuring against any occupational or other liabilities, the cost of waste minimization efforts and waste treatment, and the cost of current and projected future compliance and risk management issues would certainly need to be included.

Generally the net present value (NPV) method is used to allow initial costs and future costs to be compared equitably. Software is readily available to assist in the calculation of life cycle costs.

Reference

http://www.eere.energy.gov/femp/techassist/
softwaretools/softwaretools.html#blcc5.

ROBERT ALLENDER
ENERGY RESOURCES MANAGEMENT,
HONG KONG SAR, CHINA

Life safety code, The

The Life Safety Code began its existence in 1913, when a special committee for the National Fire Protection Association (NFPA) saw fit to develop standards governing the design of buildings for the effective, efficient, and safe egress of occupants during times of emergencies. It has been in almost constant revision since that time with a new edition appearing approximately every two years during recent times. NFPA 101 is the designation by which the Life Safety Code is otherwise known.

The code does not address general fire prevention that is normally covered by other codes and standards, nor does it provide any guidelines for the preservation of property during a fire. Its major purpose is the preservation of life and the prevention of injuries during a conflagration that may be caused by the fire, smoke or panic.

The general content of the code covers anything that could possibly impact the safe evacuation of a building during a fire emergency or panic situation and therefore is explicit in its standards for the construction, maintenance, and protection of exits and exit pathways. A side benefit of the Life Safety Code is that while protecting the safety of building occupants, it also protects the property. The code recognizes that for people to safely survive fire or panic situations they must first be able to get to an exit. Therefore the code will mandate such things as sprinkler systems and firewalls that serve to protect the property as well. The code classifies all common occupancies and their hazards and develops specific standards for each occupancy based on whether it is new or existing construction.

Reference

Life Safety Code: NFPA 101 (n.d.) http://www.nfpa.org/catalog/Home/index.asp.

JERRY LACHAPPELLE
HARRAH'S ENTERTAINMENT, INC., USA

Lighting equipment and systems

Lighting equipment consists of lamps, fixtures, and controls. Selection of the appropriate elements of equipment and integration of these into a lighting system that operates harmoniously with the interior design as well as with the lighting needs for various tasks results in a pleasant visual environment that can be operated in an efficient manner. Lighting also serves to advertise the lodging product via lighting of the building exterior and the lighting found in signage.

Lamps are the component of a lighting system that produces light. Two broad categories of lamps are incandescent and discharge lamps. Incandescent lamps produce light by means of an element heated to incandescence by the passage of an electric current. The widely used screw base lamp found in table lamps and some ceiling fixtures as well as halogen lamps used for spot or decorative lighting are incandescent lamps. Discharge lamps produce light, directly or indirectly, by an electric discharge through a gas, a metal vapor, or a mixture of several gases. Fluorescent, mercury vapor, high pressure sodium and low pressure sodium are all types of discharge lamps. Discharge lamps require a ballast to control their operation.

Lamps have a number of characteristics that define them physically as well as operationally. Physically, incandescent lamps are specified by the shape of the bulb, color of the bulb, type of base, filling gas, operational voltage, overall physical dimensions, and other such factors. Operationally, lamps are defined by such terms as lumen output (a measure of the amount of light produced), color rendering index (a measure of the spectral output of the lamp), depreciation/maintenance factor (a measure of the reduction in the lamp output over time), lifetime (defined as the time when half of a sample of lamps would have failed), and other terms as well. Also of interest is the lamp efficiency. This is expressed as the amount of light generated per unit of electrical power consumed or lumens per watt.

Lighting fixtures include items such as wall sconces, table 'lamps,' fluorescent lighting fixtures, and a variety of other items. Fixtures hold the lamps and distribute the light that is produced into the adjacent space. There is a vast variety of fixture types. Fixtures have an efficiency measure known as the coefficient of utilization that essentially measures the ratio of the amount of light delivered to the space by the amount of light produced by the lamp.

Lighting systems are installed to provide levels of illumination needed by people to perform tasks, to assist in establishing an atmosphere of security, or for aesthetic purposes. Various amounts of light are required for the human eye to effectively view items and the surroundings. These light levels are specified by groups such as the Illuminating Engineers Society of North America and by building codes. They are specified in either foot-candles (used in the United States) or lux (used more widely throughout the world). Lighting for security is of particular concern in areas such as parking lots but even in guest corridor areas the security value of lighting needs to be considered. Aesthetic illumination is done for paintings and artwork displays as well as to highlight other items in hotel environments such as the lobby and restaurants. In addition, almost any lighting system will interact with the adjacent environment and so modifications to the system (such as changing types of lamps) should be done cautiously to preserve the design intent of the facility.

Lighting controls can be as simple as a wall switch or as complex as a computer controlling a laser light show. In addition to the basic on–off wall switch or simple dimmer switches, lighting control via occupancy sensors is becoming more common. Occupancy sensors detect a human presence in a space and operate the lighting system accordingly. The result can be substantial energy savings for lighting operation. It is also possible to control lighting in locations that are potentially 'daylit' through the use of a photocell. The amount of light produced by the lighting system is modulated depending on the amount of sunlight entering the space. In the past, control of fluorescent lights by dimming was not particularly effective. Modern lamps and electronic ballasts allow for effective dimming of fluorescent lamps over a wide range of output.

Lighting equipment and systems maintenance is both similar to and different from that of other building systems. Lamps are almost never 'repaired.' When they reach the end of their useful life they are discarded. Lighting systems maintenance can consist of the cleaning of lamps as well as the cleaning of fixtures themselves. The replacement of lamps can be done on an 'as needed' basis, often the method used in guestrooms. Or, replacement can be via 'group relamping' where decisions are made to replace all lamps in a certain area at one time. This may be due to the difficulty of replacing the lamps (say high ceilings where special equipment is needed) and/or in recognition of the economies that can be achieved with this practice. One advantage of fluorescent versus incandescent lamps is that the longer life of fluorescent means substantially fewer lamp changes are required over time.

Emergency lighting is provided at properties to ensure that exit corridors and stairwells can be navigated even in a power outage. The lighting may be provided from battery powered lamps or by connection of certain lamps to the emergency power system. Battery powered lamps will only operate for an hour or so before their light output is severely reduced. Some hotels have chosen to put a circuit in the guestroom on the emergency power circuit so guests have light in the room as well, but this is relatively rare.

Fluorescent lamps and ballasts can be potential environmental hazards. Local regulations may require recycling of these. Consideration should be given to recycling whether required by law or not. Practicing group relamping can assist in developing sufficient lamp volume to make recycling more feasible.

References

http://www.iesna.org/.

http://www.lighting.philips.com/glossary/index.php#L.

http://www.energystar.gov/ia/business/Lighting.pdf.

DAVID M. STIPANUK
CORNELL UNIVERSITY, USA

Limited menus

A limited menu is typically limited in one of two senses. It may be limited in the number of menu choices offered or in the number of ways a menu ingredient is prepared/served. In the first instance the term refers to the number of menu items a restaurant has for its guest to choose from. The most limited menus in terms of choices are thought by most to be offered at quick service restaurants. 'Variety' in this setting is provided by the numerous condiments and toppings that can be applied to each order.

Full service restaurant menus are generally expected to offer more extensive menu item choices. However, this is often achieved by preparing the same ingredient in different ways, e.g., shrimp cocktail, fried shrimp, shrimp Creole, shrimp scampi, etc. The same shrimp is used in all dishes but is prepared differently and combined with different ingredients to offer variety.

Midscale restaurants that serve breakfast, lunch, and dinner offer perhaps the most extensive menu choices. Because of the wide choices of menu items, however, they typically limit variations in item preparation to less than three. Conversely, upscale restaurants have the capability of offering extensive choices in both number of menu items and in preparation methodology. When preparation is done to order, however, choices will generally be limited because of the high direct labor element that is required when foods are scratch-prepared.

Limited menus reduce the need for equipment, personnel, and extensive inventories. Cost control and quality control is much easier than in a restaurant with extensive menu offerings.

However, limited menus appeal to a narrow segment of the market.

Reference

Pavesic, D.V. (1998) *Fundamental Principles of Restaurant Cost Control.* New York: Prentice-Hall.

DAVID V. PAVESIC
GEORGIA STATE UNIVERSITY, USA

Liquidity ratios

Liquidity ratios of a business measure how well such a business is able to meet its short-term obligations. In other words, liquidity ratios represent the ability of a business to pay obligations that are expected to become due with the next year or operating cycle. The two main liquidity ratios are the current ratio and the acid test ratio.

The *current ratio* is also known as the *working capital ratio*. In accounting, current assets less current liabilities equal working capital. In ratio analysis, the current ratio is obtained by dividing current assets by current liabilities and expressing the current ratio as a multiple.

Example: Restaurant A:

Current assets

Cash	$2,000
Accounts receivable (debtors)	1,000
Marketable securities	4,000
Inventories (stock)	10,000
Prepaid expenses	3,000
Total current assets	$20,000

Current liabilities

Accounts payable (creditors)	$1,000
Notes payable	1,500
Accrued expenses	500
Income tax payable	2,000
Current portion of long-term debt	5,000
Total current liabilities	$10,000

Using the above example, the current ratio would be:

$$\text{Current ratio} = \frac{\text{Current assets}}{\text{Current liabilities}}$$

$$= \frac{20,000}{10,000}$$

$$= 2.0$$

Is 2.0 a strong ratio? Most business would like to see a 2.0 ratio. This means that for every dollar of current liabilities outstanding, the business has $2.00 (twice the amount of short-term assets) to fund current debt. However, it is prudent to determine the current ratio of the industry that the particular business belongs to. For most hospitality companies, the current ratio is often less than 2.0 as hospitality businesses do not normally carry the level of inventories that one would see in other businesses such as manufacturing concerns.

From this example, one may also assume the higher the current ratio, the better the business is. This, however, is not true. If a company has a current ratio of 4, or 8, or 10, this company has 4, 8, or 10 times of current assets to cover its current obligations. Although this may look good on the surface, one needs to examine which specific current asset account contributes to the high current assets balance. If such current assets are mainly in cash, this excess resource may be better directed to more profitable investment opportunities rather than having the cash in a bank earning minimal interest.

The other liquidity ratio is the *acid test ratio*. It is also known as the *quick* or *liquid* ratio, and is calculated by comparing the current liabilities of the business with its quick assets. Quick assets are those that are either cash or 'near' cash. Such assets are considered as 'quick' as they can normally be rapidly or 'quickly' converted into cash. Neither inventories nor prepaid expenses are included in this calculation. In the case of inventories, it takes a while for a business to convert inventories into cash. First, the business has to make a sale. If the sale is cash, that is fine. If the sale is on account, the account has to be collected first before cash is on hand. As for prepayments, they are advance payments of services such as rent or insurance which are not normally cashable items. Most ratio publications will use the following formula:

Acid-test ratio = Cash + Marketable securities + Accounts receivable/Current liabilities

Using the example of Restaurant A, the acid-test ratio, expressed also as a multiple like the current ratio, is:

$$\text{Acid-test ratio} = \frac{2000 + 1000 + 4000}{10,000}$$

$$= 0.70$$

Normally, this ratio should not be less than 1. In the example of Restaurant A, a 0.70 ratio means the restaurant can only cover its current liabilities 0.70 times over within a few days' notice. This is not a good ratio for the business as it will only be able to cover $.70 to a $1.00 of its liabilities.

Similar to the current ratio, one also would like this ratio to be around 1.0 and not to be too high. The same logic of not keeping excess resources in a current ratio also applies to the quick or acid-test ratio. If there are excess resources, such resources should be directed to investments that have a higher earning potential.

References

Coltman, M.C. and Jagels, M. (2001) *Hospitality Management Accounting*, 7th edn. New York: John Wiley & Sons.

Kotas, R. and Conlan, M. (1997) *Hospitality Accounting*, 5th edn. London: International Thomson Business Press.

Owen, G. (1998) *Accounting for Hospitality, Tourism and Leisure*, 2nd edn. London: Longman.

Weygandt, J.J., Kieso, D.E., Kimmel, P.D., and DeFranco, A.L. (2005) *Hospitality Financial Accounting*. New York: John Wiley & Sons.

AGNES LEE DEFRANCO
UNIVERSITY OF HOUSTON, USA

Local area network (LAN)

A local area network (LAN) is a communication network that links computers together within an office, a hotel, a university or other organization. It can be contrasted with a wide area network (WAN), where the computers to be linked are further apart – for instance, all the hotels in a chain might be linked by a WAN.

Each computer in a LAN is fitted with a network card, and cables link the computers to each other and to at least one server. It is now also possible to link the computers using wireless technology, linking the machines by radio and removing the need for cables to connect them. A file server is used to store software and data files which are shared by users at the various computers. A property management system (PMS) often uses a LAN, allowing transactions in different departments of the hotel to be entered on a computer within each department, to be added to a customer's bill held on the central server. The network can also be used to allow users to share expensive resources, such as a fast printer or a scanner.

References

Bocij, P. *et al.* (1999) *Business Information Systems*. London: Pearson.

Buhalis, D. (2003) *eTourism*. London: Pearson.

O'Connor, P. (2000) *Using Computers in Hospitality*, 2nd edn. London: Cassell.

JOHN NIGHTINGALE
LEEDS METROPOLITAN UNIVERSITY, UK

Lock-off

Many vacation-ownership (timeshare) resorts have 'lock-off' units consisting of two bedrooms and two bathrooms, three bedrooms and three bathrooms, or even four bedrooms and four bathrooms that by design can function as two discrete units. The advantage of this unique design is that it offers the owner the ultimate in flexibility in using their villa. The concept of a lock-off is basically adjacent units that can function as independent living units that contain separate bedrooms, kitchen facilities, dining space, living quarters, and frequently balcony facilities. The flexibility comes in three basic forms, whereby the owner may occupy the living room and one or two bedrooms while another uses the remaining and physically separate villa space. The first option allows the owner to spend two separate weeks in a year at their home resort by electing to choose the main portion of the unit during one week, while using the other week to stay in the lock-off. The second choice occurs when the owner chooses to spend one week at their home resort and exchange the other section of the villa. The last option occurs when the owner arranges two separate exchanges for a single maintenance fee.

Reference

American Resort Development Association (2002) *The Timeshare Industry Manual.* Washington, DC.

BEVERLY SPARKS
GRIFFITH UNIVERSITY, AUSTRALIA

Lock-out/tag-out

Lock-Out/Tag-Out is an United States OSHA (Occupational Safety and Health Administration) mandated program (29 CFR 1910.147) that is designed to protect employees from the uncontrolled release of hazardous energy. The term lock-out means using a lock and a device that, when in use, makes it impossible to activate a switch, circuit breaker, etc., that would energize or set a machine/process in motion endangering an employee working on the machine/process. It takes into account the total energy system sources, such as electrical, mechanical, hydraulic, pneumatic, kinetic and chemical.

Locking out to a 'zero energy state' is a planned approach for service and maintenance safety. It takes into account the total energy of a system, and eliminates the possibility of sudden or unexpected release of that energy during such service or maintenance functions.

The purpose of the lock-out/tag-out policy is to prevent personal injury and property damage due to the accidental energizing or start up of machinery, equipment, and/or process systems under repair or on which maintenance is being performed.

OSHA requires that an employer have a written Lock-Out/Tag-Out Program, the proper tools, an equipment inventory, and employee training.

Reference

Control Hazardous Energy (n.d.) http://osha. gov/SLTC/controlhazardousenergy/index. html.

JERRY LACHAPPELLE
HARRAH'S ENTERTAINMENT, INC., USA

Loyalty Circle (The)

The Loyalty Circle is a way to create customer loyalty. The three main functions on the circle are Process, Value, and Communication. With different points along the circle, there are places where the customer might exit the circle and hence the relationship. The goal of the companies is to keep the customer in the circle by executing equally well the three functions of the circle. Equality is the key to the loyalty circle. If companies perform well in creating value for instance, but do not effectively communicate with the customer, then that customer may leave the relationship.

On one side of the Loyalty Circle is the process, which is 'how the service works.' It involves all activities from both the customer's perspective and the service provider's perspective. Ideally, there should be no gaps in this process. For the customer, the process includes everything that happens from the time he or she begins buying the service (e.g., calling to make a reservation) to the time that they leave the property (e.g., picking up their car from a valet.) All interactions with employees are part of this process. For the company, the process includes all interactions between the employees and the customers, the design of the service operations, the hiring and training of service personnel, and the collection of information to understand customers' needs, wants, and expectations.

A second component of the Loyalty Circle is value creation. Value creation is subdivided into two parts: value-added and value-recovery. Value-added and value-recovery strategies are designed specifically to enhance customer perceptions of the rewards and costs associated with present and future service transactions. In general, value-added and value-recovery strategies both affect the value of the buyer–provider exchange, but this influence is exerted in different ways.

Valued added strategies increase loyalty by providing customers with more than just the core product; for example, for hotels, offering more than just a place to sleep. Value-added strategies increase the long-term value of the relationship with the service firm by offering greater benefits to customers than can be found at competing firms who charge a comparable price. Features that pertain to value-added are of six types: *financial* (e.g., saving money on future transactions, complete reimbursement if service failure); *temporal* (e.g., saving time by priority check-in); *functional* (e.g., making the process easier); *experiential* (e.g., enhancing the experience such as by getting an upgrade); *emotional* (e.g., more recognition and/or more pleasurable service experience); and/or *social* (e.g., interpersonal link with a service provider). For example, temporal value is important for business travelers who have stated that they value their time at $100 per hour and anything that saves them time saves them money.

Consider for instance, the check-in process of a hotel. Research reveals that many frequent business travelers want to go immediately to their room and do not want to wait in line to check-in. If they have to wait in line for 15 minutes, they mentally figure they have spent $25 to check-in. Waiting in line is especially annoying if the guest is a member of the hotel's frequent guest program and all the guest's information is already stored on file. Certain technologies (e.g., Bluetooth software that works with one's personal digital assistant) allow guests to check-in, receive their room number, unlock their room, and have charges automatically billed to their credit card without having to check-in with the front desk. Moving these guests to this form of check-in would have the benefit of shortening the line for those guests who want to speak with a front desk clerk. This new check-in procedure speeds up and improves the process (*functional value*) and adds value because it saves the guests' time (*temporal value*).

The importance of value-added strategies in creating customer loyalty is illustrated in a study of business travelers who both spend more than $120 per night for a hotel room and take six or more business trips per year. The study revealed that 28% of the 344 who spent more than 75 nights per year in hotels (38% of the total sample) claimed that the feature 'is a good value for the price paid' is important in the decision to stay in the same hotel chain when traveling on business. A similar percentage rated the features 'collects your preferences and uses that information to customize your current and future stays' and 'accommodates early morning check-in and late afternoon check-out' important in the decision to stay with the same chain. Both these tactics are examples of features that add value to the core product offering.

Value-recovery strategies are designed to rectify a lapse in service delivery. The goal is to insure that the customers' needs are taken care of without further inconveniences. Empowering employees to solve problems and offering 100% guarantees are examples of value-recovery strategies. The key to value-recovery strategies is that the complaints be taking seriously by the company and that processes be put in place so that the same mistakes do not happen over and over again.

The final component of the Loyalty Circle is communication. This side of the circle incorporates database marketing, newsletters, and general advertising. It involves all areas of how the company communicates with its customers. When communicating with customers, it is critical that external communications do not over-promise what the service can deliver. A gap occurs when external communications over-promise what the service can deliver. This gap is a result of inadequate management of service promises, promising unrealistic expectations and rewards in advertising or personal selling, and insufficient customer communication. It is also critical that the communiqué reflects the needs of the customer and that he or she does not receive offers in which the customer has no interest.

If marketers can focus the organization on these components they will create loyal customers who will return over and over again. If they do not focus on the components of the circle, they will be forced to focus on getting more and more customers to replace those who have left the circle.

Reference

Shoemaker, Stowe and Lewis, Robert (1999) Customer loyalty in hotels. *International Journal of Hospitality Management*, 18 (4), 345–370.

SUNA LEE
UNIVERSITY OF NEVADA, LAS VEGAS, USA

M

Maintenance fee

The amount established (or 'levied') by an owners association against owners of a common-interest subdivision for maintenance, improvements, upkeep, and management of the association's property. Assessments are generally levied to each owner/member in proportion to the ownership interest, or combined ownership interest of each owner. The manner in which the assessment will be levied will be determined upon the declaration of the common-interest owners association. Methods used to determine the proportional assessment to owners include: equal assessment of fees levied against owners of each interval or unit and assessment based upon the size of the unit owned and the number of units or intervals owned. Maintenance fees are generally assessed and collected on an annual basis at the beginning of each fiscal year. Some common-interest resorts, particularly in resort locations where maintenance costs are prohibitive, allow for quarterly or semi-annual payment of the fees. Assessments are generally divided into three categories: operating funds, reserve and replacement funds, and management fees. Some common-interest resorts allow annual property taxes to be collected as part of the maintenance fee assessment. Should an owner/member fail to pay the assessment in full or in part the association that governs the property may suspend the use rights of the member/owner until such time the payments are made. The association may also take foreclosure action as defined in the declaration governing the association.

Reference

American Resort Development Association (2002) *The Timeshare Industry Resource Manual.* Washington, DC.

MICHAEL HAUSHALTER
ORLANDO, FLORIDA, USA

Maintenance management

A key and possibly the most important managerial responsibility of the facilities area is the ongoing maintenance of building systems and equipment, the building itself, recreational facilities, and areas such as the grounds and parking facilities. Costs associated with maintenance are charged against the Property Operations and Maintenance account. These costs include labor and benefits, supplies and materials, and contract services. Although maintenance costs could be charged to the departments incurring these costs, the lodging industry typically does not do this. As such, these are therefore 'undistributed' costs.

While many maintenance tasks are performed by in-house staff, a number are provided via contract services. Contract services are often used when the activity requires special equipment (e.g. window cleaning), special skills or liability (e.g. elevator service), and licensing (e.g. pesticide application). Larger corporations often negotiate master service contracts for these services to achieve economies of operation as well as consistency in service levels.

Maintenance activities at the property level can be thought of as involving preventive and predictive activities, scheduled activities, and emergency and breakdown activities. Hotels should also have a program of specific guest-room maintenance activities.

Preventive maintenance (often abbreviated PM) is a systemized approach for maintaining the equipment in a lodging facility. Preventive maintenance ensures that the facility equipment functions properly and performs upon demand. Preventive maintenance includes: routine inspection, taking readings from recording devices, lubrication and adjustment, minor repair and part replacement, and work order initiation for more extensive problems. A properly designed preventive maintenance program may provide the following benefits: increased equipment life, increased energy efficiency, decreased service costs, and reduced inventory costs. In addition, equipment that is beginning to fail can be repaired or replaced at a time when guest inconvenience is minimized.

A preventive maintenance program is typically based on a manufacturer's recommendations for equipment servicing. A preventive maintenance program typically identifies all equipment requiring periodic maintenance and then establishes a schedule for routine inspection. Routine inspection is an integral part of any preventive maintenance program since it is the inspection that detects whether or not a piece of equipment requires scheduled maintenance, repair, or replacement. Preventive maintenance programs can be customized to conform to property size and frequency of equipment use.

Predictive maintenance entails monitoring engineering systems in order to forecast when and where system failure will arise, and inspecting, repairing, or replacing the system before that breakdown occurs. For example, in electrical systems, heat is often an indicator of possible system breakdown. Thermography can be used to detect these electrical heat build-ups giving the engineering department sufficient opportunity to repair the problem before system failure occurs. With equipment, the machine's condition is used accurately to schedule repair intervals. The machine's condition also

determines the required replacement parts. It is generally agreed that among predictive maintenance, breakdown maintenance, and emergency maintenance, predictive maintenance has the lowest cost.

Scheduled maintenance requires advanced planning and preparation and is initiated by a formal work order. Scheduled maintenance attempts to meet equipment and system needs in a timely and orderly manner. Scheduled maintenance involves more than inspection and simple cleaning and repair. During scheduled maintenance, systems and equipment are often offline for several hours or longer. As a result, coordination with other departments is critical. In addition, this type of maintenance is often costly and performed by contract service personnel.

Emergency maintenance is crisis-oriented and requires immediate attention by the engineering department. This type of maintenance generally causes a disruption in the normal engineering department schedule and may result in increased costs, lower revenues, and decreased customer satisfaction.

There are two general types of emergency maintenance: guest-initiated and employee-initiated. Guest-initiated emergency maintenance typically centers on a problem or problems in the guestroom and may affect the guest's satisfaction. If the problem appears to be minor, an engineer is dispatched to the guestroom to fix the problem in a timely manner. If the problem appears to be more extensive, the guest may be asked to move to another available room. How well the guest-initiated problem is handled may influence the guest's perception of the operation. Employee-oriented emergency maintenance may not affect guest satisfaction immediately but if left unattended to will lead to guest dissatisfaction as well as possible employee dissatisfaction. Emergency maintenance is an expensive form of maintenance for three reasons: overtime pay is often required to fix emergency maintenance problems, parts and supplies are often bought outside of the traditional purchasing system, and there are often additional costs associated with their solution (e.g., a leaking pipe may damage ceilings, walls, or cabinets).

Breakdown maintenance, like emergency maintenance, is crisis-oriented and occurs when a piece of equipment or a structural component of the facility completely fails. Breakdown maintenance is often considered the most expensive form of maintenance since in addition to the cost of repair or replacement, there is often a loss of business resulting in a decline in revenues. As a result, there is no scheduling leeway for breakdown maintenance. Breakdown maintenance is an expensive form of maintenance for similar reasons as emergency maintenance.

Guestroom maintenance is a critical maintenance activity that focuses on preventive maintenance, although emergency maintenance may be required on occasion. Guestroom maintenance includes: checking and repairing furniture, fixtures, and equipment; inspecting plumbing for leaks; checking the condition of the floor coverings and walls; and inspecting exterior windows. The guestroom is one of the most visible areas of a lodging property. A properly maintained guestroom enhances the customer's experience with the property. Noting the importance of guestroom maintenance, many lodging operations have developed formal guestroom maintenance programs. These programs typically include the following provisions: a guestroom inspection sheet, a guestroom maintenance cart containing parts and supplies typically needed to repair common guestroom problems, the dedication of one or more experienced staff members to guestroom maintenance, a schedule ensuring regular guestroom inspections, and management inspections to inspect the quality of the maintenance work.

In order to manage the delivery of maintenance services, there are various managerial tools that may be used. These can include standards and schedules for maintenance activities (e.g. guestroom preventive maintenance performed once per quarter), various record-keeping systems (e.g. information about equipment warranties, maintenance activities and costs, and names of parts suppliers), and a work order system.

The work order is a key document used by the engineering department. It is a report stating that an engineering system or piece of equipment needs to be inspected, repaired, or replaced (i.e., a request for work to be done). This document is sequentially numbered and contains the following information: a description of the problem, the location of the problem, the name of the individual who reported the problem, the date and time the problem was reported, the name of the engineer assigned to the task, the time and date the task was completed, and any comments the engineer may have concerning the task. In larger properties the Chief Engineer or an assistant issues the work orders. In smaller operations the front desk or housekeeping typically issues the work orders. The engineering department must make sure that work orders are executed in a timely fashion. If a work order cannot be fulfilled in a timely manner the engineering department needs to communicate with the department or person who reported the initial problem and alert them of when the request will be fulfilled. In addition, once the work order has been completed the engineering department should notify the department or individual that the work requested has been completed.

While maintenance management at small and medium-size properties can certainly be operated effectively using paper records, larger properties are turning to using computerized maintenance management systems. A computerized maintenance management system (CMMS) is a software application designed to provide logical, easy to use tools to manage all maintenance functions of the engineering department. A CMMS supports and enhances the responsiveness and effectiveness of the engineering department. Typically these systems provide a variety of modules, including: diagnostic and equipment history data, staff scheduling and productivity reports, scheduled and preventive maintenance tracking, work order backlog control, inventory tracking, purchase order generation, supplier information, communication within the department and with departments outside of the engineering department, and information regarding adherence to standards and regulatory compliance.

Typically, a service request is entered into the CMMS after it is received by e-mail or phone. The service request generates a work order number, which is then assigned to a maintenance engineer who then responds to the request. A request by e-mail generates a return e-mail with a brief description of the request and the work order number. This information alerts the individual requesting service that the request has been processed and assigned to an engineer. In addition, this individual has the work order number when making inquiries on the status of the request.

Some CMMS products also provide the ability to interface with handheld electronic products that are expanded versions of personal digital assistants (PDAs). These electronic products contain maintenance information for the technicians in the field, eliminating the need to carry paper printouts and allowing for electronic recording of maintenance activities and also of maintenance needs, should the technician be unable to deal with these at the current time. These may also utilize bar code scanning devices which assist in documenting the performance of maintenance activities and, under some circumstances, can also be used to conduct inventory of assets.

Computerized maintenance management systems can be challenging to implement due to the amount of information that is needed for their effective operation. There is also a need for training in their operation and periodic updates for compatibility with computer system modifications. Because of this, some operations have taken an interim move. They have elected to have their maintenance record-keeping done by contracted firms who operate the computer systems. The property receives information about scheduled and preventive maintenance activities from the contract firm, has employees complete the work and make note of any additional issues, and then returns this information to their vendor who maintains the record-keeping system.

A CMMS provides a very useful managerial tool in the hands of a knowledgeable individual. Its information collection and analysis techniques (as outlined above) can greatly assist in decision-making about staffing, equipment replacement, and maintenance issues in general. In addition,

the information collected by the CMMS can be used to allocate maintenance costs to operating department within the hotel.

Reference

Stipanuk, D. (2002) *Hospitality Facilities Management and Design*, 2nd edn. Lansing, MI: Educational Institute of American Hotel and Lodging Association, pp. 30–58.

REED FISHER
JOHNSON STATE COLLEGE, USA

Management accounting

Management accounting is used internally to a business and consists of a selection of methods and techniques that can be used to monitor and improve the profitability of a hospitality business. Systematic management reporting provides regular financial information covering short time periods (week or month) and which is analyzed to reflect the management of profit-generating centers within a business (such as rooms, or food and beverage departments in a hotel) and permits a close control of those units. It includes decision-making techniques such as models to determine optimum levels of output, e.g. room occupancy and numbers of guests, and understanding how profit varies in relation to changes in a given level of turnover (cost–volume–profit). Much of the data are drawn from the financial accounting system, but techniques such as the 'Balanced Scorecard' bring in comparative data from outside and non-accounting performance indicators.

In order to monitor management performance, a classic tool is the budget. The budgetary process involves setting targets for future performance and then later comparing actual performance against budget. The system is helpful in analyzing deviations from planned activity and is essential for the control of large, geographically dispersed organizations, since it provides a means of centralized control and coordination.

References

Harris, P.J. and Hazzard, P.A. (1992) *Managerial Accounting in the Hospitality Industry*, 5th edn. Cheltenham: Stanley Thornes.

Horngren, C.T. and Sundem, G.L. (1999) *Introduction to Management Accounting*, 11th edn. Upper Saddle River, NJ: Prentice-Hall.

PETER WALTON
ESSEC BUSINESS SCHOOL, FRANCE

Management contract

A hotel management contract stipulates that the operator of a hotel is acting fully and completely as an agent of the owner and for the owner, and assumes fully responsibility for operating and managing the hotel. Such operators can be individuals or a third party management company. Employees of such hotels are employees of the owner. Generally any losses resulting from lawsuits or judgments against a hotel operating with management contract must be absorbed by the owner. Similarly, the final financial result of the operation, be it a profit or a loss, is recorded on the owner's account, not the operator's account. For fulfilling the role of manager of the hotel on behalf of the owner, the operator receives certain fees. American hotel companies have been aggressively expanding internationally, using management contracts, because the owner or country is assuming all of the financial risk in order to develop tourism. The management company provides the management talent, standardized training programs, and name recognition.

For a hotel company the management contract is a way for a hotel chain to grow with a low level of investment. Third party management companies even have assisted the owner in some cases by providing funds such as loans to the owner to finalize the deal. Also, for the hotel company a management contract rarely requires that the operator participate in operating deficits because the owner is assuming the financial risk.

On the other hand, a hotel company operating under a management contract has little control over the transfer of ownership. An undercapitalized owner can restrict the cash needed to cover the expenses that are essential to the maintenance of quality, adversely affecting operations. While in the long term this will decrease the value of the hotel and adversely affect the owner, in the short term, the task of operating the hotel becomes difficult for the management company.

A typical management contract may contain a cancellation provision through which either party may withdraw from the contract, with penalties imposed on the party that initiates the cancellation, unless it can show that the other party has defaulted on terms that were included in the agreement. The cancellation, while requiring a fee that must be paid to the management company, although it does avoid other problems, can result in a surplus of key management personnel and a public relations problem.

Traditionally, management contract fees have been specified rates that are set each year. More recently, this arrangement has changed to a graduated fee structure tied to the financial success of a hotel. In some cases, a maximum cap on the total management fee is negotiated by the owners.

The management fee can be calculated in different ways. If it is based solely on total revenue, the operator can spend money freely, particularly on advertising. In this case, because the revenues of the property are high, a high fee is achieved, even if the hotel might not show a profit. On the other hand, calculation of the fee on the basis of the gross operating profit places pressure on the operator to manage the hotel profitably. When results are poor, the management company may find that it is not recovering its costs. A combination fee based on a combination of total revenue and gross operating profit is typically the most equitable arrangement for both the operator and the owner.

In addition to stating the fee calculation method and clarifying the responsibilities of the operator to the owner, management contracts usually contain certain other clauses including the technical services to be provided by the management company, pre-opening services, and the operational duties of the management company. During the contract negotiations stage, there are a number of issues that are usually debated.

Three key issues are contract duration, financial reporting, and contract termination. The owner usually wants a contract duration as short as possible with renewals at the owner's option, which permits the owner to change operators with minimal costs and the management company wants a long-term contract with renewals at the operator's option which gives the management company an opportunity to recover costs association with start-up such as marketing, employee training and management payroll.

The owner typically wants to maximize the number of financial reports, budget data, and financial meetings in order to better control how his/her money is being spent, while the operator may seek to minimize such information and meetings. A typical owner wants the power to approve or reject all transactions, while increased autonomy is the goal of the operator.

The owner wants the freedom to terminate a contract upon immediate written notice, while the management company under no circumstances wants the owner to be able to terminate before the expiration date.

Generally, the keys factors in the selection of a management company include cost, market strengths, lender reputation, efficiency of operations, and flexibility in contract terms and negotiation. The management company profile describes its present status and its future plans. The number of properties and the number of years it has under contract, the locations of the properties, chain affiliations, facilities, amenities, ages, market orientation, and of the owners of managed properties all are typically considered carefully by an owner.

The management company that can demonstrate greater market strength, which is a successful track record in capturing and servicing the market segments that are critical to the success of the hotel, has a distinct advantage.

Because financial lenders are often critical to an owner the reputation of the management company with financial lenders is also critical in the selection process. Lenders often are more comfortable funding projects that are operated by companies that are recognized both for their operational success in the market and for the product concepts that the hotel reflects.

Other factors that an owner may consider when selecting a management company include: efficiency and profitability of the management company and the methods for charging central services to the contract, such as accounting, reservations, engineering, architectural design, and labor relations, insurance and purchasing.

Reference

Stutts, Alan T. (2001) *Hotel and Lodging Management – An Introduction*. New York: John Wiley & Sons.

ALAN T. STUTTS
AMERICAN INTERCONTINENTAL
UNIVERSITY, USA

Management development

Management development (MD) comes in various guises: training, education, professional development, personal development, succession planning, and so on. Jansen *et al.* (2001, p. 106) suggest a definition:

> Management development is defined as a system of personnel practices by which an organization tries to guarantee the timely availability of qualified and motivated employees for its key positions. The aim of MD is to have at its disposal the right type of managers and specialists at the right moment.

In some hotel businesses, this is seen as succession management, and is often reflected through management cadet programs that attempt to groom potential, future 'managers'. The 'Hilton Elevator Program' is a good example. However, these programs focus on recruiting potential managers, rather than offering structured development for current management stock.

In many hotels, money spent on training and development tends to be skewed in favor of staff-induction, skills-based training. Fewer resources are used to develop managers within the business. Management development is often limited to providing managers (mostly the general manager) with the opportunity to go to industry conferences and meetings. Large international chain hotels often set up annual meetings for departmental managers from their property portfolio: rooms division, accountants, food and beverage, and so on. At these meetings, there is an element of development through outside specialists coming in to talk to the group on current and future issues that may impact the organization.

Jansen *et al.* (2001) suggest a four-pronged typology of management development:

- *Administrative MD* shows a lack of both organizational and personal development. This is most applicable to 'lifetime employment' where promotion tends to be by seniority.
- *Derived MD* reflects an 'up-or-out' organizational culture; if you don't move up the hierarchy fast enough, you tend to move out to another organization (promotion through redeployment).
- *Partner MD* creates an atmosphere where very strict (contracted) criteria are set for managerial development (in terms of attaining skills) and if these criteria are not met, then managers need to seek employment elsewhere.
- *Leading MD* tends to reflect hospitality organizations, where management development is seen as a purely personal attribute, not tied to organizational strategies and objectives. Management development is left solely to the discretion of the individual manager and his or her own motivations and aspirations.

Whilst this typology can be attributable to a range of hospitality businesses, it is important to note that each is derived from the underlying culture, strategies, and context of each individual organization; it is difficult to form a one-size-fits-all approach. In Japan, for instance, very hierarchical organizational structures tend to mitigate against clearly defined development programs, either within or from outside the organization.

Several authors suggest that management development is much to do with improving personal and management skills through competencies regarded as essential to management tasks. Quinn *et al.* (2003) suggest 24 competencies for management development through their Competing Values Framework model. Their proposition is that managers need to go through five levels in order to become a 'Master manager': novice stage, advanced beginner stage, competent

stage, proficient stage, and expert stage. In order to accomplish a higher level of management development, they note several steps that a manger could take for self-improvement: learn about yourself, develop a change strategy, and implement this change strategy. Therefore a manager needs to progress up the ranks (from novice to master) through a series of personal objectives and strategies, which could include performance-based assessment and feedback, education and training, and participation in high-level executive decision-making.

'A competency model is useful for building an integrated framework for developing a company's human resources system' (Chung-Herrera *et al.*, 2003, p. 19). This study suggests that MD is focused on change and change management within the business and that well-developed and integrated competency models enable a company to communicate with its employees (and managers) regarding the behavior connected with success, thereby increasing the firm's ability to achieve its business objectives in uncertain economic and social times. The study identifies a total of 99 competencies, which they have grouped into eight categories of knowledge, from self-management (the highest rated category), through critical thinking and communication to the lowest rated categories of 'interpersonal, leadership and industry knowledge' (Chung-Herrera *et al.*, 2003, p. 23).

To create and implement a management development program that allows managers to learn higher-order skills can be a financial and resource burden on many hospitality businesses. Often budgetary constraints and the availability of appropriately trained facilitators require that companies outsource such MD programs. In Australia, an MD program was set up to allow management executives within the Sheraton group to undertake an MBA, through Bond University (there are other examples). A study completed in 1995 shows that hotel managers in Canada were overwhelmingly in favor of structured MD programs and were able to secure funds for such activities as long as they were 'both short and reasonably priced' (Shaw and Patterson, 1995, p. 38). Agreement over what constitutes management development and thus what elements should be included in such a program is problematical.

The issue of promoting women and minorities, through management development, is another key component, broader than can be considered here. However, when Marriott International created a management development program some years ago, an unexpected benefit was that the company was able to identify and promote women and minorities from within the organization (Enz and Siguaw, 2003, pp. 116–117). Critically, the MD program at Marriott has made it possible for managers to focus their own development efforts in specific ways enabling the company to increase the pool of managers ready to move forward.

Establishing and implementing management development programs, whether internal or outsourced, needs careful consideration. The various costs and benefits need to be weighed against the total outcomes that an organization may gain from such programs. In most instances, MD is reserved for the larger hospitality sector companies, with smaller independent properties relying on buying-in well-developed managers and leaders through selective recruitment.

References

Chung-Herrera, B.G., Enz, C.A., and Lankau, M.J. (2003) Grooming future hospitality leaders: a competencies model. *Cornell Hotel and Restaurant Administration Quarterly*, 44 (3), 17–25.

Enz, C.A. and Siguaw, J.A. (2003) Revisiting the Best of the Best: innovations in hotel practice. *Cornell Hotel and Restaurant Administration Quarterly*, 44 (5/6), 115–123.

Jansen, P., van der Velde, M., and Mul, W. (2001) A typology of management development. *Journal of Management Development*, 20 (2), 106–116.

Quinn, R.E., Faerman, S.R., Thompson, M.P., and McGrath, M.R. (2003) *Becoming A Master Manager: A Competency Framework*, 3rd edn. New York: John Wiley & Sons.

Shaw, M. and Patterson, J. (1995) Management-development programs: A Canadian perspective. *Cornell Hotel and Restaurant Administration Quarterly*, 36 (1), 34–39.

PAUL WEEKS
SOUTHERN CROSS UNIVERSITY, AUSTRALIA

Management information system

A management information system (MIS) consists of people and equipment and contains procedures to gather, sort, analyze, evaluate, and distribute timely and accurate information needed for managerial decision-making. In the hospitality field, the main sources of an MIS are information collected by the firm on a regular basis as a routine part of business activities (internal data) and market research information from an organization's environment (external data), both stored in a database format. More advanced systems also provide features to forecast the future state of the economy and market demand for tourism products. By analyzing complex marketing data, disseminating information, and providing decision support features for tourism managers, an MIS contributes to the improvement of managerial performance. An effective MIS provides query functions for quick information retrieval on a video display terminal and delivers printed forms or reports to alert the manager when an unexpected situation – either positive or negative – has developed. The value of reporting has greatly been enhanced by recent advances in graphical display technology and by the increased interest of hospitality managers to exchange information electronically. Enhancements with more sophisticated analytical models move a management information system towards a decision support system or expert system.

References

Laudon, J.P. and Laudon K.C. (2003) *Management Information Systems*, 8th edn. Upper Saddle River, NJ: Prentice-Hall.

Wöber, K.W. (2003) Information supply in tourism management by marketing decision support systems. *Tourism Management*, 24 (3), 241–255.

KARL WÖBER
VIENNA UNIVERSITY OF ECONOMICS
AND BUSINESS ADMINISTRATION,
AUSTRIA

Management information system: methods and usage

A management information system (MIS) combines computerized systems with regular management procedures and transforms raw data into information that managers can use in day-to-day decision-making. Data can be defined as raw, unanalyzed facts. Information can be defined as data that have been put into a meaningful context for a manager. Since the quality of a manager's decisions relates to the information that is available, the better the information, the better the decisions (Ivancevich *et al.*, 1996).

Managers need information about their organizations and about the external environment to recognize problems, make assumptions, generate and choose alternatives, and implement and control their choices.

An MIS is important for effective decision-making in all aspects of management: organization, human resources, strategy, customer service, and operations. An MIS is also used for implementing organizational initiatives, such as total quality management (TQM), a system that uses both processes and people for improving inventory control, quality control, and service.

Fundamental elements of MIS functions include collecting, storing, and processing of data and then allowing managers to select various formats for presenting such data (Higgins, 1991).

Collecting data

The process of collecting data includes a wide variety of records and information used in the operation of a business – personnel records; information about customers, competitors, and suppliers; sales data; accounting data; and the like. The collecting function organizes raw data into a database (a collection of data stored in a software program).

Storing and processing data

After a database has been created, it must then be stored (usually on magnetic tape or disk) and

activated and processed by a specialized software program often referred to as a database management system (DBMS). The data require updating in order to be accurate and timely, which can be done by a computer operator, such as a manager, an accountant, or a computer programmer (depending upon the complexity of the data). In some systems, data are automatically updated because the database is permanently connected to the MIS (the computer automatically makes updates and changes as new data become available).

Once data are stored and processed into a suitable format, managers can access and analyze the data for decision-making. Organizations typically process both text (such as reports) and numbers (such as counts).

Presenting information

There are several ways effectively to present processed data to managers and others in an organization. Words can be organized into reports, outlines, lists, white paper articles, and manuscripts. Numbers can be presented in table format or in graphs. Some of the most commonly used graphic formats include bar charts (whereby vertical or horizontal bars represent values) and pie charts (whereby slices of a circle represent proportions of the whole).

In an organization, managers who are lower on the organization chart (a graphical depiction of reporting authority) are typically more concerned with information that relates to day-to-day operations. Mid-level managers are responsible for implementing plans formulated by upper-level managers and therefore require access to information that can be processed and retrieved. Top-level managers are responsible for strategic decisions and are most likely to be interested in trends and forecast information.

In deciding a manager's information needs, Kotler (2002) proposed this list of questions:

1. What types of decisions do you make regularly?
2. What type of information do you need to make those decisions?
3. What type of information do you get currently?

4. What type of information would you like to get that you do not currently get?
5. What information would you want daily, weekly, monthly, yearly, and so on?
6. What type of data analysis would you like to have available?

References

Higgins, J. (1991) *The Management Challenge.* New York: Macmillan.

Ivancevich, J., Lorenzi, P., Skinner, S., and Crosby, P. (1996) *Management: Quality and Competitiveness.* New York: Richard D. Irwin, Inc.

Kotler, P. (2002) *Marketing Management.* Englewood Cliffs, NJ: Prentice-Hall.

EDWARD A. MERRITT
CALIFORNIA STATE POLYTECHNIC
UNIVERSITY, USA

Management of change

Managing change in hospitality organizations can be defined as the reshaping of the strategy, structure, and culture of an organization over time by external forces or through using internal mechanisms. The characteristics of change in hospitality organizations can be categorized along the following two dimensions: radical versus incremental change and planned versus emergent change. One of the early models of planned change developed by Lewin (1951) involves three steps: 'unfreezing' the present pattern, 'changing' or developing a new pattern, and 'refreezing' at the new desired level. In their empirical research Okumus and Hemmington (1998) found that Lewin's three-stage model was not applicable in complex and dynamic situations in hospitality organizations. Several potential barriers and resistance to change in hospitality firms may include financial difficulties, cost of the change, fear of losing the existing customers, time limitation, priority of other businesses, lack of skills and cooperation, and internal politics. The abilities, skills, experience of managers, and active support and coordination from other management levels are the key factors in overcoming the barriers and resistance to change in hospitality organizations. It is recommended that hospitality organizations should develop a dynamic and responsive organizational structure and culture where change is seen as the norm and is accepted as part of the normal process of organizational evaluation (Okumus and Hemmington, 1998).

References

Lewin, K. (1951) *Field Theory in Social Science.* New York: Harper and Row.

Okumus, F. and Hemmington, N. (1998) Management of the change process in hotel companies: an investigation at operational level. *Journal of International Hospitality Management,* 17 (4), 363–374.

FEVZI OKUMUS
THE HONG KONG POLYTECHNIC
UNIVERSITY, HONG KONG SAR, CHINA

Management proficiency ratio

Management proficiency ratio is a set of key measures for evaluating goals and objectives. Ideally, a manager would have input into selecting the goals and objectives to be achieved, the ratios (measures) to be used for evaluation, be given the appropriate power by the organization to facilitate achievement, and be held responsible for such achievement. The ratio should be set as objective (based on counts and timed events) instead of subjective (based on feelings and impressions).

The management proficiency ratio may include ratio analysis, formulas, guidelines, and rules of thumb to help analyze and evaluate any business-related problem. For example, accounting principles and guidelines may be used as the basis for evaluating an organization's financial health. Similarly, financial and economic measures may be included as a basis for decision-making such as breakeven analysis. Finally, quantitative methods (mathematical and statistical techniques for solving managerial planning and decision-making) may be used for forecasting and validity testing. An array of these types of measures is used in creating a management proficiency ratio.

Reference

Khan, M.A. (1999) *Restaurant Franchising*. New York: John Wiley & Sons.

EDWARD A. MERRITT
CALIFORNIA STATE POLYTECHNIC
UNIVERSITY, USA

Management styles

Management is the process common across all functions of an organization by which the efforts of staff are coordinated, directed, and guided using systems and procedures towards the achievement of organizational goals. Management style is the way a manager uses their authority to achieve this, and can be a combination of factors that are internal to the individual, such as national culture, personal values, and personality and external factors such as explicit and implicit organizational rules and procedures and how these are interpreted by the manager. An example of this interplay is with the increasing globalization of the hospitality industry it is becoming more common that managers have to manage trans-culturally. Expatriate general managers are used where there is a lack of suitable local management talent and a lack of understanding of the corporate culture of the organization.

One of the earliest attempts to systematize the job of management was the work of F.W. Taylor and his '*scientific management*.' Scientific management is a form of job design that emphasizes the need to standardize tasks by dividing jobs into smaller, specialized, and highly prescribed chunks and for managers to ensure the rigorous enforcement of this highly prescribed way of working. This limits the number of tasks an operative carries out and therefore the level of skills and training required. Motivation to adhere to the standardized procedure is based on extrinsic rewards such as performance-related bonuses.

Fast food outlets often subscribe to the principles of scientific management, with speed of service delivery and standardization of product as key outputs but at the expense of deskilled jobs, with little discretion over work for employees due to technology.

The *human relations approach*, alternatively, is a school of management thinking based on the research findings of Elton Mayo, which emphasizes the importance of social processes in the workplace. As such, the research findings highlighted that people are motivated by factors other than money, with intrinsic rather than extrinsic rewards being more highly prized, even in low-skilled jobs. Also, they illustrated the importance of the group as a unit of analysis in organizational influence. They maintained that people could be influenced by the norms of their work group in relation to attitudes to work and level of productivity. Under such a regime, the manager is therefore responsible for creating an atmosphere of trust and commitment, with a high degree of teamwork and communication. Some argue that strong informal groupings exist in hospitality organizations. The key for managers is therefore to recognize them and develop a strategy which optimizes the orientation of members and the overall cohesion of the group.

The human relations approach was further developed by the work of Douglas McGregor (1960). McGregor concentrated on the manager's assumptions about human behavior and divided them into two categories; those that managed according to what he referred to as 'Theory X' and those that managed according to 'Theory Y'. Theory X managers assume that employees have an inherent dislike of work and are therefore lazy and shiftless. As a result, the manager adopts a style of management which emphasizes control to the point of coercion, with little room for empowerment, delegation or trust. Conversely, Theory Y managers believe that employees view work as natural and motivating. Unlike Theory X, which assumes that the goals of the individual and the goals of the organization are mutually exclusive. Theory Y managers see their role as creating the conditions under which these goals can be integrated. As a result, the hospitality organization can harness the creative potential of employees and create a motivating and rewarding environment in return.

The Contingency Theory perspective argues that there is no universally applicable model of management. Rather, the most useful model of management is contingent on and consistent with such factors as the type of environment in which the organization is functioning, the type of task employees are carrying out and the attributes of those employees. Therefore, according to contingency theory, the style of management that is appropriate for a small, family-run hotel with only a few employees and limited services may not be the same as the style of management which is appropriate for an international luxury resort with several hundred staff. Also, in a busy hotel kitchen when many courses have to be prepared in a very short timescale, a more autocratic, Theory X approach may achieve results more easily, and may also be accepted by staff that recognize the need for tight control and clear authority.

One of the factors that influence the role of the manager is their level within the organizational hierarchy. Katz (1974) identified three attributes or qualities that are necessary for a manager: their technical competence, their human and social skills and their conceptual ability. The appropriate mix of these three abilities will change as the level of responsibility of the manager changes. For example, at the supervisory level of management, the emphasis is likely to be on technical and social skills as the main part of the jobs overseeing operational activities and staff motivation and performance. However, as the responsibility of the manager increases, their ability to influence not only their own staff but also other areas of the business becomes more important, as does their understanding of the strategic importance of their contribution. As a result, the development of conceptual ability becomes a key factor in their personal and organizational effectiveness.

The effectiveness of any management style should be measured not only in terms of the achievement of objectives, but also in relation to the creation of a positive working environment, where creativity, responsibility and commitment flourish. When the management style is inappropriate this can result not only in poor business performance but also in poor use of human resources, with problems such as absenteeism, staff turnover, disciplinary issues and generally poor morale.

References

Katz, R. (1974) Skills of an effective administrator. *Harvard Business Review*, Sept–Oct, pp. 90–102.
McGregor, D. (1960) *The Human Side of Enterprise*. New York: McGraw-Hill.

GILLIAN KELLOCK HAY
GLASGOW CALEDONIAN UNIVERSITY, UK

Manager on duty

A lodging manager is responsible for keeping the hotel or lodging enterprise operating, efficient, and profitable. In a small enterprise with a limited staff, the general manager may oversee all aspects of operations. However, larger hotels and lodging enterprises may employ hundreds if not thousands of employees, and the general manager usually is aided by a number of assistant managers assigned to the various departments of the operations. During the absence of the general manager an assistant is typically identified as the manager on duty. The manager on duty fields concerns, questions, and issues that may arise from guests and employees. It is essential that the hotel staff have a person who they can go to with issues or concerns at all times, particularly when their department supervisor or manager may not be available. Because of its central location and focal point in a hotel or lodging enterprise often the manager on duty is an assistant who is located at the front desk or reception of the hotel. The key demands facing the manager on duty are in large part short term. The short-term demands include day-to-day operational issues of quality service and controlling costs and revenue. The manager on duty, like all operations managers, is under tremendous pressure to produce short-term positive results.

Reference

Stutts, Alan T. (2001) *Hotel and Lodging Management – An Introduction.* New York: John Wiley & Sons.

ERIC O. LONG
WALDORF ASTORIA HOTEL, USA

Marginal costs

Marginal cost describes the cost of the last unit produced. There are often considerable differences between the average cost (calculated as the total cost divided by the volume) and the marginal cost. Marginal cost is an important concept in economic analysis. The optimal production volume is achieved when marginal cost equals the price of the product. The marginal cost is then normally much higher than the average cost which implies that the volume of the optimal result will not be the volume that minimizes the average cost. Marginal cost is the theoretical basis for contribution margin pricing whereas average cost is the basis for full cost pricing. Depending on the level of analysis, marginal cost may also include fixed costs:

1. The marginal cost of serving one more customer in a restaurant is equal to the variable cost.
2. The marginal cost of keeping the restaurant open one extra hour includes variable cost as well as some fixed costs, such as energy and management salaries.
3. The marginal cost of running yet another restaurant includes variable as well as fixed costs.

At the first decision level, i.e. one more customer, the contribution margin, defined as revenue less variable cost, is equal to the marginal profit, defined as marginal revenue less marginal cost.

References

Dorward, N. (1986) The mythology of constant marginal costs. *Accountancy*, April, pp. 98–102.

Harris, P.J. (ed.) (1995) *Accounting and Finance for the International Hospitality Industry.* Oxford: Butterworth-Heinemann.

TOMMY D. ANDERSSON
GOTEBORGS UNIVERSITY, SWEDEN

Market penetration

As one component of a core set of growth strategies (see table below), a market penetration strategy seeks to *increase sales of existing products or services to existing markets*. Although this seems like a simple concept, variants of this definition are used by both marketing academics and practitioners. How a market penetration strategy is ultimately defined, applied, and measured depends on how the user of the concept defines its elements – existing products, existing markets, strategic outcomes – in terms of sales or some other desired result (Table 1).

In the strictest sense, market penetration involves existing products that are not modified in any way. Thus, a product that is in some way changed or improved, whether through different packaging or some other feature enhancement, counts as a new product. If this new product is sold to existing markets, the firm is using a product development strategy as opposed to a market penetration strategy. However, for practical management purposes, the definition of 'existing products or services' can vary widely. It might include only unmodified products or products that are modified somewhat to replace an existing product offering. Existing products might also include those in a product line or portfolio.

Similarly, there is ambiguity because market penetration can mean selling to existing *customers* or selling to the broader category of existing *markets*. A customer is a person or organizational

Table 1 Definition of market penetration

	Existing product(s)	*New or modified product(s)*
Existing market(s)	Market penetration	Product development
New market(s)	Market development	Diversification

buyer that has purchased a marketer's offering before. A market includes customers but also potential buyers who have not purchased a marketer's offering but might do so in the future. The difference between customers and markets is not inconsequential, for it can impact how a market penetration strategy is implemented. For instance, if a market penetration strategy is oriented to customers, the objective is to *induce existing buyers to buy more*; on the other hand, if the strategy is oriented to non-users within a defined market, the objective is to *attract more buyers* by turning potential buyers into actual customers. The specific means for accomplishing these different objectives are also likely to differ, as described below.

The result of a market penetration strategy is usually defined in terms of sales: unit sales, dollar sales, or market share. The latter measure – the percentage of total unit or dollar sales within a product market captured by a specific brand – is also known as 'share of wallet.' Advertising agencies also speak of market penetration in terms of brand awareness, brand recall, or some other marketing-communication metric that reflects 'share of mind.' For example, an advertiser might recommend a new campaign as part of a market penetration strategy designed to increase brand awareness from 25% of the market to 40%. As the above conceptual discussion suggests, clarity and consistency in the definition and measurement of the various elements of the strategy are key to understanding market penetration.

Tactic

A market penetration strategy can be implemented by using an array of tools in the marketing mix, most commonly aggressive pricing and sales promotion, but also advertising and distribution. These tactics are designed to accomplish one of two things, either separately or in combination: generating more frequent, greater, or novel usage on the part of existing customers; or, attracting more non-users within a market to become users (customers).

For example, in the worldwide cola war, Coca-Cola and PepsiCo bottlers constantly wage market share battles using discount pricing and special promotion tactics (e.g., coupons, sweepstakes, and in-store offers). Because the cola soft-drink category is mature with flat growth in many markets, the objective of these tactics is to steal share from the competition. In contrast, in fast-growing product categories, such as bottled water, a market penetration strategy might feature brand advertising designed to create an image and solidify market position in order to build market share by turning non-users into customers. Another example of market penetration is promotion that encourages greater or more frequent usage, such as recent marketing communication for products such as orange juice, cranberry juice, and oatmeal. After certain health benefits of these products were revealed by medical studies, advertising at both the product category and brand level encouraged consumers to increase consumption.

Discount or 'penetration pricing' – setting a price below that offered by competitors – is especially effective for building market share when buyers are price-sensitive, or when a firm employing the strategy can benefit from the cost economies achieved with higher volume production. On the other hand, such an approach can lead to ruinous price competition when competitors are willing to vigorously defend market share. In such contexts, market penetration can be better achieved by other means, such as sales promotion and advertising. For example, in the spring of 1997, McDonald's helped to boost otherwise flat growth in the United States fast food market with a sales promotion that linked McDonald's Happy Meals with Teeny Beanie Babies from the toy maker, Ty. The promotion became McDonald's most successful to date for Happy Meals and had to be cut short in many markets due to short supplies of the toys. Some customers were purchasing dozens of Happy Meals per visit, often discarding the food just to obtain the toy.

Finally, market penetration can also be achieved by employing distribution strategies. Starbucks Coffee Company is widely recognized as a leader in growth via market penetration. In July of 2003, the company opened its 1000th store in Asia and 6500th store worldwide.

However, a rival company, Dunkin' Donuts, has penetrated markets in the eastern United States even more deeply than Starbucks. By comparison, whereas one can find a Starbucks for every 15,000 residents in the company's home state of Washington, there's a Dunkin' Donuts store for every 7,500 residents in the latter company's home state of Massachusetts.

In sum, if growth is fundamental to the success of a business, and achieving this is difficult through new products or new markets, a market penetration strategy is a powerful tactic.

Reference

Friedman, L.G. (2002) *Go to Market Strategy: Advanced Techniques and Tools for Selling More Products to More Customers More Profitably.* Burlington, MA: Butterworth-Heinemann.

ROBERT KWORTNIK
CORNELL UNIVERSITY, USA

Market saturation

Market saturation is the point at which current market demand no longer supports additional units of supply – the market (actual and potential buyers) is effectively glutted. In product markets, saturation is achieved when there are no new buyers for a marketer's existing product offering. For example, if there are only 10 restaurants in a particular geographic area, and a marketer of coffee machines has already sold machines to nine of them, with the final potential buyer unwilling to purchase, the market is saturated. In such a situation, the only viable strategies for growth are to seek new, unsaturated markets or to introduce product upgrades to replace existing models as they wear out or become obsolete.

In service industries, market saturation similarly occurs when a market can no longer support an additional outlet or service provider without harming the sales of existing firms serving that market. Although the major cause of this type of market saturation is clustering of providers – too many stores located too closely together and chasing too few customers – this is often only part of the story. Changing buyer preferences, lack of innovation in the product or service mix, and intensifying competition can accelerate the effects of market saturation.

This confluence of forces in the marketing environment contributed to the problems faced by McDonald's in January of 2003, when the company reported a quarterly loss for the first time since it went public nearly 40 years earlier. McDonald's phenomenal success had been fueled by a high-growth, market penetration strategy. Revenue growth came from adding more stores – thousands per year – to satisfy the needs of underserved markets rather than from increasing sales of those stores in markets McDonald's already served. However, with more than 13,000 stores in the United States and 31,000 stores worldwide, many markets McDonald's serves had become saturated. For example, it is estimated that 7% of Americans eat at McDonald's on a daily basis. In addition, the company was negatively impacted by shifts in buyer preferences toward healthier dining, competition in the fast food category from such companies as Subway Restaurants, and a menu that had not seen a truly successful product innovation since 1983 and the introduction of the Chicken McNugget. These factors contributed to flat and even declining same-store sales in some markets, as well as complaints from franchise owners that nearby, newly opened stores were cannibalizing sales. To combat these problems, McDonald's management slowed store growth and even closed older, underperforming stores. In addition, the company focused on improving service delivery and adding new menu items such as salads in order to improve sales performance in existing markets.

Many companies, such as McDonald's, have taken the lessons learned when saturating one market and now are assessing foreign markets. For example, while the quick service restaurant leader has saturated the US market, the company estimates that on a global basis its food accounts for only 1% of daily consumption. The objective, then, is to calculate when saturation will occur in the newer markets and pair that with strategies corresponding to the company's life cycle.

Reference

Middleton, V.T.C. and Clarke, J.R. (2001) *Marketing in Travel and Tourism*. Burlington, MA: Butterworth-Heinemann.

ROBERT KWORTNIK
CORNELL UNIVERSITY, USA

Market segmentation: trends and challenges

Market segmentation is one of the fundamental principles of marketing given the fact that firms cannot normally serve all of the customers in a market because of diverse (heterogeneous) needs and preferences. The basic tenet of market segmentation is that a heterogeneous group of customers can be grouped into homogeneous groups or segments exhibiting similar wants, preferences, and buying behavior. The process enables companies to target specific market segment(s), design more suitable marketing mix variables (price, product, promotion, and distribution), and develop more effective positioning strategy. Market segmentation leads to better understanding of the customers and competitors, more effective allocation of resources, and capitalization on the opportunities (i.e. niche markets).

The segmentation procedure first involves selecting the most appropriate base to divide the overall market and the segmentation approach to be used. The segmentation bases include demographic, geographic (geodemographic), psychographic, and behavioral variables. There exists a hot debate over which segmentation base is more effective. Although this selection may be market- or product-specific and be identified based on how the segment(s) meet the criteria for effective segments (measurability, substantiality, accessibility, and actionability), the consensus and empirical evidence across fields demonstrate that the psychographic and behavioral variables are more effective than the demographic and geographic variables in terms of dividing the overall market. Particularly, two concepts have surfaced as being more powerful

bases: lifestyle and benefits sought. The lifestyle concept, classified under psychographics, has been shown to influence both buying and communication (media) behavior, which is why it is very powerful. Although the basic dimensions of the concept are activities, interests, and opinions (AIO), some other variables are often employed to form lifestyle segments such as values, aesthetic styles, and life visions. Benefit segmentation has also been found an effective base because benefits are impelling and compelling reason behind all behavior. Benefits are what the product does for the customer. Benefits which people are seeking in consuming a product or experiencing a service explain why people are looking for certain attributes or features. The reason for its wide and extensive use is that benefits sought are closely related to values, motivations, and preferences. However, most of the empirical studies on benefit segmentation do not differentiate between benefits and features or benefits realized before or after the experience (Shoemaker, 1994). The selection of appropriate base is more challenging for segmenting international markets. Although culture has often been used as a segmentation base for international markets. Most studies have ignored subcultures or just compared different nationalities due to the difficulty of measuring cultural characteristics. International market segmentation represents a good area for further research in terms of identifying the most appropriate segmentation base.

The segmentation approach can be priori *vs.* posteriori and forward *vs.* backward. An *a priori* approach is one where the segments are chosen before the data are analyzed (i.e. male/female, non-users/first-time users/repeat users, etc). An *a posteriori* approach is one where the segments are determined by the data rather than by the researcher. This approach is usually associated with cluster analysis. A *forward* segmentation approach includes grouping consumer characteristics based on their similarity in demographics, personality, attitude, and benefits sought followed by discriminating groups by consumer response, (i.e. chosen product or service). A *backward* approach, on the other hand, involves grouping consumer response based on their similarity in choice of products and services followed by discriminating groups by consumer characteristics. No matter which approach is being utilized, they have inherent weaknesses from conceptual and practical standpoints when consumers have diverse demand for products and services. First, consumer characteristics are more likely to show a relationship with broad patterns of consumer response than a specific response. Second, the relationship will often be weak and unstable over time when consumers have diverse demands and choices. Several researchers in marketing and consumer behavior have emphasized that consumers may belong to multiple segments rather than one and only one segment. Their basic argument is that identifying consumers as a member of one, and only one, segment grouping seems technically appropriate but conceptually and practically questionable. When products and services are suitable for several types of usage situations, overlapping clusters are more appropriate because hierarchical clusters requiring exclusive group membership may be misleading. For example, Baloglu *et al.* (1998) introduced an alternative perspective on lodging market segmentation and analyzed consumer response (type of hotel) and product attributes preferred (consumer characteristics) simultaneously. A follow-up assignment method showed that a large number of respondents fell into more than one segment and revealed both overlapping and unique (mutually exclusive) product-benefit segments. Although different approaches (i.e. canonical correlation) and algorithms have been applied to reveal mutually exclusive and overlapping segments, there has been limited research on this interesting topic.

In recent marketing literature, one-to-one marketing (or mass customization) and the characteristics of postmodern consumers have been debated as factors posing challenges to the segmentation practices. There are those who argue that in the postmodern era the market is fragmented, where the postmodern consumer wants to experience the diversity and exhibit multiple self-images and lifestyles for different occasions. Consumers try several or many images, brands and products, both sequentially and simultaneously. Therefore, current segmentation

practices may not be useful (Firat and Shultz, 1997). This, indeed, represents a significant challenge for marketers because it suggests that an individual may belong to different segments not only at the same time, but also at different points in time. It further justifies the need for more future research on overlapping segments in identification of multiple consumer images, benefits, and/or motivations. Perhaps the companies will be more likely to use occasion-based segmentation. Another implication is that more empirical studies will be needed to examine the stability of segments overtime, which will require longitudinal and cohort studies. Loyalty as a segmentation base (attitudinal and behavioral) may provide interesting insights to differentiate true, spurious, and latent loyal customers.

Advances in information technology and computerization now allow companies to track customers individually and customize marketing efforts. This practice, so called one-to-one marketing, mass customization, or database marketing, does not eliminate or preclude market segmentation. Hospitality firms still need to strategically develop general marketing mix variables for different segments and tactically customize some components to each customer. The practice also provides many opportunities for data mining, which is the process of searching through customer data files to detect or discover patterns to guide marketing decision-making. Although the databases are mostly limited to demographic and behavioral data, data mining represents many opportunities for future research to discover new segmentation bases, identify niche segments, and to combine segmentation and one-to-one marketing.

The most popular multivariate statistics in hospitality and tourism segmentation research have been factor-cluster analysis and discriminant analysis. The emerging statistical tools available to segmentation researchers, despite their limited use, are Neural Network models and CHAID (Chi-Square Automatic Interaction) (Mazanec, 1999; Chen, 2003). Some neural network models even allow researchers to determine a firm's optimal segments and positioning for each segment simultaneously. By using CHAID, one can identify the most appropriate segmentation variable to start with and optimum segments based on a trade-off between segment size and variance. These tools would be particularly useful in identifying the segments, modeling within segments, and data mining research.

References

Baloglu, S., Weaver, P., and McCleary, K. (1998) Overlapping market segments in the lodging industry: a canonical correlation approach. *International Journal of Contemporary Hospitality Management*, 10 (4), 159–166.

Chen, J. (2003) Developing a travel segmentation methodology. *Journal of Hospitality and Tourism Research*, 27 (3), 310–327.

Firat, A.F. and Shultz, C.J. II (1997) From segmentation to fragmentation: markets and marketing strategy in the postmodern era. *European Journal of Marketing*, 31 (3/4), 183–207.

Mazanec, J.A. (1999) Simultaneous positioning and segmentation analysis with topologically ordered feature maps: a tour operator example. *Journal of Retailing and Consumer Services*, 6 (4), 219–235.

Shoemaker, S. (1994) Segmenting the US travel market according to benefits realized. *Journal of Travel Research*, 33 (2), 8–21.

SEYHMUS BALOGLU
UNIVERSITY OF NEVADA, LAS VEGAS, USA

Market segmentation in foodservice operations

Market segmentation has become an indispensable marketing practice in industrialized countries where the notion of a mass market has all but disappeared, and buyers have come to expect some degree of customization from marketing offers. Market segmentation can be defined as the process of dividing larger, more heterogeneous markets into smaller, more homogeneous markets based on specific characteristics and wants of the buyers. Thanks to advances in information technology, marketers can more precisely identify, describe, and categorize buyers, thus making it easier to produce the right products and services for the right markets. In this way, effective market segmentation leads to efficient target marketing to groups of buyers most likely to perceive value in the marketer's offer.

It was not long ago that market segmentation was often an afterthought of the marketing process – if it was thought of at all. Firms began product or service development with an idea for a marketing offer and later sought buyers for that offer. Indeed, some entrepreneurs still think of marketing in this manner; their 'big idea' comes first, followed by the search for markets to which the big idea can be sold. Progressive marketers, however, recognize that the marketing process begins with identifying needs that are shared by certain buyers.

For example, a needs-based segmentation strategy is the foundation of marketing for restaurants in North America's emerging fast casual category (e.g., Baja Fresh and Panera Bread Company). Buyers driving the success of this category need the same basic things as customers of traditional fast food restaurants (e.g., McDonald's, Taco Bell, and Chick-fil-A) – convenient, quick, low-price meals. However, fast casual customers also want healthier, fresher foods, and a more comfortable dining experience. Furthermore, these customers are willing to pay more for these benefits. Understanding the needs unique to this segment of fast casual dining customers, identifying who is a member of this segment, and then developing a marketing offer for them depends upon effective market segmentation.

Once buyers' needs and wants are identified, market segmentation follows the process described in the figure below. It should be noted, though, that this conceptual approach to segmentation is not always practiced in real-world marketing. Typical instead is the product-driven approach of the entrepreneur described earlier (develop a product concept first, then try to find a market to fit to the concept). Another common approach is *sector marketing* or *a priori segmentation*. With sector marketing, a mass market is divided into groups of buyers before research is conducted to identify buyers' needs and wants.

For example, the marketer might divide a market based on age, income, and gender. A marketing offering is then developed for select sectors (e.g., middle-income, middle-aged men). The problem with an *a priori* approach to segmentation is that what constitutes a segment is arbitrarily determined by the marketer. Thus, buyers' needs are likely to differ within sectors (e.g., not all women in their 20s seek low-calorie desserts) or needs may be shared across different sectors (e.g., some men in their 40s do seek low-calorie desserts). For this reason, a needs-based or benefits-sought approach to market segmentation is more likely to reveal underlying, 'true' segments of buyers who will respond similarly to a marketer's offering.

Not all groups of buyers identified during the segmentation process will be viable or attractive as targets for a marketing offer. To be viable, a segment must be meet several criteria. It must be:

- *Measurable* – e.g., in terms of size and identifying characteristics
- *Meaningful* – e.g., differentiable from other segments and large enough to be served at a profit
- *Marketable* – e.g., reachable through reasonable marketing efforts given the firm's resources.

In addition, for a segment to be attractive as a target market, it must offer potential for growth and profits – but not so attractive that competition is intense.

An important part of the segmentation process is the description of segments in terms of characteristics that will be useful for marketing strategy design. This requires market research. Market segments can be described in myriad ways. Common bases for segmentation include *geographic* (e.g., from nation to neighborhood), *demographic* (e.g., age, education, income, occupation, gender, and ethnicity), *psychographic* (e.g., lifestyle as reflected in activities, interests, and opinions), and *behavioral* (e.g., product usage or media usage). The challenge is to find that combination of segmentation variables that best represents those buyers with a need met by the marketer's offering or potential offering. For example, Subway Restaurants has identified its target market segment as adults between the ages

Table 1   The market segmentation process

Determine buyer needs and wants in a specific consumption context
Segment the market based on these needs and wants
Identify shared characteristics of buyers within segments, as well as characteristics that distinguish segments
Assess the attractiveness of each market segment in terms of predefined criteria (e.g., growth rate and nature of competition)
Select those segments to pursue
Craft a clear and distinct value offer and image for each target market
Implement the positioning strategy using elements of the marketing mix 4Ps: product, price, place, and promotion

Source: Kotler, 2003

of 18 and 34 (demographic) who are heavy fast food users, eat quick meals (behavioral) and seek good-tasting options (psychographic and benefits sought).

Once market segments are described, the segmentation process turns to assessment of segments for attractiveness, followed by selection of attractive segments to target. Few organizations can afford to target all attractive segments; therefore, market targeting involves the deliberate choice of select segments to pursue based on the marketer's objectives and resources. Identification of target markets is a critical output of the segmentation process – and the most important input to marketing-strategy development (Table 1).

In summary, when a 'one-size-fits-all' approach will not satisfy buyers' individual needs, market segmentation is vital for determining which sizes will best fit groups of customers who share similar needs, thereby increasing customer satisfaction and, ultimately, profits.

Reference

Kotler, P. (2003) *A Framework for Marketing Management*, 2nd edn. Upper Saddle River, NJ: Prentice-Hall.

ROBERT KWORTNIK
CORNELL UNIVERSITY, USA

Market segmentation in hospitality

Understanding the concept of market segmentation is essential to hospitality marketing. Marketers first segment the market prior to selecting specific target markets for their hospitality establishment. Market segmentation is the act of dividing a market into distinct and meaningful groups of buyers who might merit separate products and/or marketing mixes. Once careful thought has gone into market segmentation, marketers can then identify primary (and secondary) markets they wish to target. A major assumption in the practice of market segmentation is that the marketplace is comprised of heterogeneous groups of buyers, i.e., different groups of people have different needs and wants and, thus, are attracted to different product offerings accordingly.

In hospitality, the 'purpose of the trip' is a starting point for the segmentation process. We need to first consider whether people are primarily traveling for business purposes or for leisure purposes. Within each of these categories segments emerge. The following discussion highlights some of these major segments that marketers target in hospitality.

The business travel segment

The business traveler is looking for efficiency and effectiveness in a timely manner to conduct business away from home base. Major segments in business travel include individual, corporate, and the conference and convention market. *Individual business travelers* are essentially entrepreneurs who travel to conduct business on their own behalf. Independent business professionals such as lawyers, accountants, doctors, contractors, consultants, and the like (i.e., people who do not work in the corporate environment), are typically categorized in this market segment. They are the sole decision-maker on when, where, and how they travel to conduct their personal business. Whether these individuals operate a small- or medium-sized business, the specific purpose of the trip will impact their choice of budget, midscale, or upscale accommodations. It should be noted that the term 'FIT,' or free independent traveler, is often used to identify this market. However, the FIT nomenclature does not clearly distinguish the important difference between business versus leisure travel.

Individual *corporate travelers* are those who travel to conduct business for the corporation with which they are employed. This normally implies that they are traveling on their own and not involved with group activity. Many large corporations have travel departments who make many, if not most, of the travel and accommodation decisions for their traveling employees. Indeed, travel managers for these types of corporations are a segment in themselves and are often targeted by the large chain hotel companies that seek business clientele. Similar to the individual traveler, the specific purpose of the trip, such as a sales appointment with a potential client or an intra-company business appointment, will help determine the type of accommodation they require. In other words, all business travelers are not necessarily in the same market segment. It all comes down to the particular purpose of the trip being planned.

The *conference and convention market* (also referred to as the *meetings market*) is another major segment in business travel. These are group events where people gather for a common business purpose. Conference implies smaller groups of, say, 50–150 persons, where as convention normally suggests groups of 200+ attendees. Major players include associations and corporations.

Associations are organizations that are formed to serve the common interests of its membership. CHRIE, or the Council of Hotel, Restaurant, and Institutional Education, for example, is an association made up of hospitality and tourism educators. The CHRIE annual convention is held each summer in alternating cities throughout North America. Each year the specific location is chosen by the CHRIE executive committee and members of the association can choose (or not choose) to attend the convention in any given year.

Corporations hold a multitude of conferences and conventions throughout the year for varying reasons, including regional and national sales meetings, training seminars, new product introductions, etc. Selection of personnel to attend these meetings is at the discretion of the individual organizing the event, and attendance is very often mandatory. People who plan the logistics for an event (who may or may not be the person organizing the meeting, its agenda, goals, etc.) are called meeting planners. They may work directly for the organization or may be independent contractors. Outsourcing meeting planning to independent meeting planners is becoming more pronounced in today's business environment.

The leisure travel segment

Similar to the business market, market segments in leisure travel consist largely of *individual* and *group travel*. The leisure traveler is looking for relaxation away from home or, in some instances, to attend to personal affairs such as weddings, funerals, bar mitzvahs, christenings, and so forth.

Relaxation means different things to different people. For example, for some it may be sunbathing on a sandy beach in Florida or on the Mediterranean coast in southern France. For others, it might be hiking, biking, rafting, and kayaking across Costa Rica in Latin America. Culinary tourism is on the rise, too. As noted in a recent publication, 'Cooking schools around the world are putting more emphasis on understanding the cultures that spawned them' (*Globe and Mail*, 2003). In other words, the purpose of leisure travel varies widely.

The individual travel segment is largely comprised of singles, couples, families, and mature travelers. *Single travelers* sometimes travel on their own or explore with colleagues and friends. The same holds true for *couples*. Often couples will share villa rentals, apartment rentals, and time share or vacation ownership purchases depending on the similarities of travel preferences. Honeymoon couples, needless to say, normally prefer their own accommodations(!) *Families* may travel to visit relatives, explore new destinations, and/or return each year to their favorite retreat for the annual vacation. *Mature travelers* are growing in numbers and travel for myriad reasons as do singles, couples, and families. The mature traveler is commonly defined as persons aged 50+. Mature travelers, in particular, often choose to travel with organized tour groups, which is discussed next.

Group travel is a major segment in leisure travel. This segment is largely made up of *tour groups* for leisure travelers who want their trips planned for them. Tour group operators organize the trips, which include selecting a destination, planning the itinerary, and arranging for lodging accommodations, ground transportation, meals, sightseeing, etc. Often these planned excursions are *escorted tours* which means that a representative from the tour operator travels with the group throughout the trip. Group tours vary in duration yet typically range from five- to seven-day excursions.

Segments and people

An important concept when thinking about segments is that one person can be in several segments depending on the particular purchase occasion. Segmentation derives from the purpose of travel and not individual people. A person may be a corporate traveler during the week and then a leisure traveler with his or her family on the weekend – different purpose of travel, different needs, different wants, different price sensitivities, and so forth. As noted by Theodore Levitt, renowned for his seminal work in marketing, 'If you are not thinking segments, you are not thinking' (Levitt, 1986). This line of thinking very much holds true in today's marketplace.

References

Levitt, T. (1986) *The Marketing Imagination*. New York: The Free Press, p. 127.
New recipe for culinary vacations (2003) *The Globe and Mail*, p. T8.

MARGARET SHAW
UNIVERSITY OF GUELPH, CANADA

Market segments and customer profitability analysis

In order to improve financial performance, hotel companies often target multiple customer segments by expanding their product and services.

However, offering a wide array of products and services to a large number of customer segments is likely to result in an increase in a property's support costs. Costs escalate because the complexity of operations increases as the availability of products and services expands. A property's overhead costs (classified as undistributed operating expenses) are likely to increase with both customer and product service variety. Hotels that focus on one or two well-defined customer segments, and maintain a narrow product mix, are likely to have lower support costs than those properties that offer many products to a diverse guest population. 'Customer segment profitability analysis' is similar to 'customer profitability analysis' except for the fact that customer segments, rather than individual customers, comprise the unit of analysis. It is sufficiently emphasized that 'revenue-enhancing' techniques are important in the present-day hotel market, but even more important are analytical methods that help managers determine what segments of the business are making the most substantial profit contribution to the bottom line. Therefore, from a hotel company standpoint, the main benefit of market segment profit analysis accounting is the provision of financial information for planning and decision-making, rather than as a control mechanism. As such, the information required to determine the relative profitability of segments/customers should take account of all related costs that would be affected as a result of decisions made by management.

The existing Uniform System of Accounts for Lodging Industry provides the basis for one dimension of accounting, namely recording, controlling, and benchmarking the product mix, i.e. rooms, food and beverage, but is not designed to facilitate the introduction of the second dimension, namely planning and optimizing the customer mix, i.e. market segment and customer profitability. Thus, currently, there is a mismatch between the 'provision' of information (by accountants) and the 'use' of information (by managers) at the hotel property level; as a result, accountants are producing information for departments, whilst managers are making decisions based on market segments. Following the changing emphasis in business towards market

orientation, the concept of understanding customer and market segmentation is becoming key to the improvement of hotel operating performance.

References

Burgess, C. and Bryant, K. (2001) Revenue management – the contribution of the finance function to profitability. *International Journal of Contemporary Hospitality Management*, 3 (3), 144–150.

Downie, N. (1997) The use of accounting information in hotel marketing decisions. *International Journal of Hospitality Management*, 16 (3), 305–312.

Dunn, K. and Brookes, D. (1990) Profit analysis: beyond yield management. *Cornell Hotel and Restaurant Administration Quarterly*, 31 (3), 80–90.

Noone, B. and Griffin, P. (1997) Enhancing yield management with customer profitability analysis. *International Journal of Contemporary Hospitality Management*, 9 (2), 75–84.

Srikanthan, S., Ward, K., and Meldrum, M. (1987) Segment profitability; a positive contribution. *Management Accounting*, April, 11–16.

VIRA KRAKHMAL
OXFORD BROOKES UNIVERSITY, UK

Market share

A multiple indicator

The market share is a useful indicator that helps identify the various positions (according to inventory, sales or revenues) of one company towards its direct or indirect competitors. The calculation can be a broad industry scope or a set of companies similar in product offerings, category, geographical location or target markets.

Unlike consumer goods, for which global market shares are calculated on a total potential market (i.e. the sales of Bass beers in the UK versus the total number of beer drinkers, or versus the total number of households . . .), the hotel industry uses the inventory of the number of available rooms as a basis for its fair market share calculation. (Note, available rooms are rooms that can be rented and do not include rooms that are out of service for repair or remodeling.)

Fair market share is the first basic indicator that gives the competitors' positions in terms of capacity (total number of hotels, outlets, rooms, beds available), sales or revenue that the company should achieve based on its available production capacity. Unless new competitors arrive on the market or there is a change of available products (new building, additional rooms, inventory closed for refurbishment), that number should not vary over the years.

1 Fair market share (theoretical market share) – FMS

$$\frac{\text{Number of rooms available per competitor}}{\text{Total rooms available within the defined competitors' market}}$$

Beside the importance of a company's production capacity, the fair market share analysis (FMS) does not give much information regarding its profitability. However, it becomes the standard for comparison with the market share of the actual production (profit, revenues, room nights, seat sales . . .).

2 Actual market share (realized market share) – AMS

$$\frac{\text{Number of rooms sold per competitor}}{\text{Total rooms sold by the defined competitors' market}}$$

The penetration ratio will give further an immediate indication of the company's performance on its market, by combining the two results that were obtained previously. A figure exceeding 1 or 100 indicates that the company is stealing market shares from one or more competitors. Any figure under 1 or 100 indicates on the contrary that the company is losing market shares to its competitors.

3 Penetration ratio – PenRatio

$$\frac{\text{Actual market share of a given company}}{\text{Fair market share of that same company}}$$

However, markets are expected to move according to various external and internal environmental factors, such as economic up- and downturns, competitors' strategies, and investment in communication tools. Therefore, actual market shares as well as penetration ratio need to be understood over time, as to their history and/or in a prospective format. The analysis of their variances requires rigor and structure.

4 Analysis of variances

Ideally, the market share measurement should be analyzed with related indicators such as the share of mind (the market awareness of competing products), the share of heart (the market preference for competing products), and the share of voice (the competitors' spending in advertising on a given market) (Table 1).

The strategic decisions

Behind the calculation – these formulas can easily be designed and stored in a PC file – it is important to identify and verify the source of data. The first decision refers to the choice of competitors one wishes or needs to compare to, i.e. with 1965 establishments, Accor accounts for 21% of the total lodging market in Europe. That indicates the position of the group on a global market. In this case, the figures to compare will

Table 1 Analysis of variances

Hotels	FMS (%)	2002 AMS (%)	2002 Pen Ratio	2003 AMS (%)	2003 Pen Ratio	Variance (%)
X	46.2	42.4	0.92	44.9	0.97	**6.0**
Y	30.8	35.3	1.15	32.7	1.06	**−7.5**
Z	23.1	22.4	0.97	22.4	0.97	**0.4**
Total	**100**	**100**	**1**	**100**	**1**	

be chosen between hotels, rooms or beds available for sale and compared to the total number of hotels, rooms or beds available in Europe. This number will fluctuate not because of the consumers' market, but with the closing and opening of new European Accor and non-Accor properties. That same calculation could be reduced to the 4* category, or else extended to the comparison revenue with all tourism-related industries. This analysis will provide useful indication as to the evolution of a company in a region and the effectiveness of its growth strategies in the sector. However, if used to set business objectives, the fact that data must be provided by secondary sources might represent a problem in terms of precision and regularity.

At property level the market share analysis is more often used for the purpose of setting objectives to and measuring the management and more specifically the sales and marketing department. For that more regular task and purpose, the AMS and penetration ratio are of significant importance.

The market share analysis requires that direct competitors are clearly identified for the long term (a new entrant will modify the FMS) and as to the main target markets they share. The marketing management will need to take efficient decisions regarding:

- The reason behind the *choice* of direct competitors.
- The *number* of competitors that will be taken into account (with more than six hotels to compare, the AMS analysis becomes intricate.
- The *means* of collecting accurate and regular figures for the calculation.

The issue starts with the identification of the target market and the property's perceived positioning. The perception is important here, since it is the customer's decision to choose one or the other competitor: 'If my hotel was closed or fully booked, which other hotel would my customer book?' We are not speaking about products looking after the same customer's money, but products that may offer the most similar type of experience. Although many hotels have a tendency to compare themselves to better establishments or

to the market leader, they will lose on accuracy if the calculation is not taking sharable markets into consideration. In today's highly competitive environment, and especially because lodging is a convenient ingredient of the travel package but only rarely the reason for the trip, hotels always share their customers with similar establishments, although their differentiation and positioning strategies may suggest their uniqueness in some or many aspects.

In the hotel industry, the identification of competitors relies on six main criteria:

- *Location:* One of the main reasons for choosing a hotel amongst business customers.
- *Category:* guarantees a classification according to similar features, officially approved and mutually recognized.
- *Size of the hotels:* Large hotels need to target specific business volumes, often at the expense of their ADR.
- *Price:* Customers usually select their accommodation based on a personal or corporate expense budget. Their choice will be made within a certain price range.
- *Type of hotel (usage):* The same customer may very well choose different hotels (resorts, long-stay, suite hotels, hotels with large congress facilities . . .) for different stays, depending on his/her needs and the type of experience he/she is looking for.
- *Type of customers:* Direct competitors must recognize their similarity in terms of their offer to identical customer segments. The market share analysis might be biased if a business hotel for instance, accommodating business and leisure markets, were to compare itself to hotels from the same category and in the same location but targeting only leisure segments.

Fine-tuning of the analysis may also suggest the breakdown of competitors per target market (i.e. hotel comparing the leisure market to three competitors and the business segment with two other competitors, such as when there is a strong input of one market segment in the revenue of a hotel, that is not shared with the usual competitors, but with a more distant one). That implies the exchange of information between those operators, since such calculation would require that companies assess the breakdown of room nights and revenues provided by each specific segment (possibly with congresses, airlines, where figures can be obtained from the clients, the organizational buyer). Unfortunately such data are not easy to manipulate, this type of more accurate analysis requires transparent and disciplined markets and/or conscious associations.

The market share analysis for large congress or incentive groups could even be calculated among hotels in various destinations, since the choice between two properties is usually linked to the country, thus revealing one resort hotel in Acapulco, Mexico, to be the direct competitor to a similar establishment in Bali, Indonesia.

Positioning maps (categorization maps) might prove to be useful for sorting several direct competitors, the ones that call most often for the same criteria (features, strengths and weaknesses, price ranges, target markets . . .).

Accurate data are essential to ensure an effective comparison and analysis of the long-term performance. It is no easy task to collect data from competitors and record them over the years for use. There are many problems and decisions related to these tasks that need to be addressed:

- The type of data
- The accuracy and manner of collection
- The regularity of collection
- The processing.

The first decision lies in the *identification of the type of data* needed. And if this first depends on the ratio that a company will want to calculate, it then also depends on the availability of such data on the market. The collection of data for the analysis of FMS, to identify a company's potentiality on a given market, is relatively easy. Once direct or indirect competitors have been identified, figures are available mostly from official sources.

For AMS data are more difficult to obtain, since this information reflects the hotel's daily performance, and many companies consider those figures confidential and not exchangeable. Ideally the AMS calculation is made using the following data: rooms occupied, room revenue, average daily rate (ADR), or two of those indicators that will provide the basis for calculation. It is important, however,

that the hotels concerned agree to exchange their data. A comparison of total revenues would be interesting but the industry has never been keen on exchanging this type of sensitive information.

However, further important decisions need to be taken as to:

- The inclusion of complimentary rooms, and rooms that are out of order
- VAT and other government taxes that may or may not be included in the ADR
- The removal from the inventory of rooms that are being refurbished and their later reintroduction in the number of available rooms.

The relevance of the analysis will depend on the regularity of its application and whether direct competitors provide data in a similar format.

In good economic times, when competitors perform with high occupancy levels and growth promises, the exchange of data between hotels is not problematic, and one can reasonably expect that the data are *accurate* and *reflect reality*. However, that same goodwill is not there in difficult times. Either hotels do not agree to share the information or they give erroneous figures: higher than actual figures if they perform lower than their competitors, or they do not communicate higher occupancy or revenue figure due to the accommodation of a newly found business they do not want the others to know about. In case of doubts about data provided by a competitor, the market share ratio may need to be adjusted by the collector to approach reality, thus jeopardizing the credibility of the findings.

For some markets actual figures are not exchanged, and the market share analysis needs to be based on figures collected from other secondary sources, such as the national tourism board (occupancy figures) or related official bodies, observation (number of cars in parking lots), number of seats occupied at breakfast. Obviously the calculation of indicators based on such data will be very approximate. Other companies or associations may provide data usable for part of the market, such as *Travel Quick* for bookings through a global distribution system (GDS). In this the exchange of data is known and mutually agreed by all subscribers.

For most markets, general managers usually agree to release a certain amount of information, which will then be exchanged by front office managers or sales and marketing departments on a regular basis (daily, monthly, etc.). As for other financial data, the regularity of the exchange as well as the processing and saving of those figures in the agreed and constant format, is essential for the calculation of ratios and their analysis.

Recently some European government bodies circulated information within the hotel industry requesting that operators to stop the exchange of revenue-related data in order to avoid a cartelization.

As mentioned earlier, indicators need to be evaluated over time. In this respect the seriousness of collection and *regular processing* of data is essential to guarantee their credibility. It requires that one or more staff members (often at front office level or the database manager from the sales and marketing department) are in charge of this task.

Use and misuse of market share analysis

Market share ratios are used by marketing departments for reporting and forecasting:

- *Daily* – for early bird reports discussed in the department heads morning briefing
- *Daily or weekly* – for marketing and yield management meetings that usually involve sales and reservation teams
- *Monthly* – for department heads meetings, where budgeted figures are reforecast and adjusted to the market evolution
- *Yearly* – for the preparation of marketing plans or the interpretation of year-end results.

These ratios are taken into consideration by hotel chains or consortia to compare their members within the group or within a region.

The market share is common business language and is therefore a powerful indicator to use when presenting the company's performance to owners or head offices. It is often used in public relations to communicate positive results to journalists or potential customers. The simplicity of the market share makes it easy for employees to understand. It motivates them to aim at and fight together for higher market positions.

Besides assessment of market evolution and competitors' performance, the AMS analysis also makes it possible to understand customers' sensitivity to prices. The company is able to identify, at various occupancy levels, how much market share was lost or gained due to the opposite move of the ADR, thus reflecting one or more price modifications. However, the comparison of RevPAR (revenue par available room) is the complementary assessment of the revenue performance between direct competitors. The decrease in market shares may be motivated by the loss of unprofitable market segments.

The desire for and the expansion of a company's market share need to be carefully verified as to the increase of return on investment (ROI) they can provide, that is the cost of acquiring new market shares. The expenses linked with communication, pricing or distribution strategies must remain within acceptable margins.

However, the market share analysis needs to be interpreted and quoted with great care, seeing that too often comparisons of documents issued by various competitors do not show similar results. The fact that competitors' figures cannot be checked with accuracy makes it possible to manipulate the analysis, mostly to the advantage of the hotel that imports and presents the data.

In the future, hotels will probably need to identify new ways to interpret accurate market share calculations; neutral associations or governmental organizations could prove to be useful intermediaries for that purpose.

The more classical use of global and relative market shares, as for consumer goods, may also reveal useful indicators for hotels that wish to understand their penetration of a market not restricted to their own capacity.

References

Choi, J.-G. (2003) Developing an economic indicator system (a forecasting technique) for the hotel industry. *International Journal of Hospitality Management*, January.

Kotler, P. (1999) *Marketing Management: Analysis, Planning, Implementation, and Control*, 9th edn., International edn. Upper Saddle River, NJ: Prentice-Hall.

Lewis, R.C. and Chambers, R.E. (1999) *Marketing Leadership in Hospitality: Foundations and Practices*, 3rd edn. New York: John Wiley & Sons.

Métayer, E. How to calculate Market Shares, the CEO Refresher.

DOMINIQUE FAESCH
ECOLE HÔTELIÈRE DE LAUSANNE (EHL),
SWITZERLAND

Marketing

The American Marketing Association defines marketing as 'the process of planning and executing the conception, pricing, promotion, and distribution of ideas, goods, and services, to create exchanges that satisfy individual and organizational objectives' (Bennett, 1989). Important in this definition is that marketing involves a planning process that begins before the product or service is created. In addition to the development of an idea, product, or service, marketing includes the development of pricing, promotion, and distribution plans. Finally, it is important to note that the exchanges must be satisfactory to both the customer and the organization. Marketing activities are ongoing and include continuous research about customers, their preferences, and lifestyles. Marketing requites a long-term view of business whereby change is expected, accepted, and adapted to. Adaptations necessitate cooperation among the organization's constituents, such as managers and other employees, intermediaries, and complementary businesses.

Lewis and Chambers (2000) offer an easier and sensible marketing definition. They state that marketing is 'communicating to and giving the target market customers what they want, when they want it, where they want it, at a price they are willing to pay.' This is the ultimate goal of marketing efforts in the hospitality and tourism organization.

References

Bennett, Peter (1988) *Dictionary of Marketing Terms*, Chicago: American Marketing Association, p. 115.

Lewis, Robert C. and Chambers, Richard E. (2000) *Marketing Leadership in Hospitality Foundations and Practices*, 3rd edn. New York: John Wiley & Sons.

LINDA J. SHEA
UNIVERSITY OF MASSACHUSETTS, USA

Marketing concept

The marketing concept is the idea that a business should be intuitively aware of its customers' needs and wants and practice a management style that revolves around these items. The four bases of the marketing concept are (1) customer orientation, (2) integrated company effort, (3) profit or goal orientation, and (4) social responsibility. The philosophy implies that a firm's success is dependent upon its ability to understand its customers, deliver value to its customers, have employees that are customer oriented, and be more effective and efficient than its competitors. The customer focus must extend beyond marketing personnel to all employees and managers in an organization. The result of a business that practices the marketing concept is that the business will yield favorable results and benefit from long-term profitability. Companies that follow the marketing concept do not believe they are in business to sell goods, but rather to satisfy customers. They understand the social and economic reason for operating is to fulfill and adapt to customers' ever-changing desires. These activities should be carried out in a socially responsible manner. Companies will often invest in customer satisfaction surveys and employee training to accomplish their mission.

Establishing a target market, exploring market opportunities, and conducting market research on a continuous basis are key in applying the marketing concept. It views marketing as more than a set of activities, but a way to be.

References

Lewis, Robert C. and Chambers, Richard E. (2000) *Marketing Leadership in Hospitality Foundations and Practices*, 3rd edn. New York: John Wiley & Sons.

Zeithaml, Valerie A. and Bitner, Mary Jo (2003) *Services Marketing Integrating Customer Focus Across the Firm*, 3rd edn. New York: McGraw-Hill.

STEVE SASSO
UNIVERSITY OF MASSACHUSETTS, USA

Marketing information system

A marketing information system is a routine, planned, gathering, sorting, storage, and retrieval system for market information relevant to the operation of a particular business. A marketing information system is intended to bring together disparate items of data into a coherent body of information. As Kotler's definition says, a marketing information system is more than a system of data collection or a set of information technologies:

A marketing information system is a continuing and interacting structure of people, equipment and procedures to gather, sort, analyze, evaluate, and distribute pertinent, timely and accurate information for use by marketing decision-makers to improve their marketing planning, implementation, and control.'

It is suggested that whilst the MIS varies in its degree of sophistication, a fully fledged MIS should have four main constituent parts; the internal record, marketing research, marketing intelligence, and information analysis.

Reference

Kotler, P., Bowen, J., and Makens, J. (1988) *Marketing Management: Analysis Planning and Control*. Englewood Cliffs, NJ: Prentice-Hall, p. 102.

BOMI KANG
UNIVERSITY OF NEVADA, LAS VEGAS, USA

Marketing research

Marketing research is the systematic process of collecting and analyzing information in an attempt to reduce the uncertainty surrounding marketing decisions. The first step in the marketing research process is to *define the problem*. The researcher determines the problem from the marketing manager's perspective and then translates it into a research problem. Once the research problem has been defined, the second step is to *plan the research*. Secondary data analysis is the process of reviewing existing information that is related to the research problem. Primary data analysis is the process of collecting new data that is specific to the problem at hand. Secondary data analysis is quicker and less expensive, but primary data analysis is normally more complete and accurate.

The third step in the marketing research process is to *collect the data*. The decisions made during this step involve choosing a data collection method, designing data collection forms, and determining the sampling plan. The primary data collection methods are observation, experiments, and surveys. Data collection forms can be questionnaires for surveys or some other form used to compile the results from observation or experiments. The goal of the sampling plan is to obtain information from people or sampling units that are representative of the population being studied.

The fourth step in the research process is to *analyze the data*. Descriptive analysis uses aggregate data to describe the average, or typical, respondent or sampling unit. Inferential analysis is used to test hypotheses and estimate population parameters using sample statistics. The fifth step is to *prepare the final report*. The final report should summarize the activities performed in the previous steps in a clear and concise format using visual aids where applicable.

Reference

Reid, R. and Bojanic, D. (2001) *Hospitality Marketing Management*, 3rd edn. New York: John Wiley & Sons, pp. 159–172.

DAVID BOJANIC
UNIVERSITY OF MASSACHUSETTS, USA

Mark-up

In menu pricing, mark-up refers to the traditional way operators price individual menu items above the variable costs associated with that item (also see menu pricing and pricing methods). Some menu items may have a higher food cost, such as those with considerable quantities of meat, while others have a higher direct labor component.

The price charged is rationalized as a means of returning an amount that reflects a fair return for the time, effort, and risk involved. While it is necessary to price above cost in order to produce a profit, the amount of the mark-up depends on whether the item is a commodity or a specialty good and whether the price is demand-driven or market-driven. The actual price point on the pricing continuum, which ranges between the lowest price that will achieve a profit and the highest price the market or customer will bear, is influenced by the menu item itself and over two dozen direct and indirect cost factors.

If an operator chooses to add a substantial mark-up, it is critical that the operation be on the leading edge in terms of food quality, taste, freshness, and plate presentation. Service and décor must match the price as well. Customer expectations increase proportionally with the price they pay.

Reference

Miller, Jack E. and Pavesic, David V. (1996) *Menu Pricing and Strategy*. New York: Van Nostrand Reinhold.

DAVID V. PAVESIC
GEORGIA STATE UNIVERSITY, USA

Mass customization

According to the concept of economies of scale, maximum manufacturing efficiency, and hence lowest unit cost, is achieved when a standardized product is produced in large quantities, since:

$$\text{Unit cost} = \text{Variable cost} + \text{Quantity produced/Fixed cost}$$

where the variable cost equals the cost of labor and materials per unit, and the fixed cost is equal to the cost of the infrastructure (e.g. factory) needed to allow production.

The minimum unit cost is reached when production capacity is fully utilized. The concept of economies of scale and mass production made it possible for Henry Ford to produce an affordable automobile, available in one model and one color only, the Model T. If more than one variety of product is required, maximum economies of scale cannot be achieved using traditional manufacturing techniques with production lines 'dedicated' to a single product, or which require extensive retooling or set-up to accommodate product changes.

Mass customization is a technique used by product manufacturers and service providers to resolve this 'cost *vs.* variety' dilemma in a way that allows them to achieve acceptable economies of scale (and hence lower costs), for example through the use of standardized products or platforms, while providing a considerable degree of customization (and hence differentiation), of their product or service to the individual customer or market segment. In the manufacturing industries, so-called flexible manufacturing systems (FMS, also referred to as 'lean production'), combined with information technology (IT), have greatly contributed to the feasibility of mass customization: FMS, by allowing economies of scale with even relatively small production runs, and IT by allowing customers to order through the Internet, thereby greatly reducing the administrative overhead associated with order processing. Examples of mass customization include apparel or footwear ordered from on-line merchants, the options ordered with a new automobile, online custom textbook publishing, and personal computers assembled to user specifications from a menu of choices. Examples in the service industries include checkbook printing, special meal orders on airlines, and the choice of in-room amenities offered to arriving hotel guests. In general, mass customization is more difficult to achieve in the services industries than in the manufacturing industries: indeed, how does one apply the equivalent term 'built-to-order' to a stay in a hotel room, or a flight from one city to another? Those areas which lend themselves most readily to e-commerce implementation (e.g. banking, travel, and tourism) appear to offer the greatest immediate opportunities for the use of mass customization, for example, by allowing an Internet user to personalize the Web page he sees when logging into the company's site.

Mass customization, while generally requiring substantial investments in technology, allows companies to customize products to meet the needs of relatively small customer groups (microsegmentation) at a cost far lower than that of true customization, thereby increasing their customer responsiveness, which in turn leads to increased value creation in the form of greater differentiation.

Reference

Hill, C.W. and Jones, G.R. (2001) *Strategic Management: An Integrated Approach*, 5th edn. Boston, MA: Houghton Mifflin.

ROBERT F. JENEFSKY
ECOLE HÔTELIÈRE DE LAUSANNE (EHL),
SWITZERLAND

m-Commerce

m-Commerce is any transaction with a monetary value that is conducted over a wireless telecommunication network (Barnes, 2002). Fuelled by wireless communication technologies converging portability and networking, m-Commerce is creating several new business models, e.g. m-gambling, m-advertising, m-payments, m-music, m-banking, m-education. Equipped with microbrowsers and other mobile applications, the new mobiles offer the Internet at any place, on any device, and at any time and 'always on.'

m-Commerce involves a number of players in a chain of value-adding activities that terminate with the customer. Barnes (2002) developed the m-commerce value chain model for analyzing the players with which a company willing to develop m-commerce should collaborate. Two main categories of players are identified. Infrastructure and service players including: mobile transport companies (e.g. AT&T, DoCoMo, Vodafone); mobile

services and delivery support (e.g. WAP, i-mode), security, the service platform and payment systems; mobile interface and applications. Second, players involved with content creation and aggregation, packaging firms, and mobile portals (e.g. Vizzavi).

m-Commerce offers the following value-added attributes: product/service personalization and localization, ubiquity enhancement, instant connectivity, time and place convenience. m-Commerce can be used for several hospitality operations: customer oriented m-Commerce, such as hotel reservations, m-transactions, m-concierge services; and business-oriented m-Commerce such as virtual front desk, sales force automation, m-CRM. The hospitality industry is well suited to be a beneficiary of m-Commerce. From sales, restaurant, and inventory staff, the majority of hospitality employees are involved in jobs requiring mobility. These employees rely on paper forms and manual procedures to process transactions because they cannot have direct access to computers at the location they work. This requires manual entry of information into various computer systems and generates vulnerability to data inaccuracies.

References

Barnes, S. (2002) The mobile commerce value chain: analysis and future developments. *International Journal of Information Management*, 22, 91–108.
Vos, I. and Klein, P. (2002) *The Essential Guide to Mobile Business*. Upper Saddle River, NJ: Prentice-Hall.

MARIANNA SIGALA
UNIVERSITY OF THE AEGEAN, GREECE

Media markets

The area and persons receiving media messages via media outlets such as television, radio, and newspaper are commonly referred to as media markets. Media messages come in many forms such as motion pictures, sound recordings, books, newspapers, magazines, and the Internet. In regard to marketing, these messages are in the form of advertising within the various media outlets. Media markets are frequently discussed in regard to advertising and programming because media markets identify the persons that can be reached by an advertisement or program. An organization that wishes to deliver (communicate) a message (advertisement) to a particular group of people about a new product will purchase advertising in specific media markets that reach the target market (Albarran and Arrese, 2003). In marketing, media outlets are commonly referred to as communication channels. Media markets are an important concept in marketing because these markets often provide the communication link between marketers and consumers.

Interestingly, media markets are often controlled by only a few large media conglomerates. For instance, in the United States, Clear Channel Communication owns over 1200 radio stations that reach over 100 million listeners (Fonda, 2004). This is of great concern to many consumers and watchdog groups because of the power associated with controlling a media market. The regulation of media markets in the United States is managed by the Federal Communication Commission (Baker, 2002). In 2003, media markets in the United States received extensive attention regarding the deregulation of media outlet ownership in the United States because many media markets in the United States are dominated by one or two media giants.

References

Albarran, A.B. and Arrese, A. (2003) *Time and Media Markets.* Mahwah, NJ: Lawrence Erlbaum Associates.

Baker, E. (2002) *Media, Markets, and Democracy.* New York: Cambridge University Press.

Fonda, D. (2004) The revolution in radio. *Time,* 163, 55–56. Retrieved 22 April 2004 from EBSCO Host Research Databases.

BRUMBY MCLEOD
UNIVERSITY OF NEVADA, LAS VEGAS, USA

Meeting

A meeting is a type of gathering, including:

- *Colloquium:* An academic meeting where one or more content specialists speak about a topic and answer questions.
- *Conference:* An event used by an organization to meet and exchange views, convey a message, open a debate, or give publicity to an area of opinion on a specific subject and an assembly of individuals to discuss items of mutual interest or engage in professional development by learning.
- *Convention:* A general and formal meeting of a legislative body or social or economic group to provide information on a particular situation and to establish consent on policies among the participants.
- *Congress:* The European term for a convention.
- *Panel discussion:* Three or more subject area specialists each give a brief presentation after which the audience has the opportunity to ask questions of the panellists.
- *Structured panel:* Eight to ten questions are prepared and distributed in advance to selected attendees and following each presentation, attendees ask questions of the panelists from the list. Presenters have prepared answers, eliminating the potential for misinformation.
- *Roundtables:* Tables seating 10 to 12 attendees are placed at round tables throughout the room. A key topic and an expert in that area are assigned to each table and the experts lead the discussion.
- *Seminar:* A lecture, presentation, and discussion under the guidance of an expert discussion leader allowing participants to share experiences in a particular field.
- *Symposium:* Experts discuss a particular subject and express opinions or a meeting of a number of experts in a particular field where research papers are presented and discussed by content specialists who then make recommendations.
- *Workshop:* A training session in which participants develop skills and knowledge in a given field, an event designed to stimulate intensive discussion and compensate for diverging views in a particular discipline or subject, an informal

public session of free discussion organized to take place between formal plenary sessions on a subject chosen by the participants or on a special problem suggested by the organizers.

Reference

Goldblatt, Joe and Nelson, Kathleen (2001) *The International Dictionary of Event Management*, 2nd edn. New York: John Wiley & Sons.

PATTI J. SHOCK
UNIVERSITY OF NEVADA, LAS VEGAS, USA

Meeting or event history

Meeting and event histories are critical to planning. Event histories are accurate, detailed records about the meeting. They are useful to the planning organization and the hotel or venue under consideration. Before a hotel responds to a request for a proposal, the sales manager will ask for a history of past meetings. The extent and depth of historical data needed will vary from organization to organization. Data generally collected includes attendee demographics, including age, political preferences, religious preferences, geographic differences, educational levels, gender, music tastes, food tastes, and recreation preferences.

Historical data of the meeting itself include the objectives for the meeting, location and sites of the previous three to five years, the length of previous meetings, actual guestroom usage (pick up), arrival and departure patterns, occupancy mix, no-show factor, affiliated or ancillary business, e.g. hospitality suite revenues, use of recreational facilities, outlet activity, actual meeting attendance numbers *vs.* anticipated, actual meal function numbers *vs.* guarantees and projections, attendance, both pre-registered and on-site registration patterns; the number, type, and size of all food and beverage events; pre-/post-meeting events scheduled; sleeping room information including the number of single occupancy, double occupancy, suites used; and the number and size of general sessions and break-out, concurrent sessions exhibit sales, spouse/guest events, rebates, assessments, commissions. It is important to note any significant differences between years/events. For example, if attendance in a particular year was higher or lower than normal because it was an anniversary year, this should be indicated. If the attendance was lower for some reason, such as economic changes or the location, indicate that also.

An event history can help determine if the meeting's objectives were accomplished: was the meeting successful; did the organization make money; did the attendees leave with positive feelings about the meeting, the organization, and the site? This information can be used to help plan for future meetings. What attendees liked and did not like about the meeting enables one to track the group's trends and patterns. This information also helps to develop more accurate budgets and provides a better understanding of the meeting's value to the hotel, convention center, and city.

One tracks this information through post-convention reports. After the meeting is over, one should ask for the hotel's meeting history and make sure that the information is accurate. Hotels and other suppliers can also help in obtaining information. The International Association of Convention and Visitor Bureaus' meetings and convention database should verify each year that the information is accurate and up-to-date. Meeting profiles are shared with member convention and visitors bureaus.

References

Connell, Barbara, Chatfield-Taylor, Cathy, and Collins, Martha C. (2002) *Professional Meeting Management*, 4th edn. Chicago: Professional Convention Management Association Foundation.

Hildreth, Richard A. (1990) *The Essentials of Meeting Management*. Englewood Cliffs, NJ: Prentice-Hall.

Krug, Susan, Chatfield-Taylor, Cathy, Collins, Martha C. (2000) *Convention Industry Council Manual*, 7th edn. McClean, VA.: Convention Industry Council.

SUZETTE EADDY
NATIONAL MINORITY SUPPLIER
DEVELOPMENT COUNCIL, USA

Meeting or event planner

A meeting planner is an individual whose primary responsibility is to coordinate all the details to produce a meeting. The term meeting planner may be used generically to refer to people who plan a variety of events, including meetings, exhibitions, seminars, conferences, and conventions. Regardless of the type of event, however, there are many tasks that a planner would have to complete in order for the event to be successful. The planner, either alone or as part of a team, determines the objective of the meeting, decides on a location, conducts site inspections, contracts with the hotel(s) and/or convention center, plans the educational program, books speakers, arranges transportation, plans events, parties and banquets, contracts with suppliers, such as audiovisual, florists, photographers, and manages on-site operations. Evaluations of the meeting are also the responsibility of the planner. The meeting planner is responsible for the meeting budget. Revenues may come from a variety of sources including registrations, exhibits, sponsorships, merchandising books, tee-shirts, and other memorabilia. Expenses include, but are not limited to, travel, space, food and beverage, administration, hospitality, entertainment, printing and postage, and gratuities.

References

Jedrziewski, D. (1991) *The Complete Guide for the Meeting Planner.* Cincinnati: Southwestern.

Montgomery, R. and Strick, S. (1995) *Meetings, Conventions, and Expositions: An Introduction to the Industry.* New York: John Wiley & Sons.

M.T. HICKMAN
RICHLAND COLLEGE, USA

Meeting or event timeline

A timeline is the chronological list of details and procedures essential to planning a meeting or event. This list typically begins with the present and outlines each function necessary to finalize all details of an event. The first step for planning any event is typically the development of objectives and goals while the last step would be the evaluation of the event. While there is no standard timeline formula, it is suggested to list each function and determine the necessary time needed to complete the task as it is placed in chronological order. Some meetings may take years to plan, for example a large convention for an association or a trade show that attracts tens of thousands of people. In these examples, the destination and site selection would have to be made years in advance of the actual meeting because the number of venues that could host the events is limited. The marketing of these events typically begins one year before the event will take place. Corporate meetings, on the other hand, tend to be planned in a relatively short period of time, sometimes with only a few weeks' notice.

Reference

O'Toole, W. and Mikolaitis, P. (2002) *Corporate Event Project Management.* New York: John Wiley & Sons.

DEBBI BOYNE
MEETING DEMANDS, USA
KIMBERLY SEVERT
UNIVERSITY OF CENTRAL FLORIDA, USA

Meeting or event profile

The meeting profile contains the history of the meeting or event, including facts and details regarding previous meetings, including receptions, banquets, dinners, audiovisual requirements, and recreational activities such as golf, tennis, health club, spa, etc. The profile also contains information on other sponsored functions that piggyback with the event and generate revenue for the facility. This information shows the potential for income derived from sources other than just room rates. Information that should be included is the anticipated use of foodservice outlets such as room service, cocktail lounges, and snack outlets. The meeting profile includes the spending habits of attendees based on prior years' histories and will establish the value of the meeting to the facility. The specific profile of the attendees, which outlines the expected number, their economic level, and their spending habits, as well as who is paying the bill, is vital information. The hotel can anticipate more revenue when the meeting's sponsor pays the bill. The room occupancy pattern will be of great interest to the hotel and is usually broken down into the number of single rooms, double rooms, and suites. Room pickup rate and total room night histories allow hotels to estimate the number of rooms that will be available to fill other reservation requests. High double occupancy rates are looked upon favorably and can help in negotiating lower rates. A high no-show factor is a negative, but a low no-show factor can help reduce rates.

The meeting profile should contain the length and time of stay as the arrival and departure patterns may provide the hotel with extra days for pre-meeting and post-meeting and/or weekend stays that could otherwise be difficult to sell. In some areas the season affects room rates. Peak season rates are less flexible and off-season or shoulder season dates are usually easier to negotiate. The space pattern, which is guestroom nights combined with meeting room and exhibit requirements that use the entire hotel, will usually result in a better room rate and negotiated function room rental fees. Transportation needs must also be included if off-site activities are planned. Other considerations include parking, nearby shopping, local entertainment and attractions. Information should also be included on any outside vendors for equipment, decorations, and services not supplied by or used from the property, including who they are, how many are needed, and at what cost.

Reference

Connell, B., Chatfield-Taylor, C., and Collins, M.C. (eds) (2002) *Professional Meeting Management*. Chicago: Professional Convention Management Association.

PATTI J. SHOCK
UNIVERSITY OF NEVADA, LAS VEGAS, USA

Menu mix

A restaurant's menu mix, also referred to as its 'sales mix,' is the ranking of each menu item by customer preference (popularity) by meal period. It has a direct impact on the overall food cost percentage that will be produced at the end of the month and on the profit generated by the operation.

The objective of sales mix analysis is to identify specific menu items that contribute to your profit, cost, and revenue objectives. Major contributors become featured items on the menu (using menu psychology techniques). This also works in reverse to 'hide' items that do not contribute to cost and revenue objectives.

Menu mix optimization is assessed using a variety of menu engineering techniques. The simplest of these take into account the popularity and food cost of each item relative to all other items within the menu-item category (e.g., entrées). More robust techniques include multiple variables including contribution margin, popularity, and likely degree of relative elasticity, among others, within the context of other related menu items. The key to effective menu mix analysis is to use a continuous-improvement approach and to integrate those variables that are most salient to the operators, the market, and the concept.

References

Miller, Jack E. and Pavesic, David V. (1996) *Menu Pricing and Strategy*. New York: Van Nostrand Reinhold.

Reynolds, D. (2003) *On-Site Foodservice Management: A Best Practices Approach*. Hoboken, NJ: John Wiley & Sons.

DAVID V. PAVESIC
GEORGIA STATE UNIVERSITY, USA

Menu pricing and calculation

Probably the simplest menu pricing method is to go to a competitor's foodservice operation, take the menu away, and copy the prices. Copying competitors' menu prices is, however, a dangerous practice as conditions in any two types of foodservice operations are invariably different. To determine food and beverage prices, however, a variety of factors should be considered, such as type of restaurant, meal occasion, style and level of service, competition, customer mix, and profit objective (Miller, 1980).

Menu pricing procedures often rely on some form of cost-plus pricing technique. For example, a restaurateur may establish a target food-cost percentage of 33% of food sales revenue as an operating goal. This percentage is subsequently converted to a multiplier by taking the reciprocal of the percentage (Orkin, 1978). Thus, the multiplier equals:

$$\frac{1}{0.33} = 3$$

which will multiply raw food cost by three to derive the price of a menu item. Instead of taking raw food cost, to multiply by an established pricing factor, it is also possible to use prime costs. This prime cost includes direct labor (labor involved in the actual preparation of the food

item) and raw food cost. Menu profitability, however, requires an absolute cash differential rather than a functional percentage relationship between cost and revenue. Thus, a menu item may have a preferable food-cost margin, but still make a lesser contribution to overhead expenses and net profit than another (similar popular) menu item (Table 1).

Another approach is to use a (differential) gross profit margin, for which the basic formula is:

$$\text{Food/Beverage Cost per Portion + Gross Profit} = \text{Selling Price}$$

Where the amount of profit contribution is set uniformly across all guests, hospitality firms may use:

$$\frac{\text{Sales} - \text{Food Cost}}{\text{Number of Guests}} = \text{Average Gross Profit}$$

where food costs are added to average gross profit to arrive at the menu item's price. This variation of gross margin pricing is particularly suitable for establishments where customer counts are predetermined (e.g. in a hospital foodservice). It establishes lower prices for more expensive items and vice versa (Table 2).

One way to develop individual prices for dishes, meals and drinks, is what may be described as a 'multi-stage approach' which comprises of a number of distinct steps commencing with the estimated sales for a period and ending with individual food and beverage selling prices, as illustrated in Figure 1 (Harris and Hazzard, 1992).

The initial stage includes the determination of the annual sales and average gross margin percentages that will provide a desired return on capital employed. The second stage requires the estimation of *departmental* sales mix with anticipated gross margin percentages. Stage three comprises

Table 1   Difference in food-cost ratio versus variation in contribution margin

Starter	Soup	Carpacchio
Food cost	€1.85	€2.95
Labor cost	€1.05	€1.35
Prime cost	€2.90	€4.30
Selling price	€4.55	€6.35
Food/cost ratio	41%	47%
Prime/cost ratio	64%	68%
Contribution margin	€1.65	€2.05

Table 2   Gross profit method with an average gross profit margin

Main dish	Food cost (a) (€)	Fixed mark-up (b) (€)	Differential profit margin (€) (c)	Average gross profit (€) (d)	Menu price (a + b) (€)	Menu price (a + c) (€)	Menu price (a + d) (€)
Chicken	3.45	1.45 42.0%	1.76 51.0%	2.50	4.90	5.21	5.95
T-bone steak	6.85	2.88 42.0%	2.95 43.0%	2.50	9.73	9.80	9.35
Lobster	7.45	3.13 42.0%	2.84 38.0%	2.50	10.58	10.29	9.95
Subtotal		7.46	7.54	7.50	25.21	25.30	25.25

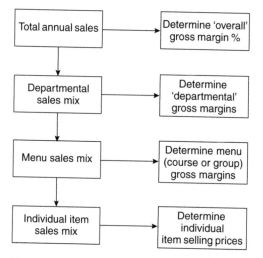

Figure 1 Food and beverages multi-stage approach (from Harris and Hazzard, 1992)

a further differentiation into departmental *menu* sales mix estimates. The last stage consists of estimating *individual* food and drink *items* as well as establishing selling prices.

Yet another method to set menu prices is via the actual pricing method, which can also be used 'backwards' (i.e. the base price method) to meet the market or going price. The method includes the establishment of food cost and total labor cost as well as the determination of variable cost, fixed cost and profit as a percentage of sales. Thus, when raw food cost is €1.70, average total labor cost is €2.15, sales is €1,700,000, (the remaining) variable cost is €250,000, fixed cost is €450,000 and profit is 15% of €1,000,000 total assets employed (e.g. €150,000), the selling price equals

$$\text{Price} = \frac{\text{Food Cost } + \text{Average Total Labour Cost}}{1 - \left(\dfrac{\text{Variable and Fixed Cost and Profit}}{\text{Sales}} \right)}$$

$$= \frac{3.85}{1 - 0.50} = 7.70$$

There is no question that a well-designed, properly priced menu is invaluable to restaurant operators having to succeed in an increasingly competitive environment (Hayes and Huffman,

1985). Due to its nature, the hotel and catering industry experiences a relatively high degree of product and service interrelationship. For example, on the one hand an à la carte menu contains a number of courses which are interdependent in so much as they constitute a complete meal. The meal, on the other hand, cannot be seen in isolation, as a restaurant itself can be an interdependent component of a hotel as it forms part of the total service offering to a guest. Therefore, hotel and tourism managers should be aware of the interdependence of departments and, thus, the pricing of accommodation, food and beverages should on no account be determined independently, but should represent a total business pricing effort (Rogers, 1976).

References

Harris, P. J. and Hazzard, P.A. (1992) *Managerial Accounting in the Hospitality Industry*, 5th edn. Cheltenham: Stanley Thornes.

Hayes, D.K. and Huffman, L. (1985) Menu-analysis: a better way? *Cornell Hotel and Restaurant Administration Quarterly*, 25 (4), 65–70.

Miller, J. (1980) *Menu Pricing and Strategy*. Boston, MA: CBI.

Orkin, E.B. (1978) An integrated menu pricing system. *Cornell Hotel and Restaurant Administration Quarterly*, 19 (2), 8–13.

Rogers, A.N. (1976) Price formation in hotels. *Hotel, Catering and Institutional Management Review*, pp. 227–237.

JEAN-PIERRE VAN DER REST
LEIDEN UNIVERSITY, THE NETHERLANDS

Menu pricing in foodservice

Pricing is a complicated process that cannot be reduced to a single quantitative formula for marking up raw food cost. While food cost percentage and gross profit return are important considerations, the pricing process is more subjective and enigmatic. *Pricing can never be reduced to a simple mark-up of cost.* It is more of an *art* than a science because it requires the consideration of a number of subjective factors. It is said that the customer, not the operator, ultimately determines the price that can be charged for any given menu item. Therefore, the operator must be able to make a profit selling menu items at the price the customer is willing to pay.

Pricing decisions are affected by the clientele, the amount of business the restaurant will generate, its location, the meal period, and even the menu item itself. If the price is perceived as too high, it may not be selected. If the price is too low, it could be viewed as low quality by the customer and also not be selected. The consumer sometimes uses price as a gauge of quality. A high price implies quality although a low price does not necessarily translate as a bargain or value.

Any attempt to apply a single mark-up to every menu item would result in over-pricing high-cost items and under-pricing low-cost items. Menu pricing methodologies are as disparate as political and theological beliefs. Cost plays an important but limited role in the pricing decision. Consider the price one would pay for a glass of iced tea in a full service restaurant or for a cup of chicken or beef bouillon in an upscale restaurant. The actual cost of the liquid in the glass and cup is probably less than $0.15. A 12–16 ounce glass of iced tea will be priced as low as $1.50, which would be an acceptable price to most customers. The cup of beef bouillon will probably be priced around $5.95 and it too would be considered acceptable to the customer. The tea has a 10% cost and the bouillon a 2.5% cost. If the bouillon were priced at $1.50, it would not be perceived as a bargain and reflect negatively on the image of the restaurant. One must also be aware of the competitor's prices and what is customary in the market for similar items. This applies to commodities like hamburgers and chicken fingers as well as to specialty items.

These examples show that each menu category – appetizers, salads, sandwiches, entrées, and desserts – must be marked up to reflect competitive prices rather than to focus narrowly on realizing a single food cost or gross profit percentage. Table 1 offers very general guidelines to the corresponding menu categories and profit mark-up opportunities.

In the broadest of terms, menu pricing can be viewed as either market-driven or demand-driven. The appropriate categorization depends on the uniqueness and monopolistic aspects of

Table 1   Profit mark-up range

	Mark-up (%)
Appetizers	20–50
Salads	10–40
Entreés	10–25
Vegetables	25–50
Beverages	10–50
Breads	10–20
Desserts	15–35

the item and the restaurant. Prices that are market-driven must be responsive to competition (e.g., items that are common). For example, an operator would be hard pressed to price a Reuben sandwich at $12.95 when the restaurant down the street offers the same items for $5.95 (assuming the associated characteristics of the restaurants are reasonably similar). Demand-driven prices are the operator's response to customers who want items for which there are few if any alternatives in the marketplace. Examples include items featuring specialty meats or rare produce.

Finally, issues integrating the aforementioned concerns with price elasticity from the market perspective affect operators' ability to price items such that they produce the greatest profit. Related factors include the current economy, socio-economic characteristics of the target market, and positioning of the restaurant. Furthermore, these factors are constantly changing and may create even more complex concerns when evaluating simultaneously.

References

Miller, J.E. and Pavesic, D.V. (1996) *Menu Pricing and Strategy.* New York: Van Nostrand Reinhold.

Pavesic, D.V. (1999) Menu pricing: 25 keys to profitable success. *Nation's Restaurant News,* 3, 91.

DAVID V. PAVESIC
GEORGIA STATE UNIVERSITY, USA

Menu psychology

The psychology of menu design uses the layout and format of the menu to call attention to particular menu items a restaurant prepares best and wants to sell more of than other menu items for reasons including profitability, check average, and ease of preparation, or because the item is a specialty of the restaurant. The concept of menu psychology was developed from merchandising techniques used by retail grocery and department stores when setting up counter or window displays. The objective is to get the shopper to stop, look, and touch, raising the probability that a purchase will be made.

When used properly, menu psychology will help the restaurant operator achieve sales, cost, and profit objectives more directly than a menu designed without such techniques. These techniques include distinctive font sizes and styles, and the incorporation of graphics, illustrations, and dot matrix screens as 'eye magnets.' Eye magnets employ any of several techniques used to 'draw the eye' of the customer to particular items.

Menu psychology approaches the menu as a marketing tool to produce a predictable menu sales mix which, when compared with forecasted customer counts, will allow for more accurate purchasing and preparation of perishable foods. Its primary purpose is to render certain menu items more noticeable, thereby increasing the odds that items featured on the menu will be ordered with greater frequency than those not emphasized in some manner or form.

Reference

Pavesic, D.V. (1999) *Menu Pricing: 25 Keys to Profitable Success* (Restaurant Manager's Pocket Handbook Series). New York: Lebhar-Friedman.

DAVID V. PAVESIC
GEORGIA STATE UNIVERSITY, USA

Merchandising

'Merchandising' is defined as 'the selection and display of goods in a retail outlet.' An increasing number of hospitality businesses are creating product ranges using their logo, name or reputation.

Whilst these will bring in additional revenue, it is likely that the promotional benefits of spreading the organization's name are actually more valuable. Destination and boutique hotels such as The Savoy, London, Gleneagles, Auchterarder, and The Scotsman Hotel, Edinburgh, offer a range of items for guests to purchase. These range from embossed dressing gowns, clothing, and tableware to beauty products and local delicacies. In-house leisure facilities are also an excellent merchandising opportunity. Examples can be found on the following websites – www.gleneagles.com/shopping; www.savoygifts.com; www.thescotsmanhotel.co.uk.

When analyzing a merchandising strategy one must assess how customers perceive the product range, offer, and ultimately the brands. Good quality and effective merchandising is essential to create the right shopping environment so as to positively affect customers' buying decisions. Merchandising begins with a complete review of the point of sale material in light of its marketplace positioning and the requirements of the in-store communication. Merchandising must also look at internal procedures of managing and communicating point of sale standards throughout the chain, as well as reviewing the current supplier base.

Reference

Collins English Dictionary (1990) London: William Collins & Sons.

ERWIN LOSEKOOT
UNIVERSITY OF STRATHCLYDE, UK

MICE

MICE is an acronym for group business organizations whose market segments are comprised of meetings, incentives, conventions, and exhibitions. The group business market segment of the hotel industry has experienced exponential growth fueled by the rapid globalization and expansion of the service industries and the continuous evolution of scientific and technological innovations. Furthermore, the creation of international trade and government agreements such as the World Trade Organization (WTO) and the North American Free Trade Organization (NAFTA) have spawned cross-border business affiliations and mergers resulting in increased business travel. Four major parties are generally involved in the group business travel industry consumption cycle:

- The individual participant in the event
- The sponsor of the event (the association or corporation)
- The intermediary (the meeting planner, travel agent or convention and visitors bureau)
- The venue (the hotel, convention/exhibition center, or municipal facility).

Although the letters of four segments of the group business industry are used for the acronym MICE, the industry is usually sub-divided into three primary market segments: meetings and conventions, incentives, and exhibitions and trade fairs.

Meetings and conventions

The two primary entities that hold meetings and conventions are associations and corporations. Their primary purposes are to communicate, to allow for personal exchange of ideas, and/or to provide the opportunity for personal interaction or networking. Meetings can involve as few as three participants, whereas conventions generally involve the attendance of several thousand participants.

An association comprises a group of people joined together for a common purpose. Its primary objective is to advance the status and image of the members, to provide for peer interaction and exchange of information and to emphasize the value of membership. Thousands of different associations exist. They can be broadly classified into the following categories: trade and professional, government, labor, avocational, scientific and medical, charitable and SMERF (social, military, educational, religious, and fraternal). Each of these associations has special function space, food and beverage, lodging, and entertainment meeting requirements. Attendance at association meetings and conventions is voluntary and is paid for by the individual participant. Therefore, it is important that the program content and the selected destination and venue appeal to its membership. Major association meetings require long lead times (3–5 years) and are often held on a rotating basis in different geographic locations.

Off-site corporate meetings are usually held at hotels or purpose-built conference centers. Whereas attendance at association meetings and conventions is voluntary, attendance at corporate meetings is mandatory. The billing for corporate meetings includes all room, meal, and entertainment expenses under one master account charged to the company. The lead time for corporate meetings is relatively short, often governed by changes in the external or internal environment (i.e. political, economic, corporate strategy). The most frequent types of corporate meetings are management meetings, training seminars, new product introductions, chair-holder meetings, professional, technical or marketing meetings.

Incentives

Incentive travel has long been recognized by companies as a motivational tool to reward its employees for the achievement of outstanding accomplishments, such as the reaching of financial targets, the development of new products, or the achievement of superior customer satisfaction. The preferred venues for incentive travel are upscale resort hotels or cruise ships that offer unique amenities and leisure programs.

Exhibitions and trade fairs

Exhibitions are increasingly held in conjunction with the annual meetings of national and international associations. They permit manufacturers and service providers to directly reach a target audience that would otherwise be difficult and expensive to contact. Exhibitions are usually closed to the general public.

A trade fair is a marketplace for commercial suppliers of products or services that are of interest to a specific profession or market segment. Trade fairs are usually held during the same period in the same location each year. There are closed trade fairs that are only open to the professional trade, and open trade fairs that are targeted to a sector of the general public (e.g. home and garden shows, bridal shows, auto shows). Large trade fairs and exhibitions are usually held in purpose-built centers.

Reference

Nykiel, Ronald (2003) *Marketing in the Hospitality Industry*. Lansing, MI: Educational Institute of the American Hotel and Lodging Association.

UDO SCHLENTRICH
UNIVERSITY OF NEW HAMPSHIRE, USA

Midscale restaurants

The first examples of 'chain' restaurant companies were those in the segment called midscale. This market niche has also gone by the terms *coffee shop, limited service,* or *family restaurants*. The term 'midscale' refers to both pricing and service components. Pricing is midscale because menu items are generally priced above the QSR level but below the casual theme segment. Service falls between traditional full service and the low-cost fast food/quick service offerings. Midscale/family coffee shops are typified by a strong identification with breakfast and lunch menu offerings, often serving these items in a 24 hour/7 day-a-week operating environment. Menu selection can be quite broad, primarily to appeal to a general population of consumers ranging from young to old, traveler to local, business to leisure, and everything in between.

This market positioning has created some significant economic pressures for the segment over the past two decades. As an analogy, when you play tennis, you can play on the baseline or you can rush the net – in other words you can win if you play aggressively or if you play defensively, but you never win if you stand in the middle of the court. For the midscale company, pricing pressure comes from being compared with the lower priced QSR players, and service pressure comes from the full serve casual theme restaurants. This segment has therefore been 'caught in the middle' and has been challenged to stay current in the market as demographics and consumer lifestyles have changed over time.

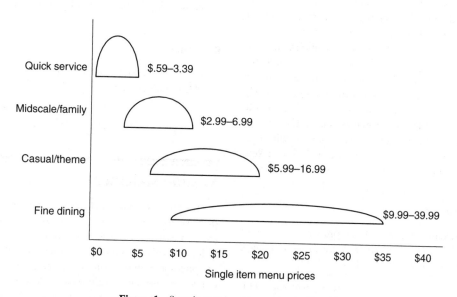

Figure 1 Sample restaurant segment price 'bands'

Reference

Muller, C. and Woods, R.H. (1994) An expanded restaurant typology. *Cornell Hotel and Restaurant Administration Quarterly*, 35 (3), 27–37.

CHRISTOPHER MULLER
UNIVERSITY OF CENTRAL FLORIDA, USA

Mini-vacation

A mini-vacation is discounted or free vacation accommodations offered as an inducement to the recipients to experience a vacation ownership resort with the understanding that acceptance of the accommodations will require the recipients to participate in a sales presentation of the host vacation ownership resort. Mini-vacations may also be offered as discounted or free accommodations in hotels in the general vicinity of the host vacation ownership resort with the understanding that acceptance of the accommodations will require the recipients to participate in a sales presentation at the host vacation ownership resort. Mini-vacations may also be offered without an understanding (un-hooked) that the recipient must participate in a vacation ownership presentation. However, in this event, should the host resort offer the accommodations with the intent of inducing the recipients to participate in the vacation ownership sales presentation during the period of use of the accommodations, the host resort must disclose this intent at the time the offering is made. Mini-vacations may, in addition to the accommodations being offered, be packaged with other ancillary benefits and services to be enjoyed by the recipients during their use of the accommodations. Such ancillary benefits may include: rental car use, meals, attraction tickets, attendance to sporting events and activities, etc.

Reference

American Resort Development Association (2002) *The Timeshare Industry Resource Manual*. Washington, DC: ARDA.

MICHAEL HAUSHALTER
ORLANDO, FLORIDA, USA

Mise en place

Organization is extremely important at any workplace. Foodservice organizations are no exception. *Mise en place* is a French phrase meaning *'everything in its place.'* In foodservice organizations, employees are often found to be spending too much time searching for things they need to perform their daily activities. In addition, employees may also be searching for food items that have been misplaced in storage areas. Most managers and employees agree that smallwares are often misplaced, for example. To minimize wasteful spending of employees' time searching for misplaced things, foodservice professionals are trained to practice *mise en place* – keeping everything where it belongs to the extent possible.

Typically in foodservice organizations, employees who close a unit at the end of the day are not expected to return the next day to open the place. In those circumstances, *mise en place* is very essential so that everyone opening in the morning knows where everything has been placed the night before. Every piece of equipment or instrument has a defined place in storage areas. It must be returned to that specific area after every use. This is one of the cardinal rules of foodservice management. *Mise en place* is often preached from the earliest days to the highest levels of training.

Reference

Baskette, M. (2001) *Chef Manager*. Columbus, OH: Prentice-Hall.

H.G. PARSA
OHIO STATE UNIVERSITY, USA

Mission statement

A Mission statement is a clear statement of intent that lists the purpose, goals, objectives, activities, and motives of an organization. In the hospitality industry a mission statement is used to articulate the philosophy and culture of an organization to employees, customers, and stakeholders. As such, mission statements have both internal and external dimensions. Internally, they are a powerful administrative and evaluative tool that communicates the vision and culture of the organization to managers and employees. Externally, they convey the image and core values of the organization to the market and thus play a key role in fashioning customers' expectations.

In an industry as dynamic as hospitality, mission statements provide perspective and continuity to the activities of the organization, whilst assisting in upholding service quality standards (Cullen, 2001). Mission statements should be structured, succinct, inspirational, engaging, and meaningful and should include clear, achievable, and measurable goals. Mission statements usually express what a company does whereas vision statements express what they would like to do or where they would like to be in the future.

Whilst mission statements aim to provide mission clarity, they should also account for a firm's strategic choice. In other words they should answer the question 'How and with what will we compete to achieve our mission?'

Reference

Cullen, N.C. (2001) *Team Power: Managing Human Resources in the Hospitality Industry*. Upper Saddle River, N J: Prentice-Hall.

BARRY O'MAHONY
VICTORIA UNIVERSITY, AUSTRALIA

Model timeshare act

In 1983, the American Land Development Association adopted a Model Timeshare Act that became the basis for subsequent state legislation. Its provisions were designed to curb scam artists while providing a framework within which reputable developers could operate. In 1994, the American Resort Development Association (ARDA) adopted a Model Vacation Club Act that recognized vacation clubs as a distinct product type and proposed a separate regulatory framework for them. Like the Model Timeshare Act, the Model Vacation Act was designed to protect consumers without imposing unreasonable limitations on legitimate developers

and marketers. In 2001, ARDA established a task force that set forth legislation to form what they chose to call 'Guiding Principles.' In other words, the task force chose to list the areas that timeshare legislation should address and include a statement of principles for each area. In many cases, the guiding principles listed have been used by ARDA for years, both formally and informally, and in other instances, they are new concepts. The Model Timeshare Act has been superseded by the American Resort Development Association's Model Vacation Club Act, and a version adopted by the National Conference of Commissioners on Uniform State Laws.

References

http://www.timesharexpo.com/timesharebasics. htm. Accessed 2 October 2003.

http://www.arda.org/model_tsgp.htm. Accessed 2 October 2003.

KURT GRUBER
ISLAND ONE RESORTS, USA

Model Vacation Club Act

The Model Vacation Club Act was adopted by the American Resort Development Association (ARDA) on 15 November 1994. In January 2001, the State Legislative Committee of ARDA formed a task force to revise and update the 1994 Model Vacation Club Act. The task force, nearing completion on the project, has recommended adoption by the State Legislative Committee of 'Guiding Principles' to be used by legislatures to develop legislation instead of specific proposed language. The Act is a proposed model act developed by the ARDA for the purpose of providing legislatures with recommended provisions for developing or amending timeshare legislation for their particular area in with respect to regulation of timeshare plans, including multi-site timeshare plans. The areas of recommended regulation include applicable definitions, scope and exemptions, subordination and financial assurances, management and assessments, reservation systems, purchaser disclosures, cancellation rights, escrow requirements, and agency governance. In the area of registration a developer may not offer, sell, or dispose of a timeshare interest unless all necessary registrations are filed and approved by the applicable state agency. An exemption to this rule applies to owners of a timeshare interest who purchase for their own personal use and later decide to offer it for resale.

Reference

http://www.arda.org/ARDAModelActGuiding Principles4-03.pdf. Accessed 2 October 2003.

KURT GRUBER
ISLAND ONE RESORTS, USA

Moment of truth

The interaction that occurs between a service provider and the guest is one of the key elements of service that define a guest's service experience. Richard Normann, of the Service Management Group, developed the term 'Moment of Truth' for any moment when an employee and customer have contact in a service operation and the guest determines his or her impression of the service quality. Jan Carlzon, CEO of Scandinavian Airlines Systems (SAS), popularized the Moment of Truth concept when reorganizing SAS to gain a competitive edge. Carlzon saw the customer as an active participant in the service experience. During a service encounter, the employee and guest both exhibit behavioral cues that allow them to form impressions and choose their reactions. A positive Moment of Truth occurs when the service provider has the ability to monitor the guest's behavioral cues and react in a way that promotes guest satisfaction along with delivering the service. In order to develop positive Moments of Truth, service operations support the staff members who have direct customer contact. By turning the organizational structure upside down, the employee with direct guest contact will be empowered to react appropriately to the customer's behavioral cues.

NICOLE MARIE HOLLAND
LONDONDERRY, NH, USA

Motivation

Motivation is the process by which people seek to achieve certain goals, which in turn satisfy a need. The word motivation is used to describe the things that motivate people, the process through which a goal satisfies a need, and the social process by which a manager seeks to influence the performance of a subordinate to increase productivity. Motivation is a key aspect of hospitality management and one of the mechanisms for tackling the high levels of labor turnover within the industry in developed countries.

The academic discussion of motivation has been dominated by a dichotomy between the study of the things that motivate – content theories – and the process by which people are motivated – process theories. Content theories of motivation focus on identifying the things or situations to which employees aspire as a way of describing motivation. Generally, they explain that people are driven to fulfill needs that are deficient or unsatisfied such as a desire for more money, promotion, responsibility or personal fulfillment. Therefore to motivate someone one must first identify their individual level of need. Content theorists believe that such needs are innate in humans. The main examples of Content theories are Maslow's Hierarchy of Needs (1943) and Herzberg's Two Factor Theory (Herzberg et al., 1959). Herzberg differentiated between the things that would prevent dissatisfaction and the things that would motivate employees. The 'dissatisfiers' tended to be extrinsic rewards or outcomes, benefits provided by the organization such as pay increases, working conditions, and interpersonal relations. It was recognized that extrinsic rewards are less effective as motivators, except in the short-term. The 'motivators' tended to be intrinsic rewards, outcomes or benefits that come from within the individual themselves, such as feelings of satisfaction, self-esteem, feelings of achievement and competence or a sense of purpose and therefore the focus of motivational effort for managers should be on providing opportunities for responsibility, autonomy, personal development, and recognition.

However, such studies have been criticized for being ethnocentric; there is an assumption that the priorities associated with different levels of need are universal, whereas there is evidence to suggest that not only are levels perceived as more or less important depending on cultural values, but some levels do not exist at all (Yu, 1999). Also, the intangible nature of the 'product' in hospitality sometimes makes it difficult to measure the performance of an employee, so the process of recognizing and rewarding employees becomes more complicated.

Process theories of motivation seek to explain the reason why people might be motivated and the individual differences evident in people's choices of goals and behaviors, rather than identifying the things that are motivators. Examples are theories such as equity theory, expectancy theory, and goal-setting theory, all of which seek to describe the cognitive processes that people follow in evaluating motivational drives. Expectancy theory (Vroom, 1964), for example, explains the process by which someone is motivated as a product of the relationship between the effort that they have to expend and the likelihood that their effort will lead to a reward that they value. For example, although people are not solely motivated by money, if a waiter recognizes that better service might lead to a bigger gratuity for them personally, they may be motivated to increase their service level. However, this situation might not be as motivating if tips are pooled and therefore the increase in their share would not be significant enough to merit extra effort as the value of the final reward is either too small or not directly related to the amount of effort (if other waiters give poor service and subsequently contribute little to pooled tips). Process theories have been criticized for being overly intellectualized; however, they do provide alternative practical insights into the motivation debate.

Some methods of increasing employee motivation have centered on redesigning the jobs and tasks that people do. *Job rotation* redesigns work by switching employees from task to task at regular intervals. This can be an attempt to relieve the boredom of low-skilled tasks, as it provides some variety in the tasks undertaken, to share responsibility for unpopular tasks or as part of a training program. For example, employees may be rotated through reception duties, bar work, restaurant work or kitchen duties, either as a way of covering for staff shortages or training on new skills. Although this increases flexibility for the organization, it does not enrich the job for the jobholder, as skills are all at a similar level and individual tasks remain the same.

Job enlargement redesigns jobs by combining a number of tasks at a similar skill level to increase the length/scope of the job. Although this can reduce boredom and increase interest in work, it does require greater knowledge, skill, and training. For example, rather than have waiters for each course or drinks order in a restaurant, they could be given responsibility for the complete ordering of a small number of tables. This would increase the length of time they are involved in their task. However, it does not necessarily make the component parts of the job any more interesting or rewarding.

Job enrichment, based on the work of Herzberg outlined above, seeks to increase the level of satisfaction of workers by addressing the factors that motivate individuals and including these in the redesigned role. Instead of increasing the job horizontally, as happens with job enlargement, the job is increased vertically, by increasing the employee's responsibility and autonomy by adding elements such as planning, organizing, and control. For example, levels of supervision can be decreased to give workers more control and responsibility over their workload, work pace, and quality of output. They can also be encouraged to take on more direct customer interaction or responsibility for a larger part of the process.

An alternative classification of motivation theories focuses on whether they are 'near to' tasks undertaken in the workplace (proximal) or at some 'distance' from it (distal). Evidence so far suggests that proximal theories such as goal setting are more powerful at motivating employees than their distal counterparts.

References

Herzberg, F., Mausner, B., and Synderman, B.B. (1959) *The Motivation to Work*, 2nd edn. New York: Chapman & Hall.

Maslow, A.H. (1943) A theory of human motivation. *Psychological Review*, 50, July, 370–396.

Vroom, V. (1964) *Work and Motivation*. Chichester: John Wiley & Sons.

Yu, L. (1999) *The International Hospitality Business: Management and Operations*. London: The Haworth Hospitality Press.

GILLIAN KELLOCK HAY
GLASGOW CALEDONIAN UNIVERSITY, UK

Multi-branding

Multi-branding is based on the process of differentiation by offering independent, unconnected brands that maximize a company's impact on the market and increase its market share. Some of the risks associated with a multi-branding strategy are loss of economies of scale, stagnation, cannibalization, and higher costs. However, multi-branding offers certain advantages in terms of positioning brands on their functional benefits and dominating niche segments with a targeted value proposition. Thus, multi-branding avoids incompatible brand associations, minimizes channel conflict, allows optimum market coverage, limits competitors' extension possibilities, and, in certain cases, defends against a price war. As the market matures, consumer needs diverge and the market becomes segmented, which leads to an increased demand for niche products and services. Several hospitality companies have resorted to multi-branding to correspond to the various market segments and niches. For example, Choice Hotels has eight different brands that include Comfort Inn, Quality Inn, Clarion and Econolodge. Similarly, Starwood Hotels and Resorts offer Westin, Sheraton, St Regis and W, which concentrate upon well-defined and diverse market segments. In the restaurant business, Darden Restaurants operates Red Lobster, Olive Garden, Bahama Breeze, and Smokey Bones, each catering to distinct market segments.

References

Aaker, David A. and Joachimsthaler, Erich (2000) *Brand Leadership*. New York: The Free Press, pp. 100–114.

Kapferer, Jean Noel (1994) *Strategic Brand Management: New Approaches to Creating and Evaluating Brand Equity*. New York: The Free Press, pp. 192–197.

ASHISH KHULLAR
UNIVERSITY OF MASSACHUSETTS, USA

Multimedia

The term multimedia describes a number of diverse technologies that allow visual and audio media to be taken and combined in new ways for the purpose of communicating. Multimedia can be defined as any combination of two or more of the following – text, graphics, sound, animation, video – which are integrated together and can be delivered in various formats including standalone (PC, CD-ROM, DVD) and networks (WWW, ISDN, cable, cellular, wireless). Fetterman and Gupta (1993, p. 34) suggest a definition within the concept of an 'all digital environment offering functional integration of different forms of media enabling the development of multimedia applications.' This incorporates the idea of seamless integration encompassing the fluid transition and control of different media through computing software. Vaughn (1994) complements this definition by including the devolving of control of multimedia applications into the hands of the end-user providing the elements of interactivity and user choice. This may be delivered not only by PCs and CDs but also by interactive TV set-top boxes and pocket devices such as mobile phones. Multimedia is currently used in the hospitality sector to enhance the in-room guest experience, for training of staff and for communicating internally and externally. More adventurous multimedia applications, such as virtual reality, are yet to be fully exploited the hospitality sector.

References

Fetterman, R.L. and Gupta, S.K. (1993) *Mainstream Multimedia – Applying Multimedia in Business*. New York: International Thomson Publishing.

Vaughn, T. (1994) *Multimedia – Making It Work.* Berkley, CA: Osborne.

HILARY C. MAIN-MURPHY
ECOLE HOTELIERE DE LAUSANNE,
SWITZERLAND

Multi-site timeshare plan

A multi-site timeshare plan is a timeshare plan that connects more than one timeshare property together through a central reservations system such that the owner of a deeded timeshare interest or a right-to-use timeshare interest at one of the properties in the plan, or the owner of a right-to-use interest in the plan as whole that is not tied to a specific timeshare property, has the right to reserve and use the accommodations and facilities at any of the properties that are part of the plan pursuant to the terms and conditions of the reservation system. Unlike exchange programs, membership and participation in the multi-site timeshare plan is mandatory, and the owner cannot use a timeshare period without accessing the reservation system. Many multi-site timeshare plans provide for a 'home resort' priority reservation right that allows owners of a deeded timeshare interest or a right-to-use timeshare interest at one of the timeshare properties to have a priority right to reserve and use an accommodation at the timeshare property of ownership before the owners of other timeshare properties that are part of the plan can make a reservation at that property. Multi-site timeshare plans are sometimes referred to as 'vacation clubs.'

References

See, e.g., *Fla. Stat.* §721.52(4) (2 October 2003).
http://www.flsenate.gov/statutes/index.cfm?
    App_mode=Display_Statute&Search_String
    =&URL=Ch0721
SEC52.HTM&Title=->2000->Ch0721->
    Section percent2052.

KURT GRUBER
ISLAND ONE RESORTS, USA

Multi-skilling

By way of a working definition 'skilling' is the term given to instilling competence for a task or activity in trainees through training. Cordery (1989) defines multi-skilling as, 'The process of increasing the skill repertoire of workers to improve their ability to work in more than one narrowly defined occupational specialty.' According to Cross (1991), multi-skilling is usually based on two principles:

- Competency within the workplace, i.e. the ability of a single individual to assess and rectify problems as they occur day to day, almost regardless of the nature of the problem
- The full utilization of capabilities, i.e. the only limitations on who does what, how and when are the skill that an individual has or can acquire, the time available to perform any new or additional tasks, and the requirements of safety.

As guest expectations and demands continuously increase in the hospitality industry employers are equipping the workforce with the relevant skills to make them able to function in any of the positions within a team. In a hotel, staff put through a multi-skilling program can regularly be re-deployed across two or more work areas such as housekeeping and bar. These staff can also be rostered to work shifts in different departments and from time to time be redeployed in the course of a shift.

References

Cordery, J. (1989) Multi-skilling: a discussion of proposed benefits of new approaches to labor flexibility within organizations. *Personnel Review*, 18 (3), 13–22.
Cross, M. (1991) Monitoring multiskilling: the way to guarantee long-term change. *Personnel Management*, 23 (3), 44–48.

FRANCES DEVINE
UNIVERSITY OF ULSTER, UK

ADRIAN DEVINE
UNIVERSITY OF ULSTER, UK

Musculoskeletal disorders

Musculoskeletal disorders (MSDs) are injuries of the muscles, nerves, tendons, ligaments, joints, cartilage, or spinal discs. Other expressions used to describe MSDs include repetitive strain injuries (RSIs), cumulative trauma disorders, overuse injuries, and repetitive motion disorders. Some common MSDs are back pain and carpal tunnel syndrome (wrist pain). MSDs are not typically the result of any instantaneous or acute event (such as a slip, trip, or fall) but reflect a more gradual or chronic development. MSD type injuries are not only very painful for the victim; they are also difficult and very expensive to treat. Musculoskeletal disorders account for nearly 70 million physician office visits in the United States annually and an estimated 130 million total health care encounters including outpatient, hospital, and emergency room visits. In the UK musculoskeletal disorders are the most common occupational illness affecting 1.1 million people a year. The US National Institute for Occupational Safety and Health (NIOSH) and the European Agency for Safety and Health at Work have developed considerable resources for the identification of hazardous work environments, recommendations for the reduction of MSDs through better workplace design, guidelines for employee training, advice on medical treatment options, and a complete program that establishes a proactive approach to the reduction of MSDs.

References

Ergonomics (n.d.): http://www.cdc.gov/niosh/ephome2.html.

Musculoskeletal disorders (n.d.) http://europe.osha.eu.int/good_practice/risks/msd/.

JERRY LACHAPPELLE
HARRAH'S ENTERTAINMENT, INC., USA

N

Net present value (NPV)

The net present value (NPV) method belongs to the discounted cash flow (DCF) methods. These are methods to support the process of selection and evaluation between different courses of action, enabling decision-makers to take financial decisions. DCF methods are normative approaches as they relate decisions to necessary conditions, for example the existence of alternatives and existence of objectives, such as the long-term goals of achieving streams of benefits in the future in return for current outlays. The use of DCF methods entails the representation of the different courses of action as current and future streams of money (or, more generally, of benefits, under the criterion of the wealth maximization). These techniques enable investment decision-makers to take into account relevant variables such as: time value of money, perception of risk, forecast of inflation, and conditions for cost of capital and opportunities for alternative investments.

The main concept of DCF methods is the time value of money, i.e. money has a different value depending upon the time it is received or paid out, and hence cash flows in future time have to be discounted. Therefore the underlying concept of NPV is that if cash to be received in the future were received now, the cash could be invested to earn interest (return), or it would not be necessary to borrow money now and to pay interest (cost of capital). In addition a future cash flow bears the risk of not being paid by the debtor (risk) and finally the nominal value of a

cash flow will correspond to a lower purchasing value in the future than now, according to the general price increase (inflation).

To make decisions it is therefore necessary to convert cash flows of different years into their present values in order to use a common value of any future cash flow, as Tables 1 and 2 show.

NPV determines the sum of future cash inflows related to a project, after having discounted them by an appropriate rate of interest and deducted the initial cash outflow.

The rate of interest used is a subjective evaluation of the risk associated with the project, the forecast of inflation, and the cost of capital.

The following example shows how to calculate the NPV of a project.

Table 1 Time value of money: the investment of $100 at a rate of 10%

Now (2004)	Year 2005	Year 2006	Year 2007
$100	$100 \times (1.1)$ $=\$110$	$100 \times (1.1)^2$ $=\$121$	$100 \times (1.1)^3$ $=\$133.1$

Table 2 How to convert future cash flows in present value: the present value of a sum of money to be received in 'n' years' time is the result of discounting

	Year 2005	Year 2006	Year 2007
Sum to be received	$220	$242	$266.2
Discounting	$220/(1.1)$	$242/(1.1)^2$	$266.2/(1.1)^3$
Present value	$200	$200	$200

Table 3 How to calculate the NPV of a project: enlarging a hotel's capacity from 150 rooms to 175 rooms at an outlay of $1 million dollars paid in 2004, rate of interest 15%

	Year 2005	Year 2006	Year 2007	Year 2008	Year 2009
Additional cash flow due to the enlargement ($)	230,000	320,000	350,000	400,000	460,000
Discounting cash flows	$230,000/1.15$	$320,000/(1.15)^2$	$350,000/(1.15)^3$	$400,000/(1.15)^4$	$460,000/(1.15)^5$
Discounted cash flows ($)	200,000	241,966	230,131	228,701	228,701

Total discounted cash inflows: $1,129,500
NPV: $1,129,500 - 1,000,000 = $129,500$

NPV is the technique that represents the impact of a project on shareholders' wealth. Therefore it is said to be the most accurate method with which to evaluate a project from a financial point of view. For this reason, and because the wide availability of computer spreadsheets makes it generally affordable, this technique is gaining in popularity.

The NPV method also allows a sensitive analysis to be carried out where the estimated selling price, cost of capital, life of the project, initial cost, operating costs, sales volume, and the estimated level of risk can be varied in order to observe their effects on the NPV.

A challenge in NPV is determining which cash flows are relevant to the analysis. To this end only expected cash flows that differ from the alternatives, have to be taken into consideration. This entails that for different subjects the relevant cash flows of a project might be different, e.g. when a company establishes a subsidiary in another country, the cash flows relevant to the subsidiary are the net cash flows that they produce, whilst the relevant cash flows to the parent company are the net remittance flows that they receive, net of withholding tax and after restrictions on remittance are applied.

References

Drury, C. (2000) *Management and Cost Accounting*, 5th edn. London: Thomson Learning.

Horngren, C.T., Foster, G., and Datar, S.M. (2000) *Cost Accounting: A Managerial Emphasis*, 10th edn. Upper Saddle River, NJ: Prentice-Hall International.

Lumby, S. and Jones, C. (1999) *Investment Appraisal and Financial Decisions*, 6th edn. London: Thomson Learning.

McLaney, E.J. (1994) *Business Finance for Decision-Makers*, 2nd edn. London: Pitman Publishing.

Moffett, M.H., Stonehill, A.I. and Eiteman, D.K. (2003) *Fundamentals of Multinational Finance*. New York: Addison-Wesley.

MARCO MONGIELLO
UNIVERSITY OF WESTMINSTER, UK

Night audit

The term night audit actually describes itself. It is an activity that occurs at night and is financial in nature. A hotel is a 24 hour, seven days a week operation. The front desk operates continuously, with three shifts per day. The night audit occurs during the last shift, which begins at night and ends in the early morning. This is called the grave shift and it is at this time when the financial day at the hotel ends and a new one begins. The night audit is performed every night and is an important part of the accounting function within a hotel. It is during the night audit that financial activities are used to review and check the accuracy and reliability of the hotel's front office financial transactions.

A special desk clerk called the night auditor performs the night audit. This person fulfills many roles. He or she is responsible for the traditional duties of a front desk clerk including checking guests in and out and performing various customer service functions. Like all desk clerks the night auditor reports to the front desk manager. However, this person also reports to the hotel's controller and has additional financial responsibilities. Because the night auditor works in the evening he or she usually has management responsibilities and may act as the manager-on-duty.

Prior to the computerization of the hotel front desk area, a hotel would have many night auditors who performed their job. Today computerized property management systems (PMS) have shortened the time it takes to do the night audit and have greatly reduced the number of auditors required to complete the task. Regardless of how it is performed, the night audit plays an important function within the hotel's financial process.

During the night audit both guest accounts and non-guest accounts are cross-referenced and reconciled. Errors and discrepancies that are discovered during the audit are corrected before the end of the shift. These steps are taken to ensure that the hotel accounts are accurate and in balance. Also during the night audit reports are generated to provide management with operating and marketing information.

The night audit function can be described in a series of steps:

- Complete outstanding posting and reconcile front desk discrepancies
- Reconcile departmental activities
- Verify room rates and post room and tax
- Prepare cash receipts for deposit
- End the day by clearing out the day's activities and backing up the system
- Prepare the night audit reports.

The first step of the night audit is to ensure that all transactions on both guest accounts and non-accounts have been posted properly. The transactions for the day are checked for accuracy and then all outstanding transactions are completed. The front desk accounts involve those transactions that occur at the front desk.

The night auditor may also handle transactions from other revenue centers in the hotel. These departments may include the gift shop, parking, telephone, and restaurants. The night auditor usually balances the front office accounts against the other departments. This process is called the trial balance. Any discrepancies discovered during this process are corrected before the night auditor can move to the next step.

The accuracy of guestroom rates is very important since most hotels generate the majority of their revenue from room rentals. Hotels have a variety of guest types who may be charged different rates for the same room type. A very important aspect of the night audit is to verify the various room rates. Once the rates are checked the night auditor can then post room and tax for each guestroom. In a computerized PMS system this step is handled with a press of a button.

At some hotels the night auditor is also responsible for preparing cash reports and deposits. This involves reconciling the cash, room charges, and credit card charges with reports from the PMS system, other point-of-sales systems or cash registers. The total revenue from each shift report is verified against the money deposited from each shift. This is a time-consuming process without a PMS or other computerized system.

The night auditor prepares to end the financial day once accounts are deemed in balance. This means that all errors have been corrected and accounts are considered to be accurate. The end of the day usually happens around 3 a.m. When using a PMS system the computer changes over the date to the next day. Quite often this step takes the computer offline. During this downtime data are compiled. When the system comes back on line the hotel begins the next day and all the accounts are totaled and reset at the new date.

The last step in the night audit process involves the preparation of the night audit reports. These reports become a snapshot or financial picture of the front desk activities and operation for the previous day. The reports summarize the day's activities and provide an insight into the hotel's operation. The information relates to revenue, receivables, financial transactions, and operating statistics. The information includes occupancy percentages, average daily room rates, yield percentages, and number of guests. Management uses the information generated by the night audit to make decisions regarding the operation of the hotel property.

The night audit is a vital process within the accounting function of a hotel operation. Hotel managers depend upon the accuracy of the documentation created by the night audit process. Whether performed manually, by computer or PMS system the night audit remains one of the most important accounting functions performed by the front desk staff.

References

Bardi, James, A. (2003) *Hotel and Front Office Management*, 3rd edn. New York: John Wiley & Sons.

Kasavana, M.L. and Brooks, R.M. (2001) *Management Front Office Operations*, 6th edn. Lansing, MI: Educational Institute of the American Hotel and Lodging Association.

Kline, Sheryl, F. and Sullivan, William (2002) *Hotel Front Office Simulation*. New York: John Wiley & Sons.

Stutts, Alan T. (2001) *Hotel and Lodging Management: An Introduction*. New York: John Wiley & Sons.

SHERYL F. KLINE
PURDUE UNIVERSITY, USA

No-show

This refers to people who have made a reservation with the hotel but fail to show up on the day of arrival or have not cancelled the reservation. No-shows create a problem for the hotel in that it makes it difficult for them to maximize their occupancy. It represents a loss of revenue for the hotel. However, guests who have guaranteed their reservation (either by paying a deposit or giving credit card information) and failed to show up on the day of arrival will be charged for the first night of the reservation. The hotel should calculate the percentage of no-shows so as to help make decisions on when (or if) to sell rooms to walk-in guests, particularly in busy periods.

Various types of travellers – corporate, group, or pleasure – have varying no-show rates. For example, corporate confirmed reservations may have a 1% overall no-show rate. Group travelers may have a 0.5% no-show rate, with no-shows all coming from one or two particular bus companies. Pleasure travelers may have a 10% no-show rate. The detailed investigation of each of these categories will suggest methods for minimizing no-show rates.

References

Abbott, P. and Lewry, S. (1991) *Front Office Procedures, Social Skills and Management*. Oxford: Butterworth-Heinemann.

Kasavana, M.L. and Brooks, R.M. (1995) *Front Office Procedures*, 4th edn. Lansing, MI: Educational Institute of the American Hotel and Motel Association.

IRENE SWEENEY
INTERNATIONAL HOTEL MANAGEMENT
INSTITUTE SWITZERLAND, SWITZERLAND

Non-controllable expenses

Non-controllable (sometimes termed uncontrollable) foodservice/restaurant expenses are costs that cannot be changed in the short term. Some fixed costs are considered non-controllable since management staff are not able to effect change in them during the short-term. Conversely, all non-controllable expenses are fixed costs. Examples of non-controllable expenses in restaurants and foodservice enterprises include rent, mortgage interest, depreciation and amortization, insurance, license fees, legal and accounting fees, and taxes. Although these amounts may change over time, the management staff of a foodservice operation usually is not responsible for negotiating new rates or making changes to these numbers; hence, they are considered non-controllable. Non-controllable expenses may include direct and indirect expenses.

Reference

Schmidgall, R.S. (1986) *Hospitality Industry Managerial Accounting*. Lansing, MI: Educational Institute of the American Hotel and Motel Association.

DEBORAH BARRASH
UNIVERSITY OF NEVADA, LAS VEGAS, USA

Nouvelle cuisine

Nouvelle cuisine ('new cookery' in French) is a culinary movement that owed its momentum to two food critics, Gault and Millau, in the early 1970s. Practitioners of nouvelle cuisine revised much of the classical food preparation methods by doing away with complicated preparations, overly rich sauces which masked the true flavor of food, rigid recipe formulae, and pretentious and elaborate rituals and service arrangements.

To counter the rigidity and obsolescence of some of classical cuisine's repertoire and to counter an increasing use of processed foods, nouvelle practitioners embraced authenticity and simplicity in preparation and cooking methods; freshness of ingredients; lightness and use of natural flavors; greatly reduced use of fat; doing away with flour-based sauces; use of rapid cooking methods, natural flavorings, grilling, steaming, and slow cooking; doing away with elaborate garnishing; and use of natural juices, stocks, and essences to make sauces. Nouvelle cuisine brought greater awareness to the public and culinary practitioners alike about the importance of good and often simple food preparations, the use of fresh and natural ingredients, uncomplicated cooking methods, and uncomplicated service.

Reference

Franck, K.A. (2003) *Food + Architecture*. London: Academy Editions.

JAKSA KIVELA
THE HONG KONG POLYTECHNIC
UNIVERSITY, SAR, CHINA

O

Occupancy, types of

Occupancy of a hotel is comprised of walk-ins, reservations, stayovers, understays, and no-show reservations. The objective of the hotel's management is to attain 100% occupancy. Careful monitoring and tracking of the types of occupancy permits hotel management to more accurately predict occupancy and effectively use management tools such as the occupancy management formula. The front office manager can obtain the data for this formula by reviewing the property management system (PMS) reservation module, which lists the groups, corporate clients, and individual guests who have made reservations for a specific time period. Also, the front office manager can check the tourism activity in the area, business events planned in other hotels, and other special events happening locally.

The occupancy management formula includes confirmed reservations, guaranteed reservations, no-show factor for these two types of reservations, predicted stayovers, predicted understays, and predicted walk-ins to determine the number of additional room reservations need to achieve 100% occupancy. The calculation: (total number of rooms available) − (confirmed reservations) × (no-show factor) − (guaranteed reservations) × (no-show factor) − (predicted stayovers) + (predicted understays) − (predicted walk-ins) gives the number of additional room reservations needed to achieve 100% occupancy.

Reference

Stutts, Alan T. (2001) *Hotel and Lodging Management – An Introduction*. New York: John Wiley & Sons.

ALAN T. STUTTS
AMERICAN INTERCONTINENTAL
UNIVERSITY, USA

Occupancy costs

Occupancy costs include all the costs of occupying a physical area. For many foodservice establishments, the most significant cost is rent. If a foodservice operation owns its own facility, however, these costs include property taxes, mortgage expenses, and property insurance expenses. In the US, the average occupancy costs are 4–10% of total revenues.

According to Deloitte & Touche (1996), each of the following should be categorized under occupancy costs on the income statement:

- Rent (including leases of land, buildings and equipment)
- Property taxes and property insurance (pro-rated accordingly if paid in lump sums)
- Real estate taxes (including those assessed by a state, county, or city government)
- Personal property taxes (such as those payable by the restaurant operator)
- Other municipal taxes (such as charges for use of sewers)
- Insurance on buildings and contents (including insurance against damage or destruction).

Depreciation, while totaled separately, is sometimes included into an aggregated line item on the income statement as 'occupancy costs and depreciation.' If such a practice is used, such depreciation should be related to costs pertaining to buildings, amortization of leasehold improvements, and furniture, fixtures, and equipment.

Reference

Deloitte & Touche LLP (1996) *Uniform System of Accounts.* Washington, DC: National Restaurant Association.

DEBORAH BARRASH
UNIVERSITY OF NEVADA, LAS VEGAS, USA

Occupancy percentage

Occupancy percentage historically revealed the success of a hotel's staff in attracting guests to a hotel. The traditional view of measuring the effectiveness of the general manager, marketing staff, and front office staff was used to answer such questions as how many rooms were sold due to the director of sales' efforts in creating attractive and enticing direct mail, radio and television ads, billboard displays, or newspapers and magazine display adds. The occupancy percentage for a hotel property is computed daily. Occupancy percentage is the number of rooms sold divided by the number of rooms available multiplied by 100. Investors have utilized occupancy percentage to determine the potential gross income of a hotel by calculating: (occupancy percentage) × (number of available hotel rooms) × (daily rate), which provides revenue per day. If revenue per day is then multiplied by the number of days in the year gross revenue from room sales annually can be determined. However, one cannot presume that occupancy is standard each night. Variations might occur on a daily basis and this must be factored into any weekly, monthly, and annual projection of gross revenue from room sales. A variation is the multiple occupancy percentage, which determines the average number of guests per room sold or occupied. This ratio is particularly

useful in forecasting food and beverage revenue and operating requirements such as the clean linen requirements. The multiple occupancy percentage is calculated by determining the number of rooms occupied by more than one guest divided by the number of rooms occupied.

Reference

Bardi, James A. (2003) *Hotel Front Office Management,* 3rd edn. New York: John Wiley & Sons.

ALAN T. STUTTS
AMERICAN INTERCONTINENTAL
UNIVERSITY, USA

Occupational safety and health

All industrialized countries have statutes and regulations aimed to protect the health and safety of working people. For example, in the United States, the US Congress in 1970 passed the Occupational and Safety Health Act to ensure worker and workplace safety. Their goal was to make sure employers provide their workers a place of employment free from recognized hazards to safety and health, such as exposure to toxic chemicals, excessive noise levels, mechanical dangers, heat or cold stress, or unsanitary conditions (Oliver, 2001). In order to establish standards for workplace health and safety, the 1970 Act also created the National Institute for Occupational Safety and Health (NIOSH) as the research institution for the Occupational Safety and Health Administration (OSHA) that oversees the administration of the Act and enforces standards in all 50 states. In Australia and other countries of British heritage most occupational health and safety legislation has incorporated elements drawn from the common law of 'torts' that all persons owe a duty of care to others requiring employers to implement and maintain a safe working environment for employees and others. As far as hospitality employees are concerned, their employers are obligated to avoid exposing them to reasonably foreseeable risks of injury.

When assessing an apparent breach of employers' duty of care, courts will consider three issues. First, whether the employer was aware of the risk of injury and if not, would a prudent employer have been aware of such a risk; second, did the employer take reasonable steps to avoid or reduce the risk; third, was the injury preventable (Woods, 2002).

References

Oliver, C. (2001) *Australian Master Human Resources Guide 2002*. Sydney: CCH Australia Ltd.

Woods, R.H. (2002) *Managing Hospitality Human Resources*, 3rd edn. Lansing, MI: Educational Institute of the American Hotel and Lodging Association.

NILS TIMO
GRIFFITH UNIVERSITY, AUSTRALIA

Off-premise contact

Off premise contacts (OPC), or 'outside property contacts', or similar terms, are used to describe those whose job it is to invite potential resort owners to visit the resort. Typically these are agents employed to generate potential sales leads from specified target groups. The off-premise contact with potential owners is chiefly concerned with generating visitors to tour the resort with the aim of generating sales of timeshare slots. The resort pays the OPC a commission for each qualified prospect making a tour of the property.

Due to the use of some high-pressure selling techniques in the past, OPCs are restricted by legislation. Limitations have been placed on who may operate, the numbers in any particular resort, the location of these contacts, the numbers operating in a resort and time when they can approach consumers. Approaches that generate people who tour the property as the result of false pretences, such as through false prize-winning schemes, are regarded as unacceptable business practice.

Recently, approaches that generate lead couples through high-pressure selling techniques are seen as counter-productive when dealing with an increasingly well-educated and sophisticated consumer base. Most of the large branded resort companies now look to sales techniques such as the 'mini-vacation', certificate programs, customer referral schemes, and telemarketing to generate interest from consumers who are more likely to be genuinely interested in making a timeshare purchase.

Reference

American Resort Development Association (2002) *The Timeshare Industry Resource Manual*. Washington, DC: ARDA.

CONRAD LASHLEY
NOTTINGHAM TRENT UNIVERSITY, UK

On change status

At check-out, along with settling the guest account, the front desk agent must change the status of the guestroom from occupied to on change, or a room from which the guest has checked out but which is not ready for the next arrival or is not ready for cleaning, and notify the housekeeping department of the departure. With an integrated property management system (PMS), departure notification may be forwarded to housekeeping automatically. Because the room is not available until housekeeping is finished with it, the on change status is typically for as short a time as possible. Thus, an effective interaction between the front office and housekeeping is key. Housekeeping and the front office must inform each other of changes in a room's status. Knowing whether a room is on change is a key to maximizing room sales. When a front desk promptly notifies housekeeping of a check-out it is a significant aid in getting early-arriving guests registered, especially during high-occupancy or sold-out periods.

Reference

Stutts, Alan T. (2001) *Hotel and Lodging Management – An Introduction*. New York: John Wiley & Sons.

ALAN T. STUTTS
AMERICAN INTERCONTINENTAL
UNIVERSITY, USA

On-line booking

The revolutionary development of the Internet in the past 15 years has meant a paradigm shift in the way central reservations are regarded. Prior to that, it was assumed that the way forward was to have ever larger central reservation networks. The largest companies controlled access to the inventory. The Internet has meant that the smallest bed and breakfast operation can now have a global presence alongside the largest names in the industry. For the larger operators it has meant a reduced cost for customers trying to access their CRS. The growth in Internet bookings (particularly in the United States where estimates quote increases from US$276 million in 1996 to US$8.9 billion in 2002), is due to a number of issues: more people online; secure transaction systems for payment on the Internet; and increased competition between online travel sites. Hotel operators are particularly keen to utilize the Internet to reduce commission payments to travel agents. Six Continents now offer 'automatic' requests for proposals through their websites.

Business travelers and administrative assistants are increasingly using the Internet, mainly to make airline, hotel, and rental car reservations. Airline reservations are the most common travel arrangements made online by either the business traveler or an administrative assistant. In a survey of 811 executives, United Airlines, Embassy Suites, and Hertz had the highest percentage of satisfied customers with their respective categories.

References

Hotel Online Special Report (2000) Number of business travelers making reservations online doubles in six months. Press Release, Hotel Online.Com.

Vallen, G.K. and Vallen, J.J. (2000) *Check-in Check-out*. Englewood Cliffs, NJ: Prentice-Hall.

ERWIN LOSEKOOT
UNIVERSITY OF STRATHCLYDE, UK

On-site foodservice

Sometimes referred to as contract catering or non-commercial foodservice, on-site foodservice comprises food outlets in business and industry, schools, universities and colleges, hospitals, skilled-nursing centers, eldercare centers, correctional facilities, recreational facilities such as stadiums and national parks, and childcare centers. The roots of on-site foodservice date back to around 3500 BC, and are apparent in the way foodservice was provided to the workforce who built the pyramids. In modern times, the importance of on-site foodservice to the economies of business and the utilization of labor was established in the factories of England and Scotland during the dawn of the industrial revolution and is omnipresent in modern business settings.

Today, the on-site segment represents some $230 billion in global revenue. Its complexity is evident in the sophistication of board plans offered by many colleges, and its similarity to traditional foodservice outlets is apparent in cafés found commonly in the corporate headquarters of companies such as Motorola and Microsoft. The high quality of food and service found in leading healthcare institutions, where foodservice often includes 24-hour room service, belies the outdated perception of bland and boring dishes. Indeed, the streamlined production systems, progressive management-development programs, and aggressive brand-management approaches used by many managed-service companies to whom many firms outsource their on-site needs underscore the evolution of on-site foodservice and its growing presence in the foodservice industry.

References

Reynolds, D. (1999) Managed-services companies: the new scorecard for on-site foodservice. *Cornell Hotel and Restaurant Quarterly*, 40 (3), 64–73.

Reynolds, D. (2003) *On-site Foodservice Management: A Best Practices Approach*. New York: John Wiley & Sons.

DENNIS REYNOLDS
WASHINGTON STATE UNIVERSITY, USA

Operating cash flow

Operating cash flow is the cash flow resulting from a firm's day-to-day operation activities of production and sales. To calculate before-tax operating cash flow, one must calculate revenues minus various operation costs. Depreciation and amortization, however, are not included because they are not cash expenses. Expenses associated with the firm's financing of its assets, such as debt interests, are also irrelevant costs because they are not operating expenses. Before-tax operating cash flow, often referred to by financial analysts as earnings before interests, taxes, depreciation, and amortization (EBITDA), is an important measure of the operating performance of a hospitality firm. In particular, since property level (unit) management has no control over a hospitality firm's fixed charges and financing costs, EBITDA is an appropriate performance measure for hospitality management. After-tax operating cash flow can be calculated as:

Operating cash flow = Earnings before interest and taxes + depreciation and amortization − taxes

Operating cash flow is an important concept in hospitality financial management because it shows whether a hospitality firm is generating enough cash flows from its business operations to cover its cash outflows. A negative operating cash flow often signals trouble for the hospitality firm.

References

Keown, A., Martin, J., Petty, W., and Scott, D. (2003) *Foundations of Finance: The Logic and Practice of Financial Management*, 4th edn. Upper Saddle River, NJ: Prentice-Hall.

Ross, S., Westerfield, R., and Jordan, B. (2004) *Essentials of Corporate Finance*, 4th edn. Boston, MA: McGraw-Hill.

ZHENG GU
UNIVERSITY OF NEVADA, LAS VEGAS, USA

Operating leverage

Operating leverage is defined as the extent to which costs are fixed within a firm's operations. A hospitality firm with higher percentage of fixed costs is said to have a higher degree of operating leverage (DOL). Operating leverage may also be perceived as the responsiveness of a hospitality firm's earnings before interests and taxes (EBIT), and hence its return on equity (ROE), to fluctuations in firm sales. The DOL is defined as the percentage change in a firm's EBIT resulting from a given percentage change in its sales.

DOL = (Percentage change in EBIT)/(Percentage change in sales)

The higher a hospitality firm's DOL, the greater the fluctuation in its EBIT as a result of changes in its sales. That is, *ceteris paribus*, a high DOL in a hospitality firm would imply that relatively small changes in its sales would lead to large changes in its operating income. Under adverse conditions, however, a small decrease in the sales of the firm will lead to a large decrease in its operating income as well as its ROE. All else remaining equal, the higher a hospitality firm's operating leverage, the greater the firm's business risk.

References

Brigham, E.F. and Gapenski, L.C. (1993). *Intermediate Financial Management*, 4th edn. Orlando, FL: The Dryden Press.

Weston, J.F. and Brigham, E.F. (1993) *Essentials of Managerial Finance*, 10th edn. Orlando, FL: The Dryden Press.

ATUL SHEEL
UNIVERSITY OF MASSACHUSETTS, USA

Operating ratios

Operating ratios are utilized to evaluate the success of the various departments of a hotel. For example payroll and related expenses tend to be the largest single expense item for the rooms division as well as the largest for the entire hotel.

Dividing the payroll and related expenses of the rooms division by the division's net room revenue yields one of the most frequently analyzed areas of front office, and that is labor cost.

Operating ratios should be compared against proper standards such as budgeted percentages. Any significant difference between actual and budgeted labor cost percentages must be carefully investigated, since payroll and related expenses represent the largest single expense category. In addition, operating ratios are compared against corresponding historical ratios and industry averages.

Another key to operating success in the lodging industry is ratio analysis. Ratio analysis is simply a mathematical expression of a relationship between two numbers. Ratio analysis is useful because it determines the lodging enterprise's ability to meet its short-term obligations; determines the lodging enterprise's ability to generate profits; and it determines the lodging enterprise's ability to meet its long-term obligations. To be useful, a ratio must be compared against some standard, of which there are typically four: comparison with a past period; comparison with an industry average; comparison with a budgeted ratio; and comparison with similar and close competitors. Management should use ratio analysis to monitor operating performance in meeting goals and objectives; to maintain effectiveness and efficiency of operation; and to identify potential problem areas when actual results fall short.

Reference

Stutts, Alan T. (2001) *Hotel and Lodging Management – An Introduction*. New York: John Wiley & Sons.

ALAN T. STUTTS
AMERICAN INTERCONTINENTAL
UNIVERSITY, USA

Operating system

An operating system is a set of software products that jointly control system resources and the multitude of processes which use these resources on a computer system. It may provide scheduling, debugging, input/output control, system accounting, compilation, storage assignment, data management, and related services. Most popular operating systems today, generally, as in hospitality, are Windows for front-end machines and Unix and its derivate Linux for mainframes, while a great many dedicated operating systems exist powering different devices. Operating system software consists of three levels of services: kernel, library, and application-level services. Linked programs that run applications are called processes. These are supported by the kernel, which provides them with needed resources. Operating systems respond to service calls from the processes and interrupts from the devices. The roles of operating systems include hiding details of hardware by creating abstractions, managing resources, and providing a pleasant user interface. Resources enable the execution of fundamental computer functions: storing programs in computer memory, executing instructions, accepting data and presenting results. The execution of various processes in time is managed by the scheduler. The user interface is a part of the operating system that allows users to communicate with it, to perform such tasks as loading programs, accessing files, and accomplishing various other tasks. The three main types of user interfaces include the command-driven, menu-driven, and graphical user interface. An easy-to-use graphical user interface relies on a pointing device such as the electronic mouse to make a selection of accomplished functions.

References

Finkel, R.A. (1996) Operating systems. *ACM Computing Surveys*, 28 (1), 201–203.
Zhou, Z. (2003) *E-Commerce and Information Technology in Hospitality and Tourism*. Clifton Park, NY: Delmar Publishers.

BOZIDAR KLICEK
UNIVERSITY OF ZAGREB, CROATIA

Organization structure and design

If organizations are to successfully implement their chosen strategy, it is essential that they devise an appropriate organization structure and design. The appropriateness of any organization structure and design is dependent upon a number of key factors: the chosen strategy, the nature of the external environment, and the organizational culture.

Structural options include 'the simple structure,' which relies upon personal and direct control and is typically found in small firms, 'the functional structure' (or 'unitary (U) form'), whereby the organization structure is shaped around the primary activities of finance, operations, marketing, and personnel (for example, the typical hotel uses this type of structure – food and beverage, rooms division, personnel and accounts), 'the multidivisional structure' (or 'M-form'), which is essentially the functional form subdivided into divisions based upon (or a combination of) products, markets, geography or processes (hotel groups frequently use this to create separate divisions for individual hotel brands). The most complex organizational structure is the 'matrix structure,' which is essentially a combination of structures such as product and geographical divisions or functional and divisional structures.

In multinational organizations, structural types are primarily driven by the degree of desired global coordination and the degree of local independence and responsiveness. This can range from low coordination and low responsiveness ('international divisions') to high coordination and high responsiveness ('transnational corporations'). The intermediate positions of high coordination/low responsiveness and low coordination/high responsiveness correspond to the structural types 'global product companies' and 'international subsidiaries,' respectively (Bartlett and Ghoshal, 1989). This is an area that proves challenging for international hotel chains that frequently strive to achieve high coordination *and* high responsiveness across their international operations.

Organization design addresses three key elements: the degree of centralization versus devolution; organizational configurations; and resource allocation and control processes. In respect of the first, the focus is essentially upon the role of the corporate center and its relationship with subsidiaries. Goold and Campbell (1987) have

suggested that the options can be arranged along a continuum with high centralization at one end and high devolution at the other. They identified three archetypal approaches that corporate parents might adopt: 'strategic planning,' whereby the center adopts the role of 'master planner' and represents the most centralized solution, 'financial control,' whereby the center adopts the role of essentially a 'shareholder/banker' and is the most devolved solution, and finally, 'strategic control,' whereby the center adopts the role of 'strategic shaper' and this represents a compromise between centralization and devolution. Fundamentally, the question to be answered here is how does the corporate center add value and not just overhead?

Organizational configurations represent an attempt to capture the complexity of organizational design that is avoided by the structural types above. This more detailed approach looks at organizations as consisting of configurations of six building blocks and associated coordinating mechanisms (Mintzberg, 1979). From these elements it is possible to develop six organizational configurations which reflect a particular combination of external (environmental) and internal situational factors confronting the organization. Each will place a particular emphasis upon one of the six building blocks and a particular coordinating mechanism. Overall, configurations provide a more holistic approach to thinking about organizations than is offered by the traditional structural types.

In addition the above factors, organization design needs to address the issue of how resources will be allocated to support the desired outcomes and how organizational performance will be controlled to ensure that the behavior of the organizational members is in line with achievement of these outcomes. With regard to the former, it is essential to identify the necessary critical success factors and to ensure resources are allocated appropriately to support them. In respect of monitoring organizational behavior, this requires the development of an appropriate system of controls. Organizations have three broad types of control available to them: 'administrative control,' which involves systems, rules and procedures; 'social control,' which relies upon the culture of the organization to shape individual behavior; and 'self-control,' whereby individuals have direct responsibility for their own behavior. Organizations such as Marriott and Disney are frequently cited as examples of organizations using strong internal cultures (social control) to influence behavior of employees ('associates' and 'cast,' respectively). Chacko (1998) suggested a 'seamless' organization structure for hotels with only two categories: guest service and internal service. This structure is exposed to create an environment where customer service quality is the organizational driver, allowing hotels to develop service quality as a true competitive advantage.

Furthermore, organizational structure is often reflected in the 'informal' structure that refers to the power, control, influence, and knowledge flow that are not officially recognized by the members of the organization, particularly top management. Personal traits such as leadership and charisma may have an impact on the power some members might have beyond their official job description and position in the organizational hierarchy. Similarly, the growing recognition of the significance of knowledge management may result in 'knowledge or expertise centers' that are not officially recognized as part of the structure, yet may be presented in the aforementioned configurations. Moreover, changes in the importance assigned to specific positions due to environmental changes or to owner preferences often result in the disruption of traditional formal organizational structures. For example, the presumably staff role of the revenue manager in many hotels often deflates the line position of the marketing and sales managers, while leaving the formal structure intact.

Recently, especially as a result of the growing impact of the Internet, a new organizational design emerged: the virtual organization. It is rather a radical form, or a 'no structure' form that eliminates in-house business functions. In the hospitality context, it refers to organizations where numerous functions are outsourced so that there are a series of project groups linked by constantly changing non-hierarchical, cobweb-like networks. The applicability of this concept to the hospitality industry is yet to be thoroughly investigated.

References

Bartlett, C. and Ghoshal, S. (1989) *Managing Across Borders: The Transnational Corporation.* Boston, MA: Harvard Business School Press.

Chacko, E.H. (1998) Designing a Seamless Hotel Organization. *International Journal of Contemporary Hospitality Management*, 10 (4), 133–140.

Goold, M. and Campbell, A. (1987) *Strategies and Styles.* London: Blackwell.

Johnson, G. and Scholes, K. (1999) *Exploring Corporate Strategy*, 5th edn. London: Prentice-Hall.

Minztberg, H. (1979) *The Structuring of Organizations.* Englewood Cliffs, NJ: Prentice-Hall.

J. STEPHEN TAYLOR
UNIVERSITY OF STRATHCLYDE, UK

Organization Timeshare Europe

The Organization Timeshare Europe (OTE) is the official trade body representing the timeshare industry within Europe. Some of Europe's operators also term this sector as 'resort ownership,' 'vacation ownership' or 'holiday ownership.' In principle all these terms refer to timeshare arrangements, but are attempting to find alternatives to the somewhat negative image of timeshare.

The OTE was formed in 1998 as the result of pooling the resources of the various national trade bodies throughout Europe. OTE's purpose is to support the pace and quality of growth of the sector. It promotes best practice across the industry and aims to raise a positive profile of timeshare organizations with customers and communities within which operations take place. The OTE has a major lobbying role with the European Union and undertakes pan-European research for the industry.

The OTE represents members across Europe, North Africa, and the Middle East. Membership includes resort developers, marketing companies, management companies, exchange companies, trustees, finance houses, resale companies and professionals such as law firms and accountants. The OTE Charter identifies objectives and establishes rules for its operation and management. Its code of ethics sets down principles and rules governing sales, marketing, resale, exchange, and points-based timeshare schemes.

The OTE policy is to advocate a balance of state intervention and self-regulation by the industry. It has lobbied European politicians to ensure restrictive legislation is not introduced before self-regulation is given a fair chance.

Reference

http://www.ote-info.com/. Accessed 3 September 2003.

CONRAD LASHLEY
NOTTINGHAM TRENT UNIVERSITY, UK

Organizational culture and climate

The effectiveness and success of an organization is not solely measured by profitability, it can also be measured by the way business is done and how the company is perceived by both its employees and the external community. These processes and formed impressions are functions of organizational culture which may be defined in several ways.

> The organization itself has an invisible quality – a certain style, a character, away are doing things – that may be more powerful than the dictates of any one person or any formal system. To understand the soul of the organization requires that we travel below the charts, rulebooks, machines, and buildings into the underground world of corporate cultures. (Kilmann, 1985, p. 63)

Schein (1985, p. 6) suggests that culture is:

> A pattern of basic assumptions – invented, discovered, or developed by a group as it learns to cope with its problems of external adaptation and internal integration – that has worked well enough to be considered valid, and therefore, to be taught to new members as

the correct way to perceive, think, and feel in relation to those problems.

For our purposes, organizational culture consists of the shared values and assumptions of how its members will behave, or more specifically it can be defined as shared philosophies, ideologies, values, beliefs, assumptions, expectations, attitudes, and norms (Kilmann *et al.*, 1985, p. 5).

It includes the following dimensions:

- *Observed behavioral regularities* when people interact, such as organizational rituals and ceremonies, and the language commonly use
- *The norms* shared by working groups throughout the organization, such as 'Ladies and Gentlemen serving Ladies and Gentlemen', from Ritz–Carlton
- *The dominant values* held by an organization such as 'service quality' or 'price leadership'
- *The philosophy* that guides and organization's policy towards employees and customers
- *The rules* of the game for getting along in the organization, or the 'ropes' that a newcomer must learn in order to become an accepted member
- *The feeling or climate* conveyed in an organization by the physical layout in which its members interact with customers or other outsiders.

Note that no dimension by itself represents the culture of the organization. Taken together, however, they reflect and give meaning to the concept of organizational culture. Top management must define these attitudes, values, and expectations that they want organizational members to share.

Multinational hotel companies will also want the same organizational culture to be reflected across all of their properties worldwide, and so they introduce training schemes and systems that not only ensure uniform quality service across the properties but also shared values and attitudes to work and the company. This culture training is designed to change people's attitudes, not the organization structure. This also assists in moving staff around their properties. Employees know that wherever they are moved within an organization there will not only be shared hard systems (financial control, reservations, etc.) but also shared values and working culture.

However, developing and managing culture in hospitality organizations is difficult. In part this is due to the nature of the industry. For example, most hotels, restaurants, and other destination organizations are small to medium-sized and owned independently. Some argue that management styles range from autocratic to non-supportive. In the former instance, culture will reflect attitudes of the owner/managers. In cases where managers are unsupportive, offer few opportunities for staff development and operate seasonally, an informal staff-driven culture often develops in a less formally structured way. These informal cultures appear in other industries but are particularly common in hospitality. Moreover, specific work groups in hotels (food production and foodservice, or reservations and reception) often have different values, cultures, criteria for rewards and organizational ceremonies and rites.

Salaman (1974) classifies these alternative organizational cultures as occupational communities and defines them as: 'People who are members of the same occupation, who work together, or who have some common form of life together, and are to some extent, separate from the rest of society' (p. 19).

These communities take either a 'cosmopolitan' or 'local' form. The former is where members do the same jobs but in hotels in different geographical areas. Local occupational communities undertake the same work in the same hotel. In either case, informal common cultures emerge which if not understood by managers are almost impossible to manage effectively.

Organizational culture is sometimes measured by organizational climate. Climate is the employee's perception of the atmosphere of the internal environment. Organizational climate is important because the employee's perception of the organization services the basis for the development of their attitudes towards it. Their attitudes in turn affect their behavior. Climate is concerned with the entire organization and all major subunits within it.

Morale is an important part of organizational climate. Morale is a state of mind based on attitudes and satisfaction with the organization and can be affected by:

- *Structure* – the degree of constraint on members, that is, the number of rules, regulations, and procedures
- *Responsibility* – the degree of control over one's own job
- *Rewards* – the degree of being rewarded for one's efforts and being punished appropriately
- *Warmth* – the degree of satisfaction with human relations
- *Support* – the degree of being helped by others and cooperation
- *Organizational identity and loyalty* – the degree to which employees identify with the organization and their loyalty to it
- *Risk* – the degree to which risk-taking is encouraged.

Organizational culture and climate are different, but related. *Climate* is a sharing of perceptions of the intangibles of the internal or real environment of the occupational community (i.e. both the small workgroup, such as chefs, and the larger workgroup, as in all the employees of the hotel), while *culture* is the values and assumptions of the ideal environment that management hopes will be instilled into all employees. Thus culture informs climate.

References

Kilmann, R.H. (1985) Corporate culture. *Psychology Today*, 11 (4), 62–68.

Kilmann, R.H., Saxton, M.J., and Serpa, R. (1985) *Gaining Control of the Corporate Culture*. San Francisco: Jossey-Bass.

Salaman, G. (1974) *Community and Occupation*. Cambridge: Cambridge University Press.

Schein, E.H. (1985) *Organizational Culture and Leadership*. San Francisco: Jossey-Bass.

PAUL REYNOLDS
UNIVERSITY OF SOUTH AUSTRALIA,
AUSTRALIA

Organizational structures, types of

Bartol, Martin, Tein, and Matthews (2001, p. 267) define organizational structure and design as 'The formal pattern of interactions and coordination that managers design to link the tasks of individuals and groups to achieve organizational goals.' Structure is important in organizations because it reduces ambiguity and clarifies task and role expectations. It also has an undeniable impact on the attitudes and behavior of organizational members and thus productivity.

The structure of individual firms varies; some are simple with only a few levels of hierarchy. These are commonly known as 'flat' organizations. Others are more complex and have a 'taller' structure with many hierarchical levels. Additionally, some hybrid organizations display characteristics of both extremes.

Flat structures are also sometimes known as 'organic' and are said to have improved communication, imperceptible chain of command, and extensive delegation of responsibility. These organizations often perform better in dynamic business environments because they respond quickly to these trading shifts. The hospitality industry tends to be dominated by this type of small to medium-sized organization.

On the other hand, larger, taller organizations have the opposite characteristics. This type is also known as a 'mechanistic' structure. The chain of command is clear, managerial decision-making tends to be slower and there is limited employee empowerment (or delegation of responsibility). These organizational types are also less likely to be as responsive to the environment as the former type. Nonetheless, they still feature strongly in the hospitality industry. For example, 'chain' hotels with 150 or more bedrooms (Novotel, Carlton Crest, Hilton, and so on) are of the highly structured type.

The structure and design of hospitality organizations is a response to four contingencies. The first is its external environment that typically includes customers, pressure groups, suppliers, competitors, government, and so on. These elements combine to produce a particular type of trading environment which is increasingly becoming difficult to predict. In fact, it is the sum of these factors which compromises the effectiveness of hospitality organization structure.

The second contingency is technology or the way the organization transforms its inputs into outputs. In the hospitality industry, there is a composite product of goods and services. The means of goods and service provision in each organization is broadly similar but differences exist. Woodward (1958) refers to these differences as the degree of routineness of production where the process appears on a continuum of unit and small batch (all frontline exchanges with customers); large and mass batch (table d'hôte items for catering functions and large events); and continuous (no true examples in the hospitality industry, however, fast food and centralized cook – chill and cook – freeze operations come close).

Contingency factor three is organizational size. There are a number of negative outcomes associated with large structures with many hierarchical levels. Interestingly, Shamir (1975) comments that as the hierarchy and complexity of hotels increases, formal communication becomes impoverished and employees have to instead rely on informal methods of communication to operate effectively. Currently across many organizational sectors even large organizations are downsizing to smaller, flatter structures. This, in part, is because of retrenchment but also an acknowledgement that simple structures are more flexible and are quick to respond to environmental dynamics.

The fourth factor is where structures are designed to match strategy. Organizational strategies vary but for simplicity's sake may categorized as 'innovation' (emphasizes introduction of major new products and services, e.g. Virgin Blue, Australia and Formule 1, France); cost-minimization (tight cost controls and avoidance of unnecessary innovation or marketing expenses, e.g. Novotel, UK and Motel 6, USA); and 'imitation' (movement into new areas only after viability has been proven, e.g. Alton Towers Theme Park, UK, Warner Brothers Theme Park, Australia and any number of franchise operations). Clearly many of these examples could appear in more than one category.

In addition to these four contingencies, there are several other design fundamentals impacting on efficiency and effectiveness. The theoretical structure of hospitality organizations is underpinned by work specialization (complexity or simplicity of tasks undertaken in a job), division of work/departmentalization (a common grouping based on the major purpose or function), chain of command and span of control which are based on authority and the number of employees that can be effectively supervised by one person. This number is said to vary depending on several variables including the nature of the organization and product, complexity of the work, and personal qualities of managers; it is therefore an inexact science.

As organizations grow in size there exists an increasing potential for inefficiency and ineffectiveness. Communication may become unclear, with corresponding sluggish response rates and the chance of increased competition between departments (i.e. sub-optimization). An organizational design said to ameliorate these problems is known as a 'matrix' structure. Simply, a set of divisional horizontal reporting relationships are imposed onto a hierarchical functional structure or where functional departments are combined with units that integrate activities of different functional departments on a project or product basis. Whilst this structure is said to have some theoretical strengths, several disadvantages include high administrative costs, role ambiguity, and an overemphasis on group decision-making.

Most basic structural design principles are communicated via an organization chart, including details of departmentalization, activity groupings, relationships, and authority. The formal relationships between different areas and members are known as 'line' and 'staff' (there are other classifications). Mullins (1996) considers the former as the downward vertical flow of authority from directors to managers, supervisors, and operatives. He considers staff (or function) to be the relationship between specialists and advisers (having no line authority) with managers and operatives, e.g. personnel manager.

The actual detail of information depends on the hospitality organization's requirements. However, these charts only show structure at one particular point in time and may often be misleading. Despite this they remain popular because they are easy to understand and provide a seemingly accurate picture of the organization. According to Lashley and Lee-Ross (2003), the way in which employees interpret jobs, operationalize tasks, and work within formal structures is the 'real' organizational structure.

References

Bartol, K., Martin, D., Tein, M., and Matthews, G. (2001) *Management: A Pacific Rim Focus*, 3rd edn. Sydney: McGraw-Hill.

Lashley, C. and Lee-Ross, D. (2003) *Organization Behaviour for Leisure Services*. Oxford: Butterworth-Heinemann.

Mullins, L. (1996) *Management and Organizational Behaviour*, 4th edn. London: Pitman.

Shamir, B. (1975) *A Study of Working Environments and Attitudes to Work of Employees in a Number of British Hotels*. PhD thesis, London School of Economics.

Woodward, J. (1958) *Management and Technology*. London: HMSO.

DARREN LEE-ROSS
JAMES COOK UNIVERSITY, AUSTRALIA

OSHA (occupational safety and health administration) [USA]

The Occupational Safety and Health Act, Code of Federal Regulations (CFR) 29 part 1900, was passed into law by the United States federal government in 1970. Its purpose is to promote worker safety and health in the United States by regulating workplace conditions and training requirements. The Act includes numerous regulations that employers and employees are required to follow. The majority of the industrialized countries have their own national organizations that have similar missions and objectives as the US OHSA.

The federal program instituted the formation of the OSHA (Occupational Safety and Health Administration), which is charged with overseeing employer compliance to current OSHA regulations, the issuance of citations for employer failures to comply, monitoring the occurrence of workplace accidents for the purpose of identifying opportunities for new regulations, and providing advice, guidance, and training for employers on how to provide a safe work environment.

Federal OSHA allows individual states to implement and maintain their own OSHA program providing that the state's program standards are as stringent as the federal program.

OSHA enforces its standards through a program of compliance officer inspections. These officers will visit an employer for one of the three following reasons:

- Accidents involving fatalities or the hospitalization of three or more employees
- Employee complaints about workplace conditions
- An ongoing program of inspecting various industries.

References

Ellis, Raymond C. (1998) *A Guide to Occupational Safety and Health Standards Compliance for the Lodging Industry*. Lansing, MI: Educational Institute of the American Hotel and Motel Association.
http://www.osha.gov.

JERRY LACHAPPELLE
HARRAH'S ENTERTAINMENT, INC., USA

Outsourcing ICT services

Outsourcing takes place when a business appoints a third party to carry out functions that were previously performed within the firm. Hospitality organizations often outsource their legal, finance, and marketing functions as well as use a certain degree of outsourcing for housekeeping, catering,

and procurement. This allows them to fluctuate resources according to demand and to hire skills for as long as they are required. Outsourcing allows the firm to build skills quickly, often to catch up or overtake the competition. In an increasingly competitive environment, outsourcing information communication technology (ICT) services can be a way of reducing costs, avoiding the risk of investing in ICT skills that may become obsolete over time, strengthening areas of weakness, and allowing firms to concentrate on their core competence. This may include a website development and hosting or even assigning the entire ICT function to a specialist company.

Application service providers (ASPs) for example deliver hospitality software applications through remote data and processing centers, in a rental or lease arrangement. These applications may include property management, reservation or customer relationship management systems. Hitherto, the adoption of ASPs has been limited. Outsourcing and ASPs can be key enablers for the hoteliers of the future.

References

McFarlan, F.W. and Nolan R.L. (1995) How to manage an IT outsourcing alliance. *Sloan Management Review*, Winter, pp. 9–23.
Paraskevas, A. and Buhalis, D. (2002) Outsourcing IT for small hotels: the opportunities and challenges of using application service providers. *Cornell Hotel and Restaurant Administration Quarterly*, 43 (2), pp. 27–39.

DIMITRIUS BUHALIS
UNIVERSITY OF SURREY, UK
RUTH OWEN
UNIVERSITY OF SURREY, UK

Outsourcing of business services

Outsourcing is basically getting another party to carry out a business process instead of doing that process in-house. The boundaries are blurred between outsourcing, subcontracting, working with a partner, even with simply purchasing. The principal distinction is that outsourcing implies transfer of ownership of that process.

The hotel industry makes great use of outsourcing on the supply side – hotel management companies depend on the willingness of hotel owners to outsource the management of their hotels to them. Traditionally, less use was made on the demand side – hotel management often prided itself on self-sufficiency, with quality being judged by number of staff per guest. This extended to both hotel management companies and to individual properties, although functions such as sales activities in foreign locations have long been outsourced to sales agents. More recently, however, outsourcing of business processes such as laundry services, security services, and limousine services has become more common.

Hospitality industry outsourcing decisions tend to be made simply as the choice to have an outside party carry out a business process because it is less expensive than doing it in-house. But as the decision to outsource becomes a more strategic one, that choice will be more to do with changing the question from 'what can we do cheaper than buy' or even 'what can we learn to do, so we don't have to buy it' to 'what matters to the customer – do that better than anyone else.' So with the growing trend for organizations to seek to maximize profits by focusing on providing those things customers find so important that they will pay a premium for them, the hospitality industry can be expected to expand those business processes it outsources from those it thinks are not its core activity to those its customers think are not its core activity.

A number of facilities services are commonly outsourced. These include landscape care, snow removal, window cleaning, pest control, elevator maintenance, and many capital project activities. Some reasons for outsourcing of these services involve cost, equipment, special skills, and licensing.

Successful outsourcing has been found to be more about managing the ongoing relationship rather than doing the initial deal.

References

Bendor-Samuel, Peter (2000) *Turning Lead into Gold*. Provo, UT: Executive Excellence Publishing.

Stipanuk, D. (2002) *Hospitality Facilities Management and Design*, 2nd edn. Lansing, MI: Educational Institute of American Hotel and Lodging Association, pp. 50–52.

ROBERT ALLENDER
ENERGY RESOURCES MANAGEMENT,
HONG KONG SAR, CHINA

Outsourcing of foodservice

Using modern business models, outsourcing stems from a resource-based view of organizations. Resource-based theorists argue that, when a service or organizational function delivers no measurable value (such as profit) but is necessary to an operation, it should be outsourced to reduce the drain on resources better allocated to profit-producing endeavors. Using the example of outsourced foodservice in factories, this makes sense: If someone else can feed a company's employees better or more efficiently than the company can, alternatives must be explored.

Outsourcing of foodservice has spawned a host of managed-services companies (also known as contract-management companies or contract feeders). Such companies manage food and related services in a multi-unit environment by relying on a trade name. Using brand management to spur growth, these companies differentiate themselves by devising proprietary systems and approaches tailored to those on-site segments they service. The similarities extend to the human resources component; employees comprise their primary asset. Indeed, managed-services companies differ from their chain brethren in maintaining few physical assets – their people are, ultimately, what they bring to the table.

Most companies in business and industry settings outsource their foodservice to managed-services companies. Similarly, more than half of all US colleges and universities already outsource foodservice. This trend toward outsourcing services that fall outside of a company's core competency is also creating opportunities for companies traditionally known as foodservice providers to offer other hospitality-related services.

Reference

Penrose, E. (1959) *The Theory and Growth of the Firm*. New York: John Wiley & Sons.

DENNIS REYNOLDS
WASHINGTON STATE UNIVERSITY, USA

Overbooking

This refers to a situation where the hotel has accepted more reservations than there are rooms available. Hotels practice overbooking to overcome the changeable number of arrivals that may occur on any given day due to no-shows, cancellations, and understays. One of the front desk goals is to achieve as high an occupancy rate as possible and practicing overbooking is a way to try to achieve this. Care has to be taken however, to make sure that you do not end up having to turn away ('walk') a guest, as this creates poor guest relations and is not good for repeat business.

The concept of overbooking is viewed with skepticism. However, US courts seem to agree that in many instances, overbooking to overcome the problem of no-shows and late cancellations may produce advantages by way of operating efficiencies that far outweigh the occasional inconveniences to guests and travelers. Courts have held hotel overbooking to be customary and justifiable practice for offsetting the losses from no-shows. The financial loss due to no-shows can be substantial. In a hotel that typically has 100 confirmed reservations (not guaranteed with a credit card) and experiences a 5% no-show rate, five rooms per night would remain unsold. With an average room rate of $70, these five rooms would cost the hotel $350 in revenue. Over a year, this would amount to $127,750. Lost revenues of this volume virtually force the hotelier to develop an aggressive occupancy management policy to manage no-shows.

References

Abbott, P. and Lewry, S. (1991) *Front Office Procedures, Social Skills and Management*. Oxford: Butterworth-Heinemann.

Bardi, James (2003) *Hotel Front Office Management*, 3rd edn. New York: John Wiley & Sons.

Kasavana, M.L. and Brooks, R.M. (1995) *Front Office Procedures*, 4th edn. Lansing, MI: Educational Institute of the American Hotel and Motel Association.

Renner, P. (1994) *Basic Hotel Front Office Procedures*, 3rd edn. New York: Van Nostrand Reinhold.

IRENE SWEENEY
INTERNATIONAL HOTEL MANAGEMENT
INSTITUTE SWITZERLAND,
SWITZERLAND

Overstay

This refers to guests who stay in the hotel beyond the date of departure that they had originally indicated. Overstays need to be carefully monitored by the front desk as the rooms may be pre-blocked for other expected guests. A way of trying to avoid this problem is by verifying at check-in when is the actual departure date of the guest. In the modern hotel it is not uncommon for the guest to initial the departure date on the registration paperwork to confirm the number of nights for which the lodging is required. Minimizing this is critical when a hotel in near full occupancy, however, overstays can represent extra revenue for the hotel when it is not operating at full occupancy.

In recent years, electronic locking systems on guestroom doors have replaced the traditional lock and key system, reducing the security problems associated with lost or unreturned keys. However, in addition they provide the front office with another tool to prevent overstays in that the key can be programmed with the number of nights the guest has access to the room and upon reaching that date the key no longer provides access and requires that the guest make contact with the front desk to clarify any requirements for additional lodging.

Reference

Kasavana, M.L. and Brooks, R.M. (1995) *Front Office Procedures*, 4th edn. Lansing, MI: Educational Institute of the American Hotel and Motel Association.

IRENE SWEENEY
INTERNATIONAL HOTEL MANAGEMENT
INSTITUTE SWITZERLAND, SWITZERLAND

P

Pay and benefits

Pay is simply the consideration arising from a contract of employment (as opposed to a contract for services associated with subcontracting) to give somebody a particular amount of money for work done for goods or services provided. Benefits are similarly defined as a regular payment made to somebody qualified to receive it. Total pay and benefits are also known collectively as a 'remuneration package' and this includes wage and non-wage payments such as bonuses and fringe benefits such as heath insurance, pension fund, sickness benefits etc.

Both definitions are understandably similar and draw attention to a number of key issues. First, there is a suggestion of equity or a fair exchange of something for something else with each outcome having benefit for both parties (money and goods and services provided); second, a notion of 'worth' attached to qualifications. With some imagination these fundamentals may be extrapolated into issues of pay structure linked to jobs and pay levels in organizations. De Cieri and Kramar (2003, p. 426) provide adequate summaries of these terms:

> [Pay structure is] the relative pay of different jobs and how much they are paid (pay level) . . . [Job structure is] the relative pay of jobs in an organization.

Overall, employees may be paid either a bi-weekly or monthly salary or a weekly wage (the latter is more common in the hospitality industry). The actual payment is a function of several factors, the two most important being the structure of the job itself and the capabilities of the individual (reflected by previous experience, competencies, and qualifications). However, to make the process equitable and easier to manage for the employer, the establishment of organizational pay policies mainly focuses on job structures. This is an effective way of standardizing treatment of workers employed in similar jobs. In many instances, employers have combined several bands or grades of jobs into fewer simpler categories; this is known as 'broad banding.' For example, in the hospitality industry most front-line workers employed at the same level receive a similar wage because jobs have been reclassified using a broad banding approach, for example, food and beverage attendants and bartenders occupy the same band.

Market and job evaluations

Employers, particularly in the hospitality industry, often make pay level and job structure decisions based on 'market pay surveys' and job evaluations. The former is based on a comparison with the going rate of pay for similar jobs in other organizations. Levine (1992) argues that external comparison is the most important way to set satisfactory levels of pay. Moreover, De Cieri and Kramar (2003) consider that this external benchmarking with other companies lessens typical problems of employee inflexibility and status consciousness associated with other approaches.

The job evaluation method of establishing pay levels is an administrative procedure used to measure job worth via 'compensable factors.' The process allows judgments to be made about pay levels of different jobs in the same organization through the use of pay grades. Potentially, these approaches allow equitable pay setting decisions to be made through inter-organizational comparisons. Indeed, employees will certainly contrast pay levels of similar jobs. Evaluations will have a positive or negative impact on worker attitudes depending whether levels are higher or lower than they expected. This matching and judging process is linked with equity theory (Adams, 1963), which in this context considers that if employees perceive that the balance between the effort that they put in to work and what they are paid is unfair, they may deliberately reduce their effort. This theory also underpins the self-explanatory terms of effort–reward bargain' and the 'felt fair principle.'

Equity in terms of wage transparency is particularly pertinent because recent changes of employment laws in many industrialized countries have instigated a shift from centralized wage fixing to bargaining at an enterprise level (see Mitchell *et al.*, 1997). In the hospitality industry, individual 'contract-making' with employees is common. This effectively does away with transparency in wage-setting advocated in equity theory. Against the advice of Adams (1993), and much wage-setting legislation (pre-1990s in Australia), opaque individual employment contracts are becoming increasingly favored whereby employers strike customized pay deals with single employees.

Minimum wage

More positively, the existence of a legal minimum wage set by statute or labor tribunal determinations attempts to protect employees from falling below the 'poverty line' in many developed economies. Similar is true of the Australian legal 'Awards' system. However, an appropriate level for each is largely a matter of political opinion. Interestingly despite these 'safety nets,' hospitality employees remain some of the lowest paid workers internationally. Employers usually justify low wages by citing high fixed costs and

a high ratio of labor to total costs (because of the labor-intense nature of the industry). In some cases this is justified as they can account for around 50% of total costs, particularly in 'luxury' enterprises. Some managers also consider that many of their workers are more than recompensed for their efforts by additional income provided through customer tipping.

Tipping, rewards, and other discretionary benefits

Tips are a small gratuity which may be given by a hotel customer in addition to the set charge (usually 10–15%) in recognition of satisfactory service, and is generally more common in close customer contact jobs such as waiting, bar, portering, and front office, as consideration for service quality. A contentious issue is whether tips should be treated as income and taxed as wages. There are variations across countries in the practice of paying tips.

Another alleged benefit system specific to hotel employees is known as the 'Total Rewards System' (TRS). Its existence in reality is debatable but Mars and Nicod (1984) insist that hotel employees are rewarded in both an official and an unofficial manner. The former exists of wages and tips whereas unofficial benefits take the forms of 'fiddles' and 'knock-offs' (financial and non-financial). Whilst the TRS may be classified as a benefit, less clandestinely, fringe or non-financial benefits refers to non-salary, wages or other cash remuneration, but additional benefits that employers offer above and beyond those in the contract of employment to induce employees to stay. Such benefits usually apply more frequently to salaried employees, covering such matters as car allowance, or cars, travel, telephone allowances etc., including subsidized meals as in the case of hotels.

As can be appreciated, management discretion plays a significant part in setting pay levels. For example, with the optional system of profit-related pay or performance-related pay, employers distribute a proportion of surplus (or profit) to employees in recognition of achieving certain output or sales-related targets. Profit pay is usually distributed annually after deductions of costs. These methods are also referred to as merit pay or bonus payments. Another scheme is known as profit sharing, whereby employees receive a share of net profits after achieving certain output or sales targets at an enterprise. There are many different schemes of this nature and they may take the form of a bonus payment or distribution of shares in the form of employee stock ownership. These are often labeled 'common interest schemes' in that they seek to bring employers and employees closer together.

References

Adams, J. (1963) Toward an understanding of inequity. *Journal of Abnormal and Social Psychology*, 67, 422–436.

De Cieri, H. and Kramar, R. (2003) *Human Resource Management in Australia: Strategy, People, Performance*. Sydney: McGraw-Hill.

Levine, H. (1992) The view from the board: the state of compensation and benefits today. *Compensation and Benefits Review*, 24.

Mars, G. and Nicod, M. (1984) *The World of Waiters*. London: Allen and Unwin.

Mitchell, R., Naughton, R., and Sorensen, R. (1997) The law and employee participation – evidence from the Federal Enterprise Agreements Process. *Journal of Industrial Relations*, 39 (2), 196–217.

Woods, R.H. (2002) *Managing Hospitality Human Resources*, 3rd edn. Lansing, MI: Educational Instutute of the American Hotel and Lodging Association.

NILS TIMO
GRIFFITH UNIVERSITY, AUSTRALIA

PBX

PBX is an abbreviation for private branch exchange. Historically, telephone systems in a hotel were manual and required all outgoing calls to be made by a hotel operator. As hotel telephone technology has advanced dial systems have been introduced, in which guests could dial their own calls. The role of the hotel operator, sometimes referred to as the PBX manager, is now almost entirely limited to servicing incoming calls and: assisting guests to answer incoming calls; directing calls to guestrooms, staff or departments of the hotel; providing information about guest services to guests; answering questions about hotel events and activities; providing paging services for hotel guests and employees; knowing what action to take when an emergency call is requested or received; and monitoring automated systems including fire alarms and telephone equipment when the engineering and maintenance department is closed.

A PBX is a telephone system within an enterprise that switches calls between enterprise users on local lines while allowing all users to share a certain number of external phone lines. The main purpose of a PBX is to save the cost of requiring a line to the telephone company's central office for each user.

The PBX is owned and operated by the enterprise rather than the telephone company (which may be a supplier or service provider). Private branch exchanges used analog technology originally. Today, PBXs use digital technology (digital signals are converted to analog for outside calls on the local loop using the standard telephone service). A PBX includes: telephone trunk (multiple phone) lines that terminate at the PBX; a computer with memory that manages the switching of the calls within the PBX and in and out of it; the network of lines within the PBX; and usually a console or switchboard for a human operator.

Reference

Stutts, Alan T. (2001) *Hotel and Lodging Management – An Introduction*. New York: John Wiley & Sons.

ALAN T. STUTTS
AMERICAN INTERCONTINENTAL
UNIVERSITY, USA

Perceived risk

As part of the decision-making process in purchasing a product customers will consider the perceived risk of the transaction. Perceived risk is classified into four categories:

- Financial
- Performance
- Physical
- Social/psychological.

Once customers realize that they need a product or service, they seek out information on the item or service that will fulfill their desire. Before purchasing the product, the customer will often consider the risk or likelihood of any negative impact that buying the product will produce and compare this to the benefit expected. Perceived risk is the extent of possible consequences versus uncertainty or likelihood that it will occur. Generally, effective marketing and advertising can reduce the perceived risk and uncertainty of a customer. However, a customer will perceive or believe what they will based upon many other factors, including sociological and psychological reasons. Ultimately, if the customer feels the perceived risk is too high, they will seek out alternative selections or simply not purchase the product or service. It is a crucial task in marketing to attempt to understand the customer's perceptions and attitudes and endeavor to lower the customer's perceived risk. Often the perceived risk is greater when it comes to purchasing a service rather than a product due to the intangible characteristics of a service.

References

Lewis, Robert C. and Chambers, Richard E. (2000) *Marketing Leadership in Hospitality Foundations and Practices*, 3rd edn. New York: John Wiley & Sons.

Zeithaml, Valerie A. and Bitner, Mary Jo. (2003) *Services Marketing Integrating Customer Focus Across the Firm*, 3rd edn. New York: McGraw-Hill Companies.

STEVE SASSO
UNIVERSITY OF MASSACHUSETTS, USA

Perceptual mapping

An easy way to illustrate how competing products are rated, relative to each other, is by generating a perceptual map, using multi-dimensional scaling (MDS) techniques. This technique is most appropriately used for two types of research questions. First, MDS and perceptual mapping can help us identify previously unrecognized issues or attributes of a product or service that lead to customer behaviors. Second, MDS and perceptual mapping can help us compare how our product performs against our competitors' products. It can also help us to identify which combination of features and/or benefits are most preferred by our customers. The end result of the analysis – the perceptual map – provides a graphic illustration of how the competitors or options compare against each other. The technique is often used in marketing to understand how our product is positioned against the competition. It is particularly useful if we wish to reposition our product to a new target market.

The first step in creating a perceptual map is to obtain customer's ratings of a variety of products (or services), or a variety of features that are available for a single product. The questions ask respondents to compare products or attributes against each other. For example, if we are looking at a single product that comes in several different colors, we would ask respondents questions such as 'which color do you prefer, red or green,' 'is the red one more similar to the orange one or the purple one,' or 'using a 10-point scale, please indicate how similar the red one is to the blue one.' A hospitality example might ask how various hotels compare on attributes such as convenient location, friendly service, overall value, or interior décor.

The data gleaned from the ratings questions are then used in a process called multi-dimensional scaling (MDS). The MDS process uses Euclidean geometry to determine each product's distance on a geometric plane from the other options under consideration. Several algorithms exist that are used to perform MDS. The algorithms 'work' by taking the 'distance' between the products or attributes – created from the differences in mean scores between the competing products on the attributes – and constructing a set of coordinates that accurately represents these distances. These coordinates are then used to plot the competing products in perceptual space (Shoemaker, 1996).

One result could be a ranking of the product against the others on a basis of 'this option is most similar to our product' through 'this product is least similar to ours.' This allows us to gain an understanding of what our true competition is, or what our customers' true preferences are.

The perceptual maps are then developed to graphically illustrate the relationship between all of the rated products. The perceptual map shows, in a two-dimensional or three-dimensional space, where the product falls, relative to all of the alternatives under consideration.

Generally speaking, there are two methods of interpretation of an MDS perceptual map. The first is subjective in nature. For example, we might look at how a group of casino hotels in Las Vegas rate against each other. Here, one looks at the distance between casinos. The closer the casinos are to each other on the perceptual map, the more they are perceived to be similar. Conversely, the further apart they are, the more dissimilar. We might find that the Station Casinos in Las Vegas are considered most similar to each other. Similarly, properties such as the Las Vegas Hilton, MGM Grand, and Luxor could be perceived to be alike.

Perceptual mapping in this instance is used to consider the properties of the casinos occupying extreme positions in the derived space and then to attempt to identify possible attributes that explain the relative positions. Using the Las Vegas casino hotel example, we might find that the casinos appearing at the top of the 'y' axis represent properties that are more geared to tourists, while casinos at the bottom of the 'y' axis are more geared to the 'locals' market. Another interpretation may be casinos on the bottom are more 'downscale', while casinos on the top are more 'upscale'. Again, interpretation of perceptual maps is subjective in nature.

The second method of interpretation of perceptual maps is termed 'property fitting.' Continuing with our Las Vegas hotel casino example, the property fitting places the attributes that the respondents used to rate the different casinos in the *same* perceptual space as the casinos, to aid in interpretation of the casinos' positioning. The attributes are placed in the same perceptual space using multiple regression

techniques. Essentially, the mean, or average, rating of each of the measured attributes is taken individually and regressed on the derived space coordinates (from the algorithm used to generate the perceptual map). One important by-product of the regressions, besides the R^2, which shows how important each variable is in defining the perceptual space, is the beta weights generated by the regression. There is one beta weight generated for each stimulus point. These beta weights are used to calculate the coordinates for the attribute vector.

The positioning of the rated casinos along with the vectors derived via property fitting is then often drawn manually on the map. Vectors are simply lines that are drawn through the 'ideal point' for a combination of factors under study, from the origin on the map. The 'ideal point' does not always mean that this is a perfect combination of attributes – it only means that this is the overall preference for the group of respondents rating the attributes or products. Each vector is a line that passes through an ideal point and the graph's origin.

Once the ideal points are established, a perpendicular line from the hotel to each vector shows the influence of these attribute vectors on the placement of the hotels. While the vectors are shown pointing only in the positive direction, it is useful to remember that they continue in the negative direction as well. Using our casino example, a casino on the negative side of the line is thought to have less of that particular attribute, while casinos on the positive side of the line are thought to have more of a particular attribute.

Once a business manager obtains the perceptual maps and has fitted the properties under study onto the map, the map may be used to determine how far away the current product is from meeting the ideal combination, as specified by the survey respondents. If the goal of the analysis is to look at repositioning a property or product, the manager would look at the placement of his or her property with relation to each vector to see how far away their property rates from the ideal. The manager might also look at products or properties against which he or she wishes to compete. The manager would determine the types of attributes (or lack of attributes)

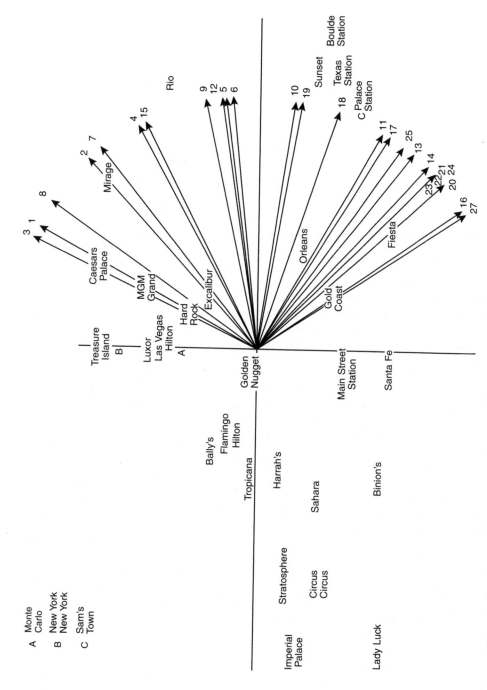

Figure 1 Sample perceptual map using customer perceptions of Las Vegas casinos. The arrows are vectors showing distance from the origin

that the competition has so the property can be redesigned to more closely resemble the desired competitive set.

References

Hair, J.A., Anderson, R.E., Tatham, R.L., and Black, W.C. (1998) *Multivariate Data Analysis*, 5th edn. Upper Saddle River, NJ: Prentice-Hall.

Shoemaker, S. (1996) Hotel positioning: an illustration. In Richard Kotas *et al.* (ed.), *The International Hospitality Business*. New York: John Wiley & Sons, pp. 339–350.

DINA MARIE V. ZEMKE
UNIVERSITY OF NEW HAMPSHIRE, USA

Performance evaluation

Performance evaluation is the process by which employees receive formal feedback on their job performance. Conducted by the employee's immediate supervisor, the evaluation is typically held within the first three to six months of employment (particularly if a probationary period has been established), and thereafter on an annual basis. Performance criteria, on which the evaluation is ideally based, are often included as part of the employee's job description or communicated as part of the employee's initial orientation. Such criteria can include both outcome measures (e.g., sales, costs, customer satisfaction ratings) and process measures (e.g., effective team player). Many organizations translate performance criteria into a standard evaluation instrument, which requires the supervisor to indicate on a scale of 1 to 5 the extent to which the employee's performance has been satisfactory. In completing this form, the supervisor may rely on his or her own observations, solicit input from others with whom the employee interacts (e.g., peers, subordinates, customers), and/or draw on operational data. Employees may also be asked to evaluate their own performance and discuss how their perceptions compare to those of their supervisor. Such discussions provide the opportunity to clarify expectations, correct misconceptions, explore barriers to successful performance, and develop a plan for continuous improvement. Performance evaluation results are ideally tied to training and development and career and succession planning decisions.

Reference

Armstrong, M. (2001) *A Handbook of Personnel Management Practice*, 8th edn. London and Milford, CT: Kogan Page.

JULIA CHRISTENSEN HUGHES
UNIVERSITY OF GUELPH, CANADA

Performance indicators

Performance indicators in the hospitality industry measure the efficiency and effectiveness of an employee's work. Managers and employees at all levels in the hospitality industry should have a clear view of work-related objectives/goals. These objectives/goals are assessed and wherever possible measured as outputs or performance using performance indicators as a tool for appraisal. Performance reviews, assessments, evaluations, ratings, and appraisals are all terms that refer to the task of assessing the progress of a workforce (Tanke, 2001). Performance indicators serve similar purpose. According to Tanke (2001), there are many purposes for the appraisal process, for example:

- To assess the quality of job performance
- To provide feedback to employees regarding job performance
- To plan future performance goals and objectives
- To establish a better knowledge of the employee so as to understand what motivates him or her.

Davidson and Griffin (2000) consider that performance behaviors are the total set of work-related behaviors that the organization expects the individual to display. Performance indicators seek to establish objective measures against which such behaviors may be assessed.

References

Tanke, M.L. (2001) *Human Resource Management for the Hospitality Industry*, 2nd edn. Melbourne: Delmar Thomson Learning.

Davidson, P. and Griffin, R.W. (2000) *Management – Australia in a Global Context*. Brisbane: John Wiley & Sons.

ASAD MOHSIN
UNIVERSITY OF WAIKATO, NEW ZEALAND

Performance measurement

The term 'performance measurement' has been in existence for a considerable time as an important component of the decision-making process. Performance measurement is utilized for different reasons: to monitor activities in business units and through time, for diagnosing problems and taking corrective action, to facilitate continuous improvement in key areas and to promote behavior in ways that would help sustain competitive advantage. Overall, performance measurement is considered to be an integral part of the management processes to identify the poor performing areas or opportunities so that better plans can be developed.

Traditionally, performance measures were mainly financial and they 'provide quantitative and common yardsticks to evaluate achievement relative to a plan or to compare parts of the company' (Emmanuel *et al.*, 1990, p. 222). Profit, return on investment, residual income figures, and their ratios are the most commonly used indicators both in manufacturing and hospitality industries. Additionally, budgetary data, in particular the comparison of budgeted and actual results, are recognized as forming the basis for evaluating overall performance, helping control future operations, and providing incentives for motivating the staff.

Although financial indicators are the generally accepted performance measures, there has been increasing recognition that implementation of financial performance measures on their own provides a limited perspective on the performance of a company. The problems associated with financial measures are the short-termism, lack of balance, past performance information relative to ongoing operations, and that results, rather than managerial efforts, are reflected. Thus, it is argued that financial measures can provide better performance information when used in conjunction with non-financial measures.

In recent years, several performance measurement approaches have been developed in order to satisfy the changing emphasis from financial measures, including the Tableau de Bord (Lebas, 1994), Balanced Scorecard (Kaplan and Norton, 1992), and the Results and Determinant Matrix (Fitzgerald *et al.*, 1991).

The Tableau de Bord is an important management control system that has been used in French enterprises for more than 45 years. Tableau de Bord literally means 'dashboard' or 'instrument panel' and was developed to monitor the progress of the business and, where necessary, take corrective action. The approach entails three-dimensional communication between managers, peers, and subordinates and is described as being 'nested' because of the high interaction between different levels of responsibility. The main objective is to give managers certain key parameters to support their decision-making. It does not give a major importance to accounting-based information and it is equally important to use operational indicators with the financial indicators. Additionally, the reporting frequency is not limited to a specific accounting cycle; information is provided as per decision-makers' requirements.

The Balanced Scorecard is a performance measurement system, devised to provide a set of measures that gives managers a fast, but comprehensive view of their business. The approach incorporates four main perspectives (Figure 1), of which 'financial measures' are the results of actions taken and the operational measures of 'customers,' 'internal business processes', and the organization's 'learning and growth' are the drivers of future financial performance.

The Balanced Scorecard puts strategy and vision at the center so that the measures are designed to pull people toward the overall vision, rather than the more traditional focus on control. It is a tool for managers to ensure that all levels of the organization understand the long-term strategy and that objectives at different levels are aligned with it. It emphasizes that financial and non-financial measures must be part of the information system at all levels of the organization. The approach enables companies to integrate

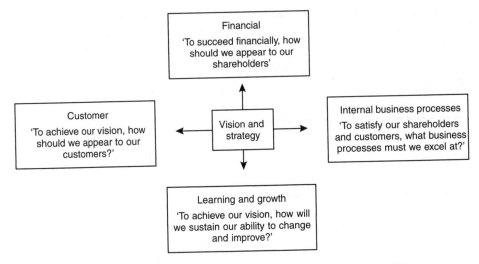

Figure 1   The Balanced Scorecard (adapted from Kaplan and Norton, 1996)

Dimensions	Types of Measure
R Competitiveness	Relative market share and position
E	Sales growth
S	Measures of the customer base
U	
L Financial	Profitability
T	Liquidity
S	Capital structure
	Market ratios
D	Reliability
E	Responsiveness
T	Aesthetics/appearance
E	Cleanliness/tidiness
R	Comfort
M	Friendliness
I	Communication
N	Courtesy
A	Competence
N	Access
T	Availability
S	Security
Flexibility	Volume flexibility
	Delivery speed flexibility
	Specification flexibility
Resource utilization	Productivity
	Efficiency
Innovation	Performance of the innovation
	Performance of the individual

Figure 2   The results and determinant matrix (adapted from Fitzgerald *et al.*, 1991)

their business and financial plans and gives companies the capacity for continuous feedback and strategic learning. It is more than an operational measurement system, but rather, it is of use as a long-term strategic management system.

Fitzgerald, Jonston, Brignall, Silvestro and Voss developed the Results and Determinants Matrix in 1991, as a result of the field research into performance measurement in service businesses in the UK. The choice of measures that are used in a business would be contingent upon the three key factors of competitive environment, competitive strategy and service type – which primarily determine the why, the what and the how of performance measurement. Additionally, they must include both financial and non-financial measures, enable a feed-forward and feedback control system and combine the internal and external dimensions of the work. These were integrated into six generic performance dimensions: competitiveness, financial, quality of service, flexibility, resource utilization and innovation (Figure 2). The dimenions fall into two conceptually different categories – the results of actions taken and the determinants of competitive success. Measures of competitiveness and financial performance reflect the 'end' or 'results' of actions previously taken and reflect the success of the chosen strategy. The remaining four dimensions are factors that determine competitive success, now and in the future, thus they are the 'means' or 'determinants' of competitive success. It is anticipated that such a framework has the capacity to recognize the key differences in the manufacturing and the service industries – such as the presence of the customer in the service delivery process, the intangibility, the heterogeneity, the simultaneity and the perishability of service. Although the dimensions of performance are specified, the actual measures of these dimensions will depend on the business type and the competitive strategy.

References

Emmanuel, C., Otley, D., and Merchant, K. (1990) *Accounting for Management Control.* London: Chapman & Hall.

Fitzgerald, L., Johnston, R., Brignall, S., Silvestro, E., and Voss, C. (1991) *Performance Measurement in Service Businesses.* London: CIMA,.

Kaplan, R.S. and Norton, D.P. (1992) The Balanced Scorecard – measures that drive performance. *Harvard Business Review*, Jan–Feb, 71–79.

Kaplan, R.S. and Norton, D.P. (1996) Using the Balanced Scorecard as a strategic management system. *Harvard Business Review*, Jan–Feb, 75–85.

Lebas, M. (1994) Managerial accounting in France: overview of past tradition and current practice. *The European Accounting Review*, 3 (3), 471–487.

MINE HAKTANIR
EASTERN MEDITERRANEAN UNIVERSITY,
TURKISH REPUBLIC OF NORTHERN TURKEY

Performance measures in foodservice/restaurants

A periodic analysis of a restaurant's financial performance is vital to effective management. Such an examination may uncover undesirable trends or indicate serious issues underlying the data. Moreover, analyzing key performance measures allows operators to gauge a given restaurant's operational health over time and against that of other similarly positioned units.

Operators choose from a variety of useful measures. The National Restaurant Association and Deloitte (2003) suggest a variance analysis for each income statement line item as a good starting point; they also identify sales per seat (for a given period) and daily seat turnover (customers divided by seats divided by days in the year) as key indicators. Gross profit per seat and net profit per seat are also useful. Other macro measures include RevPASH (revenue per available seat hour) and average check. Finally, productivity analysis is among the best performance measures when it includes multiple input and output variables. Critical inputs include major expense categories and constraint factors (e.g., number of seats), while necessary outputs include revenue, profit, and – where appropriate – guest satisfaction (Reynolds, 2003).

While each of these techniques measures overall performance effectively, operators use other measures to assess performance in specific areas. For example, labor turnover pertains to management's ability to effectively recruit, select, and retain line employees. Sales per labor hour gauges labor efficiency. 'To go' sales indicates carryout business as a percentage of total sales.

References

National Restaurant Association and Deloitte (2003) *2003 Restaurant Industry Operations Report.* Washington, DC: NRA.

Reynolds, D. (2003) *Hospitality Productivity Assessment using Data Envelopment Analysis. Cornell Hotel and Restaurant Administration Quarterly*, 44 (2), 130–138.

DENNIS REYNOLDS
WASHINGTON STATE UNIVERSITY, USA

Permission marketing

The term 'permission marketing' (also referred to as 'permission-based marketing' or 'opt-in marketing') describes marketing actions taken with the express consent of the customer, for example, through the use of e-mails. The customer's permission increases the likelihood both that the e-mail will actually reach the customer (and not, for example, be eliminated by a spam filter) and, because message content reflects interests expressed by the customer (for example in a customer profile previously established), will ultimately result in a sale. Thus, permission marketing can be described as a method which addresses both legal (e.g. privacy) issues and marketing criteria. Permission marketing can be described as marketing that is driven by customer 'pull' rather than by company 'push.' Although permission marketing can apply to direct ('snail') mail and telemarketing, its primary use is in Internet-based marketing. Indeed, the rapid growth in recent years of permission marketing can largely be attributed to the fact that, thanks to Web-based marketing tools, it has become a low-cost, high-impact tool for marketers, particularly when compared to mass (e-) mailings and other more traditional marketing techniques. Permission marketing allows marketers to come closer than ever before, and at lower cost, to the 'holy grail' of marketing – a one-to-one relationship with customers who are really interested in receiving their company's message.

Customer motivation

The rapid growth of electronic media has provided marketers with a new communications channel but at the same time has led to further fragmentation of the marketplace. An increasing number of consumers, faced with an ever greater and more bewildering choice of products and services offered via an expanded choice of media (print, TV and radio, e-mail and the Internet), have come to the realization that they can in fact gain time and often find bargains by selecting those companies that they want to hear from and telling those companies what products and services they are interested in. For example, by subscribing to the monthly e-newsletter of a major car rental company and identifying favorite destinations, a traveler can be made aware of special rental offers not available on the company's website, and thereby save money. A purchaser of books from an online bookstore will be made aware of titles of potential interest, based on his or her buying history. A visitor to a hotel reservation site will receive e-mails when special offers to favorite destinations are in effect, etc.

How permission marketing works

The starting point for a permission marketing relationship is generally via a so-called 'opt-in e-mail list' whereby a customer (current customer or prospect) grants permission to a company to contact him in the future with information about products or services of potential interest to him. Typically, the customer is asked to grant this permission by filling out a form on the company's website or on a pop-up menu which appears while the customer is accessing another website or Web portal. For example, while accessing an article on the cruise line industry in the travel section of an online newspaper, a reader may be offered a pop-up menu from a cruise line company asking him to provide his e-mail address and answer one or two questions, including one or more boxes granting the marketer permission to contact him in the future. A variety of e-marketing tools are used in order to provide the necessary customization to the information sent to the customer, as described below.

Permission marketing customization tools

On the one hand, permission marketing involves the use of 'company-side tools' which allow marketers to track customer activity and initiate marketing actions. These include:

- *Cookies:* Small files written to the user's hard drive when they visit the company's website. When the user returns to the website for a subsequent visit, the information in the cookie is used to personalize the appearance of the site, for example, by welcoming the user back by name.
- *Web log:* A file maintained on the company's Web server that tracks page visits, duration of visits, and purchasing behavior by users. This information can be utilized by the company to customize a session for an individual user: for example, an online bookstore can recommend books of potential interest to the user.
- *Real-time profiling:* Software that tracks users' movements through a website and which can be used to make real-time adjustments to Web pages ('clickstreaming') in order to optimize content to user interests.
- *Automated e-mailing:* Sending of e-mails in regular intervals (for example, 'weekly Web special' fares offered by airlines to e-newsletter subscribers).

On the other hand, companies provide 'client-side tools' which allow users to personalize their experience in using the company's website, update their user profile, and request specific information. These tools include:

- *Individualized web portals:* Users can create personalized Web pages with personal content. These portals often have names such as 'my<*company name*>.com' or similar.
- *Wireless data services:* Wireless Web portals which make use of the increasing number of Wi-Fi 'hotspots', cell phones, pagers etc. for communicating with the customer.
- *Web forms:* HTML forms which allow users to enter personal profile information directly into the company's website.
- *Fax-on-demand:* Allows users with or without an Internet connection to request information about products and services. Primarily used in the business-to-business (B2B) market, it can be fully automated.
- *E-mail:* Companies generally provide an e-mail address to which users can send requests for information or help, or send feedback, as well as to withdraw permission for direct marketing by the company.

Permission enforcement

Because the goal of permission marketing is the establishment of a long-term customer relationship based on trust, the use of specialized software by companies to create and enforce permission-based marketing policies (in particular, to allow customers to 'opt out') are an essential part of such programs.

References

Ferrell, O.C., Hartline, M.D., and Lucas, G.H. (2002) *Marketing Strategy*, 2nd edn. Mason, OH: South-Western.

Goldin, S. (1999) *Permission Marketing*. New York: Simon and Schuster.

PWC Consulting (2002) *Technology Forecast: 2002–2004, Volume 1: Navigating the Future of Software*. Menlo Park, CA: Pricewaterhousecoopers Technology Centre.

Strauss, J. and Frost, R. (2001) *E-Marketing*, 2nd edn. Upper Saddle River, NJ: Prentice-Hall.

ROBERT F. JENEFSKY
ECOLE HÔTELIÈRE DE LAUSANNE (EHL),
SWITZERLAND

Perpetual inventory

A perpetual inventory is a survey or record of an operator's goods and supplies in stock that is ongoing and kept continually up to date. It can be tracked manually or with a computerized inventory management system.

With a manual system, a bin card is placed on the front of the shelf for each of the items stored there. The bin card contains the name of the item, how it is packaged, and, preferably, the item number corresponding to the number used when ordering from the vendor. As items are removed from inventory, the date, the number of the item, and the initials of the person taking the item are recorded on the bin card. Conversely, as items are received to replace depleted stock, the amount added is recorded on the bin card, along with the date and the initials of the person who stored the items. The final column on the bin card keeps a running total of the items as they are issued for use or are replenished.

Advances in technology have allowed foodservice operators to utilize software that tracks each ingredient of each menu item to tally up-to-the minute inventory counts. When using a computerized inventory management system, as stock is received the items and their quantities are entered into the system. As items are sold, the quantities of each item are automatically subtracted from the amount in storage.

Reference

Poirer, C.C. (1999) *Advanced Supply Chain Management: How to Build a Sustained Competitive Advantage*. San Francisco: Berrett–Koehler.

NANCY SWANGER
WASHINGTON STATE UNIVERSITY, USA

Personal selling principles

All professional sales representatives (sales reps) follow a series of eight principles, or steps, to guide their actions. These principles include the following:

- *Prospecting and Qualifying*: This step includes the work done to uncover potential customers (Prospecting) who may have the need and the ability to enter a contract and to pay for the product or service (Qualifying) that the sales representative offers. This is one of the most important steps since good prospecting and qualifying leads to increased productivity and profitability of the sales rep.
- *Pre-approach*: This step requires the sales rep to gather as much information about the customer, including the 'decision-maker' in the household or firm, before setting up a meeting with the customer.
- *Approach*: This step occurs when the initial contact is made with the customer. One common approach technique is the 'cold call,' where the sales rep drops in unannounced or telephones the customer directly. Many sales reps will precede a cold call with a letter or note ahead of time if they find that prior notice of the initial contact increases the likelihood that the customer will talk with them.
- *Presentation/Demonstration*: This step occurs when the sales rep meets with the customer to present the actual product. Presentation may be conducted using proxies for the actual product, such as brochures, photographs, menus, or samples. A more powerful method of presentation in the hospitality industry is to invite the customer for a tour of the property.
- *Negotiation*: This step occurs once a formal proposal is made. Most sales involve some discussion or alteration to the original proposal. Typical points of negotiation include adding or subtracting features of the product or changing the proposed price. The good sales rep who negotiates by lowering the price will also receive concessions from the customer to reduce the amount of service provided.
- *Overcoming objections*: The customer often raises objections or questions during the Approach, Presentation/Demonstration, or Negotiation phases of a sale. The experienced sales rep will use a variety of techniques to uncover, and then overcome or address, each objection. If objections are not overcome, the sale is usually not completed and the proposal is closed. If all objections are overcome, the sale proceeds to the Closing phase.
- *Closing*: A typical proposal for services is 'closed' when the customer says 'yes' and signs the proposal, thereby creating a contract. Sales reps use various techniques to close the sale once all objections have been overcome. Techniques may range from 'hard closing,' when the sales rep pushes for a quick signature on the contract, to a 'softer' closing, where the sales rep encourages the customer to think about the proposal and does not push the customer to sign. Both 'hard' and 'soft' closing techniques are useful and the professional sales rep is adept at using the proper technique for each situation.
- *Follow-up/Account maintenance:* Truly professional sales reps know that it is important to follow up with the customer shortly after the sale is completed, both to address any lingering doubts or 'buyer's remorse' that the customer may experience as well as to uncover any misunderstandings. The follow-up phase will reinforce the wisdom of entering into the contract with the sales rep's company. Account maintenance refers to ongoing communication with the customer, both before and after the service or product has been delivered. Good account maintenance will increase the likelihood of repeat business, positive word-of-mouth advertising, and customer loyalty.

References

Kotler, P., Bowen, J., and Makens, J. (2003) *Marketing for Hospitality and Tourism*, 3rd edn. Upper Saddle River, NJ: Pearson Education.
Siguaw, J.A. and Bojanic, D.C. (2004) *Hospitality Sales: Selling Smarter*. Clifton Park, NY: Delmar Learning.

DINA MARIE V. ZEMKE
UNIVERSITY OF NEW HAMPSHIRE, USA

Personalization

A term related to several different approaches toward increasing customer loyalty through understanding needs or goals of each individual customer. This helps to find, design or obtain the perception of services or products that efficiently and with knowledge address these needs and goals. Personalization is supported through different customer interfaces: the Internet, bricks-and-mortar, call centers, and various voice/ telephony services using automatic speech recognition and text to speech or dual-tone multi-frequency. The goals of personalization are: to make a website easier to use; increase sales; create a one-to-one experience; improve customer service; save customers' time; increase customer loyalty; attract a broader audience; achieve cost savings; target advertising; and build a community. Personalization is user- or system-initiated and can facilitate the work (enabling access to information content, accommodating work goals and individual differences) or address social requirements (eliciting an emotional response and expressing identity). Mobile phone devices can be personalized with ring tones and other settings. Also, users can personalize access to information sources, and establish filters supplying personalized assistance when shopping, where the system recognizes past behavior of the consumer and recommends products to the user. Consumers now have tools to search for information and to build their own personalized tourist products, to pack their own bundles and to purchase the most suitable ones. Collecting data on past guests, hotels can recognize guests' requirements more easily and front-office personnel can efficiently identify consumers' preference and price range.

References

Buhalis, D. (2003) *eTourism: Information Technology for Strategic Tourism Management.* Harlow: Prentice-Hall.

Cingil, I., Dogac, A., and Azgin, A. (2000) A broader approach to personalization. *Communications of the ACM*, 43 (8), 136–141.

BOZIDAR KLICEK
UNIVERSITY OF ZAGREB, CROATIA

Persuasion

Persuasion is the deliberate effort to change the attitudes of one or more people. Attitudes are evaluations of people, objects or ideas. Attitudes are important to hospitality marketers because marketers assume that consumer attitudes affect consumer behaviors. Thus, marketers design advertising and promotional campaigns to change consumers' attitudes toward their product and service offerings in the hope that the altered attitudes will result in greater sales and profits.

Attitudes are most likely to predict consumer behaviors when the attitudes are highly accessible to the consumer. Accessibility refers to the strength of the association between a person, object or idea and the evaluation of that person, object or idea. One way that accessibility can be measured is by assessing reaction time. The faster a consumer responds with an evaluation (either positive or negative) to a product, the more accessible the attitude. Attitudes that are created based on direct experience with a person, object, or idea are typically highly accessible, and thus are more predictive of consumer behavior than attitudes created via advertising campaigns. Attitudes are also more likely to predict actual behaviors when both the attitude and the behavior are measured at the same level of specificity. The more behaviorally oriented the attitude question, the better it will predict behavior. For example, instead of asking consumers how much they like a particular menu item, hospitality marketers should ask how likely they are to purchase the menu item in the next month.

When trying to change attitudes, marketers typically rely on either a hard sell or a soft sell to persuade consumers. These approaches to selling correspond to two routes to persuasion identified by academic researchers. Hard selling pursues a *central route to persuasion.* Central route persuasion occurs when a consumer thinks carefully about the information intended to change his or her attitude, and is then persuaded because of the strengths of the arguments. Soft selling pursues a *peripheral route to persuasion.* Peripheral route persuasion occurs when consumers are persuaded as a result of superficial cues in the persuasive message. Attitude change via the central route tends to be longer-lasting and more resistant to counter-persuasion than attitude change via the peripheral route, so marketers should seek to persuade with hard sell arguments rather than (or in addition to) soft sell cues whenever possible.

Effective hard selling (or central route persuasion) requires strong arguments and an audience that pays attention to and understands those arguments. Thus, it is best used by marketers only when a product is distinctive in ways that are important to consumers, the consumer cares about the purchase decision enough to seek information about the available options, and the consumer is able to understand the differences between products and what they mean. Sadly, these conditions are rare.

Most of the time, products within a category are similar to one another and consumers are uninterested in carefully comparing the alternatives available to them. In these cases, marketers must rely on soft selling (or peripheral route persuasion). Peripheral route persuasion requires the presence of cues that prompt unthinking acceptance of the persuasive message as well as an audience that is either unwilling or unable to think about the objective merits of the message's position. Among those cues that prompt unthinking acceptance of advertisements are the attractiveness, status, credibility and likeableness of the product endorser/spokesperson. Other cues that induce unthinking acceptance are repetition of the message, familiarity with the brand, and pictures or music that evoke positive emotions.

A final way marketers can change consumers' attitudes is to change consumers' behaviors. For example, marketers can offer special deals or incentives to induce consumer trial of their products. Once consumers make a commitment to purchase a product, their attitude toward the product becomes more positive. This is believed to occur either because people are motivated to appear consistent to others and themselves (cognitive dissonance) or because people infer their attitudes from their behaviors (self-perception). Either way, attitudes follow behavior and reinforce that behavior in the future.

References

Cialdini, R.B. and Goldstein, N.J. (2002) The science and practice of persuasion. *Cornell Hotel and Restaurant Quarterly*, April, 40–50.

Petty, R.E. and Wegener, D.T. (1998) Attitude change: multiple roles for persuasion variables. In D.T. Gilbert, S.T. Fiske, and Lindzey, G. (eds), *The Handbook of Social Psychology*, 4th edn. New York: McGraw-Hill, pp. 323–390.

ANN LYNN
ITHACA COLLEGE, USA

Petty cash fund

A petty cash fund is usually established to cover small purchases incurred over a short time period (a week or two). Initially, a specific, limited amount (e.g., $200) of funds are removed from the operation's bank account and kept at the establishment. Over the course of the short time period, funds may be removed from petty cash to purchase small items (e.g., a box of powdered sugar from the local grocery store, a jar of olives for the bar) and the receipts are kept when money is removed from the fund. At the end of the time period, a manager or bookkeeper collects the receipts and replenishes the missing cash from the fund using money from the bank account. The receipts are used to adjust COGS and other balance sheet accounts appropriately before the next cycle begins. A given amount (e.g., $200) should remain in the fund at all times (cash + receipts) and employee advances should not be made from this fund.

Novice operators sometimes maintain a large petty cash fund. This is considered a bad practice since it needlessly presents opportunities for theft. In addition, operators can become accustomed to purchasing items with petty cash rather than planning accordingly and making such purchases using conventional distributors that usually charge lower prices.

Reference

Geller, A.N. (1992) *Internal Control: A Fraud Prevention Handbook*. Ithaca, NY: Cornell Campus Store.

DEBORAH BARRASH
UNIVERSITY OF NEVADA, LAS VEGAS, USA

PGA of America

Founded in 1916 and with more than 27,000 members across 41 geographic sections, The PGA (Professional Golfers' Association) of America claims the title as the world's largest working sports organization.

The PGA of America, with headquarters in Palm Beach Gardens, Florida (not to be confused with the PGA Tour, an organization comprised of golfers who compete in golf tournaments professionally), conducts four major golf events including the Ryder Cup Matches, the PGA Championship, the Senior PGA Championship, and the PGA Grand Slam of Golf.

The PGA of America conducts scores of programs to promote golf to people of all skill levels and backgrounds at its PGA Golf Club in Florida and across the United States. Besides conducting some 40 tournaments for its PGA Professional members, the PGA of America directs the world's largest golf tournament (the Buick Scramble), with more than 100,000 participants annually, as well as other programs reaching an estimated 500,000 people each year.

PGA Professionals, who comprise the association's membership, work in the golf industry providing golf instruction, retail, and facility management.

The PGA of America offers several gold pro classifications that assist golf course managers in determining and seeking out PGA professionals for a specific type of golf club.

Reference

PGA of America (2003) www.pga.com/about-the-pga.cfm.

EDWARD A. MERRITT
CALIFORNIA STATE POLYTECHNIC
UNIVERSITY, USA

Physical inventory

A physical inventory involves the manual counting of each item in stock on a regular basis. For accounting purposes, an inventory is conducted at the end of each calendar month or, if using the period system, at the end of each four-week period. The ending inventory numbers are then used to calculate the cost of goods sold on an income statement; these calculations are then used for related processes such as inventory-turnover analysis. Some operators take inventory on a weekly basis and may even count high-cost or very select items on a daily basis.

Inventory sheets are most effective when organized by storage area. For example, a separate sheet may be used for each of the following areas: freezer, walk-in refrigerator, dry goods, chemical stores, and beverage alcohol. Categories for inclusion on the inventory sheet are: product name, purchase unit, and purchase unit count. If the inventory is being calculated manually, the inventory sheet will also include a column for the purchase unit price and a column for recording the total of the purchase unit price multiplied by the purchase unit count. Many operations use a computer software program that calculates the value of the ending inventory after the purchase unit counts have been entered into the system. To be accurate, unit costs must be updated in the computer with each change in price from the supplier.

Reference

Piasecki, D.J. (2003) *Inventory Accuracy: People, Processes, and Technology*. Kenosha, WI: OPS Publishing.

NANCY SWANGER
WASHINGTON STATE UNIVERSITY, USA

Pluralism and unitarism

In many introductory hospitality and service industry management texts, the concept of the hospitality organization as one entity, with 'everyone serving the customer,' is common. Similarly, sections in texts on human resource management sometimes treat the hospitality workface as a homogeneous entity, without recognition of the diversity of needs and wants of the individual or the organization culture of the workgroup. This approach is called 'unitarism.' It still holds relevance for the modern manager, especially when trying to instill a culture or ethic throughout the workforce. A good example of this would be in the introduction of quality standards, where groups of employees from different areas work together to look at ways of raising standards throughout the hotel.

Unitarists would see hospitality organizations as a seamless whole where organizational members are in complete harmony, cooperate with each other, and are committed and loyal to the firm. Conflicts can be explained, for example, by poor communications or personality clashes. Troubles would be perceived as an illness and consultants would be used to provide a way forward. Additionally, problems might be blamed on 'trouble makers' or 'union militants' (although the latter culprit is less likely in hospitality organizations due to impoverished union membership). This perspective is often held by hospitality managers because it is a common 'truth' that organizations need to be this way in the 'free market' context. In a sense this view is naive because it does not recognize the power play and inherent political nature of hotels.

However, Anderson *et al.* (1998) view hospitality organizations as comprised of distinct groups that are actively autonomous and interdependent. They also consider conflict among these groups inevitable and impossible to resolve permanently. These authors conclude that inter-group conflict may only be managed temporarily. This requires responsible management of the interrelationships as well as empowerment, with equity among groups in decision-making power. The recognition that these groups have different needs and wants (and therefore require flexible management approaches) is know as a 'pluralist' perspective or simply called 'pluralism'.

Pluralism is a pragmatic, effective alternative to the unitarist approach. The approach sees conflicts of interest and disagreements between managers and workers, and workgroups with each other, as normal and inescapable. Realistic managers should:

- Accept that conflict will occur and that a greater propensity for conflict exists rather than a harmonious organizational situation (unitary perspective),

- Anticipate and resolve these conflicts by securing agreed procedures for settling disputes.

Pluralism assumes that achievement of consensus and long-term stability in management/worker relations is the best way to balance the demands of competing groups. Mechanisms and channels must therefore be designed and introduced so that the frustration and anger associated with conflict can be vented and given relief rather than harmfully repressed. Management should thus adopt policies and agree to procedures and codes which recognize that conflicting interests exist. For instance, Dann and Hornsey (1986) recognized that different workgroups (such as food and beverage production and food and beverage service) have very different approaches to work, reward, and motivation. In addition to the requirement for managers to recognize the sometimes disparate attitudes of workers and work groups, they must also recognize that they too have differing interests to their workers. Management must know this and manage accordingly, otherwise the service will suffer and customers will be compromised.

Thus, pluralists view hospitality organizations as collections of different groups with different interests, aims, and aspirations. Sometimes these groups have interests which overlap and sometimes they do not; this often brings them into conflict with other groups in the organization. It is therefore important that mechanisms for conflict regulation and resolution are high on the management agenda.

It is also important to recognize the heterogeneity of the workforce in hospitality organizations. Several authors (for instance see, Lee-Ross 1993, 1998) have commented on not only the cultural and ethnic mix, but also the mix of casual and full-time workers as well as seasonal and year-round employees. Management must be cognizant of the fact that each group has different aims, objectives, and expectations of work and loyalty to the place of work and must be managed as such rather than as a cohesive group.

There are two further perspectives which are pluralist in nature. The first is known as 'interactionist' and the second, 'radical pluralist.' Interactionists recognize conflict but view it as inevitable and potentially beneficial because changes will result. This is a realistic view of hospitality organizations because interdepartmental conflict is a common occurrence, particularly at the kitchen/restaurant interface. However, rather than being destructive, the conflict may actually be used to redesign more effective and efficient production and service systems. Of course the reality of this beneficial outcome may not always be realized because of other complex behavioral reasons. These often include interpersonal conflict based on personalities, status differentials, perceived inequity and so on (which are all facets of organizational culture).

Radical pluralists view organizations chiefly as political entities. As such, conflict is inevitable because of the never-ending struggle between management, workers, and shareholders. For example, hotel managers are required to hold shareholders' interests as paramount. Thus, high levels of employee wages and salaries detract from other stakeholders' dividends. Radical pluralists would therefore consider managers as loyal to shareholders rather than workers. Indeed, the successful 'hostile takeover bid' of the UK-based Forte group by Granada in the 1990s was fuelled by poor financial performance and dwindling shareholder dividends.

References

Anderson, J., Clément, J., and Crowder, L.V. (1998) Accommodating conflicting interests in forestry – concepts emerging from pluralism. *Unasylva*, 49 (194), 3–10.

Dann, D. and Hornsey, T. (1986) Towards a theory of interdepartmental conflict in hotels. *International Journal of Hospitality Management*, 5 (1), 23–28.

Lee-Ross, D. (1993) An investigation of 'core job dimensions' amongst seasonal seaside hotel workers. *International Journal of Hospitality Management*, 12 (2), 121–126.

Lee-Ross, D. (1998) The reliability and rationale of Hackman and Oldham's Job Diagnostic Survey and Job Characteristics Model among seasonal hotel workers. *International Journal of Hospitality Management*, 17 (4), 391–406.

PAUL REYNOLDS
UNIVERSITY OF SOUTH AUSTRALIA,
AUSTRALIA

Point of purchase promotion (POP)

Point of purchase promotion (POP), also known as point of sale advertising, refers to promotional displays positioned in the distribution channel (usually at retail) where buyers actually purchase or make the decision to purchase a product or service. Common POP display examples include:

- Banners
- Brochures
- Counter displays
- End-of-aisle displays
- Floor-stand displays
- Grocery bag advertisements
- Grocery cart advertisements
- Magnets
- Neon beverage signs
- POP coupon checkout machines
- Shelf coupon dispensers
- Shelf talkers
- Tabletop tent cards
- Video consoles
- Wall posters
- Window clings
- Window signage

POP displays are usually produced and paid for by the sponsoring manufacturer or service firm, which may also set up and maintain the display. Typically, POP displays are found in retail outlets close to where the buyer makes the decision to purchase. Though the location of POP displays may be at the point of actual exchange, such as the check-out counter, the buying decision often occurs earlier and at a different location, such as a grocery store aisle or while the customer is in a queue at a drive-through fast food restaurant. The key difference between POP displays and other forms of advertising is the relative proximity of the promotion to the actual point where the buyer–seller transaction takes place. For example, advertising in traditional media channels (newspapers, television, billboards, etc.) may take place far from the actual point of purchase. With POP displays, the promotion and purchase location coincide.

POP displays can serve a number of purposes: to build store traffic, attract attention to a specific brand, advertise a brand, or cue recall of brand advertising the buyer may have seen elsewhere. Ultimately, though, the main goal of POP displays, like that of most promotions, is to boost immediate sales. Though the POP display environment has become cluttered, studies show that well-designed and located POP displays can increase sales, sometimes dramatically. This depends on a number of factors, however, including the type of product being promoted, the nature of the decision environment (novel or repeat), and the product knowledge and brand loyalty of the buyer.

Consumer behavior research, for example, shows that many purchase decisions are stimulus-based as opposed to memory-based (Peter and Olson, 1990). Stimulus-based decisions are those for which product choice is primarily influenced by information available in the purchase environment, such as product packaging and POP displays. Memory-based decisions are primarily influenced by information retrieved from memory, such as prior experience with a brand or brand advertising seen on an earlier occasion. Stimulus-based decision-making is especially common for grocery products, for which estimates of purchase decisions made in the store are as high as 75%. Similarly, restaurant meal and beverage decisions are often stimulus-based decisions – diners infrequently approach the restaurant experience with a well-formed purchase plan in place, but instead are persuaded by information in the decision environment, including POP displays.

POP promotion has also found utility in recruiting line employees. Many foodservice operations, particularly in the quick service and fast casual segments, use a variety of POP materials to inform customers that job openings exist. The most common of these is window signage and messages printed on the sales receipt. Researchers believe the POP recruiting is effective since such messages build on the given brand. Furthermore, potential employees see what the job entails thereby creating accurate job expectations.

This tool that has recently become commonplace for most marketers will likely gain in complexity during the foreseeable future. It is also likely that crossover marketing efforts, such as those that combine Internet-based approaches with POP promotions will continue to expand the reach of companies, particularly those in the service sector.

Reference

Peter, J.P. and Olson, J.C. (1990) *Consumer Behavior and Marketing Strategy*. Homewood, IL: Irwin.

ROBERT KWORTNIK
CORNELL UNIVERSITY, USA

Point of sale (POS) functions

Any point where a sales transaction can occur in a hospitality organization, such as restaurants or bars, can be considered a point of sale (POS). Hotel integrated property management systems feature electronic POS systems (EPOS), which are equipped with a cash register and can retain and communicate data. EPOS systems are used in reception and the restaurants of a hotel and any department that cash transactions take place. EPOS systems can be linked directly to the main hotel computer system and a transaction at the restaurant can instantly debited on the room bill. In restaurants, EPOS systems have become increasingly useful as the data that is stored can be analyzed in order to perform a number of managerial functions including cost control, inventory, production efficiency, service and sales, menu engineering, and even highlight needs in staff training. For example, comparing sales of restaurant waiters can show the need for training for a particular member of staff, or can introduce incentive schemes to reward hard-working staff. Customer trends can be measured, as to type of food, average time spent in the restaurant or average expenditure. All this information can then be fed into the hotel research and intelligent systems to support decision-making.

References

Cousins, J., Foskett, D., and Shortt, D. (1995) *Food and Beverage Management*. Harlow: Longman.

Davis, B. and Lockwood, A. (1994) *Food and Beverage Management*. Oxford: Butterworth-Heinemann.

IOANNIS S. PANTELIDIS
UNIVERSITY OF SURREY, UK

Point of sale system

A point of sale (POS) system is an integrated configuration of hardware and software that connects front-of-the-house operations to the back-of-the-house accounting functions. Typical front-of-the-house equipment includes computer terminals set up to function as smart cash registers that can be programmed to help control and account for sales, timing, and inventory, while increasing efficiency. Often, these computer terminals are set up to include one or more cash drawers, barcode scanners, receipt printers (including remote location printers), touch-screen monitors, credit card readers, and pole displays.

In a POS system, a computerized cash register system replaces stand-alone cash registers. While a cash register performs the single purpose of reporting how much income is received, a POS system can report additional information such as profit, how much inventory is on the shelf, which products should be ordered, and how many individual menu items were sold for a specified period.

A POS system can help reduce theft and inventory shrinkage, reduce or increase inventory levels, monitor margins, speed guest check settlement, increase accuracy, and keep track of guests. The following points will help elucidate some of the application features of a POS system:

- *Reducing theft:* By producing customized and standardized reports, which may (or may not) include every inventory item stocked, managers can more easily monitor store inventory.
- *Reducing inventory shrinkage:* By monitoring inventory and comparing physical inventory with computerized reports, employees will have an increasing awareness of the effects of giving away inventory, retaining obsolete inventory, monitoring breakage and waste, and checking inventory at delivery.

- *Reducing or increasing physical inventory:* By watching inventory reports, employees can ensure that ordering is more precise. If an organization is seasonal, it is not likely that it will need to stock the same amount of a basic product – such as flour or sugar – in the low season as it will in the high season. Watching inventory reports helps increase efficiency.
- *Watching margins:* By reading management reports, employees of an organization may find that it sold 500 tuna sandwiches that cost $2.00 each for $6.00 each (33.3% cost of sales) and 500 minute steaks that cost $5.00 for $10.00 each (50% cost of sales). The cost of sales report would suggest that the tuna sandwich is the preferred item. However, the margin report would disclose that the minute steak delivers a higher profit margin ($2500 *vs.* $2000) and is therefore the preferred item over the tuna sandwich. Inventory reports will help an operation to stock more products that provide greater profits and fewer products that deliver fewer dollars to the bottom line.
- *Speeding guest ordering and checking out:* Computerizing speeds up ordering and checking out. Depending upon the type of service, barcode scanning (scanning a code), price lookup (ordering by number), picture ordering (ordering by line art), and the like can speed both the ordering process and the checking out process. Even if the organization does not use barcode scanning, checking out is still faster and more accurate, because the order is held in a pre-check function (allowing items to be added after the order is placed) or otherwise held open until the guest is ready to check out, which automatically ties back to pricing specified in the cash register program for each inventory item.
- *Ensuring accuracy:* Every menu item in an operation has a price associated with it. With a POS system, items are entered in single keystrokes (barcode scanning, price lookup, picture ordering, or other method) instead of open key prices (whereby a $2.95 item would be entered with three keystrokes). Similarly, entering prices by single descriptor increases accuracy, since employees will not be guessing, estimating, or otherwise entering incorrect prices for menu items.

- *Keeping track of guests:* The best customers are the organization's current guests. No matter the type of operation, organizations should try to develop a database including the name and address of their most frequent guests. Mailing to guests is a direct and effective form of advertising – even if only a postcard listing a few seasonal specials. POS systems include a database function whereby guest contact information can be collected and sorted.

A partial list of features and reports available in POS systems includes employee login screens (which can function as time clocks), zero-items-sold reports, touch screens, quantity and price prompting, stay–go–delivery options, mix-and-match pricing, multiple guest tendering, table layout design options, bulk customer e-mail addresses, employee e-mail messaging, account restrictions, department sale report by server, yearly comparison reports, gift cards, check validation, multiple A/R invoicing, credit card processing with tips, multiple receipts, split ticket functions, multiple discount levels, check authorization and signature pads, custom touch screen, invoice printing, multiple level screens, quick customer history, and others.

Reference

Rutherford, D. (2001) *Hotel Management and Operations.* New York: John Wiley & Sons.

EDWARD A. MERRITT
CALIFORNIA STATE POLYTECHNIC
UNIVERSITY, USA

Points system

A system used in the timeshare industry that employs points as a unit of use measurement to value or define the rights of a timeshare owner to reserve accommodations in a timeshare resort or resorts. Points may also be used both as a unit of use measurement and as an expression of the percentage ownership interest in the timeshare plan owned by the owner. In a point system, points are assigned to each timeshare interest or accommodation based on such factors as accommodation type, location and time of year. The timeshare owner purchases points in the system, or is assigned points based on the timeshare interest owned, which are then used to reserve and use the accommodations of the timeshare plan in accordance with the values assigned to the accommodations. The point system may be established to permit reservation and use of accommodation types different then the type purchased and for larger increments of time or for as little as a day. Some timeshare plans permit owners with points to use the points outside of the reservation system to reserve and use alternative or ancillary products such as hotels and rental cars in the same manner as hotel frequent-user programs.

References

American Resort Development Association (2002) *The Timeshare Resource Manual.* Washington, DC.

Sherles, T. and Marmorstone, J. (1994) How successful point systems begin: careful program design and point valuation. *Resort Development Operations*, April/May.

KURT GRUBER
ISLAND ONE RESORTS, USA

Portal

A Web portal is a website or service that offers a broad array of resources and services, such as search engines, e-mail lists, forums for a number of content providers who usually are located elsewhere and maintained by other parties. In hospitality management the main objective is to serve potential or actual visitors who want to access hotel websites in order to satisfy their information needs. Portals vary according to their users and services:

- Public portals are generally available and bring together information from various sources (e.g. Yahoo).
- Enterprise portals give employees access to organization-specific information and applications.
- Marketplace portals are trading platforms that connect sellers and buyers.

- Specialized portals (e.g. www.visiteuropeancities. info) offer an access path to specific information and applications for travelers.

In addition to fulfilling customers' actual needs, portals provide a platform for hospitality managers and other tourism organizations to bundle information from their websites in order to allow joint marketing initiatives. Hotel websites available in portals become more visible on the Internet and benefit from complementing their offer with additional services of other providers. Portals also open opportunities to gain valuable insights into the consumer's decision-making process by tracking the users' information needs.

References

Katz, R.N., and associates (2002) *Web Portals and Higher Education: Technologies to Make IT Personal.* San Francisco, CA: Jossey-Bass.

Wöber, K. (2003) Evaluation of DMO web sites through interregional tourism portals: a European cities tourism case example. In A.J. Frew, M. Hitz, and P. O'Connor (eds), *Information and Communication Technologies in Tourism*, ENTER 2003 Proceedings. Vienna/ New York: Springer, pp. 76–85.

KARL WÖBER
VIENNA UNIVERSITY OF ECONOMICS AND
BUSINESS ADMINISTRATION, AUSTRIA

Portion control

For each recipe produced in an operation, a precise serving size should be included to ensure consistency in quality from those who are using the recipes. Portion control can be implemented by using the appropriate weighing and measuring tools. This can be accomplished for food portions through the use of scales to weigh, or scoops, ladles, and other volumetric measuring tools such as measuring cups or measuring spoons; similarly for beverages, the use of measured pouring devices, jiggers, and shot glasses will help accomplish this outcome. Portion control will ensure that each guest receives the same amount of product each time or that the amounts used in production will be consistent.

Failure to maintain good portion control can affect customer satisfaction. For example, if a customer orders the same dish on different occasions at a given restaurant (or at different restaurants within a chain) and experiences dissimilar portion sizes, he or she may not return. Even worse, if guests sitting together order the same menu item but receive different amounts, customer satisfaction will be negatively affected. Repeated episodes across customers will eventually compromise the restaurant's long-term success. In the short term, poor portion control may lead to increased cost of goods in cases where portion sizes exceed those specified in the standardized recipes.

Reference

Knight, J.B. and Kotschevar, L.H. (1979) *Quantity Food Production: Planning and Management.* Boston, MA: CBI Publishing.

DAVID BIEL
HOUSTON'S RESTAURANTS, USA

Portion cost

Portion cost is the cost of goods purchased and consumed in preparing and delivering a given menu item to customers. It is determined through recipe costing, which is an extension of recipe standardization. Portion cost calculations are fundamental to all pricing activities.

Operators calculate portion cost by summing the cost of each ingredient in a standardized recipe and dividing this by the number of portions that the recipe produces. For example, if the cost of a recipe's ingredients totals $120 and the recipe produces 80 portions, then the portion cost is $1.50.

Effective portion costing should reflect the current cost of goods consumed in producing and delivering menu items. While prices cannot always be raised immediately following price hikes on one or more of an item's ingredients, managers must understand the effects of such cost increases on profitability. Lower portion costs obviously tend to increase profitability. Factors that affect portion cost include improper portion control (overly large portions lower profit while portions that are insensitive to customer preferences diminish customer satisfaction) and shrinkage (employee theft or incompetence depletes ingredient stocks).

Reference

Polimeni, R.S. (1994) *Schaum's Outline of Cost Accouting.* New York: McGraw-Hill.

DAVID BIEL

HOUSTON'S RESTAURANTS, USA

Positioning

Positioning is a fundamental concept in marketing. It was popularized in the early 1970s by Ries and Trout. It is intertwined with another basic marketing concept, differentiation. Differentiation is the creation of tangible or intangible differences between a company's product or service and its competition. Positioning is the set of strategies that a company develops and implements ensuring that these differences occupy a distinct and valued place in the consumer's mind relative to the competition. Positioning is based on customer perception acknowledging that perception is reality.

Positioning is useful in three general instances. First, positioning is critical in establishing a new service or product image. The new product/service does not currently exist in the consumer's mind. A company must distinguish this new product from the services/products to which it will be compared. Second, positioning is important for maintaining and reinforcing an established image in the consumer's mind. Finally, positioning can be used to reposition a product/ service in the consumer's mind. Repositioning is necessary when the current product/service position is no longer competitively sustainable or profitable.

To position an offering in the consumer's mind, a company designs and develops its offering so that the target market perceives and values the offering as distinct. Six common strategies to position an offering are: by attributes and benefits, by use or application, by product or service user, by product or service class, by competitors, and by price and quality. The most frequently used strategy is by attribute and benefit. Service organizations sometimes position themselves by focusing on the five dimensions of service quality developed by Zeithaml, Parasuraman, and Berry: reliability, responsiveness, assurance, empathy, and tangibility.

In order to position a product, marketing managers must understand the dimensions along which the target market perceives the product or service. In addition, marketing managers must understand how their customers view their offering relative to the competition. The following basic questions need to be answered: How do our customers view our offering? Who do our customers see as our closest competitors? What product or service attributes seem to be most responsible for these perceived differences? Once these questions are answered, managers can assess how well their offerings are positioned in the market. Then, and only then, can management identify the critical elements needed to differentiate their product or service.

A question remains. How can management develop an understanding of the competitive structure and dimensions of their markets? Perceptual mapping is a formal technique used to depict the competitive structure of a market. Perceptual mapping is a spatial representation in which competing alternatives are plotted in Euclidian space. Perceptual maps have the following three characteristics: pairwise distances between product/service alternatives represent perceived similarities, a vector displayed on the map indicates both the direction and magnitude of an attribute, and the axes of the map suggest the underlying dimensions that best characterize how customers differentiate between alternatives. Typically orthogonal axes (perpendicular axes) are used to represent the dimensions of the map. In addition, the axes can be rotated in order to facilitate interpretation of the mapping results.

Perceptual maps summarize and visualize the key elements of the market structure facilitating managerial decision-making. Without this knowledge companies might invest in differentiating their offerings along dimensions that do not align with customer perceptions. By concentrating on the underlying dimensions, managers gain strategic focus. In addition, the visual representation helps management hone their thinking about how their product or service is perceived.

Perceptual mapping was originally developed by psychologists to map psychological measurements of how people perceive things on multiple dimensions. The technique that was developed is referred to as multi-dimensional scaling (MDS). Marketers adapted MDS to aid in positioning products and services. MDS methods vary depending on the nature of the input data available. Three basic approaches are used: attribute-based methods, similarity-based methods, and joint-space methods. Joint-space methods include both customer perception and preference data.

Finally, perceptual maps are useful in at least four specific areas of marketing. The first is new product or service development. Mapping can locate gaps in the market, evaluate potential names, and identify segments that would find the new product/service most appealing. Second, mapping can be used to check management view's of the competition. Management's perceptions must align with customer perception to successfully position products/services. Third, perceptual maps can be used to identify whom to compete against. Often it is difficult to clearly differentiate a product/service from the competition. Mapping can highlight the competition's weaknesses and even show differences between competitive offerings that customers do not notice. Finally, perceptual mapping may be used to quantify a company's image or reputation.

Additional methods are used in product/service positioning. Matrices are developed relating attributes of the product/service to identified market segments. Bar charts and snake plots are used to visually summarize customer perceptions. Recently a methodology for measuring a firm's linear market position based on the idea that consumers holistically rank competing firms on a linear or hierarchical continuum has been introduced by Reich.

The challenge facing management is deciding which positioning strategy is optimal given the current situation. Management needs to know who its competitors are, what positions they hold,

and where its own product/service is positioned in the customer's mind. Once these questions have been answered management can focus on what position they want to win, which competitors are threats, and what resources are needed to attain and hold the targeted position. The position selected must be clearly communicated to the targeted customers. Finally, the position chosen should be sustainable and profitable.

References

Dev, C.S., Morgan, M.S., and Shoemaker, S. (1995) A positioning analysis of hotel brands based on travel manager perceptions. *Cornell Hotel and Restaurant Administration Quarterly*, 36 (6), 48–55.

Reich, A.Z. (2001) Determining a firm's linear market position. *Journal of Hospitality and Tourism Research*, 25 (2), 159–172.

Ries, A. and Trout, J. (2000) *Positioning: The Battle for Your Mind*. New York: McGraw-Hill.

Urban, G.L. (1975) PERCEPTOR: A model for product positioning. *Management Science*, 8, 858–871.

REED FISHER
JOHNSON STATE COLLEGE, USA

Pre-convention meeting

Pre-convention briefings are usually held 24 to 48 hours in advance of the beginning of a meeting, to reconfirm and review meeting logistics and discuss the fine points and any last minute changes. All meeting details should be in the hands of all participants at least 30 days prior to the meeting. The purpose of the pre-con meeting is to meet and establish rapport with the entire facility team and to clear up any procedural questions. For small meetings, a brief meeting with the convention service manager and/or catering manager may be sufficient to go over room set-ups and other requirements. A larger meeting will require key staff from each department, normally including the general manager, the executive chef, the sales manager, the accounting manager, the front desk manager, the concierge, the bell captain, the housekeeping manager, the security manager, the engineering manager, the telephone switchboard manager, the recreation manager (golf, tennis, spa, etc.), and outside suppliers such as the general service contractor, the destination management company, the audiovisual contractor, etc. Often official contractors and other suppliers are included as well. All function sheets, banquet event orders, and other instructions should be reviewed. The meeting format involves introductions of the meeting staff with the facility staff.

Topics discussed generally include a review of the contracted room block and actual room pick-up, the number of attendees expected, VIPs and special considerations such as in-room amenities, accounting arrangements to include the establishment of the master account, who is authorized to sign on the account, billing instructions, check-in procedures with review of main arrival and departure dates, transportation arrangements, business center requirements, security arrangements, expected use of food and beverage outlets and room service, shipping and receiving arrangements, anticipated use of switchboard and special telephone arrangements, housekeeping needs such as turndown service, engineering needs such as hanging banners or electrical requirements, recreational activities, and what is handled by outside contractors.

Reference

Krug, S., Chatfield-Taylor, C., and Collins, M. (eds) (1994) *The Convention Industry Council Manual*, 7th edn. McLean, VA: The Convention Industry Council.

PATTI J. SHOCK
UNIVERSITY OF NEVADA, LAS VEGAS, USA

Pre-costing

This term is used less often today than it was 25 years ago. It may also be referred to as 'pre-control' and it implies 'pre-planning.' It was first mentioned in Brodner, Maschal, and Carlson (1962). It takes a 'proactive' approach to cost control instead of a 'reactive' after-the-fact response. Pre-costing or pre-control uses forecasts, standards, and budgets to predict cost activity so that appropriate steps can be taken to prevent losses. It also relates to planned production and scheduling. Pre-costing 'promotes efficiency, provides sound sales data, coordinated purchasing, and preparation, reduces over-preparation and over-staffing, and results in reduced food and labor costs' (Brodner *et al.*, 1962). It relies on historical sales and production records as the basis for forecasting sales and production quantities. Thus, the primary concern with any related pre-costing activity is use of accurate data and quantitatively based forecasting information. Moreover, pre-costing is dependent on management's ability to ensure related production systems are in place and are maintained throughout the production process.

Reference

Brodner, J., Maschal, H.M., and Carlson, H.T. (1962) *Profitable Food and Beverage Operation*, 4th edn. New York: Ahrens.

DAVID V. PAVESIC
GEORGIA STATE UNIVERSITY, USA

Pre-/post-meeting tours

A program offered by a meeting organizer to provide for educational, recreational, and/or sightseeing tours in conjunction with a planned meeting or event. Many organizations offer their attendees the opportunity to explore the destination where they are holding a meeting by arranging pre- and post-meeting tours. Attendees can combine leisure travel with their business travel. The destination is happy to promote these programs because they mean additional room nights and revenues for the hospitality enterprises. Some organizations arrange their own tours while others may employ a tour company or destination management company that specializes in arranging tours. When planning a tour program, give careful consideration to the structured meeting or event and schedule tours so as they do not compete with the main program. It is important to insure the safety of tour participants by checking into equipment maintenance and certifications of the company hired. Tours are often priced on a per person basis with a minimum number required to make the program viable. Tours may last one day or several days. They may target families as a way to encourage attendees to bring their families with them to a meeting.

Reference

Connell, B. (ed.) (2002) *Professional Meeting Management*, 4th edn. Chicago, IL: Professional Convention Management Association Education Foundation.

DEBBI BOYNE
MEETING DEMANDS, USA
KIMBERLY SEVERT
UNIVERSITY OF CENTRAL FLORIDA, USA

Preventive maintenance

Preventive maintenance (PM) includes checking, testing, making comparisons to performance standards, and replacing low-cost items with the objective of preventing premature device or facility component failures. Preventive maintenance starts with the manufacturer's scheduled recommendations for device or component safety checks, efficiency testing, and the general wear and tear of devices and components. Property total quality management (TQM) objectives may supersede manufacturer's maintenance recommendations. In addition, routine maintenance reports of repeated device failure and repairs may indicate required changes in the preventive maintenance schedule to minimize future failures. All equipment, devices, and facility components that are accessible or operated by guests and non-maintenance employees should be included in a preventive maintenance schedule.

Increasingly hotel, lodging, restaurant, and hospitality enterprises are utilizing automated systems to assist in managing preventive maintenance. The automation of preventive maintenance provides the building management personnel with a powerful full-featured preventive maintenance system. Such systems establish preventive maintenance performance frequencies, including seasonal, specific calendar dates, high/low performance values, consideration for outages, and facility down days and weekends. Multiple preventive maintenance performance triggers may also be defined. Automated preventive maintenance enables the maintenance organization to fine tune preventive maintenance tasks by analyzing task performance. The system also provides extensive forecasting information including dates needed, labor requirements, materials, tools, etc.

Automation of the preventive maintenance function creates tasks and routines including a library of preventive maintenance procedures; conversion of job plan/job standard into PM routine, seasonal activation of PM work; fixed and float PM reset capability; tasking on-demand; and PM performance route definition.

Automation can also create maintenance schedules and meter frequencies consisting of: user-defined calendar/occurrence frequencies; accumulating, increasing, fixed, and fluctuating value meter reading types, unlimited meter types; unlimited meter triggers for each PM; complete meter reading history capability; meter reading validation formula definition; meter instrument tracking and meter rollover and swap out functionality.

Automation of the preventive maintenance function can also facilitate tracking preventive maintenance history and creating due lists.

Reference

Borsenik, Frank D. and Stutts, Alan T. (1997) *The Management of Maintenance and Engineering Systems in the Hospitality Industry*, 4th edn. New York: John Wiley & Sons.

FRANK BORSENIK
UNIVERSITY OF NEVADA, LAS VEGAS, USA

Price customization

Robert Crandall, the former chief executive of American Airlines, once said 'If I have 2000 customers on a given route and 400 different prices, I am obviously short 1600 prices.' This one sentence captures the essence of revenue management, for it argues that rather than setting prices by segment (e.g., weekend traveler *vs.* midweek traveler, business guest *vs.* leisure guest etc.), firms should price by individual customer.

Before discussing why and how a firm can set prices by individual customer, it is important to understand some critical pricing definitions. *Reference price* is the first pricing term firms need to understand. This is the price for which consumers' believe the product should sell. The reference price is formed when consumers consider such things as: the price last paid, the price of similar items, the price considering the brand name, the real or imagined cost to produce the item, and the perceived cost of product failure. The last item is of considerable importance for it reflects consumers' imaginations. For example, the reference price for a meal where one is celebrating a special occasion is higher than the reference price for a meal with some old college friends, even though the restaurant may be the same. The risk of failure is critical in the first case and less critical in the second.

The second definition one needs to understand is *reservation price*. This is defined as the maximum price the customer will pay for a product. For instance, if the customer's *reservation price* for a canned soft drink (soda) is 1 euro and the price is 1.01 euro, the customer will not buy the product. If the selling price is less than the reservation price, the customer will buy the product. Firms that price exactly to the reservation price are said to extract the entire *consumer surplus*. Firms that price less than the reservation price are said to be *leaving money on the table*. Obviously, firms do not want to leave money on the table.

The desire to set prices by individual customer further implies that each customer has a different reservation price and by selling to that price, the firm maximizes revenue because everyone will buy the product. By having a limited number of prices, there will always be some people whose reservation price is less than the selling price and hence, they will not buy. On the other hand, there will be others who would be willing to pay more, but are paying less because prices are below their reservation price.

Dolan and Simon (1997) provide a good example as to why multiple pricing works using an airline. This example, of course, is equally applicable to the hotel industry by substituting the word room for airline seat. Figure 1 shows that the airplane has 380 seats and variable cost per seat is \$100, which means that this is the minimum price the airline seat would sell for; anything less and the airline would lose money. The maximum reservation price is \$3900, which means that at \$3901 no one would buy the seat. The area of potential is represented by the triangle ABC. Basic geometry tells us that the area of a triangle is ½ the base times the height; for this example the area is \$722,000 [½ × 380 × (\$3900 − \$100)]. The goal of pricing is to capture all, or as much as possible, of this \$722,000.

Therefore, if one price was to be chosen, the optimum price would be somewhere between \$100 and \$3900. It turns out that if there is a linear sales response curve similar to Figure 1, then the optimal price is the middle between the lowest and highest price [(\$100 + \$3900)/2], which is \$2000.

Figure 2 shows that at a price of \$2000, 190 seats will be sold, as this is where the lines intercept the linear sales response curve. The area in the square formed is calculated by multiplying the base times the height. The base is equal to the sales price (\$2000) minus the variable cost (\$100), or \$1900. The height is the number of seats sold. The revenue captured is then \$361,000, or 50% of the total revenue. This means that 50% of the potential revenue was not earned. We can say the airline lost potential revenue of \$361,000. Where did this revenue go? Figure 2 provides the answer.

Note that in Figure 2 there is a group who did not buy the airline seat because their reservation price was under \$2000. This group is labeled X. There is another group who had a higher reservation price (labeled Y), but were able to buy the airline seat at a lower price. In this case, the airline left money on the table. The challenge is to transfer some of the revenue in X and Y to the firm. The firm does this by having more than one price.

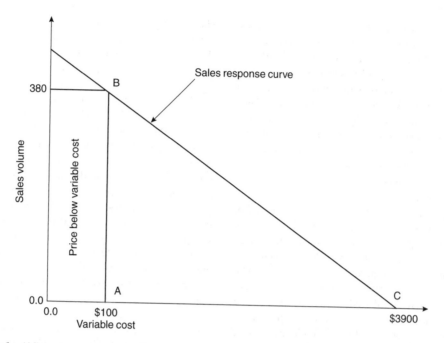

Figure 1 Airline sales response curve. The sales response curve in Figures 1 to 4 illustrates how sales change in relation to price changes. In theory, the lower the prices, the higher the sales. The SRC is rarely linear. However, because the mathematics are easier if it is linear, we present the simplest case here. The theory is the same, although the complications get more complex

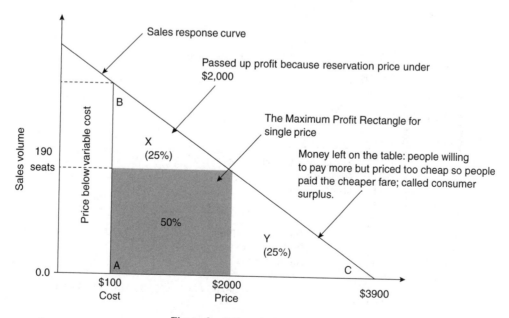

Figure 2 Airline sales response curve

In order to have more prices, however, the firm needs to create different products. In the airline industry, this is accomplished by different classes of services and restrictions on Saturday night stay, time of booking, and the like. For a hotel, a simple way to create different products is to treat rooms with a view as one type of room and rooms overlooking the parking lot as another type of room. Each room type can be priced differently. The room for a guest staying four nights is also different than a room for a one-night guest.

Figure 3 shows what happens when instead of just one price the airline adds two prices – a price for economy class and a price for business class. These prices are $1367 and $2633, which were determined at random for this example. The reader should immediately note that the areas of X and Y have decreased. This is because with a lower price some of those who were priced out initially can now afford to fly. Similarly, some of those with a higher reservation price elected to fly business instead of economy. As can be seen in Figure 3, 127 people chose to fly business and 127

chose to fly economy. Again, these numbers are determined by the intersection of the prices with the linear response curve. The revenue for business class is $321,691 [($2633 − $100) × 127]. The revenue for economy is $160,909 [($1367 − $100) × 127]. The revenue for both classes combined is $482,600, which is an increase of $121,600 from just one price.

Note again that the firm did not maximize revenue, as some flyers were able to pay less than their reservation price and others still found the lower price too expensive. This suggests that perhaps another price, and hence another category of service, could be added. This is shown in Figure 4. Specifically, the categories of service are now first class ($2950), business class ($2000), and economy class ($1050).

Figure 4 shows that each level of service (price point) has attracted 95 flyers. The revenue for economy class is $90,250 [95 × ($1050 − $100)], for business class $180,500, and for first class the revenue is $270,750. The combined total is $541,500, which means that by having three price points, the firm has captured 75% of the

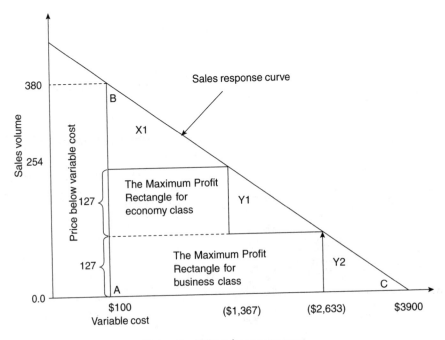

Figure 3 Airline sales response curve

total possible revenue ($541,500/$722,000). Table 1 summarizes the financial impact of multi-prices. It should be clear that if additional prices were added, more revenue would be captured.

This detailed example should convince the reader that Robert Crandall is correct when he says, 'I am obviously short 1600 prices.' The key to multiple prices is that each price must represent a different product and that those who have a high reservation price must be kept from buying less expensive products. This occurs through what is known as fences. Table 2 shows some typical fences in the hospitality industry.

In choosing fences, it is important that 'the fence' makes sense to the consumer. That is, the customer must believe that the rate he or she is paying is based on his or her choices, not on greed by the firm. For instance, the consumer needs to think 'I need to pay more because having flexibility is more important than price.'

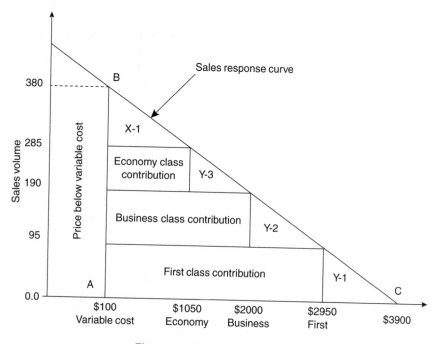

Figure 4   Airline sales response curve

Table 1   The financial impact of multiple pricing

	One Ticket price	First Class	Economy Class	First Class	Business Class	Economy Class
Price	$2,000	$2,633	$1,367	$2,950	$2,000	$1,050
Sales volume	190	127	127	95	95	95
Total passengers	190		254		285	
Increased (%)						
Passenger count from one price	NA	33.6%(254–190)/190		50%(285–190)/190		
Contribution	$361,000	$482,6000		$180,500		
Money left on table passed up	$361,000	$239,400		$180,500		

Table 2   'Potential' fences

Rule type	Advanced Requirement	Refundability	Changeability	Must Stay
Advance purchase	3-days	Non-refundable	No changes	Weekend
Advance reservation	7-days	Partially refundable (% refund or fixed$)	Change to dates of stay, but not number of rooms	Weekday
	14-days	Fully refundable	Changes, but pay fee, must still meet rules	
	21-days		Full changes, non-refundable	
	30-days		Full changes allowed	

Or, 'I am paying more because I cannot decide exactly what I want to do.'

One fence that is not listed in Table 2 is the 'loyalty fence.' This is a fence for frequent and loyal customers. The firm that offers multiple prices must be careful that the pricing decision does not destroy loyal customers' trust in the organization and hence, their loyalty. In research where loyal hotel consumers were presented with a hypothetical situation where the hotel they were loyal towards increased its rate because of anticipated demand consumers were asked how this would change their attitudes and behaviors towards the hotel. Findings indicated that 60% of the customers would inquire as to the rate the next time they called for a reservation (normally, loyal customers do not ask about rates). In addition, 35.7% would call other hotels in the area to get their prices. Clearly, the loyal guest needs to be treated differently than the guest who comes for a one-night stay.

In summary, the challenge is to determine how many different 'products' can be offered to the customer to maximize revenue. Again, these products not only include the room type, but the method and time of booking and length of stay. For a firm that can get this right, the rewards are great.

Reference

Dolan, Robert J. and Simon, Herman (1996) *Power Pricing: How Managing Price Transform the Bottom Line.* New York: The Free Press.

STOWE SHOEMAKER
UNIVERSITY OF HOUSTON, USA

Price discrimination

A pricing action may be judged as a case of price discrimination *when a seller charges competing buyers different prices for 'commodities' of like grade and quality.* Discriminatory prices might be direct, or indirect in the form of allowances (e.g., payments for advertising or other services). For differential pricing to be deemed discriminatory and illegal, however, it must substantially lessen competition in commerce or be intended to injure, destroy, or prevent competition among buyers.

Because price discrimination essentially involves charging buyers different prices for the same commodity, it is rarely found in cases involving the sale of services or other intangibles due to the inherent variability of these market offerings. Moreover, even in situations where price discrimination of commodity sales appears to have occurred, sellers have defenses against liability. The two most common are cost justification and changing conditions. With a *cost-justification defense*, sellers can argue that the costs of producing, selling, or delivering to different buyers varies, as when it costs less for a seller to service a high-volume account (e.g., chain restaurants) as opposed to a smaller buyer (e.g., an independent operator). Differential pricing in the form of quantity discounts is acceptable in such circumstances, provided the seller can produce evidence of actual differences in cost when selling to different buyers. A *changing-conditions defense* is typically argued when perishable goods are involved or some amount of time has elapsed between the sales to two or more buyers such that demand for the commodity has changed.

As the qualifiers to the basic concept of price discrimination suggest, it is difficult for buyers to prove price discrimination. The Robinson–Patman Act of 1936 was intended to address price discrimination, especially complaints by smaller, less-powerful retailers that large chain stores were obtaining favorable prices from manufacturers. However, the Robinson–Patman Act has been criticized for sometimes harming competition as opposed to promoting it; consequently, private enforcement of the act by legal channels is difficult and usually requires evidence that the intent of an act of price discrimination is predatory and designed to drive rivals out of business.

Interestingly, though the name implies an illegal marketing activity, price discrimination is not illegal *per se*, and it is widely practiced as a profit-maximizing pricing approach. When used as a marketing strategy, differential pricing goes by such names as segmented pricing or revenue management. For example, senior citizens often receive discounts at restaurants or theaters, children pay reduced fares on public transportation, and women often pay more than men for dry cleaning, haircuts, and clothing alteration. Such examples of segmented pricing work because different buyer segments have different price elasticities, though in the case of gender-based pricing, this differential willingness to pay is dubious. Similarly, airline passengers and hotel guests are likely to pay different prices for the same seat or hotel room as the customer right next to them. This revenue-managed approach to differential pricing is made possible because demand for a perishable, fixed-capacity inventory (seats on a plane or rooms in a hotel) is often time-variable – typically, customers who buy closer to the use date (e.g., business travelers) are less price-sensitive.

These examples are also not illegal because they primarily involve services as opposed to commodities of like grade and quality. Furthermore, by charging individual consumer or consumer groups differential prices, competition is usually not threatened. Thus, the Robinson–Patman Act fails to apply. This is not to say, however, that such pricing strategies are perceived as fair. Indeed, revenue-managed prices can be perceived as unfair by customers, especially when it is difficult to keep segmented buyers separate. This can occur, for example, when business and leisure travelers both purchase airline seats of the same class, and when the only variable that impacts prices paid is the timing of the purchase. In addition, some local governments have passed laws making it illegal to use gender-based segmented pricing, arguing that such a practice runs foul of human rights and gender-discrimination laws.

Reference

Philips, L. (1983) *Economics of Price Discrimination.* Cambridge: Cambridge University Press.

ROBERT KWORTNIK
CORNELL UNIVERSITY, USA

Price earnings ratio

The price earnings (P/E) ratio enables a comparison to be made between the earnings per share and the market price of the share. It is calculated as follows:

$$\text{Price/Earning} = \frac{\text{Current market price per share}}{\text{Earnings per share}}$$

This ratio can be seen as the number of years that it would take, at the current share price and rate of earnings, for the earnings from the share to cover the price of the share, and is, therefore, in effect a capitalization factor. The ratio indicates how much an investor is prepared to pay for the business earnings and is one of the most common methods of share valuation. The value of the ratio depends mostly on the past movements in earnings and interest rates and a relatively high value would suggest that the prospects for an industry are optimistic. The price earnings ratio for different hospitality enterprises may vary significantly. Typically price earnings ratios for the hospitality firms tend to be lower than averages for other industry sectors, reflecting the relative risk of the business, the stability of earnings, perceived earnings trend, and the perceived potential growth of the share price.

References

Dyson, J.R. (2003) *Accounting for Non-accounting Students*. London: FT Prentice-Hall.

Schmidgall, R.S. (2002) *Hospitality Industry Managerial Accounting*, 5th edn. Lansing, MI: Educational Institute of the American Hotel and Lodging Association.

DEBRA ADAMS
ARENA4FINANCE LTD, UK

Pricing acronyms

- *RevPAR* is an acronym for revenue per available room. The term is frequently used in revenue management regarding hotel operations.
- *RevPAC* is an acronym for revenue per available customer. The term is frequently used in revenue management regarding service operations.
- *ValuePAC* is an acronym for value per available customer. This term was only recently introduced to the hospitality literature. The term suggests that pricing should be based on the potential value a consumer presents to an organization. This potential value is based on the consumer's previous behavior.

Reference

Shoemaker, S. (2003) Future of revenue management: the future of pricing in services. *Journal of Revenue and Pricing Management*, 2, 271–279.

BRUMBY MCLEOD
UNIVERSITY OF NEVADA, LAS VEGAS, USA

Pricing methods in foodservice/restaurants

Foodservice operators traditionally choose from among a handful of menu pricing models. The first of these is the non-structured approach, known also as seat-of-the-pants pricing. More quantitative approaches in general use include the factor method, the prime-cost method, the actual-cost method, the gross-profit method, and the stochastic-modeling approach.

Non-structured pricing is the simplest approach to catering pricing. It involves a cursory examination of the competition's prices without regard to other factors. Although this method is completely inadequate, some operators still use it.

The factor method is the most common tactic used in pricing and dates back more than 100 years to hotel-restaurant operators in Europe. A 'factor' is established by dividing 1.0 by the desired food-cost percentage. (For example, a 37% food cost would result in a factor of 2.7.) The raw food cost for an item is then multiplied by the factor to produce the menu price. An item with a food cost of $2.25 would therefore be represented on the menu at a cost of $6.08. This method's simplicity makes it popular. (An alternative calculation is simply to divide the raw food cost by the desired food cost percentage.) The downside is that not every item should be marked up by the same proportion, since this would price high-cost items beyond market value. Also, low-cost items such as coffee, which normally produces a higher than usual contribution margin, would be priced too low to generate an adequate return. Finally, this method does not reflect the potentially differing labor costs associated with different items.

The prime-cost method is a variation of the factor method and integrates both raw product and labor costs. This method requires that labor costs be separated into direct labor costs (labor used for the preparation of a specific menu item) and indirect labor costs (labor used to finish the item, such as grilling, frying, etc.) for each menu item. The biggest advantage here is that this method reflects differences between labor-intensive items and prepared foods. The challenge is to make such allocations accurately, particularly since these may vary with the volume of items sold. Consider a simple example using only a single menu item. Assuming that the total direct and indirect labor costs for a steak sandwich (including the cost of benefits) is $2.60, the desired food cost is 37%, and the desired labor cost is 38%, the price of the item is calculated as:
- ($2.25 + 2.60)/(37% + 38%) = $6.47.

The actual-cost method accomplishes the vital goal of including profit as part of every price on the menu. It uses food cost dollars, total labor cost per guest, related variable cost percentage (covering such items as paper goods), fixed cost percentage (critical when space or equipment must be rented as part of the catering agreement), and the desired profit percentage. While limited to information found on the pro forma statement, this method is useful in that the inputs are more inclusive. The calculation, using fictitious numbers for a generic item, is as shown in Figure 1.

The gross-profit method is designed to indicate a specific amount of money that should be made on the basis of the number of guests served. This improves on the previously discussed methods since the focus is on gross profit; but because it is predicated on the accuracy of prior data and is specific to the number of guests, erroneous data or inaccurate forecasts can affect the pricing structure dramatically.

Assume that an operation typically sells 100 orders of an item, say a turkey sandwich with fries, and that the desired gross profit is 63%. Related data suggest that such an item at that volume should produce revenue of $1368. Thus, the targeted gross profit is $862 or $8.62 per person. Assuming food cost for the specific menu is $4.25, the price for the menu is $12.87 per person. This method underscores how important accurate sales forecasts are to the pricing function.

The stochastic-modeling approach is the only method of pricing that integrates internal and external variables, particularly demand functions such as item popularity and the market position of the caterer. In the event that off-site catering is a new venture for an on-site operator, the market

position may be intentionally undervalued in the beginning. Conversely, if the reputation of the on-site staff is already recognized in the marketplace or the products offered are unavailable elsewhere, the market position is considerable and should be reflected in the pricing algorithm.

The data necessary to price the menu using this approach is:

Oc = Percentage of sales allocated to costs other than food and labor (sometimes referred to, somewhat incorrectly, as occupation costs)

Lc = Percentage of sales allocated to labor

Pm = Percentage of menu price (MP) desired for profit mark-up (which may vary for different items)

FC = Raw food cost

Mc = A subjective determination of market sensitivity to the catering firm; this is the variable representing promotional discounts or premiums

The menu price calculation, then, is:

$$\text{Menu price} = \frac{FC}{(100\% \, MP) - (Lc + Oc + [Pm * Mc])}$$

Using a catering example, assume that a customer requests a luncheon for 100 guests with an Italian-themed menu. Market analysis performed by the caterer suggests that competing firms, particularly the one considered the best in town, promote menus appropriate for this event at a sizeable mark-up. The caterer decides on a conservative profit of 10% but also wants to include a 5% discount from the total profit to promote the business. The resulting calculation, assuming 25 and 38% for Oc and Lc, respectively, and a raw food cost of $3.92, is:

$$Oc + Lc + (Pm * Mc) = 72.5\%; \text{ therefore,}$$
$$\text{food cost is } 27.5\%$$
$$MP = FC/(MP\% \text{ available for food})$$
$$= \$3.92/27.5\% = \$14.25$$

This list of menu-pricing approaches is not exhaustive. Some computer packages simplify the process, and some integrate various additional

EP cost ($)	Selling price = X
+ Labor ($)	Var., fixed, & profit = 34%
+ Variable cost (%)	Food & labor = $4.85
+ Fixed cost (%)	Food & labor = 100% − 34%
+ Profit (%)	= .66
	.66X = $4.85
= Menu price	
	X = $4.85/.66 = $7.35
	Therefore, the menu price is $7.35

Figure 1 Determining the menu price

variables. The important thing is to understand how each of these variables functions in producing individual or whole menu prices. And as with most management functions, menu pricing blends science and art; failure to embrace both will result in less-than-optimal operating results.

References

Miller, J.E. and Pavesic, D.V. (1996) *Menu Pricing and Strategy*. New York: Van Nostrand Reinhold.

Reynolds, D. (2003) *On-Site Foodservice Management: A Best Practices Approach*. Hoboken, NJ: John Wiley & Sons.

DENNIS REYNOLDS
WASHINGTON STATE UNIVERSITY

Pricing practices in hospitality/tourism

Price is one of the four pillars of the marketing mix (4Ps) and price is the only 'P' that is directly related to revenue production. According to Cressman (1997), most managers make poor pricing decisions. Managers make bad decisions because they have inadequate or incorrect information about their customers and competitors (Monroe, 2003, p. 3). Traditional thinking and simplified methods of cost-plus pricing, room rates of dollars per $1000 construction cost may not be effective in the current competitive markets where consumers neither know nor care for cost information. In the global economy, consumers have an abundance of choices for hospitality services. Consumers prefer and practice competitive shopping from home or office using the Internet as an effective shopping tool for the desired product attributes.

Traditionally pricing decisions are made as operational-centered practices that are driven by the objective of maximizing contribution margins per unit of production. These practices no longer hold true in the market-driven economy where price is set by the consumer demand, not by the production cost. Thus market-driven and consumer-centered pricing practices are highly recommended to be able to compete in the global economy. Unfortunately, the classic economic principles of supply and demand do not work exactly in the hospitality business. For example, when Mr Herrera, a restaurant owner in Houston, Texas increased menu prices by about 40% over a 3 year period, his restaurant actually experienced an increase in revenues at a higher percentage than the price increases, indicating low resistance to price increases (Kotler *et al.*, 2003, pp. 373–374). In Ohio, USA, a privately held hotel management company with a portfolio of nationally recognized hotel brands changed its pricing practices. The senior management decided to add 95 cents at the end of each price presentation at all properties they managed (psychological pricing). As a result, this particular hotel management company realized a significant improvement in contribution margins. At the same time, interestingly, there was no change in consumer satisfaction ratings towards the concerned hotel brands. Collins and Parsa (2004) estimated that if all hotels in the United States adopted this innovative pricing strategy, the hotel industry would realize nearly an additional $700 million as net profit. These real industry examples indicate that hospitality pricing is much more complicated than simple economics, product costing, and intuition. Therefore, some of the most commonly used pricing practices in the hospitality field and the pros and cons of each method are presented below.

Competition-based pricing

This practice is more common than most people admit to in the hospitality industry. It is a strategy that is prevalent in the travel and tourism industry. It is also called 'price matching.' Airline companies often match price reductions/increases by the competition immediately. Very often hotels and restaurateurs follow the pricing strategy of the competition, with the fear that they will price themselves out of the market. It is also based on the belief that somehow the competition knows something that we don't know. In this scenario, market leaders often set the price level and others follow the lead. This practice may be adopted by any segment of the industry.

Target pricing method

This method is based on the principles that each product must contribute a certain amount of profit. Target pricing practice is based on the principle of break-even analysis. Some hotels try to reach break-even points by lowering or increasing prices as the supply and demand changes with a consideration to variable costs.

In the foodservice industry, this method is appropriate for institutional foodservice and catering where each customer is charged a set amount. Usually companies that follow this method calculate the total food cost and overhead and add a desired amount of profit. The total amount is divided by the total number of customers to arrive at a menu price for each meal. This method may or may not be appropriate for commercial restaurants as they follow à la carte pricing practices.

Cost-based approach

This approach is the most commonly used and easiest method to understand and implement in the hospitality industry. This method simply adjusts the product price to achieve a desired cost percentage. For example, some restaurants aim to achieve 30% food cost percentage. If the cost of food for a menu item is $8.00 the restaurant has to divide the food cost dollars ($8.00) with 30% to arrive at the desired menu price ($26.66 round up to $26.75 or $27.00). This method assumes that food prices remain constant and unaffected by seasonality. Though it is simple to use, this method does not take into consideration impact on consumer preferences, revenues, and price elasticity for each product.

From a marketing perspective, this method is not a prudent choice. Customers neither know nor care for product cost information. Customers are more concerned about the value they receive for the price they pay.

Line pricing

Line pricing can be practiced only by large organizations with a wide array of products offered within various product lines. It is commonly noted in the hotel industry. For example, when a hotel organization has a portfolio of hotel lines, it can set the price for each hotel line (brand) differently to match the target customers' needs and expectations. Such a pricing practice must also match the services offered by that specific hotel line. In this scenario, one may find the same hotel company practicing different pricing strategies to meet the different needs of each hotel line. As is obvious, hospitality companies that specialize in a single line of products cannot practice this strategy.

Price bundling

Price bundling takes place when a hospitality-tourism company wraps several products with one price. It is most commonly noted in the tourism industry. For example, a tour operator may wrap travel, hotel accommodations, food, entertainment, and sightseeing services with one charge. By charging one set price for several bundled services, tour operators may gain economies of scale. Bundled services are also very common in the hotel industry. It is very common for high-end hotels to offer weekend packages to include lodging, dining, and entertainment in town. Similarly, even planners may prefer to offer bundled services to improve their revenues. From the customers' perspective, price bundling is an additional service at a reduced price. Bundled products minimize the search efforts for various sources of services. Typically business travelers prefer bundled services to economize the search process.

Value pricing

This method is often followed by companies that try to create a high value image such as budget hotels and quick-service restaurants. Budget properties try to maintain value leadership by offering the lowest price possible for minimum amenities. Economy hotels try to maintain a clear 'price distance' from mid-price and high-end properties. High-end, luxury, prestige properties often take leadership roles in pricing decisions by setting the upper 'ceiling' for price points.

In the foodservice industry, this concept is treated slightly differently. Restaurants that follow this strategy tend to charge the lowest price possible but only for selected items. These items are tagged as value leaders. The rest of the menu items are priced at normal levels.

This strategy often attracts value-centered customers and customers visiting for the first time. The downside of this strategy includes resistance to periodic price increases by the value-centered loyal customers. In such a case, value leader menu items eventually become loss leaders. Often market share leaders with 'deep pockets' could afford to play this game and keep prices artificially low, as is often done by the giant retailers at the expense of small entrepreneurs. Budget and economy hotels always face the challenge of resistance for price increases from consumers.

Prestige pricing

High-end resorts, tourism attractions, and fine dining restaurants may adopt this strategy. It is based on the belief that consumers associate high prices with high quality and low prices with low quality. Restaurants that maintain a large inventory of wines follow this strategy to reflect the image of the valuable and prestigious wine collection. This strategy has limited appeal and limited usage for many mid-price and low-end hospitality firms. High-end resorts, cruise lines, exclusive tour operators, etc. follow this strategy to offer additional psychological benefits of exclusivity.

Psychological pricing

This pricing strategy emphasizes consumer psychology and attitude about pricing rather than economics. Typically consumers tend to ignore the right-most digits in making purchase decisions. Thus hospitality firms may use price endings as marketing tools. According to a paper published in the *Cornell Hotel and Restaurant Quarterly* (Parsa and Naipul, 2001), high-end restaurants prefer to use 0 endings to present high-quality *image* and low-end restaurants prefer to use 9 endings to

project *high-value image*. Some ethnic restaurants, mostly Asian, tend to avoid using digits 9 and 4 as price endings and consider even numbers as lucky numbers and odd numbers as bad luck numbers. Budget hotels and motels usually follow psychological pricing. But Collins and Parsa (2004) reported that some of the high-end hotel companies have also begun practicing psychological pricing, especially after the downturn following the 9/11 tragedy in the United States.

Point spread and price point

Point spread strategy is common across all segments of the hospitality industry. According to this strategy, companies prefer to maintain a certain point spread distance above and below the competition. If the competitor above raises prices, then a hospitality firm may try to maintain the price distance by raising prices proportionately.

In the hotel industry, the price points vary geographically. Price points for major metropolitan companies differ from medium and smaller-size cities. Similarly, price points for downtown properties vary from the rural and suburban properties. Various segments of the hotel industry try to identify the appropriate price points for their segment and try to match the pricing strategies.

In the restaurant industry, some companies try to identify the price points that their customers do not like to cross. This phenomenon is common where buffet pricing or prix fixe is practiced. Customers resist price increases under those conditions and set 'price points.' Some restaurants find that certain menu items are 'sacred cows' and cannot be touched. One hospital firm learned that the number one seller in its cafeteria was chicken wings and customers were very price-sensitive about chicken wings. This price sensitivity did not extend to other menu items. These are called 'price resistors.' Every restaurateur should know the 'price resistor' of their own operation.

Promotional pricing

This strategy is often noted in tourism–hospitality industries. It is very common to promote a product at a reduced price for a short duration to increase product trials. The primary objective of this strategy is to 'pull' consumers towards a product or service by offering temporary economic incentives. This strategy is effective only if it is supported by strong operational efficiency, effective distributional channels, and high consistency in product/service quality. It is effective only as a short-term solution. If an organization is not well prepared to deliver the goods and services as promised, promotional strategies do more harm than good. So it is not recommended when an organization is not operationally competent. In that case, more consumers may try the promoted product to take advantage of the economic incentives and may be disappointed by poor execution.

Promotional pricing is often practiced effectively in introducing a new product at an existing establishment or when entering a new market by an established brand. This strategy may also help in gaining market share from the competition but it is not recommended for those purposes. If promotional pricing is used to gain market share, it may lead to 'price wars' thus leading to economic losses for participants in an industry.

Several market-driven pricing strategies have been described. They include competition-based, target return, cost-based, price lining, bundling, value-based, prestige, psychological, point spread and price point, and promotional pricing. These market-driven and consumer-centered pricing practices are highly recommended to be able to compete in the dynamic global economy.

References

Collins, Mike and Parsa, H.G. (2004) Revenue maximization through an innovative pricing strategy in the hotel industry. *CHRIE Conference*, Philadelphia, PA.

Cressman, G.E. (1997) Snatching defeat from the jaws of victory: why do good managers make bad pricing decisions? *Marketing Management*, 6 (Summer), 9–19.

Dolan, Robert, J. and Simon, Herman (2002) *Power Pricing: How Managing Price Transforms the Bottom Line*. New York: The Free Press.

Kotler, P., Bowen, J. and Makens, J. (2003) *Marketing for Hospitality and Tourism*. Upper Saddle River, NJ: Prentice-Hall.

Monroe, Kent (2003) *Pricing: Making Profitable Decisions*, 3rd edn. New York: McGraw-Hill Irvin.

Nagle, T.T. and Holden, R.K. (1995) *The Strategy and Tactics of Pricing: A Guide to Profitable Decision-Making*, 2nd edn. Englewood Cliffs, NJ: Prentice-Hall.

Parsa, H.G. and Naipaul, S. (2001) Price endings as communication cues, and consumer response behavior: a study of the restaurant industry. *Cornell Hotel and Restaurant Administration Quarterly*, 42 (1), 26–37.

H.G. PARSA
THE OHIO STATE UNIVERSITY, USA

Pricing types

Hospitality firms use various methods to set prices for their products. Hospitality managers select different pricing approaches based on one or a combination of several factors: a firm's cost structure, competitors' prices, and customer value perceptions of hospitality products. Cost-based pricing usually involves marking-up techniques of actual variable costs (product costs) at a certain desired product cost percentage. Alternatively, pricing methods based on customer's value perceptions of hospitality products exclude the consideration of costs and attempt to provide value by offering high quality at low prices. Hospitality firms can also apply price sensitivity measurement (PSM) methods which reveal how relationships between price and quality affect customers' perceptions of value. In addition, price sensitivity measurement data combined with activity-based cost (a cost accounting system that traces overhead costs to individual products) allows for designed profits and is defined as activity-based pricing (Daly, 2002).

Furthermore, several price adjustment strategies, such as volume, and based-on-time-of-purchase discounting, as well as discriminatory pricing, are used in the hospitality industry (Kotler *et al.*, 2003). A popular example of discriminatory pricing is yield management, a pricing approach that involves charging various room rates to different market segments. Finally, many hospitality firms set their prices by considering demand and costs as secondary factors and set prices according to 'going rates' of competitors.

References

Kotler, P., Bowen, J., and Makens, J. (2003) *Marketing for Hospitality and Tourism*, 3rd edn. Upper Saddle River, NJ: Prentice-Hall.

Daly, J.L. (2002) *Pricing for Profitability: Activity-based Pricing for Competitive Advantage*. New York: John Wiley & Sons.

CAROLA RAAB
UNIVERSITY OF NEW HAMPSHIRE, USA

Primary and secondary electric power rates

Normally, hotels are on a 'secondary' electric power rate with electricity supplied at 480 volts or less. That is, the meter is set on the customer's side of a transformer that is owned by the utility company. Primary power customers take power from a utility meter that is in the line before the customer-owned transformer. Primary power may be supplied at voltages in excess of 480 volts and up to in excess of 13,400 volts.

The primary power customer pays a lower kilowatt-hour rate than secondary power customers do, but primary customers must pay for the transformer or pay for a replacement if the existing one fails. Primary power can be a dramatic energy saving for hotels that can qualify for the rate – usually only very large full service properties, large convention centers or resort properties. A majority of hotels are secondary power customers.

JIM ACKLES
THARALDSON ENERGY GROUP, USA

Prime costs

Prime costs are the most significant cost for any operation. In a foodservice operation, these costs include raw materials (food and beverage) and labor costs. The associated labor costs include labor payroll (salaried and hourly), payroll taxes, and employee benefits. In the United States, these costs typically constitute 50–70% of total revenues. Managers generally spend more time trying to manage prime costs than any other costs because they comprise such a large portion of total costs. The majority of prime costs are variable, which means that managers have some ability to control their totals in the short term.

Always expressed as a percentage of total sales, this number is considered the most important in determining profitability since controlling prime costs plays such a determining role in whether the operation can meet its financial goals. The prime costs indicator is also used often in comparing restaurants within a given segment as a barometer of unit- and corporate-level managers' operational prowess. This measure also affords operators the latitude to trade labor efficiencies realized through the use of food ingredients requiring less handing (such as par-cooked meats or shredded cheese) with increased food costs in their efforts to minimize overall prime costs.

Reference

Dittmer, P.R. (2002) *Principles of Food, Beverage, and Labor Cost Controls*. New York: John Wiley & Sons.

DEBORAH BARRASH
UNIVERSITY OF NEVADA, LAS VEGAS, USA

Private Club Advisor organization

The Private Club Advisor (PCA) organization, established in 1990, produces timely information that is specific to the private club industry that can be found in two publications: *The Private Club Advisor* and *PCA Plus*. The *Private Club Advisor* (*PCA*) has a circulation of 16,000 readers that comprise private club chief operating officers (general managers), club officers, private club owners, and club members.

The foci of the PCA are to (a) up-date club executives on trends and issues of great importance, and (b) improve the transfer of information between policy-makers (e.g., law-makers, government officials, etc.) and management so that club managers can properly implement policies. *PCA Plus* is targeted toward top-level executive members of private clubs and specifically focuses on issues surrounding daily club operations. It should also be noted that students and faculty of private club related programs can access these services and more at http://www.privateclubadvisor.com and http://www.pca-plus.com. Relative to this educational outreach to academic programs, students can learn about the characteristics of private clubs and differentiate clubs from other hospitality operations; the role of private clubs in society; and have access to discussion of contemporary issues and trends in private club management.

Reference

PCA (2004) *The Private Club Advisor*. Club Advisory Communications Corporation. St. Louis, MO.

RANDALL S. UPCHURCH
UNIVERSITY OF CENTRAL FLORIDA, USA

Private club dining types

As the private club product evolved over time, the type of club service offerings changed in direct accordance to member wishes. In particular, one area of the private clubs industry that has witnessed the most dramatic change in member desires is that of foodservice operations. In particular, the type of dining facilities has evolved from a formal to an informal dining experience. This is not to say that all private club have disbanded a formal dining experience, instead the switch has been in offering both. The enforcement of policies surrounding the club's foodservice outlets is the province of the clubhouse committee. For instance, the clubhouse committee requires the membership to dress in formal attire while being served in the formal dining room, which typifies a formal dining experience.

Conversely, the clubhouse committee loosens the dress requirements for an informal dining experience by allowing casual business attire or perhaps resort casual attire. It should be understood that this change in dining room ambience has not necessarily mandated the alteration or construction of new facilities. To the contrary, this conversion process has typically been achieved through an exchange of the table dressings and altered member dress codes.

References

Perdue, Joe (1997) *Contemporary Club Management*. Lansing, MI: Educational Institute of the American Hotel and Motel Association.
White, Ted and Gerstner, Larry (1991) *Club Operations and Management*. New York: Van Nostrand Reinhold.

ARAM SON
JAMES COOK UNIVERSITY, AUSTRALIA

Private club industry

The private club industry has a very rich history of exclusive clubs that are designed to satisfy members' social, recreational, sporting, political, professional or other preferences and purposes. The richness of this history has been traced to clubs that catered to those of aristocratic backgrounds from the 1700s onward in clubs located in England and Scotland. To affirm this need for affiliation and recreation the combination of a club setting and golf has been traced by various authors to the Royal and Ancient Golf Club of St Andrews, Scotland. Clearly this makes the private club industry one of the more established segments of the hospitality industry.

According to a study conducted by the Club Managers Association of America (CMAA), there are over 14,000 private clubs located throughout the United States. These 14,000 private clubs generate over 11.322 billion dollars each year, which is a significant economic impact. Moreover, private clubs generate 4.5 billion dollars in annual member dues, 3.795 billion dollars in food and beverage fees, an average annual club income of

4.9 million dollars, with 320 million in sales tax revenue. In addition, 302,000 people are on private club payrolls for an annual payroll of 4.4 billion dollars.

References

Brymer, R. (2004) *Hospitality and Tourism: An Introduction to the Industry.* Dubuque, IA: Kendall/Hunt Publishing.
Walker, J. (2004) *Introduction to Hospitality Management.* Upper Saddle River, NJ: Prentice-Hall.

RANDALL S. UPCHURCH
UNIVERSITY OF CENTRAL FLORIDA, USA

Private club management to leadership model

At the 2004 Club Managers Association of American (CMAA) conference held in Anaheim, California, leaders of CMAA unveiled their management to leadership model. The leadership of CMAA expects this leadership model to revolutionize the management of the private club industry by compartmentalizing the leadership process via identifying general manager leadership skills that heretofore have not been identified. It should be understood that this model is the result of a focus group of private club managers concerning what they thought were critical skills that lead to successful private club leadership.

This model is divided into three distinct components of (a) operations, (b) asset management, and (c) club culture. The operation dimension is subdivided into the skill areas of: property management, human and professional resources, management, marketing, food and beverage operations, golf/sports and recreation management, accounting and financial management, building and facilities management, and knowledge of government and external influences. The asset dimension consists of financial management skills, physical plant management of assets, and human resource asset management. The final and culminating dimension is culture as comprised of vision, history, club tradition, and governance issues.

Given that this was the rollout of this leadership model, these concepts remain to be field tested as to specific tactical strategies that result in any of the aforementioned leadership dimensions. However, many of these elements are logical and seemingly measurable.

References

Perdue, Joe (1997) *Contemporary Club Management.* Lansing, MI: Educational Institute of the American Hotel and Motel Association.
White, Ted and Gerstner, Larry (1991) *Club Operations and Management.* New York: Van Nostrand Reinhold.

ARAM SON
JAMES COOK UNIVERSITY, AUSTRALIA

Private club merchandising

The concept of merchandising is not the sole province of the retail industry. In fact, merchandising in the private club industry is a mainstay of the private club manager's arsenal leading to club member satisfaction. Private club merchandising is a comprehensive process that encompasses internal advertising, internal marketing, and the production of promotional materials, the intent being the provision of services that meet or exceed membership needs. Examples can be found in the clubhouse via menu construction that offers a wide array of food and beverage items that appeal to a vast array of member palates. The area of the club in which merchandising is the most pronounced is perhaps that of the pro shop. The products in the pro shop should indicate distinction that is sought by the membership via brand name or signature clothing and equipment. In turn, the pro shop offers advice in equipment use and in the repair of this equipment if the occasion arises. Furthermore, the pro shop further follows tried and true merchandising rules by use of adequate lighting, layout design of the merchandise, use of indirect lighting, spot lighting, and diffused lighting for visual enhancements of the products on display.

References

Perdue, Joe (1997) *Contemporary Club Management*. Lansing, MI: Educational Institute of the American Hotel and Motel Association.

White, Ted and Gerstner, Larry (1991) *Club Operations and Management*. New York: Van Nostrand Reinhold.

ARAM SON
JAMES COOK UNIVERSITY, AUSTRALIA

Private club overtime tax exemption

In the United States, overtime tax exemption for private clubs represents an exemption offered by the Internal Revenue Service relative to commission-based wage earners. As with lodging and restaurant operations, taxation issues are a constant concern to the operator and the employee. Such is the case with overtime taxes seeing that this can be very costly to the private club and viewed by the employee as a negative because the income tax ramifications often offset the desire to work overtime. According to the US Department of Labor Fact Sheet No. 20 the following three conditions, if satisfied, would qualify the private club (employer) for overtime exemption: (a) the employee is employed by the private club; (b) the employee's rate of pay exceeds one an one-half that applicable minimum wage for every hour worked in the assigned work week; and (c) more than half of the employee's total earnings consists of commissions. The benefits of exercising this ruling is twofold; first, the club becomes protected from elevated labor costs, and second, the club's employees are provided with a competitive wage in their given market. To date, this issue of overtime exemption remains unchallenged by the Internal Revenue Service.

Reference

Finan, T. (2004) *PCA Plus*. Club Advisory Communications Corporation. St Louis, MO.

RANDALL S. UPCHURCH
UNIVERSITY OF CENTRAL FLORIDA, USA

Private equity club committee types

Committees within an equity club are very influential relative to the overall operation of the private club given the role in advising the board of directors about club operations. It is important to note that participation on a club committee is entirely voluntary in nature, which often means that serving on a club committee indicates strong personal interest in the overall operation of the club. It is also important to note that members who are chosen to sit on certain committees must also have some knowledge of the charges assigned to the committee.

In this advisory function a club committee merely offers advice relative to the board of directors on club policies that are within the charge of the committee as set forth in the club's bylaws. Within these bylaws the board of directors sets the duties and responsibilities of each club committee, length of term, committee structure, and reporting structure. In order to promote majority consensus on issues, a committee's membership requires an odd number of members so a majority vote can be obtained versus a split vote.

In general, the guidelines surrounding committee structure are: (a) membership is limited to a specific number (commonly an odd number) to promote discussion and resolution of issues; (b) committees set policy relative to a specific function (e.g., membership, clubhouse policies, golf, etc.); (c) committees directly advise the board of directors; and (d) committees communicate and seek advice from club management so that pertinent issues are addressed and acted upon by the committee.

There are two basic types of committees found within a private club; first is the standing committee, and second, is the ad hoc committee. A standing committee indicates a permanent committee structure that deals with routine operations. Examples of standing committees include the: athletic committee, bylaw committee, entertainment committee, executive committee, finance and budget committee, golf course committee, house committee, membership committee, nominating committee, and strategic planning committee.

An ad hoc committee is a temporary committee that is established for the sole purpose of dealing with a pressing issue on a one-time basis. A good example of a one-time issue would be the renovation of the clubhouse.

The *athletic committee* is a standing committee of a private club that reviews, enforces, and mandates policies concerning sports activities. In this function the athletic committee establishes rules for all sports activities (e.g. hours of operation), assists the respective sports professionals in the development of an annual budget for the sports outlet in question (e.g. tennis, racquet ball, squash, etc.), assists in the development of new sports programs that fit the needs of the club's membership.

The *bylaw committee* within a private club is a pivotal standing committee that reviews, develops, amends, and appeals the club's bylaws. In doing so, the bylaw committee makes recommendations directly to the board of directors. It is critical for the bylaw committee to ensure that club bylaws are in accordance with state and national laws.

The *entertainment committee*, also known as the social committee, of a private club is charged with establishing policies that surround the club's entertainment selection. The duties of this committee include the selection of regular entertainment to special events that correspond with holidays and festivals. As such, this committee is empowered to accept or reject all entertainment applicants on behalf of the club's membership.

An *executive committee* is sometimes known as the club's steering committee. This standing committee serves as the main vehicle that collects and acts upon club operational issues as forwarded by the standing committees on issues that require a quick and efficient response that does not require the entire board to meet, discuss, and take action.

The *finance and budget committee* is a standing committee that is assigned duties and responsibilities relative to the club's financial situation. These duties range from constructing the annual operational and capital expenditure budget, tracking initiation fees and membership dues, and proper investment of club assets. In short, this committee monitors accounts receivable, payable, and investment functions of the club.

The *golf course committee*, sometimes known as the greens or the grounds committee, of a private club is charged with oversight of the golf course. The primary duties of this standing committee concern play policies, daily maintenance issues (e.g. mowing, golf car maintenance), compliance with federal chemical regulations, and long-term course condition (e.g., capital expenditures).

The *house committee*, also known as the clubhouse committee, at a private club is given the charge of developing policies and general upkeep of the clubhouse and the surrounding grounds. In most cases, the particular duties of the house committee encompass: operational policies (e.g. hours of operation), preparation of the annual budget, capital expenditure budget, and consultation on menu offerings, and beverage and wine selections.

The *standing committee*, known as the membership committee, is pivotal in controlling membership and in interpreting the club's membership bylaws. It should be understood that the membership committee reviews all membership requests, as well as current members that are seeking reclassification. Due to this role, it is not uncommon to find this committee involved in applicant review, interviewing, decision notification, and the review and construction of a membership waiting list.

The *nomination committee* (otherwise known as the nominating committee) is a standing committee of a private club that is charged with forwarding members that are interested in being elected to the board of directors. In most cases, the nomination committee is chosen by the club president and reports directly to the board of directors.

The *strategic planning committee* is a standing committee of a private club that is charged with long-range capital improvement planning. This committee is given the specific charge of developing a three- to five-year projection concerning necessary building and equipment repairs. This committee plays a very critical role because it has to interface with projected renovation projects with other standing committees such as the finance committee, and general management of the club. Last but not least, the magnitude of these decisions mandates communication with the club's board of directors relative to suggested projects.

References

Perdue, Joe (1997) *Contemporary Club Management.* Lansing, MI: Educational Institute of the American Hotel and Motel Association.

White, Ted and Gerstner, Larry (1991) *Club Operations and Management.* New York: Van Nostrand Reinhold.

SUWATHANA BHURIPANYO
COCA-COLA CO., THAILAND

Private residence club

This is a membership concept in which a distinctive bundle of services and amenities are offered and provided to members/owners of a high-end real estate development; typically second homes or condominium resorts in which the members/owners have a fractional/interval ownership interest. Shares of the fractional ownership interests are generally 1/4 to 1/13 of full interest in a given parcel or unit. Ownership of each fractional interest is usually evidenced by a deed representing a fee simple fractional interest in a specific housing unit, plus an undivided interest in the common areas. PRCs generally offer and deliver services and amenities consistent with high-end vacation resort hotels but generally not found in traditional timeshare resorts. Examples of such services and amenities found in PRCs are: bell/luggage service, valet parking, ski storage (where appropriate), room service, daily housekeeping, year-round storage of personal property, concierge service, and vacation planning services. PRCs are further defined by the 'Club' rules and regulations, unique to each PRC, that govern the reservation process, owners association, and associated fees of membership in the PRC. It should be understood that a private resident club is not a timeshare due to the percentage of interest in the underlying real estate which is drastically higher in terms of 'share' than is the timeshare product because the typical timeshare is sold as one week out of 52 weeks for a 1/52 interest.

References

Hobson Ferry and Associates (2003) Industry overview of luxury fractional and private residence club. *Land Use Economics,* October 2000.

Ragatz and Associates (2003) *Fractional Interest Symposium.* Boca Raton, FL, May 2003.

MICHAEL HAUSHALTER
ORLANDO, FLORIDA, USA

Prix fixe

The French term *prix fixe* is used to identify a meal at a set price that covers several courses (e.g., appetizer, entrée, and dessert). Used today synonymously with table d'hôte, prix fixe offerings are usually associated with upscale restaurants and haute cuisine.

Prix fixe menus offer operators a number of advantages. First, there is substantial opportunity for maximizing profit since many of the lesser courses have a lower food cost while the large number of courses equate to a high perceived value to many guests. Second, if forecasts are accurate, an operator can monitor costs very closely since there is no waste or need for overproduction. Finally, the production and delivery of multiple courses can be streamlined owing to the limited number of menu offerings (compared to an operation with a lengthy menu).

The challenge of the prix fixe format is that dining duration is long thereby reducing the opportunity for operators to increase seat turnover. Nonetheless, if adequate care is taken in the pricing and positioning strategy, prix fixe can offer an attractive alternative. It is also a valuable approach for holiday meals when offering a full menu is not logistically advantageous due to volume of guests.

Reference

Labensky, S.T., Ingram, G.G., and Labensky, S.R. (2001) *Webster's New World Dictionary of Culinary Arts.* Upper Saddle River, NJ: Prentice-Hall.

JAKSA KIVELA
THE HONG KONG POLYTECHNIC
UNIVERSITY, HONG KONG SAR, CHINA

Pro shop

The existence of a pro shop within a private club is a direct artifact of the club's membership needs for sports or recreational services and merchandise. Relative to the game of golf, this is important to note because the primary reason that people join a club is the game of golf. In order to cater to these unique needs, private club management should provide an area that is operated as a high-class boutique and it addresses player game scheduling, training, equipment, or retail needs. The operation of a private club pro shop comes in two formats; the first is where the club owns the merchandise and all members play or equipment service requests are done by club employees; and the second is where the pro shop is leased by the golf pro who in turn acts as an independent contractor. Under this latter scenario, the merchandise that is sold in the pro shop is under the control of the pro with commissions being paid to the club for use of the pro shop facilities. Under either operational format the key is in providing the highest level of product quality and member service as possible. This is an important notation because the members often will not know or care who is the primary owner of the merchandise and services, because in their minds these are the responsibility of the club, and therefore all responsibility resides with club management.

References

Perdue, Joe (1997) *Contemporary Club Management.* Lansing, MI: Educational Institute of the American Hotel and Motel Association.
White, Ted and Gerstner, Larry (1991) *Club Operations and Management.* New York: Van Nostrand Reinhold.

ARAM SON
JAMES COOK UNIVERSITY, AUSTRALIA

Product life cycle

Marketers believe each product normally goes through a life cycle stage. Although not every product experiences all stages, it is assumed that a product experiences a typical pattern of the evolution from its birth to its termination. There are four stages of a product life cycle: introduction – growth – maturity – decline. Each stage of a PLC is distinct and marketers may adjust different marketing strategies for each stage to maximize a product's value and profitability (Ryan and Riggs, 1996). In the *introduction* stage, a new product is introduced into the market. Sales growth is normally slow because the customers are not aware of the product. A firm's objective is to create product awareness. Competition is at a minimum because the product is at the 'pioneering' stage (Onkvisit and Shaw, 1989). In the *growth* stage, sales increase rapidly. Competition increases as competitors see the product's profit potential. A firm makes profits and may expand market share. At maturity stage, sales volume is stable and sale growth rate is rather slow. Heavy promotion and cost reduction are required as competitors may lower prices and introduce an improved version of the product. In the *decline* stage, sales continue to decline. A firm may maximize profit by lowering product costs or withdraw the product from the market.

References

Onkvisit, S. and Shaw, J.J. (1989) *Product Life Cycles and Product Management.* Westhaven, CT: Quorum Books.
Ryan, C. and Riggs, W.E. (1996) Redefining the product life cycle: the five-element product wave. *Business Horizons,* September–October, 33–40.

EUNHA MYUNG
UNIVERSITY OF NEVADA, LAS VEGAS, USA

Production company

A production company offers a wide variety of technical, creative, and logistical services to meet the event objectives and budget of corporate and association planners. Projects of various size and complexity can range from product launches, training programs, entertainment concerts, theme parties and galas, event marketing programs, and business meetings with video-conferencing to multi-media campaigns. An event producer essentially can provide pre-conference planning, on-site management, and production services through complete turn-key program development or à la carte offerings.

Most planners rely on a production company's expertise in event strategy and technical design to bring the most innovative products and services in audiovisual and multi-media. Lighting, sound, staging, video, graphics, and set, costume, and prop design are important elements of the presentation providing production and technical direction of the event. Additional services in scripting, voice production, speaker selection, and coaching add to the overall strategic vision of the event.

Furthermore, production companies can be an excellent partner in branding corporate identity or creating conference themes and logos. Strategic communication and marketing is critical to event success. Logistically, production companies assist with site selection, contract management, food and beverage menu creation and management, trade show sale, travel coordination, ground transportation, and other event services. Projects involving the services of a production company demand expert creativity, project management, and integration of talents to exceed expectations.

References

Goldblatt, J. (2002) *Special Events: Twenty-First Century Global Event Management*, 3rd edn. Hoboken, NJ: John Wiley & Sons.

Silvers, J.R. (2004) *Production Event Coordination*. Hoboken, NJ: John Wiley & Sons.

AMANDA KAY CECIL
INDIANA UNIVERSITY, USA

Production schedule

A production schedule shows the sequence and quantity of kitchen production for a given day. The schedule must take into account the equipment needed, the time of preparation, the quantities needed, and the staffing required to complete the production based on inventory and the delivery of needed ingredients. As stated in Knight and Kotschevar (2000), 'The production sheet is the final control needed before the menu becomes a reality by means of kitchen production. It instructs both the purchasing department and the kitchen to purchase and prepare the food items for any particular day.' The goal is to eliminate over-purchasing and over-production, the chief causes of high food costs.

The production schedule will contain the following:

- Menu item
- Quantity needed (expressed in total yield or number of portions)
- The time the production needs to start and finish.

The production schedule is necessary for a comprehensive inventory management program. Without a production schedule in place for each item, management cannot accurately identify where unnecessary food-cost expenditures are occurring. Furthermore, these schedules ensure consistency of production, which can lead to increased customer satisfaction.

Reference

Knight, J.B. and Kotschevar, L.H. (2000) *Quantity Food Production, Planning and Management*, 3rd edn. New York: John Wiley & Sons.

DAVID V. PAVESIC
GEORGIA STATE UNIVERSITY, USA

Productivity

Schroeder (1985) defined productivity as the relation between the inputs and outputs of a productive system and this definition is widely adopted in the hospitality literature. However, the intangible nature of hospitality services complicates productivity management and measurement (Jones and Lockwood, 1989). It is difficult objectively to define and measure the service outputs being provided (e.g. number of guest-nights versus number of satisfied guests). The measurement and management of inputs/outputs are also complicated because of the simultaneous production and consumption of hospitality services as well as their perishability and heterogeneity.

Witt and Witt (1989) incorporated these issues into their identification of three problems regarding productivity measurement, namely the 'definition,' 'measurement,' and '*ceteris paribus*' problems. These issues are compatible with the following generic problems of productivity management recognized in the operations management literature: the identification of appropriate inputs and outputs, measures of those inputs and outputs, and ways of measuring the relationship between inputs and outputs. In the context of hospitality productivity analysis, Reynolds (1998) provided a solution – with specific relevance to on-site food-service – that incorporates a total-factor productivity statistic.

Expanding this even further, Sigala (2004) developed and validated a systematic, three-step approach to constructing robust productivity metrics. These are analyzed in the following.

The first step in developing useful productivity metrics is to address the definition problem. The latter refers to the problems encountered when trying to identify the right inputs and outputs of a sector, which is particularly difficult when the outputs/inputs are intangible or are highly heterogeneous. The selection of inputs/outputs depends on two issues: (a) the approach to productivity definition, namely whether to take a partial or total approach; and (b) the identification of the level or unit of analysis. Partial productivity metrics focus on specific inputs that can be easily identified and measured, while a total productivity metric considers all production inputs (Figure 1).

Because of the synergy among all inputs and the fact that hospitality inputs/outputs are amalgams of tangible and intangible/qualitative elements, a multi-factor or total factor view to productivity is proposed. Indeed, because long-term customer satisfaction is perhaps the most important service output, intangible elements that are an intrinsic part of the service experience, such as management style, staff flair, and expertise, should undoubtedly be crucial components of both productivity inputs and outputs. Productivity measurement becomes even more complex when one also examines the array of factors (e.g. aesthetics, ergonomics, management and ownership, demand variability, competition, staff flexibility, and marketing practices) that face managers attempting to enhance their companies' productivity.

Overall, the first step requires managers to decide whether productivity metrics would:

- Include all inputs and outputs rather than the consideration of each input at a time (partial measures)
- Measure both tangible and intangible features of inputs/outputs whether or not partial or total productivity ratios are calculated
- Consider other factors that may be external to the control of management but can crucially affect productivity, e.g. competition
- Consider all the previous factors or a combination of them.

The second issue affecting the selection of appropriate inputs/outputs is the level or unit of analysis. Inputs/outputs that are relevant to the level of analysis (e.g. hotel department, product, market segment) should be used (Figure 2). Productivity levels are interrelated, i.e. lower productivity levels affect higher levels, while

$$\text{Total productivity metric} = \frac{\text{Sales revenue}}{\text{Labor} + \text{Materials} + \text{Overheads} + \text{Energy}}$$

$$\text{Material productivity} = \frac{\text{Sales revenue}}{\text{Material costs}}$$

$$\text{Labor productivity} = \frac{\text{Sales revenue}}{\text{Direct labor costs}}$$

Figure 1 Total *vs.* partial productivity metric

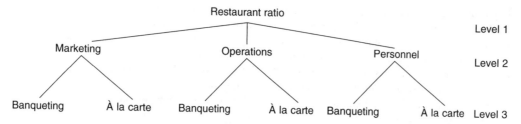

Figure 2 The levels and hierarchy of productivity metrics

productivity decisions at higher levels impact productivity performance at lower levels.

Level 1, example:

$$\frac{\text{Restaurant}}{\text{Productivity}} = \frac{SR_1 + SR_2 + SR_3 + \ldots}{\text{Costs}_1 + \text{Costs}_2 + \text{Costs}_3 + \ldots}$$

where: SR_1, SR_2, SR_3 etc. are the individual departmental sales revenues and Costs_1, Costs_2, Costs_3, etc. are the individual departmental costs.

Level 2, example:

$$\frac{\text{Marketing}}{\text{Productivity}} = \frac{MR}{\text{Costs}_1 + \text{Costs}_2 + \text{Costs}_3 + \ldots}$$

where: MR is revenue derived from marketing activities and Costs_1, Costs_2, Costs_3, etc., are marketing costs.

Level 3, examples:

$$\begin{matrix}\text{Personnel}\\\text{Productivity}\\\text{(banqueting)}\end{matrix} = \frac{\begin{array}{c}\text{Revenue resulting from}\\\text{banqueting activities}\end{array}}{\begin{array}{c}\text{Labor costs directly}\\\text{related to banqueting}\end{array}}$$

$$\begin{matrix}\text{Personnel}\\\text{Productivity}\\\text{(à la carte)}\end{matrix} = \frac{\begin{array}{c}\text{Revenue resulting from}\\\text{à la carte activities}\end{array}}{\begin{array}{c}\text{Labor costs directly}\\\text{related to à la carte}\end{array}}$$

Overall, aggregated input/output metrics can be disaggregated at any level for constructing a whole 'family'/'hierarchy' of partial (detailed) productivity ratios. Aggregated metrics tend to obscure information, however, whereas partial measures do not provide the whole picture and tend to hide information and trade-offs among other dimensions (e.g. departments, resources). Although the latter can be overcome by considering partial metrics simultaneously, this process is very laborious and sometimes may lead to conflicting results. Recognizing the disadvantages of partial productivity metrics, Brown and Dev (1999) proposed to measure productivity at an even lower level, i.e. at the individual customer level. Nowadays, Holiday Inn uses the metric revenue per available customer (RevPAC). The shift to such customer-centric productivity metrics is quite critical in the experience economy whereby company success depends on identifying, keeping, and making the most out of loyal customers.

The second step in developing useful productivity metrics is to address the second problem, i.e. the identification of suitable units of measurement. Although outputs/inputs can be measured in some way, it is difficult to identify appropriate units of measurement for this purpose. For example, there are distinctions between input metrics such as 'per member of work-force,' 'per man-hour,' and 'per £100 wages,' as the different units reflect different tangible and intangible elements. There are three main categories of measurement units, namely financial, physical (e.g. number of personnel and meals served, kilos of potatoes used), and a combination of the previous two. It is generally agreed that quantitative physical measures reflect a quantitative approach to productivity that equates productivity with production efficiency only, while a total factor approach would require more sophisticated and qualitative measures. There are, however, arguments supporting the view that the truly quantitative, aggregate, 'broad' measures (e.g. profit, sales) implicitly encapsulate intangible qualitative performance for two reasons. First, only if the intangibles are as they should be will customer levels be sustained and income earned. Second, only if the tangibles are as they should be will income and costs be controlled in such a way that profit is produced at the required rate in relation to the capital employed.

The third step in developing useful productivity metrics is to address the third problem, i.e. the use of an appropriate way to compare inputs and outputs. Sigala (2004) illustrated how the selection of this method can also be used for solving the 'ceteris paribus' problem of productivity measurement. The most common methods of comparison used in the hospitality industry are ratio analysis, multi-factor ratios, and regression analysis, but their major limitation is their inefficiency in simultaneously handling multiple inputs and outputs. As there are numerous inputs/outputs and measurement units in the industry, several ratios can be calculated. This further complicates the third problem while it stresses the need to condense several ratios into a single productivity metric. Moreover, the productivity metric that would take into consideration multiple inputs and outputs should be computed in such a way that it does not directly relate certain inputs with outputs but rather highlights the interrelationships and trade offs among all of them.

Since production function techniques consider multiple inputs and outputs simultaneously, they have been widely used for productivity studies. However, as parametric techniques, production functions assume a functional form for the technology, transforming inputs into outputs, so they suffer from specification error. On the other hand, because there is usually no known functional form for the production function, a nonparametric approach (that does not make any assumptions about the form of the production function) may be used for constructing the production function. The most heavily used nonparametric technique for measuring productivity in hospitality is data envelopment analysis (DEA). DEA constructs a frontier function in a piecewise linear approach by comparing like units with like taken from the observed dataset. Reynolds (2004) demonstrated the utility of this approach within the context of the restaurant industry by studying a small chain of restaurants.

Low productivity in hospitality is identified as a major source of concern, which is mainly attributed to a lack of understanding and application of quantitative and analytical techniques. Robust productivity measurement is very critical, though, because it can be used for several purposes. For example, it can be used strategically as a basis for making longer-term comparisons with competitors. Productivity measurement can also be used tactically, i.e. for controlling specific functions of a firm to enhance overall performance. Third, it can be used for planning purposes, as it allows management to balance and compare the different yields from a range of outputs. Finally, it can be used for other purposes, e.g. collective bargaining or staff motivation. The robustness and appropriateness of the types of productivity measurement would depend on the purpose of the measurement. Through the three-step approach to productivity measurement described here, both the theoretical issues and the practical implications regarding productivity conceptualization and measurement have been discussed. The approach also presents a baseline from which further research can be conducted.

References

Brown, J.R. and Dev, C.S. (1999) Looking beyond RevPAR; productivity consequences of hotel strategies. *Cornell Hotel and Restaurant Administration Quarterly*, April, 23–33.

Jones, P. and Lockwood, A. (1989) *The Management of Hotel Operations*. London: Cassell.

Reynolds, D. (1998) Productivity analysis in the on-site food-service segment. *Cornell Hotel and Restaurant Administration Quarterly*, 39 (3), 22–31.

Reynolds, D. (2004) Multiunit restaurant productivity assessment using data envelopment analysis. In Z. Gu (ed.), *Management Science Applications in Tourism and Hospitality*. New York: Haworth Press.

Schroeder, R.G. (1985) *Operations Management: Decision-making in the Organization's Function*. New York: McGraw-Hill.

Sigala, M. (2004) Using Data Envelopment Analysis for measuring and benchmarking productivity in the hotel sector. *Journal of Travel and Tourism Marketing*, 16 (2/3).

Witt, C.A. and Witt, S.F. (1989) Why productivity in the hotel sector is low. *International Journal of Contemporary Hospitality Management*, 1 (2), 28–33.

MARIANNA SIGALA
UNIVERSITY OF THE AEGEAN, GREECE

Professional congress organizer

A professional congress (conference) organizer (PCO) is an independent person or organization specializing in all aspects of convention and meeting management. The term PCO is commonly used in Europe and Asia for individuals or companies that offer services to inbound MICE professionals – it is synonymous with terms like independent meeting manager, meeting planner or coordinator, conference manager or event manager that are customary in North America. Furthermore, destination management companies (DMCs), primarily found in North America, are similar to PCOs in that they provide services to inbound MICE professionals. They differ in that the types of services offered by DMCs are of a more social nature than those of PCOs. The former will guide meeting planners to services that will enable convention attendees to experience the unique attributes of a particular city or region.

The services of PCOs are contracted by both associations and corporations that do not employ an in-house congress organizer, to manage either the entire event or specific tasks only. To be successful, a partnering relationship between the client and a PCO is essential whereby the PCO acts as a consultant and executor to the convention committee or client organization. The client has to clearly establish the role of the PCO by setting policies, goals, and objectives, facilitate effective communication, act on the recommendation of the PCO and monitor progress. To that extent the client typically prepares a brief for the PCO that details specifics of the event on the basis of which the PCO manages it. Important brief components include the background of the host organization, the history of the event, the objectives of the event, the proposed dates and preferred locations, the event theme, the accommodation requirements, the anticipated attendance numbers and origin of delegates, the speakers, the social program, the funding and financing, the marketing and the list of services required from the PCO. Such a brief allows invited PCOs to prepare a proposal for the event management, including a cost estimate for the services of the PCO. A PCO normally receives a management fee from the client organization, which can take the form of a flat management fee, a management fee plus per capita registration and secretarial fees, or an all-inclusive fee. The client and the PCO may also enter a profit-sharing arrangement. Furthermore, PCOs may also charge a commission to the congress center (typically 8–10% of the value of the congress to the venue), on accommodation bookings and other services provided.

On behalf of the client, PCOs need to liaise and work with various suppliers of services and products for the event, i.e., they act as an intermediary between the client and suppliers. PCOs have the ultimate responsibility for the quality and success of the event. As such, they need to carefully select suppliers based on the quality of their work and reputation, given the serious impact of supplier services on the overall success of the event and, consequently, the reputation of the PCO.

The services of PCOs are not only confined to managing the basic logistics of an event but also extend to providing leadership in the planning, coordination, and communication processes. Specific tasks include the following: conceiving a theme for the event; researching and recommending a suitable site and venue; negotiating with the venue and suppliers; interpreting venue and supplier contracts; assisting in the event program planning, including the social program and any concurrent exhibition; managing and monitoring the finances and the budget; promoting the event and delegate attendance; handling delegate registration, booking accommodation/housing, managing and executing the event on-site; finalizing bills, evaluating the event; providing final reports and event evaluations to the client at a post-conference meeting. As is evident, their job involves managing all details, activities, and interactions of a convention or meeting, from the time of conception through the event to its conclusion with the event evaluation. It is critical to pay attention to all aspects to ensure the success of the event in terms of delegate and client satisfaction and financial success.

In view of the extensive range of services provided, management and leadership skills are essential for PCOs. In particular, they should possess flexibility, excellent organizational and administrative skills in addition to verbal and written communication skills, a people-orientation that facilitates the interaction with a wide range of people and sensitivity to clients' and delegates' needs. They also need to take initiative, be highly motivated and creative, and possess an ability to handle pressure in stressful situations.

In recent years, the competition for business has intensified and in order to succeed in such a competitive environment, a PCO has to establish a reputation for excellence in service provision. Beyond addressing the client's basic requirements, a PCO needs to establish a reputation for creativity, dependability, honesty, and integrity. As PCOs often work for numerous clients at any one time, they also need to adhere to strict ethical standards, and demonstrate both discretion and confidentiality.

The position of the PCO has emerged and developed only in the past two decades. As such, professional development is accorded great importance by the various trade associations. There are numerous associations that aim to raise the professional standards of PCOs and meeting managers. The International Association of Professional Congress Organizers (IAPCO) is the professional association of PCOs. Founded in 1968, this nonprofit organization represents professional congress organizers and managers of international and national congresses, conventions, and special events. IAPCO membership offers a unique quality assurance recognized by conference clients and suppliers all over the world. In North America, the Professional Convention Management Association (PCMA) and Meeting Professional International (MPI) are important professional associations for independent meeting managers (as well as association and corporate ones), offering educational services and professional certification.

References

McCabe, V., Leiper, N., Weeks, P., and Poole, P. (2000) *The Business and Management of Conventions*. Milton, Qld: John Wiley & Sons.

Rogers, T. (1998) *Conference: A Twenty-first Century Industry*. Harlow: Addison-Wesley.

Weber, K. and Chon, K. (eds) (2002) *Convention Tourism: International Research and Industry Perspectives*. New York: Haworth Press.

KARIN WEBER
THE HONG KONG POLYTECHNIC
UNIVERSITY, HONG KONG SAR, CHINA

Profit in foodservice operations

Profit is the residual monetary return to the foodservice operator (owner or investor) and as such is the driving force behind restaurant operations. This residual return is usually predetermined. From an economic perspective, profit does not include any of the return on labor, land, or capital, but is rather the surplus (predetermined or not) remaining after the full opportunity costs of these have been met (where opportunity cost is the value of that which must be given up to acquire or achieve something). Economists distinguish two types of profit: normal profit and excess profit. Normal profit is the minimum amount of profit necessary to attract the potential foodservice operator to venture into business and to remain in it. Excess profit is any profit over and above the normal profit.

From the accounting perspective, the term 'net profit before tax' denotes the residual after deduction of all money costs: sales revenue less labor costs, rent and fees insurance, food and beverage materials, utilities, interest on money borrowed, and depreciation. 'Net profit after tax' is the residue left after deduction of company taxes (state or federal), income tax (for partnerships), and any other taxes that might be levied by the state or federal tax authorities.

Reference

Welch, P.J. and Welch, G.F. (2003) *Economics: Theory and Practice*. New York: John Wiley & Sons.

JAKSA KIVELA
THE HONG KONG POLYTECHNIC
UNIVERSITY, HONG KONG SAR, CHINA

Profit and loss statement

The profit and loss statement is generally referred to as the income statement in the United States. It provides an overview of the profit earned by the reporting entity over a specific period of time (this time period is always stated in the heading to the profit and loss statement). Net profit represents the excess of revenues over expenses for the time period in question. If expenses exceed revenues then a net loss results. At least two levels of profit are generally referred to in profit and loss statements: gross profit (which is calculated by deducting cost of sales from sales revenue) and net profit (which is calculated by deducting all expenses from all revenue). All publicly listed companies are required to present an audited profit and loss statement that pertains to their most recent financial year in their annual reports. Internally, profit and loss statements are also produced, however, on a much more frequent basis for managers as they represent an important source of information that can facilitate management's monitoring of the hotel's financial performance. An example of a profit and loss statement is presented in the figure below:

ABC HOTEL
**Profit and Loss Statement for the
year ended 31 December, 200X, in US$**

Sales Revenue		100,000
Less: Cost of Sales	25,000	
Gross Profit		75,000
Less: Other Expenses		
Administration		30,000
Depreciation	15,000	45,000
Net Profit		30,000

References

Guilding, C. (2002) *Financial Management for Hospitality Decision-makers*. Oxford: Butterworth-Heinemann.

Uniform System of Accounts for the Lodging Industry, 9th edn. (1996) Lansing, MI: Educational Institute of the American Hotel and Motel Association.

CHRIS GUILDING
GRIFFITH UNIVERSITY, AUSTRALIA

Profitability ratios

The profit made by organizations can only be effectively evaluated when compared to the amount of resources and activity required to generate it. The most common comparators are the investment required to generate the profit and the sales revenue required to earn the profit.

Net profit/income ratio

The net profit to sales ratio is the key measure of operational performance, showing the amount of profit generated from sales revenue in percentage terms. There are many variations of this ratio but the key ratio is usually presented as profit before interest and tax (PBIT) divided by sales revenue expressed as a percentage.

$$\text{Net profit ratio} = \frac{\text{PBIT}}{\text{Sales}} \times 100$$

Example:

$$\frac{\pounds 16,875}{135,000} = 14.22\%$$

This ratio reflects performance after all expenses have been taken into account, including prime costs/cost of sale and other expenses such as wages and salaries, overheads, insurance. It excludes interest and taxation as these are arguably not within managerial control and are the result of financial and treasury decisions.

This ratio is also known as net income to revenue ratio and net operating margin. This ratio forms a key part of the ROCE (return on capital employed) and combines with asset turnover to deliver overall company performance. The ratio of net profit to sales varies widely from industry to industry and within one industry sector profit margins will also vary. Some sectors may be characterized by low profit margins and high levels of asset turnover, e.g. budget hotels; where other sectors will have high profit margins, e.g. full service luxury hotels. This variability means that care should be taken when comparing profit ratios; differences in industry sectors; and accounting practices. Although this is still a key measure of performance, increasingly it is recognized that maximization of profit will lead to sub-optimal short-term decisions and inhibit long-term performance.

Return on investment

Return on investment (ROI) is a widely used measure of overall performance. There are two key approaches to ROI: first, return on total assets (ROTA) or return on capital employed (ROCE), which focus on operating efficiency of the total enterprise, and second, return on equity (ROE), which concentrates on this efficiency as translated into return to owners of the business (shareholders).

ROCE and ROTA provide overall measures of operational performance, linking profits generated to the value of assets in the business. ROCE is calculated by expressing profit before interest and tax (PBIT) as a percentage of capital employed, which is calculated by taking fixed assets (FA) plus current assets (CA) and deducting current liabilities (CL).

Example:

Fixed assets	£960, 000
Current assets	£640,000
Current liabilities	£480,000
PBIT	£224,000

$$\text{ROCE} = \frac{\text{PBIT}}{(\text{FA} + \text{CA} - \text{CL})}$$

$$= \frac{224,000}{(960,000 + 640,000 - 480,000)} \times 100$$

$$= 20\%$$

ROTA is calculated by expressing PBIT as a percentage of total assets, which is FA plus CA. Using figures from the example above:

$$\text{ROTA} = \frac{\text{PBIT}}{(\text{FA} + \text{CA})}$$

$$= \frac{224,000}{(960,000 + 640,000)} \times 100$$

$$= 8.75\%$$

ROTA compares the profit before interest and tax (PBIT) to the total value of total assets being used by the business. Total assets include fixed and current assets; as such, it excludes the effect of current liabilities which reduce the needs for operational demands on funding. The result is that ROTA will produce a lower figure for return than ROCE for the same company. In the example above, it can be seen that ROTA is 8.75% and ROCE is 20%.

ROCE relates PBIT to the total net assets, which includes fixed assets plus current assets less current liabilities. This amount represents the total investment in the business from shareholders and long-term lenders who must be receive a return, in the form of interest payments or dividends, from PBIT (and reserves). ROCE is the headline measure which is driven by a combination of operational profitability and efficiency/productivity.

It can be seen from Figure 1 that there is a triangular relationship between the ratios. The net profit ratio multiplied by the asset turnover will generate the ROCE percentage.

ROCE is the starting point for analysis of company performance. All companies must ensure that they generate a greater percentage return on investment in order to cover the cost for raising capital (weighted average cost of capital) otherwise they will not be able to afford the returns required by investors. Analysis of the two bases of the triangle will explain performance and facilitate the targeting of managerial actions.

One of the key limitations of ROCE is the difficulty of identifying a true value for fixed assets;

ROCE

PBIT ÷ Total net assets

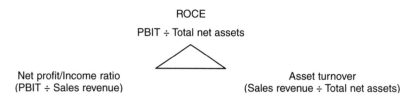

Net profit/Income ratio
(PBIT ÷ Sales revenue)

Asset turnover
(Sales revenue ÷ Total net assets)

Figure 1 Return on capital employed (ROCE) relationship

in addition to normal variations in accounting policy, care must be taken when comparing different companies.

Return on equity ratio relates the return achieved by shareholders in relation to the value of their equity to provide a measure of return on investment. It includes both dividends paid to shareholders and the retained profit which technically belongs to shareholders and which generates future capital growth. It is calculated by expressing profit after taxation (this is also referred to as profit attributable to shareholders) as a percentage of shareholders' funds. Shareholders' funds are made up of issued share capital and reserves. Based on the company's book value, it provides an overall measure of return to shareholders' investment, e.g. capital and reserves equal £50,000 and profit attributable to shareholders equals £2000, the return on equity would be 4% (2000/50,000 × 100).

It is recognized that the greater the risk, the greater the return investors will require, so when comparing ratios between different companies it is important to consider risk.

References

Adams, D. (1997) *Management Accounting for the Hospitality Industry: A Strategic Approach*. London: Cassell.

Glautier, M.W.E. and Underdown, B. (1997) *Accounting Theory and Practice*, 6th edn. London: Pitman Publishing.

Jagels, M. and Coltman, M. (2003) *Hospitality Management Accounting*, 8th edn. New York: John Wiley & Sons.

McKenzie, W. (1998) *FT Guide to Using and Interpreting Company Accounts*, 2nd edn. London: Financial Times and Pitman Publishing.

Walsh, C. (1996) *Key Management Ratios: How to Analyze, Compare and Control the Figures that Drive Company Value*. London: FT Management Masterclass series, Pitman Publishing.

HELEN ATKINSON
UNIVERSITY OF BRIGHTON, UK

Program

The program is designed to meet the goals and objectives of the attendees at an event. It may be as simple as a fundraising dinner with entertainment or as complex as a five-day convention that offers a wide variety of educational sessions, networking opportunities, special events, and organized recreation. Ideas for programming may come from the event producer, previous attendees (if it is a repeat event), sponsors, or the event planner. Many times, attendees are asked to submit their own proposals for presentations. Once all of the sessions and activities are decided upon, a printed schedule of events will be available giving details of a meeting or convention, including times, places, events, locations of function rooms, speakers, topics, bios, and other pertinent information. Selecting the right speakers, panelists and other program participants is a key to the success of the meeting. The budget will be a factor in determining the program but in particular the type of speaker(s) selected. Options include celebrities, authors, sports personalities or professional speakers. Sources for speakers include the recommendations of colleagues, speakers bureaus, professional organizations or the Internet. Ask potential speakers for a biography, testimonials, videos or CDs made before live audiences, and references.

References

Goldblatt, Joe and Nelson, Kathleen (2001) *The International Dictionary of Event Management*, 2nd edn. New York: John Wiley & Sons.

Krug, S., Chatfield-Taylor, C., and Collins, M. (eds) (1994) *The Convention Industry Council Manual*, 7th edn. McLean, VA: The Convention Industry Council.

PATTI J. SHOCK
UNIVERSITY OF NEVADA, LAS VEGAS, USA
DEBORAH BREITER
UNIVERSITY OF CENTRAL FLORIDA, USA

Promotional mix

Modern hospitality marketing calls for developing successful products and services that when priced attractively and made available to selected markets strike a responsive chord with those markets. However, today's competitive environment in hospitality companies also means taking the time continuously to communicate with both present or loyal customers and potential customers. Every company needs to build relationships and to be consistently involved in a communication and promotional role.

The communication and promotional role is built largely around a set of promotional tools called 'the promotional mix,' which most modern marketers agree should be built under the theme of an integrated marketing communication process. In other words, there should be an integrated plan of message development or relationship-building across all these promotional tools which builds a consistent integrated message of the firm and strives to build trusting relationships between the parties – the customers and the company. For every hospitality company the question is not one of whether to communicate, but of how much, in what ways, and how best to use the promotional tools to both develop a consistent message and build those long-term relationships.

The promotional planning process is no longer something that is completely turned over to an advertising agency to plan and produce. Rather, promotion in the modern marketing world is viewed as a form of communication that exists as an interactive dialogue between the customers and the company and is highly integrated into the company's marketing plan. Communication is also not a one-way process or a message going from the company to the customer. Rather, the message must be at least a two-way process. The hospitality company must answer both communication questions: 'How do we best reach our customers?' and 'How can our customers best reach us?'

Rapid changes in technology now allow firms to reach customers through traditional media such as newspapers, radio, telephone, and television, but also through new media such as the Internet and World Wide Web, computer e-mails, websites, cell phones, and pagers. Through the proliferation of media the choice of which medium to use becomes more difficult; however, the ease, the price competitiveness, and decreasing costs of communicating have motivated many hospitality companies to move from a mass communication format to a mass customization format or one-to-one dialogue. As the ability to communicate becomes more diverse, so too does the company's challenge to make the best and most meaningful impression toward building a trusting relationship with the customer.

The hospitality manager or customer contact person's dress and mannerisms, the décor, the company's communication pieces – all communicate something to the customers. Every hospitality brand contact delivers an impression that can strengthen or weaken a customer's view of the company and the choice or build some form of relationship. The whole marketing and promotion mix must be highly integrated to deliver a consistent message and to obtain a strategic position in building strong loyal customer relationships. Therefore, a hospitality firm's marketing communication effort must be integrated into what is now called an 'integrated marketing communication' (IMC) program.

An integrated marketing communication program develops a consistently clear message or set of impressions through the use of the communication tools called the promotional mix. The mix consists of paid advertising, sales promotion, publicity and public relations, direct marketing, personal selling, and interactive marketing.

Advertising

Advertising is any paid form of non-personal communication or presentation that promotes the ideas, goods, services or relationship opportunities of an identified sponsor or company. Advertising is generally accepted by the public as a standard, legitimate, publicly understood, and accepted way of communicating. Paid advertising allows a firm to repeat its message and often is used to highlight competitive differences, advantages, popularity, successes, and responsive chords with its markets. Advertising is also used to build a consistent, long-term image or position in the marketplace. Advertising can also stimulate quick sales, promote action or responsiveness, and can reach large masses of geographically dispersed customers at a relatively low-cost per exposure. Despite its advantages, advertising also has its weaknesses. It is impersonal, is largely a one-way form of communication, it is costly and not as easily or as quickly changed, and may easily be ignored by the intended audience. A critical challenge faced by hospitality managers and marketers is the ability to create awareness of the brand name through paid advertising of the firm's brand name to ensure that the hospitality brand is included in the customer's choice set or evoked set of brand choices. A study of the evoked or choice set, the impacts of advertising and prior stay of lodging properties was investigated in a study of frequent travelers (Morgan, 1991). It was found that chains whose brand names were well established in a traveler's choice or brand set most often were selected or won the traveler's business. There was little influence on the brand name recall of prior stay without ad exposure nor influence on ad exposure without prior stay. The combined effect of ad exposure and prior stay had an important impact on the brand name property selection.

Sales promotion

Sales promotion is usually a set of short-term or temporary market or sales incentives that induce or encourage the purchase, trial or sales or a hospitality product, service or membership. These sales or market incentives come in a variety of forms including promotional event, coupons, contests, price reductions, premiums refunds/rebates, bonus packs or purchase, frequency programs, point of purchase displays, and cooperative advertising. Another definition of sales promotion includes, 'a direct inducement that offers an extra value or incentive for the product [service] to the sales force, distributors, or the ultimate consumer with the primary objective of creating an immediate sale' (Belch and Belch, 2004). Key words in the promotional tool definition are an *inducement* that provides an *extra incentive* to buy, try or use. The incentive is usually the key element in this type of promotional program. Unlike paid advertising, which creates an image or a reason to buy, the sales promotion tool works best first through appeals that are financially driven by the direct price or promotional price and the incentive provides that extra value to induce the transaction or exchange. Second, a key issue in the use of this tool is that sales promotion is an acceleration tool aimed at speeding up the selling process and maximizing overall sales volume. Sales promotion can also be broken into consumer-oriented sales and trade-oriented sales promotion. Consumer-oriented sales promotions are largely sales promotional techniques aimed at the end users, the consumers. Trade-oriented sales promotions include dealer or wholesaler contests and incentives that are designed to motivate retailers and distributors to both carry the product or service and to make that extra effort to push or promote their product to the ultimate consumer.

Publicity

Publicity refers to non-personal communication about an organization, product, service, person or people or an idea that is not directly run under an identified sponsor nor is it paid for through a contractual agreement. Like advertising, the message usually reaches a massive audience and is non-personal, but unlike paid advertising, it is not a paid form of communication. Here the company attempts to get the medium(s) to cover an event or run a story about any number or specific assets of the firm to impact awareness and an image. Some useful tools in publicity would include news or press releases, press conferences, feature articles, phonographs, films and videos or DVD tapes. A major advantage is that publicity is creditable as the message is perceived to be coming from a source that is unbiased. A major disadvantage of this technique is that the message is not under the firm's control and publicity can sometimes be negative or unfavorable.

Public relations

Public relations, which is different from publicity, is when a company systematically plans and distributes information in a controlled and managed way to put forth a desired image among its various publics. The company also manages this image by evaluating public attitudes and perceptions, identifies the policies and procedures of the individual or organizational interest, and executes a program of managed information to earn public understanding and acceptance. Public relations is different than publicity in that it has a broader objective of establishing and maintaining a positive image of the company and, when necessary, acting to correct any negative perceptions. Typically, public relations is seen by many firms as more of a supportive than a primary function. But, with a more demanding public, many firms have now made public relations a major part in the IMC process.

Personal selling

Personal selling is a direct form of person-to-person communication between a buyer and a seller where the seller attempts to assist and/or persuade prospects to purchase the firm's goods or services or even continue in the purchasing cycle. The transactions have the major advantage of being highly customized to fit the given situation. On the other hand, personal selling is a rather expensive way of moving large numbers of exchanges.

Direct marketing

Direct marketing is where a firm, through the careful acquisition of highly targeted consumers, communicates directly with the targeted group to generate a response and/or transaction. Direct marketing is often perceived as direct mail, direct e-mail, and direct mail-order catalogs. It now involves not only these skills and tools, but also database management, direct selling, telemarketing, and direct response ads through direct mail. This technique or promotion tool has become more popular over the past decade, but also generates negative public opinion. With the overall growth of direct marketing have come negative backlashes, too. The volume of direct marketing has resulted in consumers seeking placement on a 'do not call' listing as a reaction to telemarketing.

Interactive marketing

The last IMC promotional tool in the mix is the youngest variable – interactive marketing. This form of communication allows for a back-and-forth flow of information whereby the actual consumers can participate in and modify the form and content of the information that is received via the Internet in real time. Unlike traditional mass media sources, consumers are allowed to perform a variety of functions such as receiving and altering images, making inquiries, visiting destinations in a virtual reality mode, responding to questions and also making/modifying/tracking purchases. The growth of the Internet is driving this promotion tool, but the Internet's popularity also can be seen as a medium unto itself to execute all the functions of the promotional mix. Live and high-speed video will further enhance how and with whom hospitality firms interact in the coming years.

Each of the components of the promotion mix – advertising, personal selling, sales promotion, publicity, public relations, direct marketing, and interactive marketing – are synchronous parts of the interactive marketing communications (IMC) program. An appropriate IMC program is an important part of the overall marketing plan for companies and organizations in the international hospitality and tourism arena.

References

Belch, George E. and Belch, Michael A. (2004) *Advertising and Promotion: An Integrated Marketing*

Communication Perspective, 6th edn. Boston, MA: Irwin-McGraw-Hill. Kotler, P.; Makens, J., and Bowen, J.T. (2003) *Marketing for Hospitality and Tourism*, 3rd edn. Upper Saddle River, NJ: Prentice-Hall.

Morgan, M.S. (1991) Traveler's Choice: The Effects of Advertising and Prior Stay. *Cornell Hotel and Restaurant Administration Quarterly*, 32 (4), 40–49.

ROD WARNICK
UNIVERSITY OF MASSACHUSETTS, USA

Property management system (PMS)

Sometimes referred to as a front office system, a property management systems (PMS) forms the core of all the computerized systems used in a hotel. While a PMS's primary functions are to track which rooms are currently occupied or vacant, and to maintain the guests' folios by recording details of all sales and payment transactions, they also act as the information hub of all the other ancillary systems used to improve customer service, and interface with reservation systems such as the CRS and Internet bookings engines to support the management of the distribution process. A PMS is now a necessity for most hotels as it would be difficult, if not impossible, to manage a hotel of 100 bedrooms or more without one.

The front office is often described as the center of all hotel activities. It not only acts as the main contact point between the hotel and the guest, but also provides information to and receives information from, practically every other department. A PMS helps manage these interactions, and adds the power, speed, discipline, and information processing capabilities of a computerized system to improve the efficiency of the process. The functions of a PMS may be broken down into four different categories.

Registration

Upon arrival, a guest must check in and be allocated a vacant room. Where the reservation system and the PMS are integrated, the guest's personal details are electronically transferred to speed up the registration process and eliminate unnecessary re-keying of data. The room is then marked as being occupied to prevent it being allocated in error to another incoming guest. While registration has traditionally occurred at the front desk, developments in technology now mean that the process can be facilitated remotely by staff using wirelessly connected handheld computers, by guests themselves at self check-in using kiosks in the lobby of the hotel, or even over the Internet prior to arrival. In the latter case, the guest can go straight to their allocated room and use their frequency card to open the electronic door lock – improving customer service for the guest and reducing pressure and costs at the front office. Irrespective of how the registration occurs, where the PMS is integrated with the other systems, the process of room allocation makes the auxiliary systems aware that a new guest has arrived and instructs each system to provide its services to the newly occupied room. For example, the telephone system will then allow calls to be made from the room's telephone, the energy-management system will blast the room with air to get it to an acceptable temperature, and the electronic door-locking system will issue a new magnetic key specifically for the new guest. A billing folio is also opened automatically for the guest so that charges can be posted to the room number. Similarly, on check-out, the processed is reversed and each of the auxiliary systems is informed that the room is no longer occupied and to not provide services to that location. All of this happens automatically and invisibly, greatly helping to enhance guest service.

Housekeeping

The housekeeping department is responsible for cleaning both the guestrooms and the public areas of the hotel. Its work needs to be closely coordinated with that of the front office. Good communication is essential as the front office needs accurate and up-to-date information on the status (vacant, occupied or dirty) of every room in order to operate effectively. Some systems facilitate this using an interface between the PMS and the telephone system. When the room attendant has finished servicing a room, a code is typed into the telephone, which alerts the PMS that the room is ready for inspection. The room can then be checked by the supervisor, and another code entered to inform the PMS that it is clean and ready for allocation to incoming guests. The PMS also assists the accommodation manager by automatically providing lists of which guests are departing or staying over. Some systems will even help equally to distribute the cleaning load between room attendants, and produce assignment sheets automatically.

Guest accounting

As has already been mentioned, a folio is automatically opened at registration to allow charges to be posted to the guest's account. This folio must always be kept accurate and up to date, ready to be produced for the guest on demand. Charges may be divided into two categories. Some charges, such as the room rate, are posted automatically by the system. This is important as, today, because of the use of yield management systems, hotels normally have many room rates, which if working manually makes it easy to accidentally post an incorrect rate, either losing revenue for the hotel or infuriating the guest! A PMS, however, should correctly identify the rate originally quoted to the guest, and post it accurately to the guest's folio. Other charges are posted as the guest uses the hotel's various services. While sometimes these are posted manually from a paper docket system, more recently the trend has been to use integrated electronic point of sales (EPOS) systems to electronically post charges directly and instantly onto the guest's account. This helps to reduce clerical errors and also prevents guests checking out without paying for services.

Night audit

Each night, routine tasks such as automatically posting the room charge to each guest's account and cross-checking the integrity of the accounting system must be performed. Traditionally carried out manually by a team of night auditors, these

tasks are routine and repetitive. However, this makes them very suitable for computerization and the night audit module automates these procedures and uses the power of the computer to ensure accuracy and reliability. Because the computerized system works at electronic speeds, the audit is completed in minutes rather than in hours.

Current trends in the PMS market include the development of ASP-based systems, which are standardized across entire hotel chains. This allows consistent guest data to be collected and managed across an entire brand – one of the essential requirements for the successful implementation of customer relationship management.

References

Bardi, C. (2002) *Hotel Front Office Management*, 3rd edn. New York: John Wiley & Sons.

Buhalis, D. (2003) *eTourism: Information Technologies for Strategic Tourism Management*. Harlow: Pearson.

Collins, G. and Malik, T. (1999) *Hospitality Information Technology: Learning How to Use It*, 4th edn. Dubuque, IA: Kendall/Hunt Publishing.

Kasavana, M.L. and Brooks, R.M. (2001) *Managing Front Office Operations*, 6th edn. Lansing, MI: Educational Institute of the American Hotel and Lodging Association.

O'Connor, P. (2003) *Using Computers in Hospitality*, 3rd edn. London: Continuum International.

PETER O'CONNOR
IMHI (CORNELL – ESSEC), FRANCE

Proprietary

Proprietary means held in private ownership. In the context of ICT, the term is used in relation to technology such as software algorithms restricted by patent or trademark, for example, Unisys' LSW, used in GIF files. Proprietary technology is therefore neither 'free' nor 'semi-free'. Hence unless specifically authorized, it is not permitted to use, copy, modify or redistribute proprietary software either for a fee or gratis because the source code is copyrighted (GNU, 2003). Since the late 1990s, the 'Open Source' movement has actively promoted 'free' software (free as in liberty rather than price), such as the Linux operating system, under the terms of the GNU General Public License (GPL), in opposition to the traditional proprietary model. In comparison with proprietary offerings, free software's source code is openly accessible to be used, modified, and redistributed. Proprietary software is used extensively in the hospitality industry for example, 'general purpose' software like Microsoft Word, used for menu production, or 'dedicated' software applications like property management systems (PMS) such as Micros' FIDELIO or ASI's general purpose FrontDesk, which help to manage interdepartmental interactions.

References

GNU (2003) Categories of free and non-free software. http://www.gnu.org/philosophy/categories.html. Accessed 14 June 2003.

O'Connor, P. (2000) *Using Computers in Hospitality*, 2nd edn. London: Cassell.

PETER SCHOFIELD
UNIVERSITY OF SALFORD, UK

Psychological contract

The psychological contract is different from the written contract; it is implicit in the relationship between employer and employee and concerns a series of mutual expectations and needs arising from the relationship (Huczynski and Buchanan, 2001). Individuals expect, for example, to be working in safe and hygienic conditions; to work with trained and disciplined colleagues; and to be treated with respect, free from bullying etc. Employers, on the other hand, are likely to expect employees to work with diligence and care; to be loyal; and to uphold the image and good name of the organization etc. (Mullins, 2002). The precise content of the obligations and expectations on both parties are difficult to define, because they change over time and may well vary between individuals. Indeed, the individual employee and the employer may not be consciously aware of the terms, but they do

have expectations of the other party. These expectations should be largely satisfied within the relationship; otherwise it will break down resulting in unplanned staff leaving or employee dismissal. This unfortunate outcome is common in hospitality because of the prior knowledge and skills employers assume (experienced) candidates possess.

References

Huczynski, A. and Buchanan, D. (2001) *Organizational Behaviour: An Introductory Text.* Harlow: Pearson Education.

Mullins, L. (2002) *Management and Organizational Behaviour.* London: Pitman Financial Times.

CONRAD LASHLEY
NOTTINGHAM TRENT UNIVERSITY, UK

Public offering statements

Most regulations governing the development, marketing, sale, and management of timeshare plans are based on concepts of disclosure to the consumer who is considering acquiring and using a timeshare interest in a timeshare plan. Consequently, applicable timeshare legislation generally requires that the developer or seller of timeshare interests deliver to the purchaser a public offering statement which summarizes the salient features of the timeshare plan, contains disclosures in conspicuous type, and attaches exhibits of important documents related to the creation and use of the timeshare plan. The summary and disclosures focus on such details as a description of the facilities and amenities of the timeshare property or properties, a description of use rights and rules and regulations governing owner use, a description of the developer and managing entity, and financial and budgetary descriptions for the property. Exhibits attached to the public offering statement include the restrictive covenants establishing the plan, the annual budget for operating the timeshare plan, and governing documents of any managing entity. Public offering statements are usually filed with the agency responsible for regulating timeshare in the jurisdiction, and an approved version must be delivered to the consumer before any applicable consumer cancellation rights can begin to run.

References

See, e.g., *Fla. Stat.* §721.07 (2 October 2003). http://www.flsenate.gov/statutes/index.cfm? App_mode=Display_Statute&Search_String =&URL=Ch0721/SEC07.HTM&Title=−> 2000−>Ch0721−>Section percent2007.

KURT GRUBER
ISLAND ONE RESORTS, USA

Public relations

Public relations refers to building good relations with the hospitality or tourism company's various publics by obtaining favorable publicity, creating and sustaining a strong corporate image, and dealing with unfounded rumors, stories, and events (Kotler *et al.*, 2003). Public relations by its very meaning connotes dealing with the public; however, the public takes many different forms of groups who may have some relationship with hospitality or tourism organizations. Usually the customers, both current and potential, are the most obvious public group, but constituents will include government agencies, suppliers, citizen action groups including environmental or cause-related groups, the media, and the financial community including bankers and investment partners. Hospitality and tourism companies must also be involved with 'internal publics,' which will include employees, board of directors or internal advisory groups, stockholders, and sub-contractors. In larger hospitality firms, public relations responsibilities may be handled by the PR department while in smaller firms it will be an extension of the marketing function of the business. Major activities would include press relations and press releases, product and service publicity, corporate or business communications, lobbying and legislative review, and counseling. PR plans are a requirement of most forward-thinking companies as well as planning for disasters and crises. In business subjected to any array of potential natural or man-made disasters, crisis management planning is a special area of preparation for the hospitality firm. PR tools that are used include: publications, events, news, speeches, public service activities, and identity media. The PR function may also include a role in the sales and marketing function of sales promotion, activities that include setting objectives and selecting and developing the appropriate consumer-promotion tools.

References

Kotler, P., Bowen, J., and Makens, J. (2003) *Marketing for Hospitality and Tourism*, 3rd edn. Upper Saddle River, NJ: Prentice-Hall.
Middleton, V.T.C. and Clarke, J. (2001) *Marketing in Travel and Tourism*, 3rd edn. Oxford: Butterworth-Heinemann.

ROD WARNICK
UNIVERSITY OF MASSACHUSETTS, USA

Purchase order

A purchase order is a sheet specifying particular products or services to be purchased from a purveyor. Product specifications are often used on purchase orders for food and beverage buys. In many cases, the purchase orders are sent out to competing companies for bid. While not all products are sent out for bid, those used on a regular basis or those that tend to have higher prices may be. Purveyors will submit bids to the purchaser, possibly along with a sample of the product for comparative purposes. In other cases, the purveyor uses the purchase order to bill the buyer for products delivered or services rendered, as the purchase order contains an official identifying number. In this case, the purchase order (in addition to product specifications) will also include the exact amount to be purchased and the price to be paid.

Many foodservice distributors offer electronic purchasing. As Cavinato and Kauffman (1999) note, such systems automate the purchase order process, thereby reducing paper handling and increasing productivity related to the purchasing process.

Reference

Cavinato, J.L. and Kauffman, R.G. (1999) *The Purchasing Handbook: A Guide for the Purchasing and Supply Professional.* New York: McGraw-Hill.

NANCY SWANGER
WASHINGTON STATE UNIVERSITY, USA

Purchasing

Purchasing is the process of buying goods necessary for the operation of a business. These purchases are made through purveyors after negotiations regarding issues such as price, quality, and delivery dates/times are completed. Those in charge of purchasing must know how inventory items are packaged and sold and identify price breaks that might be available for buying items in certain quantities (Cavinator and Kauffman, 1999).

Most companies provide the purveyor with very strict specifications regarding each item to be delivered. For example, a restaurant serving steaks may specify the following:

> New York Strip – frozen
> 12 oz. – 12 per box
> USDA Choice
> 1 1/2″ thick
> 1/4″ trim

As many inventory items are perishable, it is critical that 'just the right amount' of a particular product is in stock. Carrying too much inventory can lead to increased spoilage and theft, higher carrying costs, and overstocked storage space. An effective purchasing program utilizes par stock levels of inventory items. These par stocks are based on counts of each product used between delivery dates, plus 10–25% extra to have on hand as a safety net. Par stock specifies a reorder point – the least amount of an item that can be held in storage before ordering additional inventory. Also see distribution channels and customer relationship management.

Reference

Cavinato, J.L. and Kauffman, R.G. (1999) *The Purchasing Handbook: A Guide for the*

Purchasing and Supply Professional. New York: McGraw-Hill.

NANCY SWANGER
WASHINGTON STATE UNIVERSITY, USA

Purveyors

Purveyors are vendors or suppliers of goods and services to others. In most cases, purveyors compete for business based on price, quality, and service.

Establishing solid relationships with reputable purveyors is critical to the success of hospitality operations. Today, many view purveyors more as partners than vendors, and consider such relationships critical to long-term profitability (e.g., Brownell and Reynolds, 2002). To this end, most purveyors send out sales representatives on a regular basis to help ensure that the needs of the operator are being met. While these representatives may take orders during personal visits, technology has allowed purchasing agents to complete most of their ordering via the Internet or through the use of a fax machine.

Sometimes in an attempt to establish a relationship with or to thank purchasers for continued business, purveyors will offer 'gifts' such as tickets to athletic events, free cases of champagne, or other valued items. While this may be legal, the practice is considered by some to be unethical; it is important to determine the underlying purpose of the gift. A thank-you gift is different from a quid pro quo gift. In the latter case the purveyor expects something in return. Many companies prohibit the acceptance of gifts from purveyors, regardless of the intended purpose.

Reference

Brownell, J. and Reynolds, D. (2002) Strengthening the food and beverage purchaser–supplier partnership: behaviors that make a difference. *Cornell Hotel and Restaurant Administration Quarterly*, 43 (6), 49–61.

NANCY SWANGER
WASHINGTON STATE UNIVERSITY, USA

Qualitative *vs.* quantitative marketing research

Based on a phenomenological paradigm, qualitative research refers to observation and analysis of data that are not predetermined by the researcher. It assumes that reality is socially constructed through individual or collective definitions of the situation or environment. The goal of qualitative research is to capture the understanding of the social phenomenon as participants experience it. Therefore, qualitative research is not mainly concerned with establishing cause-and-effect relationships among variables of interest. Rather, it helps to identify new variables and questions for further research. The researcher is part of the phenomenon of interest. Another school of thought argues that qualitative research can also develop causal explanations of the phenomenon. Common qualitative research designs include ethnographies, grounded theory, case studies, participant observation, interviewing, and focus groups.

Quantitative research takes on a positivist perspective that social facts with an objective reality have nothing to do with the beliefs of individuals. The goal of quantitative research is to explain the causes of changes in social facts, primarily through objective analysis of data that are treated in magnitude. Quantitative research is more concerned with developing and empirically testing hypotheses. The researcher focuses more on established procedures rather than the individual judgment. Quantitative research attempts to reduce the amount of error in the study by designing and implementing appropriate sampling procedure (preferably random sampling) and instrumentation. Common quantitative research designs include surveys and experiments.

References

Creswell, J.W. (1994) *Research Design: Qualitative and Quantitative Approaches.* Thousand Oaks, CA: Sage Publications.

Maxwell, J.A. (1996) *Qualitative Research Design: An Interactive Approach.* Thousand Oaks, CA: Sage Publications.

Taylor, S.J. and Bogdan, R. (1984) *Qualitative Research Methods: The Search for Meanings*, 2nd edn. New York: John Wiley & Sons.

BILLY BAI
UNIVERSITY OF NEVADA, LAS VEGAS, USA

Quality control

Quality control is part of the quality management process. Quality management involves three steps: quality planning, quality control, and quality improvement (i.e., the Juran Trilogy; see Juran, 1992). Quality planning refers to steps taken to develop products and services that meet customers' needs. Based on the process control system established in the planning phase, quality control evaluates actual quality by comparing performance to quality goals and then acting on the detected differences. While planning is concerned with setting goals and establishing the means to achieve these goals, quality control is concerned with operating the business in order to meet the goals. It monitors operations in order to detect discrepancies between actual performance and quality goals, and it undertakes actions to remedy the discrepancies. To keep up with the emerging competition, quality improvement aims at raising quality performance to the next level.

In its original form, quality means conforming to factory specifications in the manufacturing industry. As the focus of the modern business environment has shifted to services and technologies, however, quality has come to suggest responsiveness to customer needs, both internal and external, in all industries. Under this renewed focus, quality can be defined in terms of two features. First, *product features* can be described as characteristics of products and services. In the hospitality industry, examples of product features may include in-room Internet access, express check-out service, or variety in food offerings. Second, quality can also be defined in terms of *freedom from deficiencies*. Examples of freedom from deficiencies may include consistently fast service delivery, the absence of customer complaints, and food consistently prepared to standards. From the customers' perspective, the better the product features and the fewer the deficiencies, the higher the quality. The two aspects of quality influence different components of a services operation. The former, product features, impact service quality by increasing customer satisfaction, allowing for premium prices, increasing market share, and most of all, increasing sales. The latter, product deficiencies, reduce errors, waste, and customer dissatisfaction and, as such, have major effects on costs. Therefore, it is essential that hospitality managers consistently monitor and control the two aspects of quality.

Controlling for quality requires that specific quality goals be set. Quality goals will drive the process of identifying customer needs and specifying product and process features. These features will, in turn, be used as quality standards against which quality will be monitored and controlled. Ideally, precise measurements should be used for quality control. In other words, in order

that all managers and line workers know exactly what they are referring to, it is necessary to express quality standards in numbers. Measurement of quality requires *a unit of measure* (a defined amount of some quality feature, such as minutes of service delivery time) and *a sensor* (a method or an instrument to calculate units, for example a clock). Hospitality products pose special challenges in quantifying quality. The units and sensors that evaluate service quality features are often subjective judgments made by human beings. Therefore, it takes multiple people to agree on the quality measurements. Furthermore, in many cases, service quality may be measured only as a composite of various features. For example, high-quality foodservice may be a composite of food quality, service efficiency, food presentation, and other features related to the total dining experience.

Several organizations promote quality control as a company-wide strategic process. One of the most traditional processes is total quality management, commonly referred to as TQM. Total quality management aims at organizational-level quality control through implementing a structured system for satisfying customers and suppliers, both internal and external, by integrating the business environment and pushing for continuous improvement and breakthroughs in development and maintenance cycles while changing organizational culture. Originating in the manufacturing sector, TQM has recently attracted hospitality organizations aiming to improve overall quality. In general, TQM programs incorporate the following attributes: executive commitment, customer and supplier involvement, process improvement, measurement, employee empowerment, open organization, training, benchmarking, flexibility, and a zero-defects mentality. The International Organization for Standardization (ISO) offers another systematized set of standards to apply to quality management. ISO is a network of the national standards institutes of 147 countries based in Switzerland, and offers ISO9000 certifications to organizations that meet standards of quality management. ISO standards are designed to fulfill the customer's quality requirements, meet applicable regulatory requirements, improve customer satisfaction, and improve performance in business organizations. Among the more than 30,000 companies that are certified, approximately 1100 are in the hotel and restaurant industries.

Beyond these standards, several awards recognize companies for their achievements in quality and business performance excellence. Established in 1987 by the US government, the Malcolm Baldrige National Quality award recognizes such companies in the United States. The criteria for the award include customer satisfaction, quality results, human resources utilization, quality assurance of products and services, leadership, planning for quality, and information and analysis. Of all the criteria, customer satisfaction is allocated the greatest weight, accounting for 30% of all points. The Framework for Business Excellence, an Australian quality award, uses similar categories and 20% of all the points are allocated to people aspects.

A notable example of a hospitality organization that has strived for quality is the Ritz–Carlton Hotel Company, LLC, which has been awarded the Malcolm Baldrige award twice in the past. They assure quality internally and monthly through a group of external specialists. This achievement marked a turning point for the hospitality industry in developing a systematic approach to customer satisfaction through quality management. This was underscored even more poignantly in 2002 when a small US restaurant chain, Pal's Sudden Service, won the award. However, such a methodological approach to quality control is yet to be a norm in many other hospitality companies. Reflecting the challenges in quantifying quality, many hospitality companies do not have precisely defined and written quality standards against which quality may be measured and controlled. Whether or not the application of a quantifiable quality control process is a viable alternative for a hospitality company remains debatable.

Reference

Juran, J.M. (1992) *Juran on Quality by Design: The New Steps for Planning Quality into Goods and Services*. New York: The Free Press.

MASAKO TAYLOR
TAYLOR ASSOCIATES, JAPAN

Quality of work life

The concept of quality of work life (QWL) deals with the issue of how rewarding or satisfying the time spent in the workplace is. As such, QWL may reflect working conditions and contextual issues such as relationships with work colleagues and the intrinsic satisfaction of the job itself.

From the work into socio-technical systems by Emery and Trist in the 1950s, social scientists identified six requirements for job satisfaction, also termed 'psychological job requirements' (Emery and Emery, 1975):

1. Adequate elbow room
2. Opportunity of learning on the job and going on learning
3. An optimal level of variety
4. Conditions where workers can and do get help and respect from their workmates
5. A sense of one's own work meaningfully contributing to society
6. A desirable future.

These factors were at the core of the QWL programs initiated in the 1970s and 1980s, such programs represented a comprehensive effort to improve the quality of the work environment by integrating employee needs with the firm's need for higher productivity.

Hales (1987) found low adoption of QWL in the UK hospitality industry especially in hotel operations; and furthermore, where QWL measures were used they were seen primarily as a means of increasing productivity rather than improving the quality of working life.

References

Emery, F.E. and Emery, M. (1975) Guts and guidelines for raising the quality of work life. In D. Gunzburg (ed.), *Bringing Work to Life*. Melbourne: Cheshire, pp. 28–37.

Hales, C. (1987) Quality of working life: job redesign and participation in a service industry: a rose by any other name? *Service Industries Journal*, 7 (3), 253–273.

RON DOWELL
SOUTHERN CROSS UNIVERSITY, AUSTRALIA

Quick service restaurant (QSR)

What the restaurant industry calls a quick service restaurant (QSR) the rest of the world refers to as 'fast food'. In all fairness, the food itself is not fast; it is the service that adds the quickness, generally taking less than five minutes from the time an order is placed until it is presented to the diner.

It can reasonably be assumed that from the time the very first person served another a meal for compensation, there has been a desire to make the production and service of food faster. Historical records do not generally document the use of 'hand-held food' throughout the ages, but at least since the Earl of Sandwich created his namesake meal so he could avoid leaving a card game, quick service has been evolving.

Early restaurants in this segment included the dining cars on transcontinental railroad trains during the end of the nineteenth century. When retired, these cars became urban diners, where short-order cooks were masters at fixing meals quickly and serving them instantly to customers sitting directly behind them at a counter. In 1922 the Ingram family created a collection of small hamburger stands, The White Castle, to efficiently serve batch-cooked sandwiches to factory workers on short lunch breaks.

Probably the best-known QSR restaurants are those bearing the name of the McDonald brothers, Maurice and Dick. Their experiments during the late 1940s in streamlined mass production of hamburgers created a new hybrid form for restaurants, one that also required the customer to provide a significant involvement in his or her own 'quick' service. This new idea caught the interest of a salesman named Ray Kroc, and the fast food industry has never looked back.

It is important to note that today all five of the world's revenue-leading restaurant companies are in the quick service segment.

References

Love, John (1995) *McDonald's: Behind the Arches*. London: Bantam Books.

Schlosser, Eric (2002) *Fast Food Nation: The Dark Side of the All-American Meal*. New York: HarperCollins.

CHRISTOPHER MULLER
UNIVERSITY OF CENTRAL FLORIDA, USA

R

Ratio analysis

A ratio represents a numeric relationship that compares one measurement with another in the form of a multiple, fraction, percentage, or rate. For example:

Multiple	5 : 1
Fraction	5/1 (or 1/5)
Percentage	500%
Rate	5 per 1 (or 5 for 1, or 5 times – expressed as 5 ✕)

Thus, for instance, in the case of a hospitality business such as a hotel, room occupancy is normally calculated as a percentage of total room capacity, whereas restaurant occupancy is often calculated as a seat turnover figure, i.e. the average number of times each seat is sold.

Ratio analysis is a tool often used to interpret information presented in financial statements. It is, therefore, important that the relationship between the elements used in ratios is clear, direct, and understandable. Although the arithmetic of ratios is usually simple, the interpretation is often more complex. As a consequence, the results of ratios are often misunderstood and, therefore, their significance is misunderstood. Thus, the benefits obtained from applying ratio analysis are dependent upon the intelligent and skilled interpretation of the user. It is through the presentation of such multiples and relationships that ratios generate new information, making the numbers more valuable, meaningful, informative, and useful.

References

Coltman, M.C. and Jagels, M. (2001) *Hospitality Management Accounting*, 7th edn. New York: John Wiley & Sons.
Owen, G. (1998) *Accounting for Hospitality, Tourism and Leisure*, 2nd edn. London: Longman.

AGNES LEE DEFRANCO
UNIVERSITY OF HOUSTON, USA

Receiving

The practice of inspecting, accepting, and routing products when they arrive on site at a foodservice facility is termed 'receiving,' as is the department typically responsible for these activities. Tight controls and rigorous management of the receiving function can help protect an operation from *shrinkage*, reduce opportunities for unsafe food handling, and save the operation money through reduced waste.

The receiving process can be broken down into a series of simple steps. First, when a delivery arrives at a facility, a member of the foodservice staff must meet it and the relevant paperwork must be obtained from the delivery driver. The delivery then needs to be checked against purchase orders to ensure that what is being delivered has been ordered. The receiver must next inspect the items for quality, quantity, and condition, which may involve weighing boxes, opening and inspecting cases or crates, and in some cases counting items piece by piece. Lastly, accepted goods need to be moved into storage quickly, particularly if the items require a refrigerated environment or have significant value. In a large foodservice facility, a full-time receiver may be employed to perform these functions, but in a smaller facility like a restaurant, the chef or manager may be responsible for checking incoming goods.

In addition to accepting and processing deliveries, the duties of a receiver may also include monitoring stock rotation through the labeling and stocking of incoming goods so that the products received first will be the first used. Bar codes and other forms of computerized material handling systems are becoming more common for large production kitchens, and the receiver's job often involves entering delivery data into these systems.

The receiving area is usually a secure room or corridor protected from the weather, located adjacent to the doorway or loading dock where delivery vehicles access the operation. The amount of space required for a receiving area will vary depending on the frequency and size of deliveries, the amount of processing that needs to take place before goods can be stored, and the number of foodservice outlets being served by a single receiver. A basic rule of thumb is that about 1 m^2 (10 ft^2) of receiving space will be required for every 10 seats or 100 meals served. For smaller operations, truck space for a single vehicle is all that is usually required, but for a hotel, hospital, or other large institutional setting where the receiving function handles more than just food products, space for three or more vehicles to unload at any one time may be needed. For these larger operations, it is common practice to depress the truck parking area (or raise the receiving dock) by approximately 1–1.2 m (3–4 ft.) so that goods may be loaded directly from the back of the truck to the receiving area. It is important to be aware of the size and types of delivery vehicles used by suppliers to ensure that the truck areas are adequately sized.

An important feature of a large receiving area is a small office where the receiver can process paperwork related to incoming orders. This office should have a window that looks out into the receiving area to monitor arrivals and goods that may not yet be in secure storage. In a smaller operation without a full-time receiver, there should be a good visual connection between the receiving door and the chef's office or the main production area of the kitchen, so that deliveries will not go unnoticed by the senior staff.

Equipment required in a receiving area includes a scale for weighing deliveries, refrigeration for holding chilled and frozen products if processing these orders is for some reason delayed or if the refrigerated storage areas are far from the receiving area, and a sink for washing soil off of vegetables as well as for washing the receiver's hands between deliveries. Pest control devices are also a valuable addition to a receiving area, as this can be a primary point of entry for insects and vermin. A well-planned receiving area also leaves circulation room and space for storing dollies or carts for moving heavy goods.

In some operations, a modest amount of repackaging may occur at the receiving area, as products might be taken out of crates or boxes and placed in sanitary containers and labeled for storage. For this reason, it is common for the receiving function to be located close to the waste handling area where empty shipping containers can be held for recycling or disposal. Larger facilities that do substantial repacking of products in the receiving area may also choose to include a hose and drain for easy cleaning between deliveries.

Because the receiving area is one setting in a foodservice operation where valuable products may be unsecured for a period of time, security and control measures are an important part of any well-run receiving department. Locked doors on refrigeration equipment, security cameras, and full-time attendance by a responsible employee are some of the measures adopted to reduce the potential for theft from the receiving function. Careful monitoring of shipping invoices and purchase orders is also important to ensure that goods being paid for are in fact those that are being delivered to and used by the operation.

Reference

Birchfield, J.C. and Sparrowe, R.T. (2003) *Design and Layout of Foodservice Facilities*. Hoboken, NJ: John Wiley & Sons.

STEPHANI K.A. ROBSON
CORNELL UNIVERSITY, USA

Recipe costing

Recipe costing is at the core of all pricing functions. In order to price a menu item properly, the first step is to calculate the cost per edible portion (EP), which is the cost per servable pound, based on the standardized recipe. One lists the recipe ingredients, quantities, and respective costs for each recipe. One then calculates the total cost of the recipe yield. This cost is then divided by the number of standardized portions to determine the cost per portion.

In order properly to cost a recipe, then, one must understand the difference between 'as purchased' (AP) price per pound and EP. For most ingredients, the cost per servable pound is always more than the AP price per pound because of trim waste and cooking shrinkage. Even convenience items like pre-mixed cookie dough will not always result in exact yields based on accurate portioning. If, for example, broken cookies cannot be sold, one needs to include an allowance for 'breakage.' If one overstates the recipe yield, the cost per portion will be understated, resulting in a food cost that cannot be achieved.

If an operator overcompensates for 'breakage,' however, overcooking or cost per portion will be overstated, resulting in menu prices much higher than those of the competition since the pricing calculations are based on erroneous cost calculations. In order for recipe yields and portion costs to be accurate and consistent, a restaurant must have standardized purchase specifications, standardized recipes, and standardized portioning controls.

Reference

Gudmundsen, L. (2002) *Math for Life and Foodservice.* Upper Saddle River, NJ: Prentice-Hall.

DAVID V. PAVESIC
GEORGIA STATE UNIVERSITY, USA

Recipe standardization

A standardized recipe is a set of instructions for producing a particular menu item in a consistent

CATEGORY ____	MENU ITEM		
YIELD ____	EQUIPMENT UTENSILS		
PORT SIZE ____			
PREP TIME ____			
COOK TIME ____	STATION(S)		
COOK TEMP			
SPECIAL NOTES/GARNISHES PRESENTATION			
INGREDIENTS	WEIGHTS	MEASURES	METHOD OF PREPARATION
SELLING PRICE ____	SOURCE		
TOTAL FOOD COST ____			
FOOD COST % ____			
CONTRIBUTION MARGIN ____			

Figure 1 Proforma for standardized recipe

manner so that the quality, quantity, and cost will be approximately the same each time it is prepared. Such a recipe lists ingredients, amounts, preparation method, cooking instructions and times, portion size, and serving instructions for a given menu item. Some standardized recipes include how leftovers are to be stored or incorporated into other recipes. They might also list the types and sizes of utensils, pots, pans, and equipment needed to produce the recipe. It is 'customized' to the ingredients, equipment, and utensils used by a specific operation. Today, standardized recipes also include plating instructions, usually including a photograph, to ensure that a given item will be plated in a consistent fashion. A typical standardized recipe pro forma is shown in Figure 1.

The standardized recipe is at the core of subsequent costing and pricing activities. It is also tied directly to the inventory-management process. Failure to use and continually maintain standardized recipes for all menu items is considered a leading cause of food-cost overages.

Reference

Gisslen, W. (2003) *Professional Cooking*. New York: John Wiley & Sons.

DAVID V. PAVESIC
GEORGIA STATE UNIVERSITY, USA

Recruitment and E-recruitment

Recruitment is the process of attracting a pool of qualified job candidates from which an appropriate selection decision can be made (Christensen Hughes, 2002). Internal recruitment strategies (e.g., promotion from within, lateral transfers) are often supported by career planning, human resource information systems (HRIS), or internal job-posting systems and are helpful for motivating, developing, and retaining employees. External recruitment approaches are useful when significant numbers of new employees are required or for introducing new ideas and skill sets to the organization. External recruitment methods have traditionally included employee referrals, walk-ins/write-ins, advertisements, headhunters/employment agencies, job fairs,

and liaising with educational institutions. Increasingly, however, recruitment has gone online. Using the company's own website to post jobs has proven particularly useful to international employers in the hospitality industry for retaining employees who are interested in relocating, for dealing with seasonality (i.e., to encourage movement between locations with opposite demand cycles), and for communicating with potential employees from outside the immediate geographic area. Potential candidates may be invited to respond to advertisements by e-mail or listservs, to submit their résumés electronically, and/or to complete an online pre-screening instrument to help assess compatibility. E-recruitment can also involve posting jobs on private employment websites and reviewing résumés posted by those looking for work.

Reference

Christensen Hughes, J. (2002) Recruitment and selection issues and strategies within international resort communities. In N. D'Annunzio-Green, G.A. Maxwell, and S. Watson (eds), *Human Resource Management: International Perspectives in Hospitality and Tourism*. London: Continuum.

JULIA CHRISTENSEN HUGHES
UNIVERSITY OF GUELPH, CANADA

Redundancy

Redundancy refers to when an employer's decision leads to the termination of the worker's employment. Grounds for redundancy are fulfilled if the employer decides that it no longer wishes the job a worker has been performing to be done by anyone; the employer's decision is not due to the ordinary and customary turnover of labor; and the termination is not due to any personal act or default of the employee (Michalandos, 2001). A job may become obsolete (or redundant) if tasks and duties are deconstructed to become internal elements of other positions so that the original occupier of that job has nothing left to perform. Additionally, redundancies may result from a substantial decrease of responsibilities, a geographical change in the location of the job, and the sale or transfer of a business.

Prior to making a redundancy decision, employers are required to justify the validity of grounds on which the decision was made and how employees to be made redundant were identified. Employers are also expected to provide evidence of whether employees were consulted and whether redundancy payments and periods of notice are appropriate.

In the hospitality industry, some redundancies have occurred through increased levels of autonomy afforded to staff. Additionally, advances in food technology have meant the replacement of traditional *chefs de parti* with fewer lower-skilled operatives.

Reference

Michalandos, M. (2001) *Australian Master Human Resources Guide 2002*. Sydney: CCH Australia.

DARREN LEE-ROSS
JAMES COOK UNIVERSITY, AUSTRALIA

Reference checks

Given the mobility and youth of hospitality industry employees, reference checks can be a valuable and low-cost source of accessing a variety of information on a potential candidate (Zwell, 2000). Reference checks are considered one of three ways to do background checks (Klinvex *et al.*, 1999). Other ways of performing background checks are to confirm candidate credentials and assess candidate training needs.

Reference checks are used to confirm past employment and assess any uncertainties about that employment – position, duties, strengths, weaknesses, competencies, reasons for leaving previous employment, and suitability for present position. Given the importance of the customer service interaction in hospitality, checks can also be used to confirm past behaviors used in service situations. Often reference checks are used to determine criminal background and credit-worthiness.

The law on reference checks varies from jurisdiction to jurisdiction; therefore, hospitality organizations should be aware of these differences. Generally information conveyed must be based on objective facts not opinions. The discussion should be related to job issues and not deal with personal information. However, opinions about the candidate, personal characteristics of the candidate, tone of voice used, the person contacted and their manner of answering questions, if legal, can provide good information about the suitability of a candidate to a hospitality employer.

References

Klinvex, K.C., O'Connell, M.S., and Klinvex, C.P. (1999) *Hiring Great People*. New York: McGraw-Hill.
Zwell, M. (2000) *Creating a Culture of Competence*. New York: John Wiley & Sons.

G. KEITH HENNING
UNIVERSITY OF CALGARY, CANADA

Reference group

A reference group is an individual(s) or group(s) that influences the shaping of an individual's opinions, beliefs, attitude, and/or behavior. There are two major types of reference groups: normative reference groups and comparative reference groups. Normative reference groups influences an individual's norms, attitudes, and values through direct interaction. Parents, teachers, associates, peers, and friends belong to this group. Comparative reference groups are aspirational groups to which an individual does not belong, but which are used as a standard for self-evaluation. Comparative reference groups serve as a reference point that an individual uses to compare himself/herself to other individuals or groups. Celebrities or heroes are examples of comparative reference groups that indirectly influence an individual's attitude or behavior.

Marketers accept the reference group as an important concept that can exercise an influence on information processing and consumer purchasing decision. A reference group or individual with high credibility such as expertise in a certain area, for example, often works as a source of information for uncertain or uninformed customers. The influence of reference groups on consumer behavior has been evidenced in the types of products and brand choice decision. Advertising is one of the marketing fields that heavily use reference group influence.

Reference

Childers, T.L. and Rao, A.R. (1992) The influence of familial and peer-based reference groups on consumer decisions. *Journal of Consumer Research*, 19 (September), 198–211.

EUNHA MYUNG
UNIVERSITY OF NEVADA, LAS VEGAS, USA

Refreshment break

Refreshment breaks are essential. A refreshment break is an energy break. It is intended to refresh and sharpen attention. It also helps alleviate the boredom that tends to develop when guests are engaged in tedious business activities during the day. Breaks provide learners with an opportunity to reflect on what they have just heard. It is common to have breaks between sessions at a meeting or convention where participants are going from one location to another. The break allows for participant movement, as well as for refreshments.

Breaks should be placed in convenient locations, which allow attendees to obtain refreshment in a relaxed atmosphere. The location of a break should relate to the purpose of the break, what is being served, the space available, and the participants' convenience.

A break can be set up in the pre-function space just outside the meeting room if the space is secure and the area is large enough to accommodate the group. If the room is large enough, the break can be set up in the back of the room, if the space is available. However, noise during set-up can be distracting to both the speaker and the audience. Attendees, realizing the break is set up prior to the meeting recess may slip back to grab

a cup of coffee. Another disadvantage is a late meeting start, due to lingerers still chatting, grabbing one last cup to take to their seat, etc. The noise of breaking down the service can be distracting. If a meeting has a number of concurrent sessions, one should have a centralized, common location for the refreshments instead of putting a station in each room.

Set-up completion should be at least 15 minutes prior to the scheduled break time, as a session may end early. At least one server should be scheduled for every 100 attendees.

Costs for breaks may be quoted per person or on a consumption basis. Paying for coffee by the gallon and pastry by the dozen is usually more economical than paying a per person price. It is advantageous to cut Danish pastries in half and only order half as many whole ones as one needs.

In these health-conscious times, fruit juice can be a welcome alternative to coffee at the morning break or to soda drinks at an afternoon break. Items can also be ordered à la carte, on a consumption basis, meaning one only pays for what is consumed. Coffee and tea can be purchased in half-gallon (2.5 litre) increments. Individual juices and bottled water (sparking and still) in addition to coffee and soda drinks should be paid for on the basis of consumption. Attendees prefer individual containers of condiments to a dish for everyone's consumption.

Refreshment breaks are typically scheduled at mid-morning and mid-afternoon when coffee, tea and/or other refreshments are served.

A general rule of thumb is a 10-minute break for every 50 minutes of instruction. Time must be allowed for participants to leave the session room, visit rest rooms, obtain their beverage and other items, eat and drink, and return to the same room or proceed to another room.

Breaks should be at least 15 minutes long and last from 15 to 30 minutes depending on the number of attendees as follows:

Up to 50 people	20 minutes
50–100 people	30 minutes
100–1000 people	30–45 minutes

SUZETTE EADDY
NATIONAL MINORITY SUPPLIER
DEVELOPMENT COUNCIL, USA

Registration

Registration is an activity that usually takes place at the hotel's reception and upon the guest's arrival at the hotel. The registration process, irrespective of the type of the hotel, can be divided in a series of activities. These activities typically include: greeting the guest, which may go a long way toward establishing a rapport with the guest in that the guest may judge all other services during a stay by this first encounter; creating a registration record; distributing a key; and finally fulfilling any special requests (such as wake up calls) that the guest might have. In some countries, it is the legal obligation of the hotel to obtain and retain information, including identification or passport number, from the hotel guest during registration. The hotel can improve the registration efficiency by acquiring the necessary information from the guest at the reservation stage. This is often regarded as an additional, or even the first in chronological terms, activity of the registration process, called the pre-registration activity.

A key report that is created as a result of registration is an arrivals report which includes the number of guests arriving by date and the type of room(s) that the guest has requested.

References

Kasavana, M.L. and Brooks, R.M. (1998) *Front Office Procedures*, 5th edn. Lansing, MI: Educational Institute of the American Hotel and Motel Association.

Dix, C. and Baird, C. (1988) *Front Office Operations*. Harlow: Longman.

CONSTANTINOS S. VERGINIS
THE EMIRATES ACADEMY OF HOSPITALITY
MANAGEMENT, UNITED ARAB EMIRATES

Registration card

The front office utilizes a registration card or the computer-based equivalent to check in guests. A typical registration card requires the guest to furnish personal data including name, billing address, length of stay, and method of settlement. From the registration card credit can be established or verified during check-in as well. While payment guarantees may be established during the reservation process in case a guest does not arrive at the hotel as expected, most credit card companies will require a swipe of the credit card in an electronic recording device or imprint on a credit card voucher in order to establish credit for the guest. The registration card is a record of the credit card information. Most governmental jurisdictions require the guest's signature on the registration card before the relationship between the hotel and the guest is considered legal. In some governmental jurisdictions there may be specific requirements printed on the card relating to the availability of safe storage for guest valuables. The registration card will also show the room rate, allowing the guest to confirm it, and a place for the guest to initial an agreement and confirmation of the rate. Such information reduces questions about the price of the room at check-out.

Reference

Stutts, Alan T. (2001) *Hotel and Lodging Management – An Introduction*. New York: John Wiley & Sons.

ALAN T. STUTTS
AMERICAN INTERCONTINENTAL
UNIVERSITY, USA

Relationship marketing

Relationship marketing is a customer-centric strategy that selectively builds long-term, mutually profitable customer relationships through interactive and individualized interactions that maximize customer lifetime value. Relationship marketing, also referred to as customer relationship management (CRM) (Parvatiyar and Sheth, 2001), and closely related to one-to-one marketing and aftermarketing (Vavra, 1992), has become one of the leading business strategies in the new millennium. In the current scenario of increased competition, disintermediation, experienced and demanding customers, globalization, limited marketing resources, and fast-changing technologies, market-oriented management is best based on a relational approach (i.e. one that does not finishes its activities after the sale is completed) rather than a transactional one. It is a common mistake for traditional marketers to be too focused on getting new customers, but to neglect to keep existing ones. This is despite the fact that it has been demonstrated that on average it is about six to eight times more expensive to gain new customers than selling to current ones. This is a 'revolving-door effect' – while trying to pull new customers through the door, the existing customers walk away. Relationship marketing is all about making customers happy and bringing them back.

The objective of relationship marketing is to selectively turn existing, new or prospective customers into loyal ones through a good understanding of needs and individual preferences, a superior service designed accordingly, and a long-term, mutually beneficial relationship (Dyche, 2001). It represents a return to the roots of traditional hospitality: knowing every customer intimately, providing one-to-one solutions to customers' requirements, and developing a continuous elation that does not expire at the end of the customer's stay. The result is to make customers feel part of the 'family' and convincing them that the hospitality company truly cares about them and their problems.

Parvatiyar and Sheth (2001) argue that there are at least three aspects that articulate the uniqueness of the concept. First, relationship marketing relates to a one-to-one relationship between the company and the customer. This implies that relationship marketing cannot be pursued in the aggregate but at the individual level Second, relationship marketing is an interactive process that is more than a transactional exchange, as not all the contacts with the customer have a transactional component. Third, relationship marketing is a value-added activity through mutual interdependence and collaboration between suppliers and customers.

Another important facet of relationship marketing is customer selectivity. That comes from the understanding that not all customers are equally profitable for a company. The hospitality company therefore must be selective in tailoring its marketing efforts by segmenting and selecting appropriate customers for specific marketing programs.

One of the key aspects for the success of a relationship marketing strategy in the hospitality industry is to understand it as a company-wide business strategy. Thus relationship marketing is much more than a mere technology solution: Technology is a core component of relationship marketing. Tools such as relational databases, data mining and data warehousing, and techniques such as collaborative filtering, expert systems and artificial intelligence are increasingly being applied for managing information on customer interactions. But technology is not the sum total of a relationship marketing strategy. Relationship marketing is a culture, a way of thinking, a set of values, and a way of doing things. True customer relationship management involves the totality of how hospitality companies approach their business and interactions with customers. It is a whole attitude towards customers and employees supported by certain systems, processes and technologies. Projects that focus on the technology tools rather than on business objectives are doomed to failure. Hospitality professionals also need to realize that.

Relationship marketing affects the whole organization; not only marketing or IT are involved with relationship marketing. Successful relationship marketing consists of a holistic business philosophy, affecting everyone in the organization, in order to align business activities and customer needs. It involves the integration of marketing, sales, customer service, front-line employees, and the back office. The front line will be key in determining customer needs, preferences, and service expectations and in providing personalized service as a result of the relationship marketing information and the support of the organizational structure. Customer-contact employees need to know how to listen, probe customers for their needs, handle objections and complaints, cross-sell, and make referrals. Back office departments, such as accounting, are key in providing support and in organizing this information.

Human resources is responsible for providing the necessary training and support structures (performance assessment, reward and recognition, etc.). Therefore the entire organization needs to be relationship marketing orchestrated.

There are four basic components of a relationship marketing system:

1. Identification of customer needs and preferences. Storage of all these data in the appropriate databases allows managers to develop a complete picture of the customer by actively gathering, organizing, and analyzing customer data.
2. Sorting of the data in order to obtain customer profiles that indicate characteristics and patterns meaningful for the organization. The analytical components of a relationship marketing strategy include data marts, decision support tools, customer behavior modeling, and analytical tools. The customer data that are captured within the 'operational' components of a relationship marketing system are stored, retrieved, and analyzed for performance management and results measurement.
3. Interaction with the customer. This includes face-to-face, telephone, mail, e-mail, interactive voice response systems, Web conferencing, and Web portals. The objective is to put in practice the customer-contact strategies designed and to obtain even more information to feed the databases through database marketing techniques (Robledo, 2002). Direct online communications with customers any time and any where, and customer service centers that help customers solve their questions, are important elements. However, in the hospitality industry the front-office contact with customers become crucial for collecting information and for personalizing the service.
4. Measurement and metrics. Periodic assessment of results in relationship marketing is needed to evaluate whether the programs are meeting expectations. Pre-determined metrics for a relationship marketing project must include measurements of increased profit, decreased spending, and increased market share. Incorporating customer-behavior-analysis

software can establish effective customer-profitability metrics.

In conclusion, relationship marketing is a critical strategy for achieving a competitive edge in the hotel industry since it gives hoteliers the opportunity to be closer to customers than ever before. It can assist in maintaining a long-lasting relationship with every customer that can contribute to the hotel's profitability. Furthermore, relationship marketing restores the personal touch that technology is often accused of destroying.

References

Dyche, J. (2001) *The Relationship Marketing Handbook: A Business Guide to Customer Relationship Management*. New York: Addison-Wesley.

Parvatiyar, A. and Sheth, J. (2001) Customer relationship management: emerging practice, process and discipline. *Journal of Economic and Social Research*, 3 (2), 1–34.

Robledo, M.A. (2002) DBM as a competitive strategy: the state of the art in the Spanish hotel industry. *Tourism*, 50, 1.

Vavra, Terry G. (1992) *Aftermarketing: How to keep Customers for Life Through Relationship Marketing*. Homewood, IL: Irwin.

Winer, R.S. (2001) A framework for customer relationship management. *California Management Review*, 43 (4), 89–107.

MARCO ANTONIO ROBLEDO
UNIVERSITY OF THE BALEARIC ISLANDS,
SPAIN

Renewable energy

Renewable energy consists of energy that is provided by the capture of solar energy, wind energy, falling water, biomass, and some other sources (such as geothermal heat). These are called renewable because they are constantly being renewed by short-term natural processes. This is in contrast to fossil energy sources such as natural gas and oil where the process of renewal takes thousand to millions of years.

Hotels fairly easily use solar energy for heating domestic water or for pool heating. Some hotels are also using solar energy with photovoltaic cells to produce electricity. Some hotels access geothermal energy through the use of ground source heat pumps and a few, in active thermal areas, are able to use geothermal heat directly. A few hotels may be using wind power to produce electricity although it is probably more likely they will buy wind-powered electricity.

Green power purchasing is an optional service at several utilities, allowing customers the option of purchasing all or part of a building's energy load from renewable energy technologies. The term 'green power' generally refers to electricity supplied from sources such as wind and solar power, geothermal, hydropower, and various forms of biomass. Participating customers usually pay a premium on their electric bill to cover the extra cost of the renewable energy.

Reference

Green Power Partnership: www.epa.gov/greenpower

TOM JONES
UNIVERSITY OF NEVADA, LAS VEGAS, USA

Renovation

Renovation is the process of improving the image of a hospitality organization by modifying its tangible product by making changes in the property's layout, such as a new extension or replacing furniture and equipment (Hassanien and Losekoot, 2002). Renovation may be essential for a number of reasons, such as improving operational efficiency, reducing costs, improving corporate image and standards, responding to new trends and technology in the market, complying with government requirements, and recovering from accidents and disasters. Through renovation, the original reputation of the property and market share can be retained. In some cases, renovating may be faster more economical than building a new property. Every hospitality organization should develop an annual renovation plan. According to Stipanuk (2002), approximately 750,000 guestrooms are renovated every year. Renovation may range from a minor renovation, which may only involve replacing furnishings, to a master renovation or restoration that involves the entire property and results in extensive changes to the physical layout, and that may take a long time to complete. A four-stage model of renovation is advocated, starting from analysis, planning, implementation, and evaluation (Hassanien and Losekoot, 2002). Certain tasks have to be undertaken and specific issues should be considered at each stage if the renovation is to be successful.

References

Hassanien, A. and Losekoot, E. (2002) The application of facilities management expertise to hotel renovation process. *Facilities*, 20 (7/8), 230–238.

Stipanuk, D.M. (2002) *Hospitality Facilities Management and Design*, 2nd edn. Lansing, MI: Educational Institute of the American Hotel and Lodging Association.

FEVZI OKUMUS
THE HONG KONG POLYTECHNIC UNIVERSITY,
HONG KONG SAR, CHINA

Request for proposal

A request for proposal, or RFP, is an invitation to submit a competitive bid soliciting hospitality services and/or products. It specifically details the major needs and requirements for meeting services or provides description of products to be procured. The document typically lists specifications and application procedures to be followed and serves as a precursor to a legal agreement.

Depending on the scope and purpose of the RFP, it may include such information as: meeting and organization name, key contacts and decision-makers, preferred dates and arrival/departure patterns, meeting goals and objectives, historical information and data, expected attendance and guest profile, number and type of hotel accommodations, meeting space needs, food and beverage requirements, exhibits or special events, tentative meeting schedule, specific contract considerations, transportation needs, proposal deadlines, and anticipated decision dates.

Recent technology advancements have allowed planners to submit RFPs directly to suppliers via the Internet. Response time and efficiency has greatly improved, allowing the planner additional time to make an educated decision. Notably, organizations such as the Convention Industry Council (CIC) and Accepted Practices Exchanges (APEX) have supported initiatives to implement an industry-wide standardized RPF to streamline processes, resulting in less duplication of effort and time and cost saving. Related terms include invitation to tender, request for quote (RFQ), bid solicitation, and invitation to bid.

References

Connell, B. (ed.) (2004) *Professional Meeting Management*, 4th edn. Chicago: Professional Conference Management Association.

Fenich, G. (2004) *Meetings, Expositions, Events and Conventions: An Introduction to the Industry*. Englewood Cliffs, NJ: Prentice-Hall.

AMANDA KAY CECIL
INDIANA UNIVERSITY, USA

Rescission

Rescission means the cancellation of a contract by mutual agreement or by law. In timeshare contracts the rescission period is fixed by the company or by statute. Also known as a 'cooling off period,' this allows a consumer to cancel a purchase contract for a timeshare property without incurring a penalty, and with full refund of any money paid up front. The right to rescission is now a universal provision in countries with substantial numbers of timeshare resorts. Purchase contracts used by companies may exceed statutory requirements, but all must provide at least the minimum time for 'cooling off.'

In the United States this period varies between states. In Mexico, the statutory cooling off period is five days. The European Union's Directive on Timeshare Arrangements stipulates a minimum of ten days across all member states, though individual countries may exceed these arrangements. The UK, for example, requires all timeshare purchase agreements to allow a 14-day period during which the purchaser may cancel the contract.

To a large extent the now universal legal requirement for a rescission period is a response to concerns about high pressure selling techniques that have been used by some unscrupulous operators in the past. The cooling off period allows the customer time to reflect on the decision made during the site visit and sales presentation. Properly targeted leads, generating couples with a genuine interest in making a purchase, minimizes the number of contracts cancelled during rescission.

Reference

American Resort Development Association (2002) *The Timeshare Industry Resource Manual*. Washington, DC: ARDA.

CONRAD LASHLEY
NOTTINGHAM TRENT UNIVERSITY, UK

Research and development in foodservice

A successful foodservice operation must continually examine its menu offerings and recipes as well as its production and service methods to ensure that it is knowledgeable about customers' needs and desires while maximizing efficiency and effectiveness. Many foodservice organizations dedicate significant resources to research and development (R&D) in their efforts to optimize their operations' potential.

Larger organizations may create a menu research and development department that creates new recipes reflecting the taste and texture profile that customers want. In some cases, this work might involve updating an existing recipe to reduce its fat or carbohydrate content, or catering to evolving customer preferences for spicier or more sophisticated flavors. Other R&D projects may include the development of completely new menu items that make use of popular ingredients, represent a fashionable cuisine, or meet specialized needs. Menu and recipe R&D teams are made up of specially trained chefs who typically have a background in food chemistry as well as specialized kitchen expertise.

The R&D process for creating a new or revised menu item combines market research to determine customer preferences and trends; recipe development and testing, often in a specialized kitchen designed for this purpose; and test-marketing the resulting item to a small subset of the operation's market prior to 'rolling out' the new item to the organization as a whole. Analyzing competitors' offerings, studying specific cuisines, and sometimes even traveling to a different region or country to taste items and identify suppliers are also part of an R&D chef's role. The time required to develop a new item to the point of being offered to a valued customer base may be months or, in extreme cases, even years.

Another area that foodservice organizations research carefully is the design of production and service systems. These systems can be categorized into three main groups: equipment selection and use; operational procedures; and facility layout and design. To evaluate equipment, operators may consult with manufacturers or with private testing agencies to identify the optimal piece of equipment for a given menu item or process as well as the best mix of time, temperature, and technique required to deliver a consistent and satisfactory product. To develop the best operational procedures, researchers may analyze the amount of physical effort required for staff to accomplish their tasks – a discipline called ergonomics – and attempt to redesign systems so that employees are able to achieve more with less physical stress. Time–motion studies are among the tools that these researchers adopt, during which activities are observed while step-saving measures are identified and tested. Lastly,

a specialized R&D team may examine more effective ways of designing a kitchen to reduce operating costs through reduced staffing, energy savings, or lower construction costs. Multi-unit foodservice operations may also research the best approach to designing the front-of-the-house so that the guest experience is maximized without compromising staff efficiency. It is common for research and development pertaining to facilities to be performed by consultants with specific training in engineering, architecture, or design.

Creating a dedicated R&D facility is a good strategy for organizations with many operational units or complex marketing or design concepts. Such a facility might include test kitchens, a chemical laboratory, an equipment testing area, and perhaps an area where different configurations of equipment or seating can be 'mocked up,' or created in life size for evaluation. It is not uncommon for R&D teams to work closely with their marketing departments to ensure a mutually clear understanding of customer desires, and therefore it is practical for a large foodservice organization to locate these two departments in close proximity.

It is important to note that the cost of comprehensive R&D in the foodservice industry is considerable. In fact, even when an item is developed through a thorough R&D process including the aforementioned steps of determining customer trends, recipe development and testing, and test marketing of the product, the resulting sales may not be adequate to cover these R&D costs – even when such costs are amortized over an extended period. Thus, R&D must be managed and measured in terms of its contribution to the overall profitability of the unit or chain.

An excellent case in point is the move by QSR leaders in the early 1990s to create healthier menu items. As Ball (2004) notes, for example, McDonald's 'McLean Deluxe,' which was intended to offer customers a lower-fat alternative to the QSR leader's standard fare, never succeeded. Following four years of R&D, the item remained on the menu for almost two years with company executives hoping to recoup at least a portion of the reported 2 million dollars spent on its R&D. Conversely, the ten years McDonald's spent on its Chicken McNuggets proved a prudent investment, as this menu item continues to sell well.

References

Ball, D. (2004) With food sales flat, Nestlé stakes future on healthier fare. *Wall Street Journal*, 18 March, B5.

Birchfield, J.C. and Sparrowe, R.T. (2003) *Design and Layout of Foodservice Facilities*. Hoboken, NJ: John Wiley & Sons.

STEPHANI K.A. ROBSON
CORNELL UNIVERSITY, USA

Reservation

Hotels around the world and of various levels of service accept advance bookings aiming to maximize their occupancy and therefore their profitability. These advance bookings are called reservations. The length of time in advance that guests reserve rooms varies from a few hours to several months depending on the type of the hotel and the season. In order for a hotel to accept reservations a manual or a computerized system must be in place. Such a system enables the hotel staff to perform the three principal steps of a reservation, namely check whether a reservation request is possible (room availability), record the reservation, and retrieve the reservation when required. There are many mediums that potential guests use in order to make a reservation, including telephone, fax, central reservation systems, global distribution systems, travel agencies, tour operators, and through the Internet to name but a few. Irrespective of the inquiry medium, before confirming a reservation the hotel must obtain a range of information from the guest. The required amount of information varies from hotel to hotel. The minimum however may include the arrival date, the length of stay, the name of the person(s), the type of room, the price, and other conditions such as check-in and check-out time.

References

Dix, C. and Baird, C. (1988) *Front Office Operations*, 4th edn. Harlow: Longman.

Kasavana, M.L. and Brooks, R.M. (1998) *Front Office Procedures*, 5th edn. Lansing, MI: Educational Institute of the American Hotel and Motel Association.

CONSTANTINOS S. VERGINIS
THE EMIRATES ACADEMY OF HOSPITALITY
MANAGEMENT, UNITED ARAB EMIRATES

Reservation file

A computer-based collection of reservation records that are compiled prior to the arrival of guests. Based on this file guests may be sent a letter or electronic confirmation to verify that a reservation has been made and that its specifications are accurate. The confirmation permits errors in communication to be corrected before the guest arrives and verifies the guest's correct mailing or electronic address for future correspondence. With current technology and an automated interface between the reservation system and a word processor, many hotels often provide confirmations in the form of letters, making the process seem more personal. The reservations software of an in-house computer system may directly interface with a central reservations network and perform many pre-arrival activities and calculations from the reservation file. In addition to automatically generating letters, electronic folios can be established from the reservation file and pre-registration transactions can be processed for guests with confirmed reservations. From the reservation file an expected arrivals list, occupancy and revenue forecasts can also be generated.

The reservation file can also facilitate automated checks, such as the video check-in. Touch screens on free-standing terminals at kiosks are being used as part of systems to check in and also check out guests without the need to use the traditional front desk. Touch-and-Go was the first system of its kind in the industry, providing the guest who had an advanced reservation and a credit card the option of avoiding the front desk at the beginning or end of the stay. The target speed for the system was to allow guests to check themselves into their own rooms in less than 90 seconds.

Reference

Stutts, Alan T. (2001) *Hotel and Lodging Management – An Introduction*. New York: John Wiley & Sons.

RICHARD NELSON
HYATT HOTELS CORPORATION, USA
ALAN T. STUTTS
AMERICAN INTERCONTINENTAL
UNIVERSITY, USA

Reference

Stutts, Alan T. (2001) *Hotel and Lodging Management – An Introduction*. New York: John Wiley & Sons.

RICHARD NELSON
HYATT HOTELS CORPORATION, USA
ALAN T. STUTTS
AMERICAN INTERCONTINENTAL
UNIVERSITY, USA

Reservation record

The reservation record identifies guests and their occupancy needs before the guest's arrival. This record enables a hotel to personalize guest service and more accurately schedule staff. In addition the reservation record can be utilized to generate multiple management reports. Typically a reservation record includes: guest name; guest home or billing address; guest telephone number including area and country codes; guest corporate address and telephone numbers as appropriate; name of and pertinent information about the person making the reservation; number of people in the party; arrival date and time; number of nights required or expected departure date; whether the reservation is guaranteed or not guaranteed with some form of payment; special requirements such as non-smoking or services for an infant or disabled guest; and additional information about transportation requirements, late arrival, room preference, etc.). Individual properties and chains may differ with respect to quoting and confirming room rates during the creation of a reservation record. Although published rates may be subject to change without notice, a rate quoted and confirmed during the reservations process must be honored. When creating the reservation record reservationists must be particularly knowledgeable about supplementary charges for extra services or amenities; minimum stay requirements in effect for the dates requested; special promotions in effect for the dates requested; applicable currency exchange rates, if quoting an international guest; applicable room tax percentages; and applicable service charges for gratuities.

Reservation reports

An effective reservation system helps maximize room sales by accurately monitoring room availabilities and forecasting rooms' revenue. Regardless of the degree of automation, the number and type of management reports available through a reservation system are functions of the hotel's needs and the system's capability and contents. Typically reservation reports include: reservation transaction report, which summarize daily reservations activity in terms of reservation record creation, modification, and cancellation; commission agent's report, which tracks the amount a hotel owes to each agent who has a contractual agreement with the hotel to book business; turnaway report, which tracks the numbers of reservation requests refused because rooms were not available for the requested dates; and revenue forecast report, which projects future revenue by multiplying predicted occupancies by applicable room rates.

In addition: expected arrival and departure lists are typically generated from reservation data to indicate the number and names of guests expected to arrive, depart or stay over; advance deposits for reservations can be identified; and reservation histories which include statistics on all aspects of the reservations process including the number of guests, occupied rooms, reservations by source, not shows, walk-ins, overstays and understays, and can be used by sales and marketing personnel to identify trends, review available products and services, and assess the impact of the hotel's marketing strategies.

Reference

Stutts, Alan T. (2001) *Hotel and Lodging Management – An Introduction.* New York: John Wiley & Sons.

ALAN T. STUTTS
AMERICAN INTERCONTINENTAL
UNIVERSITY, USA

Kotler, P., Bowen, J., and Makens, J. (2002) *Marketing for Hospitality and Tourism.* Upper Saddle River, NJ: Prentice-Hall.

IAN McDONNELL
UNIVERSITY OF TECHNOLOGY, SYDNEY,
AUSTRALIA

Reservations

An essential aspect of any hospitality business is reserving space – a hotel room, a restaurant seat, a conference room, and a banquet hall – for customers. This ensures that the customers' needs are satisfied when they require it, and the hospitality providers know the quantity of demand for their products on a daily basis, which assists in planning labor and consumable requirements for that day.

Reservations (the use of the word in this sense first appeared in 1906, according to the *Oxford English Dictionary*) can be made by the guest or client using various media – directly using the telephone, the Internet, in person, post mail, or e-mail, or via an intermediary (a travel agent or a global distrubution system) – and recorded by the firm. Recording of reservations can range from writing them manually in a bound book, which can still be seen occasionally in small hotels, *pensions* and especially in restaurants, to electronically recording them in an establishment's computer reservation system, which is generally part of its property management system (PMS).

Much useful marketing data can be gathered from the reservation records, depending on the amount of information requested from the guest, which forms the basis for much of the marketing activity of an establishment – customer relations management, yield management, market segmentation etc.

References

Buhalis, D. (2003) *eTourism: Information Technology for Strategic Tourism Management.* Harlow: Pearson Education Limited.

Reserve for replacement

The replacement reserve refers to funds in various stages of liquidity set aside by a firm and targeted for future major refurbishments and replacements of the physical assets, e.g., building exterior and interior, mechanical, electrical and plumbing systems and major equipment, where the assets' expected lives are less than the *expected property life*. The replacement reserve enables the firm to maintain property value both as an operating concern and a real estate asset, and to handle required improvements while hedging against unforeseen increases in costs of capital. There are two types of reserves: *contingency* and *capital reserves*. Contingency reserves are set aside to handle unforeseen significant expenditures. Capital reserve fund amounts are based on a reserve study of each major physical asset that can be expected to need repair or replacement at some point in the future. Reserve funds may be established using either the *line item* method or the *cash flow* method. In the line item method, funds are added for each asset listed in the reserve study. When required, funds are deducted to renovate or replace that specific item. This method requires estimating future costs and assigning funds to each of the items in the asset list. In the cash flow method, reserve funds are set at estimated levels which are expected to cover anticipated projects or contingencies.

References

Rushmore, S. (1990) *Hotel Investments – A Guide for Lenders and Owners.* Boston: Warren, Gorham, Lamont, pp. A 3–12.

Eyster, J.J. (1997) *Hotel Management Contracts in the US. Cornell Hotel and Restaurant Administration Quarterly*, 38 (3), 30. www.pwcreval.com/survey/faq.asp.

BONNIE CANZIANI
UNIVERSITY OF NORTH CAROLINA –
GREENSBORO, USA

Resident manager

This title was historically given to the senior management representative who actually resided on the property. In today's hotel environment there has been a movement away from live-in status. The title, however, has remained, and is most often given to the individual recognized as the assistant general manager of the property. The term resident manager is used to describe that person who acts on behalf of the general manager in his/her absence and who often resides permanently on the hotel property. The general manager may promote any executive to relieve the general manager of some operational duties; however, a resident manager may take on these duties without being relieved of her/his regular departmental responsibilities. In practice, the general manager may select the manager of the rooms department to be resident manager. Responsibilities of the resident manger may include serving as acting general manager in the absence of the general manager, representing the general manager on various hotel interdepartmental committees, and taking responsibility for important special projects such as major hotel renovations, VIP guests, or operating reports that require in-depth analysis for the regional or perhaps corporate offices. In some hotel and lodging properties the role of general manager and resident manager may be one and the same. While a resident manager may only work an 8-hour day because hotels and lodging establishments are open around the clock, night and weekend work is common. A resident manager may work more than 40 hours per week and if they are living in the hotel they may be called to work at any time during peak periods. During peak periods the resident manager may be expected to coordinate a wide variety of functions including front office, housekeeping, convention services, and security.

Reference

Stutts, Alan T. (2001) *Hotel and Lodging Management – An Introduction*. New York: John Wiley & Sons.

ERIC O. LONG
WALDORF ASTORIA HOTEL, USA

Resignation

Refers to when employees give notice unilaterally to employers of their intention to quit their job (or terminate their employment) with or without notice (De Cieri and Kramar, 2003). It is not always necessary to state this in writing unless it is a stipulation of the original contract of employment. Whether verbal or written, a key element of a resignation is the date from which it becomes effective. This must be explicit and understood clearly by both parties. Workers must also give an appropriate notice period; usually this is the same length as the pay period. This allows both employer and worker to make arrangements. Employers have an option of either allowing the employee to work out their notice period or paying them in lieu of notice. However, should workers refuse to work out their notice, they are not entitled to be paid for the period of notice. In some instances, failure to report for duty can be considered a repudiation of the contract of employment. Also, employees are entitled to receive other payments such as accrued annual leave (and any long service leave where appropriate), outstanding commission payments and bonuses or allowances. Resignation is distinguishable from other forms of termination such as voluntary redundancy and dismissal. The tourism and hospitality industry by nature has a large employee turnover through natural attrition and staff moving from hotel to hotel (Woods, 2001).

References

De Cieri, H. and Kramar, R. (2003) *Human Resource Management in Australia: Strategy, People, Performance*. Sydney: McGraw-Hill.

Woods, R.H. (2002) *Managing Hospitality Human Resources*, 3rd edn. Lansing, MI: Educational Institute of the American Hotel and Lodging Association.

DARREN LEE-ROSS
JAMES COOK UNIVERSITY, AUSTRALIA

Resource-based view

The resource-based view (RBV) of the firm posits that firm performance is ultimately a return on unique assets owned and controlled by the firm (Barney, 1991). This assertion is important in the context of the history of strategic management theory.

Within the classical industrial organization (IO) literature, scholars have typically assumed that firm management cannot influence industry conditions or its own performance. As firm conduct (i.e., strategy) is constrained by industry structural forces, it does not represent independent managerial action, and therefore the role of management can be ignored (Spanos and Lioukas, 2001).

A modified framework advanced by Porter (1990) departed from traditional IO theory and focused on the performance of the firm rather than the industry. For Porter, industry structure was not necessarily stable. Instead, Porter (1990) viewed market environments as partially subject to influences by firm actions, and the firm was viewed as a 'bundle of activities'. Porter also assumed that firms were identical in terms of strategically relevant resources and that any attempt to develop resource heterogeneity would have no long-term viability due to the high mobility of strategic resources among firms.

For the resource-based scholars, a firm is not a 'bundle of activities', but rather a 'bundle of unique resources' (Barney, 1991). In contrast to Porter's view, RBV focuses on the relationships between internal resources of a firm and performance, assuming that firms may be heterogeneous in relation to the resources and capabilities on which they base their strategies, and that these resources and capabilities may not be perfectly mobile across firms, resulting in heterogeneity among industry participants.

The focus of RBV categorizes resources into three main groups: physical capital resources (such as plant and equipment), human capital resources (such as training, intelligence, and experience), and organizational capital resources (such as reporting structure and coordinating systems). These resources are employed to support the firm's quest for a competitive advantage, or a sustained competitive advantage. Competitive advantage is defined as the ability to use firm resources for implementing a value-creating strategy that is not simultaneously being implemented by any competitor. Similarly, sustained competitive advantage is a competitive advantage that the competition cannot copy or simulate. More specifically, a competitive advantage becomes sustained only if it continues to exist after efforts to duplicate that advantage have failed and ceased. Therefore, the definition of sustained competitive advantage is an equilibrium definition.

RBV enables identification of firm resources capable of generating sustained competitive advantage for the firm. The initial requirement is that the resources are heterogeneous and immobile, and then they are considered relevant as strategic resources. These resources must then meet four conditions: First, they must be valuable. Resources are valuable if they can enable the firm to conceive or implement a value-creating strategy. Second, the resources have to be rare. Rarity implies that the chance that competing firms may also own them is relatively low. Third, the resources must be imperfectly imitable. Firm resources can be imperfectly imitable if the ability to obtain them depends on unique historical circumstances, or if the relationship between these resources and the firm competitive advantage is causally ambiguous, or if these resources are socially complex. Finally, the fourth requirement is that they do not have a substitute (or a strategic equivalent).

The framework offered by RBV is appealing for firms seeking sustained competitive advantage. However, the four aforementioned requirements for firm resources limit the number of resources with the potential to create a sustained competitive advantage. Hospitality organizations are seeking firm resources that may support a sustained competitive advantage. However, the research on RBV in the hospitality industry is not yet developed. Olsen, West, and Tse (1998) offer some insights into identification of firm resources capable of generating a competitive advantage. Among these are behavioral performance skills, information exchange skills, speed of transactions, employee competency, and management competency. That said, it is difficult to find examples in which these resources support a sustained competitive advantage.

Brand name is one of the popular firm assets in the hospitality industry. Many hotels use a brand name to generate a competitive position (and advantage) in their industry. However, little evidence exists to show that brand name is a firm resource that can generate a sustained competitive advantage, as it generally is not rare. Furthermore, for a given quality level, some brands are both homogeneous and mobile. A study by Israeli (2002) confirms this assertion. The study focused on brand name in an effort to evaluate whether it constitutes a firm resource capable of supporting a competitive advantage in the Israeli hospitality industry. The findings suggest that brand name is not consistent in its ability to support a request for a premium price and to generate a competitive advantage. In some geographical areas, the competition in the industry uses similar brand names with the same quality rating and thus these resources are not rare or imperfectly imitable, and they do not meet the criteria offered by Barney. The study also focused on star rating as a resource that communicates quality to customers. With respect to the star rating of hotels, which is partially dependent on historical circumstances difficult to imitate, partial evidence was found to support the argument that star rating is a resource capable of generating a competitive advantage for firms with high star rating and high ranking of quality.

References

Barney, J. (1991) Firm resources and sustained competitive advantage. *Journal of Management*, 17 (1), 99–120.

Israeli, A. (2002) Star rating and corporate affiliation: their influence on pricing hotel rooms in Israel, *International Journal of Hospitality Management*, 21 (4), 405–424.

Olsen, M.D., West, J.J., and Tse, E.C. (1998) *Strategic Management in the Hospitality Industry*. New York: Van Nostrand Reinhold.

Porter, M. (1990) *The Competitive Advantage of Nations*. New York: Macmillan.

Spanos, Y.E. and Lioukas, S. (2001) An examination into the causal logic of rent generation: contrasting Porter's competitive strategy framework and the resource-based perspective. *Strategic Management Journal*, 22, 907–934.

AVIAD ISRAELI
BEN-GURION UNIVERSITY, ISRAEL

Resource planning

Resource planning for the hospitality industry may be divided into two major streams:

- *Material resource planning (MRP):* The practice of calculating what materials are required to create a product by analyzing bill of materials data, inventory data and/or a master production schedule
- *Enterprise resource planning (ERP):* The practice of consolidating an enterprise's planning, manufacturing, sales, and marketing efforts into one management system.

Implementation of enterprise resource planning systems is not difficult. A company stores the fixed information needed to run its business – materials inventory, order lead times and quantities, safe stock levels, etc.), and adds processes such as sales, works and purchase order processing, and inventory control. The benefits of using project management techniques on ERP/MRP systems can be dramatic, but require real discipline and skill in project management. The discipline of project management requires clear definition of tasks, appropriate resources, and real deliverables that mark the end of a task. Emphasis is placed on work breakdown structures, using earned value techniques (rather than percent complete), and time sheet data entry with regular reevaluation of 'estimates to completion.' Project teams within the hospitality industry may include IT, front office, back-of-the-house and outside contractors, usually with an empowered leader for each team.

References

Jones, P. (1999) Operational issues and trends in the hospitality industry. *International Journal of Hospitality Management*, 18 (4), 427–442.

Robinson, P. (1998) *Business Excellence – the Integrated Solution to Planning and Control.* London: BPI.

MALCOLM COOPER
RITSUMEIKAN ASIA PACIFIC UNIVERSITY,
JAPAN

Responsibility centers

In a decentralized organization, tasks and responsibilities are allocated among managers in order to decentralize the decision-making process. Managers are responsible for the financial outcomes of the decisions they control. In this context, the accounting system plays a critical role in driving management behavior in order to achieve an efficient and effective use of resources. Manager performance is evaluated against goals and targets set in the budget. The accounting system is meant to 'tie' the contribution of each responsibility center to the overall profitability of the firm.

The purpose of a management control system is to guide decision-making at management level within the parameters of the financial goals of the organization. A critical part of this process is the specification of tasks and responsibilities of each manager where responsibilities are defined in financial terms. The whole activity of the firm is divided in several parts, and organizational units are charged with the responsibility of each individual segment.

A responsibility center is an organizational unit with a manager responsible for the relationship between input (resources/costs) and outcome. The combination of the outcome of each unit results in the outcome of the organization as a whole. The assumption is that if each manager achieves his or her own target, the organization as a whole achieves its financial goals.

Responsibility centers might be projected over organizational units, but always result in a hierarchy, which matches the structure of the organization. Responsibility is assigned accordingly with the decision-making power of each unit because managers are accountable only for what they can control. Therefore, responsibility is both a direct consequence of the actual control over resources and of the decision-making power assigned to a specific manager. Along with a 'concept' of responsibility, specific parameters have to be selected in order to assign goals and to measure results.

Responsibility centers are traditionally classified in five groups:

- *Cost centers:* Managers have control over variable costs and are accountable for the relationship between variable costs and the volume of output (efficiency). In a cost center, the manager is focused on resources efficiency.
- *Revenue centers:* Managers have control over sales, and they are responsible for the amount of sales achieved. In revenue centers managers are focused on generating revenues.
- *Expense centers:* Activity in this unit cannot be measured and therefore efficiency cannot be calculated. Managers are responsible for keeping the total cost of the unit below budget.

Table 1   Responsibility centers in a business unit

Type of responsibility	Controlled variables	Responsibility measure
Cost centers	Managing variable resources usage	Cost per unit
Revenue centers	Managing sales	Total revenues
Expense centers	Managing activities with non-measurable output	Total expenses
Profit centers	Prices, volume, and costs	Operating profit
Investment centers	Profit, level of investment in operating assets	Residual income, ROI

- *Profit centers:* When managers have control over price setting, they have to take into account both costs and revenues simultaneously and their achievement must be measured in terms of profit. Given that profit centers' managers are responsible for both revenues and expenses, they usually are either directly responsible for managing both revenues and costs or they have hierarchical control over cost and revenue centers.
- *Investment centers:* When managers have control over the level of investment, they have to take into account the effect of their actions on asset profitability and are therefore responsible for the relationship between profits and investments.

The responsibility can be assigned on costs and revenues independently or on profit only or, moreover, on the relation between profit and investment. Usually more comprehensive responsibility (on profit or investments) is assigned at an upper level of the organizational hierarchy.

The main issue in designing a management control structure (or responsibility structure) is the alignment between responsibility and control. Managers have to be kept responsible for those activities – more precisely the resources (revenues, expenses, assets) – over which they exert a reasonable degree of control.

In recent years, a great deal of attention has been driven toward a new kind of non-financial responsibility. In both academia and practice, a 'new structure of responsibility,' based on non-financial measures, has been designed in order to include in a manager's goals and targets the long-term effects of his or her decisions. These 'new performance measurement systems' do not change the nature of financial control. Regardless of the long-term performance goals a manager is supposed to achieve, the short-term financial targets of an entity have to be achieved. Therefore, the non-financial performance indicators, when adopted in a manager control structure, are seen as additional indicators and not as a substitution of 'traditional' financial indicators.

References

Drury, C. (2000) *Management and Cost Accounting*, 5th edn. London: Thomson Learning.

Fay, C.T., Rhoads, R.C., and Rosenblatt, R.L. (1976) *Managerial Accounting for the Hospitality Service Industries*, 2nd edn. Dubuque, IA: Wm. C. Brown.

Hilton, R.W. (2002) *Managerial Accounting: Creating Value in a Dynamic Business Environment*, 5th edn. Boston, MA: McGraw-Hill/Irwin.

PAOLO COLLINI
TRENTO UNIVERSITY, ITALY

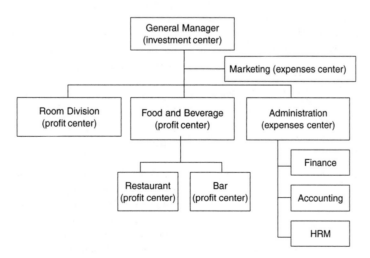

Figure 1   Responsibility centers identified in a hotel

Restaurant life cycle

Foodservice operations, like other businesses, progress through several life cycle stages: introduction, growth, maturity, and decline. These stages correspond, as shown in Figure 1, to a revenue–time function. Some restaurateurs enjoy a lengthy life cycle while others experience the four stages in less than a year. The terminality depends on understanding the differences among the different stages, progressing smoothly in the early stages while managing growth effectively, and executing successful strategies that are appropriate to the respective life cycle stage at the right time.

The introduction stage marks a restaurant's creation and launch. During the growth stage, market share and sales increase; many operators add additional units, explore franchising options, or expand the concept to include other outlets (such as on-site foodservice outlets). In the maturity stage sales stabilize, brand identity is secure, and business is predictable; at this point, markets are clearly defined. In the decline stage, sales and profit margins begin to decline, standards fall, and market share shifts away to competitors.

As Minno and Bhayana (1985) outlined, an operator's strategies and goals as well as a business's characteristics during each of these stages are quite distinct. In the introduction stage, management is highly centralized with the owner/operator making all operating decisions. Often, the entrepreneur has so much vested that he or she may fail to seek input from valuable sources such as other business operators, vendors, or employees. Correspondingly, the lack of experience in one or more key areas (human resources, financial management, marketing, etc.) often leads to losses.

In this stage, the burden to build patronage is nearly overwhelming and all efforts are directed at this primary objective. Appropriate points concerning price, value, and market position must be established. Drastic or ill-planned changes to these primary operating issues can lead to confusion for the customer, increasing the likelihood of business failure. Strategies that are required, then, include a sound pricing approach. In some cases, pricing may be lower than prevailing market prices in order to draw customers. Pricing that is too low, however, may impact profitability so strongly that sustained financial viability is compromised. Moreover, sharp jumps in prices will reduce nascent customer loyalty. Marketing during the introduction stage is the other key concern. Often high expenditures are necessary to attract first-time buyers and establish an identity in the marketplace.

A successful introduction leads to the growth stage. Here, the operation is streamlined. The menu is refined with a strong emphasis on balancing menu mix so that overall contribution margin is maximized while maintaining guests' perception of strong value. Depending on the operator's acumen, performance measures are used (e.g., productivity analysis) to assess efficiency. Revenue management techniques such as optimizing dining duration and associated serving times are also explored.

Where appropriate, the initial foodservice operation is replicated. Now, standardization is more important than ever to maintain brand equity. Whether the number of units is increased or not, the focus on standardization must include clearly articulating standards, policies, and practices.

The price, value, and positioning efforts expended in the introduction stage continue to play a vital role. Competition during the growth stage typically increases, with competitors hoping to capitalize on the concept's popularity. Effective price-value strategies employed by the restaurant will then pose barriers to competitors' success.

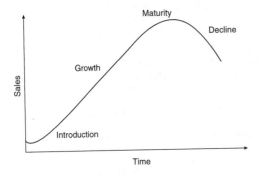

Figure 1 Relationship between sales and time by life cycle stage

Perhaps the most important concern during this stage is the shift in the entrepreneur's role. In the birth stage, the operator was the single voice in every important decision. In the growth stage, the planning becomes the most important management function due to its role in determining long-term success. Minute-to-minute direction, then, must be delegated. This requires extremely thoughtful selection processes and also requires the operator, who was so narrowly focused on day-to-day operations, to 'let go.' This change in role is sometimes difficult and, when not executed smoothly (including the hiring of effective unit managers), often leads to a reduced overall life cycle.

In the maturity stage, sales and profits stabilize, as the customer base is comprised largely of repeat guests. While brand equity is firmly established at this time, there are several factors that must be acknowledged. First, the concept may be showing signs of obsolescence. What new additions have been made to the menu? Have efforts been made to capture new market segments? Second, employees may become listless and complacent. Thus, management must consider motivational approaches that address this problem. At the same time, however, management may also become lax in enforcing the standards that have helped the unit or units thrive thus far.

Some operators respond to these issues and the potential negative effect on short-term profit by focusing almost exclusively on bottom-line results. For example, operators of restaurants in the latter point of the maturity stage may raise prices to compensate for reduced customer traffic. Such a strategy usually leads to further declines in patronage (resulting from the perceived poor value), which in turn prompts more price increases. This approach moves the operations quickly to the next stage.

The most characteristic phenomenon in the decline stage is a decrease in customer traffic and, correspondingly, sales. Competing restaurants now leverage successfully the best features of the mature restaurant and increase market share by combining these with new concepts, fresh ideas, and innovative business approaches. Regular customers cease to patronize the restaurant or chain and demonstrate their foodservice preferences by patronizing other establishments. Employee loyalty deteriorates, with the best managers and employees leaving for more attractive settings. Finally, the leadership is often confused. If still in the picture, the entrepreneur who survived the transition throughout the earlier stages may find the uncertainty now faced overwhelming and daunting.

In many cases, the decline stage marks inevitable demise. In others, however, restaurateurs progress through the life cycle understanding the need for eventual rebirth. These savvy operators observe and anticipate customers' changing tastes and dining preferences. They manage as though they are still in the growth curve and take an aggressive approach to business strategy, thereby ensuring that competitors do not take market share from them.

Ultimately, the restaurant's life cycle duration is the result of managerial prowess, entrepreneurial spirit, adequate capitalization, and a little luck. The introduction, growth, and maturity stages may lead to death, or they may lead to a fresh concept that may or may not include the same moniker. One thing is certain: the longer the business's life cycle, the more evident it becomes that change is the only stable item on the menu.

Reference

Minno, M.P. and Bhayana, R. (1985) Critical stages in the life cycle of a restaurant. *NRA News*, January, 16–20.

DENNIS REYNOLDS
WASHINGTON STATE UNIVERSITY, USA

Restaurant systems

Restaurant systems describe the information communication technology used for the effective running of the business, namely procurement, stock control, production and service, revenue control, and payroll systems. The procurement system includes the ordering and receipt of a food or beverage requisition, the selection of reputable suppliers, the creation of electronic invoices, and the acceptance of goods and the transfer of goods to stores. The stock control system facilitates storing and issuing of food or beverages, stocktaking, and receiving food or beverages. Production systems support production methods, such as cook–hold–serve, call–order, cook-to-order, batch, cook–chill, cook–freeze, standard refrigeration, sous vide, to name a few. They also provide vital information for menu engineering, and monitoring customer service in the restaurant, including reservations, loyalty schemes, and special promotions. Revenue systems include electronic points of sales and support staff record-keeping, such as commission payments, rotas, training achieved or sick leave. The introduction of computer software has enabled even small restaurants to have efficient systems at low cost and has provided significant benefits for restaurant management.

References

Davis, B. and Lockwood, A. (1994) *Food and Beverage Management.* Oxford: Butterworth-Heinemann.
Cousins, J., Foskett, D., and Shortt, D. (1995) *Food and Beverage Management.* Harlow: Longman.

IOANNIS S. PANTELIDIS
UNIVERSITY OF SURREY, UK

information provided, enabling the applicant to reflect their personality and tailor information for specific situations.

Résumés should contain information on the candidate's work-related history, including job duties, job-related accomplishments, and educational background. Especially important to the hospitality industry are indications of one's service-oriented accomplishments.

There are two basic types of résumés: chronological and experiential (or functional) (Klinvex *et al.*, 1999). Chronological résumés list applicant accomplishments in reverse chronological order. Experiential résumés list candidate accomplishments in some topical order without reference to employer. Employers are listed at the end of the experiential résumé. There appears to be a greater preference in the hospitality industry for chronological résumés.

Some research indicates that one in five résumés and applications contains false information (Klinvex *et al.*, 1999).

Reference

Klinvex, K.C., O'Connell, M.S., and Klinvex, C.P. (1999) *Hiring Great People.* New York: McGraw-Hill.

G. KEITH HENNING
UNIVERSITY OF CALGARY, CANADA

Résumé/curriculum vitae

Curriculum vitae (CV) and résumé are terms that are often used interchangeably. However, CVs are usually much longer documents with greater detail. Résumés are generally two or three pages, and therefore, more widely used in the hospitality industry.

In many hospitality organizations, résumés are supplemented by or supplanted by employment applications developed by the organization. Application form uniformity allows for greater comparability across applicants on non-personality-related dimensions. Résumés are open-ended in how they are structured and the

Revenue

For most hotels, the largest portion of revenue comes from sales of services such as accommodation and restaurant meals. Revenue can be robustly defined as occurring when there is an inflow of assets. In most cases, the asset received following a sale is cash or an increase in accounts receivable (debtors) if the sale is made on credit. Other examples of revenue that increase assets include: interest revenue (where the hotel has interest-bearing investments), dividend revenue (where the hotel has share investments), and rental revenue (where the hotel has rented out one or more properties). Under accrual accounting revenue is recognized at the time it is earned, which does not necessarily coincide with the cash receipt associated with the revenue.

It is generally held that three conditions must be met in order for revenue to be recognized. First, the seller must have passed control of the goods to the buyer, or provided the service to the consumer of the service. Second, the agreed price has to have been paid by the purchaser or it has to be deemed probable that the agreed price will be received from the purchaser. Third, it is necessary that the amount of the revenue can be reliably measured.

References

Schmidgall, R.S. (2002) *Hospitality Industry Managerial Accounting*, 5th edn. Lansing, MI: Educational Institute of the American Hotel and Lodging Association.

Uniform System of Accounts for the Lodging Industry, 9th edn. (1996) Lansing, MI: Educational Institute of the American Hotel and Motel Association.

CHRIS GUILDING
GRIFFITH UNIVERSITY, AUSTRALIA

Revenue center

A revenue center is a hotel department that generates revenues and costs that are directly related to the department. The biggest revenue center for most full service hotels is the rooms division. In addition other major revenue centers include: food and beverage serving facilities such as restaurants, bars, lounges, room service, and banqueting facilities; telephone; gift shops; newsstand; valet; laundry; barbershop or beauty salon; and recreation centers. Specialized hotels have other additional revenue centers such as health clubs, golf courses, casinos and gaming facilities, and conference facilities. It is very important for the hotel's profitability to promote all revenue centers to all arriving and in-house guests. Most hotels promote these facilities through the hotel's front desk employees (up-selling) and through printed material in strategic places within

the hotel such as elevators and the guestrooms. Each revenue center is subject to internal controls ranging from manual systems to semi-automated systems to fully automated systems.

References

Coltman, M.M. and Jagels, M.G. (2001) *Hospitality Management Accounting*, 7th edn. New York: John Wiley & Sons.

Kasavana, M.L. and Brooks, R.M. (1998) *Front Office Procedures*, 5th edn. Lansing, MI: Educational Institute of the American Hotel and Motel Association.

CONSTANTINOS S. VERGINIS
THE EMIRATES ACADEMY OF HOSPITALITY
MANAGEMENT, UNITED ARAB EMIRATES

Revenue management

The most simple and commonly used definition of revenue management is 'the business practice of selling the right inventory to the right customer at the right price at the right time so as to maximize total revenue', profit, and market share. With the emergence of Internet travel websites, the definition may be extended to include '. . . through the right channel.' Moreover, the above definition truly describes the objective of revenue management. Effective hotel revenue management is dependent on accurate demand forecasting of future arrival dates at a granular level as well as a relative understanding of the demand and rate positioning of competitors. To achieve optimal revenue performance over time, hotels must forecast total arrivals demand by rate, market segment, length of stay, and distribution channel while positioning the rates within each channel and market segment giving consideration to several factors such as seasonal market demand, citywide events, competitors' rate positioning, and demand levels. An understanding of total consumer spending habits (beyond just the room rate) by market segment will further enhance the results derived from the revenue management process.

In very simple terms, revenue managers face one of two conditions: excess demand (where forecasted demand for a given arrival date exceeds the available supply of rooms) or excess capacity (where the supply of rooms exceeds forecasted demand). The strategies deployed against these two conditions vary greatly.

When hotel capacity exceeds demand over a consecutive period of future arrival dates, the revenue management strategy is fairly simple: open run-of-house availability of all rates to all qualified market segments (negotiated entitlement rates such as AAA, AARP, discount clubs, local and national corporate accounts, etc.) of all stay patterns in all channels. When the excess capacity condition exists, optimal revenue and profitability will not be achieved if any demand from qualified segments is rejected. Retail (non-qualified market segment, i.e. consumers that pay the 'rate of the day') pricing then requires artful positioning based on the retail rates, product quality, location, brand strength, and demand levels of direct, upper, and lower tier competitors.

When hotel demand exceeds capacity, the revenue management strategy becomes more complex. The goal is to accept the demand that produces the greatest level of profitability over time. It is not just about getting the highest average rate on the night(s) with the excess demand. It is about filtering reservation requests that cross over the excess demand date(s), usually accepting the reservations with the longest lengths of stay and rejecting the reservation requests with the shorter lengths of stay. When extreme excess demand is projected, further filtering may be attempted by accepting the longest length-of-stay reservations with the highest room rate from the least expensive distribution channels. When excess demand exists, the objective is to fill as many rooms as possible on the excess capacity dates that surround the excess demand date(s) before the excess demand date(s) become overbooked to the point of having to be completely closed. To achieve this objective, revenue managers deploy length-of-stay restrictions in the distribution channels. These restrictions trigger the acceptance or rejection of all incoming reservation requests. An example of the use of this demand filtering strategy would be the deployment of a two-night length-of-stay restriction on a Saturday where extreme excess demand is projected sur-

rounded by a Friday and Sunday with projected excess capacity. The two-night minimum length of stay restriction on Saturday triggers a rejection of all Saturday one-night stay requests while accepting Saturday arrivals with a multi-night length-of-stay pattern. The restriction also allows pre-Saturday arrivals to stay through and beyond Saturday night. If the length-of-stay restriction is not deployed, less-profitable one-night reservations will be accepted until the Saturday in question becomes so overbooked that it must be closed to all reservation requests. When this occurs, all revenue from future multi-night reservation requests that include Saturday in the stay pattern – including those that benefit the surrounding excess capacity dates – will be lost.

Revenue management produces optimal results in hotels that have access to accurate granular historical information, robust forecasting tools, strong competitive intelligence, a talented director of revenue management, and a strong revenue management-focused leadership team including the general manager, director of revenue management, director of sales, director of operations, controller, and reservations manager.

Reference

Smith, B.C., Leimkuhler, J.F., and Darrow, R.M. (1992) Yield management at American Airlines. *Interfaces*, 22 (1), 8–31.

FREDERICK J. KLEISNER
WYNDHAM INTERNATIONAL, INC., USA

Revenue management in restaurants

Restaurant revenue management can be defined as selling the right seat to the right customer at the right price, and for the right duration. The determination of 'right' entails achieving both the highest revenue possible for the restaurant and also delivering the greatest value to the customer. Without that balance, revenue management-type practices will in the long-term alienate those customers who feel that the restaurant has taken advantage of them. Revenue management, or yield management, is commonly practiced in the hotel and airline industries. Companies implementing revenue management report increases in revenue of 2–5% over the results of prior procedures.

Restaurant operators have two main strategic levers that they can use to manage revenue: price and meal duration. Price is a fairly obvious target for manipulation, and many operators already offer price-related promotions to augment or shift peak-period demand (e.g., early bird specials, special menu promotions, happy hours for low-demand periods, and minimum cover charges or higher priced menu items during peak periods). More sophisticated manipulations of price include day-part pricing, day-of-week pricing, and price premiums or discounts for different types of party size, tables, and customers.

Managing meal duration is a bit more complicated. One of the difficulties of implementing revenue management in restaurants is that their explicit unit of sale is a meal (or event) rather than an amount of time – although one could argue that the true measure of the restaurant's product is time. While one can estimate a likely mean length for that meal, the actual duration is not set. By comparison, implementing revenue management is much easier for the hotel, airline, cruise line, and car rental businesses, because they sell their services for an explicitly contracted amount of time. Restaurants rarely sell tables for a fixed amount of time, and most restaurants seem reluctant to broach this topic with customers. Moreover, North American restaurateurs cannot even rely on the practice of charging for the cover, which is common in many European countries.

One of the stumbling blocks to successful implementation of restaurant revenue management is the struggle that restaurant operators face in developing internal methods of managing meal duration. In the context of managing meal duration, one should not think only of reducing diners' average meal length. Quite often the factor interfering with revenue management is the variability in meal lengths, and not just their duration. These issues can be addressed by, for example, streamlining the service-delivery process, changing reservation policies, redesigning menus, pacing service processes, and making those processes more efficient. Although customer dining time can be reduced, the issue of how customers will react to the reduction must be addressed.

Reduced dining times can have considerable revenue potential during high-demand periods. Consider a restaurant with 100 seats, a $20 average check, a one-hour average dining time, and a busy period of four hours per day. During busy periods, defined as those when customers are waiting for a table, a decrease in dining time can increase the number of customers served and the associated revenue. Under current conditions, the restaurant could theoretically serve 400 customers (240 minutes/60 minutes × 100 seats) and obtain revenue of $8000 (400 customers × $20 average check). If the average dining time could be reduced to 50 minutes, the potential number of customers served would increase to 480 (240 minutes/50 minutes × 100 seats) and the potential revenue would increase to $9600, an increase of 20%. Even small improvements beyond that reduction of, say, 2 minutes would produce appreciable savings.

References

Kimes, S. (1989) The basics of yield management. *Cornell Hotel and Restaurant Administration Quarterly*, 30 (4), 15.

Susskind, A.M., Reynolds, D., and Tsuchiya, E. (2004). An evaluation of guests' preferred incentives to shift time-variable demand in restaurants. *Cornell Hotel and Restaurant Administration Quarterly*, 45 (1), 68–84.

SHERRI KIMES
CORNELL UNIVERSITY, USA

Revenue per available room (RevPAR)

Revenue per available room or RevPAR is determined by dividing room revenue received for a specific day by the number of rooms available in the hotel for that day. Revenue per available room is used in hotels to determine the amount of dollars each hotel room produces for the overall financial success of the hotel. The profit from the sale of a hotel room is much greater than that from a similar food and beverage sale. However, the food and beverage aspect of the hotel industry is essential in attracting some categories of guests who want conference services. Hotels with strong food, beverage, banquet, and recreational facilities typically have revenue per available room well above the average daily rate. Hotels with fewer revenue centers have revenue per available room numbers closer to the average daily rate. Revenue per available room is the best way a hotel has to compare its competition and is a reflection of the way occupancy and average daily rate are being managed. Revenue per available room can alert a manager to how well the reservations department is selling during slow periods and/or how successfully reservationists are upselling hotel guests to higher rated rooms or packages during peak periods. The property management system's revenue per available room module can instantly sort through the myriad of rates and packages and provide a reservationist with instructions on how to sell to the guest in a manner that will maximize hotel revenue and occupancy.

Reference

Stutts, Alan T. (2001) *Hotel and Lodging Management – An Introduction.* New York: John Wiley & Sons.

ALAN T. STUTTS
AMERICAN INTERCONTINENTAL
UNIVERSITY, USA

Revenue per available seat hour (RevPASH)

Because it embraces capacity use and check averages, revenue per available seat-hour (RevPASH) is a much better indicator of the revenue-generating performance of a restaurant than the commonly used measures of average check per

Table 1 Various calculations of RevPASH

Restaurant	Seat occupancy (%)	Average check per person ($)	RevPASH ($)
A	40	18.00	7.20
B	60	12.00	7.20
C	80	9.00	7.20
D	90	8.00	7.20

person or food and labor margins. RevPASH indicates the rate at which revenue is generated and captures the trade-off between average check and facility use. If seat occupancy percentages increase even as the average check decreases, for instance, a restaurant can still achieve the same RevPASH. Conversely, if a restaurant can increase the average check, it can maintain a similar RevPASH with slightly lower seat occupancy.

Table 1 gives a hypothetical illustration of this principle. The four restaurants in the exhibit all have the same RevPASH ($7.20), but each achieves it in a different manner.

The easiest way to calculate RevPASH is to divide revenue for the desired time period (e.g., hour, day-part, day) by the number of seat-hours available during that interval. For example, if a 100-seat restaurant makes $1500 on Fridays between 6 and 10 p.m., its RevPASH would be $15 ($1500/[100 seats × 4 hours] or $5000/400 seat-hours).

Reference

Kimes, S.E., Chase, R.B., Choi, S., Lee, P.Y., and Ngonzi, E.N. (1998) Restaurant revenue management: applying yield management to the restaurant industry. *Cornell Hotel and Restaurant Administration Quarterly*, 39 (3), 32–39.

SHERRI KIMES
CORNELL UNIVERSITY, USA

Right-to-use ownership

A type of interest in a timeshare plan in which the owner receives the right to use the accommodations and facilities of the timeshare plan during the term of the timeshare plan but does not receive an ownership interest in the underlying property included in the timeshare plan. If the timeshare plan terminates the owner of a right-to-use interest will not have any ongoing use rights or ownership interest. The purchaser of a right-to-use ownership interest is conveyed the interest through the execution and delivery of a purchase contract which governs the purchaser's rights under the timeshare plan. Consequently, right-to-use ownership is governed by the same laws and principles applied to traditional real estate leasing transactions, such as consumer finance and taxing laws and accounting rules. Since the owner does not receive an underlying property interest, right-to-use timeshare plans may be regulated to a greater degree than deeded ownership interests, including requiring that the developer records in the applicable public records a notice to creditors and a non-disturbance agreement putting potential creditors of the developer on notice of the right-to-use purchasers' interests in the timeshare plan. This type of interest is also referred to as a timeshare license.

Reference

See, e.g., *Fla. Stat.* §721.05(35) (October 2, 2003). http://www.flsenate.gov/statutes/index. cfm?App_mode=Display_Statute&Search_ String=&URL=Ch0721/SEC05. HTM&Title=→2000→Ch0721→Section percent2005.

KURT GRUBER
ISLAND ONE RESORTS, USA

Risk–return tradeoff

The risk–return relationship is a key concept related to the valuation of stocks, bonds, and new projects. In investment, the required rate of return (RRR) has two components: reward for delaying consumption and compensation for bearing risk. The risk associated with different hospitality investments varies. Some investors may choose to invest in risky assets because those

investments generate higher returns. The higher the perceived risk associated with an investment, the greater the RRR and vice versa. An increase in the perceived risk of an investment will raise the RRR and hence lower the value of the asset or project. On the other hand, if the perceived risk associated with an asset or project decreases, the investors' RRR will be lowered and the value of the asset or project will increase.

Major national or international events can change the perceived risk of investors, hence having a significant impact on RRR and assets valuation. For example, the 9/11 terrorist attacks increased the uncertainty of the world economy and raised the perceived risk associated with investments, thus raising investors' RRR and lowering the equity value. Consequently, stock markets across the world fell sharply in the wake of those attacks.

References

Keown, A., Martin, J., Petty, W., and Scott, D. (2003) *Foundations of Finance: The Logic and Practice of Financial Management*, 4th edn. Upper Saddle River, NJ: Prentice-Hall.

Ross, S., Westerfield, R., and Jordan, B. (2004) *Essentials of Corporate Finance*, 4th edn. Boston, MA: McGraw-Hill Companies.

ZHENG GU
UNIVERSITY OF NEVADA, LAS VEGAS, USA

Role playing and simulations

Role playing is an interactive training technique in which participants experience real or exaggerated workplace situations involving the reenactment of certain parts or roles (Cannon and Gustafson, 2002, p. 169). This training technique is particularly effective for practicing and developing interpersonal skills such as hospitality employees appropriately responding to guest requests or complaints. In that employees assume the roles of guests, as well as workers, this technique helps in building empathy toward guest needs and perceptions.

Simulations also involve interactive training techniques in which there is a scaled-down enactment of reality. Typically this training approach utilizes technology such as CD-ROMs or the Internet (Cannon and Gustafson, 2002, p. 176).

Simulations offer many benefits, including providing a realistic learning experience that enhances the transfer of learning to the workplace. The duplication of the working environment also allows for training not to interrupt business operations. Many hotels now have simulated front office training programs involving computer applications in which employees are trained in the process of rooming or checking out a guest.

Reference

Cannon, D.F. and Gustafson, C.M. (2002) *Training and Development for the Hospitality Industry*. Lansing, MI: Educational Institute of the American Hotel and Lodging Association.

DEBRA F. CANNON
GEORGIA STATE UNIVERSITY, USA

Roles

Whilst role formally refers to 'an organized set of behaviors' (Ivancevich *et al.*, 1997) and is used to define the tasks and activities undertaken as part of our work (Mount and Bartlett, 1999), one of the key issues in the discussion of role is how our individual work performance and job satisfaction is shaped by our expectations with regards to role. The study of role, and its contribution to organizational behavior and effectiveness, has only emerged in the past 30 years (Bassett and Carr, 1996). In fact, these authors argue that 'role analysis, rooted in the psychology of individual differences and social psychology may offer a significant opportunity for redirection and enrichment of organization theory'. In particular, they suggest that a stronger focus on the 'role of role' will help us better understand the balance between getting the most out of our

employees and delivering to them maximum job satisfaction and job retention.

There are three aspects to role of which we must be aware because of their implications for role performance, job satisfaction, and staff turnover. They are: role ambiguity, which is a person's lack of understanding about the rights, privileges, and obligations of a job; role conflict, which refers to the conflict between what one prefers to do as an individual and what one believes one has to do in the execution of one's job role; role set, which is the set of expectations we have for the behavior of an individual in a particular role.

The sources of *role ambiguity* can be in the individual's misunderstanding of what is required of them. This confusion can lead to the individual delivering sub-standard performance at work. This could be due to the lack of clear direction from the organization and management, or a failure on the part of the individual to fully consider what is required of them. Whilst there are the unusual circumstances of some people being blissfully and carelessly ignorant of what is expected of them, most people are deeply troubled and perplexed by role ambiguity. As well, and perhaps more importantly, especially if the individual is doing his job well, this can also lead to high levels of anxiety and stress which in turn will have a negative impact upon the person's level of job satisfaction. A low level of job satisfaction may in turn lead to staff turnover (Abraham, 1997). Therefore, it is important for managers to ensure that all staff fully understand and appreciate what is expected of them in terms of the actual tasks to be completed and the standards to be achieved.

Role conflict presents as a major challenge for hospitality managers in the management of front-line hospitality staff. For many front-line hospitality workers, delivering guest satisfaction and the positive feedback from satisfied guests are major motivating forces. However, hospitality managers are required to ensure that long-term operating profits are not sacrificed just to achieve isolated instances of guest satisfaction. These conflicting goals can lead to role conflict, which in turn can challenge the individual's sense of job satisfaction. For example, a waiter may suffer role conflict if he or she feels the need to give a guest a new main course because the dish was not to the guest's liking, even though it was a perfectly good dish. From the business's point of view it is the customer's fault for making a wrong decision. However, for the waiter, the presence of an unhappy guest can directly challenge his or her sense of role as a waiter, who makes people comfortable and happy in the restaurant.

If role conflict is particularly severe, and is not properly managed by the employee, manager and organization, it can lead to high levels of staff dissatisfaction. In turn, high levels of staff dissatisfaction can lead to premature staff departure (Abraham, 1977).

The emergence of psychological assessment of employees is seen, amongst other things, as a positive step towards addressing the issue of role conflict. The notion of the psychological assessment is to gain an understanding of the attitudes and values of the individual. Obviously, if the individual has a temperament and personality that is warm, friendly and outgoing, with a high level of interdependence, then she is likely to be comfortable working in front-line hospitality. In contrast, if the person is naturally cool and aloof with a high need for independence, then it is unlikely that she will feel comfortable working in front-line hospitality. Therefore, if managers can better understand the values, attitudes and opinions of potential staff, they will be able to make better decisions about aligning people's values and attitudes with the requirements of their particular role and thus reduce the potential for role conflict.

Role set also has implications for the hospitality industry because of the role it plays in shaping our assessment of service delivery. As stated above, role set refers to the expectations we have of people who fulfill a particular role. Our understanding of the SERVQUAL Model (Parasuraman *et al.*, 1985) clearly indicates that our initial expectations play a major role in our assessment of perceived service delivery. Therefore, if hospitality workers, by way of their behavior, attitudes, and general demeanor, meet the role set held by guests and customers then the chances of achieving guest and customer satisfaction are significantly improved. In contrast, if

the hospitality worker does not live up to the role set of the position, then customer dissatisfaction is likely to occur. This again places considerable importance on the role of the manager in selecting, recruiting, and training the right staff for the role.

The integration of our understanding of these aspects of role is of significant importance for the hospitality industry. Our understanding suggests that hospitality managers must clearly and explicitly describe not just the title and function of a job, but also its role, and the expectations of an incumbent in that role. Further, in recruiting staff, the manager must be careful to ensure appropriate alignment between the individual style and characteristics of the potential incumbent with the actual style, personality and characteristics needed and expected in that role.

References

Abraham, R. (1997) Thinking styles as moderators of role stressor–job satisfaction relationships. *Leadership and Organisation Development Journal*, 18 (5), 236–243.

Bassett, G. and Carr, A. (1996) Role sets and organisation structure. *Leadership and Organisation Development Journal*, 17 (4), 37–45.

Ivancevich, J., Olekalns, M., and Matteson, M. (1997) *Organizational Behavior and Management*. Sydney: Irwin.

Mount, D.J. and Bartlett, A.J. (1999) The managerial role assessment survey: design and test of an instrument measuring Mintzberg's roles among hotel managers. *Journal of Hospitality and Tourism Research*, 23 (2), 160–175.

Parasuraman, A., Zeithaml, V.A., and Berry, L.L. (1985) A conceptual model of service quality and its implications for future research. *Journal of Marketing Practice: Applied Marketing Science*, 49 (4), 41–50.

PAUL A. WHITELAW
VICTORIA UNIVERSITY, AUSTRALIA

Room status

Before a guest arrives at the hotel the front desk needs to know the status of the rooms so as to check guests into rooms that are vacant and clean rather than inconveniencing the guest by sending them to an occupied or dirty room. Highlighted below are some of the terms used in relation to room status. It is important for both the front desk and housekeeping staff to be familiar with these terms, and information in relation to room status must be communicated to the front desk from housekeeping as soon as possible in order for room sales to be maximized.

- *Did not check out:* The guest did not actually come to the front desk to check out but had made arrangements previously to settle their account. This guest is not a skipper (explained below).
- *Do not disturb:* The guest does not want to be disturbed. Usually indicated with a sign left hanging on the guestroom door knob or electronically by a red light indicator outside the guestroom door.
- *Due out:* The guest is expected to vacate the room after the following day's check-out time.
- *Late check-out:* Hotels have a normal check-out time (usually 11 a.m. or 12 noon) and in this situation the guest has made arrangements with the front desk to check out later than this normal check-out time. Care has to be taken before this is granted to determine whether a late check-out charge should be added and the guest informed.
- *Occupied:* A guest is registered to the room and is not due to check out yet.
- *On change:* The guestroom is in the process of being cleaned. The guest has vacated the room but it is not as yet ready for resale.
- *Skipper:* This refers to a guest that has not made arrangements with the front desk to settle their accounts and has left the hotel without paying. Also known as a walk-out.
- *Sleeper:* This situation occurs when the front desk has not updated their room status information. The guest has settled their account and left the hotel but this is not recorded in the front desk records.
- *Stayover:* This refers to a room that is occupied by a guest but they are not checking out on that day. A guestroom is known as a stayover

from the date of arrival to the date of departure.

Reference

Kasavana, M.L. and Brooks, R.M. (1995) *Front Office Procedures*, 4th edn. Lansing, MI: Educational Institute of the American Hotel and Motel Association.

IRENE SWEENEY
INTERNATIONAL HOTEL MANAGEMENT
INSTITUTE SWITZERLAND, SWITZERLAND

Room types

It is important for the front desk staff to know the different characteristics of each of their room types when assigning a room to a guest. The receptionist has to make sure that the guest's needs and preferences are satisfied. Guest needs and preferences are usually indicated at the reservations stage. Walk-in guests can only be assigned a room when it has been determined if the type of room requested is available. Some of the common terms used in relation to room types are highlighted below.

- *Adjacent rooms:* Rooms that are close to each other, e.g. across the hall. This type of room is possibly suitable for families.
- *Adjoining rooms:* Two rooms beside each other with a common wall but they do not have a connecting door between them. This type of room is possibly suitable for families.
- *Connecting rooms:* Two rooms beside each other with a common wall and they do have a connecting door between them, which allows access to each room without the use of a public corridor. Also known as communicating rooms. This type of room is possibly suitable to a family with young children.
- *Double:* A room that may accommodate one or two people. It may have one double bed or two single beds in the room. In American terminology this can also be referred to as a twin.
- *Double-double:* A room that has two double beds in it. One or more people can be accommodated in this room type.

- *En suite:* A room that has bathroom facilities included within.
- *Family room:* A room that can accommodate a family. Can be a double-double, a triple, a quad or a suite. It depends on the number of people being accommodated. Family rooms can get a child's cot or a Z-bed added.
- *Junior suite:* A room that has a sitting/living area and a bed. The sleeping area can be separate from the sitting/living area but this is not always the case.
- *King:* A room that has a king-size bed, which may accommodate one or two people.
- *Mini suite:* As for junior suite above.
- *Quad:* A room that can be assigned to four people. It may have two or more beds, e.g. double-double.
- *Queen:* A room that has a queen-size bed, which can accommodate one or more people.
- *Single:* A room that is assigned to one person. It may have one or more beds in it.
- *Studio:* A single or double room with a studio bed. A studio bed usually converts to a couch during the day. In a studio room there may also be an additional bed.
- *Suite:* A room that has one or more bedrooms and a living room. All of these rooms are connected.
- *Triple:* A room that can accommodate three people. It may have two or more beds in it.
- *Twin:* A room that has two beds and may accommodate one or more people.

References

Baker, S., Bradley, P., and Huyton, J. (1994) *Principles of Hotel Front Office Operations.* London: Cassell.

Dukas, P. (1974) *Hotel Front Office Management and Operation*, 3rd edn. Dubuque, IA: Wm. C. Brown.

Kasavana, M.L. and Brooks, R.M. (1995) *Front Office Procedures*, 4th edn. Lansing, MI: Educational Institute of the American Hotel and Motel Association.

IRENE SWEENEY
INTERNATIONAL HOTEL MANAGEMENT
INSTITUTE SWITZERLAND, SWITZERLAND

Room energy management systems

The goal of a room energy management system (EMS) is automatically to reduce the energy consumption of the room HVAC unit when the room is vacant and allow the guest to set any desired temperature when the room is occupied. There are basically three types of room EMS systems:

- An infrared occupancy-based thermostat (uses motion and/or heat to sense occupancy) utilizing a setback temperature when the room is vacant (i.e. changes the set point to 78 °F 15 minutes after a guest leaves the room).
- An infrared occupancy-based thermostat (uses motion and/or heat to sense occupancy) utilizing an algorithm that returns the room to its last set point within a pre-programmed time (i.e. recovers the room to the original set point in 10 minutes) after a guest enters the room.
- An entry key-based system that requires a guest to insert a key card into a holder mounted by the room entry. The room stays in a predetermined setback temperature until the guest enters the room and inserts the room key into the slot. When a guest leaves, the guest must remove the key to exit the room and the temperature then reverts to a setback temperature.

Each system type has its advantages and disadvantages. For example, if the guest receives two keys during a stay using the key entry system, one key could be left in the slot when the guest was not in the room, defeating the savings function.

Many systems have the ability to be networked to a head end and even the hotel's PMS system. When networked, housekeeping, engineering, and the front desk can monitor rooms for occupancy, check to see if the air conditioning units are working, even see if the mini-bar has been opened. Connecting to the hotel's PMS system will dramatically improve the energy savings because two setbacks can be programmed, a less aggressive one for a rented room and a more aggressive setback for un-rented rooms.

Reference

Stipanuk, D. (2002) *Hospitality Facilities Management and Design*, 2nd edn. Lansing, MI: Educational

Institute of American Hotel and Lodging Association, pp. 242–245. www.inncom.bom.

JIM ACKLES
THARALDSON ENERGY GROUP, USA

Room rate

A hotel or lodging enterprise will usually designate a standard rate for each room. This rate is typically called the rack rate because traditionally the standard rate was the one posted on or near the room rack. The rack rate is considered the retail rate for the room.

Other room rate schedules may reflect variations of the rack rate and relate to the number of guests assigned to the room, service level, and room location. If authorized, front desk agents should know how and when to apply a special room rate during the registration process.

Rates might include: corporate rates for business people staying in the hotel or lodging enterprise; commercial rates for business people who represent a company and have infrequent patterns of travel but collectively this group can represent a major segment of the hotel's guests; complimentary rates for business promotion; group rates for a predetermined number of affiliated guests; family rates for parents and children sharing the same room; day rates for less than an overnight stay; military and educational rates because they are traveling on restricted travel expense accounts and are price-conscious; frequent traveler rates for guest's earning discounts through the hotel's frequent traveler program; and package rates that include goods and services in addition to rental of a room. Variation of the package rate is the American plan, which provides the guest with a room and typically the morning and evening meal; modified American plan, a room rate that offers one meal with the price of a room, and the European plan, which keeps food and beverage charges separate from room charges.

Room rates are often confirmed as part of the reservation process. This is becoming the preferred way of doing business by most business travelers and travel agents. Assigning rates for walk-in guests is left to the front desk agent. Front desk agents may sometimes be allowed to offer a room at a lower price than its standard rack rate. Normally, this occurs only when management deems it appropriate.

The cost structure of the hotel or lodging enterprise dictates the minimum rate for a room, and competition helps the hotel establish its maximum rate. The room rate range is the range of values between minimum and maximum rates.

Pricing is a marketing decision. Pricing is viewed in different ways by different constituencies. Liquidity issues are of concern to hotel owners, the realities of the marketplace are of primary concern to hotel mangers, and to customers pricing is what they are willing and able to pay to rent a room for the night.

Yield management, or revenue management grew in popularity in the late 1980s and into the 1990s and continues to be widely practiced today. Advanced computer technology has spurred increased usage in hotel management. Yield management in hotel vernacular is a systematic approach to pricing decisions through guestroom inventory management and respective prices allocated to each room in the inventory. The point of yield management is to use demand forecasts to determine how much to charge for rooms on a given day.

Its primary objective is revenue maximization for any given period. In other words, depending on forecasted demand for a future period, prices are adjusted to reflect that demand. It is essentially adjusting the price of available guestroom inventory to reflect the realities of the marketplace. Forecasting is key to the successful implementation of a yield management system. Most hotels target multiple markets with varying degrees of price elasticity of demand. Through computer applications hotel managers can capture the subtleties of market shifts and adjust the prices of the remaining rooms inventory to ensure that rooms do not go unsold. Conversely, when demand is higher than expected for the higher-rated rooms category, the number of available rooms in the discounted-rooms category is reduced. The goal of yield management is to select which business to accept and which business to turn away based on the relative value of each booking. Typically a hotel establishes four to six different rate categories for their transient bookings (i.e. rack no discount, 10–20% discount, 25–35% discounts, 40–50% discount, and more than 50% discount).

The art of yield management is in learning how to turn undesirable booking requests into desirable ones. This may become particularly apparent in the negotiation process for group business, which generally involves decisions about rates, dates, and space. Rates are how much the group is going to pay, dates are when the group is going to be staying, and space is how many rooms the group will use. Applying yield management principles to group business involves more than changing a group's proposal from undesirable to acceptable. One thing that typically makes business undesirable is when a hotel can sell a rate to another group at a better profit margin; and yield management is a tool that provides the hotel with an indicator based on historical and projected data of whether a better rate might be obtained and under what conditions a particular group's business becomes desirable.

Front desk agents and reservationists have the opportunity to present various room rates in a manner that reflects the positive features of the product. Knowledge of room furnishings, special features, layout, and rate ranges is necessary to maximize room rates. The front desk agent and reservationists should be trained to recognize subtle clues to a guest's needs. A front office manager should also devise an incentive program for the staff to maximize room rates. The staff with proper knowledge, vocabulary, and attitude will maximize room rates better than staff who are simply told to sell from the bottom up, a sales method that involves presenting the least expensive rate first, or from the top down, a sales method that involve presenting the most expensive rate first. These principles are important in achieving a maximum room rate.

References

Bardi, J. (2003) *Hotel Front Office Management*, 3rd edn. New York: John Wiley & Sons.

Quaint, W. and LeBruto, S. (2002) Yield management: choosing the most profi*table* reservations, in Denney G. Rutherford (ed.), *Hotel Management and Operations*, 3rd edn. New York: John Wiley & Sons.

Shaw, M. (2002) Hotel pricing, in Denney G. Rutherford (ed.), *Hotel Management and Operations*, 3rd edn. New York: John Wiley & Sons.

ALAN T. STUTTS
AMERICAN INTERCONTINENTAL
UNIVERSITY, USA

Room rate pricing

The empirical pricing literature shows that there is no single, universal approach to set a price. In essence, however, each approach is similar: a process of gathering, exchanging, and interpreting information. Pricing is an organizational process that involves discussions and negotiations between different business functions such as marketing, operations, and finance. An organization can thereby base its pricing decisions on three types of information: customer value; competition; and costs. These decisions are based not on a single type of information, but on each of the three types of information to some extent. For this reason it is better to use the terms cost-informed, competition-informed, and value-informed pricing, instead of cost-based, competition-based, and value-based pricing.

Setting room prices is a complex decision process. Faced with this complexity, hotel management used to simplify the pricing process by modeling only the most important elements affecting price. For many years, the hotel industry applied the *rule of a thousand*, which was an oversimplification of the cost-plus pricing approach. For example, if a hotel was built with 300 rooms at a cost of 20 million euros, every thousand euros spent on a hotel bedroom had a price charged of one euro per night:

$$\frac{\text{Total Cost of Investment}}{\text{Number of Rooms}}$$

$$= \frac{€20,000,000}{300} = €66,667 \text{ spent per room}$$

$$\frac{\text{Cost per Room}}{1000} = \frac{€66,667}{1000} = €66.67$$

The competitive environment, the extensive market segmentation, and increasing room occupancy instability in today's hotel industry, however, have largely rendered the rule of a thousand method obsolete. Another old 'rule of thumb', the *Hubbard formula*, established a room rate that covered all costs, including a return on capital invested. The various steps of the Hubbard formula for setting room rates are (Coltman, 2001):

- Calculation of the desired return on assets employed
- Estimation of the pre-interest and pre-tax profits
- Computation of all fixed charges and management fees
- Determination of all operating expenses
- Subtraction of operating profit from sources other than rooms e.g. food and beverage
- Calculation of total profit required from rooms to cover all costs and to provide a reasonable return on capital
- Determination of the available number of room nights in a year and the estimated occupancy rate
- Calculation of the expected room nights by multiplying available room nights by the estimated occupancy rate
- Establishment of the price per room by dividing the revenue required to cover all costs by the number of rooms expected to be sold.

This cost-plus approach (also known as bottom-up or backward-costs room pricing) makes financial sense, as the method attempts to cover costs and make profits, but it has all the traditional drawbacks of any full cost pricing system. The formula is fallacious, as no sales forecast can estimate the level of demand without taking price into consideration. It involves a circular interdependence – a price has to be assumed in order to determine price (Rogers, 1976). In the 1970s and 1980s the formula induced an increase in room rates more than the American Consumer Price Index, identifying the procedure with 'Hubbard the Horrible.' In response to the depression, hotels started to discount their rooms stock (inventory), by, e.g., placing restrictions to segment guests as to their needs, behavior, and willingness to pay, to bring in incremental revenue from price-sensitive guests.

In the late 1980s, this practice evolved into a set of *yield management techniques*, which aim to maximize rooms revenue by adjusting room rates in response to forecasted patterns of demand. Typically, the demand for rooms in each market segment is predicted and bedroom prices are adjusted to different market segments on a day-by-day basis. Hence, the focus of this technique is to keep all rooms available for guests who are likely to pay most for them, whilst at the same time selling each room for the rate above incremental cost. The commonly used measurement of efficiency in using available rooms to generate room revenue is defined as a 'yield' statistic.

Rooms pricing is an ongoing process, a practice, a strategic capability (Dutta *et al.*, 2002), that includes both the establishment and alteration of room rate prices. It requires extensive knowledge of costs, demand, competitive and market conditions as well as the company objectives. Yield management systems are therefore a base for the development of a pricing strategy (e.g. early discounting and overbooking). Yield management is a form of segmentation pricing, a differential pricing strategy. It is, thus, better to talk about yield or revenue management pricing.

Many of the hotel industry's pricing policies run counter to economic wisdom and market realities. Management fails to understand the marketing environment, to develop an appropriate room rate pricing strategy, to administer the pricing process. The most recent challenges include Internet pricing and the rising of a so-called global economy. Undoubtedly, it is the high degree of market-orientation that places pricing in hospitality establishments at the forefront of business problems and operation policies. From a managerial perspective, room price should, therefore, receive special attention as it is one of the few major variables under a hotel's control that generates income.

References

Coltman, M.C. (2001) *Hospitality Management Accounting*, 7th edn. New York: Van Nostrand Rheinhold.

Dolan, R.J. (1996) *Power Pricing: How Managing Price Transforms the Bottom Line*. New York: The Free Press.

Dutta, S., Bergen, M., Levy, D., Ritsen, M., and Zbaracki, M. (2002) Pricing is a strategic capability. *Sloan Management Review*, Spring, 61–66.

Monroe, K.B. (2003) *Pricing: Making Profitable Decisions*. New York: McGraw-Hill.

Nagle, T.T. and Holden, R.K. (1995) *The Strategy and Tactics of Pricing: A Guide to Profitable Decision-Making*. Englewood Cliffs, NJ: Prentice-Hall.

Rogers, A.N. (1976) Price formation in hotels. *Hotel, Catering and Institutional Management Review*, pp. 227–237.

JEAN-PIERRE VAN DER REST
LEIDEN UNIVERSITY, THE NETHERLANDS

Room revenue analysis

Room revenue management and analysis has been adopted since the early 1980s. It started as yield management, where hotel rooms are provided to the right customer, at the right time, at the right price, by forecasting rooms demand. The basic idea is to match the room rate and timing of the sale to the customer who will pay the most for that room inventory.

The process works as follow. First, rooms are divided into different rate levels, such as A, B, C, and D with, for instance, A being the highest rate category. A team of managers, normally including front office, reservations, and sales, will be the 'yield team' or 'revenue management team.' The team will meet periodically to assess the forecast of the hotel contracts. Rates are then opened or closed depending on demand. For example, when demand for the hotel is low, all rate categories will be opened. Staff are asked to upsell the property, such as asking if guests would prefer a room with a beach-front view. If the guest is a frequent guest, staff may also upgrade the room with better amenities and the like so that the guest can experience a better level of service and may not mind to pay more on his or her next stay and will book a better room. As demand increases, the lower rate categories will be closed, and guests will then need to pay the higher rate. The revenue of the hotel is then maximized. If the lower rate categories are not closed during the high demand days, rooms will be sold at these lower rates and the revenue of the hotel will not be maximized.

Rooms revenue management not only looks at total rooms sales but also analyzes various market groups such as meetings and conventions, tour groups, corporate, and walk-ins, on their demand patterns. Restaurants and even golf courses have also adopted the same process to better their yield of revenues.

Depending on the type of hotel, the usage can be very different. For a smaller property where there is only one product and there is not much product or price differentiation, the process can be quite simple and mostly determined by the demand. For hotels that are bigger and offer many levels of products, from a standard room without a view to a presidential suite of many rooms, there is more scope for revenue management and computer programming is often involved.

In the last few years, with technology advancements, many software companies are working with providers for property management systems, sales and catering systems, and central reservations systems to develop software and to use the Internet to better forecast demand and compile the best results for hotels. Through data mining products, new software enables hotel executives to analyze future contracts on all the room distribution channels, from direct sales to Internet sales, and thus shaping the role of revenue management in the future. Examples of the leading technology providers are Pegasus and Delphi.

It is important to note that even the best technology needs the human touch. To have a successful revenue management program, training and workshops for managers and staff are crucial. Hotels have now created revenue managers, who are part of the rooms division and who also work closely with sales, reservations, and the accounting offices. Some hotel companies even develop proprietary revenue management courses before launching new software.

References

Blank, D. (2000) Internet will shape revenue-management role. *Hotel and Motel Management*, 215 (11), 54.

Blank, D. (2002) Extended-stay segment struggles to achieve yield management. *Hotel and Motel Management*, 217 (10), 52.

Choi, S. and Kimes, Sheryl (2002) Electronic distribution channels' effect on hotel revenue management. *Cornell Hotel and Restaurant Administration Quarterly*, 43 (3), 23–31.

Enz, C. and Withiam, G. (2001) *Yield Management*. New York: Center for Hospitality Research at Cornell University.

AGNES LEE DEFRANCO
UNIVERSITY OF HOUSTON,
USA

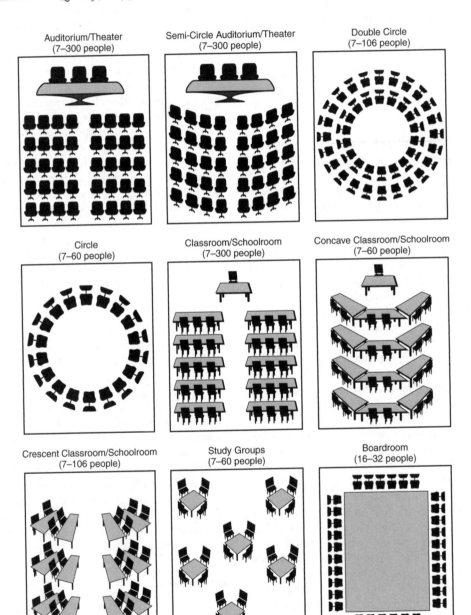

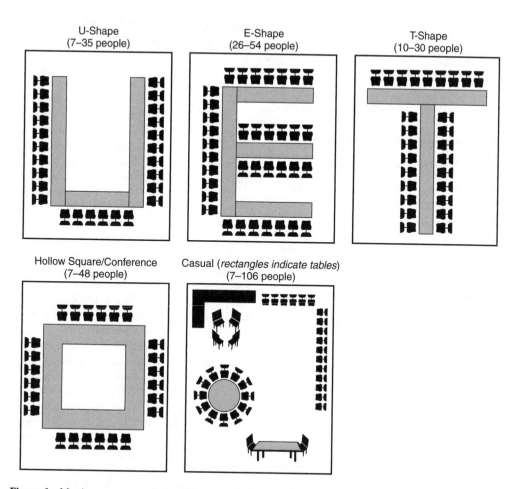

Figure 1 Meeting room set-up choices. The top of each diagram represents the front of the meeting room. Furniture arrangements are approximate and will vary. For the Auditorium/Theater style a table at the front is optional; there may also be an elevated stage

Room set-up

Set-up refers to the organized design of tables, chairs, audiovisual equipment, food and beverage stations, other furniture and equipment in a room that allows for the favorable environment of an event. There are a number of room set-up standards in the industry, including theater or auditorium style, schoolroom or classroom, reception, banquet, boardroom, hollow square, U-shape, and variations of these styles. The different room set-ups are appropriate for different types of events. Additionally, events with different types of objectives or desired outcomes may require different room sets. They each require different amounts of square footage per person. A number of criteria go into a room set-up and considerations should be made to comply with the Americans with Disabilities Act (ADA) and facility capacity requirements. Fire codes are a critical concern when designing room layouts and dictate the number of people (load) that a room can accommodate. It is also important to leave enough room around tables and chairs for the service staff. There are a number of software programs available to help with design and placement of furniture and equipment in the room.

Reference

Astroff, M.T. and Abbey, J.R. (2002) *Convention Sales and Services*. Las Vegas, NV: Waterbury Press.

DEBBI BOYNE
MEETING DEMANDS, USA

Room system automation

Hotel rooms are becoming increasingly wired, with a wide range of electronic and information technology-based systems being used to both enhance the guest experience and generate incremental revenue. They may be broken down into two categories: structural systems (such as electronic door locks, energy management systems, mechanical curtains and blinds and even to a limited extent systems that regulate air quality and smell): and guest service systems (such as in-room bars, entertainment systems that deliver music, movies or video games on demand, guest information systems, and Internet access facilities).

As technology becomes more persuasive and guests become more familiar with such facilities in their own homes, provision of such facilities will become essential if a property wants to remain competitive. However, this has major implications in terms of capital requirements and infrastructure, and the situation is further complicated by the lack of commonly accepted business models for charging the guest for use of such facilities – should they be provided free, built into the room charge or charged on a per-use or per-day basis? Opportunities also exist to personalize the guest experience by interfacing in-room systems of this kind with CRM databases to allow guestrooms to be configured precisely to match guest preferences.

References

Collins, G. and Malik, T. (1999) *Hospitality Information Technology: Learning How to Use It*, 4th edn. Dubuque, IA: Kendall/Hunt Publishing.

Levy, J. (1998) *Technical Hotel Management*. Geneva, Switzerland: www.jlevy.ch.

PETER O'CONNOR
IMHI (CORNELL – ESSEC), FRANCE

Routine maintenance

Routine maintenance consists of repairing devices and facility components within a scheduled period of time. Upon receipt of a device or facility breakdown the request is prioritized as emergency, routine or backlogged. Some examples may include: replacing electric light bulbs, guestroom equipment or furnishings repairs and adjusting thermostats in public areas. Most repairs are handled as routine and are corrected within a 24-hour time period. In addition, when the device is being repaired it should be inspected for premature wear and tear and if potential defects are found, these should be repaired and included as routine maintenance. Emergency repairs are necessary because of safety reasons or need and are corrected immediately. Backlogged maintenance is scheduled when resources become available.

Automation has increased the efficiency of managing routine maintenance. With an automated system routine inspections can be scheduled. Through a combination of software, hand-held computers, and bar codes, automated systems can plan, schedule, and track routine maintenance activities including resources, materials, and labor hours. Automation of the routine maintenance function prompts the managers of the maintenance function with the tasks required to complete a routine maintenance order. Through automation of the routine maintenance function a hospitality enterprise reduces downtime on equipment, increases equipment life, maximizes productivity of the equipment in the facility, increases the efficiency of the maintenance team and simplifies the management of routine maintenance.

Reference

Borsenik, Frank D. and Stutts, Alan T. (1997) *The Management of Maintenance and Engineering Systems in the Hospitality Industry*, 4th edn. New York: John Wiley & Sons.

FRANK BORSENIK
UNIVERSITY OF NEVADA, LAS VEGAS, USA

S

Safety

Safety involves preventing employees and customers within the hospitality property from potential death and injury, such as from accidental slips, falls, cuts, burns and so forth, as well as preventing related property damage (Enz and Taylor, 2002; Stipanuk, 2002). Hospitality organizations are semi-public places, which pose certain challenges for the safety of guests and employees. However, failing to provide a safe environment can be costly monetarily, in terms of reputation, as well as in the time required to deal with the consequences. After the events of September 11, 2001, the issue of safety has become more important. However, apart from terrorist attacks, hospitality organizations have many concerns about safety such as fires, food poisoning, infectious diseases, accidents, problems with electronic equipment, physical attacks on guests and employees. Certain safety issues need to be considered for bedrooms, baths, lifts, kitchens, restaurants, bars, discos, casinos, lobbies, swimming pools, sport areas, etc. In order to improve safety, hospitality organizations now install electronic locks, fire sprinklers, smoke detectors, and closed-circuit televisions. However, providing safety requires extensive and ongoing investment, training, and the improvement of physical conditions. Having regular fire drills and providing inductive and ongoing safety training for employees can be helpful. Special signs and written information on safety issues such as fire should be provided for both guests and employees.

References

Enz, C.A. and Taylor, M.S. (2002) The safety and security of US hotels: a post September 11 report. *Cornell Hotel and Restaurant Administration Quarterly*, 43 (3), 119–136.

Stipanuk, D.M. (2002) *Hospitality Facilities Management and Design*, 2nd edn. Lansing, MI: Educational Institute of the American Hotel and Lodging Association.

FEVZI OKUMUS
THE HONG KONG POLYTECHNIC
UNIVERSITY, HONG KONG SAR, CHINA

Sales promotion

An activity, material, or technique that stimulates interest, trial, or purchase by offering added value to or incentive for the product to resellers, salespeople or consumers. Promotion activities are generally other than advertising, publicity, and personal selling. There are at least four types of sales promotion activities in the hospitality industry.

- *Sampling:* This is an attempt to pre-sell the activity or service to the patron. For example, the base restaurant may want to promote a new dessert menu by providing an opportunity for patrons to sample a small piece of the 'dessert of the evening,' free of charge.
- *Coupons:* Coupons are used by 70% of American retailers in promoting products.

A coupon gives the patron the opportunity to participate in an activity at reduced or no cost.

- *Contests:* Contests usually provide some form of prizes. An example of a contest to promote enthusiasm and interest in a particular activity is a chilli cook-off, held at the snack bar, judged by the staff, and a featured menu for a period of time.
- *Demonstrations:* A good example would be a cooking demonstration arranged at a booth during a food festival or restaurant show, in hopes of creating interest in menu specialities or a new chef.

Reference

Food and hospitality marketing guide. Available from http://www.usmc.mil/directiv.nsf/0/2b79f4e14c004a6e85256d6b005e9d98/$FILE/NAVMC percent202770.pdf.

BOMI KANG
UNIVERSITY OF NEVADA, LAS VEGAS, USA

Schools of thought

Strategic management literature has been influenced by many disciplines such as anthropology, biology, economics, history, mathematics, military history, physics, psychology, political science, and urban planning. Therefore, as the field has evolved, different views have emerged on its nature and characteristics. Starting from the 1980s, scholars have reviewed the strategic management literature and recognized groups of authors who share similar views about strategy formulation and implementation. In their comprehensive text, Mintzberg *et al.* (1998) identify 10 schools of thought. The strategy process is viewed as a deliberate process of conception by (1) the design school, as a formal top-down rational planning process by (2) the planning school, as an analytical positioning process by (3) the positioning school, as a visionary process by (4) the entrepreneurial–leadership school, as a mental process by (5) the cognitive school, as an emergent and learning process by (6) the learning school, as a

process of power struggle and negotiation among stakeholders within and outside the organization by (7) the power school, as collective process by (8) the cultural school, as a reactive process to the external environment by (9) the environmental school. When the implications of these schools of thought are analyzed and evaluated it emerges that there are important differences and similarities among them. It is evident that some schools of thought focus on certain areas and provide more detailed explanations than others. In short, they all try to propose one best way of managing and making organizations successful in the long term.

In order to eliminate weaknesses of each school of thought and combine all these schools into a single and holistic perspective, Mintzberg *et al.* (1998) propose (10) the configurational school of thought. This school views strategy formation as a process of transformation and suggests that the strategy process is determined by time, place, and context. Rather than recommending one best way to formulate and implement strategies, this view suggests that any or all of the above schools of thought may be appropriate in different circumstances. However, it all depends on the nature, size, and maturity of the organization as well as the conditions in the external environment. Mintzberg *et al.* (1998) further categorize these schools of thought into three groupings. The first is the prescriptive schools, which include the design school, the planning school and the positioning school. The second group is called the descriptive school, which includes the entrepreneurial school, the cognitive school, the learning school, the power school, the cultural school, and the environmental school. Finally, the last group includes only the configurational–transformational school of thought.

Mintzberg *et al.* (1998) and Stacey (2000) stress that even the configurational school may have limitations and therefore one should look beyond configurations. Stacey (2000) labels this as the complexity view and claims that organizations can employ previous approaches when the internal and external environments of the company are predictable and stable and should use the complexity approach when the situation is complex and dynamic in order to challenge and, if necessary, alter the company's existing systems and mental models. The complexity school of thought suggests that for organizations to be innovative, creative and changeable, they should move away from equilibrium where they can face and experience disorder and irregularities. Organizations are viewed as adaptive systems that take the form of non-linear negative and positive feedback loops connecting individuals, groups, functions, and processes within an organization to each other, and connecting an organization to other systems in the environment. It is claimed that due to these non-linear feedback loops, any small change or development, both within or outside the organization, can have significant and unexpected implications for the firm; this is often entitled the 'butterfly effect' (Stacey, 2000).

In reality, there has been a hierarchical and integrative relationship among these approaches and they are rarely found in their pure form (Okumus and Roper, 1999). It is suggested that the development of these schools should be interpreted as a chronological evolution of the strategic management field as scholars appear to have advocated new approaches in order to eliminate the limitations of previous views (Mintzberg et al., 1998). Each school has advantages and limitations. The important point here for researchers and practicing executives is that looking at the strategy process in organizations from the perspective of different schools of thought can provide alternative explanations and understanding for complex strategic management issues and problems. In other words, each school of thought in the strategic management field can be seen as a special lens to view strategic issues, actions, and outcomes.

A number of studies in the hospitality management field identified and referred to different strategic management schools of thought. For example, Okumus and Roper (1999) identify five different schools of thought to the strategy process, which are the classical planning, emergent, cultural, contingency, configurational, and the complexity views. Edgar and Nisbet (1996) explained how the chaos theory could help hospitality organizations in decision-making and evaluating complex issues. However, when critically reviewing the strategic hospitality management literature, one dominant school of thought emerges which is the classical planning approach (Okumus, 2002). Strategy is seen more as a plan and the importance of achieving the 'fit' between the hospitality organization's external and internal environments is emphasized. Overall, there are very few studies referring to other strategic management schools of thought in the hospitality field. It is also worth noting that the strategy literature in the hospitality management field is still in its embryonic stage and there is a big gap between the generic strategy field and the strategic hospitality management field. Therefore, it is essential that scholars and researchers in the hospitality management field should specifically look at and evaluate their research questions and findings from multiple perspectives, particularly from the configurational and complexity views (Okumus, 2002). This is predominantly important as the configurational school emphasizes that the strategy process is determined by time, place, and context and the complexity view suggests that small differences and changes may lead to dramatic unexpected outcomes. It is often underlined that the hospitality industry has unique characteristics, which in turn may have some important implications on the strategy process in hospitality organizations. More research is therefore essential in the field in order to investigate how these unique characteristics of the industry impact on the strategy process in hospitality organizations. It is believed that future research can provide rich and meaningful explanations and propositions from the perspective of disparate strategic management schools of thought.

References

Edgar, D. and Nisbet, L. (1996) A matter of chaos – some issues for hospitality businesses. *International Journal of Contemporary Hospitality Management*, 8 (2), 6–9.

Mintzberg, H., Ahlstrand, B., and Lampel, J. (1998) *Strategy Safari*. London: Prentice-Hall.

Okumus, F. (2002) Can hospitality researchers contribute to the strategic management literature.

International Journal of Hospitality Management, 21 (2), 105–110.

Okumus, F. and Roper, A. (1999) A review of disparate approaches to strategy implementation in hospitality firms. *Journal of Hospitality and Tourism Research,* 23 (1), 20–38.

Stacey, R.D. (2000) *Strategic Management and Organizational Dynamics,* 3rd edn. London: Pitman Publishing.

FEVZI OKUMUS
THE HONG KONG POLYTECHNIC UNIVERSITY,
HONG KONG, SAR, CHINA

Scripts and schemas

The term 'script' refers to a schema that is retained in memory. The schema describes sequences of events or behaviors that are appropriate in a particular context. In the hospitality industry, customer scripts serve as antecedents of what customers expect to happen when they visit a hospitality operation (Shoemaker, 1998).

Scripts are developed and altered, according to the typicality of a situation. If a situation is unusual, intensive conscious processing is required to decide appropriate behaviors and actions. Since there is no script that exists for the unusual situation, little or no script processing can occur and intense conscious processing must take place. In contrast, when a situation is very familiar, little or no conscious processing occurs because the situation already is highly scripted.

Scripts are important to hospitality managers and researchers because the hospitality industry involves a wide array of situations that demand that employees and customers fluidly move from intensive conscious processing to less active processing. For service to be delivered as smoothly as possible, the actions that lead up to a service must be performed as correctly as the service itself (Shoemaker, 1998). It is therefore necessary for employees and customers to work from the same script. Managers must monitor and replace ineffective scripts. If new services are developed, or existing ones altered, the manager must ensure that employees and customers alike are 'trained' to operate according to the new script.

References

Shoemaker, S. (1998) Scripts: precursor of consumer expectations. *Cornell Hotel and Restaurant Administration Quarterly,* 37 (1), pp. 42–53.

CAROLA RAAB
UNIVERSITY OF NEW HAMPSHIRE, USA

Seasonality in foodservice

In terms of foodservice, seasonality has two meanings. The first refers to the time of year a product is in its highest period of abundance, availability, quality, and usually lowest price. Seasonality often refers to produce, but it can also refer to protein types of entrée dishes. Examples include, but are not limited to, finned fish, shellfish, wild game, and turkey.

You can buy many types of fruits and vegetables all year round, but that does not mean that they were locally grown. The concept of seasonality suggests that if a restaurant is located in Southern California, for example, and it is the spring season of the year, locally grown strawberries will cost as much as 60–70% less than at other times (when strawberries must be trucked in or shipped from remote areas), and will be more plentiful, colorful, and flavorful.

The second meaning pertains to seasonality of business. Business seasonality exists when guest counts (and correspondingly, revenue) fluctuate according to some seasonal pattern. The 'season' may be one of the four seasons of the year, or may be interpreted similarly but applied to days of the week or months of the year.

Reference

Rutherford, D. (2001) *Hotel Management and Operations.* New York: John Wiley & Sons.

EDWARD A. MERRITT
CALIFORNIA STATE POLYTECHNIC
UNIVERSITY, USA

Secondary data

Secondary data consist of information that is obtained from existing records of past data collection or from an outside source. This is in contrast to primary data, which are collected for the specific project at hand. Secondary data may be obtained internally from a company's existing records or through external sources. Secondary data can be classified as being either internal or external depending on the source of the information. This designation refers to the existence of data within an organization or outside of it.

Internal sources in the hospitality industry may include resources such as guest registration records, point-of-sale systems, internal financial reports, forecasting and budgeting reports, and hotel management's daily reports.

External sources of secondary data are numerous and diverse. Examples of external secondary data sources are the Internet, publications, government reports, public records, such as competitors' annual reports and 10-K reports; demographic records from collected national, state, or local government agencies; information available through the media, such as newspapers, magazines, or television/radio broadcasts; and data purchased through information-gathering services and consulting firms.

Internal secondary data might include such information as sales reports for a catering department, the daily audit report for a hotel, or corporate ticket purchases for a travel agency. Generally, internal data are easier to validate and obtain than external data, but both must be reviewed once discovered to ensure the information is accurate and applicable to the research being conducted. Since secondary data is not sought or gathered for the research project at hand, it is important for the researcher to scrutinize the information carefully and sometimes either disregard portions of it or its entirety. Some consideration has to be given when obtaining secondary data to its accessibility, applicability, cost, validity, and its format in relation to the format of primary data.

References

Cooper, D.R. and Schindler, P.S. (1998) *Business Research Methods*, 6th edn. Boston, MA: Irwin/McGraw-Hill.

Lewis, Robert C. and Chambers, Richard E. (2000) *Marketing Leadership in Hospitality Foundations and Practices*, 3rd edn. New York: John Wiley & Sons.

Zeithaml, Valerie A. and Bitner, Mary Jo. (2003) *Services Marketing: Integrating Customer Focus Across the Firm*, 3rd edn. New York: McGraw-Hill.

Zikmund, W.G. (2000) *Business Research Methods*, 6th edn. New York: The Dryden Press.

STEVE SASSO
UNIVERSITY OF MASSACHUSETTS, USA
DINA MARIE V. ZEMKE
UNIVERSITY OF NEW HAMPSHIRE, USA

Security

Following the 9/11 terrorist attack in the United States, security took on a new dimension for the hospitality industry globally. A troubling fact is that a suicide bomber cannot be intercepted nor deterred. Consequently, plans must be made to mitigate the damage and accelerate the response to the victims of such an attack.

The magnitude of the problem is such that efforts should be made to establish strategic alliances within the community. Liaison with the fire and police is fundamental. This should be enhanced by contact with the local office or representative of Homeland Security or the equivalent governmental entity in the country where the lodging business is located. There should be active participation within the community in emergency evacuation exercises, simulations, and special training opportunities. Avail yourself of all the assistance provided through corporate headquarters or coalitions of local facilities under a local, state or the national association.

At the property level there should be a full assessment of vulnerabilities. Are there remote entries, windows, vents, ducts, trap-doors, roof-top ventilation or elevator or other machine-room penthouses or openings? Are there persons on each work shift that know where switches are for turning off ventilating systems in the event of a chemical or bio-terrorist attack? Is the water system secured to avoid introduction of foreign materials into that system?

One should establish a comprehensive training program for *all* employees and consider the training of every employee in American Red Cross First Aid or a similar emergency training program provided in other countries. This provides a significant reservoir of trained staff in the event of a community-wide emergency where it is impossible for the usual police or fire authorities' response. It is important to complement the training with an inventory of employee skills that could be used in the event of a property-wide emergency where it becomes necessary for everyone to 'do their own thing.' Last but not least it is good practice to have a continuing emphasis on greater awareness and sensitivity on the part of staff as to what is going on throughout the property, and to make sure that communications to staff also permit a ready-response capability and a dialogue between management and employees.

Reference

Ellis, Raymond C. and Stipanuk, David M. (1999) *Security and Loss Prevention Management*, 2nd edn. Lansing, MI: Educational Institute of the American Hotel and Motel Association.

RAYMOND CLINTON ELLIS, JR
UNIVERSITY OF HOUSTON, USA

Security systems

In addition to electronic locking systems, there are other security systems that have been introduced in the lodging industry. A critical technology has been the detection of motion or presence of a person in a secured area. Microwaves may be established within a secured space that will alarm by turning on lights, providing an audible warning or silent warning to a remote site when the wave is interrupted. Infra-red technology will provide the same capability by sensing the presence of body heat.

A seismic unit may also alarm when a person or animal crosses a buried seismic detector indicating an unwanted presence in a secured location. This has been successful when protecting against intruders in the perimeter grounds of a guestroom area. Usually such a device will alarm remotely; although it could cause a floodlight to activate or an audible alarm to sound.

A significant development in an access control system was achieved in 1996. This provides an answer to unauthorized entrance from non-lobby doors and the movement of unwanted persons via stairways, emergency doors or 'employee only' doors. It protects against the propping of a door or opening from the inside to permit illegal entry and further controls unauthorized egress. Electro-magnetic pressure holds a door against any pressure less than 1500 pounds. However, in a building emergency, the alarm will immediately release the electro-magnet to permit emergency egress.

The system further includes cameras (CCTV) and elevator access systems. An added feature provides a victim alarm and distress signal for activation by a disabled person at each stairway door. A door that has been violated announces a 20 second message: 'Hotel security is on the way. Legal prosecution will be made.' A flashing strobe light signals to a central control panel and continues to operate until reset. (A procedure that requires 30 seconds only.)

Closed circuit television (CCTV) has a multitude of uses in both the front- and back-of-the-house. Due to privacy concerns it must be used judiciously. Consideration must also be given to response capability if an incident is detected by CCTV. Many systems will record only, and will not have continuous monitoring. Organizations are able to provide such monitoring from remote locations via satellite or other electronic means. This enhances the effective use of CCTV.

Reference

Ellis, Raymond C. and Stipanuk, David M. (1999) *Security and Loss Prevention Management*,

2nd edn. Lansing, MI: Educational Institute of the American Hotel and Motel Association.

RAYMOND CLINTON ELLIS, JR
UNIVERSITY OF HOUSTON, USA

Self check-out

Provides guests with an opportunity to check themselves out of the hotel from lobby terminals and/or the guestroom. A self check-out terminal might be a monitor in the lobby or a guestroom television. In either case the terminal or in-room system is interfaced with the front office computer. A guest accesses the proper folio and reviews its contents. Guests may be required to enter a credit card number or insure the accuracy of a credit card number. Settlement can be automatically assigned to an acceptable credit card as long as the guest presented a valid card at registration.

A self check-out is complete when the guest's balance is transferred to a credit card account and an itemized account statement is printed and dispensed to the guest. A self check-out system that is connected to an integrated property management system should then automatically communicate updated room status information to the front office and housekeeping and initiate action to create a guest history record.

In-room folio review and check-out utilize the room's television with a remote control or guestroom telephone access via an in-room television. The guest can confirm a previously approved method of settlement for the account since the in-room television is connected via the property management system to the front office. The property management system directs the self check-out process. Generally, guests can pick up a printed folio copy at the front desk on their way out. Similar to other self check-out technologies, in-room self check-out automatically updates room status and creates guest history records. Another advantage of in-room folio review is that guests can look at their folios at any time during their stay without having to stop by the front desk.

Reference

Stutts, Alan T. (2001) *Hotel and Lodging Management – An Introduction*. New York: John Wiley & Sons.

ALAN T. STUTTS
AMERICAN INTERCONTINENTAL
UNIVERSITY, USA

Self-development

Stewart (1996, p. 171) defines self-development as individuals improving their knowledge, skills, and abilities through their own self-directed efforts. According to Stewart, there are three critical questions that must be answered in the self-development process:

1. Where am I now?
2. Where do I want to be?
3. How will I monitor progress?

In the process of answering these three questions, the ability to engage in self-analysis including objectivity of one's own strengths and weaknesses is of great importance.

In addition to self-analysis, the learner must have the ability to formulate learning objectives, target dates for completion, and determine methods and resources to be utilized. For example, an individual desiring to one day become a hotel general manager could initiate a program centered on education and work experience in the lodging industry. One goal, in addition to the completion of a hospitality degree, may be to achieve certification through a professional industry association. Self-development is a lifelong process and, for this hotel general manager, can continue on to include attendance at professional conferences, executive education programs, and embracing leadership positions in professional associations.

Reference

Stewart, J. (1996) *Managing Change Through Training and Development*. London: Kogan Page.

DEBRA F. CANNON
GEORGIA STATE UNIVERSITY, USA

Self-service technologies

Self-service technologies (SSTs) are services produced entirely by the customer without any direct involvement or interaction with a service firm's employees. As such, these services represent the ultimate form of customer participation. Advances in technology, particularly the Internet, have allowed the introduction of a wide range of SSTs, including automated teller machines (ATMs), hotel check-in and check-out, automated car rental, and Internet shopping (Zeithaml and Bitner, 2003).

Services can be viewed along a convenience continuum, from those that are produced entirely by the firm, to those that are produced entirely by the customer (Brown, 1990). SSTs occupy the latter portion of this spectrum. Bowen (1990) even suggests segmenting customers based on their willingness to participate in the creation of a service.

The factors underlying satisfaction in customers' use of SSTs has also been examined in the literature. This research classified the SSTs as either satisfying, or dissatisfying in nature. For the dissatisfying SSTs, the service encounters usually contained an element of service failure (Meuter et al., 2000).

References

Bowen, J. (1990) Development of a taxonomy of services to gain strategic marketing insights. *Journal of the Academy of Marketing Science*, 18 (1), 43–49.

Brown, L.G. (1990) Convenience in services marketing. *Journal of Services Marketing*, 4 (1), 543–559.

Meuter, M.L., Ostom, A.L., Roundtree, R.I., and Bitner, M.J. (2000) Self-service technologies: understanding customer satisfaction with technology-based service encounters. *Journal of Marketing*, July, 50–64.

Zeithaml, V.A. and Bitner, M.J. (2003) *Services Marketing: Integrating Customer Focus across the Firm*, 3rd edn. New York: McGraw-Hill Irwin, pp. 362–363.

KARL MAYER
UNIVERSITY OF NEVADA, LAS VEGAS, USA

Semantic Web

The Semantic Web refers to a range of standards, languages, development frameworks and tool development initiatives aimed at annotating Web pages with metadata, so that intelligent agents can reason effectively about services. Agent development and website annotation are based on ontologies (consensual, shared, and formal descriptions of key concepts in given domains). The ultimate aim is to be able to handle user requests such as: 'Arrange a vacation for me, somewhere in Victoria (Australia), during March.' An intelligent agent needs to determine an appropriate time slot, make airline and hire car bookings, find a hotel, and book tours etc. The user's personal website needs to be accessed to obtain details of preferences: ranging from the general (such as their preferred airline and hire car preferences) through to trip-specific detail (such as they would like to do some surfing and visit a favorite restaurant). In addition to the user's personal website, the application needs to access tourism board promotional sites, the websites of individual tourism operators plus the likes of airline and rental car company sites.

References

Berners-Lee, T., Hendler, J., and Lassila, O. (2001) The Semantic Web. *Scientific American*, 284 (5), pp. 34–43.

Werthner, H. and Klein, S. (1999) Information technology and tourism – a challenging relationship. New York: Springer.

G. MICHAEL MCGRATH
VICTORIA UNIVERSITY, AUSTRALIA

Semi-variable costs

A semi-variable cost tends to vary partially, rather than in proportion, with the volume of activity. The difference between fixed and semi-variable costs depends wholly on the relevant range within which the analysis is made. Payroll for a hotel is an example of a semi-variable cost, where the minimum (skeleton) staff is required in order for the property to function and accept guests (fixed cost element) and additional staff are employed on an 'as needed' basis as activity increases beyond the capacity of the minimum staff level to absorb. Payroll will, thus, increase 'step-wise' with volume. It will be a fixed cost within a limited range of activity, but will have to step up to a higher level once activity increases above that range. The classification of cost types into fixed cost or semi-variable cost is not easy in practice since most costs vary with volume in one way or another. However, the main methods available to analyze semi-variable costs into their fixed and variable elements are by technical estimate (using managers' intimate knowledge of their businesses), graphical analysis (charting using a scatter-graph) and statistical cost analysis (using regression and correlation analysis).

References

Harris, P.J. (ed.) (1995) *Accounting and Finance for the International Hospitality Industry*. Oxford: Butterworth-Heinemann.

Horngren, C.T., Foster, G., and Datar, S.M. (2000) *Cost Accounting: A Managerial Emphasis*, 10th edn. London: Prentice-Hall.

TOMMY D. ANDERSSON
GOTEBORGS UNIVERSITY, SWEDEN

Service profit chain

The 'service profit chain' concept was developed through an analysis of successful service organizations. The chain illustrates relationships between service firms' profits and customer satisfaction and loyalty, as well as employee satisfaction and loyalty (Heskett *et al.*, 1994). There are three components in the service profit chain. First, work environment and hiring practices are designed to foster employee satisfaction, loyalty, and productivity. Satisfied and loyal employees drive service quality, which in turn drives customer satisfaction and then customer loyalty.

A stable base of loyal customers ultimately results in continuing profits and growth.

Customer loyalty is directly related to customer satisfaction, which is influenced by the quality of goods and services delivered to the customer and high perceived value. Employee satisfaction, loyalty, and productivity are a necessary prerequisite for the creation of customer value. Employee satisfaction is linked to the internal quality of work life in a service organization.

The service profit chain is a particularly important concept for the hospitality industry because of the positive relationship between good human resource practices and profits. Hospitality industry employees are a major component of the service product and successful management of human resources is a clear source of competitive advantage in a highly competitive business climate.

Reference

Heskett, J.L., Jones, T.O., Loveman, G.W., Sasser, W.E. Jr, and Schlesinger, L.A. (1994) Putting the service-profit chain to work. *Harvard Business Review*, 72 (2), 164–174.

CAROLA RAAB
UNIVERSITY OF NEW HAMPSHIRE, USA

Service system

The hyper-competitive global marketplace has compelled organizations to transform – not only the way that they conduct business but, more importantly, the way that they think and conceptualize their business. Today's businesses operate within the realm of infinite possibilities, where new knowledge and technology assists them to transcend the challenges of the past (Kandampully, 2003). When firms incorporate customers and employees within the business model, a radical shift occurs in the way that they perceive, orchestrate and manage their business. Services in hospitality and tourism firms manifest primarily through the contribution of people serving people. People-focused services have become the recognized value enhancement variable for successful service firms. This elevates the value of human input – both emotionally and intellectually. It is therefore imperative to seek ways to assist firms to nurture employees' mental contribution over and above their manual input. This necessitates cohesion, not only between the people who make up the organization, but also between the systems that support the activities and the processes that manifest as service.

A collective orientation, therefore, is imperative if hospitality and tourism firms are to remain focused. The conceptual underpinning of the 'service system' is to align both strategy (thoughts) and internal activities (actions) to one focus – the customer – while recognizing and acknowledging the contribution of people and technology. The benefit of the service system is the outcome of the collective efficiencies of three strategies, namely: service empowerment, service guarantees, and service recovery (Kandampully and Duddy, 2001). A cohesive service system that permeates the conceptual and internal activities will not only help firms to excel in service delivery, but will render it difficult for competing firms to emulate the outcome – thereby proffering a competitive advantage.

Service empowerment will prove efficient only if the firm's internal activities engender sufficient flexibility to permit empowered employees to undertake creative thinking and modification (service innovation) of their job tasks – and to therefore deviate from the firm's standard processes and systems – for the benefit of the customer. Managers can effectively use service empowerment to nurture competitive intelligence – within all employees and at every level of the organization – to build the firm's competitive advantage. Moreover, a service system provides the interconnected structure and the flexible pathway for empowered employees to permeate laterally and vertically across the organization to support fellow employees and also to serve customers. Empowerment, as discussed within the context of a service system, is beyond the concept of a single strategy; it is the concept of collective thinking and the creative mind of the organization. It is hence argued that empowerment should be viewed as only one part of a

holistic strategy that seeks to focus on the creativity of the human mind.

Creativity, however, should not be confined to the act of creation alone, but should extend to all other activities of the firm; for example, the ongoing update of the quality of service. Firms often fail to realize the full potential of their employees' creative innovations. Moreover, since innovation is valueless unless it directly benefits the customer, it is management's responsibility to ensure that innovation encompasses all activities involved in service delivery – where the true assessment of service takes place. As production and consumption occurs simultaneously in services, the opportunity for traditional quality control mechanisms – such as inspection prior to delivery – is limited. The service system brings together the concepts of service guarantees and service recovery to effectively manage the delivery of superior service.

The service guarantee constitutes a firm's 'blueprint' for service, defining its service promise effectively to both internal and external customers and establishing the criteria by which customers evaluate the quality of service. A service guarantee thus clarifies to employees the standards that they must exceed rather than meet, if they are to creatively innovate and render services far in advance of customers' expectations. It is the freedom creatively to 'think for the customer' that imbues employees with the motivation, pride, and satisfaction in their job that facilitates the development of the all-important relationship with the customer that leads to long-term loyalty. In this regard a service guarantee is neither a strategy nor a standard, but the firm's quality-conscious pathway that assists an organization in its metamorphosis to a service-oriented culture, where every employee takes pride in upholding the firm's promise to its customers, and transforms every moment-of-truth to a memory of superior experience.

Service managers recognize the fact that, given the high involvement of the human element in services at the production and consumption stages, mistakes are inevitable, albeit not intentional. Perfecting every service process to ensure 'zero defects' may thus not prove entirely tenable. The degree of flexibility required by employees in their endeavors to customize the service delivery may also lead to possible mistakes. It is therefore imperative to prepare for corrective action well before mistakes occur. Moreover, it is this preparedness that sets the leader apart from the others, as it clearly communicates – inside and outside – the organization's loyalty, competency, and commitment to its customers. In fact, it is when mistakes occur during the production and delivery of services that the true nature of the organization is exposed to its customers. Recovery should thus be designed into every service activity and constitute part of the core skills required by all service personnel. Service recovery enables the firm to rectify failures immediately while proffering the opportunity to learn and to prevent the occurrence of similar mistakes anywhere in the organization.

In this age of information, technology not only supports service personnel with knowledge, but it helps the entire organization to disseminate valuable information (knowledge) across international borders and create organization-wide strength through interdependency (Kandampully, 2002). However, collective efficiency will manifest only when there is interdependency between the people, processes, and systems that make up the service organization. The service system is specifically designed to create this collective focus of the three independent but interrelated strategies: namely, service empowerment, service guarantees, and service recovery.

References

Kandampully, J. and Duddy, R. (2001) Service system: a strategic approach to gain a competitive advantage in the hospitality and tourism industry. *International Journal of Hospitality and Tourism Administration*, 2 (1), 27–47.

Kandampully, J. (2002) Innovation as the core competency of a service organization: the role of technology, knowledge and networks. *European Journal of Innovation Management*, 5 (1), 18–26.

Kandampully, J. (2003) B2B relationships and networks in the Internet age. *Management Decision*, 41 (5), 443–451.

JAY KANDAMPULLY
OHIO STATE UNIVERSITY, USA

Service types

'Service' is a term that is used to describe the manner and method in which food is served to guests in foodservice operations. In former times this often constituted an elaborate and convoluted protocol, much of which is no longer in vogue, notwithstanding that some technical terms are still in use today, particularly in Europe.

When food is placed directly on plates and served to guests at the table this is referred to as service à l'assiette. When guests serve themselves from the dish on the table with serving spoons this is referred to a service à la française. When the waiter places the food onto the diner's plate this is referred to as service in the à l'anglaise style. In service à la russe, which is also known as au guéridon, the dish is first offered to the guest for viewing or approval, and then the food is served onto the diner's plate at a pedestal table or guéridon, which is located close to or beside the dining table. There are essentially seven styles or methods of service used in foodservice operations today. They are:

- Plate service
- Silver service
- Guéridon service
- Family service
- Buffet service
- Smorgasbord service
- Cafeteria service.

Plate service (service à l'assiette) and silver service

For plate service the food is plated in the kitchen and served to the guest on the plate. (This is often referred to as 'American' service.) For silver service the food is first presented on serving dishes (which may or may not be silver nowadays) to the guest and is then portioned and transferred from a serving dish onto the plate in front of the guest by using a service spoon and fork, which is commonly referred to as the service gear. (This style is also known as 'Russian' service if the portioning is performed by the food server or 'English' service if the maître d' hôtel assists.) Often, however, a combination of the two techniques can be used. The main food item, e.g. meat, can be portioned onto a plate in the kitchen and served using the plate service method and the accompaniment can then be served at the table using the silver service technique. Interestingly, in formal Chinese dining and many oriental banquets a modified version of silver service is used throughout each of the eight or twelve courses. The correct service technique in this instance is to present the dishes within each course to the guest of honor, other guests, and the host, in that order. Once presented, these are placed in the middle of the table on a carousel also known as a 'lazy Susan.' The waiter then portions and serves the food for each guest from the carousel commencing with the guest of honor, then other important guests, proceeding to the remaining guests and the host. Once this is done, the carousel table is cleared of dishes. At less formal banquets, however, once the guests have been served the remaining dishes are left at the carousel and guests are allowed to help themselves from the dishes. This then becomes similar to the family service style (see below).

It is worth noting that, traditionally, the plate service method and other forms of table service required food to be served from the left of the guest, and removal of empty plates to be done from the right of the guest. This can still be observed in more traditional restaurants and in formal service situations, e.g. state banquets. However, modern practice increasingly demands that plates be placed and cleared from the guest's right because it is believed that this method causes least disturbance to the guest.

As noted, silver service or service à l'anglaise is a method of transferring food from a service dish to the guest's plate and serving from the guest's left by using service gear, which is normally comprised of the serving spoon and fork and at times fish or carving knives. A waiter must be able to master the silver service technique using only one hand to hold the service gear (spoon and fork) while the other hand holds the service dish. It is also worth noting that very few foodservice operations offer full silver service to their guests nowadays.

Guéridon service (service à la russe)

The actual term 'guéridon' denotes a side table or service trolley (in former times, especially in Russia, a guéridon was a sideboard) which is used in the dining room in front of guests for the service and preparation of foods. Normally guéridon service – also referred to as 'French' service – requires food to be transferred from a serving dish onto the guest's plate on the guéridon, which is then served to the guest. In addition, a guéridon is often used to finish off certain dishes, e.g. to flame (flambé) them or to prepare certain desserts, or to dress salads, before being portioned and served to the guests.

Family service (service à la française)

Family service is a very simple method of serving food in which serving dishes are placed on the dining table (on a carousel in the middle of the table for Chinese service and Chinese dim sum service), allowing guests to select what they wish and to serve themselves. Family service style is predominantly used in Oriental, Middle Eastern, and Mediterranean countries.

Buffet service

For buffet and smorgasbord service, the food is usually artistically arranged on a display table (possibly more than one) and guests select what they wish from a range of hot and cold foods, soups, roasts, salads, and desserts. A proper buffet service requires service staff to serve the foods, which the guest has selected, using the silver service technique. This differs from the smorgasbord service where guests are allowed to help themselves from the smorgasbord table. It is not unusual, though, for many modern foodservice operations to allow guests to help themselves from the buffet table.

Smorgasbord service

As already noted, smorgasbord service is similar to buffet service except that the guests are allowed to serve themselves from the smorgasbord. Also, a true smorgasbord is comprised of dishes from Scandinavian countries and features hot and cold seafood delicacies, which are often smoked or pickled.

Cafeteria service

In cafeteria-style service, guests select their meals from food counters, the full length of which is known as a 'race,' and place these on their meal tray. These meals might be pre-bought or paid for at the end of the race at the cash desk prior to sitting down to consume the meal. Usually, cutlery, napkins, additional crockery and beverages are collected at the end of the race before proceeding to the cash desk. Cafeteria-style service can be found in on-site foodservice, which – depending on the venue – may also serve gourmet-style food.

Reference

Revel, J. (1982) *Culture and Cuisine*. Garden City, NY: Doubleday.

JAKSA KIVELA
THE HONG KONG POLYTECHNIC
UNIVERSITY, HONG KONG SAR, CHINA

Shrinkage

Shrinkage is the loss of assets in a foodservice operation, usually food or liquor. As Geller (1992) underscores, this loss is usually the result of inadequate internal controls.

Restaurants suffer greater losses associated with shrinkage than other businesses because the majority of assets are consumable and easily usable. For example, food and liquor has demonstrated value to employees. Furthermore, employees can use inedible assets such as plates, silverware, glassware, cleaning supplies, tablecloths, napkins, and candles at home. It is for this reason that shrinkage is the leading cause of business failure for restaurateurs.

Shrinkage also results in increased costs for the respective categories on a firm's income statement. Take, for example, the effect of stolen steaks. Since the food cost for a given period is calculated by assessing what was taken from inventory during the period, it is difficult to distinguish what was sold to guests and what was stolen; both phenomena result in reduction of inventory and an increase in the cost of goods.

Operators' best defense against shrinkage involves eliminating the opportunity for employees to steal. This extends to proper purchasing, receiving, and inventory-management practices. With such practices in place, along with effective internal controls and monitors, shrinkage can be all but eliminated.

Reference

Geller, A.N. (1992) *Internal Control: A Fraud Prevention Handbook*. Ithaca, NY: Cornell Campus Store.

DAVID BIEL
HOUSTON'S RESTAURANTS, USA

Site inspection

Site inspections are personal, careful investigation of a property, facility or area. A site inspection allows the planner to assess everything from the general condition of the hotel and meeting facilities to the attitudes of the service personnel who manage them. Site inspections should be done at least a year or two in advance for large meetings, although many associations book as far as 10 years in advance of their annual conventions.

During the site inspection planners set a time to meet with the hotel sales representative or, if several hotels will be visited, the convention and visitors bureau representative for the destination. Meeting planners determine in advance the parts of the facilities they wish to tour and set a firm schedule. They review the meeting requirements and history with department managers. During their visit they take photographs of the available space from all angles and make sure that the site meets the national regulations affecting people with disabilities (i.e. in the United States the Americans with Disabilities Act).

To facilitate the process of inspection meeting planners use a checklist and ask questions. The checklist should include the date of the site inspection, the facility name, the facility address, the main phone number, the reservations phone number, the toll free phone number, the website address, info on online reservations capabilities, a phone number for international attendees, information on the confirmation process for reservations, the deposit policy for attendees, when the property was built, when the last renovation was and when is the next planned renovation, what was or will be renovated. The contact information should include the name, direct phone line, fax number, and e-mail address for the primary contact (sales manager), general manager, catering director, convention or conference service manager, electrical services manager, audiovisual set-up department, security, and any other pertinent numbers.

Other information to gather includes the distance to the nearest airport, the distance to downtown, the distance to the convention center (if applicable), transportation options and cost from the hotel to the convention center (if applicable), traffic considerations, a listing of local entertainment, shopping centers, stores, and restaurants. Information on parking should include self parking availability on site, availability of valet parking, number of parking spaces, number of accessible spaces for handicapped drivers, cost of self parking, and cost of valet parking. Information on the number of guestrooms should be broken down into single, double, double/double or king with the number of smoking and non-smoking rooms in each category. The same breakdown should be obtained for suites and accessible rooms.

In the United States, one should also obtain the FEMA (Federal Emergency Management Agency, which determines the hotel's compliance with the Fire Safety Act and issues a certifying number) number of the property.

Other questions that should be asked include the following:

- What is the hotel's complimentary room policy?
- What is included in the standard room rate?

- What are the concierge hours? What are check-in and check-out times?
- What amenities are provided in the rooms?
- Are there mini-bars in the rooms?
- Are there irons and ironing boards in the rooms or will attendees have to call housekeeping to have them delivered?
- Does the hotel provide high-speed data ports?
- What is the fee for use of the data ports?
- Are there multiple telephone lines?
- Are there surcharges for toll-free access?
- Is there an in-room safe in every room and is there a fee to use it?
- Can guests control the in-room temperature?
- Is there a resort fee?
- Is there a charge to receive faxes?
- What is the air quality of the hotel and what is the hotel's schedule of filter cleaning?
- Is there a concierge level and what is included?
- Is there a health club, spa, pool and costs?
- What is the portage fee?
- What other charges may be added to the guest bill?
- What are the capacities, typical menus, and hours of operation of the restaurants?
- Is there room service and what are the hours of operation?
- Is there a newsstand, gift shop, business center or other outlets?
- What is the sales tax on guestrooms?
- What is the sales tax on food?
- Is there a bed tax and how much?
- What is the gratuity or service charge percentage?
- What are the catering menus?
- List of certifications and conditions from catering contracts or Banquet Event Orders.
- How many tables of each type does the hotel have in its inventory (rounds of ten, serpentine, etc)?
- What types and sizes of chairs, number of lecterns, microphones, projectors, podiums, projection stands, easels, screens, etc. are available?
- What are the hotel's liquor policies and local alcohol laws?
- What decorations are available for use?
- What are the hotel's cancellation and room attrition policies, standard dates to cut off the room block, its peak and shoulder seasons?

- What is the hotel's preferred group patterns (Sunday through Wednesday, Thursday through Sunday, etc.)?
- Does the hotel provide any promotional assistance and in what quantities (reservation cards, logo/artwork for your publications and web site, rack brochures, etc)?
- Is information available about local doctors and hospitals and the availability of child care providers?
- What sports and recreation are available on-site, nearby (such as golf courses), and what is the costs to attendees?
- Are there any local holidays or regional celebrations and festivals on the dates that are being considered?
- Will any other group be in the hotel over the same dates and if so, who are they and how many attendees do they expect?
- Is there Internet access in the guest and meeting rooms and what is the cost?
- What is the drayage policy? How good are the freight access (including the number and size of loading docks, type of loading area, truck clearance space), lift gates (number), and freight elevators (number, dimensions, weight limit). Are pads required, and what is the maximum truck size and height limit.
- Which union performs which duties?
- When is the union's contract expiration dates (to avoid potential union strikes during the meeting).
- What are the local labor jurisdictions?
- What are interior and exterior rules on signage, including sizes and locations?
- What hotels are adjacent (including the name of the hotel, the walking distance and the number of rooms available for overflow guests)?
- What client references are available, including groups of similar size, time period and market segment?
- Is there information on any anticipated ownership/franchise changes, current owners and managers of the facility, and staff turnover statistics.

In addition to asking those questions, meeting planners obtain the following documents:

- A billing application for credit or deposit arrangements for guests and group

- The hotel function room floor plan that also indicates the location of windows, doorways (dimensions), column sizes and locations, built-in screens, stages and podiums, temperature controls, air walls, storage rooms, computer hook-ups, rest rooms (number of each), and telephones (number of each)
- List of available meeting rooms with dimensions (including ceiling height), capacities in various configurations (auditorium set, classroom set, banquet set, etc.), lighting (dimmable?)
- List of rental costs, floor load capacity, type of flooring, location of electrical outlets (overhead, floor, columns), and plumbing
- List of available equipment, including forklifts, dollies, hand trucks, etc.

References

Krug, S., Chatfield-Taylor, C., and Collins, M. (eds) (1994) *The Convention Industry Council Manual*, 7th edn. McLean, VA: The Convention Industry Council.

Connell, B., Chatfield-Taylor, C., and Collins, M. (eds) (2002) *Professional Meeting Management*, 4th edn. Chicago: Professional Conference Management Association Education Foundation.

M.T. HICKMAN
RICHLAND COLLEGE, USA

Site selection

First the destination is chosen, and then a facility in that destination can be selected. The destination for a meeting must be carefully considered, looking at factors including geographic regions, accessibility, affordability, urban or suburban, resort destination, gaming destination. It is important to prepare the meeting specifications prior to opening discussions with prospective destinations. Meeting specifications include requirements for space, dates, rates, and services. Space would include sleeping rooms, suites, number of complimentary rooms per paid occupied room, number and size of meeting rooms, exhibit space, registration area, audiovisual requirements, computer and technology requirements, suitable storage space, office space, meeting dates and types of events requiring banquet space. Dates would include the meeting pattern, such as Sunday through Wednesday or Wednesday through Saturday, and required or preferred month or week of the year. Historical data from previous meetings are important to show the type of attendance expected. First-time events have the most difficulty booking space. Location specifications take into consideration the accessibility of the location by plane, train, bus and/or automobile, as well as the number of seats on all planes flying into a destination per day, month or year.

Meeting planners need to know if the attendees prefer affordable or luxury accommodations, if they want 24 hour room service, valet parking, shops, on-site business center, airport shuttle service. They must also consider the number of available hotel rooms in the city for citywide conventions or the largest number available in a single hotel for meetings that want to keep attendees together. Convention and visitors bureaus are designed to assist planners, and have specific knowledge of the destinations they represent, as well as the hotels, conference, and convention centers, non-traditional venues, and suppliers that are needed to service a meeting.

Other items that affect the site selection include room rates, the number of complimentary (comp) rooms, suites and upgrades, food and beverage, meeting/function space rental rates, and 24-hour hold.

Reference

Krug, S., Chatfield-Taylor, C., and Collins, M. (eds) (1994) *The Convention Industry Council Manual*, 7th edn. McLean, VA: The Convention Industry Council.

CYNTHIA VANNUCCI
METROPOLITAN COLLEGE, USA

Small business entrepreneurship

The majority of businesses in the hospitality industry are small. Establishment of small business is often related to the social and personal context as well as considerations of the entrepreneur. In fact, hospitality small business entrepreneurship has been identified as a vehicle through which entrepreneurs can achieve personal goals such as having fun, enriching their social life, generating jobs for family members, and educating their children. Several forms of small hospitality businesses exist including:

- Lifestyle businesses established to maintain sufficient income to ensure that the business provides the entrepreneur and his/her family with a satisfactory level of funds to enable them to enjoy their chosen lifestyle, e.g., small motels
- Self-employment businesses, such as bed and breakfasts, in which entrepreneurs express their talents and skills through serving a specific niche of customers
- Ethnic entrepreneurship, which helps overcome disadvantages of immigrants and minorities in their new environment. This can be seen in the establishment of specialty ethnic restaurants in 'ethnic enclaves' (Gold, 1992).

The aforementioned forms of hospitality small businesses are not necessarily profit-motivated and may also be established to generate a secondary source of income for the entrepreneurs. Furthermore, these forms of small businesses are characterized by a relatively high level of female entrepreneurs who combine career and home duties (Haber and Reichel, 2004).

References

Gold, S.J. (1992) Self-employment and refugee communities. In S.J. Gold, *Refugee Communities*. Newbury Park, CA: Sage Publications, pp. 167–197.
Haber, S. and Reichel, A. (2004) Identifying performance measures of small ventures – the case of the tourism industry. *Journal of Small Business Management*. (forthcoming).

SIGAL HABER
TEL-AVIV UNIVERSITY, ISRAEL

Smart card

The first smart card was developed in 1974 by independent inventor Roland Moreno. In year

2004, almost 1 billion smart cards will be produced worldwide by several large manufacturers. Smart cards are among the newest and most exciting tools in the world of information technology. The size and shape of a credit card, smart cards have many of the attributes of a miniature computer. A single card can contain multiple applications and functions that are protected by advanced security features to prevent unauthorized use.

A smart card is a card that is embedded with either a microprocessor and a memory chip or only a memory chip with non-programmable logic. The microprocessor card can add, delete, and otherwise manipulate information on the card, while a memory-chip card can only undertake a pre-defined operation. Smart cards, unlike magnetic stripe cards, can carry all necessary functions and information on the card. Therefore, they do not require access to remote databases at the time of the transaction.

Today, there are three categories of smart cards, all of which are evolving rapidly into markets and applications:

- Integrated circuit (IC) microprocessor cards
- Integrated circuit (IC) memory cards
- Optical memory cards.

References

http://java.sun.com/products/javacard/smartcards.html.
http://impactsolutions.cc/smartcard/smrtcard.htm.

BENNY CHAN
THE HONG KONG POLYTECHNIC
UNIVERSITY, HONG KONG SAR, CHINA

Smoke detectors

Smoke detectors react to the solid and liquid aerosols created by a fire. Each of the four types reacts to a specific aspect of smoke. The four major types of smoke detectors are:

- Spot-type ionization
- Spot-type, light scattering
- Line projected beam
- Air sampling.

Ionization smoke detectors have two electrically charged plates arranged in a parallel manner with an air gap between. The air is ionized by a small, low-strength radioactive source, creating a small electrical current. Smoke particles slow down the ionized air and the detector measures this change. Spot-type photoelectric smoke detectors contain a small light source that shines into the detection chamber. A light-sensitive receiver is placed at an angle to the light source so only a small amount of light is normally received. Smoke particles entering the detector chamber cause additional light to be scattered so more reaches the photosensitive receiver. Projected beam detectors contain a light source that projects a beam through a space to a receiver. When smoke crosses the beam, the amount of light reaching the receiver is reduced. When the percentage of light obscured reaches a preset threshold, an alarm sounds. Air-sampling detectors use separate detection chambers to sample air from a room. The detection chamber may use a cloud chamber to detect minute particles in the air. A second type of air-sampling detector uses a sensitive photoelectric light-scattering detector. This system uses a high-power strobe light or laser beam to detect submicro-sized particles in small concentrations.

Reference

Schifiliti, R.P. (2000) Fire alarm systems for Life Safety Code users. In R. Cote (ed.) *Life Safety Code Handbook*. Quincy, MA: National Fire Protection Association, pp. 943–966.

CAROLYN LAMBERT
PENNSYLVANIA STATE UNIVERSITY, USA

Social influence

Broadly, social influence is a change in behavior due to the real or imagined influence of other people. There are three types of social influence: informational, normative and interpersonal.

Informational social influence occurs because of people's desire to be correct and to know how best to behave in a given situation. Persuasion is the most common type of informational social influence. *Normative social influence* occurs because of people's desire to conform to social norms in order to be liked and accepted. Normative social influence occurs when people adopt the behaviors, attitudes, and values of members of a reference group. *Interpersonal social influence* occurs as the result of direct pressure from another person. Two types of interpersonal social influence are obedience and compliance.

While persuasion is the most common type of informational social influence, another example found in marketing is references to authorities. When a wine, for example, is marketed as having been rated highly by expert wine tasters, the hope is that the expert opinion will change consumer behavior. Another information technique is called the 'foot-in-the-door'. In the foot-in-the-door, consumers are presented with a small request (to which they are expected to acquiesce). Then they are presented with a large request, to which the marketer hopes they will also acquiesce. Marketers use this technique by presenting consumers with incrementally increasing requests. Soon, a casual customer becomes a regular guest. Foot-in-the-door is considered informational social influence because by complying with a small request the consumer begins to view him- or herself as the type of person who uses the product or service and this information produces subsequent behavior changes.

Normative social influence occurs when consumers are concerned with being accepted and liked by others. This type of social influence typically results in public compliance with the group's beliefs and behaviors, but not necessarily private acceptance. The likelihood that a consumer will respond to normative social influences seems to depend upon three factors: the strength, immediacy, and the number of people applying influence. Strength refers to how important the people in the group are to the consumer. Immediacy is how close the group is in time and space to the consumer. Number is simply the number of people in the group. Conformity to normative social influence increases as strength and immediacy increase. Number operates differently. Conformity to social influence levels out once the consumer perceives unanimity in the group; beyond that number, adding members to the group does not increase conformity.

Compliance is the type of interpersonal social influence most relevant to sales and other negotiation situations. Compliance is a change in behavior due to a direct request from another person. Compliance techniques rely upon consumers behaving without deliberating about their actions. Some compliance techniques rely upon unobtrusively reminding consumers of social norms. For example, tips to servers increase when the server signs his or her name to the check. This may make the server seem more personal, and remind the customer of the norm to tip. Compliance can also be achieved using various ingratiation techniques. These are tactics that increase the requester's attractiveness to the consumer. Ingratiation techniques include appearing similar, helpful, and physically attractive to customers. Reciprocity is another interpersonal social influence technique. All cultures have a norm of reciprocity – that receiving anything positive from another person requires a similar response. This norm can be used by simply giving customers token gifts such as candy. It can also be by applying the 'door-in-the face' technique. In the door-in-the-face, customers are presented by a large and unreasonable request. Then, after the customer refuses, the marketer responds with a smaller request (to which the consumer is expected to acquiesce). The reciprocity norm in this situation is invoked when the marketer backs down from an extreme request to a reasonable request. This puts pressure on the consumer to reciprocate with compliance.

Of the three types of social influence, information social influence results in long-lasting attitude and behavior change and is the type most sought after by marketers. Normative and interpersonal social influence techniques are effective at changing behavior, but their effects persist as long as the agents of the social influence are salient.

Reference

Cialdini, R.B. (2001) *Influence: Science and Practice*, 4th edn. Boston, MA: Allyn & Bacon.

ANN LYNN
ITHACA COLLEGE, USA

Socialization

Socialization is the process whereby new employees are inducted into the culture of an organization (Schultz and Schultz, 2002); norms may be regarded as those implicit standards of behavior that are accepted and shared by members of a work group. Within the hospitality context, the socialization process involves the transmission of values, beliefs, and attitudes embraced by individuals already within an organization, particularly those holding positions of power, influence, and salience. Such individuals would include hotel general managers, human resource managers, and also divisional managers. The concept of person–environment fit holds considerable explanatory power in the understanding of how employees take on their new hospitality work culture and the norms embedded within it. Socialization is regarded as the process that seeks to make this fit as precise as possible, comfortable for all, and generally enduring for the newly employed. It may also be understood as a continuous process that will periodically occur throughout a person's career in hospitality; employees are regularly required to adapt to change, whether it involves a new position in the existing organization or a new job in another hospitality organization; it can also involve organizational restructuring, or even physical relocation. In many industries such as hospitality, resocialization of some type will necessarily confront an employee. Pizam (1999) has noted that hotel jobs of the future may well become linked together in career ladders; in such a situation resocialization practices would be more efficient and smoother, and could result in less stressful experiences.

Upon entry to any hospitality organization, there is a considerable amount of detail that an individual needs to learn; this typically includes expected performance levels, recognition of superiors and codes of appropriate conduct. The notion of role as an explanatory idea is generally deemed to be of some value here, with roles regarded as the expectations of others regarding appropriate hospitality workplace behavior. These roles are invariably multifaceted: They are impersonal in that the position generally determines the role expectation and not the person; they tend to focus on task, with the requirements of the position setting role parameters; they may have a subjective and even evanescent aspect to them, with various individuals in the organization taking differing perspectives as to a new staff member's work role; they present basic facts and procedures to the newly employed that are usually required to be learned quickly, often producing major change in the individual over a short space of time; finally, a distinction is often made between a position or job, and a role, with most workers having multiple roles in any job. An individual, for instance, may be designated as hotel human resource manager, and have a responsibility for a wide range of activities including staff selection, promotion, and dismissal, for the implementation of current industrial statutes, for occupational health and safety within the hotel, as well as having a general responsibility for staff motivation, retention, and productivity.

A number of commentators (e.g. Wanous 1992) have developed schemas that suggest various stages within the socialization process, such as that of anticipatory socialization, accommodation, and then role management. Anticipatory socialization involves those many experiences encountered prior to taking up a hospitality position, yet having the effect of preparing a person for the position. A primary purpose of activities at this point involves the acquisition of both information and attitudes about the new position and its industry context. Individuals generally desire to know as much as possible about the hospitality organization and industry in which they will work. It is suggested that people in this phase are constantly monitoring their perceived suitability for the intended position; individuals often seek out information and then translate it to their circumstances, though not always accurately or thoroughly. This is a process that regularly reoccurs in any hospitality career, such as at major decision-points like promotion, transfer, organizational restructuring or redundancy. Organizational recruitment programs can play a vital role in socialization; Woods (1999) suggests that hospitality organizations need to sell to prospective employees the many advantages of working for their organization in the same way that they might market their product. If such programs are effective, new hospitality employees are more likely to experience feelings of realism and congruence. Accurate expectations about a job are held much more likely to lead to realism and congruence among new hospitality workers after their appointment.

The second stage of socialization is encountered when the person becomes a new member of the hospitality organization; it is at this point that the job may be seen in a fresh and more realistic light. A variety of activities are typically employed so as to encourage the individual to become an energetic participant in the functioning of the hotel or resort, as well as a competent and loyal member of the workgroup. In this stage stress can often be experienced by the new recruit; anxiety, engendered by the uncertainty and novelty of the context, can play a major role. Those individuals experiencing realism and congruence as a result of their anticipatory stage experiences are said to suffer less stress at this point in the process. It is, however, the case that stress, albeit at a moderate level, is rarely absent from any new staff member; the demands of a new role in the hospitality industry do present previously unencumbered situations and challenges that evoke strain in many.

Within the accommodation stage individuals are expected to establish new relationships with both co-workers and superiors. They are required to learn the various tasks associated with their role. They are, moreover, expected to develop an understanding of the hospitality organization in which they are employed, including their place and function *vis-à-vis* the various elements of the organization. Finally, there is an expectation that a self-monitoring of process will occur, and that the individual will readily seek out assistance when required. If these challenges are successfully negotiated, the individual is likely to perceive approval and acceptance on the part of their supervisors; they will also likely perceive a level of personal competence in the performance of their new job. Other positive outcomes of a successful negotiation of this stage include the clarification of role definitions and the perceived congruence as between themselves and co-workers in respect of the person–environment fit estimation. Thus a new hospitality industry employee may perceive a growing understanding of their designated function within the hotel, and also have a sense of the degree to which other more experienced employees recognize their successful socialization into the hotel's workforce.

Role management, according to commentators such as Payne and Cooper (2001), sees the individual confronting a broader set of issues, often involving a set of potential conflict situations which might exist within any hospitality organization. Two conflict situations in particular may present themselves: Conflict between the demands of work life and home life, and conflict between the new employee's workgroup and other workgroups within the hospitality organization. A major source of potential conflict is between the person's work and home life, with judgments constantly being made regarding the apportionment of time and energy devoted to the job and to the family. Both contexts may actively press their claim for a major share of the person's time. New hospitality industry employees who are unable to resolve this situation in some satisfactory manner risk conflict and distress arising, particularly at times such as the early socialization phase of a job wherein long and stressful hours may be required. Long-term conflicts in this phase may even force the person to leave the position, or indeed the hospitality industry altogether. Conflict in the role management stage involving the new person's workgroup and also other workgroups within an organization will see competing demands of loyalty, of time, of resources, and of effort placed upon the new hospitality worker; if not resolved, this source of conflict can also lead to chronic work stress later in the socialization process which, if not minimized or reduced to manageable proportions, could render the new hospitality employee less than productive and contented.

The idea of norms has been regarded as pivotal in the understanding of work socialization. Norms are shared group expectations in respect of desirable work behavior. Whilst roles may define what is expected in any position, norms define what is acceptable individual, group, sectional or even organizational conduct within the hospitality industry; roles thus may be seen to differentiate jobs, whereas norms serve to maintain that conduct deemed appropriate in any aggregate within an organization. Norms, moreover, are generally unwritten *dicta* that strongly regulate hospitality workplace conduct. Schultz and Schultz (2002), and Payne and Cooper (2001) are among those who suggest that norms have several essential components. First, there is an 'oughtness' about them, a quality similar to that of an ethical precept. Norms also encapsulate desirable behavior for an aggregation of people, as compared to individual conduct not primarily regarded as social or organizational in nature, and individual conduct regulated by law, formal codes of conduct or private ethical values. Norms are generally regulated and enforced at group level; expected hospitality workplace behavior within the group domain is often closely monitored, particularly among newer members, with implementation sanctioned by work group agreement.

The communication and establishment of norms is said to follow a multi-phase process (Dipboye *et al.*, 1994). The first step involves the articulation of the norm to the new hospitality employee in the socialization process; this is usually achieved within the context of the verbal interaction, and also by story telling and by modeling through behavior-display. An example of this may be observed in the recounting of stories by more experienced staff concerning the successful handling of problematic or angry guests. Monitoring of the newly employed is the second step; this is done so that longstanding members of the organization are able to make a judgment as to the effectiveness of the socialization process in the internalization of norms. Finally, the group of more experienced hospitality workers dispenses or withholds rewards for successful socialization and incorporation of norms. Conformity to the norms may be rewarded by way of both psychological and physical means,

and will often include the expression of approval and friendship, as well as the sharing of more tangible benefits that might be at the disposal of the group of more senior hospitality industry employees. Punishments can also be administered if a new employee is judged to have offered resistance in the adoption of group norms, and may take the form of exclusion from communications, of insulting or hostile remarks, and even by means of physical aggression in some cases.

An increasingly important issue within the socialization process, particularly for industries such as hospitality, is that of employee diversity. The idea of diversity may be understood as that considerable array of physical and cultural variety constituting the spectrum of human difference; a number of core dimensions of diversity are recognized, including age, ethnicity, gender, physical attribute, and sexual orientation. Such core human attributes can have a lifelong positive impact upon behavior and work styles. Valuing diversity, from a hospitality management perspective, can mean understanding and utilizing those dimensions different to oneself. In a globalized industry such as hospitality, an increasingly important goal ought to be the understanding, appreciation, and incorporation of a diversity of individuals within the future hospitality industry (Woods, 1999). The socializations process, as it involves an ethnically diverse workforce, may be viewed as reciprocal; not only must the hospitality manager learn about the employee's cultural background, but the new employee has a need to learn about the customs, the rituals, and the values of the organization within which he or she now works. The provision of awareness workshops and also orientation sessions is regarded as vital for new employees and also for those who are managers and co-workers. Global competition in hospitality demands of managers that they learn more about unfamiliar cultures, customs, and countries from which new employees come. An awareness of and pride in cultural heritage is now regarded as an advantage, both to the worker and also to the organization; it is thus not indicative of a failure of the socialization process, but rather a sign of the encompassing breadth of the workforce that will meet the needs of an industry whose clientele is more diverse and international that ever before. Commentators such as Holjevac (1999), Pizam (1999), and Woods (1999) have all suggested that an appropriately trained and productively functioning workforce will be a principal determinant of success for the hospitality industry of the future. A socialization process that is inclusive of diversity (Woods, 1999; Pizam, 1999), comprehensively educates (Sigala and Baum, 2003), evokes commitment and empowers (Hancer and George, 2003), and embraces quality of life dimensions (Pizam, 1999) will optimally serve the hospitality industry and its employees.

References

Dipboye, R.L., Smith, C.A., and Howell, W.C. (1994) *Understanding Industrial and Organizational Psychology.* Fort Worth, TX: Harcourt Brace College Publishers.

Hancer, M. and George, R.T. (2003) Psychological empowerment of non-supervisory employees working in full-service restaurants. *Hospitality Management,* 22 (1), 3–16.

Holjevac, I.A. (2003) A vision of tourism and the hotel industry in the 21st century. *Hospitality Management,* 22 (2), 129–134.

Payne, R.L. and Cooper, C.L. (2001) *Emotions at Work.* Chichester: John Wiley & Sons.

Pizam, A. (1999) Life and tourism in the year 2050. *Hospitality Management,* 18 (4), 331–343.

Schultz, D. and Schultz, S.E. (2002) *Psychology and Work Today.* Upper Saddle River, NJ: Pearson Education.

Sigala, M. and Baum, T. (2003) Trends and issues in tourism and hospitality higher education: visioning the future. *Tourism and Hospitality Research,* 4 (4), 367–376.

Wanous, J. (1992) *Organizational Entry: Recruitment, Selection, Orientation and Socialization of Newcomers.* Reading, MA: Addison-Wesley.

Woods, R.H. (1999) Predicting is difficult, especially about the future: human resources in the new millennium. *Hospitality Management,* 18 (4), 443–456.

GLENN ROSS
JAMES COOK UNIVERSITY, AUSTRALIA

Soft branding

The term 'soft branding' in the hotel industry refers to a branding strategy of independent hoteliers who wish to maintain their uniqueness, yet also wish to gain immediate positioning and credibility through a branded affiliation. They are able to deepen relationships with their existing customers, acquire new markets through the 'soft' brand's global distribution systems, as well as benefit from other marketing services that are normally only enjoyed by hotels that are part of larger, more standardized hotel groups. The Leading Hotels of the World, Steigenberger Reservations Service (SRS), Preferred Hotels and Resorts, Small Luxury Hotels, and Relais and Chateau all are considered 'soft brands.' These brands all have standards for membership, connectivity to electronic channels of distribution, sales initiatives, marketing programs, and participation in trade shows.

The term soft branding was first used in 1991 by Slattery (Connell, 1992) to refer to middle-of-the-road branding strategies of large hotel chain companies that found it difficult to achieve a strong consistent brand offer across all of their properties. This initial usage of this term 'soft branding,' which again referred to lower levels of product and service consistency within the same hotel company, was in contrast to 'hard branding' that referred to those hotel chains that had very consistent and highly standardized products and services. This was especially the case with those hotel chains in the US with new buildings and centralized purchasing as well as access to a fairly homogeneous workforce.

However, unlike the more pejorative term 'soft branding' of 1991, the term today refers to a certain desired inconsistency that is a common attribute promoted as individuality by the affiliation companies. These companies, however, still have specific brand identities with which an independent hotel can match its offer as well as controlled quality standards to ensure credibility for the hotelier.

All this is important because to reach optimal levels of standardization is a challenge due to the unique nature of providing a satisfying hotel experience that is oftentimes a high involvement and emotional purchase with intense and unpredictable human interactions. In Europe, for example, the challenge of achieving consistency in a chain hotel offer is even more formidable where many existing hotels are located in historical areas restricted by building codes, impacted by local economies, and constrained by regulations concerning standards for official hotel categories. This can be further complicated by cultural differences between the staff as well as within the customer segments. In contrast to the US, the hotel market in Europe is still dominated by small and medium-sized independent hotels within a fragmented market with customers that are not always seeking standardization. Therefore, more and more independent European hoteliers have been joining third party affiliations, consortia, and branded distribution companies which are again oftentimes referred to as 'soft branding' companies.

'Hard branding' still refers to large hotel chains that have highly standardized products. From the point of view of independent hoteliers who are less interested in maintaining their individuality, 'hard branding,' in the form of franchising or management contracts, also provides an opportunity for a competitive advantage in an increasingly more branded industry worldwide.

References

Connell, J. (1992) Branding hotel portfolios. *International Journal of Contemporary Hospitality Management*, 4 (1), 26.

Swig, R. (2000) *Independent Hotels: The New Brand Alternative*. Retrieved from http://www.hotel-online.com/Trends/Swig/Swig_Independent Brand.html.

SONJA HOLVERSON
ECOLE HÔTELIÈRE DE LAUSANNE (EHL),
SWITZERLAND

Software

Software is the general collective term used to describe the methods of using and controlling computers. The four main task-related categories based on the type of operating instructions provided are language software, system software, applications software, and network software. Language software provides computer programmers with a set of commands to write programs. System software includes operating systems and programs that support applications software. It controls the allocation and use of hardware resources such as memory, central processing unit (CPU) time, and disk space. Applications software comprises the programs that perform tasks computer users want to do, such as hotel reservations or client billing. Network software enables computers to communicate with each other to perform tasks such as program and data sharing or interpersonal message transmissions; this allows personnel from different departments to work together more effectively. Integrated hospitality systems which combine reservation systems (CRS), property management systems (PMS), catering information systems (CIS), back office systems, and ancillary systems for example, telephone or energy management systems, are widely used effectively to satisfy the needs of guests and hotel management.

References

Buhalis, D. (2003) *eTourism*. Harlow: Pearson.

Buhalis, D. and Schertler, W. (eds) (1999) *Information and Communication Technologies in Tourism*. New York/Vienna: Springer.

O'Connor, P. (1999) *Electronic Information Distribution in Tourism and Hospitality*. New York: CAB International.

PETER SCHOFIELD
UNIVERSITY OF SALFORD, UK

Solvency ratios

Solvency is the ability of a business to pay its debt. While liquidity ratios measure a business's ability to deal with short-term obligations, solvency ratios, therefore, measure a business's ability to pay its long-term debt. Long-term solvency is normally measured by four ratios: debt ratio, debt–equity ratio, capital gearing ratio, and interest coverage ratio.

The *debt ratio* is expressed in a percentage form of a business's total debt over its total assets:

$$\text{Debt ratio} = \frac{\text{Total debt}}{\text{Total assets}}$$

It is generally preferable to have this number in the region of 40–50%. The reason is that there are only two main methods to finance the assets of a business: If the assets are not financed by debt, they must be financed through equity. Consider the following:

$$\text{Total assets} = \text{Total liabilities} + \text{Total equity}$$

$$\$100,000 = \$45,000 + \$55,000$$

$$\text{Debt ratio} = \frac{\text{Total debt}}{\text{Total assets}}$$

$$= \frac{45,000}{100,000}$$

$$= 45 \text{ or } 45\%$$

Thus, if the debt ratio is 45%, the equity portion of the business must be 55%. This means for every $0.45 of assets that is financed through debt, the business has $0.55 of equity to pay off the debt.

This leads to the second solvency ratio, the *debt–equity ratio*, which is expressed as a multiple:

$$\text{Debt–equity ratio} = \frac{\text{Total debt}}{\text{Total equity}}$$

If there is less debt than equity, the ratio will be less than one. If there is more debt than equity, the ratio will be larger than 1.0. It is better to have a debt-equity ratio of less than 1.0. Using the previous 45% debt example, the result of the debt-equity ratio will be 0.45/0.55 or 9/11 or 0.82. If a debt–equity ratio is 1.0 that means for every dollar of debt there is a dollar (equal amount) of equity to cover such debt.

The *capital gearing ratio* is also known as the capital structure or leverage ratio. A business obtains capital through debt or equity and these two numbers are reported distinctly on the balance

sheet. Long-term debt is a liability while equity represents the investment of the owners. The capital structure ratio is therefore obtained by dividing long-term debt by the total capitalization of the business (owner's equity and long-term debt).

This ratio measures the degree to which a business depends on borrowed capital as compared to total capital. Generally, when the long-term debt exceeds 40% of total capital, the structure may become unsatisfactory. As the level of debt increases, the probability of obtaining future loans diminishes as the risk to lenders increases.

Capital gearing ratio

$$= \frac{\text{Long-term debt}}{\text{Owner's equity} + \text{Long-term debt}}$$

$$= \frac{\text{Long-term debt}}{\text{Total capitalization}}$$

Current liabilities	
Accounts payable	$1,000,000
Accrued payable	1,500,000
Notes payable	500,000
Income tax payable	2,000,000
Current portion of long-term debt	5,000,000
Total current liabilities	$10,000,000
Plus	
Deferred income taxes	$ 5,000,000
Long-term liabilities	25,000,000
Total liabilities	$40,000,000
Stockholder's equity	
Common stock	$3,800,000
Paid-in-capital	41,200,000
Retained earnings	15,000,000
Total equity	$60,000,000
Total liabilities and equity	$100,000,000

$$\text{Capital gearing ratio} = \frac{40,000,000}{100,000,000}$$

$$= 40\%$$

The *interest cover ratio*, also known as interest coverage or times-interest-earned, indicates how adequate the earnings of a business are to cover the obligations of bond/debt/loan interest.

The higher this ratio, the better the business is able to meet its interest payment.

$$\text{Interest cover ratio} = \frac{\text{Income from operations}}{\text{Interest}}$$

or:

$$\frac{\text{Earnings before Interest} + \text{Tax}}{\text{Interest}}$$

or:

$$\frac{\text{EBIT}}{\text{I}}$$

If Hotel A has earnings before interest and tax for the past period at \$10,000,000 and its interest expense was \$1,000,000, then the interest cover ratio would be:

$$\text{TIE} = \frac{10,000,000}{1,000,000}$$

$$= 10 \text{ times}$$

This ratio is expressed as a multiple form. In this case, Hotel A has a TIE of 10 times; that means it can pay its interests 10 times over with earnings before interest and tax.

References

Coltman, M.C. and Jagels, M. (2001) *Hospitality Management Accounting*, 7th edn. New York: John Wiley & Sons.

Harris, P.J. and Hazzard, P.A. (1992) *Managerial Accounting in the Hospitality Industry*, 5th edn. Cheltenham: Stanley Thornes.

Kotas, R. and Conlan, M. (1997) *Hospitality Accounting*, 5th edn. London: International Thomson Business Press.

Owen, G. (1998) *Accounting for Hospitality, Tourism and Leisure*, 2nd edn. London: Longman.

Schmidgall, R.S. (2002) *Hospitality Industry Managerial Accounting*, 5th edn. Lansing, MI: Educational Institute of the American Hotel and Lodging Association.

AGNES LEE DEFRANCO
UNIVERSITY OF HOUSTON, USA

Speaker

A person described as a speaker may be: an individual of interest or stature who can speak to the theme of the event and who presents a session on a specific topic or topics, including a convention keynote address; a general session or seminar leader, who is a topic specialist; or a trainer or workshop leader, who facilitates for group participation and interaction. A change of pace speaker may be a humorist, entertainer, sports figure, or industry insider, whose speech may be educational or interactive. Types of speakers best suited for meeting audiences include humorists, athletes, futurists, economists, local executives, politicians, media personalities, authors, etc.

When selecting a speaker the most important factors to keep in mind are the purpose and/or objective of the meeting, the message that is to be communicated, the audience mix (gender, age, socio-economic background), and the audience interest. Other factors to be considered are date, time, budget, and approximate attendance.

Speakers should be invited based on their expertise on the subject, their contribution to the program, and appropriateness for the audience, and because the person is an accomplished orator.

There are several methods that can be used for finding speakers. Speakers' bureaus, which are professional brokers or agents that represent many speakers, are one of the most important sources. Agents and speakers' bureaus have very extensive databases. Other sources include volunteer speakers, who may be members of the organization, word of mouth, other conferences and meetings, professional journals, unsolicited proposals from speakers and the Internet – online database, searchable by name, topic, location and fee structure.

How are speakers selected? By calling people whose opinion is respected, looking up biographies on the Internet or in *Who's Who* or by calling someone who knows the speaker or has a business relationship with him/her. Before booking, one should preview the speaker in person either by seeing him/her in action at another conference or by requesting a videotape of a recent live presentation. Other information that should be obtained from potential speakers includes: the extent to which they have addressed similar groups, the names of recent sponsoring organizations, biographical information, and photographs.

The speaker should be given notice in writing (with a copy to be initialed and returned) of the date, time, and place of the engagement. It is imperative to specify in writing whether the speaker should attend any function before or after the presentation, such as photo opportunities, interviews, and to make sure that this expectation is within the parameters of the fee and the travel schedule. Other items that should be communicated in writing to the speaker are:

- The meeting's theme
- What is expected of them
- The terms of the honorarium and expenses (including what if any expenses will be paid to the spouse or assistant if they attend the meeting).

Meeting planners should request from the speaker – in writing – a list of audiovisual equipment or other items the speaker may need and how the room should be set up. One should keep in mind that all technical or audiovisual requirements add extra costs.

In introducing the speaker, it is very important to pronounce the speaker's name correctly. This can be achieved by providing the phonetic pronunciation of the name to whoever is making the introduction. It is also important to spell the speaker's name correctly in the program and to read the introduction as written.

References

Connell, Barbara, Chatfield-Taylor, Cathy, and Collins, Martha C. (2002) *Professional Meeting Management*, 4th edn. Chicago: Professional Convention Management Association Foundation.

Goldblatt, Joe and Nelson, Kathleen (2001) *The International Dictionary of Event Management*, 2nd edn. New York: John Wiley & Sons.

Krug, Susan, Chatfield-Taylor, Cathy, and Collins, Martha C. (1994) *Convention Industry Council*

Manual, 7th edn. McClean, VA: Convention Industry Council.

SUZETTE EADDY
NATIONAL MINORITY SUPPLIER
DEVELOPMENT COUNCIL, USA

Special events management

The special events management field is an exciting, growing industry throughout the world. It attracts professionals who possess creative talents as well as organizational skills. As long as there have been groups of people, there have probably been special events. Events celebrate human triumphs and milestones. Events celebrate past, present, and future lives and all of the accomplishments and bittersweet moments that accent life's journey.

The event management profession descended from the field of public relations. Public relations are a major part of the marketing mix. And, according to the Public Relations Society of America (PRSA), event management is one of the fastest-growing and most important trends in the public relations profession.

Event management is a profession that requires public assembly for the purpose of celebration, education, marketing, and reunion (Goldblatt, 2002). The event management process includes the research, design, planning, coordination, and evaluation of events.

Event management is a multidisciplinary profession. The elements of most events are basically the same: entertainment, decorations, lighting, sound, special effects, catering and, quite often, transportation. Therefore, employment in the field of special events management crosses over into many hospitality positions in hotels, food and beverage, tourism, and meetings and conventions.

Event professionals enjoy a work environment where no two days are ever the same. They are in the business of creating and customizing events for clients who are in search of an interesting, unique, and memorable experience (Allen, 2000). Events also have the ability to reflect and mold our society. Hallmark events (sustainable, revivable events) such as the Olympics and the football

World Cup have become important milestones in shaping cultures around the globe.

Many event planners/producers are small business owners and, therefore, categorize events according to markets. Classifying events in this manner helps entrepreneurs focus on niche markets. The most common event markets are association, corporate, casino, cause-related, fairs, festivals and parades, retail, social, sporting, and tourism. Corporations typically spend the most money on events, but the largest market, by far, is the social market. This is because it encompasses life cycle events such as birthdays, bar/bat mitzvahs, weddings, anniversaries, and funerals.

Association events

Associations are incubators for events of all types, serving the myriad purposes for which associations exist, including leading the way for other types of event planners towards attracting participation and public awareness (Hoyle, 2002). Examples of association events are awards presentations, political rallies, community service, as well as the installation of officers/leaders, training programs, conventions, expositions, and seminars.

Corporate events

Corporate events are sponsored by a corporation for the purpose of achieving specific goals and objectives and include celebratory events such as product introductions, customer appreciation, grand openings, topping off parties, and incentive programs. The international corporate event market is the fastest-growing arena in the event industry (O'Toole and Mikolaitis, 2002).

Casino events

Special events are a huge part of the marketing that takes place in casino/hotels today. In addition to corporate events that occur on the property such as topping off parties, grand openings, and anniversaries, special events are used to attract and reward casino players. Events such as

boxing matches and rock concerts are used to attract the highest level of VIP players, while high roller parties are often utilized as a customer appreciation tool.

Slot clubs and tournaments help to increase revenue during slow periods, build customer loyalty, and develop a customer database. Slot tournaments are a perfect example of how the casino uses special events as a marketing tool. Players are encouraged to join slot clubs, where they are given a membership card. This card is used to track each member's play – number of hours and dollars spent playing the slots on the casino's property. It also has a built-in reward system that allows the customer to earn points towards meals, shows and hotel rooms, as well as receive VIP treatment.

Casino club members are invited to participate in slot tournaments, which are held monthly at most casino properties. The tournaments are highly themed, with a high-ticket prize at the end of the tournament. The tournaments have become highly competitive between casino properties, relying on the 'next' creative theme to attract players to the tournaments. The tournament ends with an awards banquet that includes themed entertainment and food.

Harrah's casinos are known for having the most sophisticated rewards program in the gaming industry because its database is linked to all Harrah's Entertainment properties nationwide. Harrah's Total Rewards card offers three levels of membership: Total Gold, Total Platinum, and Total Diamond.

Cause-related events

Many nonprofit organizations raise a huge portion of their monies from fundraising events. The Association of Fundraising Professionals (AFP) represents 26,000 members in 167 chapters throughout the United States, Canada and Mexico. The AFP has educated fundraisers for more than 40 years, while promoting philanthropy and ethical fundraising.

Make-A-Wish Foundation grants the wishes of children with life-threatening illnesses to enrich the human experience. Ronald McDonald

House Charities have awarded more than $320 million in grants worldwide. Their mission is to make an immediate and positive impact on as many children as possible by creating, funding, and supporting programs that directly improve the health and well-being of children.

Retail events

The main purpose of retail events is to introduce/sell merchandise to prospective customers. Promotions are used to attract buyers and increase sales. During the 1960s and 1970s, retail establishments could attract thousands of consumers to their stores via one-day events that included the appearance of soap opera stars and athletes. Today, retailers rely on marketing research to design long-range promotional events that use an integrated approach to attract consumers on a steady basis. Theme-restaurants are experiencing a tremendous growth. Diners in Las Vegas, New York, Orlando, and Los Angeles have as many as ten theme-restaurants from which guests can choose when visiting these destinations.

Retail establishments are utilizing special events and entertainment techniques not only to attract, but also to keep customers shopping in their stores. A well-conceived store with an entertainment focus typically sells 60% more merchandise (Miller & Associates, 2002). Recent developments include the Sony Metreon complex in San Francisco where shoppers can enjoy the maximum of entertainment and events with 15 movie screens, an Imax theater, eight restaurants, a large number of retail stores and attractions that would rival any amusement park; and The Mall of America, the first to develop the concept. The $625 million, 4.2 million square foot complex was designed to resemble a flattened 'X,' with the theme park in the center of the complex.

Sporting events

Sporting events have the ability to bring lots of visitors, and, therefore, lots of money into a community. According to the Metro Atlanta Chamber of Commerce, the total economic impact of the 1996 Olympic Games was $5.1 billion, with total out-of-state visitor spending being approximately $1.15 billion (Miller & Associates, 2000).

Sporting events are a perfect platform for corporate sponsorship. However, no other single event in the United States is more attractive to corporate America as the Super Bowl. In fact, Las Vegas shares the economic impact of the Super Bowl each year. In 1999, Las Vegas attracted 250,000 visitors for the Super Bowl compared to 150,000 out-of-towners in Miami, where the Super Bowl was hosted.

Fairs, festivals, and parades

Fairs, festivals, and parades provide many opportunities to bring communities together to celebrate various cultures and interests through performances, arts, crafts, and socializing. These events are often used to boost tourism dollars. The Kentucky Derby Festival attracts 1.5 million visitors, while the Rose Bowl Parade attracts 1 million visitors for that one-day event. New York's largest street festival, the San Gennaro Feast, featuring sausage sandwiches, calamari, pasta, to name but a few, takes place in Little Italy every September.

The Travel Industry of America (TIA) reports that more than 31 million adults attended a festival while on a trip away from home. Additionally, the Ohio Department of Tourism reports that special events are the leading motivator for Ohio day-trip tourists and overnight travelers. The TIA study revealed that event travelers traditionally travel as families, are college graduates, and have two or more wage earners in the household.

Social events

The social or life cycle market continues to grow as health conditions improve and people live longer. There was a time when celebrating a fiftieth wedding anniversary was quite rare, and today it is almost commonplace. Celebratory events such as ones that recognize the passage of time are usually ritualistic in nature.

These life cycle events are so important to clients. Today, many weddings are becoming up-scale themed events that may last for days. In 2001, an award-winning wedding was produced at a Las Vegas casino resort property that utilized 32 florists, and a 4000 man-hour set-up crew to carefully attend to the bridal couple's every wish at a cost that exceeded one million dollars.

Tourism events

Communities that do not have the facilities to attract larger events are turning to tourism events to attract visitors. Redevelopment projects are reviving many of the downtown areas of American cities after the four-decade exodus of businesses to suburban shopping centers and malls. With the redevelopment projects and funding, comes the opportunity for creating tourism events. According to the 1999 study by the Travel Industry Association of America, one-fifth of adults visited a special event (fair, festival, other) while on vacation.

One of the biggest trends in the event industry today is the merging of corporate and public events. This is accomplished through many forms of sponsorship. Sponsorship dollars, goods, or services are rendered in exchange for a return on investment (ROI). In an era of dwindling public funding for the arts, corporate sponsorship of museums is rising rapidly. In addition to the arts, corporate sponsorship plays an increasingly important role in public events. Corporate sponsorship of festivals was approximately $777 million in 2001. According to the International Events Group (IEG) sponsorship is the fastest growing form of marketing.

References

Allen, S. (2000) The future of event marketing. *Event Solutions*. September.

Goldblatt, J. (2002) *Special Events: Twenty-first Century Global Event Management*. New York: John Wiley & Sons, pp. 5–6.

Hoyle, L.H. (2002) *Event Marketing: How to Successfully Promote Events, Festivals, Conventions and Expositions*. New York: John Wiley & Sons, pp. 130–133.

Miller, R.K. and Associates (2002) *The 2002 Entertainment Cultural and Leisure Market Research Handbook*. Norcross, GA. Richard K. Miller & Associates, Inc.

O'Toole, W. and Mikolaitis, P. (2002) *Corporate Event Project Management*. New York: John Wiley & Sons, p. 1.

KATHY NELSON
UNIVERSITY OF NEVADA, LAS VEGAS, USA

Special markets

Special or niche markets have always had a prominent place in the meetings industry. These markets consist of two primary categories – *government* and *SMERF* (defined below). When combined with the two most prominent market segments – corporate and association – they make up the total mix of the meetings industry. For clarification, a market segment is the 'categorization of people, organizations or businesses by professional discipline or primary areas of interest for the purposes of sales analysis or assignment' (APEX Industry Glossary).

The term 'special market' in this case should not be confused with the same meetings industry term identifying 'Foreign countries with high potential for US travel, but without a USTTA office. US promotional activities under the guidance of Visit USA Committees. Often with the cooperation of the U.S. and Foreign Commercial Service, an agency of the US Commerce Department' (APEX Industry Glossary).

Specifically, special markets include government meetings as well as the components of a meetings industry acronym SMERF, identifying the category of meeting marketing segments consisting of *social, military, education, religious, and fraternal*. It is clear from the type of segments involved, this market encompasses much of the nonprofit sector. In general these groups hold meetings and events that are very similar to those of trade and professional associations – conventions, board and committee meetings, training and educational seminars.

- *Social meetings* are defined as 'life cycle celebrations such as weddings, bar/bat mitzvahs, anniversaries, birthdays' (APEX Industry Glossary) and class or family reunions. In addition, social clubs, fundraisers or society events also comprise this category. In many cases, volunteers, or friends and members of the family, plan most of these events with a growing number of professional of planners specializing in fundraising, family, and class reunions.
- *Military meetings* attract attendees who are affiliated with one of the armed services, or are suppliers to the armed forces. The fastest growing component of this segment is the military reunion held for the veterans of various divisions, companies or crews of the armed forces. In many cases these events are held in the towns and cities of the military bases nearby.
- *Education meetings* are those events designed for elementary, high school, and college faculty and administrators, education supporters and vendors, school sports groups, and academic disciplines where original research and opinions are shared on a given area of study and interest. Every state in the United States has a teachers' or education association holding one-day or weekend conferences, and in most cases educators are required to obtain continuing education credit by attending various classes.
- *Religious meetings* are so prominent a market segment that the industry has an association solely for religious meeting planners. The inter-faith Religious Conference Management Association (RCMA) was founded in 1972, and has over 3000 members (http://www.rcmaweb.org/). With international, national, state-wide, and district-wide organizational structures and memberships, this segment requires a wide variety of venues – from 40,000 seat arenas to small break-out rooms. Religious organizations may require their meeting planners to have a familiarity with the faith and an understanding of specific rituals and rites.
- *Fraternal* is defined as those groups where membership is based on common personal interests rather than common job or career responsibilities. Such groups as Rotary International, Lions or Elks Clubs, college fraternities and sororities, or socio-political groups such as the National Organization for Women, the National Rifle Association or the World Wildlife Federation help train their members and volunteers, build a sense of community and help to further their cause, issue or concern.

The SMERF market is much like the association market with their marketing approach to potential attendees. Attendees are often members of the organization and also non-members and/or persons with close relationships to the organization. In addition, the trade press and students and families involved in the concern or interest of the organization may be involved. In nearly all cases, attendance to the event is voluntary. Because of this, SMERF groups must provide an appealing program to attract registration. Advance notice of dates, locations, topics, program, speakers, and special events must be provided a number of times prior to the event through direct mail, advertisements, broadcast fax, email, and websites. Registration fees and procedures must be established and communicated while costs are kept low.

While each of the SMERF groups are unique to themselves, they all have three things in common:

- They tend to be very price conscious and sensitive.
- They often book meetings during the 'low' or off-season (over weekends, holidays or when demand by corporations and associations is not at its peak).
- Their meetings are often managed by volunteers who change from year to year, or from location to location of the event.

However, SMERF organizations with larger and/or complex events are increasingly turning to professional planners for their logistical and contractual expertise.

Today many hotel groups now refer to the SMERF market as a primary or special market since they fill in those dates with business not usually booked by associations or corporations. To capture this business, many hotels have sales personnel designated to sell specifically to these particular markets.

In a category unto itself, and separate from the SMERF market, is the government market segment. Government meetings bring together attendees who are civil servants, elected officials or service providers to governmental entities. (APEX Industry Glossary). These meetings are held by the agencies or departments of city, county, state or province, national or international governments. It is in this category that quasi-government meetings, such as political party conventions or lobbying groups, can also be found.

A variety of government meetings are held for the purpose of employee training, interdepartmental or inter-agency operations and programs, agency meetings with the public, legislative hearings, and retreats. Government agencies might also be involved in legislative or policy-making events. One aspect of government meetings are 'governmental conferences,' defined as technical or political events between governments with the aim of discussing national or international topics (APEX Industry Glossary).

As with the religious groups, government meetings are such a specialty that planners of government meetings have formed their own professional society – Society of Government Meeting Professionals (SGMP). Founded in 1981, the organization has over 2700 members (http://www.sgmp.org) and is primarily a US-based organization.

SMERF and government meetings remain a critical component of the hotels' marketing mix. While these groups tend to spend less overall than the corporate or association markets, these 'special markets' fill in the gap over holidays, during a soft season, and on weekends, providing properties with much needed revenue, and hotel employees with work during a downtime.

References

APEX (Accepted Practices Exchange) Industry Glossary of the Convention Industry Council. Retrieved 27 July 2004 from http://glossary.convention industry.org/alphSearch.asp?term = s.

Astroff, M.T. and Abbey, J.R. (2002) *Convention Management and Service*, 6th edn. Lansing,

MI: Educational Institute of the American Hotel and Lodging Association.

Feiertag, H. (2003) Hotels need to get a share of the SMERF market. *Hotel and Motel Management,* 218 (9), 12.

Fenich, G.G. (2004) *Meetings, Expositions, Events, and Conventions: An Introduction to the Industry.* Upper Saddle River, NJ: Pearson/Prentice-Hall.

McGee, R. (2004) Getting a fix on SMERF. *Association Meetings,* 16 (2).

WILLIAM R. HOST
ROOSEVELT UNIVERSITY, USA

Staging guide

A 'compilation of all function sheets, scripts, instructions, room set-up diagrams, directory of key personnel, forms, and other material relating to the event' is the definition of a staging guide provided by the Convention Industry Council's Accepted Practices Exchange (APEX) Terminology Panel.

A Meeting and Exhibition Specification Guide is a key component of the staging guide and is comprised of three sections:

- *The narrative*, a general overview of the meeting
- *Schedule of events*, a timetable outlining all functions that compose the overall meeting
- *Meeting event orders* (function sheets) detailing the requirements for each specific event within the meeting.

These specifications are sent to the facility 30 days prior to the meeting so the facility's convention service manager can communicate the meeting's needs to their staff.

While some planners design staging guides to be as simple as a series of check-off sheets (one for each function), others add components such as:

- Scripts that provide the written text of speakers' presentations
- Room set-up diagrams that illustrate the visual plan of each room's layout and equipment
- A directory of personnel, which will include the contact information for the organization's staff and volunteers, the facility staff and suppliers

- Forms used for the event, which might include registration form and schedule of fees; attendance history; an audiovisual flow chart showing the use of equipment throughout the day in various meeting rooms; budget; packing and shipping lists; VIP information and schedules; etc.
- A production schedule that provides a minute-by-minute timetable of the actions to be taken by various staff during the event.

The meeting planner uses the staging guide to maintain the smooth flow of the logistical and programmatic aspects of the meeting. Some planners refer to this collection of documents as their Bible or as the Production Manual.

References

Connell, B., Chatfield-Taylor, C., and Collins, M.C. (eds) (2002) *Professional Meeting Management.* Chicago: Professional Convention Management Association.

Convention Industry Council (2001) *Preliminary Report of the APEX Terminology Panel.* Retrieved from Convention Industry Council, Accepted Practices Exchange, website: http://www.conventionindustry.org/apex/Panels/Termin ology_Prelim_Report.htm.

WILLIAM R. HOST
ROOSEVELT UNIVERSITY, USA

Standard cost accounting in foodservice

Cost accounting relates the expenditure of a foodservice organization to its food and beverage sales. Cost accounts, while they can be directly related to financial accounts, are concerned with the detailed make-up of cost in identifiable output for purposes of pricing, budgeting, control of food and beverage production and service, purchasing and control of food and beverage materials, and control of labor expenditure, rather than the overall financial results of the foodservice operation.

In a standard cost system, the following accounts are always recorded at budgeted cost: food and beverage held in inventory, finished food and beverage inventory, and cost of food and beverage sold. Hence, if actual costs exceed budgeted costs the variance is unfavorable, while if actual costs are less than budgeted costs, the variance is said to be favorable. The calculation and entry of variances can be as follows:

1. Direct food and beverage materials variance equals actual direct food and beverage materials cost minus budgeted direct food and beverage materials cost.
2. Direct food and beverage materials quantity variance equals (actual quantity minus standard quantity) times standard cost.
3. Direct food and beverage materials price variance equals (standard price minus actual price) times actual quantity.
4. Show the journal entry to record the direct food and beverage materials variances.
5. Direct labor cost variance equals actual direct labor cost minus standard direct labor cost.
6. Direct labor time variance equals (actual hours minus standard hours) times standard rate.
7. Direct labor rate variance equals (actual cost per hour minus standard cost per hour) times actual hours.
8. Show the journal entry to record the direct labor variances.
9. Foodservice overhead variance equals actual foodservice overhead costs minus budgeted foodservice overhead costs.
10. Show the journal entry to record the foodservice overhead variance.
11. Show the entries to complete the standard cost accounting cycle, e.g. to record finished food and beverage goods or to record cost of food and beverage sold. Variance accounts are closed to the Cost of Goods Sold account.

Standard cost accounting has its opponents. Like most other business enterprises, foodservice operators aspire to run lean and efficient operations; however, in order to identify how lean a foodservice operation is or must be, the foodservice manager's reporting needs to move away from cost accounting, which has over the years evolved to measure profitability across a range of food and beverage products or outlets within a food-service organization. For example, in a batch-and-serve production environment such as some quick service restaurants, cost accounting tracks food and beverage inventory transactions as large batches of food and beverage goods move from the production process to the production/service process. It identifies the value added to these food and beverage materials and attempts to quantify budgeted rates as to how much labor and overhead should be absorbed into the financial statement, recording unfavor-able variances when production is under-uti-lized. There are instances, for example in large catering operations, where overproduction occurs in response to under-utilized production, and this is what a leaner approach to running foodservice operations attempts to eradicate. As the organization becomes more lean and cost-efficient, one can say that it should produce food reasonably closely to its occupancy or customer demand. Food production areas, which complete and serve all food-in-production batches, can greatly reduce inventory to the quantities of food and beverage moving through production and service to customers. In such a case, complex tracking and valuation mechanisms may no longer be necessary. Even though one has to have an inventory valuation, this can be done in a much simpler way. Once the foodservice opera-tion becomes lean, the inventory of food and beverage and non-food and beverage products can be reduced to their most optimum levels, which greatly reduces the need for tracking transactions. In addition, cost accounting does not always clearly show the tangible benefits of lean strategies such as improved production and labor planning, additional production capacity, better cash flow, and reduced storage space.

Reference

Epstein, M.J. (1978) *The Effect of Scientific Management on the Development of the Standard Cost System.* Manchester, NH: Ayer Company Publishing.

JAKSA KIVELA
THE HONG KONG POLYTECHNIC
UNIVERSITY, HONG KONG SAR, CHINA

Storage

Protecting a foodservice organization's invest-ment in inventory depends on its having effective and efficient storage facilities. Storage is a vital function that is given too little attention: Well-planned and well-managed storage areas encour-age employee productivity, reduce product loss, and improve food safety.

Storage needs vary depending on the scope and size of an operation, its menu offerings and level of service, anticipated meal volumes, the fre-quency of deliveries, and the configuration of the building. A small, chef-run restaurant in a busy urban area may require only modest refrigerated and ambient temperature storage rooms off the kitchen, while a large resort hotel in a remote loca-tion may need thousands of square meters of temperature-controlled and ambient storage for a wide range of food, beverage, service, and support products. For this reason, storage requirements for an individual operation should be determined by that facility's distinctive characteristics.

In general, storage for foodservice operations can be classified into three distinct groups: temperature-controlled storage such as refrigera-tors, freezers, and wine rooms; ambient tempera-ture (or 'dry') food storage for bulk goods and packaged items that do not require refrigeration; and non-food storage, typically for service ware, utensils and cookware, paper goods, linens, and cleaning supplies. The wise foodservice operator keeps food storage separate from non-food stor-age to ensure food safety and control access to valuable inventory.

Temperature-controlled storage may take the form of reach-in refrigerators and freezers located near the point of use, or a chilled room commonly called a *walk-in*. For storing most food products, a temperature of 36–40 °F (2–4 °C) is typical, although the amount of humidity required for optimal storage of items such as fresh fish or produce varies and thus operations with large volumes of these ingredients tend to have dedicated refrigeration for each product type. Frozen items must of course be stored at temperatures well below 32 °F (0 °C), requiring a separate storage area. It is common, particularly in smaller operations, for a frozen storage walk-in to be connected to and accessed from a refrigerated walk-in as a way of saving energy. Chilled storage rooms at temperatures of 50–60 °F (10–15 °C) may also be employed for storing wines, or for aging specialty cheeses or meats.

Dry storage areas for food and non-food items are best positioned near the point of use, which unfortunately is impractical when space is at a premium. Many operations divide these storage areas in two, with a small 'day use' storage area in the kitchen and larger storage facilities elsewhere in the building that are ideally accessed only once or twice a day. Within the scope of the entire space of an operation, storage areas should be carefully integrated with employee work stations whenever possible as a way of increasing productivity and reducing fatigue.

The ideal foodservice storage area is readily accessible from both the receiving area and the kitchen. In large operations, designers try to adopt a 'forward-flow' model (Kotschevar and Terrell, 1986) that allows supplies to move into storage at one end and out the other, into preparation and cooking areas, and from there to customers. This approach keeps kitchen staff separated from non-kitchen areas, limiting the potential for cross-contamination.

Important features of an effective storage area include sturdy shelving that makes optimal use of the volume of space available. The best storage shelving is adjustable, wheeled for easy removal for cleaning, and, if located in humid areas, resistant to corrosion. Good shelving also allows airflow around the products being stored, which is why many operations choose wire or slatted shelf units. Foodservice shelving may be purchased in a variety of lengths and heights, typically in some multiple of 15 cm, and in a range of widths, although for many operations a width of 60 cm (24 in.) is optimal as it readily accommodates typical pan sizes as well as cases or loose packaged products. Most health codes require that all food products and food contact materials be stored a minimum of 15 cm (6 in.) off the floor, favoring low racks for large, bulky items as well as more traditional storage shelves.

Lighting in storage areas needs to be bright and uniform, and should be shielded to protect products in case of a damaged lamp or bulb. In all storage areas, adequate airflow and protection from extremes of temperature or humidity need to be provided. Choosing the right floor and wall finishes will make storage areas easier to clean; tile or industrial composite floors are ideal in most storage areas, while epoxy paint is appropriate for dry storage area walls. Refrigerated storage space is typically pre-fabricated from panels, which may be steel-coated at the factory with enamel or made of stainless steel, an expensive but long-lasting and effective choice. Lastly, many operators choose to control access to storage areas, particular those areas holding valuable inventory such as alcohol or meats.

When planning a foodservice operation, management should consider storage not only for food, beverages, and service ware, but also for items that are rarely considered but are inevitably required in the course of business. These might include parts and supplies for kitchen equipment, media and receipt tapes for point-of-sale systems, festive decorations, soiled linens, or surplus furniture. Storage areas for such items are often created out of 'found space,' which may be functional but is rarely optimal.

Reference

Kotschevar, L.H. and Terrell, M.E. (1986) *Foodservice Planning: Layout and Equipment*. New York: Macmillan.

STEPHANI K.A. ROBSON
CORNELL UNIVERSITY, USA

Strategic choice

Strategic choices relate to decisions about the future of an organization and how it should respond to environmental pressures and influences (Johnson and Scholes, 2002). According to Evans, Campbell and Stonehouse (2003), strategic choice involves three stages:

1. Formulating options for future development
2. Evaluating available options
3. Selecting which options should be chosen.

As a result of the complexity of the environment, scope and scale of many hospitality and travel and tourism organizations, it is common to distinguish between various levels of strategic choices: corporate level, business level, and operational (or functional) levels. Accordingly, there are numerous strategic options to consider. For example, at the business level, i.e. staying within the realm of hospitality, it is possible to consider cost leadership, differentiation or focus strategies. A multibrand or segment hospitality organization may choose among strategies such as diversification, vertical integration or merger and acquisition. Clearly, it may choose to concentrate within the hospitality business.

Most normative approaches to strategic choice emphasize the requirement that the chosen strategy take advantage of environmental opportunities, while attempting to avoid threats. At the same time, the choice should be based on organizational strengths and unique resources that will result in a sustainable competitive position.

References

Evans, N., Campbell, D., and Stonehouse, G. (2003) *Strategic Management for Travel and Tourism.* Amsterdam: Butterworth-Heinemann.

Johnson, G. and Scholes, K. (2002) *Exploring Corporate Strategy*, 6th edn. Harlow: Pearson Education.

ARIE REICHEL
BEN-GURION UNIVERSITY,
ISRAEL

Strategic configurations

The theme in configurations is that organizational effectiveness is not attributable to a single factor, but the intercorrelation between a number of factors. Performance is thus seen as dependent upon the development of a compatible mix of organizational characteristics – a configuration – for example, a particular blend of structure, culture, and management style.

The researcher most closely associated with configurations is Miller, who focused upon

developing archetypes of strategy formation based on published studies (see Miller and Friesen, 1984). Later work, introduced the argument that change in organizations is not an incremental process, but a quantum one whereby many elements are changed concurrently – a strategic revolution.

This 'quantum theory of change' is a sharp contrast to the idea of the learning organization and its view that change is a continuous process involving small incremental adjustments. This is a controversial area in strategic management and can be paralleled with the debate in biology between Stephen Jay Gould's theory of punctuated equilibrium and the orthodoxy as represented by Charles Darwin's concept of evolutionary change.

Lashley and Taylor (1998) developed a series of configurations, or 'ideal types' for matches between the style of human resources management (HRM) in hospitality organizations and the specific nature of the service offer. This research was later extended to include operations and marketing in addition to HRM. It therefore highlights the general focus by looking for identifying compatibilities across a broad range of organizational characteristics.

References

Lashley, C. and Taylor, S. (1998) Hospitality retail operations types and styles in the management of human resources. *Journal of Retailing and Consumer Services*, 5 (3), 153–165.

Miller, D. and Friesen, P.H. (1984) *Organizations: A Quantum View.* Englewood Cliffs, NJ: Prentice-Hall.

J. STEPHEN TAYLOR
UNIVERSITY OF STRATHCLYDE, UK

Strategic direction

A strategic direction is essentially those policies required to provide a clear mandate for action, whether at the individual firm or at the community and government level. For example: a hotel may require a business strategy for investment, comprising of options identification and project requirements definition; while an industry organization may need to seek stakeholder consensus on issues and opportunities in order to set direction and define a framework for resolution in a policy/strategy document. Equally, a government, region, or city may wish to create a master plan for development of the hospitality industry within its territory.

A strategy will be embodied in an existing business approach (to customers or to suppliers), or may be developed in response to issues identified in relation to the development of a new approach to the management of the hospitality industry. Simply put, a strategic direction determines where an organization is going over the next year or more, how it is going to get there and how it will know if it got there or not. The focus is usually on the entire organization, while the focus of a business plan is usually on a particular product, service or program. There are a variety of perspectives, models, and approaches used to create strategic directions. The way that these are developed depends on the nature of the organization's leadership, its culture, the complexity of its environment, its size, and/or the expertise of planners and the other human resources it can call upon (Ansoff, 1987). For example, there are goals-based, issues-based, organic, and scenario modeling methods. Goals-based strategy development is probably the most common and starts with focus on the organization's mission (and vision/values), goals, strategies to achieve those goals, and actions (who will do what and by when). Issues-based strategy development often starts by examining issues facing the organization, strategies to address those issues, and possible action plans to address them. Organic strategy development might start by articulating the organization's vision and values and then developing action plans to achieve the vision while adhering to those values. Some strategies are scoped to one year, many to three years, and some to five to ten years into the future. Some include only top-level information and no action plans.

Quite often, an organization's strategic planners already know much of what will go into a strategic plan (this is true for business planning, too). However, development of the strategic direction greatly helps to clarify an organization's plans and to ensure that key leaders are all 'on the same wavelength.' Thus often far more important than the strategic direction, is the strategic planning process itself (Tourism Council of Australia, 1998; McNamara, 2004). Nevertheless, a good strategic direction is one that has a real impact on day-to-day decision-making and ultimately leads to business success. The criterion of business success, however, means that a business may have to wait from one to three years to say with any certainty that it has been achieved. The success of any strategic direction also depends on the people designated to carry it through. Despite how obvious this statement is, many management teams fail to consider its implications. If a strategic direction is to have a solid impact on the success of a business, it must be seen by all stakeholders to be desirable, believable, and useful for getting real work done. Failure to meet these criteria will almost certainly lead to an elegant set of direction statements that may be largely ignored.

What then is a desirable strategic direction? In simplest terms the direction set by an organization must meet the needs of all stakeholders and do so in a way they value. Each stakeholder group will define its needs in different ways depending on the relationship it has with the organization. Shareholders, for example, will look for the return on their investment while employees will look at the impact the direction will have on their jobs. Industry analysts, on the other hand, will look for clarity and the ability of the organization to implement the proposed direction. Managers and planners should begin by identifying who the stakeholders are and understanding what they need. The challenge then becomes one of addressing these needs, which does not mean that a different direction should be created for each group. Rather, a direction might be positioned differently for each stakeholder group if that is seen as desirable. The starting point is clearly to describe the business rationale underlying the strategic direction and its potential impact on stakeholders.

In creating a strategic direction, management is making a public commitment to what they see as necessary for success (Cooper and Erfurt, 2002). Any such claim needs to be believable. For example, a goal to 'Achieve $10 billion in room sales in two years' proposed by a hotel chain that currently has only $50 million in sales could safely be said to have little credibility. Such unbelievable goals are commonplace and are usually based on an attempt to have a direction that is truly desirable. Regardless of how desirable a direction may look, however, stakeholders will quickly compare it to the organization's track record and capabilities before investing time, money or energy in achieving it. Finally, the direction must be useful. A simple test of any strategic direction is to ask when it was last used to make a business decision. For organizations where the answer to this question is 'Never,' it can be predicted that strategic direction will fall by the wayside in favor of *ad hoc* responses to daily issues (Ansoff, 1987).

References

Ansoff, H.I. (1987) *Corporate Strategy*, rev edn. London: Penguin.

Cooper, M.J. and Erfurt, P.J. (2002) Ecotourism accreditation: a planning tool for Asia–Pacific countries? In K.-S. Chon, V.C.S. Cheung, and K. Wong (eds), *Proceedings of the 5th Biennial Conference on Tourism in Asia*, Hong Kong, 23–25 May. University of Houston: Haworth Hospitality Press, pp. 115–125.

Tourism Council of Australia (1998) *Code of Sustainable Practice*. Sydney: TCA.

MALCOLM COOPER
RITSUMEIKAN ASIA PACIFIC UNIVERSITY,
JAPAN

Strategic evaluation

The strategic evaluation process assesses whether the organization is achieving the desired performance and following the correct path to remain competitive into the future. Evaluation takes place at all levels of the firm. Managers obtain clear, thorough and accurate information from the frontline and throughout the organizational hierarchy. By synthesizing this information, managers compare actual outcomes with expectations established during the strategy formulation stage. The evaluation process creates a feedback loop to assess the success of implemented strategies and action plans. Poor performance usually indicates that something has gone wrong at the formulation stage, implementation stage or both. This feedback from the formulation, implementation, and evaluation cycle may become a learning process to improve planning systems or the implementation process to ensure greater success in the future.

Hospitality organizations' strategies and competitive methods should be evaluated on a frequent basis. Performance is traditionally assessed using quantitative measures such as profits or cash flow but should also be evaluated on more qualitative measures such as customer satisfaction or employee turnover rates. Managers should consider whether or not these levels of performance are satisfactory and whether they will continue at the current level into the future.

References

Olsen, M., Tse, E., and West, J. (1998) *Strategic Management in the Hospitality Industry*, 2nd edn. New York: John Wiley & Sons.

Wheelen, T.L. and Hunger, J.D. (2000) *Strategic Management and Business Policy*, 7th edn. Upper Saddle River, NJ: Prentice-Hall.

ROBERT HARRINGTON
NICHOLLS STATE UNIVERSITY, USA

Strategic formulation

Strategic formulation is the process of determining a value-based strategy that considers external opportunities and threats as well as internal capabilities and constraints. This process has generally been perceived as an analytical approach, driven by formal structure and planning systems. An on-going debate in the strategy literature has been the question of whether strategy formulation is a rational and comprehensive process (the deliberate view) or a more incremental and trial-and-error type of approach (the emergent view) (Farjoun, 2002).

The deliberate perspective is based on an early view of strategic management that assumes a predictable environment and perfect foresight by managers. The ideas underpinning the emergent approach to strategy formulation reflect the idea that strategy formulation is both a learning and maneuvering process, which allows managers to respond to the vagaries of a dynamic environment. As such, a change between what was intended (deliberate formulation) and what strategies are realized represents emerging changes. Realized strategy can be conceptualized as the combination of deliberate components (intentions defined in advance) and emergent components (the level of replacement and additive strategies) (Mintzberg et al., 1998). Consequently, an assessment of the deliberate-emergent nature of a firm's strategy formulation process should include factors that capture the complex nature of this phenomenon.

References

Farjoun, M. (2002) Towards an organic perspective on strategy. *Strategic Management Journal*, 23, 61–594.

Mintzberg, H., Ahlstrand, B., and Lampel, J. (1998) *Strategic Safari*. New York: The Free Press.

ROBERT HARRINGTON
NICHOLLS STATE UNIVERSITY, USA

Strategic groups

A strategic group is 'the group of firms in an industry following the same or similar strategy along the strategic dimensions' (Porter, 1980, 129). Strategic dimensions are essentially those decision variables which underpin the business strategies and competitive positioning of the firms within an industry. These include product market scope, distribution channels, level of product quality, degree of vertical integration, choice of technology and so on.

Research into strategic groups has primarily focused upon analyzing the differences in profitability between firms. The expectation (in line with Porter's industry structural analysis theory) that profitability differences between firms within a strategic group would be less than the differences between strategic groups has not received robust empirical support. Nonetheless, as research by Reger and Huff (1993) has demonstrated, managers within an industry typically have consistent perceptions of groupings of similar firms and the concept of strategic groups has an intuitive appeal that seems to capture the structural texture of competitive rivalry with an industry.

Within the hospitality industry the value and relevance of the strategic group concept can be readily observed in the lodging sector. For example, in terms of market levels (or, if one prefers, product quality levels), the existence of clusters of brands is evident. Indeed, customers would typically be aware of which hotel brands are competing in the luxury market segment and which are competing in the economy market segment. As such, each cluster of brands represents a distinct strategic group within the lodging industry.

References

Porter, M.E. (1980) *Competitive Strategy*. New York: The Free Press.

Reger, R.K. and Huff, A.S. (1993) Strategic groups: cognitive perspective. *Strategic Management Journal*, 14, 103–124.

J. STEPHEN TAYLOR
UNIVERSITY OF STRATHCLYDE, UK

Strategy implementation

Strategy implementation means putting the formulated strategy into action in hospitality organizations. It may also be defined as carrying out essential activities to make strategy work. Strategy implementation in the hospitality management field is often treated as a tactical activity and it is usually taken into consideration after strategy has been formulated. However, lately it has started receiving more attention since it has been realized that in hospitality organizations the main difficulty is the implementation of strategies rather than the development of them. In their studies, Okumus (2001) and Schmelzer and Olsen (1994) identified a number of implementation variables/factors such as organizational structure, culture, programs, resources, people, communication, rewards and control and constructed strategy implementation frameworks for hospitality organizations. It has been emphasized that there should be a 'strategic fit' among the above implementation variables. However, Okumus (2001) found that strategy implementation is a complex and dynamic process in which achieving a fit among the implementation variables is almost impossible. Moreover, internal context of hospitality organizations, particularly organizational structure and culture, play a key role in execution of strategy and focusing on the implementation plan and ignoring the wider context does not provide a holistic picture of the strategy implementation process and its challenges.

References

Okumus, F. (2001) Towards a strategy implementation framework. *International Journal of Contemporary Hospitality Management*, 13 (7), 327–338.

Schmelzer, C.D. and Olsen, M.D. (1994) A database strategy implementing framework for companies in the restaurant industry, *International Journal of Hospitality Management*, 13 (4), 347–359.

FEVZI OKUMUS
THE HONG KONG POLYTECHNIC
UNIVERSITY, HONG KONG SAR, CHINA

Strategy marketing planning and the marketing plan

Strategic marketing planning is a management tool used to help determine where an organization is going and how it is going to get there. The strategic planning process attempts to address three core questions:

1) Where are we?
2) Where do we want to be?
3) How are we going to get there?

Typically, the process is organization-wide or focused on a major function such as a division or a department. At the corporate level, managers use strategic planning to determine in what businesses the company should compete. At the Strategic Business Unit level, strategic planning is focused on how to compete within the industry.

The situational analysis

The first stage of strategy planning involves answering the question, 'Where are we?' This stage requires a company to identify its strengths and weaknesses by looking internally at the organization and then to identify the current or potential opportunities and threats by scanning the external environment. This activity is referred to as a SWOT analysis or situational analysis. The strengths and weaknesses of a hospitality organization may be broken down into four categories: marketing, operations, finance, and human resources. Once the organization's strengths and weaknesses are identified, some sort of scan, or review, should be conducted of the organization's environment to include the political, social, economic, demographic and technical environment. The external scan may be further broken down into a microenvironmental scan and a macroenvironmental scan. The microenvironment would include suppliers, intermediaries, stockholders, bankers, and other financial institutions, media and ad agencies, customers, and competitors. These groups directly and indirectly affect organizational decisions. The macroenvironment includes various driving forces in the environment such as changing demographics, technological advancements, and economic conditions.

By matching the company's strengths and weaknesses with the micro- and macroenvironment, the company should be able to identify the current and potential opportunities and threats.

Once the SWOT analysis is complete, broad market opportunities can be identified. There are four basic categories of market opportunities available to a firm:

- Market penetration
- Market development
- Product/service development
- Diversification.

Goals and objectives

The second stage of the strategic planning process is to decide where the organization wants to be and to establish the overall mission and objectives that will guide the strategy. Drawn from the SWOT analysis and market opportunities, the organization's strategic goals and strategies to achieve the goals must be identified. This process involves identifying or updating the organization's mission, vision and/or values statements. Mission statements are brief written descriptions of the purpose of the organization. Mission statements vary in nature from very brief to quite comprehensive, but should state for whom the organization exists, what it is supposed to do for those groups, and how it plans to do it. Many people consider the values statement and vision statement to be part of the mission statement. Vision statements are usually a compelling description of how the organization will or should operate at some point in the future and of how customers or clients are benefiting from the organization's products and services. Values statements list the overall priorities in how the organization will operate.

Once the mission, vision, and/or value statements are established, corporate and marketing objectives should be stated. At the corporate level, objectives should specify the desired target return on investment. The marketing objectives focus on market share or other measures of sales. Objectives should be designed and worded as much as possible to be specific, measurable, quantifiable, timely, and attainable.

The marketing plan

The third stage of the strategic planning process involves creating a marketing plan. The marketing plan, or 'marketing strategy,' consists of identifying the target market and developing the marketing mix. Three target markets should be identified. First, the internal market, or employees, should be defined. For the internal marketing mix, the employee is the 'customer' and the job is the 'product.' The marketing mix for the internal target market must distribute, promote, and price the 'product' to the 'customer's' satisfaction. The second target market is the external consumer market. This group includes the customers or guests who will directly benefit from the service or product being offered. The third target market is the intermediary market, which would include travel agents, meeting planners, and tour operators. Each market segment must be precisely identified using geographic, demographic, and psychographic variables.

Once the target markets have been identified, the organization must define its positioning statement. The positioning statement defines the customer's perception of the total product in light of the other competitive product and service offerings. The positioning statement must be clear, distinctive, unambiguous, and understood by all employees of the organization.

The final step of the marketing plan is to develop the marketing mix. A separate marketing mix should be created for each identified target market. The marketing mix consists of the '4Ps' – product, promotion, place, and price. Within the product considerations, a list of all product and service offerings should be compiled and the core benefits of each product/service should be listed. Next, the tangible and intangible aspects of the products and/or services should be named.

As part of the promotion mix, promotion objectives should be clearly defined and the mix of advertising, personal selling, publicity, and sales promotion should be stated. Types of media usage, such as broadcast, print, and direct mail, should be identified in addition to the specific outlets, such as radio stations and magazines. The promotion budget should be determined and promotion ideas and themes should be discussed.

Under the place mix, the distribution objectives (exclusive, selective, or intensive) must be identified. The use and selection of intermediaries should be discussed as well as strategies for increasing relationships with intermediaries.

Finally, as part of the marketing mix, pricing objectives should be established. These objectives should include list prices, rack rates, package prices, and menu prices. Pricing policies concerning discounting, quantity, seasonal fluctuations, and price discrimination practices should also be discussed.

The strategic marketing planning process involves conducting a situational analysis, establishing goals and objectives, and developing a strategic marketing plan. An effective marketing plan should enhance the hospitality organization's strengths, help overcome internal weaknesses, take advantage of the opportunities in consideration of the threats, and contribute to the organization's goals.

Reference

Shea, L.J. (2004) Strategic Marketing Planning and the Strategic Marketing Plan. Unpublished working paper. Amherst, MA: University of Massachusetts.

JENNIFER T. CONDON
NEWMARKET INTERNATIONAL, INC., USA

Submetering

Submetering refers to the function of using additional meters, other than the main meters at the boundary of the building. The purpose of submetering is to identify where utilities are used. Without submetering, there can be no valid basis for operational control and cost allocation. Likewise, there can be no way to verify efficiencies and quantify savings.

In a hotel, submetering of electricity, steam, chilled water, hot water, and cold water are all practiced. The reduced cost of chilled water metering in the past ten years has made it viable to identify where air conditioning is being used down to the level of individual rooms.

Installing submeters is significantly cheaper when done during construction or major renovation, so decisions about submetering are best made prior to

these activities. Consistency of meter readings is generally more important than absolute accuracy.

ROBERT ALLENDER
ENERGY RESOURCES MANAGEMENT,
HONG KONG SAR, CHINA

Sustainability

Sustainability implies the protection and conservation of resources for future generations, as opposed to current users' undue depletion. Behavioral standards have been developed in an effort to assist tourism and hospitality operators in developing practical environmental impact monitoring measures, or to regulate their activities (Cooper and Erfurt, 2002). Within the hospitality industry such standards are usually self-regulated unless they are mandated by law, as for example in the fire protection and health areas of operation. Underlying mandated and voluntary measures is the realization that the natural environment is not static but is itself constantly undergoing change. However, in order to take this change into account operationally there is a need to develop flexible management regimes and hospitality enterprises that are responsive to change. As the market for environmentally sensitive facilities continues to expand on a worldwide basis it is vital that local businesses meet global expectations and standards associated with sound environmental and operational practice.

References

Cooper, M.J. and Erfurt, P.J. (2002) Ecotourism accreditation: a planning tool for Asia–Pacific countries? In K.-S. Chon, V.C.S. Cheung, and K. Wong (eds), Proceedings of the 5th Biennial Conference on Tourism in Asia, Hong Kong, 23–25 May. University of Houston: Haworth Hospitality Press, pp. 115–125.

Tourism Council of Australia (1998) *Code of Sustainable Practice*. Sydney: TCA.

MALCOLM COOPER
RITSUMEIKAN ASIA PACIFIC
UNIVERSITY, JAPAN

Switch companies

Global distribution systems (GDSs) are used extensively by travel agents to make reservations for airline seats and, to a lesser degree, hotel rooms. Switch companies (sometimes called 'universal switches') act as a bi-directional translator, converting electronic messages between the unique languages used by each of the four major GDSs and the large number of proprietary central reservations systems used by the hotel companies (and vice versa). Two major switch companies currently operate in the hotel sector – THISCO (The Hotel Industry Switching Company) and Wizcom. In the absence of a switch, each hotel company would have to develop costly individual interfaces between its CRS and each of the GDSs in order to make their product available to travel agents electronically. Using a switch means that only a single interface (between the CRS and the switch itself) needs to be developed to give access to all of the major GDS systems, thus saving valuable capital for the hotel company concerned. In addition to their core functionality, most switches provide a range of additional services to their users – for example, by centralizing the payment of commissions or other fees due or by including their properties on a consumer-oriented website.

References

Emmer, R., Tauck, C., and Moore, R. (1993) Marketing hotels using global distribution systems. *Cornell Hotel and Restaurant Administration Quarterly*, December, 80–89.

O'Connor, P. (1999) *Electronic Information Distribution in Hospitality and Tourism*. Wallingford: CABI International.

PETER O'CONNOR
IMHI (CORNELL – ESSEC), FRANCE

Switching costs

These are one-time costs facing a hotel or restaurant as it contemplates switching from one supplier's product to another's. Such costs may include direct expenses as a different purchase price, modifications in equipment used (such as having to change the hotel linen cart configuration to accommodate the changing sizes of amenities) plus any related testing and retraining expenses (Porter, 1980). Good customer or volume discounts, generated over time by combining different purchases, could be lost. Indirect costs such as building or ending relationships and time factors may also be involved. For instance, it takes time for the hospitality firm (as a customer) to learn the operating habits of a supplier, i.e., with whom to speak in order to more easily fulfill requests, delivery patterns, etc. If switching costs are high, the hospitality firm must perceive a major benefit to changing suppliers – but such a benefit would have to clearly outweigh the high costs involved in such a switch. Otherwise, the firm would likely remain with the current supplier. If switching costs are low, the hospitality firm may more readily change suppliers. The goal is to build relationships with customers so that they perceive large costs in changing suppliers and are thus encouraged to continue existing relationships (Burnham *et al.*, 2003).

References

Burnham, T.A., Frels, J.K., and Mahajan, V. (2003) Consumer switching costs: a typology, antecedents, and consequences. *Academy of Marketing Science*, 31 (2), 109–127.

Porter, M.E. (1980) *Competitive Strategy*. New York: The Free Press.

CHRIS ROBERTS
UNIVERSITY OF MASSACHUSETTS, USA

Systematic risk

Systematic risk is the stock volatility caused by the capital market volatility, or the covariance of stock return with market return. This type of volatility or risk cannot be eliminated via portfolio diversification because the volatility is due to factors that affect all securities such as changes in the nation's economy, tax reform by Congress, or a change in the world energy situation (Van Horne and Wachowicz, 2001). Even if an investor holds a portfolio consisting of all the stocks in the capital market, he or she will still be exposed to systematic risk. The non-diversifiability of systematic risk determines that it should be priced on the capital market. High systematic risk should be compensated by high return, and vice versa.

For an individual investing in a hospitality firm, the systematic risk of the firm is the relevant factor in determining his or her required rate of return within the Capital Asset Pricing Model (CAPM) framework. A hospitality firm's systematic risk, denoted as beta, is measured by the slope of the characteristic line that represents the sensitivity of the firm stock's return to the overall return of the capital market.

Reference

Van Horne, J.C. and Wachowicz, J.M. (2001) *Fundamentals of Financial Management*, 11th edn. Upper Saddle River, NJ: Prentice-Hall.

HYUNJOON KIM
UNIVERSITY OF HAWAII, USA

T

Table d'hôte

The literal interpretation of *table d'hôte* is 'table or offering of the host.' It stems from a bygone period when nobility and people of means entertained their guests in their homes. A contemporary table d'hôte or 'set' menu offers a fixed price for a limited number of courses and dishes. It can also be offered for a set dining period, e.g. lunch. Table d'hôte menus may change daily, weekly, or even monthly, and they may be used in rotation, as they are for cycle menus in on-site foodservice. Table d'hôte menus offer a complete meal of three or more courses with or without a choice of dishes in each course. Guests usually pay full price for all courses whether or not they consume all of them. Some foodservice operators who offer special gourmet table d'hôte menus for events such as Christmas dinner or wedding banquets require a deposit when making reservations.

Foodservice operators prefer table d'hôte menus because they are versatile and adaptable to different occasions; production costs are easier to monitor; food materials usage and sales estimates are more accurate; more time can be spent on high-quality production and service; and higher quality food materials can be purchased because of reduced food stock needs. It should be noted, however, that many foodservice operations offer a table d'hôte menu in conjunction with an à la carte menu, thus offering diners a 'fast-track' selection, a 'value-for-money' choice, menu items that are not featured on the à la carte menu, seasonal or regional food specialties, and promotional items.

Reference

Revel, J. (1982) *Culture and Cuisine*. Garden City, NY: Doubleday & Company.

JAKSA KIVELA
THE HONG KONG POLYTECHNIC
UNIVERSITY, HONG KONG SAR, CHINA

Tables per server

Tables per server numbers indicate how many tables are assigned to each server or server station in a foodservice operation. For example, if a restaurant has 50 tables, it may assign four or five tables to each server. Typically, fine dining restaurants assign fewer tables per server than casual dining restaurants and as a result offer a higher level of service. Some foodservice managers prefer assigning a certain number of seats to each server rather than assigning a certain number of tables. In this case, all servers might have a mix of 2-tops, 4-tops, and 6-tops, but would be serving approximately the same number of guests.

As Sanders, Paz, and Wilkinson (2002) point out, one of the major factors involved in determining the appropriate number of tables per server (or servers per table in rare situations) is the use of bussers. Bussers may be employed to simply clear and reset tables; such use increases somewhat the amount of time available for the server to spend with guests. Another approach is to use bussers for most other functions besides taking the guests' orders and delivering the food. In such situations, bussers must be more fully trained since their interaction with the guest is considerable.

Reference

Sanders, E., Paz, P., and Wilkinson, R. (2002) *Service at Its Best*. Upper Saddle River, NJ: Prentice-Hall.

SHERRI KIMES
CORNELL UNIVERSITY, USA

TCP/IP

TCP and IP are protocols governing the handling and the formatting of data in an electronic communications system; they are the main protocols used on the Internet. The messages (files) exchanged over the network are divided into small units (called packets) by TCP, while IP takes care of managing the actual delivery of the data. The routing needed to accomplish this is completely transparent to the user. All is needed in order to access another system is an 'Internet address' (called IP address), a 32-bit number, normally written as 4 decimal numbers. A specific service, called DNS (domain name service), provides a database containing the correspondence between numeric addresses and alphabetic domain names. TCP/IP uses the client/server model of communication in which a computer user (a client) requests and is provided with a service by another computer (a server). This is the case, for example, in which a consumer is asking to view a hotel website. TCP/IP protocols support services such as remote login to a computer, file transfer (FTP), electronic mail and the World Wide Web. In the hospitality industry, beside these applications, many internal networks are using TCP/IP protocols to connect not only computers, but also other electronic equipment.

References

Loshin, P. (2003) *TCP/IP Clearly Explained*, 4th edn. San Francisco, CA: Morgan Kaufmann.

Tanenbaum, A.S. (2003) *Computer Networks*, 4th edn. Upper Saddle River, NJ: Prentice-Hall.

RODOLFO BAGGIO
BOCCONI UNIVERSITY, ITALY

Telephone systems

Telephone systems are used to link people together within an organization, and to the outside world. Most hotels provide telephones in guestrooms, which allow guests to ring reception or other numbers within or outside the hotel. The system usually has a private automated branch exchange (PABX) where calls are received, perhaps by a receptionist, and then transferred to the appropriate person within the organization. Many systems allow 'direct dial-in' (DDI) so that calls can be made direct to the correct extension without being processed by the receptionist.

Hotel telephone systems allow guests to make calls, recording details automatically and passing charges to the guest's bill. With the increased use of mobile phones, and the premium rates often charged by hotels, there may be reduced demand for voice telephony. However, there is a dramatic growth in the provision of Internet connections in guestrooms, allowing guests with laptop computers to access e-mail and Web browsers.

Telephone systems also allow a range of other facilities, including automatic wake-up calls and voicemail for guests. The telephone system often links to the property management system (PMS), allowing cleaners to notify the PMS that a room is clean. The PMS can also direct the telephone system to bar calls from unoccupied rooms.

References

O'Connor, P. (2000) *Using Computers in Hospitality*, 2nd edn. London: Cassell.

Smith, J. (1990) *Practical Computing – A Guide for Hotel and Catering Students*. Oxford: Butterworth-Heinemann.

JOHN NIGHTINGALE
LEEDS METROPOLITAN UNIVERSITY, UK

Tennis professional classifications

In the private club industry within the United States the importance of obtaining a certification from the United States Professional Tennis Association (USPTA) cannot be overstated. USPTA's Career Development Program offers tennis teachers three certification levels, culminating with the master professional designation.

To earn the *Professional 1* designation the individual must be 22 years or older, have successfully passed the certification exam at the Pro 1 level or higher, hold a score of 4.5 on the National Tennis Rating Program (skills test), and have three or five seasons of full-time instructional experience.

An individual holding the *Professional 2* designation must be at least 18 years old, have successfully completed an apprenticeship program or an equivalent combination of experience, successfully passed the written examination at a Pro 2 or higher, and passed the National Tennis Rating Program at 4.0 or higher.

To hold a *Professional 3* designation and individual must be at least 18 years old, have passed the written certification examination at the Pro 3 level or higher, must hold a National Tennis Rating Program score of 4.0 or higher, but is not required to have tennis-teaching experience.

The *Master Professional* must hold a Professional 1 designation for a specified period of time, have maintained continuing education hours and completed a variety of service activities as recognized by the USPTA. To receive this designation, the tennis pro must submit an application to the Master Professional review board of the USPTA for ratification and certification.

Reference

http://www.uspta.org/. Accessed 28 January 2004.

CHIEMI YAGI
UNIVERSITY EDUCATION CENTER,
UNIVERSITY OF THE RYUKYUS, JAPAN

Tennis tournaments

The importance of tennis to private clubs received its biggest influx during the 1970s when the game of tennis was at its pinnacle. As a result of this changing societal trend private club operators have been slow to add additional tennis facilities within private country club facilities. Nonetheless, for the tennis enthusiast tennis tournaments are essential to maintaining their needs for competition, social bonding, physical invigoration, and fitness concerns. The common tournaments offered at private clubs are (a) men's and women's singles, (b) men's and women's doubles, and (c) mixed doubles. To make any of these tournaments a success, the tennis pro should engage the tennis committee in securing the use of the courts for tournament play, confirming that the tournament will be sanctioned by the United States Tennis Association, deciding the hours of play, deciding which courts will be used for the tournament and which courts will remain accessible to the members, arranging publicity (if this is to be public event), and ensuring that all registrant information is completed in advance and so that rosters of play can be established. The tennis pro, tennis committee, and tennis director play a critical role in organizing the event, matching the players, establishing event timing, recording and supervising of the tournament, and finalizing the event via a tournament banquet with resultant public relation events being planned as well.

References

Perdue, Joe (1997) *Contemporary Club Management*. Lansing, MI: Educational Institute of the American Hotel and Motel Association.

White, Ted and Gerstner, Larry (1991) *Club Operations and Management*. New York: Van Nostrand Reinhold.

ARAM SON
JAMES COOK UNIVERSITY,
AUSTRALIA

Third party planner

A third party planner can be described in a couple of ways:

An independent meeting or event professional provides event or meeting services for a third party, meaning a corporation, a nonprofit, a educational institution or an association, as an outsourced vendor.

Or, another definition created by a group of meeting industry peers, describes the broader business perspective of third party planners:

Independent meeting professionals are small business owners, individuals or third party representatives that are contracted to assist, in whole or in part, in the arrangements of client meetings, events, conferences and/or exhibitions.

They may be self-employed and/or operate a division within a company specifically designed to administer various facets of design, planning, strategic consultation, support services and/or logistics for meetings, conferences, and/or exhibitions.

Two examples of third party planner applications follow:

- The meeting department of a major association based in Washington, DC regularly hires a third party to handle the details of an annual awards banquet held during the annual convention. The third party is responsible for inviting the individual award winners, the evening logistics and production, handling RSVPs separate from the convention's registration process, ordering flowers, décor and the actual award plaques, and scripting the evening's schedule. The head of the meeting department is thrilled with the consistency of the third party and saves on staff expense. He only pays for the specific service: the awards banquet.
- A Fortune 500 company has a complete meeting, travel, and event department. However, the senior VP of marketing is budgeting for a single sales and marketing retreat for his senior managers and has retained a third party, separate from the negotiated agreements within the organization, to manage the site selection process. The third party is responsible for managing the process, identifying the audience, prospecting destinations, soliciting venue availability, and negotiating a value based contract. The cost of this service is covered by a commission paid by the venue to the third party. This is a specific service that the independent will provide.

These are two, very different, examples of services provided by a third party planner; with two separate pricing models, yet both represent qualified, legitimate business within the meeting and event industry.

Third party planners types and services

The services that third parties perform range from managing small parts of an event (task or service specific), to the full service deliverable: 'soup to nuts.' Many organizations that have a small staff, choose to outsource their meeting or event services rather than hire and bring these services in-house.

Full service meeting or event planners are hired by their client organization to take the complete meeting from the very beginning – determining goals and objectives – to the end – the thank you letters and budget reconciliation.

In the case of *task or service specifics*, the third party planner may be contracted to perform a piece of the meeting or event. For example:

- Registration
- Housing only
- Site selection only
- Sponsorship development or fund raising
- Theme development
- Budgeting
- Premiums/gifts
- Menu planning/BEO (banquet event order) development
- On-site management
- Sports activities, tours, and recreation
- Agenda planning; program development

- Exhibit management
- Facilitation or training; or fundraising.

Often, a destination management company (DMC) is hired to perform specific pieces of a convention, like tours, spouse events, or other items specific to their city. They often have the best contacts in the city, can arrange for the best price and provide the greatest insight into the destination.

In international waters, a professional congress organizer (PCO) can perform those same services.

Why clients hire third parties

There seem to be two reasons that organizations outsource a meeting: either they do not have the talent within the organization to deliver the specific services needed; or the current meeting or event department is overwhelmed with other responsibilities.

In either scenario, third party planners are a great resource because they will have the skills necessary to step in and get the job done and yet will not be a competitive threat to the in-house planner.

How third parties charge for their services

In drawing up a budget for outsourcing meeting or event functions, there are a few guiding formulas that will assist in creating a framework for these costs:

- Commissions
- Service fees
  - per project
  - hourly
  - deliverables
- Cost of hiring an employee.

It is helpful to run the numbers in a variety of ways to gain a complete picture and thus arrive at the best decision.

Under a *commission* structure, a hotel pays the third party up to 10% (or more during value seasons) of the guestroom revenue generated by a meeting. Commissions are not usually paid on other revenue brought to a hotel or conference center, such as food and beverage, audiovisual or entertainment.

For example, if 75 attendees are staying at a hotel (each in a single room) for three evenings at $150 per night, the total guestroom revenue paid to the hotel will be $33,750 ($75 \times 3 \times \$150 = \$33,750$). The hotel could pay $3375 (or 10%) in commissions to the meeting management company.

Practices on accepting commissions vary among third parties. Some companies will not accept commissions under any circumstances. These companies feel strongly that clients may question their objectivity if they accept commissions. They believe that clients might think that they negotiate contracts with the vendor that pays the best commission, not the vendor that gives the client the best deal.

Some companies reduce their fee to the client by the amount of the commission. These companies see commissions as a way to provide extra savings to their clients, while still making a fair and reasonable profit. A third group of third parties views commissions as a way to increase their revenues, and accept the commission in addition to the client's fee.

Regardless of the compensation structure, thorough discussion about fees and commissions with the third party and their vendors is called for. As with any enforceable contract, agreements about commissions – such as when they are paid and to whom – should be in writing. It is also fair to discuss commissions and rebates from suppliers, asking the third party if they are compensated from any other sources.

Service fees are as straightforward as they seem – the client organization compensates the third party directly for its services. Service fees follow no standard formula, but there are several options:

- *À la carte pricing:* Based on the request for proposal (RFP), each service is given a price
- *Single price:* The entire scope of work is covered in a single price
- *Retainer:* The third party is paid a fee to guarantee that they will be available whenever the hiring organization needs the services
- *Service contract:* Negotiated contract (based on an RFP) regarding individual services that can be purchased over the course of a year.

This contract is renegotiated each year, *not* each meeting.

The third option is to consider what it would cost in terms of time, energy, and salary for personnel within the organization to manage this event, or to hire a third party onto the staff. Standard human resources formulas would consider the following as an annual cost:

	$
Salary higher-level	75,000
Benefits (35% of salary)	26,250
Overhead	10,000
Training and development	1,000
Total	112,250

SHELLEY T.I. HARRIS
THE HARRIS GROUP, USA

Timeshare financing

The development of a timeshare resort, otherwise known as a vacation ownership resort, is a capital-intensive operation from the outset that requires calculated and structured financing. The three predominant types of financing that are available to a timeshare developer are hypothecation, sales of receivables, and securitization.

Hypothecation

Hypothecation in the timeshare industry refers to the process of pledging an asset as collateral (security) for a loan. The most common usage is the phrase 'to hypothecate a mortgage,' which occurs when a borrower assigns rights to a piece of real estate (such as a hotel and the land on which it stands) or other asset (such as accounts receivable, inventory, etc.) to a lender. This asset, called the collateral, is pledged as security for a loan in addition to the promissory note (obligation to repay) that is signed by the borrower. If an asset is hypothecated, the loan is secured. If no collateral is pledged, the loan is unsecured.

In the event of a default (failure to repay) by the borrower on a secured loan, the lender has the right to seize the hypothecated asset (the collateral) and sell it, using the proceeds to repay the loan. In contrast, in the case of a default on an unsecured loan, the lender must take the borrower to court to force repayment. This may result in the borrower filing for bankruptcy protection, in which event the lender will have to wait for the bankruptcy court to determine how the remaining assets of the borrower will be divided among all of the unsecured creditors.

A single asset may be hypothecated to more than one loan. In this case, the first loan has a senior claim (first lien). The other loans have subordinated or junior claims (second lien, third lien, etc.). In the event of a default, the collateral is sold and the most senior loan gets repaid first. Subordinated claims get repaid in order and only if any proceeds remain. Once the proceeds from the collateral have been dispersed, any 'secured' lenders who have not been repaid in full must make a legal claim as an unsecured creditor. For this reason, subordinated claims provide less default protection for a lender.

Sales of receivables

Many timeshare businesses sell products and services to their customers on credit. As one example, hotels that host conventions often allow event sponsors 30 days or more to pay their bills. As another example, time share resorts often allow buyers to pay for their purchases through monthly payments made over a number of years rather than in full when the contract is signed. In both cases, selling on credit creates a receivable on the business's balance sheet and earnings on the business's income statement. Selling on credit does not, however, provide an immediate cash flow. Because businesses need cash flow to pay their own bills – the timeshare resort must pay its mortgage, its employees, and its utility bills and the timeshare resort must pay its employees and its building contractors – it may be desirable to sell receivables in order to raise cash. If a timeshare developer chooses to sell its receivables to create cash flow, it will need to make a decision; to whom to sell the receivables. A financier who specializes in the purchase of receivables is traditionally called a factor, and the sale is referred to as 'factoring the receivables.' The business may also be able to securitize certain types of receivables. Another issue to be resolved is the discount on the sale.

Securitization

Securitization in the timeshare industry is a process in which a number of financial assets (typically loans of some specific type) are sold to a legal entity called a special purpose vehicle, which then sells new securities to investors based on the assets it holds in trust. The group of loans owned by the special purpose vehicle is called the asset pool. The payments made to investors in these new securities come from the earnings of the loans in the pool. The securities created during a securitization are called *asset-backed securities* or ABS. The most common form of ABS are those created from one to four family residential (home) mortgages; these are called *mortgage-backed securities* or MBS. Other ABS are created from time share receivables, commercial real estate loans, home equity loans, automobile loans, student loans, and credit card receivables.

For lenders, the advantage of securitization is that it allows originators of loans (such as timeshare resort owners and other lenders) to sell assets that, individually, would be very illiquid (difficult to sell for an amount close to their underlying value). This allows the lender to specialize in originations, reusing the same capital over and over again as new loans are originated, sold for securitization, the proceeds of the sale used to originate a new group of loans, and so on. For example, a time share resort developer may be very good at developing a new resort, marketing it to potential buyers, evaluating the buyer's credit, and creating a receivable (loan) by which the buyer agrees to make monthly payments over a number of years. The developer, however, may not wish to have its capital tied up until the buyer makes the required payments. Securitization allows the developer to sell these receivables, take the profit from the project, and reinvest its capital back into a new resort.

Investors prefer to buy ABS rather than individual loans for two reasons. First, each ABS

share represents parts of each individual loan in the pool, so the ABS investor is well-diversified. If the investor instead bought individual loans, he or she would have to take care to build a well-diversified portfolio. Second, most ABS provide added default protection for investors. This may come from a third party insurer who agrees to make good on any defaults by the borrowers in the pool. Or the protection may come from over-collateralization, which occurs when the value of the individual loans in the pool is greater than the value of the ABS that are issued. It is also possible for a lender to sell loans to the pool with recourse. Selling 'with recourse' means that the original lender is liable if too many of the borrowers default. If the investor bought individual loans rather than ABS, he or she would have to evaluate the credit quality (the default risk) of each individual loan, an expensive and time-consuming task.

References

Anonymous (2000) Why can't my line do that? *The Kansas Banker*, 90 (11), 24–26.

Monroe, Ann (1985) Sales of receivables by big firms gain respect in public offerings, *The Wall Street Journal*, 2 December, p. 1.

Roever, W. Alexander and Fabozzi, Frank J. (2003) A primer on securitization, *Journal of Structured and Project Finance*, 9 (2), 5–17.

JAMES H. GILKESON
UNIVERSITY OF CENTRAL FLORIDA, USA

Timeshare industry

Timeshare ownership has made steps to become a mainstream travel product. The resilience of the timeshare market and continued growth based on number of units sold and the addition of an increasing number of national brands have placed the timeshare industry in a promising position. The legitimization of the timeshare industry by established brands has given timeshare an increasing amount of credibility. Currently only 12–15% of timeshares are brands, but this will change as major industry brands are looking for alternative sources of income. Sales have been driven up to nearly US$9 billion annually, with 6.2 million owners worldwide owning 9.9 million weeks.

The incentive of developing units as timeshares has been the availability of capital through financing. In a market where six out of ten timeshare units are financed through the developer by the timeshare owner, the cash-strapped hospitality industry is prompted to stand up and take notice. Currently, the enticement is the promise of longer stays at destinations. In a society that is opting for shorter vacations, vacation ownership is encouraging the lengthening of stays at individual destinations.

Development has increased in the more traditional timeshare venues (i.e. beach) and has found a new area in the emergent urban market. The leisure traveler desires more cultural options, entertainment, dining experiences, and shopping opportunities, which can be easily satisfied in a more urban location.

Growth has extended to the international arena, although to date Marriott Vacation Club International is the only international brand represented. Spain continues to be the dominant force in Europe, possibilities are being investigated in Eastern Europe and Asia. Timeshare exchange groups in conjunction with the World Travel and Tourism Commission are seeking to develop tourism policies that will help with the regulation of these emerging markets and will ignite development opportunities in these areas. There are currently 5300 resorts worldwide in 95 different countries with 1600 operating in the United States. There are 2.7 million timeshare owners in the United States and 6.2 million timeshare owners worldwide cementing the timeshare industry as a truly global concept.

The Caribbean, where there are currently 8500 timeshare units being planned, has become one of the most dynamic markets. Aruba, St Maarten, Dominican Republic, Puerto Rico, and the Bahamas have been the areas of biggest growth. The major impediment continues to be politics. Taxation and the complexities of some of the tax structures on some islands have created barriers to growth. Working with the governments to figure out amenable solutions to the tax structure and consumer protection issues will continue to be at the forefront in order to ensure that growth is not stunted in these areas.

Diversification is the rule instead of the exception in this vibrant industry. The types of units to be sold as timeshare have begun to be as diverse as the public purchasing them. The high end units sold by Four Seasons Hotels & Resorts and Ritz–Carlton Hotels have filled a niche of buyers looking to have a taste of luxury at a more reasonable cost and as the market opens there is room for more moderately priced resorts.

The traditional marketable beach location has been taken over by the desire to be close to attractions and entertainment in the United States. The largest number of new timeshares sold are attraction and entertainment locations (58%) followed by the beach locations (45%). These numbers indicate the increase in people wanting a fuller vacation experience by having the proximity to a selection of entertainment options and the opening of the timeshare market to locations that do not have close proximity to the beach.

The reasons behind purchasing timeshares units in the United States include the desire for flexibility. Overall flexibility – ability to use different locations, unit sizes, times of year, as applicable – was rated by 86% of timeshare purchasers as very important. Certainty of quality accommodations was rated 84%. Exchange opportunity with other resorts through an exchange company was rated 80%. Credibility of the timeshare company was rated 77% and liking the timeshare resort, amenities, or unit was rated by 72% as very important (Ragatz Associates, 2003; Pricewaterhousecoopers, 2002).

Less US consumers use their time at their home timeshare resort (34%) than the consumers that exchange for another location (54%). The remainder rent (4%) or give their unit away to friends or family (3%). This number indicates the ongoing necessity or effective, convenient exchange methods and the increase in demand for flexibility in the purchase of a timeshare.

The split-week use option has helped with the desired flexibility sought by US timeshare purchasers. Nearly 30% of current owners indicated that their unit was in a resort that allows them to split their week of time into two or more shorter stays. The hesitations about purchasing cover a wide range of reasons from the location of the resort to clarity of the exchange option. However, the primary reasons for hesitation to purchase include: possible future maintenance fee increase (65%), usually do not make same-day purchase decisions (63%), and price (59%). Developers will need to take today's more educated prospects into consideration in their sales practices. Price is second to being rushed to make a decision and having insurances of a stable fee payment system.

The growth has also been based on the increasing satisfaction of timeshare owners in the United States. More than half of the timeshare consumers were very satisfied with their purchase (55%), 29% were somewhat satisfied, and a minority (16%) were neutral, somewhat dissatisfied, or very dissatisfied.

Most timeshare owners are looking forward to their vacations. Seventy-seven percent of timeshare owners in the United States state that timeshare ownership has increased the degree that they look forward to vacations. The purchase of the timeshare has extended time spent on vacation. Sixty-nine percent believe it has increased the amount of time spent on vacation after the purchase of their timeshare unit. Finally, in a time where a prime motivator is education in one's travel experience timeshare ownership is proving to fulfill this need as well. Sixty-nine percent feel that their ownership has increased their learning experiences.

Most US timeshare owners own a timeshare in one resort (58%). However, an increasing number of people are buying timeshares in more than one resort. Twenty-eight percent own timeshares in two resorts and 14% own timeshares in three or more resorts. Also, 17% of the US timeshare buyers have expressed interest in buying more time in the same resort where they already own week(s). The trends indicate the number of multiple resort timeshare owners increasing thereby reiterating the positive experience that people are finding in their timeshare purchases.

The 'do not call' regulations have prompted timeshare developers in the United States to rethink their marketing tactics. Twenty-two percent of people who have made recent timeshare purchases stated that they found out about the resort via a telephone sales call. However, direct mail was mentioned by 19% of the people that had made recent timeshare purchases in listing how they had found out about the resort. This could prompt the need for a more dynamic mail campaign to alleviate leads lost through the loss of the telemarketing tool.

The resale of the timeshare unit is not the biggest part of the US timeshare industry. Although, it is about a $390 billion dollar business annually, consumer-to-consumer resales represent only 15% of the market.

The average price paid for an annual week of timeshare use in the United States has increased to $14,200 per week in 2003 from $8846 in 1997. These numbers show that not only has the US timeshare market been resilient in the post-September 11, 2001 economy, it has been thriving. The prices have been escalating at a rate of 3% annually and show no signs of slowing down.

Most timeshare buyers in the United States are female (54%), white (77%), married (56%), are 37 years old or older (57%), and have household incomes of $50,000 (63%). These numbers show that there is room for diversity amongst prospective timeshare purchasers. Education and a more cross-cultural marketing plan will only drive interest and growth in the timeshare industry. Currently, the family market is appealing based on the family-friendly atmosphere of timeshare resorts. However, by 2010 there is going to be a 29% decrease in the households with children under the age of 18 and the markets are going to need to reinvent themselves yet again. The sites that are built to be able to handle large families and have units that can become smaller through lock-off configurations will be the best bet to serve both markets.

The awareness of timeshares by people in the United States is increasing. Eighty-seven percent of households with incomes of $25,000 or greater have heard of timeshares. Sixty-eight percent of those people have a very positive, somewhat positive or neutral view of timeshares in the United States which reiterates a move in the right direction for this industry.

Most timeshare resorts in the U.S. are located in Florida (323), California (125),

South Carolina (119), Colorado (75), Hawaii (71), and North Carolina (59). As this industry matures the following states are entering the picture with greater numbers: Nevada (55), Missouri (49), Texas (49), Arizona (45), Massachusetts (45), and Virginia (40).

The expansion has been prompted by the positive impact timeshare resorts may have in the community. The result of the timeshare owner visiting more often and staying longer in a community has resulted in an increase in capital brought into the community. United States timeshare owners report that once a timeshare unit has been purchased the amount they personally spend in the resort area where their timeshare is located has increased 146% after purchasing. This is welcome addition to any community wishing to have a stable tourism economy fueled by an increase in visitation and a stabilized repeat visitation record.

The timeshare business in the United States pours $5.4 billion dollars annually into the collective communities where they are located. The average US travel party spends $1205 in the local economy during their visit on average. The maintenance of the timeshare properties in the United States contributes to the local economies as well. Annually timeshare owners pay $1.87 billion dollars in maintenance fees to maintain and operate their resorts. Much of this money is spent in the local community through contract work for repairs and other services needed to upkeep the resort property.

The constancy is key stable tourism economy that timeshare resorts bring in the United States. Ninety-two percent of the timeshare owners report using their unit themselves or allowing others to use their timeshare unit. High timeshare occupancy results in a strong year-round utilization of the product resulting in less seasonality which in turn strengthens the job market and the success of the local businesses in the United States.

The state of the timeshare industry throughout the world is promising and shows signs that it is a staple in the hospitality mix that is going to strengthen the hospitality and tourism industry's buying power, provide more options to the growing traveling public, and offer stability to the economies of the communities in which they are housed. As more people become educated about the possibilities of vacation ownership and as more brand names enter the fray there will be even bigger and better contributions from the timeshare industry to the health of the hospitality and tourism industry in the future. Key points to watch will be the effect of the baby boom generation on the market, the diversification of the timeshare product, the effect of more brand names in the timeshare arena, and the growth of the industry around the world prompting an increase in diversity among timeshare purchasers.

References

American Resort and Development Association (2004) http://www.arda.org. Accessed 11 February.

Crotts, John and Ragatz, Richard (2002) Recent US timeshare purchasers: who are they, what are they buying, and how can they be reached? *International Journal of Hospitality Management*, 21 (3), 227–238.

Interval International (2003) *Future Timeshare Buyers: 2003 Market Profile*. Miami, FL: Interval International.

Marson, Joan (2002) The timeshare oasis: in a difficult environment, timeshare offers hoteliers ancillary opportunity. *Hotels*, 36 (2), 43–46.

Pricewaterhousecoopers (2002) *A Study of the Timeshare and Vacation Ownership Industry*. Prepared for ARDA International Foundation, New York.

Ragatz Associates (2003) *Resort Timesharing in the United States*. Eugene, OR: Ragatz.

Scoviak, Mary (2003) A little bit of sunshine: consumers' unwillingness to give up their holidays and a greater need for family time continue to support cautious optimism for timeshare and fractional ownership. *Hotels*, 37 (2), 28–34.

TAMMIE KAUFMAN
UNIVERSITY OF CENTRAL FLORIDA, USA

Timeshare resales

Simply defined, a resale is a legal timeshare interest that is sold by a purchaser to a third party. If the timeshare interest is fee-simple property, an owner can dispose of it by sale, lease, or in a will within the limits set forth by applicable laws or in the purchase documents. If the product is not sold as a fee-simple interest, such as a right-to-use or vacation-club products, the owner may not have a right to resell their timeshare interest. The owner must refer to their original purchase documents to determine if a 'resales' clause exists. The concept of a 'resale' market is problematic because as a resort reaches sellout, the developer's prices rise as a reflection of product demand. As a result, the owner who purchases at a lower price early in the resort development process has bargaining power in setting the resale price. A dilemma exists when the owner sells his or her timeshare interest at a lower price, therefore entering into direct competition with the developer. Another challenge exists because the timeshare owner typically does not gain a full return on their capital due to the elevated sales and marketing costs associated with the timeshare product.

References

American Resort Development Association (2002) The *Timeshare Industry Manual*. Washington, DC: ARDA.

Trowbridge, Keith (1993) *Timesharing Today*. New York: Simon & Schuster.

BEVERLY SPARKS
GRIFFITH UNIVERSITY, AUSTRALIA

Tipping

Tips are voluntary payments made to service providers after they have delivered a service product. In American restaurants, it is customary to tip a waiter or waitress 15–20% of the check amount. These restaurant tips amount to approximately $20 billion a year and represent nearly all of US waiters' and waitresses' take-home pay. Even in countries with less generous tipping norms, tips often make up a substantial portion of servers' incomes. Thus, tipping is an important issue to restaurant servers around the globe.

It should be a concern of restaurant managers as well. Tipping affects servers' attitudes and behaviors as well as customers' dining experiences, so it should be managed to maximize employee motivation and customer satisfaction. Tipping also affects restaurants' legal responsibilities with respect to income and social security taxes, so it should be carefully monitored and recorded by managers.

Many restaurant managers rely on tips to (a) motivate servers to deliver high-quality service, (b) measure server performance, and (c) identify dissatisfied guests who need grievances addressed. These uses of tips assume that tips are strongly related to customers' perceptions of service quality. Research has not, however, supported that assumption (e.g., Lynn, 2001). In fact, customers' service ratings account for only about 4% of the variability in a restaurant's tip percentages, so tipping should not be relied upon to accomplish the previously mentioned goals.

If managers cannot rely upon tips to reflect service quality, they can nevertheless rely on good tips to help keep servers happy and motivated. Moreover, managers can increase their servers' tip incomes by providing the servers with appropriate tools and training. For example, researchers have found that servers in casual-dining restaurants earn larger tips when they introduce themselves by name, squat down next to tables, touch customers on the shoulder, smile at customers, joke and play games with customers, call customers by name, write or draw on the backs of checks, deliver checks on tip trays embossed with credit card logos, and give customers after-dinner candies. Managers who train servers to do one or more of these things and who provide servers with the appropriate tip trays and candies can increase their servers' tips by 20% or more. The effects of this increase in tips on servers' morale include reducing server turnover and improving customer service (Lynn, 1996).

In addition to employing the techniques mentioned in the previous paragraphs, servers unfortunately can also increase their tip incomes by (a) focusing on customers at the expense of their other responsibilities in the restaurant, (b) hurrying customers in order to turn tables quickly during busy nights, (c) stealing food and drinks that are given to customers free of charge, (d) ignoring or spending little time on groups considered poor tippers, (e) refusing to work during slow shifts, and (f) under-reporting their tip incomes for tax purposes. Thus, tipping may actually reward behaviors that most restaurant managers would consider undesirable and managers of tipped employees need to keep a watchful eye to identify and discourage such behavior.

In particular, restaurant managers in the United States need to monitor and record their servers' tip incomes because they are responsible for withholding income taxes on tips and for making social security contributions based on tip income. Recently, the US Supreme Court ruled that the IRS can audit restaurants (rather than individual servers in restaurants) and hold them responsible for paying social security taxes on undeclared tip income even when those unde-clared tips cannot be attributed to a particular server. This has substantially reduced the cost to the government of collecting taxes on undeclared tips and has substantially increased the costs to restaurants of under-reporting tip income. As a result, many restaurants enter into agreements with the IRS in which they work with the agency to estimate their servers' tip earnings, educate employees about tip-reporting responsibilities, and set up procedures for reporting tip income. In exchange, the IRS agrees not to audit the restau-rants' tips as long as the agreements are in effect.

References

Lynn, M. (2001) Restaurant tipping and service quality: a tenuous relationship. *Cornell Hotel and Restaurant Administration Quarterly*, 42, 14–20.

Lynn, M. (1996) Seven ways to increase your servers' tips. *Cornell Hotel and Restaurant Administration Quarterly*, 37 (June), 24–29.

WM. MICHAEL LYNN
CORNELL UNIVERSITY, USA

Total quality management (TQM)

Total quality management (TQM) was devel-oped by management theorist W. Edwards Deming in the early 1950s. Deming sought to offer a new way for US manufacturers to improve the quality of their products by reducing defects through worker participation in the planning process. US manufacturers were slow to embrace the concept but Japanese manufacturers were quick to adopt the principles, particularly in streamlining the design of automobiles.

Joseph Juran expressed his approach to total quality management in the form of a quality tril-ogy. Managing for quality involved three basic processes:

- Quality planning, or identifying the customer (both internal and external), determining their needs, designing goods and services to meet these needs at the established quality and cost goal
- Quality control, or establishing standards or critical elements of performance, identifying measures and methods of measurements, com-paring actual to standard and taking action if necessary
- Quality improvement, or identifying appropri-ate improvement projects, including organizing the team, discovering the causes and providing remedies, and finally, developing mechanisms to control the new process and hold the gains.

Juran also created the concept of cost of quality. The four elements of cost of quality are:

- Prevention cost, or those costs associated with the initial design quality
- Appraisal costs, or those costs associated with the inspection testing of raw materials, work-in-progress, finished goods, procedures for testing, training manuals, etc.
- External costs of returned merchandise, such as making repairs or refunds, credibility loss and lawsuits
- Internal costs of scrap, rework, redesign, down-time, broken equipment, reduced yields, selling products at a discount, etc.

Philip Crosby described quality as free and argued that zero defects were a desirable and achievable goal. He articulated his view of qual-ity as the four absolutes of quality management: quality means conformance to requirements; quality comes from prevention which is a result of training, discipline, example, and leadership; quality performance standard is zero defects; and quality measurement is the price of nonconformance.

Others such as Armand Feigenbaum define total quality management as an excellence-driven rather than a defect-driven concept; and Kaoru Ishikawa believed that all divisions and all employees in the organization should be involved in studying and promoting quality control. Ishikawa focused on the customer as primary in defining quality. He also advocated quality control circles. He understood the value of using teamwork in solving quality problems.

Total quality management in a hotel or lodging enterprise is a management technique that encourages managers to look with a critical eye at the processes used to deliver products and services. Managers must ask front-line employees and supervisors to question each step in the methods they use in providing hospitality for guests. Some examples might be asking guests why they are unhappy about waiting in line at check-out or why a guest might feel the table service in a hotel restaurant was rushed or why guests are dissatisfied when their room is not ready on check-in. Critical to success in total quality management is the interaction that occurs between frontline employees and their supervisors; specifically, the interaction of employees in a group setting and/or one-on-one basis to determine the basic cause of the problem and how a specific end result can be achieved. This interaction typically moves managers, supervisors, and employees into a cooperative interaction that may not have previously existed. Such interaction can be as simple as day and night shift employees who may not understand each other's activities, finding they do have common concerns about serving guests.

Total quality management in a hotel could be explained with the following example. The hotel general manager receives multiple complaints about the sloppy appearance of the hotel's lobby including furniture in disarray, ashtrays overflowing, flowers wilted and trash containers overflowing. The general manager recruits a total quality management team, which consists of a front desk agent, a housekeeper, a food server,

and the director of marketing and sales. The team meets and discusses how the lobby area could be more effectively maintained. The housekeeper indicates his colleagues are working at capacity and are permitted only 15 minutes to clean up the lobby on the day shift. The front desk agent says that she would often like to take a few minutes to leave the desk and go into the lobby to straighten the furniture, but is not allowed to leave the desk unattended. The director of marketing and sales indicates that he is embarrassed when prospective customers come into the hotel and see the lobby. He indicates that he has called housekeeping several times to have the lobby cleaned and is told it is not in the budget to have the lobby cleaned more than once daily. The food server indicates that whenever he is passing through the lobby he tries to pick up food and beverage related items and carry them to the restaurant but that his time out of the restaurant is very limited. All of the team members begin to understand the impact that the lobby appearance is having on the success of the hotel.

The team decides to look at the elements of the problem. The furniture is on wheels for ease of moving when housekeeping is cleaning. The pillows on the furniture do add a decorative look to the furniture but are usually scattered about. The housekeeper suggests they be sewn to the back and arms of the sofas. The food server asks whether ashtrays might be replaced with receptacles; and the front desk agent suggests that receptacles with a swinging lid be used to avoid misplaced litter. The director of marketing and sales wonders whether the fresh flowers might be replaced with silk flowers and plants.

The team discussion encourages each person to understand why the housekeeper cannot straighten the lobby every two or three hours and why the front desk agent cannot leave her post to take care of the problems. The employees' comments concerning furniture and appointments create a better understanding of the problem. Team members start looking at one another with more understanding and are slower to criticize on this and other issues. The problem of the lobby was resolved but more importantly the team members developed a way to look at a challenge in a more constructive manner.

Reference

George, Stephen and Weimerskirch, Arthur (1998) *Total Quality Management: Strategies and Techniques Proven at Today's Most Successful Companies.* New York: John Wiley & Sons.

WILLIAM FISHER
UNIVERSITY OF CENTRAL FLORIDA, USA

Trade show

A trade show is the exhibit of products and services that are targeted to a specific clientele and are not open to the public. It is a marketing activity that provides the exhibiting company the opportunity to do market research, talk to customers, and promote products and/or services. Trade shows are business-to-business (B2B) activities. Trade shows are usually held in convention centers but may be held in convention hotels, armories, arenas, or other venues. Some trade shows also offer educational sessions. Attendees pay a registration or entrance fee that gives them access to the show floor. Educational sessions may require a separate payment. Attendees visit the shows to learn about products, compare products, find out about new trends in their industry, and make buying decisions. Exhibitors at the shows may give away product samples, demonstrate products and/or talk to attendees about how their products can be used.

The modern trade show is a descendent of early fairs and festivals where people gathered to barter or sell goods. The Crystal Palace Exhibition that took place in Britain in 1851 is generally considered the first modern exhibition. As new types of products were introduced during the Industrial Revolution, a new method of product distribution was required. Exhibitions were that new form. Associations, which began to develop in the United States in the mid 1800s, started to organize their own exhibitions to help their members market their products. Trade shows are one type of exhibition and have become a major industry worldwide. The models for trade shows differ around the world. In the United States they tend to be short-term events, lasting from 3 to 5 days. In other parts of the world, these events may last weeks or months. Venues have been designed specifically to accommodate large trade shows that require floors that can handle tons of freight, loading docks where semi-trucks can park, roll-up doors that semi-trucks can drive through, high ceilings, and other special features.

References

Morrow, S.L. (2002) *The Art of the Show.* Dallas, TX: Education Foundation, International Association for Exhibition Management.
Robbe, D. (2002) *Expositions and Trade Shows.* New York: John Wiley.

DEBORAH BREITER
UNIVERSITY OF CENTRAL FLORIDA, USA

Trade show organizer

The individual who plans a trade show, reserves the space, markets to exhibitors, and promotes attendance by buyers is known as a trade show organizer. Several different people may actually accomplish these activities but one person would have overall responsibility for the success of the event. The organizer must create a business plan for the event that includes goals and objectives, operational plans, and evaluation methods. Somebody must negotiate contracts with a variety of suppliers. A dedicated exhibition facility, such as a convention center, might be chosen to house the event but sometimes a convention hotel can be used. Other types of venues for trade shows include arenas, armories, and civic centers. Trade show organizers may also negotiate with hotels for blocks of sleeping rooms for attendees. They may also negotiate contracts for shuttle buses to run between the convention venue and hotels. The show organizer hires a general services contractor to handle the freight for the event, create the graphics and look of the show, design the registration area, create an exhibitor services kit and act as the liaison between show management and the venue. Show management sells exhibit space to companies and businesses. Trade show organizers today are being challenged to provide greater value to their exhibitors. Private events are starting to compete for marketing dollars that exhibiting companies have to spend.

References

Morrow, S.L. (2002) *The Art of the Show*. Dallas, TX: Education Foundation, International Association for Exhibition Management.

Robbe, D. (2002) *Expositions and Trade Shows*. New York: John Wiley & Sons.

DEBORAH BREITER
UNIVERSITY OF CENTRAL FLORIDA, USA

Trade union

A trade union is an organization of employees formed to engage in collective action and membership. It is usually based on a particular industry or occupational group (De Cieri and Kramar, 2003). The goals of trade unions are usually to enable their members to pursue their industrial interests, but some unions may also seek political and social goals. Unions as 'ex parte' agents on behalf of their members generally have recognition under most industrial legislation, particularly in collective bargaining, for pursuing wage claims and grievance handling with employers. Unlike employer associations, trade unions tend to be more cohesive as they share common goals. In some countries unions are also called employee associations or guilds. Employers may also form trade unions to represent their broader interests, in the form of employer associations. Union representational rights tend to do better under pluralism.

In most industrialized countries, union representation in the hospitality industry is lower than that of other industries (Woods, 2002). Reasons usually given for this situation include split-shift work scheduling and a frantic pace of operations which limits available time for collective discussion; separate and distinct hospitality jobs mitigate formation of an holistic and cohesive work group; paternalistic management styles; high proportion of part-time, casual, and flexible forms of employment; transient nature of many hotel workers; anti-union orientation of some front-line hospitality workers, etc.

References

De Cieri, H. and Kramar, R. (2003) *Human Resource Management in Australia: Strategy, People, Performance*. Sydney: McGraw-Hill.

Woods, R.H. (2002) *Managing Hospitality Human Resources*, 3rd edn. Lansing, MI: Educational Institute of theAmerican Hotel and Lodging Association.

DARREN LEE-ROSS
JAMES COOK UNIVERSITY, AUSTRALIA

Training

Training can be identified as activities that 'help an individual acquire competence in a specific task, process or role' (Harrison, 2002, 5). Within the hospitality industry training focus is often on the development of specific skills related to behavior and performance that will ultimately have an impact on guest satisfaction. In developing training to address these areas, organizations will use a process often referred to as the training cycle. This is a continuous process involving the following activities:

- Identification and analysis of training needs
- Planning and design of training interventions
- Delivery of training interventions
- Monitoring and evaluation of outcomes.

The first stage in the process is training needs analysis. At this point the organization identifies the key skills, knowledge, attitudes, and behaviors that are required for effective performance. There are many ways in which to identify these, such as assessment methods, interviewing staff about their job, observing staff whilst carrying out specific tasks or reviewing the results of performance appraisals. Other sources of information are guest feedback and analysis of business volumes. For example, if there is an increase in complaints around the standard of breakfast service this may highlight a training need in the restaurant or kitchen areas.

When training needs have been identified the organization will then develop a training plan to address the needs. This plan will include detail on the overall objectives of training interventions, the people involved, the methods to be used (classroom style, presentations, workshops, on-the-job training etc).

The delivery of the training interventions can be through a variety of means. On-the-job training can be a mix of one or all of the following: instruction, coaching, counseling, delegation from a manager, secondment or guided processes (Wilson, 1999). In the UK, 87% of organizations use on-the-job training (CIPD, 2001). The process can be both informal and formal in structure. A formalized structure would involve the individual observing a more experienced employee carrying out job tasks. The individual would then ask questions to clarify understanding and have an attempt at the task; the individual then practices the task under supervision from the more experienced member of staff. Eventually the individual will take on more tasks and become proficient without supervision. McDonald's uses this method for training new staff members. Each staff member is allocated a 'buddy' from a special 'training squad' to work with them until they become fully trained in all job tasks. Hilton (UK) also uses a system of 'departmental trainers' who are experienced employees who will work on the job with those requiring training. This type of training is cost-effective as it is carried out at the workplace during operational hours. It is best suited for one-to-one training.

Wilson (1999) further defines off-the-job training as interventions provided either internally or externally which require the individual member of staff to be removed from the operation whilst completing their training. In-company methods used involve lectures, presentations, role-plays etc, normally within a classroom or workshop-style environment. For example, a general manager will attend a series of workshops at head office designed to improve budgeting and financial skills. External methods tend to be short and

long college courses and/or training sessions conducted by consultants or training providers. For example a head chef may be required to attend college to complete a certificate course in food hygiene. These methods are more costly in terms of time and money as individuals are being trained outside of the working environment. They are generally used for longer-term career development or for the acquisition of specialist skills and knowledge.

Some organizations have developed their training provision beyond on-the-job training to gain competitive advantage within the marketplace. By setting up corporate universities they ensure a consistent approach to the training of all staff from entry-level, hourly paid employees to development programs for managers and executives. The most well-known corporate universities are Disney and McDonald's.

The final part of the training cycle is evaluation of training outcomes. Although evaluation to test knowledge can take place throughout the training session, e.g. through question and answer sessions or tests at the end of each section before moving to the next section, the evaluation of training is generally carried out on completion of the training intervention. The Kirkpatrick Model (1967) is a popular method of evaluation: 'most trainers espouse this classic approach' (Simmonds, 2003, 171). Kirkpatrick (1967) states that evaluation takes place on four distinct levels:

- Reaction
- Learning
- Behavior
- Results.

At the most basic level, we can evaluate the trainees' reaction to the training intervention. This is often achieved by issuing post-course evaluation sheets, sometimes referred to as 'happy sheets.' Second we can identify what the participants learned from the training intervention, for example setting a task or test for them to complete both at the start and at the end of the program. Any resultant improvement would suggest that learning has taken place. Behavioral change can be measured by looking at the resultant workplace behaviors, for example asking has there been a decrease in the number of accidents since the completion of health and safety training. Finally, and probably more difficult, is the evaluation of whether the learning and change in behavior have had an impact on the organization. For example, have room sales and revenue increased as a result of sales training for the reservations team?

Within the hospitality industry customer satisfaction is a central theme and therefore there is much emphasis placed on customer service training. Dimensions of customer service include: communication skills; sensitivity to customer needs; motivation to provide service; job knowledge; situational analysis skills; understanding of clearly defined performance standards; initiative; integrity and flexibility; and thorough and timely follow-up. All of these dimensions could be identified as the skill set required of any hospitality employee and as such it would be prudent for organizations to carry out a training needs analysis related to these areas. If any needs were highlighted the organization would then design training interventions to address the needs. Such programs may include training on anticipating guest needs. This would be achieved by using role-plays to show how employees can read verbal and non-verbal behaviors to indicate whether a customer was satisfied. Additionally, they could involve activities designed to train staff in how to deal with angry customers or customers with unusual needs. On completion of training the organization could evaluate the success of the program by comparing customer satisfaction levels with those prior to the training program.

References

CIPD (2001) Annual Training Survey Report. London: Chartered Institute of Personnel and Development.

Harrison, R. (2002) *Learning and Development.* London: Chartered Institute of Personnel and Development.

Kirkpatrick, D. (1967) As cited in Simmonds, D. (2003) *Designing and Delivering Training.* London: Chartered Institute of Personnel and Development.

Simmonds, D. (2003) *Designing and Delivering Training.* London: Chartered Institute of Personnel and Development.

Wilson, J. (ed.) (1999) *Human Resource Development.* London: Kogan Page.

DEBRA F. CANNON
GEORGIA STATE UNIVERSITY, USA
SAMANTHA QUAIL
GLASGOW CALEDONIAN UNIVERSITY, UK

Turnover

Turnover occurs when an employee leaves his or her organization either voluntarily or involuntarily. Operationally, turnover is often expressed as a percentage either within a hospitality organization's department or the organization as a whole, or sometimes both. Turnover, in percentage and department/organizational terms, may differ between hospitality organizations depending on natural business seasons, the organization's location, external forces (international or domestic), and staff themselves. Turnover rate is typically expressed as an annualized percentage. While turnover rates in the hospitality industry vary considerably by country, they tend to be significantly higher than in most other industries. For example, within the US turnover in all industries was estimated at 13% in 1995, whereas in the hospitality industry it was estimated to range from 58 to 154% among staff, and 15 to 48% among management personnel' (Pizam and Ellis, 1999,113). Turnover is associated with both costs and benefits. Turnover costs include: (1) replacement costs, such as those associated with recruitment, selection, and training; (2) reduced customer service and product quality; and (3) poor morale resulting from insecurity and increased workload for remaining employees. (Deery and Shaw, 1999). On the positive side, turnover can bring resolution to performance issues, provide opportunities for promotion, and result in new skills and ideas being introduced to the organization. Some organizations have what can be described as a turnover culture in which a high rate of turnover is accepted as standard business practice and little is done to rectify the situation (Deery, 2002). High rates of voluntary turnover have been linked to many factors, including job dissatisfaction and lack of connection between subordinate and supervisor (Pizam and Ellis, 1999).

References

Deery, M. (2002) Labour turnover in international hospitality and tourism. In N. D'Annunzio-Green, G.A. Maxwell, and S. Watson (eds), *Human Resource Management: International Perspectives in Hospitality and Tourism*. London: Continuum.

Deery, M.A. and Shaw, R.N. (1999) An investigation of the relationship between employee turnover and organizational culture. *Journal of Hospitality and Tourism Research*, 23 (4), 387–400.

Pizam, A. and Ellis, T. (1999) Absenteeism and turnover in the hospitality industry. In D. Lee-Ross (ed.), *HRM in Tourism and Hospitality*. London: Cassell, pp. 109–131.

JULIA CHRISTENSEN HUGHES
UNIVERSITY OF GUELPH, CANADA

ANTHONY BRIEN
LINCOLN UNIVERSITY, NEW ZEALAND

Turnover culture

Staff turnover is generally acknowledged as particularly high within the hospitality industry. Indeed, some fast food chains have annual turnover rates in excess of 200%. Turnover culture tends to be correlated with poor communication within organizations and more autocratic styles of management. Turnover culture is a product of a number of factors, including the seasonality of employment, the limited career structure in smaller establishments, the semi- or unskilled nature of some jobs, and finally, the percentage of employees from secondary labor markets. Where the industry has faced a significant problem for certain labor-intensive or semi-skilled jobs it has tended to turn to labor from foreign countries. However, these low-skilled employees are often more motivated by extrinsic rewards such as pay and conditions and are therefore more likely to be lured to another employer by higher wages or to escape poor working conditions therefore perpetuating the problem. However, despite these industry-related turnover factors, many employees who leave a job voluntarily do not move out of the sector. Instead, it is accepted that people move from establishment to establishment with little organizational loyalty. This perpetuates a turnover culture that produces a higher level of employee churn than experienced in other sectors (Woods, 2002).

Reference

Woods, R.H. (2002) *Managing Hospitality Human Resources*, 3rd edn. Lansing, MI: Educational Institute of the American Hotel and Lodging Association.

GILLIAN KELLOCK HAY
GLASGOW CALEDONIAN UNIVERSITY, UK

U

Understay

This refers to a guest who leaves the hotel prior to the departure date that they had originally indicated. Pleasure travelers may find their tourist attraction less interesting than anticipated. Urgent business may require the corporate client to return to the office sooner than expected. It is also known as early departure or curtailment. Like overstays, this situation has to be monitored, especially in periods when the hotel is busy. Front office management review and analyze various data produced during check-out. Most of this information is financial. The data can be grouped into categories as requested by management and must include understays. Understays are lost revenue in that the hotel had not anticipated the departure and thus may be unable to sell the room to another guest to recoup the anticipated revenue. To minimize understays, upon check-in a guest is often asked to initial the departure date and thus may be charged for an early departure.

Reference

Kasavana, M.L. and Brooks, R.M. (1995) *Front Office Procedures*, 4th edn. Lansing, MI: Educational Institute of the American Hotel and Motel Association.

IRENE SWEENEY
INTERNATIONAL HOTEL MANAGEMENT
INSTITUTE SWITZERLAND, SWITZERLAND

Undistributed operating expenses

The expenses of various service or cost centers – e.g., administrative and general, information systems, human resources, marketing, security, property operation and maintenance, etc. – are normally grouped under the heading 'undistributed operating expenses.' The costs comprising the two principal subcategories of each cost center's expenses, namely payroll and related expenses and other expenses, are direct costs of their respective cost centers, but indirect costs (overhead expenses) of the property's revenue centers. Thus, in the usual departmental accounting presentation under the Uniform System of Accounts for the Lodging Industry, undistributed operating expenses are treated as overhead expenses, and there is no attempt to allocate them to revenue centers. For example, a hotel general manager's salary is included in the line item administrative and general expenses. Since the role of a hotel general manager is to manage the business as a total entity – allocating his time and managerial expertise among the various departments as needed – treating the salary as an overhead expense recognizes the reality of the function.

Thus, in the case of a hotel property, the undistributed operating expenses essentially reflect the resources put in place to support the business as a whole (including cost and revenue centers), rather than to focus on any one particular department or aspect of the property's business activities.

References

Geller, A.N. and Schmidgall, R.S. (1980) Cost allocation under the Uniform System of Accounts for Hotels. *Cornell Hotel and Restaurant Administration Quarterly*, 21 (3), 31–39.

Uniform System of Accounts for the Lodging Industry, 9th edn (1996) Lansing, MI: Educational Institute of the American Hotel and Motel Association.

PAUL BEALS
UNIVERSITY OF DENVER, USA

Uniform Resource Locator (URL)

Uniform Resource Locator (URL) – also known as Uniform Resource Identifier (URI), Uniform Resource Name (URN), and previously called Universal Resource Locator – is the global address of documents and other resources accessible on the World Wide Web. These resources include Hypertext Markup Language (HTML) pages, image files, virtual tours, or any other file supported by Hypertext Transfer Protocol (HTTP). URLs are typed into the browser window to access Web pages and are embedded within the pages themselves to provide hypertext links to other pages. The URL contains the protocol prefix, port number, domain name, subdirectory names, and file name. URLs may also be numbers but words are easier to use and remember.

To access a home page on a website, only the protocol and domain name are required. In the URL http://www.expedia.com, for example, the first part of the address indicates what protocol to use 'HTTP' while the second part, 'www.expedia.com,' specifies the IP address or domain name, thereby identifying a specific computer on the Internet where the resource is located. URLs are important as they make hospitality brands, such as Hilton.com, easy to identify and locate on the Web.

References

The National Center for Supercomputing Applications (NCSA) (2003) *A Beginner's Guide to URLs*. Availbale from: http://archive.ncsa.uiuc.edu/demoweb/url-primer.html

World Wide Web Consortium (W3C) (2003) *Architecture Domain: Naming and Addressing: URIs, URLs*. Available from: http://www.w3.org/Addressing/

JULINE E. MILLS
PURDUE UNIVERSITY, USA

Uniform system of accounts

Uniform systems of accounts are standardized charts of accounts developed to reflect the specific operating and financial characteristics of individual hospitality-industry segments. The Uniform System of Accounts for the Lodging Industry (USALI) is by far the most widespread in its use, in part because it brings order to the complexity inherent in the numerous revenue and cost centers comprising a multi-faceted lodging property, but the Uniform System of Accounts for Restaurants (USAR) and the Uniform System of Financial Reporting for Clubs are also widely used.

Uniform systems of accounts are designed to meet four distinct yet overlapping objectives:

- *Comparability:* Because uniform systems provide carefully developed formats reflecting evolving operating and financing trends in their segments, the comparisons of financial results among adopters' operations are more reliable.
- *Responsibility accounting:* Uniform systems distinguish between direct and indirect costs, thus permitting the assignment of costs to the activities – and their managers.
  - A *direct cost* is an expense that is readily and reliably assigned to a revenue-generating activity or a cost center. In the USALI, for example, the cost of food sold is readily identified if appropriate record-keeping procedures are followed, and it can reliably be assigned as a cost of generating food sales. Similarly, payroll and related expenses of both revenue centers (e.g., rooms department, food and beverage department) and cost centers (e.g., marketing, property operations, and maintenance) are direct costs because

they are the responsibility of individual revenue- and cost-center managers.

○ An *indirect cost* is an expense that cannot be readily and reliably assigned to a revenue-generating activity. For example, under the USALI, no cost of sales is assigned to the rooms division. Obviously, significant costs are incurred to generate the sale of room nights, but assigning the bricks-and-mortar (and other) costs of generating the rooms department revenue would (a) violate the objective of responsibility accounting, since the rooms division manager does not control the size of the rooms division (or its marketing budget) and (b) require the use of subjective allocation bases. Indirect costs are thus considered overhead costs, or burden. Under the USALI, operating overhead costs are termed undistributed operating expenses, while occupancy and financial overhead costs are termed fixed charges.

• *Adherence to accounting standards:* Careful use of uniform systems helps ensure that property level accounting personnel are reporting transactions according to Generally Accepted Accounting Principles (GAAP).

• *Flexibility:* Uniform systems typically contain far more classifications and accounts than are used by most adopters, but this feature permits individual operations to customize the system to their needs while preserving comparability and accuracy.

Efficient systems of accounts summarize operating results succinctly, relegating more detailed information on revenues and costs to departmental schedules. This yields an uncluttered, more usable picture of operating performance while preserving a 'drill-down' capability if greater detail is needed. Similarly, expense dictionaries provide users with guidance by categorizing into their appropriate departmental schedules the myriad transactions a hospitality operation records. Although most adopters seek above all to generate operating statements that permit performance comparisons, uniform systems of accounts provide guidance on the presentation of other financial statements, including: the balance sheet, statement of owners' equity, and the statement of cash flow. The evolution of ownership entities, changing operating characteristics, and evolving accounting standards require periodic revision of the guidelines for presenting the financial data for the industry's various sectors.

Finally, although the above discussion emphasizes the record-keeping function, an effective uniform system also provides analytical guidance. This might include procedures for the application of standard managerial accounting tools, e.g. ratio analysis, cost–volume–profit (CVP) analysis, operational budgeting and budgetary control, and allocation and apportionment of expenses (responsibility accounting) to the hospitality segment.

References

National Restaurant Association (1996) *Uniform System of Accounts for Restaurants*, 7th edn. Washington, DC: National Restaurant Association.

Schmidgall, R.S. (2002) *Hospitality Industry Managerial Accounting*, 5th edn. Lansing, MI: Educational Institute of the American Hotel and Lodging Association.

Schmidgall, R.S. (2003) *Uniform System of Financial Reporting for Clubs*, 6th rev. edn. Hospitality Financial and Technology Professionals and Club Managers Association of America.

Uniform System of Accounts for the Lodging Industry, 9th edn (1996) Lansing, MI: Educational Institute of the American Hotel and Motel Association.

PAUL BEALS
UNIVERSITY OF DENVER, USA

Uniform system of accounts for restaurants

By nature, restaurant operators are protective of their proprietary information. In other words, they are reluctant to share operating results with their neighbors for fear that it will give those neighbors a competitive advantage. For generations, this meant that every small or large restaurant had its own way of 'keeping score' financially. Unfortunately, this made it difficult for one restaurant to compare itself with others, or to compare standardized knowledge across segments, regions, or even on occasion within organizations themselves.

As the National Restaurant Association became a stronger advocate for the disparate voices of the industry, it was a driving force behind determining a standardized way to compare one restaurant with another. The outcome was the Uniform System of Accounts for Restaurants (USAR) (National Restaurant Association, 1996). Originally published in 1930, the Uniform System has undergone numerous updates and revisions over the intervening years. The Uniform System has nevertheless become the accounting basis for all restaurants, even though many larger chain organizations have adapted or altered it to suit their own particular reporting needs.

Reference

National Restaurant Association (1996) *Uniform System of Accounts for Restaurants*. Washington, DC: National Restaurant Association.

CHRISTOPHER MULLER
UNIVERSITY OF CENTRAL FLORIDA, USA

Uniform system of accounts income statement

Income statements for hotels and restaurants are organized above all to provide responsibility accounting information to users, although restaurant operating statements provide a lesser degree of detail.

The *hotel income statement* communicates the dual retail-real estate nature of lodging. In its most useful format, entitled 'Summary Statement of Income' (Uniform System of Accounts for the Lodging Industry, 1996, 33), the income statement is readily divided into three panels or levels.

The first level, summarized at the line 'Total operated departments,' reports the combined results of the property's revenue centers. Each department's revenue is recorded in the first column, while its direct costs are deducted horizontally, yielding the department's profit (loss). The individual revenue centers' results are summed and appear as a single figure captioned 'Total operated departments.' The gross margin contributed by the operating departments will depend on three factors: (1) management's ability to drive revenue, especially in departments such as the rooms division, which enjoys a high degree of operating leverage; (2) management's acumen in controlling the departments' direct costs; and (3) the hotel's sales mix, since some departments (e.g., food and beverage) are inherently less profitable than others and product offerings within the same department provide smaller (e.g., group rooms versus transient rooms) or larger (e.g., banqueting versus room service) contribution margins than others.

The second panel describes the costs of the various service centers supporting the operating departments of the hotel, and is captioned 'Undistributed operating expenses.' As the term 'undistributed' suggests, the Uniform System of Accounts for the Lodging Industry (USALI) does not allocate these costs to the revenue-generating departments. This level is summarized at the line formally called 'Income after undistributed operating expenses,' but more commonly called 'GOP' (for gross operating profit) or 'house profit.'

The third level, summarized at the 'Net income' line, is the province of ownership and reports the expenses related to the hotel's real estate component and capital structure. A common industry term for these expenses is 'fixed charges,' although some (e.g., management fees, rent) vary with sales volume. Like undistributed operating expenses, fixed charges are indirect costs that are not allocated to the hotel's revenue-generating departments.

The hotel income statement's emphasis on responsibility accounting is evident at every level. Individual department heads are responsible for driving their profit centers' revenues, as well as the departmental costs under their control. Although department heads in the cost centers (e.g., human resources, marketing, security) have no revenues attributed to their activities, they have direct responsibility for the costs their departments incur.

The hotel income statement's GOP is the line of demarcation between the hotel's retail and real estate components. The hotel's general manager is ultimately responsible for all the operating activities reflected in the financial data above this line. The entity owning the property is responsible for decisions regarding the hotel's mode of operation (e.g., self-operation versus a third party operator), the composition and cost of its assets, and its capital structure. Accordingly, these elements of cost are reported separately from operations.

In contrast to the hotel income statement, the *restaurant income statement* provides less responsibility-accounting information. In the Uniform System of Accounts for Restaurants (USAR) format only the cost of sales is presented as a direct cost of the two revenue centers, food and beverage, while labor and other expenses are treated as indirect costs. Similarly, the real estate component, reflected in the line items 'Occupancy' and 'Depreciation,' is not distinguished from the operating component. Capital-structure charges are, however, reported separately.

The limited degree of cost allocation reflects the small business nature of unit level restaurant operations but probably does not represent a significant disadvantage in the USAR's day-to-day use. The most significant costs of restaurant operations – food and beverage, wages, and operating supplies – are identified separately, allowing performance comparisons among operations on these important measures. It is also very likely that, whether at an independent restaurant or the unit level of a chain, the ultimate responsibility for controlling revenues and costs resides in a single individual, thus reducing the level of detail necessary for effective management.

References

National Restaurant Association (1996) *Uniform System of Accounts for Restaurants*, 7th edn. Washington, DC: National Restaurant Association.

Schmidgall, R.S. (2002) *Hospitality Industry Managerial Accounting*, 5th edn. Lansing, MI: Educational Institute of the American Hotel and Lodging Association.

Uniform System of Accounts for the Lodging Industry, 9th edn. (1996) Lansing, MI: Educational

Institute of the American Hotel and Motel Association.

PAUL BEALS
UNIVERSITY OF DENVER, USA

Unit week

The unit week is the traditional use period that is conveyed to and used by the purchaser of a timeshare interest. It consists of seven days in a particular accommodation in a timeshare property. A unit week generally begins and ends on the same day of the week, but that day may vary from accommodation to accommodation in the timeshare property, especially in larger resort properties where there is a need to stagger check-in times to avoid overloading the front desk. If the unit week is the unit of measurement used, there are fifty-two seven-day unit weeks created with a fifty-third unit week created for years with excess days. The fifty-third unit week can be conveyed separately, given to the purchaser of the fifty-second unit week, or retained by the developer for its own use or the use of the management company. Depending on the jurisdiction and the documents underlying the timeshare plan, the unit week may be recognized as the actual timeshare interest that is being purchased, tied to a particular timeshare interest as a fixed timeshare interest pursuant to fixed timeshare plan, or not tied to a particular timeshare interest and made available for reservation pursuant to a float timeshare plan.

Reference

American Resort Development Association (2002) *The Timeshare Resource Manual.* Washington, DC: ARDA.

KURT GRUBER
ISLAND ONE RESORTS, USA

United States Environmental Protection Agency (US EPA)

The United States Environmental Protection Agency, or US EPA, which is located in

Washington, DC, is an independent executive agency of the US federal government responsible for the formulation and enforcement of regulations governing the release of pollutants and other activities that may adversely affect the public health or environment. The EPA also approves and monitors programs established by state and local agencies for environmental protection and is also concerned with noise pollution and sponsors research into the effects of pollution on ecosystems.

The EPA also works with other nations to identify and solve transboundary pollution problems and to ensure that environmental concerns are integrated into US foreign policy, including trade, economic development, and other policies, as well as to provide technical assistance and scientific expertise to other nations.

The EPA has developed some extremely helpful programs that have assisted facilities professionals in the management of their operations. Among these are the EPA Energy Star Program (focusing on energy-efficient building equipment and operations), the WAVE Program (dealing with water conservation), and an energy benchmarking tool. EPA also has resources to assist with solid waste management and indoor air quality issues.

References

Franck, I. and Brownstone, D. (1992) *The Green Encyclopedia: An A–Z Sourcebook of Environmental Concerns and Solutions.* New York: Macmillan, p. 323.

Stevenson, Harold L. and Wyman, B. (1991) *The Facts on File Dictionary of Environmental Science.* New York: Facts on File, p. 90.

www.epa.gov

LYLE THOMPSON
BURNABY, BC, CANADA

Unsystematic risk

Unsystematic risk is the stock volatility caused by firm-specific events such as lawsuits and labor disputes. This type of volatility or risk can be diversified away because it is independent of economic, political, and other factors that affect all securities in a systematic manner (Van Horne and Wachowicz, 2001). For hospitality investors, firm-specific volatility or unsystematic risk can be eliminated by holding a well-diversified portfolio that includes both hospitality and non-hospitality stocks. Since unsystematic risk is avoidable via diversification, those hospitality investors need not be compensated for bearing it. Consequently, unsystematic risk is not a relevant factor affecting their required rate of return within the theoretical framework of Capital Asset Pricing Model (CAPM).

In reality, however, hospitality investors are unlikely to ignore unsystematic risk completely because of imperfections of capital markets (Van Horne, 1998). In the real world, market imperfections, such as transaction costs, costly information, and unequal borrowing and lending rates, limit the effectiveness with which investors are able to diversify away unsystematic risk. As a result, unsystematic risk may still need to be compensated by adding a premium to the required rate of return, thus playing some role in firm valuation.

References

Van Horne, C. (1998) *Financial Management and Policy*, 11th edn. Englewood Cliffs, NJ: Prentice-Hall.

Van Horne, J.C. and Wachowicz, J.M. (2001) *Fundamentals of Financial Management*, 11th edn. Upper Saddle River, NJ: Prentice-Hall.

HYUNJOON KIM
UNIVERSITY OF HAWAII, USA

Upscale restaurants

The most traditional segment of the restaurant and foodservice industry is fine dining. Historically, the idea of an upscale restaurant included certain key organizing principles: efficiency in the production of freshly prepared food and professionalism in service. Prices are typically the highest of any segment, because the food is almost exclusively 'hand-made,' not unlike a Rolls–Royce automobile or a man's tailored suit. Fine dining is defined by having a well-trained and professional staff of waiters, usually including a dining room managed by someone in the role of maître d'hôtel. This type of restaurant will almost always have an extensive wine list, as well as a full range of other alcoholic beverages. Meals are most often created by a culinary artiste called an executive chef, with dishes best described as consisting of elaborately and freshly prepared food.

For more than a century the kitchen production system and the dining room service system have remained basically unchanged. The fabled French chef Auguste Escoffier designed the hierarchical structure of the kitchen. His colleague, the eponymous Cesar Ritz, an equally legendary maître d'hôtel, designed the dining room. Escoffier took what was essentially a loose, craft-based system and turned it into a paramilitary food production factory. At the top of the line is an executive chef, supported by a battery of sub-chefs, cooks, and stewards called a 'kitchen brigade.' Each has a well-defined role, often specializing in just one part of the otherwise complex menu: for example, the saucier makes all of the soups and stocks, while the poissonier is responsible for anything to do with fish. Dining room service is just as efficient as the kitchen's, with captains leading teams of waiters, busboys, and food runners, supported by sommeliers (wine stewards), and other various players.

References

Kuh, Patric (2001) *The Last Days of Haute Cuisine: America's Culinary Revolution.* New York: Viking.

Spang, Rebecca L. (2000) *The Invention of the Restaurant.* Boston, MA: Harvard University Press.

CHRISTOPHER MULLER
UNIVERSITY OF CENTRAL FLORIDA, USA

Upselling

Upselling represents the efforts of reservation agents and front desk agents to convince guests to rent rooms in categories above standard rate accommodations. Hotels typically have several rate categories based on such factors as décor, size, location, view, and furnishings. Often the difference in rate between two similar guestrooms can be substantial.

To upsell, front office and reservations staff must be trained to be more than simply order-takers. They must be trained as professional sales people. These personnel must see that they can upsell rooms in much the same way that a food server can sell an extra food item. Front office staff should learn effective techniques for suggesting room options to guests. This involves knowing how and when to ask for a sale in a non-pressuring way and how to direct the sale from the guest's perspective.

Offering guestroom options is the key to the reservations and registration sales process, and it requires thoughtful planning and practice. Although the majority of upselling is conducted during the reservations process, front desk agents are likely to have similar sales opportunities with walk-in guest. Some hotels, as a matter of policy, offer registering guests more than one room option and then let them state their preferences. To create guest acceptance, the front desk agent must know how to describe the hotel's facilities and services in a positive manner. A guest will probably provide several clues about what is acceptable for his/her stay and some information might already be available on a reservation record.

Upselling to walk-in guests often holds the best opportunity to create more revenue for the hotel. In some cases, only the highest rated rooms may be available. In other cases, a good selling effort, creating the impression of additional value, will convince a guest that the increased room rate is worth the expense.

Reference

Stutts, Alan T. (2001) *Hotel and Lodging Management – An Introduction.* New York: John Wiley & Sons.

ALAN T. STUTTS
AMERICAN INTERCONTINENTAL
UNIVERSITY, USA

Urban timeshare

An urban timeshare at a fundamental level is a high-rise condominium with a penthouse exposure that is located in thriving business districts within major cities. Timeshare resort developers have been successful in certain demographic markets by pricing the urban timeshare product against other vacation long-term stay alternatives such as high-end condominiums and high-end hotels to a limited degree. To cater to this upscale, long-term, business consumer an urban timeshare must be located in an area that has access to a high volume of tourists and business clientele. Good current examples of urban timeshare locations include New York, London, and Paris.

The urban timeshare product is not for everyone. According to industry research, there are four distinct markets. These markets encompass: upscale urbanites that exchange for the purpose of meeting friends and/or relatives; people that live within a 150-mile radius that want to take advantage of the city's arts, entertainment, and retail outlets; an international tourist market that is drawn to the arts and educational offerings of the city; and businesses that have need of long-term stays for national and international travelers.

Reference

http://www.hotel-online.com/Trends/Andersen/1998_TimeshareWave.html.   Accessed   29 January 2003.

PIMRAWEE ROCHUNGSRAT
JAMES COOK UNIVERSITY, UK

Use period

A use period is the generic name given to the defined period of time in a timeshare plan during which an accommodation in a timeshare property is subject to reservation and use by the timeshare owner. Use periods can be as short as a single day or as long as a larger fractional interest, which commonly refers to more than one week of timeshare interest. The use period traditionally used in timeshare plans is the week, consisting of seven days starting and stopping on the same day, and with or without the option to split the week into a three-day and a four-day stay or into other usage increments. Depending on the jurisdiction and the documents underlying the timeshare plan, the use period may be tied to the underlying timeshare interest, such as a fixed week, or may not be tied to the underlying timeshare interest, such as a floating week. The smaller the increments of time that can be reserved and the more flexibility in the use options given to the timeshare owner with respect to use periods, the greater the cost for operating the timeshare plan and the greater the complexity of the reservation program for timeshare consumers.

Reference

American Resort Development Association (2002) *The Timeshare Resource Manual.* Washington, DC: ARDA.

KURT GRUBER
ISLAND ONE RESORTS, USA

V

Vacation exchange history

The history and evolution of vacation exchange is directly tied to the history and evolution of the timeshare industry, which dates back to the 1960s in the French Alps. Demand for the vacation pleasures of a 'second home' were extremely limited, prices were high and consumers did not want the financial burdens of year-round second property ownership. In order to expand the potential customer base, companies began marketing a concept which involved buying only specific weeks of time in a resort condominium unit.

The idea spread to the United States in the early 1970s. From the beginning it was clear the product still had one basic flaw: vacation owners were unwilling to buy an inflexible product that limited their vacation options by locking them into taking their vacation at the same time and at the same place year after year.

Timeshare owner and entrepreneur Jon DeHaan recognized that timeshare owners wanted more flexibility to take a vacation when and where they wanted. The idea of an exchange network took hold. Jon and his wife, Christel, with the support of a few key developers and ALDA (the precursor to ARDA), were convinced the exchange component was needed to facilitate timeshare sales, and in 1974 they founded RCI, the world's first exchange network.

The DeHaans originally intended to help developers of *vacation* condominiums sell new units by offering the buyers of those units' opportunities to exchange into other vacation destinations.

When the mid-1970s condo boom went bust, many developers of whole-ownership condominium properties subsequently converted their projects to timeshare. RCI was uniquely poised to enhance the attractiveness of the timeshare product by offering 'like-for-like' vacation exchanges. In 1976, Interval International was formed to compete in the timeshare exchange marketplace.

Vacation exchange allows timeshare owners the opportunity to trade their vacation week(s) for different vacation experiences at other comparable resorts around the world. The developers of timeshare resorts clearly understand the intrinsic value of affiliating their properties with an Exchange Company. The ability to exchange enhances the value of their product by adding flexibility, providing vacation alternatives, and offering additional leisure benefits and services. Industry studies validate the importance of exchange during the sales process and indicate 84.2% of timeshare owners cited the opportunity to exchange as their primary motivation to buy.

Timeshare owners typically become consumer members of the exchange company at point of sale. Since most developers treat exchange as an integral component of their timeshare plan, they agree to enroll new owners at the developer's expense for their first years(s) of membership. Thereafter, the exchange company solicits renewals directly from their members. In addition to exchange, both major exchange companies offer a variety of leisure-oriented benefits to their members, including bonus vacations, travel services, vacation insurance, and cruise exchange.

Timeshare owners 'deposit' their vacation week(s) with the exchange company. As other vacation owners deposit their weeks, the exchange company builds up an inventory of weeks that are available for vacation exchanges. The inventory pool is typically enhanced by unsold weeks deposited by resort operators and developers.

When a member deposits their week with the exchange provider, the company compares the week the depositor is relinquishing with weeks deposited by other members and provides a suitable match based on availability and value. Factors affecting the 'trading value' are: demand for the vacation time (prime time versus off-season), the size of the unit relinquished, the resort's quality rating, and how early the week was deposited in advance of the start date of the vacation week. Once the exchange provider matches an owner's request to a vacation week, the owner pays an exchange transaction fee. The exchange provider will advise the host resort of all inbound exchange guests for each applicable arrival date. Members receive a written confirmation, which includes information about the unit they confirmed and the features and amenities of the host resort.

As stated, exchange offered at the sales table is proven as a powerful inducement for new owners to buy. Developers also benefit from their exchange company affiliation when they host inbound exchange guests. These guests are highly desirable sales prospects as they already have a general understanding of vacation ownership and are on the premises at no additional cost to the developer. Existing owners who remain active members of the exchange company are equally important to developers, resort operators, and owners' associations. Satisfied owners are much more likely to continue paying off the purchase contract, stay current in their annual assessments, and refer their family and friends as sales prospects.

Since the inception of timeshare, the industry has grown dramatically. Resort developers have continued to refine their vacation products and have found creative ways to sell vacation weeks. Today's vacation ownership products include traditional fixed week intervals, floating reservation plans, fractional interests, points programs, and vacation clubs. Developers are taking advantage of other travel and leisure alternatives and showcasing them to new owners in their sales centers. Exchanging vacation weeks for cruises, airfare, car rentals, and urban hotel stays are part of today's sales presentations, yielding improved sales efficiencies.

Leading exchange providers have continued to enhance the diversity of the products they offer to their members. In 2000, RCI launched the world's first global points-based exchange system, RCI Points. This system allows timeshare owners to have their vacation ownership interests expressed as an annual quantity of points. RCI Points members can utilize their points for resort accommodations with greater flexibility in length of stay and/or size of unit. Points can also be used for airfare, rental cars, hotel stays, golf outings, and many other travel products. RCI also brought new benefits to private residence club developers and owners through the introduction of Global Registry. The Global Registry provides flexibility and added value to the luxury segment of the vacation ownership industry by providing property owners at private residence clubs access to a portfolio of fine leisure assets.

Given the importance of the exchange option, it is gratifying that, based on a recent survey, 61% of US timeshare owners report themselves 'very satisfied' with their most recent exchange vacation, while 24% are 'somewhat satisfied.' By contrast, only 9% express any level of dissatisfaction. Exchange providers will continue to find new and innovative ways to enhance their offerings and seek new ways to provide quality vacation experiences.

References

Miner, Steven (2001) *Timeshare Purchases: A Profile of Recent Activity*. Ragatz Associates/RCI, NJ.

Miner, Steven S. and Leavitt Jackman, Lisa (2000) *Increase in Weeks Owned and High Satisfaction Levels*. KPMG Peat Marwick LLP and Steven Miner Research and Appraisal.

JOY TALBOT-POWERS
RESORT CONDOMINIUMS
INTERNATIONAL, USA

Vacation ownership

The term is used to describe a method of use and ownership of vacation property in common-interests subdivisions including timeshare resorts, second homes, fractional interest resorts, membership campground interests, and recreational-subdivision lots.

'Timeshare unit' means an accommodation of a timeshare plan which is divided into timeshare periods. The smallest timeshare period is a unit week, which means that the purchaser buys one week out of 52 possible weeks.

'Timeshare plan' means any arrangement, plan, scheme, or similar device, other than an exchange program, whether by membership, agreement, tenancy in common, sale, lease, deed, rental agreement, license, or right-to-use agreement or by any other means, whereby a purchaser, for consideration, receives ownership rights in or a right to use accommodations, and facilities, if any, for a period of time less than a full year during any given year, but not necessarily for consecutive years. It is important to differentiate this from the exchange program because all timeshare plans reside with a specific developer and not an exchange company.

References

American Resort Development Association (2002) *The Timeshare Industry Resource Manual.* Washington, DC: ARDA.
http://www.flsenate.gov/Statutes/index.cfm?App_mode=Display_Statute&Search_String=&URL=Ch0721/SEC05.HTM&Title=-> 2003-> Ch0721-> Section percent2005.

MICHAEL HAUSHALTER
ORLANDO, FLORIDA, USA

VALS

VALS is one of several consumer profiling and segmentation services available through market research firms. VALS was created by Scarborough Research. The VALS system consists of eight different segments to which a consumer may belong, based on the consumer's primary motivation and his or her access to resources to fulfill their needs and motivations. These segments include Innovators, Thinkers, Achievers, Experiencers, Believers, Strivers, Makers, and Survivors.

There are many ways to use VALS. The system may be used in new product development by comparing the company's proposed targeted customer base with the profiles most closely associated with the target. VALS can offer insight into the likes and dislikes of the proposed target group, as well as offer suggestions on how best to structure and present an advertising message. VALS may also be used for existing products and services, where the current customer base is surveyed using the VALS survey to gain greater insight into the current customer. This tool may be useful in increasing sales of existing products, developing new products, and uncovering potential new customer segments.

Reference

Scarborough Research – Scarborough Consulting Business Intelligence. Available from http:// www.sric-bi.com/VALS/.

DINA MARIE V. ZEMKE
UNIVERSITY OF NEW HAMPSHIRE, USA

Value-added statement

The difference between what a hotel pays for the goods and services that it sells and the price that it sells them for represents the hotel's value-added. Preparation of a value-added statement can allow management to consider what proportion of value-added is consumed by expenses such as staff costs, rent paid, etc. As can be seen from the example below, this can be facilitated in a value-added statement by stating all elements of the statement as a percentage of the total value-added. A value-added statement should not be confused with 'economic value-added,' which can be calculated by taking an organization's operating profit minus its annual cost of capital.

ABC HOTEL
Value-Added Statement for the year
ended 31 December, 200X

	$	%
Sales revenue	85,000	
Bought-in goods and services	35,000	
Value-added	50,000	100
Applied the following way:		
To pay employees		
Wages, pensions, etc.	24,000	48
To pay providers of financial capital		
Interest on debt capital	4,500	9
Dividends	6,500	13
To pay providers of physical capital		
Lease payments	5,000	10
To pay for fixed asset maintenance and expansion	9,000	18
Depreciation	1,000	2
Retained profit		
Value-added	50,000	100

Reference

Owen, G. (1998) *Accounting for Hospitality, Tourism and Leisure*, 2nd edn. Harlow: Longman.

CHRIS GUILDING
GRIFFITH UNIVERSITY, AUSTRALIA

Value drivers

Value drivers are indicators of a company's core values. Expressed in terms of measurable operating variables or activities that approximate the potential and often intangible assets of companies, changes in value drivers significantly impact the market value of a company. For example, a hotel company's value drivers may include growth, market share, technology, level of service, and amenities. The main utility of a value driver lies in its function to measure an overall corporate performance and estimate the company's market value by adding non-financial aspects to the evaluation process. To this end, value drivers are of interest to anyone concerned with measuring corporate performance such as investors, operators, and shareholders. The significance of value drivers may be inferred from the estimation that non-financial performance accounts for as much as 35% of institutional investors' valuation for public companies (Low and Seisfeld, 1998). In this respect, value drivers have significant implications for the hospitality industry, given the intangible nature of hospitality products. They provide some critical insights into foodservice operations that often go unnoticed under the conventional accounting-based approach to property valuation often based on Uniform System of Accounts or RevPASH.

Although there is no specified list of value drivers, critical value drivers may be categorized into nine areas (Kalafut and Low, 2001):

1. *Innovation* involves a company's value in terms of its future growth. Value drivers for innovation in the hospitality industry may include, for example, R&D expenditures.
2. *Quality* reflects a company's focus toward product and service features as its core values. Specified quality standards or product features are examples of value drivers reflecting quality.
3. *Customer relations* address a company's commitment to its clients. Loyalty programs for customer relations or online reservation services may be examples of value drivers in this category.
4. *Management capabilities* reflect the value of human resources and leadership in a company. Performance appraisals for key managerial employees or the quality of executive development programs may be used as value drivers to measure management capabilities.
5. *Alliances* refer to a company's strength in terms of external resources. Value drivers in alliances may be measured in terms of the number of external alliances and joint ventures, or the market value of the alliance companies.
6. *Technologies* are the fastest growing category of value drivers. In-room Internet connections and express check-out using TV monitors are examples of technology-related value drivers.

7. *Brand value* is one of the major concerns of chain hospitality corporations. The image associated with a brand has significant impact on a company's performance. The value of the brand may be influenced by value drivers such as strength of brand image among main competitors.
8. *Quality of employees* also impacts value creation. After all, employees play a main role in service delivery in the hospitality industry. Value drivers that reflect employee quality include performance appraisals and the quality and quantity of training offered to employees.
9. *Environmental and community concerns* also affect a company's value. For example, two restaurants offering identical products and services may perform differently in different neighborhoods.

A recent study of US hospitality operations from the perspective of the operators revealed that value drivers have changed for them in the recent years (Watkins, 2003). Operators use value drivers to identify specific product features that motivate customers to purchase their products and services. While the price and location are still the dominant value drivers that attract customers, increasing numbers of customers lead to new value drivers. The findings suggest that while traditional value drivers, such as price and location, still account for approximately 70% of customers' selection criteria, approximately 30% of the selection process is led by new value drivers such as technology, loyalty points, and customization options. The study further suggests that hospitality corporations, in an effort to respond to rapidly changing market needs, are offering varieties of new value drivers such as wireless Internet access (e.g., cyber cafés) and customized frequent customer programs. However, merely adding new drivers without identifying what a company's core values are will be misleading. In order to maximize the gain from their value drivers, hospitality companies should first thoroughly understand their markets, identify the core values that differentiate them from the competition, and add or create new value drivers that are meaningful. Obviously, different value drivers influence different market segments, and the value is added only if the new drivers tap into target markets that are significant for the company.

A good example of this is McDonald's strategy in 2004. In response to concerns of obesity and possible linkages with diets high in fat, the multinational quick service giant launched a campaign surrounding a line of salads. Tying quality, brand value, and community concerns together, the firm successfully increased stock price and customer loyalty.

References

Kalafut, P.C. and Low, J. (2001) The value creation index: quantifying intangible value. *Strategy and Leadership*, 29 (5), 9–15.

Low, J. and Seisfeld. I. (1998) Measures that matter: Wall Street considers non-financial performance more than you think. *Strategy and Leadership*, 26 (2), 24–28.

Watkins, E. (2003) How guests choose hotels. *Lodging Hospitality*, 59 (20), 36–40.

MASAKO TAYLOR
TAYLOR ASSOCIATES, JAPAN

Value pricing

Value pricing is a marketing tool that bases product prices primarily on the consumer's perception of value for a given product. The application of value pricing is an effort to satisfy consumer demand for value without decreasing the quality of the product (Hayes and Huffmann, 1995). There are several value pricing strategies that a hospitality firm can apply, such as everyday value pricing, bundling, and special offers at given times.

However, value pricing can be a risky technique if hospitality firms apply it merely as a discounting strategy in order to increase their market share, hoping to achieve a profit with increased sales volumes. In order to make value pricing a financial success, hospitality operators have to learn what represents value in their customers' minds and set prices accordingly. Value pricing strategies ideally are based on knowledge of how relationships between price and quality affect perceptions of value. These relationships can be investigated by applying price sensitivity measurement (PSM) techniques. The results then can serve as the basis for successful value-pricing, as was demonstrated by Taco Bell who created its very successful 59-cents value menu based on such an analysis (Lewis and Shoemaker, 1997).

References

Hayes, D. and Huffman, L. (1995) Value pricing: how low can you go? *Cornell Hotel and Restaurant Administration Quarterly*, 36 (1), 51–56.

Lewis, R. and Shoemaker, S. (1997) Price sensitivity measurement: a tool for the hospitality industry. *Cornell Hotel and Restaurant Administration Quarterly*, 38 (2), 44–54.

CAROLA RAAB
UNIVERSITY OF NEW HAMPSHIRE, USA

Variable costs

A variable cost varies in direct proportion to the level of business activity. Thus, where the level of business increases by 10%, variable costs can be expected to rise by approximately 10%. Examples of variable costs include cost of casual labor, guest supplies, travel agents' commission, laundry in a hotel, and beverage cost of sales and the cost of raw material such as food in a restaurant. If variable costs are linear, then the cost per unit is independent of the volume (remains constant) and there are no economies or diseconomies of scale effects. When variable cost per unit is decreasing (e.g. if there are discounts for the purchases of larger quantities of raw material), there are scale advantages, but when variable cost per unit is increasing (e.g. need for more overtime work if the volume increases) there are scale disadvantages.

The balance between fixed and variable costs is open to strategic choice. Variable costs can be turned into fixed cost through automation. Fast food chains normally have comparatively high fixed costs. Purchasing semi-finished dishes may be a means to turn fixed labor costs into variable costs.

References

Horngren, C.T., Foster, G., and Datar, S.M. (2000) *Cost Accounting: A Managerial Emphasis*, 10th edn. London: Prentice-Hall International.

Schmidgall, R.S. (2002) *Hospitality Industry Managerial Accounting*, 5th edn. Lansing, MI: Educational Institute of the American Hotel and Lodging Association.

TOMMY D. ANDERSSON
GOTEBORGS UNIVERSITY, SWEDEN

Variable costs in foodservice

Total variable costs change based on the number of customers patronizing a foodservice establishment. As the number of customers increases, the total variable costs for that restaurant also increase. Conversely, if the number of customers decreases, the total variable costs decrease. However, over the short term, the variable cost per customer will not change. This means that for each customer who patronizes the establishment, total variable costs will increase by the same amount, on average. Examples of variable costs include food, beverages, and some labor costs, as well as some costs of supplies used in food production and service areas.

In larger operations, variable costs may not be as linearly correlated with guest volume as is the case in smaller restaurants. This is due to rebate programs and other economies of scale that allow larger-volume operators to reduce variable costs increasingly with guest patronage. This has ramifications for pricing strategies and breakeven analysis. It is also important in budgeting and places even more importance on the accuracy of related forecasts.

Reference

Reynolds, D. (2008) *Foodservice Management Fundamentals*. Hoboken, NJ: John Wiley & Sons.

DEBORAH BARRASH
UNIVERSITY OF NEVADA, LAS VEGAS, USA

Vending

According to the National Automatic Merchandising Association (NAMA), vending is defined as 'providing service at an unattended point of sale through the use of monetarily-driven equipment' (NAMA, 2004). Vending machines can be found in many locations, ranging from schools to businesses to medical facilities to hospitality properties.

While vending operations are very impersonal, they are also very convenient for customers whose purchasing needs fall outside of traditional business hours or where desired services and products are not otherwise available. A major advantage from an operator's perspective is the ability to provide food/drink/snack service while incurring low or no labor costs. The four most common items distributed through vending machines are candy, cigarettes, soda (soft drinks), and coffee. Through technology and innovation the industry has evolved to include such products as hot and cold entrées, frozen foods, and dairy products, which may be purchased using coins, bills, or credit cards.

NAMA (2004) estimates that the vending industry racks up US$19–28 billion in sales annually. Based on the National Restaurant Association's 'Restaurant Industry Forecast' for 2004, these numbers equate to 4.3–6.4% of total projected food and drink sales in the United States (2004).

References

National Automatic Merchandising Association (2004) Vending 101 (online). Available at http://www.vending.org/doc/vending101_english.doc. Accessed on 9 March 2004.

National Restaurant Association (2004) Restaurant Industry Forecast (on-line). Available at http://www.restaurant.org/research/ind_glance.cfm. Accessed on 9 March 2004.

NANCY SWANGER
WASHINGTON STATE UNIVERSITY, USA

Ventilation system

Ventilation contributes to human comfort. Air inside an occupied building can become stale and stagnant. In hotels, activities such as smoking and cooking tend to magnify this problem. Consequently, the air in the building needs either to be filtered or to be replaced with fresh outside air. The replacement of inside air with air from the outside will raise heating and cooling costs because this outside air must be brought to the inside air temperature; thus a good air filtration system may be a cost-effective investment. In addition, building surroundings that allow free movement of winds may have positive impact on ventilation.

Buying a ventilation system based strictly on low price is generally not a wise economic decision in the long run. A well-insulated building is always easier to ventilate than one with too little or poor insulation. The ventilation system also interacts with the heating and cooling systems. Ventilation requires air movement and this can have a cooling effect. Heated or cooled air is sometimes distributed around a building by ventilation-assisted air movement; when this occurs, the ventilation system becomes a part of the heating and/or cooling system. Thus, although the ventilation system alone is responsible for providing fresh, clean air, all the elements of the HVAC system must work together to provide the most comfortable combination of temperature, humidity, and air speed.

References

http://www.gov.on.ca/OMAFRA/english/engineer/facts/94-045.htm

Palmer, J.D. (1990) *Principles of Hospitality Engineering*. New York: Van Nostrand Reinhold.

BENNY CHAN
THE HONG KONG POLYTECHNIC
UNIVERSITY, HONG KONG SAR, CHINA

Vertical transportation

There are many ways of moving people and equipment vertically through a multi-story building. The most common method is using the stairs. Most modern commercial buildings have one or more pieces of equipment that allow them to move people and objects mechanically.

This equipment falls into the general category of vertical transportation. Vertical transportation systems that are most commonly found in the hospitality buildings include elevators, escalators, and dumbwaiters.

Elevators

Elevators are the most common type of vertical transportation equipment found in hospitality properties. They are equipped with numerous redundant safety devices, resulting in a form of transportation that is one of the safest in the world for transporting both equipment and passengers. There are three basic types of elevator equipment, each serving a different set of operational parameters – hydraulic elevators, geared elevators, and gearless elevators.

Hydraulic elevators are the most prevalent type of elevator. They are designed to be used in buildings with a relatively low vertical rise, usually serving between two and six stops. Traditional hydraulic elevators operate using a piston-and-cylinder arrangement, where a cylinder is buried in the ground beneath the elevator cab and a piston, attached to the bottom of the cab, travels up and down the cylinder to raise and lower the elevator. The piston is propelled by fluid, usually a specially formulated oil that is pumped in and out of the cylinder. This mechanical process results in a relatively slow elevator, with speeds ranging from 50–150 feet/minute (0.254–0.762 meters/second). Many new hydraulic elevators are being installed that use piston-and-cylinder arrangements that are not buried in the ground, which greatly reduces installation time and expense, since it does not require a hole to be drilled into the ground for the cylinder. The 'holeless' hydraulic elevator also reduces the risk of a hole forming in the side of the cylinder which can result in hydraulic fluid leaking into the surrounding ground.

Buildings that require greater speed and travel height typically turn to geared and gearless elevators to accomplish the task. Geared and gearless elevators do not use a piston-and-cylinder arrangement to raise and lower the elevator. Instead, the elevator cab is attached to a 'rope,' or wire cable, that travels over a grooved sheave at the top of the hoistway. The other end of the rope is attached to a counterweight that travels in the opposite direction of the elevator. Geared elevators are designed to serve mid-rise buildings (i.e., 6–20 stops) at medium speeds, ranging from 250–500 feet per minute (1.27–2.54 meters/second). Gearless elevators are designed to serve buildings with a higher rise, and usually travel at higher speeds, ranging from 400 to 1500 feet/minute (2.03–7.62 meters/second).

Escalators

Escalators are moving staircases. They are complex mechanical systems that are very effective at moving large volumes of people over relatively short distances. Some escalators are capable of moving more that 6000 passengers per hour. The escalator carries passengers from one floor to another. Escalators are the most expensive type of vertical transportation equipment, both to install as well as to maintain. The expense is due to the complexity of the equipment and the hundreds of moving parts in the system that must be maintained regularly and properly to insure safe and consistent operation.

The basic parts of an escalator include the steps, the handrail and balustrade, the truss, motors, and safety equipment. The steps are the part of the escalator that passengers stand on. The handrail is a moving rail that travels in sync with the steps. The handrail sits on top of the balustrade, which rises vertically above the steps. The balustrade may be skinned in metal or may be made of glass. The truss is the structure in which the escalator components are located and provides the support for the entire system.

A modern hotel escalator may be equipped with several safety devices to prevent injury, depending on the age of the escalator and national and local code requirements. Some of the more common devices include lighting at the top and bottom landing, lines painted on the steps to help passengers identify the edges of the steps, manually-operated emergency stop switches, stop switches that are activated in the event of equipment failure, and special panels designed to close the gap between the balustrade and the moving steps.

Dumbwaiters

Dumbwaiters are small elevators that are designed to carry materials only. Dumbwaiters are usually hoisted using a drum-style machine, where a cable is wrapped around a drum. The dumbwaiter descends when the cable is unwrapped and ascends when the drum reverses direction and rewraps the cable.

Dumbwaiters can land at floor level, or anywhere above the floor to facilitate easy loading and unloading of materials. Foodservice operations will often use dumbwaiters to transport food to service areas located on floors different from the food preparation areas, as well as to transport dirty dishes to a kitchen stewarding area on a different level. Hotels often use dumbwaiters to transport linens as well as to move room service food and beverages.

Unlike elevators, there are no safety systems built into a dumbwaiter that make it safe for passengers to ride. It is important that hotel and restaurant managers ensure that their employees do not ride in dumbwaiters.

Reference

Starkest, G.R. (ed.) (1998) *The Vertical Transportation Handbook*, 3rd edn. New York: John Wiley & Sons.

DINA MARIE V. ZEMKE
UNIVERSITY OF NEW HAMPSHIRE, USA

Virtual reality

Virtual reality is a computer simulation that offers the user the opportunity to experience different kinds of pre-produced programs, as if in real time (Williams and Hobson, 1995). It enables users to enjoy computer-generated environments that offer three-dimensional perspectives through the use of sound, sight, and touch technology. Using virtual reality, it is possible to simulate the physical environment of almost any tourism destinations or hospitality facility.

Virtual reality enables people who have the equipment to experience artificial tourism products and services at low cost. It can also provide tourism experiences to those who are unable to travel because of physical disabilities or illnesses, lack of skills, or lack of sufficient time (Bennett, 1996). There are challenges to address in giving a feeling for the social and cultural aspects of a destination or of smelling and tasting. Regarding the impact of virtual reality on the future of the hospitality industry, some commentators argue that people will have no need to visit a hospitality facility because 'virtual' conditions can provide the perfect experience. Others suggest that the chance to test or practice an experience will generate higher demand to visit the real place.

References

Bennett, M.M. (1996) Information technology and databases for tourism. In A.V. Seaton and M.M. Bennett (eds), *Marketing Tourism Products*. Oxford: International Thomson Business Press, pp. 421–443.

Williams, P. and Hobson, J.S.P. (1995) Virtual reality and tourism: fact or fantasy? *Tourism Management*, 16 (6), 423–427.

METIN KOZAK
MUGLA UNIVERSITY, TURKEY

Vortal

A vortal is a gateway to Web content on a particular subject area. A vortal may also be more simply defined as the industry-specific equivalent of the general-purpose portal (e.g. Yahoo.com) on the Web. Vortals are also known as vertical portals, VEP or vertical enterprise portals, vertical-market websites, vertical industry portals, or voice portals. Vortals can be corporate portals, business intelligence portals, Web hubs, or Interest community websites. Vortals provide information and resources including research and statistics, discussions, newsletters, online tools, and many other services that educate users about a specific industry such as travel, insurance, automobiles, food manufacturing, and healthcare. Vortals also give users a single place to communicate with and about a single industry. Some vortals may be accessible by telephone, hence the term voice portal. Examples of hospitality vortals are www.hospitalityindia.info and www.hotelshop.co.za that provide information for suppliers to the hospitality industry and their purchasers. On the consumer side, www. travelplan.it is a vortal on Italian tourism providing consumers with booking as well as national, regional, and local information on Italy.

References

Jafari, A. and Sheehan, M. (2003) *Designing Portals: Opportunities and Challenges*. Hershey, PA: Idea Group Publishing.

Wang, S. (2001) Vortal defined. *IT-specific Encyclopedia*. Available at http://whatis.techtarget.com.

JULINE E. MILLS
PURDUE UNIVERSITY, USA

Walk-in

A walk-in refers to a person who arrives at a lodging facility without a reservation. According to the American Hotel and Motel Association, a walk-in is an excellent opportunity to increase sales and occupancy. Therefore, treat the walk-in guest just as warmly as a guest who has a reservation. First ask the guest the length of his/her stay to ascertain that a room is available for the requested days. If space is available for the entire length of his/her stay then the available rate should be quoted. The walk-in guest is an excellent opportunity to practice upselling and maximizing potential revenue for the property.

A person who says they have a reservation that cannot be found would also be treated as a walk-in. In this case the front desk staff must try to minimize the loss of the reservation by moving on quickly and asking the guest for the necessary information to check him/her into the property. However, if the lodging facility is in a sold-out situation, the clerk should make every effort to find the reservation, and if it cannot be found should apologize and offer to locate the person in alternative accommodation (walking the guest).

Reference

American Hotel and Motel Association (1996) *Hospitality Skills Training Series: Front Desk Employee Guide*. Lansing, MI: Educational Institute of the American Hotel and Motel Association.

Stutts, Alan T. (2001) *Hotel and Lodging Management – An Introduction*. New York: John Wiley & Sons.

MORGAN GEDDIE
UNIVERSITY OF HOUSTON, USA

Walking the guest

When a guest arrives at a lodging facility with a guaranteed reservation and there are no rooms available the guest must be sent to a similar lodging facility at the expense of the facility that did not honor the reservation. The guest should be given free transportation to the facility and one free long-distance phone call to notify someone of the change in where they will be staying. If the guest had a reservation for more than one night, every effort should be made to move the person back to the property the next day. The key to minimizing the negative impact of walking a guest is preparation. According to the Educational Institute of the American Hotel and Motel Association (1996), when facing a sold-out situation the front desk should contact similar properties to inquire of their availability and be prepared to send a guest to a different establishment prior to their arrival. PBX should be notified so calls and messages may be forwarded to the displaced guest. If the guest returns the next day, a gesture can be made such as arranging for an upgrade on their room and placing a gift basket in the room with a letter of apology.

Reference

American Hotel and Motel Association (1996) *Hospitality Skills Training Series: Front Desk Employee Guide*. Lansing, MI: Educational Institute of the American Hotel and Motel Association.

Stutts, Alan T. (2001) *Hotel and Lodging Management – An Introduction*. New York: John Wiley & Sons.

MORGAN GEDDIE
UNIVERSITY OF HOUSTON, USA

Wall reader

A wall reader is an important part of a smart card system. A small fob or card can be held near the reader, at a distance of from 4 to 24 feet depending on the model, and an electric strike or magnetic lock opens. The reader can be mounted inside or behind the wall in areas where vandalism is a problem. Each reader has a unique identification number. Some of the readers have a keypad built in to use for programming.

Programming is easy to do and is actually done right at the reader itself, using either the proximity keys that come with the reader or by using the number buttons (keypad) built into the unit. A laptop or PC can also be used to program the system and do audit trails (who entered and when). The system can monitor who goes in and who goes out of the area, offering greater security control. In hotel operations, it can lower operation cost through fewer handling errors, decreasing production time, and minimizing excess programmed proximity cards in inventory. It is simple to use and the software allows the administrator to set usage permission for the users.

References

http://www.nokey.com/proxread.html

http://www.vttech.com/Products/products_PW.htm

BENNY CHAN
THE HONG KONG POLYTECHNIC
UNIVERSITY, HONG KONG, SAR, CHINA

Warnings to employees

Poor performing employees need to be managed carefully and fairly through separate performance appraisals with formal and documented processes. In many cases employers will also use verbal and written 'warnings' in an attempt to improve employee performance (De Cieri and Kramar, 2003).

A verbal caution given to a hospitality employee usually represents the first step of the disciplinary action process relating to management action aimed at controlling, punishing, modifying or inhibiting undesirable employee behavior (e.g. absenteeism, poor performance, inefficiency, negligence, safety violation etc.). In most instances where there is a strong human resources management (HRM) focus, there is a formal disciplinary code or procedure to be followed. In some industrial jurisdictions, disciplinary action or a disciplinary code or grievance procedure are codified either by statute or in industrial awards or determinations.

A formal warning or reprimand of a hospitality employee usually represents the second stage of the disciplinary process (Woods, 2002). Whilst there are no specific legislative guidelines in most countries, as a rule, there is a verbal warning, followed by either one or two written warnings alerting the employee that their behavior is unsatisfactory and may lead to the termination of their employment should they not improve.

References

De Cieri, H. and Kramar, R. (2003) *Human Resource Management in Australia: Strategy, People, Performance*. Sydney: McGraw-Hill.

Woods, R.H. (2002) *Managing Hospitality Human Resources*, 3rd edn. Lansing, MI: Educational Institute of the American Hotel and Lodging Association.

NILS TIMO
GRIFFITH UNIVERSITY, AUSTRALIA

Waste factor/yield

When calculating recipe and portion costs, allowances need to be made for unavoidable waste when calculating the recipe yield. Failure to do so will result in understating portion costs. Subsequently, instead of figuring on 100% yield from a recipe, assume that only 98% will be actually used, allowing 2% for evaporation, over-portioning, and quality control waste. This percentage of waste will differ depending on the menu item. There is a higher allowance for waste on items prepared from scratch than on items that are purchased pre-portioned. For example, if steaks are purchased pre-cut, there would be zero tolerance for waste and over-portioning. However, if steaks were cut in-house, the yield (number of steaks) from a primal cut of meat will vary depending on the weight of the primal cut and the skill of the butcher. Once the steaks are cut and sent to the kitchen for sale, however, there would be zero tolerance for waste or quality control. Furthermore, yield calculations are most critical for more expensive items, such as meats, since these have a more dramatic impact on cost and profit outcomes.

Reference

Mutkoski, S.A. and Schurer, M.L. (1981) *Meat and Fish Management.* North Scituate, MA: Breton.

DAVID V. PAVESIC
GEORGIA STATE UNIVERSITY, USA

Water and waste water systems

Hospitality facilities require relatively large amounts of water and create large amounts of wastewater as well. Water is used by hotels in guestroom areas for bathing and sanitary purposes. Food and beverage operations use water for food preparation, cooking, and a variety of cleaning purposes. Laundry operations are also substantial consumers of water. Grounds and landscaping can consume significant amounts of water as well. Swimming pools require a substantial amount of water when filled and ongoing amounts to replace water lost to evaporation and other losses. Finally, operations with cooling towers can evaporate large amounts of water in their operation.

Usage of water in hotels can range from 40,000 gallons per room per year for economy properties to 80,000 gallons for upscale and as much as 150,000 gallons for resort operations. The variation is primarily due to the items discussed in the paragraph above (e.g. does the property have F&B, etc.).

Water costs are typically composed of a charge for water supply and a charge for waste-water removal and treatment. In the United States, total water costs typically range from $3 to $8 per 1000 gallons – about 50% being supply charges. Water can be produced by the property itself from a well or other water source rather inexpensively. Water can also be produced by operation of a desalinization plant – a very expensive but sometimes unavoidable option. In addition to the water cost itself, the cost of hot water is increased by the cost of the fuel. The result is that hot water can cost an additional $8 to $20 per 1000 gallons.

Water systems require water at a proper pressure and in adequate quantity. Pumps may operate on the water system within the building to provide pressure and quantity as needed. The hot water system also needs water supplied at an appropriate temperature. Many hotel operations in the United States attempt to supply hot water at approx. 120 °F (48 °C) at the supply point with a target of approx. 115 °F (46 °C) at the actual point of use. Water for sanitizing purposes in F&B is generally produced at 140 °F (60 °C) with supplemental heating done at the point of use as needed.

Each usage of water within the building has requirements regarding the quality of the water. Water quality refers to the bacteriological, physical (taste, clarity, and odor), radiological, and chemical characteristics of water relative to its safety for human consumption. Standards specify maximum contaminant levels that may occur in potable (drinkable) water. Quality water standards governing potable water in the United States (US) are set forth in the Safe Drinking Water Act of 1974; it was amended in 1986 and again in 1996. The law is enforced by the US Environmental Protection Agency. If the facility's water comes from a source other than a public water utility, maintaining water quality becomes the responsibility of the hospitality manager.

If the water supplied by the water utility is potable, the operation does not need to do further treatment. However, sometimes this is not the case for the utility water or the property is supplying water from its own source. In this instance water treatment is needed. This treatment involves the removal of any suspended solids as well as some sort of treatment to kill bacteria. Bacteria are often killed using chlorine although in some locations this is done via ultra-violet radiation or ozone. Sometimes there is a need for additional treatment as well to remove some other contaminants.

A common water treatment is softening. This is done to remove calcium or magnesium from the water. Removal of these minerals allows the water to more easily create a soap lather when bathing. It also reduces the chances of a mineral buildup on plumbing fixtures and of spotting on surfaces. There are also advantages of softening for water used in other equipment, as is noted below.

Additional water treatment will be necessary for water supplied to boilers and cooling towers (CT), pools and laundry equipment in a facility. These additional specifications concern maximum allowable limits on hardness (calcium and magnesium), alkalinity, dissolved solids, suspended solids, dissolved oxygen, carbon dioxide, iron, manganese, silica, and microorganisms. If the equipment water quality is not controlled properly it can cause formation of inorganic deposits and corrosion in boiler tubes and CT, soap curd (scum), and fabric damage. Untreated or stagnant water in CT, air conditioning (AC) drip pans, fountains, hot tubs, showerheads, and faucets, etc. encourages algae formation that can foul pumps and equipment and foster bacterial growth that can lead to Legionnaire's disease. Managers are responsible for ensuring that preventative maintenance is done on all AC coils and that AC pans are clean and treated. They are also responsible for insuring that proper chemical levels are maintained at all times in spas, hot tubs, indoor fountains, and cooling towers. Showerheads and aerators should be cleaned or replaced on a schedule.

Waste water is the used water and solids from the facility flowing into a septic system or treatment plant. Storm water, surface water, and ground water are included in the definition of waste water and depending on location, may also enter a waste water treatment plant. Waste water standards define maximum contaminant allowances rather than 'quality' specifications. Of particular concern for discharged waste water is the water temperature, biological oxygen demand, and the amount of fat, oil, and grease, total suspended solids, and microorganisms present.

In facilities there are essentially two waste water systems – the sanitary sewer system and the storm sewer system. Additional subsystems may feed into these two systems. Bathroom, restroom, and other waste water discharges flow into the sanitary sewer system, which are treated by the local or regional sewage treatment facilities. Kitchen discharges also flow into this system, but must first pass through a grease trap (grease separator) for grease removal. Circulating boiler and cooling tower water discharges – 'bleed streams' – and laundry water discharges should also enter the sanitary sewer system. Chemical content of these two subsystems may have to be monitored to avoid surpassing waste water contaminant allowances.

'Gray water' or 'run-off' water from roof drains, parking lots, and other outdoor areas of the property enter the storm sewer system. This waste water may be diverted into holding ponds to be used for landscape or other outdoor watering systems. However, this water will also have contaminants that may have to be monitored.

Back flow prevention devices are installed in the main water line to a building just after the water meter. The devices are used to prevent a hotel's water system from over-pressurizing and forcing the water back into the municipality's system. This can happen if a domestic booster pump is higher pressure than the municipality's water pressure or if the municipal system were to lose pressure.

Back flow prevention devices are becoming a standard requirement in a majority of cities. Typically, annual or bi-annual testing of the device is required by the municipalities or fines can be incurred, including having the water turned off at the meter.

References

Harrison, J.F. and McGowan, W. (1997) *WQA Glossary of Terms.* Lisle: Water Quality Association.

Kemmer, F.N. (ed.) (1988) *Nalco Water Handbook.* New York/St Louis: McGraw-Hill.

Stipanuk, D.M. (2002) *Hospitality Facilities Management and Design*, 2nd edn. Lansing, MI: Educational Institute of the American Hotel and Lodging Association.

www.epa.gov/OGWDW/wot/appa.html

CONNIE E. HOLT
WIDENER UNIVERSITY, USA

Weighted average cost of capital (WACC)

The WACC calculates the overall cost of capital for a company. The funds of capital of a company are divided into equity capital (E) and debt capital (De). The costs of each of the funds are different because they bear different levels of risk for the lenders. Namely: dividend (D) is the cost of the use of equity capital provided by the shareholders, and interest (I) is the cost of the use of debt capital provided by capital lenders. The average between the rate of dividend (total dividend paid divided by equity capital) and the rate of interest (total interest paid divided by debt capital) is the average cost of capital. Such a measure can be calculated as follows:

$$\text{WACC} = I \times [\text{De}/(\text{De} + \text{E})] + D \times [\text{E}/(\text{De} + \text{E})]$$

By rearranging the formula in a few steps it is possible to demonstrate that WACC is the IRR of the overall company, coming to the following formula, where the assumption is made that dividend and interest are perpetual:

$$\text{De} + \text{E} = [D_1/(1 + \text{WACC}) + I_1/(1 + \text{WACC})] - [D_2/(1 + \text{WACC})^2 + I_2/(1 + \text{WACC})^2] - \ldots$$

$$- [D_n/(1 + \text{WACC})^n + I_n/(1 + \text{WACC})^n]$$

Therefore, the WACC is the average cost of capital employed by the company as well as the average rate of return expected by both shareholders and capital lenders – adjusted by adding the company's costs – if considered together.

The expected cost (I) of debt capital (De) – which includes bonds (B) and preferred stock (PS) – is calculated as the weighted average of:

The discount rate (K_b) that makes the present value of the sum of the future flows of interest (Cf_b) paid to the bondholders and the present value of the bond's maturity (M) equal to the net proceeds from the bonds (NP_b), where the adjustment for considering the issuing costs is included by using NP_b rather than the market value of the bond, as follows:

$$NP_b = Cf_1/(1 + K_b) + Cf_2/(1 + K_b)^2 + Cf_3/(1 + K_b)^3 + \cdots + Cf_n/(1 + K_b)^n + M/(1 + K_b)^n$$

and

the rate (K_{ps}) calculated as the preferred stock dividend (D_{ps}) divided by net proceeds from preferred stocks (NP_{ps}), where the adjustment for considering the floating costs is included by using NP_{ps} rather than the market value of the preferred stock, as follows:

$$K_{ps} = D_{ps}/NP_{ps}$$

resulting in:

$$I = K_b [B/(B + PS)] + K_{ps} [PS/(B + PS)]$$

The expected cost (D) of equity capital (E) is calculated as the sum of the risk-free rate (K_{rf}) and the gap between the risk-free rate and the expected rate of return of the market (K_m), adjusted by the stock's risk (b), as follows:

$$\text{De} = K_{rf} + b (K_m - K_{rf})$$

An easier, but less accurate, way of calculating I and De is as follows:

I = (current interest + current preferred stock dividend)/(B + PS)

De = current ordinary stock dividend/E

This simplified method assumes that the ordinary stock dividend is constant and that the nominal value of bonds, ordinary, and preferred stock is equal to their market value.

The WACC is used to discount the cash flows when the net present value (NPV) method is applied to evaluate a project. The concept underpinning this choice is known as the 'pool of funds' concept, which refers to the cash entering the company's general pool of cash, which is then used for different projects. This cash is not earmarked for use when it enters the company, and therefore the cost related to the company cash is the same for all projects, as it is impossible to track where the specific cash comes from.

Some assumptions limit the validity of the use of WACC to discount cash flows in the NPV:

- The capital structure is assumed to be constant, in order for the two funds of capital to weigh the same before and after the project.
- The level of risk of the project should be comparable to that of the company in order to be equally well represented by the WACC.
- The size of the new project must be small relative to the size of the company in order for the rate of interest and the rate of dividend to be a realistic cost of the new cash needed for the project.
- All cash flows (dividend, interest, project cash flows) should be level perpetuities in order to make the calculation stated above possible.

The WACC is also used to calculate the economic value-added of a project, which is the after tax residual operating income after a figurative cost of capital has been deducted, where the figurative cost of capital used is the WACC multiplied by the capital employed (CE) (which is the working capital plus the fixed assets).

$$\text{Figurative cost of capital} = \text{WACC} \times \text{CE}$$

For different situations the relevant WACC of a project might be different, e.g. when a company establishes a subsidiary in another country, the WACC relevant to the subsidiary is based on the cost of the capital that the company is raising in the host country (in the calculation the interest paid to the parent company should arguably be replaced with a figurative interest), whilst the relevant WACC for the parent company is based on its own sources of capital.

References

Drury, C. (2000) *Management and Cost Accounting*, 5th edn. London: Thomson Learning.

Horngren, C.T., Foster, G., and Datar, S.M. (2000) *Cost Accounting: A Managerial Emphasis*, 10th edn. Upper Saddle River, NJ: Prentice-Hall International.

Keown, A.J., Martin, J.D., Petty, J.W., and Scott, D.F. Jr (2002) *Financial Management Principles and Applications*, 9th edn. Upper Saddle River NJ: Prentice-Hall International.

Lumby, S. and Jones, C. (1999) *Investment Appraisal and Financial Decisions*, 6th edn. London: Thomson Learning.

McLaney, E.J. (1994) *Business Finance for Decision-makers*, 2nd edn. London: Pitman Publishing.

MARCO MONGIELLO
UNIVERSITY OF WESTMINSTER, UK

Table 1 How to use discount cash flows when NPV is applied WACC: project to enlarge a hotel's capacity from 150 rooms to 175 rooms, with outlay of 1 million dollars paid in 2001

Equity capital of the company Dividend = 20%	$10,000,000
Debt capital of the company Interest = 5%	$5,000,000
WACC = 20% 10,000,000 / (10,000,000 + 5,000,000) + 5% 5,000,000 / (10,000,000 + 5,000,000) = 15%	

The WACC applicable to the NPV of the project is 15%

Wireless

Wireless is a term used to describe telecommunications in which electromagnetic waves (as opposed to wire) carry a signal. Early wireless transmitters used radiotelegraphy to transmit Morse code and later voice. Information communication technology (ICT) developments

Table 1　Wireless devices: standards and descriptions

Device	Standard	Range	Description
Laptop	IEEE802.IIb	Up to 100 m	Standard for WALNs used for office, residential, and public access environments to connect a number of computers together. Operates in the 2.45 GHz frequency spectrum and enables devices to link to a network over a range of 100 m at speeds of up to 11 Mb per second. Multiple users can share the bandwidth. The closer the client adapter is to the access point, the faster the speed.
	Wi-Fi	Up to 100 m	Wi-Fi is a specification and certification for IEEE802.11b equipment based on an interoperability test plan. Wi-Fi is the seal of approval that the equipment will work with all other brands of Wi-Fi certified equipment. Wireless labeled Wi-Fi meets the WECA standards for interoperability
	IEEE802.IIa	Up to 100 m	New specification for WLANs operating in the 5 GHz frequency spectrum. Five times faster than IEEE802.IIb, enabling devices to link to a network at speeds of up to 54 Mbps. Its range is shorter at higher data rates, but because it has higher bandwidth, eight channels per access point, and uses new multiplexing technology, it can support more bandwidth-intensive applications and more users. As 802.IIa and 802.IIb are in different frequency bands and use different modulations, they do not interoperate but they can be used together in the same coverage area without conflicts
	IEEE802.IIg	Up to 100 m	Like 802.Iib it operates in the 2.4 GHz frequency, but like 802.IIa, it reaches speeds of up to 54 Mbps. Compatible with 802.IIb products, sports ranges similar to 802.IIa produce higher data rates, and shares the 802.IIb version's three channels
	HiperLAN2	Up to 100 m	New European standard for WLANs operating in the 5 GHz frequency spectrum. Delivers higher quality of service and allows voice data to be prioritised
Laptop Cellular	Bluetooth	Up to 20 m	Wireless standard for connecting PDAs, cell phones, computer mice, and other peripherals to computers based on short-range radio transmission in the 2.45 GHz frequency spectrum. Connections are secure, instant, and maintained even if devices are not within line of sight
Cellular	GSM	Up to 12 km	GSM (Global System for Mobile Communication) is the de facto wireless telephone standard in 120 countries. Operates at 900 MHz or 1800 MHz frequency band. Roaming agreements between foreign operators support usage of mobile phones around the world
	WAP	Up to 12 km	WAP (Wireless Application Protocol) is a specification for a set of communication protocols to standardize the way that wireless devices can access the Internet over GSM
	WML		WML (Wireless Markup Language), is a language that allows the text portions of HTML Web pages to be presented on cellular telephones and personal digital assistants (PDAs) operating WAP
	GPRS		General Packet Radio Services (GPRS) is a packet-based wireless communication service that promises data rates of up to 114 Kbps and always on connection to the Internet for mobile phone and computer users. The higher data rates will allow users to take part in video conferences and interact with multimedia websites and similar applications using mobile handheld devices as well as notebook computers. GPRS is based on GSM communication and it is an evolutionary step toward the UMTS
	UMTS		UMTS (Universal Mobile Telecommunications Service) is a 3G broadband, packet-based transmission of multimedia data at rates of up to 2 Mbps. Based on GSM communication standard, UMTS is the planned standard for mobile users around the world
	i-Mode		i-Mode is the packet-based service for mobile phones offered by Japan's NTT DoCoMo. i-Mode uses a simplified version of HTML, Compact Wireless Markup Language (CWML), instead of WAP's WML to enable Web browsing

Source: Adapted from Searchnetworking http://searchnetworking.techtarget.com/

have proliferated the use of wireless applications and devices, including: cellular phones and pagers; global positioning systems (GPS); cordless computer peripherals and telephones; home-remote control and monitor systems.

Wireless technology has been evolving rapidly. The development of mobile telephony over the Global System for Mobile Communication (GSM) and Wireless Application Protocol (WAP) allowed the communication of voice and data over mobile phones. General Packet Radio Service (GPRS) and Universal Mobile Telecommunications System (UMTS) as well as I-Mode in Japan have gradually introduced the 3rd Generation (3G) mobile phones and services empowering the communication of multimedia information on interactive mobile devices. In addition, wireless local area networks (WLANs) allow users to connect their laptop computer through a wireless-radio connection, whilst Bluetooth connects personal digital assistants (PDAs), cell phones, computer mice, and other peripherals over short distances. A number of wireless technologies and standards have been developed (Table 1). Figure 1 demonstrates that increasingly these technologies will be converging, enabling the mobile user to utilize a variety of systems and network applications to access a range of multimedia data. Location, distance range, speed required, cost, purpose of access, easiness to use and even style determine which combination will be used at the time.

Wireless in hotels

Hotels are taking advantage of the wireless revolution to improve their own operations and strategies and to enhance customer service. GPRS is expanding, allowing users to pay only for data packets received and allowing both faster connectivity to WAP and to Internet browsers. Wi-Fi networks are also becoming widely available, through the installation of wireless hotspots for hotel guests and employees. These hotspots allow individual users to access the network via wireless cards in their laptops or wireless-enabled Internet Protocol (IP) telephone handsets or other mobile devices such as a PDA.

From the *hotel customer's point of view*, wireless services can facilitate the reservation process, especially for last minute bookings, when a traveler has arrived at a destination with no reservation. Consumers can communicate with the hotel, alter their reservations or make special requests. Whilst at the hotel, wireless access to the Internet is becoming a critical feature for accessing work information, but also for communicating with family and friends or organizing leisure activities. This is the case for people attending meetings, conferences, and exhibitions, whereas wireless access supports easy connectivity and the ability to move around within the area. Wi-Fi or Bluetooth have enabled high-speed Internet access to become a significant benefit that can augment the hospitality product. This may work as complementary to GPRS or UMTS access over mobile networks, especially for visitors from a different country who would have had to pay expensive roaming charges. In the short to medium term, offering this service can differentiate the hotel product, improve the value for money and time for guests, and lead to competitive advantage. In the longer term, access will be widely available and will be treated as a normal utility function.

From the *hotel operations point of view*, wireless technologies play an increasingly vital role for hotels, linking together everything from point-of-sale terminals to housekeeping and security management systems. Wireless allows mobility and freedom to work more productively, for both hotel employees and guests, by allowing users to access the Internet, e-mail, instant messages, and the corporate intranet from any location. Faster communication with the workforce enables better access to information and operations. Better and up-to-date communications between departments can minimize waiting times, reduce errors and increase overall productivity. In addition, hotels can use wireless portals to expand their distribution network. Also wireless services allow additional opportunities for providing added-value and location-based services. For example, a hotel hotspot may incorporate access to a pizza delivery service to complement or outsource in its entirety the room service function. Table 2 demonstrates some best practice of wireless applications in hotels.

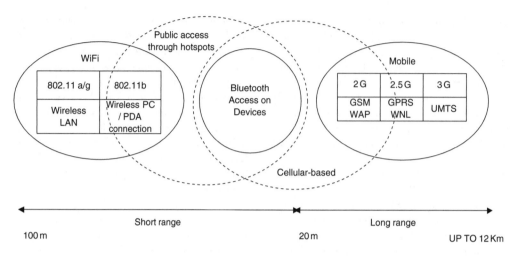

Figure 1   Convergence of wireless technologies

Table 2   Examples of best practice

Hotel chains	Applications	Applications providers
Six Continents	Mobile directions and reservations Remote check-in	Air2Web OperaPalm: Micro/Fidelio and Palm Bluetooth technology
Swissotel Hotels North America	Wireless high-speed access for all guests and meeting rooms WAP access to static guest information	
Best Western	Research locations, check availability, check frequent traveler club balance and click-to-dial reservations Online booking and m-wallet capabilities	
Hilton	Reservations, information or retrieve/cancel a reservation via any wireless PDA or mobile phone Access to loyalty programs HHonors	OpenGrid mobile solution
Marriott	Housekeeping audits of guestrooms using palms, handheld PDAs Wireless conference rooms and group meetings	Acadian Embedded Solutions; STSN- 802.11a and 802.11b (Intel Communications Fund)
Fairmont Hotels and Resorts	Wireless LAN for guests offering Web-based branded services provides interactive source for destination- based content	Cisco Systems (Wi-Fi)
Omni Hotels	Free wireless high-speed Internet service	Core Communications

Source: Adapted from mTravel.com

Wireless in hotel operational and strategic management

Hotels involve network-enabled business solutions, to improve their business functions. These include marketing and reservations, customer relationships, front and back office, training, and communications. Wireless technologies are expected to have a major impact throughout the hospitality value chain by integrating and making accessible data and processes, whilst enhancing guest experiences. Wireless Internet can also facilitate internal operations, improve effectiveness and efficiency as well as enhance guest experiences.

The wireless Internet can facilitate the innovation, adoption, and integration with existing systems. This allows further technology development, which can improve communications with employees, partners, and customers. Hotels can improve their firm infrastructure by enabling the exchange of real-time information through integrating centralized data warehouses on a comprehensive enterprise resources planning (ERP) system. Authorized members of staff access data whist on the move, making better-informed decisions, faster. Real-time communication can instigate paperless administration for planning and allocation of resources, whilst it can assist hotel mangers to share knowledge faster and to make proactive and reactive decisions. Human resources management (HRM) also benefits, as hotels can communicate more effectively with employees in the property and outside. Employees can access rota schedules and changes to programs as well as receive information on their remuneration and commissions, access training courses, and other potential benefits. Internal marketing can also be facilitated, by providing employees with information about the current status of the hotel and also special benefits for them. Wireless communications can assist a more flexible deployment of the workforce, improving productivity. Procurement also benefits as hotel buyers attending local markets access remotely real-time data, including requirements, stock levels, alternative sources, pricing, and historical data on suppliers. Wireless systems facilitate purchasing, order acceptance process, storekeeping and control functions whilst they support real-time inventory

and financial tracking for suppliers, supporting inbound logistics.

Wireless solutions bring mobility, flexibility, and productivity for hotels as they can facilitate communications using real-time data. The hotel guest is at the center and is surrounded by various applications. Integration of wireless POS (point of sales) systems and customer relationship management (CRM) gives hotels opportunities for real-time sales statistics, tracking of frequent guests/diners and personalized information. This can assist operational management and enable a wide range of proactive and reactive procedures to deal with seasonality, demand fluctuations or unexpected events. They empower hotel front-line employees, such as receptionists, waiters and chambermaids and enhance their operational efficiencies. For example, receptionists may collaborate with group leaders and check-in guests during the transfer to the hotel. Frequent customers can check-in wirelessly as soon as they arrive by using a Bluetooth-enabled device. A waiter can have access to all information related to availability of dishes, food orders, time required, kitchen delays, and bill payments at the customer's table. Housekeeping can monitor room status, cleaning process, and maintenance in real time. As this information is updated constantly, it can be followed by all relevant employees who can then adapt their schedule. Staff can reduce the time spent going forwards and backwards to their control center and dedicate more time to doing their job and serving guests.

Wireless technologies have unprecedented implications for marketing and sales. Consumers can make and change reservations anytime, anywhere, from any Internet-enabled device. Hotels will need multi-channel distribution strategies to support real-time availability with dynamic pricing to maximize their yield. Wireless-enabled devices will also provide hotel marketers with another distribution channel empowered with location-based services and customer profiling. Finally, wireless solutions can assist after-sales services such as instant feedback, update of guest history, and CRM-based marketing. Wireless technologies can also allow hotels to expand their value chains through partnerships with complementary suppliers constantly updating and differentiating their product.

Strategic developments and challenges

Wireless technologies have revolutionized the entire hotel value chain. Innovative hotels need to reengineer their processes and reexamine how to profit from emerging technologies. For example, purchases on mobile devices can add value to hotel guests through 'location/destination-based services'; whilst providing self-services through wireless technologies can mean operational and productivity gains. Hotels need to focus on the abilities of wireless technologies to enhance their competitiveness by improving their customer service and differentiation advantage, whilst reducing costs and increasing efficiency.

A number of challenges remain open. Hotels will need to readjust their business model to account for revenue lost through wired telephony/Internet and also to provide for investments required. A number of new stakeholders/partners also emerge, and they need to be addressed in the new business models. Wireless solutions will increase price transparency further. That will have implications for hotel pricing and yield management. Security of data and transactions also remains a major challenge. Finally, consumers would expect hospitality organizations to be always ready to interact, putting additional pressure on small and medium-sized enterprises that already lack expertise and capital to invest in those technologies.

Sheldon (1997) suggests that 'high-tech and high-touch' can bring efficiency, reduced costs, and the potential for higher levels of personal services. Wireless applications will propel customer-centric approaches, placing knowledge and information at the core of the competitive profile of tomorrow's hospitality enterprise (Olsen and Connolly, 2000).

References

Buhalis, D. (2003) *eTourism: Information Technology for Strategic Tourism Management*. Harlow: Pearson Education.

Computer Associates (2002) *Enabling Mobile eBusiness Success*. White paper, http://wp.bit-pipe.com/resource/org_943197149_209/ena bling_mobile_ebiz_wp_bpx.pdf.

O'Connor, P. (1999) *Electronic Information Distribution in Tourism and Hospitality*. Wallingford: CABI Publishing.

O'Connor, P. and Frew, A. (2000) Evaluating electronic channel distribution in the hotel sector: Delphi study. *Information Technology and Tourism*, 3 (3/4), 177–193.

Olsen, M. and Connolly, D. (2000) Experience-based travel: how technology is changing the hospitality industry. *Cornell Hotel and Restaurant Administration Quarterly*, February, pp. 30–40.

Porter, E.M. (1985) How information gives you competitive advantage. *Harvard Business Review*, July–August, p. 3.

Sangster, A. (2001) The importance of technology in the hotel industry. *Travel and Tourist Analyst*, 3, 43–55.

Sheldon, P. (1997) *Tourism Information Technology*. Wallingford: CABI Publishing.

Turban, E., King, D., Lee, J., Warkentin, M., and Chung, H.M. (2002) *Electronic Commerce – A Managerial Perspective*, 2nd edn. Upper Saddle River, NJ: Pearson Education, pp. 48, 858.

Zilliox, D. (2002) *The Get-Started Guide to m-Commerce and Mobile Technology*. New York: American Management Association.

DIMITRIOS BUHALIS
UNIVERSITY OF SURREY, UK
KAREN TANG
UNIVERSITY OF SURREY, UK

Wireless application protocol (WAP)

The WAP-Forum was founded in 1997 on the initiative of Ericsson, Nokia, Motorola, and Phone.com to develop a uniform and open standard for the transmission of wireless information and telephone services to mobile devices. The goal was to bypass transmission bottlenecks through a simplified transmission language. The content is represented in WML (Wireless

Markup Language) for which a WAP-capable microbrowser is needed. Cut-down Internet sites thus can be displayed on WAP browsers on mobile phones, organizers, palmtops or pagers with a standard speed of 9.6 kbit/s.

However, the appropriate devices were launched late – only in the year 2000. The initial over-hype and the technical problems meant WAP brought the mobile network operators only 1–2% of their total turnover. The reasons for the slow penetration were expensive per minute charges, insufficiently developed technologies and standards (long connection establishment times, frequent connection breakdowns, slow speed), limited offers and services, as well as bad business models of mobile service providers (Zobel, 2001). According to research by Marcussen (2002), the most relevant WAP applications for tourism and hospitality are: providing information on flight delays, the traffic situation, weather and road conditions, flight schedules, and restaurant information. Accordingly, tourists seem to be interested mostly in location-based services and schedule information. There is an opportunity therefore for hospitality organizations to benefit.

References

Marcussen, Carl (2002) *SMS, WAP, m-commerce – opportunities for travel and tourism services.* Available at http://www.crt.dk/uk/staff/chm/wap/ itb.pdf

Zobel, Jörg (2001) *Mobile Business und M- Commerce. Die Märkte der Zukunft erobern.* Munich/Vienna: Hansen.

ROMAN EGGER
SALZBURG, AUSTRIA

goals, values, wants and outlooks, career-related aspirations and desired rewards.' Goldthorpe *et al.* (1968) identified three main types of orientation to work:

- *Instrumental* – viewed as 'a means to an end' rather than the central focus of their life. Hospitality work provides opportunities as the first work experience for young people, extra income for students, and a supplement to the household income for women and so can contribute to an instrumental orientation to work.
- *Bureaucratic* – considered critical component of employee life. There is positive involvement with work issues because work is considered as a profession. Individuals may seek to enhance their hospitality career prospects by undertaking career-oriented programs, such as diplomas or degrees in hospitality management.
- *Solidaristic* – enjoyed for its associated social and group activities. There is a strong involvement with work groups such that work and non-work activities are closely linked. The existence of occupational communities within the hospitality sector means that work attitudes can be dependent on the social aspects of hospitality work.

References

Burke, R.J. and Desza, G. (1988) Career orientations, satisfaction and health among police officers: Some consequences of person–job misfit. *Psychological Reports*, 62 (2), 639–649.

Goldthorpe, J.H., Lockwood, D., Bechhofer, F., and Platt, J. (1968) *The Affluent Worker: Industrial Attitudes and Behaviour.* London: Cambridge University Press.

JOSEPHINE PRYCE
JAMES COOK UNIVERSITY, AUSTRALIA

Work orientation

The concept of work orientation refers to individuals' attitudes towards work. It emphasizes how people construe their roles and work environments. According to Burke and Deszca (1988, p. 646), work orientation draws on 'the meaning of work for individuals; it includes

Working capital

Working capital is normally defined as the monetary value of current assets less the current liabilities. When the value of the current assets exceeds the current liabilities this is known as *positive working capital*, where current assets are funded partly from the current liabilities, such as accounts payable (creditors) and bank overdrafts, and also from long-term sources of funds, such as bank loans or equity. The term *negative working capital* arises when current liabilities exceed current assets. In this case current liabilities are funding both current assets and a proportion of long-term assets. Working capital management is concerned with the management of business liquidity in order to attain a balance between profitability and risk. This balance is monitored by the current ratio.

The *current ratio* is calculated as follows:

$$\text{Current ratio} = \frac{\text{Total current assets}}{\text{Total current liabilities}}$$

The *quick ratio* (or *acid test ratio*) takes account of the fact that it may take time to convert inventory (stocks) into cash, and is calculated as follows:

$$\text{Quick ratio} = \frac{\text{Total current assets} - \text{Inventory}}{\text{Total current liabilities}}$$

Working capital is required to fund the time lag between expenditure being made for the purchase of raw materials and the subsequent collection of cash for the sale of the finished product. This is called the *working capital cycle*. If a business is operating profitably then it should, in theory, generate cash surpluses. Without cash the business will eventually become insolvent and, therefore, it is widely recognized that the way in which companies manage their optimal cash position can make a difference to shareholder value. There are two major components of the working capital cycle that use cash – inventory and accounts receivable (debtors). The main sources of cash inflow are accounts payable and, for long-term sources, equity and loans. Each element of working capital has two important dimensions, namely time and money.

Inventory management

Generally a hospitality business should seek to reduce the amount of money tied up in inventories and aim to move inventory stocks more quickly (inventory turnover):

$$\text{Inventory turnover (days)} = \left[\frac{\text{Average inventory}}{\text{Cost of goods sold}}\right] \times 365 \text{ days}$$

Managing inventories requires specific expertise. Too much inventory held ties up cash in the business but insufficient inventory available can result in lost sales and loss of customer goodwill. To manage inventory effectively it is essential to identify the fast- and slow-moving stock items within the total inventory and determine optimum stock levels. Factors to consider when determining optimum inventory levels include:

- Accurate projected usage of the product
- Frequency and availability of supply
- Relationship between products.

Specific models exist which can help the business to determine optimum stock levels but these are usually dependent on consistent annual demand for products.

Managing accounts receivable

In the hotel sector in particular, it is necessary to offer credit to customers in order to secure the business. However, slow payment of the outstanding debt can have a serious impact on the business and ultimately can lead to bad debts. An effective debtor policy should include:

- Clearly established policies for giving credit
- Procedures for checking credit-worthiness of customers
- Established credit limits for each customer
- Prompt and accurate invoicing
- Penalties for late payment
- Procedures for monitoring outstanding balances.

The monitoring of outstanding payments is commonly undertaken using the *accounts receivable ratio*:

$$\text{Accounts receivable ratio} = \frac{\text{Receivables}}{\text{Credit sales}} \times 365$$

Debtors due over 90 days should receive immediate attention and are usually clear indicators of future bad debt problems. Increasing debtor days can be an indicator of internal operational problems such as:

- Poor procedures for collecting debt
- Slow issue of invoices and statements
- Errors in invoices
- Customer dissatisfaction.

Managing accounts payable

Hospitality businesses can benefit by getting better credit terms from suppliers and increasing short-term financing. This is monitored by the *accounts payable ratio*:

$$\text{Accounts payable ratio} = \frac{\text{Payables}}{\substack{\text{Cost of sales} \\ \text{(or Purchases)}}} \times 365$$

Improved purchasing techniques not only serve to improve the profitability of the business but also improve the liquidity of the business too. In the hospitality industry a large proportion of accounts payable arise from the purchase of perishable products such as food and beverages. Effective purchasing includes:

- Coordination of the purchasing process to achieve maximum discounts and best quality
- Accurate forecasting of demand
- Understanding of stock holding and purchasing costs
- Effective alternative sources of supply
- Knowledge of delivery frequency and availability.

Managing supplier relationships is crucial to managing working capital. Slow payment to suppliers can create bad feeling and undermine the potential to work with suppliers to enhance the future profitability of the business.

Overtrading

Revenue expansion without sufficient working capital can easily overstretch the financial resources of the business. This position is called overtrading and is a common feature of growth businesses that fail, not because of insufficient product profitability, but due to insufficient liquidity to purchase current assets such as inventories. The *working capital ratio* measures the relationship between working capital and sales as a percentage:

$$\text{Working capital ratio} =$$
$$\frac{\text{Inventory} + \text{Receivables} - \text{Payables}}{\text{Sales}} \times 100$$

The faster a company expands in terms of investment, the more working capital it will require. Therefore, a company that borrows long term and invests in short-term assets such as cash and stocks is creating liquidity for the business that can create a buffer against risk in times of financial distress. Similarly, using cash to purchase long-term assets will reduce the liquidity of the business and other forms of longer-term financing should be considered, such as equity, loans or leasing.

References

Dyson, J.R. (2004) *Accounting for Non-Accounting Students*, 6th edn. London: FT Prentice-Hall.

Jagels, M. and Coltman, M. (2003) *Hospitality Management Accounting*, 8th edn. New York: John Wiley & Sons.

Owen, G. (1998) *Accounting for Hospitality, Tourism and Leisure*. London: Longman.

Schmidgall, R.S. (2002) *Hospitality Industry Managerial Accounting*, 5th edn. Lansing, MI: Educational Institute of the American Hotel and Lodging Association.

DEBRA ADAMS
ARENA4FINANCE LTD, UK

X

Xeriscape

Xeriscape was derived from the Greek word *xeros*, meaning 'dry' and 'landscape.' Xeriscape means gardening with less than average water. Xeriscape is landscape consisting primarily of native, drought-resistant species, less than average turf, and other practices that require little or no maintenance, watering or fertilization. Welsh *et al.* (2004) suggest that xeriscape landscaping incorporates seven basic principles which lead to saving water: planning and design, soil analysis, practical turf areas, appropriate plant selection, efficient irrigation, use of mulches, and appropriate maintenance. A Xeriscape-type landscape can reduce outdoor water consumption by as much as 50% without sacrificing the quality and beauty of the environment.

Xeriscape is particularly beneficial to hotels that can use anywhere from 100,000 gallons to 1,000,000 gallons of water for irrigation each month.

References

Welsh, D.F., Welch, W.C., and Duble, R.L. (2004) Landscape water conservation . . . Xeriscape http://aggie-horticulture.tamu.edu/extension/xeriscape/xeriscape.html. Accessed 28 April 2004.

Xeriscape (n.d.) www.csu.org/xeri/.

Water-Efficient Landscaping: http://www.epa.gov/OW-OWM.html/water-efficiency/final_final.pdf.

JIM ACKLES
THARALDSON ENERGY GROUP, USA

XML (extensible markup language)

XML is an open standard for describing data from the World Wide Web Consortium (www.w3.org). XML is written in Standard Generalized Markup Language (SGML), the international standard meta language for defining the structure of different types of electronic documents. It is used for defining data elements on a Web page using a similar tag structure as HTML. However, whereas HTML defines how elements are displayed by using predefined tags, XML allows the tags to be defined by the website developer, allowing Web pages to function like database records.

The design and use of XML by Web developers improves functionality, providing more flexible and adaptable information identification, as well as a more robust and verifiable file format for the storage and transmission of data on and off the Web. XML is an important development in Web design as it removes two major constraints of Web development: that of the dependence on a single, inflexible document type (HTML) and the complexity of full (SGML), whose syntax allows many powerful but hard-to-program options. XML is good for hospitality because its interoperability between hospitality businesses and distributors such as aggregators, GDS, and electronic travel agencies.

References

Harold, E. and Means, W. (2002) *XML in a Nutshell: A Desktop Quick Reference*, 2nd edn. Sebastopol, CA: O'Reilly & Associates Publishing.

XML.org (2003) *XML Beginner's Guide, FAQ, Tutorials, and Articles*. Available at http://www.xml.org/xml/resources_focus_beginnerguide.shtml.

JULINE E. MILLS
PURDUE UNIVERSITY, USA

Y

Yield management

Yield management (YM) is a management tool or technique which is currently being utilized by an increasing number of group- and independently owned hotels in order to maximize the effective use of their available capacity and ensure financial success. YM is not entirely new, and most hoteliers practice some form of YM, such as the adjusting of room rates to temper fluctuations between peak and off-peak seasons, mid-week, and weekend rates. This chapter, therefore, examines the use and application of YM in the hotel industry and hopes to demonstrate its ability to effectively maximize revenue and profit generation in this highly competitive and capital-intensive industry.

Historical development of YM from airlines to hotels

The airline industry has been credited with the development and refinement of YM following deregulation of the US airline industry in the late 1970s. The resulting heavy competition led to a price-cutting war with some airlines going out of business. Kimes (1997) cites the example of People's Express, which emerged briefly as a low-price, no-frills airline. In response, large carriers such as American and United began to offer a small number of seats at even lower fares whilst maintaining the higher-priced fares on the remainder of the seats. This strategy allowed American and United to attract the price-sensitive customers and still retain their high-paying passengers. As a result, People's Express went into bankruptcy. Consequently, YM was introduced as a method of utilizing capacity and maximizing revenue or 'yield' where airline companies sought to fill their planes with the optimum mix of passengers.

In similar highly competitive circumstances, YM began to be adopted in the hotel industry around the middle of the 1980s. At this time the industry was being confronted with excess capacity, severe short-term liquidity problems, and increasing business failure rates. Major hotel chains such as Hyatt, Marriott, Quality Inn, and Radisson endeavored to redress these difficulties by adopting YM. Opportunities for applying YM in small to medium-sized hotels are actively being developed following the report for the European Union (Arthur Andersen, 1996).

Definition

In general terms, Kimes (1997) has described YM as the process of allocating the right type of capacity or inventory unit to the right type of customer at the right price so as to maximize revenue or 'yield.' Applying this to airlines, YM can be considered to be the revenue or yield per passenger mile, with yield being a function of both the price the airline charges for differentiated service options (pricing) and the number of seats sold at each price (seat inventory control). Larsen (1988) further crystallizes the meaning of YM in the airline context by dividing it into two distinct functions: overbooking and managing discounts.

In hotels, YM is concerned with the market-sensitive pricing of fixed room capacity relative to a hotel's specific market segments. Kimes (1997) states therefore that YM in hotels consists of two functions: rooms inventory management and pricing. The goal of YM is the formulation and profitable alignment of price, product, and buyer. As such, Donaghy *et al.* (1995, 140) define YM in hotels as a 'revenue maximization technique which aims to increase net yield through the predicted allocation of available bedroom capacity to predetermined market segments at optimum price.' It is the predicted nature of YM that is the key to its ongoing successful financial management of hotels in today's increasingly competitive market. On a strategic level, Jones and Kewin (1997) have extended the definition of YM as 'a decision-making tool based on an analysis of past performance and forecast of future demand that enables the goal of revenue maximization to be achieved through the strategic management of a hotel's market positioning and the operational management of the hotel's room sales.' This definition further highlights the differentiation between the strategic and tactical role that yield management plays in managing capacity.

Preconditions and Ingredients of YM

YM suits the hotel industry, where capacity is fixed, where the demand is unstable, and where the market can be segmented (Kimes, 1997). As with many service organizations, a feature of hotels is that they have low marginal costs and usually sell their perishable product to their customers well in advance of consumption. Developing these ideas further, Kimes (1997) has outlined a number of pre-conditions for the success of YM and suggested a number of factors or ingredients which are prerequisites for the implementation of YM as a functioning, workable system.

The *preconditions* for YM include:

- *Fixed capacity:* Hotels tend to be capacity-constrained with no opportunity to inventory their products or goods. Simply put, many hotel services and products are perishable. Capacity can be changed by, for example, adding a

number of new bedrooms or a new function suite but this usually involves a large financial investment in terms of equipment and plant.

- *High fixed costs:* The industry is characterized by high fixed costs and, as explained above, the cost of adding incremental capacity can be very high and is not quickly adjusted. Adding new bedrooms to a hotel not only entails a large capital outlay but may also involve a long planning and construction period.
- *Low variable costs:* The costs incurred by, for example, selling a bedroom to a customer in otherwise unused capacity is relatively inexpensive and incurs only minor servicing costs.
- *Time-varied demand:* Since hotel capacity is fixed, organizations cannot easily adjust their capacity to meet peaks and troughs in demand. Kimes (1997) explains that when demand varies, hotels can benefit from controlling capacity when demand is high and relaxing that control when demand is low. As with airlines, utilization of reservation systems can assist in managing demand since they log requests for rooms in advance.
- *Similarity of inventory units:* As a general rule, YM systems operate in a situation where inventory units are similar. However, it should be noted that service firms like hotels can differentiate their units by, for example, offering add-on luxury features or the possibility of upgrades.

The *ingredients* for successful YM include:

- *Market segmentation:* Hotels normally have the ability to divide their customer base into distinct market segments such as leisure, business, and long and short stay. Business or corporate clients who are usually time-sensitive are willing to pay higher rates whilst leisure travelers who tend to book longer in advance are price-sensitive.
- *Historical demand and booking patterns:* Detailed knowledge of a hotel's sales and booking data per market segment should help managers predict peaks and troughs in demand and assist the hotelier in more effectively aligning demand with supply.
- *Pricing knowledge:* Kimes (1997) describes YM as a form of price discrimination. In practice, hotels operate YM systems that depend on opening and closing rate bands. In order to

stimulate demand in periods of low demand, hotels can offer discounted prices whilst during periods of high demand low rates can be closed off. Additionally, by offering a number of rates in the hotel the manager will, ideally, profitably align price, product, and buyer and increase net yield.

- *Overbooking policy:* Overbooking is an essential YM technique. Overbooking levels are not set by chance but are determined by a detailed analysis of what has happened in the past and a prediction of what is likely to happen in the future. Predicted no-shows, cancellations, and denials all form part of a complex calculation carried out in advance. In this way the risk of disappointing a customer who has booked in advance is minimized.
- *Information systems:* Effective management information is essential for successful YM whether the hotelier is operating a manual or computerized system. However, information technology can assist greatly in the sorting and manipulation of required data. The use of artificial intelligence (AI) has enormous potential for handling the complexities of YM because of its abilities in complex problem-solving, reasoning, perception, planning, and analysis of extensive data (Russell and Johns, 1997). Expert systems (ES) are 'knowledge-based' software packages that reflect the expertise in the area of the application and these types of systems have extensive capacity in dealing with non-numeric, qualitative data.

Measuring yield

Traditional methods of performance measurement in hotels such as occupancy rate and average room rate have tended to focus on the volume or value aspects of accommodation sales. However, high occupancy rates are no indication of financial success since the rate per room charged to the customer may be a highly discounted rate well below the rack rate. While the average room rate gives an indication of the level of revenue generated per sold room, it gives no indication of the actual number of rooms sold. Indeed, as the hotelier increases one, he/she tends to decrease the other. Furthermore, where

room night productivity becomes a valuation technique for sales and reservation staff, lower-paying group business will increase while higher-paying transient business is turned away (Jones and Hamilton, 1992; Orkin, 1988). YM, on the other hand, aims to optimize both occupancy and average room rate simultaneously and this can easily be seen in Orkin's (1988) Yield Efficiency Statistic:

$$\text{Yield efficiency} = \frac{\text{Revenue realized}}{\text{Rooms sold} \times \text{Average room rate}}$$
$$= \frac{\text{Rooms sold} \times \text{Average room rate}}{\text{Room rate} \times \text{Available rooms}}$$

Orkin (1988) defined revenue realized as 'actual sales receipts' and potential revenue as 'the income secured if 100% of available room are sold at full rack rates.' Therefore, a 250-bedroom hotel with a £145 rack rate which sells 190 rooms at an average of £98 yields:

$$\frac{190 \times £98}{145 \times 250} = 51.37\%$$

The nearer the percentage is to 100, the better the yield.

Yield management decision variables

Yeoman and Watson (1997) identify the variables that hotel managers use to make YM decisions. These variables are based upon the principles of forecasting, systems, procedures, strategies, and tactics.

- *Forecasting* is the foundation of yield management. This forecasting must be done on a daily basis, with 30 day, 60 day, 180 day, and 365 day projections. A continuous examination of demand and supply variables is required in order to take effective YM decisions. The factors that may affect demand and supply include past business forecasts, sales mix, special events, weather, and competitors' behavior.
- *Systems and procedures:* A computerized system manages all the variable decisions in order to recommend appropriate pricing decisions.

Appropriate systems and procedures enable the hotel manager to store, track, and make appropriate decisions.

- *Strategies and tactics:* Decisions are made in relation to pricing policy and market demand. Therefore on high demand days, management concentrates on decisions regarding average room rate. This will involve restricting access to accommodation from groups and low-spending customers. Whereas on low demand days, management is concerned with market mix in order to maximize occupancy. In both scenarios, hotel management will have to design a policy that relates to overbooking. Overbooking occurs when customers cancel accommodation, check-out early or don't show up on the day of arrival. As accommodation can only be sold once in the hotel industry, the hotel manager needs to set a level, i.e., a number of rooms, at which they are prepared to overbook. This level will depend on the forecast for the given period, anticipated no-shows, cancellations, and early check-outs.

Yield management offers hotels an opportunity for a focused methodology for improving revenue that integrates the characteristics of the hotel industry. The hotel sector is both distinct and diverse in the characteristics of the unit of inventory compared to the manufacturing sector. The benefits of YM have been drawn from the airline industry but tailored to suit the hotels. Many hotels are facing financial pressures that are focusing hotel managers to come up with imaginative and new ways of managing accommodation. YM provides that edge as a means of helping the hotel manager take decisions on how much accommodation to sell, to which customer, and at what price.

References

Arthur Andersen/European Commission DGXXIII, Tourism Unit (1996) *Yield Management in Small to Medium Sized Enterprises in the Tourism Industry*. Luxembourg: Eur-Op.

Donaghy, K., McMahon, U., and McDowell, D. (1995) Yield management – an overview. *International Journal of Hospitality Management*, 14 (2), 139–150.

Donaghy, K., McMahon-Beattie, U., and McDowell, D. (1997) Implementing yield management: lessons from the hotel sector. *International Journal of Contemporary Hospitality Management*, 9 (2 and 3), 50–54.

Jones, P. and Hamilton, D. (1992) Yield management: putting people in the big picture. *Cornell Hotel and Restaurant Administration Quarterly*, 33 (1), 88–95.

Jones, P. and Kewin, E. (1997) Yield management in UK hotels: principles and practice. Paper presented at 2nd International Yield Management Conference, University of Bath.

Kimes, S.E. (1997) Yield management: an overview. In I. Yeoman and A. Ingold (eds), *Yield Management: Strategies for the Service Industries*. London: Cassell.

Larsen, T.D. (1988) Yield management and your passengers. *Asta Agency Management*, June, 46–48.

Orkin, E.B. (1988) Boosting our bottomline with yield management. *Cornell Hotel and Restaurant Administration Quarterly*, 28 (4), 52–56.

Russell, K.A. and Johns, M. (1997) Computerized yield management systems: lessons learned from the airline industry. In I. Yeoman and A. Ingold (eds), *Yield Management: Strategies for the Service Industries*. London: Cassell.

Yeoman, I. and Watson, S. (1997) Yield management: a human activity system. *International Journal of Contemporary Hospitality Management*, 9 (2), 80–83.

IAN YEOMAN
SCOTLAND NATIONAL TOURISM AGENCY, UK
UNA MCMAHON-BEATTIE
UNIVERSITY OF ULSTER, UK

Z

Zoning codes

The objective of zoning codes is to promote the safety and welfare of the public. Topics covered in zoning codes include land use, setback, building codes, easements, parking restrictions, density, and building heights. Some include regulations for the aesthetics of buildings. The earliest zoning ordinance on record in the United States was enacted in 1913 in New York City to regulate the height, size, and layout of buildings. The motion made by the president of Manhattan Borough stressed the need to limit building heights to put a stop to congested living and street conditions. In 1916, a more comprehensive ordinance was adopted to control the density and uses of land. In the United States zoning codes are developed by a town's council and enforced by the zoning officer, sheriff or police officer. When necessary, they are interpreted by the judicial system, beginning with a Zoning Board of Appeals and then to the county, state, and federal court system.

Reference

Haar, C.M. and Kayden, J.S. (eds) (1989) *Zoning and the American Dream*. Washington, DC: Planners Press.

CAROLYN LAMBERT
PENNSYLVANIA STATE UNIVERSITY, USA

Index

Main entries are in bold type including those also appearing as sub entries under other headings. Regular type is used for all other entries.